THE LAW OF THE POLICE

ASPEN CASEBOOK SERIES

THE LAW OF THE POLICE

Rachel Harmon

Professor of Law
University of Virginia School of Law

Published by Wolters Kluwer in New York.

Wolters Kluwer Legal & Regulatory U.S. serves customers worldwide with CCH, Aspen Publishers, and Kluwer Law International products. (www.WKLegaledu.com)

To contact Customer Service, e-mail customer.service@wolterskluwer.com, call 1-800-234-1660, fax 1-800-901-9075, or mail correspondence to:

> Wolters Kluwer
> Attn: Order Department
> PO Box 990
> Frederick, MD 21705

Printed in the United States of America.

1 2 3 4 5 6 7 8 9 0

ISBN 978-1-4548-9113-0

Library of Congress Cataloging-in-Publication Data

Names: Harmon, Rachel, author.
Title: The law of the police / Rachel Harmon, Professor of Law, University of
    Virginia School of Law.
Description: New York : Wolters Kluwer, [2021] | Includes bibliographical
    references and index. | Summary: "This is a casebook covering primary
    laws and doctrines that govern local police, and evaluating the ways we
    regulate and reform police conduct"— Provided by publisher.
Identifiers: LCCN 2020051992 (print) | LCCN 2020051993 (ebook) |
    ISBN 9781454891130 (hardcover) | ISBN 9781543823301 (ebook)
Subjects: LCSH: Police regulations—United States. | Law
    enforcement—United States. | Police—United States.
Classification: LCC KF5399 . H37 2021 (print) | LCC KF5399 (ebook) |
    DDC 344.7305/2—dc23
LC record available at https://lccn.loc.gov/2020051992
LC ebook record available at https://lccn.loc.gov/2020051993

Certified Chain of Custody
Promoting Sustainable Forestry
www.sfiprogram.org
SFI-01681

SFI label applies to the text stock.

About Wolters Kluwer Legal & Regulatory U.S.

Wolters Kluwer Legal & Regulatory U.S. delivers expert content and solutions in the areas of law, corporate compliance, health compliance, reimbursement, and legal education. Its practical solutions help customers successfully navigate the demands of a changing environment to drive their daily activities, enhance decision quality, and inspire confident outcomes.

Serving customers worldwide, its legal and regulatory portfolio includes products under the Aspen Publishers, CCH Incorporated, Kluwer Law International, ftwilliam.com, and MediRegs names. They are regarded as exceptional and trusted resources for general legal and practice-specific knowledge, compliance and risk management, dynamic workflow solutions, and expert commentary.

To Bob, Stephen, Avery, and Claire,
the multistar system that shapes my path.

Summary of Contents

Table of Contents

PART TWO
INVESTIGATIVE POLICING   79

Chapter 2
Uncovering Crime   83

Chapter 3
Obtaining Testimony   147

Chapter 4
Handling and Disclosing Evidence   197

PART THREE
STREET POLICING   231

Chapter 5
Preventing Crime   235

Chapter 6
Stopping Traffic   281

Chapter 7
Making Arrests   321

Chapter 8
Using Force   361

Chapter 9
Policing Resistance   423

Chapter 10
Maintaining Order   477

Chapter 11
Federal Influence over Local Policing   521

PART FOUR
REMEDIES AND REFORMS   573

Chapter 12
The Exclusionary Rule   577

Chapter 13
Suing the Police for Damages   611

Chapter 14
Prosecuting the Police   659

Chapter 15
Suing for Reform   731

Chapter 16
Changing the Police: Beyond Litigation   797

Preface

The Origins and Purposes of **The Law of the Police**

In law review articles in 2012 and 2016, I argued that legal scholarship and law school courses were stuck in an overly narrow way of thinking about policing and the law: To that point, classes and commentators treated constitutional criminal procedure—mainly the Fourth and Fifth Amendments and their associated legal remedies—as the law of the police. When policing seemed problematic, lawyers, legal scholars, and students looked to the Supreme Court and argued for changes in constitutional doctrine to fix it. Scholars and students studied Supreme Court cases and thought they understood both policing and the project of regulating it. In fact, policing has never been limited to—or even dominated by—criminal investigation, and the law that governs it has never been written only by courts. Nor could it be.

Policing provides benefits and imposes harms—and it often distributes both unevenly. Determining how much and what kinds of policing to have, arbitrating among the competing individual and communal interests, and influencing officers who operate in a vast array of diverse institutions and environments could hardly be more complex. That project, the project of regulating the police, includes local, state, and federal actors using legislative, judicial, and administrative tools. Constitutional criminal procedure is only a part of the picture.

To get beyond the limitations of the courts-and-Constitution approach to thinking about the law governing the police, I recommended a new agenda for scholarship on policing and the law, one designed to help us better understand, develop, and evaluate legal regulation of the police. I argued that scholars should:

- Study the true extent of the harms policing produces and whether effective policing can be made less harmful.
- Consider the full web of federal, state, and local laws that govern policing both in and outside the context of criminal procedure.
- Assess the comparative roles, capacities, and incentives of the variety of government actors that regulate and influence police conduct.

By exploring these neglected areas of inquiry—harm efficiency, the real law of the police, and comparative institutional analysis—I believed we could better understand policing and how it might best be regulated. See Rachel A. Harmon, *The Problem of Policing*, 110 Mich. L. Rev. 761, 762–764 (2012); Rachel Harmon, *Reconsidering Criminal Procedure: Teaching the Law of the Police*, 60 St. Louis U. L.J. 391 (2016).

A lot has changed since 2012, helped in part by intense national attention to police killings of unarmed African American men. These deaths and the protests that followed were not the first time concern about police violence rose to center stage in the United States. Still, they helped reveal to the public (again) the harms and unfairness that plague policing. They also set in stark relief (again) the limits of constitutional law as a way of understanding how police are influenced by law and as a framework for change. In response to these events, both legal scholars and criminologists have expanded their view and, in the process, have made new progress on the agenda I had earlier suggested. Scholars have considered the harms of policing in far more depth, have explored aspects of the law regulating the police that were all but ignored previously, and have debated more thoroughly how well laws and legal institutions regulate different aspects of policing.

From these efforts has grown an academic field of policing and the law, one which explores how and how well the law regulates police interactions with the public. This field offers lessons and guidance for litigators, for legislators, for policymakers, and for anyone inside or outside of those categories who wishes to assess or change policing. Scholars are building the field, and, in a sense, governments, private lawyers, and nonprofit organizations are practicing in it. As yet, however, no one has laid out a conceptual structure for it, and no treatise or casebook is available to introduce the subject to those who wish to know more.

This book seeks to fill these gaps: It provides materials and analysis for law school classes on policing and the law. It offers a resource for lawyers, judges, police executives, elected officials, policymakers, journalists, scholars, and activists who want to understand how American law governs police interactions with the public. It also frames this new field in legal scholarship, highlighting especially the work of young scholars. Or, at least, it is a start.

A Note for Readers

This book provides primary materials—including cases, statutes, and departmental policies—and commentary and questions designed to help readers explore the law, its context, and its consequences. Among other issues, the notes and questions encourage readers to consider the form and content of the law; who is making it; and how the law may influence the costs, benefits, fairness, and accountability of policing. They also encourage readers to consider alternative forms of regulation and how to achieve them. The book is organized in four parts.

- Part One introduces local policing—its history, goals, and problems—and its relationship to law, including the many types of law and legal actors that influence the police.
- Part Two considers the law that regulates police intrusions on members of the public during criminal investigations.
- Part Three addresses the law that governs police interactions with members of the public on patrol and on the street.
- Part Four looks at legal remedies and reforms used to encourage officers and departments to change their conduct and follow the law.

Because there is no accepted course of study on policing and the law, and different professors will offer varying seminars and black-letter courses, the book is designed to be flexible, suited for courses on the law of the police generally, on civil rights remedies, on aspects of police misconduct, and on more specific topics, such as the use of force. The materials are appropriate both for students without prior experience and for students who have taken courses in criminal procedure or civil rights litigation, as most of my students have. Some subjects, such as criminal prosecution of police officers and pattern-or-practice suits against police departments, are dealt with in special depth in recognition that other materials on these subjects are scant. Professors and students may pick and choose to suit their purposes.

Students who have studied constitutional criminal procedure or civil rights litigation will recognize some of the book's cases. They are used here toward different ends, and my students consistently tell me that they feel fresh rather than repetitive. For example, although every criminal procedure casebook includes *Miranda v. Arizona*, 384 U.S. 436 (1966), many omit the dissents or include only those parts of the dissents that highlight the debate among the Justices about proper methods of constitutional interpretation. In this book, the case is edited instead to emphasize the Justices' express debate about the role of the Court in regulating the police given limited information about interrogation practices and the consequences of regulation. Case excerpts throughout the book illustrate and emphasize the role courts play in regulating policing, a subject that other courses only touch on. If anything, familiarity with the doctrines makes it easier to focus on how and how effectively they regulate policing, as opposed to whether they are good constitutional law.

A Word About Editorial Choices

- *Race.* No chapter in this book includes *race* in its title. Race affects every aspect of policing practice and its legal regulation, and it is considered throughout the book. Readers looking for focused discussions of race and the law of policing might find the following chapters especially interesting: Chapter 5, which considers stops and frisks; Chapter 6, which considers the law governing racially disparate traffic stops; and Chapter 8 on the use of force.
- *Gender.* There is no easy solution to the problem of gendered language for this book. Women serve in every role in the criminal justice system, including as police officers and as suspects. As in any text, using male nouns and pronouns to refer to people who might not be male is imprecise and risks reifying existing gender categories and dynamics. Nevertheless, policing remains overwhelmingly male: Only one in eight local police officers is a woman, and people suspected of serious crimes are even less often female. Moreover, police interactions with members of the public are gendered and sexualized in important ways, and ideas of masculinity affect the content and quality of policing. As a result, using female pronouns for hypothetical or generic parties in the text (or alternating, as some texts do) risks being both jarring and misleading. Although the text seeks to use gender-neutral language when possible, masculine pronouns are used, with apologies, to refer to hypothetical officers and suspects unless the context requires or easily permits doing otherwise.
- *Perception and reality.* The book discusses some police activities targeted at members of particular communities, such as undercover stings focused on gay men, street stops of transgender women, and traffic enforcement targeted at Latino drivers. When officers target members of a community, they

usually base their actions on their perceptions of a person's status, which may not correlate perfectly with reality. As a result, such activities often affect not only members of the targeted community but also the penumbra of people most likely to be mistaken for members. While the text often abbreviates by referring only to effects on community members, such discussions are intended to include by implication those affected by misperception.

- *Nonofficers.* Discussions of policing are plagued by another linguistic problem: how to refer to people with whom police officers interact. In the context of criminal investigation, *suspect* or *arrestee* might appropriately describe the legal role a person plays, and these terms are used some, but this book also goes beyond the law of criminal investigation. *Subject* is broader, including more of those to whom police attention is directed, such as those involved in traffic stops, but it characterizes people by police interest in them rather than by any legal or political role they inhabit in relation to the police. Many authors use *civilians* to describe nonofficers, but this word equates serving on a police force with being in the armed forces, and therefore suggests that policing is inevitably or properly militaristic, hierarchical, and armed, an assumption the book questions. I sometimes use *citizens*, which is valuable because it emphasizes the political relationship between officers and those who are policed. However, that term apparently excludes many in the country (such as noncitizen immigrants), who may be heavily policed. *Residents* is used some, but it overemphasizes where people live. I often favor *members of the public, community members*, or *members of the community* (although *nonofficer members* would be more accurate). Nevertheless, where the connotations are appropriate or *members of the community* is too cumbersome, the text uses other imperfect terms.
- *Scope.* The institutions and people that constitute the police are vast and diverse. In addition to local, municipal police officers, they include county sheriffs, state officers, tribal police, and a large variety of federal law enforcement officers, as well as private security guards, who significantly outnumber sworn police. As is discussed in Chapter 1, this book focuses on local police. Although much of the law discussed applies to other government officials who carry out policing activities, narrowing the scope to local policing allows readers to consider the impact of many different types of law on one (diverse) type of institution.
- *Omissions and alterations.* Footnotes, citations, internal quotation and alteration marks, and parentheticals have been eliminated from quotations without notation in the interest of readability. Some paragraph breaks and section numbers have been eliminated from quoted materials for the same reason. Some footnotes have been converted to in-line citations. Citation forms within quoted texts have also been changed for clarity. Other omissions and alterations are indicated, and footnotes that are preserved in sources are numbered as they are in the original. Editorial notes added to primary materials are indicated by *Ed. note.*
- *Other policing law.* Because the book focuses on aspects of the law that govern police intrusions on and interactions with the public, it does not consider in depth other kinds of law that significantly shape policing, including employment and labor law, civil service law, employment discrimination law, state regulations guiding police management and organization, and public

records and data transparency laws. Although these laws are touched on, readers should look to other sources (or future editions) for a more complete picture.

- *Transparency.* I have worked on policing matters for more than two decades as a lawyer, consultant, and academic. As a result, I have occasionally been involved in subjects discussed in the book. In an effort to be transparent about my potential biases, I have added editorial footnotes whenever I have been personally connected with events discussed. However, to limit the number of self-referential footnotes, which already seem too numerous, I have not always disclosed prior positions I have taken in writing about matters in the text, which seem less critical to evaluating the materials.
- *Future editions.* The subject of policing and the law—even when confined to police interactions with the public—is vast and ever changing. No single volume could include all aspects of it, nor stay up to date. You will likely find mistakes I have made, omissions that grate at you, areas of the law that have changed, or opinions and implications that you cannot abide. I look forward to expanding, improving, and correcting the book in future editions, and I welcome reader reactions, suggestions, and comments toward that end.

Like a photograph, a book is fixed at a moment in time. This first edition was written almost entirely before May 25, 2020, when George Floyd, a 46-year-old Black man, died under the knee of a police officer, who knelt on his neck for several minutes, even as Floyd remained prone, handcuffed, and eventually nonresponsive. Within a fortnight, widespread protests in response to this killing and others dramatically changed the tenor of conversations about public safety, policing, and the law, opening new possibilities for the future. The protests also led states to propose and pass new legislation on policing. I have tried to add some of this law to the book. Then, after the content of the book was complete, Joe Biden was elected President, protending a significant change in federal policy on policing. Given those developments, the book's tone and content may be dated even before the ink is dry. Consider this edition a first effort at providing insight into the law of the police, one that reflects its moment. The constantly changing world of policing and the law will inevitably provide new materials and perspective for editions to come.

Rachel Harmon
December 2020

Acknowledgments

This book grows out of my scholarship on the legal regulation of the police and a series of courses on policing that I have taught at the University of Virginia for more than a dozen years. My thanks go to my fellow travelers—the legal scholars and criminologists who have shared insights on policing with me in writing and in person, in public and in private. I hope they will find this book as useful as what I have learned from them. Thanks also go to the police executives and lawyers with whom I have worked. These professionals have taught me a tremendous amount, and their influence pervades the book.

I am especially grateful to the students have helped make this project possible, including the thousand or so who have served as guinea pigs in versions of my Law of the Police course. Special thanks go to Galen Bascom and Andrew Manns, who helped think through the structure of these materials early on; to Alex Boota and Alec Ward for help with content; to Juliet Buesing, for turning over her ticket; and to Michael McGuire and Chris Palermo-Re, who devoted enormous attention to drafts, even after they graduated from law school. Thanks also go to my many other dedicated research assistants: Nellie Black, DeAnza Cook, Kathleen Delsandro, James Dennison, Nathanael Eagan, Kate Ferrara, Raymond Gans, Kolleen Gladden, Megan Jones, Megan Keenan, Ashley Markson, Hutton Marshall, Ben-Yusuf Massey, Daniel Natal, Matthew Nicholls, Anna Noone, Brendan Porter, Sharon Rogart, Lauren Schnyer, and James Tomberlin. My undying affection goes to the unparalleled reference librarians at the University of Virginia School of Law, and especially Kent Olson, on whose skill and patience I utterly depend.

I am grateful to the scholars and lawyers who took precious time to comment on draft chapters, including Ron Allen, Josh Bowers, Jeffrey Bellin, Barbara Bosserman, Brandon Garrett, David Harris, Richard Leo, Ben Levin, Wayne Logan, Christy Lopez, Robert Mikos, Eric Miller, Rachel Moran, Maria Ponomarenko, Richard Schragger, Jocelyn Simonson, Christopher Slobogin, Jordan Blaire Woods, participants in the Vanderbilt Roundtable of 2018, the 2018 Law of the Police workshop at the University of South Carolina, CrimFest 2019, and the University of Chicago Public Law workshop. Super duper thanks go to Seth Stoughton and Joanna Schwartz, who provided smart and detailed comments on large chunks of the book. Thanks also to the many folks at Wolters Kluwer who touched the book and made it better.

I also appreciate Deirdre Enright, Jody Kraus, Caleb Nelson, and Bob Newman, who entertained endless conversations about the casebook, and my other family and friends, who all showed me exceptional patience; they have suffered this project for longer than I would have liked.

Any author compiling a list of acknowledgments harbors a fear of having overlooked friends, students, and colleagues who have made contributions and provided support. If I have omitted any such, I look forward to correcting the error in a future edition.

I am grateful to the following sources for permission to reprint excerpts or images:

Excerpts

Barry Friedman, et. al., Changing the Law to Change Policing: Initial Steps (2020): https://law.yale.edu/sites/default/files/area/center/justice/document/change_to_change_final.pdf.

Charles Wolf, Jr., "'Non-Market' Failures And Market Failures." The Rand Paper Series (1978). The RAND Corporation. Copyright © 1978. https://www.rand.org/pubs/papers/P6136.html.

Egon Bittner, "Florence Nightingale in Pursuit of Willie Sutton: A Theory of the Police." The Potential for Reform of Criminal Justice (Herbert Jacob ed., 1974). SAGE Publications. Copyright © 1974.

Henry F. Fradella & Michael D. White, "Stop-and-Frisk." Reforming Criminal Justice: Punishment, Incarceration, and Release, Vol. 2 (Erik Luna, ed., 1997). Arizona State University. Reprinted with permission.

James X. Dempsey, "Communications Privacy in the Digital Age: Revitalizing the Federal Wiretap Laws to Enhance Privacy." Albany Law Journal of Science and Technology, Vol. 8 (1997). Albany Law School. Reprinted with permission from the author.

National Research Council. 2003. The Polygraph and Lie Detection. https://doi.org/10.17226/10420. Reprinted with permission from the National Academy of Sciences, Courtesy of the National Academies Press, Washington, D.C.

National Research Council. 2004. Fairness and Effectiveness in Policing: The Evidence. https://doi.org/10.17226/10419. Reprinted with permission from the National Academy of Sciences, Courtesy of the National Academies Press, Washington, D.C.

National Research Council. 2014. Identifying the Culprit: Assessing Eyewitness Identification. https://doi.org/10.17226/18891. Reprinted with permission from the National Academy of Sciences, Courtesy of the National Academies Press, Washington, D.C.

National Academies of Sciences, Engineering, and Medicine. 2018. Proactive Policing: Effects on Crime and Communities. https://doi.org/10.17226/24928. Reprinted with permission from the National Academy of Sciences, Courtesy of the National Academies Press, Washington, D.C.

Rachel A. Harmon, "Federal Programs and the Real Costs of Policing." New York University Law Review, Vol. 90 (2015). New York University School of Law. Copyright © 2015.

Rachel A. Harmon, "The Problem of Policing." Michigan Law Review, Vol. 110, Issue 5 (2012). University of Michigan Law School. Copyright © 2012.

Rachel A. Harmon, "When is Police Violence Justified?" First published by Northwestern University Law Review, Volume 102, Issue 3 (2008). Northwestern University Pritzker School of Law. Copyright © 2008.

Rachel A. Harmon, "Why Arrest?" Michigan Law Review, Vol. 115, Issue 3 (2016). University of Michigan Law School. Copyright © 2016.

Rachel A. Harmon & Andrew Manns, "Proactive Policing and the Legacy of Terry." Ohio State Journal of Criminal Law, Vol. 15, No. 1 (2017). Ohio State University Moritz College of Law. Copyright © 2017.

Vincent Ostrom & Elinor Ostrom, "Public Goods and Public Choices." Alternatives for Delivering Public Services: Toward Improved Performance (E.S. Savas ed., 1977). The Diebold Institute on Public Policy Studies.

Images

#SayHerName protest signs by The All-Nite Images via Flickr. Licensed under CC BY-SA 2.0.

Axon Taser by Junglecat. Licensed under CC BY-SA 3.0.

BearCat deployed in Charlottesville, Virginia during the Unite the Right rally on August 12, 2017. Courtesy of Andrew Shurtleff. Copyright © 2017.

BolaWrap. The Washington Post / Getty Images. Copyright © 2020.

Camden police chief J. Scott Thomson, 2018. Reprinted with permission from the Camden Police Department.

"Colored Only" waiting room sign. Copyright © 2020 The National Association for the Advancement of Colored People. All Rights Reserved.

Cop Watch poster. Reprinted with permission from Justice Committee Inc.

"Cops are NOT Above the Law" banner by Ted Eytan. Licensed under CC BY-SA 2.0.

Corvette seized by New Braunfels Police Department from an alleged drug dealer and repurposed as Coptimus Prime. Courtesy of the New Braunfels Police Department.

"Defund the Police" sign painted on a Washington DC street. Photo by Tasos Katopodis/Getty Images. Copyright © 2020.

"Demilitarize the Police" sign by Johnny Silvercloud. Licensed under CC BY-SA 2.0. https://bit.ly/3mxk3EI.

Demonstrators face off with officers in front of the San Diego Police. Ariana Drehsler/AFP via Getty Images. Copyright © 2020.

Drone camera. Kaleb Kendall via StockSnap. Available at https://stocksnap.io/photo/drone-camera-ZPCZDX0CW5.

Evidence bag by WebStockReview.net. Licensed under CC BY 3.0. https://bit.ly/3oDkrDx.

Floyd plaintiffs. Leroy Downs and Devin Almonor. Reuters/Eduardo Munoz. Copyright © 2013.

Former Milwaukee police chief Edward Flynn. Courtesy of the Milwaukee Police Department.

Handcuffs used in the arrest of Henry Louis Gates, Jr. Licensed under CC0 1.0 Universal. Collection of the Smithsonian National Museum of African American History and Culture, Gift of Professor Henry Louis Gates, Jr.

James Webb's ticket. Courtesy of Nick Somberg.

Justice for Mario Woods, 2015. Courtesy of Sins Invalid and Micah Bazant with permission from Gwen Woods.

LAPD car door: "To protect and serve." George Clerk via iStock/Getty Images. Copyright © 2019.

LAPD officers conversing with homeless woman conversation during Skid Row patrol. Ricardo DeAratanha/Los Angeles Times via Getty Images. Copyright © 2006.

Man arrested by Las Vegas police. Benjamin Sibuet/123RF.COM. Copyright © 2010.

Man with "Special Prosecutors for Police Shootings" sign by Edward Kimmel. Licensed under CC BY-SA 2.0. https://www.flickr.com/photos/mdfriendofhillary/15830770487/.

Mobile ALPR camera system on police car. Licensed under CC BY.

Officer wearing face mask. Julian Wan via Unsplash. Available at https://bit.ly/3jGMm1q.

"Pedestrian movement only" sign. Courtesy of Street Roots. Available at https://bit.ly/399ibi3.

Police K-9. Charles Krupa/AP. Copyright © 2017.

Police sobriety checkpoint. Jim West / Alamy Stock Photo. Copyright © 2016.

Protestor with "We Want An Indictment" sign. Courtesy of James Head via Flickr. Available at https://bit.ly/375FdDB.

Ray Hill at first National March on Washington for Lesbian and Gay Rights. Reprinted with permission from Houston LGBT History.org and Larry Butler courtesy of J.D. Doyle.

Scene from Ferguson, Missouri after the fatal shooting of Michael Brown by the police. AP Photo/David Goldman. Copyright © 2014.

"Skin color is not reasonable suspicion" sign. Courtesy of Yvonne Sam.

Soldier firing with M16A2 machine gun. SuperStock/Alamy Stock Photo.

Sony Handycam video recorder by JesseG. Licensed under CC BY-SA 3.0. Available at https://bit.ly/35PPByK.

Stop and frisk. Rafael Ben-Ari / Alamy Stock Photo. Copyright © 2015.

Traffic Stop. Marmaduke St. John / Alamy Stock Photo. Copyright © 2005.

"Twin Cities Police Easily Startled" road sign photo, 2017. Reprinted with permission from Addy Free. Available at https://bit.ly/3lZtv3j.

"Unite the Right" Rally in Charlottesville, Virginia. Chip Somodevilla/Getty Images. Copyright © 2017.

We Stand with Monica Jones, 2013. Reprinted with permission by Monica Jones, Sex Worker Outreach Project Phoenix and Micah Bazant.

THE LAW OF THE POLICE

PART ONE

INTRODUCTION

We all want to live free from fear and violence. We want protection from others who would harm us. We want to enjoy our property and our homes without violation. We want to use public spaces freely and safely. We want justice when serious wrongs are done. Policing is one set of social activities we use to reach these goals, and it is hard to imagine a complex society without it.

At the same time, we want to live free from fear of our government and its actors. We never want to endure harassment or injury or death at the hands of law enforcement. We do not want police officers to target us for the color of our skin, our gender nonconformity, our mental disability, or our poverty. Yet policing sometimes leads to these harms. Although officers talk, solve problems, assist, and reassure, they also command and cajole, surveil and search, detain and arrest, and hurt and kill. They choose when and how to intervene, whom to suspect, and what to protect, all with enormous effect. Policing thus carries the potential both to increase our safety and to threaten it.

Although policing takes many forms, in the United States it most often is organized through local police departments, structured hierarchically, that employ patrol officers to interact directly with the public. The law empowers, constrains, and incentivizes those officers. It determines the consequences when officers and departments act outside the law.

Policing in turn shapes the law. Courts and legislatures provide new powers to the police in response to the perceived necessities of law enforcement. Or they respond to newly salient problems in policing by imposing new rules on officers and departments, constraining the tools the police may use to pursue public safety, enforce the criminal law, and maintain public order.

This book explores the law that governs the public's interactions with the police. Many of these interactions are cooperative, positive, and uncontroversial. The law typically has little to say about these interactions, and although they are important to policing, they are less central to the law of the police. Instead, this book focuses specifically on the harms the police impose in the name of public safety and how the law responds—that is, what constraints the law places on officers. Part One introduces policing and the law that governs it. Part Two looks at doctrines governing core tasks in criminal investigation, including discovering and observing criminal activity; obtaining testimony from witnesses; and handling, collecting, and disclosing evidence in preparation for criminal trials. Part Three examines the law governing activities central to street policing, including preventing crime, stopping traffic, making arrests, using force, addressing those who challenge the police, and maintaining order. Part Four considers the legal remedies and other mechanisms that are used to challenge and change police conduct.

These materials and the notes and questions that follow encourage you to think about the following questions. You might spend a few minutes now jotting answers to these questions so that you can compare your thoughts after you have learned more.

1. What do police do?
2. What social purposes do police activities serve?
3. What harms do police activities risk for individuals and groups?
4. How might variations in the source, form, and content of the law affect police conduct?
5. How might the law affect the fairness of policing?
6. How does the law influence the responsiveness of policing to communities?
7. How does the law influence what we know about policing?
8. How might the law and policing both be made better?

Above all, policing matters. It changes lives, sometimes forever.

The premise of this book is this: Policing should be effective, fair, worth its harms, and responsive to communities. The law sometimes helps policing achieve these goals, and sometimes it is an impediment. Sometimes it is hard to tell. See what you think.

Chapter 1

Understanding Policing

This chapter introduces the police and the law of policing. It also provides some analytical tools to help you as you read further. Along the way, notice how what you read affects you. Are you surprised? Confirmed in your beliefs? Intrigued? Angered? Something else?

A. Officers, Departments, and What Police Do All Day

1. The Paradigmatic Police

This book focuses almost exclusively on local policing. To understand why, it helps to know a bit more about public policing more generally.

a. Overview

Policing is only one component of the American criminal justice system, but it is the biggest: It affects the most people, it employs the most people, and it costs the most money.

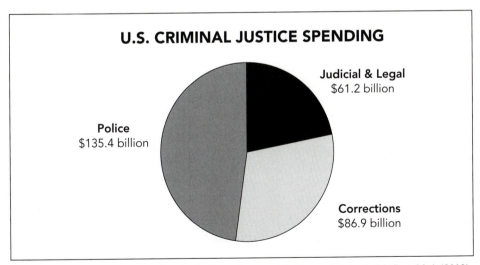

Source: Bureau of Justice Statistics, *Justice Expenditure and Employment Extracts, 2015*, at tbl. 1 (2019).

Within policing, although many kinds of public policing agencies exist in the United States, local municipal policing is what most Americans experience in their day-to-day lives.

Nat'l Research Council of the Nat'l Academies, *Fairness and Effectiveness in Policing: The Evidence*
49–51 (Wesley Skogan & Kathleen Frydl eds., 2004)

Law enforcement agencies at different levels of government have substantially different formal responsibilities, as prescribed by law, and therefore engage in different kinds of activities. Local police (municipal police departments, county police departments, and county sheriffs) have the broadest mandate: nearly all municipal and county police agencies enforce criminal laws, maintain order, and provide miscellaneous services to the public on a day-to-day basis. Because these agencies engage in routine patrol throughout the communities they serve and respond to requests for service, they are the agencies most visible to the public and also have the most direct contact with them.

At the local level, municipal law enforcement agencies provide the lion's share of police services in the United States, with a few sheriffs providing general policing services. . . .

Local law enforcement is also organized at the county level, primarily around the office of county sheriff. . . . Sheriff's departments are also unique in that they serve all three branches of the criminal justice system: law enforcement, courts, and corrections. About 98 percent of all sheriff's departments also provide bailiff and other services to the county courts, including serving summonses and other civil law matters, and about 80 percent also operate the primary jail in their counties.

State law enforcement agencies fall into two basic categories. About half are primarily responsible for traffic enforcement on highways, while the other half have general law enforcement responsibilities throughout the state. In addition, many states maintain state-level bureaus of criminal investigation with broad law enforcement responsibilities. . . . Most states also maintain other organizations with special and limited law enforcement powers, such as fish and game police, harbor police, and units that guard state buildings. . . . In addition, state agencies often cover jurisdiction anomalies or unincorporated areas and small towns that do not have their own police forces. Basic police services are provided to these areas by state law enforcement or county sheriff's departments, often under a formal contractual arrangement.

At the federal level, there are an estimated 69 law enforcement agencies[1] . . . "with arrest and firearm authority." The responsibilities

---

[1] *Ed. note:* This number is no longer accurate. See discussion below.

of federal agencies are generally very specific and defined by federal law—for example, the Customs Bureau enforces import and export laws. . . .

Law enforcement services are also provided by a number of special district police, which are independent or semi-independent of other units of government. Of these, the most important are American Indian tribal law enforcement police. As a result of the historic and unique legal status of American Indian tribes, many tribal authorities operate their own police departments (and in some cases entire criminal justice systems). These agencies are not subject to many of the state and federal laws (e.g., equal employment opportunity requirements). Little research has been conducted on tribal policing; however, a recent federal report found very high rates of criminal victimization and inadequate law enforcement protection in tribal areas.

Apart from tribal police, there are . . . other special district police departments, including . . . public school system police[,] . . . transportation system police agencies . . . and . . . campus law enforcement agencies.

Despite this variety of law enforcement agencies, when most people think of the police, they think of uniformed patrol officers who are sworn employees of local police departments—and for good reason. Local policing dominates law enforcement.

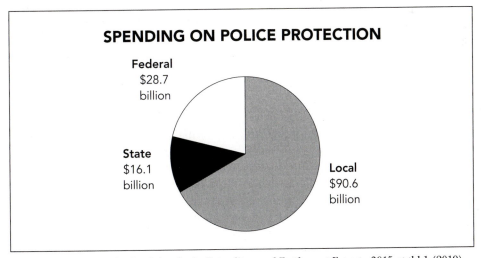

Source: Bureau of Justice Statistics, *Justice Expenditure and Employment Extracts, 2015,* at tbl.1 (2019).

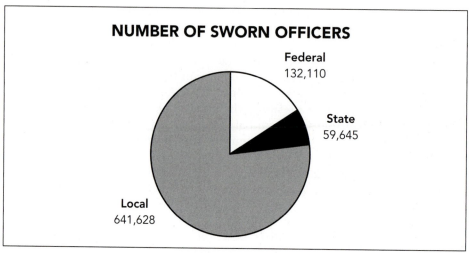

NUMBER OF SWORN OFFICERS

Federal
132,110

State
59,645

Local
641,628

Source: Shelley S. Hyland & Elizabeth Davis, Bureau of Justice Statistics, *Local Police Departments, 2016: Personnel* 1 (2019).

b.   *Federal Law Enforcement*

In contrast to the 12,261 local police departments, only 83 federal law enforcement agencies exist, and that includes Offices of Inspectors General. Even that number overstates the breadth of federal law enforcement. Overwhelmingly, federal law enforcement officers with arrest powers (of which there are 132,110) serve in just a few major agencies.

TOP 10 AGENCIES BY NUMBER OF FULL-TIME FEDERAL LAW ENFORCEMENT OFFICERS

Agency	Number of Officers	Percentage of Officers
Customs and Border Protection	43,724	33%
Federal Bureau of Prisons	19,093	14%
Federal Bureau of Investigation	13,799	10%
Immigration and Customs Enforcement	12,400	9%
Secret Service	4,729	3.5%
Drug Enforcement Administration	4,181	3%
Department of Veterans Affairs Police Department	3,839	3%
U.S. Marshals Service	3,788	3%
Bureau of Alcohol, Tobacco, Firearms, and Explosives	2,675	2%
U.S. Postal Inspection Service	1,891	1%

Source: Connor Brooks, Bureau of Justice Statistics, *Federal Law Enforcement Officers, 2016—Statistical Tables* 1 (2019).

Many other federal law enforcement agencies, including the Forest Service (592 officers), the Mint Police (292 officers), the Supreme Court Police (156 officers), and the National Aeronautics and Space Administration Police (62), are far smaller.

The National Zoological Police, founded in 1889, employs 25 sworn officers in 2020.

Moreover, federal law enforcement has far less interaction with the public, in part because they engage in different tasks. A far higher percentage of federal law enforcement officers (nearly two-thirds), compared to state or local officers, are primarily tasked with criminal investigation, and 15 percent more primarily work in corrections. Fewer than 1 in 11 federal law enforcement officers spends most of their time in ordinary patrol and police response activities. See Connor Brooks, Bureau of Justice Statistics, *Federal Law Enforcement Officers, 2016—Statistical Tables* 6 (2019).

c.   State Law Enforcement

Every state has a primary state law enforcement agency and a range of special jurisdiction agencies. Most special jurisdiction agencies focus on policing particular activities. These include fish and wildlife enforcement agencies, parks and recreation police, highway patrol, mass-transit police, and alcohol enforcement agencies. States also authorize agencies for specific geographic areas that are not political subdivisions, including university police, transit system police, and hospital police. These agencies are neither what we usually think of as state agencies nor what we usually think of as local ones.

d.   Local Police Departments and Officers

Local policing agencies and their officers far outnumber state agencies and officers, and there are far more municipal police departments than sheriffs' offices. Of the 15,322 general-purpose law enforcement agencies in the United States, local police departments, including mostly municipal and a few county departments make up 80 percent of the agencies, numbering 12,261. They employ two-thirds (468,000) of the full-time sworn officers with arrest powers (701,000). Shelley S. Hyland & Elizabeth Davis, Bureau of Justice Statistics, *Local Police Departments, 2016: Personnel* 1 (2019). Sheriffs' offices and deputies make up most of the rest.

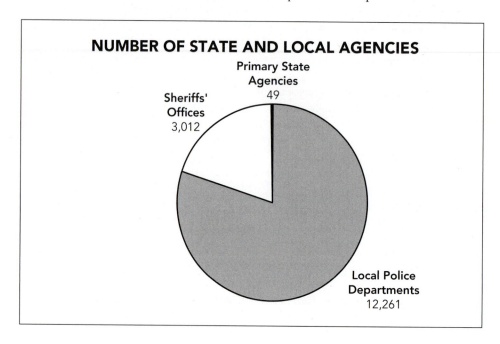

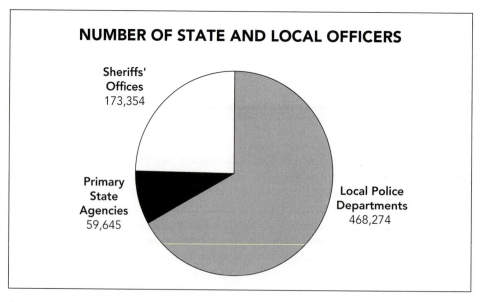

Source: Shelley S. Hyland & Elizabeth Davis, Bureau of Justice Statistics, *Local Police Departments, 2016: Personnel* 2 tbl.2 (2019). Sheriffs' office data excludes agencies without patrol and arrest powers.

Police Chiefs vs. Sheriffs

Although the same rules often also regulate state and federal law enforcement, this book focuses on the law governing local policing. Most of the law discussed applies to the activities of all local agencies that engage in general policing services and have officers with the power to arrest. That includes municipal police departments, county police departments (which are far rarer), and sheriffs' offices, which often provide policing services to unincorporated areas and small towns within a county. For simplicity, when more specificity is required in the book, the text and notes focus on departments that are organized and operated by municipalities.

As you proceed, however, it is worth remembering that governance and political accountability differ significantly for police departments and sheriffs' offices. State law authorizes the creation of municipal, and sometimes county, departments, which are run by politically appointed chiefs. That means city (or county) officials hire and fire those chiefs, and local (or county) governments set police department budgets, allowing them to require the agencies to adhere to specific goals and means set by the public officials. Those officials in turn are elected or appointed by those who are elected. Some differences might arise between municipal and county departmental accountability from differences in governmental structures and the fact that county elections tend to be of lower salience, but the basic structure of accountability for municipal and county departments is identical.

By contrast, sheriffs are state constitutional officers: Local officials cannot remove sheriffs from office, and they must fund their offices adequately, without conditioning that funding on performing in specific ways. The effect is that sheriffs are far less constrained in exercising their discretion and are far less controllable by other public officials. See James Tomberlin, Note, *"Don't Elect Me": Sheriffs and the Need for Reform in County Law Enforcement*, 104 Va. L. Rev. 113, 129, 133–134 (2018).

Of course, sheriffs have their own accountability mechanism: They are directly elected. In his study of sheriffs, James Tomberlin argues that county elections do not, in practice, operate as much of a check on sheriff conduct. Looking around the country, it is hard to disagree. Many elections are uncontested, and when there is competition, incumbents have an enormous advantage. Communities have even less information about what sheriffs do than they do about local police departments. Many complain that local police departments and officers are insufficiently accountable. Even a cursory look suggests that sheriff accountability to the public might be even more limited.

As with federal agencies, local agencies vary enormously in size. About half of all local police departments employ fewer than ten sworn officers, but agencies with more than 100 officers employ nearly two-thirds of all local officers.

LOCAL POLICE DEPARTMENTS AND SWORN OFFICERS, BY SIZE OF AGENCY, 2016

Size of Agency	Departments		Full-Time Sworn Officers	
	Number	Percent	Number	Percent
All departments	12,261	100.0	468,274	100.0
1,000 or more full-time-equivalent sworn officers	45	0.4	153,438	32.8
500–999	53	0.4	37,738	8.1
250–499	101	0.8	34,634	7.4
100–249	425	3.5	62,782	13.4
50–99	845	6.9	57,398	12.3
25–49	1,587	12.9	54,677	11.7
10–24	3,358	27.4	47,083	10.1
5–9	2,875	23.4	15,219	3.3
2–4	2,203	18.0	4,653	1.0
1	770	6.3	652	0.1

Source: Shelley S. Hyland & Elizabeth Davis, Bureau of Justice Statistics, *Local Police Departments, 2016: Personnel* 3 tbl.3 (2019). Rounding leads to percentages that total more than 100 percent.

Really, though, when you think about agencies by size, the New York City Police Department (NYPD) stands in a class of its own. The NYPD employs approximately 36,000 police officers, more than three times the size of the Chicago Police Department, which is the next largest, and 2.5 times as many officers as there are agents of the Federal Bureau of Investigation (FBI). In fact, there are more police officers in New York City than there are armed forces in any military in Central America. Beyond New York City, the following table gives you some perspective on the largest local agencies.

25 LARGEST LOCAL POLICE DEPARTMENTS IN THE UNITED STATES, BY NUMBER OF FULL-TIME SWORN OFFICERS, 2016

Name of Department	Population Served	Number of Full-Time Sworn Officers
New York City (N.Y.) Police	8,537,653	36,008
Chicago (Ill.) Police	2,704,958	11,965
Los Angeles (Cal.) Police	3,976,322	9,870
Philadelphia (Pa.) Police	1,567,872	6,031
Houston (Tex.) Police	2,254,546	5,203
Washington, D.C., Metropolitan Police	681,170	3,712

Name of Department	Population Served	Number of Full-Time Sworn Officers
Dallas (Tex.) Police	1,236,028	3,408
Miami-Dade (Fla.) Police	1,345,983	2,723
Phoenix (Ariz.) Police	1,615,017	2,689
Las Vegas (Nev.) Metropolitan Police	1,592,178	2,566
Baltimore (Md.) Police	614,664	2,524
Nassau County (N.Y.) Police	1,065,674	2,462
Suffolk County (N.Y.) Police	1,320,309	2,385
San Francisco (Cal.) Police	870,887	2,356
Detroit (Mich.) Police	672,795	2,250
San Antonio (Tex.) Police	1,492,483	2,244
Boston (Mass.) Police	673,184	2,099
Memphis (Tenn.) Police	652,717	2,012
Honolulu (Haw.) Police	992,605	1,962
Milwaukee (Wis.) Police	595,047	1,879
Baltimore County (Md.) Police	831,026	1,869
San Diego (Cal.) Police	1,406,630	1,857
Columbus (Ohio) Police	841,563	1,838
Austin (Tex.) Police	947,890	1,807
Charlotte-Mecklenburg (N.C.) Police	892,705	1,743

Source: Shelley S. Hyland & Elizabeth Davis, Bureau of Justice Statistics, *Local Police Departments, 2016: Personnel* app. tbl.1 (2019).

Agency size matters a lot in policing. Agencies with fewer police officers often cannot have the same kind of specialization or structure as larger agencies do. It should not be surprising that whereas almost all agencies in large jurisdictions have internal affairs and crime analysis units, those kinds of units are far less common in smaller departments. Similarly, nationally, about one in eight local police officers is female, and one in four local officers is Black or Hispanic, and those numbers are going up with time. See Shelley S. Hyland & Elizabeth Davis, Bureau of Justice Statistics, *Local Police Departments, 2016: Personnel* 5–6 (2019). Yet agencies in large jurisdictions have on average far more women and Black and Hispanic officers than agencies in smaller towns. See *id.*

Still, size isn't everything. An agency with 300 officers might police a struggling Rust Belt city with an eroding industrial base, entrenched poverty, budgetary cutbacks, and drug and violent crime. Or it might police a booming suburb with a large and progressive professional class, good schools, and medical care, facing conflicts arising from wealth disparity and racial divisions. Communities vary by population density; housing stock; wealth; education levels; age distributions; racial and ethnic diversity; risk of terrorism and other critical incidents; and strength of social, educational, and medical services. Agencies often vary enormously in the ratio of officers to citizens in the jurisdiction and the size of the jurisdiction. They also vary in their hiring standards, their training capacity, and their management. All those characteristics also affect the nature of policing.

2.   What Do Police Officers Do?

Reread the notes you made about what police do. How does your list compare with this description?

Nat'l Research Council of the Nat'l Academies, *Fairness and Effectiveness in Policing: The Evidence*
57–78 (Wesley Skogan & Kathleen Frydl eds., 2004)

Uniformed Patrol

The bulk of police work is conducted by uniformed officers assigned to patrol specific geographic areas (beats). Typically, roughly 60 percent of all sworn officers in city police departments are assigned to the patrol bureau, and these officers have the vast majority of police officer contacts with the general public. More than 90 percent of the local police agencies that employ 100 or more sworn officers assign at least three-fourths of their patrol force to automobile patrol. A substantial proportion of agencies employing 100 or more officers (and nearly all of the big-city agencies) assign officers to walk foot beats, with some devoting more than a third of their patrol force to such duty. Most agencies also conduct some patrol on motorcycles. . . . In the last decade or so, many agencies have added bicycles to the list of conveyances via which their officers patrol. . . .

The bulk of patrol officer contacts with the public involve responding to calls for service. Overall, 65 percent of all local police officers worked by responding to calls for service in 1999. In less specialized, smaller agencies, as many at 90 percent did so. Historically, one of the most important changes in policing has been the growth of publicly initiated, as opposed to police-initiated, interactions between police and community residents. This has been driven by the development and widespread adoption of communication systems designed to allow individuals to quickly contact the police and, in turn, for law enforcement agencies to quickly dispatch officers in response. Most important among these was the widespread adoption of a three-digit emergency number—911. . . . Widespread use of cell phones has made contacting police departments or even individual officers even easier. On the police-to-resident side of the coin, the most important advancement has been the use of computer-aided dispatch (CAD) systems that allow dispatchers to track the status and whereabouts of patrol officers and direct them to the person who is requesting assistance in an efficient fashion. . . .

About half of all calls to the police result in the dispatch of a police officer. Perhaps contrary to expectation, most of these calls do not involve either serious crimes or pressing emergencies. . . . Research indicates that between 70 and 80 percent of dispatches are based on requests for order maintenance and service, rather than criminal activities. Moreover, when officers appear on the scene, they often find a somewhat different situation from what they expected on the basis of the initial call; many calls that initially appear to involve criminal activity in fact involve no actionable offense.

The ability to easily telephone the police has affected the allocation of police personnel and the nature of patrol work itself. In the absence of a formal program to actively screen calls and make decisions on whether or not to dispatch a car in response, what the general public defines as worthy of police attention dominates police patrol work. On the positive side, this ensures that, to no small degree, the police will be highly responsive to what local residents think they need from their local police department. On the negative side, the "you call, we come" system reduces the capacity of both police chiefs and the elected officials who represent the *collectively* defined goals and purposes of the police to achieve those goals. Too many of their resources may be committed to responding to individuals' insistent calls.

Recent thinking on policing, which has been driven by community policing and increased interest in crime prevention, has placed a high priority on increasing proactive activities initiated by uniformed patrol officers. . . . Proactive or officer-initiated police work involves a number of different activities: field interrogations of pedestrians, traffic stops, checks of buildings or other areas for possible criminal activity, and informal contacts with the public. There is substantial variation in the level of officer-initiated activity in different departments. . . .

Patrol officers also spend a significant part of their unassigned time conducting what is known as "preventive patrol". Since the advent of modern police forces in the 19th century, preventive patrol has been the core police activity, designed to prevent crime by deterring potential offenders through a visible police presence, to create feelings of public safety, and to make officers available for service in local communities with uniformed patrol forces.

One important idea animating interest in problem-solving and community policing (which are discussed in detail below) is that both call for less reactive and more proactive uses of the uniformed patrol force. Of course, the idea that the police patrol operations ought to be proactive is hardly a new idea. One goal of patrol was always to spot and investigate suspicious activity as well as respond to calls for service. Such activities were justified by a strong interest in *preventing* crime as well as responding after crime had occurred. Indeed, in the late 1960s, some police departments were relying on a police tactic described as "aggressive preventive patrol" (which bears a close resemblance to what is often described as "zero tolerance policing" today). The aim was to make the police a credible presence on the street by using their powers to stop people and ask questions. The hope was that, by doing so, the police could discourage offenders from committing offenses and interrupt situations that were leading to crimes. . . .

An important question is whether the new forms of proactive policing are any different from the old forms. . . . [S]ome police departments, under the rubric of community and problem-oriented policing, have embraced strategies that look a great deal like some of the old proactive strategies of policing. Aggressive preventive patrol has been resurrected as zero tolerance policing. Directed patrol operations, in which the police simply dispatch police officers to places and times where crimes are likely to occur, have reemerged as a limited form of problem solving policing. Location oriented patrol has reemerged as "hot spot policing" in which the police identify particular locations in which crimes are likely to occur, and dispatch patrol officers to watch over the hot spot.

Yet what seems most importantly new about the proactive forms of policing recommended under the rubric of community policing has less to do with proactivity than with the creation of the "warrant" for the proactive police activity. A crucial difference between reactive and proactive policing is that individuals calling the police for help provide legitimacy for the police in reactive policing, while in proactive policing legitimacy comes from the professionalism of the police themselves, as they identify crime and other community problems. One key concept of community policing is that communities should have a role in shaping police priorities with respect to the policing of their neighborhoods. Citizen guidance emanates not just from city hall and not just from individuals calling the police. Instead, formal and informal consultations with the community give the police some guidance about priorities, allowing them to be responsive not only to individual demands or city wide mandates, but also to local neighborhood concerns. This consultation, in turn, could be expected to warrant police actions through a political agreement as well as their legal authority and professional commitments. What might be new about the way that community policing approaches the idea of proactivity, then, is not only to agree that it is important, but also to take some pains to limit and justify the form that proactive policing takes. Community policing urges community consultation to create a political warrant for proactive policing. . . .

Maintaining Order . . .

Many order maintenance activities of the police are relatively mundane. Traffic control, for instance, can be seen as a form of order maintenance to the extent that it facilitates people going about the routines of their daily lives without interruption. Special events, such as sporting events or parades, also call on the police to maintain order. The policing of overtly political events is far more complicated, however. . . . [T]he police must balance their responsibility to maintain order with the equally important responsibility to protect individual civil and political liberties, such as freedom of speech and assembly. The changing face of disorder, however, militates against simplified and universal strategies in dealing with protests or disturbances. . . . It must also be noted that some disturbances—such as rioting after athletic events—feature the impaired judgment of a number of inebriated participants; this can also create difficulty for police trying to maintain order without relying on broad use of law enforcement powers.

Providing Service

Another core feature of police activity involves the provision of miscellaneous services that are divorced from the law enforcement and order maintenance or peacekeeping functions. Research indicates that service activities constitute a major portion of what patrol officers do day in and day out, making up between one-third and one-half of all calls for service to police departments. These services include but are not limited to giving directions, answering questions from the public, monitoring crowds at public events, finding lost children, assisting motorists who have locked themselves out of their vehicles, escorting merchants to late night depositories, and ensuring that a drunk person makes it safely home. . . .

State Patrolman Schlageter helps a motorist find his destination in Castle Rock, Colorado. November 1958.

Controlling Traffic

In most large agencies, traffic enforcement is conducted primarily by officers assigned to a specialized traffic unit (although general patrol officers also make traffic stops). Traffic stops comprise the most common form of contact between police officers and the public. . . .

Preventing Crime

Developments in policing over the past 20 years have blurred the distinction between the traditional categories of law enforcement, service provision, and order maintenance. There has also been a new interest in expanding the traditional notions of the police role in crime prevention, creating a fourth general category of police activity. While many crime prevention programs include activities that have been defined along with more traditional categories, emergent ideas of crime prevention also include opportunity reduction strategies, such as target hardening, situational crime prevention, and reduction of repeat victimization. In addition, expanded crime prevention strategies often involve police mobilization of third parties to exert informal social control. . . .

Investigating Crimes

The investigation of alleged criminal incidents is a basic police function, but probably one more significant in the popular mind than in the context of everyday policing. While investigation has been emphasized in entertainment media, in practice, criminal investigation plays a relatively small role in the day-to-day activities of police departments. In large departments, investigations are generally conducted by specialized units, such as homicide, robbery, sexual assault, property crimes, and so on. In small agencies, there is little specialization of function of any sort. Criminal investigation units typically involve only about 10 percent of all sworn officers in an agency. . . .

Processing Information

In a broad sense, one of the most important roles of the police is to process information. That is to say, law enforcement agencies collect information, process it, act on it, and in some cases provide it to other agencies including the public; some of the information collected by the police is unique to their organization—for example, police reports—and plays an important role in the larger systems—for example, processing insurance claims. . . .

Specialized Services

Since the Progressive Era at the turn of the 20th century, professional police administration has emphasized the development of specialized units to carry out particular police responsibilities. The most common specialized units are those related to criminal investigation, traffic enforcement, juvenile delinquency, police community relations, crimes of vice, domestic violence, gangs, and hate crimes. Specialized bomb and arson squads and SWAT units, or specially designated and trained officers are found in most law enforcement agencies. Some community policing programs have been carried out by specialized units, while others are department-wide efforts.

The rationale for the formation of these units is both strategic and managerial. Specialization enables officers to focus their efforts on problems important to their organization and to gain special knowledge and expertise. In this respect, specialized unit officers stand in contrast to the generalist function of patrol officers. The existence of a specialized unit also signals to the wider community that police are taking a particular problem seriously.

SWAT teams are a good example. Prior to the late 1960s, police departments responded to special threat situations—such as those involving barricaded gunmen and hostages—on an ad hoc basis, simply handling the situation in whatever way seemed appropriate at the time. When several notorious incidents during the 1960s—one example is Charles Whitman's 1966 murderous sniping rampage in Austin, Texas—showed that the ad hoc approach was wanting in many regards, many police departments developed cadres of specially trained and equipped officers who could handle crisis situations in a systematic fashion. Over the years, SWAT teams have handled a myriad of assignments besides the aforementioned hostage and barricaded subject situations. These tasks include dignitary protection, responding to civil disturbances, stakeouts, and the service of search and arrest warrants that pose a greater than normal risk of injury to police officers and the public. Thus SWAT teams give police managers the ability to deal with a variety of problems that require specialized knowledge and equipment without having to go to the expense of training and equipping all of their officers.

At the same time, specialized units have often been beset by serious management problems. Overspecialization can result in inefficiencies by diverting too many officers from other core functions (especially patrol) and the development of overly complex bureaucratic structures. Specialized units also create potential problems of control and accountability. Vice units, for example, have historically been the loci of some of the worst forms of corruption. Intelligence units engaged in illegal spying on legitimate political activities. Police-community relations units created in the 1960s were often detached from the mainstream of police operations and deemed largely irrelevant to the problem they were created to solve. Some current gang units have become detached from the official channels of supervision, thereby raising serious issues related to effectiveness or accountability.

Despite the range of activities officers engage in, members of the public commonly encounter police in just a few ways. According to federal data, for example, in 2015, approximately 21 percent of U.S. residents age 16 or older—about 53.5 million persons—had contact with the police during the prior year. In 2011, 26 percent of residents had such contact. Elizabeth Davis et al., Bureau of Justice Statistics, *Contacts Between Police and the Public, 2015* 1 (2018). Residents initiated half of those contacts, mostly by reporting a crime or noncrime emergency. Police initiated the other half of contacts, overwhelmingly by pulling over a car in a traffic stop. Altogether, more than one in three people who had any contact with the police did so in the context of a traffic stop (38.2 percent), something that happened to more than 1 in 12 drivers. A similar fraction of the public who reported contact with the police (36.8 percent) had called the police to make a report about a crime or other emergency. See *id.* at 9 fig.2.

Men have more contact with the police than women, although women are more likely to call the police than men. Whites are more likely to have contact than Blacks or Hispanics, but much of that disparity comes from the fact that whites are more likely to initiate contact with the police. More males than females, Blacks than whites and Hispanics, and young drivers than older ones are pulled over by the police. See *id.* at 2 tbl.1.

Although these data provide some perspective, keep in mind that what we don't know about policing in the United States swamps what we do. What else would you want to know about policing? What might the effects be of not knowing?

B.   How the Law Generates Policing

Now that you know something about the police and policing, it is time to learn something about the law that governs them. You can think of the law of the police in two parts. Most of this book considers law that constrains police authority or that remedies violations of legal rules. But those kinds of law presume a more basic form of law about the police: the law that generates policing by authorizing and empowering officers and departments.[2]

1.   The Legal Structure of Police Authority

No one can just put out a shingle and announce that he is a police officer. How are police officers made?

a.   Step 1: The States Retain the Police Power Under the Constitution

The U.S. Constitution grants only limited powers to the federal government, and those powers do not include general regulation of crime and public order. The Tenth Amendment determines what happens to powers not given to the federal government:

> The powers not delegated to the United States by the Constitution, nor prohibited by it to the States, are reserved to the States respectively, or to the people.

U.S. Const. amend. X.

One of the powers retained by states is the police power. The police power is broader than traditional policing and notoriously difficult to define. Nevertheless, it clearly includes "the suppression of violent crime and vindication of its victims," United States v. Morrison, 529 U.S 598, 617–618 (2000), as well as state authority over the minutiae of public life, including preventing conflicts of rights and maintaining public order.[3]

b.   Step 2: State Constitutions Delegate Police Power to State Governments

State constitutions broadly delegate to state legislatures the power to legislate in the public interest and to state governors the power to ensure that laws are executed, effectively granting the police power to state governments.

---

[2] Some statutes play both roles, authorizing police to make arrests within some limits, for example, or permitting them to use force under some conditions. Such laws are discussed further in Chapters 7 and 8, which discuss arrests and the use of force.

[3] For an argument that the police power of the government has problematic, patriarchal origins and a vast scope that permits almost uncheckable power to regulate private activity, see Marcus Dirk Dubber, *The Police Power* (2005). For an argument against broadly construing the police power, see Randy E. Barnett, *The Proper Scope of the Police Power*, 79 Notre Dame L. Rev. 429 (2004).

c.   Step 3: States Create Municipalities and Empower Them to Create Police Departments

Municipal governments are political subdivisions of states created and empowered by state law. In some states, in accordance with what is known as *Dillon's Rule*, local governments have only those powers specifically granted to them by states. In most states, however, state constitutions and statutes permit some form of *municipal home rule*, which allows a local government to define its structure by charter and exercise the police power without express state legislative enactments. The degree of authority local governments may exercise varies enormously from state to state, but every state permits local governments to organize police departments and select police officers, either expressly, by statute or constitutional provision, or by virtue of a general statutory or constitutional grant of home-rule power.

d.   Step 4: State Legislatures Empower Qualified and Certified Police Officers Hired by Local Police Departments

Although states allow localities to create police departments, they retain the power to determine whom localities may choose to serve as a police officer and what powers those officers will have. Thus, state statutes set minimum qualifications for police officers regarding characteristics such as age, education, and criminal history, and they set minimum training and testing standards for officers. Legislatures also delegate the power to establish further standards to state agencies, known as Peace Officer Standards and Training councils or boards. An officer who satisfies these statutory and regulatory standards may receive state certification and, when selected by a local government to serve on a police force, may exercise the powers of a police officer, including the power to execute warrants, to conduct arrests without warrants, and to use force to do so.

e.   Step 5: Local Governments Create and Fund Police Departments and Hire Police Officers to Staff Them

Local governments create local police departments by charter and by ordinance, and then they fund them through ordinary budgetary processes. The vast majority of a department's budget is devoted to paying for personnel, and cities determine how many officers a department is permitted to hire largely through the budgeting process. Police departments then hire police officers based on standards set by the department and in accordance with local, state, and federal law regarding hiring public employees.

As you can see, creating a local police officer requires both state and local action.

2.   Building a Police Officer in Charlottesville, Virginia

To get more specific, look at how policing is authorized in Charlottesville, Virginia. The Virginia Constitution allows the General Assembly to provide for cities and empower them. Can you see how the other steps described

above are reflected in these laws? Look specifically for how Virginia determines who is qualified to be an officer, what must happen before an individual exercises the powers of a police officer, and what those powers are. In the local law, look for who exercises control over what officers do and how.

a.   Relevant Virginia Statutes

VA. CODE. ANN. §§15.2-1700 TO -1701, 15.2-1704 TO -1706

Section 15.2-1700. Preservation of peace and good order.

Any locality may provide for the protection of its inhabitants and property and for the preservation of peace and good order therein.

Section 15.2-1701. Organization of police forces.

Any locality may, by ordinance, provide for the organization of its authorized police forces. Such forces shall include a chief of police, and such officers and other personnel as appropriate.

When a locality provides for a police department, the chief of police shall be the chief law-enforcement officer of that locality. However, in towns, the chief law-enforcement officer may be called the town sergeant.

Section 15.2-1704. Powers and duties of police force.

A. The police force of a locality is hereby invested with all the power and authority which formerly belonged to the office of constable at common law and is responsible for the prevention and detection of crime, the apprehension of criminals, the safeguard of life and property, the preservation of peace and the enforcement of state and local laws, regulations, and ordinances.[4]

B. A police officer has no authority in civil matters, except (i) to execute and serve temporary detention and emergency custody orders and any other powers granted to law-enforcement officers in [statutes providing for court-ordered involuntary emergency detention for mentally ill individuals who pose a threat to themselves or others], (ii) to serve an order of protection pursuant to [statutes providing for court protection orders in cases of family abuse], (iii) to execute all warrants or summons as may be placed in his hands by any magistrate serving

---

[4] *Ed. note:* Additional state laws permit local law enforcement officers to execute warrants and summonses, Va. Code Ann. §19.2-76; direct a person to appear for the purpose of executing a warrant or summons, Va. Code Ann. §19.2-73.1; issue a subpoena requiring a person to appear to answer some misdemeanor and traffic charges, Va. Code Ann. §19.2-73.2; issue a summons in lieu of a warrant for some misdemeanor offenses, Va. Code Ann. §19.2-74; make warrantless arrests for felonies, any crime committed in the officer's presence, and some other misdemeanors, Va. Code Ann. §§19.2-81, 19.2-81.3; arrest individuals suspected of violating federal immigration laws, Va. Code Ann. §19.2-81.6. Although state statutes seem to prohibit all searches by local police officers except pursuant to a warrant, Va. Code Ann. §19.2-59, Virginia courts have recognized many exceptions to this rule.

the locality and to make due return thereof, and (iv) to deliver, serve, execute, and enforce orders of isolation and quarantine issued pursuant to §§32.1-48.09,[5] 32.1-48.012,[6] and 32.1-48.014[7] and to deliver, serve, execute, and enforce an emergency custody order issued pursuant to §32.1-48.02. . . .[8]

Section 15.2-1705. Minimum qualifications; waiver.

A. The chief of police and all police officers of any locality, all deputy sheriffs and jail officers in this Commonwealth, and all law-enforcement officers as defined in §9.1-101[9] who enter upon the duties of such office after July 1, 1994, are required to meet the following minimum qualifications for office. Such person shall (i) be a citizen of the United States, (ii) be required to undergo a background investigation including fingerprint-based criminal history records inquiries to both the Central Criminal Records Exchange and the Federal Bureau of Investigation, (iii) have a high school education or have passed a high school equivalency examination approved by the Board of Education, (iv) possess a valid driver's license if required by the duties of office to operate a motor vehicle, (v) undergo a physical examination, subsequent to a conditional offer of employment, conducted under the supervision of a licensed physician, (vi) be at least eighteen years of age, (vii) not have been convicted of or pled guilty or no contest to a felony or any offense that would be a felony if committed in the Commonwealth, and (viii) not have produced a positive result on a pre-employment drug screening, if such screening is required by the hiring law-enforcement agency or jail, where the

---

[5] *Ed. note:* This section permits the State Health Commissioner to issue orders of quarantine to prevent the transmission of communicable diseases that threaten public health. If the order covers a geographic area rather than a specific person, the Governor must first declare a state of emergency. Both law enforcement officers and health officials are permitted to deliver orders of quarantine pursuant to this section.

[6] *Ed. note:* This section permits the State Health Commissioner to issue an order of isolation for individuals reasonably suspected to be infected with a communicable disease that threatens public health if necessary to contain transmission of the disease. Both law enforcement officers and health officials are permitted to deliver orders of isolation pursuant to this section.

[7] *Ed. note:* This section permits law enforcement agencies to enforce orders of quarantine or isolation as directed by the State Health Commissioner. The State Health Commissioner may authorize agencies to detain or arrest people who have or may fail or refuse to comply with such an order. It also provides that local law enforcement officers may enforce orders of quarantine or isolation issued by the Director of the Centers for Disease Control and Prevention.

[8] *Ed. note:* This section permits the State Health Commissioner to issue orders to individuals to report to local health departments for treatment and/or custody and allows local law enforcement officers to take custody of subjects of such orders. For more on these powers, see the text box below on the power to police COVID-19.

[9] *Ed. note:* Va. Code §9.1-101 provides:

As used in this chapter or in Chapter 23 (§19.2-387 et seq.) of Title 19.2, unless the context requires a different meaning:

. . . "Law-enforcement officer" means any full-time or part-time employee of a police department or sheriff's office which is a part of or administered by the Commonwealth or any political subdivision thereof, or any full-time or part-time employee of a private police department, and who is responsible for the prevention and detection of crime and the enforcement of the penal, traffic or highway laws of the Commonwealth . . .

positive result cannot be explained to the law-enforcement agency or jail adminis-trator's satisfaction. . . .

B. Upon request of a sheriff or chief of police . . . the Department of Criminal Justice Services is hereby authorized to waive the requirements for qualification as set out in subsection A of this section for good cause shown.

Section 15.2-1706. Certification through training required for all law-enforcement officers; waiver of requirements.

A. All law-enforcement officers as defined in §9.1-101 . . . must be certified through the successful completion of training at an approved criminal justice training academy in order to remain eligible for appointment or employment. In order to obtain such certification, all entry level law-enforcement officers seeking certi-fication on or after July 1, 2003, shall successfully complete statewide certification examinations developed and administered by the Department of Criminal Justice Services. . . .

b.   Charlottesville City Charter

In 1946, the General Assembly of the State of Virginia enacted a Charter for the City of Charlottesville, which also appears in the Charlottesville City Code of 1976. It includes the following:

Section 14.—Same—Powers enumerated.

The council of the city, except as hereinbefore provided, shall have . . . power to make such ordinances, bylaws, orders and regulations as it may deem desirable to carry out the following powers which are hereby vested in them:

. . . Twentieth. Additional and incidental powers; jurisdiction beyond corporate limits. To pass all bylaws, rules and ordinances, not repugnant to the constitu-tion and laws of the state, which they may deem necessary for the good order and government of the city, the management of its property, the conduct of its affairs, the peace, comfort, convenience, order, morals, health, and protec-tion of its citizens or their property, including authority to keep a city police force. . . .

Section 18.—Conservators of the peace.

. . . [T]he chief of police and the policemen of the city shall also be conservators of the peace within the limits aforesaid, and all proper arrests may be made and war-rants of arrest executed by such chief of police and policemen.

c.   Charlottesville City Code

CHAPTER 2. ARTICLE III. CITY MANAGER

Sec. 2-149—General authority with respect to city departments and personnel.

(a) The city manager shall have charge of the appointment of competent, quali-fied officers and employees to the administrative departments of the city and shall have the power to dismiss, suspend and discipline, in accordance with duly adopted personnel regulations, all officers and employees in such departments, except as otherwise specifically provided by law. . . .

(d) The city manager shall have the power to set aside any action taken by a department head or other officer subject to his control, except as otherwise specifically provided by law.

CHAPTER 20. POLICE. ARTICLE I.—IN GENERAL

Sec. 20-1—Control of city manager.

The police force shall be under the control of the city manager for the purpose of enforcing peace and order and for the execution of the laws of the state, this Code and other ordinances of the city and the performance of such other duties as the city council may prescribe.

Sec. 20-2—Appointment of chief and other officers.

The city manager shall appoint a chief of police, such appointment to be approved by the city council. The city manager, with the advice of the chief of police, shall appoint such other officers as may be deemed necessary.

Sec. 20-3—General powers and duties of chief.

(a) The chief of police shall be the chief executive of the police department, but he shall always be subject to the orders and regulations of the city manager and the city council. He shall be under the control of the city manager and the city council for the purpose of enforcing peace and order and executing the laws of the state and ordinances of the city. It shall be the duty of the police force to respect and obey orders of the chief not in conflict with this chapter.

(b) The chief shall be responsible for the good order of the city and for the general good conduct of the members and officers of the police force. He shall cause to be served all processes directed to him by a magistrate or the judge of the district court and all orders of the city manager.

Sec. 20-4—Authority of chief to promulgate rules and regulations.

The chief of police shall have the authority to promulgate rules and regulations for the conduct of the members of the police department. Such rules and regulations shall be subject to the approval of the city manager and shall be in conformity with the laws of the state, the Charter and the provisions of this Code.

NOTES AND QUESTIONS

1. *Developing a definition.* Based on these legal provisions, what *is* a police officer? Can you come up with a functional definition?

2. *Who is in charge?* Who controls the police in Charlottesville?

3. *What do police do?* What does Charlottesville want its police to do?

4. *Responsibility vs. authority.* Va. Code §15.2-1704 makes police "responsible for" certain activities. So does the Charlottesville City Code in §20.3(b). What does that mean? Does it define the scope of police powers? The scope of their duties? Do

you know what police officers are permitted to do? Note that there is no consensus about the precise powers of a constable at common law, but it included the power to arrest and to collect and present evidence in court.

5. *Force in Virginia.* All states permit officers to use force under some circumstances. Unlike most other states, Virginia has no statute authorizing police officers to use force. Instead, common law cases reassure officers that they are permitted to use reasonable force to carry out their other duties, although the details of that permission are vague. See, e.g., Pike v. Eubank, 90 S.E.2d 821, 825 (Va. 1956); Davidson v. Allam, 130 S.E. 245, 246 (Va. 1925).

6. *Limits on civil enforcement.* In addition to the activities for which §15.2-1704(A) makes police responsible, the statute forbids police from exercising power in civil matters, except for those listed in subsection B. What do the activities in subsection B have in common? What does that tell you about policing in Virginia?

7. *Qualifications.* States vary in their qualifications for police officers. All states require a minimum age between 18 and 21. Most states require officers to be U.S. citizens. Most require a high school diploma, but no more, although some set no minimum education requirement, and a couple require some college credits. States overwhelmingly expressly preclude felons from serving as officers, and many also disqualify people convicted of misdemeanor drug offenses, crimes of moral turpitude,[10] or domestic violence offenses (which as a matter of federal law preclude an individual from possessing a firearm). See Lautenberg Amendment, 18 U.S.C. §922(g)(9). Some states disqualify those who have been dishonorably discharged from the military. In addition, as in Virginia, states often require background investigations to determine whether a potential officer is of good moral character, medical examinations, physical testing, and/or psychological screening for potential officers. How do you think these qualifications should be determined? Are there other categories of qualifications you would wish to see?

8. *Certification.* Like other states, Virginia requires that all police officers be certified (§15.2-1706). What are the conditions for certification? What purpose does certification serve? What could be required to gain certification? How might you use certification to change policing in Virginia (or elsewhere) if you wanted to do so?

9. *State requirements.* Why might Virginia require an ordinance to establish a police department? Why might it require a chief?

10. *Local government form.* Municipal governments come in a variety of forms, including mayor–council, council–manager, and commission. Charlottesville is a council–manager municipality. It is run by an elected city council, which makes policy and budgetary decisions and sets tax rates. That council hires a professional city

---

[10] Although long-standing, the *moral turpitude* standard has no fixed meaning. It often is used to describe "conduct that is inherently base, vile, or depraved, and contrary to the private and social duties many owes to his fellow men or to society in general." Navarro-Lopez v. Gonzales, 503 F.3d 1063, 1068 (9th Cir. 2007). That can include a variety of crimes from violent crimes and fraud to incest and animal fighting. For further discussion of the standard, see Julia A. Simon-Kerr, *Moral Turpitude*, 2012 Utah L. Rev. 1001 (2012).

manager to implement and administer city policy. There is a mayor, but the mayor is part of the city council and does not have independent executive functions. How might governance of policing be different in a strong-mayor form of city government in which an elected mayor has administrative authority, including the power to appoint and dismiss the police chief, and the power to prepare a city budget to be approved by the city council?

11. *Internal rules.* The Charlottesville City Code provides rules and regulations for the conduct of official city employees, including police officers. The Charlottesville Police Department also has its own policies and procedures. Internal orders in police departments are often the most important rules governing the police, and they are discussed more in Chapter 10. What would you want to see in such rules?

The Power to Police COVID-19

There is nothing natural about the power to police. It comes from the law. When you see police officers exercising power—especially new power—you should ask yourself: Where, precisely, does that power come from? What are its limits? How could that power be restricted, expanded, or changed?

Take the example of police enforcement of restrictions imposed to prevent the spread of SARS-CoV-2 and the disease it causes, COVID-19. In the spring of 2020, states imposed rules to reduce disease transmission, and officers throughout the country began responding to calls, issuing citations and summonses, making arrests, and stopping drivers at checkpoints demanding to know the purpose of their travel. Where does all this power come from? Each state has laws in place to facilitate state responses to the spread of communicable diseases that threaten public health, and when triggered, those laws can expand the power of local law enforcement. Because you are now familiar with Virginia's laws empowering the police, let's use Virginia as an example.

As Va. Code Ann. §15.2-1704 (above) indicates, local law enforcement officers are empowered by Virginia state law "to deliver, serve, execute, and enforce orders of isolation and quarantine." After the World Health Organization declared the COVID-19 outbreak a "public health emergency of international concern," and the U.S. Health and Human Services Secretary declared a national public health emergency, the Virginia Governor issued an executive order, Va. Exec. Order No. 51 (Mar. 12, 2020), declaring a state of emergency, and the Governor and State Health Commissioner together declared a public health emergency in Virginia. The Health Commissioner and Governor also issued declarations pursuant to Va. Code Ann. §32.1-13, and related statutes, which allow the State Health Commissioner broad powers to take actions to control the spread of communicable diseases. Among other restrictions, these declarations forbid restaurants, theaters, or fitness facilities from serving more than ten patrons. Under Va. Code Ann. §32.1-27, willful violations of such orders constitute a Class 1 misdemeanor. As local police officers have the power to make warrantless arrests for crimes committed in the presence of an officer, §19.2-81, and issue a summons in lieu of an arrest for Class 1 misdemeanors, §19.2-74, local police officers could arrest or summons those who failed to comply with the orders issued by the Governor and Health Commissioner.

Soon after issuing the first set of declarations, the Governor used his authority under Va. Code Ann. §44-146.17, which allows the Governor to issue orders to protect the safety and welfare of Virginians in times of emergency, to issue Va. Exec. Order No. 53 (Mar. 23, 2020), which prohibited all gatherings of ten or more people and called for the closure of all restaurants and recreational and entertainment businesses, and Va. Exec. Order No. 55 (Mar. 30, 2020), which instructed all people in Virginia to remain in their homes except for limited purposes and to maintain a social distance of at least six feet in public. Under §44-146.17, such orders have the force of law, and violations are punishable as Class 1 misdemeanors, which again gives local police the power to enforce the orders against those who fail to comply.

In sum, state law grants Virginia's Governor and State Health Commissioner the power to manage emergencies by issuing orders. Once issued, those orders effectively trigger new crimes, defined as the willful violation of those orders. And those crimes, like other crimes in Virginia, are enforceable by local police officers. In this way, the state's response to a public health emergency functionally expanded the power of local police by giving them one more basis on which to make an arrest.

C.   *The Essence of Policing*

The questions of what officers do and how police power is generated are distinct from a deeper question: What is policing for?

1.   Policing and the Capacity to Use Force

Egon Bittner, a renowned sociologist, made an influential attempt to answer this question in his article *Florence Nightingale in Pursuit of Willie Sutton: A Theory of the Police,* in *The Potential for Reform of Criminal Justice* 17–41 (Herbert Jacob ed., 1974). Bittner's theory of the police function is based on "what their existence makes available in society that, all things being equal, would not be otherwise available." As he puts it:

> My thesis is that police are empowered and required to impose or, as the case may be, coerce a provisional solution upon emergent problems without having to brook or defer to opposition of any kind, and that further, their competence to intervene extends to every kind of emergency, without any exceptions whatever. This and this alone is what the existence of the police uniquely provides, and it is on this basis that they may be required to do the work of thief-catchers and of nurses, depending on the occasion.

Id. at 18. That might seem surprising. Many of us believe that the core of policing is investigating crime and arresting criminals. That impression is not entirely accidental. *Dragnet,* which started as a radio drama in 1949 and moved to television soon afterward, was produced collaboratively with the Los Angeles Police Department and its chief, William H. Parker. In it, professional, uncorruptible Sergeant Joe Friday investigated and solved crimes. Television and movie officers have become more complex over the decades. Nevertheless, popular portrayals of the police—and the occupational self-conception of many officers—continues focus on the "endangered crime fighter who battles heroically against the ever-threatening chaos of crime." Peter K. Manning, *Police Work: The Social Organization of Policing* 26–27 (1997).
    Bittner argues against this view of the police. First, he notes police officers spend most of their time in activities other than criminal law enforcement:

> Regardless of how strenuously criminal law enforcement is emphasized in the image of the policeman and in police administration, and regardless of how important police work might actually be for keeping the administration of criminal justice in business, the activity of criminal law enforcement is not at all characteristic of day-to-day, ordinary occupational practices of the vastly preponderant majority of policemen. In other words, when one looks at what policemen actually do, one finds that criminal law enforcement is something that most of them do with the frequency located somewhere between virtually never and very rarely.

Bittner, *supra,* at 22–23. Second, police do not enforce all criminal laws:

> Relying mainly on my observations, I believe the police tend to avoid involvement with offenses in which it is assumed that the accused or suspected culprits will not try to evade the criminal process by flight. Characteristically, for example, they refer

citizens who complain about being defrauded by businesses or landlords directly to the prosecutor. . . . It is at least reasonable to suggest . . . that police interest in criminal law enforcement is limited to those offenses in which the perpetrator needs to be *caught* and where catching him *may* involve the use of physical force. The point in all this is not that the police are simply ignorant of, and uninterested in, the majority of the provisions of the penal code, but that their selectivity follows a specific principle, namely, that they feel called upon to act only when *their* special competence is required, and that special competence is related to the possibility that force *may* have to be used to secure the appearance of a defendant in court.

Id. at 24. Third, police rarely invoke criminal law in their work:

It has become commonplace to say that patrolmen do not invoke the law often. . . . According to estimates issued by the research division of the International Association of Chiefs of Police, "the percentage of the police effort devoted to the traditional criminal law matters probably does not exceed ten per cent." Reiss, who studied the practices of the patrol in a number of American metropolitan centers, in trying to characterize a typical day's work, stated that it defies all efforts of typification "except in the sense that *the modal tour of duty does not involve an arrest* of any person."

Id. at 24–25.

Rather than viewing the criminal law as the *purpose* of policing, Bittner argues that the criminal law is a *tool* of policing:

I am not aware of any descriptions of police work on the streets that support the view that patrolmen walk around, respond to service demands, or intervene in situations, with the provisions of the penal code in mind, matching what they see with some title or another, and deciding whether any particular apparent infraction is serious enough to warrant being referred for further process. While it does happen occasionally that patrolmen arrest some person merely because they have probable cause to believe that he has committed crimes, this is not the way all but a small fraction of arrests come about. In the typical case the formal charge *justifies* the arrest a patrolman makes but is *not* the *reason* for it. The actual reason is located in a domain of considerations to which Professor Wilson referred as the need "to handle the situation," and invoking the law is merely a device whereby this is sometimes accomplished. Since the persons who are arrested at a backyard game of craps are not arrested because they are gambling but because of a complex of situational factors of which no mention is made in the formally filed charge, it would seem specious to try to refine the law pertaining to the charge, since any policeman worth his salt is virtually always in a position to find a *bona fide* charge of some kind when he believes the situation calls for an arrest. In sum, if criminal law enforcement means acting on the basis of, and in accordance with, the law's provisions, then this is something policemen do occasionally, but in their routine work they merely avail themselves of the provisions as a means for attaining other objectives. . . . [P]olicemen use the provisions of the law as a resource for handling problems of all sorts, of which *no mention* is made in the formal charge.

Id. at 27.

Because criminal law is not the core police mandate, Bittner looks to a persistent feature of patrol policing to figure out what that mandate is. He notes that, whatever a police officer is assigned to do, "there exists a tacit understanding that no matter how important the post might be, it is always possible for something else to come up that can distract the patrolman's attention from it and cause him to suspend attending to the assigned task," even though no law or regulation requires him to turn from what he is doing. *Id.* at 28.

> I am saying more than merely that patrolmen, like everybody else, will suspend the performance of an assigned task to turn to some extraordinary exigency. While everybody might respond to the call of an emergency, the policeman's vocational ear is *permanently and specifically attuned* to such calls, and his work attitude throughout is permeated by preparedness to respond to it, whatever he might happen to be doing. In the case at hand, it is virtually certain that any normally competent patrolman would abandon the traffic post to which he was assigned without a moment's hesitation and without regard for the state of the traffic he was supposed to monitor, if it came to his attention that a crime was being committed somewhere at a distance not too far for him to reach in time either to arrest the crime in its course, or to arrest its perpetrator.

Id. Yet police don't rush to the scene of *every* crime in progress. And officers often rush to scenes that involve no crime.

> When I stated . . . that the patrolman will abandon his assignment to rush to the scene of a crime, I assumed without saying that the crime would be something like an act of vandalism, an assault, or a burglary. But if the crime that came to the attention of the officer had been something like a conspiracy by a board of directors of a commercial concern to issue stock with the intention of defrauding investors, or a landlord criminally extorting payments from a tenant, or a used-car dealer culpably turning back an odometer on an automobile he was preparing for sale, the patrolman would scarcely lif[t] his gaze, let alone move into action. The real reason why the patrolman moved was not the fact that what was taking place was a crime in general terms, but because the particular crime was a member of a class of problems *the treatment of which will not abide.* In fact, the patrolman who unhesitatingly left his post to pursue an assailant would have left his post with just a little hesitation to pull a drowning person out of the water, to prevent someone from jumping off the roof of a building, to protect a severely disoriented person from harm, to save people in a burning structure, to disperse a crowd hampering the rescue mission of an ambulance, to take steps to prevent a possible disaster that might result from broken gas lines or water mains, and so on almost endlessly, and entirely without regard to the substantive nature of the problem, as long as it could be said that it involved *something-that-ought-not-to-be-happening-and-about-which-someone-had-better-do-something-now!* These extraordinary events, and the directly intuited needs for control that issue from them, are what the vocational interests of patrolmen are attuned to. And in the circumstances of such events citizens feel entitled and obliged to summon the help of the police.

Id. at 29–30. The consequence is that police respond to a dizzying array of crises, and to Bittner, it can therefore be said that "no human problem exists, or is imaginable, about which it could be said with finality that this certainly could not become the proper business of the police." *Id.* at 30. This vast substantive mandate is a reflection of their unique competence:

> [W]hen it is asked on what terms this police service is made available in every conceivable kind of emergency, the usual answer is that it happens by default because policemen are the only functionaries, professionals, officials—call them what you will—who are available around the clock and who can be counted on to make

house-calls. Further, it is often said that it would be altogether better if policemen were not so often called upon to do chores lying within the spheres of vocational competence of physicians, nurses, and social workers, and did not have to be all things to all men. I believe that these views are based on a profound misconception of what policemen do. . . . Even if physicians and social workers were to work around the clock and make house-calls, the need for the police service in their areas would remain substantial, though it certainly would decline in volume. . . . Indeed, only by assuming a distinct kind of police competence can one understand why psychologists, physicians, and social workers run into problems in *their* work for which they seek police assistance. In other words, when a social worker "calls the cops" to help him with his work, he mobilizes the kind of intervention that is characteristic of police work even when it looks like social work.

Id. at 31.

According to Bittner, that unique competence has several characteristics:

First, and foremost, *the need to do something* is assessed with regard for actually existing combinations of circumstances. . . . [W]hile anything at all could become properly the business of the police, the patrolman can only decide whether anything in particular is properly his business after he "gets there" and examines it.

Second, the question whether some situational need justifiably requires police attention is very often answered by persons who solicit the service. Citizen demand is a factor of extraordinary importance for the distribution of police service, and the fact that someone did "call the cops" is, in and of itself, cause for concern. . . . [T]he determination that some development has reached a critical stage, ripe for police interest, is related to the attitudes of persons involved, and depends on common sense reasoning. For example, in a case involving a complaint about excessive noise, it is not the volume of the noise that creates hazards for life, limb, property, and the public order, but that the people involved say and otherwise show that the problem has reached a critical stage in which something-had-better-be-done-about-it. Closely connected with the feature of critical emergency is the expectation that policemen will handle the problem "then-and-there." Though it may seem obvious, it deserves stressing that police work involves no continuances and no appointments, . . . and that its scheduling derives from the natural fall of events, and not from any externally imposed order, as is the case for almost all other kinds of occupations. Firemen too are permanently on call, but the things they are called upon to do are limited to a few technical services. A policeman is always poised to move on any contingency whatever, not knowing what it might be, but knowing that far more often than not he will be expected to *do something.* . . . [H]e literally sees things in the light of the expectation that he somehow *has* to handle the situation. . . .

Third, though police departments are highly bureaucratized and patrolmen are enmeshed in a scheme of strict internal regulation, they are, paradoxically, quite alone and independent in their dealings with citizens. . . . He may call for help when there is a risk that he might be overwhelmed, and will receive it; short of such risks, however, he is on his own. . . . Connected with the expectation that he will do what needs to be done by himself is the expectation that he will limit himself to imposing provisional solutions upon problems. . . . That is, they are always trying to snatch things from the brink of disaster, to nip untoward development in the bud, and generally to arrest whatever must not be permitted to continue; and to accomplish this they sometimes arrest persons, if circumstances appear to demand it.

Fourth and finally, like everybody else, patrolmen want to succeed in what they undertake. But unlike everybody else, they never retreat. Once a policeman has defined a situation as properly his business and undertakes to do something about it, he will not desist till he prevails. That the policemen are uniquely empowered and required to carry out their decisions in the "then-and-there" of emergent problems is the structurally central feature of police work. There can be no doubt that the decisive and unremitting character of police intervention is uppermost in the minds of people who solicit it, and that persons against whom the police proceed are mindful of this feature and conduct themselves accordingly. The police duty not to retreat in the face of resistance is matched by the duty of citizens not to oppose them. . . .

. . . When . . . a citizen is ordered to move or to refrain from what he is doing, he may actually succeed in persuading the policeman to reverse himself. But contrary to judges, policemen are not required to entertain motions, nor are they required to stay their orders while the motion receives reasoned consideration. Indeed, *even* if the citizen's objection should receive favorable consideration in *subsequent* review, it would still be said that "under the circumstances" he should have obeyed. And even if it could be proved that the policeman's action was injudicious or in violation of civil liberties, he would be held to account only if it could also be proved that he acted with malice or with wanton frivolity.

In sum, what policemen do appears to consist of rushing to the scene of any crisis whatever, judging its needs in accordance with canons of common sense reasoning, and imposing solutions upon it without regard to resistance or opposition. In all this they act largely as individual practitioners of a craft.

Id. at 32–34.

What, then, fundamentally is the unique capacity of the police?

[T]he specific competence of the police is wholly contained in their capacity for decisive action. More specifically, that the feature of decisiveness derives from the authority to overpower opposition in the "then-and-there" of the situation of action. *The policeman, and the policeman alone, is equipped, entitled, and required to deal with every exigency in which force may have to be used, to meet it.* Moreover, the authorization to use force is conferred upon the policeman with the mere proviso that force will be used in amounts measured not to exceed the necessary minimum, as determined by an intuitive grasp of the situation. And only the use of deadly force is regulated somewhat more stringently.

Id. at 35. Policing then, to Bittner, is the capacity to respond to emergent problems with force.

Three points must be added in explanation of the foregoing. First, I am *not* saying the police work consists of using force to solve problems, but only that police work consists of coping with problems in which force *may have to be used.* This is a distinction of extraordinary importance. Second, it could not possibly be maintained that everything policemen are actually required to do reflects this feature. For a variety of reasons—especially because of the ways in which police departments are administered—officers are often ordered to do chores that have nothing to do with police work. . . . Third, the proposed definition of police competence *fully embraces* those forms of criminal law enforcement policemen engage in. I have mentioned earlier that the special role the police play in the administration of criminal justice has to do with the circumstance that "criminals"—as distinct from respectable and propertied persons who violate the provisions of penal codes in the course of doing business—can be counted on to try to evade or oppose arrest. Because this is so, and to enable the police to deal effectively with criminals, they are said to be empowered to use force. They also engage in criminal investigations whenever such investigations might be reasonably expected to be instrumental in making arrests. But the conception of the police role in all this is upside down. It is *not* that policemen are entitled to use force because they must deal with nasty criminals. Instead, the duty of handling nasty criminals devolves on them *because* they have the more general authority to use force *as needed* to bring about desired objectives. . . . [P]olicemen show little or no interest in all those kinds of offenders about whom it is not assumed that they need to be caught, and that force may have to be used to bring them to the bar of justice.

Id. at 35–36.

Bittner concludes with two final thoughts. First, he contends that misunderstanding by the police contributes to bad policing:

[T]he principal cause is an illusion. Believing that the real ground for his existence is the perennial pursuit of the likes of Willie Sutton[11]—for which he lacks both opportunity and resources—the policeman feels compelled to minimize the significance of those instances of his performance in which he seems to follow the footsteps of Florence Nightingale.[12] Fearing the role of the nurse or, worse yet, the role of the social worker, the policeman combines resentment against what he has to do day-in-day-out with the necessity of doing it. And in the course of it he misses his true vocation.

Id. at 40. And second, he argues that criminal law—maybe all law—plays a marginal role in legitimating the police:

The search for a proper authorizing norm for the police led to the assumption that the criminal code provided it. I have argued that this was a mistake. Criminal law enforcement is merely an incidental and derivative part of police work. They do it simply because it falls within the scope of their larger duties—that is, it becomes part of police work exactly to the same extent as anything else in which force may have to be used, and only to that extent. Whether the police should still be considered a law enforcement agency is a purely taxonomic question of slight interest. All I intended to argue is that their mandate cannot be interpreted as resting on the substantive authorizations contained in the penal codes or any other codes. I realize that putting things this way must raise all sorts of questions in the minds of people beholden to the ideal of the Rule of Law. And I also realize that the Rule of Law has always drawn part of its strength from pretense; but I don't think pretense is entitled to immunity.

Id. at 41.

---

[11] *Ed. note:* Willie Sutton was an exceptionally prolific, enduring, and quotable twentieth-century bank robber (and repeated prison escapee) who made one of the first FBI Most Wanted Fugitive lists in 1950. Sutton might be most famous for (reportedly) answering a journalist who asked him why he robbed banks by saying, "Because that's where the money is." *The Yale Book of Quotations* 739 (Fred R. Shapiro ed., 2006). He also explained in his memoir that he carried a gun during his crimes because, "You can't rob a bank on charm and personality," Willie Sutton with Edward Linn, *Where the Money Was: The Memoirs of a Bank Robber* 130 (2004) (1976), although Sutton, who later made a well-known commercial for a credit card company, might have tried.

[12] *Ed. note:* Florence Nightingale was the founder of modern nursing, a towering example of compassion, a prolific writer, and a heroic figure in nineteenth-century Britain.

NOTES AND QUESTIONS

1. *Bringing force.* Bittner argues that the police are the institution we rely on to solve emergent problems and maintain order, with force if necessary. That view explains why the police are critical because there will likely always be at least some societal problems that necessitate actors with that mandate. It explains why police are fearful: Any problem from a traffic stop to a family squabble is one in which force may need to be used and therefore one in which the officer's safety is on the line. And it explains why police can be so scary and deadly to others; they always bring the capacity and authority to use force.

2. *Bittner and the law of the police.* Bittner seems to suggest that policing at its core depends on broad discretion to apply the criminal law and almost unlimited authority to use force to overcome resistance. Is he suggesting that the law should not constrain police discretion or violence? Or does his account imply some legal limits on policing?

3. *The limits of Bittner's theory.* Bittner offers important insight into critical aspects of policing. But he does not offer a comprehensive account of the police. Instead, Bittner focuses on public policing by patrol officers in urban environments responding to public-order problems involving small numbers of individuals. That leaves out policing engaged in by private entities, by rural departments, by undercover officers and detectives, and in response to major public events, such as political protests, among other aspects of policing. Bittner also deemphasizes the role of the police as state actors, although the police derive their power from and act only at the behest of the state. As you read more about the law of the police in subsequent chapters, you might think more about how important these limitations are.

The Pathological Myth of Police as Crime Fighters

Although Bittner seems to decisively refute the conception of policing primarily as crime-fighting, that narrative has been stubbornly persistent in the decades since Bittner wrote. This image is often used to justify policing, but it also deforms policing and threatens its legitimacy.

Because the crime-fighting portrayal conflicts with reality, it makes police legitimacy precarious, subject to contestation and truth-telling. As a result, the narrative needs constant reinforcement. That reinforcement frequently takes the form of exaggerating the threat of crime, which is said to necessitate more and stronger policing. To wit, over the last 30 years, both violent and property crime have dropped dramatically in the United States. Yet year after year, a significant majority of Americans believe that there is more crime in the United States than there was a year earlier, see Gallup Historical Trends: Crime, Gallup (October 2019), and police budgets have risen accordingly.

To establish the threat of crime, police need criminals. Thus, crime-fighting police continually label and treat some people as suspects, and they often choose politically and historically vulnerable groups, especially people of color. In this ideological construction, criminals are not merely people who violate criminal laws and by doing so threaten public safety. If they were, they might be helped in other ways—with education, housing and jobs, or social services and community support. Instead, criminals are envisioned as people who place themselves outside the moral community by willfully transgressing societal rules. Thus, only coercion can contain them, and that coercion requires policing. See P.A.J. Waddington, *Policing Citizens: Authority and Rights* 23–24 (1999). You might argue that this framing contributes to the racialization of crime.

People labeled suspect are in turn likely to view the police as illegitimate. Policing distrustful communities in turn necessitates even more coercion. Additional coercion, not surprisingly, further delegitimizes policing and leads communities to fight to reveal and resist the false narrative. In this way, justifying the police as the "thin blue line" between public order and lawlessness not only conflicts with the reality of American policing, but it encourages policing that is more harmful and less fair. The image of crime-fighting police ironically threatens the legitimacy it seeks to shore up.

4. *Changes in policing and police accountability.* Bittner viewed officers on the street as alone and unwatchable. But technological changes in policing mean that today officers are accessible by radio, tracked by GPS in cars, and observed by car and body cameras, including some with real-time streaming capacity. Similarly, Bittner's officers responded to 911 calls or stumbled over emergent problems; today, police are summoned by social media and use acoustic sensors to identify gunshots as soon as they occur. Bittner imagined officers addressing violent crime and public disorder. But local police officers since have fought the War on Drugs, and more recently, wars on terrorism and illegal immigration, as well as more traditional challenges. See David H. Bayley, *The Complexities of 21st Century Policing*, 10 Policing 163, 163–169 (2016) (describing changes in policing tasks, public demands, strategies, and technologies since the 1980s). Can you think of other ways policing has changed?

5. *Changes in the police mandate.* In Bittner's description, policing represents a legitimate intrusion into public life because officers come when called or address public problems that obviously necessitate intervention. In a way, the 911 calls and visible emergencies imply consent to policing. But after Bittner wrote, several studies suggested that responding to calls and randomly patrolling do not effectively prevent crime. In response, departments began to adopt new, proactive policing strategies, in which officers seek new means of preventing and deterring criminal activity, including by approaching more people.[13] The new proactive policing raises a new question: If no one calls the police, and no visible problem exists, what justifies the harms and risks that policing necessarily entails? To answer that concern, police departments today widely engage in *community policing* and *problem-oriented policing* strategies that solicit public input and cooperation, thereby building a new mandate for police activities. But this mandate remains hotly contested, especially by those who tend to suffer more harm from officers' preventative activities, feel limited power to influence proactive police priorities, and yet receive less *you-call-and-we-come* policing, including young people; members of the LGBTQ community; members of racial, ethnic, and linguistic minorities; and people struggling with homelessness, addiction, or mental illness.

6. *More about force, race, and the police mandate.* By Bittner's account, no matter how friendly and polite an officer is, the officer ineluctably brings the power to back commands with force. That makes any encounter with an officer potentially

---

[13] Proactive policing strategies are discussed further in Chapter 5.

dangerous, even fatal. Given that, perhaps we should be more cautious about what we expect officers to address:

> Vexing social problems—homelessness, drug use, the inability to support one's children, mental illness—are presently solved by sending in men and women who specialize in inspiring fear and ensuring compliance. Fear and compliance have their place, but it can't be every place.

> When Walter Scott fled from the North Charleston police, he was not merely fleeing Michael Thomas Slager,[14] he was attempting to flee incarceration. He was doing this because we have decided that the criminal-justice system is the best tool for dealing with men who can't, or won't, support their children at a level that we deem satisfactory. Peel back the layers of most of the recent police shootings that have captured attention and you will find a broad societal problem that we have looked at, thrown our hands up, and said to the criminal-justice system, "You deal with this."

Ta-Nehisi Coates, *The Myth of Police Reform*, Atlantic (Apr. 15, 2015).

As Coates implies, assuming that Bittner is right and that police are necessary to address *some* problems, relying on the police to handle problems that could be predictably handled noncoercively changes the balance between the costs and the benefits of policing: It risks violence when noncoercive means of achieving public safety might be equally or more effective. That makes policing more harm-inefficient, that is, more harmful than achieving public safety demands. Bittner assumes that the police mandate is dictated by emergent events and unconstrainable. Do you agree? How could policing be made more harm-efficient?

Coates goes on to point out that overrelying on the police disproportionately affects the Black community: Although police always have the *capacity* to use force, police actually use force when they cannot address a situation by leveraging cooperation and consent that comes from respect for their authority. According to Coates, whereas most Americans perceive police as appropriate figures of authority,

> African Americans, for most of our history, have lived under the power of the criminal-justice system, not its authority. The dominant feature in the relationship between African Americans and their country is plunder, and plunder has made police authority an impossibility, and police power a necessity.

Id. In this view, Bittner only tells part of the story. We need a further account of how force gets operationalized and against whom.

2.   Policing as Social Control

Coates seems to agree with Bittner that the police are problem solvers, even as he invokes the violent historical role police have played in maintaining Black inequality to show why they are often distrusted in this role. Some commentators reject Bittner entirely, viewing the preservation of an unequal social order as the *raison d'être* of policing. In this view, police are not problem solvers (with the capacity to use force), as Bittner suggests. Instead, they are social-control agents (with the capacity to use force):

---

[14] *Ed. note:* On April 4, 2015, days before Coates wrote this article, Walter Scott, an unarmed Black man, was shot and killed by Michael Slager, a North Charleston (S.C.) police officer, following a traffic stop. Scott apparently ran from the traffic stop because he feared arrest for failing to pay court-ordered child support, something for which he had been jailed several times before. Video of the incident shows Slager shooting Scott in the back as Scott fled. Slager eventually pleaded guilty to federal civil rights charges and is serving 20 years in prison.

> The mandate of police patrol officers is to employ a system of rules and authoritative commands to transform troublesome, fragile situations back into a normal or efficient state whereby the ranks in society are preserved. . . . Their sense of order and the order they seek to reproduce are that of the status quo.

Richard V. Ericson, *Reproducing Order: A Study of Police Patrol Work* 7 (1982).

In early municipal policing in the United States, maintaining the status quo often meant promoting the interests of the bourgeois at the expense of the working class:

> As the major local source of state violence, the municipal police played a crucial role in the class struggle of the period, working repeatedly to break working-class resistance to corporate power, to socialize new immigrants to the demands of monopoly capitalism, to provide protection services to strikebound companies and those threatened with strikes, to control rebellious segments of the working-class population, and to control and gather intelligence in working-class communities.

Sidney L. Harring, *Policing a Class Society: The Expansion of the Urban Police in the Late Nineteenth and Early Twentieth Centuries*, in *Crime and Capitalism: Readings in Marxist Crimonology* 546, 547 (David F. Greenberg ed., 2010). The police role in suppressing labor helped justify the militarization of the police, which in turn made the police prepared to do more violence:

> The inaugural event was the Great Strike of 1877, which ran up and down the burgeoning railroad system and briefly witnessed workers running the entire city of St Louis. While federal troops were used to suppress the strike, urban property owners started to think more seriously about permanent police forces able to deploy quickly, forcefully, and on a new scale. In Chicago, a group of wealthy citizens raised $28,000, which they used to buy rifles, cannons, cavalry equipment, and a Gatling gun for public forces.

> The strike wave of 1886 further concentrated the minds of the urban bourgeoisie. Strikes now included thousands—occasionally tens of thousands—of workers, sometimes armed, and able to paralyze whole cities even when not armed. This social force required a whole new scale of violence to suppress.

Alex Gourevitch, *Why Are the Police Like This?*, Jacobin (June 12, 2020).

Of course, social order in the United States has never been defined by class alone.

> Since their inception in the mid-nineteenth century, urban police forces . . . police regulated behavior to comport to their own sense of racial, sexual, ethnic, and class order. Because police were organized by districts and because cities were spatially segregated, police forces primarily regulated social hierarchies through their regulation of space. In marginalized neighborhoods—and predominantly black neighborhoods, in particular—residents experienced a discriminatory mix of underpolicing and overpolicing.

Christopher Lowen Agee, *Crisis and Redemption: The History of American Police Reform since World War II*, J. of Urb. Hist., Apr. 2017, at 2. Although there have been moments of resistance and disruption, policing continued throughout the twentieth century to both overpolice and underserve poor communities and communities of color, in part by constructing criminality to maintain existing power relations.

Consider the arrest of Rosa Parks on December 1, 1955, when she refused to give up her seat to a white passenger on a Montgomery, Alabama, bus. At the time, the Montgomery City Code gave bus drivers "the powers of a police officer," to enable them to enforce Montgomery's bus segregation provision. The Code also made it criminal not to comply with a bus driver's order to take a seat "assigned to the race to which he belongs." Montgomery City Code, Ch. 6, §11 (1952), *invalidated by* Browder v. Gayle, 142 F. Supp. 707 (M.D. Ala.), *aff'd per curiam*, 352 U.S. 903 (1956). The driver of Parks's bus, James Blake, instructed Parks to move and summoned the police when she did not. Leroy Pierce, the first officer on the scene, responded to the call quickly because—anticipating Bittner—"if you're a good police officer and something is happening on the bus, you know somebody needs to look at it." Andrew J. Yawn, *Alabama Officer Recalls 1955 Arrest of Rosa Parks*, Associated Press (Dec. 5, 2018). The police then arrested Parks for failing to comply with Blake's order.

Arrest report for Rosa Parks, 1955.

Parks's arrest made history, sparking the Montgomery bus boycott and the legal case that ruled segregated public buses unconstitutional. See *Browder*, 142 F. Supp. 707. As Pierce put it decades later, though, "To me it was a regular, routine arrest." Yawn, *supra*. Bittner's account takes for granted how the police identify *something-that -ought-not-to-be-happening- and-about-which-someone- had-better-do-something-now*. As Parks's arrest illustrates, Montgomery police were empowered and expected to treat resistance to unjust racial ordering as a problem that needed to be solved.

Some argue that policing campaigns in recent decades—from the war on crime in the 1960s and the war on drugs in the 1980s and 1990s to proactive policing from the 1980s through the 2000s—function in much the same way, defining Black Americans as criminal to exert racial control. See Elizabeth Hinton & DeAnza Cook, *The Mass Criminalization of Black Americans: A Historical Overview*, Ann. Rev. Criminology (forthcoming 2021).

Handcuffs used to arrest Harvard University Professor Henry Louis Gates, Jr. Gates was arrested outside his home by Cambridge Police Sergeant James Crowley for disorderly conduct in July 2009. Crowley initially suspected Gates of burglary, but that suspicion was alleviated when Gates showed the officer his university identification and driver's license. The encounter nevertheless escalated in a manner many commentators view as racial: Crowley might not have as easily disrespected and arrested a white man in the same circumstances, and Gates's hostility to and distrust of the officer were connected to his experiences with the police as a Black man. The arrest became national news, and President Barack Obama invited Crowley and Gates to the White House for a private meeting known as the "Beer Summit." The handcuffs are now in the collection of the Smithsonian National Museum of African American History and Culture.

If policing serves as a form of social and racial control, as commentators suggest, then police violence takes on a different meaning. Rather than being solely situationally responsive, as Bittner's theory implies, or aberrational, as contemporary defenders of the police claim, violence becomes part of the project of putting people in their place. More specifically, police use of force against African Americans can be viewed as part of "an unbroken stream of racist violence, both official and extralegal, from slave patrols and the Ku Klux Klan to contemporary profiling practices and present-day vigilantes." Angela Y. Davis, *Freedom Is a Constant Struggle: Ferguson, Palestine, and the Foundations of a Movement* 133 (2016). This view helps contextualize calls to defund or abolish policing: If police violence serves primarily to reinforce the power of elites, then it might well pose as great a threat to safety and security to targeted communities as does (ordinary) crime, and it might be inessential to promote public safety.

3. Examining Police–Citizen Encounters

a. *A Model of Police–Citizen Encounters*

To understand policing and the law of the police, it helps to describe the dynamics of common reactive street encounters between the police and members of the public. You can think of such interactions as having several steps.

First, police engage citizens on the street only once they identify a situation as one that requires investigation or intervention, what Bittner calls *something-that-ought-not-to-be-happening-and-about-which-someone-had-better-do-something-now*. When an officer stops a driver weaving across lanes of traffic, responds to a 911 complaint about street noise, or detains a woman he believes to be soliciting clients as a prostitute, the officer is determining that the situation justifies police action.

Second, police seek to clarify and resolve the problems they identify with "provisional solutions." Often, this involves no coercion. An officer might respond to a burglary call by taking a report for future investigation or to a welfare check by talking a man down from a ledge. Even when an officer attempts to impose an unwelcome solution, he often does so by persuasion and pressure rather than command or compulsion. Sometimes, however, an officer issues commands—telling people to leave the area or to stay put—or attempts an arrest to get someone off the street or to start the criminal process against him.

Third, the person the police target reacts. Most people cooperate or comply, even if they disagree with the police. Some fail to obey an officer's directions. Some actively resist by running away, by fighting an arrest, or by threatening or harming the officer.

Fourth, perceiving or predicting noncooperation or resistance, officers respond, often with further commands, an arrest, or force.

In simpler terms, police–citizen encounters have four steps:

[1] Problem identification
[2] Solution imposition
[3] Citizen reaction
[4] Officer follow-up

In more coercive encounters, they might be listed as follows:

[1] Problem identification
[2] Coercion or command
[3] Perceived noncompliance
[4] Command, coercion, or force

In coercive encounters, steps two, three, and four are sometimes repeated and escalated. Together, this description of coercive encounters constitutes a simplified model of many police contacts with the public. For purposes of discussion, let's call it the Encounter Model.

This model will reappear in future chapters because it helps to reveal how the law permits or restricts harm during police–citizen encounters: The law determines what problems police are permitted to use coercive efforts to try to solve, what kinds of non-cooperation justify further coercion, and when and how much force is a permissible response to noncompliance. It also suggests stages at which intervention might prevent an encounter from going awry: Communities might redefine what constitutes a problem, limit coercive solutions, reconceive noncompliance, and restrict responses. But the model is not a full account of police–citizen interactions. For instance, it does not explain *why* officers or members of the public act the way they do, a matter considered in future chapters. Already, you have encountered Coates's view that police participation in racial oppression leads African Americans to be less compliant.

The model also focuses exclusively on the actions within a single encounter. Police encounters take place in a broader social context, one that shapes the understandings and actions of the participants. In recent years, several scholars have proposed accounts of the group dynamics and structural forces that shape police encounters with African Americans. Devon Carbado, for example, has emphasized the ways African Americans are pushed into repeated interactions with the police that lead to violence, which is then condoned and legitimated by law. See Devon W. Carbado, *Blue-on-Black Violence: A Provisional Model of Some of the Causes*, 104 Geo. L.J. 1479 (2016). Monica Bell has described how police disrespect and mistreatment experienced both directly and vicariously leads to legal estrangement, "a marginal and ambivalent relationship with society, the law, and predominant social norms that emanates from institutional and legal failure." Monica C. Bell, *Police Reform and the Dismantling of Legal Estrangement*, 126 Yale L.J. 2054, 2083 (2017); see also Amy E. Lerman & Vesla M. Weaver, *Arresting Citizenship: The Democratic Consequences of American Crime Control* (2014) (arguing that policing and other criminal justice contact alienates citizens from political institutions and undermines a sense of full citizenship).

Building off these accounts, but abstracting from the specific context of encounters with African Americans, one might argue:

1. Social forces (e.g., housing policies, socioeconomic factors, implicit and explicit biases) and policing practices (e.g., strategies, training, policies, and incentives) dictate how often and for what purpose officers interact with individuals.
2. The law, departments, and officer decisions determine the form those encounters take.

3. Prior experience, both individual and communal, influences how officers and citizens interpret encounters and respond to each other.
4. The law and legal institutions assess and label police encounters and determine legal consequences for them, which in turn shapes their social meaning.

Because the law operates almost exclusively at the level of individual encounters, this book often focuses on those interactions. Still, it is worth remembering that those encounters are influenced by broader forces, and that the law is part of the social backdrop against which those individual encounters take place.

b. Considering a Police–Citizen Encounter: The Arrest of Sandra Bland

Texas State Trooper Brian Encinia stopped Sandra Bland on July 10, 2015, for failing to signal a lane change. Watch the video of her stop and arrest, David Montgomery, *Sandra Bland Was Threatened with Taser, Police Video Shows*, N.Y. Times (July 21, 2015) *https://www.nytimes.com/2015/07/22/us/sandra-bland-was-combative-texas-arrest-report-says.html*, and read this transcript of their encounter. As you do so, think about the Encounter Model. Does it help you describe some of what is happening? Can you use it to identify what Encinia and Bland disagree about in terms of the legitimacy of this encounter?

1	**Encinia:**	Hello, ma'am.
	Bland:	[faint] Hi.
	Encinia:	[indistinct] the reason for your stop is that you didn't fail . . . you failed to signal the lane change. You got your driver's license and insurance with you?
5	**Bland:**	[indistinct]
	Encinia:	What's wrong?
	Bland:	[indistinct]
		[Pause. Bland hands objects to Encinia.]
10	**Encinia:**	How long have you been in Texas?
	Bland:	I got here yesterday.
	Encinia:	OK.
		[Pause.]
	Encinia:	Do you have a driver's license?
15	**Bland:**	I didn't give you my driver's license?
	Encinia:	No, ma'am.
	Bland:	[indistinct]
	Encinia:	You're OK.
		[Pause.]
20	**Encinia:**	OK. Where're you headed to now?
	Bland:	[indistinct]
	Encinia:	OK, give me a few minutes, all right?
	Bland:	[indistinct]
		[Several minutes pass during which Encinia returns to his car and
25		then returns to Bland.]
	Encinia:	You OK?

	Bland:	I'm waiting on you, you . . . this is your job. . . . I'm waiting on you whenever you want me to . . .
	Encinia:	Well, you seem very irritated.
30	Bland:	I am, I, I really am, but that's what I . . . just happened, but what I was getting a ticket for, I was getting out of your way, you were speeding up, tailing me, so I move over, and you stop me, so yeah, I am a little irritated, but that doesn't stop you from giving me a ticket, so [indistinct, overcut by radio chatter].
35	Encinia:	Are you done?
	Bland:	You asked me what's wrong, and I told you.
	Encinia:	OK.
	Bland:	So now I'm done, yeah.
	Encinia:	OK. [five-second pause] You mind putting out your cigarette, please, if you don't mind?
40		
	Bland:	I'm in my car, why would I have to put out my cigarette?
	Encinia:	Well, you can step on out now.
	Bland:	I don't have to step out of my car. . . .
	Encinia:	Step out of the car.
45		[Brief pause. Then officer opens driver's door of car.]
	Bland:	Why am I . . .?
	Encinia:	Step out of the car.
	Bland:	No, you don't, no, you don't have the right.
	Encinia:	Step out of the car.
50	Bland:	You do not, you do not have the right to do that.
	Encinia:	I do have the right. Now step out or I will remove you.
	Bland:	I refuse to say . . . I refuse to talk to you, other than to identify myself. . . .
	Encinia:	Step out or I will remove you.
55	Bland:	Why am I . . .? I am getting removed for a failure to [indistinct].
	Encinia:	Step out, or I will remove you. I am giving you a lawful order. [brief pause] Get out of the car, now, or I'm gonna remove you.
	Bland:	I'm not going, and I'm calling my [indistinct].
		[Encinia reaches into car.]
60	Encinia:	I am gonna yank you out of here.
	Bland:	OK, you gonna yank me out of my car?
	Encinia:	Get out.
	Bland:	OK, all right . . . let's, let's do this.
	Encinia:	Yeah, we're going to.
65	Bland:	Yeah.
		[Brief pause. Encinia and Bland begin to struggle.]
	Bland:	Don't touch me.
	Encinia:	Get out of the car!
	Bland:	Don't touch me, don't touch me! I'm not under arrest, you don't have the right to take me out of my car.
70		
	Encinia:	You *are* under arrest!
	Bland:	I'm under arrest for what? For what? For what?
	Encinia:	[over radio] Send me another unit. [to Bland] Get out of the car! Get out of the car, now!

75	**Bland:**	Why am I being apprehended? You're trying to give me a ticket for all of your failures?
	Encinia:	I said get out of the car.
80	**Bland:**	Why am I being apprehended, you just opened my car door, you just opened my car door, so you're gonna, you're threatening to drag me out of my own car?
	Encinia:	I am giving you a lawful order. I am gonna drag you out of here. [Encinia steps back, grabs Taser off his belt with left hand, and points it at Bland, still in car.]
	Encinia:	Get out of the car! I will light you up. Get out! Now!
85	**Bland:**	And [indistinct] me? [pause] Wow. Wow. [Bland gets out of car, holding her phone.]
	Bland:	Really, for a failure to signal, you're doing all of this for a failure to signal?
	Encinia:	[pointing toward curb] Get over there.
90	**Bland:**	Right, yeah, yeah, let's take this to court, let's do it.
	Encinia:	Go ahead.
	Bland:	For a failure to signal, yeah, for a failure to signal.
	Encinia:	Get off the phone.
	Bland:	[indistinct]
95	**Encinia:**	Get off the phone.
	Bland:	I'm not on the phone. I have a right to record; this is my property, this is my property.
	Encinia:	Put your phone down. Put your phone down.
	Bland:	Sir.
100	**Encinia:**	Put your phone down. Put your phone down, right now. Put your phone down.
	Bland:	[indistinct] For a fucking failure to signal [indistinct].
	Encinia:	Come over here.
105	**Bland:**	Y'all are, y'all are interesting, very interesting. You feeling good about yourself? You feeling good about yourself?
	Encinia:	Come over here. Come over here now. Stand right here. Stand right there.
	Bland:	. . . for a failure to signal. You feel real good about yourself, don't you? You feel good about yourself, don't you?
110	**Encinia:**	Turn around. Turn around. Turn around now.
	Bland:	What, what are you, why am I being arrested?
	Encinia:	Put your hands behind your back and turn around. Turn around.
	Bland:	Why can't you tell me why I'm . . . ?
	Encinia:	I am giving you a lawful order. I will tell you.
115	**Bland:**	Why am I being arrested?
	Encinia:	Turn around.
	Bland:	Why won't you tell me that part?
	Encinia:	I am giving you a lawful order. Turn around.
	Bland:	Why will you not tell me what's going on?
120	**Encinia:**	You are not complying.
	Bland:	I'm not complying because you just pulled me out of my car!
	Encinia:	Turn around.

	Bland:	Are you fucking kidding me, this is some bullshit, you know it is, cause you know this is straight bullshit . . .
125	**Encinia:**	[indistinct] hands behind your back.
	Bland:	. . . you pulling shit, you pulling straight shit, that's how y'all are [indistinct] some scary fucking cops, South Carolina got y'all bitch-asses scared. That's all it is. Fucking scared of a female.
	Encinia:	If you would have just listened.
130	**Bland:**	[indistinct], I'm trying to sign a fucking ticket, whatever.
	Encinia:	Stop moving! Stop moving!
	Bland:	Are you fucking serious, you . . . ooh, I can't wait 'til we go to court, oooh, I can't wait. I cannot *wait* 'til we go to court. I can't wait, oooh I can't wait. You want me to sit down now?
135	**Encinia:**	No!
	Bland:	Or you gonna drop, you gonna throw me to the floor? That'd make you feel better about yourself?
	Encinia:	Knock it off.
	Bland:	Nah, that'd make you feel better about yourself? That'd make you feel real good, wouldn't it? Oh yeah. Fucking pussy, for a failure to signal, you doing all of this, and little [indistinct], my god, they, they must've . . .
140		
	Encinia:	You were getting a warning, until now, you're going to jail.
	Bland:	No, I'm getting a . . . for what? For what?
145	**Encinia:**	You can come read, come read right . . .
	Bland:	I'm getting a warning for what?
	Encinia:	Stay right here. Stay right . . . .
	Bland:	Well, you kept pointing me over there!
	Encinia:	I said, stay right here!
150	**Bland:**	Get your fucking mouth right, let me . . . oooh, I swear on my life, y'all some pussies. A pussy-ass cop for a fucking signal, you gonna take me to jail.
	Encinia:	[over radio] I got her controlled, she's in handcuffs.
	Bland:	What a pussy, what a pussy. What a pu—you about to break my fucking wrist!
155		
	Encinia:	Stop moving!
	Bland:	I'm standing still, you keep moving me, goddammit!
	Encinia:	Stand right here! Stand right there.
	Bland:	Don't touch me! Fucking pussy for a traffic ticket you're doing all this bullshit. [indistinct brief sentence]
160		
	Encinia:	Come read right over here. This right here says a warning. You started creating a problem.
	Bland:	You asked me what was wrong!
		[Soon after this point, a second officer arrives, and Bland is detained.]

NOTES AND QUESTIONS

1. *Bittnerian policing?* Why do you think Trooper Encinia stopped Sandra Bland? What circumstances surrounding this encounter might raise questions about the legitimacy of this stop?

2. *Apply the Encounter Model.* Using the model, how would you describe what happened here?

3. *The cigarette, part 1.* Why do you think Trooper Encinia asked Sandra Bland to put out her cigarette? In Encinia's mind, was his question a request or command? What did Bland think?

4. *The cigarette, part 2.* What might Bland have intended by her response? What was Encinia's perception of that response? In a classic article on patrol policing, John Van Maanen argued that officers respond aggressively when members of the public challenge their authority to determine who poses a threat to social order and what should be done about it.

> When a police officer approaches a civilian to issue a traffic citation . . . he directly brings the power of the state to bear on the situation and hence makes vulnerable to disgrace, embarrassment, and insult that power. . . . To the patrolman, such contests are not to be taken lightly, for the authority of the state is also his personal authority. . . . To deny or raise doubt about his legitimacy is to shake the very ground upon which his self-image and corresponding views are built.
>
> . . . [T]he police will respond in particular ways to those who challenge or question their motive or right to intervene in situations that they believe demand police intervention. . . . In fact, they can be seen to push the encounter to a new level wherein any further slight to an officer, however subtle, provides sufficient evidence to a patrolman that he may indeed be dealing with a certifiable asshole and that the situation is in need of rapid clarification.

John Van Maanen, *The Asshole,* in *Policing: A View from the Street* 221, 229 (Peter K. Manning & John Van Maanen eds., 1978). According to Van Maanen, if the officer determines that the person's challenge was intentional, he will impose street justice, usually in the form of violence or an unnecessary arrest. This response has nothing to do with the original intent of the encounter. Instead, it serves to castigate the individual and enforce the officer's view of the situation. *Id.* at 231–232. Does that help make sense of what happened here? Or might there be an alternative explanation for the officer's conduct?

5. *Racial, cultural, and personal specificity.* All of us interpret other people's behavior through our own culture and experience. What police perceive as a challenge or noncompliance is shaped by their experiences with and ideas about people they police. Similarly, how police treat and interact with communities contributes to whether those communities trust the police and therefore whether they are likely to cooperate with police requests and obey police commands. Could those forces have mattered here? Encinia stated in his arrest report that he knew from Bland's "aggressive body language and demeanor" that "something was wrong"

Sandra Bland.

Trooper Brian Encinia.

during the stop, perhaps indicating criminal activity. Bland was just arriving in Texas for a job interview when she was stopped by Encinia, but she had had at least ten prior encounters with the police in Illinois and in Texas, including at least half a dozen traffic stops, and she had been charged and fined (and charged with failing to pay fines) on nearly 20 traffic and misdemeanor offenses. See Katy Smyser, *Suburban Woman Found Dead in Jail Had Previous Encounters with Police*, NBC Chicago (July 16, 2015). Bland also supported the Black Lives Matter movement, which has drawn attention to the problem of racially disparate police violence. How might your background affect how you read this interaction between Encinia and Bland?

6. *"Step out of the car."* Most of this section focuses on understanding policing rather than the details of the law, but in analyzing this encounter—and in analyzing many encounters with the police—some law helps. When Bland questioned Encinia about his authority with respect to the cigarette, he ordered her out of the car. Encinia likely thought he had clear authority to issue this latter command; the Supreme Court held in *Pennsylvania v. Mimms*, 434 U.S. 106 (1977), that an officer does not violate the Fourth Amendment when he orders a driver to get out of the car during a traffic stop, even without reason to believe that criminal activity is underway or that the occupants pose a threat to police safety, and every state allows officers to do so. As Encinia had no obvious source of authority for the cigarette command, you might interpret Encinia as issuing the second order to shift the encounter to more legally secure ground. This might be why he repeatedly refers to the order to exit the car (as opposed to the question about the cigarette) as a *lawful order*.

But if Encinia thought *Mimms* gave him constitutional cover, he might have been wrong. In *Rodriguez v. United States*, 575 U.S. 348 (2015), the Supreme Court held that extending a traffic stop for several minutes to secure backup and walk a drug dog around the vehicle violates the Fourth Amendment:

> Like a *Terry* stop, the tolerable duration of police inquiries in the traffic-stop context is determined by the seizure's "mission"—to address the traffic violation that warranted the stop, and attend to related safety concerns. Because addressing the infraction is the purpose of the stop, it may "last no longer than is necessary to effectuate th[at] purpose." United States v. Sharpe, 470 U.S. 675, 684 (1985). Authority for the seizure thus ends when tasks tied to the traffic infraction are—or reasonably should have been—completed. . . .
>
> . . . In *Mimms*, we reasoned that the government's "legitimate and weighty" interest in officer safety outweighs the "*de minimis*" additional intrusion of requiring a driver, already lawfully stopped, to exit the vehicle. . . .

Unlike a general interest in criminal enforcement, however, the government's officer safety interest stems from the mission of the stop itself. Traffic stops are "especially fraught with danger to police officers," *Arizona v. Johnson*, 555 U.S. 323, 330 (2009), so an officer may need to take certain negligibly burdensome precautions in order to complete his mission safely. On-scene investigation into other crimes, however, detours from that mission. So too do safety precautions taken in order to facilitate such detours. Thus, even assuming that the imposition here was no more intrusive than the exit order in *Mimms*, the dog sniff could not be justified on the same basis.

Id. at 354–357. Assuming Encinia was holding a written warning when he returned to the car, was he acting constitutionally when he ordered Bland out of the car? Or was his "mission" already complete? Traffic stops are discussed further in Chapter 6.

7. *How intrusive?* As *Rodriguez* suggests, in *Mimms*, the Court downplayed the driver's experience of being ordered out of the car:

[W]e are asked to weigh the intrusion into the driver's personal liberty occasioned not by the initial stop of the vehicle, which was admittedly justified, but by the order to get out of the car. We think this additional intrusion can only be described as *de minimis*. The driver is being asked to expose to view very little more of his person than is already exposed. The police have already lawfully decided that the driver shall be briefly detained, the only question is whether he shall spend that period sitting in the driver's seat of his car or standing alongside it. Not only is the insistence of the police on the latter choice not a "serious intrusion upon the sanctity of the person," but it hardly rises to the level of a "petty indignity." Terry v. Ohio, 392 U.S. 1, 17 (1968). What is at most a mere inconvenience cannot prevail when balanced against legitimate concerns for the officer's safety.

Mimms, 434 U.S. at 111. Sandra Bland does not appear to have seen the command to get of the car as a *de minimis* intrusion. What is the Supreme Court's description missing?

8. *Aftermath: Sandra Bland.* Following her arrest, Sandra Bland stayed in jail because she could not make the $5,000 bond required for release. A few days after her arrest, she was found dead in her cell, having hanged herself with a plastic bag. Although her family initially worried that she had been killed by her jailors, an autopsy confirmed that she had committed suicide. Bland's family received $1.9 million from the county where she was jailed and the Texas Department of Public Safety in a subsequent wrongful-death lawsuit.

9. *Aftermath: Brian Encinia.* Encinia was indicted by a grand jury for perjury for making a false statement about the arrest. The charge was later dropped after Encinia surrendered his license to be a Texas police officer and agreed not to work in law enforcement in the future. Encinia was also fired by the Texas Department of Public Safety for failing to remain "courteous and tactful" and "exercise patience and discretion" during the encounter; for prolonging the traffic stop "beyond the time reasonably necessary"; and for failing to follow departmental protocols governing encounters. Letter from Steven C. McCraw, Dir., Tex. Dep't of Pub. Safety, to Brian Encinia, Trooper, Tex. Dep't of Pub. Safety (Jan. 28, 2016); Letter from Steven C. McCraw, Dir., Tex. Dep't of Pub. Safety, to Brian Encinia, Trooper, Tex. Dep't of Pub. Safety (Mar. 1, 2016).

10. *Aftermath: The law.* The Sandra Bland Act amended several sections of Texas law. S.B. 1849, Leg. Sess. 85(R) (Tex. 2017). In addition to changes in how jail personnel handle individuals who might be suffering from a mental-health crisis or have an intellectual or developmental disability, the act required that all police officers receive a one-time 40-hour training course on deescalation and interacting with people with mental impairments, and training every two years on topics including civil rights, racial sensitivity, cultural diversity, deescalation, and limiting the use of force. See Tex. Occ. Code Ann. §§1701.352(b), 1701.402(b). It also required all policing agencies to adopt written policies on racial profiling, to permit members of the public to file complaints, and to audit officer uses of force and searches during traffic stops. See Tex. Code Crim. Proc. Ann. art. 2.132-2.134.

11. *Avoiding Bland's arrest.* If Sandra Bland had never been pulled over, she would not have been arrested or had force used against her. If the police officer had not issued the command for Bland to put out her cigarette and then ordered her out of the car, she likely would have grudgingly received her ticket and not been arrested or had force used against her. If Bland had complied with the officer's instructions to get out of the car, she might not have been arrested, although that is harder to tell. And if the officer had overlooked her noncompliance about getting out of the car, given that he was not concerned at the time with his own safety, with public order, or with any crime, Bland would not have been arrested or had force used against her. Right? If so, then, as the Encounter Model suggests, arrests and uses of force are generated by (1) the problems officers think need solving immediately, (2) the tools we give police to solve them, (3) the relationships individuals and communities have with the police, (4) what constitutes noncompliance that justifies a response, and (5) when we permit force to overcome noncompliance. What legal changes or other social interventions might alter these conditions?

12. *Avoiding police–citizen encounters.* Assuming that Sandra Bland committed a traffic violation worth addressing, how might the encounter have been different if the person who stopped her was not a law enforcement officer but instead a city worker without arrest power or a gun? What might be the risks and rewards of civilianizing this aspect of policing?

Here are some other typical situations to which police respond. Should they? If not, should anyone respond to these situations? If so, what training should those actors have? Should they work for the government? Should the police be present?

a. Several dozen homeless people have set up tents in a city park. Some nearby residents have complained that their presence makes the park unusable, in part because some of the occupants are visibly intoxicated and disorderly or openly use drugs. Occupying the park violates local ordinances against erecting structures on public land and staying in the park after it has closed.

b. A man runs into a fast-food restaurant waving a knife and shouting that his wife is a "spy" and that the Central Intelligence Agency is trying to kill him. He talks to himself as he wanders around the seating area scaring customers.

c. A convenience store clerk calls the police to report that a man has just taken several candy bars and over-the-counter medication bottles and left the store without paying. The store manager confronted the man, and the two are arguing in front of the store.

d. A woman calls 911. Her adult son, who suffers from schizophrenia and lives with her, is in the midst of a psychotic episode and is becoming increasingly aggressive. She fears he may soon injure her or himself.

e. Dozens of people gather and block a downtown street to hold a Black Youth Summit during the COVID-19 pandemic. They are violating city and state rules against blocking traffic without a permit and COVID-related rules that require wearing masks and social distancing in public.

f. Neighbors complain about a street corner that has become a popular place to buy and sell crack cocaine, leading to loitering, noise, littering, drug use, damage to property, and other crime.

g. A local gang of teenagers has declared a five-block area their "turf," and they have had several confrontations with interlopers from nearby gangs and two drive-by shootings.

h. A 911 caller tells a dispatcher that the couple next door has been arguing for hours and now it sounds like "he's beating the hell out of her."

Bad and Good Policing

Policing sometimes goes awry. Here are some of the most frequently noted problems with policing:

- *Disparities and discrimination.* Policing's harms are often concentrated on some communities and individuals rather than fairly distributed. African Americans, for example, "are significantly more likely to be stopped, searched, frisked, and arrested by the police than similarly situated whites." Anthony A. Braga et al., *Race, Place and Effective Policing*, 45 Ann. Rev. Soc. 535, 539 (2019). Surveillance programs have targeted Muslims, and police engage in undercover activities specifically targeted at members of the LGBTQ community. Policing can discriminate in who it protects as well as who it harms. Although racial disparities in policing are discussed throughout the book, the way the law handles discrimination claims against the police is discussed in Chapter 6.

- *Violence.* Police sometimes use force when no force is necessary, use aggressive tactics that unnecessarily escalate encounters, or use more force than the situation requires. The law regulating police use of force is discussed in Chapter 8.

- *Abuse of discretion.* Critics complain that police often abuse their power by using illegitimate criteria in deciding whom to approach, detain, question, and arrest and by treating people with disrespect during encounters. Some of the ways the law tries to control discretion are discussed in Chapter 10.

- *Privacy invasion.* Local law enforcement agencies routinely observe people with body-worn cameras, cell-site simulators, closed-circuit cameras, and facial-recognition systems, among other technologies. This surveillance threatens privacy. So does undercover policing and the use of criminal informants, who enter people's homes and lives pretending to be friends or trustworthy associates rather than agents of the state. The law governing police surveillance and deception is discussed further in Chapter 2.
- *Corruption.* Officers sometimes misuse state-granted power for "state" purposes, by planting evidence and then pretending to find it or by lying on the stand about why they stopped a suspect. They also sometimes police to profit agencies, by aggressively confiscating property from suspects or by issuing tickets to fill city coffers rather than serve public safety. Police corruption can also serve personal ends, when officers take kickbacks, steal from suspects, or participate in drug sales and burglaries. Asset forfeiture is discussed in Chapter 11.

Is good policing merely policing when none of these problems exist? Here is a possible list of qualitative characteristics of *good policing*:

- *Authorized.* Policing should be the product of democratic processes and subject to them.
- *Effective.* Policing should increase public safety, security, and order and reduce fear.
- *Beneficial.* The harms of policing and its financial costs should not exceed its benefits.
- *Harm-efficient.* Even if policing is beneficial, its harms (and financial costs) should be minimized.
- *Lawful.* Police officers should obey the law and respect individual rights.
- *Fair.* The benefits and harms of policing should be fairly distributed.
- *Legitimate.* Policing should treat people with dignity, respect, and neutrality, so as to justify their support and their obligation to act in accordance with state commands.

If this list is right, what more is there to good policing besides the absence of bad policing?

As this list suggests, good policing is a tall order: It is multifaceted, hard to measure, and a matter of degree. The list creates tensions for police officers, who are expected to fight crime and disorder with little access to their causes; enforce the law vigorously but never too much; act powerfully and yet limit coercion; and respond to any emergency immediately and in the moment, without being unfair or arbitrary, and somehow always knowing what to do. Moreover, police departments are expected to meet these standards despite limited resources, conflicting and unrealistic community expectations, and dysfunction in institutions on which they depend.

One thing is clear: Neither stopping bad policing nor generating good policing can be achieved by law alone.

D.   *Origins of Contemporary Policing in the United States*

How did contemporary local policing get started?

1.   British and Colonial Precursors to Policing

Every political community, and certainly a growing one, needs some way to address violence and enforce the law. So it was in the colonies where the first night watch was established in Boston in the early 1630s.

> When the first English colonists in America created their own law enforcement agencies, they borrowed from their English heritage. The three important institutions were the sheriff, the constable, and the watch. In the new environment of America, however, these institutions acquired distinctive American features.
>
> The sheriff was the most important law enforcement official in America. Appointed by the colonial governor, the sheriff had a very broad role that included law enforcement, collecting taxes, supervising elections, maintaining bridges and roads, and other miscellaneous duties.
>
> The constable also had responsibility for enforcing the law and carrying out certain legal duties. Initially an elective position, the constable gradually evolved into a semiprofessional appointed office. . . .
>
> The watch most closely resembled the modern-day police. Watchmen patrolled the city to guard against fires, crime, and disorder. At first there was only a night watch. As towns grew larger, they added a day watch. Boston created its first watch in 1634. Following the English tradition, all adult males were expected to serve as watchmen. Many men tried to avoid this duty, either by outright evasion or by paying others to serve in their place. Eventually, the watch evolved into a paid professional force.

Samuel Walker & Charles M. Katz, *The Police in America: An Introduction* 32 (9th ed. 2018).

In the South, these British institutions were supplemented by slave patrols.

> As early as 1704 and continuing through the antebellum period, Southern slave states used local patrols with specific responsibility for regulating the activity of slaves. Those slave patrols were comprised of citizens who did patrol duty as their civic obligation, for pay, rewards, or for exemption from other duties. The patrollers had a defined area which they were to ride in attempts to discover runaway slaves, stolen property, weapons, or to forestall insurrections. Unlike the watchmen, constables, and sheriffs who had some non-policing duties, the slave patrols operated solely for the enforcement of colonial and state laws.

Philip L. Reichel, *Southern Slave Patrols as a Transitional Police Type*, 7 Am. J. Police 51, 68 (1988). Some of these slave patrols functioned much like modern-day departments, wearing uniforms, carrying guns, and walking a beat, leading Marvin Dulaney to label them, "the first distinctly American police system," one that "set the pattern of policing that Americans of African descent would experience throughout their history in America." W. Marvin Dulaney, *Black Police in America* 2 (1996).

2.   Transition to Modern Policing — Britain

Even after independence, American cities looked to Great Britain's law enforcement organization and practices. When, in the early nineteenth century, urbanization and industrialization proved too much for traditional means of maintaining order and enforcing law in England, British Home Secretary Robert Peel proposed to Parliament, and Parliament created, the London Metropolitan Police Department (MPD). Widely viewed as the first modern police department, London's MPD made policing public, professional, and hierarchical — all qualities that Anglo-American policing retains today.

In histories of policing, law is usually treated as incidental. But policing has always been generated by and bound up with law and, critically, law dictates who exercises control over policing. It took an act of Parliament, the Metropolitan Police Act of 1829, 10 Geo. 4 c. 44, to create the London department:

An Act for Improving the Police in and Near the Metropolis (June 19, 1829)

Whereas Offences against Property have of late increased in and near the Metropolis; and the local Establishments of Nightly Watch and Nightly Police have been found inadequate to the Prevention and Detection of Crime, by reason of the frequent Unfitness of the Individuals employed, the Insufficiency of their Number, the limited Sphere of their Authority, and their Want of Connection and Co-operation with each other: And whereas it is expedient to substitute a new and more efficient System of Police in lieu of such Establishments of Nightly Watch and Nightly Police, within the Limits herein-after mentioned, and to constitute an Office of Police, which, acting under the immediate Authority of One of His Majesty's Principal Secretaries of State, shall direct and control the whole of such new System of Police within those Limits: Be it therefore enacted by the King's most Excellent Majesty, by and with the Advice and Consent of the Lords Spiritual and Temporal, and Commons, in this present Parliament assembled, and by the Authority of the same, That it shall be lawful for His Majesty to cause a new Police Office to be established in the City of Westminster, and by Warrant . . . to appoint Two fit Persons as Justices of the Peace. . . .

And be it enacted, That the Whole of the City and Liberties of Westminster, and . . . [the parts of] the Counties of Middlesex, Surrey, and Kent, as are enumerated in the Schedule to this Act shall be constituted . . . into One District, to be called "The Metropolitan Police District"; and a sufficient Number of fit and able Men shall from Time to Time, by the Directions of One of His Majesty's Principal Secretaries of State, be appointed as a Police Force for the Whole of such District, who shall be sworn in . . . to act as Constables for preserving the Peace, and preventing Robberies and other Felonies, and apprehending Offenders against the Peace; and the Men so sworn shall . . . have all such Powers, Authorities, Privileges, and Advantages, and be liable to all such Duties and Responsibilities, as any Constable duly appointed now has or hereafter may have within his Constablewick by virtue of the Common Law of this Realm, or of any Statutes made or to be made, and shall obey all such lawful Commands as they may from Time to Time receive from any of the said Justices for conducting themselves in the Execution of their Office.

And be it enacted, That the said Justices may from Time to Time, subject to the Approbation of One of His Majesty's Principal Secretaries of State, frame such Orders and Regulations as they shall deem expedient, relative to the general Government of the Men to be appointed Members of the Police Force under this Act; the Places of their Residence; the Classification, Rank, and particular Service of the several Members; their Distribution and Inspection; the Description of Arms, Accoutrements, and other Necessaries to be furnished to them; and which of them shall be provided with Horses for the Performance of their Duty; and all such other Orders and Regulations, relative to the said Police Force, as the said Justices shall from Time to Time deem expedient for preventing Neglect or Abuse, and for rendering such Force efficient in the Discharge of all its Duties; and the said Justices may at any Time suspend or dismiss from his Employment any Man belonging to the said Police Force whom they shall think remiss or negligent in the Discharge of his Duty, or otherwise unfit for the same; and when any Man shall be so dismissed, or cease to belong to the said Police Force, all Powers vested in him as a Constable by virtue of this Act shall immediately cease and determine.

And be it enacted, That if any Victualler or Keeper of any House, Shop, Room, or other Place for the Sale of any Liquors, whether spirituous or otherwise, shall knowingly harbour or entertain any Man belonging to the said Police Force, or permit such Man to abide or remain in his House, Shop, Room, or other Place during any Part of the Time appointed for his being on Duty, every such Victualler or Keeper as aforesaid, being convicted thereof before any Two Justices of the Peace, shall for every such Offence forfeit and pay such Sum, not exceeding Five Pounds, as they shall think meet. . . .

And be it enacted, That if any Person shall assault or resist any Person belonging to the said Police Force in the Execution of his Duty, or shall aid or incite any Person so to assault or resist, every such Offender, being convicted thereof before Two Justices of the Peace, shall for every such Offence forfeit and pay such Sum, not exceeding Five Pounds, as the said Justices shall think meet. . . .

NOTES AND QUESTIONS

1. *Purpose of the law.* When Peel introduced the bill, he argued that existing crime was at least in part a result of the lax system of police, in which "each parish had its own watchhouse establishment, its own watchmen, its own discipline, and its own irresponsibility; that it was left to the parochial authorities alone to devise and enforce, and control the means of protecting the property and persons of its inhabitants." The Times (London), Apr. 16, 1829, at 2. Not only were these watches incompetently performed, but even if a parish struggled to make its policing more effective, it would be quickly subverted by criminal spillover from surrounding jurisdictions. Thus, Peel argued, "The chief requisites of an efficient police were unity of design and responsibility of its agents, — both of which were not only not ensured by the present parochial watchhouse system, but were actually prevented by it." *Id.* His proposal was therefore designed to achieve "the necessity and advantage of having an efficient, vigilant, and well-regulated patrol, both by night and day, controlled by one authority, and acting under one head." *Id.* With this design, Peel became the father of modern policing.

2. *Contemporary features.* An 1829 English law seems obscure. But aspects of contemporary policing can be seen in it. Can you identify any?

3. *Policing as a judicial function.* Who controls the Metropolitan Police Department according to the law? How? Although many aspects of contemporary policing are visible in the act, the fact that the police forces are subject to judicial supervision is a holdover from earlier days, when constables effectively functioned as an extension of lower courts. As the law creating the New York Police Department below indicates, early police departments in the United States made a clearer and quicker break from this past than their English counterparts did.

3. Transition to Modern Policing—The United States

a. The First Department

In the United States in the decades after London's MPD was created, immigration and industrialization generated conflict, crime, and urban riots. American leaders turned to the London model in response. Although Boston established a day force that served as a precursor to the Boston Police Department, New York City created the first unified prevention-oriented police force modeled after London's department. Here is the New York state statute that created the New York Police Department. As you read, see how many features of modern policing and police departments you can identify in the act.

AN ACT FOR THE ESTABLISHMENT AND REGULATION OF THE POLICE OF THE CITY OF NEW-YORK, CH. 315, 1844 N.Y. LAWS 469

Article I. Of Police.

§1. The watch department, as at present organized, is hereby abolished. . . .

§2. In lieu of the watch department . . . there shall be established a day and night police of not to exceed eight hundred men, including captains, assistant captains and policemen. . . .

§5. Each ward of the city of New-York shall be a patrol district. The corporation shall provide in each patrol district, a suitable room for the accommodation of the patrol of such district, to be designated "District Head-Quarters." The patrol of each district shall consist of one captain of police, a first and second assistant captain of police. The number of policemen that each ward shall be entitled to shall be designated by an ordinance of the common council.

§6. Captains of police, assistant captains of police, and policemen, shall, in and for the city of New-York, possess all the powers now possessed by marshals appointed by the mayor of the city and county of New-York. . . .

§8. The captain, assistant captains and policemen of the district, in accordance with rules and regulations prescribed by the mayor, in conformity with the laws of the state and the ordinances of the corporation, shall watch and guard the district day and night, and protect the polls at election; and in like manner the policemen shall light the lamps and ring the alarm bells. And the police of the district, or any of them, shall perform all other duties prescribed to them by ordinance of the corporation.

§9. The captain, assistant captains and policemen shall carry a suitable emblem or device by which they may, when necessary, make themselves known.

§10. In case of the absence of the captain the duties required of him shall be performed by the first assistant captain, and in his absence, by the second assistant captain, who, while acting in such capacity, shall possess and exercise the powers and rights of such captain.

§11. At any alarm of fire, it shall be the duty of the captain of patrol nearest the scene of conflagration, forthwith to proceed to the same with one-half of the number of the policemen off duty, to be diligent in preserving order and protecting property. In case of any riot or any other sudden emergency, requiring the services of the police, on notice being given, the captain of police shall forthwith proceed to the scene of riot with the whole police off duty, or any part thereof, and be vigilant in suppressing the same.

§12. It shall be the duty of the policemen to obey such orders as they may from time to time receive from captains and assistant captains of police respecting their duty, and to report (through the captain and assistant captains,) to the chief of police, all violations of the corporation ordinances; to preserve the public peace. And it shall be the duty of the policemen . . . to report to the captain all suspicious persons, all bawdy houses, receiving shops, pawnbrokers' shops, junk shops, second-hand dealers, gaming houses, and all places where idlers, tiplers, gamblers and other disorderly suspicious persons may congregate; to caution strangers and others against going into such places, and against pick-pockets, watch stuffers, droppers, mock auctioneers, burners and all other vicious persons; to direct strangers and others the nearest and safest way to their places of destination, and when necessary to cause them to be accompanied to their destination by one of the police.

§13. All information respecting offences committed, or of suspicious persons or places, shall be communicated to the presiding justice, and made a matter of private record in the police offices, that the services of the whole department may be secured in the detection of offenders and the recovery of the property, and for the more effectual prevention of crime.

§14. The clerks in each police office shall keep a proper book or books, in which shall be entered at length a description of each and every article of stolen or other property, which shall be brought to said offices, or which shall be taken from prisoners, and what disposition has been made thereof. . . .

§16. A room shall be provided at each police court for the deposit and preservation of all property brought to said court. . . .

Article II. Of Chief Police.

. . . **§2.** The chief of police in and for the city and county of New-York, shall . . . (subordinate to the mayor) be the chief executive of the police department; he shall obey, and cause the police department under him to obey the rules and regulations prescribed by the mayor, in accordance with the laws of the United States, of this state, and the ordinances of the common council; he shall repair to the scenes of fires and riots, and take command of the police present, and may direct any or all of the police of the city of New-York to any place where their services may be deemed necessary.

§3. The chief of police shall have his office in the mayor's office.

Article III. Of Appointments and Removals.

§1. The chief of police shall be nominated by the mayor to the common council, and with their approval, shall be appointed by the mayor; the chief of police must be a citizen of the United States, a citizen of the state of New-York, an actual resident of the city and county of New-York. The above mentioned officer shall hold his office for one year, unless sooner removed from office for cause. . . .

§3. The alderman, assistant alderman and the assessors of each ward, shall nominate yearly to the mayor, one captain of police, one first assistant captain, and one second assistant captain, and as many policemen as the ward may be entitled to. The mayor may appoint all or any of the persons thus nominated. Should the mayor reject any such nominations, other persons shall in like manner be nominated to the mayor for such places. Each of said persons so nominated to the mayor, must be a citizen of the United States, a citizen of the state of New-York, and a resident of the ward for which he is nominated. . . .

§4. The captains of police shall have power to suspend Powers or policemen front office for cause. . . . In all such cases of suspension, the officer making the suspension shall, within twenty-four hours thereafter, notify the mayor of such suspension, in writing, which notice shall specify the grounds for such suspension, and contain the names of the witnesses to establish the charge. The mayor shall receive from any person, complaints for cause against the chief of police, captains, assistant captains and policemen; in each case of suspension and complaint, the mayor shall cause notice to the accused to be given, to afford him an opportunity to be heard in his defence. The mayor shall examine witnesses upon the charges, and in defence, and may for cause remove the accused from office, or restore him to duty. The testimony shall be reduced to writing, which testimony, together with the decision of the mayor thereon, shall be filed in the office of the clerk of the common council. . . .

Article IV. Compensation of Officers.

§1. The compensation of officers and patrolmen named in this law, shall be fixed by the common council. . . .

§2. No fees or compensation shall be charged or received by any officer, for the arrest of any prisoner, or for mileage, or for receiving any prisoner into the prison, or discharging him from the same; and no fees or costs shall be charged or received for the issuing of any warrant, subpoena, or other process, or for the taking of a complaint, bail, or affidavit. . . .

§10. No member of the police department, nor any magistrate or police officer, shall receive any present or reward for services rendered, or to be rendered, unless with the knowledge and approbation of the mayor, such approbation to be given in writing, and entered in a book to be kept in the mayor's office; any officer who shall receive any present or reward, in violation of this section shall be guilty of a misdemeanor, and shall also be removed from office.

NOTES AND QUESTIONS

1. *Other cities.* The same forces of urbanization, immigration, and racial conflict, combined with growing intolerance for disorder, that led New York City to create a police department soon led other cities to follow, including New Orleans and Cincinnati in 1852, Boston and Philadelphia in 1854, and Chicago and Milwaukee in 1855. By the last quarter of the nineteenth century, all major cities in the United States had police departments.

2. *Contemporary elements: example 1.* New York's department has been hierarchical since the beginning. In the law excerpted above, the ranks are chief, captain, first assistant captain, second assistant captain, and policeman. Today, the NYPD is run by the police commissioner, who is appointed by the mayor. The police commissioner has under him a first deputy commissioner, other deputy commissioners,

and a chief of department (the highest ranking uniformed member of the service). Under the chief of department, there are bureau chiefs, assistant chiefs, deputy chiefs, inspectors, captains, lieutenants, sergeants, detectives (grades third to first), police officers, probationary police officers, recruit officers, and cadets. This unified hierarchy allows a member of the public to tell an officer about a crime, confident that the officer will communicate the message to headquarters, which in turn may assign other officers to respond. What other consequences might hierarchy have?

3. *Contemporary elements: example 2.* Police officers were not then and are not now limited to addressing crime and enforcing the law. At the turn of the twentieth century,

> [p]olicemen on patrol . . . spent most of their time doing nothing at all—or in such routine activities as learning the beat or socializing with local people. Those assigned to outlying residential neighborhoods might go for days or weeks without making an arrest or engaging in law enforcement activities. Even when the police were active, they were often involved in functions only indirectly related to crime control. Police took injured persons to hospitals, mediated family quarrels, rounded up stray dogs for the city pound, returned lost children to parents, directed traffic on the downtown streets and at bridge crossings, removed dead horses from city streets, reported broken gas lamps, and performed the innumerable services that have always constituted most police work.

Mark H. Haller, *Historical Roots of Police Behavior: Chicago, 1890–1925*, 10 Law & Soc'y Rev. 303, 321 (1976). Police officers in early departments helped with soup kitchens, distributed shoes and medicine to the poor, and set up beds for homeless people in stationhouses. Today, they direct traffic, find lost children, deal with abandoned cars, manage crowds, check on the elderly, and run youth basketball programs, among many other activities.

4. *Powers and duties.* Today, the New York City Charter says this about the police department's powers and duties:

> The police department . . . shall have the power and it shall be their duty to preserve the public peace, prevent crime, detect and arrest offenders, suppress riots, mobs and insurrections, disperse unlawful or dangerous assemblages and assemblages which obstruct the free passage of public streets, sidewalks, parks and places; . . . regulate, direct, control and restrict the movement of vehicular and pedestrian traffic for the facilitation of traffic and the convenience of the public as well as the proper protection of human life and health; remove all nuisances in the public streets, parks and places; . . . and for these purposes to arrest all persons guilty of violating any law or ordinance for the suppression or punishment of crimes or offenses.

N.Y. City Charter ch. 18, §435(a). How much has police authority changed in New York? What do you see as the big differences?

5. *Police and data.* Here is another feature of policing that might not immediately jump out at you: Police officers have been recordkeepers and information producers since the beginning.

6. *Staving off misconduct.* Both the Metropolitan Act and the New York statute seem concerned with preventing and addressing misconduct by the new forces. What kinds of misconduct do the drafters seem worried about? How do they attempt to prevent misconduct? Do these statutes assume that misconduct is baked into policing?

7. *Political accountability.* The New York law places control over officers in political hands. Look at the chief's term in office and who gets to hire and fire officers. Policing in Britain remained under bureaucratic control. Consider the trade-offs between these two alternatives. On one hand, political control ensures that policing is responsive to the community's (or at least its politicians') concerns. On the other, it permits political figures to leverage the police toward political ends and to use police jobs as patronage, a recipe for corrupt and incompetent police. Indeed, for decades men in New York who wanted to work as officers paid politicians for the privilege, and police chiefs in many U.S. cities changed as often as the seasons. Bureaucratic control can reduce corruption and improve selection, but it risks policing that does not reflect community values. Departments continue today to struggle with balancing these concerns. Which means of control seems like it might work better? Why?

8. *Signaling to the public.* The New York statute provides for emblems, and the department choose a star-shaped badge, which evolved into the contemporary badge. Uniforms came to New York City officers later, in 1854. What purposes do you think badges and uniforms serve? Many states require officers to wear uniforms or badges for certain activities today. Virginia, for example, requires:

> All officers . . . who shall make any arrest, search or seizure on any public road or highway of this Commonwealth shall be dressed at the time . . . in such uniform as he may customarily wear in the performance of his duties which will clearly show him to casual observation to be an officer.

Nothing in this section shall render unlawful any arrest, search or seizure by an officer who is not in such customary uniform.

Va. Code Ann. §19.2-78. Does that help you figure out what badges and uniforms are for?

9. *Training and qualifications.* The New York Act mentions neither training nor qualifications for officers, and early members of American police departments had neither. "New policemen heard a brief speech from a high-ranking officer, received a hickory club, a whistle, and a key to the call box, and were sent out on the street to work with an experienced officer." Mark H. Haller, *Historical Roots of Police Behavior: Chicago, 1890–1925*, 10 Law & Soc'y Rev. 303, 303 (1976). As a result, by most accounts, nineteenth-century policing was largely incompetent, brutal, and corrupt.

b.   Early Police Violence

Despite early accountability mechanisms, illegal violence was institutionalized in nineteenth-century and early twentieth-century policing, including in New York, where public hostility to police practices led officers to use violence, which in turn increased distrust of the police.

> In the Irish tenement districts of the Fourth and Eighteenth wards, for example, police officers were walking targets and would only patrol in groups of three or more. To reassert control of these areas, Capt. George W. Walling organized strong-arm squads in 1853 consisting of several plainclothes officers armed with clubs made of locust wood, an extremely hard wood that could crack skulls on impact. Squad members proceeded to "beat senseless" every known gang member in the area and allegedly dispersed the criminal element. As strong-arm tactics won praise from local business interests, the department made nightsticks mandatory equipment for all officers, and patrolmen increasingly wielded their clubs as a means of preserving order and establishing authority. Many New Yorkers, however, resented this violent intrusion in their neighborhoods and would become even more antagonistic toward police.

Marilynn Johnson, *Street Justice: A History of Police Violence in New York City* 15–16 (2003). More generally, in early police departments,

> there were essentially three circumstances under which violence, as an accepted norm, became part of police procedure.
>
> First of all, many policemen believed that they should themselves, at times, mete out punishment to wrongdoers. Policemen on patrol, particularly in high-crime areas, were often expected to be able to physically dominate their beats and to handle suspicious persons or minor crimes without resort to arrest. This was particularly true before the installation of call boxes in 1880. Arrests were difficult to make. A patrolman, unable to summon assistance, had to walk his prisoner as much as a mile to the station house. . . .
>
> A second type of police violence occurred as a tactic to persuade a recalcitrant defendant to confess his guilt or to reveal the names of accomplices. Indeed, standard

interrogation in important cases, and many less important cases, was to place a suspect in the "sweat box,"[15] as it was called, for hours or days, until he broke down
under continuous questioning.

Finally, the police subculture often sanctioned violence to uphold the personal dignity of the policeman. Such violence . . . was seldom recorded; and, when reported
in newspapers, was difficult to distinguish from the random violence that some
policemen occasionally visited upon citizens.

Mark H. Haller, *Historical Roots of Police Behavior: Chicago, 1890–1925*, 10 L. & Soc'y
Rev. 303, 317–320 (1976).

Serious, even deadly, police violence was not uncommon. For example,

Between 1875 and 1920, Chicago police officers killed 307 people, accounting for
one homicide in every eighteen committed in the city. Chicago policemen claimed
three times as many victims as local gangsters during this era. In a city renowned
for its bloody strikes, local law enforcers killed almost two and half times as many
Chicagoans as died in labor conflict.

Jeffrey S. Adler, *Shoot to Kill: The Use of Deadly Force by the Chicago Police, 1875–1920*,
38 J. of Interdisc. Hist. 233, 237 (2007). According to Jeffrey Adler, a dramatic rise
in armed robberies left Chicagoans fearful and calling for more aggressive policing.
The police department adopted more deadly police strategies in response, including ordering officers to "shoot to kill," and rewarding them when they did so, even
when they fired into crowds, killed innocent people, or shot fleeing suspects in the
back. See *id.* at 241–249.

In Chicago, deadly force was usually deemed legal. But many forms of brutality
by officers in early departments clearly violated the law. Still, officers were largely
immune from legal sanction.

In the case of police use of violence, as in other violations of law by policemen,
there was little recourse for an aggrieved citizen. Very early, the police developed a
group loyalty that required policemen to rally to the defense of an officer in trouble.
Top officials of the department told new recruits that, if they could not say something good about fellow officers, they should remain silent. . . . When charges were
brought against a policeman, conviction was difficult for a number of reasons. As
one city hall official told a reporter in 1905, "It is well nigh impossible to convict a
favored policeman of any offense. . . . If ten witnesses testify to a certain set of facts,

---

[15] *Ed. note:* "The sweat box is a small cell completely dark and arranged to be heated till the prisoner, unable to endure the temperature, will promise to answer as desired. Or refusal to answer may
be overcome by whipping, by beating, with rubber hoses, clubs, or fists, or by kicking, or by threats, or
promises." Nat'l Commn. on Law Observance and Enforcement, *Report on Lawlessness in Law Enforcement*
47 (1931). In 1910, the President of the International Association of the Chiefs of Police described sweat
boxes after the Civil War, involving a cell "in close proximity to a stove, in which a scorching fire was built
and fed with old bones, pieces of rubber shoes, etc., all to make great heat and offensive smells, until the
sickened and perspiring inmate of the cell confessed in order to get released." *Id.* at 38–39. Well into the
twentieth century, the sweat box was used often in close conjunction with other methods for pressuring
or torturing suspects into confessing crimes. Together, these methods are often known as *the third degree.*
Interrogation methods are discussed further in Chapter 3.

> and their testimony is unshaken, the defendant puts twenty police witnesses on the stand to testify to an entirely different set of facts."

Haller, *supra*, at 320. Alexander "Clubber" Williams, for example, an officer famous for brutality over his 30-year career in the NYPD, received more than 350 formal complaints against him and faced 18 charges for assaulting members of the public, as well as police board hearings and civil suits. Yet he was never convicted and was repeatedly promoted by the department, retiring as an inspector. See Johnson, *supra*, at 44–45. It seems Williams was not wrong when he said, "There is more law in the end of a nightstick than in a decision of the Supreme Court." *The Law of a Nightstick*, N.Y. Tribune, Sep. 25, 1898, at 31.

Today, although police violence remains a serious problem, some of the casual violence that early departments engaged in has been replaced with formalized state coercion through arrests and incarceration. What consequences might there be from trading violence for control?

The Line from Slave Patrols to Policing Today

Southern departments emerged largely at the same time northern departments did, but they often evolved out of slave patrols. These new departments addressed problems resulting from industrialization and immigration like their northern counterparts. But far more than in the north, southern departments existed to maintain racial order, dealing with, as one mayor put it, "a vagabond freed element in our midst, and constantly pouring into the city, together with the influx of 'roughs' coming by every steamer." Edward L. Ayers, *Vengeance and Justice: Crime and Punishment in the 19th-Century American South* 173 (1984). These threats made it "a matter of necessity to keep up at any cost an efficient Police Force for our protection." *Id.*

New departments enforced Black Codes and, later, Jim Crow laws. They funneled Black people into chain gangs and the convict lease system, which, after slavery, became newly important forms of white control. In the late nineteenth and early twentieth centuries, police colluded with lynch mobs, sometimes participating in killings. See *id.* at 245–246. Later, the police turned African Americans out of so-called sundown towns, the all-white municipalities in the United States that excluded African Americans, pressuring or forcing them to leave before nightfall.

Southern police departments also helped to transmute white oppression into Black criminality. "By making African American predators the new face of public disorder and the new focus of the beefed-up criminal justice system, city officials pandered to jittery voters, affirmed their commitment to white supremacy, and demonstrated their crime-fighting zeal." Jeffrey S. Adler, *Less Crime, More Punishment: Violence, Race, and Criminal Justice in Early Twentieth-Century America*, 102 J. Am. Hist. 34, 43 (2015). This pattern continued during the twentieth century, and not just in the south. In a historical review, Elizabeth Hinton and DeAnza Cook argue that criminal law enforcement strategies throughout the twentieth century have functioned to target and control Black Americans. For instance,

> in the wake of the mainstream civil rights movement in the 1950s and 1960s, federal, state, and local law enforcement forces regularly mobilized against civil

rights protestors, black power militants, and urban activists dubbed by authorities as domestic insurgents. Law enforcement officials justified the occupation,
patrol, and surveillance of "high risk," low-income neighborhoods of color with
mounting media and government reports of mass protest, fear of crime, and civil
violence in the late 1960s. . . .

. . . National law enforcement programs that originated in the mid-1960s laid the
groundwork for the implementation of proactive policing reforms in the "high
risk" neighborhoods identified by police and set the stage for community-based
policing experiments and crime prevention tactics . . . into the twenty-first century. The War on Gangs waged during the Clinton administration consolidated
the federal aims and objectives of the preceding Wars on Crime and Drugs. . . .

Despite the numerous complexities and nuances spotlighted by this richer, fuller
historical overview of policing and punishment in America, it is impossible to
disentangle institutional racism in America—past and present—from the simultaneous development of the nation's criminal legal system.

Elizabeth Hinton & DeAnza Cook, *The Mass Criminalization of Black Americans: A
Historical Overview*, 4 Ann. Rev. Criminology (forthcoming 2021).

   In light of this history, many draw a direct line from early slave patrols to contemporary racialized policing practices. As Bryan Stevenson put it, "The presumptive identity of black men as 'slaves' evolved into the presumptive identity of 'criminal,' and we
have yet to fully recover from this historical frame." Bryan Stevenson, *A Presumption
of Guilt: The Legacy of America's History of Racial Injustice*, in *Policing the Black
Man: Arrest, Prosecution, and Imprisonment* 3, 12 (Angela J. Davis ed., 2017).

   Although some contemporary police leaders resist talking about the past, many
others see acknowledging this history as critical to building trust between police
departments and communities of color today. As Stockton, California, police chief Eric
Jones has said, "There was a time where police . . . used to be dispatched to keep
lynchings 'civil.' That's a fact of our history that we have to at least acknowledge. Now,
I didn't do that. These officers didn't do that. But the badge we wear still does carry
the burden, and we need to at least understand why those issues are deep-rooted
in a lot of our communities." Stockton Police Department, *Chief Eric Jones Talking
Police/Community Relations at Progressive Community Church*, Facebook (July 17,
2016). Do you want your police department to acknowledge its historical role in racial
oppression? How?

4.   The Role of Law in Policing over Time

Both because there was less law and because early American policing was less controlled by the law that existed, legal norms mattered less in early policing than they
do today.

   Not only were policemen untrained in law, but they operated within a criminal
   justice system that generally placed little emphasis upon legal procedure. Most
   of those arrested by the police were tried before local police justices, who rarely
   had legal training. Those arrested seldom had attorneys, so that no legal defense

was made. Thus, there were few mechanisms for introducing legal norms into the street experiences and crime control activities of policemen. . . . Democratic sensitivities rather than legal norms were expected to guide police behavior and check abuses. . . . [P]olicemen and other criminal justice personnel developed informal systems of operation that reflected their own subculture and organizational needs. These informal methods of operation bore, at best, only an indirect relationship to the formal legal system.

Mark H. Haller, *Historical Roots of Police Behavior: Chicago, 1890–1925*, 10 Law & Soc'y Rev. 303, 303–304 (1976).

By the 1890s, however, it became harder to ignore complaints about police incompetence, corruption, violence, and lawlessness. States began to take minor, largely ineffectual, steps to address problems in policing with new legislation including, for example, statutes criminalizing excessive force and the coercive interrogation methods known as the third degree. But no state meaningfully enforced laws against corruption or abuse, and police officials often defended apparently illegal investigative techniques as essential. Reformers focused more on improving police professionalism through training, institutional changes, and greater public scrutiny than subjecting the police to greater legal controls.

Starting in the 1930s, commentators and public officials focused on bureaucratic legal reforms for the police, albeit initially with limited effect. State and federal courts excluded some confessions obtained through brutal methods, a practice the Supreme Court blessed when it decided *Brown v. Mississippi*, 297 U.S. 278 (1936), a case that initiated federal constitutional scrutiny of local police practices. In addition, some states passed bills expanding statutory regulation of the police, including through the use of the exclusionary rule in criminal cases and hiring standards and civil service requirements intended to improve the quality of officers. In 1939, the U.S. Department of Justice created the Civil Liberties Unit, and with it began federal civil rights prosecutions of local police officers.

In the 1960s, the federal courts' role in shaping local policing expanded dramatically. In *Mapp v. Ohio*, 367 U.S. 643 (1961), the U.S. Supreme Court, led by Chief Justice Earl Warren, applied the Fourth Amendment rule excluding unconstitutionally obtained evidence to the states, starting a new era in policing. The Warren Court, frustrated with state governance of policing and racial injustice in the criminal process, interpreted constitutional criminal procedure rights expansively to regulate police conduct. Although the Supreme Court later retrenched, many reformers long continued to view constitutional rights enforced by courts as the primary mechanism for addressing police misconduct.

Over the last decade or so, scholars, reformers, and public officials have highlighted the limits of constitutional litigation and court regulation of the police, and have turned their focus to strengthening state, local, and community-based democratic and regulatory control over the police. This shift was hastened by concern over police shootings of Black men, especially the 2014 death of Michael Brown, an unarmed Black teenager, at the hands of a police officer in Ferguson, Missouri. The protests that followed Brown's death and subsequent police shootings revealed a national crisis in policing that inspired new—often local—efforts at police reform.

It was also encouraged by the 2016 election of President Donald Trump, which signaled a turn away from federal scrutiny of local police practices and federal efforts at reform. In the years since, states have become more active in regulating the police, including by changing use-of-force rules and strengthening state criminal remedies for misconduct. Local reformers have developed new mechanisms for community input and oversight of officers. That process again received a dramatic push in the aftermath of the killing of George Floyd, another unarmed Black man, in Minneapolis in May 2020.

Although the law governing the police has expanded with time, scholars disagree about how much all that law actually influences policing. Lawyers tend to assume that well-crafted laws will effectively shape officer conduct and that problems in policing can be addressed with improved rules and remedies. Examples of their efforts appear in every chapter of this book. And normatively speaking, in a liberal society, policing *should* be subject to the *rule of law*. Policing should be legally authorized by legitimate institutions and constrained by specific rules guiding officer conduct. But legal rules designed to change policing are filtered through police departments and social, political, and legal institutions that can, in practice, limit their effect. As you read, consider what might make law more powerful in shaping policing.

Technology and Policing

Technological changes have transformed how officers communicate, travel, collect and utilize information, and use force, all with significant consequences. It would be hard to summarize the effects of technology on policing succinctly, but four effects might be worth noting here.

First, technology has changed how officers and members of the community engage each other. For example, telephones, the 911 universal-emergency-number system, and cellphones have each made it easier for the public to call on the police. The spread of cars both justified police interventions and made it easier for police to respond. See Sarah A. Seo, *Policing the Open Road: How Cars Transformed American Freedom* (2019); Samuel Walker, *Popular Justice: A History of American Criminal Justice* 189–191 (1980). But cars have also removed police from the streets, so that they no longer walk the beat, a change that community-policing strategies have sought to mitigate.

Second, surveillance, transportation, forensic, analytic, and communication technologies promote officer efficiency. GPS tracking devices, drones, and closed-circuit cameras, among other devices, have made surveillance more intrusive and less resource-intensive. Computer-aided dispatch, crime geomapping, and predictive-policing strategies take advantage of computing technology to determine where police officers should go. See Andrew G. Ferguson, *The Rise of Big Data Policing: Surveillance, Race, and the Future of Law Enforcement* (2017). Car- and phone-based computers give officers more information in the field than ever before, and FirstNet, a new law enforcement wireless communications network, is improving communication among agencies and officers.

Third, technology in both police and private hands has transformed police accountability. Police are no longer unwatched or unwatchable. Instead, radios, computer-aided dispatch systems, GPS in cars, dashboard-mounted and body-worn cameras, and citizen-held cameras help track and record what officers do. See I. Bennett Capers, *Crime, Surveillance, and Communities*, 40 Fordham Urb. L.J. 959 (2013) (describing ways technology can improve policing accountability).

Finally, technologies of force have changed the consequences of antagonizing or resisting the police. For much of the twentieth century, police officers had two basic options: Striking weapons, such as batons, could be used to subdue a suspect without killing him, but only when the suspect was within reach and only by risking officer safety. Firearms, by contrast, allowed force at a distance and with less risk, but they were far more lethal. In recent decades, departments have adopted an expanding array of less-lethal technologies for using force against individual suspects and for crowd control at some distance, including rubber bullets, oleoresin capsicum (OC) spray devices (pepper spray), and conducted-energy devices, such as Tasers.

Each new technology brings with it risks and rewards, and together technological changes have transformed policing, sometimes in unexpected ways, often creating new challenges for the law.

E.   Policing as a (Heavily Regulated) Public Good

The brief historical materials above provide some perspective on *how* publicly provided local policing became the paradigmatic form of policing in the United States and how additional law developed to shape and restrain it. But legal history provides a limited perspective on *why* we organize policing this way. This question can be broken down further: (1) Why is policing publicly provided? (2) Why is it mostly local? (3) Why do we have so much regulation of local policing beyond the local political process?

Although economists rarely consider policing in any detail, economics provides one useful way of answering these questions. The following nontechnical excerpt by Ostrom and Ostrom describes what economists call *public goods*, which, because of their nature, will not be adequately provided by private markets. It helps to explain why policing is both public and local.

1.   The Nature of Public Goods

Vincent Ostrom & Elinor Ostrom, *Public Goods and Public Choices*

in *Alternatives for Delivering Public Services: Toward Improved Performance* 7, 9–27 (E.S. Savas ed., 1977)

The Nature of Public Goods

People have long been aware that the nature of goods has a bearing upon human welfare. Aristotle, for example, observed: "that which is common to the greatest number has the least care bestowed upon it." Within the last two decades an extensive literature has developed on the character-istics that distinguish public or collective goods from private or individual goods. In this discussion we shall consider exclusion and jointness of use or consumption as two essential defining characteristics in distinguishing between private and public goods. . . .[16]

Exclusion

Exclusion has long been identified as a necessary characteristic for goods and services to be supplied under market conditions. Exclusion occurs when potential users can be denied goods or services unless they meet the terms and conditions of the vendor. If both agree, goods or services are supplied at a price. A *quid pro quo* exchange occurs. The buyer acquires the good and the seller acquires the value specified.

Where exclusion is infeasible, anyone can derive benefits from the good so long as nature or the efforts of others supply it. The air we breathe can be viewed as a good supplied by nature, so exclusion is difficult to attain. A view of a building—whether seen as a "good" or a "bad"—is supplied by the efforts of others and is not subject to exclusion in normal circumstances. Air, noise, and water pollution are "bads" that an individual cannot exclude or avoid except at a cost; conversely, an individual cannot be excluded from receiving a good when the pollution level is reduced.

Jointness of Use or Consumption

Another attribute of goods or services pertains to jointness of use or consumption. No jointness of consumption exists when consumption by one person precludes its use or consumption by another person. In that case consumption is completely subtractible. A loaf of bread consumed by one person is not available for consumption by another; it is subtracted from the total that was originally available. A good having *no* jointness of consumption and with which exclusion *is* feasible is defined as a purely private good. Jointness of consumption, on the other hand, implies that the use or enjoyment of a good by one person does not foreclose its use or enjoyment by others; despite its use by one person, it remains available for use by others in undiminished quantity and quality. A weather forecast is an example of a joint consumption good.

Few, if any, joint consumption goods are perfectly nonsubtractible. The use and enjoyment of gravity as a force which firmly keeps ou[r] feet on the ground may illustrate the case of perfect *nonsubtractibility*, but most joint consumption goods are instead subject to *partial subtractibility*. At certain

---

[16] *Ed. note:* What the Ostroms call *jointness* and *exclusion* other economists usually call *rivalrous* and *excludable.* In that language, a public good is one that is both *nonexcludable* and *nonrivalrous.* The precise terminology matters less than recognizing the concepts when you see them.

thresholds of supply, one person's use of a good subtracts *in part* from its use and enjoyment by others. Congestion begins to occur. Each further increase in use impairs the use of the good for each other person in the community of users. Highways, for example, become subject to congestion when the addition of more users causes delays and inconveniences for others. . . .

. . . In the same way we can think of exclusion as applying in degrees. A walled city can attain a high degree of exclusion by controlling admission to those who wish to reside, enter, and do business with the city. Even in the unwalled city, jurisdictional boundaries may be a way for distinguishing between residents and nonresidents where some public goods and services are primarily for the joint benefit of persons living within those boundaries. A weak form of partial exclusion may exist in such circumstances.

Exclusion, and jointness of consumption, are independent attributes. . . . If these defining characteristics are then arrayed in a simple matrix, four logical types of goods are revealed as indicated in figure 1.

FIGURE 1

	Alternative use	Joint use
Feasible exclusion	**Private goods:** Bread, shoes, automobiles, haircuts, books, etc.	**Toll goods:** Theaters, night clubs, telephone service, toll roads, cable TV, electric power, library, etc.
Infeasible exclusion	**Common pool resources:** Water pumped from a groundwater basin, fish taken from an ocean, crude oil extracted from an oil pool	**Public goods:** Peace and security of a community, national defense, mosquito abatement, fire protection, streets, weather forecasts, public TV, etc.

. . . Most governmental services . . . are of the public good, toll good, or common pool resource types. . . . In this discussion we shall focus more upon the type characterized as public goods because they pose the more difficult problems in the operation of a public economy. . . .

Measurement

Since public goods are difficult to package or unitize they are also difficult to measure. Quantitative measures cannot be calculated like bushels of wheat or tons of steel. Qualitative measures such as the amount of dissolved oxygen in water, victimization rates, and traffic delay can be used to measure important characteristics of goods subject to joint consumption, but such measures cannot be aggregated in the same way that gross production can be calculated for a steel factory or for the steel industry as a whole.

The task of measuring performance in the production of public goods will not yield to simple calculations. Performance measurement depends instead upon estimates in which indicators or proxy measures are used as estimates of performance. . . .

Some Implications for Organization

. . . If a public good is supplied by nature or the efforts of other individuals, each individual will be free to take advantage of the good since he cannot be excluded from its use or enjoyment. . . . [He or she] has an incentive to take advantage of whatever is freely available without paying a price or contributing a proportionate share of the effort to supply a public good. . . . If some are successful in pursuing a holdout strategy, others will have an incentive to follow suit. The likely short-run consequence is that voluntary efforts will *fail* to supply a satisfactory level of public goods. Individuals furthering their own interest will fail to take sufficient account of the interests of others and the joint good will inexorably deteriorate.

. . . Therefore, to supply many public goods and services, it is necessary to have recourse to some form of collective action in which sanctions can be used to foreclose the holdout problem and to compel each individual to pay his share of the burden. . . . Potential recourse to coercion in levying taxes and preventing holdouts will be . . . important. . . .

The Organization of a Public Economy . . .

Some Basic Assumptions and Terms . . .

A public good, as defined above, is a good or service subject to joint use or consumption where exclusion is difficult or costly to attain. . . . Governments, like households, might be viewed first as *collective consumption units*. Once the collective consumption aspects of governmental organization have been identified, we can then turn to the production side. Governmental agencies and private enterprises can be viewed as potential production units concerned with the supply and delivery of public goods and services. . . . [A] governmental unit operating as a collective consumption unit may contract with another governmental agency or a private enterprise to produce public services for its constituents.

Collective Consumption Units . . .

Whereas the income received for providing a private good conveys information about the demand for that good, taxes collected under the threat of coercion say little about the demand for a public good or service. Payment of taxes indicates only that taxpayers prefer paying taxes to going to jail. Little or no information is revealed about user preferences for goods procured with tax-supported expenditures. As a consequence, the organization of collective consumption units will need to create alternative mechanisms to prices for articulating and aggregating demands into collective choices reflecting individuals' preferences for a quantity and/or quality of public goods or services.

An appropriately constituted collective consumption unit would include within its jurisdictional boundary the relevant beneficiaries who share a common interest in the joint good or service and would exclude those who do not benefit. The collective consumption unit would be empowered to make operational decisions without requiring unanimity: this is necessary to foreclose holdouts. It would hold a limited monopoly position on the consumption side. It would have authority to exercise coercive sanctions, but it need not meet the criterion sometimes used to define a government as exercising a monopoly over the legitimate use of force for a society as a whole.

The choice of particular voting rules, modes of representation and rules applicable to making operational decisions about taxes, expenditures and levels of service need to be viewed from a constitutional perspective where the consequences of such rules are estimated in choosing a particular structure of organization. The set of rules most likely to produce decisions which take account of citizen-consumer interests is preferred. Citizens are presumed to be the best judges of their own interests. Such rules provide mechanisms for articulating and aggregating demand in the absence of market prices and for translating demand into decisions about the level of service to be procured. . . .

Production Units

A production unit, by contrast, would be one which can aggregate technical factors of production to yield goods and services meeting the requirements of a collective consumption unit. The organization of an appropriate production unit will require a manager who can assume entrepreneurial responsibility for aggregating factors of production and organizing and monitoring performance of a production team that would supply the appropriate level of a good or service.

A collective consumption unit may supply a public good or service through its own production unit. In that case, the collective consumption unit and the production unit would serve the same population. Yet, the constitution of the two units may be essentially separable. . . .

TABLE 3.   OPTIONS FOR OBTAINING PUBLIC SERVICES

A government which serves as a collective-consumption unit may obtain the desired public goods by:

1. Operating its own production unit

   Example: A city with its own fire or police department

2. Contracting with a private firm

   Example: A city that contracts with a private firm for snow removal, street repair, or traffic-light maintenance

3. Establishing standards of service and leaving it up to each consumer to select a private vendor and to purchase service

   Example: A city that licenses taxis to provide service, refuse collection firms to remove trash

4. Issuing vouchers to families and permitting them to purchase service from any authorized supplier

   Example: A jurisdiction that issues food stamps, rent vouchers, or education vouchers, or operates a Medicaid program

5. Contracting with another government unit

   Example: A city which purchases tax assessment and collection services from a county government unit, sewage treatment from a special sanitary district, and special vocational education services from a school board in an adjacent city

6. Producing some services with its own unit and purchasing other services from other jurisdictions and from private firms

   Example: A city with its own police patrol force, that purchases laboratory services from the county sheriff, joins with several adjacent communities to pay for a joint dispatching service, and pays a private ambulance firm to provide emergency medical transportation

---

NOTES AND QUESTIONS

1. *Policing as a public good.* Is policing really a public good? Under what conditions might policing be excludable? Subtractable?

2. *Policing as a private good.* Not all policing is provided publicly. By many estimates, there are more private security workers than public ones. Private security guards patrol malls and gated communities, and they transport money in armored cars, among other activities. What do these examples of private policing tell us about when policing is most and least a public good? For discussions of private policing and its implications for public policing, see, e.g., Elizabeth E. Joh, *Conceptualizing the Private Police*, 2005 Utah L. Rev. 573; David A. Sklansky, *Private Police and Democracy*, 43 A. Crim. L. Rev. 89 (2006).

3. *Private–public policing.* Sometimes public policing works jointly with private policing. Thus, cities license and register alarm companies and work with them to vet alarm calls and prevent false alarms. Cities hire private companies to operate red-light cameras and issue citations and share the revenue. What do examples of public–private partnerships tell us? States also sometimes authorize private entities to run police departments with arrest powers. See, e.g., Va. Code Ann. §19.2-13. How would the Ostroms think about the Kings Dominion Park Police Department in Virginia, or the Yale (University) Police Department in Connecticut? See Seth W. Stoughton, *The Blurred Blue Line: Reform in an Era of Public & Private Policing*, 44 Am. J. Crim. L. 117 (2017) (discussing the relationship between private and public policing).

Likely, the most famous public–private policing partnership is fictional, that between the Gotham City Police Department, under the leadership of Commissioner James W. Gordon, and the city's vigilante, known as Batman. Commissioner Gordon effectively institutionalized Batman's role in public policing when he installed a bat symbol searchlight on the roof of Gotham City police headquarters to enable the department to solicit Batman's help. See Bob Kane & Jack Shiff, *Case of the*

Costume-Clad Killers, Detective Comics, No. 60 (DC Comics Feb. 1942). But the relationship has long been complicated by persistent corruption in the Gotham City Police Department and Batman's unorthodox crime-fighting methods. For more on Gotham City policing, see Ed Brubaker et al., *Gotham Central* (omnibus ed., DC Comics 2016), and Chuck Dixon et al., Batman: GCPD Nos. 1-4 (DC Comics 1996).

4. *What is the good of policing?* What precisely is the *good* at issue in policing? Call response? Public safety? Freedom from fear? How you define the good at issue could make a big difference in what and how much policing you think communities should provide. For example, what if we see public safety as a good that includes both safety from private harm and security from government overreach and oppression? Would that lead to less intrusive ways of achieving safety? See Tracey L. Meares, *Policing: A Public Good Gone Bad*, Bos. Rev. (Aug. 1, 2017).

5. *Common interest in policing.* Ostrom and Ostrom argue that public goods should be organized by those "who share a common interest in the joint good or service." What defines that group for policing? Geographic contiguity? Economic interdependence? Crime conditions? Trust in the police?

6. *Local vs. national consumption units.* Most countries organize policing nationally rather than locally. Just as modern police departments were getting off the ground, John Stuart Mill argued in favor of central superintendence of policing on the ground that effectiveness in crime control, consistency in punishment, and equal justice between individuals are too important to be left to local governments that may be inadequate to the challenge. See John Stuart Mill, *Considerations on Representative Government* 279–280 (1861). Should we make the federal government the collective consumption unit for policing? What about having national standards that govern qualifications, management, and conduct?

7. *Federal consumption units.* Although most policing is local, the federal government is the collective consumption unit for some important aspects of policing. The FBI focuses on stopping terrorism, corruption, and organized crime, among other activities. The DEA handles drug trafficking. The Secret Service fights counterfeiting. And so on. In addition, many states operate as the collective consumption unit for some complex criminal investigations and state highway patrol. What might explain the divisions?

8. *Big-city policing.* If common interests in policing are truly local—so much so that more than 8,500 police departments in the United States serve towns with populations of fewer than 10,000—why do big cities have only one primary policing agency? The NYPD polices 8.5 million people spread over 300 square miles. The Jacksonville (Fla.) Sheriff's Office (which provides law enforcement for the City of Jacksonville and Duval County, Florida) serves 900,000 people spread across nearly 750 square miles. And the Juneau (Alaska) Police Department serves 32,000 people over an area bigger than Delaware. Should these departments be broken up? Does it surprise you that experts regularly argue instead for consolidating police departments to improve service?

9. *Local elections and policing.* Are local governments really so good at aggregating preferences and serving collective interests? Voter turnout in local elections is abysmally low, often around 25 percent of voters, and incumbency rates are exceptionally high. Would it be any better to use state and federal elections? More people vote, but those voters are concerned about a far broader range of issues. See Roderick M. Hills, Jr., *Is Federalism Good for Localism? The Localist Case for Federal Regimes*, 21 J. L. & Pol. 187, 189–192 (2005).

10. *Police production units.* Ostrom and Ostrom suggest that even if you think municipalities are the appropriate collective consumption unit for policing, we might still consider *producing* policing in other ways. Indeed, quite a few small juris-dictions contract with other law enforcement agencies, often county sheriffs' offices, for policing services. How might these two alternative approaches affect community control over policing?

2.   Nonmarket Failures and State and Federal Regulation of Local Police

Local governments (empowered by state law) generate most policing and exercise the greatest control over it. Local elections choose public officials who in turn hire, fire, and supervise police chiefs; influence departmental rules; and deter-mine department budgets. And yet most of the law described in this book is fed-eral and state law that seeks to facilitate, change, or restrain some aspect of local policing. Why is there so much federal and state law that seeks to influence local policing? Sociologists, historians, and political theorists might all provide differ-ent explanations for this phenomenon. Continuing with the economic theme, one way to think about federal and state law on policing is as a form of regulation.

Government regulation is often used to mitigate problems with private mar-kets: Because manufacturers do not factor the costs of pollution into production decisions, we regulate air and water pollution. Because private markets generate normatively unacceptable disparities in income and wealth, we develop welfare pro-grams to redistribute resources. Might state and federal government law influenc-ing the police similarly be a tool to mitigate systematic problems with the public provision of goods by local political processes?

Although providing policing publicly and locally solves a basic problem — private markets would not generate enough policing — public provision of public goods also causes some notable problems. First, when we provide a good publicly, we use elections to figure out how much and what kind of policing to have. But elec-tions are notoriously bad at revealing and aggregating public preferences. Second, even when we understand what people want, public officials do not always have sufficient incentive to give it to them.

In his article *Market and Non-Market Failures,* 7 J. Pub. Pol'y 43 (1987), Charles Wolf, Jr., describes *nonmarket failures* that result from the conditions of supply and demand when governments produce goods.

First, Wolf argues that several factors are likely to lead to an overinflated *demand.* Here are the ones that might be most relevant to policing:

3. The Structure of Political Rewards

In the political process, which mediates these heightened public demands for remedial government action, rewards often accrue to legislators and governmental officials who articulate and publicize problems and legislate proposed solutions, without assuming responsibility for implementing them.

4. The High Time-Discount of Political Actors

In part as a consequence of this reward structure, and of the short terms associated with elected office, the rate of time-discount of political actors tends to be higher than that of society. The result is often an appreciable disjuncture between the short time horizons of political actors, and the longer time required to analyze, experiment, and understand a particular problem or market shortcoming, in order to see whether a practical remedy exists at all. Hence, future costs and future benefits tend to be heavily discounted or ignored, while current or near term benefits and costs are magnified. . . .

5. Decoupling Between Burdens and Benefits

Finally, a distortion of non-market demand often arises from the decoupling between those who receive the benefits, and those who pay the costs, of government programs. The classical free-rider problem is a special case of decoupling: benefits are extended to all, or to specified groups, regardless of whether any particular member pays. Where benefits and costs are borne by different groups, incentives toward political organization and lobbying by prospective beneficiaries predictably lead to demands that may be politically effective yet economically inefficient. . . .

This decoupling between beneficiaries and victims can explain the absence of government intervention, as well as its presence. For example, in the case of gun control in the United States, prospective beneficiaries, namely the public at large, are numerous and dispersed, while those who would incur the costs of control are concentrated and well-organized, i.e., the National Rifle Association. Even though the aggregate social benefits from gun control may exceed the costs that would be imposed on the gunners, control by government does not occur. . . .

Two different aspects of this decoupling phenomenon are worth distinguishing. What might be called micro-decoupling arises where the benefits from an existing or prospective government program are concentrated in a particular group, while the costs are broadly dispersed among the public, as taxpayers or consumers. The beneficiaries thus have stronger incentives, and may make politically more effective efforts, to initiate, sustain or expand a particular program, than the victims have or make to oppose it. The result may be a government program or regulation that is inefficient (aggregate costs exceed benefits), or inequitable, or both. . . .

The second type of decoupling, macro-decoupling, . . . arises because political power rests with the voting majority, while a minority provides most of the tax base. The result is an opportunity and incentive to expand redistributive programs since the demand depends on the majority, while the supply of revenues comes from the minority. Whereas micro-decoupling implies that a well-organized minority can exploit the majority, macro-decoupling implies that the majority can exploit the minority.

The result of macro-decoupling, in the absence of restraint by the majority, can be erosion of the mainsprings of investment, innovation and growth, if the lower-income majority's temptation to redistribute before-tax income weakens the upper-income minority's incentive to invest and innovate. . . .

Both types of decoupling may contribute to excess demand for government activities (programs, regulations, redistribution) — "excess" either in the sense that they entail greater social costs than benefits, or that they are not sustainable because they diminish incentives for productivity and growth in the economy. It is also possible that conditions affecting the demand for non-market activities may sometimes result in insufficient demand. For example, the special type of macro-decoupling associated with free-riding for a public good, like national security, together with the high time-discounts of political actors, may lead to less than optimal resource allocations for defense purposes.

Id. at 55–58.

Can you see how these forces might affect policing? For example, might a politician hype crime and push for policing strategies with swift and visible, if weak, effect—such as making many low-level arrests—rather than invest in education and employment opportunity to lower criminality in the future?

As Wolf describes it, *micro-decoupling* exists when a group benefits disproportionately from the production of a public good and can organize to influence it. In this vein, consider that officers receive concentrated benefits from additional policing in the form of secure jobs, good pay, and overtime. Officers might also have a strong interest in how policing is carried out. For example, Chapter 8 discusses how permissive rules about officer uses of force might lower officers' risk of getting injured or killed at the price of an increased risk to members of the public with whom they interact. Might officers' interests lead some communities to adopt socially inefficient use-of-force rules? Can you see how state and federal limits on force might mitigate this effect?

Micro-Decoupling and Police Unions

Although police unionization started in the late nineteenth century to improve police pay and working conditions, it strengthened dramatically in the late 1960s. Officers felt attacked by civil rights leaders who drew attention to police brutality and racism and by federal courts that limited investigative and arrest powers. They feared unfair investigations for misconduct and civilian review boards that could punish rank-and-file officers for departmental practices. And they organized accordingly.

Today, most states permit or require localities to bargain collectively with police unions, and police unions represent over half a million police officers. States tend to define the scope of collective bargaining broadly, permitting officers to negotiate on any "matters of wages, hours, and other conditions of employment," often including disciplinary procedures. Stephen Rushin, *Police Union Contracts*, 66 Duke L.J. 1191, 1205 n.63, 1206 (2017) (collecting examples of state statutes).

Police unions have helped improve wages for officers and given them a role in internal governance. Moreover, they often help bring about organizational change by bringing members on board. Many see this officer buy-in as critical to meaningful change in policing. Nevertheless, police unions often stand firm against police reforms; collective bargaining slows and taxes departmental change; and police union contracts often prevent managerial decisions and reforms that could improve policing. For example, a contract that requires assignment exclusively by seniority would prevent a manager from assigning an officer to an immigrant community because he speaks the residents' language.

Police unions have been especially effective in stymying officer accountability. In his study of 178 police union contracts, Stephen Rushin found that 88 percent "contained at least one provision that could thwart legitimate disciplinary actions against officers engaged in misconduct." Stephen Rushin, *Police Union Contracts*, 66 Duke L.J. 1191,

1224 (2017). More specifically, 28 percent of the contracts delay interrogations of officers by a substantial period of time; 19 percent mandate that supervisors provide officers with all evidence hours or days before an interrogation; 49 percent require the destruction of disciplinary records after a period of time; 18 percent prohibit the investigation of anonymous complaints; 26 percent disqualify complaints after a set period of time; and 65 percent permit or require arbitration in adjudicating officer appeals of disciplinary measures. See *id.* at 1227–1238.

Police unions and associations have also helped embed accountability resistance into state law, by successfully advocating for Law Enforcement Officer Bills of Rights (LEOBRs). LEOBRs often limit investigations against officers; delay interviews of officers after critical incidents and ensure that questioning takes place in conditions favorable to officers; provide for substantial disclosures to officers who are investigated; limit civilian participation in investigations; and prohibit departments from communicating openly to the public. For example:

> Maryland's LEOBR prevents localities from punishing officers for any "brutality" unless someone files a complaint within 366 days. It also allows the removal of civilian complaints from officer personnel files after three years. Louisiana's LEOBR provides officers with up to thirty days to secure counsel before investigators can interview them about alleged misconduct. In Florida, the LEOBR requires investigators to provide an officer under investigation with all evidence related to the investigation before beginning an interrogation. This includes the name of all complainants, physical evidence, incident reports, GPS locational data, audio evidence, and video recordings. In Illinois, the LEOBR bars the consideration of anonymous civilian complaints. And in Delaware, the LEOBR bars municipalities from requiring officers to disclose personal assets as a condition of employment. These only scratch the surface of the protective procedures offered by LEOBRs to police officers facing internal investigations.

Stephen Rushin, *Police Disciplinary Appeals*, 167 U. Pa. L. Rev. 545, 561–562 (2019); see also, e.g., Del. Code Ann. tit. 11, §9202; Fla. Stat. §112.532(1)(d); 50 Ill. Comp. Stat. 725/3.8(b); La. Stat. Ann. §40:2531(4)(a); Md. Code Ann., Pub. Safety §§3-104(c), 3-110(a).

Does all this tell you about micro-decoupling in policing? What effects on policing might unions ultimately have?

In Wolf's analysis, *macro-decoupling* often happens when the benefits go to everyone in a community while the costs of the public service are concentrated on a minority of residents providing most of the tax base. Arguably, policing involves a different form of macro-decoupling: The public safety benefits of policing are widely distributed, but nonfinancial costs of police-initiated encounters are concentrated on groups who are disproportionately stopped, ticketed, searched, arrested, or questioned. These costs are unlikely to be fully internalized in local elections. Several of those groups cannot vote and rarely get heard in the political process—think convicted felons, young people, and undocumented immigrants. Other groups disproportionately affected by policing vote and organize less effectively than others—think people who are poor, homeless, or members of politically weak racial and ethnic minorities. Might we have socially inefficient policing because policing's true costs do not get reflected in public decisions about how much and what kinds of policing to have? As you read more about the law of the police, think about whether federal and state laws could, should, or do mitigate this effect.

Second, Wolf suggests that conditions of nonmarket *supply* are also likely to produce inefficient public services:

1. Difficulty in defining and measuring output

Non-market outputs are often hard to define in principle, ill-defined in practice, and extremely difficult to measure as to quantity, or to evaluate as to quality. This, of course, is why non-market outputs are measured in the national accounts as the value of the inputs used in producing them.

Non-market outputs are usually intermediate products which are, at best, only proxies for the intended final output: for example, restrictions or prohibitions on the distribution of drugs and foods by the Food and Drug Administration; licenses issued or rejected by the Federal Communications Commission; forces and equipment developed and deployed by the military services; and cases processed and payments disbursed by health and welfare agencies.

The quality of non-market output is especially hard to ascertain, in part because information is lacking about output quality—information that would, in the case of marketed outputs, be transmitted to producers by consumer choices. Consider, for example, the difficulty of determining whether the quality of education, or welfare programs, or environmental regulation, or food and drug regulation, is better or worse now than five or six years ago. . . . In general, measuring non-market outputs by their inputs is accepted because direct measurement of the output value is so difficult.

2. Single-source production

Non-market outputs in government are usually produced by a single agency whose exclusive cognizance (monopoly) in a particular field is legislatively mandated, administratively accepted, or both. . . . Thus, the absence of sustained competition contributes to the difficulty of evaluating the quality of non-market output.

3. Uncertainty of production technology

The technology of producing non-market outputs is frequently unknown, or, if known, is associated with considerable uncertainty and ambiguity. An example of uncertain technology in the educational domain is provided by the Coleman report and other studies of student performance according to standardized test scores. These studies leave very little in the variance of student academic performance to be accounted for by such variables as class size or expenditures per pupil or teacher/pupil ratios, once proper allowance has been made for the social and economic status of students and their families. Yet we know very little about how to produce education, and indeed what precisely the product consists of. . . .

4. Absence of bottom-line and termination mechanism

Non-market output is generally not connected with any bottom line for evaluating performance comparable to the profit-and-loss statement of market output. Closely related to this absence of a bottom line is the absence of a reliable mechanism for terminating non-market activities when they are unsuccessful.

Id. at 60–62. Wolf's concerns—measuring outputs, assessing quality, limited competition, and uncertainty of production—are all serious issues in policing. Communities have especially struggled with determining the relevant output of policing. How do we know whether a department is doing a good job?

Traditionally, communities have used crime rates, arrests, citations, clearance rates, and response times to evaluate policing. Policing has limited effect on crime rates, though, which go up and down for reasons that have nothing to do with cops, and the other measures do not closely correlate with public safety, fail to capture important police activities, and overlook quality issues, such as whether policing is discriminatory or abusive. As an alternative, Mark Moore and Anthony Braga have argued that police departments should measure whether the police:

1. reduce criminal victimization;
2. call offenders to account by solving crimes and arresting suspects;
3. reduce fear and enhance personal security;
4. guarantee safety in public spaces, including in traffic, parks, and schools, maintaining space for political activity;
5. use financial resources fairly, efficiently, and effectively;
6. use force and authority fairly, efficiently, and effectively; and
7. satisfy customer preferences and achieve legitimacy with the policed.

Mark H. Moore & Anthony A. Braga, *Measuring and Improving Police Performance: The Lessons of Compstat and Its Progeny*, 26 Policing 439, 444–445 (2003). How can communities attempt to measure these outcomes?

According to Wolf, these supply and demand conditions in public goods lead to systematic problems: Public goods are likely to be produced inefficiently, using more resources and imposing more harm than necessary. The agencies that produce them are likely to develop internal standards for performance that diverge from public goals. Government service provision is likely to have unintended side effects—externalities—that are not taken into account in decisions about how much and what kind of service to provide. And public goods are likely to disproportionately serve those with power or privilege, exacerbating inequality. See Wolf, *supra*, at 66. Do you see how these might affect policing?

Many people believe that a national crisis exists in local policing. They see too much policing that is harmful, unresponsive, or unfair. We govern that policing first and foremost through local political processes. Still, this book considers a wide array of state and federal rules, remedies, and programs that seek to influence policing and those processes. As you read further, perhaps you will form your own opinion about whether those laws do or could offer a way out.

PART TWO

INVESTIGATIVE POLICING

Every community expects its police department to address crime by responding to calls that report a crime, identifying and classifying criminal activity, collecting physical and testimonial evidence, and turning over criminal suspects to courts for prosecution. In fact, communities often use police call-response times and crime-clearance rates to evaluate police performance.

Still, as Chapter 1 indicates, crime response is only one relatively small component of policing. Police departments devote far greater resources to patrolling beats (where officers encounter minor offenses often but rarely stumble over serious crimes) and responding to calls for service (which often have nothing to do with criminal activity). In the most recent available data, two-thirds of local police officers were assigned to patrol operations. Fewer than one-sixth were devoted to criminal investigations. See Brian A. Reaves, U.S. Dep't of Justice, *Local Police Departments, 2013: Personnel, Policies, and Practices* 2 (2015).

Why start with the law governing police activities that use few officers and departmental resources? Even if policing crime is not most of what officers do, it is central to how police perceive themselves and to what most communities want from the police. Crime wrongly deprives people of their lives and livelihoods, and it causes family and social disruption. When the government fails to solve crimes, to adjudicate criminal guilt, and to express the state's condemnation for crimes, victims feel disrespected and communities lose faith in the government. In addition, when policing fails in its crime-related functions, individuals may take matters into their own hands and refuse to cooperate with the police in the future, making further crime both more likely and more difficult to solve.[1]

Of course, police efforts to address crime threaten freedom and security, too. Police find criminals and bring them to account by breaking into houses and cars, taking personal property, tricking or intimidating people into revealing private thoughts and activities, and holding people against their will. Those activities can look awfully similar to the crimes police purport to address. Perhaps, then, it is no surprise that criminal investigation is more heavily regulated than directing traffic or finding missing persons.

Criminal investigation also has outsized influence on the law governing the police. Much of contemporary law governing policing is developed in the context of

---

[1] A rich academic literature attempts to theorize and measure aspects of this phenomenon. See Tom R. Tyler, *Why People Obey for Law* (2006), for a key contribution. For a less technical argument along these lines, see Jill Leovy, *Ghettoside: A True Story of Murder in America* (2015).

criminal investigation, facilitating or limiting police power to investigate crime and detain offenders. Even when the law governs other police activities, such as what officers can do on patrol, police officers' role as criminal investigators informs the thinking of those who make legal rules for the police, including courts and legislatures. For all these reasons, understanding the law governing criminal investigation is critical to understanding the law of the police.

Much of the time, police take on serious crime *reactively*. When a witness or victim calls 911 to report a crime and ask for assistance, a dispatcher usually sends a patrol officer. That officer provides aid to any victims, assesses the nature of any crime, collects obvious physical evidence, ensures that witnesses stick around, and, if necessary, calls for additional resources, such as an investigator. Afterward, the patrol officer prepares a report. When an investigator—often a detective—is sent to the scene, that person talks to suspects and collects physical evidence from them, canvasses the area for additional witnesses, and makes sure the crime scene is documented and processed further for evidence. Later the detective might examine the physical evidence and arrange for any necessary testing; interview victims, suspects, and witnesses; and follow other leads. All of this is done with three goals in mind: determining the nature of the offense; identifying (and arresting) perpetrators; and building a case for criminal prosecution.

Alternatively, police look for hidden crimes *proactively*. Aware that a pattern of criminal activity is occurring or that a crime is likely to occur, they try to discover or even witness it, often by using surveillance, undercover officers, and informants.

Do Detectives Solve Crime?

On television and in movies, police detectives invest unlimited resources to determine who committed a violent crime, and 99 times out of 100, they succeed and lead the chastened criminal away in handcuffs by the end of the hour. Reality is more complex.

First, it is not detectives who solve most crimes. Instead, when a serious crime is cleared[2] by the police, it is usually because the suspect is obvious or identified immediately by a victim or witness.

Second, detectives do not investigate most crimes thoroughly. New crimes pile up behind old ones, and detectives often have little time to investigate very much. This is especially true of crimes other than homicide. This helps to explain, for example, why only about one-third of rapes and even fewer robberies are solved each year.

---

[2] A crime is *cleared* in federal crime statistics, and therefore in the view of police departments and scholars, if a perpetrator is arrested and charged, or if a perpetrator is identified but special circumstances (such as his death) prevent arrest or prosecution.

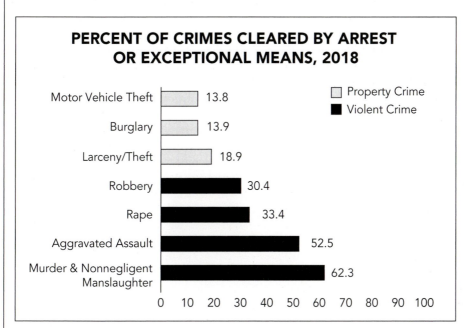

PERCENT OF CRIMES CLEARED BY ARREST OR EXCEPTIONAL MEANS, 2018

Motor Vehicle Theft	13.8
Burglary	13.9
Larceny/Theft	18.9
Robbery	30.4
Rape	33.4
Aggravated Assault	52.5
Murder & Nonnegligent Manslaughter	62.3

☐ Property Crime
■ Violent Crime

0 10 20 30 40 50 60 70 80 90 100

Source: FBI, *2018 Crime in the United States.*

Third, detectives often fail to solve crimes they investigate. For instance, police departments investigate homicides more thoroughly than other serious crimes. But more homicides today are committed by strangers, often in connection with drug trafficking or gangs. Those crimes are harder to solve than crimes against family members or crimes of passion, and they depend on community cooperation and adequate resources. Thus, despite DNA and forensic advances and falling murder rates nationally, fewer than two-thirds of homicides are solved, a rate that has been largely stable for years. In many large cities, far fewer killings are solved in part because detective workloads are too high.

The next three chapters consider the law governing police criminal investigation. Chapter 2 looks at laws that regulate police surveillance, undercover work, and the use of informants, all of which are used to discover and solve hidden crime. Chapter 3 considers the law that affects how police gain testimonial evidence from criminal suspects and witnesses, including the law of interrogations and eyewitness identifications. These activities are especially important in solving reported crimes. Chapter 4 considers the law that regulates police when they gather physical evidence and that requires police to disclose evidence to prosecutors and prosecutors to disclose information about the police to defendants. In each of these chapters, constitutional criminal procedure provides a core piece of the puzzle, but other legal rules also play important roles in governing police conduct.

A couple of key lessons emerge from these chapters. First, the investigative process is regulated unevenly by the law. Some aspects of criminal investigation, such as entries into homes and interrogating suspects, are heavily regulated. Other aspects, such as the use of undercover officers or interviews of witnesses, are barely regulated at all. Second, federal constitutional law structures the law in this area, although state statutes and constitutional doctrines and local ordinances raise standards and fill gaps. Third, constitutional regulation is not obviously more protective or more capable of achieving a fair balance between public safety and individual freedom than other forms of regulation. Although the Warren Court erected new limits on criminal investigation, the Supreme Court has carved away at many doctrines since. Today, constitutional criminal procedure sometimes seems hulking and decrepit, casting a long shadow over police investigation without offering much shelter for those it is intended to protect.

Chapter 2

Uncovering Crime

Many crimes have no witnesses or victims to call the police. Neither a politician taking a bribe nor the businessman offering it, the drug seller nor the drug buyer, the prostitute assaulted by a violent john nor the john himself, will report their crimes. If police are to address drug distribution, gang activity, prostitution, gambling, and corruption, among other criminal activities, they cannot depend solely on traditional reactive enforcement. Tackling secret criminal activity means finding it.

How do police find these criminals, who typically go to great lengths to avoid getting caught? Unlike when they engage in patrol policing, thought to be effective because of its visibility, officers investigating these crimes must often trade in *stealth* and *deception*. That is, police officers attempt to observe crime surreptitiously, by engaging in covert surveillance or monitoring of criminal behavior. Or they try to observe crime sneakily by pretending to be a criminal participant or by persuading a criminal participant to act on behalf of the police. The more that law enforcement targets hidden crimes, by fighting a "war on drugs" for example, the more the police will need to use surveillance and informants in their investigative work.

These strategies trigger a wealth of concerns, including that they invade privacy. This chapter considers the law that addresses, or fails to address, the trade-offs involved in invisibly intruding on individuals to uncover crime. The first section considers Fourth Amendment regulation of surveillance. The second section compares federal privacy statutes with constitutional law. The third section looks at state and local surveillance regulations that go beyond federal law and constitutional doctrine. And the last considers the far more limited legal regulation of undercover officers and informants. By the end of the chapter, you will know some basic Fourth Amendment doctrine that governs police searches and seizures. You will be able to identify some of the advantages and disadvantages of using courts and Congress to regulate privacy intrusions by the police. You will also learn something about covert policing and the rarely studied and very limited law that addresses it.

Why Do Police Address Unreported Crime?

You might well ask why the police look for unreported crimes. Some might contend that *all* crimes should be investigated and punished, but the traditional law enforcement argument for focusing resources on hidden crime is something like this.

First, although many crimes happen behind closed doors, they can have an unwelcome public component. Prostitutes walk avenues soliciting clients late at

---

night. Groups of men stand on street corners and in public parks dealing drugs. Neighborhood residents often call the police about these activities, complaining about their visible manifestations and secondary effects on public order.

Second, some apparently victimless crimes impose significant social costs. Corruption undermines faith in the political process, and opioid disbursement sometimes kills. Police often face public pressure to prevent these harms and help hold accountable those who cause them.

Third, police leaders believe that enforcing criminal statutes against vice and other hidden crimes helps reduce serious crime. Drug dealing can breed violence when participants fight over territory or deals gone wrong, and drug users might burgle and steal to pay for drugs. Gangs might invade homes, commit murders, and organize armed robberies in addition to selling guns and drugs. In this view, addressing drug and gang activity is critical to preventing serious crime, a priority for all police departments.

Do you accept these arguments? What more would you want to know to evaluate them?

A.   *Fourth Amendment Regulation of Police Surveillance*

1.   The Fourth Amendment

By all accounts, the Fourth Amendment is the single most important legal rule governing police conduct today. It states:

> The right of the people to be secure in their persons, houses, papers, and effects, against unreasonable searches and seizures, shall not be violated, and no Warrants shall issue, but upon probable cause, supported by Oath or affirmation, and particularly describing the place to be searched, and the persons or things to be seized.

U.S. Const. amend. IV.

2.   Warren Court Era Regulation of Police Surveillance

By its language and doctrine, the Fourth Amendment governs all government searches or seizures, not just those designed to uncover crime by stealth. Still, many Fourth Amendment cases have been decided in this context, and the Fourth Amendment functions as an important constraint on surreptitious policing. The next case lays down the analytical framework that has dominated the Court's thinking about the Fourth Amendment for more than 50 years. In reading it, consider whether you can identify what assumptions the Court is making about police motives and other efforts to keep police in check.

KATZ v. UNITED STATES
389 U.S. 347 (1967)

MR. JUSTICE STEWART delivered the opinion of the Court.

The petitioner was convicted . . . under an eight-count indictment charging him with transmitting wagering information by telephone from Los Angeles to Miami and Boston in violation of a federal statute. At trial the Government was permitted, over the petitioner's objection, to introduce evidence of the petitioner's end of telephone conversations, overheard by FBI agents who had attached an electronic listening and recording device to the outside of the public telephone booth from which he had placed his calls. In affirming his conviction, the Court of Appeals rejected the contention that the recordings had been obtained in violation of the Fourth Amendment, because "[t]here was no physical entrance into the area occupied by [the petitioner]." We granted certiorari in order to consider the constitutional questions thus presented.

The petitioner had phrased those questions as follows:

> "A. Whether a public telephone booth is a constitutionally protected area so that evidence obtained by attaching an electronic listening recording device to the top of such a booth is obtained in violation of the right to privacy of the user of the booth."

> "B. Whether physical penetration of a constitutionally protected area is necessary before a search and seizure can be said to be violative of the Fourth Amendment to the United States Constitution."

We decline to adopt this formulation of the issues. In the first place the correct solution of Fourth Amendment problems is not necessarily promoted by incantation of the phrase "constitutionally protected area." Secondly, the Fourth Amendment cannot be translated into a general constitutional "right to privacy." That Amendment protects individual privacy against certain kinds of governmental intrusion, but its protections go further, and often have nothing to do with privacy at all. Other provisions of the Constitution protect personal privacy from other forms of governmental invasion. But the protection of a person's *general* right to privacy—his right to be let alone by other people—is, like the protection of his property and of his very life, left largely to the law of the individual States.

Because of the misleading way the issues have been formulated, the parties have attached great significance to the characterization of the telephone booth from which the petitioner placed his calls. The petitioner has strenuously argued that the booth was a "constitutionally protected area." The Government has maintained with equal vigor that it was not. But this effort to decide whether or not a given "area," viewed in the abstract, is "constitutionally protected" deflects attention from the problem presented by this case. For the Fourth Amendment protects people, not places. What a person knowingly exposes to the public, even in his own home or office, is not a subject of Fourth Amendment protection. But what he seeks to preserve as private, even in an area accessible to the public, may be constitutionally protected.

. . . No less than an individual in a business office, in a friend's apartment, or in a taxicab, a person in a telephone booth may rely upon the protection of the Fourth Amendment. One who occupies it, shuts the door behind him, and pays the toll that permits him to place a call is surely entitled to assume that the words he utters into the mouthpiece will not be broadcast to the world. To read the Constitution more narrowly is to ignore the vital role that the public telephone has come to play in private communication.

The Government contends, however, that the activities of its agents in this case should not be tested by Fourth Amendment requirements, for the surveillance technique they employed involved no physical penetration of the telephone booth from which the petitioner placed his calls. It is true that the absence of such penetration was at one time thought to foreclose further Fourth Amendment inquiry, Olmstead v. United States, 277 U.S. 438 (1928); Goldman v. United States, 316 U.S. 129 (1942), for that Amendment was thought to limit only searches and seizures of tangible property. But "[t]he premise that property interests control the right of the Government to search and seize has been discredited." Warden v. Hayden, 387 U.S. 294, 304 (1967). . . . Indeed, we have expressly held that the Fourth Amendment governs not only the seizure of tangible items, but extends as well to the recording of oral statements overheard without any "technical trespass under . . . local property law." Silverman v. United States, 365 U.S. 505, 511 (1961). Once this much is acknowledged, and once it is recognized that the Fourth Amendment protects people—and not simply "areas"—against unreasonable searches and seizures, it becomes clear that the reach of that Amendment cannot turn upon the presence or absence of a physical intrusion into any given enclosure.

We conclude that the underpinnings of *Olmstead* and *Goldman* have been so eroded by our subsequent decisions that the "trespass" doctrine there enunciated can no longer be regarded as controlling. The Government's activities in electronically listening to and recording the petitioner's words violated the privacy upon which he justifiably relied while using the telephone booth and thus constituted a "search and seizure" within the meaning of the Fourth Amendment. The fact that the electronic device employed to achieve that end did not happen to penetrate the wall of the booth can have no constitutional significance.

The question remaining for decision, then, is whether the search and seizure conducted in this case complied with constitutional standards. In that regard, the Government's position is that its agents acted in an entirely defensible manner: They did not begin their electronic surveillance until investigation of the petitioner's activities had established a strong probability that he was using the telephone in question to transmit gambling information to persons in other States, in violation of federal law. Moreover, the surveillance was limited, both in scope and in duration, to the specific purpose of establishing the contents of the petitioner's unlawful telephonic communications. The agents confined their surveillance to the brief periods during which he used the telephone booth,[14]

---

[14] Based upon their previous visual observations of the petitioner, the agents correctly predicted that he would use the telephone booth for several minutes at approximately the same time each morning. The petitioner was subjected to electronic surveillance only during this predetermined period. Six recordings, averaging some three minutes each, were obtained and admitted in evidence. They preserved the petitioner's end of conversations concerning the placing of bets and the receipt of wagering information.

and they took great care to overhear only the conversations of the petitioner himself.[15]

Accepting this account of the Government's actions as accurate, it is clear that this surveillance was so narrowly circumscribed that a duly authorized magistrate, properly notified of the need for such investigation, specifically informed of the basis on which it was to proceed, and clearly apprised of the precise intrusion it would entail, could constitutionally have authorized, with appropriate safeguards, the very limited search and seizure that the Government asserts in fact took place. . . .

. . . Yet the inescapable fact is that this restraint was imposed by the agents themselves, not by a judicial officer. They were not required, before commencing the search, to present their estimate of probable cause for detached scrutiny by a neutral magistrate. They were not compelled, during the conduct of the search itself, to observe precise limits established in advance by a specific court order. Nor were they directed, after the search had been completed, to notify the authorizing magistrate in detail of all that had been seized. In the absence of such safeguards, this Court has never sustained a search upon the sole ground that officers reasonably expected to find evidence of a particular crime and voluntarily confined their activities to the least intrusive means consistent with that end. Searches conducted without warrants have been held unlawful "notwithstanding facts unquestionably showing probable cause," Agnello v. United States, 269 U.S. 20, 33 (1925), for the Constitution requires "that the deliberate, impartial judgment of a judicial officer . . . be interposed between the citizen and the police. . . ." Wong Sun v. United States, 371 U.S. 471, 481–482 (1963). "Over and again this Court has emphasized that the mandate of the [Fourth] Amendment requires adherence to judicial processes," United States v. Jeffers, 342 U.S. 48, 51 (1951), and that searches conducted outside the judicial process, without prior approval by judge or magistrate, are *per se* unreasonable under the Fourth Amendment—subject only to a few specifically established and well-delineated exceptions.

It is difficult to imagine how any of those exceptions could ever apply to the sort of search and seizure involved in this case. Even electronic surveillance substantially contemporaneous with an individual's arrest could hardly be deemed an "incident" of that arrest. Nor could the use of electronic surveillance without prior authorization be justified on grounds of "hot pursuit." And, of course, the very nature of electronic surveillance precludes its use pursuant to the suspect's consent.

The Government does not question these basic principles. Rather, it urges the creation of a new exception to cover this case. It argues that surveillance of a telephone booth should be exempted from the usual requirement of advance authorization by a magistrate upon a showing of probable cause. We cannot agree. Omission of such authorization

"bypasses the safeguards provided by an objective predetermination of probable cause, and substitutes instead the far less reliable procedure of an after-the-event justification for the . . . search, too likely to be subtly influenced by the familiar shortcomings of hindsight judgment." Beck v. Ohio, 379 U.S. 89, 96 (1964).

[15] On the single occasion when the statements of another person were inadvertently intercepted, the agents refrained from listening to them.

And bypassing a neutral predetermination of the *scope* of a search leaves individuals secure from Fourth Amendment violations "only in the discretion of the police." *Id.* at 97.

These considerations do not vanish when the search in question is transferred from the setting of a home, an office, or a hotel room to that of a telephone booth. Wherever a man may be, he is entitled to know that he will remain free from unreasonable searches and seizures. The government agents here ignored "the procedure of antecedent justification . . . that is central to the Fourth Amendment," a procedure that we hold to be a constitutional precondition of the kind of electronic surveillance involved in this case. Because the surveillance here failed to meet that condition, and because it led to the petitioner's conviction, the judgment must be reversed.

It is so ordered.

MR. JUSTICE MARSHALL took no part in the consideration or decision of this case.

[The concurring opinion of Justice Douglas, with whom Justice Brennan joined, is omitted.]

MR. JUSTICE HARLAN, concurring. . . .

. . . My understanding of the rule that has emerged from prior decisions is that there is a twofold requirement, first that a person have exhibited an actual (subjective) expectation of privacy and, second, that the expectation be one that society is prepared to recognize as "reasonable." Thus a man's home is, for most purposes, a place where he expects privacy, but objects, activities, or statements that he exposes to the "plain view" of outsiders are not "protected" because no intention to keep them to himself has been exhibited. On the other hand, conversations in the open would not be protected against being overheard, for the expectation of privacy under the circumstances would be unreasonable.

The critical fact in this case is that "[o]ne who occupies . . . [a telephone booth] shuts the door behind him, and pays the toll that permits him to place a call is surely entitled to assume" that his conversation is not being intercepted. The point is not that the booth is "accessible to the public" at other times, but that it is a temporarily private place whose momentary occupants' expectations of freedom from intrusion are recognized as reasonable. . . .

[The concurring opinion of Justice White and the dissenting opinion of Justice Black are omitted.]

NOTES AND QUESTIONS

1. *Applying the* Katz *test.* Before *Katz,* an officer who wanted to know whether the Fourth Amendment applied to his conduct could ask himself whether he was about to physically invade a protected area. That test focused on where the officer was and what he was doing. After *Katz,* he is required to ask about the social meaning of the suspect's actions and expectations. As Anthony Amsterdam described it in his classic article, *Perspectives on the Fourth Amendment,* 58 Minn. L. Rev. 349, 403–404 (1974),

> How in the devil is a policeman engaged in an investigation supposed to decide whether the form of surveillance that he proposes to use, if not restricted by the fourth amendment, would curtail the liberties of citizens to a compass inconsistent

with a free society? And, even if that were a question that a policeman could practicably answer, I would frankly not want the extent of my freedom to be determined by a policeman's answer to it.

Katz would seem to give officers little usable guidance about whether their activities are covered by the Fourth Amendment.

2. *Does the form of test matter?* Even if police cannot easily apply *Katz*, once courts determine that bugging a public phone booth or squeezing a passenger's bag on a Greyhound bus is a search, police understand the rules for that activity going forward. Because officers use the same investigative techniques repeatedly, officers generally know whether they are doing something regulated by the Fourth Amendment before they do it. However, new investigative techniques and technologies are constantly developing, and uncertainty about their status can last a long while. Police departments were obtaining historical cell-site location information about suspects for about a decade before the U.S. Supreme Court ruled that doing so is a search within the meaning of the Fourth Amendment in *Carpenter v. United States*, 138 S. Ct. 2206 (2018). Does that make the *Katz* test more problematic?

How police react to uncertainty depends on what happens if they get it wrong. When *Katz* was decided, the exclusionary rule was strong: A department unsure whether an activity required a warrant (because it constituted a search) might well have gotten the warrant to ensure the evidence would be admissible rather than risk exclusion. Given available exceptions to the exclusionary rule today, the department might make a different choice. See Chapter 12 for more discussion of the exclusionary rule.

3. *Bringing property back in.* Although *Katz* minimized the importance of property rights in Fourth Amendment analysis, recent cases have reinvigorated their importance. In *United States v. Jones*, 565 U.S. 400 (2012), the Supreme Court held that the government searched a suspect when it attached a GPS tracking device to the suspect's vehicle and monitored the device for 28 days. Rather than applying *Katz*, the majority opinion ruled that the government's actions constituted a common law trespass and therefore a search. The *Jones* majority characterized *Katz* as supplementing rather than replacing property analysis in Fourth Amendment law. Is that how you read *Katz*? The Court reiterated the *Jones* approach in *Florida v. Jardines*, 569 U.S. 1 (2013), when it concluded that taking a drug-sniffing dog to a suspect's front porch was a search because the officers entered the suspect's property without permission. The Court found that because such an intrusion constitutes a search under *Jones*, it was unnecessary to decide whether the suspect's reasonable expectation of privacy was violated.

Property analysis does not make Fourth Amendment law more accessible to police officers: *Jones*'s outcome was based on eighteenth-century trespass law. In *Jardines*, the Court cited almost no law in determining that the officers were engaged in a search within the meaning of *Jones*. Instead, it relied on its own interpretation of the scope of the customary license implicitly granted to those who approach a home by way of the front porch. More recently, in *Carpenter v. United States*, 138 S. Ct. 2206 (2018), Justice Gorsuch argued (in a dissent) that contemporary state and federal legislation, state common law, and property rights at the founding (along with their modern analogues) might all be relevant in determining whether the Fourth Amendment applies to a police activity. *Id.* at 2267–2271 (Gorsuch, J., dissenting). Moreover, after *Jones* and *Jardines*, police officers who want to know whether the

Fourth Amendment regulates their activity must ask themselves *both* the *Katz* question (whether an activity would violate a person's reasonable expectation of privacy) and the *Jones* question (whether it would constitute a trespass or physical intrusion on houses, persons, papers, or effects within the original meaning of the Fourth Amendment).

4. *Where are the police?* Although the first half of *Katz* revamps the law governing police investigative techniques, it barely mentions the police and says nothing about crime, criminals, or police strategies and goals. It does not describe how difficult it is to uncover illegal sports betting or the resource constraints police face. Instead, it talks about the meaning of individual privacy and telephone booths. How might the absence of policing (and the presence of privacy) affect the Court's thinking?

5. *What the Fourth Amendment requires.* If a police investigative activity satisfies the test established in the first part of *Katz*, or the test later established in *Jones*, indicating that the activity is a search or seizure within the meaning of the Fourth Amendment, then the text of the Fourth Amendment requires that the activity be *reasonable.* The second part of *Katz* rules that to be reasonable, unless an exception exists, a search or seizure must be reviewed in advance by a judge. In this "procedure of antecedent justification," *Katz*, 389 U.S. at 359, an officer describes to a judge the place he wants to search, the things he is looking for, and the evidence obtained so far. Then, if satisfied, the judge issues a *warrant* finding *probable cause* that a crime has been committed and that evidence, fruits, or instrumentalities of the crime will be found at the location to be searched.

6. *Why warrants?* Why does the Court suggest it is so important that judges set limits in advance on police searches? The law rarely requires preclearance. Usually, people act, and if they violate the law, they can be subject to legal consequences afterward. This option exists for searches: If an officer engages in a search without a warrant and discovers evidence, a defendant can argue in his criminal case that the evidence was unconstitutionally obtained, and he will have a lawyer representing his interests when he does so. That is what happened in *Katz*. Why does the Court think that is not good enough? Might officers reason differently about what justified a search, or courts assess legality differently, after they know what was found in the search?

7. *Another argument for preclearance.* A second argument exists for preclearance that the Court does not mention in *Katz*. To identify it, think about what must happen for a search to be reviewed by a court because a defendant brings a suppression motion in a criminal case.[1] Which police actions will never be reviewed in this process?

8. *Who does the Court distrust?* *Katz*'s rhetoric suggests that the Court distrusts police to self-regulate and sees state judges who review warrants as a solution to the

---

[1] A suppression motion, also called a motion to suppress, is a request by a party to exclude evidence from a trial, that is, to disallow the other party from introducing it. Probably the most common basis for suppressing evidence is arguing that the government obtained it in violation of the Fourth Amendment. Suppression motions in criminal cases are usually made *in limine*, that is, before the trial begins. Motions in limine allow evidentiary questions to be resolved outside the presence of the jury, and they often occur sufficiently before the trial to allow both parties to reevaluate and prepare their case in light of the evidence that is likely to be admitted. In criminal cases, a motion in limine to exclude tangible evidence, statements, or identification evidence can often effectively resolve the case. Without this evidence, it might be nearly impossible to convict the defendant. With it, a jury might be unlikely to doubt his guilt. For this reason, once the court rules on a motion in limine challenging evidence as unconstitutionally obtained, the case can often be resolved by dismissal or by guilty plea rather than by trial.

problem of police overreach. But reading between the lines, couldn't you read *Katz* as distrusting state courts to regulate the police effectively in suppression hearings? How do warrants make state courts more effective?

9. *Procedural solutions to state regulatory failures. Katz* is not the only case in which the Warren Court[2] imposed a procedural mechanism to correct the limits of state regulation of law enforcement. One might see *Mapp v. Ohio*, 367 U.S. 643 (1961), and *Miranda v. Arizona*, 384 U.S. 436 (1966), in similar terms.[3] In *Mapp*, the Court viewed state remedies for constitutional violations by local police as inadequate and stepped in with the exclusionary rule. In *Miranda*, the Court viewed (primarily) state court efforts to hold police accountable for obtaining involuntary confessions insufficient, so it required that officers warn suspects of their rights and obtain waivers before confessions.

Why Criminal Procedure Dominates the Law of the Police

In *Mapp v. Ohio*, 367 U.S. 643 (1961), the Supreme Court ruled that evidence obtained by the police in violation of the Fourth Amendment is inadmissible in a state criminal trial. This ruling gives criminal defendants an *incentive* to contest police conduct because doing so offers the prospect of excluding damning evidence. It also gives them a *process* by which to do it, a motion in limine to suppress evidence found by the police. Subsequent cases similarly allow criminal defendants to challenge evidence discovered in violation of the Fifth, Sixth, and Fourteenth Amendments, further allowing defendants to challenge police conduct during investigations.

Mapp's exclusionary rule might not have transformed the law if not for *Gideon v. Wainright*, 372 U.S. 335 (1963). The *Gideon* Court recognized a Sixth Amendment right to appointed counsel for indigent criminal defendants, ensuring that criminal defendants have the *means* to challenge police misconduct. When police officers try to use illegally obtained evidence, defense lawyers who know what they are doing will challenge police conduct in court.

By contrast, when an officer uses too much force or discriminates, a victim against whom no charges are brought usually has no recourse but to bring a civil lawsuit against the officer or department. Potential *civil* plaintiffs have no right to a lawyer; there is no civil equivalent to *Gideon*. Lawyers work for these civil plaintiffs because they are promised a portion of any damages awarded or expect to receive court-awarded attorneys' fees if the plaintiff wins. Lawyers therefore tend to cherry-pick the most promising, sympathetic, high-damages, and low-cost cases, leaving some potential plaintiffs out in the cold.

Because of the opportunities afforded criminal defendants, suppression motions challenging searches, seizures, and interrogations in criminal cases are far more common than civil suits against police and their departments. As a result, the law governing evidence-producing investigative practices is better developed than other law governing the police.

---

[2] The Supreme Court from 1953 to 1969, when Earl Warren was Chief Justice, is known as the Warren Court. The Warren Court is famous for expansive interpretation of individual constitutional rights, including with respect to policing, and its decisions are discussed throughout this book.

[3] *Mapp* appears in Chapter 12 and *Miranda* in Chapter 3.

3.   Modern Constitutional Regulation of Police Efforts to Uncover Crime

Although *Katz* suggests that exceptions to the warrant requirement will be rare and well defined, post-*Katz* Fourth Amendment cases have identified many exceptions to the warrant rule. In the next case, the Court considers the scope of an exception and illustrates the contemporary Supreme Court's take on using Fourth Amendment doctrine to regulate policing. As you read, notice how the Court's tone and concerns have changed since *Katz*.

KENTUCKY v. KING
563 U.S. 452 (2011)

JUSTICE ALITO delivered the opinion of the Court.

It is well established that "exigent circumstances," including the need to prevent the destruction of evidence, permit police officers to conduct an otherwise permissible search without first obtaining a warrant. In this case, we consider whether this rule applies when police, by knocking on the door of a residence and announcing their presence, cause the occupants to attempt to destroy evidence. The Kentucky Supreme Court held that the exigent circumstances rule does not apply in the case at hand because the police should have foreseen that their conduct would prompt the occupants to attempt to destroy evidence. We reject this interpretation of the exigent circumstances rule. The conduct of the police prior to their entry into the apartment was entirely lawful. They did not violate the Fourth Amendment or threaten to do so. In such a situation, the exigent circumstances rule applies.

I

A

This case concerns the search of an apartment in Lexington, Kentucky. Police officers set up a controlled buy of crack cocaine outside an apartment complex. Undercover Officer Gibbons watched the deal take place from an unmarked car in a nearby parking lot. After the deal occurred, Gibbons radioed uniformed officers to move in on the suspect. He told the officers that the suspect was moving quickly toward the breezeway of an apartment building, and he urged them to "hurry up and get there" before the suspect entered an apartment.

In response to the radio alert, the uniformed officers drove into the nearby parking lot, left their vehicles, and ran to the breezeway. Just as they entered the breezeway, they heard a door shut and detected a very strong odor of burnt marijuana. At the end of the breezeway, the officers saw two apartments, one on the left and one on the right, and they did not know which apartment the suspect had entered. Gibbons had radioed that the suspect was running into the apartment on the right, but the officers did not hear this statement because they had already left their vehicles. Because they smelled marijuana smoke emanating from the apartment on the left, they approached the door of that apartment.

Officer Steven Cobb, one of the uniformed officers who approached the door, testified that the officers banged on the left apartment door "as loud as [they] could" and announced, "'This is the police'" or "'Police, police, police.'" Cobb said that "[a]s soon as [the officers] started banging on the door," they "could hear people inside moving," and "[i]t sounded as [though] things were being moved inside the apartment." These noises, Cobb testified, led the officers to believe that drug-related evidence was about to be destroyed.

At that point, the officers announced that they "were going to make entry inside the apartment." Cobb then kicked in the door, the officers entered the apartment, and they found three people in the front room: respondent Hollis King, respondent's girlfriend, and a guest who was smoking marijuana. The officers performed a protective sweep of the apartment during which they saw marijuana and powder cocaine in plain view. In a subsequent search, they also discovered crack cocaine, cash, and drug paraphernalia.

Police eventually entered the apartment on the right. Inside, they found the suspected drug dealer who was the initial target of their investigation.

B

. . . [A] grand jury charged respondent with trafficking in marijuana, first-degree trafficking in a controlled substance, and second-degree persistent felony offender status. Respondent filed a motion to suppress the evidence from the warrantless search, but the Circuit Court denied the motion. . . . Respondent then entered a conditional guilty plea, reserving his right to appeal the denial of his suppression motion. The court sentenced respondent to 11 years' imprisonment.

The Kentucky Court of Appeals affirmed. . . .

The Supreme Court of Kentucky reversed. As a preliminary matter, the court observed that there was "certainly some question as to whether the sound of persons moving [inside the apartment] was sufficient to establish that evidence was being destroyed." But the court did not answer that question. Instead, it "assume[d] for the purpose of argument that exigent circumstances existed."

To determine whether police impermissibly created the exigency, the Supreme Court of Kentucky announced a two-part test. First, the court held, police cannot "deliberately creat[e] the exigent circumstances with the bad faith intent to avoid the warrant requirement." Second, even absent bad faith, the court concluded, police may not rely on exigent circumstances if "it was reasonably foreseeable that the investigative tactics employed by the police would create the exigent circumstances." Although the court found no evidence of bad faith, it held that exigent circumstances could not justify the search because it was reasonably foreseeable that the occupants would destroy evidence when the police knocked on the door and announced their presence.

We granted certiorari.

II

A . . .

The text of the [Fourth] Amendment . . . expressly imposes two requirements. First, all searches and seizures must be reasonable. Second, a warrant may not be issued unless probable cause is properly established and the scope of the authorized search is set out with particularity.

Although the text of the Fourth Amendment does not specify when a search warrant must be obtained, this Court has inferred that a warrant must generally be secured. "It is a 'basic principle of Fourth Amendment law,'" we have often said, "'that searches and seizures inside a home without a warrant are presumptively unreasonable.'" Brigham City v. Stuart, 547 U.S. 398, 403 (2006). But we have also recognized that this presumption may be overcome in some circumstances because "[t]he ultimate touchstone of the Fourth Amendment is 'reasonableness.'" *Id.* at 403. Accordingly, the warrant requirement is subject to certain reasonable exceptions.

One well-recognized exception applies when "'the exigencies of the situation' make the needs of law enforcement so compelling that [a] warrantless search is objectively reasonable under the Fourth Amendment." Mincey v. Arizona, 437 U.S. 385, 394 (1978).

This Court has identified several exigencies that may justify a warrantless search of a home. Under the "emergency aid" exception, for example, "officers may enter a home without a warrant to render emergency assistance to an injured occupant or to protect an occupant from imminent injury." *Brigham City*, 547 U.S. at 403. Police officers may enter premises without a warrant when they are in hot pursuit of a fleeing suspect. See United States v. Santana, 427 U.S. 38, 42–43 (1976). And—what is relevant here—the need "to prevent the imminent destruction of evidence" has long been recognized as a sufficient justification for a warrantless search. *Brigham City*, 547 U.S. at 403.

B

Over the years, lower courts have developed an exception to the exigent circumstances rule, the so-called "police-created exigency" doctrine. Under this doctrine, police may not rely on the need to prevent destruction of evidence when that exigency was "created" or "manufactured" by the conduct of the police.

In applying this exception for the "creation" or "manufacturing" of an exigency by the police, courts require something more than mere proof that fear of detection by the police caused the destruction of evidence. An additional showing is obviously needed because, as the Eighth Circuit has recognized, "in some sense the police always create the exigent circumstances." United States v. Duchi, 906 F.2d 1278, 1284 (8th Cir. 1990). That is to say, in the vast majority of cases in which evidence is destroyed by persons who are engaged in illegal conduct, the reason for the destruction is fear that the evidence will fall into the hands of law enforcement. Destruction of evidence issues probably occur most frequently in drug cases because drugs may be easily destroyed by flushing them down a toilet or rinsing them down a drain. Persons in possession of valuable drugs are unlikely to destroy them unless they fear discovery by the police. Consequently, a rule that precludes the police from making a warrantless entry to prevent the destruction of evidence whenever their conduct causes the exigency would unreasonably shrink the reach of this well-established exception to the warrant requirement.

Presumably for the purpose of avoiding such a result, the lower courts have held that the police-created exigency doctrine requires more than simple causation, but the lower courts have not agreed on the test to be applied. . . .

III

A

Despite the welter of tests devised by the lower courts, the answer to the question presented in this case follows directly and clearly from the principle that permits warrantless searches in the first place. As previously noted, warrantless searches are allowed when the circumstances make it reasonable, within the meaning of the Fourth Amendment, to dispense with the warrant requirement. Therefore, the answer to the question before us is that the exigent circumstances rule justifies a warrantless search when the conduct of the police preceding the exigency is reasonable in the same sense. Where, as here, the police did not create the exigency by engaging or threatening to engage in conduct that violates the Fourth Amendment, warrantless entry to prevent the destruction of evidence is reasonable and thus allowed. . . .

B

Some lower courts have adopted a rule that is similar to the one that we recognize today. But others, including the Kentucky Supreme Court, have imposed additional requirements that are unsound and that we now reject.

Bad faith. Some courts, including the Kentucky Supreme Court, ask whether law enforcement officers " 'deliberately created the exigent circumstances with the bad faith intent to avoid the warrant requirement.' " King v. Commonwealth, 302 S.W.3d 649, 656 (Ky. 2010).

This approach is fundamentally inconsistent with our Fourth Amendment jurisprudence. "Our cases have repeatedly rejected" a subjective approach, asking only whether "the circumstances, viewed *objectively,* justify the action." *Brigham City,* 547 U.S. at 404. Indeed, we have never held, outside limited contexts such as an "inventory search or administrative inspection . . . , that an officer's motive invalidates objectively justifiable behavior under the Fourth Amendment." Whren v. United States, 517 U.S. 806, 812 (1996).

The reasons for looking to objective factors, rather than subjective intent, are clear. Legal tests based on reasonableness are generally objective, and this Court has long taken the view that "evenhanded law enforcement is best achieved by the application of objective standards of conduct, rather than standards that depend upon the subjective state of mind of the officer." Horton v. California, 496 U.S. 128, 138 (1990).

Reasonable foreseeability. Some courts, again including the Kentucky Supreme Court, hold that police may not rely on an exigency if " 'it was reasonably foreseeable that the investigative tactics employed by the police would create the exigent circumstances.' " *King,* 302 S.W.3d at 656. Courts applying this test have invalidated warrantless home searches on the ground that it was reasonably foreseeable that police officers, by knocking on the door and announcing their presence, would lead a drug suspect to destroy evidence.

Contrary to this reasoning, however, we have rejected the notion that police may seize evidence without a warrant only when they come across the evidence by happenstance. . . .

Adoption of a reasonable foreseeability test would also introduce an unacceptable degree of unpredictability. For example, whenever law enforcement officers knock on the door of premises occupied by a person who may be involved in the drug trade, there is *some* possibility that the occupants may possess drugs and may seek to destroy them. Under a reasonable foreseeability test, it would be necessary to quantify the degree of predictability that must be reached before the police-created exigency doctrine comes into play. . . .

We have noted that "[t]he calculus of reasonableness must embody allowance for the fact that police officers are often forced to make split-second judgments—in circumstances that are tense, uncertain, and rapidly evolving." Graham v. Connor, 490 U.S. 386, 396-397 (1989). The reasonable foreseeability test would create unacceptable and unwarranted difficulties for law enforcement officers who must make quick decisions in the field, as well as for judges who would be required to determine after the fact whether the destruction of evidence in response to a knock on the door was reasonably foreseeable based on what the officers knew at the time.

Probable cause and time to secure a warrant. Some courts, in applying the police-created exigency doctrine, fault law enforcement officers if, after acquiring evidence that is sufficient to establish probable cause to search particular premises, the officers do not seek a warrant but instead knock on the door and seek either to speak with an occupant or to obtain consent to search.

This approach unjustifiably interferes with legitimate law enforcement strategies. There are many entirely proper reasons why police may not want to seek a search warrant as soon as the bare minimum of evidence needed to establish probable cause is acquired. Without attempting to provide a comprehensive list of these reasons, we note a few.

First, the police may wish to speak with the occupants of a dwelling before deciding whether it is worthwhile to seek authorization for a search. They may think that a short and simple conversation may obviate the need to apply for and execute a warrant. See Schneckloth v. Bustamonte, 412 U.S. 218, 228 (1973). Second, the police may want to ask an occupant of the premises for consent to search because doing so is simpler, faster, and less burdensome than applying for a warrant. A consensual search also "may result in considerably less inconvenience" and embarrassment to the occupants than a search conducted pursuant to a warrant. *Id.* Third, law enforcement officers may wish to obtain more evidence before submitting what might otherwise be considered a marginal warrant application. Fourth, prosecutors may wish to wait until they acquire evidence that can justify a search that is broader in scope than the search that a judicial officer is likely to authorize based on the evidence then available. And finally, in many cases, law enforcement may not want to execute a search that will disclose the existence of an investigation because doing so may interfere with the acquisition of additional evidence against those already under suspicion or evidence about additional but as yet unknown participants in a criminal scheme. . . .

Standard or good investigative tactics. Finally, some lower court cases suggest that law enforcement officers may be found to have created or manufactured an exigency if the court concludes that the course of their investigation was "contrary to standard or good law enforcement practices (or to the policies or practices of their jurisdictions)." United States v. Gould, 364 F.3d 578, 591 (5th Cir. 2004). This approach fails to provide clear guidance for law enforcement officers and authorizes courts to make judgments on matters that are the province of those who are responsible for federal and state law enforcement agencies.

C

Respondent argues for a rule that differs from those discussed above, but his rule is also flawed. Respondent contends that law enforcement officers impermissibly create an exigency when they "engage in conduct that would cause a reasonable person to believe that entry is imminent and inevitable." In respondent's view, relevant factors include the officers' tone of voice in announcing their presence and the forcefulness of their knocks. But the ability of law enforcement officers to respond to an exigency cannot turn on such subtleties.

Police officers may have a very good reason to announce their presence loudly and to knock on the door with some force. A forceful knock may be necessary to alert the occupants that someone is at the door. Furthermore, unless police officers identify themselves loudly enough, occupants may not know who is at their doorstep. Officers are permitted—indeed, encouraged—to identify themselves to citizens, and "in many circumstances this is cause for assurance, not discomfort." United States v. Drayton, 536 U.S. 194, 204 (2002). Citizens who are startled by an unexpected knock on the door or by the sight of unknown persons in plain clothes on their doorstep may be relieved to learn that these persons are police officers. Others may appreciate the opportunity to make an informed decision about whether to answer the door to the police.

If respondent's test were adopted, it would be extremely difficult for police officers to know how loudly they may announce their presence or how forcefully they may knock on a door without running afoul of the police-created exigency rule. And in most cases, it would be nearly impossible for a court to determine whether that threshold had been passed. The Fourth Amendment does not require the nebulous and impractical test that respondent proposes.

D

For these reasons, we conclude that the exigent circumstances rule applies when the police do not gain entry to premises by means of an actual or threatened violation of the Fourth Amendment. This holding provides ample protection for the privacy rights that the Amendment protects.

When law enforcement officers who are not armed with a warrant knock on a door, they do no more than any private citizen might do. And whether the person who knocks on the door and requests the opportunity to speak is a police officer or a private citizen, the occupant has no obligation to open the door or to speak. When the police knock on a door but the occupants choose not to respond or to speak, "the investigation will have reached a conspicuously low point," and the occupants "will have the kind of warning that even the most elaborate security system cannot provide." United States v. Chambers, 395 F.3d 563, 577 (6th Cir. 2005) (Sutton, J., dissenting). And even if an occupant chooses to open the door and speak with the officers, the occupant need not allow the officers to enter the premises and may refuse to answer any questions at any time.

Occupants who choose not to stand on their constitutional rights but instead elect to attempt to destroy evidence have only themselves to blame for the warrantless exigent-circumstances search that may ensue.

IV . . .

Like the court below, we assume for purposes of argument that an exigency existed. Because the officers in this case did not violate or threaten to violate the Fourth Amendment prior to the exigency, we hold that the exigency justified the warrantless search of the apartment.

The judgment of the Kentucky Supreme Court is reversed, and the case is remanded for further proceedings not inconsistent with this opinion.

It is so ordered.

[The dissenting opinion of Justice Ginsburg is omitted.]

NOTES AND QUESTIONS

1. *Comparing tone in* Katz *and* King. *Katz* is still good law, but the Court's tone seems to have changed in the 44 years between *Katz* and *King.* Consider the Court's view of the warrant requirement. *Katz* instructed that a search without a warrant is "*per se* unreasonable under the Fourth Amendment—subject only to a few specially established and well-delineated exceptions." 389 U.S. at 357. *King* states, "this Court has inferred that a warrant must generally be secured . . . subject to certain reasonable exceptions." 563 U.S. at 459. Does this shift reflect the fact that more exceptions have been recognized by the time of *King?* Or does it reflect a more fundamental change in the Court's understanding of the doctrine? What makes you think so?

2. *Supreme Court* vis-à-vis *lower courts.* The *King* decision came only after several state supreme courts and most federal appellate courts formulated tests to limit police use of the exigent-circumstances exception to the warrant requirement. Why did all these different courts invent those tests? It seems likely they saw cases in which police relied on the exigency exception to search homes in ways the courts considered unnecessary or overly intrusive. Does the *King* Court address their concern?

3. *Courts as regulators redux.* Look at the *King* Court's reasons for rejecting each limit placed on the exigency exception by state and federal appellate courts. Two themes predominate. First, police need freedom from restrictive rules to investigate crime effectively. Second, courts are not likely to be good at regulating the police. Whereas the *Katz* Court worried more about police invading privacy, the *King* Court worried that police might be stymied in their fight against crime. Both *Katz* and *King* were concerned with the reliability of judges as regulators of the police, but their concerns point in opposite directions: The *Katz* Court worried that judges too often fail to hold police to account, but the *King* Court worried that courts too often restrict police when what they need is flexibility and freedom. The Court also appears to view its own role differently over time: The *Katz* Court regulates the police through state courts, but the *King* Court protects police from intrusive state courts.

4. *Testilying.* Reading *King* and other Fourth Amendment cases, it is easy to forget that courts have no magical way to determine what happened during a search or seizure. They depend almost entirely on officer testimony.[4] In its investigation of corruption in the NYPD in the mid-1990s, the Mollen Commission concluded based on interviews with officers that false police statements in testimony or reports was "probably the most common form of police corruption facing the criminal justice system, particularly in connection with arrests for possession of narcotics and guns. Several officers also told us that the practice of police falsification in connection with such arrests is so common in certain precincts that it has spawned its own word: 'testilying.' " Commn. to Investigate Allegations of Police Corruption and

---

[4] For some Fourth Amendment questions, such as whether the suspect's actions constituted probable cause of criminal activity, the suspect's testimony might also be helpful. But determining the sufficiency of an exigency justifying a home entry rarely requires courts to hear from the suspect, as what matters is usually what the officers perceived from the outside.

the Anti-Corruption Procedures of the Police Dep't, Commission Report, *Anatomy of Failure: A Path for Success* 36 (1994). While false statements are sometimes used to cover up abuse or corruption, falsification often serves what officers perceive as legitimate law enforcement ends, including convicting a guilty person despite a search or arrest that might not have satisfied the Fourth Amendment. See *id.* at 36–37. For a canonical academic discussion of false testimony by police officers, see Christopher Slobogin, *Testilying: Police Perjury and What to Do About It*, 67 U. Colo. L. Rev. 1037 (1996). If an officer testifies falsely about the circumstances justifying an exigency, using what was found during the search to make his testimony sound credible, how could a court know?

5. *Tailoring.* Even if an officer does not lie about what he perceived, he might tailor his testimony to accord with the law. Might the testimony that supported the apartment entry in *King* be an example? To use the exigency exception to the warrant requirement for entering a home, an officer must have reason to believe that people inside are going to destroy evidence. (That requirement is unchanged by the *King* decision.) The *King* Court quotes from and summarizes patrol officer Steven Cobb's testimony at the suppression hearing about the circumstances of the entry. Here it is in fuller form:

A.   As we got into the hallway, about midway, there was a very strong odor of burnt marijuana inside the breezeway.
     As we got closer to the back left apartment, we could tell that it seemed to be the source of that, almost as if the door had been slammed right there. Detective Maynard made contact with the door, announced our presence, banged on the door as loud as we could, announced, "Police, police, police." I had reason to believe—. . . .

Q.   How do you know it was burnt marijuana?

A.   Through training and experience. . . .

Q.   What did you observe or hear when you-all banged on that door?

A.   As soon as we started banging on the door, Detective Maynard turned to Sergeant Simmons to let him know that we could hear people inside moving. It sounded as—things were being moved inside the apartment. We had obviously felt at that point that someone had just gone into the apartment. So. . . .

Q.   What kind of movement did you hear inside?

A.   Things were being moved around inside the apartment.

Q.   What did you-all do once you heard these things being moved around in the apartment?

A.   We knew that that there was possibly something that was going to be destroyed inside the apartment. . . .

Q.   Why did you think something could be destroyed in the apartment?

A.   Just based upon the nature of what it is we were there for. Crack cocaine can easily be destroyed because of its size.

Joint Appendix at 22–24, Kentucky v. King, 563 U.S. 452 (2011) (No. 09-1272), 2010 WL 4628574.

When cross-examined by King's attorney, Cobb explained further:

Q.   What was your basis for believing you could enter the apartment that these defendants were in?

A.   There was a crime occurring inside and also possible destruction of evidence.

Q.   And isn't it true that you actually wrote in your report that "We could hear persons inside the apartment and noises possibly consistent"—is that right—"possibly consistent with the destruction of potential evidence"?

A.   Yes, I wrote "possibly consistent with destruction of potential evidence."

Q.   You've testified previously to Ms. Williams that there was movement. What is it about that movement that was unique to allow you to discern that that was possibly consistent with destruction of physical evidence?

A.   It's consistent with my experience of people who do destroy evidence inside apartments or other structures when we're outside.

Q.   Is it consistent with your experience that people who live in apartments move around in them?

A.   Do people move in apartments?

Q.   Sure.

A.   Yes, people move in apartments.

Q.   (Inaudible) regularly that don't commit crimes move around in their apartment?

A.   Most people answer the door when the police knock at the door also.

Q.   That wasn't really what I asked. I was asking you if it's common, in your experience, that people move around in their apartment, and I'm asking you—you said that you have expertise that says it's consistent or possibly consistent—

A.   I said I had experience.

Q.   Okay. I'm asking you what that experience is that made you be able to discern between possibly consistent with destruction of evidence and normal use of an apartment?

A.   What is the difference?

Q.   Yes, sir.

A.   Between movement you can hear inside? We announced our presence at the door, told them we were police, and after that, it's been through my experience, when we've made that—when we've done that before, we have had people who have destroyed evidence inside, it's the same kind of movements we've heard inside.

Id. at 40–42.

Courts tend to defer to this kind of police testimony, as the court did in this case. The Supreme Court has encouraged them to do so, most notably in *Terry v. Ohio*, 392 U.S. 1, 27 (1968), which instructs courts to give due weight "to the specific reasonable inferences which [the officer] is entitled to draw from the facts in light of his experience" in deciding whether the officer acted reasonably. See Anna Lvovsky, *The Judicial Presumption of Police Expertise*, 130 Harv. L. Rev. 1995 (2015) (considering the history and practice of judicial deference to police claims of experience and expertise). Does this judicial deference change how you think about the Court's ruling? How so?

6. *What exigency?* If King and his friends *were* trying to destroy evidence, they could not have been worse at it. When the police entered, all three defendants were in the living room. No one was reaching for the 25 grams of marijuana sitting on the coffee table in front of them. No one was heading for the kitchen, where police found enough cocaine on a counter to get a couple of hundred people high. And one of King's buddies had not even bothered to put down the marijuana joint he was smoking. What do you make of that?

What Happens to All Those Drugs?

After police find drugs and collect them into evidence, they line warehouse shelves in evidence lockups and crime laboratories stored, often for years, until they are no longer needed. Then what?

The drugs mostly get burned. Some agencies do it themselves. Others use hospitals or crematories. Several state agencies rely on industrial factories. In Detroit, the state police use a metal forging plant's high temperature furnace. Ohio state police used to do the same, vaporizing drugs with molten steel in a local factory, but when the factory worried that emissions could lead to positive drug tests for employees, the police switched to a company that specializes in hazardous materials. See Kantele Franko, *Report: Police Methods for Destroying Drug Evidence Vary*, Police One (May 25, 2014).

Agency choices are complicated by an array of federal, state, and local environmental and safety rules on burning things. In Missouri, for example, departments that want to destroy drugs are required to seek permits from the Missouri Department of Natural Resources's Air Pollution Control Program. See Mo. Code Regs. Ann. tit. 10, §10-6.060. Among other requirements, those permits mandate burning drugs at a temperature of no less than 1,400 degrees Fahrenheit and require extensive record keeping. By contrast, in West Virginia, burning drugs in an open fire pit is fine. This means that, in addition to being familiar with criminal law and criminal procedure rules; First Amendment law; and labor, employment, and discrimination law, law enforcement agencies have to be familiar with federal and state environmental codes and regulations.

Agencies also have to foot the bill for all this burning, often including construction costs for incinerators. But because they can often use assets seized in connection with drug crimes to pay for destroying their drugs, drug dealers help.

Seized powder cocaine.

7. *The government's interest.* Although the Court explains that an exception to the warrant requirement is justified if the "needs" of law enforcement are "so compelling" under the circumstances that a warrantless entry is reasonable, the Court never explains why the risk that drugs will be destroyed is so compelling. In this case, in addition to the marijuana on the coffee table and the cocaine in the kitchen, officers also found two marijuana pipes, a marijuana roach, $2,500 in cash, three cell phones, scales with cocaine residue, and other drug paraphernalia. See Joint Appendix at 25–30, Kentucky v. King, 563 U.S. 452 (2011) (No. 09-1272), 2010 WL 4628574. What precisely is the government's interest in finding the drugs? Assuming most or all of the drugs were rinsed down the drain, what would the government lose?

8. *Fourth Amendment as a tax.* Despite the rhetoric in *Katz*, in practice, magistrates overwhelmingly approve warrant applications with only minimal review. Still, warrants slow things down, leading officers to choose other investigative activities (for which no warrant is required) before engaging in activities that require a warrant. In a way, the Supreme Court's Fourth Amendment doctrine creates a differential pricing scheme for police investigative activities: Some require no justification or warrant; some probable cause but no warrant; some probable cause and a warrant. When police investigate a crime, they are likely to start with "cheap" low-hassle and low-litigation-risk activities, including consent searches and activities that are not a search within the meaning of the Fourth Amendment, such as the buy–bust in *King.* If those activities confirm suspicion and provide probable cause, officers will engage in more "expensive" activities, including activities that require a warrant. See William J. Stuntz, *Unequal Justice,* 121 Harv. L. Rev. 1969, 2017–2019 (2008).

If the Supreme Court took care to impose greater burdens on more intrusive activities, Fourth Amendment doctrine might make policing more harm-efficient, so that it imposed investigative harms on suspects only when the societal interests in protecting officers and proving the crime, and the likelihood of discovering useful evidence, justified those harms. Under current doctrine, however, some intrusive activities, such as sting operations with wired informants, are entirely "untaxed." Also, keep in mind that the government can lower its "taxes" by hiring more magistrates and allowing officers to get warrants by telephone, radio, or email, making expensive activities much cheaper for officers. Cf. Missouri v. McNeely, 569 U.S. 141, 154 (2013).

9. *Facing the police.* The Court suggests that the officers who knocked on King's door did "no more than any private citizen might do," and that King and his compatriots had "only themselves to blame" when officers then kicked in the door. *King,* 563 U.S. at 469–470. Go back to the facts of *King.* The officers did not politely knock on the door and request entry; they banged on the door as loud as they could and shouted that they were the police. Who in that situation would believe that they could "stand on their constitutional rights"? *Id.* at 470. Moreover, the officers did not enter after they overheard someone say, "Let's get rid of this stuff before they come back with a warrant." Instead, they broke in almost immediately after banging on the door because they heard "motion." Is the only way to exert constitutional rights to stay silent and stock-still? Cf. Berghuis v. Thompkins, 560 U.S. 370 (2010) (requiring suspects to speak unambiguously to invoke their Fifth Amendment right to remain silent).

10. *Comfort or threat?* The Court also suggests that many people will be reassured to realize that an unexpected knock on the door is the police. Perhaps. But

many Americans experience the police differently. For example, in light of experiences with police harassment and violence today and the historical role police have played in enforcing slavery, segregation, and racism, some Black Americans fear the police more than they are comforted by them. See, e.g., Nikole Hannah-Jones, *Taking Freedom: Yes, Black America Fears the Police. Here's Why*, Pac. Standard (May 8, 2018). The same is true for undocumented immigrants, who fear being targeted rather than protected by the police, even when they are victims of crime. See Cora Engelbrecht, *Fewer Immigrants Are Reporting Domestic Abuse. Police Blame Fear of Deportation*, N.Y. Times (Jun. 3, 2018). How should Fourth Amendment doctrine take into account that some people find the police reassuring and others find them frightening?

4.   Modern Constitutional Regulation of Surveillance Technologies

King involves a decidedly low-tech intrusion, breaking into a home without a warrant. The police also often use technological methods of surveillance to uncover crime because these methods make crime detection "quicker, easier, and more certain," all while making it more invisible. See Berger v. New York, 388 U.S. 41, 63 (1967). For years, the Court mostly resisted considering these implications of technological advances when assessing Fourth Amendment protections. The Court's decision in *United States v. Knotts*, 460 U.S. 276 (1983), provides an example. Narcotics agents believed that Tristan Armstrong was obtaining chemicals for an illegal drug-manufacturing operation. With the consent of a company that provided Armstrong some of the chemicals, the agents installed a radio transmitter, known colloquially as a beeper, in a container of chloroform (sometimes used in methamphetamine manufacturing) before Armstrong received it. The transmitter enabled the agents to track Armstrong when he delivered the chloroform to Darryl Petschen and then to track Petschen when he drove the drum to a cabin owned by Leroy Knotts. The officers used this information as part of their search warrant application for the cabin, and the search revealed a drug-manufacturing lab. Knotts was convicted after the district court rejected his argument that monitoring the beeper violated his Fourth Amendment rights. The Supreme Court affirmed:

> A person travelling in an automobile on public thoroughfares has no reasonable expectation of privacy in his movements from one place to another. When Petschen traveled over the public streets he voluntarily conveyed to anyone who wanted to look the fact that he was traveling over particular roads in a particular direction, the fact of whatever stops he made, and the fact of his final destination when he exited from public roads onto private property.

> Respondent Knotts, as the owner of the cabin and surrounding premises to which Petschen drove, undoubtedly had the traditional expectation of privacy within a dwelling place insofar as the cabin was concerned. . . .

> But no such expectation of privacy extended to the visual observation of Petschen's automobile arriving on his premises after leaving a public highway, nor to movements of objects such as the drum of chloroform outside the cabin in the "open fields." Hester v. United States, 265 U.S. 57 (1924).

> Visual surveillance from public places along Petschen's route or adjoining Knotts' premises would have sufficed to reveal all of these facts to the police. The fact that the officers in this case relied not only on visual surveillance, but also on the use of

the beeper to signal the presence of Petschen's automobile to the police receiver, does not alter the situation. Nothing in the Fourth Amendment prohibited the police from augmenting the sensory faculties bestowed upon them at birth with such enhancement as science and technology afforded them in this case. . . .

We have recently had occasion to deal with another claim which was to some extent a factual counterpart of respondent's assertions here. In *Smith v. Maryland*, 442 U.S. 735 (1979), we said:

> "This analysis dictates that [Smith] can claim no legitimate expectation of privacy here. When he used his phone, [Smith] voluntarily conveyed numerical information to the telephone company and 'exposed' that information to its equipment in the ordinary course of business. In so doing, [Smith] assumed the risk that the company would reveal to police the numbers he dialed. The switching equipment that processed those numbers is merely the modern counterpart of the operator who, in an earlier day, personally completed calls for the subscriber. [Smith] concedes that if he had placed his calls through an operator, he could claim no legitimate expectation of privacy. [Citation omitted.] We are not inclined to hold that a different constitutional result is required because the telephone company has decided to automate." *Id.* at 744–745.

Respondent does not actually quarrel with this analysis. . . . Insofar as respondent's complaint appears to be simply that scientific devices such as the beeper enabled the police to be more effective in detecting crime, it simply has no constitutional foundation. We have never equated police efficiency with unconstitutionality, and we decline to do so now. . . .

. . . Admittedly, because of the failure of the visual surveillance, the beeper enabled the law enforcement officials in this case to ascertain the ultimate resting place of the chloroform when they would not have been able to do so had they relied solely on their naked eyes. But scientific enhancement of this sort raises no constitutional issues which visual surveillance would not also raise. A police car following Petschen at a distance throughout his journey could have observed him leaving the public highway and arriving at the cabin owned by respondent, with the drum of chloroform still in the car. This fact, along with others, was used by the government in obtaining a search warrant which led to the discovery of the clandestine drug laboratory.

Knotts, 460 U.S. at 281–285.

The Court has started to see things differently. Justice Sotomayor described some of the implications of technological change for Fourth Amendment doctrine in her concurrence in *United States v. Jones*, 565 U.S. 400 (2012):

> [P]hysical intrusion is now unnecessary to many forms of surveillance. With increasing regularity, the government will be capable of duplicating the monitoring undertaken in this case by enlisting factory- or owner-installed vehicle tracking devices or GPS-enabled smartphones. . . .

> In cases involving even short-term monitoring, some unique attributes of GPS surveillance relevant to the *Katz* analysis will require particular attention. GPS monitoring generates a precise, comprehensive record of a person's public movements that reflects a wealth of detail about her familial, political, professional, religious, and sexual associations. The government can store such records and efficiently mine them for information years into the future. And because GPS monitoring is cheap

in comparison to conventional surveillance techniques and, by design, proceeds surreptitiously, it evades the ordinary checks that constrain abusive law enforcement practices: "limited police resources and community hostility." Illinois v. Lidster, 540 U.S. 419, 426 (2004).

Awareness that the Government may be watching chills associational and expressive freedoms. And the government's unrestrained power to assemble data that reveal private aspects of identity is susceptible to abuse. The net result is that GPS monitoring—by making available at a relatively low cost such a substantial quantum of intimate information about any person whom the government, in its unfettered discretion, chooses to track—may alter the relationship between citizen and government in a way that is inimical to democratic society.

I would take these attributes of GPS monitoring into account when considering the existence of a reasonable societal expectation of privacy in the sum of one's public movements. . . . I do not regard as dispositive the fact that the government might obtain the fruits of GPS monitoring through lawful conventional surveillance techniques. . . .

More fundamentally, it may be necessary to reconsider the premise that an individual has no reasonable expectation of privacy in information voluntarily disclosed to third parties. E.g., Smith. v. Maryland, 442 U.S. 735, 742 (1979); United States v. Miller, 425 U.S. 435, 443 (1976). This approach is ill suited to the digital age, in which people reveal a great deal of information about themselves to third parties in the course of carrying out mundane tasks. . . . I would not assume that all information voluntarily disclosed to some member of the public for a limited purpose is, for that reason alone, disentitled to Fourth Amendment protection.

Id. at 414–418 (Sotomayor, J., concurring).

A few years after Jones, the majority of the Court took a similar position in Carpenter v. United States, 138 S. Ct. 2206 (2018), which required police to obtain a warrant for historical cell-site location information. The Court explained:

A person does not surrender all Fourth Amendment protection by venturing into the public sphere. . . . Prior to the digital age, law enforcement might have pursued a suspect for a brief stretch, but doing so "for any extended period of time was difficult and costly and therefore rarely undertaken." United States v. Jones, 565 U.S. 400, 429 (2012) (Alito, J., concurring). For that reason, "society's expectation has been that law enforcement agents and others would not—and indeed, in the main, simply could not—secretly monitor and catalogue every single movement of an individual's car for a very long period." Id. at 430.

Allowing government access to cell-site records contravenes that expectation. Although such records are generated for commercial purposes, that distinction does not negate Carpenter's anticipation of privacy in his physical location. Mapping a cell phone's location over the course of 127 days provides an all-encompassing record of the holder's whereabouts. As with GPS information, the time-stamped data provides an intimate window into a person's life, revealing not only his particular movements, but through them his "familial, political, professional, religious, and sexual associations." Id. at 415 (Sotomayor, J., concurring).

These location records hold for many Americans the privacies of life. And like GPS monitoring, cell phone tracking is remarkably easy, cheap, and efficient compared to traditional investigative tools. With just the click of a button, the Government can access each carrier's deep repository of historical location information at practically no expense.

In fact, historical cell-site records present even greater privacy concerns than the GPS monitoring of a vehicle we considered in *Jones*. Unlike the bugged container in *Knotts* or the car in *Jones*, a cell phone—almost a "feature of human anatomy," Riley v. California, 573 U.S. 373, 385 (2014)—tracks nearly exactly the movements of its owner. . . . Accordingly, when the Government tracks the location of a cell phone it achieves near perfect surveillance, as if it had attached an ankle monitor to the phone's user. . . .

Accordingly, when the Government accessed CSLI from the wireless carriers, it invaded Carpenter's reasonable expectation of privacy in the whole of his physical movements.

The Government's primary contention to the contrary is that the third-party doctrine governs this case. In its view, cell-site records are fair game because they are "business records" created and maintained by the wireless carriers. . . .

The Government's position fails to contend with the seismic shifts in digital technology that made possible the tracking of not only Carpenter's location but also everyone else's, not for a short period but for years and years. Sprint Corporation and its competitors are not your typical witnesses. Unlike the nosy neighbor who keeps an eye on comings and goings, they are ever alert, and their memory is nearly infallible. There is a world of difference between the limited types of personal information addressed in *Smith* and *Miller* and the exhaustive chronicle of location information casually collected by wireless carriers today. The Government thus is not asking for a straightforward application of the third-party doctrine, but instead a significant extension of it to a distinct category of information.

Id. at 2217–2219.

NOTES AND QUESTIONS

1. *Change over time.* What changed between *Knotts* and *Carpenter*?

2. *Implications.* New surveillance technologies come online often. Now some police departments use unmanned aerial vehicles, commonly called drones, to observe public behavior. Federal and state statutory regulation of drones is discussed later in the chapter. For the moment, consider that an inexpensive drone can track a car or a fugitive without ever getting close. Imagine a police chief considering purchasing several drones. Among other uses, he wants officers to employ drones for traffic enforcement and following cars for investigatory purposes. He asks you whether he is likely to need a warrant to use them. What do you say? How might *Knotts*, *Jones*, and *Carpenter* apply to drone surveillance?

3. *Applications.* In advising the chief, note that the Fourth Amendment is intrusion-specific, not technology-specific. The implications of the Fourth Amendment vary according to the ways in which technology is used. No matter what the Fourth Amendment has to say about using a drone to follow a car or a person along public streets and sidewalks, using the same drone to check out whether someone is growing marijuana in his yard requires a different analysis: Under the Fourth Amendment, police officers are not permitted to enter a backyard to look around without a warrant, see United States v. Dunn, 480 U.S. 294 (1987); Oliver v. United States, 466 U.S. 170 (1984), but two cases allow officers to fly over backyards and

look down, see Florida v. Riley, 488 U.S. 445 (1989); California v. Ciraolo, 476 U.S. 207 (1986). How similar do you imagine drones are (in constitutional terms) to manned aircraft? Who would you expect to decide that question? The Court? The Federal Aviation Administration?

4. *Consequences of technology.* Technology mitigates two obstacles to police surveillance: keeping it secret and keeping it going. If an officer "gets made," he is unlikely to discover much evidence, so staying hidden is key. The officers in *Knotts* could follow less closely knowing they could use the beeper to pick up the trail again. Similarly, police officers have limited resources, and it takes multiple teams of officers to follow a suspect reliably by car or on foot. A beeper makes that less resource intensive, and a GPS less so still. CSLI makes following in real time largely unnecessary. Similarly, hovering over a backyard in a helicopter is expensive and impossible to miss from the ground. By contrast, unmanned drones cost a tiny fraction of what planes or helicopters cost; they are easier to use and store; and they are far stealthier. Is it a good thing to make policing more efficient in this way? Should this kind of efficiency matter for Fourth Amendment doctrine?

B. *Regulating Surveillance: Courts and Congress*

Although Congress has limited power over local police officers, many high-tech means of securing evidence sufficiently affect interstate commerce so as to place them within congressional purview. Congress has exercised this power in a couple of dozen privacy statutes that set conditions on police access to some kinds of information. These laws shape police use of bank records, emails, cable subscriber information, and children's online activities, among many other kinds of information.

Congress does not enact its privacy statutes in a vacuum. Inevitably, it reacts to how the courts are regulating the same kind of privacy. Usually, Congress acts only after the Supreme Court determines that an evidence-gathering technique is not protected by the Fourth Amendment. Occasionally, as in the case of wiretaps, Congress supplements Fourth Amendment protection with statutory law. To illustrate the way Congress reacts to the courts, and the courts to Congress, two privacy statutes (the Wiretap Act and the Pen Register Act) are discussed below, along with the Supreme Court cases to which Congress reacted in passing them. As you will see, interbranch interaction goes in both directions: Just as Congress responds to courts, the Supreme Court also interprets the Fourth Amendment with an awareness that legislatures can and sometimes do respond to its rulings.

1. Federal Statutes in an Area Regulated by the Fourth Amendment

Six months before the Supreme Court decided *Katz v. United States*, 389 U.S. 347 (1967), it decided *Berger v. New York*, 388 U.S. 41 (1967). Although the Court waited until *Katz* to fully reject its previous framework for analyzing Fourth Amendment cases, *Berger* was an important step along the way to expanding the scope of the Fourth Amendment.

Berger was convicted of conspiring to bribe the Chairman of the New York State Liquor Authority based on recordings made by a listening device in a co-conspirator's office. The device was installed pursuant to an order issued by a trial court judge, as provided for in a New York statute regulating wiretapping, N.Y. Code Crim. Proc. §813–a. Before ruling on the constitutionality of the statute, the Court considered the problem of wiretapping:

> Eavesdropping is an ancient practice which at common law was condemned as a nuisance. 4 William Blackstone, *Commentaries* 168. At one time the eavesdropper listened by naked ear under the eaves of houses or their windows, or beyond their walls seeking out private discourse. The awkwardness and undignified manner of this method as well as its susceptibility to abuse was immediately recognized. Electricity, however, provided a better vehicle and with the advent of the telegraph surreptitious interception of messages began. As early as 1862 California found it necessary to prohibit the practice by statute. Statutes of California 1862, p. 288, CCLX II. During the Civil War General J. E. B. Stuart is reputed to have had his own eavesdropper along with him in the field whose job it was to intercept military communications of the opposing forces. . . .
>
> The telephone brought on a new and more modern eavesdropper known as the "wiretapper." Interception was made by a connection with a telephone line. This activity has been with us for three-quarters of a century. Like its cousins, wiretapping proved to be a commercial as well as a police technique. . . . During prohibition days wiretaps were the principal source of information relied upon by the police as the basis for prosecutions. In 1934 the Congress outlawed the interception without authorization, and the divulging or publishing of the contents of wiretaps by passing §605 of the Communications Act of 1934. New York, in 1938, declared by constitutional amendment that "[t]he right of the people to be secured against unreasonable interception of telephone and telegraph communications shall not be violated," but permitted by *ex parte* order of the Supreme Court of the State the interception of communications on a showing of "reasonable ground to believe that evidence of crime" might be obtained. N.Y. Const. art. I, §12.
>
> Sophisticated electronic devices have now been developed (commonly known as "bugs") which are capable of eavesdropping on anyone in almost any given situation. They are to be distinguished from "wiretaps" which are confined to the interception of telegraphic and telephonic communications. Miniature in size ($\frac{3}{8}'' \times \frac{3}{8}'' \times \frac{1}{8}''$) — no larger than a postage stamp — these gadgets pick up whispers within a room and broadcast them half a block away to a receiver. It is said that certain types of electronic rays beamed at walls or glass windows are capable of catching voice vibrations as they are bounced off the surfaces. Since 1940 eavesdropping has become a big business. . . .
>
> As science developed these detection techniques, lawmakers, sensing the resulting invasion of individual privacy, have provided some statutory protection for the public. . . . In sum, it is fair to say that wiretapping on the whole is outlawed, except for permissive use by law enforcement officials in some States; while electronic eavesdropping is — save for seven states — permitted both officially and privately. And, in six of the seven States, electronic eavesdropping ("bugging") is permissible on court order.

Berger, 388 U.S. at 45–49.

The Court concluded that the Fourth Amendment protects conversations as well as tangible objects and that capturing a conversation by electronic means constitutes a search. Although the listening device that captured Berger's conversation was installed pursuant to New York's eavesdropping statute, the Court found that the statute did not provide sufficient protection to satisfy the Fourth Amendment's reasonableness requirement for searches:

> While New York's statute satisfies the Fourth Amendment's requirement that a neutral and detached authority be interposed between the police and the public, the broad sweep of the statute is immediately observable. It permits the issuance of the order, or warrant for eavesdropping, upon the oath of the attorney general, the district attorney or any police officer above the rank of sergeant stating that "there is reasonable ground to believe that evidence of crime may be thus obtained. . . ." Such a requirement raises a serious probable cause question under the Fourth Amendment. . . .
>
> The Fourth Amendment commands that a warrant issue not only upon probable cause supported by oath or affirmation, but also "particularly describing the place to be searched, and the persons or things to be seized." New York's statute lacks this particularization. It merely says that a warrant may issue on reasonable ground to believe that evidence of crime may be obtained by the eavesdrop. . . . The need for particularity and evidence of reliability in the showing required when judicial authorization of a search is sought is especially great in the case of eavesdropping. By its very nature eavesdropping involves an intrusion on privacy that is broad in scope. . . .
>
> . . . It is true that the statute requires the naming of "the person or persons whose communications, conversations or discussions are to be overheard or recorded. . . ." But this does no more than identify the person whose constitutionally protected area is to be invaded rather than "particularly describing" the communications, conversations, or discussions to be seized. As with general warrants this leaves too much to the discretion of the officer executing the order. Secondly, authorization of eavesdropping for a two-month period is the equivalent of a series of intrusions, searches, and seizures pursuant to a single showing of probable cause. . . . During such a long and continuous (24 hours a day) period the conversations of any and all persons coming into the area covered by the device will be seized indiscriminately and without regard to their connection with the crime under investigation. Moreover, the statute permits, and there were authorized here, extensions of the original two-month period—presumably for two months each—on a mere showing that such extension is "in the public interest." . . . This we believe insufficient without a showing of present probable cause for the continuance of the eavesdrop. . . . Finally, the statute's procedure, necessarily because its success depends on secrecy, has no requirement for notice as do conventional warrants, nor does it overcome this defect by requiring some showing of special facts. . . . Nor does the statute provide for a return on the warrant thereby leaving full discretion in the officer as to the use of seized conversations of innocent as well as guilty parties. In short, the statute's blanket grant of permission to eavesdrop is without adequate judicial supervision or protective procedures.

Id. at 54–60. With respect to the risks of regulating eavesdropping, the Court noted:

> It is said with fervor that electronic eavesdropping is a most important technique of law enforcement and that outlawing it will severely cripple crime detection. . . .
>
> In any event we cannot forgive the requirements of the Fourth Amendment in the name of law enforcement. This is no formality that we require today but a

fundamental rule that has long been recognized as basic to the privacy of every home in America. While "[t]he requirements of the Fourth Amendment are not inflexible, or obtusely unyielding to the legitimate needs of law enforcement," *Lopez v. United States*, 373 U.S. 427, 464 (1963) (Brennan, J., dissenting), it is not asking too much that officers be required to comply with the basic command of the Fourth Amendment before the innermost secrets of one's home or office are invaded. Few threats to liberty exist which are greater than that posed by the use of eavesdropping devices. Some may claim that without the use of such devices crime detection in certain areas may suffer some delays since eavesdropping is quicker, easier, and more certain. However, techniques and practices may well be developed that will operate just as speedily and certainly and—what is more important— without attending illegality.

Id. at 60–63.

In dissent, Justice Harlan argued:

The Court in recent years has more and more taken to itself sole responsibility for setting the pattern of criminal law enforcement throughout the country. Time-honored distinctions between the constitutional protections afforded against federal authority by the Bill of Rights and those provided against the action by the Fourteenth Amendment have been obliterated, thus increasingly subjecting state criminal law enforcement policies to oversight by this Court. Newly contrived constitutional rights have been established without any apparent concern for the empirical process that goes with legislative reform. And overlying the particular decisions to which this course has given rise is the fact that, short of future action by this Court, their impact can only be undone or modified by the slow and uncertain process of constitutional amendment.

Today's decision is in this mold. Despite the fact that the use of electronic eavesdropping devices as instruments of criminal law enforcement is currently being comprehensively addressed by the Congress and various other bodies in the country, the Court has chosen, quite unnecessarily, to decide this case in a manner which will seriously restrict, if not entirely thwart, such efforts, and will freeze further progress in this field, except as the Court may itself act or a constitutional amendment may set things right.

In my opinion what the Court is doing is very wrong, and I must respectfully dissent.

Id. at 89–90 (Harlan, J., dissenting).

Although congressional action is far more common when the Court does not regulate a matter than when it does, Justice Harlan was wrong in thinking that the Court's action in restricting wiretaps would "seriously restrict, if not entirely thwart" Congress. Congress responded to *Berger* and *Katz* with Title III of the Omnibus Crime Control and Safe Streets Act of 1968, Pub. L. No. 90-351, 82 Stat. 197 (1968). The law, known as the Federal Wiretap Act or Title III, prohibits any person from intercepting, procuring, disclosing, or using any wire, oral, or electronic communications. An exception exists that permits law enforcement to intercept a person's communications but only with a court order based on probable cause that the person has committed one of the crimes specified in the act and that evidence of that crime will be found in the wiretap. In addition, court orders for wiretaps are permitted under the statute only as a last resort, when other investigative techniques will not work, and law enforcement has to "minimize" capture of innocent conversations.

Remedies for violations of the Act include civil damages, fines, imprisonment, evidentiary exclusion, and injunction. In 1986, in light of widespread use of cellular and cordless phones, pagers, personal computers, and more, Congress amended Title III with the Electronic Communications Privacy Act (ECPA), which extended its rules to wireless voice communications and other computer-to-computer electronic communications, including email.

Congress intended Title III as powerful protection for private communications. Things did not turn out exactly as expected. Here is an assessment from 1997:

(1) Wiretapping is no longer confined to violent and major crimes. . . . [T]he list of offenses for which wiretapping is permitted has been expanded steadily . . .—from the original 26 in 1968 to 95 in 1996. The original list was largely limited to espionage and treason, violent crimes, and offenses typically associated with organized crime. . . . [W]iretapping is now authorized for cases involving false statements on passport applications and loan applications or involving "any depredation" against any property of the United States. . . . Wiretapping is used only rarely in cases involving homicide, kidnapping, or terrorism. In 1996, 71% of wiretaps nationwide were in drug cases.

(2) The yearly number of federal, state and local law enforcement wiretaps has gone up steadily, from 564 in 1980 to 1,149 in 1996. . . . Judges rarely deny wiretap applications. In 1996, only one wiretap application was denied; 1,149 were approved. For seven years in a row, 1989 through 1995, no judge, state or federal, denied a single government request for wiretapping. In that period, judges approved 6,598 wiretap orders in criminal cases. . . .

(3) While *Katz* indicated approval of wiretaps of short duration, the longest wiretap in 1996 lasted 420 days. The average length of intercepts has increased steadily, from an average of 21 days in 1980, to an average of 38 days in 1996. The average number of calls intercepted per wiretap has also increased steadily, from 1,058 per intercept in 1980 to 1,969 in 1996.

(4) The courts authorize electronic surveillance even when law enforcement agencies have not exhausted all other reasonably available techniques. . . . Representative of the judicial attitude is the conclusion of one court that the purpose of the statutory exhaustion requirement is "simply to inform the issuing judge of the difficulties involved in the use of conventional techniques."

(5) The minimization requirement also has not been strictly enforced by the judiciary. In *Scott v. United States*[, 436 U.S. 128 (1978)], the Supreme Court held that the complete recording of all conversations on a phone line belonging to the woman with whom the subject of the order was living was acceptable. Law enforcement agents in that case had made essentially no efforts to minimize the interception of nonpertinent calls, despite the high proportion of calls on the line that were nonpertinent. . . . [L]ower courts have read the case as effectively eliminating the requirement to minimize the recording of innocent conversations. . . .

(6) Defendants' after-the-fact challenges to the authorization or conduct of surveillance are rarely sustained. Between 1985 and 1994, judges nationwide granted 138 suppression motions while denying 3,060, for a 4.3% suppression rate.

James X. Dempsey, *Communications Privacy in the Digital Age: Revitalizing the Federal Wiretap Laws to Enhance Privacy*, 8 Alb. L.J. Sci. & Tech. 65, 76-77 (1997).

NOTES AND QUESTIONS

1. *Berger's logic.* Why does the Court reject New York's effort to regulate wiretaps? As Justice Harlan's dissent indicates, when the Court interprets the Fourth Amendment, it self-consciously makes judgments about not only what the words of the Constitution require but also what other institutional actors might do, whether they might better manage the problem.

2. *Statutes vs. constitutional rights.* What might this account suggest about the strengths and weaknesses of statutory rather than constitutional restraint on police activity? What does it say about how Congress and the courts interact as regulators of the police?

3. *Did the Wiretap Act work?* Does the increasing number of wiretaps and low rate of wiretap authorization denials necessarily mean that wiretaps are inadequately regulated?

4. *Updated numbers.* Dempsey's summary is dated, but more recent numbers support the trend he describes. According to reporting by the federal courts, wiretap applications continued to rise dramatically through 2015, when they reached a high of 4,148 intercept applications, all of which were granted, and nearly 80 percent of which involved narcotics offenses. The applications are overwhelmingly for mobile devices, and the number of communications intercepted has gone up dramatically over time, as has the average length of the intercepts. Since 2015 wiretaps applications have dropped some, but they are still far higher than they were in the 1990s.

2.   Federal Statutes in Areas Unregulated by the Fourth Amendment

Most federal privacy statutes are passed after the Court makes clear that the Fourth Amendment does not apply to law enforcement information gathering of a particular kind. Here is a case concluding that a police activity is not a search. As you read, think about the consequences of the Court's ruling.

SMITH v. MARYLAND
442 U.S. 735 (1979)

Mr. Justice Blackmun delivered the opinion of the Court.

This case presents the question whether the installation and use of a pen register[1] constitutes a "search" within the meaning of the Fourth Amendment, made applicable to the States through the Fourteenth Amendment.

---

[1] "A pen register is a mechanical device that records the numbers dialed on a telephone by monitoring the electrical impulses caused when the dial on the telephone is released. It does not overhear oral communications and does not indicate whether calls are actually completed." United States v. New York Tel. Co., 434 U.S. 159, 161 n.1 (1977). A pen register is "usually installed at a central telephone facility [and] records on a paper tape all numbers dialed from [the] line" to which it is attached. United States v. Giordano, 416 U.S. 505, 549 n.1 (1974) (opinion concurring in part and dissenting in part). See also *New York Tel. Co.*, 434 U.S. at 162.

I

On March 5, 1976, in Baltimore, Md., Patricia McDonough was robbed. She gave the police a description of the robber and of a 1975 Monte Carlo automobile she had observed near the scene of the crime. After the robbery, McDonough began receiving threatening and obscene phone calls from a man identifying himself as the robber. . . . On March 16, police spotted a man who met McDonough's description driving a 1975 Monte Carlo in her neighborhood. By tracing the license plate number, police learned that the car was registered in the name of petitioner, Michael Lee Smith.

The next day, the telephone company, at police request, installed a pen register at its central offices to record the numbers dialed from the telephone at petitioner's home. The police did not get a warrant or court order before having the pen register installed. The register revealed that on March 17 a call was placed from petitioner's home to McDonough's phone. On the basis of this and other evidence, . . . [p]etitioner was indicted in the Criminal Court of Baltimore for robbery. By pretrial motion, he sought to suppress "all fruits derived from the pen register" on the ground that the police had failed to secure a warrant prior to its installation. The trial court denied the suppression motion, holding that the warrantless installation of the pen register did not violate the Fourth Amendment. . . . The pen register tape (evidencing the fact that a phone call had been made from petitioner's phone to McDonough's phone) . . . [was] admitted into evidence against him. Petitioner was convicted, and was sentenced to six years. . . .

II

A

. . . In determining whether a particular form of government-initiated electronic surveillance is a "search" within the meaning of the Fourth Amendment, our lodestar is *Katz v. United States,* 389 U.S. 347 (1967). . . .

. . . Th[e *Katz*] inquiry, as Mr. Justice Harlan aptly noted in his *Katz* concurrence, normally embraces two discrete questions. The first is whether the individual, by his conduct, has "exhibited an actual (subjective) expectation of privacy," *id.* at 361 (Harlan, J., concurring) — whether, in the words of the *Katz* majority, the individual has shown that "he seeks to preserve [something] as private." *Id.* at 351. The second question is whether the individual's subjective expectation of privacy is "one that society is prepared to recognize as 'reasonable,'" *id.* at 361 (Harlan, J., concurring) — whether, in the words of the *Katz* majority, the individual's expectation, viewed objectively, is "justifiable" under the circumstances. *Id.* at 353.

B

In applying the *Katz* analysis to this case, it is important to begin by specifying precisely the nature of the state activity that is challenged. The activity here took the form of installing and using a pen register. . . . Petitioner's claim . . . is that . . . the State, as did the Government in *Katz,* infringed a "legitimate expectation of privacy" that petitioner held. Yet a pen register differs significantly from the listening device employed in *Katz,* for pen registers do not acquire the *contents* of communications. . . .

Given a pen register's limited capabilities, therefore, petitioner's argument that its installation and use constituted a "search" necessarily rests upon a claim that he had a "legitimate expectation of privacy" regarding the numbers he dialed on his phone.

This claim must be rejected. . . . All telephone users realize that they must "convey" phone numbers to the telephone company, since it is through telephone company switching equipment that their calls are completed. All subscribers realize, moreover, that the phone company has facilities for making permanent records of the numbers they dial, for they see a list of their long-distance (toll) calls on their monthly bills. In fact, pen registers and similar devices are routinely used by telephone companies "for the purposes of checking billing operations, detecting fraud, and preventing violations of law." United States v. New York Tel. Co., 434 U.S. 159, 174–175 (1977). . . . Although most people may be oblivious to a pen register's esoteric functions, they presumably have some awareness of one common use: to aid in the identification of persons making annoying or obscene calls. . . . [I]t is too much to believe that telephone subscribers, under these circumstances, harbor any general expectation that the numbers they dial will remain secret.

Petitioner argues, however, that, whatever the expectations of telephone users in general, he demonstrated an expectation of privacy by his own conduct here, since he "us[ed] the telephone *in his house* to the exclusion of all others." . . . Regardless of his location, petitioner had to convey that number to the telephone company in precisely the same way if he wished to complete his call. The fact that he dialed the number on his home phone rather than on some other phone could make no conceivable difference, nor could any subscriber rationally think that it would.

Second, even if petitioner did harbor some subjective expectation that the phone numbers he dialed would remain private, this expectation is not "one that society is prepared to recognize as 'reasonable.'" *Katz*, 389 U.S. at 361. This Court consistently has held that a person has no legitimate expectation of privacy in information he voluntarily turns over to third parties. In [*United States v.*] *Miller*, for example, the Court held that a bank depositor has no "legitimate 'expectation of privacy'" in financial information "voluntarily conveyed to . . . banks and exposed to their employees in the ordinary course of business." 425 U.S. 435, 442 (1976). . . .

Because the depositor "assumed the risk" of disclosure, the Court held that it would be unreasonable for him to expect his financial records to remain private.

This analysis dictates that petitioner can claim no legitimate expectation of privacy here. When he used his phone, petitioner voluntarily conveyed numerical information to the telephone company and "exposed" that information to its equipment in the ordinary course of business. In so doing, petitioner assumed the risk that the company would reveal to police the numbers he dialed. The switching equipment that processed those numbers is merely the modern counterpart of the operator who, in an earlier day, personally completed calls for the subscriber. Petitioner concedes that if he had placed his calls through an operator, he could claim no legitimate expectation of privacy. We are not inclined to hold that a different constitutional result is required because the telephone company has decided to automate. . . .

We therefore conclude that . . . [t]he installation and use of a pen register . . . was not a "search," and no warrant was required. The judgment of the Maryland Court of Appeals is affirmed.

It is so ordered.

[The dissenting opinions of Justices Stewart and Marshall are omitted.]

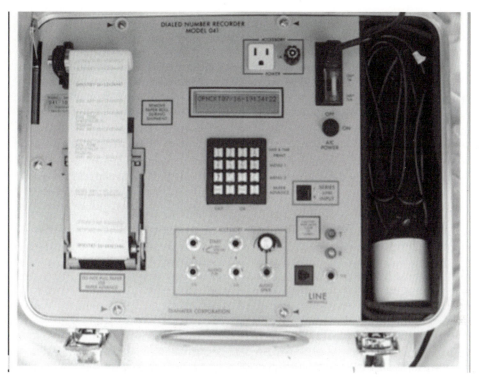

A pen register.

If the *Smith* Court had held that using a pen register is a "search" within the meaning of the Fourth Amendment, law enforcement presumably would be required to seek a warrant based on probable cause that a crime had been committed and that evidence of the crime would be found using the pen register. But that is not what happened. Instead, Congress passed the Pen Register Act as part of the Electronic Communications Privacy Act (ECPA) in 1986, Pub. L. No. 99-508, 100 Stat. 1848. As you read the act, look especially carefully at §3122. What precisely must an application for an order include? What must a court find to issue an order? What is the remedy if an officer violates the act?

PEN REGISTER ACT, 18 U.S.C. §§3121–3127

§3121. General prohibition on pen register and trap and trace device use; exception

(a) In General. — Except as provided in this section, no person may install or use a pen register or a trap and trace device without first obtaining a court order under section 3123 of this title or under the Foreign Intelligence Surveillance Act of 1978. . . .

(d) Penalty. — Whoever knowingly violates subsection (a) shall be fined under this title or imprisoned not more than one year, or both.

§3122. Application for an order for a pen register or a trap and trace device

(a) Application.—

(1) An attorney for the Government may make application for an order or an extension of an order under section 3123 of this title authorizing or approving the installation and use of a pen register or a trap and trace device under this chapter, in writing under oath or equivalent affirmation, to a court of competent jurisdiction.

(2) Unless prohibited by State law, a State investigative or law enforcement officer may make application for an order or an extension of an order under section 3123 of this title authorizing or approving the installation and use of a pen register or a trap and trace device under this chapter, in writing under oath or equivalent affirmation, to a court of competent jurisdiction of such State.

(b) Contents of Application.—An application under subsection (a) of this section shall include—

(1) the identity of the attorney for the Government or the State law enforcement or investigative officer making the application and the identity of the law enforcement agency conducting the investigation; and

(2) a certification by the applicant that the information likely to be obtained is relevant to an ongoing criminal investigation being conducted by that agency.

§3123. Issuance of an order for a pen register or a trap and trace device

(a) In General.—

(1) Attorney for the government.—Upon an application made under section 3122(a)(1), the court shall enter an ex parte order authorizing the installation and use of a pen register or trap and trace device anywhere within the United States, if the court finds that the attorney for the Government has certified to the court that the information likely to be obtained by such installation and use is relevant to an ongoing criminal investigation. . . .

(2) State investigative or law enforcement officer.— Upon an application made under section 3122(a)(2), the court shall enter an ex parte order authorizing the installation and use of a pen register or trap and trace device within the jurisdiction of the court, if the court finds that the State law enforcement or investigative officer has certified to the court that the information likely to be obtained by such installation and use is relevant to an ongoing criminal investigation. . . .

(b) Contents of Order.—An order issued under this section—

(1) shall specify—

(A) the identity, if known, of the person to whom is leased or in whose name is listed the telephone line or other facility to which the pen register or trap and trace device is to be attached or applied;

(B) the identity, if known, of the person who is the subject of the criminal investigation;

(C) the attributes of the communications to which the order applies, including the number or other identifier and, if known, the location of the telephone line or other facility to which the pen register or trap and trace device is to be attached or applied, and, in the case of an order authorizing installation and use of a trap and trace device under subsection (a)(2), the geographic limits of the order; and

(D) a statement of the offense to which the information likely to be obtained by the pen register or trap and trace device relates. . . .

(c) Time Period and Extensions. —

(1) An order issued under this section shall authorize the installation and use of a pen register or a trap and trace device for a period not to exceed sixty days.

(2) Extensions of such an order may be granted, but only upon an application for an order under section 3122 of this title and upon the judicial finding required by subsection (a) of this section. The period of extension shall be for a period not to exceed sixty days.

(d) Nondisclosure of Existence of Pen Register or a Trap and Trace Device. — An order authorizing or approving the installation and use of a pen register or a trap and trace device shall direct that—

(1) the order be sealed until otherwise ordered by the court; and

(2) the person owning or leasing the line or other facility to which the pen register or a trap and trace device is attached or applied, or who is obligated by the order to provide assistance to the applicant, not disclose the existence of the pen register or trap and trace device or the existence of the investigation to the listed subscriber, or to any other person, unless or until otherwise ordered by the court.[5]

NOTES AND QUESTIONS

1. *Pen Register Act vs. the Fourth Amendment.* Compare what would be required if using a pen register constituted a search under the Fourth Amendment with what Congress required under the Pen Register Act. The act's requirements are not as rigorous as what the Constitution would demand, right? On the other hand, given that the Court held that the use of a pen register is *not* a search, the act is far more rigorous than no regulation at all.

2. *Remedies.* Unlike the Court, which faces substantial institutional constraints on remedies, Congress can design remedies as it sees fit, including civil damages remedies, the exclusionary rule, administrative remedies, or criminal prosecution. (It still depends on courts or administrative agencies to impose them.) Some criticize Congress for not creating an exclusionary remedy for violations of the Pen Register Act. If you were a Congressmember, what would you want to know before you decided the appropriate remedy for violating the act?

3. *The Pen Register Act in an electronic age.* The above version of the Pen Register Act includes changes made following the 9/11 terrorist attacks. USA PATRIOT Act, Pub. L. No. 107-56, §216, 115 Stat. 272 (2001). Those changes made clear for the first time that the Pen Register Act also applies to internet communications. Under the current version of the act, the police can serve a pen register order on an internet service provider. Pursuant to such an order, the police can gather email header information other than the subject line (including the addresses of the email senders and recipients, the time the email was sent, and the size of the email); the IP

---

[5] *Ed. note:* 18 U.S.C. §3125, omitted here, provides for installation of a pen register or a trap-and-trace device without an order if certain emergencies exist and an order is sought within 48 hours.

addresses of computers involved in an information exchange over the internet; and perhaps information about the sites a computer visits on the internet (though not the page on the site that was visited).

4. *Other privacy statutes.* The Pen Register Act was a (delayed) response to *Smith.* Several other federal privacy laws were similarly passed after it became clear that the information at issue was not protected by the Fourth Amendment, including the Fair Credit Reporting Act (FCRA), Pub. L. No. 91-508, 84 Stat. 1127 (1970); the Family Educational Rights and Privacy Act of 1974 (FERPA), Pub. L. No. 93-380, §513, 88 Stat. 484, 571–574; the Video Privacy Protection Act (VPPA) of 1988, Pub. L. No. 100-618, 102 Stat. 3195; and the Driver's Privacy Protection Act of 1994 (DPPA), Pub. L. No. 103-322, tit. XXX, 108 Stat. 1796, 2099–2102. See Daniel J. Solove, *Fourth Amendment Codification and Professor Kerr's Misguided Call for Judicial Deference,* 74 Fordham L. Rev. 747 (2005) (discussing statutes). All these laws permit law enforcement some access to the protected information, sometimes on a request or administrative subpoena, sometimes only with a court order or grand jury subpoena. For a discussion of the law enforcement provisions in federal privacy statutes, see Erin Murphy, *The Politics of Privacy in the Criminal Justice System: Information Disclosure, the Fourth Amendment, and Statutory Law Enforcement Exemptions,* 111 Mich. L. Rev. 485 (2013).

3.   Comparative Competence — Congress and the Court

Do courts or legislatures do a better job at regulating police access to private information? There is some debate. Many scholars have argued that only courts using constitutional rights can adequately protect privacy. Orin Kerr disagrees, at least when law enforcement is using rapidly changing technology. Then, he contends, judges should act cautiously:

> Courts tend to be poorly suited to generate effective rules regulating criminal investigations involving new technologies. In contrast, legislatures possess a significant institutional advantage in this area over courts. While courts have successfully created rules that establish important privacy rights in many areas, it is difficult for judges to fashion lasting guidance when technologies are new and rapidly changing. The context of judicial decisionmaking often leaves the law surprisingly unclear. Courts lack the institutional capacity to easily grasp the privacy implications of new technologies they encounter. Judges cannot readily understand how the technologies may develop, cannot easily appreciate context, and often cannot even recognize whether the facts of the case before them raise privacy implications that happen to be typical or atypical. Judicially created rules also lack necessary flexibility; they cannot change quickly and cannot test various regulatory approaches. As a result, judicially created rules regulating government investigations tend to become quickly outdated or uncertain as technology changes. The context of legislative rule-creation offers significantly better prospects for the generation of balanced, nuanced, and effective investigative rules involving new technologies. In light of these institutional realities, courts should proceed cautiously and with humility, allowing some room for political judgment and maneuvering in a setting that is in such flux.

Orin S. Kerr, *The Fourth Amendment and New Technologies: Constitutional Myths and the Case for Caution,* 102 Mich. L. Rev. 801, 858–859 (2004).

Daniel Solove disagrees with Kerr. He argues that legislative protections are often inadequate substitutes for protections derived from constitutional interpretation. First, the privacy statutes mostly lack exclusionary rules and are therefore inadequately enforced. Second, their coverage is spotty: There are gaps in existing statutes, and many intrusive technologies, such as GPS, are never regulated. Third, the protections of the statutes often pale in comparison to those afforded by search warrants based on probable cause. See Daniel J. Solove, *Fourth Amendment Codification and Professor Kerr's Misguided Call for Judicial Deference*, 74 Fordham L. Rev. 747, 762–766 (2005). Perhaps this is not surprising given that law enforcement groups tend to lobby legislatures more effectively than privacy advocates. See Peter P. Swire, *Katz Is Dead, Long Live Katz*, 102 Mich. L. Rev. 904 (2004).

As for institutional capacity, Solove argues that expert testimony and amici briefs can sufficiently inform courts. *Id.* at 772. In my past work, I have been less Pollyannaish than Solove about court capacity to obtain knowledge and formulate rules for the police:

> Most Fourth Amendment questions are contested in state criminal cases in which neither party is likely to have adequate resources or incentives to effectively litigate significant empirical questions, and even a civil plaintiff hoping for compensation after a violent arrest cannot cost-effectively litigate many matters. Courts also often know so little about the institutional structures, occupational norms, market pressures, political influences, and nonconstitutional laws that shape police conduct that they cannot ask the right questions in making judgments about the police. Even when courts are able to engage in effective empirical analysis, they have little opportunity or ability to adjust a doctrine as the facts and social science underlying the doctrine evolve. As a result, courts have a systematic and profound disability in ensuring that doctrine accurately reflects the expected effects of criminal procedure rulings on the behavior of police.

Rachel A. Harmon, *The Problem of Policing*, 110 Mich. L. Rev. 761, 773–774 (2012).

Is the incapacity of courts inevitable? Andrew Crespo does not think so. He has argued that courts could be much more informed about policing if they used the treasure trove of data that criminal cases produce about law enforcement activities and their outcomes. Specifically, he argues that warrant affidavits and returns, postarrest affidavits, and suppression hearing transcripts provide an internal repository of information about law enforcement that could dramatically improve the courts' capacity to regulate law enforcement effectively—if only they would take advantage of it. See Andrew Manuel Crespo, *Systemic Facts: Toward Institutional Awareness in Criminal Courts*, 129 Harv. L. Rev. 2049 (2016).

Maybe, but institutional capacity is not the only problem that courts face as regulators. Courts use constitutional rights to regulate the police, and constitutional rights have a kind of inflexibility with respect to protection and remedies that legislation does not. Consider:

> Ideal regulation of the police would provide a normative framework for properly balancing individual and societal interests. It would specify the conditions under which the police *should*, rather than *may*, harm individual interests for the greater good. It would ensure that the quality of our lived experience is not impoverished but rather enhanced by law enforcement activities. Ideal regulation would take into account considerations such as how harmful any police action is to individuals and communities, as well as how it compares to other means of producing law and order in terms of cost, harm, effectiveness, and officer safety.
>
> While constitutional rights accommodate both individual and societal interests, they cannot approach the ideal balance between these interests. The well-known process by which constitutional rights are articulated and enforced instead dictates

that rights can provide only a limited analysis of police conduct. First, rights establish only minimum standards for law enforcement. . . .

Second, because rights are categorical once they are defined, that "ceiling" must be lower and more generous to law enforcement than a true measure of the interests at stake. . . .

Third, because rights are held and enforced by individuals, usually with respect to specific actions, they do a poor job of measuring aggregate costs and benefits of law enforcement activity or its effects on the quality of life in society. . . .

. . . [A]dequately protecting individual and communal interests requires regulatory efforts . . . in the form of nonconstitutional regulation that ensures adequate justification for harm to important interests left unvindicated by constitutional law.

Harmon, *supra*, at 776–778.

Note that this argument assumes that courts will enforce constitutional rights by articulating specific rules to govern police conduct. But, as John Rappaport points out, this approach—providing detailed guidance aimed directly at officers in the field—is only one option for courts. If they do not know the appropriate rules or they lack the flexibility needed to set them, courts can simply identify the relevant constitutional values and shift the burden of developing rules to legislatures, police departments, and other policymakers. See John Rappaport, *Second-Order Regulation of Law Enforcement*, 103 Calif. L. Rev. 205 (2015). The Court did a version of this in its inventory search cases: "inventories pursuant to standard police procedures are reasonable," South Dakota v. Opperman, 428 U.S. 364, 372 (1976). See also Colorado v. Bertine, 479 U.S. 367 (1987) (approving an inventory search according to "standardized criteria"). Because courts do not often engage in this "second-order regulation," it is hard to tell how well it actually works. But maybe the regulation of policing through constitutional rights isn't so inflexible after all.

Even if courts cannot achieve an "ideal balance" between individual and societal interests, such that legislative (and administrative) regulation is needed, this is hardly an argument for leaving courts out of the process altogether. Crespo reiterates long-standing arguments about the value of rights when he points out that, whatever their limitations in enforcing constitutional rights, courts are more likely than other policymakers to protect the interests of those underrepresented in the political process:

> The courts, to be sure, have not always been stalwart protectors of underrepresented groups. And the shortcomings of appointed counsel in the criminal justice system are undeniable and often severe. Still, insofar as *comparative* institutional assessments go, a reform agenda that would marginalize the judicial fora in which already marginalized groups are currently most able to be heard should cause some concern.

Crespo, *supra*, at 2063.

Maybe there is no easy answer. There is, however, one fundamental difference between the courts and Congress that ensures that courts will long keep considering these questions: Courts cannot avoid deciding cases. Trial courts (and many intermediate appellate courts) have no discretion over their dockets; criminal cases come to them daily. Even with certiorari, the Supreme Court inevitably finds itself under pressure to decide the limits of permissible law enforcement conduct. The courts can choose whether or not to regulate law enforcement conduct under the Fourth Amendment, but they cannot stay silent entirely. Congress, by contrast, can sit on its hands.

Perhaps this explains why even Supreme Court Justices who favor legislative regulation over court action sometimes favor court action over no action at all. In his concurrence for four Justices in *United States v. Jones*, 565 U.S. 400 (2012), Justice Alito cited Orin Kerr's article to argue, "In circumstances involving dramatic technological change, the best solution to privacy concerns may be legislative. A legislative body is well situated to gauge changing public attitudes, to draw detailed lines, and to balance privacy and public safety in a comprehensive way." *Id.* at 429–430 (Alito, J., concurring). Nevertheless, Justice Alito concurred with the Court's decision about law enforcement use of a GPS device to monitor a car:

> To date . . . Congress and most States have not enacted statutes regulating the use of GPS tracking technology for law enforcement purposes. The best that we can do in this case is to apply existing Fourth Amendment doctrine and to ask whether the use of GPS tracking in a particular case involved a degree of intrusion that a reasonable person would not have anticipated.

Id. at 430.

Justice Alito took the issue one step further in his solo concurrence in *Riley v. California*, 573 U.S. 373 (2014). He stated that he would gladly reconsider how the Fourth Amendment applied to cell phone searches incident to arrest "if either Congress or state legislatures, after assessing the legitimate needs of law enforcement and the privacy interests of cell phone owners, enact legislation." *Id.* at 407–408 (Alito, J., concurring in part and concurring in the judgment). Still, he voted with the majority, which, in the absence of congressional action, required the police to get a warrant to search a cellphone after an arrest.

C.   State and Local Regulation of Surveillance

Although federal constitutional doctrine and statutes provide much of the law governing police efforts to develop evidence of criminal activity, state constitutional law, state statutes, and local ordinances also regulate police surveillance in important ways.

1.   State Constitutional Law

Every state has a state constitutional provision that limits police authority to search and seize evidence. Some of these follow the Fourth Amendment verbatim. See, e.g., Alaska Const. art. I, §14. Others diverge in their language and scope. Here are a few:

ARIZONA CONST. ART. II, §8

No person shall be disturbed in his private affairs, or his home invaded, without authority of law.

MISSOURI CONST. ART. I, §15

That the people shall be secure in their persons, papers, homes, effects, and elec-tronic communications and data, from unreasonable searches and seizures; and no warrant to search any place, or seize any person or thing, or access electronic data or communication, shall issue without describing the place to be searched, or the person or thing to be seized, or the data or communication to be accessed, as nearly as may be; nor without probable cause, supported by written oath or affirmation.

NEW HAMPSHIRE CONST. ART II-B

An individual's right to live free from governmental intrusion in private or personal information is natural, essential, and inherent.

Of course, "a State is free as a matter of its own law to impose greater restric-tions on police activity than those this Court holds to be necessary upon federal constitutional standards." Oregon v. Hass, 420 U.S. 714, 719 (1975). Still, many state courts, whatever the precise language of the analogous provision in the state constitution, interpret their "Fourth Amendments" in lockstep with federal constitutional law.

Other state constitutional provisions are interpreted to grant more protection from the police than does federal constitutional doctrine, often with significant effect. Sometimes this means expanding the scope of the state provision to reach activities not (or not yet) recognized as searches or seizures within the meaning of the Fourth Amendment. For example, before the Supreme Court ruled in *Carpenter v. United States*, 138 S. Ct. 2206 (2018), several states already considered the warrant-less collection of cell-site location information a violation of their respective state constitutions. See, e.g., Commonwealth v. Augustine, 4 N.E.3d 846 (Mass. 2014); State v. Earls, 70 A.3d 630 (N.J. 2013). Alternatively, states may place stricter limits on activities already regulated as searches and seizures under federal constitutional law, including by rejecting federally recognized exceptions to the warrant require-ment. For example, in interpreting Article 14 of the Massachusetts Declaration of Rights, the Supreme Judicial Court of Massachusetts rejected the Supreme Court's approach to police-created exigency from *Kentucky v. King*, 563 U.S. 452 (2011):

> Our interpretation of art. 14 frequently aligns with the United States Supreme Court's interpretation of the Fourth Amendment. However, . . . [i]n the present case, balancing the interests of law enforcement with the rights of people to be protected from warrantless searches in the home, we conclude that art. 14 provides greater protection than the Fourth Amendment in these circumstances and that under art. 14 the police cannot avail themselves of the exigency exception to the warrant requirement when it was foreseeable that their actions would create the exigency, even if their conduct was lawful.

Commonwealth v. Alexis, 112 N.E.3d 796, 803–804 (Mass. 2018). What might be the consequences of having varying state constitutional law?

2.   State Statutes and Local Ordinances

State law also regulates police surveillance in other ways, sometimes against a back-drop or regulatory structure created by federal law.

a. *Drones*

Take, for example, police use of drones. Drones have quickly become widely available. They often come equipped with multiple cameras, high-powered zoom lenses, thermal imaging, and high-definition recording capacity. Consumers use them recreationally; businesses use them for aerial photography and thermal imaging; and broadcast media use them to view sporting events. Law enforcement has not been immune to the trend: Drones tailored for law enforcement offer a flexible and inexpensive alternative to other aerial methods of surveillance. Local law enforcement agencies use drones to find missing people, to locate suspects, to document accident scenes, to improve situational awareness during public events or entries into buildings, and to gather information about people and places.

Congress responded to the rapid proliferation of drones in the FAA Modernization and Reform Act of 2012, Pub. L. No. 112-95, 126 Stat. 11. Although much attention focused on the commercial and recreational implications of the act's directive for regulation of civil drone use (§332), the act also directed the Federal Aviation Administration (FAA) to facilitate governmental drone use by public-safety agencies (§334).

When the FAA implemented regulations as required by the 2012 act and subsequent reauthorizations, it did little to set law enforcement apart from civilian drone users. Like civilian users, police departments have two basic options: use small drones close to the ground with visual line-of-sight operations and other restrictions, or seek a Certificate of Authorization (COA) to go beyond these limits. *Operate a Drone, Start a Drone Program*, Fed. Aviation Admin. (Feb. 14, 2019). Neither option is ideal for law enforcement: The restrictions on non-COA use of drones—including rules forbidding nighttime use, 14 C.F.R. §107.29, and flying over people other than the operator, *id.* §107.39—substantially limit the usefulness of drones. Acquiring a COA requires submitting an application to the FAA seeking approval for specific periods of time and precise uses.

The FAA also recognizes state and local authority to regulate law enforcement drone operations consistent with the federal framework. Office of the Chief Counsel, Fed. Aviation Admin., *State and Local Regulation of Unmanned Aircraft Systems (UAS) Fact Sheet* 3 (2015). Many states have passed statutes restricting law-enforcement use of drones further than the federal regulations do. Here are two concise examples:

OR. REV. STAT. §837.320

Section 837.320 Allowable use of unmanned aircraft systems; warrants

(1) A law enforcement agency may operate an unmanned aircraft system, acquire information through the operation of an unmanned aircraft system, or

disclose information acquired through the operation of an unmanned aircraft system, if:

> **(a)** A warrant is issued authorizing use of an unmanned aircraft system; or

> **(b)** The law enforcement agency has probable cause to believe that a person has committed a crime, is committing a crime or is about to commit a crime, and exigent circumstances exist that make it unreasonable for the law enforcement agency to obtain a warrant authorizing use of an unmanned aircraft system.

(2) A warrant authorizing the use of an unmanned aircraft system must specify the period for which operation of the unmanned aircraft system is authorized. In no event may a warrant provide for the operation of an unmanned aircraft system for a period of more than 30 days. Upon motion and good cause shown, a court may renew a warrant after the expiration of the 30-day period.

IOWA CODE §321.492B

Section 321.492B. Use of unmanned aerial vehicle for traffic law enforcement prohibited.

The state or a political subdivision of the state shall not use an unmanned aerial vehicle for traffic law enforcement.

Some cities and counties have also regulated drones in either stand-alone ordinances or as part of broader regulation of surveillance technology. Here is an example:

SEATTLE, WASH., MUN. CODE §14.18.020

Section 14.18.020 Council approval for acquisition of surveillance technologies

A. Unless exempted or excepted from the requirements of this Chapter 14.18 pursuant to Section 14.18.030, any City department intending to acquire surveillance technology shall, prior to acquisition, obtain Council ordinance approval of the acquisition and a surveillance impact report for the technology. A City department that directs a non-City entity to acquire or operate surveillance technology on the City's behalf is bound by the requirements of this Chapter 14.18 to the same extent as if the department were acquiring the surveillance technology.

NOTES AND QUESTIONS

1. *Comparing the laws.* What does each of these statutes or ordinances do? How are they likely to affect law enforcement operations? Chapter 1 suggested that good policing should be authorized, effective, beneficial, harm-efficient, lawful, fair, and legitimate. Which of these aims does each of the above laws promote?

2. *Form of the law.* Similar to Iowa, other states disallow drone use for some purposes, such as general criminal investigation (at least without a warrant), but allow it for others, such as to counter the risk of a terrorist attack, to prevent imminent harm to life, to locate a missing person, or to photograph public gatherings. See, e.g., N.C. Gen. Stat. §15A-300.1. How does that approach differ from Oregon's?

3. *Uses of drones.* Although police use drones to check whether marijuana is being grown in a field, to track down an escaped inmate, or to provide real-time intelligence about a hostage situation, they also use drones to monitor accident scenes and engage in search-and-rescue operations—uses no one finds intrusive. That is not true for wiretaps or bugs, which are always intrusive. If you were advising a state legislator interested in drafting new legislation, how would you encourage her to take into account the multiple possible uses of the technology?

4. *Purposes of regulation.* Federal regulation of drones has so far been more concerned with ensuring safe use of airspace than with protecting privacy. How might that matter to the patchwork of regulation we end up with? Should FAA restrictions intended to protect airspace preempt local efforts to restrict police practices? Who can best consider the trade-offs involved in using drones for law enforcement purposes?

b. *Automated License-Plate Readers*

Automated license-plate readers (ALPRs) are computer-controlled camera systems, mounted on a police vehicle or stationary post, that capture images of passing vehicles' license plates; record the time, date, and location at which the image was captured; and convert the images to digital license plate numbers. The images sometimes show a vehicle's driver and passengers. These images can be compared with state and federal databases to identify stolen vehicles or to find a person subject to an arrest warrant. The images can also be stored so that the department can later determine a vehicle's location on a particular date or to track the movements of a particular car.

Mobile ALPR camera system on police car.

Critics worry that ALPRs can collect a vast amount of data on the movements of entirely innocent people. They worry that ALPRs might be used disproportionately against people in low-income communities or communities of color. They also worry that ALPRs can be used to chill First Amendment activities. For example, the NYPD used an ALPR to record the license plates of everyone parked near a mosque as part of its Muslim surveillance program. See *NYPD Defends Tactics Over Mosque Spying; Records Reveal New Details on Muslim Surveillance*, Huff Post (Apr. 25, 2012).

Under *United States v. Knotts*, 460 U.S. 276, 281 (1983), individuals have no reasonable expectation of privacy in their movements in public. Nor do they have an expectation of privacy in their license plates. See, e.g., United States v. Walraven, 892 F.2d 972, 974 (10th Cir. 1989). As a consequence, courts and police departments have long assumed that police may follow individuals or record license plates at a location without any suspicion that a person is engaged in criminal activity. Police departments adopted ALPRs on the assumption that they are functionally equivalent to an officer recording license plates one at a time.

In *Carpenter v. United States*, 138 S. Ct. 2206 (2018), the Court recognized that people can have a reasonable expectation of privacy in the whole of their movements even when they do not have a reasonable expectation of privacy in a single observation of their location. This raised doubts about long-standing assumptions about how Fourth Amendment doctrine applies to ALPRs. Already, lower courts are taking note. In a recent decision, Massachusetts's highest court concluded, using *Carpenter*, that the widespread use of ALPRs could implicate Fourth Amendment interests:

> With enough cameras in enough locations, the historic location data from an ALPR system . . . would invade a reasonable expectation of privacy and would constitute a search for constitutional purposes. Like [cell-site location information (CSLI)] data, ALPRs allow the police to reconstruct people's past movements without knowing in advance who police are looking for, thus granting police access to "a category of information otherwise [and previously] unknowable." See Carpenter v. United States, 138 S. Ct. 2206, 2218 (2018). Like both CSLI and GPS data, ALPRs circumvent traditional constraints on police surveillance power by being cheap (relative to human surveillance) and surreptitious.

> Of course, the constitutional question is not merely an exercise in counting cameras; the analysis should focus, ultimately, on the extent to which a substantial picture of the defendant's public movements are revealed by the surveillance. For that purpose, where the ALPRs are placed matters too. ALPRs near constitutionally sensitive locations—the home, a place of worship, etc.—reveal more of an individual's life and associations than does an ALPR trained on an interstate highway. A network of ALPRs that surveils every residential side street paints a much more nuanced and invasive picture of a driver's life and public movements than one limited to major highways that open into innumerable possible destinations. For while no ALPR network is likely to be as detailed in its surveillance as GPS or CSLI data, one well may be able to make many of the same inferences from ALPR data that implicate expressive and associative rights.

> Similarly, with cameras in enough locations, the hot list feature could implicate constitutional search protections by invading a reasonable expectation of privacy in one's real-time location. If deployed widely enough, ALPRs could tell police someone's precise, real-time location virtually any time the person decided to drive, thus

making ALPRs the vehicular equivalent of a cellular telephone "ping." Of course, no matter how widely ALPRs are deployed, the exigency exception to the warrant requirement would apply to this hot list feature.

Finally, like carrying a cellular telephone, driving is an indispensable part of modern life, one we cannot and do not expect residents to forgo in order to avoid government surveillance.

Commonwealth v. McCarthy, 142 N.E.3d 1090, 1104–1105 (Mass. 2020). Nevertheless, the Court ruled that four cameras at two fixed locations on major bridges did not trigger constitutional protection. *Id.* at 508–509. Other courts might similarly be reluctant to find actual ALPR practices a search, given that *Carpenter* emphasized the personal, detailed, and encyclopedic nature of the historical cell-site location information at issue in the case, qualities that ALPR data does not share to the same degree.

For the moment, then, federal constitutional doctrine is at best uncertain in its regulation of collecting and storing ALPR data. Because ALPRs do not affect airspace or other federal interests as drones do, there is also no federal regulatory equivalent to FAA rules for ALPRs. Should states and localities weigh in?

So far, few states regulate ALPRs. California, however, passed a law doing just that. As you look at this statute, consider what the California legislature was trying to achieve. Does it want ALPRs to be used less often? Or is it looking to achieve other goals? What kind of protection does it offer?

CAL. CIV. CODE §§1798.90.51, .52, .54, .55

§1798.90.51. Automated license plate recognition end-user "ALPR" operator duties; maintenance of reasonable security procedures; implementation of usage and privacy policy

An ALPR operator shall . . .

(b) (1) Implement a usage and privacy policy in order to ensure that the collection, use, maintenance, sharing, and dissemination of ALPR information is consistent with respect for individuals' privacy and civil liberties. The usage and privacy policy shall be available to the public in writing, and . . . shall be posted conspicuously on that Internet Web site.

(2) The usage and privacy policy shall, at a minimum, include all of the following:

(A) The authorized purposes for using the ALPR system and collecting ALPR information. . . .

(C) A description of how the ALPR system will be monitored to ensure the security of the information and compliance with applicable privacy laws.

(D) The purposes of, process for, and restrictions on, the sale, sharing, or transfer of ALPR information to other persons. . . .

(F) A description of the reasonable measures that will be used to ensure the accuracy of ALPR information and correct data errors.

(G) The length of time ALPR information will be retained, and the process the ALPR operator will utilize to determine if and when to destroy retained ALPR information.

§1798.90.52. Accessing or providing access to ALPR information by ALPR operator; maintenance of record of access; use of information for authorized purposes only

If an ALPR operator accesses or provides access to ALPR information, the ALPR operator shall . . .

(a) Maintain a record of that access. At a minimum, the record shall include all of the following:

(1) The date and time the information is accessed.

(2) The license plate number or other data elements used to query the ALPR system.

(3) The username of the person who accesses the information, and, as applicable, the organization or entity with whom the person is affiliated.

(4) The purpose for accessing the information. . . .

§1798.90.54. Civil action for harm caused by violation of title; award

(a) In addition to any other sanctions, penalties, or remedies provided by law, an individual who has been harmed by a violation of this title, including, but not limited to, unauthorized access or use of ALPR information or a breach of security of an ALPR system, may bring a civil action in any court of competent jurisdiction against a person who knowingly caused the harm.

(b) The court may award a combination of any one or more of the following:

(1) Actual damages, but not less than liquidated damages in the amount of two thousand five hundred dollars ($ 2,500).

(2) Punitive damages upon proof of willful or reckless disregard of the law.

(3) Reasonable attorney's fees and other litigation costs reasonably incurred.

(4) Other preliminary and equitable relief as the court determines to be appropriate.

§1798.90.55. Public meeting requirement; selling, sharing, or transfer of ALPR information by public agency prohibited

Notwithstanding any other law or regulation:

(a) A public agency that operates or intends to operate an ALPR system shall provide an opportunity for public comment at a regularly scheduled public meeting of the governing body of the public agency before implementing the program. . . .

NOTES AND QUESTIONS

1. *Content of this regulation.* What does this California statute do? The purpose of considering this statute is to highlight the choices states make about the form of regulation when they address police use of technology. Critics worry that collecting ALPR data is intrusive, indiscriminate, and often inaccurate. Police departments

find ALPRs useful. What did California do about these competing concerns? What alternatives to this statute can you imagine?

2. *Effects.* Imagine you read the ALPR policy your local agency issues in response to this statute, and you don't like it: Your agency's policy allows ALPRs to be used to find traffic violators and those who have unpaid fines, when you think it should be used only for more serious offenses, such as abducted children and car thefts. What would you do? Would you have been as likely to act if the agency had no policy or if the policy were unavailable to the public?

3. *Facial recognition.* Technology moves on. Police departments are already using facial recognition software to identify people in person, in photos, and on video. The software uses specific details about a person's face to compare one image to pictures of faces in a database of identified individuals. The software then calculates the likelihood that the submitted image matches a person in the database. Increasingly, facial recognition software can identify people in cars. As cameras become more prevalent and the technology gets better, facial recognition might make ALPRs largely unnecessary. Yet facial recognition raises many of the concerns that ALPRs raise, and then some. Critics worry that facial recognition systems are error-prone — and disproportionately so for African Americans, ethnic minorities, women, and young people. They also worry that facial recognition software can chill First Amendment activity by eliminating the traditional anonymity individuals have in crowds. For example, during protests over the death of Freddie Gray's death in police custody, the Baltimore Police Department scraped social media accounts for pictures of protesters and ran those pictures through facial recognition software to identify and arrest protesters with outstanding warrants. So far, beyond a few city ordinances, police use of facial recognition software remains largely unregulated. See, e.g., Somerville, Mass., Ordinance No. 2019-16; Nashville, Tenn., Code §13.08.080.

4. *Is privacy all it's cracked up to be?* Although many critics worry that high-tech surveillance makes policing more intrusive, Bennett Capers has argued — leveraging real incidents of racialized policing — that this surveillance can also make policing fairer by redistributing the harms of policing more evenly:

> [H]aving access to at-a-distance weapons scanners, facial recognition software, and Big Data can mean the difference between "[y]oung + [b]lack . . . = [p]robable [c]ause" and race-blind policing. It would certainly mean a drastic reduction in the number of stopped minorities and indeed a reduction in the number of all stops. . . . Facial recognition technology combined with Big Data would tell the police that the brown driver repeatedly circling the block in fact works in the neighborhood and is probably looking for a parking space and that the clean-cut white dude reading a paper on a park bench is in fact a sex offender who, just by being near a playground, is violating his sex offender registration. . . . It would tell them, in a way that is less intrusive or embarrassing, whether someone is a troublemaker casing a neighborhood or a student returning home with a bag of Skittles and an iced tea; a loiterer up to no good, or a father waiting to pick up his children from school; a burglar about to commit a home invasion or a Harvard professor entering his own home; a thug with a gun, or police chief; a trespasser attempting to enter the Capitol Building, or Republican senator; a mugger looking for his next victim, or the future United States Attorney General; a thief about to burgle a laboratory or the world renowned astrophysicist Neil DeGrasse Tyson, guilty only of "JBB (just being black)."

I. Bennett Capers, *Race, Policing, and Technology*, 95 N.C. L. Rev. 1241, 1277–1278 (2017).[6] As Capers sees it, adopting surveillance technology means that everyone would be monitored, but fewer people would be seriously harmed as a result, and those harms would be inflicted less often because of a person's skin color. Are you convinced?

A Problem: Social Media Scraping

The Civil Rights Union of Northern Utopia City (CRUNUC) has asked for your advice. During the successful prosecution of a Northern Utopia teenager for a gang-related shooting, it came out in court that the Northern Utopia City Police Department (NUCPD) has recently begun scraping information from social media using commercial software designed to help law enforcement agencies identify gang members and activities. With the software's help, NUCPD's gang unit searches online photos for gang clothing and hand signs that indicate gang membership in or near Northern Utopia City and social media chatter about revenge shootings or participation in other criminal activities. These leads help the officers decide whom to investigate further with surveillance or undercover work. Although CRUNUC recognizes that identifying individuals involved in violent criminal acts is a good thing, it is worried that social media surveillance undermines privacy, chills free association, and might lead to discriminatory targeting of racial and religious minority communities. So far, the courts that have considered the issue have held that people do not have a reasonable expectation of privacy when engaging in social networking online, and CRUNUC is skeptical that courts will accept First Amendment or Fourteenth Amendment arguments either. CRUNUC would like to advocate for appropriate regulation. What should they seek? Can you recommend a four-point plan?

D.   Covert Policing: Undercover Officers and Informants

When reading *Kentucky v. King*, did you notice what the officers were doing before they entered King's apartment? Several officers were engaged in an undercover *buy–bust* operation outside King's apartment complex. In a buy–bust (or controlled buy), an officer or an informant buys drugs, and then the seller is arrested.

1.   An Introduction to Covert Policing

Sometimes, police find that using surveillance techniques to uncover hidden crime is impracticable, ineffectual, or inefficient, in part because surveillance activities often

---

[6] In footnotes, Capers explains several of these well-known references. For example, the kid running is a reference to *Illinois v. Wardlow*, 528 U.S. 119, 125 (2000), which permitted flight in a high-crime area to constitute reasonable suspicion. The student with the Skittles and iced tea refers to Trayvon Martin, an unarmed Black youth who was shot by a self-appointed neighborhood watchman. The Harvard professor is Henry Louis Gates, Jr., who was arrested outside his own home for disorderly conduct after an officer suspected him of burglary. The Senator was Tim Scott, who reported being targeted by the Capitol police. See Capers, *supra*, at 1277–1278 nn. 218–225.

require a warrant or court order. But there are other ways to gather information about hidden criminal activity. To learn things known only to those closest to a criminal operation, police may use *cooperators*, who provide information to police out of a desire to see justice done. More often, and more controversially, they use *informants*,[7] who provide information in exchange for leniency in a criminal case, cash, or some other benefit, or *undercover officers*, officers who pretend to be criminals to infiltrate a criminal organization or report on criminal activity. This section considers the legal rules that govern the use of informants and undercover work by the police.[8]

a.   Characteristics of Covert Policing

Informants and undercover officers share several important characteristics that you should keep in mind as you think about the kind of law that should govern their use in policing.

First, unlike crime witnesses, informants and undercover officers engage in activities on behalf of the government repeatedly overtime.

Second, undercover work is fundamentally deceptive. It depends on criminal participants believing the personas that informants or undercover officers present instead of realizing their true identities working for the government.

Third, because many kinds of crime are easiest to detect and prove with evidence gathered during their commission, informants and undercover officers encourage suspects to engage in criminal activity while the officers or informants are present. Some of these activities cannot otherwise be observed by nonparticipants.

b.   Concerns About Covert Policing

These three characteristics of covert policing—its use of ongoing relationships, its reliance on deception, and the presence of officers or informants during criminal acts—lead to several concerns.

1. *Undercover and informant work is often intrusive.* These investigations seek to get around common obstacles to policing by inserting government agents in homes and conversations in which they would be otherwise unwelcome. Communities might find this intrusiveness worth its costs for serious crimes that are otherwise difficult to investigate. But police often use informants for

---

[7] These terms are sometimes used differently. For example, in federal parlance, a *cooperating witness* is usually someone who agrees to testify in a legal proceeding, and a *confidential informant* is someone who the government expects to provide useful and credible information about criminal activity in the future.

[8] This section mostly focuses on informants involved in evidence gathering outside of jails and prisons rather than jailhouse informants, who are used to obtain information about criminal activity after a suspect is taken into custody. Jailhouse informants raise even greater concerns about reliability, disclosure, and prosecutorial involvement in evidence gathering, and they are sometimes subject to additional regulation by policy, statute, or rules of evidence. See, e.g., Conn. Gen. Stat. Ann. §54-860-p (requiring data collection, tracking, and reliability hearings for jailhouse informants); Tarrant County (Tex.) Criminal District Attorney's Office Jailhouse Informant Procedure (2016) (creating central index of jailhouse informants). For a small sample of the interesting commentary available on jailhouse informants, see, e.g., Myrna S. Raeder, *See No Evil: Wrongful Convictions and the Prosecutorial Ethics of Offering Testimony by Jailhouse Informants and Dishonest Experts*, 76 Fordham L. Rev. 1413, 1419 (2007); Alexandra Natapoff, *The Shadowy World of Jailhouse Informants: Explained*, The Appeal (July 11, 2018); Katie Zavadski & Moiz Syed, *30 Years of Jailhouse Snitch Scandal*, ProPublica (Dec. 4, 2019).

less serious criminal activity, such as gun possession offenses and low-level drug offenses.

2. *Undercover and informant work is sometimes unreliable or corrupt.* Informants who are rewarded for information may provide untrue information to keep the rewards coming. As one court put it, "Our judicial history is speckled with cases where informants falsely pointed the finger of guilt at suspects and defendants, creating the risk of sending innocent persons to prison." United States v. Bernal-Obeso, 989 F.2d 331, 333 (9th Cir. 1993). In addition, informants might stay loyal to criminal associates, providing them with information about the police. Or they might take advantage of opportunities for personal gain, for example, by stealing drugs or money during an operation. Similarly, without adequate supervision, undercover officers might use drugs, get too close to criminals, or act corruptly in the course of their work.

3. *Undercover and informant work is often dangerous for those involved.* Officers and informants have been killed during covert operations. The risk of physical harm seems especially troubling with respect to informants. Informants are often a less resource-intensive alternative to infiltrating a criminal organization with an officer. But informants usually receive no training, are often young, and may be pressured to engage in risky activities by the threat of long sentences. Informants also face the risk of being *burned*—that is, exposed as a cooperator by law enforcement, either intentionally or unintentionally—and suffering retribution as result.

4. *Undercover and informant work sometimes turns criminal.* Undercover officers sometimes participate in crimes to hide their status. Informants, who often receive leniency for past criminal activity, are often permitted to continue criminal activity while working for the government.

5. *Undercover and informant work potentially alienates communities.* Good policing is generally candid and transparent. Undercover work obviously violates those principles. That can lead to community distrust. Similarly, when police departments permit some offenders to remain at large and turn community members against each other, they could corrode trust in policing and undermine the community's sense of security. These effects are likely to be worse in communities already suffering disproportionately from crime. See Alexandra Natapoff, *Snitching: Criminal Informants and the Erosion of American Justice* 43, 103 (2009).

6. *Undercover operations can be discriminatory.* Police departments and officers sometimes also use undercover operations to target populations that they consider objectionable. For example, police departments have long widely engaged in sting operations in which undercover officers suggestively approach gay and gender-nonconforming men to target them for low-level crimes, such as lewd conduct or indecent exposure, in parks and other public places. These stings may take place when no one complains about lewd behavior or when complaints are made about both gay and straight activities. In 2017, plaintiffs brought a §1983 claim as a class-action lawsuit against the Port Authority of New York and New Jersey, the Port Authority Police Department (PAPD), and four individual officers alleging that undercover

PAPD officers target men the officers perceive as gay or gender nonconform-ing by entering men's bus terminal restrooms, staring at one while using a urinal, and when the individual looks back, arresting him on baseless charges of lewd conduct or public exposure. See Class Action Complaint, Holden v. The Port Authority of New York and New Jersey (S.D.N.Y. 2017) (No. 1:17-CV-02192).

7. *Undercover and informant work sometimes distort law enforcement decision making.* Ideally, covert policing is used only when lawful, when its benefits outweigh its harms, and when its risks are minimized. However, undercover police officers often receive freedom from direct supervision, lucrative overtime pay, and reputational prestige for engaging in covert work, which could lead them to overvalue the benefits of this policing tactic. Agencies, which often do not carefully track the use of criminal informants or their produc-tivity, might assume that the informants are more valuable than they are. Moreover, because asset forfeiture laws often permit departments to keep cash and other property seized from drug dealers, departments might favor covert policing strategies that lead to forfeited property over other types of policing. See, e.g., Megan O'Matz & John Maines, *Cops. Cash. Cocaine. How Sunrise Police Make Millions Selling Drugs*, S. Fla. Sun Sentinel (Sept. 29, 2014) (describing how one department secured almost $6 million in forfei-ture funds through covert techniques, in part by luring drug buyers to the jurisdiction with discounts on cocaine).[9]

The fact that covert policing is often inadequately documented and super-vised could aggravate all of these issues. Undercover officers and informants often work based on informal orders and arrangements, without written agree-ments that might limit the purpose and scope of their activities. Agencies often fail to track their use or their productivity. Moreover, an emphasis on secrecy often means both limited supervision and very little disclosure to the public, which rarely has the opportunity to weigh in on covert policing. Altogether, policing through informants and undercover agents is a perfect storm for harm-inefficient policing: The activities pose substantial individual and distributional harms; incentives encourage police to engage in the activities at a level dispro-portionate to the public-safety benefits they yield; and conditions inhibit public scrutiny and political control.

---

[9] After investigative reporting revealed that the Sunrise (Fla.) Police Department used reverse stings excessively to profit from asset forfeiture, the department claimed to have given up the practice. But, in a bizarre twist, the department's ongoing stings ensnared a corrupt officer from the NYPD, revealing the department's ongoing operations. See Megan O'Matz et al., *Sunrise Police Halt Stings — City Officials Blame Disruption of Drug-Selling Operation on Newspaper Investigation*, S. Fla. Sun Sentinel (Oct. 13, 2013). Phillip Leroy, a two-time NYPD precinct "Cop of the Year," was arrested in Sunrise trying to purchase ten kilos of cocaine and sentenced to ten years in federal prison. Leroy cooperated with the police and prosecutors, and his sentence was later reduced to seven years. Paula McMahon, *Ex-NYC Cop Gets Prison Term Cut for $200,000 Cocaine Deal in Sunrise*, S. Fla. Sun Sentinel (Mar. 15, 2017). Asset forfeiture is described in more detail in Chapter 11.

"A Devil's Deal"

No informant relationship has gone awry more spectacularly than that between notorious mobster James "Whitey" Bulger and his FBI handler, John Connolly, Jr.

In the early 1960s, J. Edgar Hoover responded to the threat posed by La Cosa Nostra, a Sicilian mafia in Boston, by assembling the Organized Crime Strike Force within the FBI. The Strike Force fought organized crime using the "Top Echelon Criminal Informant Program," which focused on developing high-level informants within criminal organizations. Agent Connolly quickly built a reputation for developing great sources, and in the 1970s, Whitey Bulger became one of his informants.

Bulger and Connolly grew up together in a housing project in South Boston, but lost touch while Bulger served nine years in prison for a string of bank robberies. They reconnected after Bulger returned to Boston and joined the Winter Hill Gang, a local organized-crime syndicate, in which he quickly rose to leadership. Bulger agreed to share information with the FBI, and in exchange, Connolly promised that the FBI would turn a blind eye to Bulger's criminal activities. Both sides were long satisfied with the arrangement: Bulger informed on rivals, letting the FBI eliminate them, which enabled him to consolidate his power; and the FBI prided itself on its success in eradicating the Italian mafia.

In the process, however, Bulger compromised Connolly and, eventually, Connolly's supervisor, John Morris. Bulger gave them vacations and gifts worth hundreds of thousands of dollars, and paid Connolly a piece of the gang's narcotics revenues. Connolly kept Bulger well informed about law enforcement activities, and Connolly and Morris covered up 11 murders and various racketeering and extortion schemes that Bulger carried out while acting as an informant.

Ultimately, other law enforcement agencies built a case against Bulger without the FBI's help, and in 1994, they obtained a sealed indictment against him. Although retired, Connolly heard about the charges and leaked word to Bulger, who fled. Bulger remained a fugitive for more than 16 years, appearing on the FBI's Ten Most Wanted Fugitives list just behind Osama bin Laden. Only in 1997 did the FBI publicly reveal that Bulger had been an informant.

In 2002, Connolly was sentenced to ten years in prison for helping Bulger. He was later given an additional 40 years for providing information that assisted mobsters in carrying out a murder. Morris received immunity for testifying against Connolly.

In response to the fallout, the FBI revised its guidelines for using informants in 2001, mandating increased scrutiny of potential informants and prohibiting criminal activity outside narrow boundaries. Nevertheless, a 2005 report by the DOJ Office of the Inspector General found that, overwhelmingly, the FBI violated the new guidelines in its cases.

Bulger was finally apprehended outside his apartment in Santa Monica, California, in 2011 and brought to trial. He was convicted of 31 charges and received more than two consecutive life sentences. In 2018, when he was 89 years old and confined to a wheelchair, Bulger was beaten to death with a padlock and his body mutilated in an assassination carried out by other prisoners.

For a detailed account of the relationship-gone-wrong written by the journalists who first uncovered it, see Dick Lehr & Gerard O'Neill, *Black Mass: The Irish Mob, the FBI, and a Devil's Deal* (2000).

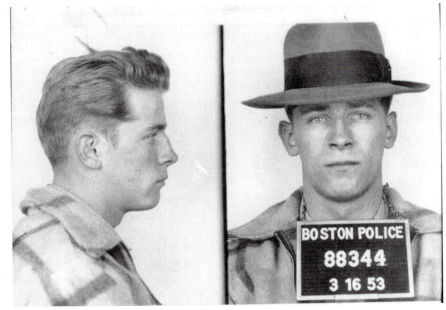

A 1953 booking photo of James (Whitey) Bulger.

2. Covert Policing and Constitutional Law

How does Fourth Amendment doctrine respond to concerns about covert policing?

UNITED STATES v. WHITE
401 U.S. 745 (1971)

MR. JUSTICE WHITE announced the judgment of the Court and an opinion in which THE CHIEF JUSTICE, MR. JUSTICE STEWART, and MR. JUSTICE BLACKMUN join.

In 1966, respondent James A. White was tried and convicted under two consolidated indictments charging various illegal transactions in narcotics. . . . The issue before us is whether the Fourth Amendment bars from evidence the testimony of governmental agents who related certain conversations which had occurred between defendant White and a government informant, Harvey Jackson, and which the agents overheard by monitoring the frequency of a radio transmitter carried by Jackson and concealed on his person. . . . The prosecution was unable to locate and produce Jackson at the trial and the trial court overruled objections to the testimony of the agents who conducted the electronic surveillance. The jury returned a guilty verdict and defendant appealed. . . .

Katz v. United States, 389 U.S. 347 (1967), . . . swept away doctrines that electronic eavesdropping is permissible under the Fourth Amendment unless physical invasion of a constitutionally protected area produced the challenged evidence. In that case government agents, without petitioner's consent or knowledge, attached a listening device to the outside of a public telephone booth and recorded the defendant's end of his telephone conversations. In declaring the recordings inadmissible in evidence in the absence of a warrant authorizing the surveillance, the Court . . . held that the absence of physical intrusion into the telephone booth did not justify using electronic devices in listening to and recording Katz' words, thereby violating the privacy on which he justifiably relied while using the telephone in those circumstances.

The Court of Appeals understood *Katz* to render inadmissible against White the agents' testimony concerning conversations that Jackson broadcast to them. We cannot agree. Katz involved no revelation to the Government by a party to conversations with the defendant nor did the Court indicate in any way that a defendant has a justifiable and constitutionally protected expectation that a person with whom he is conversing will not then or later reveal the conversation to the police.

Hoffa v. United States, 385 U.S. 293 (1966), which was left undisturbed by *Katz*, held that however strongly a defendant may trust an apparent colleague, his expectations in this respect are not protected by the Fourth Amendment when it turns out that the colleague is a government agent regularly communicating with the authorities. In these circumstances, "no interest legitimately protected by the Fourth Amendment is involved," for that amendment affords no protection to "a wrongdoer's misplaced belief that a person to whom he voluntarily confides his wrongdoing will not reveal it." *Hoffa*, 385 U.S. at 302. . . .

. . . For constitutional purposes, no different result is required if the agent instead of immediately reporting and transcribing his conversations with defendant, either (1) simultaneously records them with electronic equipment which he is carrying on his person, Lopez v. United States, 373 U.S. 427 (1963); (2) or carries radio equipment which simultaneously transmits the conversations either to recording equipment located elsewhere or to other agents monitoring the transmitting frequency. On Lee v. United States, 343 U.S. 747 (1952). If the conduct and revelations of an agent operating without electronic equipment do not invade the defendant's constitutionally justifiable expectations of privacy, neither does a simultaneous recording of the same conversations made by the agent or by others from transmissions received from the agent to whom the defendant is talking and whose trustworthiness the defendant necessarily risks. . . .

Inescapably, one contemplating illegal activities must realize and risk that his companions may be reporting to the police. If he sufficiently doubts their trustworthiness, the association will very probably end or never materialize. But if he has no doubts, or allays them, or risks what doubt he has, the risk is his. . . . Given the possibility or probability that one of his colleagues is cooperating with the police, it is only speculation to assert that the defendant's utterances would be substantially different or his sense of security any less if he also thought it possible that the suspected colleague is wired for sound. At least there is no persuasive evidence that the difference in this respect between the electronically equipped and the unequipped agent is substantial enough to require discrete constitutional recognition, particularly under the Fourth Amendment which is ruled by fluid concepts of "reasonableness."

Nor should we be too ready to erect constitutional barriers to relevant and probative evidence which is also accurate and reliable. An electronic recording will many times produce a more reliable rendition of what a defendant has said than will the unaided memory of a police agent. It may also be that with the recording in existence it is less likely that the informant will change his mind, less chance that threat or injury will suppress unfavorable evidence and less chance that cross-examination will confound the testimony. Considerations like these obviously do not favor the defendant, but we are not prepared to hold that a defendant who has no constitutional right to exclude the informer's unaided testimony nevertheless has a Fourth Amendment privilege against a more accurate version of the events in question. . . .

The judgment of the Court of Appeals is reversed.

[The opinion of Justice Brennan, concurring in the result; the statement of Justice Black, concurring in the judgment; and the dissenting opinions of Justices Douglas, Harlan, and Marshall are omitted.]

NOTES AND QUESTIONS

1. *Surveillance, informants, and undercover agents.* It is not an accident that the policing techniques at issue in *White* so often go together.

> Undercover informants, those willing to pose as co-schemers, accomplices, or confidants of criminal suspects, are the lifeblood of innumerable investigations and prosecutions. They offer police and prosecutors the prospect of gaining admissible, incriminating, and extremely persuasive evidence: damning statements that suspects make to those whom they mistakenly trust. At the same time, however, informants are notoriously unreliable, and their use threatens the moral legitimacy of law enforcement. . . . Informants thus pose a formidable challenge. They are necessary but can never be fully trusted.

> Law enforcement officials navigate the horns of this dilemma daily. They strive to obtain real-time incriminating statements from unwitting suspects without having to rely completely on questionable information or testimony from informants whom juries may reasonably view as dishonest, unreliable, or repugnant. A first possible solution is to introduce an undercover law enforcement officer into the relationship with the suspect. This provides a more credible witness to the suspect's statements—one who is not being paid a bounty or trying to avoid or mitigate punishment. A second and even more attractive solution, often undertaken in conjunction with the first, is to secretly record conversations with the suspect. Whether operated by an undercover law enforcement official or an informant, a recording device removes doubt about what the suspect really said and places the jury's focus at trial squarely on the suspect's own words and deeds rather than on an informant's reliability. . . . It is no wonder that law enforcement officials revere the use of undercover agents and recording devices: They solve the informant quandary.

Steven D. Clymer, *Undercover Operatives and Recorded Conversations: A Response to Professors Shuy and Lininger,* 92 Cornell L. Rev. 847, 847–848 (2007). Notice that informant Harvey Jackson was (conveniently) unavailable for trial—perhaps the best thing that could have happened to the prosecutors who charged White. The government was able to record the conversations with White only because Jackson was present. Then they were able to use the recordings at trial, without putting Jackson on the stand to testify or be subjected to cross-examination about his own criminal history or the deal he made with the government. Does *White* encourage police to engage in one intrusive method to make up for the weaknesses of another?

2. *Deception and the Fourth Amendment.* After *White*, it is clear that undercover officers and informants do not engage in a search or seizure within the meaning of the Fourth Amendment when they enter or search houses or observe activities and listen to conversations that would otherwise be private. As a consequence, covert policing need not be reasonable and does not require a warrant or probable cause.[10] But see Laurent Sacharoff, *Trespass and Deception*, 2015 B.Y.U. L. Rev. 359 (2015) (arguing that entry by deception can constitute a trespass by deception that should be recognized as a search).

3. *Covert policing and the Fifth Amendment.* Informants and undercover agents are also exempt from *Miranda*'s restrictions on custodial interrogations. *Miranda* doctrine ordinarily requires that suspects interrogated while in police custody receive warnings about their constitutional rights and waive those rights for their statements to be introduced in a criminal case. Otherwise, statements given in response to police questioning are considered to have been given involuntarily and are therefore inadmissible against the defendant. See Miranda v. Arizona, 384 U.S. 436 (1966). Nevertheless, in *Illinois v. Perkins*, 496 U.S. 292 (1990), the Court concluded:

> Conversations between suspects and undercover agents do not implicate the concerns underlying *Miranda*. The essential ingredients of a "police-dominated atmosphere" and compulsion are not present when an incarcerated person speaks freely to someone whom he believes to be a fellow inmate. . . . *Miranda* forbids coercion, not mere strategic deception by taking advantage of a suspect's misplaced trust in one he supposes to be a fellow prisoner.

Id. at 296–297. Pursuant to *Perkins*, an undercover agent or informant may question an incarcerated suspect without triggering the protections of *Miranda*. While the government cannot use an undercover agent to subvert the Sixth Amendment right to counsel by soliciting admissions from a suspect without counsel present, Maine v. Moulton, 474 U.S. 159 (1985); United States v. Henry, 447 U.S. 264 (1980), the right to counsel applies only once the suspect has already been charged with a crime and is specific to that crime. It therefore has a limited effect on undercover operations to identify suspects and uncover criminal activity. What might be the practical consequence of *Perkins*?

4. *Covert policing and due process.* Federal constitutional rules require that the government turn over to criminal defendants material exculpatory evidence, including evidence that affects a trial witness's credibility. Giglio v. United States, 405 U.S. 150, 153–154 (1972) (citing Brady v. Maryland, 373 U.S. 83, 87 (1963)).[11] This obligation applies to evidence that an informant received a benefit for his testimony or that an undercover officer had engaged in misconduct on the job. The defendant can then use the evidence to cross-examine the informant or officer about his work. Courts perceive this combination of disclosure and cross-examination as the primary check

---

[10] While the Fourth Amendment does not apply to officers and informants who lie about their identity, it generally does apply to government agents who admit their identity but lie about their legal authority to conduct a search or seizure. Bumper v. North Carolina, 391 U.S. 543 (1968). It also generally applies to agents who lie about their reasons for conducting a search or seizure in a way that improperly induces consent — for example, by invoking an emergency. See, e.g., United States v. Bosse, 898 F.2d 113 (9th Cir. 1990).

[11] The government's disclosure obligations with respect to witness credibility are discussed further in Chapter 4.

on problems posed by covert policing. See Hoffa v. United States, 385 U.S. 293, 311 (1966). But this system protects only people who are charged in a criminal case in which an informant or undercover agent is called to testify—and only then if the arrangement is documented and turned over to the defense. Moreover, although cross-examination may protect against unreliability, and perhaps corruption, it does nothing to check many other risks of covert policing.

5. *Covert policing and entrapment.* The common law defense of *entrapment* has a bit more bite than constitutional criminal procedure when it comes to regulating under-cover behavior. But only a bit. Because entrapment is a criminal defense, not a consti-tutional doctrine, every criminal system has its own law of entrapment. Under federal law and the law of most states, entrapment is an affirmative defense to criminal charges if (and only if) a government agent induced the defendant to commit the crime *and* the defendant lacked any predisposition to commit the offense. See, e.g., Mathews v. United States, 485 U.S. 58, 63 (1988). In practice, proving inducement is not easy because merely offering an opportunity to commit a crime (e.g., by offering to sell the suspect drugs at a discounted rate) is not inducement. Instead, the government agent must usually appeal to sympathy or personal relationships or harass or coerce the defendant into committing the offense. Nor is it easy to establish that a defendant lacked a predisposition, given that he "readily availed himself of the opportunity to per-petrate the crime." *Mathews*, 485 U.S. at 63. Given the lack-of-disposition requirement, entrapment cases frequently turn into jury referenda on the defendants' character and therefore do not effectively regulate police conduct.[12] What might an entrapment defense look like if it were designed solely to prevent government overreaching?

3.   State Regulation of Covert Policing

Without state or city regulation, departments have no legal obligation to vet the background of informants or undercover officers, minimize safety risks to them, evaluate the intrusive-ness of covert policing, develop and make public written policies on covert policing, document arrangements with informants, or track and disclose the use and effectiveness of covert activities. Nevertheless, overwhelmingly, states have no statutes that regulate covert policing. One notable exception is

Rachel Hoffman.

---

[12] Some federal courts have also recognized a common law due process defense for *outrageous government conduct* even when a defendant has the predisposition to commit a crime. This recognition is based on a comment in a Supreme Court opinion reaffirming the predisposition requirement for entrapment. United States v. Russell, 411 U.S. 423, 431–432 (1973) ("While we may some day be pre-sented with a situation in which the conduct of law enforcement agents is so outrageous that due process principles would absolutely bar the government from invoking judicial processes to obtain a convic-tion, the instant case is distinctly not of that breed."). However, most federal courts reject the defense's existence, and the Supreme Court has not ruled directly on the issue. Even federal courts that have recognized the defense have rarely applied it to dismiss an indictment or overturn a conviction. Since the defense has little practical relevance, it is not surprising that police officers are largely unaware of it.

Florida, which passed the first statute regulating the use of confidential informants in 2009, after an informant named Rachel Hoffman was killed during a drug sting.

Hoffman was 23 years old and had just graduated from Florida State University when police caught her with marijuana, ecstasy, and Valium in her apartment. The police told Hoffman that she was facing prison time on felony charges unless she led the police to large amounts of hard drugs or guns. She agreed to cooperate and wore a wire when she went to buy cocaine, 1,500 ecstasy pills, and a small handgun from someone she knew to sell drugs. The police lost track of Hoffman during the encounter, and according to later reports, when the criminals involved found her wire, they shot Hoffman five times in the chest and head, killing her. See Sarah Stillman, *The Throwaways*, New Yorker (Aug. 27, 2012).

The statute passed in response is known as Rachel's Law. As you read the law, consider who it regulates, what it requires of them, and which problems with informants it addresses.

RACHEL'S LAW, FLA. STAT. §914.28

914.28. Confidential informants . . .

(3) A law enforcement agency that uses confidential informants shall:

(a) Inform each person who is requested to serve as a confidential informant that the agency cannot promise inducements such as a grant of immunity, dropped or reduced charges, or reduced sentences or placement on probation in exchange for serving as a confidential informant. . . .

(c) Provide a person who is requested to serve as a confidential informant with an opportunity to consult with legal counsel upon request before the person agrees to perform any activities as a confidential informant. . . .

(d) Ensure that all personnel who are involved in the use or recruitment of confidential informants are trained in the law enforcement agency's policies and procedures. . . .

(e) Adopt policies and procedures that assign the highest priority in operational decisions and actions to the preservation of the safety of confidential informants, law enforcement personnel, target offenders, and the public.

(4) A law enforcement agency that uses confidential informants shall establish policies and procedures addressing the recruitment, control, and use of confidential informants. The policies and procedures must state the:

(a) Information that the law enforcement agency shall maintain concerning each confidential informant;

(b) General guidelines for handling confidential informants;

(c) Process to advise a confidential informant of conditions, restrictions, and procedures associated with participating in the agency's investigative or intelligence gathering activities;

(d) Designated supervisory or command-level review and oversight in the use of a confidential informant;

(e) Limits or restrictions on off-duty association or social relationships by agency personnel involved in investigative or intelligence gathering with confidential informants;

(f) Guidelines to deactivate confidential informants, including guidelines for deactivating communications with confidential informants. . . .

(5) A law enforcement agency that uses confidential informants shall establish policies and procedures to assess the suitability of using a person as a confidential informant by considering the minimum following factors:

(a) The person's age and maturity . . . ;

(d) Whether the person is a substance abuser or has a history of substance abuse or is in a court-supervised drug treatment program;

(e) The risk of physical harm to the person, his or her immediate family, or close associates as a result of providing information or assistance, or upon the disclosure of the person's assistance to the community;

(f) Whether the person has shown any indication of emotional instability, unreliability, or of furnishing false information;

(g) The person's criminal history or prior criminal record; and

(h) Whether the use of the person is important to or vital to the success of an investigation. . . .

(7) A state or local law enforcement agency that uses confidential informants shall perform a periodic review of actual agency confidential informant practices to ensure conformity with the agency's policies and procedures and this section.

(8) The provisions of this section and policies and procedures adopted pursuant to this section do not grant any right or entitlement to a confidential informant or a person who is requested to be a confidential informant, and any failure to abide by this section may not be relied upon to create any additional right, substantive or procedural, enforceable at law by a defendant in a criminal proceeding.

NOTES AND QUESTIONS

1. *Second-order regulation.* The enacted version of Rachel's Law instructs *law enforcement agencies* to adopt policies and procedures governing undercover work. John Rappaport labels this approach *second-order regulation*, which "speaks not directly to officers in the field, but to the political policy makers who oversee those officers, and who in turn promulgate first-order rules of their own." John Rappaport, *Second-Order Regulation of Law Enforcement*, 103 Calif. L. Rev. 205, 210 (2015). Why might a legislature instruct departments to make rules for undercover work rather than make rules themselves? Is the state punting the problem or ensuring that local administrators adequately govern this kind of work?

2. *Who should regulate undercover work?* Undercover work and informant use could have many potential regulators, including courts, legislatures, juries, and command staff. What special knowledge about the costs and benefits of undercover work and the normative values that should constrain it might each type of regulator bring to the table? Which type of actor is most likely to be motivated to regulate covert policing in the public interest? Can you think of other actors and ways of regulation that might help protect against government overreach in sting operations?

3. *Changing the law.* Policing's harms often concentrate on politically weak individuals and groups. As a result, those harms are often inadequately recognized and reflected in regulation of policing. Even when efforts are made to mitigate a

problem, well-organized law enforcement interests often argue that restrictions on the police would stymie effective law enforcement. As a consequence, policing can be more intrusive than it is socially valuable. Sometimes, however, a problem in policing becomes so widespread, so salient, or so severe that something gets done.

Law enforcement largely opposed Rachel's Law, which nevertheless passed unanimously (although somewhat revised) after Hoffman's tragic death received widespread media attention. North Dakota passed a law on confidential informants in 2017 after Andrew Sadek, a state college student, was murdered while acting as an informant for police, working to reduce drug charges. Andrew's Law restricts the use of juvenile and student informants; requires training for law enforcement officers who use confidential informants; mandates written agreements with informants; and instructs the Peace Officers Standards and Training Board to write further regulations protecting informants. See N.D. Cent. Code §29-29.5.

Once one state (or county or city) imposes additional regulation on law enforcement and nothing terrible happens, law enforcement arguments that similar regulation will hurt crime control hold less sway in other jurisdictions. Those state and local governments find it even easier to regulate when they face a tragic event of their own. Does this suggest a path for spreading innovative police regulation? If you were advising a group concerned about a harmful policing practice that is largely unregulated, what might you advise them to do?

Crime by the Police

Police departments don't just buy drugs; sometimes they sell them, using confiscated drugs from old cases. Occasionally, police even are permitted to make drugs. Not long ago, the Albuquerque Police Department got a court order allowing it to use heroin, methamphetamine, crack cocaine, and powder cocaine from its evidence unit, and to make crack cocaine—all to sell to users in order to arrest them. See Gabrielle Burkhart, *Albuquerque Police on Narcotic Operation: 'We're Not Out There Making Drugs'*, KRQE (May 16, 2016). That should make you wonder: How is it *legal* for police officers to buy—much less sell or make—drugs? What about committing other crimes to ensnare criminals or maintain an officer's cover?

As Elizabeth Joh points out, there are three layers of legal protection for officers who commit crimes while undercover:

1. *Nonenforcement.* They are almost never charged by prosecutors.
2. *Elemental defense.* Sometimes officers conducting undercover activities do not satisfy the mens rea requirements for applicable crimes.
3. *Public-authority defense.* States and the federal government recognize, either by statute or common law, a public-authority defense. The defense exempts officers from liability for conduct authorized by departments as a means of gathering evidence of crime.

See Elizabeth E. Joh, *Breaking the Law to Enforce It: Undercover Police Participation in Crime*, 62 Stan. L. Rev. 155, 168–171 (2009). With respect to the last layer of protection, some states recognize the defense without a statute, and states with statutes often provide only general guidance about what is permitted. By contrast, Iowa's statute outlining the requirements for invoking a public-authority defense is quite specific.

IOWA CODE §704.11

704.11 Police activity.

1. A peace officer or person acting as an agent of or directed by any police agency who participates in the commission of a crime by another person solely for the purpose of gathering evidence leading to the prosecution of such other person shall not be guilty of that crime or of the crime of solicitation as set forth in section 705.1, provided that all of the following are true:

> **a.** The officer or person is not an instigator of the criminal activity.

> **b.** The officer or person does not intentionally injure a nonparticipant in the crime.

> **c.** The officer or person acts with the consent of superiors, or the necessity of immediate action precludes obtaining such consent.

> **d.** The officer's or person's actions are reasonable under the circumstances.

2. This section is not intended to preclude the use of undercover or surveillance persons by law enforcement agencies in appropriate circumstances and manner. It is intended to discourage such activity to tempt, urge or persuade the commission of offenses by persons not already disposed to commit offenses of that kind.

Given universal nonprosecution, courts have rarely had to determine the legal limits of police authority to commit crimes, including under this statute. Because the law is underdeveloped, in practice, the same departments that authorize officers to commit criminal acts also set the limits on that authority. How should departments determine what types of undercover criminal activity are appropriate? How should communities ensure that they do? Departments usually do not collect even basic data about undercover activities, and if they do, they do not share it with the public. How else might community members hear about undercover work? How should they?

---

4.   Departmental Policies on Covert Policing

As the previous section suggests, constitutional and statutory regulation of covert policing is thin. Most regulation of these practices comes from departments themselves, many of which set rules and procedures for undercover and confidential informant work. Consider this example from Portland, Oregon:

PORTLAND, OR., POLICE BUREAU DIRECTIVES MANUAL §0660.33

0660.33, Informants . . .

Policy:

1. The Police Bureau recognizes the use of informants is essential in many types of investigations. The Bureau recognizes the need for flexibility in using informants, as well as the potential for harm and abuse. To minimize the potential for abuse, the Bureau recognizes that close adherence to procedures by investigators and supervisors are necessary. In the interest of maintaining consistency and the highest levels of accountability within the informant program, the Drugs and Vice Division Manager will exercise approval authority for all Bureau informants.

2. Members using informants will maintain a professional relationship with the informant in accordance with Directive 310.00, Conduct, Professional, and will do so with knowledge and approval of the command of the unit to which they are assigned. Procedures will ensure maximum benefit in the use and handling of this type of information source while minimizing risk of abuse.

3. Members obtaining information from informants, or other such sources, will use that information for law enforcement purposes in accordance with existing statutes, case law and Bureau procedures.

4. Members paying and using informants for case development purposes and members who supervise and manage the Informant Program, must receive Bureau approved training before taking such action. . . .

5. Members will control the activities of informants and use informants with a clear investigative goal. Informants are to be used as a means to an end. They are not partners in the investigative process.

NOTES AND QUESTIONS

1. *Purpose.* What are the goals of this policy? What values is it designed to protect? Or to say it another way, what problems might this policy be designed to avoid?

2. *Is it well-tailored?* How well do Portland's rules address the risks for informants? What about for those against whom informants produce evidence?

3. *Informant policies vs. undercover policies.* This is Portland's informant policy. Portland also has a policy governing undercover work, but like most such policies, it is largely oriented toward keeping undercover officers safe. Still, it forbids undercover officers from "commit[ting] criminal offenses for the purpose of disguising that he/she is a police officer." See Portland, Or., Police Bureau Directives Manual §0640.95(f).

4. *Public disclosure of undercover rules.* One advantage of internal policies is that they can be subject to local public debate. That can only happen if there are rules and they are accessible to the public. But there are also legitimate concerns that disclosing undercover practices could make covert policing less safe. How could departments balance these competing concerns?

5. *Other information.* For communities to weigh in on policies about undercover officers and informants, they need information about how the department uses these tools. If you were advising community members concerned about covert policing, what information would you encourage them to ask for? What information should departments be required to gather and disclose to the public? See Elizabeth E. Joh, *Breaking the Law to Enforce It: Undercover Police Participation in Crime,* 62 Stan. L. Rev. 155, 159 (2009) (arguing for more information about "authorized criminality" because "[g]reater transparency increases accountability").

6. *How stringent?* Portland has a more developed informant policy than most cities. Many have none at all. Still, if Oregon passed Rachel's Law, would Portland's ordinance satisfy it? What gaps do you see? Are they worth regulating?

7. *Why departments?* Are there good reasons policies on informants and undercover work might differ in different departments? Are there other advantages to department-level regulation rather than state restrictions?

8. *Final word on policing by deception.* If police acting as police are watching or listening to criminals by entering houses or listening in on private conversations, they usually need probable cause and, often, a warrant. But if an officer (or a criminal reporting to an officer) tricks someone into letting him in the door to do the same, he faces little regulation, even if he commits crimes along the way. Weird, right?

A Problem: Undercover Social Media Policing

Central Utopia City Police Department (CUCPD) Chief Earl Earnest is concerned that his department's social media investigations could draw public ire. Although CUCPD officers do not engage in broad social media monitoring, his officers sometimes set up social media accounts under false names to investigate criminal suspects and their friends. For example, when CUCPD got an anonymous tip that one man with a large Instagram following was involved in a string of home burglaries, an officer made a request to follow using an account with a fake identity. The suspect accepted the request, making the photos the suspect had posted accessible. The officer found pictures of the suspect with stolen items, leading to the suspect's prosecution and conviction for the burglaries. More recently, even without information that a particular individual might be involved, officers have begun to insinuate themselves in social networks and monitor them to uncover drug dealing, child-pornography distribution, and acquisition of guns by convicted felons. Chief Earnest has asked you for a brief summary of the legal and policy implications of these activities. What do you say?

Chapter 3

Obtaining Testimony

Police talk to many people in the course of their work. During those conversations, they gather information about situations they confront ("Did you see what happened?"), build relationships with people in the community ("How are you doing today?"), and assess potential suspects ("What are you doing here?"). In criminal investigations, police conversations focus on two goals: identifying the person who committed an offense and obtaining evidence that can be used in bringing that person to justice.

A conversation with a victim or potential witness is often called an *interview*. In many cases, witness interviews are the only means to figure out the nature of a crime and determine who committed it. A conversation with a criminal suspect to gather information and to solicit a confession is often labeled an *interrogation*. As the Supreme Court has pointed out, "A confession is like no other evidence. Indeed, 'the defendant's own confession is probably the most probative and damaging evidence that can be admitted against him.'" Arizona v. Fulminante, 499 U.S. 279, 296 (1991) (quoting Bruton v. United States, 391 U.S. 123, 139–140 (1968) (White, J., dissenting)).

In both interviews and interrogations, officers face three major obstacles: getting *any* information from those who are reluctant, getting *complete* information, and getting *accurate* information. Unfortunately, guided by tradition and intuition, police sometimes use techniques to overcome these obstacles that cause problems of their own. Since modern policing started in the nineteenth century, police have at times beaten or coerced confessions out of suspects; contaminated the testimony they obtain; and relied on improbable confessions, unreliable witness identifications, and incredible witness statements. As a result, innocent people have been convicted and guilty ones set free.

This chapter describes the legal doctrines that regulate police efforts to obtain testimony. The first section addresses the Due Process Clause, which prohibits involuntary confessions from being introduced in criminal trials. The next two sections consider *Miranda v. Arizona*, 384 U.S. 436 (1966), and its impact on police conduct in the interrogation room. The last section looks at obtaining eyewitness testimony, including identifications.

Reading this chapter will familiarize you with basic involuntariness, *Miranda*, and witness identification doctrine. These doctrines offer an opportunity to compare several different regulatory regimes that have developed over time in American law to address a closely related set of problems in policing. The example of *Miranda* also offers some perspective on how doctrines might affect police behavior. Along the way, you might also end up more skeptical of common police methods of detecting lies and gathering evidence through interrogations, interviews, and suspect identifications.

A.   Introduction to the Problem of Interrogations

1.   The Reid Technique

By most accounts, the most widely trained on and used interrogation technique in the United States is the Reid Technique, a method developed and trademarked by John E. Reid & Associates, Inc.[1] Examining the technique reveals some common interrogation practices and their problems.

Before an officer interrogates a suspect, the Reid Technique encourages him to collect information about the crime and the suspect to assess the likelihood that the suspect is guilty. Then the officer engages in a *behavior analysis interview*, in which he asks nonaccusatory questions to obtain background information and to "elicit behavior symptoms of truth or deception." Only then does the officer interrogate the suspect. The *interrogation* is structured as a near monologue in which the officer accuses the suspect of the crime and discourages him from speaking until he is ready "to tell the truth" and produce a court-admissible confession.

According to training materials, a Reid interrogation has nine stages:

1. *Confront the suspect.* "Our investigation proves that you are the person who shot the victim."
2. *Develop the theme.* The officer provides a moral justification for the crime that minimizes the suspect's responsibility and describes getting to the truth as "the most important thing."
3. *Discourage denials.* The officer discourages the suspect from explaining or denying the crime, cutting him off if necessary, and reasserts the suspect's guilt and the theme. According to the technique, innocent suspects speak without permission, their denials will strengthen with time, and they will remain sincere, steadfast, and adamant in asserting their innocence. Thus, the investigator can be confident that any suspect who does not act in these ways when discouraged from denying guilt is guilty.
4. *Overcome objections.* Guilty suspects will try to reassert control over the interrogation with objections. The officer handles objections by reshaping them to reinforce the theme.
5. *Retain the suspect's attention.* The officer tries to ensure the suspect is listening but not focusing on possible punishment, which would reinforce a resolve to deny the crime. Officers are encouraged to move very close to the suspect to keep his attention.
6. *Handle passivity.* When the suspect seems defeated or starts to cry, the officer should sympathize but also intensify his efforts to offer a justification for committing the crime and urge him to admit the truth.
7. *Present an incriminating question.* Once the suspect seems ready, the officer offers the suspect a question about the crime with two alternatives, both of which indicate guilt. One choice makes the crime more understandable; the other makes it more outrageous: "Did you react suddenly, or did you go there to kill him? I think you just reacted in the moment." The question is phrased so that the suspect merely has to nod or say "yes" to acknowledge guilt.

---

[1] *Ed note.* I received brief training on the Reid Technique as a prosecutor for the U.S. Department of Justice and sometimes informally used aspects of the technique while questioning suspects between 1998 and 2006.

8. *Reinforce the admission and obtain details.* The officer reinforces the admission, "That's what I thought all along," and then asks brief, focused questions that solicit details a bit at a time. "Was it your gun or someone else's gun?" Once the questioning is further along, the officer can ask questions to undermine the justification the officer has suggested and ask more open-ended questions to solicit a fuller confession.

9. *Reduce it to writing.* After the officer gets an account with sufficient detail, the officer makes the confession permanent by having the suspect write it down, by writing it down himself, by having a transcription made, or by audio- or videotaping a statement.

Not all officers are trained in or use the Reid Technique, but most officers use at least some of these strategies, sometimes learning them from peers on the job. Yet social scientists agree that the Reid Technique can contaminate suspect statements and lead to false confessions, in part because it inaccurately presumes that police can use behavioral clues to reliably distinguish false denials of guilt from true denials. Once officers decide that a person is guilty, the technique teaches officers to overwhelm suspects' resistance and convince them that they are better off confessing, a practice that can lead even some innocent suspects to confess. See, e.g., Alan Hirsch, *Going to the Source: The New Reid Method and False Confessions*, 11 Ohio St. J. Crim. L. 803 (2014) (summarizing evidence on the Reid Technique).

Can Officers Tell Who Is Lying?

Ask any police officer (or prosecutor, for that matter), and he will tell you that he knows when someone is lying. The research disagrees. When people attempt to detect deception based on verbal, vocal, and nonverbal behavioral indicators, they do so at a rate not much better than chance. See Charles F. Bond, Jr. & Bella M. DePaulo, *Accuracy of Deception Judgments*, 10 Personality & Soc. Psychol. Rev. 214, 214 (2006). Training and experience improve the situation only a little. See Valerie Hauch et al., *Does Training Improve Detection of Deception? A Meta-Analysis*, 43 Comm. Res. 283, 309 (2016). As a result, police interrogators are little better than anyone else, but they are much more confident about their deception-detection skills.

Scholars fantasize about a world in which brain-imaging technology will enable us to label someone a liar with more confidence. Right now, that technology gets results that are only slightly better than polygraphs, which are only somewhat better than flipping a coin (see below). See Giorgio Ganis, *Deception Detection Using Neuroimaging*, in *Detecting Deception: Current Challenges and Cognitive Approaches* 105, 114 (Pär Anders Granhag et al. eds., 2015).

It turns out that there is no reliable way to distinguish a suspect's truths from his lies. So far, the best method is the same way people do it in ordinary life, by identifying internal inconsistencies and conflicts with external sources, such as physical evidence and witness statements. Pete Blair et al., *Content in Context Improves Deception Detection Accuracy*, 36 Hum. Comm. Res. 423, 424–425 (2010). Interrogations might be improved by more strategic use of these methods. Until techniques get better, however, good investigators should be humble about their abilities to detect lies.

2.   Coercive Interrogation

Before contemporary police departments existed, magistrates carried out most criminal investigations, including interrogating suspects. As police departments developed, officers took over, and the public began to demand that the police solve crimes and generate evidence for convictions. Because officers had little training for the task, they often turned to abusive interrogation techniques to produce confessions, which served as the primary evidence in many criminal cases.

Critics complained about physically and psychologically harsh interrogation methods, which became known colloquially as *the third degree*, arguing that they undermined human dignity and constituted government abuse. The police often denied that the practice existed.

Thomas F. Byrnes (left), NYPD Detective Bureau Chief, supervising an interrogation in 1884.

During the early twentieth century, journalists and lawyers repeatedly investigated interrogation practices. Most prominently, in 1931 the Wickersham Commission published *The Third Degree*. See Zechariah Chafee, Jr., et al., *The Third Degree*, in Nat'l Commn. on Law Observance & Enforcement, *Report on Lawlessness in Law Enforcement* (1931). *The Third Degree* documented cases and concluded that abusive interrogations were widespread. For much of the twentieth century, coercive interrogation techniques stood out as among the worst problems in policing.

Today, other problems in policing are more salient in the public mind, but intimidating, coercive, and even brutal interrogation techniques sometimes continue to take place. Throughout the 1970s and 1980s, for example, former Chicago Police Commander Jon Burge led torturous interrogations of dozens of mostly African-American suspects, who were suffocated, electrocuted, burned, and forced into rounds of Russian roulette. United States v. Burge, 711 F.3d 803, 806 (7th Cir. 2013).[2]

Critics of the Reid Technique emphasize the risk of false confessions, but coercive and brutal interrogations do harm even when there is no confession or the confession is true. The process of interrogation itself can "exact[] a heavy toll on individual liberty." Miranda v. Arizona, 384 U.S. 436, 455 (1966).

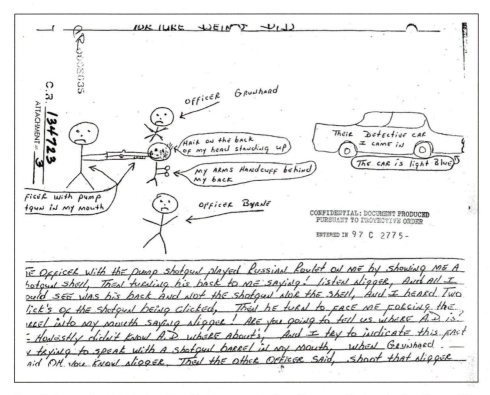

Darrell Cannon's affidavit describes his interrogation by officers working under Jon Burge. The officer with the shotgun was later identified as Lt. Peter Dignan. Cannon recounts how Dignan shoved the shotgun into Cannon's mouth and pulled the trigger as other officers shouted, "Blow the nigger's head off!" Cannon also states that a cattle prod was used on his genitals.

B.   *Due Process and Voluntary Confessions*

Although a few states regulated police interrogation during the early twentieth century by banning abuse or excluding confessions resulting from abuse under evidence law, these weakly enforced regulatory efforts made little impact. The U.S. Supreme Court stepped in for the first time in *Brown v. Mississippi*, 297 U.S. 278 (1936). The facts surrounding the confession at issue were undisputed:

> On that night, one Dial, a deputy sheriff, accompanied by others, came to the home of Ellington, one of the defendants, and requested him to accompany them

---

[2] Eventually, Burge was convicted of perjury and obstruction of justice for lying under oath about the abuse and sentenced to 54 months' imprisonment. *Burge*, 711 F.3d at 808.

to the house of the deceased, and there a number of white men were gathered, who began to accuse the defendant of the crime. Upon his denial they seized him, and with the participation of the deputy they hanged him by a rope to the limb of a tree, and having let him down, they hung him again, and when he was let down the second time, and he still protested his innocence, he was tied to a tree and whipped, and still declining to accede to the demands that he confess, he was finally released and he returned with some difficulty to his home, suffering intense pain and agony. The record of the testimony shows that the signs of the rope on his neck were plainly visible during the so-called trial. A day or two thereafter the said deputy, accompanied by another, returned to the home of the said defendant and arrested him, and departed with the prisoner towards the jail in an adjoining county, but went by a route which led into the State of Alabama; and while on the way, in that State, the deputy stopped and again severely whipped the defendant, declaring that he would continue the whipping until he confessed, and the defendant then agreed to confess to such a statement as the deputy would dictate, and he did so, after which he was delivered to jail.

The other two defendants, Ed Brown and Henry Shields, were also arrested and taken to the same jail. On Sunday night, April 1, 1934, the same deputy, accompanied by a number of white men, . . . came to the jail, and the two last named defendants were made to strip and they were laid over chairs and their backs were cut to pieces with a leather strap with buckles on it, and they were likewise made by the said deputy definitely to understand that the whipping would be continued unless and until they confessed, and not only confessed, but confessed in every matter of detail as demanded by those present; and in this manner the defendants confessed the crime, and as the whippings progressed and were repeated, they changed or adjusted their confession in all particulars of detail so as to conform to the demands of their torturers. When the confessions had been obtained in the exact form and contents as desired by the mob, they left with the parting admonition and warning that, if the defendants changed their story at any time in any respect from that last stated, the perpetrators of the outrage would administer the same or equally effective treatment.

Id. at 281-282. Once the confessions were obtained by these near lynchings, the defendants were indicted, appointed counsel, and tried the next day. The only evidence presented at trial was the confessions, which the defendants testified were tortured out of them. A deputy sheriff, as a state witness, admitted the whippings, and no witness denied them. The Mississippi Supreme Court upheld the convictions.

The U.S. Supreme Court held the convictions unconstitutional:

Because a State may dispense with a jury trial, it does not follow that it may substitute trial by ordeal. The rack and torture chamber may not be substituted for the witness stand. . . . The due process clause requires "that state action, whether through one agency or another, shall be consistent with the fundamental principles of liberty and justice which lie at the base of all our civil and political institutions." Hebert v. Louisiana, 272 U.S. 312, 316 (1926). It would be difficult to conceive of methods more revolting to the sense of justice than those taken to procure the confessions of these petitioners, and the use of the confessions thus obtained as the basis for conviction and sentence was a clear denial of due process.

Id. at 285-286.

In this way, *Brown* subjected local police interrogations to constitutional scrutiny. Over time, the Court applied similar reasoning to deprivations of sleep and continuous questioning, Ashcraft v. Tennessee, 322 U.S. 143 (1944); to lengthy incommunicado interrogations, Spano v. New York, 360 U.S. 315 (1959); and to threats of physical violence, Beecher v. Alabama, 389 U.S. 35 (1967). Over time, the Court made clear that the Due Process Clause makes it unconstitutional to admit an *involuntary* confession against a suspect in a criminal trial, where involuntariness is assessed by examining the totality of the circumstances under which the confession was produced. See Clewis v. Texas, 386 U.S. 707 (1967).

NOTES AND QUESTIONS

1. *Involuntariness as a standard.* According to the Supreme Court, involuntariness is not a measure of a specific quality of the interrogation. Instead, it is a "convenient shorthand" for "a complex of values" that prohibit the use of some confessions and vary "according to the particular circumstances of the case." Blackburn v. Alabama, 361 U.S. 199, 206–207 (1960). As the Court has acknowledged, under that approach, officers cannot easily know what techniques are allowed, and lower courts provide no clear or consistent guidance about what makes a confession involuntary. See Dickerson v. United States, 530 U.S. 428, 444 (2000); Haynes v. Washington, 373 U.S. 503, 515 (1963). Is it surprising that courts only rarely find confessions involuntary and that the involuntariness test has proven a weak check on the police? Could a clearer values test work better? How?

2. *Promises.* Although there are no bright-line rules, under the involuntariness standard, courts often allow police to make promises to suspects, offering them drug treatment or release of a family member in exchange for a confession. They also allow generic promises of leniency, "I'll put in a good word," even if no leniency results. More specific promises of leniency generally do not make a confession involuntary if the promises are kept. But courts are a little more skeptical about specific promises of leniency that induce a suspect to confess when the promises are not kept by the government. See Paul Marcus, *It's Not Just About* Miranda*: Determining the Voluntariness of Confessions in Criminal Prosecutions*, 40 Val. U. L. Rev. 601, 613 (2006) (collecting cases). Can you see a difference?

3. *Threats.* Beatrice Lynumn confessed to possessing and selling marijuana "because the police told me they were going to send me to jail for 10 years and take my children, and I would never see them again." Her children were three and four years old at the time, and their father was dead. In *Lynumn v. Illinois*, 372 U.S. 528, 532 (1963), the Supreme Court held, without much explanation, that the confession was involuntary. What if the police had strong evidence against her such that, unless she cooperated, their threats were likely true? Should officers be barred from inducing a confession by describing the potential dire consequences of failing to confess? See, e.g., Lindsey v. Smith, 820 F.2d 1137 (11th Cir. 1987) (confession voluntary despite threat of capital murder charge). What if the officer is wrong about what can happen? See State v. Strain, 779 P.2d 221 (Utah 1989) (confession not necessarily involuntary despite improper threat of execution and guarantee of non-death-penalty charge if defendant confessed). Should it matter if the officer believes what he tells the suspect?

4. *Lies.* Lying in interrogations is so common you might say that "deception is the new coercion." Michael J. Z. Mannheimer, *Fraudulently Induced Confessions*, 96

Notre Dame L. Rev. __ (forthcoming 2021). Most courts allow officers to deceive a suspect about the officer's sympathies ("I'm on your side"), about the evidence ("Your DNA was found on the victim"), and about the seriousness of the offense ("You're lucky the victim is still alive"). A few courts won't allow officers to fabricate physical evidence, see, e.g., State v. Cayward, 552 So. 2d 971, 972 (Fla. Dist. Ct. App. 1989); State v. Patton, 826 A.2d 783 (N.J. 2003); and more are skeptical about false promises of leniency, see, e.g., Smith v. State, 944 F.2d 284 (6th Cir. 1991), *aff'd,* 509 U.S. 933 (1993). Although courts disagree about what kinds of deception are permissible and why, by any measure, a stunning amount of deception is allowed. See Mannheimer, *supra* (collecting cases). Michael Mannheimer argues that deceptive practices should only violate due process if they cause a suspect to falsely, but reasonably, believe that the benefits of confessing outweigh the costs. He thinks lies about evidence and interrogations by undercover officers do not violate due process under this test. See *id.* Do you agree?

5. *Suspect protection or police regulation?* While the Court has often described voluntariness as assessing whether the defendant's "will was overborne," see, e.g, Arizona v. Fulminante, 499 U.S. 279, 288 (1991), in *Colorado v. Connelly,* 479 U.S. 157 (1986), the Court has also held that confessions are not involuntary unless there is "a substantial element of coercive police conduct" in producing the confession, because the involuntariness standard is intended to deter police misconduct rather than protect suspects. See *id.* at 164. Under this standard, a confession driven by delusion is not involuntary if the officers do nothing to coerce the suspect, even if they are aware of the suspect's mental state. Similarly, after *Connelly,* if Bob's coconspirator tells him that he will kill Bob's young son if Bob does not confess, Bob's resulting confession is voluntary and admissible because it was not induced by *police* coercion. See *id.* at 166. What does that tell you about the purpose of the involuntariness standard? If the standard is intended to regulate the police rather than protect defendants, as *Connelly* suggests, is it well designed? How might it be improved?

Bright-Line Rules

The Court's decisions indicate that voluntariness is always a totality-of-the-circumstances analysis. But if a police officer beats a suspect who then confesses, is it really necessary to consider all the conditions surrounding the interrogation? See Eve Brensike Primus, *The Future of Confession Law: Toward Rules for the Voluntariness Test*, 114 Mich. L. Rev. 1, 35–38 (2015). Should any of these circumstances make a confession involuntary without further inquiry?

- Pointing a gun at the suspect
- Withholding medical treatment
- Threatening to charge a spouse
- Interrogating a suspect for 12 hours
- Interrogating a suspect for six hours

- Denying a suspect access to food or a bathroom for four hours
- Falsely telling a suspect that confessing may lead the government to drop charges
- Telling a suspect if he does not confess, officers will tell others that he "snitched" on someone else

Bright-line guidelines could improve consistency across cases and make it easier for police to learn and apply the rules (although perhaps no officer should need to be told that pointing a gun at a suspect makes a confession involuntary). Perhaps more important, clear rules would pressure departments to ensure that officers live up to them.

You might wonder whether specific interrogation rules are practical. For decades in Great Britain, the police have been subject to the Police and Criminal Evidence Act 1984, c. 60, as amended (PACE), and *Code C: Revised Code of Practice for the Detention, Treatment and Questioning of Persons by Police Officers* (2019) (the Interrogation Code) issued by the Home Office (the British equivalent of the U.S. Department of Justice). PACE and the Interrogation Code require the police to audio-record interrogations, to inform suspects about their rights, to provide access to counsel, and to offer special protections to juveniles and other vulnerable people, among other provisions. They also forbid interrogators from requiring a suspect to stand, Interrogation Code §12.6; and require that suspects be given regular meals and short refreshment breaks every two hours, Interrogation Code §12.8. Statements taken in violation of the act may be excluded at trial.

Does Great Britain's example suggest that the United States should create bright line rules for voluntariness or alternatives to constitutional regulation? Although states could pass detailed codes regulating police interrogations, no state has.

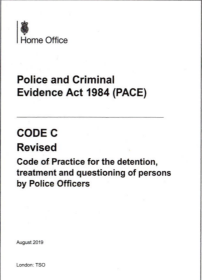

Home Office

Police and Criminal Evidence Act 1984 (PACE)

CODE C
Revised
Code of Practice for the detention, treatment and questioning of persons by Police Officers

August 2019

London: TSO

6. *Right and remedy.* Involuntariness cases protect the right to a fair criminal trial, a procedural right. The government can avoid violating that right, even after the police coerce a confession, by not introducing the confession into evidence. A trial court can similarly prevent a violation by suppressing the confession. An appellate court can cure any violation by reversing the conviction. This approach helps to ensure that the defendant is not convicted without due process. Would you expect it also to discourage police coercion? Explain.

7. *Coercion without confession.* What if a police officer strong-arms a suspect, but the suspect never confesses, or the suspect confesses, but the government never introduces the confession at trial? The Due Process Clause also has a substantive sphere. However, "only the most egregious official conduct" can be said to be sufficiently "arbitrary, or conscience shocking" so as to violate the substantive due process right. County of Sacramento v. Lewis, 523 U.S. 833, 846–847 (1998). An interrogated person can sue an officer or police department for damages. However, he must establish that the police interrogation practices *shocked the conscience,* a higher standard than *involuntariness.* See Chavez v. Martinez, 538 U.S. 760 (2003). Moreover, he has no right to counsel, and he faces substantial practical and legal barriers to success, discussed in Chapter 13. Few plaintiffs succeed. Who is most likely to refuse to confess even when coerced? Does it bother you that those individuals have such a limited remedy?

8. *Totality-of-the-circumstances tests and legal development.* When the Supreme Court decides that police conduct makes a confession involuntary, it sends a clear message to officers not to engage in that conduct. But the Supreme Court rarely decides involuntariness cases, and the totality of the circumstances test may help to explain why. Only around 3 percent of petitions for a writ of certiorari filed with the U.S. Supreme Court are granted, fewer than 150 each year. Rule 10 of the Rules of the Supreme Court states the considerations the Court uses in evaluating those petitions. It suggests that the Court will decide cases when state supreme courts, federal courts of appeals, or both disagree on an important federal question, when a decision has flouted the Supreme Court, or when a decision has teed up an important federal question that the Supreme Court has not yet decided. By contrast, it states, "A petition for a writ of certiorari is rarely granted when the asserted error consists of erroneous factual findings or the misapplication of a properly stated rule of law." U.S. S.Ct. R. 10. The Supreme Court decided many of its voluntariness cases during the 1960s, when the Court granted certiorari more generously in death penalty cases even when none of these conditions were clearly met. Consider what lower courts conclude when they decide whether a confession is involuntary. Can you see why the Supreme Court rarely hears voluntariness cases now? What consequences might that have for the law of interrogations?

9. *State voluntariness law.* States are required to enforce federal constitutional standards for voluntariness. They also enforce state constitutional law, which may bar a confession considered voluntary by federal standards. Although some states purport to apply a standard more protective of suspects than federal law, at the end of the day, they similarly, overwhelmingly, find confessions voluntary. See, e.g., State v. Kelekolio, 849 P.2d 58 (Haw. 1993); State v. Downey, 259 S.W.3d 723, 733–734 (Tenn. 2008). Why do states, like the federal government, protect this constitutional value with a scheme that does so little work?

C.   The Privilege Against Self-Incrimination and Police Interrogations

Frustrated with how ineffectively the fact-specific voluntariness standard regulated police questioning, the Warren Court famously took a new approach to interrogations in *Miranda v. Arizona,* 384 U.S. 436 (1966). The version below is edited to highlight the Court's response to the challenge of regulating police misconduct using constitutional law, rather than to emphasize constitutional doctrine. Even edited, the case remains substantial. Given the significance of the decision in the pantheon of U.S. Supreme Court cases, and its express consideration of the role of the Court in governing the police, it is well worth the time.

MIRANDA v. ARIZONA
384 U.S. 436 (1966)

Mr. Chief Justice Warren delivered the opinion of the Court.

The cases before us raise questions which go to the roots of our concepts of American criminal jurisprudence: the restraints society must observe consistent with the Federal Constitution in prosecuting individuals for crime. . . .

Our holding . . . briefly stated . . . is this: the prosecution may not use statements, whether exculpatory or inculpatory, stemming from custodial interrogation of the defendant unless it demonstrates the use of procedural safeguards effective to secure the privilege against self-incrimination. By custodial interrogation, we mean questioning initiated by law enforcement officers after a person has been taken into custody or otherwise deprived of his freedom of action in any significant way. As for the procedural safeguards to be employed, unless other fully effective means are devised to inform accused persons of their right of silence and to assure a continuous opportunity to exercise it, the following measures are required. Prior to any questioning, the person must be warned that he has a right to remain silent, that any statement he does make may be used as evidence against him, and that he has a right to the presence of an attorney, either retained or appointed. The defendant may waive effectuation of these rights, provided the waiver is made voluntarily, knowingly and intelligently. If, however, he indicates in any manner and at any stage of the process that he wishes to consult with an attorney before speaking there can be no questioning. Likewise, if the individual is alone and indicates in any manner that he does not wish to be interrogated, the police may not question him. The mere fact that he may have answered some questions or volunteered some statements on his own does not deprive him of the right to refrain from answering any further inquiries until he has consulted with an attorney and thereafter consents to be questioned.

I.

The constitutional issue we decide in each of these cases is the admissibility of statements obtained from a defendant questioned while in custody or otherwise deprived of his freedom of action in any significant way. In each, the defendant was questioned by police officers, detectives, or a prosecuting attorney in a room in which he was cut off from the outside world. In none of these cases was the defendant given a full and effective warning of his rights at the outset of the interrogation process. In all the cases, the questioning elicited oral admissions, and in three of them, signed statements as well which were admitted at their trials. They all thus share salient features—incommunicado interrogation of individuals in a police-dominated atmosphere, resulting in self-incriminating statements without full warnings of constitutional rights.

An understanding of the nature and setting of this in-custody interrogation is essential to our decisions today. The difficulty in depicting what transpires at such interrogations stems from the fact that in this country they have largely taken place incommunicado. From extensive factual studies undertaken in the early 1930's, including the famous Wickersham Report to Congress by a Presidential Commission, it is clear that police violence and the "third degree" flourished at that time. . . . The use of physical brutality and violence is not, unfortunately, relegated to the past or to any part of the country. Only recently in Kings County, New York, the police brutally beat, kicked and placed lighted cigarette butts on the back of a potential witness under interrogation for the purpose of securing a statement incriminating a third party. People v. Portelli, 15 N.Y. 2d 235 (1965).

The examples given above are undoubtedly the exception now, but they are sufficiently widespread to be the object of concern. Unless a proper limitation upon custodial interrogation is achieved—such as these decisions will advance—there can be no assurance that practices of this nature will be eradicated in the foreseeable future. . . .

. . . [W]e stress that the modern practice of in-custody interrogation is psychologically rather than physically oriented. . . . Interrogation still takes place in privacy. Privacy results in secrecy and this in turn results in a gap in our knowledge as to what in fact goes on in the interrogation rooms. A valuable source of information about present police practices, however, may be found in various police manuals and texts which document procedures employed with success in the past, and which recommend various other effective tactics. These texts are used by law enforcement agencies themselves as guides.[3] . . .

The officers are told by the manuals that the "principal psychological factor contributing to a successful interrogation is *privacy*—being alone with the person under interrogation." The efficacy of this tactic has been explained as follows:

> "If at all practicable, the interrogation should take place in the investigator's office or at least in a room of his own choice. The subject should be deprived of every psychological advantage. In his own home he may be confident, indignant, or recalcitrant. . . . Moreover his family and other friends are nearby, their presence lending moral support. In his own office, the investigator possesses all the advantages. The atmosphere suggests the invincibility of the forces of the law."

To highlight the isolation and unfamiliar surroundings, the manuals instruct the police to display an air of confidence in the suspect's guilt and from outward appearance to maintain only an interest in confirming certain details. The guilt of the subject is to be posited as a fact. The interrogator should direct his comments toward the reasons why the subject committed the act, rather than court failure by asking the subject whether he did it. Like other men, perhaps the subject has had a bad family life, had an unhappy childhood, had too much to drink, had an unrequited desire for women. The officers are instructed to minimize the moral seriousness of the offense, to cast blame on the victim or on society. These tactics are

---

[3] *Ed. note:* Although the footnotes have been removed for length, the Court cites and quotes from the Reid Technique manual and one other major manual in this section. The Reid Technique has been revised in some respects since *Miranda* was decided, but its core remains intact.

designed to put the subject in a psychological state where his story is but an elaboration of what the police purport to know already—that he is guilty. Explanations to the contrary are dismissed and discouraged.

The texts thus stress that the major qualities an interrogator should possess are patience and perseverance. One writer describes the efficacy of these characteristics in this manner:

"... Where emotional appeals and tricks are employed to no avail, he must rely on an oppressive atmosphere of dogged persistence. He must interrogate steadily and without relent, leaving the subject no prospect of surcease. He must dominate his subject and overwhelm him with his inexorable will to obtain the truth. . . ."

The manuals suggest that the suspect be offered legal excuses for his actions in order to obtain an initial admission of guilt. Where there is a suspected revenge-killing, for example, the interrogator may say:

"Joe, you probably didn't go out looking for this fellow with the purpose of shooting him. My guess is, however, that you expected something from him and that's why you carried a gun—for your own protection. You knew him for what he was, no good. Then when you met him he probably started using foul, abusive language and he gave some indication that he was about to pull a gun on you, and that's when you had to act to save your own life. That's about it, isn't it, Joe?"

Having then obtained the admission of shooting, the interrogator is advised to refer to circumstantial evidence which negates the self-defense explanation. This should enable him to secure the entire story. . . .

When the techniques described above prove unavailing, the texts recommend they be alternated with a show of some hostility. One ploy often used has been termed the "friendly-unfriendly" or the "Mutt and Jeff" act:

"... In this technique, two agents are employed. Mutt, the relentless investigator, who knows the subject is guilty and is not going to waste any time. He's sent a dozen men away for this crime and he's going to send the subject away for the full term. Jeff, on the other hand, is obviously a kindhearted man. He has a family himself. He has a brother who was involved in a little scrape like this. He disapproves of Mutt and his tactics and will arrange to get him off the case if the subject will cooperate. He can't hold Mutt off for very long. The subject would be wise to make a quick decision. The technique is applied by having both investigators present while Mutt acts out his role. Jeff may stand by quietly and demur at some of Mutt's tactics. When Jeff makes his plea for cooperation, Mutt is not present in the room."

The interrogators sometimes are instructed to induce a confession out of trickery. . . . [T]he interrogator may take a break in his questioning to place the subject among a group of men in a line-up. "The witness or complainant (previously coached, if necessary) studies the line-up and confidently points out the subject as the guilty party." Then the questioning resumes "as though there were now no doubt about the guilt of the subject." . . .

The manuals also contain instructions for police on how to handle the individual who refuses to discuss the matter entirely, or who asks for an attorney or relatives. The examiner is to concede him the right to remain silent. . . . After this psychological conditioning, however, the officer is told to point out the incriminating significance of the suspect's refusal to talk:

> "Joe, you have a right to remain silent. That's your privilege and I'm the last person in the world who'll try to take it away from you. If that's the way you want to leave this, O.K. But let me ask you this. Suppose you were in my shoes and I were in yours and you called me in to ask me about this and I told you, 'I don't want to answer any of your questions.' You'd think I had something to hide, and you'd probably be right in thinking that. That's exactly what I'll have to think about you, and so will everybody else. So let's sit here and talk this whole thing over."

Few will persist in their initial refusal to talk, it is said, if this monologue is employed correctly. . . .

Even without employing brutality, the "third degree" or the specific stratagems described above, the very fact of custodial interrogation exacts a heavy toll on individual liberty and trades on the weakness of individuals. . . .[24]

In these cases, we might not find the defendants' statements to have been involuntary in traditional terms. Our concern for adequate safeguards to protect precious Fifth Amendment rights is, of course, not lessened in the slightest. In each of the cases, the defendant was thrust into an unfamiliar atmosphere and run through menacing police interrogation procedures. . . . To be sure, the records do not evince overt physical coercion or patent psychological ploys. The fact remains that in none of these cases did the officers undertake to afford appropriate safeguards at the outset of the interrogation to insure that the statements were truly the product of free choice.

It is obvious that such an interrogation environment is created for no purpose other than to subjugate the individual to the will of his examiner. This atmosphere

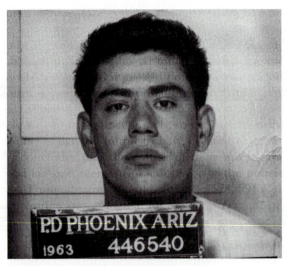

Booking photo of Ernesto Miranda.

[24] Interrogation procedures may even give rise to a false confession. The most recent conspicuous example occurred in New York, in 1964, when a Negro of limited intelligence confessed to two brutal murders and a rape which he had not committed. . . .

carries its own badge of intimidation. To be sure, this is not physical intimidation, but it is equally destructive of human dignity.[26] The current practice of incommunicado interrogation is at odds with one of our Nation's most cherished principles—that the individual may not be compelled to incriminate himself. Unless adequate protective devices are employed to dispel the compulsion inherent in custodial surroundings, no statement obtained from the defendant can truly be the product of his free choice. . . .

II. . . .

. . . We are satisfied that all the principles embodied in the privilege apply to informal compulsion exerted by law-enforcement officers during in-custody questioning. . . . As a practical matter, the compulsion to speak in the isolated setting of the police station may well be greater than in courts or other official investigations, where there are often impartial observers to guard against intimidation or trickery. . . .

Our decision in *Malloy v. Hogan*, 378 U.S. 1 (1964), . . . squarely held the privilege applicable to the States, and held that the substantive standards underlying the privilege applied with full force to state court proceedings. . . .

III.

. . . We have concluded that without proper safeguards the process of in-custody interrogation of persons suspected or accused of crime contains inherently compelling pressures which work to undermine the individual's will to resist and to compel him to speak where he would not otherwise do so freely. In order to combat these pressures and to permit a full opportunity to exercise the privilege against self-incrimination, the accused must be adequately and effectively apprised of his rights and the exercise of those rights must be fully honored.

It is impossible for us to foresee the potential alternatives for protecting the privilege which might be devised by Congress or the States in the exercise of their creative rule-making capacities. Therefore we cannot say that the Constitution necessarily requires adherence to any particular solution for the inherent compulsions of the interrogation process as it is presently conducted. . . . We encourage Congress and the States to continue their laudable search for increasingly effective ways of protecting the rights of the individual while promoting efficient enforcement of our criminal laws. However, unless we are shown other procedures which are at least

---

[26] The absurdity of denying that a confession obtained under these circumstances is compelled is aptly portrayed by an example in Professor Sutherland's recent article, *Crime and Confession*, 79 Harv. L. Rev. 21, 37 (1965):

> "Suppose a well-to-do testatrix says she intends to will her property to Elizabeth. John and James want her to bequeath it to them instead. They capture the testatrix, put her in a carefully designed room, out of touch with everyone but themselves and their convenient 'witnesses,' keep her secluded there for hours while they make insistent demands, weary her with contradictions of her assertions that she wants to leave her money to Elizabeth, and finally induce her to execute the will in their favor. Assume that John and James are deeply and correctly convinced that Elizabeth is unworthy and will make base use of the property if she gets her hands on it, whereas John and James have the noblest and most righteous intentions. Would any judge of probate accept the will so procured as the 'voluntary' act of the testatrix?"

as effective in apprising accused persons of their right of silence and in assuring a continuous opportunity to exercise it, the following safeguards must be observed.

At the outset, if a person in custody is to be subjected to interrogation, he must first be informed in clear and unequivocal terms that he has the right to remain silent. . . . [S]uch a warning is an absolute prerequisite in overcoming the inherent pressures of the interrogation atmosphere. . . . Further, the warning will show the individual that his interrogators are prepared to recognize his privilege should he choose to exercise it.

The Fifth Amendment privilege is so fundamental to our system of constitutional rule and the expedient of giving an adequate warning as to the availability of the privilege so simple, we will not pause to inquire in individual cases whether the defendant was aware of his rights without a warning being given. . . .

The warning of the right to remain silent must be accompanied by the explanation that anything said can and will be used against the individual in court. This warning is needed in order to make him aware not only of the privilege, but also of the consequences of forgoing it. . . . Moreover, this warning may serve to make the individual more acutely aware that he is faced with a phase of the adversary system — that he is not in the presence of persons acting solely in his interest.

The circumstances surrounding in-custody interrogation can operate very quickly to overbear the will of one merely made aware of his privilege by his interrogators. Therefore, the right to have counsel present at the interrogation is indispensable to the protection of the Fifth Amendment privilege under the system we delineate today. . . .

Accordingly we hold that an individual held for interrogation must be clearly informed that he has the right to consult with a lawyer and to have the lawyer with him during interrogation under the system for protecting the privilege we delineate today. . . .

In order fully to apprise a person interrogated of the extent of his rights under this system then, it is necessary to warn him not only that he has the right to consult with an attorney, but also that if he is indigent a lawyer will be appointed to represent him. . . .

Once warnings have been given, the subsequent procedure is clear. If the individual indicates in any manner, at any time prior to or during questioning, that he wishes to remain silent, the interrogation must cease. . . . If the individual states that he wants an attorney, the interrogation must cease until an attorney is present. . . .

This does not mean, as some have suggested, that each police station must have a "station house lawyer" present at all times to advise prisoners. It does mean, however, that . . . [i]f authorities conclude that they will not provide counsel during a reasonable period of time in which investigation in the field is carried out, they may refrain from doing so without violating the person's Fifth Amendment privilege so long as they do not question him during that time.

If the interrogation continues without the presence of an attorney and a statement is taken, a heavy burden rests on the government to demonstrate that the defendant knowingly and intelligently waived his privilege against self-incrimination and his right to retained or appointed counsel. . . .

An express statement that the individual is willing to make a statement and does not want an attorney followed closely by a statement could constitute a waiver. But a valid waiver will not be presumed simply from the silence of the accused after warnings are given or simply from the fact that a confession was in fact eventually obtained. . . .

Whatever the testimony of the authorities as to waiver of rights by an accused, the fact of lengthy interrogation or incommunicado incarceration before a statement is made is strong evidence that the accused did not validly waive his rights. . . . Moreover, any evidence that the accused was threatened, tricked, or cajoled into a waiver will, of course, show that the defendant did not voluntarily waive his privilege. . . .

The warnings required and the waiver necessary in accordance with our opinion today are, in the absence of a fully effective equivalent, prerequisites to the admissibility of any statement made by a defendant. No distinction can be drawn between statements which are direct confessions and statements which amount to "admissions" of part or all of an offense. . . . Similarly . . . no distinction may be drawn between inculpatory statements and statements alleged to be merely "exculpatory." If a statement made were in fact truly exculpatory it would, of course, never be used by the prosecution. . . .

The principles announced today deal with the protection which must be given to the privilege against self-incrimination when the individual is first subjected to police interrogation while in custody at the station or otherwise deprived of his freedom of action in any significant way. . . .

Our decision is not intended to hamper the traditional function of police officers in investigating crime. When an individual is in custody on probable cause, the police may, of course, seek out evidence in the field to be used at trial against him. . . . In such situations the compelling atmosphere inherent in the process of in-custody interrogation is not necessarily present.

In dealing with statements obtained through interrogation, we do not purport to find all confessions inadmissible. . . . There is no requirement that police stop a person who enters a police station and states that he wishes to confess to a crime, or a person who calls the police to offer a confession or any other statement he desires to make. Volunteered statements of any kind are not barred by the Fifth Amendment and their admissibility is not affected by our holding today. . . .

IV.

A recurrent argument made in these cases is that society's need for interrogation outweighs the privilege. . . . In announcing these principles, we are not unmindful of the burdens which law enforcement officials must bear, often under trying circumstances. . . . The limits we have placed on the interrogation process should not constitute an undue interference with a proper system of law enforcement. . . . Although confessions may play an important role in some convictions, the cases before us present graphic examples of the overstatement of the "need" for confessions. In each case authorities conducted interrogations ranging up to five days in duration despite the presence, through standard investigating practices, of considerable evidence against each defendant. . . .

Over the years the Federal Bureau of Investigation has compiled an exemplary record of effective law enforcement while advising any suspect or arrested person, at the outset of an interview, that he is not required to make a statement, that any statement may be used against him in court, that the individual may obtain the services of an attorney of his own choice and, more recently, that he has a right to free counsel if he is unable to pay. . . .

The practice of the FBI can readily be emulated by state and local enforcement agencies. The argument that the FBI deals with different crimes than are dealt with by state authorities does not mitigate the significance of the FBI experience. . . .

It is also urged upon us that we withhold decision on this issue until state legislative bodies and advisory groups have had an opportunity to deal with these problems by rule making. . . . Congress and the States are free to develop their own safeguards for the privilege, so long as they are fully as effective as those described above in informing accused persons of their right of silence and in affording a continuous opportunity to exercise it. In any event, however, the issues presented are of constitutional dimensions and must be determined by the courts. . . . Where rights secured by the Constitution are involved, there can be no rule making or legislation which would abrogate them.

V.

Because of the nature of the problem and because of its recurrent significance in numerous cases, we have to this point discussed the relationship of the Fifth Amendment privilege to police interrogation without specific concentration on the facts of the cases before us. . . . In each instance, we have concluded that statements were obtained from the defendant under circumstances that did not meet constitutional standards for protection of the privilege. . . .

MR. JUSTICE CLARK, dissenting in Nos. 759, 760, and 761, and concurring in the result in No. 584.

. . . I am unable to join the majority because its opinion goes too far on too little, while my dissenting brethren do not go quite far enough. Nor can I join in the Court's criticism of the present practices of police and investigatory agencies as to custodial interrogation. The materials it refers to as "police manuals" are, as I read them, merely writings in this field by professors and some police officers. . . . Moreover, the examples of police brutality mentioned by the Court are rare exceptions to the thousands of cases that appear every year in the law reports. The police agencies — all the way from municipal and state forces to the federal bureaus — are responsible for law enforcement and public safety in this country. I am proud of their efforts, which in my view are not fairly characterized by the Court's opinion.

I.

The *ipse dixit* of the majority has no support in our cases. Indeed, the Court admits that "we might not find the defendants' statements [here] to have been involuntary in traditional terms." . . . Now, the Court fashions a constitutional rule that the police may engage in no custodial interrogation without additionally advising the accused that he has a right under the Fifth Amendment to the presence of counsel during interrogation and that, if he is without funds, counsel will be furnished him. . . . Such a strict constitutional specific inserted at the nerve center of crime detection may well kill the patient. Since there is at this time a paucity of information and an almost total lack of empirical knowledge on the practical operation of requirements truly comparable to those announced by the majority, I would be more restrained lest we go too far too fast.

II.

Custodial interrogation has long been recognized as "undoubtedly an essential tool in effective law enforcement." Haynes v. State of Washington, 373 U.S. 503, 515 (1963). Recognition of this fact should put us on guard against the promulgation of doctrinaire rules. . . .

The rule prior to today—as Mr. Justice Goldberg, the author of the Court's opinion in *Escobedo*, stated it in *Haynes v. Washington*—depended upon "a totality of circumstances evidencing an involuntary . . . admission of guilt." . . .

I would continue to follow that rule. . . .

Mr. Justice Harlan, whom Mr. Justice Stewart and Mr. Justice White join, dissenting.

I believe the decision of the Court represents poor constitutional law and entails harmful consequences for the country at large. How serious these consequences may prove to be only time can tell. . . .

The Court's new rules aim to offset the[] minor pressures and disadvantages intrinsic to any kind of police interrogation. The rules do not serve due process interests in preventing blatant coercion since . . . they do nothing to contain the policeman who is prepared to lie from the start. The rules work for reliability in confessions almost only in the Pickwickian sense that they can prevent some from being given at all. . . .

What the Court largely ignores is that its rules impair, if they will not eventually serve wholly to frustrate, an instrument of law enforcement that has long and quite reasonably been thought worth the price paid for it.[13] There can be little doubt that the Court's new code would markedly decrease the number of confessions. . . .

How much harm this decision will inflict on law enforcement cannot fairly be predicted with accuracy. Evidence on the role of confessions is notoriously incomplete. . . . We do know that some crimes cannot be solved without confessions, that ample expert testimony attests to their importance in crime control, and that the Court is taking a real risk with society's welfare in imposing its new regime on the country. The social costs of crime are too great to call the new rules anything but a hazardous experimentation.

While passing over the costs and risks of its experiment, the Court portrays the evils of normal police questioning in terms which I think are exaggerated. Albeit stringently confined by the due process standards interrogation is no doubt often inconvenient and unpleasant for the suspect. However, it is no less so for a man to be arrested and jailed, to have his house searched, or to stand trial in court, yet all this may properly happen to the most innocent given probable cause, a warrant, or an indictment. Society has always paid a stiff price for law and order, and peaceful interrogation is not one of the dark moments of the law. . . .

. . . There is now in progress in this country a massive re-examination of criminal law enforcement procedures on a scale never before witnessed. . . . There are

---

[13] This need is, of course, what makes so misleading the Court's comparison of a probate judge readily setting aside as involuntary the will of an old lady badgered and beleaguered by the new heirs. With wills, there is no public interest save in a totally free choice; with confessions, the solution of crime is a countervailing gain, however the balance is resolved.

also signs that legislatures in some of the States may be preparing to re-examine the problem before us.

It is no secret that concern has been expressed lest long-range and lasting reforms be frustrated by this Court's too rapid departure from existing constitutional standards. . . . [T]he legislative reforms when they come would have the vast advantage of empirical data and comprehensive study, they would allow experimentation and use of solutions not open to the courts, and they would restore the initiative in criminal law reform to those forums where it truly belongs. . . .

Mr. Justice White, with whom Mr. Justice Harlan and Mr. Justice Stewart join, dissenting. . . .

. . . [T]he Court concedes that it cannot truly know what occurs during custodial questioning, because of the innate secrecy of such proceedings. It extrapolates a picture of what it conceives to be the norm from police investigatorial manuals. . . . Insofar as appears from the Court's opinion, it has not examined a single transcript of any police interrogation, let alone the interrogation that took place in any one of these cases which it decides today. Judged by any of the standards for empirical investigation utilized in the social sciences the factual basis for the Court's premise is patently inadequate. . . .

. . . Even if one were to postulate that . . . some . . . confessions are coerced and present judicial procedures are . . . inadequate to identify the confessions that are coerced and those that are not, it would still not be essential to impose the rule that the Court has now fashioned. Transcripts or observers could be required, specific time limits, tailored to fit the cause, could be imposed, or other devices could be utilized to reduce the chances that otherwise indiscernible coercion will produce an inadmissible confession.

. . . [E]ven if one assumed that there was an adequate factual basis for the conclusion that all confessions obtained during in-custody interrogation are the product of compulsion, the rule propounded by the Court will still be irrational, for, apparently, it is only if the accused is also warned of his right to counsel and waives both that right and the right against self-incrimination that the inherent compulsiveness of interrogation disappears. But if the defendant may not answer without a warning a question such as "Where were you last night?" without having his answer be a compelled one, how can the Court ever accept his negative answer to the question of whether he wants to consult his retained counsel or counsel whom the court will appoint? . . .

All of this makes very little sense in terms of the compulsion which the Fifth Amendment proscribes. . . . [T]he Court not only prevents the use of compelled confessions but for all practical purposes forbids interrogation except in the presence of counsel. . . .

IV. . . .

The most basic function of any government is to provide for the security of the individual and of his property. These ends of society are served by the criminal laws which for the most part are aimed at the prevention of crime. Without the reasonably effective performance of the task of preventing private violence and retaliation, it is idle to talk about human dignity and civilized values.

The modes by which the criminal laws serve the interest in general security are many. First the murderer who has taken the life of another is removed from the streets, deprived of his liberty and thereby prevented from repeating his offense. . . .

Secondly, the swift and sure apprehension of those who refuse to respect the personal security and dignity of their neighbor unquestionably has its impact on others who might be similarly tempted. . . .

Thirdly, the law concerns itself with those whom it has confined. The hope and aim of modern penology, fortunately, is as soon as possible to return the convict to society a better and more law-abiding man than when he left. . . .

The rule announced today will measurably weaken the ability of the criminal law to perform these tasks. . . . There is, in my view, every reason to believe that a good many criminal defendants who otherwise would have been convicted on what this Court has previously thought to be the most satisfactory kind of evidence will now, under this new version of the Fifth Amendment, either not be tried at all or will be acquitted if the State's evidence, minus the confession, is put to the test of litigation.

I have no desire whatsoever to share the responsibility for any such impact on the present criminal process.

In some unknown number of cases, the Court's rule will return a killer, a rapist or other criminal to the streets and to the environment which produced him, to repeat his crime whenever it pleases him. As a consequence, there will not be a gain, but a loss, in human dignity. The real concern is not the unfortunate consequences of this new decision on the criminal law as an abstract, disembodied series of author-itative proscriptions, but the impact on those who rely on the public authority for protection and who without it can only engage in violent self-help with guns, knives and the help of their neighbors similarly inclined. There is, of course, a saving fac-tor: the next victims are uncertain, unnamed and unrepresented in this case.

Nor can this decision do other than have a corrosive effect on the criminal laws as an effective device to prevent crime. A major component in its effectiveness in this regard is its swift and sure enforcement. The easier it is to get away with rape and murder, the less the deterrent effect on those who are inclined to attempt it. . . .

NOTES AND QUESTIONS

1. *What the doctrine does.* *Miranda* makes warnings and waivers prerequisites to admitting at trial statements made by defendants as a product of custodial inter-rogation. It also gives suspects some control over the interrogation room itself by requiring that questioning must stop, at least temporarily, if the defendant clearly invokes his rights. List the interrogation techniques that trouble the majority. Which does *Miranda* discourage? What is left?

2. *How* Miranda *works.* Assuming rational action, suspects confess because they believe the expected value of confessing is greater than the expected value of refusing to confess. Even an innocent person might confess to a crime if the gap in expected value between refusing to confess and confessing is large enough. See Richard J. Ofshe & Richard A. Leo, *The Decision to Confess Falsely: Rational Choice and Irrational Action,* 74 Denv. U. L. Rev. 979 (1997). During interrogations, police influ-ence both *actual* costs and benefits of these alternatives and suspects' *perceptions* of those costs and benefits. Beating a suspect to get him to confess increases the actual short-term costs of refusing to confess. Telling him that you will hold him until he confesses increases the perceived costs of continuing to refuse. Offering the suspect

MIRANDA WARNING

1. YOU HAVE THE RIGHT TO REMAIN SILENT.
2. ANYTHING YOU SAY CAN AND WILL BE USED AGAINST YOU IN A COURT OF LAW.
3. YOU HAVE THE RIGHT TO TALK TO A LAWYER AND HAVE HIM PRESENT WITH YOU WHILE YOU ARE BEING QUESTIONED.
4. IF YOU CANNOT AFFORD TO HIRE A LAWYER, ONE WILL BE APPOINTED TO REPRESENT YOU BEFORE ANY QUESTIONING IF YOU WISH.
5. YOU CAN DECIDE AT ANY TIME TO EXERCISE THESE RIGHTS AND NOT ANSWER ANY QUESTIONS OR MAKE ANY STATEMENTS.

WAIVER

DO YOU UNDERSTAND EACH OF THESE RIGHTS I HAVE EXPLAINED TO YOU?
HAVING THESE RIGHTS IN MIND, DO YOU WISH TO TALK TO US NOW?

A *Miranda* card for officers.

leniency increases the actual long-term benefits of confessing, at least if the offer is true. Involuntariness doctrine effectively restricts some methods of increasing the expected value gap. What do *Miranda* warnings do? What about the power *Miranda* gives to suspects to end the interrogation by invoking their rights? How might that affect the costs and benefits of talking or refusing to talk?

3. *The problem with policing.* The *Miranda* opinion assumes that some officers are so interested in convicting criminals that they engage in prolonged, isolated, and manipulative interrogations to obtain confessions. Even assuming this is the primary problem with police during criminal investigations, no police officer is born valuing criminal convictions more than the rights and dignity of suspects. If some do now, how might that have happened?

4. *Solutions for policing.* One way to read *Miranda* is that the Court felt forced to impose its prophylactic scheme at least in part because (state) courts did not use the involuntariness standard to properly control the police. In *Miranda*, as in *Mapp v. Ohio*, 367 U.S. 643 (1961), discussed in Chapter 12, and *Katz v. United States*, 389 U.S. 347 (1967), discussed in Chapter 2, the Warren Court can be read as imposing procedural requirements to force state courts to regulate the police better. Assuming the Court was right about policing and state courts, what else might the Court have done?

5. *Known unknowns.* Although the majority in *Miranda* attempts to describe police practices far more thoroughly than it does in other criminal procedure cases, all the Justices agree that they know little about what police do or about how *Miranda*'s protections might affect convictions and crime control. The majority reasons that:

(a) police-dominated, incommunicado interrogations can produce involuntary confessions;
(b) confessions induced under these conditions are common;
(c) the *Miranda* scheme will protect suspects from involuntary confessions; and
(d) the *Miranda* scheme will not undermine crime control, which will proceed without some confessions.

Justice Clark rejects (b) as unsupported and inconsistent with his intuition, and rejects (d) as too risky given the unknowns. Justice Harlan rejects both (a) and (d). Justice White finds (a) unsupported, (c) illogical, and (d) unlikely. Their debate provides a useful reminder: All regulation gets made with limited information. Courts have an especially hard time developing that information, and they have no choice but to decide cases in the meantime.

6. Miranda*'s consequences.* Law enforcement, which initially viewed *Miranda* as a bitter pill, now widely accepts it: It offers clear guidance and manageable burdens. Moreover, around 80 percent of suspects waive their rights and make statements that can be used against them after they are warned. Indeed, "[n]ext to the warning label on cigarette packs, *Miranda* is the most widely ignored piece of official advice in our society." Patrick A. Malone, *"You Have the Right to Remain Silent":* Miranda *After Twenty Years,* 55 Am. Scholar 367, 368 (1986). So the

dissenters' fears were never realized. Some would argue that neither were the majority's hopes:

> First, the warnings are so full of omissions and inaccuracies that they actually constitute deception by police officers to arrestees. Second, *Miranda* warnings perversely assist those least in need; wealthy suspects and recidivists. Almost everyone else . . . waives their *Miranda* rights, a move that is virtually never in their self-interest, and demonstrates that the *Miranda* decision did nothing to alleviate whatever inherent compulsion is part of the custodial interrogation experience. . . . Though police continue to employ the same tactics they used prior to *Miranda*, the fact that the warnings were read essentially guarantees that any subsequent statements are admitted as voluntary. . . .

Susan R. Klein, *Transparency and Truth During Custodial Interrogations and Beyond*, 97 B.U. L. Rev. 993, 1004 (2017). Still, because of *Miranda*, officers are better trained in constitutional law, less likely to mislead suspects about their rights, and subject to more monitoring in the interrogation room. How should we decide if *Miranda* has been successful? What more would you want to know before opining?

Miranda Doctrine Since *Miranda*

Whatever the initial import of *Miranda*, subsequent Supreme Court cases have notably reduced its scope and effects.

- *Custody. Miranda* applies only to *custodial* interrogation, and the Court has interpreted custody narrowly. When a suspect is detained in an ordinary traffic or pedestrian stop, he is not free to leave, but he is not in custody. See Berkemer v. McCarty, 468 U.S. 420, 437–438 (1984). Usually, custody requires an arrest, and sometimes, even that is not enough: Prisoners are often not in custody for the purposes of *Miranda*. See Howes v. Fields, 565 U.S. 499, 508–512 (2012).
- *Interrogation.* The Court appears to define interrogation more broadly, applying it "not only to express questioning, but also to any words or actions on the part of the police . . . that the police should know are reasonably likely to elicit an incriminating response." Rhode Island v. Innis, 446 U.S. 291, 301 (1980). However, the Court has narrowly applied this test. See *id.* at 294–295; Arizona v. Mauro, 481 U.S. 520 (1987). Even express questioning is not covered by *Miranda* if it is carried out by an undercover officer. See Illinois v. Perkins, 496 U.S. 292 (1990).
- *Invocation.* Although an officer must stop an interrogation if the suspect invokes his right to counsel or right to silence, only an "unambiguous" invocation has effect. If a suspect says only, "Maybe I want a lawyer," officers have no obligation to clarify and are free to continue questioning. See Berghuis v. Thompkins, 560 U.S. 370, 381–382 (2010); Davis v. United States, 512 U.S. 452, 459 (1994).
- *Waivers.* Although *Miranda* purported to make waivers difficult to establish, the Court has more recently held that if a suspect is given warnings, understands them, and does not unambiguously invoke his rights, his subsequent

Dickerson v. United States, 530 U.S. 428, 443–444 (2000). Is Justice Rehnquist suggesting that *Miranda* is constitutional *because* it is toothless?

This low-key fight over §3501 raises some questions.

1. *Best regulator.* If we were starting from scratch, which branch would be best situated to handle the problem of police interrogations? Why?
2. *Court vs. Congress.* Should the Court have waited for Congress? Once *Miranda* was decided, was §3501 a legitimate response to test the Court's resolve?
3. *Career vs. political.* What should happen when career prosecutors resist the President's appointees? What about when a U.S. Attorney (who serves at the pleasure of the President) disagrees with the U.S. Attorney General (who serves at the pleasure of the President)?
4. *Courts vs. the executive branch.* Did the Fourth Circuit overstep when it ruled on a question that no party had argued and no court had considered to issue an opinion that was at least in tension with, if not one that overturned, *Miranda*? Or did it merely prevent Main Justice from thwarting Congress?

The U.S. Supreme Court's ruling in *Dickerson* ended the free-for-all, clearly establishing the constitutionality and stability—although not the scope and impact—of *Miranda*.

D.   Interrogation After Miranda

If police read *Miranda* warnings to defendants and generally respect their rights when they invoke them, how do police continue to obtain confessions at such a high rate? They avoid invocations and they secure waivers. How do they do *that*?

1.   Deception and the Neutron Proton Negligence Intelligence Test

Miranda permits a significant amount of manipulation and trickery. The Supreme Court has "never read the Constitution to require that the police supply a suspect with a flow of information to help him calibrate his self-interest in deciding whether to speak or stand by his rights." Moran v. Burbine, 475 U.S. 412, 422 (1986). Thus, police interrogation techniques are designed to ensure that even if defendants understand their rights, they do not understand their interests.

For an illustration, consider *People v. Smith*, 150 P.3d 1224 (Cal. 2007). Defendant Robert Lee Smith was convicted of murdering his ex-girlfriend, Michelle Dorsey, and her brother, James Martin. Smith was sentenced to death. According to evidence at trial, Smith shot Dorsey and Martin with the help of a 14-year-old boy, Joseph A., to access the cash in Dorsey's safe ($100). The police twice interrogated Smith. The first interview began on the evening of March 25, 1991, and lasted six hours, concluding during the early morning hours of March 26. The second interview took place on the afternoon of March 26, less than 12 hours after the conclusion of the first interview, and lasted for an hour and a half.

During the first interview, Smith initially denied any involvement or knowledge of the murders. Later in the interview, he acknowledged that he was present but denied killing the victims. Instead, he claimed that two men came to the apartment to rob Dorsey and had killed Dorsey and Martin with the help of Joseph. Smith admitted only that he helped after the killings and took some of the money.

During the second interrogation, after the police had interviewed Joseph, Smith admitted that he and Joseph had planned to rob Dorsey and that no one else was present, but he claimed that Joseph had shot both victims. At trial, the defense pursued—and the jury apparently rejected—a theory consistent with Smith's second statement, claiming that the boy, rather than Smith, was the killer.

On appeal, Smith claimed that admitting his confessions at trial violated his constitutional rights because his statements were involuntary and unreliable. Among his arguments, Smith maintained that he had been misled about the availability of counsel during his interrogation. According to the record, defendant had asked the detective who advised him of his rights, "[I]f I don't talk to you now, how long will it take for me to talk to you 'fore a person sent a lawyer to be here?" Before the detective could answer the question, Smith told the detective, "I could wait 'til next week sometime." Detective Kimura said, "Maybe, yeah." Smith then told the detective, "I'll talk to you now. I don't got nothing to hide." Smith contended that this left him with the impression that he might have to wait a week before counsel would be available to him. The court rejected his claim:

> Contrary to defendant's contention that Detective Kimura "lied" about the availability of counsel, Detective Kimura did not actively mislead defendant. Detective Kimura never told defendant that it would take a week for counsel to be appointed, but merely responded equivocally to defendant's statement that he could wait up to a week for counsel to be appointed. The detective never represented to defendant that it actually would take up to a week for counsel to be appointed.
>
> Although defendant posits that Kimura should have corrected defendant's assumption that it could take up to a week to get counsel, he cites no authority for the proposition that a suspect who has received and understood the *Miranda* advisements cannot properly waive his Fifth Amendment rights if he labors under any misapprehension of the mechanics of when and how counsel is appointed. Indeed, several federal circuit courts have held that a suspect's *Miranda* waiver remains valid even if interrogating officers mislead the suspect about how long it will take to appoint counsel.

Smith, 150 P.3d at 1240.

Miranda and the Right(s) to Counsel

When lawyers talk about the right to counsel, they usually mean the *Sixth Amendment* right to counsel. The Sixth Amendment states, "In all criminal prosecutions, the accused shall enjoy the right . . . to have the Assistance of Counsel for his defence." U.S. Const. amend. VI. Once the Sixth Amendment right to counsel applies, deliberately obtaining a confession from a suspect without a lawyer present or a waiver of the right to counsel violates that right. See Massiah v. United States, 377 U.S. 201 (1964). Because the first thing most lawyers tell their clients is to shut up, confessions are rarer after that point, except as part of a deal. But the Sixth Amendment right to counsel "attaches" only after a defendant is charged with a crime and judicial proceedings begin, usually when he shows up for his first appearance.

Miranda effectively creates a mini right to counsel under the Fifth Amendment that may apply before then. Unlike the Sixth Amendment, however, *Miranda's* mini right to counsel does not guarantee a lawyer; it only guarantees that if a suspect unambiguously asks for a lawyer, and he does not initiate a conversation with the police, he will not be

> questioned in custody without one. See Oregon v. Bradshaw, 462 U.S. 1039 (1983). Thus, police interrogate many suspects after they are taken into custody and removed from family and friends, but before the initial appearance, when the Sixth Amendment right kicks in, and *Miranda* does not usually stop them.

Smith also argued that his confession was coerced because during the second interrogation the detectives conducted a fictitious "Neutron Proton Negligence Intelligence Test":

> In the first step of the "test," the detectives sprayed defendant's hands with soap and patted them with a paper towel. In the second step, they used a field test kit used for testing substances suspected of being cocaine, which the detectives knew inevitably would turn color. Detective Kimura told defendant that the test had provided proof that defendant had recently fired a gun. Defendant continued to deny shooting Dorsey and Martin. However, defendant did admit that only he and Joseph were involved in the murders, and that the two other men he had said were involved in the crimes had not been present.

Id. at 1238. This admission was obviously important at trial because it suggested that, by Smith's own account, either he or a 14-year-old boy must have committed the murders. Nevertheless, the court rejected his claim that the sham test rendered his statements involuntary:

> Police deception "does not necessarily invalidate an incriminating statement." People v. Maury, 68 P.3d 1, 51 (Cal. 2003). Courts have repeatedly found proper interrogation tactics far more intimidating and deceptive than those employed in this case. See, e.g., Frazier v. Cupp, 394 U.S. 731, 739 (1969) (officer falsely told the suspect his accomplice had been captured and confessed); People v. Jones, 949 P.2d 890 (Cal. 1998) (officer implied he could prove more than he actually could); People v. Thompson, 785 P.2d 857 (Cal. 1990) (officers repeatedly lied, insisting they had evidence linking the suspect to a homicide); In re Walker, 518 P.2d 1129 (Cal. 1974) (wounded suspect told he might die before he reached the hospital, so he should talk while he still had the chance); People v. Watkins, 85 Cal. Rptr. 621 (Cal. Ct. App. 1970) (officer told suspect his fingerprints had been found on the getaway car, although no prints had been obtained); Amaya–Ruiz v. Stewart, 121 F.3d 486, 495 (9th Cir. 1997) (suspect falsely told he had been identified by an eyewitness). Indeed, at least one [California] Court of Appeal has approved of the particular practice used in this case. People v. Parrison, 187 Cal. Rptr. 123 (Cal. Ct. App. 1982) (police falsely told suspect a gun residue test produced a positive result).
>
> After examining the circumstances surrounding the "Neutron Proton Negligence Intelligence Test," it does not appear that the tactic was so coercive that it tended to produce a statement that was involuntary or unreliable. In any event, we also note that the officers' tactic in using the fake test was unsuccessful in eliciting a confession; defendant never confessed to having been the shooter, but instead steadfastly denied having shot the gun.

Id. at 1241–1242. Smith also claimed that his personal background included physical, psychological, and sexual abuse; mental illness; and significant brain damage that disabled him from giving a voluntary statement. The Court reasoned that this background was irrelevant to voluntariness unless the police also engaged in misconduct. *Id.* at 1239.

NOTES AND QUESTIONS

1. *Con games.* By allowing suspects to stop interrogations, and yet leaving alone trickery, *Miranda* would seem to encourage officers to avoid coercion that leads to invocation and instead use manipulation, as in *Smith*. Richard A. Leo, who has long studied interrogations and the effects of *Miranda*, has described post-*Miranda* interrogation as a confidence game.

> . . . Like confidence men, police interrogators attempt to induce compliance from their suspects by offering them the hope of a better situation in exchange for incriminating information. The interrogator exercises power through his ability to frame the suspect's definition of the situation, exploiting the suspect's ignorance to create the illusion of a relationship that is symbiotic rather than adversarial. . . .

> . . . No longer premised on force or duress, police power inside the interrogation room is based on, and limited by, the social psychology of persuasion.

Richard A. Leo, Miranda*'s Revenge: Police Interrogation as a Confidence Game*, 30 Law & Soc'y Rev. 259, 264–265, 284–285 (1996). Is that a problem? Is there something wrong with manipulation that produces true, lawful, and uncoerced confessions?

In Heironymus Bosch's painting *The Conjurer*, circa 1502, a magician keeps the audience's attention, while a collaborator relieves one man of his money.

2. Miranda *and involuntariness.* Although *Miranda* supplements rather than replaces due process protections, *Smith* and cases like it suggest that courts evaluate more skeptically claims that confessions are involuntary when the suspect has received *Miranda* warnings. To courts, "it seems self-evident that one who is told he is free to refuse to answer questions is in a curious posture to later complain that his answers were compelled." United States v. Washington, 431 U.S. 181, 188 (1977). The Supreme Court has encouraged this trend. In *Berkemer v. McCarty,* 468 U.S. 420, 433 n.20 (1984), it noted, "We do not suggest that compliance with *Miranda* conclusively establishes the voluntariness of a subsequent confession. But cases in which a defendant can make a colorable argument that a self-incriminating statement was 'compelled' despite the fact that the law enforcement authorities adhered to the dictates of *Miranda* are rare." Similarly, in *Missouri v. Seibert,* 542 U.S. 600, 608–609 (2004), the Court said, "[G]iving the warnings and getting a waiver has generally produced a virtual ticket of admissibility; maintaining that a statement is involuntary even though given after warnings and voluntary waiver of rights requires unusual stamina, and litigation over voluntariness tends to end with the finding of a valid waiver." See also Michael J. Zydney Mannheimer, Gideon, Miranda, *and the Downside of Incorporation,* 12 Ohio St. J. Crim. L. 401, 430–432 (2015) (describing how "[t]his curious dictum has been treated as a normative gloss on the doctrine," leading to a "presumption of non-coercion," sometimes even in cases of egregious police conduct). In this way, a case intended to provide additional regulation of the police has ended up replacing a substantive measure of police coercion with an easy-to-satisfy procedural safe harbor.

3. *False confessions.* Neither *Miranda* doctrine nor the Due Process Clause concerns itself with whether the confession is *true,* and no constitutional right bars having a false confession introduced at trial. Instead, courts rely on juries to decide how reliable confessions are. According to the Supreme Court, "A fundamental premise of our criminal trial system is that the *jury* is the lie detector. Determining the weight and credibility of witness testimony, therefore, has long been held to be the part of every case that belongs to the jury, who are presumed to be fitted for it by their natural intelligence and their practical knowledge of men and the ways of men." United States v. Scheffer, 523 U.S. 303, 313 (1998). In this sense, confessions are like other witness statements.

Still, anyone who cares about public safety and criminal justice should care very much about whether a defendant's statements are true since false confessions may lead innocent people to be convicted and guilty people to remain unadjudicated. Although no one can say how often deceptive techniques lead to false confessions, techniques that confront a malleable suspect with allegedly incontrovertible evidence of guilt sometimes lead suspects to believe that they must have committed the crime, even though they do not remember doing so. Young and mentally impaired suspects seem especially vulnerable. See Saul M. Kassin et al., *Police-Induced Confessions: Risk Factors and Recommendations,* 34 Law & Hum. Behav. 3, 15–17 (2010). Will juries know that? Should the police be forbidden from using interrogation techniques that can produce false confessions? What law should govern such techniques?

Where Do False Confessions Come From?

False confessions are not just a product of police pressure; they are a product of police construction. Studying 40 confessions that DNA testing later proved false, Brandon Garrett found that

> innocent people not only falsely confessed, but they also offered surprisingly rich, detailed, and accurate information. Exonerees told police much more than just "I did it." In all cases but two . . . police reported that suspects confessed to a series of specific details concerning how the crime occurred. Often those details included reportedly "inside information" that only the rapist or murderer could have known. We now know that each of these people was innocent and was not at the crime scene.

Brandon L. Garrett, *The Substance of False Confessions*, 62 Stan. L. Rev. 1051, 1054 (2010). Those details made the confessions especially powerful. In many cases Garrett studied, police testified at trial that they had not provided the crime details to the defendant, and prosecutors argued to the jury that only the person who had committed the crime could have known the specific, nonpublic facts in the defendant's confession. Nevertheless, in most of these cases, the details clearly came from the police. See *id.* at 410–415.

Sometimes providing details for false confessions might be intentional, but officers can also contaminate confessions by accident. They might ask a leading question ("So you went in the window, right?"), which provides the right answer, or they might ask a forced-choice question ("Did you use a belt or a rope?"), which gives suspects a 50–50 chance of guessing, and then unintentionally telegraph which response they are looking for, or they might just ask about a detail again and again, until the suspect gets it "right." They might show the suspect evidence, such as crime-scene photographs, that reveals details that the suspect then reaches for when pressured to confess. Or an officer might confront a suspect with evidence to persuade him that resistance is futile ("Let us tell you what we know"), only to forget later that they had done so. See James L. Trainum, *"I Did It"—Confession Contamination and Evaluation*, Police Chief (June 2014). Can you think of interrogation rules and practices that could mitigate the risk of contaminated statements?

---

4. *Alternatives to deception.* Some law enforcement organizations have replaced techniques based on deception, accusatory questions, minimizations of blameworthiness, and assumptions of guilt with new strategies. The "PEACE" model of interrogation (Preparation and Planning; Engage and Explain; Account; Closure; and Evaluation), was developed in the United Kingdom and has been adopted in New Zealand, Norway, and Canada. Instead of lying, psychological coercion, or reliance on behavioral cues to detect deception, it calls for explaining honestly the purpose of the interview, actively listening to the interviewee, and giving the interviewee a chance to provide a full account before challenging statements with valid evidence. See Brent Snook et al., *The Next Stage in the Evolution of Interrogations: The PEACE Model*, 18 Can. Crim. L. Rev. 219, 230–235 (2014) (describing the PEACE model). After the Bush Administration drew criticism for coercively interrogating suspected

terrorists after 9/11, the Obama Administration organized the High-Value Detainee Interrogation Group (HIG), an interagency team of interrogators, which developed a technique of its own. The HIG technique is similar to PEACE in focusing on preparation, rapport, and using information strategically. It also added "cognitive load" strategies intended to trip up liars without coercion or deception. See Christopher Slobogin, *Manipulation of Suspects and Unrecorded Questioning: After Fifty Years of Miranda Jurisprudence, Still Two (or Maybe Three) Burning Issues*, 97 B.U. L. Rev. 1157, 1161–1162 (2017); High-Value Detainee Interrogation Group, Fed. Bureau of Investigation, *Interrogation Best Practices* (Aug. 26, 2016). Neither technique is common in local law enforcement. What could change that? What would you want to know before you decided whether these techniques should be adopted widely or required?

5. *State law on recording interrogations.* All of the regulation of interrogations assumes that courts and juries can determine what happened in the interrogation room. But even officers trying to be honest are likely to remember fewer promises, threats, and false statements than they actually made during an interrogation. See Saul M. Kassin et al., *Police Reports of Mock Suspect Interrogations: A Test of Accuracy and Perception*, 41 Law & Hum. Behav. 230 (2017). Audio- or videotaping interrogations can mitigate this problem by revealing deception, coercion, and promises of leniency, or establishing their absence.

According to federal courts, neither the *Miranda* doctrine nor the Due Process Clause require recording interrogations. Cf. Christopher Slobogin, *Toward Taping*, 1 Ohio St. J. Crim. L. 309 (2003) (arguing that taping interrogations is constitutionally required). Still, half of the states mandate, either by statute or state constitutional law, that the police record at least some custodial interrogations. (In two more (small) states, Hawaii and Rhode Island, all law enforcement agencies have agreed to record custodial interrogations, and in other states, many police departments require recording as a matter of agency policy.)

Among states that have them, however, recording laws vary in their scope and strength. Few states require recording for all offenses, and some laws are limited to a narrow range of crimes. With respect to remedies, a few states mandate by statute that unrecorded statements be excluded at trial; others create a rebuttable presumption against admitting the statement; and some leave the matter to the court. Two states impose a recording requirement but do not impose any remedy, at least by statute. See Brandon L. Bang et al., *Police Recording of Custodial Interrogations: A State-by-State Legal Inquiry*, 20 Int'l J. of Pol. Sci. & Management 3 (2018) (surveying state laws). A wide array of national organizations from the NAACP to the Major Cities Chiefs Association endorse recording interrogations. In 2014, the FBI reversed its long-standing opposition and began recording. Why might states still be reluctant to require recordings or impose stronger laws?

6. *Is the world better with Miranda?* Let's say that the police techniques in *Smith* are more likely because of *Miranda*. Given what you know, is the interrogation room likely a better place with *Miranda* than without it? What kind of information about interrogations would help you to decide?

2. Lie Detection

The Neutron Proton Negligence Intelligence Test at issue in *People v. Smith* sounds ridiculous. But subjecting suspects to a pseudo-scientific test, telling them it contradicts their story, and then using that to interrogate them further is not against the law, and it is not uncommon. In fact, one could argue that it is standard operating procedure. It is called a polygraph test.

Polygraph testing combines interrogation with physiological measurements obtained using the polygraph, or polygraph instrument, a piece of equipment that records physiological phenomena—typically, respiration, heart rate, blood pressure, and electrodermal response (electrical conductance at the skin surface). A polygraph examination includes a series of yes/no questions to which the examinee responds while connected to sensors that transmit data on these physiological phenomena by wire to the instrument, which uses analog or digital technology to record the data. Because the original analog instruments recorded the data with several pens writing lines on a moving sheet of paper, the record of physiological responses during the polygraph test is known as the polygraph chart. . . .

A polygraph *test* is part of a polygraph *examination*, which includes other components. A critical one . . . is the pretest interview. This interview typically has multiple purposes. It explains the test procedure to the examinee. . . . The pretest interview shapes the expectations and emotional state of the examinee during the test. It may be used to convince the examinee that the polygraph instrument will detect any deception. This process often involves a demonstration in which the examinee is asked to lie about an unimportant matter, and the examiner shows the instrument's ability to detect the lie; these demonstrations sometimes involve deceiving the examinee. . . .

A polygraph test and its result are a joint product of an interview or interrogation technique and a psychophysiological measurement or testing technique. It is misleading to characterize the examination as purely a physiological measurement technique. Polygraph examiners' training implicitly recognizes this point in several ways. It provides instruction on the kind of atmosphere that is to be created in the pretest interview, advises on techniques for convincing examinees of the accuracy of the test, and offers guidance (in different ways for different test formats) for selecting comparison questions. Examiners are advised to control these details—sometimes following carefully specified procedures—because they can affect test results.

Polygraph examination procedures often explicitly combine and interweave testing and interviewing. When a polygraph chart indicates something other than an ordinary nondeceptive response to a relevant question, the examiner typically pursues this response with questioning during the course of the examination. For example, the examiner may say, "You seem to be having a problem in the area of X [the relevant item]" and ask the examinee if he or she can think of a reason for having a strong physiological reaction to that question.

Nat'l Research Council of the Nat'l Academies, *The Polygraph and Lie Detection* 12–17 (2003).

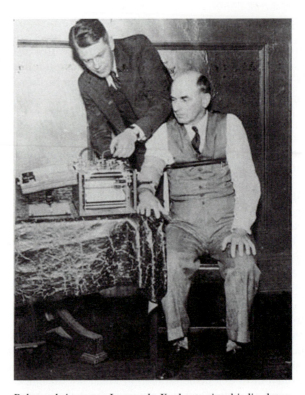

Polygraph inventor Leonarde Keeler testing his lie detector on a man who previously served as a witness in the 1935
trial of Bruno Hauptmann. Hauptmann was convicted of
abducting and murdering the young son of aviator Charles
Lindbergh and his wife Anne Morrow Lindbergh and was
executed in 1936.

Despite the white coats polygraph examiners often wear, these tests are not
grounded in good science. According to the National Research Council of the
National Academy of Sciences,

> Almost a century of research in scientific psychology and physiology provides little
> basis for the expectation that a polygraph test could have extremely high accuracy.
> Although psychological states often associated with deception (e.g., fear of being
> judged deceptive) do tend to affect the physiological responses that the polygraph
> measures, these same states can arise in the absence of deception. Moreover, many
> other psychological and physiological factors (e.g., anxiety about being tested) also
> affect those responses. Such phenomena make polygraph testing intrinsically sus-
> ceptible to producing erroneous results. This inherent ambiguity of the physiolog-
> ical measures used in the polygraph suggests that further investments in improving
> polygraph technique and interpretation will bring only modest improvements in
> accuracy.

Id. at 2. Nor do polygraphs play out that well in practice. While the National
Research Council concluded that the polygraphs produce results that are above
chance when questioning individuals about specific past events, it also noted that the
research is extremely limited. Inevitably, the tests produce both false positives and

false negatives, and there is virtually no standardization of protocols. Instead, the polygraph tests conducted in the field depend greatly on the practices of individual examiners. "Thus, even if laboratory-based estimates of criterion validity are accurate, the implications for any particular field polygraph test are uncertain." *Id.* at 204.

For these reasons, prosecutors consistently and successfully fight defendants' efforts to introduce negative polygraph results in criminal cases. Yet the police often ask suspects to submit to polygraph examinations. Why? Because polygraphs serve as an effective interrogation tool, whether or not they work at detecting lies. As the National Research Council notes:

> One role of the polygraph test is to help elicit admissions from people who believe, or are influenced to believe, that it will accurately detect any deception they may attempt. This role is demonstrated most clearly when a polygraph examination is terminated because of an admission before any charts are done. Such an examination can be thought of as an interrogation interview conducted in the presence of a polygraph. In this case, the polygraph test has a useful role independently of whether it can accurately detect deception: it is effective if the examinee believes it can detect deception. Admissions of this kind provide evidence of the value of the polygraph examination for investigative purposes, but they do not provide evidence that the polygraph test accurately detects deception.

Id. at 22. The use of polygraphs as an interrogation technique is so common, it has been called "the fourth degree." David T. Lykken, *A Tremor in the Blood: Uses and Abuses of the Lie Detector* 242 (1998). Polygraphers gently question suspects about their "lies" and the suspects make statements. "If all polygraphs were stage props it is likely that just as many admissions or confessions would be elicited." *Id.* at 246.

Another way to look at this is that the polygraph examination functions in much the same way as the Neutron Proton Negligence Intelligence Test in *Smith.* It cloaks a police-driven interrogation in a white lab coat and disguises the state's role behind the persuasive and mechanical authority of science. Cf. Andrea Roth, *Trial by Machine*, 104 Geo. L.J. 1245, 1276–1277 (2016) (discussing the role of machines, including polygraphs, in criminal adjudication). Courts universally reject evidence that a defendant passed or failed a polygraph in criminal cases. See United States v. Scheffer, 523 U.S. 303 (1998). Yet they often admit polygraph-driven confessions.

E.   *Obtaining Evidence from Witnesses: Eyewitness Identifications*

Police can seek confessions only from suspects they have already identified. How do they identify suspects? The officer might arrive at a crime scene while the perpetrator is still present, victims or witnesses who know the perpetrator might identify him immediately, or physical evidence might lead to a particular suspect. Many serious crimes, however, cannot be solved unless a witness who did not previously know the suspect identifies him.

1.   Identifications: The Basics

There are three basic methods for having a witness identify a perpetrator. *Photo arrays* are the most common. Witnesses are presented with photographs, either sequentially or all together, and asked whether they recognize anyone. The photographs include the suspect and *fillers*, which are pictures of other individuals who match characteristics witnesses have identified in the perpetrator. One typical array, often called a "six pack," includes six headshot photos arranged in two rows of three on a single page. A *live lineup* similarly presents the suspect and fillers selected for similar physical characteristics, such as gender, race, hair length and color, facial hair, and height. A *showup* is a procedure in which the police show only one person to a witness and ask whether the witness recognizes that person. It often occurs shortly after a crime at or near the crime location. Once a witness identifies a suspect, that identification is frequently used to support an arrest and to help the government prove the identity of the criminal at trial.

Photo array used to identify Juan Balderas, including a witness's signature over Balderas's face. Balderas is the only person shown in a black hoodie with a dark mark on his face, which is how the witness described the perpetrator before the lineup. The witness initially expressed uncertainty, saying that Balderas "could be the shooter." The next day, after the officer went back to her and coached her, she became positive Balderas was the right man. More than eight years later, she testified at Balderas's trial that she was sure that Balderas was the shooter. No fingerprints, DNA, or other physical evidence linked Balderas to the crime, but Balderas was arrested in possession of the murder weapon, and a fellow gang member (who later recanted) testified against him in exchange for lesser charges in an unrelated capital murder case. Balderas was convicted and sentenced to death. Although courts expressed concern about the suggestiveness of the lineup, they affirmed his conviction. Balderas continues to proclaim his innocence from death row. See Casey Tolan, *Lining Up a Conviction*, Tex. Observer (Feb. 16, 2017).

Eyewitness identifications are far from infallible, and eyewitnesses often do not know whether their identification is reliable or not.

> [M]any factors influence the visual perceptual experience: dim illumination and brief viewing times, large viewing distances, duress, elevated emotions, and the presence of a visually distracting element such as a gun or a knife. Gaps in sensory input are filled by expectations that are based on prior experiences with the world. Prior experiences are capable of biasing the visual perceptual experience and reinforcing an individual's conception of what was seen. We also have learned that these qualified perceptual experiences are stored by a system of memory that is highly malleable and continuously evolving, neither retaining nor divulging content in an informational vacuum. The fidelity of our memories to actual events may be compromised by many factors at all stages of processing, from encoding to storage to retrieval. Unknown to the individual, memories are forgotten, reconstructed, updated, and distorted. Therefore, caution must be exercised when utilizing eyewitness procedures and when relying on eyewitness identifications in a judicial context.

Nat'l Research Council of the Nat'l Academies, *Identifying the Culprit: Assessing Eyewitness Identification* 1 (2014). As this suggests, a witness sometimes gets an identification wrong because of conditions relating to the crime or the witness's opportunity to view the perpetrator: A witness might be stressed by the nature of the events or distracted by the presence of a gun. The perpetrator's face might be obscured by a mask or a hood. Or the witness might see the perpetrator from far away or in low light.

Cross-Race Identifications

In eyewitness identification, own-race bias describes the phenomenon in which faces of people of races different from that of the eyewitness are harder to discriminate (and thus harder to identify accurately) than are faces of people of the same race as the eyewitness. In the laboratory, this effect is manifested by higher hit rates and lower false alarm rates (higher diagnosticity ratio) in the recognition of an observer's own race relative to hits and false alarms for recognition of other races. Own-race bias occurs in both visual discrimination and memory tasks, in laboratory and field studies, and across a range of races, ethnicities, and ages. Recent analyses revealed that cross-racial (mis)identification was present in 42 percent of the cases in which an erroneous eyewitness identification was made. . . .

Although the existence of own-race bias is generally accepted, the causes for this effect are not fully understood. Some possible explanations are rooted in in-group/out-group models of human behavior (e.g., favoritism in which decisions regarding members of one's own "group" are regarded as having greater importance than decisions regarding members of a different "group") and differential perceptual expertise that results from different degrees of exposure to and familiarity with same versus other races.

Nat'l Research Council of the Nat'l Academies, *Identifying the Culprit: Assessing Eyewitness Identification* 96–97 (2014). The problem of own-race bias in cross-race identifications can easily reinforce other inequities and disparities in policing. Before a witness makes an identification, police disproportionately scrutinize and arrest Black individuals.

When it comes time to make an identification, studies suggest that own-race bias is strongest when white witnesses attempt to identify Black individuals. Officers, too, who are mostly white, could suffer from own-race bias when they set up identifications and choose dissimilar fillers that further reduce witness accuracy. Juries that are also predominantly white might then overvalue white cross-race identifications because of their own stereotypes of Black criminality. And so on. Racial biases, combined with apparently neutral police activities, can easily make trials less accurate and do so disproportionately in the cases of individuals already suffering unfairly in the criminal process.

Although the police cannot control factors related to the witness's original look at the perpetrator, many other factors that influence the reliability of eyewitness identifications are within law enforcement control. These factors, often called *system variables*, include "the type of presentation (e.g., lineup) used, the likeness of non-suspect lineup participants (fillers) to the suspect, the number of fillers, and the suspect's physical location in the presentation," as well as whether "images are presented—simultaneously (as a group) or consequentially (one at a time)," and "the nature of the instructions and feedback provided before and after the identification procedure." *Id.* at 16–17. Officers can unwittingly steer eyewitnesses toward an identification ("We've got him, but we need you to point him out") or increase the confidence of an uncertain witness ("You did great").

In these ways, police practices can undermine the reliability of initial identifications and contaminate future identifications, which in turn can leave violent criminals on the street and lead innocent individuals to be convicted. The Innocence Project has collected many such cases, including these two described on its website:

- Malcolm Alexander was sentenced to life without parole in Louisiana in 1980 for rape. He served 38 years before he was exonerated on the basis of DNA testing of hairs found at the crime scene. The victim's assailant had been behind her for the entirety of the crime but she "tentatively" selected Alexander out of a photo array more than four months after the crime. Police conducted a physical lineup three days later, with Alexander the only person in both the lineup and the photo array. The victim made a "possible" identification of Alexander that was subsequently recorded as a statement that she was 98 percent sure it was Alexander. The actual perpetrator was never identified.
- Antonio Beaver was sentenced to 18 years for robbery in Missouri in 1997. The victim claimed that her assailant was a clean-shaven Black man wearing a baseball cap, who was 5'10" and possessed a gap in his teeth. A detective subsequently arrested Beaver six days later on the basis of a composite sketch, despite Beaver being 6'2", with a full mustache and chipped teeth. Beaver was identified in a live lineup of four people, in which only he and another man had on baseball caps and he was the only person with noticeable teeth defects. After more than a decade, Beaver

was exonerated when a blood stain left by the assailant was DNA tested, leading to the positive identification of the actual perpetrator.

Indeed, according to the Innocence Project, mistaken identifications were present in more than 70 percent of the wrongful convictions in the United States subsequently overturned by postconviction DNA evidence. They were more often a factor than any other cause of wrongful convictions. Because DNA evidence is available in few criminal cases, many convictions could have resulted from mistaken identifications that have never been identified.

2. Constitutional Regulation

a. The U.S. Supreme Court's First Pass—Sixth Amendment Right to Counsel

The Court's first major pass at regulating police identification procedures came through the Sixth Amendment. In *United States v. Wade*, 388 U.S. 218, 227–235 (1967), the Court held that criminal defendants have the right to counsel at postindictment lineups:

> The Government characterizes the lineup as a mere preparatory step in the gathering of the prosecution's evidence, not different—for Sixth Amendment purposes—from various other preparatory steps, such as systematized or scientific analyzing of the accused's fingerprints, blood sample, clothing, hair, and the like. We think there are differences which preclude such stages being characterized as critical stages at which the accused has the right to the presence of his counsel. Knowledge of the techniques of science and technology is sufficiently available, and the variables in techniques few enough, that the accused has the opportunity for a meaningful confrontation of the Government's case at trial through the ordinary processes of cross-examination of the Government's expert witnesses and the presentation of the evidence of his own experts. The denial of a right to have his counsel present at such analyses does not therefore violate the Sixth Amendment; they are not critical stages since there is minimal risk that his counsel's absence at such stages might derogate from his right to a fair trial.
>
> But the confrontation compelled by the State between the accused and the victim or witnesses to a crime to elicit identification evidence is peculiarly riddled with innumerable dangers and variable factors which might seriously, even crucially, derogate from a fair trial. The vagaries of eyewitness identification are well-known; the annals of criminal law are rife with instances of mistaken identification. . . . A major factor contributing to the high incidence of miscarriage of justice from mistaken identification has been the degree of suggestion inherent in the manner in which the prosecution presents the suspect to witnesses for pretrial identification. . . . And the dangers for the suspect are particularly grave when the witness' opportunity for observation was insubstantial, and thus his susceptibility to suggestion the greatest.
>
> Moreover, "[i]t is a matter of common experience that, once a witness has picked out the accused at the line-up, he is not likely to go back on his word later on, so that in practice the issue of identity may (in the absence of other relevant evidence) for all practical purposes be determined there and then, before the trial." Williams & Hammelmann, *Identification Parades, Part I*, 1963 Crim. L. Rev. 479, 482.
>
> The pretrial confrontation for purpose of identification may take the form of a lineup, also known as an "identification parade" or "showup," as in the present case,

or presentation of the suspect alone to the witness. . . . It is obvious that risks of suggestion attend either form of confrontation and increase the dangers inhering in eyewitness identification. But as is the case with secret interrogations, there is serious difficulty in depicting what transpires at lineups and other forms of identification confrontations. . . . For the same reasons, the defense can seldom reconstruct the manner and mode of lineup identification for judge or jury at trial. Those participating in a lineup with the accused may often be police officers; in any event, the participants' names are rarely recorded or divulged at trial. . . . In any event, neither witnesses nor lineup participants are apt to be alert for conditions prejudicial to the suspect. And if they were, it would likely be of scant benefit to the suspect since neither witnesses nor lineup participants are likely to be schooled in the detection of suggestive influences. . . . Moreover, any protestations by the suspect of the fairness of the lineup made at trial are likely to be in vain; the jury's choice is between the accused's unsupported version and that of the police officers present. In short, the accused's inability effectively to reconstruct at trial any unfairness that occurred at the lineup may deprive him of his only opportunity meaningfully to attack the credibility of the witness' courtroom identification. . . .

Insofar as the accused's conviction may rest on a courtroom identification in fact the fruit of a suspect pretrial identification which the accused is helpless to subject to effective scrutiny at trial, the accused is deprived of that right of cross-examination which is an essential safeguard to his right to confront the witnesses against him. . . . [I]n the present context, where so many variables and pitfalls exist, the first line of defense must be the prevention of unfairness and the lessening of the hazards of eyewitness identification at the lineup itself.

NOTES AND QUESTIONS

1. *Are identifications different?* *Wade* is premised on the idea that witness identifications are significantly different from other forms of police evidence collection before trial, including witness interviews that produce a description of the crime and suspect. Do you agree? Is cross-examination a sufficient method of ensuring that those methods do not go awry? What is the alternative? Constitutionalizing all evidence collection?

2. *What can counsel do?* How does the Court think counsel who attend lineups can check suggestive and unreliable police practices? Do you agree with the Court's reasoning?

3. *Legislative alternatives.* In a part not excerpted above, the *Wade* Court, like the *Miranda* Court, invited legislative alternatives to constitutional doctrine. In justifying court action, it said, "Legislative or other regulations, such as those of local police departments, which eliminate the risks of abuse and unintentional suggestion at lineup proceedings and the impediments to meaningful confrontation at trial may also remove the basis for regarding the stage as 'critical.' But neither Congress nor the federal authorities have seen fit to provide a solution." If a state now regulates witness identifications by requiring them to be recorded or by regulating identification procedures, could the government then argue there is no right to counsel at witness identifications?

4. *Impact of* Wade. Subsequent cases have limited the impact of *Wade*. Most notably, *Wade* applies only to postindictment lineups. Kirby v. Illinois, 406 U.S. 682, 690 (1972). It also applies only to live lineups, and not to photo arrays. United States v. Ash, 413 U.S. 300, 321 (1973). Investigators can often determine the type

and timing of lineups, and in practice most identifications happen by photos or in lineups before indictment. The reality is that *Wade* is easily and often avoided by the police. Does it remain valuable? How?

b.   The U.S. Supreme Court's Second Pass—The Due Process Clause and Evidence Reliability

In *Manson v. Brathwaite*, 432 U.S. 98 (1977), the Court built on prior cases to rule that the Due Process Clause requires excluding evidence produced by an unnecessarily or impermissibly suggestive identification procedure, but only if the evidence is also unreliable. The Court instructed lower courts to use five factors in evaluating the reliability of an identification:

1. The opportunity of the witness to view the criminal at the time of the crime;
2. The witness's degree of attention;
3. The accuracy of his prior description of the criminal;
4. The level of certainty demonstrated at the confrontation; and
5. The time between the crime and the confrontation.

Against these factors is to be weighed the corrupting effect of the suggestive identification itself. *Id.* at 114.

c.   The Scientific Consensus

The science of eyewitness identifications has grown rapidly since the 1970s, and the research has not borne out the *Manson* Court's intuitions about what contributes to reliability. As the National Research Council put it:

> The *Manson v. Brathwaite* test . . . evaluates the "reliability" of eyewitness identifications using factors derived from prior rulings and not from empirically validated sources. It includes factors that are not diagnostic of reliability and treats factors such as the confidence of a witness as independent markers of reliability when, in fact, it is now well established that confidence judgments may vary over time and can be powerfully swayed by many factors. The best guidance for legal regulation of eyewitness identification evidence comes not, however, from constitutional rulings, but from the careful use and understanding of scientific evidence to guide fact-finders and decision makers.

Nat'l Research Council of the Nat'l Academies, *Identifying the Culprit: Assessing Eyewitness Identification* 44 (2014). Instead, the National Research Council recommended best practices to law enforcement agencies to improve identifications, including training all officers on eyewitness identification, implementing double-blind lineup and photo array procedures, standardizing the instructions given to witnesses, documenting verbatim the witness's stated confidence at the time of the identification, and videotaping the identification process. *Id.* at 105–109. A 2020 review of the scientific evidence on law enforcement practices that can undermine witness identifications made nine recommendations for law enforcement:

1. Conduct a recorded, prelineup interview documenting the witness's description of the suspect, circumstances of the viewing, and familiarity with the suspect.
2. Attempt an identification only if there is documented, preidentification evidence pointing to the suspect.
3. Use double-blind identification procedures in which neither the administrator nor the witness knows the identity of the suspect in the lineup.
4. Use only one suspect per lineup and use at least five fillers who match the suspect adequately so that he does not stand out.
5. Avoid providing eyewitnesses information about whether a suspect has been arrested or will be present in the lineup. Instead, instruct witnesses before the identification that the administrator does not know which person is the suspect, that the culprit may not be present, that the witness should state that they do not know if they are unable to make a decision, that they will be asked about their confidence, and that investigation will continue even if the witness does not make an identification.
6. Record the witness's confidence immediately after an identification decision (whether or not the witness identifies the suspect).
7. Video-record the entire procedure.
8. Avoid having the same eyewitness attempt to identify the same suspect in a subsequent procedure.
9. Avoid showups.

Gary L. Wells et al., *Policy and Procedure Recommendations for the Collection and Preservation of Eyewitness Identification Evidence*, 44 Law & Hum. Behav. 3, 8–9 (2020).

d.   The U.S. Supreme Court Avoids a Third Pass

In the face of growing scientific consensus, even before the National Research Council report and 2020 review on eyewitness identifications, many hoped the Court would reconsider the *Manson* factors for reliability and revise its thinking on regulating witness identifications when it took a case on the issue in 2011.[4] Instead, the Court reiterated the *Manson* factors and narrowed the applicability of the Due Process Clause by concluding that the totality of the circumstances test established in *Manson* and prior cases does not apply if the "the suggestive circumstances were not arranged by law enforcement officers." Perry v. New Hampshire, 565 U.S. 228, 232 (2012).

In *Perry*, the police interviewed a witness in her apartment. When asked for a description of the person she saw breaking into cars, she pointed out her window and identified the suspect, who was standing outside at the crime scene next to a police officer who had detained him. As the Court noted, "there were reasons to question the accuracy of [the witness's] identification: The parking lot was dark in some locations; Perry was standing next to a police officer; Perry was the only

---

[4] Although *Perry v. New Hampshire* was decided before the National Research Council issued its report, Keith Findley points out that the best practices recommended were already well-established in other reports, were accepted by state attorneys general and state commissions and, as noted below, had already been implemented in significant part as a matter of law in some states. Keith A. Findley, *Implementing the Lessons from Wrongful Convictions: An Empirical Analysis of Eyewitness Identification Reform Strategies*, 81 Mo. L. Rev. 377, 387–388 (2016).

African-American man in the vicinity; and [the witness] was unable, later, to pick Perry out of a photographic array." *Perry*, 565 U.S. at 235. The police had not asked her whether Perry was the person she saw and did not move her near the window. As a result, the fact that the identification took place under suggestive circumstances did not violate Perry's right to due process. The Court held:

> The Constitution, our decisions indicate, protects a defendant against a conviction based on evidence of questionable reliability, not by prohibiting introduction of the evidence, but by affording the defendant means to persuade the jury that the evidence should be discounted as unworthy of credit. Constitutional safeguards available to defendants to counter the State's evidence include the Sixth Amendment rights to counsel, compulsory process, and confrontation plus cross-examination of witnesses. Apart from these guarantees, we have recognized, state and federal statutes and rules ordinarily govern the admissibility of evidence, and juries are assigned the task of determining the reliability of the evidence presented at trial. Only when evidence "is so extremely unfair that its admission violates fundamental conceptions of justice," Dowling v. United States, 493 U.S. 342, 352 (1990), have we imposed a constraint tied to the Due Process Clause.

Perry, 565 U.S. at 237. That last constraint does not kick in unless the police arrange the suggestive procedures, which in *Perry* they did not.

NOTES AND QUESTIONS

1. *Bad for eyewitness identifications; good for enthusiasts of constitutional police regulation? Perry* and the rest of constitutional regulation of witness identification have been widely criticized as failures, and many would like to see eyewitness identifications better regulated by constitutional law. But could those interested in regulating the police see this decision differently?

The Court in *Perry* emphasized that its prior due process rulings on witness identifications were primarily intended "to deter law enforcement use of improper lineups, showups, and photo arrays in the first place." *Perry*, 565 U.S. at 241. Similarly, *Wade*'s imposition of counsel for postindictment lineups was intended to prevent "police rigging" of witness identifications. *Id.* at 242. Because *Perry* was a case with no police misconduct, the Court viewed other constitutional trial protections and nonconstitutional legal rules as adequate to protect the suspect's interests. *Perry* therefore can be read as an opinion in which a majority of the Court clearly reaffirms the use of constitutional law, under both the Due Process Clause and the Sixth Amendment, as a tool for influencing police behavior and preventing misconduct. Right?

2. *Is there a difference?* If so, call Justice Sotomayor skeptical about the Court's capacity to set standards that will lead lower courts to carve out police misconduct from other causes of suggestive identifications. She criticized the Court's opinion for "enshrin[ing] a murky distinction—between suggestive confrontations intentionally orchestrated by the police and, as here, those inadvertently caused by police actions." *Perry*, 565 U.S. at 250 (Sotomayor, J., dissenting). Does the Court's long experience setting standards for other constitutional criminal procedure doctrines give her cause?

3.   State Law and Departmental Policies

Although scientific research has not informed the Supreme Court's constitutional regulation of witness identifications, it has influenced the states. In a few, state courts have stepped in, requiring jury instructions or restricting the admissibility of some eyewitness evidence as a matter of state constitutional law, see State v. Henderson, 27 A.3d 872 (N.J. 2011), or state evidentiary law, see, e.g., State v. Lawson, 291 P.3d 673 (Or. 2012). Eighteen other states have passed statutes regulating eyewitness identification procedures. Consider how well these two statutes live up to the scientific consensus on best practices.

CAL. PENAL CODE §859.7

§859.7. Conducting photo lineups and live lineups with eyewitnesses; regulations developed to ensure reliable and accurate suspect identifications; requirements; application to field show up procedures; effect on admissibility of evidence standards

(a) All law enforcement agencies and prosecutorial entities shall adopt regulations for conducting photo lineups and live lineups with eyewitnesses. The regulations shall be developed to ensure reliable and accurate suspect identifications. In order to ensure reliability and accuracy, the regulations shall comply with, at a minimum, the following requirements:

> **(1)** Prior to conducting the identification procedure, and as close in time to the incident as possible, the eyewitness shall provide the description of the perpetrator of the offense.
>
> **(2)** The investigator conducting the identification procedure shall use blind administration or blinded administration during the identification procedure. . . .
>
> **(4)** An eyewitness shall be instructed of the following, prior to any identification procedure:
>
> > **(A)** The perpetrator may or may not be among the persons in the identification procedure.
> >
> > **(B)** The eyewitness should not feel compelled to make an identification.
> >
> > **(C)** An identification or failure to make an identification will not end the investigation.
>
> **(5)** An identification procedure shall be composed so that the fillers generally fit the eyewitness' description of the perpetrator. In the case of a photo lineup, the photograph of the person suspected as the perpetrator should, if practicable, resemble his or her appearance at the time of the offense and not unduly stand out. . . .
>
> **(7)** Only one suspected perpetrator shall be included in any identification procedure.
>
> **(8)** All eyewitnesses shall be separated when viewing an identification procedure.
>
> **(9)** Nothing shall be said to the eyewitness that might influence the eyewitness' identification of the person suspected as the perpetrator.
>
> **(10)** If the eyewitness identifies a person he or she believes to be the perpetrator, all of the following shall apply:

(A) The investigator shall immediately inquire as to the eyewitness' confidence level in the accuracy of the identification and record in writing, verbatim, what the eyewitness says.

(B) Information concerning the identified person shall not be given to the eyewitness prior to obtaining the eyewitness' statement of confidence level and documenting the exact words of the eyewitness.

(C) The officer shall not validate or invalidate the eyewitness' identification.

(11) An electronic recording shall be made that includes both audio and visual representations of the identification procedures. Whether it is feasible to make a recording with both audio and visual representations shall be determined on a case-by-case basis. When it is not feasible to make a recording with both audio and visual representations, audio recording may be used. When audio recording without video recording is used, the investigator shall state in writing the reason that video recording was not feasible.

(b) Nothing in this section is intended to affect policies for field show up procedures. . . .

(d) Nothing in this section is intended to preclude the admissibility of any relevant evidence or to affect the standards governing the admissibility of evidence under the United States Constitution. . . .

WIS. STAT. §175.50

175.50 Eyewitness identification procedures

. . . **(2)** Each law enforcement agency shall adopt written policies for using an eyewitness to identify a suspect upon viewing the suspect in person or upon viewing a representation of the suspect. The policies shall be designed to reduce the potential for erroneous identifications by eyewitnesses in criminal cases. . . .

(4) In developing and revising policies under this section, a law enforcement agency shall consider model policies and policies adopted by other jurisdictions.

(5) A law enforcement agency shall consider including in policies adopted under this section practices to enhance the objectivity and reliability of eyewitness identifications and to minimize the possibility of mistaken identifications, including the following:

(a) To the extent feasible, having a person who does not know the identity of the suspect administer the eyewitness' viewing of individuals or representations.

(b) To the extent feasible, showing individuals or representations sequentially rather than simultaneously to an eyewitness.

(c) Minimizing factors that influence an eyewitness to identify a suspect or overstate his or her confidence level in identifying a suspect, including verbal or nonverbal reactions of the person administering the eyewitness' viewing of individuals or representations.

(d) Documenting the procedure by which the eyewitness views the suspect or a representation of the suspect and documenting the results or outcome of the procedure.

NOTES AND QUESTIONS

1. *Best practices?* Do these statutes ensure that police policies on eyewitness identification will comport with best practices outlined above? How do they succeed? Fail?

2. *Multiple approaches.* How do these statutes differ from each other?

3. *Costs and benefits.* Clearly, we should work to ensure that innocent people are never convicted. But it would be hard to support a law that eliminated wrongful convictions by preventing all rightful ones. Bringing guilty people to justice reaffirms commitment to law, vindicates the interests of victims, and protects public safety. Much of the research on eyewitness identification focuses on improving the accuracy of identifications that are made. What if best practices also reduce some percentage of accurate identifications? How should states considering evidence-based reforms factor in concerns about the accuracy, efficiency, and fairness of the criminal justice system as a whole?

4. *Remedies.* What is the remedy if a department violates these statutes? Some states are more explicit. For example, Florida's statute requiring officers to follow blind identification procedures and to issue instructions to the eyewitness states this about remedies:

> **(4) Remedies.** — All of the following remedies are available as consequences of compliance or noncompliance with any requirement of this section:
>
>> **(a) 1.** A failure on the part of a person to comply with any requirement of this section shall be considered by the court when adjudicating motions to suppress eyewitness identification.
>>
>> **2.** A failure on the part of a person to comply with any requirement of this section is admissible in support of a claim of eyewitness misidentification, as long as such evidence is otherwise admissible.
>
>> **(b)** If evidence of compliance or noncompliance with any requirement of this section is presented at trial, the jury shall be instructed that the jury may consider credible evidence of compliance or noncompliance to determine the reliability of eyewitness identifications.

Fla. Stat. §92.70. States more typically permit a trial judge to consider the failure to follow the state law in considering the admissibility of an identification and to inform the jury about the failure. Few require excluding the identification evidence at trial. What about for defendants who plead guilty after an identification that does not comply with recognized best practices? Should those individuals have a remedy? Does it matter if they are innocent or not?

5. *Showups.* Although other statutes limit them, California's statute expressly exempts showups. Why distinguish showups?

> A showup is a procedure in which a single suspect is presented for identification within a short time after and in close proximity to the scene of the crime. The rationale for using this inherently suggestive procedure is that police want to obtain an identification of the offender while the witness's memory is fresh, or where, for logistical and legal reasons, they cannot construct a photo array or live lineup. "Research indicates, however, that showups produce higher rates of mistaken identification than do simultaneous lineups or sequential lineups, even when the witness is tested soon after the witnessed event." Wells, *Systemic Reforms* at 628. For this reason, most courts generally view showups with disfavor, although they nonetheless tend to permit them. Police tend to like showups, both because

they are easy to conduct quickly, and because they can use them even where they lack probable cause to detain the person while they conduct a photo array or live lineup.

Keith A. Findley, *Implementing the Lessons from Wrongful Convictions: An Empirical Analysis of Eyewitness Identification Reform Strategies*, 81 Mo. L. Rev. 377, 398–399 (2016). Given this, why might the statute avoid addressing showups?

6. *California's path to §859.7.* California began studying eyewitness identifications in 2004 when it appointed a commission to identify safeguards against wrongful convictions. In 2006, the commission recommended legislation to create a task force to develop guidelines for eyewitness identification policies and procedures, and the California legislature passed such a bill, but Governor Arnold Schwarzenegger vetoed it as unclear. In 2007, another California commission on criminal justice reform outlined best practices for eyewitness identifications for law enforcement agencies and recommended legislation. The legislature again acted. It passed a bill calling for two state agencies to develop evidence-informed guidelines, which would be transmitted back to the legislature for further action. S.B. 756, 2007-08 Leg., Reg. Sess. (Cal. 2007). Again, the governor vetoed the legislation as going "too far." Gov. Arnold Schwarzenegger, Veto Message on S.B. 756 (Oct. 13, 2007). The governor's veto message asserted (in direct conflict with the language of the bill) that the bill would require local law enforcement agencies to adopt whatever guidelines the state agencies recommended, and it reasoned, "Law enforcement agencies must have the authority to develop investigative policies and procedures that they can mold to their unique local conditions and logistical circumstances rather than be restricted to methods created that may make sense from a broad statewide perspective." *Id.* Effectively, Governor Schwarzenegger vetoed a bill to study and develop guidelines that could inform legislation because it intruded too heavily on local authority. The issue was left to local jurisdictions, and the results were "spotty." Most departments failed to adopt best practices. See Findley, *supra*, at 422–423. It took several more years, several more efforts, and several more statutes in other states before Section 859.7 passed. It was signed by Governor Jerry Brown on September 30, 2018, and went into effect on January 1, 2020. Can we glean anything about the challenges of reform from this story?

7. *What kind of regulation?* California and Wisconsin and almost all other states with eyewitness identification statutes require that police departments adopt policies. Virginia's guidelines might be the simplest. Its statute, passed in 2005 after a series of high-profile DNA exonerations involving eyewitness errors, states in full:

POLICIES AND PROCEDURES FOR LAW ENFORCEMENT TO CONDUCT IN-PERSON AND PHOTO LINEUPS

The Department of State Police and each local police department and sheriff's office shall establish a written policy and procedure for conducting in-person and photographic lineups.

Va. Code. Ann. §19.2-390.02. Even in some states without statutes, agencies have issued model policies for police departments. In some jurisdictions, police departments have revised eyewitness identification policies on their own. As this description suggests, there are four state approaches to regulating witness identifications:

1. Leave the matter to departments.
2. Support departmental reform through training and model policies.
3. Mandate that agencies adopt policies.
4. Mandate or restrict identification procedures.

What might be some advantages and disadvantages of each approach? Do you have intuitions about the best approach? Are those views specific to eyewitness identifications or generalizable to other police practices? Does it matter that far more research has been done on eyewitness identifications than other police practices? Note that none of these approaches determines whether departmental policy will be translated effectively into officer practice. Can the law help with that?

8. *Regulatory success or regulatory failure?* Most experts complain that police practices on eyewitness identifications have changed too slowly and unevenly to be deemed a real win, and that the law has not gone far enough to help. Still, far more progress has been made toward improving identifications than reducing racial disparities in traffic and pedestrian stops or reducing the use of excessive force, areas where law reform has been more sporadic. Compared to those, identification reform can only be described as a roaring success.

Or look at what you already know about the law of interrogations. Problems with interrogations have been well known since the beginning of the twentieth century. Although the U.S. Supreme Court stepped in early in *Brown v. Mississippi*, 297 U.S. 278 (1936), and forcefully in *Miranda v. Arizona*, both regimes are viewed almost universally as failures. Neither offers much opportunity for future development either in the Supreme Court or in federal legislative action. State legislatures have had little to add, and state courts only a little more. Why might problems with interrogations and identifications be different? Here are some possibilities. Interrogations involve:

- Less consensus about the nature of the problem.
- Less research about best practices.
- Best practices that are less easily summarized and harder to adopt.
- Problems that hurt the guilty as well as the innocent.

What might the contrast teach us about reforming the police through law?

Fixing Witness Interviews

Police interview thousands of witnesses each day, and the information they derive often plays an important role in determining whether police solve the crime and bring the right person to justice. Witness recall in interviews is often partial or inaccurate even without poor interviewing methods. Just as with identifications, improper interview techniques can increase inaccuracy, limit the information police obtain, and contaminate witness memory for the future. Researchers have long agreed that officers should do the following:

- Encourage witnesses to disclose information through simple, open-ended questions that allow witnesses to provide a narrative rather than using suggestive or yes/no questions.
- Reduce interruptions and distractions.

- Build rapport with witnesses.
- Instruct witnesses not to guess about information and to report uncertainty.

Yet officers continue to interview witnesses with leading, complex, and staccato questions, with regular interruptions and with a confrontational style, because they believe these techniques are more effective. See Dana Hirn Mueller et al., *Productive and Counterproductive Interviewing Techniques: Do Law Enforcement Investigators Know the Difference?*, 21 Psychol., Pub. Pol'y & L. 295, 296, 300 (2015).

Unlike interrogations and identifications, witness interviews are almost entirely unregulated by law. Many agencies have no policies on interviews and take no other steps to ensure that officers follow best practices. If a criminal justice reform group came to you and asked for a strategy to improve witness interviews, what would you recommend? Are there any legal reforms you think might be warranted?

Chapter 4

Handling and Disclosing Evidence

According to the Uniform Crime Reports data collected by the FBI, violent crime rates in the United States are down more than 50 percent since their heights in the early 1990s. Still, crime remains a significant social problem. More than a million Americans are victims of violent crimes each year. In addition, more than 7 million burglaries, larcenies, motor vehicle thefts, and arsons occur annually. Those crimes hurt individuals and undermine the quality of life in communities, and some suffer far more than others. For example, in 2018, Black respondents to the National Crime Victimization Survey reported suffering serious crimes at a rate more than 40 percent higher than non-Hispanic whites did. Income effects are even greater: People in low-income households experienced violent crime at several times the rate of their richer peers. See Rachel E. Morgan & Barbara A. Oudekerk, *U.S. Bureau of Justice Statistics, Criminal Victimization, 2018*, at 10 (2019).

Addressing crime means both preventing it before it occurs and bringing perpetrators to justice afterward. The next chapter considers some contemporary crime prevention efforts by the police. Like the last two, this chapter considers an aspect of police efforts to bring perpetrators to justice: To classify a crime, identify the culprit, and ensure that justice is done, our criminal justice system relies on evidence, including physical evidence left at the scene by the victim and perpetrator. That evidence can include fingerprints, semen, blood, fibers, weapons, documents, illegal drugs, cash, paraphernalia, computers, phones, and so on. That evidence must be collected, packaged, documented, stored, and secured by a law enforcement agency; analyzed and perhaps scientifically examined; and then used by the prosecutor, and sometimes by the defense, in court. Although many participants in the criminal justice system interact with evidence, police play a special role in recognizing and collecting evidence, ensuring its integrity, and making it available for use.

To a significant degree, police handle evidence based on what could happen in court. A police officer documents narcotics found during a traffic stop in anticipation of a defense attorney's motion to suppress. Police collect evidence at a murder scene looking ahead to the government's need to prove guilt beyond a reasonable doubt. They store, preserve, and document evidence so as to follow court rules that govern authentication and identification and to stand up to any cross-examination about its reliability and integrity. In this way, the police solve and help prove crimes in the manner court proceedings encourage.

Notably, however, anticipating court proceedings sometimes focuses officers on convicting those charged at the expense of identifying the right suspect or protecting others from false accusations. Thus, although police treatment of evidence ideally helps bring the guilty to justice, vindicate victims, make trials fairer, and deter future criminal activity, things are not always ideal. Police sometimes fail to collect evidence, inadequately preserve and test it, or fail to share it with prosecutors, keeping it out of a defendant's hands. At their worst, officers lie, generating evidence that imprisons the innocent, frees the guilty, and undermines faith in government.

This chapter considers legal doctrines that purport to mitigate these risks. The first section considers the police role in collecting and turning over evidence to defendants. The second considers the limited constitutional obligations officers have to preserve and test evidence. The third considers damages actions against officers for failing to disclose evidence to prosecutors. The last section considers the law that governs access to and disclosure of evidence that could be used to impeach officers at trial.

As you will see, the law is not extensive, yet it highlights how law governing the adjudicative process might (or might not) affect the policing that comes before it; it demonstrates how actors with no direct power over the police—namely, prosecutors—can nevertheless function as indirect regulators of them; and it illustrates some of the limits of individual constitutional rights in exposing and deterring police misconduct.

A.   Police as Producers of Discoverable Evidence

1.   Police Role in Disclosure to Defendants

One way the Due Process Clause ensures that criminal defendants get a fair trial is by requiring the government to turn over favorable, material evidence in its possession. This duty is often referred to as the government's "Brady obligation," named after the Supreme Court case *Brady v. Maryland*, 373 U.S. 83 (1963), in which the Court clearly articulated the right. The Supreme Court has imposed the burden of satisfying this right primarily on prosecutors, but, by natural implication, the *Brady* doctrine reaches police conduct as well. In this excerpt from a more recent case, the Court overviews the *Brady* doctrine and the police role in it:

> The prosecution's affirmative duty to disclose evidence favorable to a defendant can trace its origins to early 20th-century strictures against misrepresentation and is of course most prominently associated with this Court's decision in *Brady v. Maryland*, 373 U.S. 83 (1963). *Brady* held "that the suppression by the prosecution of evidence favorable to an accused upon request violates due process where the evidence is material either to guilt or to punishment, irrespective of the good faith or bad faith of the prosecution." 373 U.S. at 87. . . .
>
> In . . . *United States v. Bagley*, 473 U.S. 667 (1985), the Court disavowed any difference between exculpatory and impeachment evidence for *Brady* purposes. . . . *Bagley* held that regardless of request, favorable evidence is material, and constitutional error results from its suppression by the government, "if there is a reasonable probability that, had the evidence been disclosed to the defense, the result of the proceeding would have been different." 473 U.S. at 682. . . .
>
> While the definition of *Bagley* materiality in terms of the cumulative effect of suppression must accordingly be seen as leaving the government with a degree of discretion, it must also be understood as imposing a corresponding burden. On the one side, showing that the prosecution knew of an item of favorable evidence unknown to the defense does not amount to a *Brady* violation, without more. But

the prosecution, which alone can know what is undisclosed, must be assigned the consequent responsibility to gauge the likely net effect of all such evidence and make disclosure when the point of "reasonable probability" is reached. This in turn means that the individual prosecutor has a duty to learn of any favorable evidence known to the others acting on the government's behalf in the case, including the police. But whether the prosecutor succeeds or fails in meeting this obligation (whether, that is, a failure to disclose is in good faith or bad faith), the prosecution's responsibility for failing to disclose known, favorable evidence rising to a material level of importance is inescapable.

The State of Louisiana would prefer an even more lenient rule. It . . . suggested below that it should not be held accountable under *Bagley* and *Brady* for evidence known only to police investigators and not to the prosecutor. . . . In the State's favor it may be said that no one doubts that police investigators sometimes fail to inform a prosecutor of all they know. But neither is there any serious doubt that "procedures and regulations can be established to carry [the prosecutor's] burden and to insure communication of all relevant information on each case to every lawyer who deals with it." Giglio v. United States, 405 U.S. 150, 154 (1972). Since, then, the prosecutor has the means to discharge the government's *Brady* responsibility if he will, any argument for excusing a prosecutor from disclosing what he does not happen to know about boils down to a plea to substitute the police for the prosecutor, and even for the courts themselves, as the final arbiters of the government's obligation to ensure fair trials.

Kyles v. Whitley, 514 U.S. 419, 432–438 (1995).

NOTES AND QUESTIONS

1. Brady *summary.* As *Kyles* indicates, the *Brady* doctrine obligates prosecutors to turn material, favorable evidence over to defendants before trial. Favorable evidence includes both evidence that negates guilt and evidence that can be used to impeach the government's trial witnesses. "[E]vidence is material only if there is a reasonable probability that, had the evidence been disclosed to the defense, the result of the proceeding would have been different." United States v. Bagley, 473 U.S. 667, 682 (1985). If material, favorable evidence is not turned over to a defendant and a conviction results, the conviction must be overturned. *Kyles,* 514 U.S. at 435–436.

What Does Exculpatory Evidence Look Like?

Here are some common forms of evidence that can be favorable to defendants:

Exculpatory Evidence

- Suggests that the defendant was misidentified
- Suggests that the defendant was elsewhere at the time of the crime
- Suggests that the defendant had a legal defense (e.g., self-defense)
- Indicates that a witness failed to identify the defendant, identified someone else as the culprit, or was uncertain in identifying the defendant
- Suggests that the crime was less serious than charged (e.g., no weapon)
- Can be used to impeach a government witness

Here are some kinds of evidence that fit into that last category:

Impeachment Evidence

- Evidence that conditions during the crime or a witness's capacity to perceive did not permit the witness's stated perceptions
- Prior inconsistent or false statements by a witness
- Promises of leniency or other inducements made to a witness
- Prior criminal convictions or bad acts that suggest untruthfulness
- Reputation for untruthfulness
- Evidence of drug or alcohol use
- Evidence indicating bias or motive to testify against the defendant

2. *Does* Brady *work?* As a scheme for ensuring fair trials, *Brady* has problems. How well a penalty deters depends largely on how severe the penalty is and how swiftly and certainly it is imposed. *Brady* violations are difficult to discover, and the legal standard of materiality is highly malleable, so even when prosecutors violate *Brady*, they are unlikely to face consequences. When they are "punished" for *Brady* violations, it is only by having their convictions overturned. They rarely get disciplined and effectively never get prosecuted or face damages actions for *Brady* violations. When a conviction is reversed, it is often years or decades after the original violation. Ethical prosecutors still try to follow *Brady*, but they likely underestimate how favorable or material evidence is and often lack systematic means for ensuring that they collect and disclose all relevant evidence. For one description of *Brady*'s problems, see Daniel S. Medwed, Brady'*s Bunch of Flaws*, 67 Wash. & Lee L. Rev. 1533 (2010). Many wrongful conviction cases have involved *Brady* violations, and that comes as no surprise because the *Brady* doctrine does little to incentivize compliance.

3. *Disclosure beyond* Brady. *Brady* establishes a constitutional baseline for disclosing evidence to defendants. State and local statutes, rules of criminal procedure, and rules of professional conduct for prosecutors often require more. For example, almost every state follows Model Rule of Professional Conduct §3.8(d), which requires turning over *all* favorable evidence and characterizes favorable evidence broadly. Some state statutes go further still. Florida, for example, permits defendants to take depositions of individuals with relevant information, including informal depositions of law enforcement witnesses. See Fla. R. Crim. P. 3.220(b)(1)(A). North Carolina requires that prosecutors share "any other matter or evidence obtained during the investigation of the offenses alleged to have been committed by the defendant." N.C. Gen. Stat. §15A-903(a)(1)(a). See Darryl K. Brown, *Discovery*, in 3 *Reforming Criminal Justice* 147, 155–158 (Erik Luna ed. 2017) (providing an overview of discovery rules and variation among the states). However, these rules tend to be no more aggressively enforced than *Brady*.

4. Brady *and the police*. What does all this have to do with policing? As *Kyles* suggests, prosecutors and police work together. The police collect most criminal evidence, so if they do not find or keep exculpatory evidence and give it to prosecutors, prosecutors cannot disclose it to defendants. *Brady*'s success depends on either police having an independent incentive to collect, preserve, and turn over exculpatory evidence or prosecutors (or other government actors) creating that incentive

for them. Given that the risk of overturned convictions seems insufficient to motivate prosecutors to comply fully with *Brady*, it is hard to imagine that the same threat will motivate police officers, who receive far fewer professional benefits for convictions and suffer far less reputational harm for long-delayed reversals. If *Brady* is to ensure that police provide favorable evidence to prosecutors, it will likely be because prosecutors can influence the police.

5. *Police and prosecutors.* Except when police officers commit crimes, prosecutors have little direct power over them. Daniel Richman describes the relationship between law enforcement and prosecutors at the federal level this way:

> At its heart, the relationship between federal prosecutors and federal enforcement agents is a bilateral monopoly. Prosecutors are the exclusive gatekeepers over federal court, but they need agents to gather evidence. Agencies control investigative resources, but they are not free to retain separate counsel. If agents want criminal charges to be pursued against the target of an investigation, they will have to convince a prosecutor to take the case.

Daniel Richman, *Prosecutors and Their Agents, Agents and Their Prosecutors*, 103 Colum. L. Rev. 749, 758 (2003). The relationship at the local level is not much different. Local prosecutors usually wait on local police to bring them cases, but then the prosecutors decide whether and what to charge. In the process, prosecutors evaluate both the sufficiency of the investigation and the legality of the police conduct. Because prosecutors want officers to bring them good cases, they care about officers' views. Because officers want prosecutors to bring charges they care about, they care about prosecutors' preferences. See also Kate Levine, *Who Shouldn't Prosecute Police Officers*, 101 Iowa L. Rev. 1447, 1465–1470 (2016) (describing the relationship between local police and prosecutors). More generally, because prosecutors and police work closely together, they care about their relationships. Perhaps prosecutors can use those informal ties and the power to decline cases to encourage the police to collect and turn over *Brady* evidence.

6. *Brady's complications.* Motivating the police might not be enough. *Brady* is complicated. An officer might not recognize exculpatory evidence found in interview notes, electronic records, radio transmissions, interactions with forensic analysts, deals other officers have with informants, and personnel files. Even in traditional physical, testimonial, and documentary evidence, officers might easily overlook statements by witnesses that do not support their theory of a case, not realizing that they are evidence at all, much less that they are exculpatory. They might fail to record a neighbor who heard nothing or a witness who gets confused in preparing for trial, preventing the officers from later turning over the evidence. What might be necessary to improve officers' capacity to comply with *Brady*?

7. *A problem: Val and Steve.* When Officer Helen Hammond responds to a 911 call about a domestic dispute, Hammond finds Val and Steve, who are married. They are both intoxicated and have obviously just been in an altercation: Val's face is swollen and bruised, and Steve has abrasions on his forearms and knuckles. Initially, Val tells Hammond that a stranger broke into the house and assaulted her before running away. Hammond does not believe this and when she takes Val out to her patrol and asks her to consider her own safety, Val breaks down and admits that Steve had beaten her. Hammond arrests Steve for domestic battery. In Hammond's arrest report, she writes, "During field interview, Victim reluctantly stated that her husband

had assaulted her." She does not record Val's quickly abandoned lie, thinking it unimportant. At Steve's preliminary hearing, the prosecutor turns over Hammond's report with the initial discovery packet and makes a plea offer to a domestic violence diversion program, which Steve accepts. Has the *Brady* rule been violated?

8. Brady *systems.* Departments that do better at collecting exculpatory evidence establish well-functioning systems for ensuring that officers are trained in *Brady's* complexities and evidence is recorded, tracked, and disclosed. Can prosecutors push departments to develop such systems? If a police chief told you that he wanted to make sure that officers turned over all exculpatory evidence to prosecutors in every case, what would you recommend he do?

9. Brady *in Portland.* For decades after *Brady* was decided, police officers knew next to nothing about it. Even now, many departments lack effective systems to ensure that officers understand and comply with their discovery obligations. For instance, a 2017 independent review of police bureau practices in Portland, Oregon, found that the department had no written policy on *Brady,* no *Brady* system in place, and *never* conducted *Brady* training for officers, leading to limited understanding and spotty compliance. See Mary H. Caballero & Constantin Severe, Independent Police Review, *Policy Review: Portland Police Bureau Compliance with* Brady v. Maryland (2017). That was after nearly a decade in which *Brady* and its violations were the subject of intense scrutiny in legal circles. Should courts require departments to implement systems to ensure *Brady* compliance? How might states require them to do so?

10. *Open files.* Most commentators think *Brady* does not work very well. There are many proposals for expanding discovery beyond *Brady,* such as allowing defense lawyers to see all of the evidence in criminal cases, what is known as an *open-files policy.* Some prosecutors' offices have adopted open-files policies, except when necessary to protect a victim or witness, without apparent problem. Still, this solution has little impact on the police role in discovery: Open-files policies allow defendants access to prosecutor files, not to police files. Can you think of disadvantages to extending the rule to police files? How might a community interested in opening police files to scrutiny make that happen?

11. *Police and favorable evidence. Brady* requires *turning over* favorable evidence within the government's control, but neither *Brady* nor any other constitutional rule requires the government to fully and fairly investigate crimes so that it *collects* potentially favorable evidence. With limited exceptions discussed later in this chapter, flaws in police investigation are mostly addressed through cross-examination at trial. Can you think of advantages or disadvantages of this approach? How might we help to ensure that officers engage in full and fair investigations?

12. *Police and prosecutors redux.* If prosecutors can influence the police to turn over evidence favorable to the accused, what else might they use their influence to encourage the police to do? Some elected progressive prosecutors have used their declination power to end prosecutions for low-level offenses and reduce penalties for some more serious ones. Could prosecutors use that same approach more aggressively to regulate policing? In early 2020, for example, San Francisco District Attorney Chesa Boudin announced that, to reduce racial bias in policing and improve police–community relations, his office would not bring charges for contraband found during consent searches during pretextual traffic stops. See MJ Johnson, *DA Boudin to Stop Charging for Contraband at Traffic Stops, Gang Enhancements,* S.F. Examiner (Feb. 28, 2020). Presumably, a district attorney could similarly refuse

to charge crimes if an officer uses excessive force, if the officer makes an arrest when a summons would have been sufficient, if the officer violates the department's body-camera policy during the interaction, and so on. Can you think of advantages and disadvantages of using prosecutorial declination policy in this way?

Police Backlash Against Progressive Prosecutors

Brady envisions prosecutors regulating police officers. Do the police also regulate prosecutors? Sometimes they try. When Rachael Rollins, the district attorney of Suffolk County, Massachusetts, ran for office, she announced her intention to decline prosecuting more than a dozen low-level offenses. Once she was elected, police chiefs and union officials took center stage in pushing back against her. The National Police Association, for example, filed a state bar complaint against her, accusing her of violating rules of professional conduct by declining to prosecute cases. Other progressive prosecutors have faced similar pressure. Rollins wrote about it in an opinion piece:

> In Chicago, when State's Attorney Kim Foxx announced that her office would no longer charge shoplifting cases involving under $1,000 as felonies, Kevin Graham, the head of the city's Fraternal Order of Police, attacked her publicly, saying: "We need to have a prosecutor who is going to charge people when they commit a crime. If there's no charges and nobody goes to jail, then obviously the law doesn't mean anything."
>
> In Baltimore, after State's Attorney Marilyn Mosby announced that her office would no longer prosecute marijuana possession offenses, Gary Tuggle, the interim police commissioner at that time, instructed his officers to continue making arrests and explained that he felt marijuana possession drives violent crime.
>
> When Dallas District Attorney John Creuzot said he would stop prosecuting low-level theft and other offenses, Texas Governor Greg Abbott tweeted that Creuzot "stokes crime."
>
> I've felt this pushback at home, too. Michael Leary, president of the Boston Police Patrolmen's Association (BPPA), recently said, without any evidence, that as a result of prosecutorial reforms, "Crime will go up. Shootings will occur." . . .
>
> The old guard insists that criminal justice is a zero sum game, as if remedying systemic injustices, including racial and economic unfairness, requires a corresponding decrease in public safety. . . . But make no mistake: This is not a battle between safety and justice; it is a battle between two competing visions of public safety. . . .
>
> Like Mosby, I believe in prioritizing the offenses that cause serious physical harm or death rather than misspending our limited resources on low-level offenses. Murders, shootings, and sexual assaults should be our highest priority; offenses like drug possession, loitering, and driving on a suspended license should not.

Rachel Rollins, *The Public Safety Myth*, Daily Appeal (Aug. 29, 2019). Should police try to check the use of discretion by elected prosecutors? Would you think differently if the police were instead pushing back against prosecutors who were refusing to enforce gun control laws?

2. Constitutional Rules on Preserving and Collecting Evidence

The Supreme Court has always framed the *Brady* obligation as one that accrues to prosecutors. Although it has never directly addressed whether the police also have an independent obligation to disclose evidence under *Brady*, the Court has allowed the possibility that defendants have other due process rights against the police with respect to evidence.

a. *Preserving Evidence* — California v. Trombetta

In *California v. Trombetta*, 467 U.S. 479, 486–491 (1984), the Supreme Court unanimously held that due process does not require police officers to preserve breath samples from breathalyzer tests so that defendants can analyze them before they are admitted in a criminal prosecution:

> We have . . . never squarely addressed the government's duty to take affirmative steps to preserve evidence on behalf of criminal defendants. The absence of doctrinal development in this area reflects, in part, the difficulty of developing rules to deal with evidence destroyed through prosecutorial neglect or oversight. Whenever potentially exculpatory evidence is permanently lost, courts face the treacherous task of divining the import of materials whose contents are unknown and, very often, disputed. Moreover, fashioning remedies for the illegal destruction of evidence can pose troubling choices. In nondisclosure cases, a court can grant the defendant a new trial at which the previously suppressed evidence may be introduced. But when evidence has been destroyed in violation of the Constitution, the court must choose between barring further prosecution or suppressing — as the California Court of Appeal did in this case — the State's most probative evidence. . . .

> Given our precedents in this area, we cannot agree . . . that the State's failure to retain breath samples for respondents constitutes a violation of the Federal Constitution. To begin with, California authorities in this case did not destroy respondents' breath samples in a calculated effort to circumvent the disclosure requirements established by *Brady v. Maryland* and its progeny. In failing to preserve breath samples for respondents, the officers here were acting "in good faith and in accord with their normal practice." Killian v. United States, 368 U.S. 231, 242 (1961). The record contains no allegation of official animus towards respondents or of a conscious effort to suppress exculpatory evidence.

> More importantly, California's policy of not preserving breath samples is without constitutional defect. Whatever duty the Constitution imposes on the States to preserve evidence, that duty must be limited to evidence that might be expected to play a significant role in the suspect's defense. To meet this standard of constitutional materiality, evidence must both possess an exculpatory value that was apparent before the evidence was destroyed, and be of such a nature that the defendant would be unable to obtain comparable evidence by other reasonably available means. Neither of these conditions is met on the facts of this case.

> Although the preservation of breath samples might conceivably have contributed to respondents' defenses, a dispassionate review of the Intoxilyzer and the California testing procedures can only lead one to conclude that the chances are extremely low that preserved samples would have been exculpatory. The accuracy of the Intoxilyzer has been reviewed and certified by the California Department of Health. To protect suspects against machine malfunctions, the Department has developed test procedures that include two independent measurements (which must be closely correlated

for the results to be admissible) bracketed by blank runs designed to ensure that the machine is purged of alcohol traces from previous tests. In all but a tiny fraction of cases, preserved breath samples would simply confirm the Intoxilyzer's determination that the defendant had a high level of blood-alcohol concentration at the time of the test. Once the Intoxilyzer indicated that respondents were legally drunk, breath samples were much more likely to provide inculpatory than exculpatory evidence.

Even if one were to assume that the Intoxilyzer results in this case were inaccurate and that breath samples might therefore have been exculpatory, it does not follow that respondents were without alternative means of demonstrating their innocence. Respondents and amici have identified only a limited number of ways in which an Intoxilyzer might malfunction: faulty calibration, extraneous interference with machine measurements, and operator error. Respondents were perfectly capable of raising these issues without resort to preserved breath samples. . . .

We conclude, therefore, that the Due Process Clause of the Fourteenth Amendment does not require that law enforcement agencies preserve breath samples in order to introduce the results of breath-analysis tests at trial.

An officer testing a suspect's breath for alcohol.

When the Police Investigate the Police

Sometimes evidence is needed to determine *who* committed a crime. Often, though, the who is obvious, and the question is *whether* a crime was committed at all. That is especially true when an officer uses force: He might have acted in self-defense, he might have used force justified in subduing a suspect, or he might have committed a crime. Accurately determining which is critical in achieving justice for the officer and the person harmed, protecting the integrity of the justice system, and maintaining faith in government.

When the public sees a video that looks like murder, and prosecutors announce that it is not a crime, the public wonders whether that assessment was impartial or instead biased by the close relationships prosecutors have with the police. For this reason, many reformers have called for *independent investigations* of police misconduct, by which they mean special prosecutors to review police killings or serious assaults on civilians. Several states have passed or are considering such laws.

However, just as for other crimes, prosecuting a police officer depends on properly collecting and preserving evidence in addition to assessing it. By the time a prosecutor is involved, the evidence might be so badly compromised that accurate determination of an officer's culpability is impossible to assess. If an officer involved in a shooting is allowed to remove his clothes, wash his hands, and handle his own gun; if civilian and officer witnesses are allowed to leave before their statements are taken; or if the scene is not properly documented and preserved, we might never know whether the officer committed a murder or not. Although agencies have some rules for officers following a critical incident, unless they enforce strong, clear policies that ensure proper preservation of evidence and testimony, and ensure that independent investigators respond rapidly to the scene, communities and victims will not later be able to trust determinations about whether the officer's conduct violated the law.

Of course, independence alone does not guarantee fairness or neutrality. The Minnesota Bureau of Criminal Apprehension (BCA) investigates most police shootings in the state. Despite its apparent independence, sympathy for law enforcement seems to have compromised its investigation of the fatal shooting of 911 caller Justine Ruszczyk by Minneapolis police officer Mohamed Noor. The BCA failed to take statements from officers at the scene or document statements made by Noor. It allowed the only witness to the actual shooting—Noor's partner—three days to collect himself before he was questioned at a location of his choice (over coffee and doughnuts), and failed to interview civilian witnesses for months. It neglected to preserve physical evidence, including the squad car Noor shot Ruszczyk from, allowing it to return to service. See Jon Collins & Riham Feshir, *Noor Trial: Questions Resurface Over BCA's Cop-Friendly Approach*, MPRNews (Apr. 25, 2019). In the end, Noor was convicted of third-degree murder and manslaughter, but acquitted of intentional second-degree murder. Many other officers are never charged at all. For more on investigating and prosecuting police officers, see Chapter 14. In the meantime, consider what more should be done.

b.   *Testing and Maintaining Evidence*—Arizona v. Youngblood

In 1983, a middle-aged man abducted and sexually assaulted a ten-year-old boy. The boy was treated at a hospital, where doctors collected semen samples from his rectum and mouth, and the police took his clothing. More than a week later, the boy identified Larry Youngblood in a lineup, and Youngblood was arrested. The police tested the semen evidence but produced no information about the culprit's identity. They did not test the boy's underwear or T-shirt and, in fact, failed to refrigerate them, allowing the evidence to degrade over time. Only several years later did a police criminologist examine the clothing: Although there was semen staining on the clothing, the evidence was too degraded to provide useful information. Youngblood's defense was that the boy had misidentified him, and experts testified at trial that if the clothing had been properly preserved and tested, it might have identified the culprit, proving Youngblood's innocence. The police fully complied with *Brady*, as they made all of the relevant evidence available to the defendant before trial. Youngblood alleged that the officers nevertheless violated the Due Process Clause by failing to test and preserve the evidence. The U.S. Supreme Court disagreed:

> Our most recent decision in this area of the law, *California v. Trombetta*, 467 U.S. 479 (1984), arose out of a drunk-driving prosecution in which the State had introduced test results indicating the concentration of alcohol in the blood of two motorists. The defendants sought to suppress the test results on the ground that the State had failed to preserve the breath samples used in the test. We rejected this argument for several reasons: first, "the officers here were acting in 'good faith and in accord with their normal practice,' "; second, in the light of the procedures actually used the chances that preserved samples would have exculpated the defendants were slim; and, third, even if the samples might have shown inaccuracy in the tests, the defendants had "alternative means of demonstrating their innocence." In the present case, the likelihood that the preserved materials would have enabled the defendant to exonerate himself appears to be greater than it was in *Trombetta*, but here, unlike in *Trombetta*, the State did not attempt to make any use of the materials in its own case in chief.
>
> Our decisions in related areas have stressed the importance for constitutional purposes of good or bad faith on the part of the Government when the claim is based on loss of evidence attributable to the Government. . . .
>
> The Due Process Clause of the Fourteenth Amendment, as interpreted in *Brady*, makes the good or bad faith of the State irrelevant when the State fails to disclose to the defendant material exculpatory evidence. But we think the Due Process Clause requires a different result when we deal with the failure of the State to preserve evidentiary material of which no more can be said than that it could have been subjected to tests, the results of which might have exonerated the defendant. Part of the reason for the difference in treatment is found in the observation made by the Court in *Trombetta* that "[w]henever potentially exculpatory evidence is permanently lost, courts face the treacherous task of divining the import of materials whose contents are unknown and, very often, disputed." Part of it stems from our unwillingness to read the "fundamental fairness" requirement of the Due Process Clause, as imposing on the police an undifferentiated and absolute duty to retain and to preserve all material that might be of conceivable evidentiary significance in a particular prosecution. We think that requiring a defendant to show bad faith on the part of the police both limits the extent of the police's obligation to preserve evidence to reasonable bounds and confines it to that class of cases where the interests of justice most clearly require it, *i.e.*, those cases in which the police themselves by their conduct indicate that the evidence could form a basis for exonerating the defendant. We therefore hold that unless a criminal defendant can show bad faith on the part of the police, failure to preserve potentially useful evidence does not constitute a denial of due process of law.
>
> In this case, the police collected the rectal swab and clothing on the night of the crime; respondent was not taken into custody until six weeks later. The failure of the police to refrigerate the clothing and to perform tests on the semen samples

can at worst be described as negligent. None of this information was concealed from respondent at trial, and the evidence—such as it was—was made available to respondent's expert who declined to perform any tests on the samples. The Arizona Court of Appeals noted in its opinion—and we agree—that there was no suggestion of bad faith on the part of the police. It follows, therefore, from what we have said, that there was no violation of the Due Process Clause.

Arizona v. Youngblood, 488 U.S. 51, 56–58 (1988).

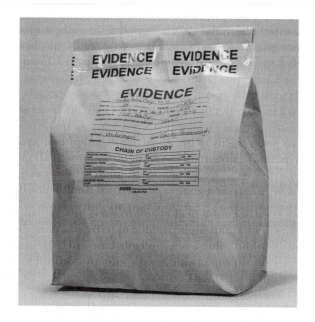

NOTES AND QUESTIONS

1. Trombetta *and* Youngblood *claims.* In the course of rejecting constitutional claims against the police, *Youngblood* and *Trombetta* described in it suggest the possibility of such claims in other cases. What would you tell a defense lawyer to look for to determine whether the defendant had a due process claim for evidence handling? Can you describe facts that you think might establish a due process claim against the police under each of these cases?

2. *Youngblood was innocent.* Youngblood spent time in and out of prison after his arrest, while his case bounced around the courts. In 2000, at Youngblood's lawyers' request, the police used new technology to conduct DNA tests on the clothing evidence degraded by police neglect. Those tests proved Youngblood innocent, and he was released from prison. The tests also led to the real culprit, and in 2002, Walter Cruise was convicted of the crime. Had the evidence been properly preserved and tested, then it is reasonably likely that Youngblood would not have been convicted, and the real perpetrator would have been caught. Does that affect your thinking about the value of these claims?

3. *Labs and police departments.* Most crime laboratories and evidence-storage facilities operate as divisions of police departments. See Sandra Guerra Thompson, *Cops in*

Lab Coats: Curbing Wrongful Convictions Through Independent Forensic Laboratories 181–183 (2015). How might that arrangement affect how evidence is handled?

4. *What determines police action?* Given how weak a constraint constitutional law is on police decisions about evidence, it seems unlikely that it significantly influences officers. What do you imagine does shape how officers handle evidence?

5. *Bad faith.* *Trombetta* and *Youngblood* bar claims unless the police act in bad faith. Why? As Grey's Law pithily states, "Any sufficiently advanced incompetence is indistinguishable from malice."[1] Wouldn't *Youngblood*, who spent nine years in prison for a crime he did not commit, say so? Why the difference from *Brady*, which recognizes constitutional violations even for evidence accidentally withheld?

6. *Fabrication of evidence.* Police may fail to preserve evidence by accident, but the same is not true of fabricating evidence. Officers sometimes claim to smell marijuana to justify a search, "find" drugs by planting them during a traffic stop, or drop a gun near a person after shooting them. They tamper with physical evidence, lie on a report, or coerce a witness statement. For an example, consider former Jackson County Sheriff's Office Deputy Zachary Wester. Wester faces criminal charges on more than 70 counts of racketeering, misusing public office, perjury, fabricating physical evidence, possessing controlled substances, false imprisonment, and other crimes. He allegedly kept drugs and drug paraphernalia in his squad car and planted it on unsuspecting drivers during traffic stops, after which he arrested them. His innocent victims spent time in jail, lost jobs, had marriages break up, and lost custody of their children because of their arrests and charges. Prosecutors have dropped 119 cases that relied on his testimony or arrests, but those charges still stay on criminal records. See Jeff Burlew, *Accused Drug-Planting Deputy Slapped with Two Dozen New Charges*, Tallahassee Democrat (Feb. 10, 2020); Meagan Flynn, *A Florida Cop Planted Meth on Random Drivers, Police Say: One Lost Custody of His Daughter*, Wash. Post (July 11, 2019). Why might an officer do such a thing? One former prosecutor suggested that the state attorney's office not only did not stop Wester, it made the problem worse: Prosecutors were pressured to rack up conviction statistics, which were then mailed on postcards to voters. As a result, they had every incentive to look the other way when police evidence did not add up. See Katie Rose Quandt, *Floridians Are Suing a Cop Fired for Planting Drugs in Their Vehicles*, The Appeal (Jun. 17, 2019).

7. *Fabrication of evidence: The law.* As Wester's case suggests, planting evidence can violate state law. It can also violate the Constitution. If an officer plants or lies about evidence and then makes an arrest based on that fabrication, he conducts an arrest without probable cause, violating the Fourth Amendment. An officer similarly violates the Fourth Amendment if he lies in a warrant application leading to an arrest or lies in a criminal complaint leading a person to be held for trial. See Manuel v. City of Joliet, 137 S. Ct. 911 (2017). If an officer lies instead about the existence of evidence or fabricates trial evidence that leads to a conviction, he violates the Due Process Clause. See, e.g., Limone v. Condon, 372 F.3d 39 (1st Cir. 2004); Castellano v. Fragozo, 352 F.3d 939 (5th Cir. 2003). What if an officer fabricates evidence that never gets used at trial? If he testifies, failing to disclose the fabrication might violate *Brady*, even if he never told anyone. Do you see why? Still, how could he get caught?

---

[1] Grey's Law is a corollary of Hanlon's Razor, which states, "Never attribute to malice that which is adequately explained by stupidity." The origins of both rules are disputed.

What of Victims?

Defendants are not the only ones concerned with how police collect and preserve evidence. Some victims claim that the police discriminate in how vigorously they investigate crimes ensuring that their attackers are never prosecuted. For example, women in a half-dozen cities have sued police departments claiming that the police denied them equal protection of the law in violation of the Fourteenth Amendment by failing to collect, preserve, and test physical evidence when they reported sexual assaults. See Valeriya Safronova & Rebecca Halleck, *They Reported Rape, and then Sued the Police*, N.Y. Times (May 24, 2019) at A13. In other cities, families of murder victims claim that police fail to thoroughly investigate those crimes against people of color. An equal protection violation is difficult to prove, but it is likely these victims' only constitutional option. All the due process rights discussed in this chapter belong to criminal defendants, not to crime victims. What should victims without an equal protection claim do when police investigation fails them?

---

3.   Damages Actions for *Brady* Claims

If a person denied material exculpatory evidence is convicted and serves time, releasing him and reversing his conviction might not be enough to remedy the damage done or to deter future violations. Can he sue for civil damages actions under 42 U.S.C. §1983?

Plaintiffs face a problem: Although the Supreme Court has charged prosecutors with fulfilling the government's *Brady* obligations, prosecutors are *absolutely* immune for actions "intimately associated with the judicial phase of the criminal process," Imbler v. Pachtman, 424 U.S. 409, 430 (1976), including not turning over evidence. This immunity exists even if prosecutors' misconduct was deliberate. See Van de Kamp v. Goldstein, 555 U.S. 335, 863 (2009). As a result, plaintiffs cannot bring civil damages actions against prosecutors when their *Brady* rights are violated.

By contrast, police officers receive only *qualified* immunity under §1983 for their actions. Although they are shielded from civil liability under many circumstances, they may be sued if they violate a defendant's *clearly established* right. See Harlow v. Fitzgerald, 457 U.S. 800 (1982), discussed further in Chapter 13. That makes them more appealing defendants than prosecutors. Yet *Brady* has been traditionally framed primarily as an obligation of prosecutors, not police officers.

When is a police officer liable for failing to provide exculpatory evidence? Courts disagree. *Brady* makes suppressing material evidence a constitutional violation, irrespective of whether the government acts in good or bad faith. But *Trombetta* and *Youngblood* suggest that due process claims against the police require bad faith. Courts are faced with a question: Are civil suits for *Brady* violations against police officers more like other *Brady* claims or more like other claims against police officers for evidence handling? The Supreme Court has not ruled on the issue, but consider the following opinion from the Sixth Circuit.

MOLDOWAN v. CITY OF WARREN
578 F.3d 351 (6th Cir. 2009)

SECOND AMENDED OPINION

CLAY, CIRCUIT JUDGE.

. . . Moldowan's claims arise out of his arrest, criminal prosecution, conviction, and retrial for the 1990 abduction and brutal sexual assault of Maureen Fournier. After new evidence came to light and a key prosecution witness recanted her testimony, the Michigan Supreme Court reversed Moldowan's conviction in 2002. On retrial, in February 2003, Moldowan was acquitted of all charges and released, having served nearly twelve years in prison. . . .

A. Factual Background

On the morning of August 9, 1990, . . . Fournier [was] abducted from the City of Warren, brutally assaulted and raped, and left on a street in Detroit.

Because Fournier had been abducted from Warren, the matter was turned over to the Warren Police Department ("Department"), and the case was assigned to Detective [Donald] Ingles. Given the extent of Fournier's injuries, officers had to wait two days before they could interview her regarding the attack. . . . During the interview, Fournier reported that she had been abducted . . . by four Caucasian males, all of whom she knew. Fournier stated that, while she was walking down the street, she was approached by Moldowan, who was her ex-boyfriend, thrown into a white or light-colored van, and brutally beaten and raped by three of the four assailants. Fournier identified her attackers as Michael Cristini, Jim Cristini, Tracy Tapp, and Moldowan. Fournier's sister, Colleen Corcoran, confirmed Fournier's claims that Moldowan previously had assaulted and threatened Fournier.

After completing their investigation, the police arrested and charged all four individuals. The police subsequently dropped the charges against Tapp based on his alibi. . . .

On September 17–18, 1990, the Macomb County Circuit Court held a preliminary examination to determine whether sufficient evidence existed to proceed to trial. During that hearing, Fournier testified that, prior to the assault, she had dated and lived with Moldowan for more than a year before their relationship ended when he was arrested for assaulting her. Fournier and her sister both testified that, prior to the attack, Moldowan had been abusive toward Fournier and threatened her. In describing the assault, Fournier testified that she had been walking . . . when a van pulled alongside her. Fournier testified that Moldowan got out of the van, grabbed her, and dragged her into the van, where she was beaten and raped. As a result of the assault, Fournier suffered significant injuries that required extensive abdominal surgery. . . .

At the conclusion of the examination, the court dismissed Jim Cristini as a defendant, but bound over Moldowan and Michael Cristini on all counts. A jury trial was held . . . during which Fournier and Corcoran offered substantially the same testimony they provided during the preliminary examination. Fournier also testified that she had never been in the Detroit neighborhood where EMS found her, and that she had never frequented a crack house in the area. . . .

In presenting their defense, Cristini and Moldowan offered alibi witnesses. . . . The defense also presented testimony from a witness who claimed that she observed several males in the street where Fournier was found, and that the males were both Caucasian and African-American. . . .

On May 10, 1991, the jury convicted Moldowan and Cristini of kidnaping, assault with intent to commit murder, and two counts of criminal sexual conduct in the first degree. . . .

After trial, a private investigator hired by Moldowan's family located a witness, Jerry Burroughs, who reported that, on the morning of August 9, 1990, he saw four African-American males standing around a naked white female who was lying in the street, and that he saw the four men leave in a light-colored van. Burroughs further recounted that, approximately one week after the assault, he overheard two of those same men talking about the incident and bragging that they had participated in the assault. Burroughs also indicated that he had seen Fournier in that neighborhood several times that summer frequenting a crack house in the area. . . .

On the basis of this new evidence and discredited testimony, Moldowan again sought review of his conviction. The Michigan Supreme Court eventually reversed Moldowan's conviction, and remanded the matter for a new trial. . . .

On retrial, in February 2003, Moldowan was acquitted of all charges and released. All told, Moldowan spent nearly twelve years in prison. . . .

1. Counts IX, X, XI, XII — *Brady* Claims (Ingles)

Moldowan asserts a number of claims against Detective Ingles . . . based on Ingles' alleged failure to disclose exculpatory evidence. In particular, Moldowan contends that Ingles was required to disclose exculpatory statements from Burroughs. . . .

Moldowan's allegations, although asserted under various constitutional provisions, present claims under *Brady v. Maryland,* 373 U.S. 83 (1963). . . . The question we confront here is whether Detective Ingles' alleged suppression of Burroughs' statements violated the same "legal norm" underlying the due process violation recognized in *Brady*. We hold that it does.

Detective Ingles argues that Moldowan cannot demonstrate that the Due Process Clause imposes on the police a clearly established obligation to disclose exculpatory information. Superficially, that argument has some appeal. To the extent that *Brady* imposes an obligation on the state to disclose exculpatory evidence to the defense, courts consistently have determined that this duty falls squarely on the prosecutor, not the police. . . . In fact, the Supreme Court has placed the responsibility to manage the state's disclosure obligations solely on the prosecutor despite acknowledging that "no one doubts that police investigators sometimes fail to inform a prosecutor of all they know." Kyles v. Whitley 514 U.S. 419, 438 (1995).

This well-established rule, however, does not resolve whether the police have a concomitant or derivative duty under the constitution to turn potentially exculpatory material over to the prosecutor. In fact, Moldowan acknowledges that the duty to "disclose" exculpatory materials to defense counsel rests on the prosecutor alone, but nevertheless maintains that the police have an analogous, but just as constitutionally-significant, obligation to turn such materials over to the prosecutor's office. Underlying Moldowan's argument is the valid concern that, if the police have no constitutional obligation in this regard, then the state could sidestep its constitutionally-mandated disclosure obligations by maintaining an unstated, but nevertheless pervasive, wall of separation between the prosecutor's office and the police with regard to the existence of potentially exculpatory evidence. Ignoring the burdens that the Constitution places on the police in this context also creates a very serious risk that police officers who conceal or withhold evidence that falls within *Brady*'s ambit will never be held accountable for the independent "deprivation of any rights, privileges, or immunities secured by the Constitution," 42 U.S.C. §1983, that their conduct causes.

As the concurrence correctly notes, however, the Supreme Court already has addressed the first of these concerns, at least to a certain extent, by imposing on the prosecutor "a duty to learn of any favorable evidence known to the others acting on the government's behalf in the case, including the police." *Kyles*, 514 U.S. at 437. . . .

Contrary to Detective Ingles' suggestion, however, this does not imply that the police have no role to play in ensuring that the state complies with its obligations under *Brady*, or that the police cannot commit a constitutional violation analogous to the deprivation recognized in *Brady*. On the contrary, . . . [b]ecause prosecutors rely so heavily on the police and other law enforcement authorities, the obligations imposed under *Brady* would be largely ineffective if those other members of the prosecution team had no responsibility to inform the prosecutor about evidence that undermined the state's preferred theory of the crime. As a practical matter then, *Brady*'s ultimate concern for ensuring that criminal defendants receive a "fundamentally fair" trial, demands that "*Brady*'s protections also extend to actions of other law enforcement officers such as investigating officers," White v. McKinley, 519 F.3d 806, 814 (8th Cir. 2008). . . .

In addition to this practical justification, it is evident that the constitutional principles recognized in *Brady* apply just as equally to similar conduct on the part of police, and thus support our recognizing that the police can commit a constitutional deprivation analogous to that recognized in *Brady* by withholding or suppressing exculpatory material. . . . As far as the Constitution is concerned, a criminal defendant is equally deprived of his or her due process rights when the police rather than the prosecutor suppresses exculpatory evidence because, in either case, the impact on the fundamental fairness of the defendant's trial is the same. . . .

In addition to these practical justifications and constitutional considerations, the police's obligation to turn over material and exculpatory evidence also follows inexorably from the Supreme Court's recognition that the police have a constitutional duty to preserve such evidence. In *California v. Trombetta*, 467 U.S. 479 (1984), the Supreme Court observed that "[w]hatever duty the Constitution imposes on the States to preserve evidence, that duty must be limited to evidence that might be expected to play a significant role in the suspect's defense." *Id.* at 488. The Court recognized that same duty in *Arizona v. Youngblood*, 488 U.S. 51 (1988), confirming that the Constitution imposes at least a limited "obligation" on the police "to preserve evidence . . . [that] could form the basis for exonerating the defendant." *Id.* at 58. If the Constitution imposes a "duty" and "obligation" on the police to preserve such evidence, that duty, no matter how limited, certainly must preclude the police from concealing that exact same information from the prosecutor, the defense, and the courts. Why else would the police be required to *preserve* such evidence if they had no attendant obligation to *reveal* its existence? *Brady* and *Trombetta* would impose hollow obligations indeed if the Constitution did not also preclude police officers from concealing the same evidence that they are not permitted to destroy and that the prosecutor is required to disclose.

The concurrence argues that the police cannot share in the state's obligations under *Brady* because "the *Brady* duty is uniquely tailored to prosecutors" in that it requires the disclosure of exculpatory evidence that is constitutionally "material," and thus requires the exercise of "a judgment that prosecutors, not police officers, are trained to make." This argument misses the point. We agree that determining whether a particular piece of evidence is "material," . . . requires the exercise of legal judgment that the prosecuting attorney is better trained, not to mention better positioned, to make. However, that implies only that the prosecutor should be assigned the responsibility of determining what evidence ultimately should be *disclosed* to the defendant; it does not imply, as our colleague suggests, that the police cannot be expected to recognize and determine what evidence should be preserved and turned over to the prosecutor. On the contrary, the Supreme Court already has assumed as much in concluding that the police have a constitutionally-significant "duty" to "preserve evidence . . . that might be expected to play a significant role in the suspect's defense." *Trombetta*, 467 U.S. at 488–89. If the police can be expected to recognize what evidence must be preserved, certainly it is not too burdensome to demand that they simply turn that same information over to the prosecutor's office.

For most of the same reasons we have laid out here, virtually every other circuit has concluded either that the police share in the state's obligations under *Brady*, or that the Constitution imposes on the police obligations analogous to those recognized in *Brady*. . . .

. . . [W]e next must determine whether, taking the facts alleged by Moldowan as true, Moldowan can make out a violation of this right. At Moldowan's retrial, Jerry Burroughs testified that he witnessed four African-American males standing in the street around Fournier's body in the early morning hours of August 9, 1990. Burroughs also testified that he witnessed one of the men kick her, and that shortly thereafter he saw the men drive away from the scene in a light-colored van. Burroughs also testified that he later overheard two of the men he saw standing around Fournier's body talking about the incident and claiming involvement in the assault. Burroughs testified that he reported this information to a police officer, but the officer "just acted like I [was] saying nothing." Although Burroughs could not remember the name of the officer with whom he spoke, Moldowan claims that it must have been Detective Ingles. It is without question that Detective Ingles did not report any such information to the Macomb County Prosecutor, or to defense counsel for that matter.

Construing these facts in the light most favorable to Moldowan, it is evident that Burroughs' statements cast serious doubt on, if not entirely discredit, Fournier's identification of Moldowan as one of her attackers, an issue that undoubtedly was one of the most important elements of the state's case. Burroughs' statements thus should have been disclosed to the defense as they undoubtedly "would tend to exculpate" Moldowan.

Defendants contend that, even if we were to conclude that the legal norms underlying *Brady* can support an analogous or derivative claim against a police officer, Moldowan cannot prevail on the facts presented here because he cannot show that Detective Ingles withheld these statements in "bad faith." . . .

Although this Court has not addressed the issue directly, at least two of our sister circuits have suggested that, in order to assert such a claim against the police, at least under §1983, a defendant-turned-plaintiff must demonstrate that the police acted in "bad faith." See, e.g., Porter v. White, 483 F.3d 1294 (11th Cir. 2007); Villasana v. Wilhoit, 368 F.3d 976, 980 (8th Cir. 2004). At least one other circuit, however, previously held that no such showing of bad faith is required. . . .

. . . We acknowledge that a number of courts, including the Supreme Court, have held that a showing of bad faith is required to prevail on a claim that the police deprived a defendant of due process by concealing or withholding evidence that is only "potentially useful." But, where the police are aware that the evidence in their possession is exculpatory, the Supreme Court's decisions in this area indicate that the police have an *absolute* duty to preserve and disclose that information. The critical issue in determining whether bad faith is required thus is not whether the evidence is withheld by the prosecutor or the police, but rather whether the exculpatory value of the evidence is "apparent" or not. . . .

Unlike the destruction or concealment of merely "potentially useful" evidence, the loss of "materially exculpatory" evidence directly threatens the fundamental fairness of a criminal trial, and thus undoubtedly implicates the Due Process Clause. In "that class of cases," *Youngblood* says, "the interests of justice" simply impose a higher burden on state actors, including the police. That is true regardless of whether the defendant is asserting a failure-to-preserve or a failure-to-disclose claim, and regardless of whether the claim is being asserted against the prosecutor or the police. . . .

Simply put, where the evidence withheld or destroyed by the police falls into that more serious category, the defendant is not required to make any further showing regarding the mental state of the police. As the Court explained in *Youngblood*, "[t]he presence or absence of bad faith by the police for purposes of the Due Process Clause must necessarily turn on the police's knowledge of the exculpatory value of the evidence at the time it was lost or destroyed." *Id.* at 56 n.*. . . .

. . . Where the exculpatory value of a piece of evidence is "apparent," the police have an *unwavering* constitutional duty to preserve and ultimately disclose that evidence. The failure to fulfill that obligation constitutes a due process violation, regardless of . . . whether a criminal defendant or §1983 plaintiff can show that the evidence was destroyed or concealed in "bad faith." The reason no *further* showing of animus or bad faith is required is that, where the police have in their possession evidence that they know or should know "might be expected to play a significant role in the suspect's defense," *Trombetta*, 467 U.S. at 488, the destruction or concealment of that evidence can *never* be done "in good faith and in accord with their normal practice," Killian v. United States, 368 U.S. 231, 242 (1961). Consequently, requiring a criminal defendant or §1983 plaintiff to show a "conscious" or "calculated" effort to suppress such evidence would be superfluous. . . .

KETHLEDGE, CIRCUIT JUDGE, concurring in the judgment in part, and dissenting in part.

Moldowan puts many labels on his claims, but his claim against Officer Ingles is essentially that he should have disclosed, presumably to the prosecutor, the fact and contents of Jerry Burroughs' alleged statement to Ingles. I agree with the majority's conclusion that, under the standard of review applicable here, Moldowan is entitled to proceed with that claim. But I respectfully disagree with how the majority gets there.

I.

A. . .

. . . By its terms, . . . *Brady* applies to prosecutors, not police officers. . . .

The imposition of that same absolute duty on police officers, therefore, would represent an extension of *Brady* that the Supreme Court itself has not made in the 46 years since it rendered the decision. I do not think the omission is fortuitous. Not only by its terms, but also by its content, the *Brady* duty is uniquely tailored to prosecutors. It applies to exculpatory evidence that is "material"; and the Supreme Court says that "[s]uch evidence is material 'if there is a reasonable probability that, had the evidence been disclosed to the defense, *the result of the proceeding* [that is, the criminal trial] *would have been different.*'" Strickler v. Greene, 527 U.S. 263, 280 (1999). Whether a particular piece of evidence would have changed the result of a criminal trial, of course, is a judgment that prosecutors, not police officers, are trained to make. . . .

The extension is also unnecessary. . . . [T]o comply with *Brady*, "*the individual prosecutor* has a duty to learn of any favorable evidence known to the others acting on the government's behalf in the case, including the police." Kyles v. Whitley, 514 U.S. 419, 437 (1995). And any breach of that duty, no matter how diligent the prosecutor's efforts, entitles the criminal defendant to a new trial. . . . Moreover, as discussed below, no one disputes that police officers already have an independent duty—though not a *Brady* duty—not to conceal materially exculpatory evidence in bad faith. Thus, as a practical matter, extending *Brady* to police officers would accomplish little with respect to the fairness of criminal trials that current law does not already accomplish.

What that extension would accomplish, rather, is a significant increase in lawsuits against police officers. Prosecutors enjoy absolute immunity for actions taken in their official capacities, see Imbler v. Pachtman, 424 U.S. 409, 413–16 (1976), whereas police officers do not. Police officers, therefore, would become the special object of attention from criminal defendants who believe that allegedly exculpatory evidence should have been, but was not, disclosed to their counsel prior to trial. And in this respect the police would present a large target. Police officers, particularly ones like Ingles who investigate violent crime in the field, obtain a great deal of information in the course of an investigation. Some of what they obtain, like shell casings, is tangible, but much of it, like things they may have seen or heard in the course of their activities, is not. As a practical matter, an officer cannot preserve, and thus pass on to the prosecutor, *everything* he sees, hears, or learns in the course of investigating a crime. He instead has to exercise judgment about what seems important and what does not. But if an officer bears an absolute duty to disclose materially exculpatory evidence, *all* of the information thus filtered by an officer's judgment, even in the purest good faith, potentially becomes the basis of a lawsuit against him. An officer's failure to recognize an exculpatory clue, for example, and thus to pass it on to the prosecutor, would be a violation of the Due Process Clause. That the officer was merely negligent, or even that no reasonable officer could have understood the clue's significance at the time, would be no defense; the *Brady* duty is absolute. So if the clue could have changed the result of the criminal defendant's first trial, the defendant would not only get a second one; he would be entitled to have the officer pay him for his troubles as well. . . .

C.

1.

. . . The standard that I would apply—and the one the Eighth and Eleventh Circuits apply—is the one that the Supreme Court has so far *always* applied to determine officer liability in the "area of constitutionally guaranteed access to evidence": namely, bad faith. Arizona v. Youngblood, 488 U.S. 51, 55 (1988). This standard requires proof that the officer engaged in a "conscious effort to suppress exculpatory evidence." California v. Trombetta, 467 U.S. 479, 488 (1984). . . .

2.

There remains the question whether Moldowan's claim against Ingles can proceed under *Youngblood*'s bad-faith standard. . . . [W]hen viewed in the light most favorable to Moldowan, and as a whole, Burroughs' testimony could be read to mean that he told Ingles that two other men had essentially admitted to committing the crime Ingles was investigating.

There is no direct evidence that Ingles withheld Burroughs' statement in bad faith. And I think courts should be wary of inferring bad faith from the mere fact of an officer's failure to disclose evidence, lest the bad-faith standard become in practice an absolute one. But I think that, under the circumstances present here, a jury could infer bad faith from Ingles' failure to disclose Burroughs' statement—whose existence, to be fair, Ingles disputes—to the prosecutor. Of course, a jury would be free *not* to make that inference, in part because they might choose to understand Burroughs' testimony in a light less favorable to Moldowan, or not to believe it at all. Given our standard of review, however, we are not so free. I therefore agree that Moldowan is entitled to proceed with his claim against Ingles.

3.

As that bottom-line agreement suggests, my disagreement with the majority may prove larger in theory than in practice. To establish an officer's conscious suppression of materially exculpatory evidence—and thus his bad faith—a plaintiff must prove, among other things, "the police's knowledge of the exculpatory value of the evidence at the time" the criminal defendant says it should have been disclosed. And therein lies the common ground between my approach and that of the majority. Notwithstanding its rather extended defense of imposing an absolute duty of disclosure upon police officers, . . . the majority . . . holds that a police officer does not breach his duty of disclosure unless the "'exculpatory value'" of the undisclosed evidence is "'apparent'" to him. . . .

Thus, in the end, the majority extends *Brady*'s duty of absolute disclosure to police officers, but limits the scope of that duty to evidence whose materially exculpatory value was known to the particular officer sued. I think the better approach would be simply to apply the Supreme Court's bad-faith rule, rather than a modified version of an absolute rule designed for prosecutors. In practice, however, the latter rule will probably operate as the functional equivalent of the former. . . .

NOTES AND QUESTIONS

1. *Why?* Do you think the officers in *Moldowan* wanted an innocent man to go to prison? Why do you think this injustice happened?

2. *Circuit diversity.* As the *Moldowan* majority opinion notes, all federal circuit courts to consider the issue permit some police liability for *Brady* violations. Most have held that negligent suppression is not sufficient to establish liability. Among those circuits that reject negligence claims, there is a further split as to the proper culpability standard. Some require bad faith. See Owens v. Baltimore City State's Attorney's Office, 767 F.3d 379, 396–397 (4th Cir. 2014); Villasana v. Whilhoit, 368 F.3d 976, 980 (8th Cir. 2004). Some require deliberate action or reckless indifference. See Tennison v. City and County of San Francisco, 570 F.3d 1078, 1088 (9th Cir. 2009). And some have not yet established a standard. See Porter v. White, 483 F.3d 1294, 1304, 1308 n.11 (11th Cir. 2007).

3. *Pity the police?* Judge Kethledge worries in his opinion about opening the floodgates to civil claims against the police. Judge J. Harvie Wilkinson similarly has worried that recognizing broad liability for police officers who do not turn over a piece of exculpatory evidence could "multiply exponentially litigation against even conscientious officers." Jean v. Collins, 221 F.3d 656, 661 (4th Cir. 2000) (en banc) (Wilkinson, C.J., concurring). In evaluating their worry, consider that federal courts of appeals largely reject §1983 claims in cases where exculpatory material was not disclosed but no conviction resulted. See Sunil Bhave, *The Innocent Have Rights Too: Expanding* Brady v. Maryland *to Provide the Criminally Innocent with a Cause of Action Against Police Officers Who Withhold Exculpatory Evidence*, 45 Creighton L. Rev. 1, 14–25 (2011) (discussing cases). Moreover, in *Heck v. Humphrey*, 512 U.S. 477 (1994), the Supreme Court forbid §1983 damages actions for claims challenging a conviction or sentence unless the defendant had already gotten the conviction or sentence overturned, a difficult and often unsuccessful process. The *Heck* rule applies to *Brady* claims. As a result of these obstacles, *Brady* civil suits are possible for only the subset of criminal cases in which police officers caused favorable evidence not to be turned over; there is a reasonable probability that the outcome would have been different if that evidence had been disclosed; the defendants were convicted; and the guilty verdict was overturned or invalidated in some fashion. Are §1983 suits against officers for *Brady* violations really likely to be so common? And if they were, what would that mean?

4. *Dividing police and prosecutors.* Judge Wilkinson in his concurrence in *Jean v. Collins*, 221 F.3d 656, 661 (4th Cir. 2000), also worried that §1983 litigation would *divide* the prosecution team:

> To hold officers responsible under §1983 for internal miscommunications that *Kyles* and *Giglio* charge the prosecution with preventing is to have §1983 suits and *Brady* doctrine heading in diametrically opposed directions. Moreover, the §1983 suit could well set up a continual exercise in finger-pointing between prosecutors and police over whose fault it was that the evidence never reached the defendant. Making internal communications between prosecutors and police the customary subject of §1983 litigation would thrust the federal courts deep into the operations of state prosecutors' offices, a breach of federalism principles for which the Due Process Clause of the Constitution provides no warrant.

That is one possibility. Given that prosecutors are immune from suit and police officers are not, might prosecutors instead take the fall for the police? Might they be encouraged to do so given that the municipality, not the officer, will usually pay the damages when an officer is found liable? Do you think collusion is likely? Why?

5. *Evaluating* Moldowan. Is the majority in *Moldowan* doing an end run around the Supreme Court's decision to place the *Brady* responsibility on prosecutors? Or is it instead following the Supreme Court's underlying goal of protecting fair trials by ensuring that police officers and cities that indemnify them have a financial incentive to comply with *Brady*? Or neither?

B.   *Police Officers as the Subjects of Discovery*

As the above sections discuss, the *Brady* doctrine gives defendants a due process right to exculpatory evidence. Under *Giglio v. United States*, 405 U.S. 150, 154 (1972), that right extends to impeachment evidence, which is used to question the credibility of a trial witness. Police officers are repeat witnesses at trial. What information about police officers should the government be required to turn over to defendants?

MILKE v. RYAN
711 F.3d 998 (9th Cir. 2013)

KOZINSKI, CHIEF JUDGE.

In 1990, a jury convicted Debra Milke of murdering her four-year-old son, Christopher. The judge sentenced her to death. The trial was, essentially, a swearing contest between Milke and Phoenix Police Detective Armando Saldate, Jr. Saldate testified that Milke, twenty-five at the time, had confessed when he interviewed her shortly after the murder; Milke protested her innocence and denied confessing. There were no other witnesses or direct evidence linking Milke to the crime. The judge and jury believed Saldate, but they didn't know about Saldate's long history of lying under oath and other misconduct. The state knew about this misconduct but didn't disclose it, despite the requirements of *Brady v. Maryland*, 373 U.S. 83, 87 (1963), and *Giglio v. United States*, 405 U.S. 150, 153–155 (1972). Some of the misconduct wasn't disclosed until the case came to federal court and, even today, some evidence relevant to Saldate's credibility hasn't been produced, perhaps because it's been destroyed. In the balance hangs the life of Milke, who has been on Arizona's death row for twenty-two years.

Facts

On the last evening of his short life, Christopher Milke saw Santa Claus at the mall. He woke up the next morning begging his mother to let him go again. Debra agreed and sent Christopher to the mall with her roommate, James Styers. On the way, Styers picked up his friend, Roger Scott. But instead of heading to the mall, the two men drove the boy out of town to a secluded ravine, where Styers shot Christopher three times in the head. Styers and Scott then drove to the mall, where they reported Christopher as missing.

Sunday morning, less than a day into the missing-child investigation, police began to suspect Styers and Scott. It was supposed to be Detective Saldate's day off, but the homicide sergeant in charge of the case called him in. . . . Soon after Saldate's appearance, Scott broke. He led the detectives to Christopher's body and told them where he and Styers had thrown the unspent ammunition. According to Saldate, Scott said along the way that Debra Milke had been involved. Detective Saldate seized on the statement and flew by helicopter to Florence, Arizona, where Milke had gone to stay . . . after she learned of Christopher's disappearance.

In Florence, . . . Saldate placed Milke under arrest and read out her *Miranda* rights. According to Saldate, when Milke started to tell him that she'd complained about Christopher to Styers but never realized Styers would hurt the boy, Saldate shut her down: "I immediately, of course, told her that wasn't the truth and I told her I wasn't going to tolerate that, that I wasn't there to listen to lies, nor did I have the time."

With that, Saldate claims, Milke opened up to him about the most intimate details of her life. He testified that, in the span of just thirty minutes, Milke knowingly waived her rights to silence and counsel, reminisced about her high school years when she was "in love with life," feigned tears, calmed down, narrated her failed marriage to Mark Milke—his drug and alcohol abuse and his arrests—recounted how she'd gotten pregnant while on birth control and contemplated an abortion, even making an appointment for one, discussed her fear that Christopher was becoming like his father, confessed to a murder conspiracy, characterized the conspiracy as a "bad judgment call" and solicited Saldate's opinion about whether her family would ever understand. (His view: No.)

By the end of the interview, Saldate had more than just cinched the case against Milke; he'd helped her emotionally. According to Saldate, Milke said she was "starting to feel better and was starting to get some of her self-esteem back." . . .

Milke has always denied involvement in the murder, and her account of the interrogation differs substantially from Saldate's. Milke testified that she told Saldate she didn't understand the *Miranda* warnings and that, when Saldate asked if she wanted the interrogation taped, she said: "No, I need a lawyer." According to Milke, Saldate ignored her request, instead putting his hands on her knees and proceeding with the interrogation; he then embellished and twisted Milke's statements to make it sound like she had confessed.

The jury had no independent way of verifying these divergent accounts. Saldate didn't record the interrogation, even though his supervisor instructed him to do so. Saldate didn't bring a tape recorder to the interview, nor did he ask anyone to witness the interrogation by sitting in the room or watching through a two-way mirror. Saldate also skipped the basic step of having Milke sign a *Miranda* waiver. Not even Saldate's interview notes made it into court: Saldate testified that he destroyed them after writing his official report three days after the interrogation.

The jury thus had nothing more than Saldate's word that Milke confessed. Everything the state claims happened in the interrogation room depends on believing Saldate's testimony. Without Saldate's testimony, the prosecution had no case against Milke, as there was no physical evidence linking her to the crime and neither of her supposed co-conspirators—Styers and Scott—would testify against her. But Saldate was an experienced witness and his account of Milke's purported confession proved convincing. The jury found Milke guilty of murder, conspiracy to commit murder, child abuse and kidnapping. The judge sentenced her to death.

Normally that would be the end of the matter. Right or wrong, a jury's credibility determinations are entitled to respect. But the Constitution requires a fair trial, and one essential element of fairness is the prosecution's obligation to turn over exculpatory evidence. This never happened in Milke's case, so the jury trusted Saldate without hearing of his long history of lies and misconduct.

The Appendix contains summaries of some of Saldate's misconduct and the accompanying court orders and disciplinary action. This history includes a five-day suspension for taking "liberties" with a female motorist and then lying about it to his supervisors; four court cases where judges tossed out confessions or indictments because Saldate lied under oath; and four cases where judges suppressed confessions or vacated convictions because Saldate had violated the Fifth Amendment or the Fourth Amendment in the course of interrogations. And it is far from clear that this reflects a full account of Saldate's misconduct as a police officer. All of this information should have been disclosed to Milke and the jury, but the state remained unconstitutionally silent.

Discussion. . . .

. . . Brady *Claim on the Merits*

Due process imposes an "inescapable" duty on the prosecutor "to disclose known, favorable evidence rising to a material level of importance." Kyles v. Whitley, 514 U.S. 419, 438 (1995). Favorable evidence includes both exculpatory and impeachment material that is relevant either to guilt or punishment. See United States v. Bagley, 473 U.S. 667, 674–676 (1985); *Giglio*, 405 U.S. at 154. The prosecutor is charged with knowledge of any *Brady* material of which the prosecutor's office or the investigating police agency is aware.

A *Brady* violation has three elements. First, there must be evidence that is favorable to the defense, either because it is exculpatory or impeaching. Second, the government must have willfully or inadvertently failed to produce the evidence. Third, the suppression must have prejudiced the defendant.

1. *Favorable evidence*. . . . Saldate's personnel file contained an internal investigation report showing he had been suspended for five days. The report explains that Saldate stopped a female motorist who had a faulty taillight and possibly an outstanding warrant. He let her go without checking her warrant. Let her go isn't quite accurate. Saldate suggested they move to a less conspicuous spot and then followed her to it. Once there, he leaned into her car, "took liberties" with her and acted in a manner "unbecoming an officer." She offered to meet him later for an "act of sexual intercourse." Saldate showed up for the rendezvous, but the woman didn't. Instead, someone—perhaps the woman, once she got free of Saldate—reported Saldate's misconduct to the police.

Questioned by investigators, Saldate steadfastly lied about the incident until he failed a polygraph test. "[Y]our image of honesty, competency, and overall reliability must be questioned," one of Saldate's supervisors wrote in a report signed by the city manager and the chief of police. The facts of Saldate's misconduct, his lies to the investigators and this assessment by his supervisor would certainly have been useful to a jury trying to decide whether Saldate or Milke was telling the truth. Not only does the report show that Saldate has no compunction about lying during the course of his official duties, it discloses a misogynistic attitude toward female civilians and a willingness to abuse his authority to get what he wants. All of this is highly consistent with Milke's account of the interrogation.

The court orders Milke's lawyers uncovered are also favorable evidence that was available to the state but the prosecution did not disclose. As Milke argued to the state post-conviction court, the orders show that Saldate "has lied under oath in order to secure a conviction or to further a prosecution." Those cases all involved the Maricopa County Attorney's Office and the Phoenix Police Department—the same agencies involved in prosecuting Milke. . . .

. . . Had Milke been able to present Saldate's menagerie of lies and constitutional violations, her allocution may well have resonated with the sentencing judge and persuaded her to spare Milke's life. Indeed, the trial judge herself acknowledged that she was considering "legitimate questions concerning guilt" as a mitigating factor, only to find she had no such questions about guilt. Had the judge known about Saldate's documented misconduct, she may well have developed such "legitimate questions concerning guilt."

2. *Suppression.* The second element of a *Brady* violation is the willful or inadvertent failure of the prosecutor to disclose evidence favorable to the defendant. We have long held that the government has a *Brady* obligation "to produce any favorable evidence in the personnel records" of an officer. United States v. Cadet, 727 F.2d 1453, 1467 (9th Cir. 1984). . . .

The state is charged with the knowledge that there was impeachment material in Saldate's personnel file. After all, the state eventually produced some of this evidence in federal habeas proceedings and has never claimed that it could not have disclosed it in time for Milke's trial. There can be no doubt that the state failed in its constitutional obligation of producing this material without any request by the defense.

The state also had an obligation to produce the documents showing Saldate's false and misleading statements in court and before grand juries, as well as the documents showing the Fifth Amendment and Fourth Amendment violations he committed during interrogations. The prosecutor's office no doubt knew of this misconduct because it had harmed criminal prosecutions. The police must have known, too.

. . . [E]ven as Milke's attorney was working hard to stave off a death sentence and win a new trial or judgment notwithstanding the verdict, the prosecutor's office and the police were actively dealing with Saldate's misconduct in another murder case. . . .

. . . [I]t must have occurred to Rood or *someone* in the prosecutor's office or the police department (or both) that Saldate was also the key witness in the high-profile case against Debra Milke—a case where the defendant was still at trial, actively fighting for her life. Yet no one saw fit to disclose this or any of the other instances of Saldate's misconduct to Milke's lawyer.

Even if there somehow weren't actual knowledge of Saldate's misconduct, inadvertent failure to disclose is enough for a *Brady* violation. . . .

3. *Prejudice.* To find prejudice under *Brady* and *Giglio*, it . . . suffices that there be "a reasonable probability of a different result" as to either guilt or penalty. Prejudice exists "when the government's evidentiary suppression undermines confidence in the outcome of the trial." *Kyles*, 514 U.S. at 434.

Milke's alleged confession, as reported by Saldate, was the only direct evidence linking Milke to the crime. But the confession was only as good as Saldate's word, as he's the only one who claims to have heard Milke confess and there's no recording, written statement or any other evidence that Milke confessed. Saldate's credibility was crucial to the state's case against Milke. It's hard to imagine anything more relevant to the jury's—or the judge's—determination whether to believe Saldate than evidence that Saldate lied under oath and trampled the constitutional rights of suspects in discharging his official duties. If even a single juror had found Saldate untrustworthy based on the documentation that he habitually lied under oath or that he took advantage of women he had in his power, there would have been at least a hung jury. Likewise, if this evidence had been disclosed, it may well have led the judge to order a new trial, enter judgment notwithstanding the verdict or, at least, impose a sentence less than death. . . .

Also at issue was Saldate's claim — again, unsupported by evidence — that Milke waived her *Miranda* rights and didn't ask for a lawyer. Beyond its effect on Saldate's credibility, evidence of Saldate's falsifications and his disregard of *Miranda*, would have been highly relevant to the determination of whether Milke's alleged confession had been lawfully obtained. The suppression of evidence of Saldate's lies and misconduct thus qualifies as prejudicial for purposes of *Brady* and *Giglio*.

III. Conclusion

Milke is entitled to habeas relief. . . .
[Appendix listing Saldate's misconduct omitted]

CHIEF JUDGE KOZINSKI, concurring:[2]
This is a disturbing case. There's no physical evidence linking Debra Milke to the crime, and she has maintained her innocence since the day she was arrested. Neither of the men who actually did the killing testified against Milke. Roger Scott refused to testify because his "testimony would not be what he felt was the truth." After spending many years on death row, James Styers continued to insist that "Debbie had nothing to do with it and thats [sic] the truth." The *only* evidence linking Milke to the murder of her son is the word of Detective Armando Saldate, Jr. — a police officer with a long history of misconduct that includes lying under oath as well as accepting sexual favors in exchange for leniency and lying about it.

Equally troubling are Saldate's unorthodox interrogation methods. Saldate has obtained confessions from people who were intoxicated, hospitalized and on pain medication. Saldate once ordered a juvenile to be detained in an interrogation room, where he was handcuffed to a table, even though the police had "no information linking the Defendant" to a crime. The trial court suppressed the resultant murder confession and called the illegal detention "a show of flagrant misconduct." . . . In another case, Saldate admitted interrogating a suspect who was strapped to a hospital bed, incoherent after apparently suffering a skull fracture.

Then there's Saldate's practice of disregarding the right to remain silent when invoked by suspects he's questioning. . . . In Milke's case, Saldate testified that he doesn't have to stop talking to suspects just "because they asked for an attorney. That would be ridiculous. . . ." What I find ridiculous is that this man — with his track record of trampling basic constitutional rights — is sent to interrogate a suspect without a tape recorder, a video recorder, a witness or any other objective means of documenting the interrogation. . . .

---

[2] *Ed. note:* Yes, Judge Kozinski concurred with his own majority opinion. Doing so is unusual, but not unheard of. See, e.g., K.T. v. Royal Caribbean Cruises, Ltd., 931 F.3d 1041 (11th Cir. 2019) (Carnes, C.J.); *id.* at 1047 (Carnes, C.J., concurring); Ciraolo v. City of New York, 216 F.3d 236 (2d Cir. 2000) (Calabresi, J.); *id.* at 242 (Calabresi, J., concurring); Cheong v. Antablin, 946 P.2d 817 (Cal. 1997) (Chin, J.); *id.* at 1078 (Chin., J., concurring) ("Obviously, I concur in the majority opinion I have authored.").

No civilized system of justice should have to depend on such flimsy evidence, quite possibly tainted by dishonesty or overzealousness, to decide whether to take someone's life or liberty. The Phoenix Police Department and Saldate's supervisors there should be ashamed of having given free rein to a lawless cop to misbehave again and again, undermining the integrity of the system of justice they were sworn to uphold. As should the Maricopa County Attorney's Office, which continued to prosecute Saldate's cases without bothering to disclose his pattern of misconduct.

Indeed, given Saldate's long history of trampling the rights of suspects, one wonders how Saldate came to interrogate a suspect in a high-profile murder case by himself, without a tape recorder or a witness. And how could an interrogation be concluded, and a confession extracted, without a signed *Miranda* waiver? In a quarter century on the Ninth Circuit, I can't remember another case where the confession and *Miranda* waiver were proven by nothing but the say-so of a single officer. Is this par for the Phoenix Police Department or was Saldate called in on his day off because his supervisors knew he could be counted on to bend the rules, even lie convincingly, if that's what it took to nail down a conviction in a high-profile case?

It's not just fairness to the defendant that calls for an objectively verifiable process for securing confessions and other evidence in criminal cases. We all have a stake in ensuring that our criminal justice system reliably separates the guilty from the innocent. Letting police get away with manufacturing confessions or planting evidence not only risks convicting the innocent but helps the guilty avoid detection and strike again. . . .

I would reverse the district court's finding that Milke knowingly waived her rights under *Miranda* and *Edwards v. Arizona*, 451 U.S. 477 (1981). The "confession," if it was obtained at all, was extracted illegally. There can be no serious claim that admission of the confession was harmless. I would therefore set aside Milke's conviction on the separate ground that it relied on an illegally-obtained confession that probably never occurred, and bar use of the so-called confession during any retrial of Milke.

NOTES AND QUESTIONS

1. *Impeachment evidence against police officers.* As *Milke* suggests, Milke could have undermined Saldate's testimony if she knew he had lied in the past. Parties often cross-examine witnesses by confronting them with their prior untruthful acts. For officers, defendants raise instances in which the officer lied under oath, filed a false report, covered up misconduct by another officer, cheated, or stole. Defendants can also confront officers with other acts of misconduct, such as uses of excessive force or relevant racial, religious, or other bias. But they need to learn of the acts first, which requires that someone keep records and turn them over to the defense.

2. *Access to officers' personnel files.* As *Milke* indicates, police misconduct is *Brady/Giglio* material. In recent years, some of the fiercest debates about *Brady* have taken place over how much access defendants should have to police personnel files. These files include department records on officers' performance, misconduct incidents, and disciplinary findings. Because that information can be used to impeach an officer's trial testimony, defendants claim that they should have access to those files. Yet

many state laws restrict access to police files, and in practice these laws often dictate defendants' access to police misconduct records, despite the constitutional issues at stake. A dozen states make misconduct records publicly available, and another 15 or so make them available on a limited basis; for example, when a misconduct investigation has resulted in discipline against an officer. Some, however, are far more restrictive, limiting most access to records. Through these laws, states accommodate the competing concerns of officer privacy and safety interests on one hand with the public's interest in transparency and the defendant's right to exculpatory evidence in individual cases, on the other. See Rachel Moran, *Police Privacy*, 10 U.C. Irvine L. Rev. 153 (2019). (For an excellent but dated resource on public access to misconduct records in the states, see Robert Lewis et al., *Is Police Misconduct a Secret in Your State?*, WYNC (Oct. 15, 2015).) *Brady* is a constitutional right, right? How can these state laws constrain it in this way?

3. *Obligation to investigate.* Even if prosecutors have access, some do not routinely look at police files for disciplinary records, and defendants may never see those records as a result. Despite language in *Kyles* that puts the onus on prosecutors, some authorities have expressly concluded that prosecutors have no affirmative obligation to seek out *Brady* evidence, at least when it comes to police witnesses with histories of misconduct. See, e.g., People v. Garrett, 18 N.E.3d 722, 732 (N.Y. 2014); see also Comm. on Ethics & Prof'l Responsibility, Am. Bar Assoc., Formal Opinion 09-454, *Prosecutor's Duty to Disclose Evidence and Information Favorable to the Defense* 4 (2009) (concluding that Model Rule of Professional Conduct 3.8 "does not establish a duty to undertake an investigation in search of exculpatory evidence"). But see, e.g., State v. Theodosopoulos, 893 A.2d 712, 714 (N.H. 2006) (requiring prosecutor to review police personnel files).

4. *A problem: Jimmy.* Sgt. Landsman, a patrol supervisor, learns that one of his officers, Jimmy, has been falsely telling dispatchers that he is responding to "flag downs" (service initiated by a city resident approaching or hailing a patrol car) when he is actually visiting his girlfriend while on duty. Sgt. Landsman tells Jimmy to cut it out and assigns him to a foot-patrol beat that will be harder to leave. Jimmy later arrests a drug dealer for a street sale. The State's Attorney's Office discloses Jimmy's investigation report and personnel record, which notes his assignment change but does not specify a reason. Has a *Brady* or *Giglio* violation occurred?

5. *Scope of impeachment evidence against officers.* Disciplinary records are not the only evidence that might be used to cross-examine police officers. What about allegations of misconduct that were never substantiated? What if the department never investigated? Some courts allow officers to be cross-examined about off-duty conduct. Should an officer be required to disclose an extramarital affair? After all, an affair arguably shows a willingness to cheat and lie in one context, which might suggest a willingness to cheat and lie in another. Would you want to become an officer knowing you were legally obligated to disclose that kind of personal wrongdoing? Or would you trust that no one would find out? What about off-duty conduct that suggests bias or unfairness, such as a Facebook post that advocates "Death to Islam" in a case involving a Muslim defendant? Or an Instagram picture that says, "It's a good day for a chokehold"? For additional examples, google the Plain View Project, which has collected Facebook posts by police officers. The issues are complex.

An officer's social media post collected by the Plain View Project.

6. *Police as repeat players.* Other witnesses face embarrassing cross-examination too, but at least arguably, officers are different. An informant put on the stand might be embarrassed by a deal with the government or a prior conviction, but that embarrassment eases when a verdict is issued. By contrast, police testify again and again as a part of their jobs, which creates greater opportunity to create and uncover *Giglio* material. Once impeachment evidence against a police officer is released, it might not easily go away. In fact, defense attorneys sometimes create repositories of police misconduct information, and some make the records public, including New York Legal Aid Society's Cop Accountability Project database. Several news sites have also done major exposés of police misconduct information. See, e.g., Steve Reilly & Mark Nichols, *Hundreds of Police Officers Have Been Labeled Liars. Some Still Help Send People to Prison,* USA Today (Oct. 17, 2019). Perhaps even worse for officers with a past, district attorneys' offices keep lists of officers who are so tainted that prosecutors do not want to use them at trial. Being on a *Brady* list (see box below)

can be career-killing. Even if the list is not made public, it can mean reassignment to what is sometimes informally called a *liars' squad*, some unappealing administrative unit where departmental command staff sticks officers who cannot go to court.

7. *Police privacy and criminal defendants.* Unsurprisingly, then, the fight over access to personnel files is fierce. Unions and officers fight hard in courts, in legislatures, and in the media to limit access and to discourage *Brady* lists. According to Jonathan Abel, all of this has consequences for defendants:

> The cumulative effect of all these impediments is that personnel files and all the impeachment material they contain are often ignored with impunity. In too many places, the belief persists that these files can go unexamined without violating *Brady*—that these files are somehow beyond the reach of the *Brady* doctrine. This view lacks firm footing in good law or good policy, and the sooner it is discarded, the better.

Jonathan Abel, Brady*'s Blind Spot: Impeachment Evidence in Police Personnel Files and the Battle Splitting the Prosecution Team,* 67 Stan. L. Rev. 743, 808 (2015). Rachel Moran argues that limiting access to personnel files distorts criminal trials:

> On the one hand, our data collection systems and evidentiary doctrines allow the government nearly instant access to a defendant's entire history of encounters with the law, disincentivize defendants from testifying on their own behalf, and give prosecutors myriad means to introduce evidence suggesting that the defendant is, based on prior misdeeds, more likely to be guilty of the charged crime. On the other hand, the law perversely prevents defendants from casting doubt on the credibility of police officers by making police misconduct records confidential and, in many cases, inaccessible to defendants. This unequal distribution of access and ability to utilize information creates trials where the jury is exposed to extensive evidence suggesting the accused is not credible, but remains naive to any reasons to question the credibility of the defendant's primary accuser, the police officer.

Rachel Moran, *Contesting Police Credibility*, 93 Wash. L. Rev. 1339, 1342–1343 (2018).

What should be done about the array of local practices, state legislation, and court rulings that have undermined *Brady* with respect to impeachment evidence against police officers? What does the existence of this array suggest about the challenges of regulating the police through constitutional rights more generally?

8. *Turning tide?* Several states have revised their statutes to allow more access to personnel files. California's new rule took effect in 2019. See 2018 Cal. Stat. ch. 988, §2 (amending Cal. Penal Code §832.7). In 2020, New York repealed N.Y. Civ. Rights Law §50-a, one of the most restrictive personnel-file-access laws in the nation. See 2020 N.Y. Laws ch. 96 (repealing N.Y. Civ. Rights Law §50-a). The law, passed in 1976, denied access to personnel files even to prosecutors, except by court order. Critics called for changing the law many times over the decades since. Their cries became especially loud after Daniel Pantaleo killed Eric Garner, a 43-year-old unarmed Black man, during an arrest for selling loose cigarettes on Staten Island in 2014. As a video of the incident shows, when Garner pulled his arms away, Pantaleo grabbed Garner around the neck and wrestled him to the ground. Garner repeatedly told officers, "I can't breathe," as officers pressed his head into the ground before he fell unconscious. See "I Can't Breathe"; Eric Garner Put in Chokehold by NYPD Officer—Video, Guardian (Dec. 4, 2014). The NYPD invoked §50-a to avoid disclosing the misconduct history of

Pantaleo, who—according to leaked documents—had more than a dozen allegations against him and four complaints sustained by the New York City Civilian Complaint Review Board.

Although thousands of people protested around the country chanting Garner's dying words, and a bill to repeal §50-a was introduced each year between 2015 and 2019, the law held. The Police Benevolent Association of New York City fiercely opposed reform and spent more than $1.4 million on campaign contributions and lobbying fees during the same period. See Greg B. Smith, *Police Union Poised to Tap War Chest to Shield Cop Discipline Records*, AMNY (Jun. 1, 2020). Then, on May 25, 2020, Minneapolis police officer Derek Chauvin, an officer with his own history of sustained complaints, knelt on George Floyd's neck for minutes, killing him, while Floyd, echoing Garner, repeatedly said, "I can't breathe." This time, hundreds of thousands of protesters marched nationwide, and within weeks, the New York legislature repealed its long-standing statute.

Prosecutor Do Not Call or *Brady* Lists

The *Brady* doctrine does not stop officers from testifying but, if followed, it ensures that some will face devastating cross-examination if they do. No lawyer relishes calling a witness the jury is unlikely to believe because doing so can cast doubt on the lawyers and the rest of their case. To avoid putting forward incredible witnesses and to maintain the integrity of trials, some prosecutors maintain lists of officers they consider too tainted to testify, known as *Brady* lists, *Giglio* lists, liars' lists, or Do Not Call lists.

Brady lists help ensure that prosecutors are not surprised when they prepare for trial. They also encourage police command staff to avoid assigning listed officers to make arrests or investigate cases because having those officers involved could make cases unprosecutable. *Brady* lists might also discourage police misconduct by amplifying its practical and reputational effects. Cf. Rachel A. Harmon, *The Problem of Policing*, 110 Mich. L. Rev. 761, 805 (2012) (discussing *Giglio* as establishing a form of prosecutorial regulation of police misconduct). But *Brady* lists are problematic, too.

First, *process*. *Brady* lists are an informal means for shaping officer conduct. There are no legal standards for putting officers on such lists, and few mechanisms ensure that decisions to do so are fair, accurate, or unbiased. The process is not transparent, and little opportunity exists for appeal or review. Officers have alleged that they landed on *Brady* lists as retaliation for politically opposing a district attorney or investigating corruption in the prosecutors' office. Some jurisdictions are responding to complaints by establishing clear guidelines for officers' inclusion on a *Brady* list.

Second, *access*. In Philadelphia, public defenders successfully sued the district attorney's office to turn over its *Brady* list to the defenders. The list was soon published in a newspaper. See Mark Fazlollah et al., *Under Court Order, District Attorney Krasner Releases List of Tainted Police*, Phila. Inquirer (Apr. 26, 2019). Similarly, the Los Angeles Sheriff's Department kept an internal *Brady* list, and although the department was initially barred by a California court from turning the list over to the district attorney's office after the deputies' union sued, the California Supreme Court held that the department was allowed to disclose impeachment material in an officer's confidential personnel files. See Assn. for L.A. Deputy Sheriffs v. Superior Court, 447 P.3d 234 (Cal. 2019).

Third, *consequences*. *Brady* lists are usually created to prevent prosecutors from using easily impeached officers at trial and to encourage police departments to avoid building cases that depend on those officers. For officers, though, the lists can compound the consequences of prior misconduct in ways that seem unfair. Imagine an officer who lies about probable cause in a police report and is disciplined but not fired by his department in a process subject to extensive procedural protections and review. If the prosecutor's office later puts this officer on a *Brady* list, command staff might feel pressure to move him to an administrative assignment to avoid undermining cases, which is in effect a further demotion for the same conduct. Officers worry that police chiefs and prosecutors can use *Brady* lists to collude to achieve outcomes that legal protections and collective-bargaining agreements otherwise protect against. See Jonathan Abel, *Brady's Blind Spot: Impeachment Evidence in Police Personnel Files and the Battle Splitting the Prosecution Team*, 67 Stan. L. Rev. 743, 781–782 (2015).

Officers have fought hard to avoid professional damage from *Brady* lists, and several states have passed laws to prevent "punitive" action against officers because their names have been placed on such a list. See, e.g., Cal. Gov't Code §3305.5; Md. Code. Ann., Pub. Safety §3-106.1. Although those laws might be intended to mitigate the harms of *Brady* lists, they also arguably put police departments between a rock and a hard place. State and local law and collective-bargaining agreements can make it hard for a department to demote or fire an officer for misconduct, so police departments are often stuck with officers who have extensive histories of misconduct and lying. If prosecutors will not use those officers at trial, departments cannot give them assignments that require them to testify. What should departments do with such officers? Is it so clear that an officer should face no further consequences if he accumulates so much baggage that he cannot be used in court? Cf. Jonathan Abel, *Brady's Blindspot: Impeachment Evidence in Police Personnel Files and the Battle Splitting the Prosecution Team*, 67 Stan. L. Rev. 743, 745 (2015) (discussing the "difficult situation for police management, which may find itself stuck with an officer who cannot testify because the prosecutor does not trust her, but who also cannot be terminated because the officer fought off her termination through arbitration"). Before you feel too sorry for police chiefs burdened with such officers, consider that they can mitigate the problem by developing better systems to prevent lying and misconduct in the first place, and *Brady* lists might help pressure them to do so.

9. *Destroying misconduct records.* Recall from *Kyles* that the *Brady* obligation extends to "favorable evidence known to the others acting on the government's behalf in the case." In response to California's 2019 law making certain law enforcement misconduct records accessible to the public, several California agencies have begun destroying records. See Liam Dillon & Maya Lau, *Transparency Law Fought with Lawsuits, Shredders,* L.A. Times (Jan. 10, 2019), at B1. In fact, many departments have a policy of doing so. When Stephen Rushin studied 178 collective-bargaining agreements in large cities, he found that 87 had language requiring departments to purge personnel files of complaints or disciplinary action, often after one to three years. Stephen Rushin, *Police Union Contracts,* 66 Duke L. J. 1191, 1230–1231 (2017). In the Phoenix Police Department, over five years, 90 percent of records of sustained misconduct had

been erased, often far earlier than required by the contract. Justin Price, *Phoenix Police Routinely "Purge" Officer Discipline Records, Keep Misconduct Secret*, Ariz. Republic (Aug. 27, 2019). If personnel records are destroyed or transferred to other city departments, are they *known* to the police department? Doesn't that sound like an end run around *Kyles*? Can police unions collectively bargain away defendants' constitutional rights?

10. *The costs of destroying records.* Purged files have many other accountability consequences beyond *Brady*. If their records are purged, officers can receive promotions and excellent performance evaluations despite relatively recent serious misconduct. Purging records can also make patterns of misconduct in a department nearly invisible, even to department leadership. See Rushin, *supra*, at 1231–1232. And the Phoenix investigation revealed that 16 sergeants and lieutenants had investigated 156 complaints against subordinates, even after they were themselves disciplined for misconduct and included on prosecutorial *Brady* lists. Price, *supra*. What does that say about police accountability?

11. Brady *and accountability.* Fights over the government's obligation to turn disciplinary records over to defendants have helped bring attention to the laws and collective-bargaining agreements that make disciplinary records inaccessible. Still, maybe *Brady* is also a distraction. Although disciplinary records can be useful to impeach an officer's testimony, far more is at stake in public access to these records: They are, in fact, *personnel* records, which describe and affect individual officers. They are also *government* records, which can provide a window into how and when a department holds officers accountable for their actions, which tells the public something important about a department's commitment to transparency and accountability. Is there a risk that battling about them in the context of discovery, where the individual constitutional rights of defendants take center stage, could distort public policy debate over this (and other) aspects of policing?

PART THREE

STREET POLICING

How do police departments try "to protect and to serve?"[1] Although policing could include many activities, since the invention of the emergency-call system in the late 1960s, departments have largely organized according to the *standard model.* This model is built around what are sometimes known as the "three Rs": random patrol, rapid response, and reactive investigation. See Lawrence W. Sherman, *The Rise of Evidence-Based Policing: Targeting, Testing, and Tracking,* 42 Crime & Just. 377, 378 (2013). Local officers (1) engage in patrol to prevent crime and address crime and disorder as it arises; (2) while on patrol, respond to calls for service from members of the public; and (3) when a service call uncovers a potential crime, investigate, make arrests, collect evidence, and, sometimes, turn the case over to detectives. Although many departments now also proactively address specific crime and order problems, such as violent-crime hot spots, drug dealing in local parks, or prostitution, most local police departments continue to devote the majority of their resources to the standard model.

---

[1] The phrase "to protect and to serve" is the motto of the Los Angeles Police Department. It originated in 1955 as the winning entry in a contest for officers. The goal was to create a motto "that in a few words would express some or all the ideals to which the Los Angeles police service is dedicated." *To Protect and to Serve,* L.A. Police Beat, Dec. 1963, at 3. After the phrase served for a few years as the motto for the police academy, a city ordinance was passed in 1963 adopting it formally for the department as a whole. Many departments around the country have adopted a version of the motto since.

Part Two of the book looked at some of the rules governing criminal investigations, including those that arise in response to crime reports, the third "R." This part of the book considers the legal rules that govern *police interactions on the street*, which often arise in the context of the first two "Rs." Local police officers mostly patrol geographic beats, largely in cars, although also on foot, bicycles, and motorcycles. They respond to calls about public behavior, stop and question pedestrians, conduct traffic stops, check buildings and other areas, monitor large gatherings, and engage in informal interactions with members of the public.

Why engage in this kind of street policing? There are three primary reasons:

1. *Criminal-law enforcement.* By policing geographic beats, police make themselves available to respond quickly to calls about criminal activity and sometimes witness criminal activity firsthand. This allows police to stop crimes in progress and rapidly apprehend criminals.

2. *Crime prevention.* By being present in communities, police deter crime. With the appearance of omnipresence, officers hope to change the calculus of criminal activity, both by decreasing the perceived likelihood that would-be criminals will succeed and by increasing the perceived risk that those who commit crimes will be caught and sanctioned.

3. *Order maintenance and community caretaking.* Police officers on the streets are available to deal with noncriminal (or low-level criminal) threats to safety and order. These activities are commonly labeled order maintenance and community caretaking. Officers engaged in *order maintenance* manage the use of public spaces, stopping activities that the community prohibits and handling conflicts, complaints, and other public dangers. It is in this capacity that police address fights, protests, verbal harassment, aggressive panhandling, noise issues, people who are drunk and disorderly in public, people experiencing mental-health crises, or people urinating on the sidewalk. Traffic control and enforcement by patrol officers also can serve as a form of order maintenance.[2] *Community caretaking* activities are closely related. However, rather than addressing public disorder, patrol officers engaged in community caretaking often handle private threats to personal safety or property that do not appear to violate the law: They assist when cars crash; check on people who might need medical aid; and help to address situations, like a water leak, that could destroy property.

How do police perform these tasks? Command staff at departments set priorities and determine the objectives that they want officers to pursue. Supervisors tell officers what to do each day. Officers hit the street attempting to fulfill those expectations and to deal with other situations as they arise, sometimes helping to facilitate noncoercive solutions, sometimes briefly detaining and questioning people about their activities, and sometimes arresting people they believe to have violated the law.

A multifaceted legal regime governs patrol activities. State criminal law, traffic law, and local ordinances determine what members of the public are forbidden from doing. State criminal procedure statutes and common law doctrines authorize

---

[2] Traffic direction and stops may serve any of the functions of street policing: law enforcement, crime prevention, or order maintenance. It also may be used pretextually to uncover crime proactively, a subject discussed in Chapter 6. As this example suggests, the lines between these categories are fluid.

police to engage in stops, searches, tickets and summons, or arrests to enforce those rules and to use force, if necessary, to carry out those activities. Federal constitutional law, along with state constitutional law and statutes, sets some boundaries on police power on the streets: The Fourth Amendment imposes conditions and limits on detentions and arrests, and it regulates the force police may use to effect them. The Equal Protection Clause prohibits officers and departments from making policing decisions based on race or other protected characteristics. The First Amendment restricts police from using criminal prohibitions to stop or retaliate against some kinds of speech and political behavior. The vagueness doctrine, derived from Fifth and Fourteenth Amendment due process, sets some limits on how states grant officers authority and discretion. The next several chapters consider the laws that govern some of the major tools and challenges of street policing.

Chapter 5

Preventing Crime

This chapter considers the primarily constitutional rules that govern one of the most common tools officers use to police the streets: brief detentions in the form of pedestrian stops. These rules not only regulate many street encounters between the police and members of public, they have contributed to a transformation in American policing.

Police use brief encounters with members of the public to solicit information, identify criminal suspects and activities, enforce low-level criminal prohibitions, deter gun and drug crimes, and more. For some, these quick, routine encounters are a mark of good policing. They connect officers with the public and enable officers to identify and resolve problems early, and they offer reassurance about public safety. For others, especially those who experience them often, stops seem a means of harassing, humiliating, and discriminating against groups, and they reinforce skepticism about police motives and legitimacy. This skepticism can morph into outrage when those stopped are thrown against a wall, sexually assaulted while being frisked, verbally abused, or otherwise degraded before being allowed to go. As with other aspects of policing, the harms of stops are not evenly distributed: People of color, sexual and gender minorities, teenagers, and low-income people, among others, are more likely to be targeted.

This chapter starts with *Terry v. Ohio*, 392 U.S. 1 (1967), in which the Supreme Court held that the Fourth Amendment regulates, though only loosely, police–citizen encounters on the street. The next section considers contemporary policing strategies, which broadly fit under the umbrella of proactive policing. *Terry* has both legitimated and shaped these strategies, as illustrated by *Floyd v. City of New York*, 959 F. Supp. 2d 540 (S.D.N.Y. 2013). The end of the chapter uses *Floyd* as an opportunity to consider questions about the role of constitutional law and litigation in governing preventative policing on the street.

At the end of this chapter, you should be able to describe the Fourth Amendment doctrine that governs brief police–citizen encounters and identify some concerns about the doctrine. You should also be able to distinguish traditional patrol policing from proactive policing strategies that rely on programmatic stops and frisks, and you should be familiar with the special concerns these strategies raise. Finally, you should be able to describe several ways that litigation can influence policing policy, beyond determining the constitutionality of specific police practices.

A.   *Legitimating Brief Encounters*

As you read, identify specifically what the Court allows during an encounter and why.

TERRY v. OHIO

392 U.S. 1 (1967)

MR. CHIEF JUSTICE WARREN delivered the opinion of the Court.

This case presents serious questions concerning the role of the Fourth Amendment in the confrontation on the street between the citizen and the policeman investigating suspicious circumstances.

Petitioner Terry was convicted of carrying a concealed weapon and sentenced to the statutorily prescribed term of one to three years in the penitentiary. Following the denial of a pretrial motion to suppress, the prosecution introduced in evidence two revolvers and a number of bullets seized from Terry and a codefendant, Richard Chilton, by Cleveland Police Detective Martin McFadden. At the hearing on the motion to suppress this evidence, Officer McFadden testified that while he was patrolling in plain clothes in downtown Cleveland at approximately 2:30 in the afternoon of October 31, 1963, his attention was attracted by two men, Chilton and Terry, standing on the corner of Huron Road and Euclid Avenue. He had never seen the two men before, and he was unable to say precisely what first drew his eye to them. However, he testified that he had been a policeman for 39 years and a detective for 35 and that he had been assigned to patrol this vicinity of downtown Cleveland for shoplifters and pickpockets for 30 years. He explained that he had developed routine habits of observation over the years and that he would "stand and watch people or walk and watch people at many intervals of the day." He added: "Now, in this case when I looked over they didn't look right to me at the time."

. . . He saw one of the men leave the other one and walk southwest on Huron Road, past some stores. The man paused for a moment and looked in a store window, then walked on a short distance, turned around and walked back toward the corner, pausing once again to look in the same store window. He rejoined his companion at the corner, and the two conferred briefly. Then the second man went through the same series of motions, strolling down Huron Road, looking in the same window, walking on a short distance, turning back, peering in the store window again, and returning to confer with the first man at the corner. The two men repeated this ritual alternately between five and six times apiece—in all, roughly a dozen trips. At one point, while the two were standing together on the corner, a third man approached them and engaged them briefly in conversation. This man then left the two others and walked west on Euclid Avenue. Chilton and Terry resumed their measured pacing, peering and conferring. After this had gone on for 10 to 12 minutes, the two men walked off together, heading west on Euclid Avenue, following the path taken earlier by the third man.

By this time Officer McFadden . . . suspected the two men of "casing a job, a stick-up," and that he considered it his duty as a police officer to investigate further. He added that he feared "they may have a gun." Thus, Officer McFadden . . . approached the three men, identified himself as a police officer and asked for their names. . . . When the men "mumbled something" in response to his inquiries, Officer McFadden grabbed petitioner Terry, spun him around so that they were facing the other two, with Terry between McFadden and the others, and patted down the outside of his clothing. In the left breast pocket of Terry's overcoat Officer McFadden felt a pistol. He reached inside the overcoat pocket, but was unable to remove the gun. At this point, . . . the officer . . . removed Terry's overcoat completely, removed a .38-caliber revolver from the pocket and ordered all three men to face the wall with their hands raised. Officer McFadden proceeded to pat down the outer clothing of Chilton and the third man, Katz. He discovered another revolver in the outer pocket of Chilton's overcoat, but no weapons were found on Katz. . . . Officer McFadden seized Chilton's gun, asked the proprietor of the store to call a police wagon, and took all three men to the station, where Chilton and Terry were formally charged with carrying concealed weapons. . . .

"Pickpockets' nemesis," Detective Martin McFadden.

After the court denied their motion to suppress, Chilton and Terry waived jury trial and pleaded not guilty. . . . We granted certiorari to determine whether the admission of the revolvers in evidence violated petitioner's rights under the Fourth Amendment, made applicable to the States by the Fourteenth. We affirm the conviction.

I. . . .

. . . Unquestionably petitioner was entitled to the protection of the Fourth Amendment as he walked down the street in Cleveland. The question is whether in all the circumstances of this on-the-street encounter, his right to personal security was violated by an unreasonable search and seizure.

We would be less than candid if we did not acknowledge that this question thrusts to the fore difficult and troublesome issues regarding a sensitive area of police activity—issues which have never before been squarely presented to this Court. Reflective of the tensions involved are the practical and constitutional arguments pressed with great vigor on both sides of the public debate over the power of the police to "stop and frisk"—as it is sometimes euphemistically termed—suspicious persons.

On the one hand, it is frequently argued that in dealing with the rapidly unfolding and often dangerous situations on city streets the police are in need of an escalating set of flexible responses, graduated in relation to the amount of information they possess. For this purpose it is urged that distinctions should be made between a "stop" and an "arrest" (or a "seizure" of a person), and between a "frisk" and a "search." Thus, it is argued, the police should be allowed to "stop" a person and detain him briefly for questioning upon suspicion that he may be connected with criminal activity. Upon suspicion that the person may be armed, the police should have the power to "frisk" him for weapons. If the "stop" and the "frisk" give rise to probable cause to believe that the suspect has committed a crime, then the police should be empowered to make a formal "arrest," and a full incident "search" of the person. This scheme is justified in part upon the notion that a "stop" and a "frisk" amount to a mere "minor inconvenience and petty indignity," which can properly be imposed upon the citizen in the interest of effective law enforcement on the basis of a police officer's suspicion.

On the other side the argument is made that the authority of the police must be strictly circumscribed by the law of arrest and search as it has developed to date in the traditional jurisprudence of the Fourth Amendment. It is contended with some force that there is not—and cannot be—a variety of police activity which does not depend solely upon the voluntary cooperation of the citizen and yet which stops short of an arrest based upon probable cause to make such an arrest. The heart of the Fourth Amendment, the argument runs, is a severe requirement of specific justification for any intrusion upon protected personal security, coupled with a highly developed system of judicial controls to enforce upon the agents of the State the commands of the Constitution. Acquiescence by the courts in the compulsion inherent in the field interrogation practices at issue here, it is urged, would constitute an abdication of judicial control over, and indeed an encouragement of, substantial interference with liberty and personal security by police officers whose judgment is necessarily colored by their primary involvement in "the often competitive enterprise of ferreting out crime." Johnson v. United States, 333 U.S. 10, 14 (1948). This, it is argued, can only serve to exacerbate police–community tensions in the crowded centers of our Nation's cities.

In this context we approach the issues in this case mindful of the limitations of the judicial function in controlling the myriad daily situations in which policemen and citizens confront each other on the street. The State has characterized the issue here as "the right of a police officer . . . to make an on-the-street stop, interrogate and pat down for weapons (known in street vernacular as 'stop and frisk')." But this is only partly accurate. For the issue is not the abstract propriety of the police conduct, but the admissibility against petitioner of the evidence uncovered by the search and seizure. Ever since its inception, the rule excluding evidence seized in violation of the Fourth Amendment has been recognized as a principal mode of discouraging lawless police conduct. See Weeks v. United States, 232 U.S. 383, 391–393 (1914). Thus its major thrust is a deterrent one, and experience has taught that it is the only effective deterrent to police misconduct in the criminal context, and that without it the constitutional guarantee against unreasonable searches and seizures would be a mere "form of words." Mapp v. Ohio, 367 U.S. 643, 655 (1961). The rule also serves another vital function — "the imperative of judicial integrity." . . . Thus in our system evidentiary rulings provide the context in which the judicial process of inclusion and exclusion approves some conduct as comporting with constitutional guarantees and disapproves other actions by state agents. A ruling admitting evidence in a criminal trial, we recognize, has the necessary effect of legitimizing the conduct which produced the evidence, while an application of the exclusionary rule withholds the constitutional imprimatur.

The exclusionary rule has its limitations, however, as a tool of judicial control. It cannot properly be invoked to exclude the products of legitimate police investigative techniques on the ground that much conduct which is closely similar involves unwarranted intrusions upon constitutional protections. Moreover, in some contexts the rule is ineffective as a deterrent. . . . Doubtless some police "field interrogation" conduct violates the Fourth Amendment. But a stern refusal by this Court to condone such activity does not necessarily render it responsive to the exclusionary rule. Regardless of how effective the rule may be where obtaining convictions is an important objective of the police, it is powerless to deter invasions of constitutionally guaranteed rights where the police either have no interest in prosecuting or are willing to forgo successful prosecution in the interest of serving some other goal.

Proper adjudication of cases in which the exclusionary rule is invoked demands a constant awareness of these limitations. The wholesale harassment by certain elements of the police community, of which minority groups, particularly Negroes, frequently complain,[11] will not be stopped by the exclusion of any evidence from any criminal trial. Yet a rigid and unthinking application of the exclusionary rule, in futile protest against practices which it can never be used effectively to control, may exact a high toll in human injury and frustration of efforts to prevent crime.

---

[11] The President's Commission on Law Enforcement and Administration of Justice found that, "[i]n many communities, field interrogations are a major source of friction between the police and minority groups." President's Comm'n on Law Enforcement and Admin. of Justice, *Task Force Report: The Police* 183 (1967). It was reported that the friction caused by "[m]isuse of field interrogations" increases "as more police departments adopt 'aggressive patrol,' in which officers are encouraged routinely to stop and question persons on the street who are unknown to them, who are suspicious, or whose purpose for being abroad is not readily evident." *Id.* at 184. While the frequency with which "frisking" forms a part of field interrogation practice varies tremendously with the locale, the objective of the interrogation, and the particular officer, L. Tiffany, D. McIntyre & D. Rotenberg, *Detection of Crime: Stopping and Questioning, Search and Seizure, Encouragement and Entrapment* 47–48 (1967), it cannot help but be a severely exacerbating factor in police-community tensions. This is particularly true in situations where the "stop and frisk" of youths or minority group members is "motivated by the officers' perceived need to maintain the power image of the beat officer, an aim sometimes accomplished by humiliating anyone who attempts to undermine police control of the streets." *Id.*

No judicial opinion can comprehend the protean variety of the street encounter, and we can only judge the facts of the case before us. Nothing we say today is to be taken as indicating approval of police conduct outside the legitimate investigative sphere. Under our decision, courts still retain their traditional responsibility to guard against police conduct which is over-bearing or harassing, or which trenches upon personal security without the objective evidentiary justification which the Constitution requires. When such conduct is identified, it must be condemned by the judiciary and its fruits must be excluded from evidence in criminal trials. And, of course, our approval of legitimate and restrained investigative conduct undertaken on the basis of ample factual justification should in no way discourage the employment of other remedies than the exclusionary rule to curtail abuses for which that sanction may prove inappropriate.

Having thus roughly sketched the perimeters of the constitutional debate over the limits on police investigative conduct in general and the background against which this case presents itself, we turn our attention to the quite narrow question posed by the facts before us: whether it is always unreasonable for a policeman to seize a person and subject him to a limited search for weapons unless there is probable cause for an arrest. . . .

II.

Our first task is to establish at what point in this encounter the Fourth Amendment becomes relevant. That is, we must decide whether and when Officer McFadden "seized" Terry and whether and when he conducted a "search." There is some suggestion in the use of such terms as "stop" and "frisk" that such police conduct is outside the purview of the Fourth Amendment because neither action rises to the level of a "search" or "seizure" within the meaning of the Constitution. We emphatically reject this notion. It is quite plain that the Fourth Amendment governs "seizures" of the person which do not eventuate in a trip to the station house and prosecution for crime — "arrests" in traditional terminology. It must be recognized that whenever a police officer accosts an individual and restrains his freedom to walk away, he has "seized" that person. And it is nothing less than sheer torture of the English language to suggest that a careful exploration of the outer surfaces of a person's clothing all over his or her body in an attempt to find weapons is not a "search." Moreover, it is simply fantastic to urge that such a procedure performed in public by a policeman while the citizen stands helpless, perhaps facing a wall with his hands raised, is a "petty indignity."[13] It is a serious intrusion upon the sanctity of the person, which may inflict great indignity and arouse strong resentment, and it is not to be undertaken lightly. . . .

In this case there can be no question, then, that Officer McFadden "seized" petitioner and subjected him to a "search" when he took hold of him and patted down the outer surfaces of his clothing. We must decide whether at that point it was reasonable for Officer McFadden to have interfered with petitioner's personal

---

[13] Consider the following apt description: "[T]he officer must feel with sensitive fingers every portion of the prisoner's body. A through search must be made of the prisoner's arms and armpits, waistline and back, the groin and area about the testicles, and entire surface of the legs down to the feet." L. L. Priar & T. F. Martin, *Searching and Disarming Criminals*, 45 J. Crim. L., Criminology & Police Sci. 481 (1954).

security as he did.[16] And in determining whether the seizure and search were "unreasonable" our inquiry is a dual one—whether the officer's action was justified at its inception, and whether it was reasonably related in scope to the circumstances which justified the interference in the first place.

III.

If this case involved police conduct subject to the Warrant Clause of the Fourth Amendment, we would have to ascertain whether "probable cause" existed to justify the search and seizure which took place. However, that is not the case. . . . [W]e deal here with an entire rubric of police conduct—necessarily swift action predicated upon the on-the-spot observations of the officer on the beat—which historically has not been, and as a practical matter could not be, subjected to the warrant procedure. Instead, the conduct involved in this case must be tested by the Fourth Amendment's general proscription against unreasonable searches and seizures.

Nonetheless, the notions which underlie both the warrant procedure and the requirement of probable cause remain fully relevant in this context. In order to assess the reasonableness of Officer McFadden's conduct as a general proposition, it is necessary "first to focus upon the governmental interest which allegedly justifies official intrusion upon the constitutionally protected interests of the private citizen," for there is "no ready test for determining reasonableness other than by balancing the need to search [or seize] against the invasion which the search [or seizure] entails." Camara v. Municipal Court, 387 U.S. 523, 534–535, 536–537 (1967). And in justifying the particular intrusion the police officer must be able to point to specific and articulable facts which, taken together with rational inferences from those facts, reasonably warrant that intrusion. The scheme of the Fourth Amendment becomes meaningful only when it is assured that at some point the conduct of those charged with enforcing the laws can be subjected to the more detached, neutral scrutiny of a judge who must evaluate the reasonableness of a particular search or seizure in light of the particular circumstances. And in making that assessment it is imperative that the facts be judged against an objective standard: would the facts available to the officer at the moment of the seizure or the search "warrant a man of reasonable caution in the belief" that the action taken was appropriate? Anything less would invite intrusions upon constitutionally guaranteed rights based on nothing more substantial than inarticulate hunches, a result this Court has consistently refused to sanction. . . .

Applying these principles to this case, we consider first the nature and extent of the governmental interests involved. One general interest is of course that of effective crime prevention and detection; it is this interest which underlies the recognition that a police officer may in appropriate circumstances and in an appropriate

---

[16] We thus decide nothing today concerning the constitutional propriety of an investigative "seizure" upon less than probable cause for purposes of "detention" and/or interrogation. Obviously, not all personal intercourse between policemen and citizens involves "seizures" of persons. Only when the officer, by means of physical force or show of authority, has in some way restrained the liberty of a citizen may we conclude that a "seizure" has occurred. We cannot tell with any certainty upon this record whether any such "seizure" took place here prior to Officer McFadden's initiation of physical contact for purposes of searching Terry for weapons, and we thus may assume that up to that point no intrusion upon constitutionally protected rights had occurred.

manner approach a person for purposes of investigating possibly criminal behavior even though there is no probable cause to make an arrest. It was this legitimate investigative function Officer McFadden was discharging when he decided to approach petitioner and his companions. . . .

The crux of this case, however, is not the propriety of Officer McFadden's taking steps to investigate petitioner's suspicious behavior, but rather, whether there was justification for McFadden's invasion of Terry's personal security by searching him for weapons in the course of that investigation. We are now concerned with more than the governmental interest in investigating crime; in addition, there is the more immediate interest of the police officer in taking steps to assure himself that the person with whom he is dealing is not armed with a weapon that could unexpectedly and fatally be used against him. Certainly it would be unreasonable to require that police officers take unnecessary risks in the performance of their duties. American criminals have a long tradition of armed violence, and every year in this country many law enforcement officers are killed in the line of duty, and thousands more are wounded. Virtually all of these deaths and a substantial portion of the injuries are inflicted with guns and knives.

In view of these facts, we cannot blind ourselves to the need for law enforcement officers to protect themselves and other prospective victims of violence in situations where they may lack probable cause for an arrest. When an officer is justified in believing that the individual whose suspicious behavior he is investigating at close range is armed and presently dangerous to the officer or to others, it would appear to be clearly unreasonable to deny the officer the power to take necessary measures to determine whether the person is in fact carrying a weapon and to neutralize the threat of physical harm.

We must still consider, however, the nature and quality of the intrusion on individual rights which must be accepted if police officers are to be conceded the right to search for weapons in situations where probable cause to arrest for crime is lacking. Even a limited search of the outer clothing for weapons constitutes a severe, though brief, intrusion upon cherished personal security, and it must surely be an annoying, frightening, and perhaps humiliating experience. . . . However, . . . [o]ur evaluation of the proper balance that has to be struck in this type of case leads us to conclude that there must be a narrowly drawn authority to permit a reasonable search for weapons for the protection of the police officer, where he has reason to believe that he is dealing with an armed and dangerous individual, regardless of whether he has probable cause to arrest the individual for a crime. The officer need not be absolutely certain that the individual is armed; the issue is whether a reasonably prudent man in the circumstances would be warranted in the belief that his safety or that of others was in danger. And in determining whether the officer acted reasonably in such circumstances, due weight must be given, not to his inchoate and unparticularized suspicion or "hunch," but to the specific reasonable inferences which he is entitled to draw from the facts in light of his experience.

IV.

We must now examine the conduct of Officer McFadden in this case to determine whether his search and seizure of petitioner were reasonable, both at their inception and as conducted. He had observed Terry, together with Chilton and another man, acting in a manner he took to be preface to a "stick-up." We think on the facts and circumstances Officer McFadden detailed before the trial judge a reasonably prudent man would have been warranted in believing petitioner was armed and thus presented a threat to the officer's safety while he was investigating his suspicious behavior. The actions of Terry and Chilton were consistent with McFadden's hypothesis that these men were contemplating a daylight robbery—which, it is reasonable to assume, would be likely to involve the use of weapons—and nothing in their conduct from the time he first noticed them until the time he confronted them and identified himself as a police officer gave him sufficient reason to negate that hypothesis. . . . [T]he record evidences the tempered act of a policeman who in the course of an investigation had to make a quick decision as to how to protect himself and others from possible danger, and took limited steps to do so.

The manner in which the seizure and search were conducted is, of course, as vital a part of the inquiry as whether they were warranted at all. . . .

We need not develop at length in this case, however, the limitations which the Fourth Amendment places upon a protective seizure and search for weapons. . . . Suffice it to note that . . . [t]he sole justification of the search in the present situation is the protection of the police officer and others nearby, and it must therefore be confined in scope to an intrusion reasonably designed to discover guns, knives, clubs, or other hidden instruments for the assault of the police officer.

The scope of the search in this case presents no serious problem in light of these standards. Officer McFadden patted down the outer clothing of petitioner and his two companions. He did not place his hands in their pockets or under the outer surface of their garments until he had felt weapons, and then he merely reached for and removed the guns. . . . Officer McFadden confined his search strictly to what was minimally necessary to learn whether the men were armed and to disarm them once he discovered the weapons. He did not conduct a general exploratory search for whatever evidence of criminal activity he might find.

V.

We conclude that the revolver seized from Terry was properly admitted in evidence against him. At the time he seized petitioner and searched him for weapons, Officer McFadden had reasonable grounds to believe that petitioner was armed and dangerous, and it was necessary for the protection of himself and others to take swift measures to discover the true facts and neutralize the threat of harm if it materialized. The policeman carefully restricted his search to what was appropriate to the discovery of the particular items which he sought. Each case of this sort will, of course, have to be decided on its own facts. We merely hold today that where a police officer observes unusual conduct which leads him reasonably to conclude in light of his experience that criminal activity may be afoot and that the persons with whom he is dealing may be armed and presently dangerous, where in the course of investigating this behavior he identifies himself as a policeman and makes reasonable inquiries, and where nothing in the initial stages of the encounter serves to dispel his reasonable fear for his own or others' safety, he is entitled for the protection of himself and others in the area to conduct a carefully limited search of the outer clothing of such persons in an attempt to discover weapons which might be used to assault him. Such a search is a reasonable search under the Fourth Amendment, and any weapons seized may properly be introduced in evidence against the person from whom they were taken.

Affirmed.

MR. JUSTICE BLACK concurs in the judgment and the opinion except where the opinion quotes from and relies upon this Court's opinion in *Katz v. United States* and the concurring opinion in *Warden v. Hayden.*

MR. JUSTICE HARLAN, concurring.

While I unreservedly agree with the Court's ultimate holding in this case, I am constrained to fill in a few gaps, as I see them, in its opinion. I do this because what is said by this Court today will serve as initial guidelines for law enforcement authorities and courts throughout the land as this important new field of law develops. . . .

. . . Since the question in this and most cases is whether evidence produced by a frisk is admissible, the problem is to determine what makes a frisk reasonable. . . .

In the first place, if the frisk is justified in order to protect the officer during an encounter with a citizen, the officer must first have constitutional grounds to insist on an encounter, to make a forcible stop. Any person, including a policeman, is at liberty to avoid a person he considers dangerous. If and when a policeman has a right instead to disarm such a person for his own protection, he must first have a right not to avoid him but to be in his presence. That right must be more than the liberty (again, possessed by every citizen) to address questions to other persons, for ordinarily the person addressed has an equal right to ignore his interrogator and walk away; he certainly need not submit to a frisk for the questioner's protection. I would make it perfectly clear that the right to frisk in this case depends upon the reasonableness of a forcible stop to investigate a suspected crime.

Where such a stop is reasonable, however, the right to frisk must be immediate and automatic if the reason for the stop is, as here, an articulable suspicion of a crime of violence. Just as a full search incident to a lawful arrest requires no additional justification, a limited frisk incident to a lawful stop must often be rapid and routine. There is no reason why an officer, rightfully but forcibly confronting a person suspected of a serious crime, should have to ask one question and take the risk that the answer might be a bullet. . . .

. . . Officer McFadden's right to interrupt Terry's freedom of movement and invade his privacy arose only because circumstances warranted forcing an encounter with Terry in an effort to prevent or investigate a crime. Once that forced encounter was justified, however, the officer's right to take suitable measures for his own safety followed automatically.

Upon the foregoing premises, I join the opinion of the Court.

MR. JUSTICE WHITE, concurring. . . .

. . . I think an additional word is in order concerning the matter of interrogation during an investigative stop. There is nothing in the Constitution which prevents a policeman from addressing questions to anyone on the streets. Absent special circumstances, the person approached may not be detained or frisked but may refuse to cooperate and go on his way. However, given the proper circumstances, such as those in this case, it seems to me the person may be briefly detained against his will while pertinent questions are directed to him. Of course, the person stopped is not obliged to answer, answers may not be compelled, and refusal to answer furnishes no basis for an arrest, although it may alert the officer to the need for continued observation. In my view, it is temporary detention, warranted by the circumstances, which chiefly justifies the protective frisk for weapons. Perhaps the frisk itself, where proper, will have beneficial results whether questions are asked or not. If weapons are found, an arrest will follow. If none are found, the frisk may nevertheless serve preventive ends because of its unmistakable message that suspicion has been aroused. But if the investigative stop is sustainable at all, constitutional rights are not necessarily violated if pertinent questions are asked and the person is restrained briefly in the process.

MR. JUSTICE DOUGLAS, dissenting. . . .

The opinion of the Court disclaims the existence of "probable cause." If loitering were in issue and that was the offense charged, there would be "probable cause" shown. But the crime here is carrying concealed weapons; and there is no basis for concluding that the officer had "probable cause" for believing that that crime was being committed. Had a warrant been sought, a magistrate would, therefore, have been unauthorized to issue one, for he can act only if there is a showing of "probable cause." We hold today that the police have greater authority to make a "seizure" and conduct a "search" than a judge has to authorize such action. We have said precisely the opposite over and over again.

In other words, police officers up to today have been permitted to effect arrests or searches without warrants only when the facts within their personal knowledge would satisfy the constitutional standard of probable cause. . . . The term "probable cause" rings a bell of certainty that is not sounded by phrases such as "reasonable suspicion." Moreover, the meaning of "probable cause" is deeply imbedded in our constitutional history. . . .

To give the police greater power than a magistrate is to take a long step down the totalitarian path. Perhaps such a step is desirable to cope with modern forms of lawlessness. But if it is taken, it should be the deliberate choice of the people through a constitutional amendment. . . .

There have been powerful hydraulic pressures throughout our history that bear heavily on the Court to water down constitutional guarantees and give the police the upper hand. That hydraulic pressure has probably never been greater than it is today.

Yet if the individual is no longer to be sovereign, if the police can pick him up whenever they do not like the cut of his jib, if they can "seize" and "search" him in their discretion, we enter a new regime. The decision to enter it should be made only after a full debate by the people of this country.

NOTES ON *TERRY* DOCTRINE

1. *The law of* Terry. Reading the opinion carefully, you might see that *Terry* does three things to the law of the police. First, it acknowledges the possibility of seizures short of "technical arrests" (stops) and searches short of "full-blown searches" (frisks). *Terry*, 392 U.S. at 19. Second, it holds that an officer may frisk a person to detect weapons if the police are investigating criminal activity and reasonably conclude that the person detained may be armed and dangerous. Third, it develops a framework for addressing those Fourth Amendment questions that are not answerable by invoking warrants and probable cause; that is, "balancing the need to search or seize against the invasion which the search or seizure entails." *Id.* at 21.

2. *Justice Harlan's gloss.* Now look at how Justice Harlan's concurrence builds on the majority opinion with three refinements. First, he argues that a frisk is permissible only when the officer is conducting a legal stop, and the stop must be justified by "articulable suspicion" (later called "reasonable suspicion") that criminal activity is afoot. *Id.* at 31 (Harlan, J., concurring). Second, he contends that if an officer has reasonable suspicion that a suspect is armed and dangerous, he may conduct a frisk immediately; he need not ask questions first. Finally, he argues that if the reasonable suspicion that justified the stop is suspicion that a suspect has been involved in a crime of violence, then that, without more, constitutes reasonable suspicion that the person is armed and dangerous, justifying an immediate search. In this way, Justice Harlan envisioned two types of justifications for frisks: the first, that the reason for the stop was suspicion of a crime of violence; the second, that the words, actions, or appearance of the suspect either before or during the stop indicates that he is armed and dangerous, making a frisk constitutional at that time.

3. *Basic stop-and-frisk law since* Terry. Justice Harlan's gloss on the majority opinion in *Terry* has become the law of the land. As the doctrine now stands, an officer may briefly detain a person to ask questions (a stop) if the officer has reasonable suspicion that the person is involved with criminal activity. See Adams v. Williams, 407 U.S. 143 (1972). The officer is also permitted to conduct a limited search of the person from outside of his clothes (a frisk) if (and only if) the officer also has reasonable suspicion that the suspect is armed and dangerous. See Minnesota v. Dickerson, 508 U.S. 366 (1993). Though the measure of suspicion is the same, the two types of suspicion are different and may be based on separate facts.

NOTES AND QUESTIONS ON *TERRY*'S CONTEXT

1. *Social context for* Terry. Serious crime tripled over the course of the 1960s, changing the United States from a society in which people could walk down almost any street in the middle of the night to a place where many were truly and reasonably afraid. Yet the number of people being imprisoned went down significantly over the same period. These competing trends contributed to public concern over Warren Court decisions such as *Mapp v. Ohio*, 367 U.S. 643 (1961), and *Miranda v. Arizona*, 384 U.S. 436 (1966), that seemed (to some) to restrain the police and coddle criminals just when crime levels justified more aggressive urban policing.

At the same time, by the late 1960s, as an outgrowth of the civil rights movement, activists and communities were bringing new attention to racism in policing. Policing became a flashpoint for several of the urban riots of the late 1960s, including most famously the Watts riots in Los Angeles in 1965, which started with a traffic stop and ended with 34 people killed and more than 1,000 injured over six days. These riots had multiple meanings. On one hand, they illustrated growing, widespread frustration about policing. On the other, the riots themselves contributed to a sense of disorder and fear that seemed to others to justify the policing strategies the critics opposed. This fear was exacerbated by footage from television news helicopters, which put images of violent rioters in homes around the country. Can you see any similarities in what you know of responses to today's protests against policing?

Buildings burning during Watts riots, August 1965.

The Supreme Court could not have been ignorant of these competing concerns. It decided *Terry* in one of the most tumultuous years in U.S. history, 1968,[1] and in the weeks leading up to the Court's decision, both Baltimore and Washington, D.C., suffered days of riots following the assassination of civil rights leader Martin Luther King, Jr., riots in which (especially in Washington) concerns about policing played a role. Do you see any of this social context reflected in the *Terry* opinion? If so, where?

2. *Legal context for* Terry: *the end of vagrancy.* When the Court considered *Terry,* brief street detentions had long been part of the toolkit police used to manage conduct perceived as undesirable or suspicious. Broad vagrancy and loitering statutes and municipal codes in every state made it criminal to be idle, indigent, itinerant,

---

[1] During the months between when *Terry* was argued in December 1967, and when it was decided in June 1968, among other events, North Korea seized the USS Pueblo, killing one crewman and imprisoning dozens of others; North Vietnamese communists launched the Tet Offensive; police opened fire on students at South Carolina State protesting segregation, killing three and wounding dozens more; more than 15,000 Latino students walked out of class in Los Angeles in protest; Martin Luther King, Jr., was fatally shot, and riots ensued in more than 100 cities; police engaged in a shootout with Black Panthers in Oakland and killed Bobby Hunton, a teenager, as he tried to surrender; Congress passed and Lyndon Johnson signed the Fair Housing Act; students took over Columbia University for a week, an event that ended in mass arrests and injuries; activists raided Selective Service offices; Andy Warhol was shot and seriously injured; and Robert F. Kennedy was assassinated after winning the California presidential primary.

impudent, or immoral. Cf. Papacrhistou v. City of Jacksonville, 405 U.S. 156 (1972). An officer facing a suspicious or objectionable person would almost always have probable cause that the person had violated such a statute, allowing the officer discretion to make an arrest. With the discretion to arrest came the ability to simply detain and question the person to determine whether to arrest or to mitigate the situation without doing so. In this way, vagrancy statutes gave officers enormous authority to investigate, harass, and move people along consistent with the Fourth Amendment.

As the vagrancy statutes fell to constitutional challenges during the 1960s, the legal status of this common police activity became uncertain. States, police departments, and scholars looked for alternative ways to ensure that police could continue to manage the streets, including through statutes that allowed two-hour detentions of criminal suspects. *Terry* is important because it "represents the first time the legal system really faced the question of how to rein in street policing, how to use legal tools to make the police behave reasonably on the ground." William J. Stuntz, Terry*'s Impossibility*, 72 St. John's L. Rev. 1213, 1216 (2012). For more on the use and long demise of vagrancy statutes, see Risa Goluboff, *Vagrant Nation: Police Power, Constitutional Change, and the Making of the 1960s* (2016).

3. *Legal context for* Terry: *interest balancing in Fourth Amendment law.* As Justice Douglas points out in his dissent, for years before *Terry*, the Fourth Amendment had one standard of proof to justify a search or seizure: probable cause. In the absence of vagrancy statutes, which prohibited a vast amount of often vaguely defined behavior, officers could not count on having probable cause to deal with many kinds of suspicious or ambiguous conduct. The two choices before the Court seemed to be either to require probable cause of criminal activity (limiting police discretion to make investigative stops) or to declare the activity beyond the boundaries of the Fourth Amendment (leaving investigative stops unregulated). Just a year before *Terry*, in *Camara v. Municipal Ct.*, 387 U.S. 523 (1967), and *See v. City of Seattle*, 387 U.S. 541 (1967), the Court faced a similar dilemma with respect to housing and safety inspections. Rather than choose one of the above alternatives, the Court expanded its account of Fourth Amendment reasonableness to accommodate the public interest at issue on the grounds that reasonableness permits "some accommodation between public need and individual rights." *Camara*, 387 U.S. at 534. In this way, *Camara* and *See* helped lay the groundwork for *Terry*'s interest-balancing framework, used to decide Fourth Amendment questions that are not easily addressed by requiring probable cause that a crime has been committed.

Still, fitting *Terry* into the *Camara* and *See* framework took some work. The opinion in *Camara* reaffirmed the importance of warrants, even as it made them easier to obtain in the administrative context. Moreover, *Camara* and *See* involved regulatory activities without criminal sanctions. Between *Camara* and *Terry*, the Court in *Katz v. United States*, 389 U.S. 347 (1967), reemphasized, in the criminal context, the importance of warrants based on probable cause that a crime had been committed. Fourth Amendment doctrine was changing, making *Terry* possible, but until the Court decided *Terry*, the extent of the change was unknown.

NOTES AND QUESTIONS ON STOPS AND FRISKS

1. *The Court contemplates reality.* As you will see later in this chapter, the *Terry* doctrine has facilitated racial discrimination in policing. But the *Terry* opinion is a

rare example of the Court acknowledging the intrusiveness of police practices and the different experience of policing that people of color have in this country. How well does the Court capture those concerns? Address them?

2. *The (nonfinancial) costs of regulation.* How does the Court see the harms of regulating the police? Why does the Court take those harms to be worth paying?

3. Terry *on frisks.* Law professor Seth Stoughton, who served as a police officer before he went to law school, has reflected that, as an officer, he found frisks forgettable and mundane, "a relatively minor facet of each encounter." Seth Stoughton, Terry v. Ohio *and the (Un)Forgettable Frisk*, 15 Ohio St. J. Crim. L. 19, 31 (2017). By contrast, the *Terry* Court casts frisks as a significant intrusion on bodily integrity, one that is humiliating and severe. This description stands in stark contrast to many Fourth Amendment opinions, which describe policing practices in ways that minimize their significance.[2] Even so, Stoughton and others think the *Terry* Court significantly understated the experience of being frisked. Stoughton points out that names like "pat-downs" fail to convey how "deliberatively invasive" frisks can be. *Id.* at 27–28. Paul Butler has likened *Terry* frisks to torture, sexual assault, and public terrorism of Black men, a form of domination that is "designed to humiliate and control." Paul Butler, *Chokehold: Policing Black Men* 84, 106 (2017). And others have argued that *Terry* frisks can be especially traumatizing to those with mental disorders or those who have previously experienced sexual assault. See Susan A. Bandes et al., *The Mismeasure of* Terry *Stops: Assessing the Psychological and Emotional Harms of Stop and Frisk to Individuals and Communities*, 37 Behavioral Sci. L. 176, 182 (2019).

4. *Frisk law since* Terry. Given that frisks are so intrusive, it might surprise you to learn that lower courts have allowed frisks far more automatically than the *Terry* opinion seemed to envision. Courts have slipped from allowing frisks automatically for people suspected of crimes that *necessarily* or *commonly* involve weapons and threats of violence, like armed robbery, to allowing automatic frisks for people suspected of crimes that *can but usually do not* involve weapons or violence, such as minor drug crimes and burglary, without any individualized basis for believing that the suspect is armed and dangerous. See David A. Harris, *Particularized Suspicion, Categorical Judgements: Supreme Court Rhetoric Versus Lower Court Reality Under* Terry v. Ohio, 72 St. John's L. Rev. 975, 1002 (1998). Similarly, *Terry* is ambiguous about what *armed and dangerous* means. Instead of requiring officers to have reasonable suspicion that a suspect is armed *and* dangerous, courts often permit officers to infer that a suspect is dangerous because the officer reasonably suspects he is armed or armed because the officer reasonably suspects that he is dangerous. You can see how these expansions might occur: Each judge decides a suppression motion after an officer testifies that he feared for his safety, conducted a frisk, and found a weapon or contraband. Each appellate panel evaluates the judge's ruling only after a conviction. Is that the kind of "hydraulic pressure" that Justice Douglas feared would lead courts to "water down constitutional guarantees and give the police the upper hand"? *Terry*, 392 U.S. at 39 (Douglas, J., dissenting).

---

[2] For an example, see the discussion of Sandra Bland's traffic stop and the Supreme Court's description of police orders to exit a car in *Pennsylvania v. Mimms*, 434 U.S. 106 (1977), in Chapter 1.

A frisk.

5. *Stop law since* Terry. In footnote 16 of the *Terry* opinion, the Court defines a Fourth Amendment seizure as taking place "[o]nly when the officer, by means of physical force or show of authority, has in some way restrained the liberty of a citizen." In this way, the Court distinguishes *voluntary encounters* with the police from *investigative stops*, in which someone has his liberty restrained but the restraint does not amount to a full arrest. However, after an encounter between a police officer and a member of the public, it can be hard to tell whether a person was stopped or instead had a consensual encounter. This question usually comes to court when the interaction escalates and results in an officer finding contraband or evidence that the government attempts to use in a criminal case. In that context, individuals often claim they were seized without reasonable suspicion to stop them, making the contraband the product of an illegal seizure. Officers argue instead that the encounter was voluntary, requiring no individualized suspicion at its start.

Here is the Court's summary of its guidance to lower courts trying to distinguish seizures regulated by the Fourth Amendment from consensual encounters that are not:

> When the actions of the police do not show an unambiguous intent to restrain or when an individual's submission to a show of governmental authority takes the form of passive acquiescence, there needs to be some test for telling when a seizure occurs in response to authority, and when it does not. The test was

devised by Justice Stewart in United States v. Mendenhall, 446 U.S. 544 (1980), who wrote that a seizure occurs if "in view of all of the circumstances surrounding the incident, a reasonable person would have believed that he was not free to leave." *Id.* at 554. Later on, the Court adopted Justice Stewart's touchstone, but added that when a person "has no desire to leave" for reasons unrelated to the police presence, the "coercive effect of the encounter" can be measured better by asking whether "a reasonable person would feel free to decline the officers' requests or otherwise terminate the encounter." Florida v. Bostick, 501 U.S. 429, 435–436 (1991).

Brendlin v. California, 551 U.S. 249, 255 (2007).

That sounds reasonable, doesn't it? You might be surprised by what passes this test. For example, in *INS v. Delgado*, 466 U.S. 210 (1984), the Court found no seizure under this test when armed immigration agents stood guard at the doors of a factory while other agents questioned workers inside. Similarly, in *United States v. Drayton*, 536 U.S. 194 (2002), the Court found no seizure when armed officers were posted at the front and back of a bus, while another officer approached and questioned the passengers individually without indicating that they were free not to cooperate. The Court noted that the officer conducting the questioning "did not brandish a weapon or make any intimidating movements," and he spoke to passengers "in a polite, quiet voice." *Id.* at 204. Moreover, because "most law enforcement officers are armed," a fact "well known to the public," the Court reasoned that "[t]he presence of a holstered firearm thus is unlikely to contribute to the coerciveness of the encounter." *Id.* at 205. Do you agree?

Note as well that so long as an officer does not convey that you are not free to leave within the meaning of this doctrine, he can approach you in the street and ask, without any reason or suspicion, "What is your name? What are you doing here? Would you turn out your pockets? Do you mind if I look in your bag?" In this kind of encounter, as Justice White points out, you are (at least theoretically) free to "go on [your] way" and refuse to answer the questions. *Terry*, 392 U.S. at 34 (White, J., concurring). But under *Drayton*, the officer has no obligation to tell you that. How free would you feel under these circumstances? Why would an officer do this without a reason to believe that "crime may be afoot"? Who are they likely to do it to?

6. *Reactions to the law of stops.* How could the Court think people being systematically questioned on a bus with multiple armed officers would feel free to disregard the police and go about their business? The Court's view seems to be that if there is no overt evidence of governmental coercion, then interactions should be treated as voluntary and consensual, however intrusive or unfair they may feel to those who are targeted. The alternative to this approach to evaluating police–citizen interactions would limit officer power on the basis of the sense of obligation many people experience when questioned by police, even though that sense is not fully within officers' control.

Although officers do not generate *all* of the pressure people feel to cooperate with the police, they do not try to eliminate it either. Instead, they use it to their advantage. "In the real world . . . few people are aware of their fourth amendment rights, many individuals are fearful of the police, and police officers know how to exploit this fear." Tracey Maclin, *Decline of the Right of Locomotion: The Fourth Amendment on the Streets*, 75 Cornell L. Rev. 1257, 1301 (1991). This is particularly true for Black men, who have special reason to fear the police and distrust that officers will respect their rights. See Tracey Maclin, *Black and Blue Encounters—Some Preliminary Thoughts about Fourth Amendment Seizures: Should Race Matter?*, 26 Val. U. L. Rev. 243 (1991).

In some sense—given that some encounters are coercive, some are not, and it isn't easy to tell the difference—the question is who should bear the risk of uncertainty? The Court has put that risk squarely on those who interact with the police. Many critics would prefer to see more of it shifted to the government. What doctrinal changes might achieve that?

7. *Reasonable suspicion.* Before police do engage in a stop within the meaning of *Terry*, they need individualized reasonable suspicion. Here, too, the courts have been generous to the police. Courts often accept vague and not-very-suspicious conduct as a justification for stops, and they do not always require that officers clearly articulate the crime they suspected. Rather than develop "a substantive review of the criteria of 'reasonable suspicion,'" courts focus on "the reasoning of the officers at the scene (based on a post-hoc account) pursuant to a specific fact, and whether that reasoning was, well, reasonable to an experienced officer." Jeffrey Fagan, Terry's *Original Sin*, 2016 U. Chi. Legal F. 43, 55. Is this approach to evaluating reasonable suspicion an inevitable consequence of *Terry*?

8. *Stop and identify.* Although many people feel significant pressure to answer police questions, Justice White contended that a person could refuse to do so during a lawful stop without justifying an arrest. But many states have stop-and-identify statutes that allow officers to demand that lawfully stopped suspects disclose their identities and explain their actions. Failing to tell an officer who you are can be the basis for an arrest and prosecution. See, e.g., Ala. Code §15-5-30; Colo. Rev. Stat. §16-3-103(1); Neb. Rev. Stat. §29-829; R.I. Gen. Laws §12-7-1. The Supreme Court upheld such a statute against both Fourth and Fifth Amendment challenges in *Hiibel v. Sixth Judicial District Court of Nevada*, 542 U.S. 177 (2004).

NOTES AND QUESTIONS ON ASSESSING *TERRY*

1. *Assessing* Terry. People who study law for a living overwhelmingly hate the *Terry* opinion.

> [I]n the legal academy, the decision is infamously reviled. It is typically depicted at best as a pragmatic reconciliation of civilian and law enforcement interests that naively believed that police discretion could be meaningful[ly] cabined in ex-post determinations of whether a quantum of suspicion was "reasonable." At worst, it stands as the Warren Court's abandonment of its rights-protective and racial justice commitments in the face of increasing crime rates and adverse public response to *Mapp* and *Miranda.*

Jennifer E. Laurin, Terry, *Timeless and Time-Bound*, 15 Ohio St. J. Crim. L. 1, 1 (2017). Ouch. There are a few dissenters, see, e.g., Lawrence Rosenthal, *Pragmatism, Originalism, Race, and the Case against* Terry v. Ohio, 43 Tex. Tech. L. Rev. 299 (2010); Stephen A. Saltzburg, Terry v. Ohio: *A Practically Perfect Doctrine*, 72 St. John's L. Rev. 911 (1998), but not very many. Still, Jennifer Laurin argues that despite whatever mischief the doctrine has done, critics of the Court's opinion in *Terry* are too harsh:

> Assigning fault to *Terry* for the full impact of its legacy risks falling into the all-too-common legal academic trap of centering the importance of judicial decision-making at the expense of grappling with the far messier and more contingent political, sociological, and institutional forces that enter the mix once the judicial ink is dry.

Laurin, *supra*, at 3. According to Laurin, subsequent court decisions, changes in policing, and growing incarceration (in part as a product of the war on drugs) have magnified the effects of *Terry* many-fold in ways the Court could not possibly have predicted. *Id.* The implication is that although *Terry* today permits significant intrusions on limited suspicion with little scrutiny by courts, it isn't the *Terry* Court's fault. Looking at the opinion, what do you think? Heroic effort to manage policing on the street with limited tools? Or judicial cover for freeing the police from law? Something else entirely?

2. *What went wrong?* Why exactly is the *Terry* doctrine problematic? Many critics suggest it sets a standard that does not constrain police discretion enough. But maybe the problem goes deeper than that. David Smith suggests that

> [p]erhaps . . . a policy like stop and search *cannot be effectively regulated through the law* and its embodiment in the criminal justice system. A law on stop and search is essentially permissive; like the law against obstructing a police officer it represents a resource that the police may use. We can argue about whether the police exceed their statutory power—I say they do—but this is ultimately irrelevant since there is no conceivable way in which such a vague (and necessarily vague) criterion as "reasonable suspicion" can be made to constitute an effective constraint. In this field, the law is just a source of presentational rules which exist to put an acceptable face on practices we prefer not to look at squarely.

David J. Smith, *The Framework of Law and Policing Practice*, in *The Police: Powers, Procedures and Proprieties* 85, 93 (John Benyon & Colin Bourn eds. 1986). If you agree, what should the law do? Not regulate stops and frisks? If you disagree and think courts or legislatures can set effective standards to constrain stops, do you also think they could keep officers from disrespecting and degrading those they stop? Or do you think those complaints are not legal ones?

3. *Institutional competence.* Rarely has the Court openly expressed so much concern about its own legitimacy as it did in *Terry*. What does the Court say about itself as a regulator of the police? Does this account accord with the Court's role as regulator in *Katz v. United States* and *Miranda v. Arizona*? (*Katz* is discussed at length in Chapter 2, and *Miranda* in Chapter 3.) If the Court is "powerless to deter invasions" when police are not seeking evidence, why did it regulate stops and frisks at all? And if the Court cannot guarantee civil rights, who should? Do you find it ironic that constitutional standards can be constrained by the very actors meant to be regulated? Or just pragmatic?

4. *Write* Terry's *alternate histories.* Imagine the *Terry* Court had decided that all stops and frisks are seizures and searches that require probable cause. How might the law and policing look different today? What if the Court had decided that stops and frisks are not searches and seizures within the meaning of the Fourth Amendment? What might have happened then?

5. *Returning to the Encounter Model.* Chapter 1 described a model of police encounters in which [1] officers see problems in the world that need a response; [2] they employ a range of provisional solutions to those problems, including some coercive ones; [3] the individuals to whom those solutions are applied react, sometimes with noncompliance; and [4] officers engage in further, often coercive steps to get the job done. Consider stops and frisks separately in light of the model. How might you think about a stop? What about a frisk? What is different about a frisk from other police activities in this category?

"Stop and Frisk 2.0" or "Walking While Trans"

Many surveys, anecdotal reports, and court cases suggest that LGBTQ people suffer disproportionate encounters, disrespect, harassment, and violence at the hands of the police. See Christy Mallory et al., The Williams Institute, *Discrimination and Harassment by Law Enforcement Officers in the LGBT Community* (2015) (collecting data and reports). One of the most frequent complaints is that the police stop and arrest transgender women for "walking while trans." According to women who have been stopped, officers empowered by broad laws that criminalize prostitution detain transgender women of color frequently, assuming they are engaged in sex work. In a case that received national attention, Monica Jones, an African-American student, trans activist, and advocate for sex worker rights, was arrested after she accepted an undercover police officer's offer to give her a ride during a prostitution-related sting. Jones was found guilty of "manifesting prostitution" under Phoenix, Ariz., Mun. Code §23-52(A)(3), which makes a person guilty of a misdemeanor who:

> Is in a public place, a place open to public view or in a motor vehicle on a public roadway and manifests an intent to commit or solicit an act of prostitution. Among the circumstances that may be considered in determining whether such an intent is manifested are that the person: repeatedly beckons to, stops, or attempts to stop or engage passersby in conversation; repeatedly stops or attempts to stop motor vehicle operators by hailing, waving, or any other bodily gesture; inquires whether a potential patron, procurer, or prostitute is a police officer; searches for articles that would identify a police officer; or requests the touching or exposure of genitals or female breast.

Although Jones's conviction was vacated on appeal, the ordinance remains on the books. See Megan Cassidy, *Transgender Activist's Conviction in Prostitution Case Thrown Out*, Ariz. Republic (Jan. 26, 2015). New York State has a statute that similarly defines loitering for the purpose of engaging in prostitution. See N.Y. Penal Law §240.37(2). Consider the scope of police authority to stop and arrest under these laws. Some argue that the NYPD uses New York's law to engage in "stop and frisk 2.0," detaining women for little more than hanging out in the street at night or being provocatively dressed. Karina Piser, *The Walking While Trans Ban Is "Stop and Frisk 2.0,"* Nation (Feb. 19, 2020). Although police departments may be able to disrupt discrimination against sexual and gender minorities by adopting and enforcing policies and practices that forbid it and by better training their officers, only legislative or judicial action can get rid of criminal laws that facilitate this discrimination.

Artist's poster supporting Monica Jones.

B.   *The Legacy of* Terry

1.   The World That *Terry* Wrought

Contemporary policing strategies have been built on the backbone of *Terry*. This excerpt helps to explain how.

Rachel A. Harmon & Andrew Manns, *Proactive Policing and*
the Legacy of Terry
15 Ohio St. J. Crim. L. 49, 55–58 (2017)

   Much of urban policing today looks very different not only from the investigative policing the Court describes in many Fourth Amendment cases, but also from . . . the patrol policing that *Terry* portrays. . . . McFadden's actions were preventative only in the limited sense that he stopped a crime that was about to happen, but they were fundamentally reactive in the sense that he waited for an indication of some problematic activity before he thought to intervene. One can think of McFadden's policing as an extreme form of rapid response: he addressed crime so quickly that he caught it even before it occurred. That was precisely what his department wanted him to do when they placed him on the streets of Cleveland. In the standard model of policing, officers are widely assigned to random preventative patrol to resolve disorder, catch criminals, and stop crime as it unfolds.

Traditional patrol still exists, but overwhelmingly departments now also engage in policing that is preventative in a deeper sense. Contemporary policing utilizes strategies designed to deter criminal behavior before it is contemplated. As early as the late 1960s, Albert J. Reiss, Jr. and David Bordua distinguished policing based on a request for service from police-initiated or "proactive" policing. But proactive policing did not develop fully or spread widely in its contemporary form until the 1980s and 1990s, after a series of reports in the 1970s and early 1980s raised serious doubts about the effectiveness of the traditional patrol model. The newer forms of proactive strategies are premised on the idea that, if the desirable outcome of policing is public safety and order, officers should be out there *preventing* problems from emerging, not just stopping them when they do.

Contemporary proactive law enforcement, also sometimes called, "the new policing," is not a single police activity or departmental strategy. Instead, it includes a collection of innovative strategies, based on new criminological theories about how crime arises and how it can be stopped. Hot Spots policing focuses police attention on very small areas that suffer persistent and frequent crime. Predictive policing depends on collections of public and government data and analytical algorithms to identify individuals, groups, or locations that are likely to be involved in future crime. Stop, Question, and Frisk (SQF) seeks to deter street criminal activity, such as drug and gun possession or violence, by raising the expected cost of engaging in them. In Problem-Oriented Policing, departments address clusters of similar incidents using a structured technique for identifying and addressing quality of life problems with the community. Broken Windows policing seeks to reduce urban disorder that might indicate an unmonitored neighborhood, in order to reduce crime. And Zero Tolerance policing targets visible, minor street crime as a means to prevent more serious criminal activity.

As these brief descriptions suggest, proactive strategies are diverse in theory. They are also heterogeneous in the ways they are implemented. Across the United States, departments leverage new technologies, community partnerships, and the substantial legal authority available to the police in a range of ways to prevent crime, sometimes combining more than one proactive strategy. Despite this variety, however, very often proactive policing has in practice meant aggressively stopping and frisking individuals on the street in order to deter (rather than uncover or directly stymie) criminal activity. Departments often apply Hot Spots and Predictive Policing by concentrating enforcement in the form of stops and frisks in the areas and against the people identified. They implement Stop, Question, and Frisk by heavily embracing its eponymous activities. When Problem-Oriented Policing identifies a problem, departments sometimes use intense enforcement in the form of stops and frisks as a method of addressing it. Broken Windows and Zero Tolerance Policing so often target stops and frisks on those involved in low-level crime and disorder that the strategies are conflated with Stop, Question, and Frisk.

In this way, proactive policing depends critically on the policing power permitted in *Terry,* and it does so in a manner unimaginable to the *Terry* Court. Once *Terry* put a constitutional Good Housekeeping Seal of approval on stops and frisks, they became a legitimate tool in the police toolkit, one that could be used in a forward-looking way, and with any frequency, so long as officers complied with the constitutional rules. Thus, today, stops are carried out strategically to address long-term problems rather than immediate ones. One might reasonably call *Terry* the foundation on which proactive policing is built.

Of course, *Terry* is not alone in providing support for programmatic, proactive enforcement. Proactive strategies, especially Zero Tolerance and Broken Windows Policing, often depend on aggressive arrests for minor crimes as well as street stops. Wide-ranging codes of misdemeanor offenses help make that possible. So do some of the Court's more recent Fourth Amendment cases, most notably, *Whren v. United States,* which allows pretextual arrests, and *Atwater v. City of Lago Vista,* which allows arrests even for minor fine-only offenses; these are arguably almost as helpful to some proactive strategies as *Terry.* But if *Terry* is not the only case that facilitates proactive policing, it remains the first and most important one. *Whren* was only decided in 1996, and *Atwater* in 2001, long after the major proactive policing strategies developed and began to be adopted. By contrast, *Terry* was the legal framework around which proactive strategies formed. Proactive policing is made possible by *Terry,* and *Terry* as a result remains central to the contemporary policing project, even as the project has departed from the kind of policing that the *Terry* decision described.

––––––––––––

For a discussion of the effectiveness, legality, and community effects of proactive policing, see Nat'l Acads. of Scis., Eng'g & Med., *Proactive Policing: Effects on Crime and Communities* (David Weisburd & Malay K. Majmundar eds. 2018).

2. Proactive Policing in New York City

Most large cities embraced proactive policing, but none more thoroughly than New York. This excerpt provides one account of how this came about:

> Like many cities across the United States, New York experienced a major spike in violence, crime, and disorder in the 1980s. Much of the violence in New York was driven by the emergence of crack cocaine and competition for the drug market. Homicides climbed steadily from 1,392 in 1985 to 2,262 in 1990.[3] At the same time, the city and subway system were struggling with rampant social and physical disorder. Marijuana, heroin, cocaine, and crack cocaine were regularly and openly being sold on street corners, blocks, and city parks. . . .
>
> The New York Transit Authority appointed William Bratton as chief of the transit police to address crime and disorder in the subway system. Chief Bratton partnered with criminologist George Kelling to develop an enforcement strategy based on Wilson

––––––––––––

[3] *Ed. note:* For comparison, you might find it interesting that the NYPD recorded 292 murders in 2017 and 289 murders in 2018, the fewest in 70 years.

and Kelling's "broken windows" theory.[67] This broken-windows–based strategy targeted low-level offenses (e.g., turnstile jumping), as well as social and physical disorder through frequent arrests and removals from the subway system. Over the next two years, the level of disorder dropped dramatically, and felony offenses declined by 30%.

New York City Mayor Rudolph Giuliani appointed William Bratton to become the commissioner of the NYPD in 1994, and [u]nder Bratton . . . and his successors . . . , SQF emerged as one of the primary strategies not only to achieve order-maintenance by targeting disorder and quality-of-life offenses (e.g., replicating the subway strategy on a larger scale), but also as a means of reducing gun violence through the seizure of illegal firearms and through the intensive investigation of gun-related incidents. Importantly, the aggressive manner in which NYPD officers used SQF [Stop, Question, and Frisk] to achieve these ends ignored the principles of community policing, causing community resentment, rather than fostering police-community collaboration. This, in turn, contributed to critics charging that the NYPD over-enforced quality-of-life infractions through a zero-tolerance approach because officers could easily justify the stops under the reasonable suspicion standard. Nonetheless, the aggressive use of SQF as a department-wide strategy had the endorsement of Mayor Rudolph Giuliani (1994–2001) and Mayor Michael Bloomberg (2002–2013). Thus, SQF enjoyed political support for a considerable period of time and under two successive administrations that spanned nearly 20 years.

Henry F. Fradella & Michael D. White, *Stop-and-Frisk*, in 2 *Reforming Criminal Justice* 51, 61–64 (Erik Luna ed., 2017).

Although SQF grew out of Bratton's interest in broken-windows policing, Jeffrey Bellin has pointed out that the two approaches are different:

Broken Windows as policing theory and the "order maintenance" policies designed to implement it are conceptually distinct from the NYPD's programmatic use of stop-and-frisk to detect and deter public gun-carrying. "Order maintenance" dictates that officers arrest subway fare evaders, graffiti artists, illegal vendors, prostitutes, and other minor offenders, to reassure the public that the authorities control the streets. As described in George Kelling and James Q. Wilson's seminal article, "Broken Windows," the apparent "order" that results assuages residents' fears (an important development in itself) and immunizes the area from further "urban decay" and "criminal invasion." Programmatic stop and frisk is a different approach. According to city officials, the NYPD uses stop-and-frisk to find guns and deter gun-carrying, a goal that is theoretically forwarded when people are stopped and searched regardless of whether they are committing any breach of public order. Indeed, NYC Stop and Frisk seems strikingly unconcerned with the neighborhood perception of order that is so central to Broken Windows theory. If anything, the program creates disorder where there was peace, with police stopping and searching people who most often turn out to be neither carrying a gun nor engaged in criminal activity. A program of mass "stop and frisk" is not geared toward reversing neighborhood perceptions of disorder, but instead aims to decrease actual incidents of gun-carrying and resulting violence citywide.

---

[67] See George L. Kelling & James Q. Wilson, *Broken Windows: The Police and Neighborhood Safety*, Atlantic Monthly (Mar. 1982), at 29. Broken windows theory posits that minor forms of social and physical disorder cause a breakdown in informal social control as citizen investment in an area diminishes. As citizens withdraw from the area, the level of disorder increases and the risk for more serious types of crime to emerge becomes greater. The theory suggests that police focus enforcement efforts on disorder and quality-of-life offenses as a mechanism for reengaging law-abiding citizens' commitment to the area. Under Chief Bratton, the transit police adopted a broken-windows-based strategy in the subway system.

Jeffrey Bellin, *The Inverse Relationship Between the Constitutionality and Effectiveness of New York City "Stop and Frisk,"* 94 B.U. L. Rev. 1495, 1504–1505 (2014).

Interestingly, mass SQF was never a formal policy or strategy of the department. Instead, it developed as Bratton increased officers on the streets, encouraged them to interdict people for low-level offenses, rewarded supervisors for demonstrable activity in high-crime areas (in the data-driven management process known as Compstat), and sought to control guns. Stops and frisks became a way to show that the police were actively addressing crime. When those stops and frisks failed to find many guns, the justification for them increasingly focused on the idea that they deterred rather than caught criminal activity. See *id.* at 1505–1517. In this way, SQF illustrates how effectively institutional incentives (as much or more than formal policies and strategies) give shape to policing on the street.

3. The Wages of Proactive Policing: *Floyd v. City of New York*

In 2008, the Center for Constitutional Rights filed a federal class action lawsuit against the City of New York, challenging the constitutionality of its proactive policing practices. After a trial in March 2013, the district court issued two opinions and orders, one on liability and one on remedies. The liability decision alone is 198 pages long. This excerpt comes from the introduction and executive summary to that opinion.

FLOYD v. CITY OF NEW YORK
959 F. Supp. 2d 540 (S.D.N.Y. 2013)

SHIRA A. SCHEINDLIN, DISTRICT JUDGE: . . .

I. Introduction

New Yorkers are rightly proud of their city and seek to make it as safe as the largest city in America can be. New Yorkers also treasure their liberty. Countless individuals have come to New York in pursuit of that liberty. The goals of liberty and safety may be in tension, but they can coexist—indeed the Constitution mandates it.

This case is about the tension between liberty and public safety in the use of a proactive policing tool called "stop and frisk." The New York City Police Department ("NYPD") made 4.4 million stops between January 2004 and June 2012. Over 80% of these 4.4 million stops were of blacks or Hispanics. In each of these stops a person's life was interrupted. The person was detained and questioned, often on a public street. More than half of the time the police subjected the person to a frisk.

Plaintiffs—blacks and Hispanics who were stopped—argue that the NYPD's use of stop and frisk violated their constitutional rights in two ways: (1) they were stopped without a legal basis in violation of the Fourth Amendment, and (2) they were targeted for stops because of their race in violation of the Fourteenth Amendment. Plaintiffs do not seek to end the use of stop and frisk. Rather, they argue that it must be reformed to comply with constitutional limits. Two such limits are paramount here: *first,* that all stops be based on "reasonable suspicion" as defined by the Supreme Court of the United States; and *second,* that stops be conducted in a racially neutral manner.

I emphasize at the outset, as I have throughout the litigation, that this case is not about the effectiveness of stop and frisk in deterring or combating crime.

This Court's mandate is solely to judge the *constitutionality* of police behavior, *not* its effectiveness as a law enforcement tool. Many police practices may be useful for fighting crime—preventive detention or coerced confessions, for example—but because they are unconstitutional they cannot be used, no matter how effective. "The enshrinement of constitutional rights necessarily takes certain policy choices off the table." District of Columbia v. Heller, 554 U.S. 570, 636 (2008).

This case is also not primarily about the nineteen individual stops that were the subject of testimony at trial. Rather, this case is about whether the City has a *policy* or *custom* of violating the Constitution by making unlawful stops and conducting unlawful frisks.

. . . In light of the very active and public debate on the issues addressed in this Opinion—and the passionate positions taken by both sides—it is important to recognize the human toll of unconstitutional stops. While it is true that any one stop is a limited intrusion in duration and deprivation of liberty, each stop is also a demeaning and humiliating experience. No one should live in fear of being stopped whenever he leaves his home to go about the activities of daily life. Those who are routinely subjected to stops are overwhelmingly people of color, and they are justifiably troubled to be singled out when many of them have done nothing to attract the unwanted attention. Some plaintiffs testified that stops make them feel unwelcome in some parts of the City, and distrustful of the police. This alienation cannot be good for the police, the community, or its leaders. Fostering trust and confidence between the police and the community would be an improvement for everyone. . . .

II. Executive Summary

Plaintiffs assert that the City, and its agent the NYPD, violated both the Fourth Amendment and the Equal Protection Clause of the Fourteenth Amendment of the United States Constitution. In order to hold a municipality liable for the violation of a constitutional right, plaintiffs "must prove that 'action pursuant to official municipal policy' caused the alleged constitutional injury." Cash v. Cty. of Erie, 654 F.3d 324, 333 (2d Cir. 2011) (quoting Connick v. Thompson, 563 U.S. 51, 60 (2011)). "Official municipal policy includes the decisions of a government's lawmakers, the acts of its policymaking officials, and practices so persistent and widespread as to practically have the force of law." *Thompson*, 563 U.S. at 61.

The Fourth Amendment protects all individuals against unreasonable searches or seizures. The Supreme Court has held that the Fourth Amendment permits the police to "stop and briefly detain a person for investigative purposes if the officer has a reasonable suspicion supported by articulable facts that criminal activity 'may be afoot,' even if the officer lacks probable cause." United States v. Swindle, 407 F.3d 562, 566 (2d Cir. 2005) (quoting United States v. Sokolow, 490 U.S. 1, 7 (1989)). "Reasonable suspicion is an objective standard; hence, the subjective intentions or motives of the officer making the stop are irrelevant." United States v. Bayless, 201 F.3d 116, 133 (2d Cir. 2000). The test for whether a stop has taken place in the context of a police encounter is whether a reasonable person would have felt free to terminate the encounter. " '[T]o proceed from a stop to a frisk, the police officer must reasonably suspect that the person stopped is armed and dangerous.' " United States v. Lopez, 321 Fed. App'x 65, 67 (2d Cir. 2009) (quoting Arizona v. Johnson, 555 U.S. 323, 326–327 (2009)).

The Equal Protection Clause of the Fourteenth Amendment guarantees to every person the equal protection of the laws. It prohibits intentional discrimination based on race. Intentional discrimination can be proved in several ways, two of which are relevant here. A plaintiff can show: (1) that a facially neutral law or policy has been applied in an intentionally discriminatory manner; or (2) that a law or policy expressly classifies persons on the basis of race, and that the classification does not survive strict scrutiny. Because there is rarely direct proof of discriminatory intent, circumstantial evidence of such intent is permitted. . . .

The following facts, discussed in greater detail below, are uncontested:

- Between January 2004 and June 2012, the NYPD conducted over 4.4 million *Terry* stops.
- The number of stops per year rose sharply from 314,000 in 2004 to a high of 686,000 in 2011.
- 52% of all stops were followed by a protective frisk for weapons. A weapon was found after 1.5% of these frisks. In other words, in 98.5% of the 2.3 million frisks, no weapon was found.
- 8% of all stops led to a search into the stopped person's clothing, ostensibly based on the officer feeling an object during the frisk that he suspected to be a weapon, or immediately perceived to be contraband other than a weapon. In 9% of these searches, the felt object was in fact a weapon. 91% of the time, it was not. In 14% of these searches, the felt object was in fact contraband. 86% of the time it was not.
- 6% of all stops resulted in an arrest, and 6% resulted in a summons. The remaining 88% of the 4.4 million stops resulted in no further law enforcement action.
- In 52% of the 4.4 million stops, the person stopped was black, in 31% the person was Hispanic, and in 10% the person was white.
- In 2010, New York City's resident population was roughly 23% black, 29% Hispanic, and 33% white.
- In 23% of the stops of blacks, and 24% of the stops of Hispanics, the officer recorded using force. The number for whites was 17%.
- Weapons were seized in 1.0% of the stops of blacks, 1.1% of the stops of Hispanics, and 1.4% of the stops of whites.
- Contraband other than weapons was seized in 1.8% of the stops of blacks, 1.7% of the stops of Hispanics, and 2.3% of the stops of whites.
- Between 2004 and 2009, the percentage of stops where the officer failed to state a specific suspected crime rose from 1% to 36%.

. . . I have made the following findings with respect to the expert testimony.

With respect to plaintiffs' Fourth Amendment claim, I begin by noting the inherent difficulty in making findings and conclusions regarding 4.4 million stops. Because it is impossible to *individually* analyze each of those stops, plaintiffs' case was based on the imperfect information contained in the NYPD's database of forms ("UF-250s") that officers are required to prepare after each stop. The central flaws in this database all skew toward underestimating the number of unconstitutional stops that occur: the database is incomplete, in that officers do not prepare a UF-250 for every stop they make; it is one-sided, in that the UF-250 only records the officer's version of the story; the UF-250 permits the officer to merely check a series of boxes, rather than requiring the officer to explain the basis for her suspicion; and many of the boxes on the form are inherently subjective and vague (such as "furtive movements"). Nonetheless, the analysis of the UF-250 database reveals that *at least* 200,000 stops were made without reasonable suspicion.

The actual number of stops lacking reasonable suspicion was likely far higher, based on the reasons stated above, and the following points: (1) Dr. Fagan was unnecessarily conservative in classifying stops as "apparently unjustified." For example, a UF-250 on which the officer checked only Furtive Movements (used on roughly 42% of forms) and High Crime Area (used on roughly 55% of forms) is not classified as "apparently unjustified." The same is true when only Furtive Movements and Suspicious Bulge (used on roughly 10% of forms) are checked. Finally, if an officer checked only the box marked "other" on either side of the form (used on roughly 26% of forms), Dr. Fagan categorized this as "ungeneralizable" rather than "apparently unjustified." (2) Many UF-250s did not identify *any* suspected crime (36% of all UF-250s in 2009). (3) The rate of arrests arising from stops is low (roughly 6%), and the yield of seizures of guns or other contraband is even lower (roughly 0.1% and 1.8% respectively). (4) "Furtive Movements," "High Crime Area," and "Suspicious Bulge" are vague and subjective terms. Without an accompanying narrative explanation for the stop, these checkmarks cannot reliably demonstrate individualized reasonable suspicion.

With respect to plaintiffs' Fourteenth Amendment claim, I reject the testimony of the City's experts that the race of crime suspects is the appropriate benchmark for measuring racial bias in stops. The City and its highest officials believe that blacks and Hispanics should be stopped at the same rate as their proportion of the local criminal suspect population. But this reasoning is flawed because the stopped population is overwhelmingly innocent—not criminal. There is no basis for assuming that an innocent population shares the same characteristics as the criminal suspect population in the same area. Instead, I conclude that the benchmark used by plaintiffs' expert—a combination of local population demographics and local crime rates (to account for police deployment) is the most sensible.

Based on the expert testimony I find the following: (1) The NYPD carries out more stops where there are more black and Hispanic residents, even when other relevant variables are held constant. The racial composition of a precinct or census tract predicts the stop rate *above and beyond* the crime rate. (2) Blacks and Hispanics are more likely than whites to be stopped within precincts and census tracts, even after controlling for other relevant variables. This is so even in areas with low crime rates, racially heterogenous populations, or predominately white populations. (3) For the period 2004 through 2009, when any law enforcement action was taken following a stop, blacks were 30% more likely to be arrested (as opposed to receiving a summons) than whites, for the same suspected crime. (4) For the period 2004 through 2009, after controlling for suspected crime and precinct characteristics, blacks who were stopped were about 14% more likely—and Hispanics 9% more likely—than whites to be subjected to the use of force. (5) For the period 2004 through 2009, all else being equal, the odds of a stop resulting in any further enforcement action were 8% *lower* if the person stopped was black than if the person stopped was white. In addition, the greater the black population in a precinct, the less likely that a stop would result in a sanction. Together, these results show that blacks are likely targeted for stops based on a lesser degree of objectively founded suspicion than whites.

With respect to both the Fourth and Fourteenth Amendment claims, one way to prove that the City has a custom of conducting unconstitutional stops and frisks is to show that it acted with deliberate indifference to constitutional deprivations caused by its employees—here, the NYPD. The evidence at trial revealed significant evidence that the NYPD acted with deliberate indifference.

As early as 1999, a report from New York's Attorney General placed the City on notice that stops and frisks were being conducted in a racially skewed manner. Nothing was done in response. In the years following this report, pressure was placed on supervisors to increase the number of stops. Evidence at trial revealed that officers have been pressured to make a certain number of stops and risk negative consequences if they fail to achieve the goal. Without a system to ensure that stops are justified, such pressure is a predictable formula for producing unconstitutional stops. As one high ranking police official noted in 2010, this pressure, without a comparable emphasis on ensuring that the activities are legally justified, "could result in an officer taking enforcement action for the purpose of meeting a quota rather than because a violation of the law has occurred."

In addition, the evidence at trial revealed that the NYPD has an unwritten policy of targeting "the right people" for stops. In practice, the policy encourages the targeting of young black and Hispanic men based on their prevalence in local crime complaints. This is a form of racial profiling. While a person's race may be important if it fits the description of a particular crime suspect, it is impermissible to subject all members of a racially defined group to heightened police enforcement because some members of that group are criminals. The Equal Protection Clause does not permit race-based suspicion.

Much evidence was introduced regarding inadequate monitoring and supervision of unconstitutional stops. Supervisors routinely review the *productivity* of officers, but do not review the facts of a stop to determine whether it was legally warranted. Nor do supervisors ensure that an officer has made a proper record of a stop so that it can be reviewed for constitutionality. Deficiencies were also shown in the training of officers with respect to stop and frisk and in the disciplining of officers when they were found to have made a bad stop or frisk. Despite the mounting evidence that many bad stops were made, that officers failed to make adequate records of stops, and that discipline was spotty or non-existent, little has been done to improve the situation.

One example of poor training is particularly telling. Two officers testified to their understanding of the term "furtive movements." One explained that "furtive movement is a very broad concept," and could include a person "changing direction," "walking in a certain way," "[a]cting a little suspicious," "making a movement that is not regular," being "very fidgety," "going in and out of his pocket," "going in and out of a location," "looking back and forth constantly," "looking over their shoulder," "adjusting their hip or their belt," "moving in and out of a car too quickly," "[t]urning a part of their body away from you," "[g]rabbing at a certain pocket or something at their waist," "getting a little nervous, maybe shaking," and "*stutter[ing]*." Another officer explained that "usually" a furtive movement is someone "hanging out in front of [a] building, sitting on the benches or something like that" and then making a "quick movement," such as "bending down and quickly standing back up," "going inside the lobby . . . and then quickly coming back out," or "all of a sudden becom[ing] very nervous, very aware." If officers believe that the behavior described above constitutes furtive movement that justifies a stop, then it is no surprise that stops so rarely produce evidence of criminal activity.

I now summarize my findings with respect to the individual stops that were the subject of testimony at trial. Twelve plaintiffs testified regarding nineteen stops. In twelve of those stops, both the plaintiffs and the officers testified. In seven stops no officer testified, either because the officers could not be identified or because the officers dispute that the stop ever occurred. I find that nine of the stops and frisks were unconstitutional—that is, they were not based on reasonable suspicion. I also find that while five other stops were constitutional, the frisks following those stops were unconstitutional. Finally, I find that plaintiffs have failed to prove an unconstitutional stop (or frisk) in five of the nineteen stops. The individual stop testimony corroborated much of the evidence about the NYPD's policies and practices with respect to carrying out and monitoring stops and frisks. . . .

In conclusion, I find that the City is liable for violating plaintiffs' Fourth and Fourteenth Amendment rights. The City acted with deliberate indifference toward the NYPD's practice of making unconstitutional stops and conducting unconstitutional frisks. Even if the City had not been deliberately indifferent, the NYPD's unconstitutional practices were sufficiently widespread as to have the force of law. In addition, the City adopted a policy of indirect racial profiling by targeting racially defined groups for stops based on local crime suspect data. This has resulted in the disproportionate and discriminatory stopping of blacks and Hispanics in violation of the Equal Protection Clause. Both statistical and anecdotal evidence showed that minorities are indeed treated differently than whites. For example, once a stop is made, blacks and Hispanics are more likely to be subjected to the use of force than whites, despite the fact that whites are more likely to be found with weapons or contraband. I also conclude that the City's highest officials have turned a blind eye to the evidence that officers are conducting stops in a racially discriminatory manner. In their zeal to defend a policy that they believe to be effective, they have willfully ignored overwhelming proof that the policy of targeting "the right people" is racially discriminatory and therefore violates the United States Constitution. One NYPD official has even suggested that it is permissible to stop racially defined groups just to instill fear in them that they are subject to being stopped at any time for any reason—in the hope that this fear will deter them from carrying guns in the streets. The goal of deterring crime is laudable, but this method of doing so is unconstitutional. . . .

To address the violations that I have found, I shall order various remedies including, but not limited to, an immediate change to certain policies and activities of the NYPD, a trial program requiring the use of body-worn cameras in one precinct per borough, a community-based joint remedial process to be conducted by a court-appointed facilitator, and the appointment of an independent monitor to ensure that the NYPD's conduct of stops and frisks is carried out in accordance with the Constitution and the principles enunciated in this Opinion, and to monitor the NYPD's compliance with the ordered remedies.

NOTES AND QUESTIONS

1. *Problems with stop-and-frisk policing.* What precisely are the legal problems with SQF? What evidence did the Court use to find that SQF violated the Constitution?

2. *Causes of constitutional violations.* Judge Scheindlin highlights factors within the department that she believes led to constitutional violations in New York. What are those factors? How would you fix them?

3. *Problems with data.* All the data Judge Scheindlin relied on was produced by NYPD officers. She assumes that it necessarily undercounts illegal stops. Why? Is it possible that because supervisors did not actively review UF-250 forms, officers had little incentive to document accurately the reasons why they stopped a suspect? If so, then some of the stops that appear illegal based on the documents might actually have been based on reasonable suspicion. Should that matter? How should we deal with evaluating police conduct when most of the evidence about that conduct is so heavily influenced by police data collection practices? Might technology help change this situation?

4. *Proactive policing and race.* In theory, deterrence-oriented proactive policing and discriminatory policing need not go together but, inevitably, legal challenges to the aggressive use of stops and frisks or misdemeanor arrests in federal court have involved allegations that police intentionally and disproportionately targeted men of color. Is proactive policing inevitably racist? Or are racial issues in proactive policing simply the product of whatever racial problems policing (or society) otherwise has?

At the very least, strategies such as NYPD's SQF seem to encourage police to act in ways that exacerbate racial bias in policing. Instead of targeting worrisome *conduct* when police see it, aggressive low-level deterrence strategies such as SQF target worrisome *people* and then look for behavior that will justify their actions. From the beginning, critics feared this would lead to discrimination. When James Q. Wilson and George Kelling published *Broken Windows: The Police and Neighborhood Safety* in *The Atlantic Monthly* in 1982, they were already well known for providing intellectual justifications for tough-on-crime criminal justice policies that discounted the concerns of Black communities. Up-and-coming police historian DeAnza Cook has described how their new theory was perceived at the time:

> The fundamental problem with Wilson and Kelling's proposition rests with their absolute deference to officer discretion as a valid mechanism for ensuring fairness and justice in the policing process. . . . When asked to consider the possibility that increasing police discretion could lead to "police . . . becom[ing] agents of neighborhood bigotry," the men responded "We can offer no wholly satisfactory answer to this important question. We are not confident that there is a satisfactory answer except to hope that by their selection, training, and supervision, the police will be inculcated with a clear sense of the outer limit of their discretionary authority."

> Unsurprisingly, broken windows critics found Wilson and Kelling's concession grossly unsatisfying. Opponents to order maintenance strategies claimed that Wilson and Kelling severely underestimated the negative externalities of increasing police discretionary authority. Moreover, they insisted that Wilson and Kelling's lack of regard for racial, ethnic, or cultural biases in American policing demonstrated their glaring ignorance toward the plight of African Americans (and other urbanites of color) battling with police misconduct throughout this period.

DeAnza A. Cook, *Policing the Black Urban Underclass: The Untold Story of Broken Windows Policing and the Order Maintenance Police Reform Movement, 1967-1994,* at

67–68 (April 2017) (unpublished B.A. thesis, University of Virginia) (on file with author). Despite activists' concerns, as departments adopted broken-windows policing, they did little to monitor racial bias. As *Floyd* suggests, even after it became clear that the critics' fears about broken-windows policing were being realized, the NYPD doubled down on its stop-and-frisk program rather than pull back from it or confront the disproportionate impact it was having on people of color. See *Floyd,* 959 F. Supp. 2d at 658.

A stop and frisk in New York City.

5. *What crime?* In *Terry,* Officer McFadden had an articulable reason to believe a specific and serious crime was about to occur. Few would say that McFadden should have stood back and done nothing at all. When stops and frisks are encouraged as a means to deter crime, the suspicious activity is far less likely to have that specificity, severity, or immediacy. Indeed, more than one-third of officers did not indicate on their UF-250 forms what crime they suspected. If the Supreme Court were to reemphasize that an officer must suspect a *particular* crime, would that meaningfully limit the use of proactive stop-and-frisk strategies? How might it affect policing if the Court held *Terry* stops were permissible only when officers have reasonable suspicion of a felony?

6. *The exclusionary rule as a remedy.* The NYPD used SQF to deter rather than solve crimes, so it thought the program successful even though 88 percent of the stops did not result in any further enforcement action. That also means that only 12 percent of stops and frisks could have possibly ended up in court. Even that 12 percent overwhelmingly involved misdemeanor charges, which are often dismissed and get little screening from prosecutors, defense attorneys, or judges. See Issa Kohler-Hausmann, *Misdemeanorland: Criminal Court and Social Control in an Age of Broken Windows Policing* (2018); Alexandra Natapoff, *Punishment Without Crime: How Our Massive Misdemeanor System Traps the Innocent and Makes America More Unequal* (2018). On the rare occasion when a judge scrutinizes a stop, courts rely mostly on what the officer testifies he perceived in assessing the legality of stops, as it is from the officer's perspective that lawfulness is evaluated. Does *Floyd* prove the *Terry* Court right about the shortcomings of the exclusionary rule?

7. *Programmatic policing and the Fourth Amendment.* Beyond the problems created by depending on the exclusionary rule to drive judicial review of stops, some critics doubt that employing the *Terry* framework to evaluate NYPD's stop-and-frisk practices makes sense as a way to protect Fourth Amendment values:

> Is it not the case that a mass of stops and frisks is simply an aggregation of individual incidents? The answer, in short, is *no.* When policing agencies engage in an organizationally determined practice of stopping certain "sorts" of people for the stated purpose of preventing or deterring crime, as the NYPD did, they are engaging in what I call a "program." The stops that flow from these programs are not individual incidents that grow organically—endogenously—out of a collection of individual investigations occurring between an officer and a person that the officer believes to be committing a crime. Rather, programmatic stops are imposed from the top down and are exogenous to the fabric of community-police relations. In *Terry,* the Court dictated a framework to assess the constitutionality of police action in the endogenous context, but proactive policing of crime does not fit that model. Because proactive policing is carried out differently from the one-off intervention into a crime in progress that *Terry* concerned, those who are subject to it experience it differently. . . .
>
> . . . *Floyd* lays bare the reality of urban policing: stop-and-frisk is carried out systematically, deliberately, and with great frequency. . . . [D]espite the fact that most stops likely are constitutional when measured individually under *Terry,* when a mass of stops are considered in the aggregate, the data make clear that police are not investigating people that they suspect to be committing particular crimes in progress but are instead proactively policing people that they suspect *could* be offenders.

Tracey L. Meares, *Programming Errors: Understanding the Constitutionality of Stop-and-Frisk as a Program, Not an Incident,* 82 U. Chi. L. Rev. 159, 162–164 (2015).

In the same vein, Aziz Huq argues that, while Fourth Amendment doctrine focuses on "the motivations and beliefs of specific, individual officers," SQF's "distinctive moral wrong is inextricably related to [its] programmatic quality, not the happenstance of individual officers' motives. . . . When operationalized at a large scale . . . SQF is an important link in the reproduction of social and racial stratification." Aziz Z. Huq, *The Consequences of Disparate Policing: Evaluating Stop and Frisk as a Modality of Urban Policing,* 101 Minn. L. Rev. 2397, 2400–2402 (2017).

If Meares and Huq are right, should the Court develop a new Fourth Amendment standard for measuring the reasonableness of stops and frisks carried out as part of a proactive program? What would that standard look like? How competent are courts likely to be at assessing a *program's* reasonableness? What is the alternative?

8. *Unintended consequences.* *Terry* does not seem intended to produce SQF. Was it nevertheless a predictable result? When Chief Justice Warren's opinion in *Terry* was circulated among the justices, Justice Fortas worried that the "'detailed description of what the cops can get away with might incite them to greater use of the latitude described!'" Risa Goluboff, *Vagrant Nation: Police Power, Constitutional Change, and the Making of the 1960s* 211–212 (2016) (quoting Letter from Justice Abe Fortas to Chief Justice Earl Warren). If Justice Fortas foresaw that much, is the world *Floyd* describes so surprising? Or is it fairer to say that, although the Court knew it was giving a loaded handgun to the police, it did not know how easily that gun could be converted into an automatic weapon?

The Harms of Police Stops

William Stuntz argued that there are four harms that might be associated with an unreasonable *Terry* stop and frisk:

> The first is a harm to the victim's privacy—the injury suffered if some agent of the state rummages around in the victim's briefcase, or examines the contents of his jacket pockets. The second is what Sherry Colb nicely labels "targeting harm," the injury suffered by one who is singled out by the police and publicly treated like a criminal suspect. Third is the injury that flows from discrimination, the harm a black suspect feels when he believes he is treated the way he is treated because he is black. Fourth is the harm that flows from police violence, the physical injury and associated fear of physical injury that attends the improper police use of force.

William J. Stuntz, Terry's *Impossibility*, 72 St. John's L. Rev. 1213, 1218 (1998).

Stuntz might have accurately identified some harms associated with *Terry* stops, but his list is far from exhaustive. What about the degradation that comes from having one's body touched? The cost of being made late to work? The price of staying off the street for fear of getting stopped? Federal data for 2015 show 40 percent of all those stopped by the police on the street felt their stop was illegitimate, and nearly 20 percent felt that police behaved improperly. Among Black Americans who were stopped, 50 percent felt the stop was illegitimate, and 40 percent felt the officer's conduct was improper. See Elizabeth Davis & Anthony Whyde, BJS, *Contacts Between Police and the Public, 2015*, 14–15 (2018). People who have experienced *Terry* stops often describe feeling vulnerable, humiliated, discriminated against, disrespected, powerless, manhandled, violated, and traumatized by their encounters with the police. See, e.g., Ctr. for Constitutional Rights, *Stop and Frisk: The Human Impact* (2012).

Moreover, Stuntz's list focuses only on the costs that illegal *Terry* stops exact on the *individual*. What about the harm done when children see their parents treated this way? Or the effects in neighborhoods when stops and frisks are so common that community residents feel under siege? Aziz Huq argues that SQF leads neighborhoods to experience a decline in what Robert Sampson calls "collective efficacy," the communal capacity of residents to achieve common objectives and maintain social control. See Aziz Huq, *The Consequences of Disparate Policing: Evaluating Stop and Frisk as a Modality of Urban Policing*, 101 Minn. L. Rev. 2397, 2432–2438 (2017) (quoting Robert J. Sampson, *Neighborhood Effects, Casual Mechanisms, and the Social Structure of the City*, in *Analytic Sociology and Social Mechanisms* 227, 232 (P. Demeluenaere ed., 2011)).

Even more important, why do Stuntz (and Judge Scheindlin in *Floyd*) assume that only *illegal* stops have these costs? Don't the costs of *all* 4.4 million stops count if we are evaluating whether SQF was worthwhile? And shouldn't we also consider all of the secondary harms of legal stops?

And what of the benefits? Apparently, these are limited. According to a 2018 assessment by the National Academy of Sciences—unlike other proactive policing strategies such as hot-spots policing, problem-oriented policing, third-party policing, and focused-deterrence policing, all of which studies show to have a significant positive effect on aspects of crime—studies of widespread use of SQF programs have mixed outcomes, at best. See Nat'l Acads. of Scis., Eng'g & Med., *Proactive Policing: Effects on Crime and Communities* 148–149, 170–175 (David Weisburd & Malay K. Majmundar eds., 2018).

4. Applying *Terry*: Two Stops from *Floyd v. City of New York*

In addition to considering the city's program as a whole, Judge Scheindlin evaluated 19 individual plaintiffs' stops and frisks, and she found 12 of them were unconstitutional. Here are her findings on two of them. As you read these findings, think about whether they help illustrate some of the ways unconstitutional stops and frisks can occur.

a. Leroy Downs

i. *Findings of Fact*

Leroy Downs is a black male resident of Staten Island in his mid-thirties. On the evening of August 20, 2008, Downs arrived home from work and, before entering his house, called a friend on his cell phone while standing in front of a chain link fence in front of his house. Downs used an earpiece connected to the phone by a cord, and held the cell phone in one hand and the black mouthpiece on the cord in the other.

Downs saw a black Crown Victoria drive past and recognized it as an unmarked police car. The car stopped, reversed, and double-parked in front of Downs's house. . . . Two white plainclothes officers, later identified as Officers Scott Giacona and James Mahoney, left the car and approached Downs. One officer said in an aggressive tone that it looked like Downs was smoking weed. They told him to "get the [fuck] against the fence," then pushed him backwards until his back was against the fence. Downs did not feel free to leave.

Downs explained that he was talking on his cell phone, not smoking marijuana, that he is a drug counselor, and that he knows the captain of the 120th Precinct. Without asking permission, the officers patted down the outside of his clothing around his legs and torso, reached into his front and back pants pockets and removed their contents: a wallet, keys, and a bag of cookies from a vending machine. The officers also searched his wallet.

After the officers failed to find any contraband, they started walking back to the car. Downs asked for their badge numbers. The officers "laughed [him] off" and said he was lucky they did not lock him up. Downs said he was going to file a complaint, and one of them responded by saying, "I'm just doing my [fucking] job." Charles Joseph, a friend of Downs who lives on the same block, witnessed the end of the stop. After the officers drove away, Downs walked to the 120th Precinct to file a complaint.

Downs told Officer Anthony Moon at the front desk that he wanted to make a complaint and described what had happened. Officer Moon said that he could not take the complaint because Downs did not have the officers' badge numbers, and that Downs should file a complaint with the CCRB [Civilian Complaint Review Board]. As Downs left the station he saw the two officers who stopped him driving out of the precinct in their Crown Victoria, and he wrote down its license plate number on his hand.

Downs then returned to the station. He tried to give Officer Moon the license plate information, but Officer Moon said that he should give the information to the CCRB instead. Downs waited at the station until he saw the two officers come through the back door with two young black male suspects.

Downs pointed out the two officers to Officer Moon and asked him, "Can you get their badge numbers?" Officer Moon talked to the officers and then told Downs "maybe you can ask them." At that point, Downs went outside again and took a picture of the license plate on the Crown Victoria, which was the same number he had written on his hand.

Eventually, Downs spoke with a supervisor, who said he would try to get the officers' badge numbers and then call Downs. The call never came. Having spent a few hours at the station, Downs went home.

The next day, Downs submitted a complaint to the CCRB. Five months later, Officers Mahoney and Giacona both testified under oath to the CCRB that they had no memory of stopping and frisking Downs—an assertion that was "not entirely credited" by the CCRB. . . . The CCRB substantiated Downs's complaint that Officers Mahoney and Giacona failed to provide their badge numbers. The CCRB found the complaints that the officers stopped Downs without reasonable suspicion and used profanity unsubstantiated. The CCRB found Downs's allegation of a search into his pants pockets "unfounded," based in part on Joseph's testimony that he did not witness a search. The CCRB substantiated the complaint against Officer Moon for failing to process Downs's complaint.

Neither Officer Mahoney nor Officer Giacona received any discipline as a result of the CCRB's recommendations. Instead, each lost five vacation days for failing to make a memo book entry for the Downs stop. They also failed to prepare a UF-250 for the stop, but received no discipline for this. Officer Mahoney has since been promoted to Sergeant.

Officers Mahoney and Giacona testified that they have no recollection of the Downs stop. Like the CCRB, I do not find their denials of recollection credible.

Downs testified that he has been stopped "[m]any times" other than the stop on August 20, 2008.

ii. Mixed Findings of Fact and Law

Downs was stopped when the officers told him to "get the [fuck] against the fence." The officers lacked reasonable suspicion to stop Downs. The officers seized Downs based on a glimpse of a small object in Downs's hand from the window of their passing car. The officers' hunch, unaided by any effort to confirm that what they glimpsed was contraband, was too unreliable, standing alone, to serve as a basis for a *Terry* stop.

Moreover, whatever legal justification the officers might have had for the stop dissipated shortly after they approached Downs. The absence of any physical evidence, smoke or marijuana smell, and Downs's explanation that he was talking on his mouthpiece, negated any ground for reasonable suspicion. Just as an officer may not reach into the pocket of a suspect after a frisk has negated the possibility that the pocket contains a dangerous weapon or immediately perceptible contraband, so an officer may not persist in stopping a person after the suspicion giving rise to the stop has been negated. Officers Mahoney and Giacona violated Downs's rights under the Fourth Amendment by stopping him based on a hunch, and continuing to detain him after it became clear that he had not been smoking marijuana.

The officers further violated the Fourth Amendment by frisking Downs without any objective basis for suspecting that he was armed and dangerous. Nothing about the suspected infraction—marijuana use—in combination with the facts summarized above provides reasonable suspicion that Downs was armed and dangerous.

The officers further violated Downs's Fourth Amendment rights by searching his pockets and wallet after the frisk. Such a search would only have been justified if the officers' frisk of the outer surfaces of Downs's pockets gave rise to reasonable suspicion that his pockets contained a dangerous weapon, or if the frisk made it *immediately apparent* that an object in his pockets was a form of contraband. Nothing in Downs's pockets could have provided reasonable suspicion that he was armed;

nor could it have been immediately apparent from the patdown that Downs's pockets contained contraband.

b. Devin Almonor

i. *Findings of Fact*

Devin Almonor is a sixteen-year-old black male high school student living in Manhattan. In 2010, Almonor was thirteen years old. He was approximately five foot ten and weighed approximately 150 pounds.

On March 20, 2010, a Saturday, around 8:45 p.m., Almonor left his house to walk his friend Levon Loggins to the bus stop at 145th Street and Amsterdam. After Loggins boarded the bus, Almonor began to walk home along Hamilton Place toward a bodega where he planned to meet his brother Malik. A group of males was standing outside the bodega and, after talking to friends outside, Almonor continued home with another individual.

Around 10:00 p.m., Officer Brian Dennis and Sergeant Jonathan Korabel were driving an unmarked vehicle in the vicinity of Hamilton Place in response to nine 911 calls describing a group of about forty youths fighting, throwing garbage cans, and setting off car alarms. A few calls indicated the possibility that weapons were involved. The calls suggested that the youths were dispersing when marked cars arrived and then returning. When the officers arrived at Hamilton Place there were garbage cans in the middle of the street and car alarms still going off. The only description they had of the individuals was that they were young black males.

The officers briefly observed Almonor and another individual walking on Hamilton Place in the direction from which the calls originated. The individuals crossed 141st Street. The officers—two white males in plainclothes—pulled up alongside Almonor, at which point Almonor retreated onto the sidewalk. After the officers exited the car and approached Almonor, Officer Dennis grabbed Almonor's arm and said: "Police." Almonor pulled away and within moments, Officer Dennis pushed Almonor down on the hood of the police car because he was not "satisfied [that Almonor] did not have something in his waist."

Together the officers handcuffed Almonor. Without explanation, Officer Dennis patted Almonor down from his feet to his torso, during which Almonor was saying, "What are you doing? I'm going home. I'm a kid." The officers did not recover anything—Almonor only had a cell phone in his right front pocket and a few dollars.

The officers did not ask Almonor his name until after he was handcuffed. Almonor did not have ID but identified himself as "Devin Al." Almonor told the officers that he was thirteen years old and was going home, which was a few blocks away. At some point, though not initially, Almonor gave the officers his full address. The officers did not ask for Almonor's phone number or whether his parents were home—instead the officers put Almonor in the back of the patrol car, took him to the precinct, and placed him in the juvenile room because of the possibility that he was thirteen.

After Almonor was released, Officer Dennis completed a handwritten UF[-]250 form and a juvenile report. The suspected crime was criminal possession of a weapon, and the circumstances of the stop indicated on the form were "fits description" and "furtive movements." The "suspicious bulge" box was not checked and Officer Dennis testified that he did not see a suspicious bulge that night. No contemporaneous document noted that Almonor was touching his waistband. The juvenile report form indicated that Almonor was "resisting arrest," although Almonor was never arrested. The next morning, Officer Dennis filled out a computerized UF-250 and another juvenile report worksheet, both of which noted a suspicious bulge.

ii. Mixed Findings of Fact and Law

Almonor was stopped when the officers approached him on the sidewalk, and Officer Dennis grabbed Almonor's arm and said: "Police." Even if credited, Almonor's alleged furtive movements—looking over his shoulder and jaywalking—in combination with the generic description of young black male does not establish the requisite individualized suspicion that Almonor was engaged in criminal activity. The officers could have approached Almonor and asked him some questions, but instead chose to physically restrain and handcuff him first, and ask questions later. The circumstances did not justify any restraint of Almonor's liberty, much less immediate physical restraint and the use of handcuffs.

Even if the officers had possessed the requisite basis to stop Almonor—which they did not—they had no basis to frisk him. While some of the 911 calls suggested that some youths involved in the fighting may have had weapons, that alone does not establish individualized suspicion that Almonor was armed and dangerous. No contemporaneous document indicates a suspicious bulge, and Almonor was not in possession of anything that would have created a suspicious bulge. Almonor's actions did not indicate that he was armed.

Finally, not only were Almonor's Fourth Amendment rights violated at the inception of both the stop and the frisk, but the officers made no effort to minimize the intrusion on his liberty. Instead, they used the most intrusive methods at their disposal, thereby exacerbating the violation of his rights.

Floyd, 959 F. Supp. 2d at 625–630.

Floyd plaintiffs Leroy Downs and Devin Almonor.

NOTES AND QUESTIONS

1. *Leroy Downs.* Can you list everything that bothers you about Downs's encounter with police? What aspects of it could constitutional law even plausibly address? What does Downs's effort to complain tell you?

2. *Devin Almonor.* Why did the police approach Almonor? Why was this encounter illegal? What if a bystander identified Almonor as one of the rowdy youths? What would you think of this encounter then?

3. *How to prevent stops.* Assuming most stops like Downs's and Almonor's never get into court, how should we address them?

5. Police Forms and Police Conduct

Here is a copy of Appendix A to Judge Scheindlin's opinion: a blank UF-250, the form mentioned in the opinion and used by NYPD at the time to record stops and frisks conducted by officers. In looking at the form, consider how it translates the law of *Terry* into guidance to officers on the streets. What impact might the form have?

STOP, QUESTION AND FRISK REPORT WORKSHEET
PD344-151A (Rev. 11-02)

(COMPLETE ALL CAPTIONS)

Pct. Serial No. ___
Date ___ Pct. Of Occ. ___

Time Of Stop ___ | Period Of Observation Prior To Stop ___ | Radio Run/Sprint # ___

Address/Intersection Or Cross Streets Of Stop ___

☐ Inside ☐ Transit | Type Of Location
☐ Outside ☐ Housing | Describe: ___

Specify Which Felony/P.L. Misdemeanor Suspected ___ | Duration Of Stop ___

What Were Circumstances Which Led To Stop?
(MUST CHECK AT LEAST ONE BOX)

☐ Carrying Objects In Plain View Used In Commission Of Crime e.g. Slim Jim/Pry Bar, etc.
☐ Fits Description.
☐ Actions Indicative Of "Casing" Victim Or Location.
☐ Actions Indicative of Acting As A Lookout.
☐ Suspicious Bulge/Object (Describe)
☐ Other Reasonable Suspicion Of Criminal Activity (Specify)

☐ Actions Indicative Of Engaging In Drug Transaction.
☐ Furtive Movements.
☐ Actions Indicative Of Engaging In Violent Crimes.
☐ Wearing Clothes/Disguises Commonly Used In Commission Of Crime.

Name Of Person Stopped ___ | Nickname/Street Name ___ | Date Of Birth ___

Address ___ | Apt. No. ___ | Tel. No. ___

Identification: ☐ Verbal ☐ Photo I.D. ☐ Refused ☐ Other (Specify) ___

Sex: ☐ Male ☐ Female | Race: ☐ White ☐ Black ☐ White Hispanic ☐ Black Hispanic ☐ Asian/Pacific Islander ☐ American Indian/Alaskan Native

Age ___ | Height ___ | Weight ___ | Hair ___ | Eyes ___ | Build ___

Other (Scars, Tattoos, Etc.) ___

Did Officer Explain Reason For Stop ☐ Yes ☐ No | If No, Explain: ___

Were Other Persons Stopped/Questioned/Frisked? ☐ Yes ☐ No | If Yes, List Pct. Serial Nos. ___

If Physical Force Was Used, Indicate Type:
☐ Hands On Suspect
☐ Suspect On Ground
☐ Pointing Firearm At Suspect
☐ Handcuffing Suspect
☐ Suspect Against Wall/Car
☐ Drawing Firearm
☐ Baton
☐ Pepper Spray
☐ Other (Describe)

Was Suspect Arrested? ☐ Yes ☐ No | Offense ___ | Arrest No. ___

Was Summons Issued? ☐ Yes ☐ No | Offense ___ | Summons No. ___

Officer In Uniform? ☐ Yes ☐ No | If No, How Identified? ☐ Shield ☐ I.D. Card ☐ Verbal

Was Person Frisked? ☐ Yes ☐ No IF YES, MUST CHECK AT LEAST ONE BOX
☐ Inappropriate Attire, Possibly Concealing Weapon
☐ Verbal Threats Of Violence By Suspect
☐ Knowledge Of Suspect's Prior Criminal Behavior/Use Of Weapon
☐ Violent Crime Suspected
☐ Other Reasonable Suspicion of Weapons (Specify)

Was Person Searched? ☐ Yes ☐ No IF YES, MUST CHECK AT LEAST ONE BOX
☐ Outline Of Weapon
☐ Other Reasonable Suspicion of Weapons (Specify)

Was Weapon Found? ☐ Yes ☐ No If Yes, Describe:
☐ Machine Gun ☐ Other (Describe)

☐ Pistol/Revolver ☐ Rifle/Shotgun ☐ Assault Weapon ☐ Knife/Cutting Instrument

☐ Furtive Movements
☐ Actions Indicative Of Engaging In Violent Crimes

☐ Hard Object ☐ Admission Of Weapons Possession

Was Other Contraband Found? ☐ Yes ☐ No If Yes, Describe Contraband And Location ___

Demeanor Of Person After Being Stopped ___
Remarks Made By Person Stopped ___

Additional Circumstances/Factors: (Check All That Apply)
☐ Report From Victim/Witness
☐ Area Has High Incidence Of Reported Offense Of Type Under Investigation
☐ Time Of Day, Day Of Week, Season Corresponding To Reports Of Criminal Activity
☐ Suspect Associating With Persons Known For Their Criminal Activity
☐ Proximity To Crime Location
☐ Other (Describe)

☐ Refusal To Comply With Officer's Direction(s)
☐ Leading To Reasonable Fear For Safety
☐ Violent Crime Suspected
☐ Suspicious Bulge/Object (Describe)

☐ Evasive, False Or Inconsistent Response To Officer's Questions
☐ Changing Direction At Sight Of Officer/Flight
☐ Ongoing Investigations, e.g., Robbery Pattern
☐ Sights And Sounds Of Criminal Activity, e.g., Bloodstains, Ringing Alarms

Pct. Serial No. ___ | Additional Reports Prepared Complaint Rpt No. ___ | Juvenile Rpt. No. ___ | Aided Rpt. No. ___ | Other Rpt. (Specify) ___

REPORTED BY: Rank, Name (Last, First, M.I.) ___ | Tax# ___ | Command ___
Print ___ Signature ___

REVIEWED BY: Rank, Name (Last, First, M.I.) ___ | Tax# ___ | Command ___
Print ___ Signature ___

Now compare the revised form adopted by the NYPD as part of reforms mandated by the opinion and order in *Floyd*. See Order Approving Recommendation Regarding Electronic Stop Report Form at 3, Floyd v. City of New York, 959 F. Supp. 2d 540 (S.D.N.Y. 2013) (No. 08-CV-1034).

(COMPLETE ALL CAPTIONS)

STOP REPORT
PD 383-151 (03-16)

Pct. Serial No. | ICAD No.
Date of Occ. | Pct. Of Occ.
Time Of Stop | Period Of Observation Prior To Stop | Duration Of Stop
Address/Intersection Or Cross Streets Of Stop

□ Inside □ Transit □ Housing   Type Of Location (Describe:)
□ Outside □ Trespass Affidavit Program
Stop Was: □ Self-Initiated □ Based on Radio Run □ Based on C/W on Scene
Officer in Uniform?   If no, how identified?   □ Shield   □ I.D. Card
□ Yes □ No   □ Verbal
Crime Suspected (e.g., Robbery, Burglary, Criminal Trespass, etc.)

Check All Factors That Led to Stop and Explain in the Narrative Section
□ Concealing or Possessing a Weapon   □ Casing Victim or Location
□ Engaging in a Drug Transaction   □ Matches a Specific Suspect Description
□ Acting as a Lookout   □ Proximity to the Scene of a Crime
□ Identified Crime Pattern (Pattern No.____) □ Other (Describe in "Narrative" Section)

Name Of Person Stopped | Nickname/Alias/Preferred Name | Date Of Birth
Address | Apt. No. | Tel. No.
Identification: □ Verbal   □ Photo I.D.   □ Refused
□ Other (Describe)
Sex: □ Male   Race: □ White □ Black □ Hispanic White □ Hispanic Black
□ Female   □ Asian/Pacific Islander □ American Indian/Alaskan Native
              □ Middle Eastern/Southwest Asian
Age | Height | Weight | Hair | Eyes | Build
Other (Scars, Tattoos, Outer Garments, Etc.)

Did Officer Explain Reason For Stop?   Information Card Given to Person Stopped?
□ Yes □ No   □ Yes □ No
If You Answered No to Either of the Previous Two Questions, Explain the Reasons in the Narrative Section on the Rear Side.
Were Other Persons Stopped/ □ Yes   Total No. Stopped   Pct. Serial Nos.
Questioned/Frisked?   □ No
Did a Body-Worn Camera (BWC) Capture □ Yes   Body-Worn Camera was Worn by:
the Event in Whole or in Part   □ No   □ Reporting Officer □ Another MOS
Body-Worn Camera Serial Number

Actions Taken to Stop and/or Detain Prior to Arrest   □ Verbal Command/Instruction
□ Impact Weapon   □ Drawing/Pointing Firearm   □ Physical Force/Restraint
□ Handcuff Suspect □ O.C. Spray   □ CEW   □ Other (Describe)
Was Suspect Arrested?   Offense   Arrest No.
□ Yes □ No
Was Summons Issued?   Offense   Summons No.
□ Yes □ No
Demeanor of Person After Being Stopped | Remarks Made by Person Stopped

Narrative (Describe the Circumstances That Led to the Stop)

Was Person Frisked? □ Yes □ No   IF YES, INDICATE BASIS FOR FRISK:
Was Person Searched? □ Yes □ No   IF YES, INDICATE BASIS FOR SEARCH:
□ Object Observed Suspected of Being a Weapon
□ Violent Crime
□ Hard Object Resembling Weapon
□ Outline of Weapon
□ Statement by Suspect
□ Suspect Known to Carry Weapons
Was Weapon Found? □ Yes □ No   If Yes, Specify: □ Firearm □ Knife/Cutting Instrument □ Other (Describe)
Was Other Contraband Found? □ Yes □ No   If Yes, Describe Contraband and Location
□ Search Incident to an Arrest
□ Admission Of Weapons Possession
Narrative (Describe the Circumstances That Led to the Frisk and/or Search, if Conducted, Include Area Searched)

Was Other Contraband Found? □ Yes □ No

Reporting MOS (Rank, Name Printed)   Signature   Tax No.   Pct. Serial No.

Supervisory Action (Must Complete):   Supervisor on Scene During Stop?   □ Yes □ No
Encounter Reviewed With Officer?   Sufficient Basis for Stop?   □ Yes □ No
Report Accurate and Complete?   Sufficient Basis for Frisk? □ Yes □ No
Corresponding Activity Log Entry Reviewed? □ Yes □ No   Sufficient Basis for Search? □ Yes □ No
Reviewing Supervisor (Rank, Name Printed)   Signature

Command   Date
Command   Tax No.   Date

Follow-Up Action (If Appropriate):   □ □
Report Corrected...... □   □ Training...............
Instruction............. □   □ Disciplinary Action
□ N/A
□ N/A

Command   Time

The law governing stops and frisks stayed the same in New York City, and both forms purported to ensure that the police documented compliance with that law. Might this new form change the practical import of the legal doctrine by changing the way the law is operationalized? What other consequences might the new form have?

C.   Law and Litigation as a Check on Proactive Policing

1.   Can Constitutional Law Regulate Proactive Policing?

As both Judge Scheindlin and the *Floyd* plaintiffs would admit, hundreds of thousands of the stops performed by the NYPD during the height of the stop-and-frisk policy *were* based on sufficient suspicion, even if many others were not. Could New York or any other city ever develop a practice of using *Terry* stops and frisks on a large scale in a way that effectively deters crime and yet is still constitutional?

Some say no:

> NYC Stop and Frisk, if conceptualized as a program to deter gun-carrying, necessarily depends on stopping people without individualized suspicion. . . . If a frisk can be avoided by avoiding criminal activity such as trespassing, public marijuana smoking or public urination, people can comfortably carry guns unlawfully so long as they obey (or think they will obey) other laws while doing so. Thus, a high volume of arbitrary frisks is essential to effectively deterring gun possession.

Jeffrey Bellin, *The Inverse Relationship Between the Constitutionality and Effectiveness of New York City "Stop and Frisk,"* 94 B.U. L. Rev. 1495, 1538 (2014). Bellin also argues that given resource constraints, stop-and-frisk strategies require demographic profiling on the basis of race. *Id.* at 1500.

Others say yes:

> Imagine . . . [e]ach officer . . . understood that she could not make a nonconsensual street stop without the relevant reasonable articulable suspicion of criminality, and that she could not make that stop " 'because of,' not merely 'in spite of' " the perceived racial identity of the individual to be stopped. . . . Consistent with the weak *Terry* rule, it may well be possible for a police force to conduct a very large volume of stops. Consistent with *Feeney*,[4] those stops might be constitutionally valid even if they were distributed in a way that deepens racial stratification. Indeed, racial disparities are particularly likely to *persist* if police sincerely believe that African Americans commit a disproportionate share of offenses and thus ought to comprise a higher per-capita rate of street stops. The application of conventional constitutional doctrine under the Fourth Amendment and the Equal Protection Clause, therefore, is consistent with preservation of SQF at its present volume and as characterized by current racial disparities.

Aziz Huq, *The Consequences of Disparate Policing: Evaluating Stop and Frisk as a Modality of Urban Policing*, 101 Minn. L. Rev. 2397, 2443–2444 (2017).

Either way, doesn't it seem that constitutional law might be an inadequate measure of whether proactive policing is good policy?

> It is the nature of constitutional rights, and especially Fourth Amendment rights, not to weigh individual interests fairly against those of the government. Rights are always framed as a ceiling on government action rather than an account of what police officers should do to ensure that law enforcement is worth the harms it imposes. Thus, even if Fourth Amendment reasonableness purports to engage in balancing of government and individual interests, in the end, it tells the police what they cannot do, not what they should. In addition, those rights are likely to be more permissive to law enforcement than a fair weighing of the interests would reflect, both because they are set in advance by inexpert judges bent on preserving law enforcement flexibility and because they are designed to accommodate the needs of courts applying them as well as the police. Finally, since rights are held and enforced by individuals, usually with respect to specific actions, they do not do a good job of measuring—and can sometimes obscure—aggregate costs

---

[4] *Ed. note: Pers. Adm'r of Mass. v. Feeney*, 442 U.S. 256, 279 (1979), requires that to establish the discriminatory purpose required for an Equal Protection Clause violation, plaintiffs must establish that the government decisionmaker "selected or reaffirmed a particular course of action at least in part 'because of,' not merely 'in spite of,' its adverse effects upon an identifiable group."

and benefits of policing, something communities care enormously about. Thus, it should come as no surprise that doctrines defining the scope of constitutional rights might permit stops and frisks that are socially very costly.

The Court often assumes that resource constraints are sufficient to check against police officers inappropriately capitalizing on permissive Fourth Amendment doctrines to tread upon individuals when the circumstances do not warrant an intrusion. Specifically, the Court imagines that when criminal conduct is minor or especially equivocal, an officer would usually have no interest in pursuing it, even when allowed by the Constitution to do so. Thus, formulating constitutional law to protect against that problem is thought to be unnecessary. In proactive policing, however, pursuing equivocal conduct can have outsized deterrence benefits. . . . Thus, not only is the Fourth Amendment likely to be permissive compared to a full weighing of privacy, autonomy, and bodily integrity interests at stake in stops and frisks, but one of the usual checks against the abuse of that freedom—limited resources—does not apply to proactive policing. . . .

Constitutional law, and in particular the Fourth Amendment, is no better suited to evaluate proactive policing's benefits than it is to check its costs. Although the Court nominally balances the individual and government interests, it does not consider how well law enforcement strategies serve the government interest at issue. Thus, the Court does not consider whether an intrusive policing practice is effective or whether it is more effective than less intrusive alternatives, i.e., whether it is harm efficient, when deciding whether the practice is reasonable for purposes of the Fourth Amendment. . . . [T]he consequence is that Fourth Amendment doctrine is devoid of the kind of analysis that might indicate whether a policing practice is reasonable in the important sense of being worth doing.

All this leaves us in the following position. The *Terry* Court accommodated law enforcement's need to respond to incident-specific events by legitimizing stops and frisks under a new standard, requiring less suspicion than probable cause. Since then, that tool has been turned into a diffuse weapon, like a form of tear gas, in proactive policing. It imposes largely temporary harms in order to deter and control. Neither the *Terry* opinion itself nor subsequent case law gives courts a way to easily check this use of *Terry*, which is no surprise in light of the structure and limits of the law. While some departments have likely violated the Constitution in implementing proactive stops and frisks, well-designed proactive policing programs that utilize stops and frisks probably could pass constitutional muster. *Terry* has therefore facilitated an important shift in policing in the United States, one that has the potential to promote public safety but also impose significant costs, and one which constitutional law is unlikely to regulate well.

Rachel A. Harmon & Andrew Manns, *Proactive Policing and the Legacy of* Terry, 15 Ohio St. J. Crim. L. 49, 63–65 (2017).

If you were the emperor of New York City, and your police commissioner proposed a new proactive program of aggressively stopping and frisking pedestrians in the 5 percent of two-block areas in the city with the highest rates of gun violence, how would you decide whether the idea is a good one?

2. The Aftermath of *Floyd*: Litigation and the Political Process

Reported stops are down dramatically since *Floyd*—more than 98 percent, from 685,000 in 2011 to 11,238 in 2018. See Tenth Report of the Independent

Monitor: Corrected Report Filed: January 7, 2020, at 3, Floyd v. City of New York, 959 F. Supp. 2d 540 (S.D.N.Y. 2013) (No. 08-CV-1034).[5]

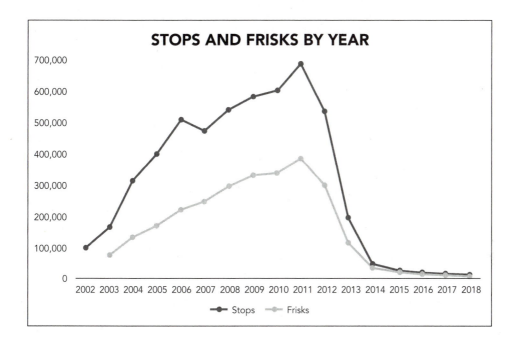

In light of such numbers, *Floyd* is often celebrated as a constitutional-litigation success story. After all, the plaintiffs won, and then SQF ended in New York City. The actual history is a little more complicated.

The trial in *Floyd* started in March 2013 during a mayoral campaign in New York City. Near the start of the trial, Bill de Blasio—a candidate in the Democratic primary race for mayor of New York—was running fourth or fifth among primary candidates. See Rebecca Kaplan, *Bill de Blasio Wins New York City Mayoral Race in Landslide,* CBS News (Nov. 6, 2013). When the trial drew attention to stop and frisk, de Blasio capitalized on it, relentlessly criticizing the police department's SQF program. After the district court decided the case in August, the issue helped catapult de Blasio to victory in both the September primary and the November general election.

After his election, Mayor de Blasio announced changes to the department's stop-and-frisk policy, and stops and frisks in New York City declined. Equally important, under de Blasio's leadership, the city dropped its appeal in *Floyd,* leaving both the liability decision and the district court's remedy in place. The police department's five unions sought to intervene to continue the city's appeal, but after this effort was rejected by the courts in late 2014, the city began the remedial process ordered by Judge Scheindlin.

So, who or what really ended SQF? What do the *Floyd* decision, de Blasio's victory, and the change in policy tell us about the relative roles of politics and courts in changing policing?

---

[5] Although the data for both years may be incomplete, making the precise decrease impossible to determine, there is no question that the decrease is dramatic.

Litigation helped end SQF in another way, too. It produced data. *Floyd* was not the first suit against the NYPD concerning stops and frisks. In March 1999, the Center for Constitutional Rights, which was also involved in *Floyd*, filed a class-action lawsuit challenging the NYPD Street Crime Unit's stop-and-frisk practices on both Fourth Amendment and Equal Protection Clause grounds. See Daniels v. City of New York, 198 F.R.D. 409 (S.D.N.Y. 2001). *Daniels* settled, and that settlement required the NYPD to better collect and release the UF-250s—the forms on which police recorded *Terry* stops and frisks. See Stipulation of Settlement, Daniels v. New York, No. 99-CV—1695 (S.D.N.Y. Sept. 24, 2003). Those UF-250s became the basis for the expert analysis that persuaded the court in *Floyd*. Journalists also used them to highlight issues with stops and frisks. *The New York Times* created an interactive tool that permitted New Yorkers to compare stop-and-frisk statistics by block. As a result, New Yorkers knew much more about stops and frisks when they voted than they otherwise would have.

But if litigation is so helpful, why didn't *Daniels* prevent the hundreds of thousands of unconstitutional stops discussed in *Floyd*? Although the NYPD disbanded the Street Crime Unit in 2002 and settled the *Daniels* litigation in 2003, the NYPD was clearly not chastened. In fact, it was at about that time that NYPD began to increase dramatically the numbers of stops and frisks it carried out. Why might the *Floyd* litigation have contributed to ending stops and frisks when the *Daniels* litigation could not?

One possible explanation is that the public is often more sympathetic to policing reform when crime rates are low. This is a chart of major felony offenses in New York City over the relevant period.

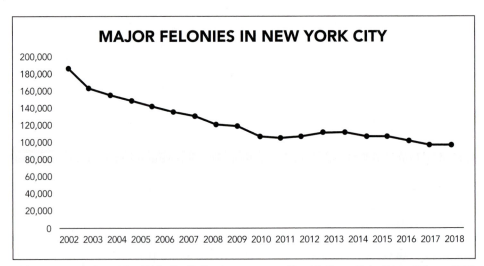

This data comes from New York City Police Department, *Citywide Seven Major Felony Offenses 2000-2018* (2019), *https://perma.cc/G65L-Q37K*. This chart illustrates the change in the *number* of murders and manslaughters, rapes, robberies, felony assaults, burglaries, grand larcenies, and grand larcenies of a motor vehicle in each year. The population of New York City increased over this period from 8,008,278 in 2000 to an estimated 8,398,758 in July 2018. See New York City Department of City Planning, Population—Decennial Census—Census 2000; United States Census Bureau, QuickFacts: New York City, New York. Thus, the *crime rate* per 100,000 New Yorkers actually dropped more sharply than the slope of this line.

Can you articulate why crime rates might matter?

Assuming litigation can drive policy change, *should* it be used that way? The American Bar Association's Model Rules of Professional Conduct prohibit lawyers from bringing a claim "unless there is a basis in law and fact for doing so that is not frivolous, which includes a good faith argument for an extension, modification or reversal of existing law." See Model Rules of Profl. Conduct R. 3.1 (Am. Bar Assn. 2016). If an organization believes that Fourth Amendment law has been misinterpreted by the Supreme Court to permit law enforcement conduct that should not be allowed, and if it believes that suing could help shift policy and public opinion on the matter, is it ethical to bring a lawsuit challenging police conduct even if the organization also recognizes that its arguments are inconsistent with current doctrine and likely to lose in court?

Despite the history of NYPD's SQF practice, programmatic stop-and-frisk policies continue to have their defenders. Moreover, police departments adopt other strategies, both proactive and reactive, that increase the aggregate harms of policing to achieve public safety benefits. What lessons do you draw from New York City's experience?

Chapter 6

Stopping Traffic

More than 20 million Americans are stopped by the police each year while driving, making traffic encounters the most common way the public experiences the police. Why are traffic stops so common? Driving is dangerous: Even with traffic enforcement, more than 2 million people are injured, and more than 30,000 are killed in traffic accidents each year. Ticketing cars for violations can increase compliance with motor vehicle laws, which in turn improves traffic safety. Fewer drunk drivers mean fewer accidents and deaths behind the wheel; enforcing seat belt laws increases belt use and makes accidents less often fatal.

For decades, however, traffic enforcement has served a second function: crime control. In addition to deterring some would-be criminals by making policing visible to the public, stopping cars allows the police to look for criminal activity. They might observe illegal weapons or decide that suspicious behavior justifies investigating further. Officers often stop traffic violators primarily for the purpose of engaging in additional investigation.

Studies since the 1970s have supported the idea that aggressive traffic enforcement can reduce gun crime, burglaries, car thefts, and even homicides without either displacing crime to other areas or alienating communities. See, e.g., Lawrence W. Sherman et al., *The Kansas City Gun Experiment* (1995). Officers are frequently reminded that the Southern California Strangler, Randy Kraft; serial killer Ted Bundy; the Son of Sam killer, David Berkowitz; and Oklahoma City bomber Timothy McVeigh were all caught as a result of traffic (or, in Berkowitz's case, parking) enforcement. Although traffic enforcement has sometimes been used to reduce violent crime, in recent decades, traffic enforcement for crime control has overwhelmingly targeted drug crime as part of the war on drugs. Declared by President Nixon, and strengthened by President Reagan, the war on drugs dramatically expanded resources available to local law enforcement agencies for antidrug efforts, including drug interdiction on the roads. Overwhelmingly, police departments today make investigatory stops part of their strategy of crime control and especially drug-crime control.

Officers can only use traffic stops to pursue crime because state law grants the police enormous discretion. State laws authorize officers to enforce traffic codes by stopping cars, and warning, ticketing, or arresting officers, and those traffic codes regulate driving behavior and vehicle conditions in such detail that almost any driver may be stopped. An ordinary traffic stop may be relatively brief and unintrusive:

> A police officer, witnessing the commission of a driving infraction (e.g., exceeding the speed limit or failure to use a required signal before a turn), or observing a defect with a vehicle's equipment (e.g., a cracked taillight or a non-working headlight) or its required licensing items (plates, stickers or the like), any of which

may violate the criminal law, may order the driver to pull over. Once stopped, the officer typically approaches the vehicle, addresses the driver, and requests the driver's license, vehicle registration, and (usually) required proof of insurance. The officer takes these documents back to the police car and uses the police radio or an in-car computer to run checks on the driver and the stopped vehicle. Regarding the driver, the officer checks for active arrest warrants and for his or her history of driving citations, accumulated points, and/or license suspensions. As for the vehicle, the officer attempts to ascertain whether the vehicle's registration and tags are current and proper, and to learn whether the vehicle has been reported stolen. Assuming that these checks come back "clean," the officer then decides whether to issue one or more citations to the driver, or instead warn the driver to avoid the conduct that caught the officer's attention or to fix problems with the vehicle. This usually takes 20 to 30 minutes.

David Harris, *Racial Profiling, in* 2 *Reforming Criminal Justice* 117, 125–126 (Erik Luna ed., 2017). Nevertheless, state law, supported by permissive constitutional doctrines, often allows additional intrusions, including ordering people out of the car, searching them, arresting them, or subjecting them to force.

A traffic stop in Roseville, Minnesota. Roseville, along with several nearby cities, started voluntarily collecting and publishing data on traffic stops, including demographic data, after the 2016 fatal police shooting of Philando Castile.

Because traffic violations are widespread and police resources are limited, officers do not stop every lawbreaker or investigate further everyone they stop. Instead, they inevitably pick and choose among violators. In light of widespread racial disparities in those stopped and investigated, many see traffic enforcement as a tool of racial discrimination.

Determining whether disparities result from discrimination can be difficult. Still, the largest analysis to date concluded that bias leads officers to stop Black drivers significantly more than others and to search Black and Latino drivers on less suspicion than whites. See Emma Pierson et al., *A Large-Scale Analysis of Racial Disparities in Police Stops Across the*

United States, 4 Nature Hum. Behav. 736 (2020). Other research suggests that officers are also more disrespectful to Black motorists. See Rob Voigt et al., *Language from Police Body Camera Footage Shows Racial Disparities in Officer Respect,* 114 Proceedings Natl. Acad. Sci. 6521 (2017). Police sometimes use subjective, often racial and racially coded, drug courier profiles to decide when to investigate a driver. This kind of policing inflicts a double whammy: It subjects men of color to intense police scrutiny on the roads, and it does so outside of the view of many other voters, making the full harms of policing nearly invisible in the political process. Given the low yield on drug interdiction, many reasonably question whether investigative stops make sense. See Derek A. Epp et al., *Suspect Citizens: What 20 Million Traffic Stops Tell Us About Policing and Race* 12–13 (2018). In communities where disparities are extreme, some have suggested that traffic enforcement functions as "a modern-day version of the slave pass," in which Black drivers can be stopped and forced to account for themselves at any time. Thomas B. Harvey & Janea Stacier, *Policing in St. Louis: "I Feel Like a Runaway Slave Sometimes,"* in *The Cambridge Handbook of Policing in the United States* 56 (Tamara Lave & Eric J. Miller eds., 2019).

This chapter isolates some of the laws and legal doctrines that expressly address investigatory stops and racial disparities in traffic enforcement. It starts with Fourth Amendment law governing pretextual activities by the police. The second section considers Equal Protection Clause challenges to racially disparate policing. The last section looks at several federal and state statutes that might prohibit disparate or racially targeted policing beyond the limits of the Fourth Amendment and the Equal Protection Clause. After reading this chapter, you should be able to identify the limits of federal constitutional law in regulating street policing that disproportionately affects racial minorities, and you should understand the different roles state and federal law might play in regulating racially targeted policing.

A.   *The Fourth Amendment and Pretextual Policing*

1.   **Permitting Pretext**

The Fourth Amendment is the primary constraint on stops, frisks, searches, arrests, and uses of force in policing, including in the traffic context. How does it handle concerns about race?

WHREN v. UNITED STATES
517 U.S. 806 (1996)

JUSTICE SCALIA delivered the opinion of the Court. . . .

I

On the evening of June 10, 1993, plainclothes vice-squad officers of the District of Columbia Metropolitan Police Department were patrolling a "high drug area" of the city in an unmarked car. Their suspicions were aroused when they passed a dark Pathfinder truck with temporary license plates and youthful occupants waiting at a stop sign, the driver looking down into the lap of the passenger at his right. The truck remained stopped at the intersection for what seemed an unusually long time—more than 20 seconds. When the police car executed a U-turn in order to head back toward the truck, the Pathfinder turned suddenly to its right, without signaling, and sped off at an "unreasonable" speed. The policemen followed, and in a short while overtook the Pathfinder when it stopped behind other traffic at a red light. They pulled up alongside, and Officer Ephraim Soto stepped out and approached the driver's door. . . . When Soto drew up to the driver's window, he immediately observed two large plastic bags of what appeared to be crack cocaine in petitioner Whren's hands. Petitioners were arrested, and quantities of several types of illegal drugs were retrieved from the vehicle.

Petitioners were charged in a four-count indictment with violating various federal drug laws. . . . At a pretrial suppression hearing, they challenged the legality of the stop and the resulting seizure of the drugs. They argued that . . . Officer Soto's asserted ground for approaching the vehicle—to give the driver a warning concerning traffic violations—was pretextual. . . .

II

The Fourth Amendment guarantees "[t]he right of the people to be secure in their persons, houses, papers, and effects, against unreasonable searches and seizures." Temporary detention of individuals during the stop of an automobile by the police, even if only for a brief period and for a limited purpose, constitutes a "seizure" of "persons" within the meaning of this provision. An automobile stop is thus subject to the constitutional imperative that it not be "unreasonable" under the circumstances. As a general matter, the decision to stop an automobile is reasonable where the police have probable cause to believe that a traffic violation has occurred.

Petitioners accept that Officer Soto had probable cause to believe that various provisions of the District of Columbia traffic code had been violated. They argue, however, that . . . the use of automobiles is so heavily and minutely regulated that total compliance with traffic and safety rules is nearly impossible, a police officer will almost invariably be able to catch any given motorist in a technical violation. This creates the temptation to use traffic stops as a means of investigating other law violations, as to which no probable cause or even articulable suspicion exists. Petitioners, who are both black, further contend that police officers might decide which motorists to stop based on decidedly impermissible factors, such as the race of the car's occupants. To avoid this danger, they say, the Fourth Amendment test for traffic stops should be, not the normal one . . . of whether probable cause existed to justify the stop; but rather, whether a police officer, acting reasonably, would have made the stop for the reason given.

. . . Not only have we never held, outside the context of inventory search or administrative inspection . . . that an officer's motive invalidates objectively justifiable behavior under the Fourth Amendment; but we have repeatedly held and asserted the contrary. . . .

We think these cases foreclose any argument that the constitutional reasonableness of traffic stops depends on the actual motivations of the individual officers involved. We of course agree with petitioners that the Constitution prohibits selective enforcement of the law based on considerations such as race. But the constitutional basis for objecting to intentionally discriminatory application of laws is the Equal Protection Clause, not the Fourth Amendment. Subjective intentions play no role in ordinary, probable-cause Fourth Amendment analysis. . . .

III . . .

It is of course true that in principle every Fourth Amendment case, since it turns upon a "reasonableness" determination, involves a balancing of all relevant factors. With rare exceptions not applicable here, however, the result of that balancing is not in doubt where the search or seizure is based upon probable cause. . . .

Petitioners urge as an extraordinary factor in this case that the "multitude of applicable traffic and equipment regulations" is so large and so difficult to obey perfectly that virtually everyone is guilty of violation, permitting the police to single out almost whomever they wish for a stop. But we are aware of no principle that would allow us to decide at what point a code of law becomes so expansive and so commonly violated that infraction itself can no longer be the ordinary measure of the lawfulness of enforcement. And even if we could identify such exorbitant codes, we do not know by what standard (or what right) we would decide, as petitioners would have us do, which particular provisions are sufficiently important to merit enforcement.

For the run-of-the-mine case, which this surely is, we think there is no realistic alternative to the traditional common-law rule that probable cause justifies a search and seizure. . . .

NOTES AND QUESTIONS

1. *Doctrine.* *Whren* rules that traffic stops are constitutional if objective suspicion exists for them, even if the officer was actually motivated by another purpose. This permits officers to use traffic stops to investigate other crimes for which they do not have sufficient suspicion to justify a search or seizure, and it prohibits courts from considering motive, even unconstitutional motives, in evaluating whether a stop complies with the Fourth Amendment. Thus, a search or a seizure may be racially discriminatory and still reasonable within the meaning of the Fourth Amendment.

Criminal Investigation During Traffic Stops

Whren allows traffic stops to serve as a basis for investigating more serious crimes. This power would be of far less use if not for a vast traffic code and other Supreme Court opinions that facilitate criminal investigation during the course of a stop. Here are just a few of the rulings that help officers investigate once they make a lawful stop:

Schneckloth v. Bustamonte, 412 U.S. 218 (1973)	Officers may ask for consent to search without suspicion or telling the driver he has the right to refuse.
United States v. Robinson, 414 U.S. 218 (1973)	Officers may conduct a full search of a person arrested for any offense, including a minor traffic offense.
Pennsylvania v. Mimms, 434 U.S. 106 (1977)	Officers may order a driver out of a vehicle during a stop.
Texas v. Brown, 460 U.S. 730 (1983)	Officers may shine light into a car to better look inside.
Berkemer v. McCarty, 468 U.S. 420 (1984)	Officers may question the occupants of a vehicle during a traffic stop without giving them *Miranda* warnings.

United States v. Sharpe, 470 U.S. 675 (1985)	Officers may stop a car based on the lesser standard of reasonable suspicion rather than probable cause.
Colorado v. Bertine, 479 U.S. 367 (1987)	Officers may conduct an inventory search of an impounded vehicle without suspicion.
California v. Acevedo, 500 U.S. 565 (1991)	Officers may search a car and containers found within it without a warrant based on probable cause that evidence or contraband is inside.
Atwater v. Lago Vista, 532 U.S. 318 (2001)	Officers may make a custodial arrest for a fine-only traffic offense.
Illinois v. Caballes, 543 U.S. 405 (2005)	Officers may walk a dog around a car to sniff for drugs and search the car if the dog "alerts."
Arizona v. Gant, 556 U.S. 332 (2009)	Officers may search a car after an arrest with reason to believe evidence of the crime of arrest will be found.

Officers may not take advantage of these rulings unless states authorize them to engage in these activities. With few exceptions, however, states allow the police the full range of constitutionally permitted powers. Even so, overwhelmingly, traffic stops proceed without a drug dog, a consent search, or an arrest. Officers use their authority selectively, usually to look for drugs, often based on little more than the age, race, and gender of the person stopped. As a consequence, as Justice Sotomayor noted in her dissent in *Utah v. Strieff*, 136 S. Ct. 2056, 2069–2070 (2016), "Although many Americans have been stopped for speeding or jaywalking, few may realize how degrading a stop can be when the officer is looking for more." Uneven use of permissive Supreme Court rulings means that Americans drive away from traffic stops with divergent perspectives on the costs and benefits of policing.

A traffic stop in Las Vegas, Nevada.

2. *Does* Whren *matter?* Ask criminal procedure professors which Supreme Court opinions they hate most, and *Whren* will almost inevitably be in the top three. But how much would the world change if *Whren* were reversed? After all, it is near impossible to prove pretext. One way to tell is to look at the two states that have experimented with greater protection than the Fourth Amendment demands. First, a few years after *Whren*, the Washington Supreme Court concluded that biased stops, as well as stops made to investigate criminal activity unrelated to driving, violated the state constitution. See State v. Ladson, 979 P.2d 833 (Wash. 1999). An examination of post-*Ladson* cases, however, found courts largely unwilling to find stops pretextual or biased. See Margaret M. Lawton, *The Road to* Whren *and Beyond: Does the "Would Have" Test Work?*, 57 DePaul L. Rev. 917, 935–937 (2008). Then, in 2008, New Mexico rejected *Whren* as a matter of state constitutional law. See State v. Ochoa, 206 P.3d 143 (N.M. Ct. App. 2008). A look at New Mexico found results like those in Washington: Despite an apparently exacting standard, New Mexican courts seem to find pretext mainly when an officer testifies that his actions were, in fact, pretextual. See Margaret M. Lawton, *State Responses to the* Whren *Decision*, 66 Case W. Res. L. Rev. 1039, 1051 (2016).

3. *Does* Whren *matter? Take 2.* Are appellate cases really the way to tell whether *Whren* matters? In 2012, in *State v. Arreola*, the state supreme court weakened the rule from *Ladson*, concluding that stops motivated primarily by an unconstitutional purpose were permissible. State v. Arreola, 290 P.3d 983, 991–992 (Wash. 2012). Thus, Washington law is once again close to *Whren*. Several teams of researchers have attempted to use this development to study whether changes in pretext doctrine altered racial profiling practices in Washington. If so, that might suggest something about the impact of *Whren*. So far, those studies have had mixed results. Assuming such studies establish that overruling *Whren would* reduce racial disparities in traffic stops, should the Court change gears?

4. *Does* Whren *matter? Pretext and violence.* After *Whren*, police officers need not distinguish traffic safety stops from those motivated by criminal law enforcement. In a study on danger and traffic stops, Jordan Blair Woods found that blurring the line between the two encourages officers to overestimate the dangers associated with ordinary stops: Because they fear violence from drug dealers, they overreact to minor driver resistance. It also led officers to underestimate the risks of investigatory stops. That left officers surprised by resistance, also contributing to overreaction. See Jordan Blair Woods, *Policing, Danger Narratives, and Routine Traffic Stops*, 117 Mich. L. Rev. 635, 704 (2019). Could *Whren* make traffic stops more dangerous for officers and suspects? Is *that* an argument for overturning *Whren*?

5. *Does* Whren *matter? One more view.* Because *Whren* allows pretextual traffic stops, departments all over the country expressly adopt strategies that include them. They train officers to do such stops and reward them when they carry them out effectively. That is, *Whren* gives pretextual stops legitimacy. If *Whren* were reversed, even if no court ever rejected a stop as pretextual, departments would be less likely to promote them. In this way, reversing *Whren* could reduce such stops, even if courts failed to enforce a constitutional prohibition on pretext.

2.   Race and Pretextual Policing

Although race is not a big issue in the opinion, when *Whren* was decided, critics immediately focused on its racial consequences, arguing that the Court's reasoning "fails
to consider a factor that often stands at the core of pretextual traffic stops and makes
those encounters particularly unreasonable—race." Tracey Maclin, *Race and the Fourth
Amendment*, 51 Vand. L. Rev, 333, 340 (1998). David Harris described the consequences
this way:

> In the most literal sense, no driver can avoid violating *some* traffic law during a short
> drive, even with the most careful attention. Fairly read, *Whren* says that any traf-
> fic violation can support a stop, no matter what the real reason for it is; . . . *Whren*
> changes the Fourth Amendment's rule that police must have a reason to forcibly
> interfere in our business—some basis to suspect wrongdoing that is more than a
> hunch. Simply put, that rule no longer applies when a person drives a car.

> This alone should worry us, but the second police practice *Whren* approves is in fact far
> worse. It is this: Police will *not* subject *all* drivers to traffic stops in the way *Whren* allows.
> Rather, if past practice is any indication, they will use the traffic code to stop a hugely dis-
> proportionate number of African-Americans and Hispanics. . . . [T]he stopping of black
> drivers, just to see what officers can find, has become so common in some places that
> this practice has its own name: African-Americans sometimes say they have been stopped
> for the offense of "driving while black." . . . And once police stop a car, they often search
> it, either by obtaining consent, using a drug sniffing dog, or by some other means. In
> fact, searching cars for narcotics is perhaps *the* major motivation for making these stops.

> . . . Yet the Court paid little attention to these obvious implications of its decision.
> *Whren* is more than a missed opportunity for the Court to rein in some police prac-
> tices that strike at the heart of the ideas of freedom and equal treatment; *Whren*
> represents a clear step in the other direction—toward authoritarianism, toward
> racist policing, and toward a view of minorities as criminals, rather than citizens.

David A. Harris, *"Driving While Black" and All Other Traffic Offenses: The Supreme Court
and Pretextual Traffic Stops*, 87 J. Crim. L. & Criminology 544, 545–547 (1997).

To see what an investigatory stop looks like, watch the police body-camera footage documenting the stop of 18-year-old Tae-Ahn Lea in August 2018, after he allegedly made a "wide turn" onto a street: Louisville Metro PD Falsely Alert K-9 to Conduct an Illegal Search, YouTube (Feb. 11, 2019), *https://www.youtube.com/watch?v=9CCQv-i6UBI.*

After asking Lea for his license, officers ordered him out of the car and frisked him. They asked for permission to search the car, and when he refused, accused him of being nervous, hiding something from the police, and having an "attitude." Officers walked a dog around the car, rooted through the passenger compartment, and let the dog into the interior of the car and the trunk. The officers claimed that the dog alerted on the car, and they handcuffed Lea, searching him and his car further. They found nothing. In the end, while Lea was still in handcuffs and had been kept at the scene for more than 25 minutes, an officer who had been curt to Lea and hostile to his mother asked him, "If you don't mind my asking, why do you, like, have this negative attitude toward the police? What's the deal? What has ever happened in your life personally? Can you give me a good explanation?" The officer's questions suggest that he had no idea how his actions affected those who experienced them.

Many who are stopped pretextually understand what is happening. How often do you think officers stop cars for wide turns or bring drug dogs when they do? That contributes to the embarrassment and intrusion those who are stopped experience. For people of color, pretextual stops have additional meaning. Because racial disparities pervade policing, and police have played a historical role in enforcing racial injustice, Black and Latino drivers uniquely suffer what Sherry Colb has called "targeting harm." Sherry F. Colb, *Innocence, Privacy, and Targeting in Fourth Amendment Jurisprudence*, 96 Colum. L. Rev. 1456, 1464 (1996). They are left to wonder, "Why me? Why have the police singled me out . . .? . . . What gave them the gut feeling that I am a criminal?" *Id.* at 1486.

African Americans and Latinos have developed a shared knowledge of the investigatory stop: how to know when one has been stopped in such a way, how to endure the experience, and how to go on with life. This racial difference in police practices and people's lived experience and shared knowledge of these practices is why black people commonly rate stops that they have experienced as unfair, while whites are generally more sanguine about the stops that *they* have experienced. It is a key reason why, compared to whites, African Americans so distrust the police.

Charles R. Epp et al., *Pulled Over: How Police Stops Define Race and Citizenship* 8 (2014). For African Americans especially, traffic stops also induce fear: "Black people in this country are acutely aware of the danger traffic stops pose to Black lives." Jamison v. McClendon, No. 3:16-CV-595-CWR-LRA (S.D. Miss. Aug. 4, 2020). What other harms result from disparate policing? For example, what costs might someone incur to avoid encounters with the police? What about people who are not stopped? Are they harmed by disparate stops?

Although *Whren* might facilitate these harms, it also keeps them out of court. In doing so, Devon Carbado has argued, *Whren* helps "(e)race" the Fourth Amendment. Devon W. Carbado, *(E)racing the Fourth Amendment*, 100 Mich. L. Rev. 946, 1033–1034 (2002).

Police departments sometimes expressly scrutinize men of color as part of drug courier profiles, surveil Arab Americans while looking for terrorism, or target Latinos for immigration enforcement. When police use race or ethnic appearance as one factor among others in deciding to stop or search someone, we call it *racial profiling*. See David A. Harris, *Racial Profiling, in* 2 *Reforming Criminal Justice* 117, 118 (Erik Luna ed., 2017). Even before *Whren*, the Supreme Court concluded that although race alone is not sufficient to justify a stop, officers may use race as a factor in determining whether someone is suspicious, at least in the context of immigration enforcement. See United States v. Brignoni-Ponce, 422 U.S. 873, 886 (1975). Officers therefore use race in assessing whether a suspect is sufficiently suspicious to stop and courts allow them to do so. See, e.g., United States v. Ramos, 629 F.3d 60 (1st Cir. 2010); United States v. Weaver, 966 F.2d 391 (8th Cir. 1992).

A protest sign.

Other racial disparities arise from more subtle uses of race:

> Implicit social cognition research demonstrates that implicit biases can affect whether police interpret an individual's ambiguous behaviors as suspicious. For instance, studies repeatedly reveal that people evaluate ambiguous actions performed by non-Whites as suspicious and criminal while identical actions performed by Whites go unnoticed. . . . [A]n officer will likely be unaware that nonconscious biases affected his or her interpretation of ambiguous behavior. Thus, an officer who acts on his suspicions can easily point to the specific facts that he believes made him feel suspicious without even realizing that implicit biases affected how he interpreted the behavior.

L. Song Richardson, *Police Efficiency and the Fourth Amendment*, 87 Ind. L.J. 1143, 1145 (2012). Similarly, research shows that people focus more on the behavior of young Black men, perhaps because they find them threatening. *Id.* at 1150–1151. Given the scope of criminal and traffic codes, police are likely to find illegal, or at least suspicious, behavior when they watch for it. Again, unconscious processes might lead officers to target people of color without realizing that they are doing so.

Even if a police officer does not have sufficient suspicion to detain or search you, he may ask, "Can you tell me what you're doing here?" or "Do you mind if I look in your bag?" As long as an officer's actions would not convey to a reasonable person that he is not free to leave, Supreme Court doctrine does not consider these activities to be seizures within the meaning of the Fourth Amendment. See, e.g., United States v. Drayton, 536 U.S. 194 (2002) (officers conducting drug interdiction on bus had not seized passengers by asking to search their bags or their persons); United States v. Mendenhall, 446 U.S. 544 (1980) (woman in airport questioned by DEA agents and asked to show her ticket and ID had not been seized within the meaning of the Fourth Amendment). Some argue that this test fails to consider how different people experience the police. Cynthia Lee puts it this way:

> A young black male who has grown up in South Central Los Angeles knows that if he is stopped by a police officer, he should do whatever the officer says and not talk back unless he wants to kiss the ground. This young man may not feel free to leave or terminate the encounter with the officer, but if the reviewing court believes the average (white) person would have felt free to leave, then the encounter will not be considered a seizure and the young black male will not be able to complain that his Fourth Amendment rights have been violated.

Cynthia Lee, *Reasonableness with Teeth: The Future of Fourth Amendment Reasonableness Analysis*, 81 Miss. L.J. 1133, 1152 (2012). What should courts do about this problem? Should courts be permitted to consider the race of the suspect in determining whether a person has been seized?

Although some of the most egregious disparities are racial, and this chapter focuses largely on race, officers might also target people because of their perceived color, ethnicity, religion, national origin, age, sex, gender identity and expression, sexual orientation, immigration status, primary language, disability, housing status, occupation, or socioeconomic status. Would changing *Whren* entail permitting Fourth Amendment challenges to police officers who acted for any of these reasons?

Whren seems to be here to stay. How else could communities use the law to prevent pretextual stops if they wanted to? Section C, *infra*, looks at state laws that forbid the use of race in traffic stops. Some states also limit criminal investigation once a person is stopped, for example, by prohibiting police inquiries not reasonably related to the purposes of the stop, see State v. Arreola-Botello, 451 P. 3d 939 (Or. 2019), or forbidding consent searches without reasonable suspicion, see State v. Carty, 790 A.2d 903 (N.J. 2002). Other suggestions include decriminalizing and civilizing traffic enforcement, just as many communities have done with parking enforcement, see Jordan B. Woods, *Decriminalization, Police Authority, and Routine Traffic Stops*, 62 UCLA L. Rev. 672, 756–760 (2015); randomizing encounters with the police, see Bernard E. Harcourt & Tracey L. Meares, *Randomization and the Fourth Amendment*, 78 U. Chi. L. Rev. 809 (2011); using technological alternatives, such as red-light cameras, for traffic enforcement, see Elizabeth E. Joh, *Discretionless Policing: Technology and the Fourth Amendment*, 95 Calif. L. Rev 199 (2007); and, someday, requiring autonomous vehicles to be programmed to follow traffic laws, see Jordan Blair Woods, *Autonomous Vehicles and Police De-escalation*, 114 Nw. U. L. Rev. Online 74, 86 (2019). Do you like any of these alternatives? Does it matter to you that, without the discretion to use one criminal offense to target another, some crimes might be harder to detect and solve?

Checkpoints

Not all traffic stops are a product of police discretion. Checkpoints stop either all vehicles or vehicles on a regular interval (e.g., every sixth car), often to assess whether drivers are under the influence of alcohol. Studies suggest that sobriety checkpoints reduce crashes. See, e.g., Alena Erke et al., *The Effects of Drink-Driving Checkpoints on Crashes—A Meta-Analysis*, 41 Accident Analysis & Prevention 914 (2009). By minimizing discretion, checkpoints also reduce "targeting harm" and discrimination. Cf. I. Bennett Capers, *Race, Policing, and Technology*, 95 N.C. L. Rev. 1241, 1283 (2017) (arguing that subjecting everyone to the same surveillance "gets us closer to equality before the law"). But they do so by having officers delay and disturb drivers who are not suspected of breaking any law. The Supreme Court thinks this trade-off is constitutionally reasonable and has approved regularized vehicle checkpoints for drunk driving, Mich. Dept. of State Police v. Sitz, 496 U.S. 444, 455 (1990), as well as for detecting undocumented immigrants, United States v. Martinez-Fuerte, 428 U.S. 543 (1976); and in dictum, for checking driver's licenses, Delaware v. Prouse, 440 U.S. 648, 663 (1979), although not for using drug-sniffing dogs to detect narcotics, City of Indianapolis v. Edmond, 531 U.S. 32 (2000). Many scholars disagree with the Court's permissive take on checkpoints, arguing either that stops without individualized suspicion should be more heavily scrutinized under constitutional law, see, e.g., Eve B. Primus, *Disentangling Administrative Searches*, 111 Colum. L. Rev. 254, 261–262 (2011), or that state administrative law should regulate them further, see Christopher Slobogin, *Policing as Administration*, 165 U. Pa. L. Rev. 1, 31 (2016). Moreover, around a quarter of states have not provided statutory authority for sobriety checkpoints, and even where they are allowed, they are relatively uncommon. Why do you imagine that is? Which is more important: ensuring that everyone equally bears the burdens of creating public safety or ensuring that government intrusions are based on individualized suspicion, which presumably makes policing more harm efficient? Why do you think so?

A police sobriety checkpoint on Vegas Valley Drive in Las Vegas, Nevada.

B. The Fourteenth Amendment—Equal Protection and Race

1. Challenging Traffic Stops

In *Whren*, the Court steered those who believe that police officers have targeted them on the basis of their race away from the Fourth Amendment and toward the Equal Protection Clause. How do those challenges tend to fare? This case is an example.

CHAVEZ v. ILLINOIS STATE POLICE
251 F.3d 612 (7th Cir. 2001)

KANNE, CIRCUIT JUDGE.

In this civil rights lawsuit, a putative class action, plaintiffs claim that the drug interdiction unit of the Illinois State Police (ISP), Operation Valkyrie, has a practice of stopping, detaining, and searching African-American and Hispanic motorists based on their race and without legally sufficient cause or justification. The allegation before us, at its core, is that the ISP engages in the practice of racial profiling. Racial profiling is generally understood to mean the improper use of race as a basis for taking law enforcement action. Challenges to the practice of racial profiling have become increasingly prevalent; indeed, this suit is part of a larger effort to challenge the practice nationwide. Defendants-appellees deny that they engage in racial profiling, and claim that they instruct their officers not to use race in determining which motorists to stop, detain, and search.

Plaintiffs filed suit in August 1994 . . . and sought damages as well as declaratory and injunctive relief. They based their claims upon the Equal Protection Clause of the Fourteenth Amendment. . . .

I. History

A. *Operation Valkyrie*

The Illinois State Police run a drug interdiction program entitled "Operation Valkyrie." The program is "designed to acquaint patrol officers with techniques which will enhance their capability to detect and apprehend drug couriers . . . while focusing on the enforcement of highway safety regulations." *Operation Valkyrie: An Officer's Guide to Drug Interdiction Techniques* i. Since its inception in 1990, the ISP has assigned more than one hundred officers to Valkyrie teams that operate in eleven of the ISP's twenty-one districts. . . . Master Sergeant Michael Snyders, the former statewide Operation Valkyrie Coordinator, testified that Valkyrie officers only stop vehicles for traffic enforcement reasons (i.e. for traffic violations or other threats to traffic safety). Once a vehicle is stopped, he explained, Valkyrie officers look for indicators of drug trafficking. These indicators are numerous—indeed there is a list of twenty-eight factors in the Operation Valkyrie training manual—and include such things as too little or too much luggage for the stated length of trip, maps from drug source cities or states, and air freshener. Officers are also trained to look for verbal and non-verbal signs of stress and deception, such as nervousness and an overly friendly demeanor. Snyders testified that when Valkyrie officers observe these indicators, they are trained to request consent to search the vehicle. In 1992, Valkyrie officers requested permission to search in approximately fourteen percent of motorist stops, and when requested, over ninety-eight percent of motorists granted consent.

Plaintiffs allege that race plays into the Valkyrie officers' decision to stop a motorist—what we will term "pre-stop profiling"—and into the decision to detain or search a motorist. . . . As evidence of this, plaintiffs assert that certain ISP drug interdiction training materials emphasize, through statistics, images, and examples, the alleged predominance of Hispanics among those highway travelers carrying illegal drugs. They also point to the testimony of Trooper Robert Cessna, who testified that a motorist's race is one "indicator" that "you've got to keep in mind." . . .

The ISP presented evidence that Valkyrie officers are taught not to use race in determining what motorists to stop, detain, and search. The training manual for Operation Valkyrie states that the "[ISP] has never endorsed, condoned or promoted the use of any profiling system in its interdiction program." See *Operation Valkyrie: An Officer's Guide to Drug Interdiction Techniques* i. Training sessions also included presentment of a videotape which emphasizes that drug couriers look "pretty much like everyone else," that it is difficult to characterize smugglers on the basis of nationality. . . .

B. *The Stops and Searches*

1. *The Stop and Search Involving Peso Chavez*

Peso Chavez's claim evolved out of the stop, search, and arrest of a white motorist, George Koutsakis. In November 1992, an Illinois state trooper, and Valkyrie officer, stopped Koutsakis for exceeding the sixty-five mile per hour speed limit.

Koutsakis was driving a red or burgundy rental car bearing California license plates, and had open maps, a mobile phone, and fast food wrappers in his vehicle. While the trooper was in the process of issuing a warning ticket, a second Valkyrie officer arrived (Trooper Graham) and walked his drug-detecting canine around the vehicle. The dog alerted, indicating the presence of drugs, and the subsequent search of Koutsakis's vehicle uncovered over two hundred pounds of marijuana in the trunk. Koutsakis's criminal defense attorney, Nancy Hollander, suspected that state troopers were stopping motorists based on skin tone or travel patterns. . . . As part of her criminal defense strategy, she thus hired Chavez, a private investigator and New Mexico resident, to recreate the circumstances leading to Koutsakis's stop and arrest.

Chavez, who is Hispanic, emulated the circumstances surrounding Koutsakis's stop and arrest, to see if he would be stopped by the Illinois State Police. He rented a red car with California license plates. On February 18, 1993, he placed open maps, fast food wrappers, a cellular phone, and a gym bag in the car, and proceeded to Interstate 80 ("I–80"). Katherine Austin, a white female from the Public Defenders' Office, followed closely behind him in a separate car. . . . When Chavez's vehicle passed State Trooper Larry Thomas, parked on the east-bound shoulder of I–80 at mile post fifty-three, Trooper Thomas decided to follow it. Thomas followed Chavez's vehicle for approximately twenty-four miles, or almost one-half hour, though he could not explain why he decided to do so. Chavez was not speeding; he traveled no faster than sixty miles per hour, although the speed limit was sixty-five. At one point, Thomas drove alongside Chavez's vehicle and looked him in the face. Thomas learned that the car was a rental car after he had a license plate check run through the dispatcher.

Thomas stopped Chavez at about mile post seventy-seven, allegedly because Chavez failed to signal a lane change. Chavez testified that he did signal and denied committing any traffic violation. Austin, who had been following Chavez, agreed. Defendants conceded for the purposes of summary judgment that Chavez did not violate any traffic laws. Thomas approached the car and noticed several items inside, including Chavez's small suitcase, several fast food bags, and an atlas. He also saw Chavez's hands shaking and thought Chavez was nervous. Thomas requested Chavez's driver's license and registration, and returned to his squad car.

Thomas was subsequently joined by Sergeant Dan Gillette, who had been monitoring traffic at mile post seventy-seven. Gillette claims that Thomas told him there was something funny about Chavez, that he smelled air freshener in the car and that he did not see any luggage. . . . To Gillette, Chavez appeared nervous and deceptive regarding his destination. Gillette also testified that he saw a road atlas and fast food wrappers in the car, and thought the car was too clean to have come from Albuquerque. Gillette returned to Thomas's vehicle and Thomas informed him that Chavez's license and registration were valid and that Chavez had no criminal history. Gillette told Thomas that he was still suspicious due to the numerous indicators of drug trafficking.

Thomas issued Chavez a warning ticket based on the alleged failure to signal, and returned Chavez's license and registration once he signed the citation. Thomas then asked Chavez for permission to search his car. Chavez did not consent to the search and stated that he wanted to leave. Based on the indicators, Gillette felt there was sufficient reason to detain Chavez for a canine walk around, and thus the officers detained Chavez to await the arrival of a canine unit.

When Trooper Graham arrived with his police dog, Krott, Thomas asked Chavez if he would consent to a canine walk-around. Gillette testified that Chavez did not consent, though Thomas's report said he did. The dog did not alert on the first walk-around. . . .

The troopers conducted a second walk-around. Graham testified that this time the canine alerted. . . . Gillette asked Chavez to go sit in Officer Thomas's vehicle. Gillette, Graham, and Trooper Robert Cessna . . . then proceeded to search Chavez's car. . . . [T]he officers did not find any contraband. Finally, thirty-five to fifty-five minutes after he was stopped, Thomas told Chavez he was free to go. Thomas completed a field report regarding the search of Chavez's vehicle and listed Chavez's race as "white," despite the fact that the report contained a listing for Hispanic. . . .

2. The Stops and Searches Involving Gregory Lee

Gregory Lee, who is African-American, testified that he was unjustifiably stopped, searched, and detained three times in 1993. In late summer or early fall of 1993, Lee was driving west on I–80 with his wife, who is also African-American, when an ISP officer stopped them. Lee says that he had not violated any traffic law. The officer requested consent to search the vehicle, and Lee gave his consent. The officer instructed Lee and his wife to step out of the car. He patted down Lee and indicated that he would pat down Mrs. Lee but then turned and searched the trunk instead. The officer found no contraband, and no ticket or warning was issued.

In March 1993, Lee was driving on I–80 near Orland Park, Illinois, with his friend, Mike, who is also African-American. ISP Trooper Robert Lauterbach stopped Lee and told him he was speeding, which Lee alleges is false. Trooper Lauterbach asked for Lee's license and then asked him to step out of the car. Once Lee stepped out, the officer brought him back to the rear of the car and at the same time asked Mike to step out of the car. Lee asked the trooper what the problem was and the trooper said something about them looking suspicious. The officer patted them down; at some point, an unidentified second officer arrived. Lauterbach ordered Lee and his friend to kneel on the roadside, behind Lee's vehicle, with their hands on their heads. While they were kneeling, Lauterbach searched the car without Lee's consent — he searched the front and back seat and the glove box — but found no contraband. The officer then returned Lee's license and keys and allowed Lee and his friend to go. No warning or ticket was issued.

In August 1993, Lee was driving on I–80, at the intersection of I–57, when he was stopped by ISP Trooper Dale Fraher. Lee got out of the car and asked the officer if there was a problem. Fraher claimed that Lee's car wheel was wobbling and that there was a problem with the license plate registration sticker, though plaintiff denies that there was anything wrong with either. After asking for and receiving Lee's drivers' license, Fraher asked if he could search Lee's car, twice stating that one can never tell with "you people." Lee consented; Fraher searched the car but found no contraband. Fraher then returned Lee's license and allowed Lee to go without issuing a ticket or warning. . . .

II.   Analysis . . .

D.   The Fourteenth Amendment Equal Protection Claims . . .

Plaintiffs assert that the ISP and individual ISP officers utilize impermissible racial classifications in determining whom to stop, detain, and search. Were this proven, it would amount to a violation of the Equal Protection Clause of the Fourteenth Amendment. See Whren v. United States, 517 U.S. 806, 813 (1996). . . .

. . . To show a violation of the Equal Protection Clause, plaintiffs must prove that the defendants' actions had a discriminatory effect and were motivated by a discriminatory purpose. See Pers. Adm'r of Mass. v. Feeney, 442 U.S. 256, 272–274 (1979); Arlington Heights v. Metro. Housing Dev. Corp., 429 U.S. 252, 264–266 (1977); Washington v. Davis, 426 U.S. 229, 239–242 (1976). We examine each element in turn.

1. Discriminatory Effect

To prove discriminatory effect, the plaintiffs are required to show that they are members of a protected class, that they are otherwise similarly situated to members of the unprotected class, and that plaintiffs were treated differently from members of the unprotected class. Chavez and Lee may show that the ISP treated them differently than other similarly situated individuals by naming such individuals or through the use of statistics, an issue which we explore in greater depth below.

a. Naming a Similarly Situated Individual

Lee did not attempt to name a similarly situated individual who was not stopped or searched. Chavez alleges that Katherine Austin—the white female from the public defender's office who was following him at the time of his stop—was a similarly situated individual treated differently. To determine whether Austin was similarly situated to Chavez we "must look at all relevant factors, the number of which depends on the context of the case." Radue v. Kimberly-Clark Corp., 219 F.3d 612, 617 (7th Cir. 2000). . . .

Defendants allege that George Koutsakis—the individual stopped by the ISP whom Chavez was emulating—was a similarly situated individual who was treated the same as Chavez. The district court agreed, and determined that Chavez failed to show that he was treated any differently than a similarly situated white motorist. The district court found that Austin was not similarly situated because she was female, drove a different color car with a non-California plate, did not have the same items visible in her car, and did not receive a warning ticket. . . .

We do not agree with the district court's treatment of this issue. The relevant inquiry is whether a similarly situated individual was treated differently than the plaintiff, not whether one white motorist was subjected to the same unlawful treatment. Allowing defendants to escape liability for discriminating against Hispanics simply because they occasionally mistreat white motorists would dismantle our equal protection jurisprudence. The fact that Koutsakis was also stopped is simply irrelevant to the inquiry of whether Chavez has shown that a similarly situated individual was treated differently.

Quite to the contrary of defendants' and the district court's assertions, Chavez and Austin were similarly situated in all pertinent respects. Both were driving down the same stretch of I–80 at the same time, and neither committed a traffic violation (defendants have conceded that Chavez did not commit a violation for the purpose of summary judgment). The factors that distinguish Austin from Chavez do not prevent her from being similarly situated. First, the ISP cannot legally decide whom to stop on the basis of gender any more than they can do so on the basis of race, thus the fact that Austin is female is not pertinent. Second, nothing in the record indicates that Trooper Thomas stopped Chavez because he was driving a red car, or because he was driving a rental car, or because it was a car with California plates.

To the contrary, the ISP asserts that Valkyrie officers do not stop motorists on the basis of these variables, and plaintiffs have agreed. Third, the objects inside Chavez's vehicle that raised officer suspicion—i.e. the small suitcase, fast food bags, and atlas—were not visible until after Chavez was pulled over, thus they could not have been the basis for the stop. Finally, the fact that Thomas was engaged with Chavez does not prevent Austin from being similarly situated. The whole point of the plaintiffs' claim is that after thirty minutes of trailing the two vehicles, Thomas stopped Chavez, who is Hispanic, rather than Austin, who is white.

We thus find that Austin is a similarly situated individual of an unprotected class who was treated differently than Chavez. That Lee has not been able to name a similarly situated individual treated differently does not, however, end our review of his claims. Plaintiffs attempt to show that similarly situated individuals were treated differently than both Chavez and Lee through the use of statistics. . . .

b. Use of Statistics to Show Discriminatory Effect

The Supreme Court has long noted the importance of statistical analysis "in cases in which the existence of discrimination is a disputed issue." *Int'l Bhd. of Teamsters v. United States*, 431 U.S. 324, 339 (1977). While few opinions directly acknowledge that statistics may be used to prove discriminatory effect, the Court has repeatedly relied on statistics to do just that. See, e.g., *Yick Wo v. Hopkins*, 118 U.S. 356, 374 (1886); *Hunter v. Underwood*, 471 U.S. 222, 227 (1985). . . . The statistics proffered must address the crucial question of whether one class is being treated differently from another class that is otherwise similarly situated. . . .

The Supreme Court's decision in *United States v. Armstrong*, 517 U.S. 456, did not depart from this precedent. *Armstrong* settled a dispute among the circuits by holding that criminal defendants bringing selective prosecution claims must show that similarly situated individuals were not prosecuted, in order to obtain discovery in support of their claim. . . . The district court in this case correctly determined that the Supreme Court rejected the statistics proffered by the plaintiffs in *Armstrong*. The statistics were rejected, however, not because plaintiffs can never use statistics to prove discriminatory effect, but because the particular statistics presented to the Court did not address the relevant issue. The criminal defendants in *Armstrong* introduced an affidavit claiming that "in every one" of the twenty-four cases handled by the public defender's office in 1991 for violations of 21 U.S.C. §§841 and 846, the defendant was African-American. See *Armstrong*, 517 U.S. at 459. The Court explained: "The study failed to identify individuals who were not black and could have been prosecuted for the offenses for which respondents were charged, but were not so prosecuted." *Id.* at 470. . . . In light of *Armstrong*, statistics demonstrating that whites stopped for traffic violations were not detained and searched, even those who displayed indicators of drug trafficking, while similarly situated African-American or Hispanic drivers were detained and searched, would be sufficient to show discriminatory effect. . . .

Even if *Armstrong* is read to require a criminal defendant in a selective prosecution case to provide the precise name of a similarly situated defendant who was not prosecuted (a possible but unnecessary reading), the rationale behind such a requirement does not apply with equal force in the context of a civil racial profiling claim. . . .

First, the *Armstrong* court noted that "[t]he similarly situated requirement does not make a selective-prosecution claim impossible to prove." *Armstrong*, 517 U.S. at

466. In a civil racial profiling case, however, the similarly situated requirement might be impossible to prove. In a meritorious selective prosecution claim, a criminal defendant would be able to name others arrested for the same offense who were not prosecuted by the arresting law enforcement agency; conversely, plaintiffs who allege that they were stopped due to racial profiling would not, barring some type of test operation, be able to provide the names of other similarly situated motorists who were not stopped.

A second distinction between this case and *Armstrong* is the factual context. The opinion in *Armstrong* allotted much of its analysis to discussing the nature of selective prosecution claims and the considerations inherent in such claims. The analysis is narrowly focused on the constitutional implications of interfering with the prosecutorial function, a factor at the heart of a criminal defendant's claim of selective prosecution, but not directly at issue in a plaintiff's civil claim of racial profiling. . . .

. . . This case is thus not like *Armstrong*. Therefore, plaintiffs do not have to provide the court with the name of an individual who was not stopped; instead they may attempt to use statistics to show that the ISP treated them differently than other motorists who were similarly situated. While it is true that statistics alone rarely state a violation of equal protection — indeed, only in the Title VII or jury venire context is this possible, as discussed *infra* — they can be sufficient to establish discriminatory effect.

c. The Plaintiffs' Statistics

Given our foregoing conclusions, we must now examine the statistics proffered by the plaintiffs. The pertinent inquiry is whether Operation Valkyrie troopers stop, detain, and search African-American and Hispanic motorists when the troopers do not stop, detain, and search similarly situated white motorists. . . .

The ISP does not keep a comprehensive record of all motorists stopped; there is no database that tracks every stop, the race of the parties involved, and whether a search took place. This is ultimately the type of information that would be useful in a suit such as this, as it would clearly indicate what percentages of African-American and Hispanic motorists were being stopped and searched on Illinois highways. . . .

The Valkyrie field reports are the source for the bulk of the plaintiffs' statistics, and were the basis of the equal protection claims they presented to the district court. Plaintiffs assert that the number of Valkyrie field reports issued to Hispanic and African-American motorists is more than two standard deviations over the expected norm, based upon the representation of each of these groups in the population. Such a finding, if based upon appropriate statistical analysis, would be statistically significant.

We are reluctant, however, to derive any conclusions about the racial breakdown of those motorists stopped, detained, and searched by Valkyrie officers based upon the Valkyrie field reports. First of all, plaintiffs have not told us how many Valkyrie field reports there are, or how many were analyzed. One record document indicates that there were 306 field reports completed by Valkyrie officers in 1992; plaintiffs then conducted a "random sample" of this data. There is no indication of the total number of stops this is being compared to, thus it is impossible to tell if this sample size is sufficiently large to be reliable. Further, the field reports (and particularly the Valkyrie field reports) are completed on a selective basis after limited types of enforcement activity. This type of non-random sample might undermine the reliability of the statistics.

While the citations and warnings database—which includes all citations and warnings issued by ISP officers—could potentially provide a more accurate estimation of the numbers of motorists stopped, detained, and searched, this database does not record the race of the motorist. The numbers of Hispanics represented can be estimated through an analysis of Hispanic surnames, but there is no mechanism for calculating the numbers of whites or African-Americans issued citations or warnings. Without comparative racial information, plaintiffs cannot prove that they were stopped, detained, or searched, when similarly situated whites were not.

The limitations of the field reports and citations and warnings databases only scratch the surface of potential problems with the proffered statistics. The crux of the matter lies in the population benchmarks. . . . [T]he plaintiffs compared the numbers derived from the Valkyrie field reports with the representation of whites, African-Americans, and Hispanics ostensibly in the Illinois population and on Illinois roads. We find that these population benchmarks cannot provide an adequate backdrop for assessing the racial composition of drivers faced by Valkyrie officers, and thus cannot indicate whether Valkyrie officers disproportionately stop, detain, and search Hispanics and African-Americans.

The first benchmark used by the plaintiffs was the 1990 Census. It is widely acknowledged that the Census fails to count everyone, and that the undercount is greatest in certain subgroups of the population, particularly Hispanics and African-Americans. We further note that the preliminary data from the 2000 Census indicates that the number of Hispanics and Latinos living in the United States has increased by 57.9% over the past ten years. . . . This recent data is simply another indication that the 1990 Census may not have accurately represented the Hispanic and African-American populations in Illinois for the relevant period.

. . . Even if it were entirely accurate, however, Census data can tell us very little about the numbers of Hispanics and African-Americans driving on Illinois interstate highways, which is crucial to determining the population of motorists encountered by the Valkyrie officers. . . .

Perhaps to address this problem, the plaintiffs also relied upon the 1990 Nationwide Personal Transportation Survey (NPTS). This is a nationwide telephone survey conducted every five years by the Federal Highway Administration of the U.S. Department of Transportation, aimed at providing a "picture of passenger travel in the United States." . . . Clearly, the NPTS was not intended to provide and cannot accurately provide racial breakdowns for the population of motorists on Illinois roads. . . .

. . . These population baselines are simply insufficient to determine the racial makeup of motorists on Illinois highways. Thus, without reliable data on whom Valkyrie officers stop, detain, and search, and without reliable data indicating the population on the highways where motorists are stopped, detained, and searched, we cannot find that the statistics prove that the Valkyrie officers' actions had a discriminatory effect on the plaintiffs.

2. Discriminatory Intent

We have found that Chavez has proven that defendants' actions had a discriminatory effect on him but that Lee, who relied solely on the plaintiffs' statistics, has not. Even if we had determined that Lee proved effect, however, both plaintiffs must still prove discriminatory intent in order to establish a violation of the Equal Protection

Clause. See Washington v. Davis, 426 U.S. 229, 242 (1976). . . . "'Discriminatory purpose' . . . implies more than . . . intent as awareness of consequences. It implies that the decisionmaker . . . selected or reaffirmed a particular course of action at least in part 'because of' . . . its adverse effects upon an identifiable group.'" McClesky v. Kemp, 481 U.S. 279, 298 (1987).

Plaintiffs offer little evidence specific to their case that would support an inference that racial considerations played a part in their stops, detentions, and searches. Instead they argue that their statistics compel an inference of purposeful discrimination. We will consider the nonstatistical evidence first, construed in the light most favorable to the plaintiffs.

. . . During the stop and search of Gregory Lee, it is asserted that Trooper Fraher justified the stop by saying that one can never tell with "you people." Trooper Cessna, a participant in the search involving Peso Chavez, said in his deposition that he was trained that a motorist's race is one "indicator" that "you've got to keep in mind." . . . Selected ISP drug interdiction training materials emphasize the alleged predominance of Hispanics among those highway travelers carrying illegal drugs; [t]hrough affidavit testimony one trooper said that ISP officers are not prohibited from considering race as a factor, and another stated that race can be a permissible factor to consider in deciding what motorists to stop (for example, in the context of an all-points bulletin or in deciding to conduct a *Terry* stop); and [f]rom 1990 to 1994 Snyders reviewed monthly statistics showing that African-American and Hispanic motorists comprised more than sixty percent of motorists searched by Valkyrie officers in District Six.

. . . Other evidence weighs against drawing a conclusion of discriminatory intent. As part of his investigation in the Koutsakis case, Chavez submitted a written memo to Nancy Hollander detailing the February 18, 1993 stop and search; he stated that none of the troopers said anything which "appeared to be racially motivated." Further, Trooper Thomas listed Chavez's race as "white" on the field report regarding Chavez's stop and search, even though there was a listing for "Hispanic." There is nothing in the record to indicate that Thomas thought Chavez was Hispanic and simply decided to list his race as white in an attempt to disguise his motivations.

Lee offers specific evidence of racial animus during his stop: the statements made by Trooper Fraher that one can never tell with "you people." While we certainly do not approve of racially insensitive remarks, such comments do not by themselves violate the Constitution. . . . Lee has not proffered any evidence of racial animus on the part of the other officers who allegedly stopped and searched him. . . .

. . . [P]laintiffs have not shown that the ISP required or encouraged Valkyrie officers to racially profile. There is actually evidence to the contrary. The first page of the *Operation Valkyrie Officer's Guide to Drug Interdiction Techniques* states:

> The success of the Valkyrie program is directly linked to its eschewment from the use of any form of violator profiles. The Illinois State Police has never endorsed, condoned or promoted the use of any profiling system in its interdiction program. Criminal elements exist in virtually every racial, national, tribal, religious, linguistic and cultural group. An officer whose enforcement stops are based on ethnicity is guilty of civil rights violations and is subject to prosecution in the federal courts. Criminality transcends any perceived racial, ethnic or socio-economic parameters; to focus on a single segment of society is to limit your enforcement opportunities.

Operation Valkyrie: An Officer's Guide to Drug Interdiction Techniques at i. Even a stringent review of the tapes of Officer Snyders' training sessions shows that, during the sessions, Snyders discourages the use of race as an indicator as "counterproductive." . . .

Just because the official policy is to decry racial profiling, however, does not automatically mean that defendants are free from reproach. . . . In this case, though, we do not think that the one ISP document referencing the high number of Hispanics involved in the drug trade visibly undermined the message that racial profiling was illegal and to be avoided.

Plaintiffs' non-statistical evidence does not prove that the defendants intended to discriminate against Chavez when they stopped and searched him. Nor is there sufficient evidence to conclude that the three different troopers who stopped Lee did so with intent to discriminate. We thus turn to plaintiffs' statistical evidence.

Only in "rare cases [has] a statistical pattern of discriminatory impact demonstrated a constitutional violation," *McCleskey*, 481 U.S. at 293 n.12, though "the Court has accepted statistics as proof of intent to discriminate in certain limited contexts." *Id.* at 293. . . . None of these situations, however, are before us. Instead, plaintiffs ask us to rely on their statistics, which allegedly show discriminatory effect, to conclude that the ISP and the individual officer-defendants are intentionally discriminating against the plaintiffs. In this context, statistics may not be the sole proof of a constitutional violation and neither Chavez nor Lee have presented sufficient non-statistical evidence to demonstrate discriminatory intent.

The plaintiffs have thus not met their burden of showing that the ISP or its individual officers purposefully discriminated against them. Because plaintiffs have not proven the prima facie elements of an equal protection claim under the Fourteenth Amendment, we will affirm the district court's grant of summary judgment in favor of the defendants. . . .

III. Conclusion

Notwithstanding the disposition of this case, we recognize the destructive effects of racial and ethnic profiling by any police agency. Plaintiffs have not proven that the Operation Valkyrie officers of the Illinois State Police stop, detain, and search African-American and Hispanic motorists on the basis of racial or ethnic profiling. Yet, unfortunately, the oft-cited public perception that race and ethnicity play a role in law enforcement decisions on Illinois highways will no doubt remain. The ISP has asserted throughout this litigation that they do not condone race-based law enforcement action; much of the evidence in this case indicates that they endeavor to conduct police activity through means that respect constitutional rights. How to change public perception and demonstrate compliance with constitutional requirements is a matter the State of Illinois may wish to consider. . . .

NOTES AND QUESTIONS

1. *The Constitution.* The Fourteenth Amendment's Equal Protection Clause provides: "No state shall . . . deny to any person within its jurisdiction the equal protection of the laws." U.S. Const. amend. XIV, §1. Plaintiffs tend to argue that police conduct violates the Equal Protection Clause in one of three ways: (1) the police acted pursuant to law or policy that contains an *express racial classification*; (2) the police applied a *facially neutral* law or policy in an *intentionally discriminatory manner*; or

(3) the police engaged in *selective enforcement,* targeting individuals for policing with discriminatory intent and disparate effect on a protected class. The last two categories are closely related, and both require proof of discriminatory effect and discriminatory intent.

2. *Discriminatory effect.* In *United States v. Armstrong,* 517 U.S. 456, 465 (1996), the U.S. Supreme Court required criminal defendants alleging that they had been selectively prosecuted to demonstrate "that similarly situated individuals of a different race were not prosecuted," a rule that some courts of appeals have also applied to selective enforcement claims about policing. How does the *Chavez* Court handle this issue? How are selective prosecution and enforcement similar or different? Do you agree with the Court that plaintiffs will have more trouble finding similarly situated people in the policing context? Should that matter to whether the rule applies?

3. *Discriminatory intent.* As *Chavez* indicates, plaintiffs also must show discriminatory purpose. Officers do not need to have a negative attitude toward the targeted racial group. But they must have "selected or reaffirmed a particular course of action at least in part 'because of,' not merely 'in spite of,' its adverse effects upon an identifiable group." Pers. Adm'r of Mass. v. Feeney, 442 U.S. 256, 279 (1979). What does it mean to act *because of* harm to an identifiable group? Why might an officer act toward a group because of their race without having a negative attitude? What if the officer had an unfounded belief about members of that group? Where might that belief come from?

4. *Establishing discrimination by statistics.* Plaintiffs who allege racial discrimination through selective enforcement usually have limited *direct evidence* that the police acted *because of* race so they use statistical evidence of racial disparities to try to establish both disparate treatment and discriminatory intent. But racial disparities in policing can have complicated causes. Plaintiffs (and their experts) commonly use two kinds of statistical analysis, discussed in the following two notes, to sort those causes out. Both have their problems.

5. *Benchmark studies.* The first statistical method for proving discrimination compares how likely Black people (or another population) are to be stopped (or searched or arrested) to the likelihood that members of other groups are treated the same way.

> Benchmark studies effectively compare interracial differences in the likelihood of being stopped, employing data on the underlying racial composition of the population at risk of being stopped in conjunction with police stop data to estimate these conditional probabilities. Of course, much debate surrounds what constitutes the appropriate population benchmark. Broad benchmarks are subject to the criticism that the researcher is not properly identifying the population at risk, and overly narrow benchmarks are subject to the criticism that the definition of who is at risk may itself be a function of racial animus.

> For example, suppose the outcome of interest was arrest-related deaths. One might argue that those at risk were those who were arrested by the police, making the race of the arrested population the relevant benchmark. However, differential arrest rates across races may reflect geographic differences in enforcement or racial bias in arrest decisions of law enforcement. To the extent that different enforcement practices contribute to racial disparities in arrest rates, using the racial composition of arrests to benchmark deaths in custody would understate the racial disparities in the risk of dying while being arrested, independent of any racial disparity in offending.

If one were interested in inequality more broadly, inclusive of how differences in poverty, educational resources, geographic segregation and isolation, and the nation's social history contribute to disparities in adverse outcomes, one might prefer the broader benchmark based on representation of the general population. However, this broader benchmark would be inappropriate for isolating the degree to which racial disproportionality in the outcomes of interest is due to disparate treatment by the police, as the societal and environmental factors included in the broader, general population benchmark will contribute to racial disparities in offending that are independent of policing practice.

Nat'l Acads. of Scis., Eng'g & Med., *Proactive Policing: Effects on Crime and Communities* 256–257 (2018).

6. *Outcome measures.* The second statistical method to prove discrimination is to look at the outcomes of police–citizen interactions.

Researchers performing outcome-based tests reason that, to the extent that the productivity of stopping, and perhaps searching, an identified demographic group differs from the productivity associated with other groups, the police would enhance public safety by either diverting resources away from the group in question (if the productivity rate for the group is below the average for all stops) or policing this group more intensively (if the productivity rate is above the average). . . .

. . . If the hit rate for stops made of Black people is lower than that for stops made of White people, then the common interpretation is that Black people are being held to a less stringent or lower evidentiary standard by police officers when making decisions whether to stop and search an individual. However, it is easy to generate a simple hypothetical example where suspects differ in their observable signals of culpability, where there are differences across race in the proportions that display these signals, where officers hold one group to a differential evidentiary standard, yet where the hit rates are equal across groups.

Further, if the average propensity to offend is higher among one racial group and the distributions of the offending propensity vary across racial groups, one cannot predict a priori what hit rates would be in the presence of racial animus. For example, if Black people are more likely to offend than White people, animus-driven, racially biased treatment by the police may generate higher hit rates for Blacks, equal hit rates across racial groups, or lower hit rates for searches of Black people.

Id. at 257–260.

7. *Sorting out the causes of disparities.* As these descriptions suggest, proving that disparities in policing result from discrimination can be difficult in part because racial disparities in policing arise from other causes, including from prior *nonpolice* discrimination. For example, if childhood lead exposure and high unemployment lead to higher offending rates, as many social scientists argue, then historical discrimination that causes those social conditions will produce racial disparities even with neutral policing. Similarly, if violence is higher where African Americans live because of economic and housing discrimination, police departments concentrate resources in high-violent–crime areas, and exposure to the police leads to increased enforcement risk, then disparities in policing are likely even if the police do not discriminate. Even prior discrimination *by the police* can complicate the picture. If African Americans fear the police because the police have targeted them for harassment and abuse, they may act nervously or defiantly in their encounters with the police. That behavior in turn becomes a seemingly neutral basis for stopping,

searching, and sometimes arresting them. Although experts try to separate background effects from discriminatory policing using statistical evidence, courts seldom accept it as proof of discriminatory intent. Ironically, other discrimination makes it more difficult for a court to find an equal protection violation. See McClesky v. Kemp, 481 U.S. 279 (1987); see also Aziz Z. Huq, *The Consequences of Disparate Policing: Evaluating Stop and Frisk as a Modality of Urban Policing*, 101 Minn. L. Rev. 2397, 2452–2456 (2017).

8. *Proving intent by multiple means.* If plaintiffs have direct evidence of intent, they often present it alongside statistical evidence, as in *Chavez*. In *Floyd v. City of New York*, 959 F. Supp. 2d 540 (S.D.N.Y. 2013), also discussed in Chapters 5 and 15, the district court found that the NYPD's stop, question, and frisk (SQF) program violated the Equal Protection Clause based not only on statistical evidence, but also because testimony indicated that NYPD officials had promoted an unwritten policy of targeting "the right people," and because the department was warned of the racial disparities and ignored them. *Id.* at 560–562. The Department of Justice similarly accused the Baltimore Police Department (BPD) of discriminating in carrying out its aggressive zero-tolerance policy because of "overwhelming statistical evidence of racial disparities in BDP's stops, searches, and arrests"; statements by officers and supervisors indicating animus, such as a supervisor's instruction to arrest "all the Black hoodies" in a neighborhood; and the department's indifference in the face of evidence of discrimination. See U.S. Dept. of Justice, Civil Rights Div., *Investigation of the Baltimore City Police Department* 48, 66 (2016).

9. *Evaluating intent.* Even our ability to evaluate racist intent is complicated by historical and social context.

> For instance, *symbolic racism*, as defined in David O. Sears, *Symbolic Racism*, in *Eliminating Racism: Profiles in Controversy* 53, 56 (Phyllis A. Katz & Dalmas A. Taylor eds. 1988), involves the belief that prejudice against Black people is no longer a problem in U.S. society today, that the overrepresentation of Black Americans in low-income, low-educated, and high-crime groups is primarily due to their own personal shortcomings, and that Black people in general demand too much from society at large and have also "gotten more than they deserve." A core part of symbolic racism, as described by Sears, is therefore the belief that if a Black person received less favorable treatment, it was likely because they objectively deserved less favorable treatment. Holding such a view would presumably influence whether one believed that indirect evidence established the discriminatory purpose necessary to prove an Equal Protection violation.

Nat'l Acads. of Scis., Eng'g & Med., *Proactive Policing: Effects on Crime and Communities* 97 (2018). What should we do about the possibility that judges and juries have such views?

10. *Should intent be required?* Plaintiffs only rarely win equal protection challenges against police departments for racial profiling during traffic stops in part because of the intent requirement. Although the intent requirement arises from ordinary Equal Protection Clause jurisprudence, combined with *Whren*, it places large disparities in policing beyond constitutional reach. Might the intent requirement distort how we understand racial disparities in policing?

> The search for discriminatory intent is a distraction. Few people, and virtually none in positions of authority, frankly acknowledge racist intent. . . . [I]t matters little if

we somehow know whether the officer merely recognized that Joe was black or *actually* thought, "I'm going to check out that black guy *because* he's black." The distinction is exceedingly fine and virtually unknowable, yet constitutional law gives any police stop a free pass unless it can be shown that the officer *did* think such a thing.

. . . Instead, attention should focus on institutionalized practice: how the structure of incentives, training, and policy in contemporary policing makes it more likely that officers will act on the basis of bigotry or implicit stereotypes, leading to racial disparities in outcomes.

Charles R. Epp et al., *Pulled Over: How Police Stops Define Race and Citizenship* 7 (2014). What would it mean to give attention to "institutionalized practice"? Is that something constitutional law, or other law, can do?

2.   Obtaining Evidence of Discrimination

The *Chavez* plaintiffs seem to have lost largely because they lacked adequate statistical evidence of discrimination. Why did they lack that evidence? Assuming the department had discriminated against them, what would have to change to enable them to prove it?

Sometimes plaintiffs cannot get evidence that would support their claims because it does not exist. Almost all evidence about police conduct is produced by officers and agencies. Although state statutes and court settlements require some police departments to collect information about low-level activities such as stops, many departments are not required to and do not keep track of the perceived race of suspects.

Even if the evidence exists, plaintiffs might not be entitled to it. As the *Chavez* court notes, in *United States v. Armstrong*, 517 U.S. 456 (1996), the Supreme Court held that plaintiffs must meet a rigorous standard of proof in selective-prosecution claims before they are entitled to discovery. Specifically, they must make "a credible showing of different treatment of similarly situated persons." *Id.* at 470. Some courts import the *Armstrong* standard into the selective-enforcement context. See, e.g., United States v. Hare, 820 F.3d 93, 97–101 (4th Cir. 2016) (using *Armstrong*'s standard as a "starting point"); United States v. Alcaraz-Arellano, 441 F.3d 1252 (10th Cir. 2006) (applying *Armstrong*); United States v. Dixon, 486 F. Supp. 2d 40, 45 (D.D.C. 2007) (applying *Armstrong* and collecting cases). But see United States v. Sellers, 906 F.3d 848, 854–856 (9th Cir. 2018) (rejecting *Armstrong* and applying less rigorous discovery standard to selective-enforcement claims); United States v. Washington, 869 F.3d 193, 219–221 (3d. Cir. 2017) (same); United States v. Davis, 793 F.3d 712, 719–721 (7th Cir. 2015) (same). How high a hurdle is this likely to be in policing cases? Can you imagine ways to overcome it?

Let's say a police chief wants to know whether racial disparities exist in his department so that he can mitigate them if they do. He institutes a rule requiring officers to record information on stops. Should plaintiffs be entitled to that evidence to prove an Equal Protection Clause violation? If so, what department would collect that information voluntarily? What city attorney would allow them to do so? Which is more important: not discouraging police departments from finding and solving racial disparities or giving plaintiffs who might have been wronged evidence to help them prove it?

Although the *Chavez* litigation was unsuccessful, it helped spur a state law that mandates that officers collect data on traffic stops, including the reason for the stop and the race of the person stopped. See 625 Ill. Comp. Stat. 5/11-212 (2018); see also Rachel A. Harmon & Andrew Manns, *Proactive Policing and the Legacy of* Terry, 15 Ohio St. J. Crim. L. 49, 66–69 (2017) (discussing the relationship between litigation and legislation).

3. Equal Protection Remedies

Even assuming a plaintiff wins, remedies can be a problem in equal protection cases. The *Chavez* plaintiffs brought suit for both injunctive relief and damages. Plaintiffs often seek *damages* for equal protection violations for their mental and emotional distress, humiliation, embarrassment, anxiety, and pain arising from discriminatory treatment. See, e.g., Fifth Amended Class Action Complaint for Declaratory Relief, Injunctive Relief and Damages, Rodriguez v. California Highway Patrol, 89 F. Supp. 2d 1131 (N.D. Cal. 2000) (No. C-99-20895-JF/EAI). But as Pamela Karlan points out, "innocent victims" of police misconduct are unlikely to bring suit, and "guilty victims" will be unsympathetic to juries, so damages may not be high. See Pamela S. Karlan, *Race, Rights, and Remedies in Criminal Adjudication*, 96 Mich. L. Rev. 2001, 2011 (1998).

Plaintiffs also seek *declaratory* and *injunctive* relief, but few can get by the barrier erected in *City of Los Angeles v. Lyons*, 461 U.S. 95 (1983), discussed in detail in Chapter 15.[1] In addition, courts on rare occasion permit motions to *dismiss criminal charges* based on selective enforcement. However, the Supreme Court has never clarified whether this is an appropriate remedy for selective prosecution or enforcement actions, and such motions are effectively never granted. See United States v. Armstrong, 517 U.S. 456, 461 n.2 (1996). Might plaintiffs win and still lose? And if they do, might that leave these constitutional violations undeterred?

There is another option. When the *Whren* Court ruled that racial discrimination by the police does not violate the Fourth Amendment, it also made the Fourth Amendment exclusionary rule inapplicable to that discrimination, even when it produces criminal evidence. Some scholars argue that the Court should develop a new equal protection exclusionary rule. See, e.g., Brooks Holland, *Safeguarding Equal Protection Rights: The Search for an Exclusionary Rule Under the Equal Protection Clause*, 37 Am. Crim. L. Rev. 1107 (2000); Pamela S. Karlan, *Race, Rights, and Remedies in Criminal Adjudication*, 96 Mich. L. Rev. 2001, 2004 (1998).

That might sound unrealistic, but Massachusetts has done it as a matter of state constitutional law. The Supreme Court held that "if a defendant can establish that a traffic stop is the product of selective enforcement predicated on race, evidence seized in the course of the stop should be suppressed unless the connection between the unconstitutional stop by the police and the discovery of the challenged evidence has 'become so attenuated as to dissipate the taint.'" See Commonwealth v. Lora, 886 N.E.2d 688, 699–700 (Mass. 2008). Still, most states

---

[1] The U.S. Department of Justice also may seek injunctive relief for Equal Protection Clause violations and violations of Title VI under 42 U.S.C. §12601 without facing the standing obstacles of *Lyons*. Its use of this authority is also discussed in Chapter 15.

do not take this approach, and given the U.S. Supreme Court's recent hostility to evidentiary exclusion, it is hard to imagine a similar federal move. Even if it happened, how much would this matter? Equal protection doctrine makes proving discrimination difficult and expensive, because of the need for statistical evidence and analysis. Is the possibility of evidentiary exclusion likely to remedy or deter equal protection violations?

Despite the obstacles to proving police discrimination, private plaintiffs and the U.S. Department of Justice have brought suits that include equal protection claims against many major departments, including those of Baltimore, Chicago, Milwaukee, New York, and Philadelphia. Few of these discrimination claims have been tested thoroughly in court, and those that have often have not fared well. See, e.g., United States v. Johnson, 122 F. Supp. 3d 272, 351–352 (M.D.N.C. 2015). And yet, many suits settle for injunctive relief. Why might departments settle these lawsuits? What effect might this pattern have on the development of the law? If you were advising a nonprofit that wanted to make discrimination less likely in the future, what would you encourage it to ask for in these settlements?

Equal Protection *by* the Police

As in *Chavez*, most equal protection claims about policing argue that the government owed the plaintiffs equal protection from being selectively targeted by the police. But communities often also suffer violence and disorder when the police selectively fail to protect them. Some scholars emphasize that this, too, is a violation of the Equal Protection Clause. See, e.g., Lawrence Rosenthal, *Policing and Equal Protection*, 21 Yale L. & Pol'y Rev. 53, 87 (2003).

Some of the strongest claims against police for discrimination by underenforcement have been about discrimination on the basis of gender rather than race. When the U.S. Department of Justice investigated the University of Montana's Office of Public Safety and the Missoula (Mont.) Police Department for engaging in patterns or practices of violating constitutional rights, it argued:

> The Equal Protection Clause of the Fourteenth Amendment to the United States Constitution prohibits intentional sex discrimination, including selective or discriminatory enforcement of the law.
>
> In addition to affirmative discrimination against members of protected groups, a *failure* to take action on behalf of these individuals can constitute unlawful discrimination. See Bell v. Maryland, 378 U.S. 226, 311 (1964) (Goldberg, J. concurring). . . . The courts have applied this principle to police under-enforcement of the law where such deliberate under-enforcement adversely impacts women. . . .
>
> Differential treatment of women premised on sex-based stereotypes, such as stereotypes about the role women should play in society or how they should behave, also violates the Equal Protection Clause. See, e.g., United States v. Virginia, 518 U.S. 515, 5l7 (1996) (holding invalid explicit sex classification and stating that "generalizations about 'the way women are,' estimates of what is appropriate for most women, no longer justify denying opportunity to women[.]"). Thus, where a law enforcement agency's failure to adequately

respond to sexual assault is premised, at least in part, on sex-based stereotypes, that failure violates the Equal Protection Clause.

[University of Montana's Office of Public Safety (OPS)] serves as the first responder to on-campus reports of sexual assault, the vast majority of which are made by women. Our investigation showed that OPS does not adequately respond to reports of sexual assault, and that its policies and training related to sexual assault response are insufficient and, until recently, nonexistent. Our investigation showed further that there is no legitimate law enforcement or other reason for these inadequacies. Rather, these gaps in policy and training appear particularly unwarranted given the prevalence of sexual assaults against college women nationwide. The deficiencies in UM's law enforcement response to campus sexual assaults are unnecessary and have a disparate impact on women. . . . In addition, OPS' failure to implement adequate policies and training, together with statements by OPS officers, reflect sex-based stereotypes and thus constitute discrimination barred by the Equal Protection Clause of the Fourteenth Amendment.

Letter from Thomas E. Perez, Assistant Attorney Gen., Civil Rights Div., & Michael W. Cotter, U.S. Attorney for the Dist. of Mont., to Royce C. Engstrom, President, Univ. of Mont. (May 9, 2013), at 5–7.

The Department of Justice made similar allegations against the New Orleans Police Department (NOPD):

Inadequate policies and procedures, deficiencies in training, and extraordinary lapses in supervision have contributed to a systemic breakdown in NOPD handling of sexual assault investigations. NOPD has misclassified large numbers of possible sexual assaults, resulting in a sweeping failure to properly investigate many potential cases of rape, attempted rape, and other sex crimes. Additionally, in situations where the Department pursued sexual assault complaints, the investigations were seriously deficient, marked by poor victim interviewing skills, missing or inadequate documentation, and minimal efforts to contact witnesses or interrogate suspects. The documentation we reviewed was replete with stereotypical assumptions and judgments about sex crimes and victims of sex crimes, including misguided commentary about the victims' perceived credibility, sexual history, or delay in contacting the police.

U.S. Dept. of Justice, Civil Rights Div., *Investigation of the New Orleans Police Department* 43 (2011). For additional argument in favor of treating underenforcement as an equal protection violation, see Deborah Tuerkheimer, *Underenforcement as Unequal Protection*, 57 B.C. L. Rev. 1287 (2016). Can you imagine other circumstances in which bias could influence how police officers handle victims? Should a single instance in which an officer refuses to take a complaint because the victim is a member of a protected class be subject to an equal protection challenge? How difficult are such claims likely to be to prove?

4. Suspect Descriptions

Traditional equal protection law requires that *express racial classifications* by the government be subjected to *strict scrutiny*: the government must "demonstrate with clarity that its 'purpose or interest is both constitutionally permissible and substantial, and that its use of the classification is necessary . . . to the accomplishment of its purpose.'" Fisher v. Univ. of Texas at Austin, 570 U.S. 297, 309 (2013) (quoted in Fisher v. Univ. of Tex. at Austin, 136 S. Ct. 2198, 2208 (2016)). But strict scrutiny is almost never applied to policing. Courts mostly refuse to treat police decisions, even those that take race into consideration, as "racial classifications" within the meaning of the Equal Protection Clause.

For an example of a court rejecting an express racial classification claim, see *Brown v. City of Oneonta*, 221 F.3d 329 (2d Cir. 2000). After an elderly woman told police that she was attacked in her home by a Black man she could not otherwise describe, the police conducted a "sweep" in which they attempted to question every Black male student at a nearby university. The police collected names of Black male students and stopped and questioned more than 200 "non-white persons" over the next few days. No suspect was arrested. The U.S. Court of Appeals for the Second Circuit concluded that the plaintiffs "were not questioned solely on the basis of their race. They were questioned on the altogether legitimate basis of a physical description given by the victim of a crime." *Id.* at 337. For this reason, the court considered the police action a facially neutral decision, one for which—in light of the suspect description by the victim—the plaintiffs could not show that the police had discriminatory animus.

When the court of appeals denied rehearing in banc, several judges dissented, arguing that police use of a racial description to target suspects is an express racial classification that requires strict scrutiny, at least if the police "set[] aside all but the racial elements in the victim's description" and use only race in identifying targets for further investigation. Brown v. City of Oneonta, 235 F.3d 769, 781 (2d Cir. 2000) (Calabresi, J., dissenting from denial of rehearing in banc). But other courts of appeals have treated the issue similarly, refusing to treat police conduct based on a victim's description of a suspect as a racial classification. See Monroe v. City of Charlottesville, 579 F.3d 380, 388 (4th Cir. 2009).

Although the use of suspect descriptions does not trigger strict scrutiny, occasionally a police policy does. In *Hassan v. City of New York*, 804 F.3d 277 (3d Cir. 2015), plaintiffs alleged that the NYPD intentionally subjected Muslim individuals, businesses, and institutions to pervasive surveillance after 9/11 on the basis of their religion. The U.S. Court of Appeals for the Third Circuit reversed a trial-court dismissal of the suit, holding that "even if NYPD officers were subjectively motivated by a legitimate law-enforcement purpose . . . they've intentionally discriminated if they wouldn't have surveilled Plaintiffs had they not been Muslims." *Id.* at 298. According to the Court, such a program must pass strict scrutiny to survive equal protection analysis. *Id.* at 301. The case subsequently settled, so no court ever ruled whether the program satisfied that test.

5.   Equal Protection Problems

a.   A Speed Trap

Sheriff Rainey is engaged in a "speed trap" operation by the side of an interstate highway. Using a rear-mounted radar gun, he can determine the speed of a car as it approaches from the rear, before he can see the driver. Because he cannot pull over everyone who speeds, Sheriff Rainey has decided that he will pull over only Black drivers, who he believes are more likely than other drivers to be engaged in drug trafficking, as well as anyone exceeding the speed limit by more than 20 miles per hour. During the first hour, Rainey clocks several cars going 10 to 15 miles per hour over the speed limit. As each car passes, however, Rainey sees that the drivers are white, and he does not pull them over. At the beginning of the second hour, James, a Black teenager driving home from college, passes Sheriff Rainey while driving 11 miles per hour over the limit. Rainey pulls him over and, unable to develop probable cause to search the car, writes James a ticket for speeding.

1. Has Sheriff Rainey violated the Fourth Amendment? The Equal Protection Clause?
2. Does your analysis change at all if James had been driving only 3 miles per hour over the speed limit? What if he were driving 20 miles per hour over?
3. Assume that James is able to obtain strong evidence of Rainey's plan, his failure to stop the white speeders, and a history of racist remarks about Black people. Will he be able to get the speeding ticket dismissed? Can he sue Rainey for monetary damages in federal court? On what theories?

b. A Stop-and-Frisk Surge

Chief Burrell is under pressure from the city council to reduce the number of shootings in his city. He has credible information showing that most of the shootings are the product of conflict between gangs composed almost exclusively of Black teenagers in low-income, mostly Black neighborhoods. In response, he plans to triple the number of officers patrolling in those neighborhoods and to instruct them to conduct *Terry* stops of young Black men whenever they can develop proper reasonable suspicion for doing so. He emphasizes that the reasonable suspicion must be sufficient in every case and orders all officers who will be participating in this "surge" to retrain on the law of *Terry* stops immediately. Chief Burrell has asked you for advice about the Equal Protection Clause implications of his plan. If there are problems, how could he change his instructions to fix them?

c. A Resisting-Arrest Charge

Officer Scott implicitly associates Black people with negative characteristics like aggression, rudeness, and lack of intelligence. He is not consciously aware of these associations and does not think of himself as a racist, even in his most private thoughts. However, his attitudes cause him to react with greater anger to Black people he arrests when they do not immediately allow themselves to be placed in handcuffs than to people of other races who do the same. As a result, over the course of his career, 90 percent of the "resisting arrest" charges he has filed have been against Black arrestees, although they represent only 40 percent of the number of people he has arrested. All the charges survived probable-cause hearings, and most resulted in convictions. Officer Scott recently arrested Joe, who is Black, for domestic violence. Joe loudly protested his arrest and initially resisted being cuffed. Scott charged Joe with resisting arrest. Joe's public defender was able to obtain Officer Scott's resisting-arrest statistics in discovery. What claims might Joe be able to bring? How are they likely to fare?

d.   School-Shooter Screening

Deputy Barnes is the resource officer at a large public high school. After a recent high-profile mass shooting at another school in the state, the school district installed metal detectors at the school's entrance, which all students must pass through on entering the building. If a student activates the metal detector — which frequently happens — it is Deputy Barnes's job to scan the student's body with a "wand," which can locate precisely what object is triggering the walk-through detector. Because this process is time-consuming and has never turned up a weapon, Deputy Barnes eventually begins simply waving most students who trigger the metal detector through into the building, without using the wand. However, because he has read that virtually all school shooters are white teenage boys, he never waves them through and instead always performs the wand test on them. Students notice this pattern, and several parents of white boys bring suit against Deputy Barnes under §1983. What is the likely result?

e.   Finding a Sexual Assault Suspect

Detective Reynolds is the night-shift violent crimes investigator in the Central Park Precinct in New York City. Late one night, he receives a 911 dispatch report of a robbery and sexual assault of a female pedestrian. The victim did not get a good look at her attacker but reports that he was a Latino man not older than 30, he brandished a pistol, and he stole her iPhone and credit cards. Because there are only a few exits from the park, Reynolds orders patrol officers to block off each of them and frisk all Latino men who appear to be under 50 years old for a gun before allowing them to leave the park. All others are allowed to leave the park without delay.

1. Luis, a 26-year-old Latino man, is stopped, questioned, and frisked on his way out of the park. Nothing is found, and he is released within five minutes. Have the police violated his rights under the Equal Protection Clause?
2. Thomas, a 65-year-old Latino man, is stopped and frisked by officers who ignore their instructions. The frisk uncovers a gun for which Thomas has no permit. He is arrested and charged with unlawful possession of a firearm. Will his lawyer likely be able to get the evidence suppressed? Have his rights under the Equal Protection Clause been violated?
3. Robert, who is 22 and committed the assault and robbery, is frisked on his way out of the park. A revolver is discovered in his waistband, and he is arrested for gun possession. In a search incident to his arrest, the victim's cell phone, still in its distinctive case, is discovered in his jacket pocket. He is charged with robbery and sexual assault. Will the evidence be suppressed?

C.   Statutes That Prohibit Discrimination

Statutes can prohibit discrimination in street policing and traffic enforcement even when constitutional law does not.

1.   Federal Statutes

Several federal statutes forbid police departments that receive federal funds from discriminating in programs using those funds. Here are two examples.

TITLE VI OF THE CIVIL RIGHTS ACT OF 1964, 42 U.S.C. §2000D

No person in the United States shall, on the ground of race, color, or national origin, be excluded from participation in, be denied the benefits of, or be subjected to discrimination under any program or activity receiving Federal financial assistance.

OMNIBUS CRIME CONTROL AND SAFE STREETS ACT OF 1968, 34 U.S.C. §10228(C)(1)

No person in any State shall on the ground of race, color, religion, national origin, or sex be excluded from participation in, be denied the benefits of, or be subjected to discrimination under or denied employment in connection with any programs or activity funded in whole or in part with funds made available under this chapter.

NOTES AND QUESTIONS

1. *Limitations on Title VI.* Title VI permits the Department of Justice to stop funding police departments that discriminate in the use of their federal funding. Although the statute creates a private cause of action, private plaintiffs who sue under Title VI must establish both discriminatory effect and discriminatory intent, making private claims no broader than equal protection claims brought pursuant to 42 U.S.C. §1983. See Alexander v. Sandoval, 532 U.S. 275 (2001). Although the Department of Justice may bring actions without establishing intent, federal regulations implementing the statute discourage the Department of Justice from cutting off funding under Title VI except as a last resort. See 28 C.F.R. §50.3(a). As a consequence, although Title VI is sometimes enforced along with the Department of Justice's pattern-or-practice authority under 34 U.S.C. §12601, which permits suits by the Department of Justice for civil rights violations such as discrimination, or occasionally used to secure changes in departmental policies, it is rarely used against police departments otherwise.

2. *Limitations on the Safe Streets Act.* The discrimination provisions of the Safe Streets Act operate in most respects like Title VI but apply to only a limited set of federal funding programs. Although private plaintiffs may bring claims, they must first exhaust their administrative remedies by filing a complaint with the Department of Justice, and all efforts to deprive agencies of federal funding face procedural barriers. Claims resulting in stopping federal funds to police departments under the Safe Streets Act are rare.

3. *Why so weak?* No one would suggest that either Title VI or the Safe Streets Act has much influence over police departments. Take Title VI. Most people who believe they are racially profiled by the police know nothing about Title VI. Even when someone complains to the Department of Justice, their allegations are primarily investigated by the Office of Civil Rights (OCR) within the Office of Justice Programs (OJP). OJP's mission is to provide grants, technical assistance, and other resources to support state and local crime-fighting efforts, and it considers OCR

a compliance office rather than a part of its programming. Under the Obama Administration, which took a more aggressive approach to enforcing civil rights statutes than the Trump Administration, OCR received fewer than 100 complaints a year and claimed to achieve voluntary compliance from every police department it investigated between late 2008 and mid-2013. Thus, the Department of Justice deprived no police department of federal funds during the period. Is it plausible to believe that none of the thousands of law enforcement agencies receiving federal funds then—or now—have a traffic enforcement practice with discriminatory effect? Why might this statute not work very well?

4. *Grant conditions and reform.* The answer matters: Many advocates for changes in police practices today have proposed adding further conditions to federal grants to force departmental reform. The proposed George Floyd Justice in Policing Act of 2020, for example, includes provisions requiring that any law enforcement agency receiving grants "maintain[ ] adequate policies and procedures designed to eliminate racial profiling" and "ha[ve] eliminated any existing practices that permit or encourage racial profiling." George Floyd Justice in Policing Act of 2020, H.R. 7120, 116th Cong. §331(a) (2020) (as passed by the House, June 25, 2020). Are those conditions likely to be more effective than Title VI and the Safe Streets Act? The proposed act also conditions various grants on agencies engaging in racial-bias training and on cities passing laws banning no-knock warrants in drug cases and chokeholds, among other requirements. Are those conditions different? Are there legal or institutional changes that might make Title VI or new conditions on grant programs to law enforcement agencies more effective?

5. *Other statutes.* These are not the only statutes that forbid discrimination in policing. The Violence Against Women Act prohibits discrimination by recipients of funds administered by the Office on Violence Against Women, a component of the U.S. Department of Justice that distributes formula and discretionary grants to strengthen law enforcement responses to domestic violence and sexual assault. See 34 U.S.C. §12291(b)(13)(A). In addition, the Americans with Disabilities Act prohibits all state and local governments and agencies from discriminating against people with disabilities because of their disabilities. See 42 U.S.C. §12132. Section 504 of the Rehabilitation Act applies similar requirements to any program or activity that receives federal funding. See 29 U.S.C. §794(a). Again, enforcement against police departments for street-policing activities under these statutes is uncommon.

6. *What is missing?* In the 1980s and 1990s, police departments used highway traffic stops aggressively as a means of finding drug traffickers in the ongoing war on drugs. Although departments denied that these stops were based on race, concerns grew about racial profiling, and the evidence revealed in several lawsuits gave credence to critics' complaints about interdiction practices. See, e.g., Memorandum of Agreement Between the U.S. Dept. of Justice and the Montgomery County Department of Police (Jan. 14, 2000); Consent Decree, United States v. New Jersey, No. 99-5970 (D.N.J. Dec. 30, 1999); State v. Soto, 734 A.2d 350 (N.J. Super. Ct. Law. Div. 1996); Wilkins v. Md. State Police, No. 93-468 (D. Md. Feb. 12, 1993). By 2000, states had started to pass laws requiring data collection and reporting, and although early attempts had failed, the nation seemed to be moving toward a federal racial profiling law. Law enforcement organizations increasingly agreed with civil rights groups that police should not target people because of their race. In early 2001, President George W. Bush declared to Congress that racial profiling is "wrong, and

we will end it in America," President George W. Bush, Address Before a Joint Session of Congress on Administration Goals (Feb. 27, 2001), in *2001 Public Papers of the President* 140, 143. The End Racial Profiling Act was first introduced that June. See Introduction of End Racial Profiling Act of 2001, 147 Cong. Rec. 10,095 (2001) (statement of Rep. Conyers); 147 Cong. Rec. 10,063 (2001) (statement of Sen. Feingold). Then the Twin Towers were brought down on September 11, 2001. After the attacks, Americans feared terrorism above all else, and some law enforcement officials and politicians embraced antiterrorism strategies that profiled individuals based on national origin or religion. Although there have been several attempts since, including in the George Floyd Justice in Policing Act of 2020, H.R. 7120, 116th Cong. §§321–335 (2020) (as passed by the House, June 25, 2020), there is still no federal statute banning racial profiling in policing.

2. State Statutes

Some states have attempted to prevent racial profiling by statute. Below are some examples. As you read, consider precisely what these statutes forbid and how they try to achieve their aims.

MONT. CODE ANN. §44-2-117

§44-2-117. Racial profiling prohibited — definitions — policies — complaints — training

(1) A peace officer may not engage in racial profiling.

(2) The race or ethnicity of an individual may not be the sole factor in:

    (a) determining the existence of probable cause to take into custody or arrest an individual; or

    (b) constituting a particularized suspicion that an offense has been or is being committed in order to justify the detention of an individual or the investigatory stop of a motor vehicle.

(3) Each law enforcement agency shall adopt a policy on race-based traffic stops that:

    (a) prohibits the practice of routinely stopping members of minority groups for violations of vehicle laws as a pretext for investigating other violations of criminal law;

    (b) provides for periodic reviews by the law enforcement agency and collection of data that determine whether any peace officers of the law enforcement agency have a pattern of stopping members of minority groups for violations of vehicle laws in a number disproportionate to the population of minority groups residing or traveling within the jurisdiction of the law enforcement agency;

    (c) if the review under subsection (3)(b) reveals a pattern, requires an investigation to determine whether any peace officers of the law enforcement agency routinely stop members of minority groups for violations of vehicle laws as a pretext for investigating other violations of criminal law.

(4) (a) Each municipal, county, consolidated local government, and state law enforcement agency shall adopt a detailed written policy that clearly defines the elements constituting racial profiling. Each agency's policy must prohibit

racial profiling, require that all stops are lawful . . . and require that all stops are documented according to subsection (3) of this section.

. **(b)** The policy must include a procedure that the law enforcement agency will use to address written complaints concerning racial profiling. . . .

(5) Each municipal, county, consolidated local government, and state law enforcement agency shall require for all of its peace officers cultural awareness training and training in racial profiling. The training program must be certified by the Montana public safety officer standards and training council. . . .

(7) If an investigation of a complaint of racial profiling reveals that a peace officer was in direct violation of the law enforcement agency's written policy prohibiting racial profiling, the law enforcement agency shall take appropriate action against the peace officer consistent with applicable laws, rules, ordinances, or policies.

(8) For the purposes of this section, the following definitions apply:

(a) "Minority group" means individuals of African American, Hispanic, Native American, Asian, or Middle Eastern descent. . . .

(c) "Racial profiling" means the detention, official restraint, or other disparate treatment of an individual solely on the basis of the racial or ethnic status of the individual.

(9) The department of justice shall make available to the public information regarding the degree of compliance by municipal, county, consolidated local government, and state law enforcement agencies with the requirements of this section.

(10) Each law enforcement agency in this state may use federal funds from community-oriented policing services grants or any other federal sources to equip each vehicle used for traffic stops with a video camera and voice-activated microphone.

PROHIBITION OF PROFILING PRACTICES ACT, N.M. STAT. ANN. §§29-21-2–4

§29-21-2. Profiling practices prohibited

A. In conducting a routine or spontaneous investigatory activity, including an interview, a detention, a traffic stop, a pedestrian stop, a frisk or other type of bodily search or a search of personal or real property, or in determining the scope, substance or duration of the routine or spontaneous investigatory activity, a law enforcement agency or a law enforcement officer shall not rely on race, ethnicity, color, national origin, language, gender, gender identity, sexual orientation, political affiliation, religion, physical or mental disability or serious medical condition, except in a specific suspect description related to a criminal incident or suspected criminal activity, to select a person for or subject a person to the routine or spontaneous investigatory activity.

B. In conducting an investigatory activity in connection with an investigation, a law enforcement agency or a law enforcement officer shall not rely on race, ethnicity, color, national origin, language, gender, gender identity, sexual orientation, political affiliation, religion, physical or mental disability or serious medical condition, except to the extent that credible information, relevant to the locality or time frame, links a person with those identifying characteristics to an identified criminal incident or criminal activity.

§29-21-3. Policies and procedures; required

A. A law enforcement agency shall:

(1) maintain written policies and procedures designed to eliminate practices by its law enforcement officers that violate the provisions of Section 2 . . . ; and

(2) provide training to its law enforcement officers, during orientation and at least once every two years, that the law enforcement agency determines will assist its law enforcement officers in adhering to . . . the Prohibition of Profiling Practices Act and to the law enforcement agency's policies and procedures.

B. As part of a law enforcement agency's administrative complaint procedures, the law enforcement agency shall, at a minimum:

(1) investigate a complaint alleging its law enforcement officer violated the provisions of Section 2 . . . ;

(2) take appropriate measures to discipline a law enforcement officer, including facilitating mediation or other restorative justice measures, when it is determined that the law enforcement officer violated the provisions of Section 2 of the Prohibition of Profiling Practices Act;

(3) provide appropriate forms for submitting the complaint against its law enforcement officer;

(4) publish the policies and procedures designed to eliminate practices that violate the provisions of Section 2 . . . ; and

(5) submit a redacted copy of the complaint and the disposition to the attorney general, which shall disclose the nature and disposition of the complaint but shall not disclose personal identifying information of a law enforcement officer or complainant. . . .

§29-21-4. Independent oversight; complaints; confidentiality

The attorney general shall establish independent procedures for receiving, and for maintaining a record of, complaints alleging profiling by a law enforcement officer or agency. The attorney general may initiate an investigation of a complaint alleging a violation, or a systematic pattern of violations, of the provisions of Section 2 . . . and take necessary actions as the attorney general deems appropriate. . . .

KAN. STAT. ANN §§22-4606, 22-4609, 22-4611

§22-4606. Racial and other profiling; definitions

As used in this act: . . .

(d) "Racial or other biased-based policing" means the unreasonable use of race, ethnicity, national origin, gender or religion by a law enforcement officer in deciding to initiate an enforcement action. It is not racial or other biased-based policing when race, ethnicity, national origin, gender or religion is used in combination with other identifying factors as part of a specific individual description to initiate an enforcement action. . . .

§22-4609. Same; prohibited as basis for making stop, search or arrest

It is unlawful to use racial or other biased-based policing in:

(a) Determining the existence of probable cause to take into custody or to arrest an individual;

(b) constituting a reasonable and articulable suspicion that an offense has been or is being committed so as to justify the detention of an individual or the investigatory stop of a vehicle; or

(c) determining the existence of probable cause to conduct a search of an individual or a conveyance. . . .

§22-4611. Same; complaints, office of attorney general, procedure; civil action

(a) Any person who believes such person has been subjected to racial or other biased-based policing by a law enforcement officer or agency may file a complaint with the law enforcement agency. The complainant may also file a complaint with the office of the attorney general. The office of the attorney general shall review and, if necessary, investigate the complaint and may find there is insufficient evidence of racial or other biased-based policing or may forward the complaint for further review and possible action to the Kansas commission on peace officers' standards and training. The commission shall review and, if necessary, further investigate the complaint. The commission may take action on the officer's certification or other corrective action as allowed by its governing statutes and rules and regulations. The commission shall consult with the head of the law enforcement agency before taking final action regarding discipline of any law enforcement officer or other disposition of the complaint. . . .

(c) Upon disposition of a complaint as provided for in subsection (a) the complainant shall have a civil cause of action in the district court against the law enforcement officer or law enforcement agency, or both, and shall be entitled to recover damages if it is determined by the court that such officer or agency engaged in racial or other biased-based policing. The court may allow the prevailing party reasonable attorney fees and court costs.

NOTES AND QUESTIONS

1. *Scope of laws.* What do the laws above actually ban? Do they all mean the same thing by "profiling"? How do these laws compare with the federal statutes and federal constitutional law?

2. *Remedies.* How do these laws seek to deter and remedy violations?

3. *Limited data.* What data do these statutes require agencies to report?

4. *Summary of state laws.* Around half of states have some law on racial profiling. Eleven states ban the practice. But many laws provide no specific remedy. Only two statutes—Kansas's and Rhode Island's—create a private cause of action. Instead, most statutes require departments to adopt policies concerning profiling, specify training for officers, and mandate at least some data collection (although often solely about complaints). See Elizabeth O'Connor Tomlinson, *Cause of Action for Racial Profiling Under State Laws,* 71 Causes of Action 2d 757 (2016). Few states require police departments to record and retain information about the number of motor vehicle stops they do, the justification for the stops, the result of the stops, and the perceived race or ethnicity of the people they stop. Nebraska requires the most comprehensive data. See Neb. Rev. Stat. §20-504. At least two other states have handled racial profiling by

executive order. See Wis. Exec. Order No. 387 (Dec. 27, 1999); Wis. Exec. Order No. 1 (Mar. 6, 2001); Ariz. Exec. Order No. 2006-12 (Aug. 22, 2006).

5. *Alternative approaches.* Five states ban profiling but create no private right of action and require no data collection. Eight states do not ban profiling but require at least some data collection. Do you see these as alternative approaches to handling the issue? What do you see as the trade-offs between them?

6. *Why some states and not others?* Why might some states have strong racial profiling laws and others have weak or no prohibitions on the practice? You might think that racial diversity could drive a state to confront the issue, but that explanation fails: Montana is one of the least racially diverse states in the nation, and it has a law, but New York and Hawaii, two of the most diverse states, do not have statutes. Conversely, New Mexico, one of the most racially diverse states in the nation, has a law, whereas Maine and Vermont, which are two of the least racially diverse, do not. Do you have other hypotheses for why states act aggressively or decline to act? How would you test them?

7. *Assessment of state laws.* When the NAACP looked at state racial profiling laws in 2014, it concluded that

> not one adequately meets all the provisions required for an effective law, making them inadequate tools to significantly curb the practice of racial profiling. Most state laws do not include a definition of profiling that is inclusive of all significantly impacted groups. They also tend to lack a ban on pretextual stops of pedestrians and motorists—where officers use minor violations such as not using a seat belt or jay walking as a pretext to search for illegal contraband. In addition, most state laws do not include a provision allowing individuals to seek court orders to stop police departments from engaging in racial profiling or obtain remedies for violations.

> State laws tend to vary widely, from that of Connecticut and Rhode Island, which are amongst the most comprehensive—yet Connecticut lacks a specific private right of action and Rhode Island lacks a good enforceable definition—to that of Kentucky, which basically lacks all of the necessary components for a good law.

Nat'l Assn. for the Advancement of Colored People, *Born Suspect: Stop-and-Frisk Abuses & the Continued Fight to End Racial Profiling in America* 19 (2014). The NAACP argues that for a law to be effective it must include the following:

- Comprehensive definition of and ban on racial profiling
- Ban on pretextual stops of both pedestrians and motorists
- Criminalization of violations and specific penalties
- Requirement of mandatory data collection for all stops and all searches
- Requirement of regular publishing of data
- Creation of an independent commission to address complaints about profiling
- Creation of an individual right of action that includes equitable relief
- Provision of funds for training and in-car and body-worn cameras to monitor traffic stops

Id. at app. II. Do you agree that each of these is both a good idea and necessary to prevent racial profiling? How do the statutes above fare by these measures?

8. *One more problem.* Sergeant Connors is on patrol when dispatch broadcasts a description of a suspect in a strong-arm robbery committed a few blocks from his location. The description contains several points of detail about height, age, and clothing, but due to static, the only thing Connors is able to make out clearly is that the suspect is a Black male. A few moments later, he spots Earl, a 45-year-old Black man, walking alone on a deserted sidewalk. Connors activates his police lights and detains Earl for 30 minutes while detectives bring the victim to their location to attempt a live identification. When the victim arrives, he is certain that Earl is not the man who robbed him, and Earl is released. Did Connors's actions violate Earl's constitutional rights under the Equal Protection Clause? Which, if any, of the state antiprofiling statutes did Connors violate?

Reducing Racial Disparities Without the Law

Given how weak the legal doctrines are that regulate disparities and discrimination under the law, you might consider how police departments can address concerns without legal intervention. In its report on traffic stops by the Metropolitan Nashville Police Department (MNPD), for example, the Policing Project made the following recommendations for addressing community concern about disparities in traffic stops:

- Reduce the number of traffic stops.
- Acknowledge Black residents have been disproportionately affected by MNPD's stop practices.
- Monitor racial disparities on an ongoing basis.
- Redeploy officer resources toward more effective crime-fighting tools.
- Consider adopting a Neighborhood Policing strategy.
- Post its department policies online.
- Conduct a review of certain key policies such as use of force.
- Conduct a review of training around use of force, traffic stops, and procedural justice.
- Adopt a body-camera policy with attention to transparency regarding the release of body-camera footage.

Policing Project at NYU School of Law, *An Assessment of Traffic Stops and Policing Strategies in Nashville* (2018). None of these strategies required changing the law. Can you think of other ways departments might address concerns about disparities in policing?

Chapter 7

Making Arrests

"You're under arrest." Everyone recognizes these words. Although police officers use other techniques to handle the problems they encounter and to enforce the law—persuasion, brief detentions, and citations, among them—the legal authority to make arrests (backed by force) arguably defines contemporary policing. Traditionally, arrests have served three main purposes: taking custody of dangerous people, ensuring that suspects show up in court to answer charges, and interrupting people engaged in ongoing crimes they might otherwise continue.

Whatever its justification, every arrest causes harm. Arrests stop suspects in their tracks and place them in state custody, thus interfering with their liberty and autonomy. Officers search and question arrestees, so arrests inevitably interfere with privacy. When officers use force to make the arrest, they threaten bodily integrity as well, sometimes injuring arrestees or even killing them. Arrests also trigger a cascade of adverse consequences largely outside police control, including booking fees and court fines, housing and immigration issues, and the creation of a long-lasting arrest record. These are good reasons to consider limiting arrests and the police power to carry them out. As you read, consider how (and how well) the law balances allowing police departments and officers to pursue law enforcement goals using arrests against the harms and risks that arrests entail.

A. The Power to Arrest

Local police officers get to make arrests only because state law empowers them to do so. States create the power to arrest in two parts. First, they pass statutes that define crimes and violations, subjecting those who violate them to penalties. Second, states authorize police officers to arrest those suspected of violating those laws. That authority to arrest is usually found in two types of statutes and court decisions: those that allow police officers to execute *arrest warrants* and those that allow police officers to make *warrantless arrests.* An arrest warrant is a judicial command to qualified officers to take a named person into state custody to answer for state law violations. A warrantless arrest happens when an officer takes a person into custody to answer for a crime without such an order. State laws widely permit warrantless arrests in public for felonies, for misdemeanors and lesser offenses that take place in the presence of the officer, for breaches of the peace, for domestic violence offenses, and sometimes for other crimes.

Of course, such state legal authority operates only within any constraints imposed by constitutional law. Recall the language of the Fourth Amendment:

> The right of the people to be secure in their persons, houses, papers, and effects, against unreasonable searches and seizures, shall not be violated, and no warrants shall issue, but upon probable cause, supported by oath or affirmation, and particularly describing the place to be searched, and the persons or things to be seized.

An arrest is a quintessential *seizure* within the meaning of the Fourth Amendment. All arrests must therefore be reasonable. According to Fourth Amendment doctrine, the reasonableness requirement restrains state power to authorize arrests in four ways:

- It dictates the minimum amount of suspicion government must have before it can authorize an arrest, requiring that all arrests be based on *probable cause* that the person committed a crime.
- It specifies that under some circumstances arrests require a warrant so that a judge can determine that probable cause exists before the arrest occurs.
- It limits how arrestees are treated after they are arrested, restricting searches, seizures of property, and the length of their detention before they see a judge.
- It limits how much force an officer may use to make an arrest happen.

The last of these issues is considered in Chapter 8. The others are discussed below.

Defining an Arrest

You may be surprised to learn that there is no agreement about precisely what constitutes an arrest. Some statutes label handcuffing a suspect or issuing a traffic ticket an arrest. Others do not call a detention an arrest even if the suspect is hauled off to jail and charged with a crime so long as he is almost immediately let go.

Even within Fourth Amendment law, the definition of an arrest changes with time and context. Before *Terry v. Ohio*, 392 U.S. 1 (1968), all Fourth Amendment seizures were considered arrests, no matter how long they lasted or whether the person was carted off to jail. *Terry* changed that, distinguishing between *arrests* and *stops*. The first requires probable cause that a person committed a crime and the second only reasonable suspicion.

Since *Terry*, the Court treats any detention that exceeds the permissible scope of a *Terry* stop (which usually must be brief and stationary) as an arrest for Fourth Amendment purposes, even if the suspect is not told he is under arrest and no arrest record is created. See *Dunaway v. New York*, 442 U.S. 200 (1979). But in *Knowles v. Iowa*, 525 U.S. 113 (1998), the Court concluded that traffic stops in which officers issue citations in lieu of arrests, which are based on probable cause and may exceed the scope of a *Terry* stop, do not constitute arrests within the meaning of the doctrine that allows officers to conduct searches incident to arrest. The takeaway: What constitutes an arrest to courts depends on what legal questions are asked.

However courts or states define arrests, the full significance of an arrest comes from its common components. It is not unreasonable to say that an arrest occurs whenever the police, on the basis that a person has committed a criminal offense or violation: (1) handcuff the suspect and deprive him of his freedom; (2) transport him against his will to a police station or jail; (3) process him, taking identifying information and generating a permanent criminal record; and (4) detain him until he is released or sees a judge or magistrate. Rachel A. Harmon, *Why Arrest?*, 115 Mich. L. Rev. 307, 311 (2016).

If you are most interested in the long-term consequences of arrests, you may worry most about the creation of arrest records. Cf. James Jacobs, *The Eternal Criminal Record* (2015). If instead you are most interested in police use of force, then perhaps the most important aspects of an arrest are securing a suspect and moving him from a place of his choosing to a jail cell. To secure and move a suspect necessitates either the *arrestee's cooperation*, however reluctant, or *force by an officer* to stop him, handcuff him, put him in the car, and take him to the stationhouse. In this way, arrests and force are inextricably linked.

B. *Probable Cause and Warrants*

1. Probable Cause

The U.S. Supreme Court has long made clear that every arrest requires *probable cause* that the suspect has committed a crime. But the Court has been less clear about precisely what probable cause is. Here is the Court's clearest explanation:

> Guilt in a criminal case must be proved beyond a reasonable doubt and by evidence confined to that which long experience in the common-law tradition, to some extent embodied in the Constitution, has crystallized into rules of evidence consistent with that standard. These rules are historically grounded rights of our system, developed to safeguard men from dubious and unjust convictions, with resulting forfeitures of life, liberty and property.

> However, if those standards were to be made applicable in determining probable cause for an arrest or for search and seizure, . . . few indeed would be the situations in which an officer, charged with protecting the public interest by enforcing the law, could take effective action toward that end. Those standards have seldom been so applied.

> In dealing with probable cause, however, as the very name implies, we deal with probabilities. These are not technical; they are the factual and practical considerations of everyday life on which reasonable and prudent men, not legal technicians, act. The standard of proof is accordingly correlative to what must be proved.

"The substance of all the definitions" of probable cause "is a reasonable ground for belief of guilt." McCarthy v. De Armit, 99 Pa. St. 63, 69 (1881). And this "means less than evidence which would justify condemnation" or conviction, as Marshall, C.J., said for the Court more than a century ago in *Locke v. United States*, 11 U. S. 339, 348 (1813). Since Marshall's time, at any rate, it has come to mean more than bare suspicion: probable cause exists where "the facts and circumstances within their [the officers'] knowledge and of which they had reasonably trustworthy information [are] sufficient in themselves to warrant a man of reasonable caution in the belief that" an offense has been or is being committed. Carroll v. United States, 267 U. S. 132, 162 (1925).

These long-prevailing standards seek to safeguard citizens from rash and unreasonable interferences with privacy and from unfounded charges of crime. They also seek to give fair leeway for enforcing the law in the community's protection. Because many situations which confront officers in the course of executing their duties are more or less ambiguous, room must be allowed for some mistakes on their part. But the mistakes must be those of reasonable men, acting on facts leading sensibly to their conclusions of probability. The rule of probable cause is a practical, nontechnical conception affording the best compromise that has been found for accommodating these often opposing interests. Requiring more would unduly hamper law enforcement. To allow less would be to leave law-abiding citizens at the mercy of the officers' whim or caprice.

Brinegar v. United States, 338 U.S. 160, 174–176 (1949).

NOTES AND QUESTIONS

1. *How clear is probable cause?* Since *Brinegar*, the Court has not added much to help explain probable cause. Instead, it has reiterated that probable cause is nontechnical, is judged from the totality of the circumstances, and does not require that officers rule out innocent explanations for facts. See, e.g., District of Columbia v. Wesby, 138 S. Ct. 577 (2018). Do you understand probable cause now? Should officers? For most arrests, an officer makes the first assessment of probable cause, and a suspect could spend some time in jail before a judge checks the officer's judgment.

2. *What is probable cause?* What does probable cause measure? Why does that matter in justifying an arrest? How does this requirement protect criminal suspects from the police?

3. *Why probable cause?* Read the last paragraph again. The Court views probable cause as a balance between protecting individuals from unfounded charges and allowing officers to enforce the law. In this reasoning, the Court assumes that the state's interest in crime control and effective law enforcement is the same as its interest in making arrests. What if the police can now start the criminal process and control crime without arrests (a topic discussed more below)? Does that suggest that a stricter standard should determine when officers may make an arrest? A preponderance of the evidence, perhaps?

Changing the standard would upend the law in every state, and as the Court points out, the probable cause standard has an impressive pedigree. "A longstanding, widespread practice is not immune from constitutional scrutiny. But neither is it to be lightly brushed aside. This is particularly so when the constitutional standard is as amorphous as the word 'reasonable,' and when custom and contemporary norms necessarily play such a large role in the constitutional analysis." Payton v. New York, 445 U.S. 573, 600 (1980). Which way does that cut for probable cause?

Note that although Fourth Amendment cases often read as if they determine what *officers* may do, they actually determine what *states* may authorize officers to do. Any state could impose a suspicion standard more stringent than probable cause for arrests, although no state has.

4. *Probable cause and crime definition.* The probable cause requirement purports to *limit* the power to arrest. Scholars argue that this does not describe how Fourth Amendment law works in practice: "With probable cause, a police officer *may* arrest, but *he need not do so unless he wishes to do so.* Thus, the term 'constraint' is something of a misnomer — or, at least, it is incomplete. Probable cause does not so much *constrain* as it *empowers.* It is a safe harbor." Josh Bowers, *Probable Cause, Constitutional Reasonableness, and the Unrecognized Point of a "Pointless Indignity"*, 66 Stan. L. Rev. 987, 1032 (2014). How protective the safe harbor is turns out to be a product of two factors: (1) the rigor of probable cause as a measure of evidence, and (2) the scope of the criminal code to which probable cause necessarily refers. "[I]f a code were made broad enough, police could pick and choose between many prospective offenders under even the most rigid plausible definition of probable cause. Conversely, if probable cause were defined as a mere possibility or a hunch, police could pick and choose between many prospective offenders under even the narrowest plausible criminal code." *Id.* at 1033. Do you see why?

Flip through any state's vast criminal code, and you will see that it broadly defines many of the crimes, especially the minor ones. Given that and what you learned from *Brinegar*, how much is probable cause likely to limit arrests? What can you say about probable cause as a standard for constraining police arrest conduct? The substantive law differs among jurisdictions, both as to its specific terms and what it criminalizes. Does this mean that the police power to arrest also differs? See Wayne A. Logan, *Contingent Constitutionalism: State and Local Criminal Laws and the Applicability of Federal Constitutional Rights*, 51 Wm. & Mary L. Rev. (2009).

2. (No) Warrants

When Fourth Amendment doctrine requires a warrant, it demands that a judge assess the basis for and limits of a search or seizure in advance. When no warrant is required, an officer may make this assessment on his own in the field and execute the search or seizure, and any judicial review will occur only after the intrusion. Although the Supreme Court requires warrants for many searches, it is far less demanding about warrants for arrests. As a result of the next case, police officers — rather than courts — almost always are permitted to determine whether sufficient cause exists to take someone into custody. As you read this case, consider whether you are satisfied with the Court's reasoning about why.

UNITED STATES v. WATSON
423 U.S. 411 (1976)

MR. JUSTICE WHITE delivered the opinion of the Court. . . .

I

The relevant events began on August 17, 1972, when an informant, one Khoury, telephoned a postal inspector informing him that respondent Watson was in possession of a stolen credit card and had asked Khoury to cooperate in using the card to their mutual advantage. . . . [T]he inspector asked Khoury to arrange to meet with Watson. . . . [O]n August 23, Khoury met with Watson at a restaurant designated by the latter. Khoury had been instructed that if Watson had additional stolen credit cards, Khoury was to give a designated signal. The signal was given, the officers closed in, and Watson was forthwith arrested. . . .

. . . Watson was convicted of illegally possessing . . . two cards seized from his car.

A divided panel of the Court of Appeals for the Ninth Circuit reversed. . . . [N]otwithstanding its agreement with the District Court that Khoury was reliable and that there was probable cause for arresting Watson, the court held the arrest unconstitutional because the postal inspector had failed to secure an arrest warrant although he concededly had time to do so. . . .

II . . .

Contrary to the Court of Appeals' view, Watson's arrest was not invalid because executed without a warrant. . . .

. . . [T]here is nothing in the Court's prior cases indicating that under the Fourth Amendment a warrant is required to make a valid arrest for a felony. Indeed, the relevant prior decisions are uniformly to the contrary.

. . . Just last Term, while recognizing that maximum protection of individual rights could be assured by requiring a magistrate's review of the factual justification prior to any arrest, we stated that "such a requirement would constitute an intolerable handicap for legitimate law enforcement" and noted that the Court "has never invalidated an arrest supported by probable cause solely because the officers failed to secure a warrant." Gerstein v. Pugh, 420 U.S. 103, 113 (1975).

The cases construing the Fourth Amendment thus reflect the ancient common-law rule that a peace officer was permitted to arrest without a warrant for a misdemeanor or felony committed in his presence as well as for a felony not committed in his presence if there was reasonable ground for making the arrest. This has also been the prevailing rule under state constitutions and statutes. . . .

The balance struck by the common law in generally authorizing felony arrests on probable cause, but without a warrant, has survived substantially intact. It appears in almost all of the States in the form of express statutory authorization. . . .

. . . Law enforcement officers may find it wise to seek arrest warrants where practicable to do so, and their judgments about probable cause may be more readily accepted where backed by a warrant issued by a magistrate. But we decline to transform this judicial preference into a constitutional rule when the judgment of the Nation and Congress has for so long been to authorize warrantless public arrests on probable cause rather than to encumber criminal prosecutions with endless litigation with respect to the existence of exigent circumstances, whether it was practicable to get a warrant, whether the suspect was about to flee, and the like.

Watson's arrest did not violate the Fourth Amendment, and the Court of Appeals erred in holding to the contrary. . . .

Reversed.

Mr. Justice STEVENS took no part in the consideration or decision of this case.

Mr. Justice POWELL, concurring. . . .

On its face, our decision today creates a certain anomaly. There is no more basic constitutional rule in the Fourth Amendment area than that which makes a warrantless search unreasonable except in a few "jealously and carefully drawn" exceptional circumstances. . . . In short, the course of judicial development of the Fourth Amendment with respect to searches has remained true to the principles so well expressed by Mr. Justice Jackson:

> "Any assumption that evidence sufficient to support a magistrate's disinterested determination to issue a search warrant will justify the officers in making a search without a warrant would reduce the Amendment to a nullity and leave the people's homes secure only in the discretion of police officers. . . . When the right of privacy must reasonably yield to the right of search is, as a rule, to be decided by a judicial officer, not by a policeman or government enforcement agent." Johnson v. United States, 333 U.S. 10, 14 (1948).

Since the Fourth Amendment speaks equally to both searches and seizures, and since an arrest, the taking hold of one's person, is quintessentially a seizure, it would seem that the constitutional provision should impose the same limitations upon arrests that it does upon searches. Indeed, as an abstract matter an argument can be made that the restrictions upon arrest perhaps should be greater. A search may cause only annoyance and temporary inconvenience to the law-abiding citizen, assuming more serious dimension only when it turns up evidence of criminality. An arrest, however, is a serious personal intrusion regardless of whether the person seized is guilty or innocent. Although an arrestee cannot be held for a significant period without some neutral determination that there are grounds to do so, no decision that he should go free can come quickly enough to erase the invasion of his privacy that already will have occurred. Logic therefore would seem to dictate that arrests be subject to the warrant requirement at least to the same extent as searches.

But logic sometimes must defer to history and experience. . . . There is no historical evidence that the Framers or proponents of the Fourth Amendment, outspokenly opposed to the infamous general warrants and writs of assistance, were at all concerned about warrantless arrests by local constables and other peace officers. . . .

Moreover, a constitutional rule permitting felony arrests only with a warrant or in exigent circumstances could severely hamper effective law enforcement. Good police practice often requires postponing an arrest, even after probable cause has been established, in order to place the suspect under surveillance or otherwise develop further evidence necessary to prove guilt to a jury. . . .

[The opinion of Justice Stewart, concurring in the result, is omitted.]

Mr. Justice Marshall, with whom Mr. Justice Brennan joins, dissenting. . . .

II

. . . The common-law rule was indeed as the Court states it. . . . To apply the rule blindly today, however, makes as much sense as attempting to interpret Hamlet's admonition to Ophelia, "Get thee to a nunnery, go," without understanding the meaning of Hamlet's words in the context of their age.[3] For the fact is that a felony at common law and a felony today bear only slight resemblance, with the result that the relevance of the common-law rule of arrest to the modern interpretation of our Constitution is minimal.

. . . Only the most serious crimes were felonies at common law, and many crimes now classified as felonies under federal or state law were treated as misdemeanors. . . .

> At common law an assault was a misdemeanor and it was still only such even if made with the intent to rob, murder, or rape. Affrays, abortion, barratry, bribing voters, challenging to fight, compounding felonies, cheating by false weights or measures, escaping from lawful arrest, eavesdropping, forgery, false imprisonment, forcible and violent entry, forestalling, kidnapping, libel, mayhem, maliciously killing valuable animals, obstructing justice, public nuisance, perjury, riots and routs, etc. were misdemeanors. . . .

Horace L. Wilgus, *Arrest Without a Warrant*, 22 Mich. L. Rev. 541, 572–573 (1924).

To make an arrest for any of these crimes at common law, the police officer was required to obtain a warrant, unless the crime was committed in his presence. Since many of these same crimes are commonly classified as felonies today, however, under the Court's holding a warrant is no longer needed to make such arrests, a result in contravention of the common law.

Thus the lesson of the common law, and those courts in this country that have accepted its rule, is an ambiguous one. . . .

. . . [T]he Court's unblinking literalism cannot replace analysis of the constitutional interests involved. . . .

III

My Brother Powell concludes: "Logic . . . would seem to dictate that arrests be subject to the warrant requirement at least to the same extent as searches." I agree. . . .

. . . A warrant is required in the search situation to protect the privacy of the individual, but there can be no less invasion of privacy when the individual himself, rather than his property, is searched and seized. Indeed, an unjustified arrest that forces the individual temporarily to forfeit his right to control his person and movements and interrupts the course of his daily business may be more intrusive than an unjustified search. . . .

A warrant requirement for arrests would, of course, minimize the possibility that such an intrusion into the individual's sacred sphere of personal privacy would

---

[3] Nunnery was Elizabethan slang for house of prostitution. 7 Oxford English Dictionary 264 (1933).

occur on less than probable cause. . . . Surely there is no reason to place greater trust in the partisan assessment of a police officer that there is probable cause for an arrest than in his determination that probable cause exists for a search. . . .

We come then to . . . whether a warrant requirement would unduly burden legitimate law enforcement interests. . . . I believe . . . that the suggested concerns are wholly illusory. Indeed, the argument that a warrant requirement for arrests would be an onerous chore for the police seems somewhat anomalous in light of the Government's concession that "it is the standard practice of the Federal Bureau of Investigation (FBI) to present its evidence to the United States Attorney, and to obtain a warrant, before making an arrest." In the past, the practice and experience of the FBI have been taken as a substantial indication that no intolerable burden would be presented by a proposed rule of procedure. Miranda v. Arizona, 384 U.S. 436, 483–486 (1966). There is no reason to accord less deference to the FBI practice here.[13] . . .

In sum, the requirement that officers about to arrest a suspect ordinarily obtain a warrant before they do so does not seem unduly burdensome, at least no more burdensome than any other requirement that law enforcement officials undertake a new procedure in order to comply with the dictates of the Constitution. . . .

Thus, the practical reasons marshaled against an arrest warrant requirement are unimpressive. . . . And given the significant protection our citizens will gain from a warrant requirement, accepted Fourth Amendment analysis dictates that a warrant rule be imposed. . . .

NOTES AND QUESTIONS

1. *What are warrants for?* Say *Watson* were reversed, and arrest warrants were required for felony arrests made in public. Getting a warrant slows officers down, but they almost always get one if they ask for it. Does that mean warrants don't matter? Maybe not:

> In many cases, getting a warrant means a day's worth of paperwork plus sitting around the courthouse, all for a five-minute meeting with the magistrate. The effective screen in such a procedure may not be the magistrate, but the long wait: such queuing costs may tend to discourage officers from using warrants save in cases where (1) finding the evidence is very important, (2) it cannot be found *without* a warrant (that is, a warrantless search would plainly be illegal), and (3) the evidence is sure to be there.

William J. Stuntz, *Warrants and Fourth Amendment Remedies*, 77 Va. L. Rev. 881, 908 (1991). Since Stuntz wrote, warrants have become easier to obtain, including by telephone and email. How does that change their value?

2. *Searches vs. arrests.* After *Watson*, searches presumptively require a warrant under the Fourth Amendment, but arrests do not. Why? Which is more unsettling: having your backpack searched in public or getting arrested in public? Are there details that matter to your choice?

3. *Warrants for misdemeanors.* *Watson* involved a warrantless arrest for a *felony*. The case does not address *misdemeanors*. Although the Court has never squarely

---

[13] The *Miranda* Court rejected as irrelevant the argument that the FBI deals with crimes different from those dealt with by state authorities. 384 U.S. at 486.

ruled on whether misdemeanors require warrants, the matter is all but decided: All states permit arrests without warrants for some misdemeanors, and courts have had little trouble with such arrests as a matter of federal constitutional law.

4. *Immediate review.* Before it decided *Watson*, the Court ruled in *Gerstein v. Pugh*, 420 U.S. 103 (1975), that a person arrested without a warrant is entitled to a "prompt" (although informal and nonadversarial) judicial determination of probable cause. In fact, a *Gerstein* hearing looks a lot like the warrant process: An officer presents the grounds for an arrest, and the magistrate decides whether they constitute probable cause to hold the suspect. If no probable cause exists, the suspect must be released. Subsequently, the Court announced that, absent exceptional circumstances, *Gerstein* hearings must occur within 48 hours of an arrest. County of Riverside v. McLaughlin, 500 U.S. 44 (1991). In practice, they often happen more quickly. There is no similar process for immediate review when an officer *searches* without a warrant. Why might such hearings matter?

5. *Exceptions to the (no) warrant rule.* Although *Watson* makes warrants unnecessary for arrests in public, officers need an arrest warrant to enter a suspect's home to arrest him absent exigent circumstances. Payton v. New York, 445 U.S. 573, 603 (1980). The Supreme Court has made clear that the interest protected in such circumstances is not the autonomy interest at stake in all arrests. Instead, it is the privacy interest in one's home, which is neutralized by the securing of an arrest warrant (that justifies entry and thus viewing of the home interior). See New York v. Harris, 495 U.S. 14 (1990). If an officer has no legal way into a home, he can always wait for his quarry to step outside and arrest him then.

6. *Consequences of differential warrant rules.* Because getting a warrant is a hassle, requiring warrants only for arrests in homes probably encourages officers to make more arrests on the street. What consequences might this have? Where are officers more likely to arrest the wrong person? Which kind of arrest would you expect to be more dangerous for officers? For suspects? For bystanders?

7. *Exigencies and arrests.* Not even Justice Marshall thought that all arrests should require warrants. Instead, he thought officers would often face exigent circumstances justifying an immediate arrest despite the warrant requirement. But if exceptions would be common, then a warrant rule would not protect suspects all that much, would it? And such a rule likely would generate a bunch of litigation over whether a warrant was required where none was had. Are these good arguments against Marshall's view?

8. *Arguments from federal practice.* Justice Marshall points to federal agents, who regularly get warrants for arrests, as evidence that a warrant rule would not hamper local law enforcement. Can you think of reasons federal and local arrest practices might be notably different?

9. *State constitutional law.* Every state has a constitutional equivalent to the Fourth Amendment. Those state provisions may constrain state lawmaking on warrants even when federal constitutional law does not. For example, the New Mexico Supreme Court has interpreted the state constitution to require warrants for all felony arrests absent exigent circumstances, contrary to the reasoning of *Watson*. See Campos v. State, 870 P.2d 117 (N.M. 1994) (interpreting N.M. Const. art. II, §10); see also State v. Paananen, 357 P.3d 958, 965 (N.M. 2015) (reiterating holding in *Campos*).

More recently, the Idaho Supreme Court interpreted its state constitution to allow warrantless misdemeanor arrests only for crimes an officer witnesses. See State v. Clarke, 446 P.3d 451, 457 (Idaho 2019). As the Idaho court acknowledged, this ruling could have serious consequences for domestic violence victims because misdemeanor domestic violence assaults are usually completed by the time an officer arrives. When an officer does not arrest, violence may resume after he departs. See *id.* at 457–458. Does this consequence change how you think about the warrant rule? How so? Domestic violence arrests are discussed more in Chapter 11.

10. *The history of arrest law.* Fourth Amendment history is rarely as clear and influential to the Court as it is in *Watson.* How much should that history matter? As Chapter 1 describes, police departments did not come about until well into the nineteenth century. In the Framing Era, night watchmen and constables were mainly volunteers and they had little discretionary authority to arrest compared to modern-era police. See Thomas Y. Davies, *The Fictional Character of Law-and-Order Originalism: A Case Study of the Distortions and Evasions of Framing-Era Arrest Doctrine in* Atwater v. Lago Vista, 37 Wake Forest L. Rev. 239 (2007). Also, should it matter that during the Framing Era, compared to today, far more felonies were eligible for capital punishment? If yes, why?

Are Warrants Protective or Threatening?

All of the justices in *Watson* assume that arrest warrants offer protection. But arrest warrants have a dark side: They generate police authority. When an arrest warrant exists for a person, every officer who encounters that person has judicial permission to take him into custody no matter what he is doing at the moment. You might be unsettled to discover how many permission slips are out there.

> Outstanding warrants are surprisingly common. When a person with a traffic ticket misses a fine payment or court appearance, a court will issue a warrant. When a person on probation drinks alcohol or breaks curfew, a court will issue a warrant. The States and Federal Government maintain databases with over 7.8 million outstanding warrants, the vast majority of which appear to be for minor offenses. Even these sources may not track the "staggering" numbers of warrants, " 'drawers and drawers' " full, that many cities issue for traffic violations and ordinance infractions. Dept. of Justice, Civil Rights Div., *Investigation of the Ferguson Police Department* 47, 55 (2015) (Ferguson Report). The county in this case has had a "backlog" of such warrants. The Department of Justice recently reported that in the town of Ferguson, Missouri, with a population of 21,000, 16,000 people had outstanding warrants against them.
>
> Justice Department investigations across the country have illustrated how these astounding numbers of warrants can be used by police to stop people without cause. In a single year in New Orleans, officers "made nearly 60,000 arrests, of which about 20,000 were of people with outstanding traffic or misdemeanor warrants from neighboring parishes for such infractions as unpaid tickets." Dept. of Justice, Civil Rights Div., *Investigation of the New Orleans Police Department* 29 (2011). In the St. Louis metropolitan area, officers "routinely" stop people—on the street, at bus stops, or even in court—for no reason other than "an officer's desire to check whether the subject had a municipal arrest warrant pending." *Ferguson Report*, at 49, 57. In Newark, New Jersey, officers stopped 52,235 pedestrians within a 4-year period and ran warrant checks on 39,308 of them. Dept. of Justice, Civil Rights Div., *Investigation of the Newark Police Department* 8, 19, n. 15 *2069 (2014). The Justice Department analyzed these warrant-checked stops and reported that "approximately 93% of the stops would have been considered unsupported by articulated reasonable suspicion." *Id.* at 9 n.7.

Utah v. Strieff, 136 S. Ct. 2056, 2068–2069 (2016) (Sotomayor, J., dissenting). These warrants are often both unnecessary—because giving a person a new court date and reminding him to attend is often sufficient to bring him to court—and ineffectual—because most bench warrants are never executed. They nevertheless have a significant impact on policing.

In *Utah v. Strieff*, the Court held that an officer's discovery of a preexisting warrant makes the exclusionary rule inapplicable to (usually drug-related) evidence discovered from a suspect during a search incident to arrest, even if the initial stop was unconstitutional because the officer lacked reasonable suspicion. *Id.* at 2063. This decision gives the police an incentive to stop someone they are interested in illegally and run a warrants check, hoping to turn up a warrant that provides the basis for an arrest, and many departments engage in a systemic practice of running warrants. See *id.* at 2069 (Sotomayor, J., dissenting). If a warrant is discovered, the person can be arrested, and the lack of suspicion for the stop is irrelevant. If there is no warrant, the pedestrian—distressed although he might now be—is permitted to go on his way.

The practice of issuing warrants for minor forms of noncompliance and then allowing officers to check for them reinforces existing disparities in the criminal justice system:

> Warrant enforcement plays a critical role in cementing class and race disparity in the criminal justice system by creating "arrest feedback." Not only do arrests generate warrants and vice versa, but warrant enforcement can also generate new criminal cases. Over time, police warrant enforcement and courts' warrant-issuing practices are recursive, producing mutually reinforcing demographic effects. Where there are a disproportionately high number of outstanding warrants for poor and minority defendants, police will target those communities for warrant enforcement. In the course of doing so, police will likely identify new criminal cases. This feedback supplies its own self-supporting rationale because the demographic profile of those with outstanding warrants reaffirms preexisting, racialized notions about crime-prone neighborhoods and communities.

Nirej Sekhon, *Dangerous Warrants*, 93 Wash. L. Rev. 967, 972 (2018).

Arrest warrants are easily issued, and they do not fade or spoil. Unless courts issue warrants more selectively and quash old warrants more easily, the number of people subject to the whims of officers is ever-increasing, and the Court's longstanding idea of warrants as a layer of judicial protection between police officers and citizens is less and less credible.

C. Constitutional Arrest Law Beyond Warrants and Probable Cause

As the previous section suggests, the Fourth Amendment requires probable cause for all arrests and no warrants for most of them. Is that enough? Being arrested is traumatic and costly, and can be injurious, or even fatal. Should probable cause *always* be sufficient to justify an arrest? As you read the next case, remember that courts can decide only what constitutional law allows states to do. When the Supreme Court permits arrests, as it does in the following case, the broader question about what role arrests should play in contemporary policing remains.

Gail Atwater was stopped for violating Texas's seatbelt law, a misdemeanor punishable by a fine of no more than $50, and she was arrested at the scene. Texas law authorizes police officers to choose between making an arrest and issuing a citation for such violations. Atwater sued, arguing that—despite probable cause to believe she had violated the seatbelt law—conducting an arrest violated her Fourth Amendment rights.

ATWATER v. CITY OF LAGO VISTA
532 U.S. 318 (2001)

JUSTICE SOUTER delivered the opinion of the Court.

The question is whether the Fourth Amendment forbids a warrantless arrest for a minor criminal offense, such as a misdemeanor seatbelt violation punishable only by a fine. . . .

. . . [H]istory, if not unequivocal, has expressed a decided, majority view that the police need not obtain an arrest warrant merely because a misdemeanor stopped short of violence or a threat of it. . . . [Nevertheless, Atwater] asks us to mint a new rule of constitutional law on the understanding that when historical practice fails to speak conclusively to a claim grounded on the Fourth Amendment, courts are left to strike a current balance between individual and societal interests by subjecting particular contemporary circumstances to traditional standards of reasonableness. Atwater accordingly argues for a modern arrest rule . . . forbidding custodial arrest, even upon probable cause, when conviction could not ultimately carry any jail time and when the government shows no compelling need for immediate detention.

If we were to derive a rule exclusively to address the uncontested facts of this case, Atwater might well prevail. She was a known and established resident of Lago Vista with no place to hide and no incentive to flee, and common sense says she would almost certainly have buckled up as a condition of driving off with a citation. In her case, the physical incidents of arrest were merely gratuitous humiliations imposed by a police officer who was (at best) exercising extremely poor judgment. Atwater's claim to live free of pointless indignity and confinement clearly outweighs anything the City can raise against it specific to her case.

But we have traditionally recognized that a responsible Fourth Amendment balance is not well served by standards requiring sensitive, case-by-case determinations of government need, lest every discretionary judgment in the field be converted into an occasion for constitutional review. Often enough, the Fourth Amendment has to be applied on the spur (and in the heat) of the moment, and the object in implementing its command of reasonableness is to draw standards sufficiently clear and simple to be applied with a fair prospect of surviving judicial second-guessing months and years after an arrest or search is made. Courts attempting to strike a reasonable Fourth Amendment balance thus credit the government's side with an essential interest in readily administrable rules.

At first glance, Atwater's argument may seem to respect the values of clarity and simplicity, so far as she claims that the Fourth Amendment generally forbids warrantless arrests for minor crimes not accompanied by violence or some demonstrable threat of it (whether "minor crime" be defined as a fine-only traffic offense, a fine-only offense more generally, or a misdemeanor). But the claim is not ultimately so simple. . . .

One line, she suggests, might be between "jailable" and "fine-only" offenses, between those for which conviction could result in commitment and those for which it could not. The trouble with this distinction, of course, is that an officer on the street might not be able to tell. It is not merely that we cannot expect every police officer to know the details of frequently complex penalty schemes, but that penalties for ostensibly identical conduct can vary on account of facts difficult (if not impossible) to know at the scene of an arrest. Is this the first offense or is the suspect a repeat offender? Is the weight of the marijuana a gram above or a gram below the fine-only line? Where conduct could implicate more than one criminal prohibition, which one will the district attorney ultimately decide to charge? And so on.

But Atwater's refinements would not end there. She represents that if the line were drawn at nonjailable traffic offenses, her proposed limitation should be qualified by a proviso authorizing warrantless arrests where "necessary for enforcement of the traffic laws or when [an] offense would otherwise continue and pose a danger to others on the road." . . .

. . . Atwater's general rule . . . promise[s] very little in the way of administrability. It is no answer that the police routinely make judgments on grounds like risk of immediate repetition; they surely do and should. But there is a world of difference between making that judgment in choosing between the discretionary leniency of a summons in place of a clearly lawful arrest, and making the same judgment when the question is the lawfulness of the warrantless arrest itself. It is the difference between no basis for legal action challenging the discretionary judgment, on the one hand, and the prospect of evidentiary exclusion or (as here) personal §1983 liability for the misapplication of a constitutional standard, on the other. Atwater's rule therefore would not only place police in an almost impossible spot but would guarantee increased litigation over many of the arrests that would occur. . . .

. . . An officer not quite sure that the drugs weighed enough to warrant jail time or not quite certain about a suspect's risk of flight would not arrest, even though it could perfectly well turn out that, in fact, the offense called for incarceration and the defendant was long gone on the day of trial. Multiplied many times over, the costs to society of such underenforcement could easily outweigh the costs to defendants of being needlessly arrested and booked, as Atwater herself acknowledges.

. . . Many jurisdictions . . . have chosen to impose more restrictive safeguards through statutes limiting warrantless arrests for minor offenses. It is of course easier to devise a minor-offense limitation by statute than to derive one through the Constitution, simply because the statute can let the arrest power turn on any sort of practical consideration without having to subsume it under a broader principle. It is, in fact, only natural that States should resort to this sort of legislative regulation, for . . . it is in the interest of the police to limit petty-offense arrests, which carry costs that are simply too great to incur without good reason. . . .

. . . [T]he country is not confronting anything like an epidemic of unnecessary minor-offense arrests. That fact caps the reasons for rejecting Atwater's request for the development of a new and distinct body of constitutional law.

Accordingly, we confirm today what our prior cases have intimated: the standard of probable cause "applie[s] to all arrests, without the need to 'balance' the interests and circumstances involved in particular situations." Dunaway v. New York, 442 U.S. 200, 208 (1979). If an officer has probable cause to believe that an individual has committed even a very minor criminal offense in his presence, he may, without violating the Fourth Amendment, arrest the offender. . . .

Justice O'Connor, with whom Justice Stevens, Justice Ginsburg, and Justice Breyer join, dissenting. . . .

. . . While probable cause is surely a necessary condition for warrantless arrests for fine-only offenses, any realistic assessment of the interests implicated by such arrests demonstrates that probable cause alone is not a sufficient condition. . . .

A custodial arrest exacts an obvious toll on an individual's liberty and privacy, even when the period of custody is relatively brief. The arrestee is subject to a full search of her person and confiscation of her possessions. United States v. Robinson, 414 U.S. 218 (1973). If the arrestee is the occupant of a car, the entire passenger compartment of the car, including packages therein, is subject to search as well. See New York v. Belton, 453 U.S. 454 (1981).[1] The arrestee may be detained for up to 48 hours without having a magistrate determine whether there in fact was probable cause for the arrest. See County of Riverside v. McLaughlin, 500 U.S. 44 (1991). Because people arrested for all types of violent and nonviolent offenses may be housed together awaiting such review, this detention period is potentially dangerous. And once the period of custody is over, the fact of the arrest is a permanent part of the public record. Cf. Paul v. Davis, 424 U.S. 693 (1976).

We have said that "the penalty that may attach to any particular offense seems to provide the clearest and most consistent indication of the State's interest in arresting individuals suspected of committing that offense." Welsh v. Wisconsin, 466 U.S. 740, 754 n.14 (1984). If the State has decided that a fine, and not imprisonment, is the appropriate punishment for an offense, the State's interest in taking a person suspected of committing that offense into custody is surely limited, at best. This is not to say that the State will never have such an interest. A full custodial arrest may on occasion vindicate legitimate state interests, even if the crime is punishable only by fine. Arrest is the surest way to abate criminal conduct. It may also allow the police to verify the offender's identity and, if the offender poses a flight risk, to ensure her appearance at trial. But when such considerations are not present, a citation or summons may serve the State's remaining law enforcement interests every bit as effectively as an arrest.

Because a full custodial arrest is such a severe intrusion on an individual's liberty, its reasonableness hinges on "the degree to which it is needed for the promotion of legitimate governmental interests." Wyoming v. Houghton, 526 U.S. 295, 300 (1999). In light of the availability of citations to promote a State's interests when a fine-only offense has been committed, I cannot concur in a rule which deems a full custodial arrest to be reasonable in every circumstance. Giving police officers constitutional carte blanche to effect an arrest whenever there is probable cause to believe a fine-only misdemeanor has been committed is irreconcilable with the Fourth Amendment's command that seizures be reasonable. Instead, I would require that when there is probable cause to believe that a fine-only offense has been committed, the police officer should issue a citation unless the officer is "able to point to specific and articulable facts which, taken together with rational inferences from those facts, reasonably warrant [the additional] intrusion" of a full custodial arrest. Terry v. Ohio, 392 U.S. 1, 21 (1968). . . .

---

[1] *Ed. note: New York v. Belton* was reinterpreted by *Arizona v. Gant,* 556 U.S. 332 (2009), to allow a narrower range of vehicle searches incident to arrest. As this change suggests, the precise toll of an arrest is something that is itself, at least in part, a product of constitutional doctrine.

While clarity is certainly a value worthy of consideration in our Fourth Amendment jurisprudence, it by no means trumps the values of liberty and privacy at the heart of the Amendment's protections. . . .

. . . The *per se* rule that the Court creates has potentially serious consequences for the everyday lives of Americans. A broad range of conduct falls into the category of fine-only misdemeanors. In Texas alone, for example, disobeying any sort of traffic warning sign is a misdemeanor punishable only by fine, as is failing to pay a highway toll, and driving with expired license plates. Nor are fine-only crimes limited to the traffic context. In several States, for example, littering is a criminal offense punishable only by fine.

To be sure, such laws are valid and wise exercises of the States' power to protect the public health and welfare. My concern lies not with the decision to enact or enforce these laws, but rather with the manner in which they may be enforced. Under today's holding, when a police officer has probable cause to believe that a fine-only misdemeanor offense has occurred, that officer may stop the suspect, issue a citation, and let the person continue on her way. Or, if a traffic violation, the officer may stop the car, arrest the driver, search the driver, see *Robinson*, 414 U.S. at 235, search the entire passenger compartment of the car including any purse or package inside, see *Belton*, 453 U.S. at 460, and impound the car and inventory all of its contents, see Colorado v. Bertine, 479 U.S. 367, 374 (1987); Florida v. Wells, 495 U.S. 1, 4–5 (1990). Although the Fourth Amendment expressly requires that the latter course be a reasonable and proportional response to the circumstances of the offense, the majority gives officers unfettered discretion to choose that course without articulating a single reason why such action is appropriate.

Such unbounded discretion carries with it grave potential for abuse. . . .

The Court neglects the Fourth Amendment's express command in the name of administrative ease. In so doing, it cloaks the pointless indignity that Gail Atwater suffered with the mantle of reasonableness. I respectfully dissent.

NOTES AND QUESTIONS

1. *Atwater's "pointless indignity."* If Atwater's arrest was not justified by any government interest, why was it constitutional? Whose interests is the Court serving?

2. *Just a seatbelt violation.* Clearly, the arrest in *Atwater* was for a very minor crime as measured by the penalty. So? Atwater was driving a pickup truck with children ages three and five in the front seat unbelted. On a previous occasion, the same officer stopped her and found her three-year-old in an unsafe position in the vehicle, something Atwater had acknowledged at the time. *Atwater*, 532 U.S. at 324. You might argue that an officer could reasonably believe that she was endangering her kids and would continue to do so unless she was arrested. Should that be enough to justify Atwater's arrest? Under what rule or logic? What could the officer have done instead?

3. *Assessing arrests.* To the Court, limiting arrests might prevent the "pointless indignity and confinement" of some needless arrests, but only at the cost of increased litigation, uncertainty, and underenforcement of criminal offenses. Given that it finds "pointless" arrests should not be limited, perhaps it is no surprise that it does not consider the costs and benefits of "pointful" arrests for jailable offenses at all. Is it so obvious that the benefits of most arrests, even for serious crimes, outweigh the costs? If the police issue a summons, most people will show up and the

others could be found, if they are worth finding. Couldn't we equally easily eliminate uncertainty and litigation by eliminating all arrests? And might we still be able to enforce criminal laws without them?

4. *What people are arrested for.* The Court suggested that there is no evidence of an *Atwater* problem. That depends what you think the problem is. Most arrests are not driven by petty revenge, and they are for offenses with penalties greater than small fines. But more than 10 million people are arrested each year in this country. In the most recent year for which data are available, about 5 percent of them were charged with violent crimes. Arrests for gambling, liquor law violations, drunkenness, disorderly conduct, vagrancy, and curfew violations are way down in recent years, yet nearly 1 million people were arrested for those offenses. More than half a million people were taken into custody for simple marijuana possession. Driving while intoxicated accounted for another million arrests. See Fed. Bureau of Investigation, Crime in the United States 2018: Persons Arrested; *id.* at Table 29. What is the difference between all of those arrests and the one in *Atwater*? How do we know if all of those arrests are necessary? And necessary to do what?

5. *Incentives for minor offense arrests?* Was Justice Souter correct in his intuition that police lack incentive to arrest for minor criminal offenses? Consider that an arrest allows for a search incident to arrest of the individual, their "grabbable area," and possibly their car if they are a "recent occupant." Those searches incident to arrest are unavailable to an officer who issues a ticket and lets the suspect go on his way. See Knowles v. Iowa, 525 U.S. 113 (1998). Arrests also stop conduct quickly and certainly. Tickets do not.

6. *Effect of nonconstitutional arrest limits?* In *Atwater*, Justice Souter suggested that state statutory limits on police arrest authority are preferable to a constitutional rule. In *Virginia v. Moore*, 553 U.S. 164 (2008), decided seven years after *Atwater*, the Supreme Court held that violating state statutory limits on arrests does not, in itself, make the arrest unreasonable for federal Fourth Amendment purposes. As in *Atwater*, for an arrest to be constitutionally reasonable, *Moore* reasoned that police only need probable cause to believe that the arrestee committed an offense in their presence. "A State is free to prefer one search-and-seizure policy among the range of constitutionally permissible options, but its choice of a more restrictive option does not render the less restrictive ones unreasonable, and hence unconstitutional." *Id.* at 174. *Moore* is further discussed below.

7. *Drug arrests.* In 2018, drug offenses accounted for more than 15 percent of all arrests. See *id.* A recent study looked at several years of data and found that nearly three-quarters of state and local drug arrests were for marijuana offenses, often for very small amounts of the drug. See Joseph E. Kennedy et al., *Sharks and Minnows in the War on Drugs: A Study of Quantity, Race and Drug Type in Drug Arrests,* 52 U.C. Davis L. Rev. 729, 743–744 (2018). Even when officers arrested people suspected of possessing hard drugs, the arrestees were hardly kingpins: 45 percent of crack cocaine arrests, 44 percent of heroin arrests, 44 percent of methamphetamine and amphetamine arrests, and 38 percent of powder cocaine arrests were for possessing or selling *a quarter gram of drugs or less*—less than what bakers call a pinch. Nearly two-thirds of hard-drug arrests were for a gram or less, which means less than a quarter of a teaspoon. What do those numbers tell you? Should constitutional law limit such arrests? How could it? Are there other ways we can avoid those arrests either by restricting them by law or by discouraging officers from carrying them out?

8. *Decriminalization and arrest authority.* In several states, marijuana possession has been legalized or decriminalized (e.g., deemed an "infraction"). If possession is legal, police cannot make an arrest (although they can still make an arrest for a related crime, such as smoking the drug in public). If possession is decriminalized, the law favors or requires enforcement by tickets or summons rather than arrests. Yet in some jurisdictions that have decriminalized possession, police continue to make arrests for possessing small amounts of marijuana. Citing *Atwater* and *Moore*, reviewing courts have condoned such arrests (and searches incident to arrest on which they are based). See Wayne A. Logan, *After the Cheering Stopped: Decriminalization and Legalism's Limits*, 24 Cornell J. L. & Pub. Policy 319 (2014). Why might arrest practices be so unyielding?

9. *Pretextual arrests. Atwater* indicates that probable cause is not only a necessary condition for arrests, it is a sufficient one. According to *Whren v. United States*, 517 U.S. 806 (1996), decided a few years before *Atwater,* that is true whatever the officer's actual reason for making an arrest. "Subjective intentions play no role in ordinary, probable-cause Fourth Amendment analysis." *Id.* at 813. (*Whren* is excerpted and discussed further in Chapter 6.) Unless an officer violates the Equal Protection Clause, which forbids an officer from intentionally discriminating in making arrests, or the First Amendment, which bars using arrests to retaliate against individuals for exercising their First Amendment rights, *Whren* and *Atwater* allow police to use arrests to solve almost any problem, from rowdy behavior that annoys neighbors to mouthing off that annoys only an officer.

10. *"Exorbitant codes."* In *Whren v. United States,* 517 U.S. 806 (1996), the petitioners, who had been stopped by police for a variety of very minor traffic offenses, argued that the "multitude of applicable traffic and equipment regulations is so large and so difficult to obey perfectly that virtually everyone is guilty of violation, permitting the police to single out almost whomever they wish for a stop." *Id.* at 818. Writing for a unanimous Court, Justice Scalia rejected the argument, stating:

> [W]e are aware of no principle that would allow us to decide at what point a code of law becomes so expansive and so commonly violated that infraction itself can no longer be the ordinary measure of the lawfulness of enforcement. And even if we could identify such exorbitant codes, we do not know by what standard (or what right) we would decide, as petitioners would have us do, which particular provisions are sufficiently important to merit enforcement. For the run-of-the-mine case, which this surely is, we think there is no realistic alternative to the traditional common-law rule that probable cause justifies a search and seizure.

Id. at 818-819.

Arrests and COVID-19

The COVID-19 pandemic that hit the United States in early 2020 had many implications for law enforcement. Here are some of the ways it affected arrests.

New reasons to arrest

Throughout the country, businesses shuttered and people sheltered in place in response to state and local emergency orders designed to prevent the spread of

COVID-19. Under the law of most states, violating such emergency orders constitutes a crime. Although officers first used persuasion and citations to encourage compliance, they sometimes arrested people for engaging in ordinary activities such as walking on the street, staying on a playground, and sitting on a beach. COVID-19 also inspired arrests for new versions of old crimes. During his arrest for an unrelated offense, one Jersey City resident allegedly claimed he was infected with coronavirus, coughed on police officers, and said, "If I'm going to die, you're going to die." He was charged with two counts of second-degree terroristic threats during an emergency, two counts of aggravated assault on a police officer, two counts of throwing bodily fluid at an officer, criminal mischief, and harassment. Press Release, Gurbir S. Grewal, Attorney General of the State of New Jersey, and Colonel Patrick Callahan, Superintendent of the New Jersey State Police, AG Grewal and Colonel Callahan Issue Daily COVID-19 Enforcement Update (Apr. 16, 2020).

New reasons not to arrest

Arrests put officers in close contact with suspects. As one reserve officer put it, "During my time on patrol, I put my hands into strangers' pockets during searches; ran my fingers inside waistbands, bra bands and shoes; put handcuffs onto wrists and held those I was arresting by the arm as I escorted them to the patrol car. People coughed, sneezed, vomited and bled on me. Sometimes, they shoved me or spat at me." Rosa Brooks, *Police Officers Nationwide Need to Consider Going Hands-Off During This Crisis*, Wash. Post (Apr. 24, 2020). During the booking process and once jailed, suspects invariably share close space with police staff and other arrestees. To mitigate risks for both law enforcement and suspects, police in cities across the country decided to issue citations for misdemeanors for which they would usually have conducted arrests. See, e.g., Tyler J. Davis, *"Prisons and Jails Are Literally Petri Dishes": Inmates Released, Arrests Relaxed Across Iowa Amid Fears of Coronavirus*, Des Moines Register (Mar. 23, 2020); Liz Kellar, *Cite and Release, Not Jail, for Some over COVID-19 Concerns*, Union (Nevada Cty., Calif.) (Mar. 18, 2020); Nichole Manna, *Fort Worth Police Will Give Citations for Low-Level Crimes Amid Coronavirus Outbreak*, Fort Worth Star-Telegram (Mar. 17, 2020). In some cities, police departments avoided arrests even for felonies. In Philadelphia, for example, the department stopped taking into immediate custody those caught committing motor vehicle thefts and burglaries, among other crimes. See Memorandum from Danielle M. Outlaw, Philadelphia Police Commissioner, to Philadelphia Police Department (Mar. 17, 2020).

Fewer offenses

Even where law enforcement practices remained stable during the COVID-19 pandemic, crime did not. Keeping people off the streets reduced crime opportunities, and most crime rates declined across the country. Arrests fell with crime rates. Crimes such as domestic violence, which often happen behind closed doors, did not see this effect, however. See Kenny Jacoby et al., *Crime Rates Plummet Amid the Coronavirus Pandemic, But Not Everyone Is Safer in Their Home*, USA Today (Apr. 4, 2020).

Fewer officers

Many stayed home during the peak of the pandemic. But the police never stop, and officers went to work, exposing themselves to heightened risk of infection both from other officers and from members of the public. At one point during the spring of 2020, nearly one in five Detroit police officers were quarantined because of exposure to coronavirus, and dozens (including the chief) were infected. Joe Guillen & Gina Kaufman, *How the Coronavirus Spread Through the Detroit Police Department*, Detroit Free Press (Mar. 28, 2020). In the NYPD, nearly one in five officers were out sick, thousands of officers tested positive for COVID-19, and some died. See Ben Chapman, *New York Police Fight Coronavirus in Department as 1 in 5 Go Out Sick*, Wall St. J. (Apr. 8, 2020). Other cities were hit nearly as hard. In many places, fewer officers meant fewer arrests.

Changes in the use of force

When a suspect resists arrest, officers typically use their hands or sometimes a baton to control him, but those techniques require close physical contact. Police can gain control of a suspect using methods that require less contact, such as conducted energy devices (CEDs), which are extremely painful and sometimes injurious, and guns, which are often fatal. A less harmful alternative to grappling with a suspect or shooting him (with a CED or gun) is pepper spray, also known as oleoresin capsicum (OC) spray, which is commonly used at a few feet away. Pepper spray does not usually cause lasting harm, and when successful, it distracts suspects and reduces resistance, allowing an officer to move in and quickly gain control. But pepper spray causes swelling of mucus membranes and a severe burning sensation in the eyes, skin, and respiratory tract. It triggers coughing, sneezing, and tearing, which could expose those present to coronavirus, if a suspect or others affected are infected. If officers avoid pepper spray for this reason, they might use other more injurious force or be injured themselves. If officers use chemical agents during the pandemic, they could cause more injury and harm through infection than usually are associated with that kind of force.[2]

As the COVID-19 crisis revealed, arrest practices change, sometimes on a dime, when circumstances warrant it. Maybe whether, when, and how police make arrests is more malleable than the Supreme Court's case law suggests.

D.   *Evaluating Arrests*

States or localities could ban arrests tomorrow or greatly restrict them. Should they? More generally, you might wonder, how should we evaluate arrests or any other coercive or intrusive police practice?

---

[2] During the protests following George Floyd's death in May 2020, for example, nearly 100 law enforcement agencies used tear gas against demonstrators. See K.K. Rebecca Lai et al., *Here Are the 99 U.S. Cities Where Protesters Were Tear-Gassed*, N.Y. Times (Jun. 17, 2020). In addition to the usual risks associated with these uses of force, tear gas might have worsened the spread of coronavirus among protesters. Police usually use tear gas to disperse crowds rather than facilitate arrests.

We often assume that if a long-standing practice is constitutional and law enforcement wants to do it, it should be allowed. However, constitutional reasoning is limited by text, precedent, history, and the need to make rules that apply everywhere. Moreover, constitutional law focuses on justice for the individual. Therefore, Supreme Court cases never provide a full account of the interests at stake in policing practices.

As Richard Bierschbach and Stephanos Bibas point out,

> We have a host of legal and conceptual tools for trading off liberty versus security for an individual arrest, or retribution versus rehabilitation for a particular defendant. At the other end of the spectrum, legislatures can make the bird's-eye, highest-level decisions to trade off funding for prisons against that for hospitals, schools, and roads. But legislatures cannot micromanage how others will implement their high-level policy choices. For the most part, legislatures pass overbroad criminal laws, delegating almost all of the implementation issues to police, prosecutors, and judges, who lack much guidance or coordination. And we have few doctrinal or regulatory tools to force such mid- and low-level actors to internalize the full social costs (and, in some cases, the net benefits) of their enforcement or sentencing approaches to drug crimes, high-crime neighborhoods, poor minority communities, and so forth. . . .
>
> What might it mean to apply such tools to the problem of criminal justice, to force our fragmented system to grapple with the overall costs it imposes? One could ask the same question of other well-known approaches to managing externalities and regulatory burdens and benefits, such as cost-benefit analysis. These tools cannot magically solve the problem of overpunishment, and we are not suggesting otherwise. But drawing on them can help frame the problem as requiring not only individual justice, but also systemic regulation. This, in turn, might at least encourage more productive thinking about how best to ration criminal justice as a resource and confront its full social and distributional consequences.

Richard A. Bierschbach & Stephanos Bibas, *Rationing Criminal Justice*, 116 Mich. L. Rev. 187, 190–191 (2017). Bierschbach and Bibas suggest that assessing harmful criminal justice practices requires multiple levels of analysis, both individual and societal. Chapter 1 argued that, among other benchmarks *good policing* must satisfy, it must be effective, worth its costs, harm efficient, and fair to individuals. Do these standards capture their concerns? If they come close, perhaps they suggest that at a minimum a coercive government practice, such as the standard use of arrests to detain criminal suspects, should

1. serve important public goals;
2. impose harms no greater than its benefits;
3. not unfairly burden individuals or groups; and
4. be reasonable in imposing harms in light of alternatives.

See Rachel A. Harmon, *Justifying Police Practices: The Example of Arrests*, in *The Cambridge Handbook of Policing in the United States* 164 (Tamara R. Lave & Eric K. Miller eds., 2019). Given what you know so far, how would you evaluate arrests by these criteria?

As for serving important public goals, according to the Court, "Arrest ensures that a suspect appears to answer charges and does not continue a crime, and it safeguards evidence and enables officers to conduct an in-custody investigation."

Virginia v. Moore, 553 U.S. 164, 173 (2008). In other words, arrests serve state interests by providing a reliable start for the criminal process, an effective way to stop problematic conduct, and a useful time to collect evidence from criminal suspects. Assuming that arrests effectively achieve these aims, satisfying the first test, the following discussion might provide you with more grist for analyzing the other three criteria.

Arrests to Prevent Crime

Although the Supreme Court has not highlighted the *deterrence* value of arrests, some departments conduct misdemeanor arrests for disorderly behavior usually ignored or dealt with through warnings and citations because the department believes that arrests prevent future crime. Such arrests are often carried out as part of a proactive strategy, such as zero-tolerance or broken-windows policing. Such arrests impose substantial aggregate harm and often generate racial disparities, so they might not be worth their costs, fair, and reasonable in light of alternatives, as the above criteria require. Even if they are, however, academic consensus increasingly indicates that they do not satisfy the first test: They do not serve their purported purpose.

Most studies on the matter suggest that more police officers mean less crime. See, e.g., Ming-Jen Lin, *More Police, Less Crime: Evidence from US State Data*, 29 Int'l Rev. L & Econ 73 (2009); Emily G. Owens, *COPS and Crime*, 91 J. Pub. Econ. 181 (2007). But how? Not primarily by arresting people for low-level crimes. See, e.g., Emily G. Owens, *COPS and Cuffs*, in *Lessons from the Economics of Crime: What Reduces Offending* 17 (Philip J. Cook et al. eds., 2013); Bernard E. Harcout & Jens Ludwig, *Broken Windows: New Evidence from New York City and a Five-City Social Experiment*, 73 U. Chi. L. Rev. 271 (2006). Instead, reviews of the research have repeatedly concluded that police stop crime by deterring would-be criminals with their presence, rather than by detaining them. In contrast to other more focused law enforcement strategies, widespread arrests do not appear to lower crime. See, e.g., Nat'l Acads. of Scis., Eng'g & Med., *Proactive Policing: Effects on Crime and Communities* 176 (David Weisburd & Malay K. Majmundar eds., 2018); Aaorn Chalfin & Justin McCrary, *Criminal Deterrence: A Review of the Literature*, 55 J. Econ. Lit 5, 23 (2017); Anthony A. Braga et al., *Can Policing Disorder Reduce Crime? A Systematic Review and Meta-Analysis*, 52 J. Research in Crime & Delinquency 567, 581 (2015).

---

1.   The Social Costs of Arrests

Arrests have many consequences:

> In the near term, arrests are often frightening and humiliating. Arrestees lose income during the arrest, and sometimes their jobs when they do not show up for work. They pay arrest fees, booking fees, and perhaps attorney's fees, if they hire a lawyer for their first appearance. If a suspect's car is towed because of an arrest during a traffic stop, he loses the value of the time it takes to find his car, travel to the impound lot, and secure the vehicle's release, as well as the impound fees. An arrest can affect child custody rights, it can trigger deportation, and it can

get a suspect kicked out of public housing. Over the long term, individuals with arrest records may have worse employment and financial prospects. And all of these consequences can occur even if the arrestee is never convicted of a crime.

As compared to simply charging someone with a crime and giving him a summons to appear in court, arrests may increase the chances that a suspect will be detained prior to trial. That in turn is linked to higher prison sentences, which compound the deprivation of liberty caused by the arrest itself. . . . [A]rrestees lose privacy. They are questioned about their home address, birth place, and medical and psychological conditions. They are likely to be photographed and fingerprinted, and to have their clothing and personal property taken. They will often be subjected to a strip search and a health screening when they enter jail, which can include X-rays for tuberculosis and blood tests for gonorrhea or AIDS. Their DNA may be taken and uploaded to the National DNA Index.

Even the initial decision to arrest carries a risk of potentially serious repercussions. . . . [E]very arrest involves a confrontation between a suspect and a police officer that can go badly awry. Once a police officer attempts an arrest, he is authorized to use force, sometimes deadly force, to enforce that decision. As a result, arrests always risk and sometimes lead to injury or death. That risk is likely to be far lower when an officer hands the suspect a citation and permits him to go on his way.

Rachel A. Harmon, *Why Arrest?*, 115 Mich. L. Rev. 307, 313–315 (2016). That list does not include secondary costs to families and communities. Note that many of the consequences of arrests have little to do with the police:

A number of actors outside the criminal justice system, such as immigration enforcement officials, public housing authorities, public benefits administrators, employers, licensing authorities, social service providers, and education officials, among others, routinely receive and review arrest information. . . .

In each of these contexts, it is the fact of an arrest itself—not only a subsequent conviction—that triggers a regulatory decision, such as deportation, eviction, loss of a professional license, or loss of custody.

Eisha Jain, *Arrests as Regulation*, 67 Stan. L. Rev. 809, 810–811 (2015). As Jain points out, arrests are not an especially good indicator that someone has a violent or unreliable character, but they are an easily available one. *Id.* at 815; see also Anna Roberts, *Arrests as Guilt*, 70 Ala. L. Rev. 987 (2019) (arguing that arrests often erroneously are treated as markers of guilt).

Arrest practices can also have invisible, unexpected consequences because established arrest practices lead individuals to take costly steps to avoid arrests. For example, some states use the mere possession of condoms as sufficient evidence to arrest and prosecute people for prostitution and related offenses. This practice discourages individuals at risk of arrest for those offenses—including sex workers, transgender people, and LGBTQ youth—from carrying or sharing condoms, endangering their sexual and reproductive health and undermining effective HIV prevention.

If I took a lot of condoms, they would arrest me. If I took few or only one, I would run out and not be able to protect myself. How many times have I had unprotected sex because I was afraid of carrying condoms? Many times.

Human Rights Watch, *Sex Workers at Risk: Condoms as Evidence of Prostitution in Four US Cities* 24 (2012). This practice is a particularly powerful disincentive for transgender women of color, who are at high risk of police profiling for prostitution offenses. See *id.* at 20, 23 ("To the police, all transgenders are prostitutes."). In this way, this police practice leads to hidden individual suffering, societal harm, and distributional unfairness.

2.   Incentives to Arrest

It is difficult to assess the full costs and benefits of arrests. Nevertheless, one might worry about whether arrests as a whole are beneficial if arrests are frequently carried out for reasons unrelated to core law enforcement interests such as taking custody of dangerous people, starting the adjudicative process, and stopping people from ongoing criminal or disruptive behavior. Presently, arrests take place for many other reasons. For example, officers often have *institutional* incentives to make an arrest: In many departments, arrests are used formally or informally as an indicator that an officer is doing his job and that the department is pursuing its mission. Arrests also give officers the power to do searches for evidence incident to the arrest, which allows them to find other crimes.

Departments also have what Elina Treyger labels *collateral* incentives to make arrests that serve law enforcement interests only indirectly:

> Under Secure Communities, fingerprints taken at arrest by any local law enforcement agency (LEA) are automatically screened against the Department of Homeland Security's (DHS) database of known and potential immigration violators. Federal and state DNA collection laws provide for the involuntary collection of DNA samples from some arrestees, which are screened against databases containing DNA samples from arrestees and convicts as well as forensic samples from unsolved crime scenes.
>
> . . . [A]n arrest by local LEAs anywhere in the country now carries with it the potential of promptly identifying and deporting immigration violators. And an arrest for a qualifying offense in most states now carries with it the potential to solve a cold case or deter a recidivist offender from future crimes for which DNA might be recovered. . . . The incentives set up by these screening regimes are "collateral" because (i) they hold out benefits that are largely uncorrelated with the suspect's probability of guilt for the crime of arrest, and (ii) the probability of reaping these benefits is largely independent of the suspect's guilt of, or prosecution for, the crime of arrest. To the extent law enforcers value the prospect of screening, the automatic availability of such makes arrests of some suspects more attractive than others, for reasons unconnected with their guilt, culpability, or the state's interest in pursuing charges for the crime of arrest.

Elina Treyger, *Collateral Incentives to Arrest*, 63 Kan. L. Rev. 557, 558–559 (2015).

The Court in *Virginia v. Moore*, 553 U.S. 164 (2008), suggested that collecting evidence is a legitimate reason to conduct an arrest. Current law permits officers a full search incident to arrest of the person and the immediately grabbable area, a protective sweep of the house or car where the person is arrested, and sometimes an inventory search of the arrestee's car or belongings. The government may often obtain fingerprints and DNA, and it may photograph scars, tattoos, and other (sometimes) incriminating physical characteristics. The officer may ask ordinary booking questions and, with *Miranda* warnings, may conduct more extensive custodial interrogations. Because these activities are largely unavailable (without a warrant) if the officer issues a citation instead of making an arrest, they might give officers additional reasons to make arrests. Some commentators view collecting evidence as a legitimate consequence of arrests, but not a legitimate reason to conduct them. Do you agree? If so, what could be done to prevent that?

3. Arrests and Race

Simply put, the costs of arrests are not fairly distributed. Black people are arrested at more than twice the rate of white people. For minor crimes for which officers exercise considerable discretion, such as marijuana possession and open-container violations, the racial disparities among arrestees are even higher. As the National Academy of Sciences summarizes the data,

> In the early 1970s, when drug arrest rates were low, blacks were about twice as likely as whites to be arrested for drug crimes. The great growth in drug arrests through the 1980s had a large and disproportionate effect on African Americans. By 1989, arrest rates for blacks had climbed to 1,460 per 100,000, compared with 365 for whites. Throughout the 1990s, drug arrest rates remained at historically high levels. It might be hypothesized that blacks may be arrested at higher rates for drug crimes because they use drugs at higher rates, but the best available evidence refutes that hypothesis. . . .
>
> In recent years, drug-related arrest rates for blacks have been three to four times higher than those for whites. In the late 1980s, the rates were six times higher for blacks than for whites. The recent relative decrease in racial disparity in drug arrests did not result from reduced police emphasis on black sellers but from increases in total drug arrests and greater emphasis on crimes related to marijuana. Marijuana arrestees are preponderantly white and are much less likely than heroin and cocaine arrestees to wind up in prison. Absolute numbers of blacks arrested for trafficking in cocaine and heroin have not fallen significantly; they simply make up a smaller percentage of overall arrest numbers that are rising.

Nat'l Research Council of the Nat'l Academies, *The Growth of Incarceration in the United States: Exploring Causes and Consequences* 50, 60 (Jeremy Travis et al. eds., 2014). The rates look even worse when non-Hispanic whites are separated from Hispanic whites, who have a higher rate of arrest. Racial disparities are also greater for juveniles than for adults. See Ojmarrh Mitchell & Michael Caudy, *Examining Racial Disparities in Drug Arrests*, 32 Just. Q. 288 (2015). In recent years, misdemeanor arrests in many jurisdictions have dropped significantly, but racial disparities remain. See, e.g., Meredith Patten et al., *Trends in Misdemeanor Arrests in New York, 1980 to 2017* 14 (2018).

Although the causes of racial disparities in arrests are hotly disputed, most experts believe that racial disparities cannot be explained by differences in offending. Whatever the causes of disparities today, you should note that arrest disparities have historically often been the product of intentional discrimination. Consider, for example, this account of policing in New Orleans:

> Beginning in the late 1920s, police officials launched dragnets in response to reports of black-on-white crime. . . . [T]his strategy . . . reached its apogee in 1943, with the late-night on-street murder of the shipyard worker John Sansone. No one

witnessed the shooting of Sansone, but a white nurse heard the gunshot, peered out a second-floor window, and saw "a man who appeared to be a colored man" near the fallen worker. The police superintendent "ordered the arrest of all Negroes found prowling the streets late at night." Although the police failed to apprehend Sansone's killer, they detained one thousand African American men, filed weapons charges against those carrying concealed dirks and revolvers, filed loitering or vagrancy charges against those without "legitimate occupations," and held those who failed "to carry with them their draft cards" for federal authorities. All at once the dragnets demonstrated the crime-fighting resolve of the police, calmed white fears of social disorder, and funneled African American men into police stations and penal facilities.

Jeffrey S. Adler, *Less Crime, More Punishment: Violence, Race, and Criminal Justice in Early Twentieth-Century America,* 102 J. Am. Hist. 34, 43 (2015). Might the law of arrests facilitate discrimination?

Not only are African Americans arrested more often, but those arrests may have greater consequences for them. For example, Devon Carbado and Patrick Rock argue that arrests lead to police violence, and more so for Black men than for others:

> First, in the context of executing an arrest, police officers almost always employ some form of force—handcuffing the person and forcing him into the back of a patrol car. This process can be more or less violent depending on how the officer manages it. Second, an officer may believe that exercising force in the context of an arrest will create a disincentive for the person being arrested to act out in any way en route to the police station. Third, the simple fact of arrest, or the way in which the officer executes it, could engender resistance on the part of the person being arrested. That, in turn, could escalate the officer's use of force. Finally, the fact that arrests of black men occur against the background of stereotypes of black men as violent and dangerous likely compounds each of the preceding dynamics.

Devon W. Carbado & Patrick Rock, *What Exposes African Americans to Police Violence?,* 51 Harv. C.R.-C.L. L. Rev. 159, 173–174 (2016).

Reformers and academics usually invoke force during arrest as a reason to restrict or punish the uses of *force* (although courts rarely endorse such arguments), but perhaps it is equally an argument against the *arrests.* Some research suggests that racial disparities in the use of force actually stem from disparities in arrests, indicating that minimizing arrests might be more consequential than targeting force directly. See Emily K. Weisburst, *Police Use of Force as an Extension of Arrests: Examining Disparities Across Civilian and Officer Race,* 109 AEA Papers & Proc. 2019 152 (2019).

Still, reducing arrests and reducing disparities in arrests are not the same thing. Cities have had a far easier time achieving the first than they had in achieving the second. See, e.g., Meredith Patten et al., *Trends in Misdemeanor Arrests in New York, 1980 to 2017* 14 (2018) (finding declines in the rates of misdemeanor arrests generally, but with little difference in the rates of arrests for non-Hispanic Blacks and Hispanics compared to non-Hispanic whites); *compare* Fed. Bureau of Investigation, Crime in the United States 2018: Persons Arrested at Table 32, *and id.* at Table 43A, *with* Fed. Bureau of Investigation, Crime in the United States 2009: Persons Arrested at Table 43 (revealing a 29 percent decrease in total reported arrests from 2009 to 2018 but little to no change in the rate of arrests between white and Black persons in the same time period).

4. Alternatives to Arrest: Citations and Diversion

Assessing arrests requires considering whether the government could achieve the same objectives in less intrusive ways. Experts largely focus on two alternatives to arrests: issuing a citation or summons and diverting a suspect to community services.

If you ever have received a traffic ticket, you know that suspects can be, and often are, charged and adjudicated without ever being arrested. A traffic ticket is a *citation* (sometimes called a *summons*) issued in lieu of an arrest for a minor offense. It orders you to appear in court to answer charges, sometimes with the option to admit guilt and pay a fine instead of showing up in court. In a sense, a citation demands self-arrest. If you fail to appear (or pay) as required, a court will issue a bench warrant for your arrest by an officer. History shows us that most people show up and most of the rest are easily found, although often we do not bother looking. The Constitution never requires an arrest, but citations are not always an option under state law.

According to the National Conference of State Legislatures, all states permit citations in lieu of arrest for at least some misdemeanor crimes or petty offenses, either by statute or by state rules of criminal procedure. Eight states also permit citations for some felonies, and seven do not specify the offense categories for which citations may be issued. See Nat'l Conference of State Legislatures, *Citation in Lieu of Arrest* (Mar. 18, 2019). In the laws permitting citations, more than half of states create a presumption that officers should issue citations rather than make arrests in some circumstances, but little opportunity usually exists to review or remedy an officer's decision to make an arrest instead. The other states give officers broad discretion to arrest or cite. Whatever their rules of *permission*, states overwhelmingly *prohibit* citations in lieu of arrest if any of the following factors is present:

- There are reasonable grounds to believe the person will not appear in court or the person has previously failed to appear.
- There are reasonable grounds to believe the person poses a danger to persons or property or that the offense will continue.
- The person has outstanding warrants.
- A legitimate investigation or prosecution would be jeopardized by release.
- The person requires physical or behavioral health care—for example, because he is intoxicated.

Id. In addition, although it is not mentioned by the National Conference of State Legislatures, many states forbid citations when a suspect does not sign the citation or does not have reliable identification. Given the wide circumstances in which citations are forbidden and the broad discretion most states give to officers, is it fair to say that state law favors arrest over citation? Should the law be more restrictive with respect to arrests? Who should determine whether an arrest is worth doing: Lawmakers? Departments? Officers? What criteria should they use?

IMPORTANT:
READ **NOTICE** ON REVERSE SIDE.

000 24813052 VIRGINIA UNIFORM SUMMONS

DEPARTMENT OF STATE POLICE

YOU ARE SUMMONED TO APPEAR IN THE (CITY OF / COUNTY OF)
Albemarle

☐ GENERAL DISTRICT COURT (TRAFFIC)
☐ GENERAL DISTRICT COURT (CRIMINAL)
☐ JUVENILE & DOMESTIC RELATIONS DISTRICT COURT

ADDRESS
501 East Jefferson St
Charlottesville, VA 22902

ON _____, 20 18 AT ___ ☐ A.M. ☐ P.M.
FOR VIOLATION OF ☐ STATE ☐ COUNTY ☐ CITY ☐ TOWN

LAW SECTION _____ DESCRIBE CHARGE:

COMMERCIAL MOTOR VEHICLE ☐ YES ☐ NO
HAZARDOUS MATERIALS ☐ YES ☐ NO
RESULTED IN FATALITY ☐ YES ☐ NO
HIGHWAY SAFETY CORRIDOR ☐ YES ☐ NO

I PROMISE TO APPEAR AT THE TIME AND PLACE SHOWN ABOVE. SIGNING THIS SUMMONS IS NOT AN ADMISSION OF GUILT. I CERTIFY THAT MY CURRENT MAILING ADDRESS IS AS SHOWN BELOW

SIGNATURE

YOU MUST APPEAR AT TRIAL (JUVENILES MUST APPEAR WITH PARENT/ LEGAL GUARDIAN).

☑ YOU MAY AVOID COMING TO COURT ONLY IF THIS BLOCK IS CHECKED AND ALL INSTRUCTIONS ON DEFENDANT'S COPY ARE FOLLOWED.

ONLY CALL 434 932 4004 IF MORE HELP IS NEEDED.

MAILING ADDRESS: ☑ SAME AS ABOVE AT RIGHT
☐ CHANGE FROM D.L.

WAIVER OF A TRIAL (PLEA OF GUILTY)

BY SIGNING BELOW, I CERTIFY THAT I HAVE READ THE NOTICE AND I AM ENTERING MY WRITTEN RATHER THAN PERSONAL APPEARANCE IN THE COURT CASE RESULTING FROM THE VIOLATION CHARGED ON THIS SUMMONS. I UNDERSTAND THAT I HAVE A RIGHT TO A TRIAL WHICH I AM GIVING UP. I ALSO UNDERSTAND THAT MY PLEA OF GUILTY WILL HAVE THE SAME FORCE AND EFFECT AS A FINDING OF GUILTY BY A JUDGE AND THAT A RECORD OF MY GUILTY PLEA TO AN OFFENSE PERTAINING TO THE OPERATION OF A MOTOR VEHICLE WILL BE SENT TO THE VIRGINIA DEPARTMENT OF MOTOR VEHICLES (OR TO THE LICENSING AUTHORITY WHICH ISSUED MY LICENSE). I FURTHER UNDERSTAND THAT IF ANY OF THE BLOCKS TO THE RIGHT LABELED "COMMERCIAL MOTOR VEHICLE", "HAZARDOUS MATERIALS", "RESULTED IN FATALITY", "HIGHWAY SAFETY CORRIDOR" OR "CDL HOLDER" ARE CHECKED "YES", MY PLEA IS AN ADMISSION THAT, AT THE TIME OF THE VIOLATION CHARGED, I WAS OPERATING A COMMERCIAL MOTOR VEHICLE, CARRYING HAZARDOUS MATERIALS, DRIVING IN A HIGHWAY SAFETY CORRIDOR, WAS A CDL HOLDER, AND/OR THE VIOLATION RESULTED IN A FATALITY, AS INDICATED BY THE "YES" CHECK MARKS. UNDERSTANDING ALL THIS, I PLEAD GUILTY TO THE VIOLATION CHARGED, WAIVE MY RIGHT TO A TRIAL, AND ENCLOSE THE FINE, COSTS AND FEES PRESCRIBED.

SIGNATURE

DATE

IF ACCUSED IS A JUVENILE

IF ACCUSED IS UNDER 18 YEARS OF AGE, THE ACCUSED'S PARENT OR LEGAL GUARDIAN MUST ALSO SIGN, IN PERSON AT THE COURT, OR IF THE FORM IS MAILED TO THE COURT, PARENT'S OR LEGAL GUARDIAN'S SIGNATURE MUST BE NOTARIZED.

SIGNATURE OF PARENT/GUARDIAN   DATE

SWORN AND SUBSCRIBED TO BEFORE ME THIS DATE.

☐ NOTARY PUBLIC ☐ CLERK ☐ MAGISTRATE   DATE

CITY/COUNTY   STATE

MY COMMISSION EXPIRES:

CASE NO.

NAME LAST FIRST MIDDLE

JURISDICTION OF OFFENSE DATE OF OFFENSE DAY OF WEEK TIME ☐ A.M. ☐ P.M.

002 ROUTE NUMBER/STREET

DIRECTION ACCIDENT ☐ YES ☐ NO WEATHER

LOCATION OF OFFENSE:

ARREST DATE ARREST LOCATION

OFFICER CODE/BADGE NO.
TPR PALMER 7938

P.O. BOX/STREET CITY/TOWN STATE ZIP

PRETRIAL WAIVER AND PREPAYMENT INSTRUCTIONS

1. CALCULATE THE AMOUNT OWED FROM PREPAYABLE OFFENSE INFORMATION SHEET IF GIVEN A COPY BY THE ARRESTING OFFICER, OTHERWISE:
   A. PROMPTLY CALL THE TELEPHONE NUMBER LISTED ABOVE.
   B. IF YOU HEAR A PRE-RECORDED MESSAGE, LISTEN TO THE ENTIRE MESSAGE, OTHERWISE, TELL THE PERSON ANSWERING THE TELEPHONE THAT YOU WISH TO WAIVE TRIAL AND "PREPAY" THE FINE, COSTS AND FEES. STATE THE EXACT CHARGE DESCRIPTION AND LAW SECTION NUMBER (IF ANY) WRITTEN ON THE SUMMONS. DISTRICT COURTS ACCEPT PERSONAL CHECKS AND CREDIT CARDS BUT, IF YOU WISH TO PAY BY CREDIT CARD, YOU SHOULD ASK THE COURT WHICH TYPE OF CREDIT CARD IT ACCEPTS.
   C. WRITE DOWN THE AMOUNT TO BE PAID AND ANY SPECIAL INSTRUCTIONS.
2. SIGN AND DATE THE WAIVER OF A TRIAL ON THIS SUMMONS. ALSO COMPLETE PROCEDURE "IF ACCUSED IS A JUVENILE" IF YOU ARE CHARGED WITH A MOTOR VEHICLE OFFENSE AND ARE UNDER AGE 18.
3. PROMPTLY MAIL OR DELIVER TO THE COURT THIS SUMMONS WITH PAYMENT ATTACHED. PAYMENT MUST BE RECEIVED BY THE COURT BEFORE THE TRIAL DATE. TIMELY DELIVERY BY MAIL IS AT THE SENDER'S RISK.

DEFENDANT'S COPY - PG. 2   VUS REV. 7-01-15

READ NOTICE ON REVERSE.

IF PREPAYMENT IS MADE, ATTACH PAYMENT HERE.

A Virginia traffic summons.

Note that although each citation is less costly than an arrest (at least initially), citations take a lot less officer time than an arrest, so officers could potentially reduce the costs of each encounter and make it up in volume, thereby imposing greater social cost overall. Sometimes, this risk is described as *net-widening*. Additional citations bring more people into the criminal justice system and risk subjecting more people to bench warrants for failure to appear. Those warrants in turn extend police discretion and permit discriminatory policing, a process Justice Sotomayor described passionately in her dissent in *Utah v. Strieff*, 136 S. Ct. 2056 (2016). See also Alexandra Natapoff, *Misdemeanor Decriminalization*, 68 Vand. L. Rev. 1055 (2015) (discussing the net-widening effects of making misdemeanor offenses nonjailable). How should we deal with the concern that citations intended to reduce the intrusiveness of policing could backfire? For discussion of the increasing reliance of police on readily accessible, expansive computer databases containing arrest warrants and other information used in investigations, see Wayne A. Logan, *Policing Police Access to Criminal Justice Data*, 104 Iowa L. Rev. 619 (2019).

Although citations provide an alternative to arrests as a means of bringing a criminal charge, they cannot replace arrests used to maintain order or stop disruptive behavior from continuing. Often, police officers can discourage disruptive conduct just by showing up. However, sometimes an officer's presence is not enough, especially when criminal conduct grows out of problems such as homelessness, mental illness, or drug or alcohol use. In some communities, police divert individuals to a drop-off center or call on social services providers, thereby avoiding an arrest, but these alternatives are not always available. See Robin Engel et al., *The Power to Arrest: Lessons from Research* 76–106 (2019).

Some communities are attempting more comprehensive diversion programs to limit arrests. In 2016, for example, the Albany (N.Y.) Police Department launched Law Enforcement Assisted Diversion (LEAD) expressly to prevent arrests for crimes related to drug and alcohol use and mental illness. The program allows officers to refer people to coordinated community-based services that focus on harm reduction. The goals of LEAD include improving public health, reducing the number of people entering the criminal justice system, reducing racial disparities in arrests, and strengthening the relationship between law enforcement and the broader community. Initial data suggest that the program is keeping at least some people out of jail.

If communities aggressively pursue alternatives to arrest, maybe permissive constitutional and statutory rules governing arrest matter less. On the other hand, if alternatives exist, perhaps permissive legal approaches are no longer justified, and communities would be far more likely to invest in generating cost-effective, harm-efficient alternatives to arrests, if courts and states limited the arrest power. Which should come first (if either should come at all)?

Your Turn: Avoiding Arrests

Citations and diversion are hardly the only ways to avoid arrests. Recall the Encounter Model from Chapter 1. It suggests that, simplified, we can imagine police–citizen encounters in four steps: [1] an officer identifies a problem that justifies intervention;

[2] the officer attempts to impose an initial solution; [3] the citizen reacts, sometimes negatively; and [4] the officer follows up, sometimes more coercively.

Arrests often happen at step two. They can also occur at step four, as officers sometimes use arrest to address perceived noncompliance. But arrests might be avoided at any step in the model. Take five minutes and brainstorm ways states and communities could (1) limit the problems to which officers respond; (2) encourage officers to use alternatives to arrest; (3) prevent (or reclassify) resistance and noncompliance; or (4) change how police react to perceived noncompliance.

Now imagine you are a consultant to Americans Against Arrests (AAA), a coalition of policymakers, community activists, and police officers who strongly support public safety goals, but nevertheless believe that many arrests are unnecessary and pose undue costs and risks to officers and the public. They have asked you to advise them on the following questions:

- Which strategies might be the easiest to achieve?
- Which might reduce arrests most substantially?
- Which might compromise public safety or order?
- Which are likely to require legal changes?
- Who should they work to persuade?
- What data might help?

5.   Reducing Arrests

Does reducing arrests make sense? If so, how should it be done? Some alternatives to arrests require state law reform. Some require local policy changes or resources investment. Still, police departments often change arrest practices themselves. In fact, police departments can dramatically increase or decrease arrests, simply by deciding to do so, without any new law. For example, when a department adopts a zero-tolerance strategy that emphasizes low-level arrests, arrests will go up. By contrast, when departments decide to restrict authority to arrest or stop using arrests as a measure of productivity, arrests go down.

In New York City, for example, the misdemeanor arrest rate rose 213 percent from 1980 to 2010, and then declined 39 percent from 2010 to 2017, largely as a result of police practices, even as nonviolent-crime reports consistently dropped through both periods. Meredith Patten et al., *Trends in Misdemeanor Arrests in New York 1980 to 2017*, at 17, 63 (2018). Similarly, Robin Engel et al. have described the Cincinnati Police Department's successful attempts to use proactive-policing strategies to reduce crime *and* arrests simultaneously after budget cuts reduced available jail space by more than one-third. See Robin S. Engel et al., *The Impact of Police on Criminal Justice Reform: Evidence from Cincinnati, Ohio*, 16 Criminology & Pub. Pol'y 375 (2017). Especially for low-level offenses for which arrests are discretionary, you might even say that policing, not criminal activity, produces arrests.

Moreover, departments decide not only *how many* people get arrested, but *who* those people are. Why? "[E]nforcement opportunities far exceed enforcement resources and departments have substantial discretion to selectively apply those resources." Nirej S. Sekhon, *Redistributive Policing*, 101 J. Crim. L. & Criminology 1171, 1212 (2011). That means that departmental decisions about where they deploy officers and what priorities officers pursue can lead to disparities in arrests. Problematically, those disparities are sometimes used to justify further targeting:

> Arrests play a contradictory and circular role in proactive policing. They are often held out both as proof of the need for crime control and as evidence of police enforcement's efficacy. This contradiction is apparent with narcotics enforcement, where a high minority-arrest rate is used to show that the minority-offense rate is high. . . . The self-reinforcing nature of arrest rates . . . likely entrenches the institutional arrangements that reproduce racial disparity.

Id. at 1194. Sekhon argues that the "law should regulate police departments' geographic deployment, enforcement priority, and tactical policies in order to minimize disparate impact on minority offenders." *Id.* at 1220. He would task prosecutors and courts with preventing racially disparate arrests. Is that realistic? There are many barriers to effective regulation by these actors. What about communities themselves? Right now, departmental decisions about geographic deployment, tactics, and enforcement priorities are subjected to little public scrutiny. Are there ways to change that so that communities could weigh in more on matters that affect the distributive consequences of policing?

Prosecutors also play a role in reducing arrests. When prosecutors prosecute prostitution charges based on little more than possession of condoms, as Human Rights Watch alleges they do in New York City, Washington, D.C., Los Angeles, and San Francisco, they encourage officers to stop, question, and detain individuals who are likely to possess condoms, such as gay youths and transgender people. See Human Rights Watch, *Sex Workers at Risk: Condoms as Evidence of Prostitution in Four US Cities* (2012).

By contrast, when prosecutors announce that they will decline prosecutions for trespassing, marijuana possession, or shoplifting, as Suffolk County District Attorney Rachael Rollins has, they signal to police officers not to make arrests for those offenses. Cf. Adam M. Gershowitz, *Prosecutorial Dismissals as Teachable Moments (and Databases) for the Police*, 86 Geo. Wash. L. Rev. 1525 (2018) (suggesting ways prosecutors could more effectively discourage unnecessary arrests).

E.   State Law Regulating Arrests and Its Consequences

As you have seen, federal constitutional law is permissive. So long as states require that arrests are based on probable cause to believe a person has committed a crime, federal law has little to say about police authority to make arrests. Might state constitutional law have more bite?

1.   State Constitutional Law

In some states, the answer is clearly yes. This case from New Mexico provides one example of a state constitutional constraint on arrests.

STATE v. RODARTE

125 P.3d 647 (N.M. Ct. App. 2005)

PICKARD, JUDGE. . . .

Background

The undisputed facts are as follows. On August 1, 2003, Hobbs police officer Antonio De La Fuente stopped the vehicle in which Defendant was a passenger for running a stop sign. As the officer approached the driver's side of the car, he saw Defendant attempt to place something under his seat, and he noted a wet spot on the passenger's side floorboard. When Officer De La Fuente asked Defendant what was under the seat, Defendant put both of his hands under the seat and appeared to attempt to push something further back under the seat.

Officer De La Fuente then ordered Defendant out of the vehicle and called for backup. When his backup arrived, Officer De La Fuente looked underneath the passenger's seat and found a partially empty bottle of beer. When the officer asked Defendant's age, Defendant replied that he was eighteen. Officer De La Fuente also noted that Defendant exhibited several indicia of intoxication, including blood-shot, watery eyes. Based on this information, the officer arrested Defendant on suspicion of being a minor in possession of alcohol and transported him to the Hobbs City Jail. Subsequently, Officer De La Fuente searched the backseat of the patrol car where Defendant had been sitting and found a white, powdery residue on the seat itself and a folded dollar bill containing a similar substance. The substance was later found to be cocaine.

Defendant was charged with possession of a controlled substance . . . , tampering with evidence . . . , and being a minor in possession of alcohol. . . . Defendant moved to suppress all the contraband. . . . The trial court denied Defendant's motion and found Defendant guilty of all three offenses. The only issue Defendant raises on appeal is whether his arrest was permissible under the New Mexico Constitution. . . .

Discussion . . .

Relying on *Atwater v. City of Lago Vista*, 532 U.S. 318 (2001), the State argues that probable cause that Defendant was a minor in possession of alcohol was all that was required to make an arrest. We disagree. Over the past two decades, our courts have interpreted Article II, Section 10 of the New Mexico Constitution to guarantee a "broad right" to be "free from unwarranted governmental intrusions." State v. Gutierrez, 863 P.2d 1052, 1065 (N.M. 1993). This interpretation has often provided significantly greater protections than those afforded under the Fourth Amendment.

The "ultimate question" in all cases invoking Article II, Section 10 is reasonableness. In determining reasonableness, our courts have "avoided bright-line, per se rules." State v. Paul T., 993 P.2d 74, 78 (N.M. 1999). . . .

The greater search and seizure protections afforded by Article II, Section 10 of the New Mexico Constitution and the disfavor that our courts have shown for bright-line categorical rules lead us to adopt the rule proposed by Justice O'Connor in *Atwater*. First, we find Justice O'Connor's rule to be the one most consistent with prior New Mexico cases interpreting Article II, Section 10. . . . We hold that, under Article II, Section 10, probable cause that a non-jailable offense has been committed does not automatically make arrest reasonable, and that for such arrests to be reasonable, there must be " 'specific and articulable facts which, taken together with rational inferences from those facts, reasonably warrant [the additional] intrusion' of a full custodial arrest." *Atwater*, 532 U.S. at 366 (O'Connor, J., dissenting).

We also find this standard to be appropriate because we agree with Justice O'Connor that when a non-jailable offense has been committed, the balancing of governmental and individual interests will generally weigh heavily in favor of the individual, such that it will often be unreasonable to make an arrest. In this case, there do not appear to have been any circumstances that made it necessary for the officer to arrest Defendant. There is no suggestion that Defendant acted in a violent or confrontational manner. He was not driving the vehicle, and he appears to have complied with all of the officer's requests. In these circumstances, a citation would likely have "serve[d] the State's . . . law enforcement interests every bit as effectively as an arrest." See *Atwater*, 532 U.S. at 365 (O'Connor, J., dissenting). Thus, under the standard we have adopted, Defendant's arrest was unreasonable because there were no circumstances justifying the officer's choice to arrest Defendant rather than issue a citation.

We also side with Justice O'Connor in believing that our interpretation of Article II, Section 10 will not create undue administrative difficulties or lead to underenforcement. . . . We believe that protecting those interests and preventing the official abuses of the misdemeanor arrest power detailed by Justice O'Connor justify imposing the simple requirement that officers be able to articulate why it is necessary to arrest a subject for a non-jailable offense.

We also note that it appears as though the majority of state courts that have addressed the question of whether *Atwater* should be followed as a matter of state constitutional law have decided that it should not. See, e.g., State v. Askerooth, 681 N.W.2d 353, 361–363 (Minn. 2004) (en banc); State v. Bauer, 36 P.3d 892 (Mont. 2001); State v. Bayard, 71 P.3d 498 (Nev. 2003) (per curiam); State v. Brown, 792 N.E.2d 175 (Ohio 2003). We do not deem it critical that the reasoning of some of these cases may have been supported by local statutes or rules. In addition, a case that considered these cases and declined to adopt their reasoning did so because, contrary to the situation in New Mexico, that jurisdiction's settled law was that the state constitutional provision was "co-extensive with the Fourth Amendment." State v. Mondaine, 178 S.W.3d 584, 589 (Mo. Ct. App. 2005). . . .

. . . [T]he State cites two New Mexico statutes that appear to allow warrantless arrests for non-jailable misdemeanors. . . . But . . . all arrests must be reasonable, and statutory authority does not automatically make an arrest reasonable. Because we have concluded that arrests for non-jailable offenses are unreasonable under Article II, Section 10 of the New Mexico Constitution in the absence of specific and articulable facts that warrant an arrest, we construe both statutes to apply to situations that meet that standard. . . .

In sum, we note that our holding today mandates only the following: when an individual has not committed an offense that our Legislature has deemed significant enough to warrant a loss of liberty, that individual should not be deprived of his or her liberty through arrest unless there is a legitimate reason for the deprivation.

NOTES AND QUESTIONS

1. *Responding to* Atwater. How does it seem that the *Atwater* decision affected the court in New Mexico? Why does the Court reject *Atwater*?

2. *Nevada's approach.* The following Nevada decision, cited in *Rodarte*, uses somewhat different reasoning to reach a similar conclusion:

> In Nevada, the Legislature has not forbidden warrantless arrests for minor traffic offenses. Nev. Rev. Stat. §484.795 requires officers to perform an arrest in certain situations and provides the officer with discretion to make an arrest or issue a citation in all other situations. The discretionary provision of Nev. Rev. Stat. §484.795 states that when a "person is halted by a peace officer for any violation of [NRS Chapter 484] and is not required to be taken before a magistrate, the person may, in the discretion of the peace officer, either be given a traffic citation, or be taken without unnecessary delay before the proper magistrate." . . .
>
> . . . Although the Legislature has given officers "discretion" in determining when to issue a citation or make an arrest for a traffic code violation, that discretion is not unfettered. Discretion "means power to act in an official capacity in a manner which appears to be *just and proper* under the circumstances." Black's Law Dictionary 419 (5th ed. 1979). . . . An officer abuses his or her discretion when the officer exercises discretion in an arbitrary or unreasonable manner. . . .
>
> We hold that an arrest made in violation of Nev. Rev. Stat. §484.795 violates a suspect's right to be free from unlawful searches and seizures under Nev. Const. art. I, §12, even though the arrest does not offend the Fourth Amendment. An officer violates Nev. Rev. Stat. §484.795 if the officer abuses his or her discretion in making a full custodial arrest instead of issuing a traffic citation. We adopt the test set forth by the Montana Supreme Court in State v. Bauer, 36 P.3d 892 (Mont. 2001), for determining the proper exercise of police discretion to arrest under Nev. Rev. Stat. §484.795. To make a valid arrest based on state constitutional grounds, "an officer's exercise of discretion must be reasonable." Reasonableness requires probable cause that a traffic offense has been committed and circumstances that require immediate arrest. Absent special circumstances requiring immediate arrest, individuals should not be made to endure the humiliation of arrest and detention when a citation will satisfy the state's interest. Such special circumstances are contained in the mandatory section of Nev. Rev. Stat. §484.795 or exist when an officer has probable cause to believe other criminal misconduct is afoot. This rule will help minimize arbitrary arrests based on race, religion, or other improper factors and will benefit law enforcement by limiting the high costs associated with arrests for minor traffic offenses.

State v. Bayard, 71 P.3d 498, 501–503 (Nev. 2003); see also State v. Harris, 916 So. 2d 284 (La. 2005) (finding arrest for littering to violate state constitution when "[t]here was no indication by the officer that the defendant was a threat to himself or anyone else").

3. *How are they different?* What circumstances might justify an arrest in New Mexico but not Nevada? Nevada but not New Mexico? How might these limits affect policing in these states? How could state legislatures respond to each of these court decisions?

4. *Reasonable reasons to arrest.* In *Bayard*, the Nevada court indicated that an arrest is reasonable if it comports with the circumstances that require arrests in Nev. Rev. Stat. §484.795, now Nev. Rev. Stat. §484A.730. That statute specifies that officers

must arrest if a suspect fails to provide satisfactory evidence of identity, if there are reasonable grounds to believe the person will fail to appear, or if the person is driving under the influence of alcohol or drugs. In effect, the *Bayard* Court upholds the constitutionality of that statute. Do you think state law should mandate arrests in those circumstances? If not, do you think such arrests should nevertheless be considered reasonable and therefore constitutional? How would you describe the role that courts and legislatures should play in determining when arrests should occur?

5. *Public understanding.* Do you think most New Mexicans and Nevadans know when officers may lawfully arrest them? Do you know the arrest law in your state? Why might that matter?

2. The Federal Consequences of State Limits on Arrests

As a matter of state statute, common law, or constitutional law, states are free to authorize remedies, such as evidentiary exclusion or damages, when an officer exceeds his lawful power to arrest. Might there also be federal constitutional consequences when local officers violate state law? The following Supreme Court case takes up this question in relation to Va. Cod Ann. §19.2-74, which prohibits arrests for many misdemeanors unless specific conditions exist. What should happen when an officer violates this law?

VIRGINIA v. MOORE
553 U.S. 164 (2008)

JUSTICE SCALIA delivered the opinion of the Court.

We consider whether a police officer violates the Fourth Amendment by making an arrest based on probable cause but prohibited by state law.

I

On February 20, 2003, two city of Portsmouth police officers stopped a car driven by David Lee Moore. They had heard over the police radio that a person known as "Chubs" was driving with a suspended license, and one of the officers knew Moore by that nickname. The officers determined that Moore's license was in fact suspended, and arrested him for the misdemeanor of driving on a suspended license, which is punishable under Virginia law by a year in jail and a $2,500 fine. The officers subsequently searched Moore and found that he was carrying 16 grams of crack cocaine and $516 in cash.

Under state law, the officers should have issued Moore a summons instead of arresting him. Driving on a suspended license, like some other misdemeanors, is not an arrestable offense except as to those who "fail or refuse to discontinue" the violation, and those whom the officer reasonably believes to be likely to disregard a summons, or likely to harm themselves or others. Va. Code Ann. §19.2-74. The intermediate appellate court found none of these circumstances applicable, and Virginia did not appeal that determination. . . .

Moore was charged with possessing cocaine with the intent to distribute it in violation of Virginia law. He filed a pretrial motion to suppress the evidence from the arrest search. Virginia law does not, as a general matter, require suppression of evidence obtained in violation of state law. Moore argued, however, that suppression was required by the Fourth Amendment. The trial court denied the motion, and after a bench trial found Moore guilty of the drug charge and sentenced him to a 5-year prison term, with one year and six months of the sentence suspended. The conviction was . . . finally reversed . . . by the Virginia Supreme Court. The Court reasoned that since the arresting officers should have issued Moore a citation under state law, and the Fourth Amendment does not permit search incident to citation, the arrest search violated the Fourth Amendment. We granted certiorari.

II

The Fourth Amendment protects "against unreasonable searches and seizures" of (among other things) the person. In determining whether a search or seizure is unreasonable, we begin with history. We look to the statutes and common law of the founding era to determine the norms that the Fourth Amendment was meant to preserve.

We are aware of no historical indication that those who ratified the Fourth Amendment understood it as a redundant guarantee of whatever limits on search and seizure legislatures might have enacted. . . .

. . . No early case or commentary, to our knowledge, suggested the Amendment was intended to incorporate subsequently enacted statutes. None of the early Fourth Amendment cases that scholars have identified sought to base a constitutional claim on a violation of a state or federal statute concerning arrest. . . .

. . . [A]s Moore adduces neither case law nor commentaries to support his view that the Fourth Amendment was intended to incorporate statutes, this is "not a case in which the claimant can point to 'a clear answer [that] existed in 1791 and has been generally adhered to by the traditions of our society ever since.'" Atwater v. Lago Vista, 532 U.S. 318, 345 (2001).

III

A

When history has not provided a conclusive answer, we have analyzed a search or seizure in light of traditional standards of reasonableness "by assessing, on the one hand, the degree to which it intrudes upon an individual's privacy and, on the other, the degree to which it is needed for the promotion of legitimate governmental interests." Wyoming v. Houghton, 526 U.S. 295, 300 (1999). That methodology provides no support for Moore's Fourth Amendment claim. In a long line of cases, we have said that when an officer has probable cause to believe a person committed even a minor crime in his presence, the balancing of private and public interests is not in doubt. The arrest is constitutionally reasonable.

Our decisions counsel against changing this calculus when a State chooses to protect privacy beyond the level that the Fourth Amendment requires. . . .

In *California v. Greenwood*, 486 U.S. 35 (1988), we held that search of an individual's garbage forbidden by California's Constitution was not forbidden by the Fourth Amendment. "[W]hether or not a search is reasonable within the meaning of the Fourth Amendment," we said, has never "depend[ed] on the law of the particular State in which the search occurs." *Id.* at 43. While "[i]ndividual States may surely construe their own constitutions as imposing more stringent constraints on police conduct than does the Federal Constitution," *id.*, state law did not alter the content of the Fourth Amendment.

We have applied the same principle in the seizure context. Whren v. United States, 517 U.S. 806 (1996), held that police officers had acted reasonably in stopping a car, even though their action violated regulations limiting the authority of plainclothes officers in unmarked vehicles. We thought it obvious that the Fourth Amendment's meaning did not change with local law enforcement practices—even practices set by rule. While those practices "vary from place to place and from time to time," Fourth Amendment protections are not "so variable" and cannot "be made to turn upon such trivialities." *Id.* at 815. . . .

B

We are convinced that the approach of our prior cases is correct, because an arrest based on probable cause serves interests that have long been seen as sufficient to justify the seizure. Arrest ensures that a suspect appears to answer charges and does not continue a crime, and it safeguards evidence and enables officers to conduct an in-custody investigation.

Moore argues that a State has no interest in arrest when it has a policy against arresting for certain crimes. That is not so, because arrest will still ensure a suspect's appearance at trial, prevent him from continuing his offense, and enable officers to investigate the incident more thoroughly. State arrest restrictions are more accurately characterized as showing that the State values its interests in forgoing arrests more highly than its interests in making them, or as showing that the State places a higher premium on privacy than the Fourth Amendment requires. A State is free to prefer one search-and-seizure policy among the range of constitutionally permissible options, but its choice of a more restrictive option does not render the less restrictive ones unreasonable, and hence unconstitutional.

If we concluded otherwise, we would often frustrate rather than further state policy. Virginia chooses to protect individual privacy and dignity more than the Fourth Amendment requires, but it also chooses not to attach to violations of its arrest rules the potent remedies that federal courts have applied to Fourth Amendment violations. Virginia does not, for example, ordinarily exclude from criminal trials evidence obtained in violation of its statutes. Moore would allow Virginia to accord enhanced protection against arrest only on pain of accompanying that protection with federal remedies for Fourth Amendment violations, which often include the exclusionary rule. States unwilling to lose control over the remedy would have to abandon restrictions on arrest altogether. This is an odd consequence of a provision designed to protect against searches and seizures.

Even if we thought that state law changed the nature of the Commonwealth's interests for purposes of the Fourth Amendment, we would adhere to the probable-cause standard. In determining what is reasonable under the Fourth Amendment, we have given great weight to the "essential interest in readily administrable rules." *Atwater*, 532 U.S. at 347. . . .

Incorporating state-law arrest limitations into the Constitution would produce a constitutional regime no less vague and unpredictable than the one we rejected in *Atwater*. The constitutional standard would be only as easy to apply as the underlying state law, and state law can be complicated indeed. . . . *Atwater* differs from this case in only one significant respect: It considered (and rejected) federal constitutional remedies for *all* minor-misdemeanor arrests; Moore seeks them in only that *subset* of minor-misdemeanor arrests in which there is the least to be gained—that is, where the State has already acted to constrain officers' discretion and prevent abuse. Here we confront fewer horribles than in *Atwater*, and less of a need for redress.

Finally, linking Fourth Amendment protections to state law would cause them to "vary from place to place and from time to time," *Whren*, 517 U.S. at 815. . . .

We conclude that warrantless arrests for crimes committed in the presence of an arresting officer are reasonable under the Constitution, and that while States are free to regulate such arrests however they desire, state restrictions do not alter the Fourth Amendment's protections. . . .

[The opinion of Justice Ginsburg, concurring in the judgment, is omitted.]

NOTES AND QUESTIONS

1. *History in Fourth Amendment reasoning.* *Watson* was a rare case in which the Supreme Court has found the historical evidence supporting a police practice sufficiently clear to inform its reasoning. *Atwater* and *Moore* are more typical: It is common for the Court to turn to history and find it ambiguous. That hardly seems surprising given how different policing practices and criminal procedure looked at the founding. Without historical answers, the Court turns to other criteria to assess the constitutionality of police practices. What are those other criteria?

2. *Illegal but reasonable.* Under *Virginia v. Moore*, an arrest that violates state law is nevertheless reasonable as a matter of constitutional law. Why? Are you persuaded by Justice Scalia's arguments? For example, the Court argues that finding Moore's arrest unconstitutional would cause the Fourth Amendment to "vary from place to place." Doesn't Fourth Amendment law already vary because of the probable cause requirement? One state's penal code might criminalize an act that another state does not. State courts also vary in their standards for what constitutes probable cause. Is the variation Justice Scalia is concerned about here different?

3. *Federal solutions to state law problems.* As the Court notes, Virginia law does not require suppressing evidence produced by officers who make arrests in violation of its catch-and-release statute. Instead, state tort law permits someone arrested in violation of state law to sue the officer for civil damages, and departments may discipline officers for violating state law, although both remedies are rare. Still, by most accounts, Virginia officers follow the state's arrest law most of the time. So, might these remedies be enough? After all, if the state faced a rash of illegal arrests, the legislature could step in and establish an exclusionary remedy. The state already provides for evidentiary exclusion for violations of other criminal procedure statutes. See Va. Code Ann. §19.2-60.1 (prohibiting police departments from using a drone without a warrant except in limited circumstances and specifying that "[e]vidence obtained through utilization of an unmanned aircraft system in violation of this section is not admissible in any criminal or civil proceeding"). Is Justice Scalia right on this point?

4. *Arrest law through suppression law.* Unlike *Atwater*, which is a civil suit for damages, *Moore* and *Rodarte* are about whether the state may use evidence found incident to an arrest on a minor charge against the arrestee to bring a different, more serious criminal charge, typically a gun or drug charge. The exclusionary rule offers arrestees an *opportunity* to challenge the arrest and therefore the evidence; the more

serious charges give them *motivation* to challenge the officer's conduct. In this way, the law governing suppression helps drive the law of arrest, and in court the law of arrest is usually refined in the context of evidentiary exclusion. What effects could that have on the development of arrest law? One possibility is that courts may be less receptive to illegal-arrest claims: When an appellate court rules in favor of a criminal defendant who claims that evidence should have been suppressed, it reverses a criminal conviction for a reason unrelated to the defendant's guilt. When it rules in favor of a plaintiff after a lower court grants a motion to dismiss in a civil suit, it merely allows the case to move forward to trial. See Nancy Leong, *Making Rights*, 92 B.U.L. Rev. 405, 437 (2012). Remedies not only make rights meaningful but shape their content as well.

Chapter 8

Using Force

Recall from Chapter 1 Egon Bittner's argument that police exist "to impose or . . . coerce a provisional solution upon emergent problems without having to brook or defer to opposition of any kind." Egon Bittner, *Florence Nightingale in Pursuit of Willie Sutton: A Theory of the Police*, in *The Potential for Reform of Criminal Justice* 17, 18 (Herbert Jacob ed., 1974). Policing, in this view, is the way in which we solve problems and enforce state commands in real time, without which threats to individual safety, public order, and private property would continue. When police face noncompliance and resistance that threatens their lives or their ability to make an arrest or otherwise "solve" a problem, they sometimes use force in response, either to overcome the opposition or to protect their own welfare.

Police uses of force, however, threaten public safety even as they purport to enhance it. They injure and kill immediately, shattering lives. Over time, they undermine community trust, which in turn can make policing less effective. One study, for instance, found that a single high-profile beating of an unarmed Black man in Milwaukee dramatically reduced calls reporting crimes in Black neighborhoods in the year after the beating was reported. See Matthew Desmond, *Police Violence and Citizen Crime Reporting in the Black Community*, 81 Am. Soc. Rev. 857, 858 (2016). They are also unfairly distributed: For young men of color, police use of force is among the leading causes of death. See Frank Edwards et al., *Risk of Being Killed by Police Use of Force in the United States by Age, Race–Ethnicity, and Sex*, 116 Proc. Nat'l Acad. Sci. 16793 (2019).

How much force the law permits could well be the most important topic in policing and the law. Police officers routinely use low-level force against suspects to carry out stops, searches, and arrests, and they sometimes use high levels of force, including deadly force, to detain suspects or stop them in their tracks. Horrified by uses of force seen as unnecessary and discriminatory, some communities have taken to the streets (and the internet) to protest police-involved fatal shootings of people of color. Others believe that, with few exceptions, officers use force only when necessary and proper to facilitate policing and protect their own safety and that of others.

The law governing force cannot decide who is right; it decides only what is legal. That matters because, as Dylan Rodriguez, a professor and founding member of Critical Resistance, has said, "[I]t's not police brutality if the state sanctions the violence. At that point, we move from calling it police brutality to calling it policing." Critical Resistance, *Dylan Rodriguez, "It's Not Police Brutality,"* YouTube (Sept. 13, 2017). By deciding what is police brutality and what is simply policing, the law helps define both the role of the police and the relationships between police and their communities.

As they do with other coercive powers, local police officers get their authority to use force from state law, usually by statute. That authority is bounded by state and federal constitutional law. Police departments translate the legal limits on the use of force into guidance for officer conduct—and add further limits on the use of force—through training and departmental policies and procedures. This chapter starts with Fourth Amendment law because many states and police departments permit officers to use force up to the federal constitutional line; constitutional doctrine structures officers' understanding of force; and many of the legal remedies for the illegal use of force depend on the federal constitutional standard. The chapter then considers the ways state regulation of force and police department policies build on top of the constitutional "floor."

As you read this chapter, keep in mind that the law on the use of force plays a limited role in determining how much force the police use: It dictates only the legality of force during an encounter. This part of the law does not determine what community resources are devoted to the problems that lead to encounters; what police are tasked to do; what resources and skills they bring to the street; how they are supervised and guided; what we know about how much force they use; and whether they are held accountable when they violate the law. Yet those decisions are likely to be at least as critical in determining when, whether, and how much the police use force. If you are interested in the project of preventing force, you need to go much further. Still, the law on force is a good place to start.

A.   Fourth Amendment

1.   Deadly Force

Perhaps surprisingly, the Supreme Court has considered the constitutionality of police use of force only rarely. *Tennessee v. Garner*, 471 U.S. 1 (1985), is the first case in which the Court takes on the issue directly. As you read *Garner*, ask yourself this: According to the Court, what conditions must exist before an officer may use force against a suspect? What interests may police use force to protect? Assuming the officer is protecting one of those interests, what limits the amount of force he can use?

TENNESSEE v. GARNER

471 U.S. 1 (1985)

JUSTICE WHITE delivered the opinion of the Court.

This case requires us to determine the constitutionality of the use of deadly force to prevent the escape of an apparently unarmed suspected felon. We conclude that such force may not be used unless it is necessary to prevent the escape and the officer has probable cause to believe that the suspect poses a significant threat of death or serious physical injury to the officer or others.

I

At about 10:45 p.m. on October 3, 1974, Memphis Police Officers Elton Hymon and Leslie Wright were dispatched to answer a "prowler inside call." Upon arriving at the scene they saw a woman standing on her porch and gesturing toward the adjacent house. She told them she had heard glass breaking and that "they" or "someone" was breaking in next door. While Wright radioed the dispatcher to say that they were on the scene, Hymon went behind the house. He heard a door slam and saw someone run across the backyard. The fleeing suspect, who was appellee-respondent's decedent, Edward Garner, stopped at a 6-feet-high chain link fence at the edge of the yard. With the aid of a flashlight, Hymon was able to see Garner's face and hands. He saw no sign of a weapon, and, though not certain, was "reasonably sure" and "figured" that Garner was unarmed. He thought Garner was 17 or 18 years old and about 5'5" or 5'7" tall.[2] While Garner was crouched at the base of the fence, Hymon called out "police, halt" and took a few steps toward him. Garner then began to climb over the fence. Convinced that if Garner made it over the fence he would elude capture,[3] Hymon shot him. The bullet hit Garner in the back of the head. Garner was taken by ambulance to a hospital, where he died on the operating table. Ten dollars and a purse taken from the house were found on his body.

In using deadly force to prevent the escape, Hymon was acting under the authority of a Tennessee statute and pursuant to Police Department policy. The statute provides that "[i]f, after notice of the intention to arrest the defendant, he either flee or forcibly resist, the officer may use all the necessary means to effect the arrest."[5] The Department policy was slightly more restrictive than the statute, but still allowed the use of deadly force in cases of burglary. . . .

Garner's father . . . brought this action in the Federal District Court for the Western District of Tennessee, seeking damages under 42 U.S.C. §1983 for asserted violations of Garner's constitutional rights. . . .

II

Whenever an officer restrains the freedom of a person to walk away, he has seized that person. While it is not always clear just when minimal police interference becomes a seizure, there can be no question that apprehension by the use of deadly force is a seizure subject to the reasonableness requirement of the Fourth Amendment.

---

[2] In fact, Garner, an eighth-grader, was 15. He was 5' 4" tall and weighed somewhere around 100 or 110 pounds. App. to Pet. for Cert. A5.

[3] When asked at trial why he fired, Hymon stated:

"Well, first of all it was apparent to me from the little bit that I knew about the area at the time that he was going to get away because, number 1, I couldn't get to him. My partner then couldn't find where he was because, you know, he was late coming around. He didn't know where I was talking about. I couldn't get to him because of the fence here, I couldn't have jumped this fence and come up, consequently jumped this fence and caught him before he got away because he was already up on the fence, just one leap and he was already over the fence, and so there is no way that I could have caught him." App. 52.

He also stated that the area beyond the fence was dark, that he could not have gotten over the fence easily because he was carrying a lot of equipment and wearing heavy boots, and that Garner, being younger and more energetic, could have outrun him. *Id.* at 53–54.

[5] Although the statute does not say so explicitly, Tennessee law forbids the use of deadly force in the arrest of a misdemeanant. See Johnson v. State, 114 S.W.2d 819 (Tenn. 1938).

A

A police officer may arrest a person if he has probable cause to believe that person committed a crime. . . . To determine the constitutionality of a seizure "[w]e must balance the nature and quality of the intrusion on the individual's Fourth Amendment interests against the importance of the governmental interests alleged to justify the intrusion." United States v. Place, 462 U.S. 696, 703 (1983). . . . Because one of the factors is the extent of the intrusion, it is plain that reasonableness depends on not only when a seizure is made, but also how it is carried out. . . .

B

The same balancing process . . . demonstrates that, notwithstanding probable cause to seize a suspect, an officer may not always do so by killing him. The intrusiveness of a seizure by means of deadly force is unmatched. The suspect's fundamental interest in his own life need not be elaborated upon. The use of deadly force also frustrates the interest of the individual, and of society, in judicial determination of guilt and punishment. Against these interests are ranged governmental interests in effective law enforcement. It is argued that overall violence will be reduced by encouraging the peaceful submission of suspects who know that they may be shot if they flee. Effectiveness in making arrests requires the resort to deadly force, or at least the meaningful threat thereof. "Being able to arrest such individuals is a condition precedent to the state's entire system of law enforcement." Brief for Petitioners 14.

Without in any way disparaging the importance of these goals, we are not convinced that the use of deadly force is a sufficiently productive means of accomplishing them to justify the killing of nonviolent suspects. The use of deadly force is a self-defeating way of apprehending a suspect and so setting the criminal justice mechanism in motion. If successful, it guarantees that that mechanism will not be set in motion. And while the meaningful threat of deadly force might be thought to lead to the arrest of more live suspects by discouraging escape attempts, the presently available evidence does not support this thesis. The fact is that a majority of police departments in this country have forbidden the use of deadly force against nonviolent suspects. If those charged with the enforcement of the criminal law have abjured the use of deadly force in arresting nondangerous felons, there is a substantial basis for doubting that the use of such force is an essential attribute of the arrest power in all felony cases. . . .

The use of deadly force to prevent the escape of all felony suspects, whatever the circumstances, is constitutionally unreasonable. It is not better that all felony suspects die than that they escape. Where the suspect poses no immediate threat to the officer and no threat to others, the harm resulting from failing to apprehend him does not justify the use of deadly force to do so. It is no doubt unfortunate when a suspect who is in sight escapes, but the fact that the police arrive a little late or are a little slower afoot does not always justify killing the suspect. A police officer may not seize an unarmed, nondangerous suspect by shooting him dead. The Tennessee statute is unconstitutional insofar as it authorizes the use of deadly force against such fleeing suspects.

It is not, however, unconstitutional on its face. Where the officer has probable cause to believe that the suspect poses a threat of serious physical harm, either to the officer or to others, it is not constitutionally unreasonable to prevent escape by using deadly force. Thus, if the suspect threatens the officer with a weapon or there is probable cause to believe that he has committed a crime involving the infliction or threatened infliction of serious physical harm, deadly force may be used if necessary to prevent escape, and if, where feasible, some warning has been given. . . .

III

A

It is insisted that the Fourth Amendment must be construed in light of the common-law rule, which allowed the use of whatever force was necessary to effect the arrest of a fleeing felon, though not a misdemeanant. . . .

. . . Because of sweeping change in the legal and technological context, reliance on the common-law rule in this case would be a mistaken literalism that ignores the purposes of a historical inquiry.

B

It has been pointed out many times that the common-law rule is best understood in light of the fact that it arose at a time when virtually all felonies were punishable by death. . . . Courts have also justified the common-law rule by emphasizing the relative dangerousness of felons.

Neither of these justifications makes sense today. Almost all crimes formerly punishable by death no longer are or can be. And while in earlier times "the gulf between the felonies and the minor offences was broad and deep," 2 Frederick Pollock & F.W. Maitland, *The History of English Law* 467 n.3 (2d ed. 1909), today the distinction is minor and often arbitrary. Many crimes classified as misdemeanors, or nonexistent, at common law are now felonies. These changes have undermined the concept, which was questionable to begin with, that use of deadly force against a fleeing felon is merely a speedier execution of someone who has already forfeited his life. They have also made the assumption that a "felon" is more dangerous than a misdemeanant untenable. Indeed, numerous misdemeanors involve conduct more dangerous than many felonies.

There is an additional reason why the common-law rule cannot be directly translated to the present day. The common-law rule developed at a time when weapons were rudimentary. Deadly force could be inflicted almost solely in a hand-to-hand struggle during which, necessarily, the safety of the arresting officer was at risk. Handguns were not carried by police officers until the latter half of the last century. Only then did it become possible to use deadly force from a distance as a means of apprehension. As a practical matter, the use of deadly force under the standard articulation of the common-law rule has an altogether different meaning—and harsher consequences—now than in past centuries. . . .

C

In evaluating the reasonableness of police procedures under the Fourth Amendment, we have also looked to prevailing rules in individual jurisdictions. The rules in the States are varied. . . .

It cannot be said that there is a constant or overwhelming trend away from the common-law rule. . . . Nonetheless, the long-term movement has been away from the rule that deadly force may be used against any fleeing felon, and that remains the rule in less than half the States.

This trend is more evident and impressive when viewed in light of the policies adopted by the police departments themselves. Overwhelmingly, these are more restrictive than the common-law rule. . . . In light of the rules adopted by those who must actually administer them, the older and fading common-law view is a dubious indicium of the constitutionality of the Tennessee statute now before us.

D

Actual departmental policies are important for an additional reason. We would hesitate to declare a police practice of long standing "unreasonable" if doing so would severely hamper effective law enforcement. But the indications are to the contrary. There has been no suggestion that crime has worsened in any way in jurisdictions that have adopted, by legislation or departmental policy, rules similar to that announced today. . . .

Nor do we agree with petitioners and appellant that the rule we have adopted requires the police to make impossible, split-second evaluations of unknowable facts. We do not deny the practical difficulties of attempting to assess the suspect's dangerousness. However, similarly difficult judgments must be made by the police in equally uncertain circumstances. Nor is there any indication that in States that allow the use of deadly force only against dangerous suspects the standard has been difficult to apply or has led to a rash of litigation involving inappropriate second-guessing of police officers' split-second decisions. . . . Finally, as noted above, this claim must be viewed with suspicion in light of the similar self-imposed limitations of so many police departments.

IV. . .

The dissent argues that the shooting was justified by the fact that Officer Hymon had probable cause to believe that Garner had committed a nighttime burglary. While we agree that burglary is a serious crime, we cannot agree that it is so dangerous as automatically to justify the use of deadly force. The FBI classifies burglary as a "property" rather than a "violent" crime. Although the armed burglar would present a different situation, the fact that an unarmed suspect has broken into a dwelling at night does not automatically mean he is physically dangerous. This case demonstrates as much. In fact, the available statistics demonstrate that burglaries only rarely involve physical violence. During the 10-year period from 1973–1982, only 3.8% of all burglaries involved violent crime.

V

. . . We hold that the statute is invalid insofar as it purported to give Hymon the authority to act as he did. . . .

The judgment of the Court of Appeals is affirmed, and the case is remanded for further proceedings consistent with this opinion.

So ordered.

[The dissenting opinion of Justice O'Connor, with whom Chief Justice Burger and Justice Rehnquist joined, is omitted.]

NOTES AND QUESTIONS

1. *Getting to* Garner. Traditionally, if an officer used excessive force in conducting an arrest or dealing with a suspect, the victim could file a civil suit or criminal complaint for assault under state law, just as the victim of an illegal search could bring a trespass action. The officer could defend himself using common law and statutory defenses, such as self-defense or a public authority defense, and state law would determine the outcome. In 1936, the Supreme Court ruled unconstitutional a conviction resting solely on a confession obtained by torture. See Brown v. Mississippi, 297 U.S. 278 (1936). Still, constitutional challenges to police violence were rare until the Supreme Court made the federal civil action for deprivations of constitutional rights, 42 U.S.C. §1983, viable as a means to challenge the constitutionality of local government action. See Monell v. Dept. of Soc. Servs., 436 U.S. 658 (1978); Monroe v. Pape, 365 U.S. 167 (1961). Once this occurred, cases such as *Garner*, which develop federal constitutional law governing force, became almost inevitable. Now almost all constitutional challenges to police uses of force come up in damages actions under §1983. One of the consequences of this shift is that, although state remedies for excessive force still exist and are utilized by plaintiffs, federal civil actions are more common and federal constitutional law dominates the thinking about when officers can use force and how much they can use when they do so.

2. Garner*'s rule.* When does the Court say an officer may use deadly force, consistent with the Fourth Amendment, to prevent an escape?

3. *Applying the Encounter Model.* One way to help you see what is at stake in this case is to apply the model for police–citizen interactions outlined in Chapter 1. Recall that the model suggests that [1] police officers identify problems; [2] they impose provisional solutions on those problems, often with coercion or commands; [3] citizens react to those interventions; and [4] officers respond to perceived noncompliance, sometimes with further coercion or force. Applying this model to *Garner* would look something like this: [1] What problem did Officer Hymon identify? [2] What solution did he choose to solve it and with what legal authority? [3] How did Edward Garner react to the officer's provisional solution? [4] How did Officer Hymon respond to Garner's reaction, and what legal authority supported this response? When we examine the case using the Encounter Model, the legal question becomes this: Is this kind of response constitutionally permitted for this kind of reaction, under the circumstances created by this problem and the initial provisional solution imposed? What is the Court's answer?

4. *Defining deadly force.* Garner rules on the permissibility of *deadly* force. Courts and statutes usually define deadly force the way the Model Penal Code does, as force that creates a substantial risk of death or serious bodily harm, whether either one actually results. See Model Penal Code §3.11(2) (defining deadly force); Smith v. City of Helmet, 394 F.3d 689, 706 (9th Cir. 2005) (noting that police forces throughout the country and courts in several federal circuits include in their definitions of deadly force conduct that poses a "substantial risk of serious bodily injury"). To be clear, deadly force need not result in death.

5. *Danger in* Garner*: Part 1.* The Court rejects the use of deadly force against *nondangerous* or *nonviolent* suspects; that is, suspects who "pose[] no immediate threat to the officer and no threat to others." *Garner*, 471 U.S. at 11. In Part II.B of the opinion, the Court adopts what might be considered a nonintuitive description of what satisfies this test: A suspect is dangerous in the Court's view if either he "threatens the officer with a weapon *or* there is probable cause to believe that

has committed a crime involving the infliction or threatened infliction of serious physical harm." *Id.* (emphasis added). Officers and departments largely invoke the first alternative: They explain the use of deadly force in terms of an immediate threat to the officer. But what about the second possibility, that the suspect poses a threat to others because he is fleeing a violent crime? The *Garner* Court effectively asserts—without explanation—that suspects who commit, or even threaten, violence during their alleged crimes are so dangerous to the public that deadly force is permissible to detain them if they run away. Is this a reasonable assertion? Consider a batterer who kills his partner in a domestic violence incident or a teenager who pushes down a woman on the street and grabs her purse. Imagine these suspects run away when police try to arrest them. Are they really dangerous if they run? Is it constitutional to kill them? Should it be?

6. *Danger in* Garner*: Part 2.* What does it mean to pose a threat to an officer? In Seth W. Stoughton et al., *Evaluating Police Uses of Force* 33 (2020), the authors argue that a suspect poses an immediate threat to an officer when he demonstrates an *ability*, *opportunity*, and *intent* to cause harm. What if the officer can avoid the threat by taking cover? Or by allowing the suspect to run away? What if the suspect grabs a bystander but immediately releases him and continues to run away? What if a suspect is visibly armed but does not reach for his weapon? What if he shouts threats at an officer but is visibly unarmed? What does *Garner* suggest about these circumstances?

7. Garner *and suspect resistance.* Garner describes the rule for *fleeing* suspects. But lower courts apply *Garner's* rule to uses of deadly force against *resisting* suspects as well. Can you see why? Compare the interests at stake in the case of a suspect who turns to fight an officer attempting to arrest him and a suspect who flees. When do you think deadly force is permissible against a resisting suspect under *Garner*?

8. *The power of law. Garner* set a clear rule for when officers are permitted to shoot, and the possibility of civil liability gave departments an incentive to train and encourage officers to follow that rule. Subsequent studies showed that departments changed their policies to conform to *Garner* and that they shot fewer suspects after *Garner* was decided, including in Memphis. Perhaps even more notably, although the Court in *Garner* did not discuss race—both Garner and Hymon were Black—the benefits of *Garner* in Memphis accrued primarily to Black suspects, and in the period after the opinion, racial disparities in shootings—which were dramatic before *Garner*—were largely eliminated. See Jerry R. Sparger & David J. Giacopassi, *Memphis Revisited: A Reexamination of Police Shootings after the* Garner *Decision,* 9 Just. Q. 211, 215–221 (1992). Why might that have happened?

States also changed the availability of state law criminal defenses after *Garner*, away from the common law rule and toward *Garner's* rule, although nothing in *Garner* necessitates this outcome. As a result, officers who use force under the circumstances that *Garner* makes unconstitutional may also be subject to criminal prosecution in most state courts, in addition to the financial liability they can face if the victims pursue remedies available under federal law. See Chad Flanders & Joseph Welling, *Police Use of Deadly Force: State Statutes 30 Years After Garner,* 35 St. Louis U. Pub. L. Rev. 109, 110–112 (2015).

9. *Form and clarity.* The *Garner* rule is not perfectly perspicuous, but it is clearer and more definite than any decision the Court has made on the use of force before or since: State laws and policies that permit using deadly force against nondangerous fleeing suspects are unconstitutional. Could that clarity explain some of the case's impact?

2. Jumping the Gun

When is an officer's life *immediately* threatened by a suspect? In the original 1977 release of *Star Wars: A New Hope*, Greedo, a Rodian bounty hunter, finds Han Solo in Tatooine's Mos Eisley, a "wretched hive of scum and villainy." After Greedo forces Solo to a cantina table at blaster-point and shares that he has looked forward for quite some time to collecting the bounty Jabba the Hutt has placed on Solo's head, Solo shoots Greedo, killing him.

Apparently, *Star Wars* director George Lucas felt the scene was too morally ambiguous, making Solo look too much like a cold-blooded killer and too little like John Wayne: "[W]hen you're John Wayne, you don't shoot people [first]—you let them have the first shot," Lucas said in a 2015 interview. Hank Stuever, *George Lucas: To Feel the True Force of 'Star Wars,' He Had to Learn to Let It Go*, Wash. Post (Dec. 5, 2015). He reedited the scene for the 1997 rerelease of the movie. In the revised version, Greedo shoots first and—defying both physics and logic—somehow misses Solo at point-blank range. Han Solo then returns fire, killing Greedo.[1] Fans objected to the change, which toned down Solo's roguish badassery. Putting character objections aside, and ignoring the fact that it is hard to imagine Solo as a law enforcement officer, would you argue that Greedo threatened Solo sufficiently in the original version to justify Solo's use of force under the rule laid down in *Garner*? What details support your reasoning? Does your answer suggest that *Garner* permits force that seems cold-blooded, at least to some?

Police officers sometimes shoot even before Han Solo did in the original cut; they don't wait to see the gun. In one study of shootings by Los Angeles County Sheriff's deputies, for example, officers who shot suspects they *thought* were reaching for their waistbands were wrong nearly two-thirds of the time because the suspects turned out to be unarmed. See Merrick J. Bobb et al., Police Assessment Res. Ctr., *The Los Angeles County Sheriff's Department 30th Semiannual Report* 63 (2011). This kind of evidence suggests that officers are pulling the trigger before threats are manifesting themselves, and they are killing suspects as a result.

Often, this is what officers are trained to do. As every officer knows, if he waits until a gun is pointed at him and an armed suspect is intent on killing him, the officer usually will not be able to react quickly enough to defend himself. See J. Pete Blaire et al., *Reasonableness and Reaction Time*, 14 Police Q. 323, 336 (2011) ("The process of perceiving the suspect's movement, interpreting the action, deciding on a response, and executing the response for the officer generally [takes] longer than it [takes] the suspect to execute the action of shooting, even though the officer already ha[s] his gun aimed at the suspect."). Do not forget that the Los Angeles County study suggests that a third of the suspects whom deputies thought were reaching for their waistbands were, in fact, armed. Because "action beats reaction," *Action vs. Reaction: The Shoot-First Fallacy*, PoliceOne (Feb. 24, 2020), officers are taught to consider using deadly force against suspects who refuse to follow orders accordingly. To do otherwise is to risk

---

[1] Several other cuts of the film have been released since with further adjustments to the scene. In a DVD version released in 2004, the timeframe was compressed so Greedo fires first, but much closer to when Han fires. In 2011's Blu-ray release, Lucas again shaved down the interval between when Greedo first fires and when Han fires back. And in late 2019, Disney, which now owns the rights to the film, released a version made by Lucas (before he sold the rights) in which Han and Greedo fire at the same time. See Alex Horton, *The Han and Greedo Shooting Scene Changed Again (and Probably Not the Way You Wanted)*, Wash. Post (Nov. 13, 2019).

"deadly hesitation," something that police defenders claim results from overscrutinizing police conduct. See Doug Wyllie, A *Plague of Deadly Hesitation, De-Motivation, and De-Policing in America*, Police: Patrol (Aug. 17, 2018). George Lucas's character might be able to defy physics, but mortal police officers cannot.

Although *Garner* does not suggest that officers are allowed to shoot people who *might* be a risk, lower courts and juries are giving officers the benefit of the doubt, largely because the Supreme Court has encouraged them to do so. *Graham v. Connor*, 490 U.S. 386, 396 (1989), discussed more below, tells courts and juries to focus on whether a reasonable officer under the circumstances—in the heat of the moment and without the benefit of 20/20 hindsight—would have concluded that a threat existed. Should that change? The Supreme Court arguably faces a difficult public policy trade-off: Requiring an officer to wait until he sees a gun pointed at him before using deadly force could decrease the number of dead suspects at the price of more dead officers.

Nonetheless, some critics think that some rebalancing has to occur. Nearly a thousand people were shot and killed by the police in 2019, *Fatal Force 2019*, Wash. Post (June 25, 2020), and only 48 officers were killed by suspects, Fed. Bureau of Investigation, *2019 Law Enforcement Officers Killed and Assaulted: Officers Feloniously Killed*. Moreover, although the number of officers assaulted or killed in recent years has gone down substantially, the number of nonofficers killed has remained relatively stable. But what do those numbers really mean? According to the *Washington Post*'s data, the people killed by the police were overwhelmingly armed. Only 46 of the 992 victims were reported to be unarmed at the time they were killed (although the status of a couple of dozen more is unknown). Numbers aside, is this what constitutional law amounts to: calibrating the ratio of police to civilian deaths?

Critics of the police sometimes argue that officers accept the risk when they put on the uniform. Police proponents, meanwhile, sometimes argue that suspects accept the risk by not complying with the police. What are the implications of those arguments? If suspects are scared of officers, they might resist less often, but they might also be deterred from living freely and exercising their constitutional rights. If officers are too fearful to engage suspects, they might carry out fewer police shootings, but policing inadequately can impose social harm and cost lives, too.

The trade-off between officer lives and suspect lives is more complicated still because the people whom police kill are not randomly distributed throughout the population. They are disproportionately men of color. Whatever choices a society might make if it were fairly internalizing the costs of achieving public safety, concentrating those costs based on race is morally wrong and socially inefficient.

What is a civilized society to do? Like Fourth Amendment law, state self-defense law allocates risk between a potential attacker and a potential defender. Historically, however, self-defense law is more stringent about the necessity and immediacy of the threat than deadly force law is. That is, although self-defense law—like Fourth Amendment law—recognizes that "[d]etached reflection cannot be demanded in the presence of an uplifted knife," Brown v. United States, 256 U.S. 335, 343 (1921) (opinion of Holmes, J.), self-defense law—unlike Fourth Amendment law—requires the knife to be uplifted. Cf. Kisela v. Hughes, 138 S. Ct. 1148 (2018) (holding that an officer who shot a woman holding a knife at her side was entitled to qualified immunity). Perhaps there should be more consideration of whether police use of force should be subject to the same rule. See Rachel A. Harmon, *When Is Police Violence Justified?*, 102 Nw. U. L. Rev. 1119, 1123 (2008) (arguing that use-of-force doctrine should be refined using the conceptual structure of self-defense law).

Whatever the rule, the best way to reduce police use of force is not to restrict force in the moment. It is to prevent the moment when an officer faces a noncompliant suspect and perceives a threat. Recall the Encounter Model of police–citizen encounters in Chapter 1. It suggests that force occurs when [1] an officer identifies a problem; [2] the officer attempts to solve it with a command, stop, or arrest; [3] the citizen reacts; and [4] the officer perceives noncompliance and uses force to respond. Considering the steps in the model, make two lists:

1. The ways we can prevent deadly force by preventing the officer from engaging the subject.
2. The ways we can prevent deadly force by changing the encounter.

While you are at it, make a third list: the ways we can prevent death from resulting by mitigating what happens after the encounter has gone awry.

As you read the rest of the chapter, consider which of those strategies could be influenced by changing the constitutional law standard on the use of force.

Shootings and Fear

From the moment they enter basic training, officers are told that their most important job is to go home at the end of their shifts. They are also repeatedly hammered with the idea that every person they encounter constitutes a potential threat. To make the message more visceral, recruits are shown gruesome videos of officers being killed in the line of duty because they failed to identify a threat or hesitated to use force to counter that threat. And officers are trained to shoot, even before a threat is fully realized, because it is "better to be judged by twelve than carried by six." As Seth Stoughton has argued, "In most police shootings, officers don't shoot out of anger or frustration or hatred. They shoot because they are afraid. And they are afraid because they are constantly barraged with the message that they should be afraid, that their survival depends on it." Seth Stoughton, *How Police Training Contributes to Avoidable Deaths*, Atlantic (Dec. 12, 2014). If so, can different training still protect officers and yet reduce shootings? Stoughton thinks it might help to give officers a more realistic perspective on the threats they face because, in truth, policing is safer than it has ever been. *Id.* Is it too much to hope that officers can be trained to be vigilant, realistic, and use less force, all at the same time?

Reducing fear also means taking officer wellness seriously. Policing is incredibly stressful, and officers who suffer mentally and emotionally as a result of their work are more dangerous to the community. As one member of the President's Task Force on 21st Century Policing commented, "Hurt people can hurt people." President's Task Force on 21st Century Policing, *Final Report of the President's Task Force on 21st Century Policing* 61 (2015). Stressed officers are also dangerous to themselves: A record number of officers committed suicide in 2019, several times more than died at the hands of suspects. Protecting both officers and community members therefore means improving programs that support officer emotional and physical health and reduce stress on them and their families. That creates a further challenge for the law: Should states protect officers who seek help for mental health and substance abuse issues from professional consequences to encourage them to seek treatment? Or should states impose those consequences to protect the public from officers who might do more harm? The lives of both officers and those they encounter are at stake.

An unofficial sign posted in St. Paul, Minnesota, in 2017, in response to several police shootings.

3.   Reasonable Force

Lower courts took the *Garner* decision to establish a bright-line rule that deadly force could be used constitutionally only against fleeing dangerous felons. Four years later, in *Graham v. Connor*, 490 U.S. 386 (1989), the Court addressed police uses of force during seizures more broadly, including uses of nondeadly force and uses of force against suspects who do not flee. *Graham* involved a civil damages action brought under 42 U.S.C. §1983 for injuries by Dethorne Graham after police handcuffed and held him to investigate a convenience store robbery.

Here is what happened:

> On November 12, 1984, Graham, a diabetic, felt the onset of an insulin reaction. He asked a friend, William Berry, to drive him to a nearby convenience store so he could purchase some orange juice to counteract the reaction. Berry agreed, but when Graham entered the store, he saw a number of people ahead of him in the

checkout line. Concerned about the delay, he hurried out of the store and asked Berry to drive him to a friend's house instead.

Respondent Connor, an officer of the Charlotte, North Carolina, Police Department, saw Graham hastily enter and leave the store. The officer became suspicious that something was amiss and followed Berry's car. About one-half mile from the store, he made an investigative stop. Although Berry told Connor that Graham was simply suffering from a "sugar reaction," the officer ordered Berry and Graham to wait while he found out what, if anything, had happened at the convenience store. When Officer Connor returned to his patrol car to call for backup assistance, Graham got out of the car, ran around it twice, and finally sat down on the curb, where he passed out briefly.

In the ensuing confusion, a number of other Charlotte police officers arrived on the scene in response to Officer Connor's request for backup. One of the officers rolled Graham over on the sidewalk and cuffed his hands tightly behind his back, ignoring Berry's pleas to get him some sugar. Another officer said: "I've seen a lot of people with sugar diabetes that never acted like this. Ain't nothing wrong with the M.F. but drunk. Lock the S.B. up." Several officers then lifted Graham up from behind, carried him over to Berry's car, and placed him face down on its hood. Regaining consciousness, Graham asked the officers to check in his wallet for a diabetic decal that he carried. In response, one of the officers told him to "shut up" and shoved his face down against the hood of the car. Four officers grabbed Graham and threw him headfirst into the police car. A friend of Graham's brought some orange juice to the car, but the officers refused to let him have it. Finally, Officer Connor received a report that Graham had done nothing wrong at the convenience store, and the officers drove him home and released him.

At some point during his encounter with the police, Graham sustained a broken foot, cuts on his wrists, a bruised forehead, and an injured shoulder; he also claims to have developed a loud ringing in his right ear that continues to this day. He commenced this action under 42 U.S.C. §1983 against the individual officers involved in the incident, all of whom are respondents here, alleging that they had used excessive force in making the investigatory stop, in violation of "rights secured to him under the Fourteenth Amendment to the United States Constitution and 42 U.S.C. §1983."

Graham, 490 U.S. at 388–390.

Before *Graham,* most courts evaluated constitutional excessive force claims against public officials under the Fourteenth Amendment's Due Process Clause. The *Graham* Court, however, emphasized that the analysis instead should start with the specific constitutional right allegedly infringed by the challenged conduct: the Fourth Amendment.

Where, as here, the excessive force claim arises in the context of an arrest or investigatory stop of a free citizen, it is most properly characterized as one invoking the protections of the Fourth Amendment, which guarantees citizens the right "to be secure in their persons . . . against unreasonable . . . seizures" of the person. This much is clear from our decision in *Tennessee v. Garner.* . . . Though the complaint alleged violations of both the Fourth Amendment and the Due Process Clause, we analyzed the constitutionality of the challenged application of force solely by reference to the Fourth Amendment's prohibition against unreasonable seizures of the person, holding that the "reasonableness" of a particular seizure depends not only on *when* it is made, but also on *how* it is carried out. Today we make explicit what was implicit in *Garner*'s analysis, and hold that *all* claims that law enforcement officers have used excessive force—deadly or not—in the course of an arrest, investigatory stop, or other "seizure" of a free citizen should be analyzed under the Fourth Amendment and its "reasonableness" standard, rather than under a "substantive due process" approach. Because the Fourth Amendment provides an explicit textual source of constitutional protection against this sort of physically intrusive governmental conduct, that Amendment, not the more generalized notion of "substantive due process," must be the guide for analyzing these claims.

Determining whether the force used to effect a particular seizure is "reasonable" under the Fourth Amendment requires a careful balancing of "'the nature and quality of the intrusion on the individual's Fourth Amendment interests'" against the countervailing governmental interests at stake. Our Fourth Amendment jurisprudence has long recognized that the right to make an arrest or investigatory stop necessarily carries with it the right to use some degree of physical coercion or threat thereof to effect it. See Terry v. Ohio, 392 U.S. 1, 22–27 (1968). Because "[t]he test of reasonableness under the Fourth Amendment is not capable of precise definition or mechanical application," Bell v. Wolfish, 441 U.S. 520, 559 (1979), however, its proper application requires careful attention to the facts and circumstances of each particular case, including the severity of the crime at issue, whether the suspect poses an immediate threat to the safety of the officers or others, and whether he is actively resisting arrest or attempting to evade arrest by flight.

The "reasonableness" of a particular use of force must be judged from the perspective of a reasonable officer on the scene, rather than with the 20/20 vision of hindsight. The Fourth Amendment is not violated by an arrest based on probable cause, even though the wrong person is arrested, nor by the mistaken execution of a valid search warrant on the wrong premises. With respect to a claim of excessive force, the same standard of reasonableness at the moment applies: "Not every push or shove, even if it may later seem unnecessary in the peace of a judge's chambers," Johnson v. Glick, 481 F.2d 1028, 1033 (2d Cir. 1973), violates the Fourth Amendment. The calculus of reasonableness must embody allowance for the fact that police officers are often forced to make split-second judgments—in circumstances that are tense, uncertain, and rapidly evolving—about the amount of force that is necessary in a particular situation.

As in other Fourth Amendment contexts, however, the "reasonableness" inquiry in an excessive force case is an objective one: the question is whether the officers' actions are "objectively reasonable" in light of the facts and circumstances confronting them, without regard to their underlying intent or motivation. An officer's evil intentions will not make a Fourth Amendment violation out of an objectively reasonable use of force; nor will an officer's good intentions make an objectively unreasonable use of force constitutional.

Graham, 490 U.S. at 394–397.

NOTES AND QUESTIONS

1. *Graham's rule.* What precisely is the post-*Graham* rule about when officers may use force consistent with the Fourth Amendment? How much guidance does the decision give officers?

2. *Poor Graham.* What were the officers doing?

The conduct of the officers reads like a classically botched job, in which the officers lacked or ignored training on how to respond to a disabled person. They were investigating behavior that struck them as suspicious—Graham had walked into and then out of the convenience store in his search for something to stabilize his blood sugar—not any particular crime.

Brandon Garrett & Seth Stoughton, *A Tactical Fourth Amendment*, 103 Va. L. Rev. 211, 230–231 (2017). The officers did not have to make any immediate decisions. "[T]hey had ample opportunity to verify that he was diabetic and to treat him as he went in and out of consciousness." *Id.* at 231. Should all that have factored into the Court's analysis?

3. *Severity of the crime: Part 1.* The only instruction the Supreme Court gives lower courts and police officers about reasonableness is the factors it mentions: "the severity of the crime at issue, whether the suspect poses an immediate threat to the safety of the officers or others, and whether he is actively resisting arrest or attempting to evade arrest by flight." *Graham*, 490 U.S. at 396. How helpful are these factors? Imagine an officer is arresting a suspected serial killer who is following the officer's commands to the letter. Does *Graham* suggest the officer could use force based on the severity of the suspected crime? Why should officers ever use force against someone who is complying with their commands? Why isn't a threat to a person or the success of an arrest the *sine qua non* of constitutional uses of force?

4. *Severity of the crime: Part 2.* Now imagine a person pulled over for a seatbelt violation shows a gun and threatens to shoot the officer. If the officer kills the suspect, does it matter that the stop was for a seatbelt violation?

5. *Severity of the crime: Part 3.* Suppose an officer seeking to contain a volatile protest crowd decides to arrest one woman for jaywalking, and she resists by sitting on the ground and clamping her arms to her sides. Under *Graham*'s rule, may the officer wrestle with the woman, risking injury and pain, to forcibly handcuff her? Should he be allowed to do so? Should *any* arrest justify nondeadly[2] force to achieve it?

6. *Timing and the use of force.* Two of the four *Graham* factors—whether an "*immediate* threat to the safety of the officers" existed and whether someone was "*actively resisting*" when force was used—imply that timing is relevant to a court's use-of-force analysis. But *Graham*'s vague "totality of the circumstances" approach might ultimately give short shrift to timing by suggesting it is just one of many factors to be considered. If there is no *immediate* and *ongoing* threat to a government interest, why should force ever be permitted? Chris Rock has joked, "If the police have to come and get you, they're bringing an ass-kicking with them." Chris Rock Show, *FUNNY! – How Not to Get Your Ass Kicked by the Police – Chris Rock*, YouTube (Aug. 22, 2014). But that can't possibly be the constitutional rule. Some courts clearly recognize the importance of timing. See, e.g., Abraham v. Raso, 183 F.3d 279, 294 (3d Cir. 1999) ("A passing risk to a police officer is not an ongoing license to kill an otherwise unthreatening suspect."); Ellis v. Wynalda, 999 F.2d 243, 247 (7th Cir. 1993) ("When an officer faces a situation in which he could justifiably shoot, he

---

[2] Note that although courts and commentators often refer to *nondeadly* force, the term used throughout most of the chapter, police officers, police departments, and policing scholars often use the term *less lethal* force in recognition of the fact that even methods of force that do not usually cause death sometimes do so.

does not retain the right to shoot any time thereafter with impunity"). But it is hard to see that *Graham* helps courts reach this conclusion.

7. *Policies after* Graham. *Garner*'s clear rule led to changes in departmental policies, training, and practices prohibiting the use of deadly force against non-dangerous fleeing felons. How should police departments react to *Graham*? Some departments adopted one-sentence use-of-force policies after *Graham*, indicating that all uses of force should be "objectively reasonable in light of the facts and circumstances confronting the officer." See Brandon Garrett & Seth Stoughton, *A Tactical Fourth Amendment*, 103 Va. L. Rev. 211, 285–286 (2017) (describing the "real pull" *Graham* has on department policies). Other departments adopted detailed policies specifying the precise circumstances in which different levels of force are permissible.

8. Graham*'s aftermath*. Before the Court's decision, Graham sued the City of Charlotte, N.C., and the individual officers involved in the incident. The case went to trial in federal district court. After Graham presented his evidence, the defendants moved for a directed verdict. Construing the evidence in the light most favorable to the plaintiff, the court granted the motion, see Graham v. City of Charlotte, 644 F. Supp. 246, 247 (W.D.N.C. 1986), and the Court of Appeals affirmed, 827 F.2d 954 (1987). After the Supreme Court vacated and remanded the case, it was again tried, and the jury found for the officers. Perhaps the jury believed that the officers' actions were reasonable. Or perhaps instead the jury did not believe — after the defendants introduced *their* evidence — that the events occurred in the way the courts described when construing the evidence in the light most favorable to the plaintiff. Most use-of-force cases come to the Supreme Court on summary judgment when the facts have not yet been litigated. Ultimately, however, if a case progresses beyond the summary judgment stage, it is up to the jury to decide what to believe.

Graham's Potential Feedback Loops

It seems plausible that if a police department uses force a lot in a community, people in the community may begin to fear and distrust the police, and they eventually might resist arrests more often than people do elsewhere. If an officer who polices that community knows his department's practices and how the community responds to those practices, is it reasonable for him to interpret ambiguous conduct by those community members as more threatening?

Consider Chicago. After an extensive investigation, the U.S. Department of Justice (DOJ) found in 2017 that, as a result of departmental deficiencies, Chicago police officers engaged in a widespread pattern or practice of using excessive force and discriminating on the basis of race, leading communities of color to distrust the police. See U.S. Dept. of Justice, *Investigation of the Chicago Police Department* (2017). If you were representing a Chicago officer who shot an unarmed Black teenager during a traffic stop in a high-crime neighborhood when the teenager reached into his jacket, wouldn't you use that report's description of distrust to argue that your client reasonably perceived a threat? Does that mean that a community could be *legally* subjected to more force because its police department has a history of using more force against it? Relatedly, some commentators argue that through social conditioning and overestimating the correlation between race and crime, officers end up unconsciously biased against Black men, perceiving them as criminal and dangerous. This bias, the commentators suggest, causes the officers to use more force against Black men in ambiguous encounters, for example, when a man reaches toward his waistband. See Joshua Correll et al., *The Police Officer's Dilemma: Using Ethnicity to Disambiguate Potentially Threatening Individuals*, 83 J. Personality & Soc. Psychol. 1314 (2002). Imagine a Black man who reasonably fears being subjected to excessive force as a result of that bias. He wants to record his interactions with the police, as the ACLU has encouraged him to do. See *ACLU Apps to Record Police Conduct*, Am. Civil Liberties Union. When that man reaches toward his pocket for his cell phone, he might be misperceived by officers as dangerous because an officer could mistake a cell phone for a gun.

Could this explain what happened to Stephon Clark? On March 18, 2018, two Sacramento Police Department officers found Clark, a 22-year-old they suspected of vandalizing cars, after he climbed a fence into a dark yard. Officers approached Clark with guns drawn, shouting, "Show me your hands!" Within seconds, the officers shot and killed Clark. Clark was a Black man suspected of a crime, approached by officers who were pointing guns at him. They believed he was holding a gun, although he had only a cell phone. The yard he had climbed into was his own. See Christoph Koettl, *What We Learned from the Videos of Stephon Clark Being Killed by Police*, N.Y. Times (June 7, 2018).

Thermal image of Stephon Clark running from police before he was shot, Sacramento, March 18, 2018. *Source: https://www.youtube.com/watch?v=A4eafRzWPiM.*

4. Minimizing Force

Did you notice anything missing from the *Graham* factors?

Consider that the Court does not require officers to try to avoid circumstances that are likely to lead to force being used, to use force only as a last resort, or to use only the minimum amount of force necessary under the circumstances. Where is the preference for verbal warnings that *Garner* mentioned? Should these factors be considered by lower courts in figuring out whether an officer behaved reasonably?

A few states have adopted minimization, de-escalation, last-resort, and warning requirements as a matter of state law. For example, Tennessee and Delaware permit deadly force[3] only after other reasonable means of arresting a suspect have been exhausted. Del. Code Ann. tit. 11, §467(c); Tenn. Code Ann. §40-7-108. Iowa authorizes deadly force "only . . . when a person cannot be captured any other way." Iowa Code Ann. §804.8.

Some would make similar requirements a matter of federal law. Almost two dozen congressmembers cosponsored the Police Exercising Absolute Care with Everyone Act of 2019 (PEACE Act), H.R. 4359, 116th Cong. (2019). The bill would permit federal law enforcement officers to use deadly force only when "necessary, as a last resort, to prevent imminent and serious bodily injury or death to the officer or another person . . . and reasonable alternatives to the use of such force have been exhausted." *Id.* §2(b). In addition, nondeadly force could be used only if "necessary and proportional in order to effectuate an arrest" and "only after exhausting reasonable alternatives to the use of such force." *Id.* §2(a). More important, the bill would prohibit local departments from receiving Edward Byrne Memorial Justice Assistance Grants, one of the largest sources of federal funding for local police departments, unless they adopt similar requirements. *Id.* §3. The PEACE Act was reintroduced as part of the George Floyd Justice in Policing Act of 2020, H.R. 7120, 116th Cong. (2020).

The United Nations, through its nonbinding Principles on the Use of Force and Firearms, advocates similar rules. Paragraph 4 states, "Law enforcement officials, in carrying out their duty, shall, as far as possible, apply non-violent means before resorting to the use of force and firearms. They may use force and firearms only if other means remain ineffective or without any promise of achieving the intended result." U.N. Secretary-General, *Eighth United Nations Congress on the Prevention of Crime and the Treatment of Offenders*, 113, U.N. Doc. A/CONF.144/28/Rev.1 (1990).

Critics argue that transforming these aspirations into policies and laws will endanger officers:

> De-escalation practices have been used for generations in policing, but they have been historically applied on a case-by-case basis. . . . Officers should not have to make a choice between compromising their own safety and complying with policy. . . . While de-escalation is a tool in every officer's toolbox, policy should not mandate that it be the first tool out of the box in all situations. Until more is known about the true impact

---

[3] Although *Graham* involved a nondeadly use of force, the totality-of-the-circumstances objective reasonableness standard applies to all uses of force, both deadly and nondeadly. See Kisela v. Hughes, 138 S. Ct. 1148, 1152 (2018); County of Los Angeles v. Mendez, 137 S. Ct. 1539, 1547 (2017).

on officer safety of de-escalation mandates, government leaders should be cautious in their blanket acceptance of these policies.

Brian Landers, *Are De-Escalation Policies Dangerous?*, Police (Oct. 14, 2017); accord Int'l Assn. of Chiefs of Police, *National Consensus Policy and Discussion Paper on Use of Force* 9 (2017) ("By overemphasizing the importance of de-escalation, officers might hesitate to use physical force when appropriate, thereby potentially resulting in an increase in line-of-duty deaths and injuries. . . . [D]e-escalation is not appropriate in every situation. . . ."). How should courts, legislatures, and communities decide whether to consider minimization efforts in assessing the reasonableness of force?

Minimization requirements might suggest that officers should always try less injurious means of gaining compliance before more injurious ones. But that raises a different issue: whether the force is likely to work. When it acknowledged that deadly force can be self-defeating, the *Garner* Court expressly considered how well the level of force it was evaluating would achieve the government's goals. But the *Graham* Court does not include this in its analysis.

Take oleoresin capsicum (OC) spray, colloquially known as pepper spray, which has been used in almost every police department for years. It is easy to carry, and it is easy to teach officers to use. It rarely causes lasting injury to suspects (unlike batons or conducted energy devices (CEDs), such as Tasers). In addition, because it can be used from several feet away, it protects officers from the injuries likely to occur when grappling with suspects. Some departments are starting to give up OC spray, however, because it also frequently fails to achieve its objectives. Even when OC spray hits the suspect properly and has its expected *effect*, that is, *pain*, it often fails to produce the intended *consequence*, that is, *submission*. Moreover, it often misses the suspect or blows back on the officer. Other pain-compliance techniques, such as baton strikes to large muscles, also might fail to achieve their goals, especially when used against someone who is high, drunk, or just very motivated. Should this factor into a reasonableness analysis?

What if a failed attempt to employ force could exacerbate the situation? A Taser used in probe mode[4] often automatically incapacitates a person, but only if the Taser is successfully deployed. That requires that both probes hit the suspect, that they are far enough apart for the charge to flow through a substantial amount of muscle, that they penetrate clothes to within an inch of the skin, and that the wires and darts stay intact during the shock. Some major departments find that Tasers are unsuccessful nearly half of the time. Even Axon, the company that makes Tasers, has sometimes admitted that devices might not work up to 20 percent of the time. See Curtis Gilbert, *When Tasers Fail*, APM Reports

---

[4] Tasers and other brands of CEDs can generally be used in two modes. In the first, *probe mode*, two probes are shot from the weapon and (if successful) attach to a person's skin or clothing several inches or more apart, completing a circuit and sending a high-voltage electrical current that causes temporary neuromuscular incapacitation. In the second, *drive-stun mode*, the weapon is pushed against the person's body without firing the probes. Because the two contact points are close together on the weapon, the electrical charge causes intense pain but not the same kind of muscular incapacitation. In drive-stun mode, therefore, a Taser is generally considered a pain-compliance rather than an incapacitation technique.

(May 9, 2019). When a Taser fails, the suspect might become enraged or the officer could become flustered, and the encounter can escalate, leading the officer to shoot the suspect. See Angela Caputo et al., *Tased, Then Shot*, APM Reports (May 9, 2019).

An Axon Taser.

Should courts include the potential futility of force in their reasonableness analysis? If they do, departments will train officers to consider this factor more carefully. Or should officers instead be expected always to try less injurious forms of force before more injurious forms, even if the lesser forms of force might not work? If you think courts cannot make this kind of judgment, what prepares them to decide whether the use of force is reasonable in other scenarios?

5. Split-Second Syndrome

Consider the following scenarios:

- An officer responds to a call about a man asleep in a car with a gun on his lap in a mall parking lot. The officer approaches the car with his gun drawn and bangs on the driver-side window. The man awakens, surprised, and lifts his hands—holding the gun. Cf. Sam Levin, *Six California Officers Fire Shots at Rapper Who Had Been Asleep in Car, Killing Him*, Guardian (Feb. 13, 2019).
- An officer responds to a 911 call about a suicidal person locked in a room with a weapon and orders the person to come out. The person does come out—still holding the weapon. Cf. Sevier v. City of Lawrence, 60 F.3d 695 (10th Cir. 1995).
- Officers enter a residence without knocking, and a resident draws a gun in response. See Dickerson v. McClellan, 101 F.3d 1151 (6th Cir. 1996).
- An officer steps in front of a moving vehicle. Cf. Fraire v. City of Arlington, 957 F.2d 1268 (5th Cir. 1992).
- An officer fails to identify himself in confronting a suspect. See St. Hilaire v. City of Laconia, 71 F.3d 270 (1st Cir. 1995).

Any of these actions by police can lead suspects to act in ways that appear to pose an immediate threat to the officer. As a result, officers have predictably killed people at least some of whom they were trying to help.

The opinion in *Graham* shows sympathy for officers who act in the moment when it emphasizes "that police officers are often forced to make split-second judgments—in circumstances that are tense, uncertain, and rapidly evolving—about the amount of force that is necessary in a particular situation." 490 U.S. at 397. James J. Fyfe, one of the twentieth century's leading criminologists focused on the use of force, argues that the Court misunderstands both the nature of policing and what should be expected of officers. He calls this form of analysis *split-second syndrome*.

> The split-second syndrome is based on several assumptions. First, it assumes that since no two police problems are precisely alike, there are no principles that may be applied to the diagnosis of specific situations. Thus, no more can be asked of officers than that they respond as quickly as possible to problems, devising the best solutions they can on the spur of the moment. . . .
>
> Second, because of these stresses and time constraints, a high percentage of inappropriate decisions should be expected, but any subsequent criticism of officers' decisions—especially by those outside the police, who can have no real appreciation of the burdens upon officers—is an unwarranted attempted to be wise after the event. . . .
>
> Finally, the split-second syndrome holds that assessments of the justifiability of police conduct are most appropriately made on the exclusive basis of the perceived exigencies of the moment when a decision had to be taken. So long as a citizen has, intentionally or otherwise, provoked the police at that instant, he, rather than the police, should be viewed as the cause of any resulting injuries or damage. . . .
>
> But such an analysis lends approval to unnecessary violence, and to failure of the police to meet their highest obligation: the protection of life. Split-second analysis of police action focuses attention on diagnoses and decisions made by the police during one frame of an incident that began when the police became aware that they were likely to confront a violent person or situation. It ignores what went before. . . .
>
> . . . [I]nstead of asking whether an officer ultimately had to shoot or fight his way out of perilous circumstances, we are better advised to ask whether it was not possible for him to have approached the situation in a way that reduced the risk of bloodshed and increased the chances of a successful and nonviolent conclusion. . . .
>
> . . . Application of these principles requires that officers diagnose the most critical problems they face—those that may require the use of extreme force—*before* they occur, and that they attempt to apply to their resolution techniques of tactical knowledge and concealment. . . .
>
> We should pay less attention to the outcomes of potentially violent situations than to questions of whether officers respond to them in ways likely to reduce the potential for violence. If we do not . . . we reward and encourage an operating-style that eschews advance diagnosis, planning and training, and relies on officers' ability to make the most critical decisions under the worst possible conditions.

James J. Fyfe, *The Split-Second Syndrome and Other Determinants of Police Violence*, in *Critical Issues in Policing: Contemporary Readings* 517, 526–530 (Roger G. Dunham & Geoffrey P. Alpert eds., 7th ed. 2015).

Clearly, an officer's conduct leading up to a use of force sometimes contributes to making force necessary. Is this preforce conduct relevant after *Graham?* Federal appellate courts disagree. Some circuits refuse to consider an officer's prior conduct in evaluating a use of force, limiting their analyses to the moments when force is used. Other circuits consider limited preforce conduct some of the time. A couple of other circuits include the officers' conduct leading to the use of force as part of the totality of the circumstances.[5] Several circuits have been inconsistent in their approach. Even when courts consider preseizure conduct, they usually look only at conduct that "is 'immediately connected' to the suspect's threat of force." Allen v. Muskogee, 119 F.3d 837, 840 (10th Cir. 1997). That leaves out most of the officer and departmental decisions that set the stage for force.

The Supreme Court waded into the debate in *County of Los Angeles v. Mendez,* 137 S. Ct. 1539 (2017). There, the Court rejected a Ninth Circuit rule under which an officer who made a seizure using force judged to be reasonable under the circumstances could still be liable for injuries under an excessive-force theory if an antecedent Fourth Amendment violation contributed to his need to use force. The Court held the Fourth Amendment provided no basis for the rule — that "[a] different Fourth Amendment violation cannot transform a later, reasonable use of force into an unreasonable seizure." *Id.* at 1544. The Court did not resolve the debate about preseizure conduct, however. In a footnote, it declined to address the question of whether assessing the totality of the circumstances for a use of force includes "taking into account unreasonable police conduct prior to the use of force that foreseeably created the need to use it." *Id.* at n.*. Just three years earlier, however, in *Plumhoff v. Rickard,* 572 U.S. 765, 777 (2014), the Supreme Court considered the reasonableness of a use of force "[u]nder the circumstances at the moment when the shots were fired," perhaps signaling its view of the matter.

The Human Costs of Police Tactics

There may be no more poignant and tragic reminder of the harms of failing to think first than the November 2014 shooting of Tamir Rice. Tamir was a 12-year-old African-American boy shot by Cleveland police officer Timothy Loehmann. Beforehand, Tamir was playing with a toy pistol at a recreation center two blocks from his house. The 911 operator received a call reporting a Black male with a gun. Although the caller also noted that the gun might be fake and the male a juvenile, those impressions were not relayed

---

[5] For examples of cases in the first category, see *Marion v. City of Corydon,* 559 F.3d 700, 705 (7th Cir. 2009) ("Pre-seizure police conduct cannot serve as a basis for liability under the Fourth Amendment; we limit our analysis to force used when a seizure occurs."); *Salim v. Proulx,* 93 F.3d 86, 92 (2d Cir. 1996) (calling actions leading up to the force "irrelevant"). For an example of a case in the second category, see *Billington v. Smith,* 292 F.3d 1177, 1189 (9th Cir. 2002) (ruling that intentional or reckless preforce conduct that violates the Constitution can render the subsequent use of force unconstitutional). For examples of cases in the third category, see *Abraham v. Raso,* 183 F.3d 279, 291 (3d Cir. 1999) (explaining that the "totality of the circumstances" cannot exclude all "context and causes" before the moment the seizure is accomplished for the use of force); *St. Hilaire v. City of Laconia,* 71 F.3d 20, 26–27 (1st Cir. 1995) (concluding that "court[s] should examine the actions of the government officials leading up to the seizure" but nonetheless rejecting the broad proposition that officers have a duty to avoid creating situations that increase the likelihood of using force).

to Loehmann and his partner. Instead, they were told that a Black male "keeps pulling a gun out of his pants and pointing it at people." Timothy J. McGinty, *Cuyahoga County Prosecutor's Report on the November 22, 2014 Shooting Death of Tamir Rice* 2–3 (2015).

Tamir Rice.

The officers drove quickly up to the gazebo where Tamir sat, and the car slid to a stop within a few feet of Tamir. Officer Loehmann immediately got out of his patrol car, and as he did, Tamir walked toward the officers and moved his right arm toward his waist. Less than two seconds after arriving on the scene, Loehmann fired two shots from a distance of less than ten feet. One of these shots hit Tamir. The boy died at the hospital soon afterward. For a video of the incident, see News 5 Cleveland, *Full Video: Tamir Rice Shooting Video* (Dec. 3, 2014), YouTube, *https://youtu.be/dw0EMLM1XRI.*

Although Loehmann claimed he shouted to Tamir to drop the gun through the closed car door, Tamir was not holding a weapon at the time and no witnesses heard warnings or commands. See McGinty, *supra*, at 66. Still, according to Loehmann's subsequent statement, "The suspect had a gun, had been threatening others with the weapon and had not obeyed our command to show us his hands. He was facing us. This was an active shooter situation." Statement of Timothy Loehman, Police Officer, Cleveland, Ohio, Police Dept. (Nov. 30, 2014). In a later interview, Loehmann reiterated that he and his partner were in "immediate danger" because they were "sitting ducks." Safia Samee Ali, *Tamir Rice Shooting: Newly Released Interview Reveals Cop's Shifting Story*, NBC News (Apr. 26, 2017).

The county prosecutor considered and rejected criminal charges. He concluded that Tamir's death was "the culmination of a tragic confluence of events," because the officers did not know that Tamir might be a juvenile or the gun fake. McGinty, *supra*, at 69. But because Tamir unexpectedly moved in the officers' direction and reached in the direction of his own waistband, the shooting, the prosecutor decided, was reasonable under the circumstances. *Id.* at 69–70.

There are factual disputes about what precisely happened in the two-second interaction, but even taking the facts in the light most favorable to the officers, Tamir's death seems entirely avoidable. Because no one else was nearby and no gun was in Tamir's hands at the time the officers arrived, there was no immediate threat to the public. The officers could have slowed things down and made themselves safer before making any decision about using force either by maintaining distance between themselves and Tamir or by taking cover and giving commands (and a chance to comply). Instead, the officers made no effort to assess or resolve the situation before rushing Tamir. When they pulled up to Tamir, they made it almost inevitable that any movement made by the boy, who had been reported to be armed, would seem like a threat. Does narrow constitutional framing prevent courts from considering seemingly relevant questions about the government's use of force?

6.   *Graham, Garner,* and Heavily Policed Populations

Graham instructs lower courts to analyze any allegation that an officer has used excessive force during an arrest under the Fourth Amendment's reasonableness standard. Some argue that *Graham*'s focus on individual interactions has problematic consequences:

> By individualizing police violence and scaling it down from a structural matter steeped in centuries of racial tensions to an individual dispute between officer and citizen, the Fourth Amendment has been used to depoliticize, deracialize, decontextualize, and ahistoricize a distinctive racial justice issue concerning the disproportionate use of force against people of color. This individualizing dynamic not only warps our understanding of the causes and consequences of police violence, but often leaves victims without any remedy.

Osagie K. Obasogie & Zachary Newman, *The Futile Fourth Amendment: Understanding Police Excessive Force Doctrine Through an Empirical Assessment of* Graham v. Connor, 112 Nw. U. L. Rev. 1465, 1469–1470 (2018). As Obasogie and Newman suggest, Fourth Amendment doctrine assesses specific interactions at the cost of obscuring the way social and cultural forces shape police violence. Should social and cultural factors be considered in deciding what force is reasonable? How?

Populations who are subject to disproportionate policing also often raise distinctive issues with respect to the use of force. Scholars have especially elaborated on ways that police practices, legal permissiveness, and preexisting discrimination combine to produce disproportionate police use of force against African Americans. Devon Carbado, for example, argues that legal, social, psychological, and organizational factors work together to produce systematic violence by officers against African Americans in the following way:

1. A variety of social forces (including, but not limited to, broken-windows policing, racial stereotypes, racial segregation and gentrification, and Fourth Amendment law) converge to make African Americans vulnerable to ongoing police surveillance and contact.

2. The frequency of this surveillance and contact exposes African Americans to the possibility of police violence.
3. Police culture and training encourage that violence.
4. When violence occurs, a range of legal actors in civil and criminal processes translate that violence into justifiable force.
5. The doctrine of qualified immunity makes it difficult for plaintiffs to win cases against police officers, and when plaintiffs win such cases, police officers rarely suffer financial consequences because their local government indemnifies them.
6. The conversion of violence into justifiable force, the qualified immunity barrier to suing police officers, and the frequency with which cities and municipalities indemnify police officers reduce the risk of legal sanction police officers assume when they employ excessive force. This reduction in the risk of legal liability diminishes the incentive for police officers to exercise care with respect to when and how they deploy violent force.

Devon W. Carbado, *Blue-on-Black Violence: A Provisional Model of Some of the Causes,* 104 Geo. L.J. 1479, 1483–1484 (2016). What role does the law governing the use of force play in this model?

African Americans are not the only people made vulnerable to police violence by structural factors. Latinos may be profiled as potential illegal immigrants. LGBTQ people are sometimes perceived as disorderly. People who are homeless often cannot help but violate misdemeanor laws or be suspected of doing so, and so on. Any of these factors can subject members of these groups to additional police violence. Should Fourth Amendment law take notice? If so, in what ways?

The almost 20 percent of Americans with some kind of disability face special risks of police violence. First, people with disabilities encounter the police more than other people as victims of crime, as offenders, and as people whose behavior confuses others or requires medical attention. Moreover, during those encounters, people with disabilities face a heightened threat of police violence because their conditions can lead to behavior that—although predictable and understandable in the context of the disability—is easily misinterpreted by officers or others as suspicious, threatening, or resistant. The facts of *Graham* provide only one example. Here are some others:

- A person who is deaf might not drop an object or weapon because he cannot hear the commands, and an officer might mistake an attempt to communicate by sign language as aggressive.[6]
- A person with a tremor could have an unsteady gait or slurred speech that can be mistaken for intoxication.
- A person with an intellectual disability might not be able to process instructions quickly enough to respond to a shouting officer, who might interpret inaction as noncooperation.
- A person with autism might pull away from being touched or engage in repetitive flapping of hands, leading an officer to perceive resistance or a threat.

---

[6] In addition, when an officer handcuffs a deaf person, especially behind the back, the officer often effectively prevents the person from communicating at all.

- A person who suffers from mental illness might not understand that an officer is trying to help and could be reactive, anxious, or enraged, triggering a violent response.

People with severe mental illness and intellectual disabilities are among the most vulnerable. Hundreds of people with such disabilities are fatally shot by police officers each year, often after their families call the police for help. Traditional police tactics often aggravate these encounters. As one advocate put it, "'Police are taught to be assertive and aggressive, to close in on a person, to raise their voices, to intimidate people who may pose threats, and, sometimes, maybe that works.'" Peter Holley & Wesley Lowery, *The Chicago Shootings and Why So Many Police Calls Involving the Mentally Ill End in Death*, Wash. Post (Dec. 29, 2015). However, those same tactics backfire, say, "for someone hearing voices telling them that, say, the FBI or CIA is hunting them—a common delusion for people suffering from schizophrenia. . . . 'It's going to accentuate the delusion that they're under threat,'" and predictably lead people to respond aggressively. *Id.*

Even if the people with disabilities or family and friends try to explain behavior, officers cannot always process the information in the moment, and they are trained to address problematic conduct and react to threats.

In addition to Fourth Amendment law, Title II of the Americans with Disabilities Act protects people with disabilities. The act prohibits the government from discriminating against people with disabilities in providing services, programs, and facilities, and it also requires reasonable accommodation for people with disabilities. 42 U.S.C. §12132 (2018). The statute applies to all state and local governments and their departments, including police departments and 911 services. But the Supreme Court has refused to address whether and how Title II applies to arrests and other policing activities. See City & Cty. of San Francisco v. Sheehan, 575 U.S. 600 (2015). Is verbal deescalation a reasonable accommodation? What about having a crisis intervention team to handle interactions with people in distress? Is failing to train officers to interact with people with autism or deaf people a kind of intentional discrimination? A de facto one?

Some departments are developing training and partnerships with non-law-enforcement service providers and mental health specialists to improve their ability to recognize and handle encounters with people with disabilities. Advocacy groups call frequently for mandating additional training. But given the variety of people with whom the police interact, it seems unlikely that police officers could ever be fully prepared for the array of challenges they will encounter. How should the law handle it when they are not?

Most commentators focus on the disproportionate threat police pose to Black men. Emphasizing one injustice can sometimes hide another.

Kimberlé Williams Crenshaw & Andrea J. Ritchie, *Say Her Name: Resisting Police Brutality Against Black Women*
1 (2015)

The August 9th, 2014 police killing of 18-year-old Michael Brown sparked a smoldering nationwide movement against police violence and, more broadly, against anti-Black racism. As Mike Brown, Eric Garner, and Tamir Rice have become household names and faces, their stories have become an impetus for public policy debates on the future of policing in America.

However, 2014 also marked the unjust police killings of a number of Black women, including Gabriella Nevarez, Aura Rosser, Michelle Cusseaux, and Tanisha Anderson. . . .

The lack of meaningful accountability for the deaths of unarmed Black men also extended to deaths of unarmed Black women and girls in 2015. Just as the officers who killed Mike Brown and Eric Garner escaped punishment for these homicides, officers who killed Black women and girls were not held accountable for their actions. Joseph Weekley, who killed a sleeping, seven-year-old Aiyana Stanley-Jones, escaped prosecution after a jury failed to convict him in his second trial. Dante Servin, an off-duty officer who shot Rekia Boyd in the back of the head, was cleared by a judge of all charges. Other officers faced no charges whatsoever, such as those who killed Mya Hall, a Black transgender woman.

None of these killings of Black women, nor the lack of accountability for them, have been widely elevated as exemplars of the systemic police brutality that is currently the focal point of mass protest and policy reform efforts. The failure to highlight and demand accountability for the countless Black women killed by police over the past two decades, including Eleanor Bumpurs, Tyisha Miller, LaTanya Haggerty, Margaret Mitchell, Kayla Moore, and Tarika Wilson, to name just a few among scores, leaves Black women unnamed and thus underprotected in the face of their continued vulnerability to racialized police violence.

The resurgent racial justice movement in the United States has developed a clear frame to understand the police killings of Black men and boys, theorizing the ways in which they are systematically criminalized and feared across disparate class backgrounds and irrespective of circumstance. Yet Black women who are profiled, beaten, sexually assaulted, and killed by law enforcement officials are conspicuously absent from this frame even when their experiences are identical. When their experiences with police violence are distinct—uniquely informed by race, gender, gender identity, and sexual orientation—Black women remain invisible.

A vigil in memory of Black women and girls killed by the police held in New York City on May 20, 2015.

7. Applying *Graham* and *Garner*

After reading the following descriptions and watching the listed videos, analyze the following incidents using *Graham* and *Garner*.[7]

Problem 1. Officer Michael Slager of North Charleston, South Carolina, shot Walter Scott on April 4, 2015. Slager pulled over a Mercedes-Benz in North Charleston for a broken brake light. After giving the officer his license, Scott, the 50-year-old Black man who had been driving the car, jumped out of the car and fled into a grassy lot. Slager pursued on foot. According to Slager, the two struggled, and Scott attempted to grab Slager's Taser. Scott then began to run from Slager. Slager shot Scott eight times in the back as he ran, killing him. See ABC News, *WARNING: Graphic Violence - Real-Time Events of Walter Scott Shooting,* YouTube (Apr. 9, 2015), *https://youtu.be/ym4tE0SQCZY.*

Problem 2. Officer Michael Nyantakyi of Richmond, Virginia, shot Marcus-David Peters on May 14, 2018. Driving away from a long day at work, Peters, a 24-year-old Black man rear-ended another car and fled the scene. Officer Nyantakyi pursued Peters until Peters crashed again. Peters, having an apparent mental crisis, climbed out of his car window naked and ran screaming toward the nearby interstate, where he was hit by a passing vehicle. When Peters noticed Nyantakyi nearby holding a weapon, he charged toward the officer, shouting expletives and threatening to kill him. The officer tried to stop Peters with his Taser but one of the prongs failed to make adequate contact, and the Taser was ineffective in incapacitating Peters. Peters continued to charge Nyantakyi. Nyantakyi then shot Peters twice, leading to his death. See Kristine Phillips, *"Marcus Needed Help, Not Death": Body-cam Video Shows Police Officer Fatally Shooting Naked Man,* Wash. Post (May 27, 2018), *https://www.washingtonpost.com/news/post-nation/wp/2018/05/27/marcus-needed-help-not-death-body-cam-video-shows-police-officer-fatally-shooting-naked-man/.*

Problem 3. Officer Betty Shelby of Tulsa, Oklahoma, shot Terence Crutcher on September 16, 2016. Shelby was responding to a call when she came across a man on foot and an SUV in the middle of the road. Crutcher, a 40-year-old Black man, walked toward Shelby and, according to Shelby's attorney, ignored her questions. Shelby drew her firearm and ordered Crutcher to get on his knees, but—again, according to Shelby's attorney—Crutcher did not respond and began walking back toward his SUV with his hands in the air. By this time, other officers had arrived on the scene. When Crutcher got back to his car and appeared to reach toward the window, Shelby fired her gun and another officer discharged his Taser. Crutcher died the next day of his injuries. See Wall Street Journal, *Police Release Footage of Deadly Tulsa Shooting,* YouTube (Sept. 20, 2016), *https://youtu.be/LJd4ThiQjEg.*

8. Handcuffs and Force During Searches

The U.S. Supreme Court has decided only one case concerning the use of force during a search rather than an arrest. Iris Mena sued the police after she was detained in handcuffs during a search of a house that she and several others occupied. As you

---

[7] These videos are disturbing. While lawyers need to be able to apply legal doctrine to specific fact patterns, including scenarios caught on videos, some readers may choose to rely on the descriptions alone. You can practice the concepts in *Graham* and *Garner* either way, and after all, many uses of force are never recorded and are described only by witnesses.

read, consider how the Court's analysis compares to the force cases you have read so far. What threat does handcuffing Mena address?

MUEHLER v. MENA
544 U.S. 93 (2005)

CHIEF JUSTICE REHNQUIST delivered the opinion of the Court.

Respondent Iris Mena was detained in handcuffs during a search of the premises that she and several others occupied. Petitioners were lead members of a police detachment executing a search warrant of these premises. She sued the officers under 42 U.S.C. §1983 . . . .

* * *

Based on information gleaned from the investigation of a gang-related, driveby shooting, petitioners [Officers] Muehler and Brill had reason to believe at least one member of a gang — the West Side Locos — lived at 1363 Patricia Avenue. They also suspected that the individual was armed and dangerous, since he had recently been involved in the driveby shooting. As a result, Muehler obtained a search warrant for 1363 Patricia Avenue that authorized a broad search of the house and premises for, among other things, deadly weapons and evidence of gang membership. In light of the high degree of risk involved in searching a house suspected of housing at least one, and perhaps multiple, armed gang members, a Special Weapons and Tactics (SWAT) team was used to secure the residence and grounds before the search.

At 7 a.m. on February 3, 1998, petitioners, along with the SWAT team and other officers, executed the warrant. Mena was asleep in her bed when the SWAT team, clad in helmets and black vests adorned with badges and the word "POLICE," entered her bedroom and placed her in handcuffs at gunpoint. The SWAT team also handcuffed three other individuals found on the property. The SWAT team then took those individuals and Mena into a converted garage, which contained several beds and some other bedroom furniture. While the search proceeded, one or two officers guarded the four detainees, who were allowed to move around the garage but remained in handcuffs. . . .

The search of the premises yielded a .22 caliber handgun with .22 caliber ammunition, a box of .25 caliber ammunition, several baseball bats with gang writing, various additional gang paraphernalia, and a bag of marijuana. Before the officers left the area, Mena was released.

In her §1983 suit against the officers she alleged that she was detained "for an unreasonable time and in an unreasonable manner" in violation of the Fourth Amendment. . . . After a trial, a jury, pursuant to a special verdict form, found that Officers Muehler and Brill violated Mena's Fourth Amendment right to be free from unreasonable seizures by detaining her both with force greater than that which was reasonable and for a longer period than that which was reasonable. The jury awarded Mena $10,000 in actual damages and $20,000 in punitive damages against each petitioner for a total of $60,000.

The Court of Appeals affirmed the judgment. . . . We granted certiorari, and now vacate and remand.

* * *

In *Michigan v. Summers*, 452 U.S. 692 (1981), we held that officers executing a search warrant for contraband have the authority "to detain the occupants of the premises while a proper search is conducted." *Id.* at 705. Such detentions are appropriate, we explained, because the character of the additional intrusion caused by detention is slight and because the justifications for detention are substantial. We made clear that the detention of an occupant is "surely less intrusive than the search itself." . . . *Id.* at 701. Against this incremental intrusion, we posited three legitimate law enforcement interests that provide substantial justification for detaining an occupant: "preventing flight in the event that incriminating evidence is found"; "minimizing the risk of harm to the officers"; and facilitating "the orderly completion of the search," as detainees' "self-interest may induce them to open locked doors or locked containers to avoid the use of force." *Id.* at 702–703.

Mena's detention was, under *Summers*, plainly permissible . . . because a warrant existed to search 1363 Patricia Avenue and she was an occupant of that address at the time of the search.

Inherent in *Summers'* authorization to detain an occupant of the place to be searched is the authority to use reasonable force to effectuate the detention. See Graham v. Connor, 490 U.S. 386, 396 (1989) ("Fourth Amendment jurisprudence has long recognized that the right to make an arrest or investigatory stop necessarily carries with it the right to use some degree of physical coercion or threat thereof to effect it."). Indeed, *Summers* itself stressed that the risk of harm to officers and occupants is minimized "if the officers routinely exercise unquestioned command of the situation." 452 U.S. at 703.

The officers' use of force in the form of handcuffs to effectuate Mena's detention in the garage, as well as the detention of the three other occupants, was reasonable because the governmental interests outweigh the marginal intrusion. The imposition of correctly applied handcuffs on Mena, who was already being lawfully detained during a search of the house, was undoubtedly a separate intrusion in addition to detention in the converted garage. The detention was thus more intrusive than that which we upheld in *Summers*.

But this was no ordinary search. The governmental interests in not only detaining, but using handcuffs, are at their maximum when, as here, a warrant authorizes a search for weapons and a wanted gang member resides on the premises. In such inherently dangerous situations, the use of handcuffs minimizes the risk of harm to both officers and occupants. Though this safety risk inherent in executing a search warrant for weapons was sufficient to justify the use of handcuffs, the need to detain multiple occupants made the use of handcuffs all the more reasonable.

Mena argues that, even if the use of handcuffs to detain her in the garage was reasonable as an initial matter, the duration of the use of handcuffs made the detention unreasonable. The duration of a detention can, of course, affect the balance of interests under *Graham*. However, the 2- to 3-hour detention in handcuffs in this case does not outweigh the government's continuing safety interests. As we have noted, this case involved the detention of four detainees by two officers during a search of a gang house for dangerous weapons. We conclude that the detention of Mena in handcuffs during the search was reasonable. . . .

JUSTICE KENNEDY, concurring.

I concur in the judgment and in the opinion of the Court. It does seem important to add this brief statement to help ensure that police handcuffing during searches becomes neither routine nor unduly prolonged.

The safety of the officers and the efficacy of the search are matters of first concern, but so too is it a matter of first concern that excessive force is not used on the persons detained, especially when these persons, though lawfully detained under *Michigan v. Summers*, 452 U.S. 692 (1981), are not themselves suspected of any involvement in criminal activity. The use of handcuffs is the use of force, and such force must be objectively reasonable under the circumstances. Graham v. Connor, 490 U.S. 386 (1989).

The reasonableness calculation under *Graham* is in part a function of the expected and actual duration of the search. If the search extends to the point when the handcuffs can cause real pain or serious discomfort, provision must be made to alter the conditions of detention at least long enough to attend to the needs of the detainee. This is so even if there is no question that the initial handcuffing was objectively reasonable. The restraint should also be removed if, at any point during the search, it would be readily apparent to any objectively reasonable officer that removing the handcuffs would not compromise the officers' safety or risk interference or substantial delay in the execution of the search. The time spent in the search here, some two to three hours, certainly approaches, and may well exceed, the time beyond which a detainee's Fourth Amendment interests require revisiting the necessity of handcuffing in order to ensure the restraint, even if permissible as an initial matter, has not become excessive.

That said, under these circumstances I do not think handcuffing the detainees for the duration of the search was objectively unreasonable. . . . Where the detainees outnumber those supervising them, and this situation could not be remedied without diverting officers from an extensive, complex, and time-consuming search, the continued use of handcuffs after the initial sweep may be justified, subject to adjustments or temporary release under supervision to avoid pain or excessive physical discomfort. . . .

[The opinion of Justice Stevens, with whom Justice Souter, Justice Ginsburg, and Justice Breyer joined, concurring in the judgment, is omitted.]

NOTES AND QUESTIONS

1. *Preemptive force.* Graham and *Garner* suggest that force is permissible to effect arrests and protect officers and others from criminal suspects when these suspects indicate that they intend to resist, flee, or threaten others. If Mena, a young unarmed woman, only five feet two inches tall, was not suspected of criminal activity and posed no apparent danger, why exactly does the Court think it is reasonable to handcuff her? The Court seems to suggest that a high-risk search pursuant to a warrant establishes the *potential* for resistance to officers, and that possibility justifies the preemptive use of force. When else might preemptive force be justified under this logic?

2. Graham *factors?* Although the Court cites *Graham*, it does not mention the *Graham* factors in analyzing the use of force against Mena. What considerations did the Court use instead? What do you think about the Court's approach?

3. *Handcuffs as force. Mena* is often overlooked as a use-of-force case because the only use of force was the application of handcuffs, and because it relied more on a search case, *Summers*, than use-of-force cases. But handcuffing matters. More than 10 million people are arrested each year, and officers regularly handcuff anyone they arrest, even if the arrest is for a fine-only traffic violation or a minor misdemeanor. Even if they are never arrested, many more are handcuffed during traffic and *Terry* stops, and during searches of cars and homes, even when those searches

relate to nonviolent offenses. How would you analyze handcuffing a person during an arrest under *Graham*? Under *Mena*? Imagine a traffic stop for rolling through a stop sign. When the officer runs the driver's license, he finds the driver has an outstanding arrest warrant for failing to pay child support. The driver acknowledges the problem and agrees to come with the officer. Is handcuffing him reasonable?

To illustrate how ordinary handcuffing is, consider that, after a few incidents in which officers were captured on video handcuffing children, some less than ten years old, the Washington, D.C., Police Department announced in 2020 that it had changed its handcuffing policies: Officers will no longer handcuff children age 12 and younger, except in situations deemed dangerous to the child or the public. See Clarence Williams & Fenit Nirappil, *D.C. Police Will No Longer Handcuff Children 12 and Younger*, Wash. Post (Jan. 28, 2020). Is it surprising that this required a policy change?

4. *Challenging handcuffs.* After *Mena*, most federal court challenges to handcuffing come in the form of claims that officers injured a suspect by using handcuffs for too long or applying them too tightly. See, e.g., Morrison v. Board of Trustees, 583 F.3d 394 (6th Cir. 2009). Courts sometimes rely on Justice Kennedy's concurrence in *Mena* to shape their analysis. See, e.g., Mlodzinski v. Lewis, 648 F.3d 24 (1st Cir. 2011). What guidance does the concurrence provide?

5. *A problem.* Officer Tom Simmons pulls over Javier Gomez for speeding. When Gomez refuses to allow Simmons to search the car, the two exchange words, and Simmons pulls Gomez out of the car. The officer roughly places handcuffs on Gomez, tightening them quickly and harshly, and places Gomez in the back of his patrol car. Simmons repeatedly ignores Gomez's pleas to lower the windows and loosen the handcuffs. Although Simmons arrested Gomez for resisting arrest, the state later drops the charge. Gomez now alleges that Simmons intentionally applied the handcuffs unusually tightly to cause pain to Gomez, and that Gomez suffers continuing nerve damage in the hands and wrists. How would you analyze Gomez's excessive force claim? Cf. Sebastian v. Ortiz, 918 F.3d 1301 (11th Cir. 2019).

6. *Threat of force.* While handcuffing Mena, the officers also pointed a gun at her. Can't this be construed as a *threat* of force? Why does the Court assume *that* is constitutional?

9. Defining Force

Physicists define force as any push or pull on an object that results from its interaction with another object, but there is no standard definition of force in the law. In *Garner*, shooting a suspect constituted force. In *Graham*, struggling with a suspect and taking him down to the ground constituted force. What definition of force is the Court using in *Mena*?

In *California v. Hodari D.*, 499 U.S. 621 (1991), which did not involve a use of force, the Court reasoned that at common law "the mere grasping or application of physical force, . . . whether or not it succeed[s] in subduing the arrestee," constituted an arrest, the "quintessential" seizure under the Fourth Amendment. *Id.* at 624. All it takes for a person to be seized, in this view, is "the slightest application of physical force" or "a laying on of hands." *Id.* at 625–626. Are these kinds of seizures also "force" within the meaning of Fourth Amendment doctrine? If so, does that mean that an officer who touches a suspect's shoulder as he talks to him uses force, but an officer who fires warning shots or shoots and misses does not? Given *Hodari D.*, it might surprise you that federal courts of appeals are divided as to whether even shooting and hitting a fleeing person multiple times constitutes a seizure if that person escapes immediate custody, a matter the Supreme Court will soon decide. See Torres v. Madrid, 769 Fed. Appx. 654 (10th Cir.), *cert. granted*, 140 S. Ct. 680 (2019).

Departments are all over the map on what constitutes a use of force for internal recordkeeping and policy purposes. Many do not consider handcuffing and effecting simple control holds to be uses of force, although they are force for purposes of the Fourth Amendment. Others include even officer presence and verbal commands as uses of force, although these clearly are not force as the Court sees it. That means that even if one had data from different departments about the use of force, comparing the departments' use of force is nearly impossible. Should departments employ a standard definition of force? How might that come about?

And what about threats? The *Garner* Court saw a *warning* as a way of mitigating the use of deadly force. But isn't a warning when no force follows just a *threat*? Threats are not *force* for Fourth Amendment purposes, but they may nevertheless constitute a seizure. Does that mean that constitutionally speaking, "Stop!" and "Stop or I'll shoot!" are the same? States vary in their approaches to threats. Some permit threats of force only when that force would be justified, either expressly by statute or by implication. Others allow a threat of deadly force even when only nondeadly force is permissible.

Courts have also struggled with unintentional harms. If an officer *strikes* a suspect with his car, he uses force against him. What about an officer who *accidentally crashes* his car into a bystander while chasing a suspect? According to the Supreme Court, he does not *seize* the bystander within the meaning of the Fourth Amendment. See Brower v. County of Inyo, 489 U.S. 593, 595-597 (1989). Seizures must be willful. They occur "only when there is a governmental termination of freedom of movement *through means intentionally applied*." *Id.* at 597 (emphasis in original). Therefore, accidental force need not be reasonable within the meaning of the Fourth Amendment, although the victim may have a civil damages action under state tort law or for a violation of the Fourteenth Amendment.

What about unintentional targets? Neither an officer who swings his baton and misses nor an officer who accidentally hits a person with his baton has used force in a Fourth Amendment sense. What about when an officer tries to strike one person but connects with another? Criminal and tort law often handle this issue through the doctrine of transferred intent, sometimes loosely described as the theory that "[t]he intention follows the bullet." State v. Batson, 96 S.W.2d 384, 389 (Mo. 1936). In Fourth Amendment law, the Court has indicated, "A seizure occurs even when an unintended person or thing is the object of the detention or taking." *Brower*, 489 U.S. at 596. To some courts, *Brower* suggests that, just as an officer who goes into the wrong apartment has searched the surprised homeowner, Maryland v. Garrison, 480 U.S. 79 (1987), and an officer who arrests the wrong man has seized him, Hill v. California, 401 U.S. 797 (1971), an officer who shoots at one suspect but hits another has used force against his victim, and his actions must therefore be reasonable. The reasonableness calculus in these situations requires courts to look not only at the justification for targeting the proper suspect in the first place, but also at the risk that someone else might suffer a collateral intrusion. See *Garrison*, 480 U.S. at 88. Other courts, by contrast, have held that the Fourth Amendment does not apply to physical injuries inadvertently inflicted by an officer on an unintended target. See, e.g., Claybrook v. Birchwell, 199 F.3d 350, 359 (6th Cir. 2000). How might this difference affect officers' behavior?

10.   Force During Pursuits and Beyond

In *Scott v. Harris*, 550 U.S. 372 (2007), the Court confronted an officer's use of deadly force against a fleeing motorist. The facts, according to the Court, were these:

> In March 2001, a Georgia county deputy clocked respondent's vehicle traveling at 73 miles per hour on a road with a 55-mile-per-hour speed limit. The deputy activated his blue flashing lights indicating that respondent should pull over. Instead, respondent sped away, initiating a chase down what is in most portions a two-lane road, at speeds exceeding 85 miles per hour. The deputy radioed his dispatch to report that he was pursuing a fleeing vehicle, and broadcast its license plate number. Petitioner, Deputy Timothy Scott, heard the radio communication and joined the pursuit along with other officers. In the midst of the chase, respondent pulled into the parking lot of a shopping center and was nearly boxed in by the various police vehicles. Respondent evaded the trap by making a sharp turn, colliding with Scott's police car, exiting the parking lot, and speeding off once again down a two-lane highway.
>
> Following respondent's shopping center maneuvering, which resulted in slight damage to Scott's police car, Scott took over as the lead pursuit vehicle. Six minutes and nearly 10 miles after the chase had begun, Scott decided to attempt to terminate the episode by employing a "Precision Intervention Technique ('PIT') maneuver, which causes the fleeing vehicle to spin to a stop." Having radioed his supervisor for permission, Scott was told to "go ahead and take him out." Instead, Scott applied his push bumper to the rear of respondent's vehicle. As a result, respondent lost control of his vehicle, which left the roadway, ran down an embankment, overturned, and crashed. Respondent was badly injured and was rendered a quadriplegic.
>
> Respondent filed suit against Deputy Scott and others under 42 U.S.C. §1983, alleging, *inter alia*, a violation of his federal constitutional rights, viz. use of excessive force resulting in an unreasonable seizure under the Fourth Amendment. In response, Scott filed a motion for summary judgment based on an assertion of qualified immunity. The District Court denied the motion.

Pursuit video in *Scott v. Harris* shows Harris's car careening off the road after Scott rammed it.

Scott, 550 U.S. at 374–376. Before ruling on the constitutionality of Scott's conduct, the Court considered and rejected the version of events adopted by the court below based on its own review of a videotape that captured some of the events in question:

> The videotape quite clearly contradicts the version of the story told by respondent and adopted by the Court of Appeals. For example, the Court of Appeals adopted respondent's assertions that, during the chase, "there was little, if any, actual threat to pedestrians or other motorists, as the roads were mostly empty and [respondent] remained in control of his vehicle." Indeed, reading the lower court's opinion, one gets the impression that respondent, rather than fleeing from police, was attempting to pass his driving test. . . .
>
> The videotape tells quite a different story. There we see respondent's vehicle racing down narrow, two-lane roads in the dead of night at speeds that are shockingly fast. We see it swerve around more than a dozen other cars, cross the double-yellow line, and force cars traveling in both directions to their respective shoulders to avoid being hit. We see it run multiple red lights and travel for considerable periods of time in the occasional center left-turn-only lane, chased by numerous police cars forced to engage in the same hazardous maneuvers just to keep up. Far from being the cautious and controlled driver the lower court depicts, what we see on the video more closely resembles a Hollywood-style car chase of the most frightening sort, placing police officers and innocent bystanders alike at great risk of serious injury.

Id. at 378–380.[8]

The Court therefore reviewed the constitutionality of Scott's actions in light of this assessment of the facts and concluded that it was "quite clear that Deputy Scott did not violate the Fourth Amendment." *Id.* at 381. In reaching its conclusion, the Court expressly refused to apply the test from *Garner*, describing it as "an application of the Fourth Amendment's 'reasonableness' test, to the use of a particular type of force in a particular situation." *Id.* at 382. The Court also chose not to cite or consider the factors mandated in *Graham*. Instead, the Court applied the balancing test described in *Terry* and later rearticulated in *United States v. Place*, 462 U.S. 696 (1983):

> Although respondent's attempt to craft an easy-to-apply legal test in the Fourth Amendment context is admirable, in the end we must still slosh our way through the factbound morass of "reasonableness." Whether or not Scott's actions constituted application of "deadly force," all that matters is whether Scott's actions were reasonable.
>
> In determining the reasonableness of the manner in which a seizure is effected, "[w]e must balance the nature and quality of the intrusion on the individual's Fourth Amendment interests against the importance of the governmental interests alleged to justify the intrusion." United States v. Place, 462 U.S. 696 (1983). Scott defends his actions by pointing to the paramount governmental interest in ensuring public safety, and respondent nowhere suggests this was not the purpose motivating Scott's behavior. Thus, in judging whether Scott's actions were reasonable, we must consider the risk of bodily harm that Scott's actions posed to respondent in light

---

[8] To watch the video yourself, go to *Media Sources*, Supreme Court of the U.S., *https://www .supremecourt.gov/media/media.aspx.*

of the threat to the public that Scott was trying to eliminate. Although there is no obvious way to quantify the risks on either side, it is clear from the videotape that respondent posed an actual and imminent threat to the lives of any pedestrians who might have been present, to other civilian motorists, and to the officers involved in the chase. It is equally clear that Scott's actions posed a high likelihood of serious injury or death to respondent — though not the near *certainty* of death posed by, say, shooting a fleeing felon in the back of the head, see Tennessee v. Garner, 471 U.S. 1, 4 (1985), or pulling alongside a fleeing motorist's car and shooting the motorist. So how does a court go about weighing the perhaps lesser probability of injuring or killing numerous bystanders against the perhaps larger probability of injuring or killing a single person? We think it appropriate in this process to take into account not only the number of lives at risk, but also their relative culpability. It was respondent, after all, who intentionally placed himself and the public in danger by unlawfully engaging in the reckless, high-speed flight that ultimately produced the choice between two evils that Scott confronted. Multiple police cars, with blue lights flashing and sirens blaring, had been chasing respondent for nearly 10 miles, but he ignored their warning to stop. By contrast, those who might have been harmed had Scott not taken the action he did were entirely innocent. We have little difficulty in concluding it was reasonable for Scott to take the action that he did.

But wait, says respondent: Couldn't the innocent public equally have been protected, and the tragic accident entirely avoided, if the police had simply ceased their pursuit? We think the police need not have taken that chance and hoped for the best. Whereas Scott's action — ramming respondent off the road — was *certain* to eliminate the risk that respondent posed to the public, ceasing pursuit was not. First of all, there would have been no way to convey convincingly to respondent that the chase was off, and that he was free to go. Had respondent looked in his rearview mirror and seen the police cars deactivate their flashing lights and turn around, he would have had no idea whether they were truly letting him get away, or simply devising a new strategy for capture. Perhaps the police knew a shortcut he didn't know, and would reappear down the road to intercept him; or perhaps they were setting up a roadblock in his path. Given such uncertainty, respondent might have been just as likely to respond by continuing to drive recklessly as by slowing down and wiping his brow.

Second, we are loath to lay down a rule requiring the police to allow fleeing suspects to get away whenever they drive *so recklessly* that they put other people's lives in danger. It is obvious the perverse incentives such a rule would create: Every fleeing motorist would know that escape is within his grasp, if only he accelerates to 90 miles per hour, crosses the double-yellow line a few times, and runs a few red lights. The Constitution assuredly does not impose this invitation to impunity-earned-by-recklessness. Instead, we lay down a more sensible rule: A police officer's attempt to terminate a dangerous high-speed car chase that threatens the lives of innocent bystanders does not violate the Fourth Amendment, even when it places the fleeing motorist at risk of serious injury or death.

The car chase that respondent initiated in this case posed a substantial and immediate risk of serious physical injury to others; no reasonable jury could conclude otherwise. Scott's attempt to terminate the chase by forcing respondent off the road was reasonable, and Scott is entitled to summary judgment. The Court of Appeals' judgment to the contrary is reversed.

Id. at 383–386.

The Court reprised the *Scott* approach to high-speed chases a few years later in *Plumhoff v. Rickard*, 572 U.S. 765 (2014), a qualified immunity case. Donald Rickard sped away from a traffic stop after the officer asked him to step out of the car, and the police pursued him in a chase that exceeded 100 miles per hour. After Rickard's car collided with several police cruisers, came to a stop, then began to move and forced an officer to jump out of the way, officers shot at Rickard's car 15 times. The car crashed, and Rickard and his passenger were killed. The Court found there to be no constitutional violation:

> Rickard's outrageously reckless driving posed a grave public safety risk. And while it is true that Rickard's car eventually collided with a police car and came temporarily to a near standstill, that did not end the chase. Less than three seconds later, Rickard resumed maneuvering his car. Just before the shots were fired, when the front bumper of his car was flush with that of one of the police cruisers, Rickard was obviously pushing down on the accelerator because the car's wheels were spinning, and then Rickard threw the car into reverse in an attempt to escape. Thus, the record conclusively disproves respondent's claim that the chase in the present case was already over when petitioners began shooting. Under the circumstances at the moment when the shots were fired, all that a reasonable police officer could have concluded was that Rickard was intent on resuming his flight and that, if he was allowed to do so, he would once again pose a deadly threat for others on the road. . . .
>
> . . . [I]t is beyond serious dispute that Rickard's flight posed a grave public safety risk, and here, as in *Scott*, the police acted reasonably in using deadly force to end that risk.

Id. at 776–777.

NOTES AND QUESTIONS

1. *New law?* How would you have analyzed the facts of *Scott* under the standards laid out in *Garner* and *Graham*? How is *Scott* different? Does it make new law? How?

2. *Is* Scott *a bright-line rule?* If Harris "endanger[ed] human life" during his late-night chase on nearly deserted roads, with few officers in pursuit and apparently no pedestrians around, *Scott*, 550 U.S. at 380, it would be rare that a use of force during any car chase failed to pass muster under *Scott*'s logic. It seems that the Court's conclusion is something close to a bright-line rule permitting deadly force in vehicle pursuits, absent improbable circumstances. There is one obvious exception: the famous police chase of O.J. Simpson in a white Ford Bronco on June 17, 1994. The car kept its emergency flashers on as it traveled slowly and methodically on a cleared expressway, while a Los Angeles officer spoke to Simpson by cell phone. Even after *Scott*, it is unlikely that police could have reasonably used deadly force to end *that* pursuit.

3. *Police pursuits.* Force aside, *Scott*'s permissive stance toward pursuits matters. Officers conduct tens of thousands of vehicle pursuits each year. Inevitably, when officers give chase, there are crashes, and more than 300 people die in pursuit-related incidents each year, mostly by accident. That number peaked to over 400 fatalities the year *Scott* was decided. Most are suspects or passengers. About a third are bystanders. Only about 1 percent of the people killed are police officers. See Brian A. Reaves, Bureau of Justice Statistics, *Police Vehicle Pursuits, 2012-2013*, at 6 (2017).

4. *Disparities in pursuits.* Neither pursuits nor the deaths associated with them are evenly distributed. Some analysis suggests that African Americans are substantially more likely to be killed during a chase and more likely to be chased for a minor offense, such as an illegally tinted window or a seatbelt violation. Although it is hard to establish whether the racial disparities represent bias, it is notable that Black drivers represent a higher proportion of drivers chased in the daytime, when their skin color is more visible to officers making a decision about whether to pursue. Still, disparities exist both day and night. See Thomas Frank, *Black People Are Three Times Likelier to Be Killed in Police Chases,* USA Today (Dec. 1, 2016).

5. *Bystanders.* The Court explicitly considers the threat that fleeing suspects posed to uninvolved members of the public in *Scott* and *Plumhoff,* as well as in *Garner,* in determining when force is constitutionally permissible. But officers' uses of force threaten the public as well, especially in the pursuit context. When an officer rams a moving vehicle or shoots into it, the driver is likely to lose control, potentially crashing into the nearby drivers or pedestrians who are intended to be protected by the use of force. When an officer shoots into a moving vehicle to stop it, he might easily kill a child passenger or a pedestrian with a stray bullet. Does the Court assume that uses of force are more likely to protect uninvolved members of the public than to threaten them? Or that departments and officers should have the discretion to decide? Or is it failing to consider a significant issue?

6. *Letting suspects go as a matter of law.* The *Garner* Court reasoned that it is better to let some suspects escape than to kill them. The *Scott* Court tells us police do not have to allow suspects to escape to avoid the use of deadly force. Why the difference?

7. *Saving time.* Dangerous driving aside, if the officers had stopped chasing Harris and he had escaped, they likely could have found him later. But that later search would have taken time and effort. Is that enough to justify using deadly force against him?

8. *Letting suspects go as a matter of policy.* Many departments restrict high-speed chases, despite *Scott,* because pursuits are dangerous for officers, bystanders, and suspects alike. See Brian A. Reaves, Bureau of Justice Statistics, *Police Vehicle Pursuits, 2012–2013* at 1, 6 (2017). Increasingly, departments are regulating foot pursuits, too. Although many analysts argue that restrictive use-of-force policies do not increase crime and can build community trust, a few departments have found prohibitory pursuit policies problematic. In Tampa, for example, the department put a moratorium on vehicle chases unless the fleeing suspect was a violent felon. Within two years of adopting the policy, auto thefts skyrocketed. The department reversed its policy, allowing officers to chase most felony suspects again, and auto thefts declined thereafter. See Dean Scoville, *Duty Dangers: Vehicle Pursuits,* Police (Jan. 12, 2012). What if prohibiting pursuits or restricting force during pursuits increases (or decreases) crime? Would that matter to the Court? Should it? Note that the Court cannot reverse course as easily as Tampa did. Does that justify *Scott?*

9. *Culpability.* The *Scott* Court also cited Harris's culpability as a factor justifying the use of force. Why is a suspect's *culpability* relevant to whether force can reasonably be used against him under the Fourth Amendment? After all, police use force to *subdue* criminals, not to *punish* them. Given that police officers overwhelmingly use force against people suspected of criminal activity who resist or flee the police, is considering culpability just a thumb on the scale for more force? Is the Court worried that, without a caution to consider their culpability, officers (or judges after

the fact) will be likely to overvalue suspects' lives? Commentators and critics of the police often worry about the opposite, that officers undervalue life—especially Black lives. Hence the phrase "Black Lives Matter."

Blaming the Victim

Defenders of the police often argue that suspects can avoid being killed by the police by complying with police commands. But it is far from clear that compliance is enough. Perhaps some suspects are perceived as threatening no matter what they do. Philando Castile, a 32-year-old Black man, was pulled over in Falcon Heights, Minnesota, by Officer Jeronimo Yanez. Castile's girlfriend and her four-year-old daughter were also in the car. When the officer asked Castile for his license and registration, Castile told the officer politely and calmly that he had a firearm. Yanez repeatedly told Castile not to pull out the weapon, but the officer still feared that Castile was doing exactly that when Castile moved to reach for his driver's and gun licenses. Despite Castile's apparent attempts to assure Yanez that he was not reaching for the gun, Yanez shot Castile seven times, allegedly in fear for his life. Other suspects have been shot before they have had a chance to comply with commands or before they were aware that law enforcement was present. Although Officer Yanez was charged with manslaughter and dangerous discharge of a firearm for shooting Castile, he was acquitted of all charges.[9]

---

10. *The law of force after* Scott: *Part 1.* In *Scott,* Justice Scalia seems to try to sweep away the common law distinction between deadly force and nondeadly force recognized in *Garner.* He is even more dismissive of *Graham's* reasonableness factors; he doesn't even cite them. Does Justice Scalia explain why he is trying to remake use-of-force doctrine? Whatever his reasons, it seems that he largely failed. Although *Scott* was the Court's first major use-of-force case in decades, lower courts continued to treat deadly force and nondeadly force differently for the purposes of constitutional law, using *Garner* to guide the use of deadly force and *Graham* to guide the use of nondeadly force.[10] Unless a car chase is involved, most courts usually relegate *Scott* to a "see also" citation. Why does the Court go out of its way to try to eliminate what little structure constitutional use-of-force analysis had? Why might lower courts have resisted that change?

11. *The law of force after* Scott: *Part 2.* It isn't just lower courts that have marginalized *Scott.* After *Scott,* many police departments have retained use-of-force policies that distinguish between deadly and nondeadly force, *à la Garner,* and they have *added* policies restricting officer authority to engage in high-speed chases and to use force during pursuits. See Brian A. Reaves, Bureau of Justice Statistics, *Police Vehicle Pursuits, 2012–2013* at 5 (2017).

---

[9] Two videos of the Philando Castile shooting have been made public: one from the dashcam of the officer's patrol car and another streamed through Facebook Live by Castile's girlfriend, who began filming after Castile was shot. Both are deeply disturbing, and watching them is likely unnecessary to understand this point.

[10] All states also treat nondeadly force and deadly force differently.

Even the Supreme Court treats *Scott* as a case of limited applicability. Look at *Plumhoff* again. The Court cites *Graham* and *Garner* as cases establishing the Fourth Amendment standard, and it treats *Scott* as an application of that standard to a set of (very similar) facts. The *Plumhoff* Court never mentions culpability, despite *Scott*'s emphasis on it. Instead, it focuses exclusively on the idea that in both cases, the suspects "posed a grave public safety risk." *Plumhoff*, 572 U.S. at 776. And in case you didn't yet get the message, Justice Alito concludes that, "as in *Scott*, the police acted reasonably in using *deadly* force." *Id.* at 777 (emphasis added). In other cases, the Court relies on *Graham* and *Garner*, maintains the deadly–nondeadly distinction, and rarely and barely mentions *Scott*. See, e.g., Kisela v. Hughes, 138 S. Ct. 1148 (2018); County of Los Angeles v. Mendez, 137 S. Ct. 1539 (2017); White v. Pauly, 137 S. Ct. 548 (2017). Why might *Garner* have changed both the law and policing while *Scott* did neither?

12. *Rule specificity.* From *Garner* to *Graham* to *Scott*, the Court sets *decreasingly* rule-like standards for guiding police uses of force. This indeterminacy has important legal consequences:

> While the Court has declared some uses or degrees of force within bounds or beyond the pale, it has failed to provide a principled basis for determining when police uses of force are reasonable under the Fourth Amendment. This has had the effect of stunting the development of the law in the lower federal courts: While the intuition of federal judges usually leads to results that seem reasonable and are consistent with the Court's doctrine, the reasoning in these cases is ad hoc, often inconsistent, and sometimes ill-considered. Because the doctrine on police violence is underdeveloped, the outcomes of future cases are largely unpredictable, even by the Supreme Court's own measure. This unpredictability turns out to be of enormous consequence to federal civil rights litigation. Under the doctrine of qualified immunity, officers are not civilly liable under federal civil rights law for using excessive force unless the unlawfulness of their conduct is apparent from prior case law. Since current Fourth Amendment doctrine is often too indeterminate to permit officers to determine the lawfulness of a particular use of force ex ante from past Supreme Court and lower federal opinions, qualified immunity plays an overly expansive role in determining the outcome of excessive force litigation. Thus, the indeterminate nature of the Court's doctrine leads many unconstitutional uses of force to go uncompensated and undeterred.

Rachel A. Harmon, *When Is Police Violence Justified?*, 102 Nw. U. L. Rev. 1119, 1123 (2008). Nancy Leong found evidence of this unpredictability when she thoroughly studied federal appellate Fourth Amendment cases, including those addressing the use of force. See Nancy Leong, *Making Rights*, 92 B.U. L. Rev. 405, 447 (2012) (finding that appellate courts "tend either to evaluate police procedures at such a minute level of detail that future courts have difficulty extracting a principle on which to decide a future case or to apply these general principles unelaborated").

13. *Factbound cases and certiorari.* The same indeterminacy that denies lower courts guidance can also forestall further regulation of the police by the Supreme Court itself. In granting certiorari on questions of constitutional law, the Court looks for disagreements between lower federal courts and state supreme courts. It resists granting cert in cases involving merely erroneous factual analysis or the misapplication of a properly stated rule of law. See Sup. Ct. R. 10. By suggesting that every

use-of-force case involves wading through a "factbound morass," Justice Scalia comes close to announcing that the Court should be closed to use-of-force cases; if every case is specific to its facts, there is unlikely to be a split among courts that is worth resolving. He intended this message: When Justice Scalia called the morass *factbound*, he was not just using a nice turn of phrase. He was expressly invoking the term that is used by lawyers in briefs to the Court and internally by clerks in cert pool memos to argue against granting a cert petition. Cf., e.g., Matthew L.M. Fletcher, *Factbound and Splitless: The Certiorari Process as Barrier to Justice for Indian Tribes*, 51 Ariz. L. Rev. 933 (2009) (discussing the use of the terms *factbound* and *splitless* in cert pool memos).

Contrast the Court's rare consideration of the reasonableness of police uses of force with its enthusiasm for overturning lower court decisions refusing officers qualified immunity in cases involving uses of force. In these opinions, the Court has repeatedly, some might say fiercely, emphasized the importance of correcting lower courts in order to shield officers from litigation and liability in the face of constitutional uncertainty. Yet it has refused to determine whether the force was constitutional or develop the standard further, leaving questions about the constitutionality of force open. See, e.g., City of Escondido v. Emmons, 139 S. Ct. 500 (2019); Kisela v. Hughes, 138 S. Ct. 1148 (2018); White v. Pauly, 137 S. Ct. 548 (2017); Mullenix v. Luna, 136 S. Ct. 305 (2015). In a world in which nearly 1,000 people are killed by the police each year and the public is consumed by concern about police violence, why is the Supreme Court avoiding these questions?

The Power of Law

When lower courts apply *Graham* and *Garner* to produce clear instruction, officers and departments respond. In *Armstrong v. Village of Pinehurst*, 810 F.3d 892 (4th Cir. 2016), the Fourth Circuit used *Graham* and its own precedents to assess an officer's repeated use of a Taser to subdue a noncompliant but nonviolent man. The court could have issued a fact-specific ruling that left officers with little guidance. After all, the facts of the case were distinctive and might easily have limited any holding by the court:

> [W]hen Officer Gatling deployed his taser, Armstrong was a mentally ill man being seized for his own protection, was seated on the ground, was hugging a post to ensure his immobility, was surrounded by three police officers and two Hospital security guards, and had failed to submit to a lawful seizure for only 30 seconds. A reasonable officer would have perceived a static stalemate with few, if any, exigencies—not an immediate danger so severe that the officer must beget the exact harm the seizure was intended to avoid.

Id. at 906. Instead, the court engaged in its analysis of the facts only after it established a more general rule that "a police officer may *only* use serious injurious force, like a taser, when an objectively reasonable officer would conclude that the circumstances present a risk of immediate danger that could be mitigated by the use of force. At bottom, 'physical resistance' is not synonymous with 'risk of immediate danger.'" *Id.* at 905.

This directive helped departments in the Fourth Circuit understand when using Tasers is legal in a way a fact-specific holding could not. As part of a larger study of Taser use, Reuters analyzed the change in Taser use in the Fourth Circuit's five states after *Armstrong* was decided. It found that cities developed more restrictive Taser policies and used Tasers significantly less often.

Police Department	Drop in Taser Deployments
Baltimore (Md.)	47%
Virginia Beach (Va.)	65%
Greensboro (N.C.)	60%
Charleston (S.C.)	55%
Huntington (W. Va.)	52%
Norfolk (Va.)	95%

Jason Szep et al., *Special Report: "Breathe, Ronald, Breathe": The Court Case Curbing Taser Use*, Reuters (Aug. 23, 2017). Another report similarly found that Taser use dropped substantially in almost all large departments and many small ones in Virginia after the opinion. See Mark Bowes, *Police Taser Use in Va. Drops—in Some Cases Dramatically in Wake of 2016 Court Decision*, Richmond Times-Dispatch (Apr. 25, 2017).

Of course, it isn't clear what officers used instead of Tasers. If officers talked people into handcuffs or waited suspects out, this decline might represent a notable success. If officers instead struggled with suspects or used batons, and both suspects and officers suffered more injuries, maybe the decrease is actually bad news. Either way, the law seems to have affected how often and when Tasers are used, at least in the cities studied.

11.   Why Didn't He Just Shoot Him in the Leg?

The plaintiffs in *Plumhoff* also argued that, even if deadly force had been permissible, the use of force was nonetheless excessive because the officer fired 15 shots. The Court rejected this contention:

> It stands to reason that, if police officers are justified in firing at a suspect in order to end a severe threat to public safety, the officers need not stop shooting until the threat has ended. As petitioners noted below, "if lethal force is justified, officers are taught to keep shooting until the threat is over."
>
> Here, during the 10-second span when all the shots were fired, Rickard never abandoned his attempt to flee. Indeed, even after all the shots had been fired, he managed to drive away and to continue driving until he crashed. This would be a different case if petitioners had initiated a second round of shots after an initial round had clearly incapacitated Rickard and had ended any threat of continued flight, or if Rickard had clearly given himself up. But that is not what happened.

Plumhoff, 572 U.S. at 777.

Officers in a high-stress situation are also unlikely to be able to target an extremity effectively, except perhaps the upper legs. Even if they could, a suspect hit in an arm or leg might not be immediately incapacitated by being shot. Indeed, the same is true for a person shot in the torso. As a result, a gravely injured suspect can remain a threat to officers and others.[11] See, e.g., Anthony J. Pinizzotto, Harry A. Kern & Edward F. Davis, *One-Shot Drops: Surviving the Myth*, 73 FBI L. Enforcement Bull. 14, 16, 20 (2004).

The most famous (in law enforcement) incident illustrating the problem was a 1986 shootout in Miami. When half a dozen FBI agents attempted to stop two bank robbers, one of the suspects managed to kill two agents and injure several others *after* he had received fatal bullet wounds but before he fell unconscious. In the aftermath of that shooting, police around the country changed their guns and ammunition to make it easier to kill suspects when they shoot them, and they newly emphasized ending the threat in training. Does that affect your view of whether 15 shots is too many? Is this another example of the way the law effectively allocates risk between officers and members of the public?

Despite tactical and legal arguments, communities have been horrified by the 41 bullets fired by NYPD officers at Amadou Diallo in 1999 as Diallo reached for his wallet; the 50 bullets fired into Sean Bell's car by NYPD officers on the morning of Bell's wedding in 2006 after Bell crashed into a plainclothes officer; and the (at least) 377 rounds fired in Miami in 2013 at two then-unarmed men who earlier robbed a drugstore, shot an officer, stole a police car, crashed another stolen vehicle, and when the shots were fired, refused to get out of the car and were seen moving their hands. How should we address the gap between community sentiment and the law?

At least one department has backed away from the traditional just-keep-firing training, earning a lot of criticism from officers. The San Francisco Police Department started to train police recruits to shoot two rounds and then stop and reassess before shooting again after its officers shot Mario Woods, a man holding a knife, 21 times in a controversial shooting. The shooting was captured on video by middle school children passing by on a bus. Although Woods repeatedly ignored officers' orders, he appeared to be walking away from them at the time of the shooting. The video can be found at Lawclerk Burris, *Mario Woods Shooting Previously Unreleased Courtesy of the Law Office of John L. Burris*, YouTube (Dec. 11, 2015), *https://youtu.be/ADr7I8mOHNA*. What difference would it have made if Mario Woods had been shot twice instead of 21 times?

A better outcome would have been if Mario Woods were never shot at all. That might seem hard—he was armed and refusing to submit—but other departments have managed to do it. The Camden County Police Department faced a similar incident in November 2015. An emotionally disturbed man with a knife threatened patrons in a restaurant and then walked out onto the street. When officers responded, more than half a dozen officers on foot and several police cars cleared the street and created a rolling perimeter to follow the man. For several minutes, they gave repeated clear and calm instructions to the man to drop the knife. Then they attempted to Tase him. When the Taser did not work, officers continued to follow the man until he—eventually—dropped the knife. Then they took him into custody. See Rebecca Everett, *How N.J.'s Most Dangerous City Is Trying to Stop Police Shootings*, NJ.com (Aug. 22, 2017), *https://www.nj.com/camden/2017/08/how_njs_most_dangerous_city_is_trying_to_stop_poli.html*. If this man had not dropped his knife, would killing him have been constitutional? At what point?

---

[11] Even beyond shooting practices, the risk that a gravely injured suspect can kill an officer costs suspects their lives. Some officers are trained not to approach an armed (or potentially armed) suspect even after he has been incapacitated in a shooting until it is clear that the person poses no threat. That precaution to protect officer safety delays medical treatment for suspects, and some suspects who might otherwise survive a shooting die as a result.

If it is possible to avoid shooting him, should that avoidance be constitutionally required? If you watch the Camden video, you will see the huge investment the department made to avoid shooting the suspect. Before the day of the incident, officers were trained and equipped to reduce force. When the particular incident was reported, the department dedicated many of its officers to resolving it, and for an extended period of time, too. What about a smaller department without so many officers? Without money to do deescalation training? Without resources to give officers access to multiple nonlethal weapons? To stop an armed suspect, such officers would likely face a starker choice between putting themselves at risk by grappling with him and protecting themselves by shooting him. How should the Court incorporate that kind of practical concern in setting standards for uses of force? Should reasonable force vary by department? Over time?

B. State Law on the Use of Force

The Fourth Amendment does not *authorize* the use of force against individuals; it sets constitutional *limits* on the force that states may authorize police officers to use. Within those limits, states define the rules of engagement in policing.

1. General Use-of-Force Statutes

Utah's statutes authorizing police officers to use force are reasonably typical.

UTAH CODE ANN. §§76-2-403 TO -404

§76-2-403. Force in arrest.

Any person is justified in using any force, except deadly force, which he reasonably believes to be necessary to effect an arrest or to defend himself or another from bodily harm while making an arrest.

§76-2-404. Peace officer's use of deadly force.

(1) A peace officer, or any person acting by the officer's command in providing aid and assistance, is justified in using deadly force when:

(a) the officer is acting in obedience to and in accordance with the judgment of a competent court in executing a penalty of death under Subsection 77-18-5.5(2), (3), or (4);

(b) effecting an arrest or preventing an escape from custody following an arrest, where the officer reasonably believes that deadly force is necessary to prevent the arrest from being defeated by escape; and

(i) the officer has probable cause to believe that the suspect has committed a felony offense involving the infliction or threatened infliction of death or serious bodily injury; or

(ii) the officer has probable cause to believe the suspect poses a threat of death or serious bodily injury to the officer or to others if apprehension is delayed; or

(c) the officer reasonably believes that the use of deadly force is necessary to prevent death or serious bodily injury to the officer or another person.

(2) If feasible, a verbal warning should be given by the officer prior to any use of deadly force under Subsection (1)(b) or (1)(c).

How close is Utah's standard to federal constitutional law?

Interestingly, some states appear to authorize more force than federal constitutional law permits. Florida law, for example, states that an officer "is justified in the use of *any* force . . . [w]hich he or she reasonably believes to be necessary to defend himself or herself or another from bodily harm while making the arrest," or "when necessarily committed in arresting felons fleeing from justice." Fla. Stat. §776.05. That statute would appear to allow deadly force in response to nonserious threats and to detain nondangerous felons.[12] Do you see how that departs from constitutional standards?

Other states authorize significantly less force than constitutional law would allow. Tennessee, for instance, permits "deadly force to effect an arrest only if all other reasonable means of apprehension have been exhausted or are unavailable, and where feasible, the officer has given notice of the officer's identity as such and given a warning that deadly force may be used unless resistance or flight ceases," as well as requiring the conditions specified in *Garner*. Tenn. Code. Ann. §39-11-620(b). Iowa permits the use of deadly force only "when a person cannot be captured any other way and either . . . [t]he person has used or threatened to use deadly force in committing a felony[, or t]he peace officer reasonably believes the person would use deadly force against any person unless immediately apprehended." Iowa Code Ann. §804.8. Though most states have separate deadly and nondeadly-force statutes, as Utah does, some, including Tennessee, have statutes governing only deadly force.

2.   Special Use-of-Force Statutes

Less commonly, states regulate specific issues in the use of force, often by requiring departments to develop policies and provide training rather than stepping directly into the regulatory fray. Consider this Georgia statute, known as the TASER and Electronic Control Weapons Act.

GA. CODE ANN. §35-8-26

§35-8-26. TASER and electronic control weapons . . .

(c) A law enforcement unit authorizing the use of electronic control weapons or similar devices shall establish lawful written policies and directives providing for the use and deployment of such weapons and devices that are consistent with the training requirements established by the Georgia Peace Officer Standards and Training Council. The policies and directives required by this subsection shall be issued prior to the issuance of such devices.

---

[12] Although Florida broadly authorizes using force against fleeing felons, officers do not have a defense against civil actions for the wrongful use of deadly force unless the force satisfies restrictions similar to those imposed by *Garner*. See Fla. Stat. §776.05(3).

(d) Prior to the official use of electronic control weapons or similar devices, peace officers authorized by the officer's law enforcement unit to use such devices shall be required to satisfactorily complete a course of instruction and certification requirements approved by the council. All persons certified to use electronic control weapons shall complete an update or refresher training course of such duration and at such time as may be prescribed by the council in order for their electronic control weapons certification to remain in force and effect.

(e) A department head authorizing the use of an electronic control weapon or similar device or a peace officer using an electronic control weapon or similar device in violation of this Code section shall be subject to disciplinary action as provided for in this chapter. The council is authorized to withdraw or suspend the certification to operate an electronic control weapon of any person for failure to meet the update or refresher requirements specified in this Code section or for violation of any portion of this chapter relating to conditions which may lead to the withdrawal, suspension, or probation of a peace officer's certification.

(f) The Georgia Public Safety Training Center shall provide council approved training to peace officers for the use of electronic control weapons and similar devices.

A couple of states also have laws banning chokeholds and many states have considered them since George Floyd was killed when an officer knelt on his neck in May 2020. Here is Colorado's new law:

COLO. REV. STAT. §18–1–707(2.5)

(a) A peace officer is prohibited from using a chokehold upon another person.

(b) **(I)** For the purposes of this subsection (2.5), "chokehold" means a method by which a person applies sufficient pressure to a person to make breathing difficult or impossible and includes but is not limited to any pressure to the neck, throat, or windpipe that may prevent or hinder breathing or reduce intake of air.

(II) "Chokehold" also means applying pressure to a person's neck on either side of the windpipe, but not to the windpipe itself, to stop the flow of blood to the brain via the carotid arteries.

NOTES AND QUESTIONS

1. *Authorizing force through defenses.* States often define permissible force indirectly. Like anyone else, police officers are subject to state criminal laws. Just as state statutes provide justification defenses to those acting in self-defense or in defense of others, they also frequently provide a defense to police officers who use force under specified circumstances. Rather than passing statutes that authorize police use of force, most states effectively provide permission to use force through these defenses. Utah's law is an example. Justification defense statutes are further discussed in Chapter 14.

2. *State law and constitutional laws.* What could happen to an officer who complies with Florida's law but violates federal constitutional law? What about an officer who violates Tennessee's law but complies with federal constitutional law?

3. *Preclusive statutes.* Georgia's use-of-force law also states: "No law enforcement agency of this state or of any political subdivision of this state shall adopt or promulgate any rule, regulation, or policy which prohibits a peace officer from using that degree of force to apprehend a suspected felon which is allowed by the statutory and

case law of this state." Ga. Code. Ann. §17-4-20(d). Does that statute help explain Georgia's distinctive Taser law? What are the advantages and disadvantages of state prohibition on local restrictions on police use of force?

4. *Indirect means of regulating force.* States and cities also look for ways to regulate police practices that frequently lead to force, such as no-knock warrant execution, or the use of military equipment. What else should states interested in reducing force consider?

5. *States without statutes.* Eight states have no statutes specifying when officers may use force; they rely on the common law instead. Given the attention surrounding the law of force after the May 2020 death of George Floyd, this might well change. At the moment, however, in several of those states, the case law on when force is authorized is not well developed, with few or no court decisions explaining the standard. What might explain why so few cases involving state law limits on the use of force arise?

Oddly, in assessing common law authority, some states without statutes turn to federal constitutional law. For example, the South Carolina Supreme Court approved a jury instruction that said " 'a law enforcement officer may use whatever force is necessary to effect the arrest of a felon including deadly force, if necessary to effect that arrest,' " as "the current and correct law of South Carolina." But in coming to that conclusion, the state high court cited only *Garner*, a *federal* constitutional case (and one that seems to contradict, rather than support, the state court's point). See Sheppard v. State, 594 S.E.2d 462, 472–473 (S.C. 2004). Similarly, a Virginia court looked to *Graham* "for guidance" when evaluating a tort claim against an officer for assault. See Gray v. Rhoads, 55 Va. Cir. 362 (Va. Cir. Ct. 2001). Doesn't it seem odd for a state court to look to federal constitutional law (which diverges from the common law) to understand the content of common law authority to use force? How much weight should state courts give to federal constitutional law in interpreting state use-of-force rules, whether there is a statute or not?

6. *Enforcement.* What do these statutes tell you about how they are enforced? What kind of enforcement would you want to see?

7. *Do they work?* Activists have demanded, and states have proposed, bills changing the law on force in the wake of controversial deaths at the hands of police officers. Could a state pass a restrictive law and find no reduction in the use of force? Why might that occur? Does it surprise you that Tennessee has a higher rate of fatal police uses of force per capita than Florida does? See Seth W. Stoughton et al., *Evaluating Police Uses of Force* 87–89 (2020). *Fatalities* are influenced by some factors unrelated to how much force was used, including access to medical aid. Still, the contrast is suggestive. What data would help you determine whether state law changes the force the police use?

8. *Use-of-force politics.* California's Assembly Bill 392 (AB 392) took effect on January 1, 2020. The statute was proposed and passed in the aftermath of the controversial 2018 shooting of Stephon Clark, described in a box earlier in the chapter. The shooting led to large protests in Sacramento and beyond. AB 392 is the legislation that survived the fierce political battle that followed, in which competing bills were proposed, rejected, revised, and sometimes linked to each other. Among other provisions, AB 392 restricts the use of force to that which an officer reasonably believes is necessary; it forbids the use of force against those who pose a threat of harm only to themselves; and it requires consideration of the officer's preforce conduct in evaluating whether a use of force is necessary.

Although the bill eventually passed overwhelmingly, the legislation faced shifting support and opposition from those concerned about the issue. Law enforcement unions fiercely opposed the legislation initially but softened their vehemence when the bill was revised to eliminate a requirement that officers exhaust other options before using force, as well as provisions that would have made it easier to prosecute officers. Once it became clear that the bill would pass, law enforcement groups moved from opposing the legislation to being neutral toward it.

Some activist groups moved along an opposite trajectory. The Black Lives Matter Global Network (BLM) initially cosponsored the bill with other community and civil rights organizations. But BLM withdrew its support when the bill was watered down:

> The bill was initially written to do three things: 1) change the police use-of-force standard from "reasonable" to "necessary," 2) require de-escalation by police officers, and 3) hold officers who violate these criminally liable. Amendments to the bill significantly weaken all three of these provisions, and, by virtually all analyses, provides the greatest guidance during litigation or after someone has been killed by police, instead of working to prevent police killings and the devaluation of human life within our communities, which was our intention. . . .

> Unfortunately, as now written, AB 392 does not provide the kind of substantive change that we imagined when the process began. While we are aware that AB 392 will likely pass without us, we feel compelled to take a strong stance consistent with our commitment to our communities to ensure police accountability and divestment from the police.

Black Lives Matter Global Network Withdraws Support from California's AB 392, Black Lives Matter (May 29, 2019). The ACLU of Southern California disagreed with BLM. It had also helped to sponsor the bill and lobbied heavily in its favor, claiming that, even in its final state, the bill would save lives by raising the standard for the use of deadly force. The ALCU even encouraged its members to send thank-you notes to legislators after it was passed. See *California Act to Save Lives (AB 392)*, Am. Civil Liberties Union. What would you want to know (e.g., about alternatives, implementation, or remedies) before deciding what you think of the law?

Constitutional rules are constrained by precedent and interpretive traditions, but they require agreement among only a handful of justices. State laws can say almost anything, but they inevitably involve political debate and compromise. How might these disparate methods for producing use-of-force standards affect the rules that result?

C.   *Agency Use-of-Force Policies*

State laws can be the basis for criminal and civil remedies, and—obviously—they have statewide effect. But they are often slow to change, and they tend to be non-specific, providing only general guidance about how and when force may be used.

Agency policies on the use of force vary much more than state statutes do. Many departments have permissive policies, tied closely to the language of *Graham* and *Garner*. Others provide restrictive guidance about when and how officers may use force in elaborate policies that go on for more than a dozen pages.

Local policies can in turn feed back into state law. For example, the "necessary" force standard adopted in California via AB 392, discussed above, had already been adopted by both Seattle and San Francisco in departmental policies. Both cities claimed to have reduced the number of force incidents following the change, which was used as an argument in favor of the state bill when it was debated.

Although agency policies do not give private actors a cause of action, members of the public can file complaints when officers violate policy, and officers in turn can be disciplined or fired for doing so. Policies are also the basis for officer training and supervision, so they can have a significant effect on police behavior.

The process for developing policies and the role of agency policies in constraining officer discretion is considered in Chapter 10. Still, use-of-force policies raise some special issues that are discussed here. As you read, consider what you think of the comparative advantages and disadvantages of using departmental policies to influence what officers do.

1.   A Force Continuum

One traditional approach to guiding police use of force is to create a *force matrix* or a *force continuum*, a graphical representation that matches defined levels of resistance to the defined levels of force with which that resistance may be met. Such a chart might specify that officers can use no more than a "come along" hold or handcuffs for a compliant suspect; pain-compliance or open-hand tactics to overcome passive resistance; more serious less-lethal weaponry (such as Taser) against a suspect who punches at or wrestles with an officer; and deadly force against someone who poses a deadly threat to the officer. Here is the Philadelphia Police Department's version:

USE OF FORCE DECISION CHART

DEADLY FORCE

Officer Options: Firearm

Offender Behavior: Objectively reasonable belief that there is an immediate threat of death or serious bodily injury

ESCALATION   DE-ESCALATION

LESS LETHAL FORCE

Officer Options: Elecronic Control Weapon (ECW), ASP/Baton
Offender Threat: Physically Aggressive or Assaultive behavior with immediate likelihood of injury to self or others

MODERATE/LIMITED FORCE

Officer Options: Physical Control Holds, OC Spray
Offender Threat: Resisting and Non-Compliant

NO FORCE

(Use of Force Report not required)
Officer Options: Verbal Commands, Officer Presence
Offender Threat: Obedient, Compliant, Non-Aggressive

Use the option that represents the minimal amount of force necessary to reduce the immediate threat

Philadelphia Police Dept., Directive 10.2, Use of Moderate/Limited Force 4 (Sept. 18, 2015).

2. Reform Proposals

Policies are important because they provide guidance for officers *before* they use force and a basis for holding them accountable *afterward*. Policies have also become an important outward-facing indicator of agency values and practices, one about which communities often have something to say. Although there are as many reform proposals for police use-of-force policies as there are groups critical of police practices, these reforms advocated by Campaign Zero have been frequently cited:

CAMPAIGN ZERO, POLICY SOLUTIONS, LIMIT USE OF FORCE

Establish standards and reporting of police use of deadly force

A. Authorize deadly force **only** when there is an **imminent** threat to an officer's life or the life of another person and such force is strictly unavoidable to protect life as required under International Law. Deadly force should only be authorized after all other reasonable means have been exhausted.

B. Require that an officer's tactical conduct and decisions leading up to using deadly force be considered in judgements of whether such force was reasonable.

C. Require officers give a verbal warning, when possible, before using deadly force and give people a reasonable amount of time to comply with the warning. . . .

Revise and strengthen local police department use of force policies

Revised police use of force policies should . . . require officers to:

- **restrict** officers from using deadly force unless all reasonable alternatives have been exhausted
- **use** minimum amount of force to apprehend a subject, with specific guidelines for the types of force and tools authorized for a given level of resistance
- **utilize** de-escalation tactics (verbalization; creating distance, time and space; tactical repositioning, etc.) whenever possible instead of using force
- **carry** a less-lethal weapon
- **ban** using force on a person for talking back or as punishment for running away
- **ban** chokeholds, strangleholds (i.e. carotid restraints), hog-tying and transporting people face down in a vehicle
- **intervene** to stop other officers who are using excessive force and report them to a supervisor
- **have** first aid kits and immediately render medical assistance to anyone in police custody who is injured or who complains of an injury

End traffic-related police killings and dangerous high-speed police chases

Prohibit police officers from:

- **shooting** at moving vehicles
- **moving** in front of moving vehicles
- **high-speed** chases of people who have not and are not about to commit a violent felony

3.   A Progressive Use-of-Force Policy

Many agency use-of-force policies remain permissive and nonspecific. But the pressure to change is growing. To see the impact of community concern, you might look at departmental policy reforms carried out in Camden, New Jersey. Scott Thomson, the then chief, is widely recognized for being progressive and innovative. He guided the adoption of a policy that garnered support from both the New Jersey ACLU and the Fraternal Order of Police. It is 18 pages long, making it too long to include here. But this is how it starts:

CAMDEN CTY., N.J., POLICE DEPARTMENT POLICY ON USE OF FORCE (2013) (REVISED 2019)

Purpose

1. The primary purpose of this directive is to ensure officers respect the sanctity of life when making decisions regarding use of force. Sworn law enforcement officers have been granted the extraordinary authority to use force when necessary to accomplish lawful ends. That authority is grounded in the responsibility of officers to comply with the laws of the State of New Jersey regarding the use of force and to comply with the provisions of this directive. Equally important is law enforcement's obligation to prepare individual officers in the best way possible to exercise that authority.

In situations where law enforcement officers are justified in using force, the utmost restraint should be exercised. Use of force should never be considered routine. In exercising this authority, officers must respect the sanctity of all human life, act in all possible respects to preserve human life, do everything possible to avoid unnecessary uses of force, and minimize the force that is used, while still protecting themselves and the public.

Policy

2. This directive applies to all officer uses of force. This directive establishes guidelines for officers with regard to use of force. This directive applies to all uses of force, whether officers are on- or off-duty. This directive complements the Critical Decision-Making model (CDM) that is the core of the Department's use of force training. CDM provides officers with an organized way of making decisions about how they shall act in any situation, including situations that may involve potential uses of force.

3. This directive recognizes constitutional principles, but aspires to go beyond them. The Fourth Amendment requires that an officer's use of force be "objectively reasonable." Graham v. Connor, 490 U.S. 386 (1989). Under this standard, an officer may only use force that a reasonable officer would when facing similar circumstances. The objectively reasonable standard acknowledges the difficult decisions that officers are forced to make under rapidly evolving and often unpredictable circumstances, but it does not provide specific guidance on what to do in any given situation.

The Constitution provides a "floor" for government action. This Department aspires to go beyond *Graham* and its minimum requirements. Sound judgment and the appropriate exercise of discretion will always be the foundation of police officer decision making in the broad range of possible use of force situations. It is not possible to entirely replace judgment and discretion with detailed policy provisions. Nonetheless, this directive is intended to ensure that de-escalation techniques are used whenever feasible, that force is only used when necessary, and that the amount of force used is proportionate to the situation that an officer encounters.

The Department's core use of force principles are as follows:

CORE PRINCIPLE #1: Officers may use force only to accomplish specific law enforcement objectives.

CORE PRINCIPLE #2: Whenever feasible, officers should attempt to de-escalate confrontations with the goal of resolving encounters without force. Officers may only use force that is objectively reasonable, necessary, and as a last resort.

CORE PRINCIPLE #3: Officers must use only the amount of force that is proportionate to the circumstances.

CORE PRINCIPLE #4: Deadly force is only authorized as a last resort and only in strict accordance with this directive.

CORE PRINCIPLE #5: Officers must promptly provide or request medical aid.

CORE PRINCIPLE #6: Employees have a duty to stop and report uses of force that violate any applicable law and/or this directive.

4. Officers will be disciplined for violations of this directive. This directive is not intended to create or impose any legal obligations or bases for legal liability absent an expression of such intent by a legislative body, court, or agency. Nevertheless, officers have an affirmative, individual duty to ensure compliance with this directive and with applicable state and federal laws. This applies to the officer's own conduct, as well as observation or knowledge of the conduct by other employees. This directive reinforces the responsibility of officers to take those steps possible to prevent or stop illegal or inappropriate uses of force by other officers. Actions inconsistent with this directive may result in disciplinary action, up to and including termination. At the same time, officers whose actions are consistent with the law and the provisions of this directive will be strongly supported in any subsequent review of their conduct regarding the use of force.

Camden Police Chief J. Scott Thomson, 2018.

4.   The Role of Unions

Although the Camden policy is exceptional in both its directness and restrictiveness, other departments also restrict the use of force in ways that go far beyond state statutes. For example, as noted above, several major police departments require officers to use deadly force only when necessary. Others require that officers use only the minimum force necessary in nondeadly situations as well. Many prohibit the use of specific kinds of force or force under specific conditions. Still, many do not, and unions often resist use-of-force policy changes that limit officer discretion.

Unions might not have the right under most states' law to collectively bargain over changes to use-of-force policies. State statutes typically define the scope of collective-bargaining agreements broadly, permitting negotiation on "matters of wages, hours, and other conditions of employment." See Stephen Rushin, *Police Union Contracts*, 66 Duke L.J. 1191, 1205 n.63 (2017) (collecting state statutes regulating public-employee collective bargaining). Nonetheless, this breadth does not include managerial prerogatives—"issues of 'policy' which are exclusively reserved to government discretion." Deborah Tussey, Annotation, *Bargainable or Negotiable Issues in State Public Employment Relations*, 84 A.L.R. 3d 242, 255–256 (1978). At least some courts have held that use-of-force policies are exempted from bargaining for this reason. See San Jose Peace Officer's Association v. City of San Jose, 144 Cal. Rptr. 3d 638, 645 (Cal. Ct. App. 1978).

Still, unionization affects the use of force. Whether or not they are required to do so, cities bring unions into discussions over use-of-force policies, because rank-and-file buy-in is important to making changes more than nominal. Moreover, unions *do* collectively bargain over all sorts of matters that make use-of-force policies effective, including how complaints are taken, when they are investigated, how officers are treated in those investigations, what kinds of discipline are permissible for violations, what kinds of appeal are available, how long disciplinary records are kept, and for what purpose they may be used.

Unions also resist reforms that are not embedded in formal policies. For example, in April 2019, Minneapolis Mayor Jacob Frey banned "warrior-style" training for police officers on the ground that "fear-based" training exaggerated officers' sense of the threat the public poses and was in "direct conflict" with community policing values. In response, the union representing the city's 900 rank-and-file officers offered free warrior-style training to any officer that wanted it as long as Frey remained mayor. Frey doubled down, insisting that any officer found to have received the training without preapproval would be disciplined. Ultimately, the union complied with the ban. See Libor Jany, *Minneapolis Police Union Offers Free "Warrior" Training, in Defiance of Mayor's ban*, Star Tribune (Apr. 24, 2019). Just over a year later, the Minneapolis police department would become the epicenter of nationwide outrage over police use of force: On May 25, 2020, Minneapolis officers arrested George Floyd after a 911 call reporting his use of a counterfeit $20 bill. Video footage of officer Derek Chauvin kneeling for minutes on Floyd's neck (including several minutes after he was nonresponsive) quickly went viral and sparked nationwide protests. See Evan Hill et al., *8 Minutes and 46 Seconds: How George Floyd Was Killed in Police Custody*, N.Y. Times (May 31, 2020).

Perhaps the combination of formal and informal influence exerted by police unions explains why one study found that sheriff's offices with collective-bargaining agreements had more violent misconduct than those that did not collectively bargain. Dhammika Dharmapala et al., *Collective Bargaining Rights and Police Misconduct: Evidence from Florida* 5 (University of Chicago Public Law & Legal Theory Working Paper No. 655, Aug. 2019). Can you think of any ways to mitigate union power to hinder police reform? Or is that the wrong goal?

5.   Public Safety Without Policing: Reform, Defund, or Abolish?

Nearly a thousand people are killed by the police each year. Many times that number are seriously injured. Although the social consequences of police violence are distributed somewhat more broadly, the physical toll is unfairly concentrated in communities of color and other vulnerable populations. Naturally, all kinds of stakeholders are searching for ways to reduce the use of force while maintaining public safety.

Efforts to reduce the use of force—through regulation as permissive as the Supreme Court's Fourth Amendment jurisprudence or as restrictive as Camden's departmental policy—have largely depended on a critical premise: Despite the enormous cost that force exacts, policing is so critical to achieving community goals that policing, and some violence along with it, must be allowed, even if it necessarily produces significant harm. But what if that premise is wrong?

To some, attempting to limit the use of force misses the point. These activists believe that policing, as it is practiced in the United States, inevitably threatens public well-being more than it enhances it—at least in many communities. The costs, they say, will always outweigh the benefits. So rather than improve policing, they seek to undermine and dismantle policing altogether.

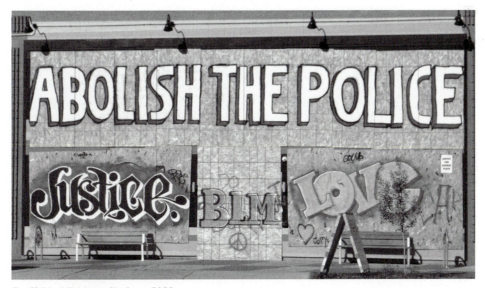

Graffiti in Minneapolis, June 2020.

The proposed solutions are varied. The Movement for Black Lives, for example, advocates a "divest-invest" strategy that includes the "reallocation of funds at the federal, state, and local level from policing and incarceration . . . to long-term strategy strategies such as education, local restorative justice services, and employment programs." See *A Vision for Black Lives: Police Demands for Black Power, Freedom, and Justice*, New Economy Coalition (Aug. 2016). Critical Resistance counsels its members to oppose any reform strategy that fails to reduce the tools, technologies, or funding for the police— including many reforms that other groups support, such as requiring the use of body cameras, adopting community policing strategies, improving officer training, and establishing civilian review boards. The #NoCopAcademy in Chicago fought to fund youth and community programs with money that Chicago's mayor had proposed to use for a police training center. The Audre Lorde Project's Safe Neighborhood Campaign teaches communities to build and practice their own intervention and safety strategies, including community-led deescalation and rapid response to violence, as an alternative to calling the police. In each case, rather than seeking to repair policing, these organizations argue for *abolishing* policing and replacing it with community-based alternatives for preventing and addressing threats to public safety and order. They also seek the reallocation of resources heretofore dedicated to policing to accomplish these goals.

Don't Call the Police?

Whether or not cities reduce or eliminate policing, some community groups are discouraging people from calling the police. Here is one flowchart they are distributing.

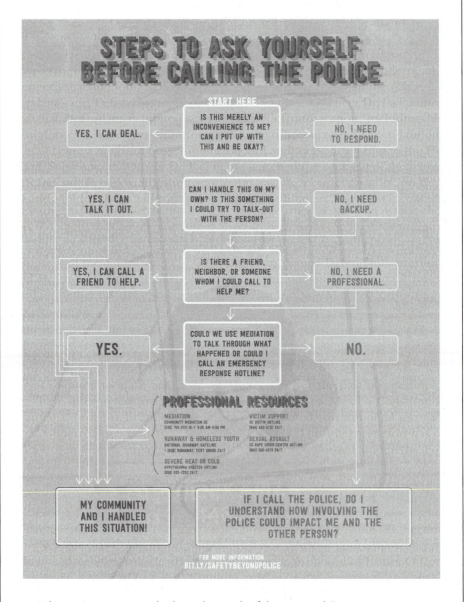

What are some potential risks and rewards of this approach?

For several years, a growing group of scholars has celebrated these abolition-minded activists and sought to provide theoretical support for their work. Amna Akbar, for example, draws on community abolitionist efforts to criticize legal scholarship that "remains largely fixated on investing in the police to recalibrate and relegitimate their social function," despite decades of reform failure. Amna A. Akbar, *An Abolitionist Horizon for (Police) Reform*, 108 Cal. L. Rev. (2020) (forthcoming). She advocates giving up "law as a reliable demarcation device for proper and improper police violence" in favor of work to "contest and then shrink the role of the police, ultimately seeking to transform our political, economic, and social order to achieve broader social provision for human needs." *Id.* at 105–106; see also Amna A. Akbar, *Toward a Radical Imagination of Law*, 93 N.Y.U. L. Rev. 405 (2018) (comparing the Movement for Black Lives' platform to the U.S. Department of Justice's reform efforts in Ferguson and Baltimore).

Others defend abolition against its skeptics, arguing that community-based public safety is a realistic (if still developing) goal. See, e.g., Allegra M. McLeod, *Envisioning Abolition Democracy*, 132 Harv. L. Rev. 1613, 1619–1620 (2019); see also Meghan G. McDowell & Luis A. Fernandez, *"Disband, Disempower, and Disarm": Amplifying the Theory and Practice of Police Abolition*, 26 J. Critical Criminology 373 (2018) (surveying the efforts of abolitionist collectives to build the capacities of communities to function without the police).

Abolitionism has taken on a new resonance. After George Floyd's death in May 2020, protests swept the nation, and calls to abolish the police became more mainstream. Abolitionists pointed out that at the time of Floyd's death, Minneapolis had already adopted many of the policies recommended by reformers, and more than 100 years of efforts to make policing less violent did not stop Chauvin from killing Floyd. See Mariame Kaba, *Yes, We Mean Literally Abolish the Police*, N.Y. Times (June 12, 2020). The Minneapolis City Council initially heeded the abolitionists' calls, pledging to dismantle the city's police department and rethink its system of producing public safety, though it is not clear how or whether that pledge will be fulfilled.

Still, not everyone is convinced. Many view abolitionism as utopian fantasy and, certainly, questions remain. Can communities fully replace state actors in stopping ongoing violence or property damage? Might there be new distributional concerns arising from abolition, given that some members of society are disproportionately vulnerable to interpersonal violence and less capable of self-help? If some policing remains, won't the legal project of determining when police officers may use force persist as well? Even with these unanswered questions, though, many commentators who do not think policing can be entirely eliminated agree with abolitionists that the police should play a less robust role in our society than they currently do. Especially if we build more efficacious communities, perhaps we could safely have far less coercive policing than we do now.

Some advocates of less policing have coalesced around the call to *defund* the police. Although defunding means different things to different people, all seem to agree with abolitionists that "[t]he surest path toward a future free of the violence of policing is one that aims to eliminate contact between those violent forces and the people it targets." Rachel Herzing, *Big Dreams and Bold Steps Toward a Police-Free Future*, Truthout (Sept. 16, 2015). Thus, defunding advocates call for shrinking the policing mandate so that armed officers will not be directing traffic, responding to noise complaints, or handling conflict over public spaces, such as those involving people experiencing homelessness. To get from here to there, defunding advocates insist on cutting police department budgets—including by slashing the number of officers—and devoting those resources to community-based means for preventing and addressing many of the public order problems police now handle. These calls have also resonated: More than a dozen cities have proposed or pledged some form of defunding, and more are considering the issue. See Sarah Holder, *The Cities Taking Up Calls to Defund the Police,* Citylab (June 9, 2020).

Sixteenth Street near the White House, Washington, D.C., June, 2020.

Skeptics worry that defunding the police could undermine both police accountability—which helps reduce the use of force—and public safety. See, e.g., Stephen Rushin & Roger Michalski, *Police Funding,* 72 Fla. L. Rev. 1 (2020). Instead of abolishing or defunding police departments, *reformers* look to reduce the use of force by strengthening legal and administrative remedies for police misconduct; limiting the use of force by state law; and strengthening departmental policies, training, supervision, and disciplinary mechanisms. Still, reformers widely agree that communities will be safer from crime, disorder, *and* police violence if they improve housing equity, employment, and services to address mental-health and addiction problems and reassign to civilians many activities now carried out by sworn officers.

What do you think? Is reforming use-of-force law tinkering at the margins rather than dismantling the police power to do harm? And if so, is that a feature or a bug? Or, to say it another way, don't you agree that communities would be better off if they could achieve the same level of safety and order with less (and less coercive) policing? How should we go about getting there?

D. *Applying Federal and State Law*

1. Real-World Problem: James Blake's Arrest

In September 2015, James Blake was standing in front of a Manhattan hotel waiting for a car. At the same time, detectives from an NYPD identity-theft task force were on the scene to arrest suspects involved in a credit card fraud scheme to purchase $3,000 of luxury sneakers expected to be delivered to the hotel. When the courier delivered the goods, the man who accepted delivery was immediately arrested. The courier identified Blake—standing about eight feet away—as the other man involved in the scheme. (Blake also looked like the photo of the suspect given to police by the defrauded vendor.) Based on this, a plainclothes officer approached and arrested Blake by tackling him. According to Blake's testimony in a later disciplinary trial for the arresting officer, the officer never identified himself or gave Blake any other kind of warning before throwing him to the ground and handcuffing him. You can see the arrest in this video: *Surveillance Video of James Blake Arrest*, N.Y. Times (Sept. 11, 2015), *http://www.nytimes.com/video/nyregion/100000003905322/surveillance-video-of-james-blake-arrest.html.*

James Blake, seconds before he was tackled.

Was the officer's use of force legal under state and federal law? The following New York statutes might be relevant in answering that question.

§35.05 Justification; generally.

[C]onduct which would otherwise constitute an offense is justifiable and not criminal when:

1. Such conduct is required or authorized by law or by a judicial decree, or is performed by a public servant in the reasonable exercise of his official powers, duties or functions. . . .

N.Y. Penal Law §35.05.

§35.10 Justification; use of force generally.

The use of physical force upon another person which would otherwise constitute an offense is justifiable and not criminal under any of the following circumstances: . . .

6. A person may, pursuant to the ensuing provisions of this article, use physical force upon another person in self-defense or defense of a third person, or in defense of premises, or in order to prevent larceny of or criminal mischief to property, or in order to effect an arrest or prevent an escape from custody. Whenever a person is authorized by any such provision to use deadly physical force in any given circumstance, nothing contained in any other such provision may be deemed to negate or qualify such authorization.

N.Y. Penal Law §35.10.

§35.30 Justification; use of physical force in making an arrest or in preventing an escape.

1. A police officer or a peace officer, in the course of effecting or attempting to effect an arrest, or of preventing or attempting to prevent the escape from custody, of a person whom he or she reasonably believes to have committed an offense, may use physical force when and to the extent he or she reasonably believes such to be necessary to effect the arrest, or to prevent the escape from custody, or in self-defense or to defend a third person from what he or she reasonably believes to be the use or imminent use of physical force; except that deadly physical force may be used for such purposes only when he or she reasonably believes that:

(a) The offense committed by such person was:

(i) a felony or an attempt to commit a felony involving the use or attempted use or threatened imminent use of physical force against a person; or

(ii) kidnapping, arson, escape in the first degree, burglary in the first degree or any attempt to commit such a crime; or

(b) The offense committed or attempted by such person was a felony and that, in the course of resisting arrest therefor or attempting to escape from custody, such person is armed with a firearm or deadly weapon; or

(c) Regardless of the particular offense which is the subject of the arrest or attempted escape, the use of deadly physical force is necessary to defend the police officer or peace officer or another person from what the officer reasonably believes to be the use or imminent use of deadly physical force.

N.Y. Penal Law §35.30.

Blake was the wrong man. It turns out that Blake, who is biracial, is a former U.S. tennis star. The car he was waiting for was scheduled to take him to the U.S. Open tennis tournament, where he was making paid television appearances. Should these personal details factor into your analysis? (Clearly, they made Blake's story a public one. It is unlikely you would know his name if he had been a salesman waiting for an Uber.)

What about the fact that James Frascatore, the white officer who tackled Blake, was a defendant in two other lawsuits alleging excessive use of force in 2013? See Ray Sanchez et al., *James Blake Mistake: NYPD Releases Video of Him Being Thrown to the Ground*, CNN (Sept. 12, 2015). How might this use of force have been avoided?

Use-of-Force Data

Although existing evidence suggests that police officers use force only rarely in their interactions with members of the public, we know very little about how often, how much, or what kinds of force police officers use. Departments are the primary source of that data, but because there are no national standards on defining force, collecting use-of-force data, or sharing it, we have no national data and only uneven local information about police violence.

A federal statute requires the U.S. Attorney General to collect data on police officers' use of excessive force and to publish an annual summary of this data. See 34 U.S.C. §12602 (originally enacted as part of the Violent Crime and Law Enforcement Act of 1994, Pub. L. No. 103-322, §210402, 108 Stat. 1796, 2071). But the Department of Justice has consistently violated this law. Although the National Institute of Justice and the Bureau of Justice Statistics made some initial efforts after the statute was enacted, the Department of Justice has never developed national guidelines for local data collection or allocated resources to collect the data. Nor has it issued the required reports.

In 2019, the FBI launched a new means of collecting data on the use of force, labeled the National Use-of-Force Data Collection. Law enforcement departments across the country can submit data to the FBI via a web application. Participation in this data collection is voluntary, though, and most departments do not participate. Moreover, the data collected are limited to uses of force that result in death or serious bodily injury or in which a gun was fired. The FBI also has not established definitions for the use of force, which would promote consistency in data collection across departments. By contrast, the FBI has provided clear definitions for major crimes, ensuring that data collected from agencies for the Uniform Crime Reports are in fact uniform.

A few states have begun to generate data about the use of force, including Texas, California, and New Jersey. All of these states require some data reporting to state agencies, either by statute or by regulation. But these efforts are limited and still in their infancy. Several nonprofit organizations, including the Center for Policing Equity and the International Association of Chiefs of Police, have invited departmental reporting on police uses of force. All these efforts are also voluntary, and none of them is complete enough to be very useful.

Private news efforts have done a bit better. *The Washington Post* has compiled a fatal-force database, which attempts to describe every fatal shooting by a police officer in the line of duty since January 1, 2015. The data are compiled by scouring local news reports or other open sources. The database documents 999 people shot and killed by the police in 2019. *Fatal Force 2019*, Wash. Post (June 25, 2020).

Although the Fatal Force database is helpful in the absence of better data, it can also distort our understanding of policing. The database reports only *fatal shootings* by the police. It does not include *deaths* caused by other intentional uses of force, such as car-stop techniques. It also does not include *nonfatal shootings* (or other less lethal uses of force by officers). In that way, the database does not present a complete picture. What makes an incident *deadly* is that someone dies, which is often as much a product of whether officers at the scene were properly trained and equipped to perform aid, and whether an adequate trauma center is located nearby, as it is a result of the number of bullets fired. In short, *death data* tell us only a little about the use of *deadly force*, which properly includes *any force* that creates a serious *risk* of death, whether or not somebody dies.

In any case, deadly force is—by any measure—a tiny proportion of the force used by the police. And even if we had data about how much force police use all told, we still would not know how much of that force is *excessive*. That kind of information is even more difficult to come by, as it requires operationalizing fact-specific legal judgments. See Rachel A. Harmon, *Evaluating and Improving Structural Reform in Police Departments*, 16 Criminology & Pub. Pol'y 617, 620 (2017).

Calls for better data on policing date back (at least) to 1931 and President Hoover's National Commission on Law Observance and Enforcement (popularly known as the Wickersham Commission). Those calls have been echoed ever since, including by the President's Task Force on 21st Century Policing, the most recent national commission on policing, in its 2015 final report. So far, they remain unheeded.

Data alone does not change policing. Still, it is hard to reduce the use of force if we do not know much about when police use force, how much they use, and against whom they use it. Data on pedestrian stops and searches are similarly problematic. You might wonder: What do we really know about police coercion? How can we govern what we don't understand?

What would you propose to help mitigate the data problem?

Chapter 9

Policing Resistance

As you have seen in earlier chapters, the law permits and police officers exercise enormous coercive authority in the name of public order and safety. What happens when members of the public decide that officers act illegally, unfairly, or too harmfully to justify? Some head to courts or seek legislative or policy change. Others, however, take to the streets, challenging officers as they work, documenting police interactions on video and sharing them with the world, and gathering to protest police conduct.

In a free society, these forms of popular criticism of the government are essential. Yet they present a challenge. Popular resistance can go too far—when it is violent, for example, or when it prevents officers from performing critical tasks. Police therefore need discretion to manage those who would oppose them. But police frequently suppress criticism simply because it is unwelcome. They invoke legitimate goals—public safety and order—and use policing tools—commands, arrests, and force—to overpower those who draw attention to problems in policing rather than to promote social well-being.

This chapter considers how the law regulates police resistance to popular resistance, and thus how the law facilitates and interferes with public efforts to protest the police. The first section looks at how the law addresses bystander challenges to police conduct. What happens when someone intervenes in an arrest or stop? Looking at the legal limits on "contempt of cop" arrests that punish individuals for disrespect helps us to see what the police may and may not do to interlopers.

The second section considers the policing of political protests and the limits on police restrictions on group demonstrations. Political protests criticize many things other than the police. Nevertheless, protests against the police raise the stakes: The subjects of criticism are the same individuals and institutions tasked with the hands-on job of protecting protesters and, at the same time, keeping them within bounds, both geographic and legal.

The third section considers protection for civilian recording of police–citizen encounters. Smartphones have changed our ability to document and share, and therefore contest, police conduct, and in doing so, they raise distinctive legal concerns.

In each case, the First Amendment provides the primary legal protection for critics of policing; the Fourth Amendment matters; and states, localities, and departments may go further in making space for the people to be heard. After reading this chapter, you should be able to identify basic forms of police resistance to criticism, the First Amendment and Fourth Amendment doctrines that constrain them, and the kinds of close cases that bedevil the courts.

A.   Policing Confrontation

Street policing takes place in public. When officers control traffic, break up a fight, or respond to complaints of a disorderly crowd, they often do so in the presence of unco-operative participants and unhelpful onlookers. Some of these people object to police practices by confronting officers. Police need authority to protect their own safety and fulfill important public goals during these confrontations. To give it to them, state laws and local ordinances are designed to empower the police: They broadly prohibit dis-orderly conduct; breaching the peace; disobeying a dispersal order; and all kinds of resisting, impeding, interfering with, delaying, or obstructing an officer. But criticizing the government by speaking truth to power and calling out injustice is one of our most prized freedoms, and police officers can easily use these broadly worded criminal prohi-bitions to make arrests meant to suppress and retaliate against this criticism.

1.   Arrests for Interference

How much does the First Amendment constrain how police use these statutes to respond to those who oppose them? The next case and the notes that follow will help you answer this question.

CITY OF HOUSTON v. HILL
482 U.S. 451 (1987)

JUSTICE BRENNAN delivered the opinion of the Court.

This case presents the question whether a municipal ordinance that makes it unlawful to interrupt a police officer in the performance of his or her duties is uncon-stitutionally overbroad under the First Amendment.

I

Appellee Raymond Wayne Hill is a lifelong resident of Houston, Texas. At the time this lawsuit began, he worked as a paralegal and as executive director of the Houston Human Rights League. A member of the board of the Gay Political Caucus, which he helped found in 1975, Hill was also affiliated with a Houston radio station, and had carried city and county press passes since 1975. He lived in Montrose, a "diverse and eclectic neighborhood" that is the center of gay political and social life in Houston.

The incident that sparked this lawsuit occurred in the Montrose area on February 14, 1982. Hill observed a friend, Charles Hill, intentionally stopping traffic on a busy street, evidently to enable a vehicle to enter traffic. Two Houston police officers, one of whom was named Kelley, approached Charles and began speaking with him. According to the District Court, "shortly thereafter" Hill began shouting at the officers "in an admitted attempt to divert Kelley's attention from Charles Hill."[1] Hill first shouted: "Why don't you pick on somebody your own size?" After

---

[1] Hill testified that his "motivation was to stop [the officers] from hitting Charles." He also explained: "I would rather that I get arrested than those whose careers can be damaged; I would rather that I get arrested than those whose families wouldn't understand; I would rather that I get arrested than those who couldn't spend a long time in jail. I am prepared to respond in any legal, nonaggressive or nonviolent way, to any illegal police activity, at any time, under any circumstances."

Officer Kelley responded: "[A]re you interrupting me in my official capacity as a Houston police officer?" Hill then shouted: "Yes, why don't you pick on somebody my size?" Hill was arrested under Houston Code of Ordinances §34–11(a), for "wilfully or intentionally interrupt[ing] a city policeman . . . by verbal challenge during an investigation." Charles Hill was not arrested. Hill was then acquitted after a non-jury trial in Municipal Court.

Code of Ordinances, City of Houston, Texas, §34–11(a) (1984), reads:

"Sec. 34–11. Assaulting or interfering with policemen.

"(a) It shall be unlawful for any person to assault, strike or in any manner oppose, molest, abuse or interrupt any policeman in the execution of his duty, or any person summoned to aid in making an arrest."

Following his acquittal in the Charles Hill incident, Hill brought the suit in the Federal District Court for the Southern District of Texas, seeking (1) a declaratory judgment that §34–11(a) was unconstitutional both on its face and as it had been applied to him, (2) a permanent injunction against any attempt to enforce the ordinance, (3) an order expunging the records of his arrests under the ordinance, and (4) damages and attorney's fees under 42 U.S.C. §§1983 and 1988.

At trial, Hill introduced records provided by the city regarding both the frequency with which arrests had been made for violation of the ordinance and the type of conduct with which those arrested had been charged. . . . Finally, Hill introduced evidence regarding his own experience with the ordinance, under which he has been arrested four times since 1975, but never convicted.

The District Court held that Hill's evidence did not demonstrate that the ordinance had been unconstitutionally applied.[4] The court also rejected Hill's contention that the ordinance was unconstitutionally vague or overbroad on its face. . . .

A panel of the Court of Appeals reversed. The city's suggestion for rehearing en banc was granted, and the Court of Appeals, by a vote of 8–7, upheld the judgment of the panel. . . .

The city appealed. . . . We noted probable jurisdiction, and now affirm.

II

The elements of First Amendment overbreadth analysis are familiar. Only a statute that is substantially overbroad may be invalidated on its face. New York v. Ferber, 458 U.S. 747, 769 (1982). . . . "[I]n a facial challenge to the overbreadth and vagueness of a law, a court's first task is to determine whether the enactment reaches a

---

[4] The facts of Hill's other three arrests as found by the District Court are as follows. On August 31, 1975, Hill intentionally interrupted two Houston police officers as they made a traffic arrest. During the arrest, Hill wrote down license plate numbers, and then walked to within an arm's length of one of the officers on the side nearest the officer's revolver. The officer asked Hill to leave, but Hill instead moved closer. Hill was arrested, tried, and found not guilty.

In 1977, after observing vice-squad cars parked near a bookstore, Hill entered the store and announced on the public address system that police officers were present and that patrons should prepare to show their identification. The patrons promptly left the store, thereby frustrating the investigation. Hill was arrested for interfering with the investigation, but the case was subsequently dismissed.

Finally, on October 3, 1982, eight months after the lawsuit began, Hill was arrested for refusing to leave the immediate area of a car with an unknown and unconscious person inside. The arresting officers failed to appear in Municipal Court, however, so the charge against Hill was dismissed.

substantial amount of constitutionally protected conduct." Hoffman Estates v. The Flipside, Hoffman Estates, Inc., 455 U.S. 489, 494 (1982). Criminal statutes must be scrutinized with particular care; those that make unlawful a substantial amount of constitutionally protected conduct may be held facially invalid even if they also have legitimate application. E.g., Kolender v. Lawson, 461 U.S. 352, 359 n.8 (1983).

The city's principal argument is that the ordinance does not inhibit the exposition of ideas, and that it bans "core criminal conduct" not protected by the First Amendment. In its view, the application of the ordinance to Hill illustrates that the police employ it only to prohibit such conduct, and not "as a subterfuge to control or dissuade free expression." Since the ordinance is "content-neutral," and since there is no evidence that the city has applied the ordinance to chill particular speakers or ideas, the city concludes that the ordinance is not substantially overbroad.[7]

We disagree with the city's characterization for several reasons. First, the enforceable portion of the ordinance deals not with core criminal conduct, but with speech. As the city has conceded, the language in the ordinance making it unlawful for any person to "assault" or "strike" a police officer is pre-empted by the Texas Penal Code. . . . Accordingly, the enforceable portion of the ordinance makes it "unlawful for any person to . . . in any manner oppose, molest, abuse or interrupt any policeman in the execution of his duty," and thereby prohibits verbal interruptions of police officers.

Second, contrary to the city's contention, the First Amendment protects a significant amount of verbal criticism and challenge directed at police officers. "Speech is often provocative and challenging. . . . [But it] is nevertheless protected against censorship or punishment, unless shown likely to produce a clear and present danger of a serious substantive evil that rises far above public inconvenience, annoyance, or unrest." Terminiello v. Chicago, 337 U.S. 1, 4 (1949). In *Lewis v. City of New Orleans*, 415 U.S. 130 (1974), for example, the appellant was found to have yelled obscenities and threats at an officer who had asked appellant's husband to produce his driver's license. Appellant was convicted under a municipal ordinance that made it a crime " 'for any person wantonly to curse or revile or to use obscene or opprobrious language toward or with reference to any member of the city police while in the actual performance of his duty.' " *Id.* at 132. We vacated the conviction and invalidated the ordinance as facially overbroad. Critical to our decision was the fact that the ordinance "punishe[d] only spoken words" and was not limited in scope to fighting words that " 'by their very utterance inflict injury or tend to incite an immediate breach of the peace.' " *Id.* at 133. Moreover, in a concurring opinion in *Lewis*, Justice Powell suggested that even the "fighting words" exception recognized in *Chaplinsky v. New Hampshire*, 315 U.S. 568 (1942), might require a narrower application in cases involving words addressed to a police officer, because "a properly trained officer may reasonably be expected to 'exercise a higher degree of restraint' than the average citizen, and thus be less likely to respond belligerently to 'fighting words.' " 415 U.S. at 135.

The Houston ordinance is much more sweeping than the municipal ordinance struck down in *Lewis*. It is not limited to fighting words nor even to obscene or opprobrious language, but prohibits speech that "in any manner . . . interrupt[s]" an officer. The Constitution does not allow such speech to be made a

---

[7] The city's threshold argument that Hill lacks standing is without merit. . . . Hill has shown "a genuine threat of enforcement" of the ordinance against his future activities. . . . We . . . agree with the Court of Appeals that "Hill's record of arrests under the ordinance and his adopted role as citizen provocateur" give Hill standing to challenge the facial validity of the ordinance.

crime.[11] The freedom of individuals verbally to oppose or challenge police action without thereby risking arrest is one of the principal characteristics by which we distinguish a free nation from a police state.[12]

The city argues, however, that even if the ordinance encompasses some protected speech, its sweeping nature is both inevitable and essential to maintain public order. The city recalls this Court's observation in *Smith v. Goguen*, 415 U.S. 566, 581 (1974):

> "There are areas of human conduct where, by the nature of the problems presented, legislatures simply cannot establish standards with great precision. Control of the broad range of disorderly conduct that may inhibit a policeman in the performance of his official duties may be one such area requiring as it does an on-the-spot assessment of the need to keep order."

The city further suggests that its ordinance is comparable to the disorderly conduct statute upheld against a facial challenge in *Colten v. Kentucky*, 407 U.S. 104 (1972).

This Houston ordinance, however, is not narrowly tailored to prohibit only disorderly conduct or fighting words, and in no way resembles the law upheld in *Colten*. Although we appreciate the difficulties of drafting precise laws, we have repeatedly invalidated laws that provide the police with unfettered discretion to arrest individuals for words or conduct that annoy or offend them. . . . In *Lewis*, Justice Powell elaborated the basis for our concern with such sweeping, dragnet laws:

> "This ordinance, as construed by the Louisiana Supreme Court, confers on police a virtually unrestrained power to arrest and charge persons with a violation. Many arrests are made in 'one-on-one' situations where the only witnesses are the arresting officer and the person charged. All that is required for conviction is that the court accept the testimony of the officer that obscene or opprobrious language had been used toward him while in the performance of his duties. . . .

---

[11] Justice Powell suggests that our analysis of protected speech sweeps too broadly. But . . . today's decision does not leave municipalities powerless to punish physical obstruction of police action. For example, Justice Powell states that "a municipality constitutionally may punish an individual who chooses to stand near a police officer and persistently attempt to engage the officer in conversation while the officer is directing traffic at a busy intersection." We agree, however, that such conduct might constitutionally be punished under a properly tailored statute, such as a disorderly conduct statute that makes it unlawful to fail to disperse in response to a valid police order or to create a traffic hazard. E.g., Colten v. Kentucky, 407 U.S. 104 (1972). What a municipality may not do, however, and what Houston has done in this case, is to attempt to punish such conduct by broadly criminalizing speech directed to an officer—in this case, by authorizing the police to arrest a person who in *any* manner verbally interrupts an officer.

[12] This conclusion finds a familiar echo in the common law. See, e.g., The King v. Cook, 11 Can. Crim. Cas. Ann. 32, 33 (B.C. County Ct. 1906) ("Cook . . . a troublesome, talkative individual, who evidently regards the police with disfavour and makes no secret of his opinions on the subject . . . [told] some persons in a tone of voice undoubtedly intended for [the officer's] ears, that the arrested man was not drunk and the arrest was unjustifiable. Now up to this point he had committed no crime, as in a free country like this citizens are entitled to express their opinions without thereby rendering themselves liable to arrest unless they are inciting others to break the law; and policemen are not exempt from criticism any more than Cabinet Ministers"); Levy v. Edwards, 1 Car. & P. 40, 171 Eng. Rep. 1094 (Nisi Prius 1823) (where constable breaks up fight between two boys and proceeds to handcuff one of them, third party who objects by telling constable " 'you have no right to handcuff the boy' " has done no wrong and may not be arrested); cf. Ruthenbeck v. First Criminal Judicial Court of Bergen Cty., 147 A. 625 (N.J. 1929) (vacating conviction for saying to police officer "You big muttonhead, do you think you are a czar around here?"). The freedom verbally to challenge police action is not without limits, of course; we have recognized that "fighting words" which "by their very utterance inflict injury or tend to incite an immediate breach of the peace" are not constitutionally protected. *Chaplinsky*, 315 U.S. at 572.

"Contrary to the city's argument, it is unlikely that limiting the ordinance's application to genuine 'fighting words' would be incompatible with the full and adequate performance of an officer's duties. . . . [I]t is usually unnecessary [to charge a person] with the less serious offense of addressing obscene words to the officer. The present type of ordinance tends to be invoked only where there is no other valid basis for arresting an objectionable or suspicious person. The opportunity for abuse, especially where a statute has received a virtually open-ended interpretation, is self-evident."

Houston's ordinance criminalizes a substantial amount of constitutionally protected speech, and accords the police unconstitutional discretion in enforcement. The ordinance's plain language is admittedly violated scores of times daily, yet only some individuals—those chosen by the police in their unguided discretion—are arrested. Far from providing the "breathing space" that "First Amendment freedoms need . . . to survive," NAACP v. Button, 371 U.S. 415, 433 (1963), the ordinance is susceptible of regular application to protected expression. We conclude that the ordinance is substantially overbroad, and that the Court of Appeals did not err in holding it facially invalid. . . .

[The concurring opinion of Justice Blackmun is omitted.]

[The opinion of Justice Scalia, concurring in the judgment, is omitted.]

JUSTICE POWELL, with whom JUSTICE O'CONNOR joins, and with whom THE CHIEF JUSTICE joins as to Parts I and II, and JUSTICE SCALIA joins as to Parts II and III, concurring in the judgment in part and dissenting in part. . . .

III

I agree with the Court's conclusion that the ordinance violates the Fourteenth Amendment, but do not join the Court's reasoning.

A

The Court finds that the ordinance "deals not with core criminal conduct, but with speech." This view of the ordinance draws a distinction where none exists. The terms of the ordinance—"oppose, molest, abuse or interrupt any policeman in the execution of his duty"—include general words that can apply as fully to conduct as to speech. It is in this respect that *Lewis v. City of New Orleans*, 415 U.S. 130 (1974), is clearly distinguishable. In that case the New Orleans ordinance made it a breach of the peace for:

"'any person wantonly to curse or revile or to use obscene or opprobrious language toward or with reference to any member of the city police while in the actual performance of his duty.'" *Id.* at 132 (quoting New Orleans Ordinance 828 M.C.S. §49–7).

On its face, the New Orleans ordinance criminalizes only the use of language. . . . By contrast, the ordinance presented in this case could be applied to activity that involves no element of speech or communication. For example, the ordinance evidently would punish individuals who—without saying a single word—obstructed an officer's access to the scene of an ongoing public disturbance, or indeed the scene of a crime. Accordingly, I cannot agree with the Court that this ordinance punishes only speech.

I do agree that the ordinance can be applied to speech in some cases. And I also agree that the First Amendment protects a good deal of speech that may be directed at police officers. On occasion this may include verbal criticism, but I question the implication of the Court's opinion that the First Amendment generally protects verbal "challenge[s] directed at police officers." A "challenge" often takes the form of opposition or interruption of performance of duty. In many situations, speech of this type directed at police officers will be functionally indistinguishable from conduct that the First Amendment clearly does not protect. For example, I have no doubt that a municipality constitutionally may punish an individual who chooses to stand near a police officer and persistently attempt to engage the officer in conversation while the officer is directing traffic at a busy intersection. Similarly, an individual, by contentious and abusive speech, could interrupt an officer's investigation of possible criminal conduct. A person observing an officer pursuing a person suspected of a felony could run beside him in a public street shouting at the officer. Similar tactics could interrupt a policeman lawfully attempting to interrogate persons believed to be witnesses to a crime.

In sum, the Court's opinion appears to reflect a failure to apprehend that this ordinance—however it may be construed—is intended primarily to further the public's interest in law enforcement. To be sure, there is a fine line between legitimate criticism of police and the type of criticism that interferes with the very purpose of having police officers. But the Court unfortunately seems to ignore this fine line and to extend First Amendment protection to any type of verbal molestation or interruption of an officer in the performance of his duty.

B

Despite the concerns expressed above, I nevertheless agree that the ambiguous terms of this ordinance "confe[r] on police a virtually unrestrained power to arrest and charge persons with a violation. . . . The opportunity for abuse, especially where a statute has received a virtually open-ended interpretation, is self-evident." *Lewis*, 415 U.S. at 135-136 (Powell, J., concurring in result). . . . People have been charged with such crimes as "Failure to remain silent and stationary," "Remaining," "Refusing to remain silent," and "Talking." Hill v. City of Houston, 789 F.2d 1103, 1113-1114 (5th Cir. 1986) (en banc). Although some of these incidents may have involved unprotected conduct, the vagueness of these charges suggests that, with respect to this ordinance, Houston officials have not been acting with proper sensitivity to the constitutional rights of their citizens. When government protects society's interests in a manner that restricts some speech the law must be framed more precisely than the ordinance before us. Accordingly, I agree with the Court that the Houston ordinance is unconstitutional.

. . . In view of the difficulty of drafting precise language that never restrains speech and yet serves the public interest, the attempts of States and municipalities to draft laws of this type should be accorded some leeway. I am convinced, however, that the Houston ordinance is too vague to comport with the First and Fourteenth Amendments. . . .

[The dissenting opinion of Chief Justice Rehnquist is omitted.]

NOTES AND QUESTIONS

1. Colten, Lewis, *and* Hill.   At the time the Court considered Hill's claims, it had already decided *Lewis v. City of New Orleans*, 415 U.S. 130 (1974), and *Colten v. Kentucky*, 407 U.S. 104 (1972). *Lewis* concerned the arrest and conviction of Mallie Lewis, a woman whose son had just been arrested by the police. As Lewis and her husband were driving from the scene of the arrest to the police station, hoping to figure out why their son had been arrested, they were pulled over. According to the officer's trial testimony, during the stop, Lewis said to the officer, "[Y]ou god damm m.f. police—I am going to Giarrusso [the Superintendent of Police] to see about this." The officer arrested her under a New Orleans breach-of-the-peace ordinance that made it a crime to "curse or revile or use obscene language toward or with reference to any member of the city police while in the actual performance of his duty." The Supreme Court overturned the ordinance because it was not limited to fighting words.

Here are the facts of *Colten*:

> Appellant Colten and 15 to 20 other college students gathered at the Blue Grass Airport outside Lexington, Kentucky, to show their support for a state gubernatorial candidate and to demonstrate their lack of regard for Mrs. Richard Nixon, then about to leave Lexington from the airport after a public appearance in the city. When the demonstration had ended, the students got into their automobiles and formed a procession of six to 10 cars along the airport access road to the main highway. A state policeman, observing that one of the first cars in the entourage carried an expired Louisiana license plate, directed the driver, one Mendez, to pull off the road. He complied. Appellant Colten, followed by other motorists in the procession, also pulled off the highway, and Colten approached the officer to find out what was the matter. The policeman explained that the Mendez car bore an expired plate and that a traffic summons would be issued. Colten made some effort to enter into a conversation about the summons. . . . In order to avoid Colten and to complete the issuance of the summons, the policeman took Mendez to the patrol car. Meanwhile, other students had left their cars and additional policemen, . . . stopped their cars in the traffic lane abreast of the students' vehicles. . . . A state police captain asked on four or five occasions that the group disperse. At least five times police asked Colten to leave. A state trooper made two requests, remarking at least once: 'Now, this is none of your affair . . . get back in your car and please move on and clear the road.' In response to at least one of these requests Colten replied that he wished to make a transportation arrangement for his friend Mendez and the occupants of the Mendez car, which he understood was to be towed away. Another officer asked three times that Colten depart and when Colten failed to move away he was arrested for violating Kentucky's disorderly conduct statute. . . .
>
> . . . Colten was tried, convicted, and fined $10.

407 U.S. at 106–108. Colten claimed that the conviction violated his constitutional rights. The Court rejected his First Amendment claim, reasoning:

> Colten insists that in seeking to arrange transportation for Mendez and in observing the issuance of a traffic citation he was disseminating and receiving information. But this is a strained, near-frivolous contention and we have little doubt that Colten's conduct in refusing to move on after being directed to do so was not, without more, protected by the First Amendment. Nor can we believe that Colten, although he was not trespassing or disobeying any traffic regulation himself, could not be required

to move on. He had no constitutional right to observe the issuance of a traffic ticket or to engage the issuing officer in conversation at that time. The State has a legitimate interest in enforcing its traffic laws and its officers were entitled to enforce them free from possible interference or interruption from bystanders, even those claiming a third-party interest in the transaction. Here the police had cause for apprehension that a roadside strip, crowded with persons and automobiles, might expose the entourage, passing motorists, and police to the risk of accident. We cannot disagree with the finding below that the order to disperse was suited to the occasion. We thus see nothing unconstitutional in the manner in which the statute was applied.

Id. at 109–110. Given *Hill, Lewis,* and *Colten,* what limits exist on police discretion to arrest individuals who oppose them pursuant to state and local law? Why does *Colten* differ from *Hill* and *Lewis?*

2. *Applying the Encounter Model.* Review the Encounter Model from Chapter 1, and then reread the relevant portion of the ordinance in *Hill.* Ordinances that criminalize interfering with or impeding the police, disobeying a lawful order, resisting arrest, and the like may be mixed in with other misdemeanor laws that criminalize vandalism or obstructing a sidewalk in a city's code. The model can help you see how these laws differ. Ordinary criminal statutes authorize arrests ([2] solutions) for people who impose or risk specific harms ([1] problems), such as—at the low end—spraying graffiti or blocking traffic. But an ordinance like the one at issue in *Hill* kicks in only when an officer is addressing a [1] problem with a [2] solution that is met with someone's [3] noncompliance, such as refusing an order to disperse. These ordinances authorize officers to arrest people (a [4] follow-up) who oppose them in the relevant ways at step [3]. Can you see the difference? Read in this context, *Hill, Colten,* and similar cases, are about the limits that the First Amendment imposes on what kinds of [3], that is, what opposition, the police may respond to with [4] an arrest, even if the state or locality authorizes that arrest.

3. *The law of gadflies.* Ray Hill was an early gay-rights activist and lifelong all-around dissenter.[1] Lewis Colten was a college kid attending a political rally. Mallie Lewis was a mom worried when her African-American son was arrested by

[1] Hill lived a colorful and extraordinary life. Born in 1940, Hill served as a Baptist evangelist as a teenager and the quarterback of his high school's football team, before in the late 1950s he (unsuccessfully) tried to take his boyfriend to his senior prom. He visited Havana in 1959 to support the Cuban Revolution. He served briefly as the secretary of the Houston chapter of the NAACP. He organized Houston's first gay pride parade and first LGBT organization. He served 4 years of a 160-year sentence for burglary in the early 1970s. He socialized with Tennessee Williams, Truman Capote, Edward Albee, and Harvey Milk. He brought together thousands to protest when Anita Bryant spoke in Houston and helped organize the first march on Washington for gay rights in 1979 after Milk's assassination. He served for decades as a radio deejay, and ran *The Prison Show,* allowing family members to communicate with people who were incarcerated. He protested sex stings of gay men and was arrested again at age 71 when he confronted officers during a strip club raid. He played a leading role in organizing the legal battle that resulted in gay-rights milestone, *Lawrence v. Texas,* 539 U.S. 558. After *Hill* was decided, Hill adopted the title given to him by the Court in footnote 7—"citizen provocateur"—on his business cards, and before Hill's death in 2018, he asked that the citation for *Houston v. Hill* be written on his tombstone. See Ben McGrath, *The Improbable Life of Ray Hill,* New Yorker (Dec. 1, 2018); Joey Guerra, *Ray Hill Galvanizes Houston's LGBT Community,* Houston Chron. (Oct. 8, 2016); Brian Rogers, *Houston Man Whose Case Advanced Gay Rights Dies,* Houston Chron. (Dec. 27, 2011); James Pinkerton, *Activist Blames Officers for Arrest at Houston Strip Club,* Houston Chron. (Dec. 12, 2011).

white officers—without explanation—in the Deep South. What do these people have in common? In his *Letter from a Birmingham Jail*, Martin Luther King, Jr., said,

> Just as Socrates felt that it was necessary to create a tension in the mind so that individuals could shake off the bondage of myths and half-truths and rise to the realm of creative analysis and objective appraisal, so must we see the need for nonviolent gadflies to create the kind of tension in society that will help men rise from the dark depths of prejudice and racism to the majestic heights of understanding and brotherhood.

Martin Luther King, Jr., *Letter from a Birmingham Jail*, The Christian Century, June 12, 1963, at 768. King was speaking about civil disobedience rather than confronting injustice through speech. Still, police officers manifest state power on the street. Gadflies challenge how that power is used. The First Amendment is the law of gadflies.

Ray Hill at first national march on Washington for lesbian and gay rights.

4. *Fighting words.* As *Hill* suggests, traditionally, the First Amendment does not protect "fighting words," which have a direct tendency to inflict injury, to cause a violent reaction, or to incite an immediate breach of the peace. What does the Court say about fighting words spoken to police officers? Since *Hill*, many courts refuse to apply the "fighting words" doctrine to insults to officers.

Either they conclude that officers should exercise greater restraint than average citizens, as *Hill* suggests, or that contemporary norms of speech are so permissive that whatever has been said is insufficiently provocative. See, e.g., Stearns v. Clarkson, 615 F.3d 1278, 1280–1284 (10th Cir. 2010) (remarking belligerently that an officer is "probably the mother f***** that shot my dad" is not using fighting words); Greene v. Barber, 310 F.3d 889 (6th Cir. 2002) (calling an officer an "asshole" is not using fighting words); United States v. Poocha, 259 F.3d 1077 (9th Cir. 2001) (clenching fists, sticking out one's chest, and yelling "fuck you" is not using fighting words); Marttila v. City of Lynchburg, 535 S.E.2d 693 (Va. Ct. App. 2000) (calling officers "fucking pigs" and "fucking jokes" who "should be at a fucking donut shop" is not using fighting words). Occasionally, however, courts permit arrests and convictions for similar comments. See, e.g., McCormick v. City of Lawrence, 325 F. Supp. 2d 1191 (D. Kan. 2004), aff'd 130 F. App'x 987 (10th Cir. 2005) (yelling "Motherfuckers," "Fuck heads," "Fucking pigs," "Why don't you run around the track, chubby?," "Hey chubby, what's your name?," "Hey fatty," "Hey fat ass," and "Leave her the fuck alone," at officers constituted fighting words); State v. Matthews, 111 A.3d 390 (R.I. 2015) (calling two officers in close proximity "motherfuckers," "queers," and "fags" and threatening to kill them and "kick their asses" was constitutionally unprotected fighting words). What language, if any, should constitute fighting words when directed at a police officer?

5. *Threats.* Like fighting words, *true threats*, those "where the speaker means to communicate a serious expression of an intent to commit an act of unlawful violence to a particular individual or group of individuals," also lack First Amendment protection. See Virginia v. Black, 538 U.S. 343, 359 (2003). That means some threats against officers are arrestable and some are not. In 2018, the Fifth Circuit Court of Appeals voided as overbroad a Louisiana statute because it prohibited not only true threats against officers ("Don't arrest me or I'll hit you"), but also threats of nonviolent consequences ("Don't arrest me or I'll sue you"). See Seals v. McBee, 898 F.3d 587 (5th Cir. 2018). The latter type of threat is protected by the First Amendment.

6. *Words and acts: Part 1.* What do the examples in Powell's *Houston v. Hill* concurrence indicate about words that are "indistinguishable from conduct"? How are these handled under the majority's rule? An Oakland County sheriff's deputy wrote James Webb a ticket for violating a misdemeanor noise ordinance by playing N.W.A.'s song "Fuck tha Police" near the officer as he conducted a traffic stop. Although the officer claimed on the ticket that the violation was for playing the song at "extremely high volume," in court, the officer admitted that he objected to the song's vulgarity. Although Webb faced a potential $500 fine and 93 days in jail, a jury found Webb not guilty in nine minutes. See *Jury Finds Man Facing Jail After Playing 'F the Police' Not Guilty,* FOX 2 Detroit (Dec. 11, 2018). But what if the jury had convicted Webb on the basis of the music's volume? What if the officer had said the song distracted him from his duties? Would the arrest have been constitutional?

James Webb's ticket.

7. *Problem 1.* An officer responding to a child-welfare call approached a couple in a fast food restaurant to investigate. Barry Buttinsky, a bystander, walked over and instructed the couple not to talk, telling them, "The police ruin peoples' lives." When the officer led the couple outside, Buttinsky followed. He got within an arm's length of the group and interrupted their conversation, asking the man whether he was okay, whether he wanted an attorney, and whether he wanted the interaction recorded. The officer instructed Buttinsky to butt out and back away, but Buttinsky

refused. He was arrested and charged with disorderly conduct. Was Buttinsky's arrest constitutional? See *State v. Biondolillo*, 55 A.3d 1034 (N.H. 2012); see also *King v. Ambs*, 519 F.3d 607 (6th Cir. 2008).

8. *Problem 2.* An officer was administering field sobriety tests to a driver on the side of an urban road when Ira Interloper began shouting to the driver that he did not have to cooperate with the police. He also pumped his fist in the air, yelling, "Power to the people!" After the officer arrested the driver and put him in the patrol car, the officer approached Interloper and told him to walk away. Interloper refused and raised his fist in the air. After repeating the order several times, the officer arrested Interloper for "knowingly refusing to comply with an order of an officer made in the performance of official duties." The officer would later testify that Interloper's activities made it harder for the officer and the driver to pay attention to traffic during the field sobriety tests. Was Interloper's arrest constitutional? Cf. *State v. Hookstra*, 630 N.W.2d 469 (Neb. Ct. App. 2001).

9. *Words and acts: Part 2.* The Supreme Court recognizes that words that are indistinguishable from conduct might not be protected by the First Amendment. What about *conduct* that is indistinguishable from *words*? There are dozens of cases involving people who have been arrested "giving the finger" to an officer. Courts overwhelmingly find vulgar gestures of disrespect to be protected speech. See, e.g., *Cruise-Gulyas v. Minard*, 918 F.3d 494 (6th Cir. 2019) (middle finger); *Duran v. City of Douglas*, 904 F.2d 1372, 1378 (9th Cir. 1990) (unspecified obscene gestures); *Clark v. Coleman*, 448 F. Supp. 3d 559 (W.D. V. 2020) (middle finger); *Nichols v. Chacon*, 110 F. Supp. 2d 1099 (W.D. Ark. 2000), aff'd, 19 F. App'x 471 (8th Cir. 2001) (middle finger). Given how many cases there are, why might police still arrest people for making obscene gestures?

10. *Why bystanders?* Ray Hill, Lewis Colten, and Mallie Lewis were not suspects when they encountered the police. They were bystanders. Why might First Amendment cases involve bystanders more often than those who the police initially target? To answer this, think about how free-speech challenges to police conduct during an arrest can reach a court. First, if an arrestee is prosecuted, he may argue in defense that the arrest violated the First Amendment. But the government can avoid the challenge simply by dropping the charges. Officers will not care much about the dismissals, because police use these arrests primarily to remove the gadfly (or retaliate against him) rather than trigger the criminal process.

Alternatively, an arrestee may, like Ray Hill, bring a civil suit challenging the arrest, because the First Amendment generally prohibits government officials retaliating against individuals for engaging in protected speech. However, to prevail on such a claim, the plaintiff must demonstrate that retaliatory motive *caused* the injury rather than merely accompanied it. *Hartman v. Moore*, 547 U.S. 250, 256 (2006). In 2019, the Supreme Court reasoned that, as officers frequently must make "split-second judgments" about whether to arrest,[2] courts should be highly reluctant to

---

[2] Do not take the Supreme Court's premise—that arrest decisions are and must be made in an instant—for granted. Although an officer might have to make a quick initial determination about whether to take a suspect into immediate custody, once a suspect is in handcuffs, officers have more time, and they frequently check identification, determine whether the suspect has outstanding warrants, and speak to a supervisor, before deciding whether to complete the arrest. The actual decision to charge a suspect, transport him, and book him is far from instantaneous. For more on arrests, see Chapter 7.

second-guess their motives. Instead, if an officer has probable cause for the arrest, that is "weighty evidence" that the suspect's conduct rather than the officer's animus caused it to happen. Nieves v. Bartlett, 139 S. Ct. 1715, 1724 (2019). Thus, the Court ruled, in run-of-the-mill cases, a plaintiff cannot make out a retaliatory arrest claim unless he shows the officer had *no* probable cause to make the arrest. See *id.* at 1725. This probable-cause bar usually prevents the initial targets of police action—the Charles Hills of the world—from bringing a retaliatory arrest claim if they are arrested, because their problematic conduct is what triggered the officer's interest. Given this, it is not surprising that most First Amendment challenges come from bystanders.

11. *Retaliatory arrest claims by bystanders.* Of course, the probable-cause bar on retaliatory arrest claims limits claims by bystanders as well: Officers can usually point to *some* crime the bystander has committed. To address this concern, the Court in *Nieves v. Bartlett* recognized an exception to "when a plaintiff presents objective evidence that he was arrested when otherwise similarly situated individuals not engaged in the same sort of protected speech had not been." 139 S. Ct. 1715, 1727 (2019). This rule is intended to allow suits "where officers have probable cause to make arrests, but typically exercise their discretion not to do so," such as for jaywalking, which "is endemic but rarely results in arrest." *Id.* Is that exception enough? What other practical obstacles might exist for legal claims against officers for retaliatory arrests?

The Thin Line Between the First and Fourth Amendments

As a limit on state criminalization of noncompliance and resistance, the First Amendment polices the distinction between legitimate and illegal antagonism directed toward the police. But it is not the only law that does so, and you might reasonably consider it secondary to the Fourth Amendment in this regard. By determining what constitutes a reasonable search or seizure, the Fourth Amendment affects the scope of legitimate resistance to the police in three ways:

Criminalizing noncompliance

The Fourth Amendment determines when a state may *criminalize noncompliance* with its efforts to stop, search, or arrest a person. For example, in *Birchfield v. North Dakota*, 136 S. Ct. 2160, 2172 (2016), a case involving blood and breath tests for alcohol, the Court noted:

> [T]he criminal law may not compel a motorist to submit to the taking of a blood sample or to a breath test unless a warrant authorizing such testing is issued by a magistrate. If, on the other hand, such warrantless searches comport with the Fourth Amendment, it follows that a State may criminalize the refusal to comply with a demand to submit to the required testing, just as a State may make it a crime for a person to obstruct the execution of a valid search warrant.[3]

---

[3] The Court has not resolved the question whether this principle entails a constitutional right to resist patently illegal arrests. Such a rule would conflict with laws in most states permitting charges for resisting unlawful arrest.

If an officer may not constitutionally conduct a search and may not arrest some-one who refuses to participate in that search, force used to overcome resistance to that search would also violate the Fourth Amendment.

Using force to overcome noncompliance

The Fourth Amendment determines *how much force* police officers may use to *overcome acts of noncompliance* that are disallowed. Under current doctrine, an officer may constitutionally use deadly force to subdue someone who threatens serious bodily harm or death while resisting or fleeing from an arrest. See Tennessee v. Garner, 471 U.S. 1 (1985). If the person resisting police action poses less of a threat, less force is permissible. As the Ninth Circuit has explained, the amount of force police may legitimately use depends on the nature of the resistance:

> Following the Supreme Court's instruction in *Graham* [*v. Connor*, 490 U.S. 386 (1989)], we have drawn a distinction between passive and active resistance. . . . "Resistance," however, should not be understood as a binary state, with resistance being either completely passive or active. Rather, it runs the gamut from the purely passive protestor who simply refuses to stand, to the individual who is physically assaulting the officer. We must eschew ultimately unhelpful blanket labels and evaluate the nature of any resistance in light of the actual facts of the case. . . . Even purely passive resistance can support the use of some force, but the level of force an individual's resistance will support is dependent on the factual circumstances underlying that resistance.

Bryan v. MacPherson, 630 F.3d 805, 830 (9th Cir. 2010). For more on the law governing the use of force, see Chapter 8.

Asserting constitutional rights

The Fourth Amendment determines what constitutes consent to search and what conversations with police are considered voluntary. These rules effectively determine *how resistant suspects must be to assert their constitutional rights* not to be searched, detained, or questioned. When members of the public are passive, intimidated, or ignorant, they may unintentionally acquiesce to government intrusion:

> [C]hallenging the police is not just a constitutional right: it is *the way* in which we assert our legal rights against the government in the context of policing. The Court, in cases like *Florida v. Bostick, Schneckloth v. Bustamonte,* and *Salinas v. Texas,* tells us that refusing to comply or cooperate with police authority is not just the *primary* way to assert our Fourth and Fifth Amendment rights. It is the *only* way: these constitutional rights *are* the right to walk away, to refuse to consent, and to decline to speak. The choice is to insist upon those rights or to waive them. If a civilian does *not* challenge the police, if she complies with police questioning, then the Court treats compliance as consent or cooperation, and the Fourth and Fifth Amendments' protections do not kick in. Acquiescence, compliance, or cooperation vitiates the protections provided by the Constitution.

Eric J. Miller, *Encountering Resistance: Contesting Policing and Procedural Justice,* 2016 U. Chi. Legal F. 295, 302–303.

Along with the First Amendment then, the Fourth Amendment tells us when we *may not* resist, when we *may* resist, and when we *must* resist. Do you think most people can intuit these rules? Or do you think many of us find ourselves damned if we resist the police and damned if we don't?

2.   Contempt of Cop

When officers arrest people or use force against them for talking back, acting disrespectfully, or criticizing the police, people often colloquially call it *contempt of cop*. Extensive anecdotal evidence supports the idea that police use arrests and force against those who criticize them. See, e.g., Christy E. Lopez, *Disorderly (mis) Conduct: The Problem with "Contempt of Cop" Arrests* (2010); see also U.S. Dept. of Justice, *Investigation of the Baltimore City Police Department* 116–119 (2016) (finding that Baltimore officers routinely arrested and used force against individuals for being critical or disrespectful). The limited available research corroborates those anecdotes: Studies indicate that officers are more likely to arrest and use force against individuals who are disrespectful and noncompliant. See, e.g., Robin S. Engel et al., *Citizens' Demeanor, Race, and Traffic Stops, in Race, Ethnicity, and Policing: New and Essential Readings* 287 (Stephen K. Rice & Michael D. White eds. 2010).

For an example of an especially blatant contempt-of-cop arrest, watch the video in this article: Ben Kelly, *S.F. Cop Arrests Skater: Did He Cross the Line?*, TransWorld SKATEboarding (Sept. 28, 2009), *https://skateboarding.transworld.net/news/sf-cop-arrests-skater-did-he-cross-the-line/*. It shows San Francisco police officer Noel Schwab arresting skateboarder Zach Stow. Schwab had originally intended only to give Stow a citation for violating San Francisco's skateboarding ban, but he changed his mind when Stow called him a "fucking dick." Schwab is transparent about his reason for making the arrest: "Now I'm gonna act like a fucking dick. You're under arrest for skateboarding in the City and County of San Francisco. . . . When I'm here to cut you a break, you need to keep your mouth shut and you need to listen." Officer Schwab told bystanders as he walked Stow away in handcuffs, "Say goodbye to your friend. He wants to be a jackass, so he can go to jail." The incident escalated from there, and bystanders claimed that Schwab also used excessive force against Stow. The police department claimed that Stow was arrested because he could not produce identification. See Justin Berton, *S.F. Skateboarder vs. SFPD Officer*, SFGate (Sept. 30, 2009).[4] Was Stow's arrest unconstitutional? Would he have been able to make out a retaliatory arrest claim?

---

[4] Eight years later, Schwab resigned while he was being investigated for exchanging bigoted text messages with other officers. See Vivian Ho, *SF Police Officer Reportedly Fired for Anti-Muslim Text Message*, SFGate (Apr. 3, 2017).

San Francisco police officer Noel Schwab arresting Zach Stow.

Stow was arrested for contempt of cop; Walter Scott was killed. Scott, an unarmed Black man, fled a traffic stop for a brake light violation. According to Slager, when he ordered Scott to stop running, Scott yelled back, "Fuck the police." Slager tased Scott twice, the two struggled on the ground, then Slager shot Scott five times in the back as he ran away. See United States v. Slager, 912 F.3d 224, 228, 237 (4th Cir. 2019).

History, Race, and Contempt of Cop

In thinking about the problem of contempt-of-cop arrests and violence, consider that how people react to the police can be influenced by their experiences, and their community's experiences, with the police. For example, the Department of Justice's investigation into the Ferguson (Mo.) Police Department described the following incident:

> In June 2014, an African-American couple who had taken their children to play at the park allowed their small children to urinate in the bushes next to their parked car. An officer stopped them, threatened to cite them for allowing the children to "expose themselves," and checked the father for warrants. When the mother asked if the officer had to detain the father in front of the children, the officer turned to the father and said, "you're going to jail because your wife keeps running her mouth." The mother then began recording the officer on her cell phone. The officer became irate, declaring, "you don't videotape me!" As the officer drove away with the father in custody for "parental neglect," the mother drove after them, continuing to record. The officer then pulled over and arrested her for traffic violations. When the father asked the officer to show mercy, he responded, "no more mercy, since she wanted to videotape," and declared "nobody videotapes me." The officer then took the phone, which the couple's daughter was holding. After posting bond, the couple found that the video had been deleted.

U.S. Dept. of Justice, *Investigation of the Ferguson Police Department* 27 (2015).

Until the 1960s, Ferguson was an all-white "sundown town": African Americans were permitted in it only by day. Only in the late 1960s did the first Black families move in, and then only in a trickle. Instead, they lived in nearby Kinloch with dilapidated housing and poorly funded schools. After federal courts ordered Ferguson's schools integrated in 1975, the African-American community in Ferguson grew to 14 percent of the population in 1980, 25 percent in 1990, 52 percent in 2000, and 67 percent by 2010, pushed by housing policies in the highly segregated St. Louis area. See Richard Rothstein, Econ. Policy Inst., *The Making of Ferguson: Public Policies at the Root of its Troubles* 3 (2014).

When Ferguson changed demographically, its power structure remained stubbornly white, and in June 2014, when this interaction occurred, African Americans lacked meaningful representation on the school board, in the police department, and on the city council. The city provided municipal services unequally and heavily policed African-American residents, in part as a regressive revenue-raising scheme. In the year this couple was stopped, more than 86 percent of traffic stops in Ferguson were against African Americans, as were 93 percent of the arrests that resulted. But police often failed to respond to serious crime in Black neighborhoods. See Editorial Board, Opinion, *The Death of Michael Brown*, N.Y. Times (Aug. 12, 2014). The Justice Department report found that the police in Ferguson engaged in "a pattern of stops without reasonable suspicion and arrests without probable cause in violation of the Fourth Amendment, infringement on free expression, as well as retaliation for protected free expression, . . . and excessive force in violation of the Fourth Amendment." U.S. Dept. of Justice, *supra*, at 2–3.

Even the officer's invocation of child neglect is racially loaded. Police officers are one of the top sources of referrals to child protective services, and child protective services have long disproportionately separated Black families. In 2014, nationally, African-American children were represented in foster care at nearly twice their rate in the general population. See Children's Bureau, U.S. Dept. of Health & Human Servs., *Racial Disproportionality and Disparity in Child Welfare* (2016).

How might this context have mattered during the encounter? Do you think the officer would have interacted with a white couple the same way?

How can communities work to avoid contempt-of-cop arrests? One way is to change officer training and supervision about arrests and handling disrespect. Alternatively, social psychology research indicates that people perceive police as more legitimate when police (1) allow people to tell their side of the story; (2) seem to make rule-based and unbiased decisions; (3) treat people with respect; and (4) demonstrate benevolent motives. Researchers call this collection of traits procedural justice,[5] and they argue that officers gain more compliance if they act in

[5] When police executives talk about *procedural justice*, they are using the term as social psychologists use it, not as most legal scholars and political philosophers do. Social psychologists look at how police conduct affects individual perceptions of the police and work backward from there to call the actions that produce perceptions of legitimacy *procedural justice*. By contrast, political philosophers and legal scholars

procedurally just ways. See Jason Sunshine & Tom R. Tyler, *The Role of Procedure Justice and Legitimacy in Shaping Public Support for Policing*, 37 L. & Soc'y Rev. 513 (2003); see also President's Task Force on 21st Century Policing, *Final Report of the President's Task Force on 21st Century Policing* 10 (2015). Many departments have adopted procedural justice training toward this end.

Whatever other reasons exist for treating people with respect, other scholars contest the claim that officer conduct generates compliance as procedural justice advocates expect. See Daniel S. Nagin & Cody W. Telep, *Procedural Justice and Legal Compliance*, 13 Annu. Rev. L. & Soc. Sci. 5 (2017). Nevertheless, most agree that *disrespect* by police increases the odds that the people police deal with will be noncompliant. See *Id.*, at 11; Wesley G. Skogan, *Asymmetry in the Impact of Encounters with Police*, 16 Policing & Soc. 99, 118 (2006). Is that what happened with Noel Schwab and Zach Stow? Perhaps encouraging officers to be respectful could mitigate the contempt that leads to contempt-of-cop arrests. When it doesn't, should the law take into account whether an officer's conduct might have contributed to noncooperation? If so, how?

3. Expanding the Right to Challenge the Police

As you have now seen, state and local governments criminalize many kinds of opposition to the police, and First Amendment doctrine carves out only narrow spaces in which officers must tolerate resistance and interference. Fourth Amendment law limits permissible citizen resistance by allowing legal responses to it, including the use of force. Is this the way constitutional law *should* treat resistance?

Over the last several years, a group of criminal-procedure scholars has criticized the law governing the police, and especially Fourth Amendment doctrine, for its approach to citizen resistance. These professors—who might be called "new resistance" scholars—use democratic theory to advocate for constitutional rules that respect greater levels of contestation in police–citizen interactions.

Alice Ristroph argues it is time to "reevaluate the doctrinal significance of resistance or nonsubmission." Alice Ristroph, *The Constitution of Police Violence*, 64 UCLA L. Rev. 1182, 1190 (2017). Jocelyn Simonson advises, "Scholars and reformers should recognize that promoting public participation in criminal justice must include facilitating the ability of civilians to observe, record, and contest police practices and constitutional norms. To seek only collaboration, at the expense of dissent, is to miss out on an important piece of the puzzle that is popular police accountability." Jocelyn Simonson, *Copwatching*, 104 Calif. L. Rev. 391, 394 (2016).

Eric Miller puts it this way:

> Mature democracies are both participatory and contestatory, providing their citizens with, not only a voice in the decision-making process, but also the ability to demand a response from public officials. . . .

---

view procedural fairness or justice as a normative quality of a decisionmaking process or political institution, however it is perceived. See Nat'l Research Council, *Proactive Policing: Effects on Crime and Communities* 114 (2018). See also Eric J. Miller, *Encountering Resistance: Contesting Policing and Procedural Justice*, 2016 U. Chi. L. F. 295, 356–357 (criticizing the focus on procedural justice in policing as about "a civilian's *psychological* feelings of obligation and credit-worthiness toward the officer or the law" rather than "the *actual* lawfulness of police directives or the *actual* normative or democratic validity of the law" in a way that allows the state to "exploit these feelings of credit-worthiness to its benefit").

> . . . [C]ontestation is one way in which we hold the state and its agents responsible, by ensuring that the state provides justifications for its activities. Without the ability to demand justifications from the state or its officials, we cannot force them to defend the legal and political propriety of their conduct.

Eric J. Miller, *Encountering Resistance: Contesting Policing and Procedural Justice*, 2016 U. Chi. Legal F. 295, 296, 298.

And Bennett Capers asks us to

> imagine if citizenship talk in criminal procedure opinions recognized the value of dissent. Right now, the message from Court opinions is that citizens should want to assist the police, should want to cooperate, should want to come forward with any information they know about themselves or others. . . . Imagine opinions that allow room for citizens, including black and brown citizens, to talk back. That allow room for individuals to be oppositional, to question authority, and to challenge the law itself, without fear of repercussion. To be clear, I am not suggesting language that would give individuals the right to physically resist arrest or to disobey a lawful order. But I am suggesting that individuals should, in general, have the right to speak, or not speak, as they choose. To be "uppity" and "belligerent" and oppositional. To "take a knee," as NFL players and others have recently done to protest racialized policing. To even say, in the immortal words of Jay-Z, "you gon' need a warrant for that." To say, in the immortalized words of Eric Garner, "Every time you see me, you want to mess with me. I'm tired of it. It stops today." And to not have to worry about having to say, moments afterwards, "I can't breathe."

I. Bennett Capers, *Criminal Procedure and the Good Citizen*, 118 Colum. L. Rev. 653, 710–711 (2018).

The views of these scholars contrast with a common argument you hear from police officers:

> [I]f you don't want to get shot, tased, pepper-sprayed, struck with a baton or thrown to the ground, just do what I tell you. Don't argue with me, don't call me names, don't tell me that I can't stop you, don't say I'm a racist pig, don't threaten that you'll sue me and take away my badge. Don't scream at me that you pay may salary, and don't even *think* of aggressively walking toward me.

Sunil Dutta, *I'm a Cop. If You Don't Want to Get Hurt, Don't Challenge Me*, Wash. Post. (Aug. 19, 2014). That sentiment has a surprisingly long history. In 1898, an article in the *New York Tribune* recommended against remonstrating with an abusive policeman because "the average policeman is constitutionally averse to taking 'back talk' even of the mildest sort." *The Law of the Nightstick*, N.Y. Trib., Sept. 25, 1898, at 31. If a citizen resists, "it is sure to result in physical damage, and not to the policeman either." *Id.*

To protect resistance, the new resistance scholars mostly look to Fourth Amendment law. Ristroph argues flight, without more, should not be treated as suspicious, making it easier for people to walk away from the police. Ristroph, *supra*, at 1242. Miller believes officers should be required to explain their reasons for following, stopping, questioning, and arresting suspects. Miller, *supra*, at 336–337. Capers thinks the police should be required to tell people when they have the right to refuse to cooperate. Capers, *supra*, at 708. As modest as these reforms seem, they all conflict with settled Fourth Amendment doctrine, so the Court is unlikely to impose them. Are there alternative ways the law might respect resistance?

Simonson thinks so. She turns to First Amendment law, rather than Fourth, and argues for broad interpretation of the First Amendment right to record video of the police in public. She argues recording is not just speech, but a form of contestation. Thus, to protect "First Amendment values of self-government, self-realization, and protecting dissent," civilians must be allowed "to intrude into the sphere of police work with their cameras and smartphones up until the point that they physically interfere with that work." Jocelyn Simonson, *Beyond Body Cameras: Defending a Robust Right to Record the Police*, 104 Geo. L.J. 1559, 1574 (2016).

Assuming you agree with Simonson, why limit protection to citizens who are holding a camera? Could the First Amendment offer broader protection to resisters in ways beyond recording? Presumably, if the Supreme Court resolved the question left open in *Hill* and ruled that *no* words directed at the police constitute "fighting words," fewer people would be arrested for purely verbal opposition. Similarly, if the Court recognized the right to discourage others from complying with police requests, lower courts would consistently protect those who do so. Both of those clarifications are consistent with existing doctrine. If you were designing a legal strategy to achieve these First Amendment reforms, what would it look like? How else might the law protect resistance? Might you look at state law?

All of these reforms involve nonviolent resistance. Should the law permit violence as well? At common law, an arrestee could invoke a provocation defense if he killed his would-be arrester resisting a patently unlawful arrest. Although most arrests at common law were by private citizens, in many states, the common law rule evolved into a broad right to resist illegal arrest, including by government officials. During the second half of the twentieth century, as legal remedies for illegal police conduct became more available, and the dangers of violent self-help became more apparent, many states eliminated the right to resist unlawful police arrests.

The tide might be turning back, at least a little. Some academics have advocated returning to the common law rule to allow citizens to contest aggressive policing. See, e.g., Craig Hemmens & Daniel Levin, *Resistance Is Futile: The Right to Resist Unlawful Arrest in an Era of Aggressive Policing*, 46 Crime & Delinq. 472 (2000); SpearIt, *Firepower to the People! Gun Rights and the Law of Self-Defense to Curb Police Misconduct*, 85 Tenn. L. Rev. 189 (2017). Violent self-help has also grown more politically palatable. Since 2005, the National Rifle Association (NRA) has helped persuade more than half of states to expand lawful self-defense in public in Stand Your Ground laws and court decisions. In 2012, it also supported an expanded right to resist the police, at least in Indiana, which passed a law giving residents the right to use deadly force against officers who illegally enter their homes. See Ind. Code §35-41-3-2.[6] What do you think would happen if more states permitted people to resist illegal entries? Or if more people resisted arrests that they believed to be unlawful?

---

[6] The NRA has long maintained a close relationship with police officers, offering equipment, training, and discounted membership. Many officers strongly support the organization (although some chiefs and officers also see NRA support for putting guns in civilian hands as an ongoing threat to officers' lives). Given this relationship, it is unclear whether the NRA will advocate for further expansions to the right to resist the police.

4.   First Amendment Rights of Police Officers

Officers are not always the speech regulators. Sometimes they are the speakers. When officers wish to speak out against departments or about policing, they present a dilemma analogous to citizens who confront officers on the street: On one hand, officer speech may serve as an important check on the government if, for example, officers reveal waste, corruption, or abuse. Yet departments, like officers, sometimes resist criticism and transparency, in the case of departments, by disciplining or firing officers who speak out. That suggests that officer speech might need protection. On the other hand, what officers say may undermine or interfere with police operations, including by stirring community distrust. This gives departments a legitimate reason to regulate officer speech.

The problem of balancing officers' free-speech rights against the government's interests has been around as long as police departments themselves. In 1892, Justice Holmes, then sitting on the Supreme Judicial Court of Massachusetts, quipped that an officer fired for his political activities "may have a constitutional right to talk politics, but he has no constitutional right to be a policeman." McAuliffe v. City of New Bedford, 29 N.E. 517, 517 (Mass. 1892). First Amendment law is now somewhat more protective of officers who speak out. Still, officers' free-speech rights are quite limited. Here is the Fourth Circuit's summary of the state of the doctrine:

> The legal framework governing public employee speech claims is well known. Public employees may not "be compelled to relinquish the First Amendment rights they would otherwise enjoy as citizens to comment on matters of public interest." Pickering v. Bd. of Educ., 391 U.S. 563, 568 (1968). Underlying this principle is the recognition that "public employees are often the members of the community who are likely to have informed opinions as to the operations of their public employers." City of San Diego v. Roe, 543 U.S. 77, 82 (2004) (per curiam). Nonetheless, a citizen who accepts public employment "must accept certain limitations on his or her freedom." Garcetti v. Ceballos, 547 U.S. 410, 418 (2006). Government employers enjoy considerable discretion to manage their operations, and the First Amendment "does not require a public office to be run as a roundtable for employee complaints over internal office affairs." Connick v. Myers, 461 U.S. 138, 149 (1983).
>
> Courts begin the First Amendment inquiry by assessing whether the speech at issue relates to a matter of public concern. See *Pickering*, 391 U.S. at 568. If speech is purely personal, it is not protected and the inquiry is at an end. If, however, the speech is of public concern, courts must balance "the interests of the [employee], as a citizen, in commenting upon matters of public concern and the interest of the State, as an employer, in promoting the efficiency of the public services it performs through its employees." *Id.*; see also *Connick*, 461 U.S. at 142.

Liverman v. City of Petersburg, 844 F.3d 400, 406–407 (4th Cir. 2016).

The rise of social media has significantly increased conflict over what police officers have to say. Although allowing officers to speak their minds can contribute to transparency about policing, it can also undermine public confidence in the police. In 2017, a group named the Plain View Project collected social media posts from thousands of police officers. These posts were filled with racism, religious animosity, language that devalued human life and dignity, and support for police violence. Many of the posts talked about "exterminating" people suspected of crimes, used racial epithets, and trivialized constitutional rights. For an example of an officer's post, see Chapter 4. To see additional posts, visit the Plain View Project website at *https://www.plainviewproject.org/data.* What can (and should) departments do?

Some police departments have adopted social media policies, some of which officers have challenged in court. In *Liverman v. City of Petersburg*, 844 F.3d 400 (4th Cir. 2016), for example, the Fourth Circuit assessed a department social media policy that included the following:

> "Negative comments on the internal operations of the Bureau, or specific conduct of supervisors or peers that impacts the public's perception of the department is not protected by the First Amendment free speech clause. . . .

> Officers may comment on issues of general or public concern (as opposed to personal grievances) so long as the comments do not disrupt the workforce, interfere with important working relationship or efficient work flow, or undermine public confidence in the officer."

Id. at 404. The Court of Appeals used ordinary First Amendment principles to analyze the policy:

> Although regulations on social media use may appear to present novel issues, . . . such questions are amenable to the traditional analysis set forth in *Connick* and *Pickering*. Indeed, the particular attributes of social media fit comfortably within the existing balancing inquiry: A social media platform amplifies the distribution of the speaker's message—which favors the employee's free speech interests—but also increases the potential, in some cases exponentially, for departmental disruption, thereby favoring the employer's interest in efficiency. What matters to the First Amendment analysis is not only the medium of the speech, but the scope and content of the restriction.

> Here we deal with a broad social networking policy setting forth the parameters of public employee speech. In *United States v. Nat'l Treasury Employees Union (NTEU)*, 513 U.S. 454 (1995), the Supreme Court addressed how courts should apply *Pickering* when a generally applicable statute or regulation (as opposed to a post-hoc disciplinary action) operates as a prior restraint on speech. . . . [T]he Court held that "the Government's burden is greater with respect to this statutory restriction on expression than with respect to [the] isolated disciplinary action[s]" in *Pickering* and its progeny. *Id.* at 467, 468. Accordingly, "[t]he Government must show that the interests of both potential audiences and a vast group of present and future employees in a broad range of present and future expression are outweighed by that expression's 'necessary impact on the actual operation' of the Government." *Id.* at 468 (quoting *Pickering*, 391 U.S. at 571). Further, the government "must demonstrate that the recited harms are real, not merely conjectural, and that the regulation will in fact alleviate these harms in a direct and material way." *Id.* at 475.

Id. at 407.

Reasoning that the above policy prohibited almost any criticism of the police department, the Fourth Circuit panel held that the policy was both facially overbroad and unconstitutional as applied to two officers who posted criticism of the department's promotion practices on Facebook. The Court rejected as hypothetical the Chief's concern that the speech prohibitions could harm community trust for the police department. *Id.* at 408–409.

Now consider this excerpt from the Philadelphia Police Department social media policy:

> I. Employees are prohibited from using ethnic slurs, profanity, personal insults; material that is harassing, defamatory, fraudulent, or discriminatory, or other content or communications that would not be acceptable in a City workplace under City or agency policy or practice.
>
> J. Employees are prohibited from displaying sexually explicit images, cartoons, jokes, messages or other material that would be considered in violation of the City Policy Preventing Sexual Harassment in City Government.

Philadelphia Police Department, Directive 6.10: Social Media and Networking §4 (July 6, 2012). This policy applies even to the use of personal social media accounts that do not display the officer's rank or any indicia of a relationship with the department, and even if the offensive content is posted off-duty using privately owned property. *Id.* at §5.

Imagine you work in the Philadelphia law department. An officer is challenging the city's social media policy, and the district court has indicated that it agrees with the Fourth Circuit's description of the law. Your boss wants your analysis about how to best defend the Philadelphia policy under *Liverman*, although he recognizes that it is not controlling in the Third Circuit. What would you say? The police commissioner is also considering expanding the policy to prohibit advocating unconstitutional violence against suspects. May she do so?

B. Policing Protest

The previous section explored *individual* rights to criticize and resist the police. This section looks at the law protecting *collective* challenges to the police — and other government and private action — in the form of political protests.

1. The Law of Protests

When police manage political protests, as the NYPD did near the Republican National Convention in 2004, both First and Fourth Amendment rights are implicated.

MARCAVAGE v. CITY OF NEW YORK
689 F.3d 98 (2d Cir. 2012)

Dennis Jacobs, Chief Judge:

Michael Marcavage and Steven Lefemine ("Plaintiffs"), protesters at the 2004 Republican National Convention at Madison Square Garden, were arrested after they failed to comply with police instructions to move along from an area where demonstrating was prohibited and to one designated for protesting. They brought this suit under 42 U.S.C. §1983 against the New York City Police Department ("NYPD"), the Police Commissioner, three NYPD officers, and others (collectively, "Defendants"), seeking . . . money damages. Plaintiffs claim the NYPD's policy around the convention violated the First Amendment and that Plaintiffs' arrest violated the Fourth Amendment. This appeal is taken from a judgment of the United States District Court for the Southern District of New York granting summary judgment in favor of Defendants. We conclude that the restriction on speech was a reasonable time, place, and manner restriction, and that the arrests were supported by probable cause.

Background

The Convention. The 2004 Republican National Convention ("the Convention") was held from August 30 to September 2 at Madison Square Garden ("the Garden") in midtown Manhattan. The security planners of the NYPD understood that political conventions are potential terrorist targets and therefore prepared for the possibility that groups and individuals would engage in criminal conduct that could significantly endanger public safety. The NYPD was also responsible for accommodating commuters, businesses, and residents in the vicinity. . . . The NYPD anticipated that there would be a volume of protest activity not seen in New York City in decades, including potentially hundreds of thousands of protesters throughout the city.

The Garden sits atop Pennsylvania Station ("Penn Station"), one of the transportation hubs of New York City. . . . The vicinity is ordinarily congested by vehicular and pedestrian traffic; a major event at the Garden can bring thousands of additional pedestrians.

The complex is a superblock bordered by Seventh and Eighth Avenues to the east and west, and by 31st and 33rd Streets to the south and north. . . .

The NYPD implemented a three-zone system outside the Garden: a demonstration area, a frozen area (with no pedestrian traffic), and a no-demonstration area.

In the "frozen zone"—the Seventh Avenue sidewalk adjacent to the Garden between 31st and 33rd Streets—barriers were erected and all pedestrian traffic was prohibited.

Directly across Seventh Avenue from the frozen zone was the "no-demonstration" zone between 31st and 33rd Streets. People on that east sidewalk were not permitted to protest, distribute leaflets, or congregate in that area, even if they remained in motion and kept up with the flow of pedestrian traffic. NYPD officers advised people in the vicinity of the Garden to go to the demonstration zone if they wanted to protest.

The "demonstration zone" was the full width of Eighth Avenue, extending south from 31st Street. Within the demonstration zone, expressive activity was permitted at any time during the Convention. The NYPD issued sound permits and constructed a stage for demonstrators at the north end of the demonstration area, near the 31st Street intersection, closest to the Garden. Thousands of protesters used the demonstration area.

Madison Square Garden, which sits atop Penn Station, and
the surrounding Manhattan streets.

The Protest. On September 1, 2004, Plaintiffs were standing in the no-
demonstration zone between 32nd and 33rd Streets, holding anti-abortion
signs—one sign was four by six feet, the other was three by five. Plaintiffs were
approximately five feet from the facade of the Pennsylvania Hotel, where (they contend) they were outside the flow of pedestrian traffic. After 10 to 15 minutes, they
were approached by police officers.

The officers repeatedly told Plaintiffs they could not protest there, and
directed them to the demonstration zone. Plaintiffs objected that the demonstration zone was not within sight and sound of the Convention attendees and that
they did not want to be in the demonstration zone lumped with other demonstrators. . . . All told, Plaintiffs were ordered to leave 17 times by three different
police officers before they were informed that they were blocking traffic and
placed under arrest.

Marcavage and Lefemine were charged with disorderly conduct, and
Marcavage was also charged with resisting arrest. All charges . . . were ultimately
dismissed. . . .

Discussion. . . .

II

Plaintiffs contend that the no-demonstration zone along Seventh Avenue was an unreasonable time, place, and manner restriction, and therefore violated the First Amendment.

Preliminarily, we consider [1] whether Plaintiffs were engaged in First Amendment protected activity [2] in a traditional public forum, and [3] if the restriction on speech was unrelated to content. See Ward v. Rock Against Racism, 491 U.S. 781, 790–791 (1989).

First, Plaintiffs' display of a political sign constituted political speech, which "is entitled to the fullest possible measure of constitutional protection." See Members of the City Council v. Taxpayers for Vincent, 466 U.S. 789, 816 (1984).

Second, Plaintiffs were carrying out their expressive activity in a traditional public forum. "Sidewalks, of course, are among those areas of public property that traditionally have been held open to the public for expressive activities," United States v. Grace, 461 U.S. 171, 179 (1983), and the sidewalks of New York are the "prototypical" traditional public forum, Schenck v. Pro–Choice Network of W. N.Y., 519 U.S. 357, 377 (1997). . . .

Third, as Plaintiffs concede, the restraint on expressive activity was content neutral. This concession is well-taken. A regulation is content neutral when it is "justified without reference to the content of the regulated speech." City of Renton v. Playtime Theatres, Inc., 475 U.S. 41, 48 (1986). The restriction on expressive activity was not aimed at the content of the message; no demonstrating of any kind was allowed in that zone.

Since Plaintiffs were engaged in expressive activity in a public forum and the regulation was content neutral, the restriction on speech near the Convention is properly characterized as a time, place, and manner restriction. Such restrictions are permissible if they " '[1] are justified without reference to the content of the regulated speech, [2] . . . are narrowly tailored to serve a significant governmental interest, and [3] . . . leave open ample alternative channels for communication of the information.' " *Ward*, 491 U.S. at 791. Defendants bear the burden of demonstrating that the regulation was constitutional. United States v. Playboy Entm't Grp., Inc., 529 U.S. 803, 816–817 (2000).

Since the restriction was content neutral, the decisive issues are narrow tailoring and alternative channels.

A

Whether the NYPD's policy was narrowly tailored to serve a significant government interest depends on the importance of the government's interest and the breadth of the speech restriction.

1

Government "certainly has a significant interest in keeping its public spaces safe and free of congestion." Bery v. City of New York, 97 F.3d 689, 697 (2d Cir. 1996). And "there can be no doubting the substantial government interest in the maintenance of security at political conventions." Bl(a)ck Tea Soc'y v. City of Boston, 378 F.3d 8, 12 (1st Cir. 2004).

Plaintiffs contend that Defendants adduced insufficient evidence to support these interests and instead relied on unspecific, generic security rationales.

The record amply establishes non-security reasons for banning protesters from occupying a crowded sidewalk. The considerable interests of the "millions of residents, visitors, and workers must be balanced" against the interest of protesters. See Concerned Jewish Youth v. McGuire, 621 F.2d 471, 478 (2d Cir. 1980). The stretch of Seventh Avenue in front of the Garden is a crowded thoroughfare even without major sports or political events at the Garden, with commuters, shoppers, tourists, residents, and other people passing through. . . . The City had the requisite significant interest in keeping that channel clear for pedestrians.

The government interest in security is also significant. In the Fourth Amendment context, we have held that "no express threat or special imminence is required before we may accord great weight to the government's interest in staving off considerable harm." MacWade v. Kelly, 460 F.3d 260, 272 (2d Cir. 2006). "All that is required is that the 'risk to public safety [be] substantial and real' instead of merely 'symbolic.'" *Id.* (quoting Chandler v. Miller, 520 U.S. 305, 322–323 (1997)). These principles also apply in the First Amendment context. Because "security protocols exist to deal with hypothetical risks"—and "security planning is necessarily concerned with managing potential risks, which sometimes necessitates consideration of the worst-case scenario"—it is "appropriate" for governments to consider possible security threats and the role that protesters may play in causing such threats or inadvertently preventing the authorities from thwarting or responding to such threats. Citizens for Peace in Space v. City of Colo. Springs, 477 F.3d 1212, 1223–1224 (10th Cir. 2007). "As long as a designed security protocol reduces a plausible and substantial safety risk, it directly and effectively advances a substantial government interest." *Id.* at 1224.

The police had to design measures to cope with a security challenge that was altogether extraordinary. The Convention was in the middle of New York City, adjacent to Penn Station. Fifty thousand attendees were expected for the Convention itself. Protesters of different persuasions would descend. Vehicle and pedestrian traffic would be rerouted along two main arteries. The national conventions that year were the first following the 2001 terror attacks. The President was coming, as well as the Vice President and a host of other government officials. These facts, taken together, bespeak a significant—indeed, compelling—government interest in security.

2

The Government must also show that its policy was "narrowly tailored" to achieve that significant government interest. *Ward,* 491 U.S. at 791.

A regulation is narrowly tailored "'so long as [it] . . . promotes a substantial government interest that would be achieved less effectively absent the regulation,'" and is "not substantially broader than necessary to achieve the government's interest." *Id.* at 799–800.

The no-demonstration zone was narrowly tailored to achieve significant government interests. The restricted zones were confined to a two-block stretch of Seventh Avenue and were in place only during the four days of the Convention. And the policy was tailored to meet the congestion and security challenges that the Convention presented. The frozen zone was limited to the sidewalk immediately in front of a single side of the Garden. The no-demonstration zone was limited to the opposite sidewalk, which had to be kept unobstructed to accommodate the heavy pedestrian traffic that usually occupies both sides. . . .

Plaintiffs argue that the no-demonstration zone was not narrowly tailored because protesters were barred even from forms of expression that did not increase congestion, such as carrying a sign while keeping up with the flow, or standing to one side. It may be, as Plaintiffs suggest, that a no-standing zone or no-large-sign zone would have been a less restrictive alternative, but "narrowly tailored" does not mean the "least restrictive or least intrusive means." *Ward,* 491 U.S. at 798. "[R]estrictions on the time, place, or manner of protected speech are not invalid 'simply because there is some imaginable alternative that might be less burdensome on speech.'" *Id.* at 797. A regulation is narrowly tailored "so long as [it] . . . promotes a substantial government interest that would be achieved less effectively absent the regulation" and is "not substantially broader than necessary." *Id.* at 799–800.

The no-demonstration zone does not burden *substantially* more speech than necessary, even if alternatives are conceivable. Even if protesters kept walking, they would occlude pedestrian passage, especially when they picketed back and forth. Policing a less than clear-cut regulation also would risk the fact or appearance of selective enforcement based on content, and would result in the "substantial, additional burdens of . . . maintaining supervision of the protestors . . . and generally providing enough manpower in close proximity to the protestors to quickly handle any protest that turned violent." *Citizens for Peace in Space,* 477 F.3d at 1223. . . .

Finally, Plaintiffs contend that justifications based on security and congestion are premised on large numbers of protesters whereas Plaintiffs are just two people standing out of the way. We disagree. The policy "should not be measured by the disorder that would result from granting an exemption solely to [Plaintiffs]" because if these two plaintiffs were allowed a dispensation, "so too must other groups," which would then create "a much larger threat to the State's interest in crowd control" and security. See Int'l Soc'y for Krishna Consciousness, Inc. v. Lee, 505 U.S. 672, 685 (1992). Plaintiffs' approach would also vest line-level officers with power and discretion to determine when the number of protesters exceeds some unspecified permissible number, whether to aggregate small groups of protesters who may not agree, and to decide which group came first and should be allowed to stay while others must leave.

In short, the NYPD's small no-demonstration zone on a two-block strip of Seventh Avenue was narrowly tailored to address the threats to sidewalk congestion and security created by an event the size and spectacle of a national convention in midtown Manhattan.

B

It remains to decide whether the regulation "leave[s] open ample alternative channels for communication of the information." *Ward,* 491 U.S. at 791.

Although an alternative channel for communication must be available, it is clear that "[t]he First Amendment . . . does not guarantee [protesters] access to every or even the best channels or locations for their expression." Carew–Reid v. Metro. Transp. Auth., 903 F.2d 914, 919 (2d Cir. 1990). . . . "All that is required is that an alternative channel be ample—i.e., an "adequate" channel for communication. Deegan v. City of Ithaca, 444 F.3d 135, 144 (2d Cir. 2006). . . .

In this Circuit, an alternative channel is adequate and therefore ample if it is within "close proximity" to the intended audience. In *United for Peace & Justice v. City of New York,* the city denied a permit to march past the United Nations headquarters and instead granted a permit for a stationary protest at a nearby park—on the other side of a major avenue, and two blocks north of the entrance to the United Nations. 323 F.3d 175, 177 (2nd Cir. 2003). Because the protesters were permitted to demonstrate in "close proximity to the United Nations," the restriction on their march comported with the First Amendment. *Id.*

Plaintiffs' chief argument on appeal is that the demonstration zone was inadequate because it was not within "sight and sound" of the intended audience, which they identify as the delegates. Although this may be a relevant consideration in some instances, none of the cases cited by Plaintiffs establishes "sight and sound" as a constitutional requirement. . . .

Whether an alternative channel is adequate cannot be determined "in an objective vacuum, but instead" requires "practical recognition [of] the facts." *Citizens for Peace in Space,* 477 F.3d at 1226. Here, the manifold risks ranged from pedestrian gridlock to assassination. Under such circumstances, a demonstration zone one avenue from the primary entrance to the Garden was an ample alternative channel for protesters, such as Plaintiffs.

Because the NYPD's limitation on speech around the Convention was content neutral, was narrowly tailored to achieve a substantial government interest, and allowed an ample alternative channel of communication, it was a permissible time, place, and manner restriction on speech. Accordingly, the district court correctly dismissed Plaintiffs' First Amendment claim.

III

Both Plaintiffs were arrested for disorderly conduct, and Marcavage was also arrested for resisting arrest. Plaintiffs contend that their arrest violated the Fourth Amendment. Defendants counter that probable cause existed. . . .

Defendants contend there was probable cause to arrest Plaintiffs for disorderly conduct,[4] obstruction of governmental administration (under New York Penal Law §195.05[5] and New York City Charter §435(a)[6]), and failure to comply with lawful orders to disperse. A Fourth Amendment claim turns on whether probable cause existed to arrest for any crime, not whether probable cause existed with respect to each individual charge. See Devenpeck v. Alford, 543 U.S. 146, 153–156 (2004). Accordingly, Defendants prevail if there was probable cause to arrest Plaintiffs for any single offense.

Probable cause supported the arrests for obstruction of governmental administration. Plaintiffs rejected 17 directives (by three officers) to leave the no-demonstration zone, insisting on a constitutional right to demonstrate where they stood. We need not decide whether Plaintiffs had to obey an unconstitutional order, because we have held that the order was constitutional.

. . . Plaintiffs' Fourth Amendment claim was correctly dismissed.

---

[4] A person is guilty of disorderly conduct when, with intent to cause public inconvenience, annoyance or alarm, or recklessly creating a risk thereof: . . . (5) He obstructs vehicular or pedestrian traffic; or (6) He congregates with other persons in a public place and refuses to comply with a lawful order of the police to disperse. . . .

N.Y. Penal Law §240.20(5)–(6) (McKinney 2010).

[5] A person is guilty of obstructing governmental administration when he intentionally obstructs, impairs or perverts the administration of law or other governmental function or prevents or attempts to prevent a public servant from performing an official function, by means of intimidation, physical force or interference, or by means of any independently unlawful act. . . .

N.Y. Penal Law §195.05 (McKinney 2010).

[6] The police department . . . shall have the power and it shall be their duty to preserve the public peace, prevent crime, detect and arrest offenders, suppress riots, mobs and insurrections, disperse unlawful or dangerous assemblages and assemblages which obstruct the free passage of public streets, sidewalks, parks and places; . . . regulate, direct, control and restrict the movement of vehicular and pedestrian traffic for the facilitation of traffic and the convenience of the public as well as the proper protection of human life and health; remove all nuisances in the public streets, parks and places; . . . and for these purposes to arrest all persons guilty of violating any law or ordinance for the suppression or punishment of crimes or offenses.

N.Y.C. Charter §435(a).

NOTES AND QUESTIONS

1. *First Amendment law overview.* Just to clarify: Protests and demonstrations are *speech* within the meaning of the First Amendment, and as *Marcavage* indicates, streets, sidewalks, and parks are *public forums* where the government's ability to restrict expressive conduct is limited:

> [T]he government may enforce reasonable time, place, and manner regulations as long as the restrictions "are content-neutral, are narrowly tailored to serve a significant government interest, and leave open ample alternative channels of communication." Perry Education Assn. v. Perry Local Educator's Assn., 460 U.S. 37, 45 (1983). Additional restrictions such as an absolute prohibition on a particular type of expression will be upheld only if narrowly drawn to accomplish a compelling governmental interest.

United States v. Grace, 461 U.S. 171, 177 (1983). That sounds pretty protective. What does *Marcavage* tell you about how the standard is being applied? How hard is it for a department to justify imposing restrictions on protesters?

2. *Who decides?* Reading Supreme Court cases, one gets the idea that decisions about protesting are made by municipal officials—who decide on permits—and by prosecutors—who decide on charges against protesters—and then reviewed by courts, which determine whether their actions are constitutional. *Marcavage* reflects another reality, that police departments often dictate who gets to speak and when. In *Marcavage*, the NYPD's decisions were made in advance and in writing. More often, police officers and departments make critical decisions about managing protests in real time. They decide where protesters may go, what commands they must follow, and whether they must disperse. Although these decisions are subject to the same First Amendment doctrine as preplanned government decisions, courts are more forgiving in evaluating officer conduct, and remedies are more limited, when the decisions are made during protests. The practical scope of constitutional rights is more often determined in the street than in court.

3. *Government interests.* In *Marcavage*, the government identified obviously weighty interests: the security of the U.S. President (and other political figures) and access to and traffic around the heart of this country's most populous city. What about less dramatic government interests? Courts have allowed reasonable restrictions to prevent "unwelcome noise," Ward v. Rock Against Racism, 491 U.S. 781, 796 (1989); maintain public parks "in an attractive and intact condition," Clark v. Community for Creative Non-Violence, 468 U.S. 288, 296 (1984); avoid "burden on the essential flow of traffic," Grayned v. City of Rockford, 408 U.S. 104, 116 (1972); maintain free egress and ingress to a country courthouse, Cameron v. Johnson, 390 U.S. 611, 617 (1968); allow access to health care facilities, Hill v. Colorado, 530 U.S. 703, 715 (2000); protect "esthetic interests," Members of City Council v. Taxpayers for Vincent, 466 U.S. 789, 807 (1984); and ensure an "undisrupted school session conducive to the students' learning," *Grayned*, 408 U.S. at 119. The severity of the speech restrictions justified by these government interests is a matter of degree, so minor traffic delays would not necessarily justify shutting down a political protest, see, e.g., Jones v. Parmley, 465 F.3d 46, 58 (2d Cir. 2006), and restrictions must all be narrowly tailored. Still, it seems the Court is permissive in allowing government interests to weigh against free speech.

4. *Speech and crime.* Did you notice what Marcavage was charged with? States criminalize disruption and noncompliance in a variety of ways, including (1) statutes prohibiting specific public conduct, such as blocking a roadway; (2) more flexible

statutes, such as prohibitions on disorderly conduct; (3) police-specific crimes, such as resisting arrest; and (4) mass-gathering crimes, which in New York include riot, inciting to riot, and criminal anarchy. This array of crimes allows officers broad discretion, at least within the constraints of the First Amendment, which prohibits states from criminalizing activities that protesters have a right to do. Thus, states may not punish peaceful protesters for disturbing the peace. See Cox v. Louisiana, 379 U.S. 536 (1965). And they may not stop speech because of the disruptive reaction of listeners. See Edwards v. South Carolina, 372 U.S. 229 (1963); Terminiello v. City of Chicago, 337 U.S. 1 (1949). But states may punish violence and property damage, which is not protected speech, and they may arrest someone for speech that makes violence imminent. See *Terminiello*, 337 U.S. at 4.

5. *Unlawful assembly.* Police often use state laws against *unlawful assembly* to end demonstrations once rocks and bottles start flying. See John Inazu, *Unlawful Assembly as Social Control*, 64 UCLA L. Rev. 2 (2017) (discussing the history of unlawful assembly laws). Such laws allow officers to make otherwise lawful conduct criminal. Under New York's law, for example:

> A person is guilty of unlawful assembly when he assembles with four or more other persons for the purpose of engaging or preparing to engage with them in tumultuous and violent conduct likely to cause public alarm, or when, being present at an assembly which either has or develops such purpose, he remains there with intent to advance that purpose.

N.Y. Penal Law §240.10. Police declare an unlawful assembly when a protest turns violent, at which point the demonstrators lose their First Amendment protection. Grayned v. City of Rockford, 408 U.S. 104, 116 (1972). At that point, the officers command people to leave the area, then arrest those who fail to depart.

6. *Police commands and due process.* Police conduct during protests must comply with Fourteenth Amendment due process requirements as well as the commands of the First Amendment. Due process demands that individuals have *fair notice* of what conduct the government forbids or requires, a requirement that applies with extra vigor when government action is limiting speech. See FCC v. Fox Television Stations, Inc., 567 U.S. 239, 253–254 (2012). Notice is often an issue when police issue orders during a protest, including by announcing an unlawful assembly.

For instance, after former St. Louis (Mo.) police officer Jason Stockley was acquitted in 2017 of murdering Anthony Lamar Smith in 2011, St. Louis was rocked by several days of protests, some of which turned violent. Police responded with unlawful assembly declarations, dispersal orders, and arrests. Some protesters sued, and Judge Catherine Perry issued a preliminary injunction against the St. Louis Police Department prohibiting officers from using chemical agents against protesters

> in the absence of probable cause to arrest the person and without first issuing clear and unambiguous warnings that the person is subject to arrest and such chemical agents will be used and providing the person sufficient opportunity to heed the warnings and comply with lawful law enforcement commands.

Ahmad v. City of St. Louis, No. 4:17 CV 2455 CDP, 2017 WL 5478410, at *18 (E.D. Mo. Nov. 15, 2017). The judge also enjoined issuing orders or using agents

> without first: specifying with reasonable particularity the area from which dispersal is ordered; issuing audible and unambiguous orders in a manner designed to

notify all persons within the area that dispersal is required and providing sufficient warnings of the consequences of failing to disperse . . .; providing a sufficient and announced amount of time which is proximately related to the issuance of the dispersal order in which to heed the warnings and exit the area; and announcing and ensuring a means of safe egress from the area that is actually available to all persons.

Id. She made an exception for when people "at the scene present an imminent threat of violence or bodily harm to persons or damage to property, or where law enforcement officials must defend themselves or other persons or property against imminent threat of violence." *Id.* Although preliminary injunctions are unusual, fights about adequate notice of police-issued rules in protests are not.

7. *Speech and the Fourth Amendment.* Marcavage and Lefemine raised Fourth Amendment claims as well as First Amendment ones. It is not unusual for protesters to complain that police arrested them without probable cause or used excessive force. These Fourth Amendment claims get complicated during protests: What if a person fails to comply with a dispersal order because other protesters make it difficult to leave? Is a protester who is in a crowd *seized* when an officer uses tear gas or a flashbang? The courts have offered no easy answers. See Renée Paradis, Note, *Carpe Demonstratores: Towards a Bright-Line Rule Governing Seizure in Excessive Force Claims Brought by Demonstrators,* 103 Colum. L. Rev. 316, 334–341 (2003) (discussing cases).

8. *Individuals and groups.* Consider that declaring an unlawful assembly or using tear gas against a crowd affects every person present, including those who were never violent, who never heard the command to disperse, or who were trying to leave the area. If First Amendment, Fourth Amendment, and Fourteenth Amendment rights are individual rights, not collective ones, how can a person lose the right to speak, the right to notice, or the right to be free from excessive force because another protester threw a brick? How should departments (and courts) ensure that rights are adequately protected? Or do the challenges of managing chaos and violence require more flexibility for law enforcement than the individual-rights framework permits?

9. *Civil disobedience.* Not all arrests during protests are unwelcome. Some protesters break the law intentionally, driven by conscience to let their lives—following the advice of Henry David Thoreau—"be a counter friction to stop the machine." Henry David Thoreau, *Civil Disobedience,* in *Walden and Other Writings of Henry David Thoreau* 667, 677 (Brooks Atkinson ed., 1992) (1849). Civil disobedience carried out "openly, lovingly, and with a willingness to accept the penalty," Martin Luther King, Jr., *Letter from a Birmingham Jail,* Christian Century 769 (June 12, 1963), may be conducted with the cooperation of the police. In some protests, arrests are negotiated and planned in advance—making them safer and more orderly. But that cooperation is far less common in protests against the police.

Law or Politics?

Despite the constraints of the First, Fourth, and Fourteenth Amendments, police have substantial discretion during protests to give commands and to enforce them, to make arrests for minor offenses or to let people continue to gather, and to tolerate disorder or to tamp it down. As a result, political scrutiny is often the primary remedy against problematic protest policing.

After the Charlottesville (Va.) City Council voted to remove two statues of confederate generals, Charlottesville famously faced a series of protests, known as the "Summer of Hate." The summer culminated in the large August 12, 2017, Unite the Right rally, in which hundreds of white nationalists and neo-Nazis, and even more counterprotesters, marched on the town. Poor planning, coordination, and execution by city officials, the Charlottesville Police Department, and the Virginia State Police left the city unprepared and ineffectual. The police let violent clashes go unabated, and tragedy ensued when white supremacist James Alex Fields, Jr., deliberately rammed his car into a group of counterprotesters, killing Heather Heyer and injuring others. See Timothy J. Heaphy, *Final Report: Independent Review of the 2017 Protest Events in Charlottesville, Virginia* (2017).[7]

Unite the Right rally on August 12, 2017, in Charlottesville, Virginia.

Although individual protesters, including Fields, faced criminal charges and civil damages actions, much of the fallout for the city was political rather than legal: The police chief, the city manager, and the mayor all lost their jobs over the summer's events, as did the head of the state police.

Personnel changes seem a weak remedy to those who are silenced or injured at a protest. These changes, however, sent a clear message about the community's views about speech, protest safety, and policing, a message that inevitably will influence future decisions about protests. In the absence of more strenuous legal protections for protesters, political messages might be as likely as the law to influence how much noise protesters are permitted to make. The law may purport to value free speech, but the practical scope of free speech rights may be determined in another arena.

[7] *Ed. note:* I served as an expert for the Independent Review and participated in drafting the report.

2. Protests Against the Police

Policing protests presents a real challenge: Too much policing can suppress speech and trigger violence. Too little can lead to lost lives and damaged property, as it did in Charlottesville. Police departments take very different approaches to this dilemma, from aggressively arresting and containing protesters to permitting all but serious disorder and violence, all within the limits of the First Amendment. When demonstrators criticize policing, the stakes are raised: Police departments are both the subject of the protest and its regulator. How departments handle such protests varies substantially.

Protest against police violence in Seattle in June 2020, days after George Floyd was killed by Minneapolis police officers.

When St. Louis protested Jason Stockley's acquittal for the death of Anthony Lamar Smith, for example, the protests were largely peaceful, with protesters holding "Black Lives Matter" signs and chanting, "Stop killing us." However, when violence broke out on the third night, officers made arrests. As they did, the officers chanted at protesters, "Whose streets? Our streets," a perversion of an iconic rallying cry for people claiming the right be heard in public spaces. The St. Louis police chief echoed his officers' tone when he proudly declared, "The police owned tonight," and, "We're in control." See Mitch Smith et al., *Protesters Descend on St. Louis, and Police Respond: "We're in Control,"* N.Y. Times (Sept. 18, 2017); *More Than 80 Arrested After Protest Violence Downtown; "Police Owned Tonight," Chief Says,* St. Louis Post-Dispatch (Sept. 18, 2017).

Contrast the St. Louis approach with the approach of the Metro Nashville Police Department in the aftermath of a grand jury's decision not to indict police officer Darren Wilson for killing Michael Brown in Ferguson, Missouri, in 2014. Police Chief Steve Anderson allowed protesters to shut down an interstate for 25 minutes without a permit rather than conduct mass arrests. When members of the community complained about the inconvenience, Chief Anderson responded:

> In Nashville, if you want to come to a public forum and express your thoughts, even if they're against the government, you're going to get your First Amendment protection, and you're going to be treated fairly by the police officers involved. . . . That's what we do here in Nashville.

Kriston Capps, *Some Law-Enforcement Agencies Are Handling Protests Right*, CityLab (Dec. 11, 2014).

In protests against the police, protesters already distrust, resent, and fear law enforcement. The police — angered by the message — often seek to suppress rather than facilitate the exercise of constitutional rights. Not surprisingly, violence sometimes results. It has long been this way: In 1886, the Haymarket Riot began as a protest against police violence during a labor strike and ended when someone bombed the police arriving to disperse the crowd. During several periods in the twentieth century, conflicts over police harassment and systemic racism helped spur urban riots, including in 1992, when Los Angeles burned after officers who beat Rodney King were acquitted. The pattern has continued into the twenty-first century: In 2014, violent protests erupted in response to a spate of high-profile police killings of unarmed Black men, including Michael Brown in Ferguson, Missouri, and Eric Garner in New York City; and in the spring of 2020, sometimes-violent protests against police brutality and racism took place in more than 140 cities in the days after Minneapolis police officer Derek Chauvin killed George Floyd by kneeling on Floyd's neck.

In 2020, some chiefs and officers marched with or facilitated protesters. Many others reacted forcefully, especially when protests turned destructive or violent. In just a few weeks, police carried out more than 10,000 arrests and injured hundreds of people with pepper spray, rubber bullets, tear gas, flashbangs, and batons. See, e.g., Michael Sainato, *"They Set Us Up": US Police Arrested over 10,000 Protesters, Many Non-Violent*, Guardian (Jun. 8, 2020). As has happened before, protests spurred by police violence were also marred by it: Dozens of videos from all over the country showed police attacking, gassing, and shooting rubber bullets at peaceful protesters. See Shawn Hubler & Julie Bosman, *A Crisis That Began With an Image of Police Violence Keeps Providing More*, N.Y. Times (July 8, 2020).

As you think about clashes between police and crowds protesting policing and the law, you might keep separate two different sets of concerns. The first concerns police operations *within the law*. As you have seen, the law provides some, but limited, restrictions on protest policing. Officers still choose whether to facilitate protests or use their power to thwart them. They decide how much community disruption will be tolerated, whether to communicate with demonstrators in advance, when to make lawful arrests, and what force to use to clear crowds and detain individuals. Different members of communities often have radically different views about how police should handle disruptive protests. Given that, how should policing policy on protests get made, implemented, and evaluated? What role does the law have to play in establishing these processes?

Second, police sometimes operate *outside the law*, raising questions about what should happen when they do. How should departments receive and respond to complaints during ongoing clashes? Which are the best legal remedies for deterring First, Fourth, and Fourteenth Amendment violations? What can protesters do in real time?

Can Protesters Be Sued When the Police Get Hurt?

In *Marcavage*, the protesters sued the police. What happens when the police sue the protesters? The First Amendment not only protects speech against criminal liability; it protects it against civil liability as well. In *NAACP v. Clairborne Hardware Co.*, 458 U.S. 886 (1982), white merchants in Mississippi sued a local NAACP chapter, its leaders, and its members for organizing a boycott that interfered with their businesses.

> Petitioners withheld their patronage from the white establishment of Claiborne County to challenge a political and economic system that had denied them the basic rights of dignity and equality that this country had fought a Civil War to secure. While the State legitimately may impose damages for the consequences of violent conduct, it may not award compensation for the consequences of nonviolent, protected activity.

Id. at 918. By contrast, unprotected conduct during a protest—such as throwing a brick at a police officer or burning a car—can be the basis for criminal charges and civil damages.

What about when a protest includes both protected and unprotected activities, as many protests do? Are leaders liable for acts of violence done during a protest? Not in *Claiborne Hardware*. Although Charles Evers, a local NAACP leader, gave an impassioned speech supporting the boycott, and some participants in the boycott coerced, intimidated, and threatened people to stop them from going to the boycotted establishments, the Supreme Court held that Evers was not liable for the consequences of his speech because he did not authorize, ratify, or incite tortious conduct. The Court cautioned "extreme care" in attaching civil liability to protest conduct. *Id.* at 916.

Still, in 2019, the Fifth Circuit court of appeals read *Claiborne Hardware* to allow a suit to go forward against DeRay Mckesson, a Black Lives Matter leader who organized a 2016 protest that blocked a highway in front of the Baton Rouge (La.) Police Department headquarters. See Doe v. Mckesson, 945 F.3d 818 (5th Cir. 2019). According to the court, "Doe's complaint does allege that Mckesson directed the demonstrators to engage in the criminal act of occupying the public highway, which quite consequentially provoked a confrontation between the Baton Rouge police and the protesters, and that Officer Doe's injuries were the foreseeable result of the tortious and illegal conduct of blocking a busy highway." *Id.* at 829. Because ordering the highway to be blocked was unprotected speech, in that it violated a reasonable time, place, and manner restriction on protests, the court held that Mckesson could be sued for the harm to Doe.

What consequences could this case have for protests? Are civil damages necessary to deter violence against officers? Or are they too great a deterrent against speech in protests?

The original panel decision in *Doe* was unanimous, 922 F.3d 604, as was the opinion issued after the panel rehearing, 935 F.3d 253. After the entire Fifth Circuit denied rehearing en banc, the panel withdrew its opinion issued after rehearing and issued yet another one, reaching the same conclusion. 945 F.3d 818. This time, however, one member of the panel, Judge Willett, changed his mind and dissented:

> In Hong Kong, millions of defiant pro-democracy protesters have taken to the streets, with demonstrations growing increasingly violent. In America, political uprisings, from peaceful picketing to lawless riots, have marked our history from the beginning—indeed, from *before* the beginning. . . .
>
> Officer Doe put himself in harm's way to protect his community (including the violent protestor who injured him). And states have undeniable authority to punish protest leaders and participants who *themselves* commit violence. The rock-hurler's personal liability is obvious, but I do not believe that Mckesson's is. . . .
>
> . . . Doe's skeletal complaint does not plausibly assert that Mckesson forfeited First Amendment protection by inciting violence. . . . And *Claiborne Hardware*, among our most significant First Amendment cases, insulates nonviolent protestors from liability for others' conduct when engaging in political expression, even intentionally tortious conduct, not intended to incite immediate violence. The Constitution does not insulate violence, but it does insulate citizens from responsibility for *others'* violence.
>
> "Negligent protest" liability against a protest leader for the violent act of a rogue assailant is a dodge of *Claiborne Hardware* and clashes head-on with constitutional fundamentals. Such an exotic theory would have enfeebled America's street-blocking civil rights movement, imposing ruinous financial liability against citizens for exercising core First Amendment freedoms.
>
> Dr. King's last protest march was in March 1968, in support of striking Memphis sanitation workers. It was prelude to his assassination a week later, the day after his "I've Been to the Mountaintop" speech. Dr. King's hallmark was nonviolent protest, but as he led marchers down Beale Street, some young men began breaking storefront windows. The police moved in, and violence erupted, harming peaceful demonstrators and youthful looters alike. Had Dr. King been sued, either by injured police or injured protestors, I cannot fathom that the Constitution he praised as "magnificent"—"a promissory note to which every American was to fall heir"—would countenance his personal liability.

Id. at 845–847. Does that change your views?

Although the Fifth Circuit let the suit proceed against Mckesson, it affirmed the district court's decision to dismiss Doe's claims against the Black Lives Matter Network Inc. and #BlackLivesMatter. It turns out that you cannot sue an informal organization with no property, no membership, no dues, and no governing agreement. You can't sue a hashtag either.

C. Policing Citizen Recording

Bearing witness to policing has always been important to police accountability. Observers who share what they know inform the political process. Since the mid-2000s, however, witnessing has taken on intensified meaning, as increasingly those who observe the police also commonly record them, creating permanent, rewatchable accounts of police–citizen interactions that can be distributed widely. Far more people now meaningfully see aspects of policing that used to be largely hidden. Moreover, filming has become a form of *contestation* as well as a form *documentation*: If you watch many videos, you will hear those recording the police again and again challenging the conduct they see. The process of recording can interfere with policing, giving police reason to check some observers. Yet, officers have often gone much further in trying to stop those brandishing these digital "weapons." They have often not borne witnessing well.

1. First Amendment Protection for Filming the Police

How does the law address the conflict between those who would film the police and the officers who would stop them? Under what circumstances is there a First Amendment right to film the police?

FIELDS v. CITY OF PHILADELPHIA
862 F.3d 353 (3d Cir. 2017)

AMBRO, CIRCUIT JUDGE

In 1991 George Holliday recorded video of the Los Angeles Police Department officers beating Rodney King and submitted it to the local news. Filming police on the job was rare then but common now. With advances in technology and the widespread ownership of smartphones, "civilian recording of police officers is ubiquitous." Jocelyn Simonson, *Copwatching*, 104 Cal. L. Rev. 391, 408 (2016). These recordings have both exposed police misconduct and exonerated officers from errant charges. However, despite the growing frequency of private citizens recording police activity and its importance to all involved, some jurisdictions have attempted to regulate the extent of this practice. Individuals making recordings have also faced retaliation by officers, such as arrests on false criminal charges and even violence.

This case involves retaliation. Richard Fields and Amanda Geraci attempted to record Philadelphia police officers carrying out official duties in public and were retaliated against even though the Philadelphia Police Department's official policies recognized that "[p]rivate individuals have a First Amendment right to observe and record police officers engaged in the public discharge of their duties." . . .

Every Circuit Court of Appeals to address this issue (First, Fifth, Seventh, Ninth, and Eleventh) has held that there is a First Amendment right to record police activity in public. See Turner v. Lieutenant Driver, 848 F.3d 678 (5th Cir. 2017); Gericke v. Begin, 753 F.3d 1 (1st Cir. 2014); Am. Civil Liberties Union of Ill. v. Alvarez, 679 F.3d 583 (7th Cir. 2012); Glik v. Cunniffe, 655 F.3d 78 (1st Cir. 2011); Smith v. City of Cumming, 212 F.3d 1332 (11th Cir. 2000); Fordyce v. City of Seattle, 55 F.3d 436 (9th Cir. 1995). Today we join this growing consensus. Simply put, the First Amendment protects the act of photographing, filming, or otherwise recording police officers conducting their official duties in public.

I. Background

In September 2012, Amanda Geraci, a member of the police watchdog group "Up Against the Law," attended an anti-fracking protest at the Philadelphia Convention Center. She carried her camera and wore a pink bandana that identified her as a legal observer. About a half hour into the protest, the police acted to arrest a protestor. Geraci moved to a better vantage point to record the arrest and did so without interfering with the police. An officer abruptly pushed Geraci and pinned her against a pillar for one to three minutes, which prevented her from observing or recording the arrest. Geraci was not arrested or cited.

One evening in September 2013, Richard Fields, a sophomore at Temple University, was on a public sidewalk where he observed a number of police officers breaking up a house party across the street. The nearest officer was 15 feet away from him. Using his iPhone, he took a photograph of the scene. An officer noticed Fields taking the photo and asked him whether he "like[d] taking pictures of grown men" and ordered him to leave. Fields refused, so the officer arrested him, confiscated his phone, and detained him. The officer searched Fields' phone and opened several videos and other photos. The officer then released Fields and issued him a citation for "Obstructing Highway and Other Public Passages." These charges were withdrawn when the officer did not appear at the court hearing.

Fields and Geraci brought 42 U.S.C. §1983 claims against the City of Philadelphia and certain police officers. They alleged that the officers illegally retaliated against them for exercising their First Amendment right to record public police activity and violated their Fourth Amendment right to be free from an unreasonable search or seizure. . . .

The District Court . . . granted summary judgment in favor of Defendants on the First Amendment claims. . . . [T]he District Court . . . decided that Plaintiffs' activities were not protected by the First Amendment because they presented no evidence that their "conduct may be construed as expression of a belief or criticism of police activity." Fields v. City of Philadelphia, 166 F. Supp. 3d 528, 537 (E.D. Pa. 2016). When confronted by the police, Plaintiffs did not express their reasons for recording. Their later deposition testimony showed that Geraci simply wanted to observe and Fields wanted to take a picture of an "interesting" and "cool" scene. *Id.* at 539. In addition, neither testified of having an intent to share his or her photos or videos. *Id.* The District Court thus concluded that, "[a]bsent any authority from the Supreme Court or our Court of Appeals, we decline to create a new First Amendment right for citizens to photograph officers when they have no expressive purpose such as challenging police actions." *Id.* at 542. . . .

III. Order of Analysis

Defendants ask us to avoid ruling on the First Amendment issue. Instead, they want us to hold that, regardless of the right's existence, the officers are entitled to qualified immunity and the City cannot be vicariously liable for the officers' acts. We reject this invitation to take the easy way out. Because this First Amendment issue is of great importance and the recording of police activity is a widespread, common practice, we deal with it before addressing, if needed, defenses to liability. . . .

IV. The First Amendment Right to Record

The District Court concluded that Plaintiffs engaged in conduct only (the act of making a recording) as opposed to expressive conduct (using the recording to criticize the police or otherwise comment on officers' actions). It did so by analogy, applying the "expressive conduct" test used to address symbolic speech: "Conduct is protected by the First Amendment when the nature of the activity, combined with the factual context and environment in which it was undertaken, shows that the activity was sufficiently imbued with elements of communication to fall within the First Amendment's scope." *Fields*, 166 F. Supp. 3d at 534 & n.34.

We disagree on various fronts. Foremost is that the District Court focused on whether Plaintiffs had an expressive intent, such as a desire to disseminate the recordings, or to use them to criticize the police, *at the moment when* they recorded or attempted to record police activity. This reasoning ignores that the value of the recordings may not be immediately obvious, and only after review of them does their worth become apparent. The First Amendment protects actual photos, videos, and recordings, see Brown v. Entm't Merchants Ass'n, 564 U.S. 786, 790 (2011), and for this protection to have meaning the Amendment must also protect the act of creating that material. There is no practical difference between allowing police to prevent people from taking recordings and actually banning the possession or distribution of them. See *Alvarez*, 679 F.3d at 596 ("Restricting the use of an audio or audiovisual recording device suppresses speech just as effectively as restricting the dissemination of the resulting recording"). As illustrated here, because the officers stopped Ms. Geraci from recording the arrest of the protestor, she never had the opportunity to decide to put any recording to expressive use.

Plaintiffs and some *amici* argue that the act of recording is "inherently expressive conduct," like painting, writing a diary, dancing, or marching in a parade. Regardless of the merits of these arguments, our case is not about people attempting to create art with police as their subjects. It is about recording police officers performing their official duties.

The First Amendment protects the public's right of access to information about their officials' public activities. It "goes beyond protection of the press and the self-expression of individuals to prohibit government from limiting the stock of information from which members of the public may draw." First Nat'l. Bank of Bos. v. Bellotti, 435 U.S. 765, 783 (1978). Access to information regarding public police activity is particularly important because it leads to citizen discourse on public issues, "the highest rung of the hierarchy of First Amendment values, and is entitled to special protection." Snyder v. Phelps, 562 U.S. 443, 452 (2011). That information is the wellspring of our debates; if the latter are to be " 'uninhibited, robust, and wide-open,' " *Snyder*, 562 U.S. at 452 (quoting N.Y. Times Co. v. Sullivan, 376 U.S. 254, 270 (1964)), the more credible the information the more credible are the debates.

To record what there is the right for the eye to see or the ear to hear corroborates or lays aside subjective impressions for objective facts. Hence to record is to see and hear more accurately. Recordings also facilitate discussion because of the ease in which they can be widely distributed via different forms of media. Accordingly, recording police activity in public falls squarely within the First Amendment right of access to information. As no doubt the press has this right, so does the public. See

PG Publ'g Co. v. Aichele, 705 F.3d 91, 99 (3d Cir. 2013); Branzburg v. Hayes, 408 U.S. 665, 684 (1972).

Bystander videos provide different perspectives than police and dashboard cameras, portraying circumstances and surroundings that police videos often do not capture. Civilian video also fills the gaps created when police choose not to record video or withhold their footage from the public.

The public's creation of this content also complements the role of the news media. Indeed, citizens' gathering and disseminating "newsworthy information [occur] with an ease that rivals that of the traditional news media." 2012 U.S. D.O.J. Letter to Baltimore Police Department. See also *Glik*, 655 F.3d at 78 ("The proliferation of electronic devices with video-recording capability means that many of our images of current events come from bystanders with a ready cell phone or digital camera rather than a traditional film crew, and news stories are now just as likely to be broken by a blogger at her computer as a reporter at a major newspaper."). In addition to complementing the role of the traditional press, private recordings have improved professional reporting, as "video content generated by witnesses and bystanders has become a common component of news programming." The Reporters Committee for Freedom of the Press and 31 Media Organizations *Amicus* Br. 11. And the inclusion of "bystander video enriches the stories journalists tell, routinely adding a distinct, first-person perspective to news coverage." *Id.* at 12.

Moreover, the proliferation of bystander videos has "spurred action at all levels of government to address police misconduct and to protect civil rights." See Nat'l Police Accountability Proj. *Amicus* Br. 1. These videos have helped police departments identify and discipline problem officers. They have also assisted civil rights investigations and aided in the Department of Justice's work with local police departments. And just the act of recording, regardless what is recorded, may improve policing. See *Glik*, 655 F.3d at 82–83. Important to police is that these recordings help them carry out their work. They, every bit as much as we, are concerned with gathering facts that support further investigation or confirm a dead-end. And of particular personal concern to police is that bystander recordings can "exonerate an officer charged with wrongdoing." *Turner*, 848 F.3d at 689.

We do not say that all recording is protected or desirable. The right to record police is not absolute. "[I]t is subject to reasonable time, place, and manner restrictions." Kelly v. Borough of Carlisle, 622 F.3d 248, 262 (3d Cir. 2010). But in public places these restrictions are restrained.

We need not, however, address at length the limits of this constitutional right. Defendants offer nothing to justify their actions. Fields took a photograph across the street from where the police were breaking up a party. Geraci moved to a vantage point where she could record a protestor's arrest, but did so without getting in the officers' way. If a person's recording interferes with police activity, that activity might not be protected. For instance, recording a police conversation with a confidential informant may interfere with an investigation and put a life at stake. But here there are no countervailing concerns.

In sum, under the First Amendment's right of access to information the public has the commensurate right to record—photograph, film, or audio record—police officers conducting official police activity in public areas.

V. Qualified Immunity

Having decided the existence of this First Amendment right, we now turn to whether the officers are entitled to qualified immunity. We conclude they are.

Government actors are entitled to qualified immunity unless they violated a constitutional right "so clearly established that '*every reasonable official* would have understood that what he is doing violates that right.'" Zaloga v. Borough of Moosic, 841 F.3d 170, 175 (3d Cir. 2016) (quoting Reichle v. Howards, 566 U.S. 658, 659 (2012)). "In other words, existing precedent must have placed the statutory or constitutional question *beyond debate*." *Id.* (quoting *Reichle*, 566 U.S. at 664).... To determine whether the right is clearly established, we look at the state of the law when the retaliation occurred, here in 2012 (Geraci) and 2013 (Fields). See *id.*

... At issue here is Plaintiffs' ability to record the police carrying out official duties in public. We have never held that such a right exists, only that it might. . . .

... [W]e cannot say that the state of the law at the time of our cases (2012 and 2013) gave fair warning so that every reasonable officer knew that, absent some sort of expressive intent, recording public police activity was constitutionally protected. Accordingly, the officers are entitled to qualified immunity. . . .

[Judge Nygaard's opinion, concurring in part and dissenting in part, is omitted.]

NOTES AND QUESTIONS

1. *Defending the right.* The Third Circuit joins five others — the First, Fifth, Seventh, Ninth, and Eleventh — in finding a First Amendment right to record the police. None have rejected its existence. In *Turner v. Lieutenant Driver*, 848 F.3d 678 (5th Cir. 2017), the Fifth Circuit made this argument in favor of the right:

"[T]he First Amendment goes beyond protection of the press and the self-expression of individuals to prohibit government from limiting the stock of information from which members of the public may draw." First Nat'l Bank of Boston v. Bellotti, 435 U.S. 765, 783 (1978). News-gathering, for example, "is entitled to first amendment protection, for 'without some protection for seeking out the news, freedom of the press could be eviscerated,'" In re Express–News, 695 F.2d 807, 808 (5th Cir. 1982) (quoting Branzburg v. Hayes, 408 U.S. 665, 681 (1972)), even though this right is not absolute. The Supreme Court has also recognized a First Amendment right to "receive information and ideas," Va. State Bd. of Pharmacy v. Va. Citizens Consumer Council, Inc., 425 U.S. 748, 757 (1976) (internal quotation marks omitted), and there is "an undoubted right to gather news from any source by means within the law." Houchins v. KQED, Inc., 438 U.S. 1, 11 (1978) (internal quotation marks omitted). Furthermore, the Supreme Court has long recognized that the First Amendment protects film. A corollary to this principle is that the First Amendment protects the act of making film, as "there is no fixed First Amendment line between the act of creating speech and the speech itself." Am. Civil Liberties Union v. Alvarez, 679 F.3d 583, 596 (7th Cir. 2012) (citing Anderson v. City of Hermosa Beach, 621 F.3d 1051, 1061–1062 (9th Cir. 2010)). Indeed, the Supreme Court has never "drawn a distinction between the process of creating a form of pure speech (such as writing or painting) and the product of these processes (the essay or the artwork) in terms of the First Amendment protection afforded. Although writing and painting can be reduced to their constituent acts, and thus described as conduct, we have not attempted to disconnect the end product from the act of creation." Anderson, 621 F.3d at 1061–1062.

Id. at 688–689.

In *American Civil Liberties Union of Illinois v. Alvarez*, 679 F.3d 583 (7th Cir. 2012), the Seventh Circuit reasoned:

> Audio and audiovisual recording are media of expression commonly used for the preservation and dissemination of information and ideas and thus are "included within the free speech and free press guaranty of the First and Fourteenth Amendments." Burstyn v. Wilson, 343 U.S. 495, 502 (1952). Laws that restrict the use of expressive media have obvious effects on speech and press rights; the Supreme Court has "voiced particular concern with laws that foreclose an entire medium of expression." City of Ladue v. Gilleo, 512 U.S. 43, 55 (1994).

> The act of *making* an audio or audiovisual recording is necessarily included within the First Amendment's guarantee of speech and press rights as a corollary of the right to disseminate the resulting recording. The right to publish or broadcast an audio or audiovisual recording would be insecure, or largely ineffective, if the antecedent act of *making* the recording is wholly unprotected, as the State's Attorney insists.

Id. at 595. Are the Fifth and Seventh Circuits' arguments the same? Do they make the same argument as the Third Circuit in *Fields*? The right to record is unlike usual speech rights in that it focuses on observing rather than expressing. Why are so many judges persuaded it exists?

2. Fields *vs.* Colten. In *Colten v. Kentucky*, 407 U.S. 104 (1972), quoted earlier in this chapter, the Court upheld the arrest of Lewis Colten, who followed officers engaged in a traffic stop. The Supreme Court rejected Colten's First Amendment claim, reasoning:

> He had no constitutional right to observe the issuance of a traffic ticket or to engage the issuing officer in conversation at that time. The State has a legitimate interest in enforcing its traffic laws and its officers were entitled to enforce them free from possible interference or interruption from bystanders, even those claiming a third-party interest in the transaction.

Id. at 109. How is *Colten* different from *Fields*? Or has the law changed? Do the arguments courts have made in favor of a First Amendment right differentiate meaningfully between watching and filming?

3. *Time, place, and manner restrictions.* The right to record is, like other First Amendment rights, subject to reasonable time, place, and manner restrictions. Clearly, an officer could, consistent with the First Amendment, stop someone who tried to insert himself and his camera between an officer and an arrestee. But if police officers may regularly order bystanders back, then the right might be pretty limited. How many feet away would someone have to be before his First Amendment right kicked in? Not surprisingly, now that many courts agree that a First Amendment right to record exists, litigation is turning to what the government may do to restrict the right.

4. *First Circuit on limiting the right.* When Carla Gericke's friend was ordered out of his car during a traffic stop, Gericke stood 30 feet away and told the officers she was filming them. Although she was never asked not to record, the police later demanded her camera. She refused to give it to them, and they arrested her, charging her with disobeying a police order, obstructing a government official, and unlawfully intercepting oral communications. The police also seized her camera. According to the First Circuit,

The circumstances of some traffic stops, particularly when the detained individual is armed, might justify a safety measure—for example, a command that bystanders disperse—that would incidentally impact an individual's exercise of the First Amendment right to film. Such an order, even when directed at a person who is filming, may be appropriate for legitimate safety reasons. However, a police order that is specifically directed at the First Amendment right to film police performing their duties in public may be constitutionally imposed only if the officer can reasonably conclude that the filming itself is interfering, or is about to interfere, with his duties. . . .

Importantly, an individual's exercise of her First Amendment right to film police activity carried out in public, including a traffic stop, necessarily remains unfettered unless and until a reasonable restriction is imposed or in place. This conclusion follows inescapably from the nature of the First Amendment right, which does not contemplate self-censorship by the person exercising the right. Such a restriction could take the form of a reasonable, contemporaneous order from a police officer, or a preexisting statute, ordinance, regulation, or other published restriction with a legitimate governmental purpose.

Gericke v. Begin, 753 F.3d 1, 8 (1st Cir. 2014). Since in Gericke's version of events, she did not receive an order to stop filming or to leave the scene, "her right to film remained unfettered," and a jury could find that the police violated her First Amendment rights. If a police chief asked you to advise her about how to translate this ruling into some bullet points for officers as they patrol, what would you say? Should they assume *Gericke* is limited to traffic stops?

5. *Pinning down "interference."* In *Gericke*, the reasonableness of the government's restrictions seems to turn on whether the filming "interferes" with police activities. What kind of recording should be taken to interfere with the police? Is officer discomfort or distraction enough? Jocelyn Simonson argues that the right to record should exist "up to the point that the act of filming presents a concrete, physical impediment to a police officer or to public safety." Jocelyn Simonson, *Beyond Body Cameras: Defending a Robust Right to Record the Police*, 104 Geo. L.J. 1559, 1563 (2016). Is that consistent with *Gericke*? Does that mean that officers should allow multiple would-be videographers to stand within a few feet of them as they make an arrest? Could you see why officers might object?

6. *Recording ordinances.* Some cities are passing ordinances that define restrictions on recording. For example, in April 2020, Tucson passed an ordinance recognizing a free-speech right to record public police activities. Still, officers are permitted to "restrict individuals from physically entering crime scenes or areas immediately surrounding where such enforcement activity, investigations, and other police-related activities are taking place," and it is a misdemeanor to enter such an area or refuse to comply with an officer's direction to leave one. Tucson, Az., Code §11-70.3. According to Tucson's mayor, the ordinance was necessary to curb people from harassing officers and interfering with police activities. How much does Tucson's ordinance protect videographers? How would you write an ordinance on recording the police?

7. *Government interests.* In *Gericke*, the Court assumes the government may impose time, place, and manner restrictions to protect officer safety or to allow officers to perform their duties unimpeded. Are there other interests that officers may limit recording to protect? Can the police prohibit bystanders from filming a murder victim until the victim's family has been notified? Or prohibit bystanders from

filming a home search pursuant to a "sneak and peek" search warrant that permits the officers to enter surreptitiously? Or prohibit filming a rape victim as she reports the crime to an officer?

8. *Recording without a record.* While Gericke was trying to record her friend's traffic stop, she realized that her camera was not working. Still, she continued to point it at the officer, and the officer was unaware that the camera had failed. The Court concluded that an individual has the right to record even if her camera is not working, noting that her "First Amendment right does not depend on whether her attempt to videotape was frustrated by a technical malfunction." *Id.* at 3 n.2. If the right to record does not turn on capturing images, what does it turn on? Is it a right to observe? To observe visibly? To observe with an object in hand?

9. *Right to record vs. the right to speak.* Justin Marceau and Alan Chen point out that even if recording is expressive, it does not collapse into a right to speak, and it cannot be treated the same as other expressive acts protected by the First Amendment. See Justin Marceau & Alan K. Chen, *Free Speech and Democracy in the Video Age,* 116 Colum. L. Rev. 991 (2016). Unlike speaking, recording is largely non-rivalrous: When one person records, he does not prevent anyone else from exercising the same right and does not interfere with most other social activities. See *id.* at 1046–1047. This is unlike a political protest, for example. Two demonstrations cannot parade on the same route without interfering with each other. That is why cities issue permits. Marceau and Chen argue that, given this difference, the right to record should be treated as analytically and doctrinally distinct from a First Amendment right to expressive speech. What might be different under these two rights? Which right was Gericke exercising?

The iPhone and YouTube

Consumer camcorders first became available in the mid-1980s, but they were too expensive and cumbersome to have much of an impact on policing. Even after the consumer camera market picked up in the late 1980s and early 1990s, videos of unplanned events were rare. George Holliday's recording of the beating of Rodney King is a dramatic exception. Although early smartphone models were available in the 1990s, a dramatic shift happened with the iPhone launch in 2007. The iPhone, along with its successors and its competitors, finally put a tiny video camera in almost every American's pocket, making spontaneous police activities easily recordable, and therefore visible, to anyone with a computer. The spread of the iPhone was not immediate or universal. Within a few years, though, the device transformed public understanding of the police.

But smartphones alone did not cause the change. When George Holliday recorded the beating of Rodney King in 1991, he had no way to show it to the public. Instead, he gave it to a local news station, KTLA, which broadcast the video. The footage was picked up by CNN the next day. Although CNN had been on the air for more than a decade at the time, it had only recently become a major force in television, due in large part to its reporting from inside Iraq during the first Persian Gulf War. The war ended just days before Rodney King was beaten, leaving CNN and other 24-hour news stations scrambling for content. Holliday's video helped fill airtime. If Rodney King had been beaten a few weeks earlier, it is possible his name would never have been known and his beating never witnessed by the nation. Even today, traditional news media—in print and on TV—are limited by space and time constraints and editorial preferences. They pick and choose the stories that will be presented to their audiences.

By the time the iPhone came around, however, citizen videographers were no longer dependent on news media to decide that a story was important enough to be aired. With the launch of YouTube at the end of 2005, for the first time, anyone could share videos with the world without professional mediation. The iPhone might never have mattered to policing if not for the invention of platforms through which people could distribute videos.

Today, YouTube.com is the most popular website in the world. It receives more visits each month (8.64 billion) than there are people on earth (about 7.8 billion). See Joshua Hardwick, *Top 100 Most Visited Websites by Search Traffic (as of 2019)*, ahrefsblog (Jun. 25, 2019). And it is only one service that allows anyone to offer a video to an audience.

Years before the iPhone or YouTube were created, Seth Kreimer presciently used the term "technologies of protest" to describe the power of internet-related technologies to facilitate political resistance, including technologies he expected would make it cheaper to disseminate information. See Seth F. Kreimer, *Technologies of Protest: Insurgent Social Movements and the First Amendment in the Era of the Internet*, 150 U. Pa. L. Rev. 119 (2001). Today, the smartphone remains the most visible technology of resistance for policing. But YouTube, other video-sharing sites, and the rise of social media have been critical in making citizen video a form of news, a locus for debate, and a means of seeking to change policing.

People watching stores burn in Ferguson, Missouri on November 25, 2014, after St. Louis County grand jury decided not to indict Ferguson police officer Darren Wilson in the August 2014 killing of Michael Brown, an unarmed African-American man. Protests responding to the grand jury's decision quickly turned violent. Cars were smashed, stores were looted, and more than a dozen buildings were set on fire.

2.   The Meanings of Police Videos

How does filming the police promote accountability?

a.   *Reducing Disputes*

Video often reduces disputes about what happened during an encounter. Traditionally, there have often been no independent witnesses to police interactions. Because courts and juries favor police testimony, victims of misconduct often could not prove their account of events. Video helps level the playing field. This impact can be especially important for people whose words alone have traditionally lacked credibility in court. "For many of these private people, especially women, people of color or other relatively powerless people in society, video surveillance is the modern day white witness." Lolita Buckner Innis, *Video Surveillance as White Witnesses*, Ain't I a Feminist Legal Scholar Too? (Sept. 30, 2012). In this way, videos can help support administrative complaints about police misconduct, facilitate civil suits, and lead to criminal charges against officers. They also can eliminate frivolous complaints and lawsuits against officers and mitigate public concern about controversial police action.

Some worry that the power of videos to resolve disputes can have a downside. What happens when there is no recording? " 'We are almost asking black people to prove they didn't deserve this. . . . We don't ask white people where the video is after mass shootings.' " See Joanna Stern, *They Used Smartphone Cameras to Record Police Brutality—and Change History*, Wall St. J. (June 13, 2020) (quoting Allissa Richardson). Does the existence of video make it harder for victims of police misconduct to prove unrecorded conduct? Should videos of the police lead us to rethink the role credibility plays in evaluating police action?

Often video neither clearly vindicates citizens nor clearly incriminates officers. Still, it might limit a dispute's scope. You might not want to watch the various videos of the killing of Oscar Grant, a 22-year-old African American man, in an Oakland subway station in 2009. They are deeply disturbing. They show Bay Area Rapid Transit police officer Johannes Mehserle drawing his pistol and shooting Grant in the back as he lay face down on the ground under police control. The events were captured by several bystanders holding cellphones. Following public outrage, prosecutors charged Officer Mehserle with second-degree murder.

The shooting and the events that led up to it remain controversial, and the videos are subject to interpretation. Nevertheless, by showing Officer Mehserle's apparent surprise when he shot Grant, the videos likely helped support his defense at his criminal trial, which was that he had not intended to shoot Grant. See Demian Bulwa, *Mehserle's "Surprised and Shocked" Reaction*, SFGate (May 20, 2009). According to his testimony, Mehserle thought he was holding his Taser but had pulled his gun by mistake. Mehserle was found guilty of involuntary manslaughter and not guilty of second-degree murder and voluntary manslaughter. He was sentenced to two years in prison. Demian Bulwa, *Johannes Mehserle Sentenced to 2-Year Minimum Term*, SFGate (Nov. 6, 2010). The videos might have helped Mehserle avoid a worse outcome at trial. On the other hand, without the videos, perhaps Mehserle would never have been charged at all.

b. Revealing Policing

Videos of police interactions can also show people who do not regularly encounter police officers something about the nature and quality of their work. This in turn can influence what communities demand of their police. Video of George Floyd's killing in Minneapolis and of police violence during protests after his death transformed the political conversation about policing in just a few weeks. Within days, Minnesota introduced 48 bills on law enforcement, Iowa banned chokeholds, and New York repealed a law that restricted public access to police disciplinary records that had been controversial for decades. See Weihua Li & Humera Lodhi, *Which States Are Taking on Police Reform After George Floyd*, Marshall Project (Jun. 18, 2020).

Still, there are reasons to be cautious. First, as Jessica Silbey puts it, "Film is particularly persuasive . . . because of its apparent indexical relationship to reality. When we watch film, we trust that it is capturing an event, place, or person as filmed." Jessica Silbey, *Cross-Examining Film*, 8 U. Md. L.J. Race, Religion, Gender & Class 17, 23 (2008). But that trust might not always be well-founded:

> [F]ilm is a constructed medium. The camera always presents a certain point of view and a frame that includes some images and excludes others. Films are depicted in artificial light and color. From the earliest emergence of film technology, filmmakers and critics recognized that the appearance of reality in films is an illusion based upon conventions of representation, much like the convention of perspective in two-dimensional drawings or the conventions of light and dark in oil paintings. These conventions produce images that resemble and represent reality, but are not reality in fact.

Id. at 18.

In this vein, officers sometimes argue that video leads them to be judged unfairly. Even legal acts might look terrible on film, almost any act can be misinterpreted, and video does not usually come with legal and policy explanations attached. Those who take video can choose between disseminating it and deleting it, so the videos the public sees could misrepresent how officers usually behave. Arrests and interactions that go smoothly never go viral. Moreover, video can be edited, altered, and redacted. It can be manipulated from prior images or created out of whole cloth. It can also be slowed down or sped up, zoomed in or backed out, broken up or mixed together, and otherwise "enhanced."

To see an example of how perspective and editing matter, compare two clips of University of California, Davis, police officers pepper spraying students during an Occupy protest in 2011. First, watch Aggie Studios, *UC Davis Protestors Pepper Sprayed*, YouTube (Nov. 18, 2011), *https://youtu.be/6AdDLhPwpp4*. Then, watch an alternate view of the pepper spraying at UCDCollegeRepublican, *Occupy Protestors Blockade UC Davis Police*, YouTube (Nov. 30, 2011), *https://youtu.be/TDd_TYotrxw*. Do the alternate views affect your perception of this encounter?

Second, even if video fairly reveals the nature of policing, it is not an unmitigated good. Videos of police officers killing George Floyd, Alton Sterling, Philando Castile, Terence Crutcher, Eric Garner, and others have been watched millions of times on the internet and on television. Many see watching these videos as a form of bearing witness. Indeed, this book has counseled you to watch several videos of police encounters in order to analyze them. But watching videos can also function as a form of racial-violence voyeurism, more like snuff films and public lynchings than political dialogue. See Jade E. Davis, *Black Men Being Killed Is the New Girls Gone Wild*, Medium (Apr. 10, 2015). Moreover, watching them can be harmful, especially for Black Americans:

> In the African American community, individual life chances are recognized as inextricably tied to the race as a whole. So when black people watch a video of police violence against another black person, they see themselves or their loved ones in that person's place, knowing that the same fateful encounter could very well happened to them.

Kia Gregory, *How Videos of Police Brutality Traumatize African Americans and Undermine the Search for Justice*, New Republic (Feb. 13, 2019). Kia Gregory argues that the damage to African Americans worsens when the videos are treated as entertainment and when justice for victims of the violence does not come. She concludes:

> The advent of new technologies has allowed us to chronicle and testify to a horribly entrenched truth: The American justice system continually, daily devalues black bodies. It has only been forced to reckon with the reality of its own bias when a flash of video shows, in soul-wrenching detail, the ease with which a life can be extinguished. This revelation comes at a cost to the well-being of African Americans across the country who are exposed to these images at the swipe of a finger or the click of a mouse. And so far, with precious little to show by way of significant and lasting reform, the cost has been too high.

Id. Is Gregory right? Is video more harmful than helpful? What does that mean for those who would advocate a strong right to record? Or for those—including readers of this book—who watch videos to assess policing and the law that governs it? Maybe video is more complicated than it first appears.

Finally, so far, citizen video has mainly contributed to public understanding of the police by telling anecdotes, that is, by displaying individual events. Because people record and post unusual incidents, it can be hard to draw broader conclusions about police practices from these stories. That will change soon. Advancing facial-recognition software and artificial-intelligence systems based on machine learning are improving our ability to decipher visual images *en masse*. This software will make police videos visual data that can say something about policing as an enterprise, especially as citizen recordings are combined with other sources of information. What new challenges for the law might such technologies raise? What opportunities might they offer?

c. Contesting Police Action

Recording the police does not just document the police; it confronts them. For example, organized groups of "copwatchers" patrol neighborhoods and record police encounters, often challenging officer conduct as they do. These citizens seek to *deter misconduct* by intervening in real time and to *improve accountability* by commenting on it later. In contrast to those who provide input into policing through cooperative mechanisms, such as civilian review boards or community meetings, copwatchers function as a form of hostile civil engagement with—but not all-out antagonism to—the police. See Jocelyn Simonson, *Copwatching*, 104 Calif. L. Rev. 391, 406–411, 436–438 (2016).

A poster for the Cop Watch project of the Justice Committee, a grassroots organization in New York City.

You could see individuals with cameras the same way. Some covertly document police conduct. But many either stand as silent, but visible, monitors, or they challenge the police as they record them, providing immediate feedback to officers, perhaps more emphatically than they could without a camera in hand. Whereas all these recorders *gather* information about police conduct, those who conspicuously observe or actively confront the police also *express* information: They announce, "We are watching." In this view, filming the police does not "*lead*[] to citizen discourse on public issues," as the *Fields* court indicates, 862 F.3d at 359; it *is* citizen discourse on public issues, part of "[t]he freedom of individuals verbally to oppose or challenge police action without thereby risking arrest," City of Houston v. Hill, 482 U.S. 451, 462–463 (1987).

3. Resisting Recording

For years, as citizen recordings became more common, some police resisted. Resistance mostly took three forms: (1) arrest the person for filming, (2) physically stop the person from filming or seize or destroy the camera, and (3) arrest the person for some other crime.

In the first case, police charged people filming them with violating state eaves-dropping or wiretapping statutes. In jurisdictions that recognize the right to record, using such laws against those who reasonably record violates the First Amendment. See American Civil Liberties Union of Illinois v. Alvarez, 679 F.3d 583 (7th Cir. 2012); Glik v. Cunniffe, 655 F.3d 78 (1st Cir. 2011).

The second approach might similarly violate the First Amendment—if an officer interferes with First Amendment activity or seizes a camera to retaliate against someone for exercising the right to record. It may also violate the Fourth Amendment because taking or destroying a camera without a warrant can be an illegal seizure.

To understand the Fourth Amendment issues at play, it helps to know that, ordinarily, an officer may seize an object without a warrant if the officer has probable cause to believe that the property "holds contraband or evidence of a crime" and "the exigencies of the circumstances demand it or some other recognized exception to the warrant requirement is present." United States v. Place, 462 U.S. 696, 701 (1983). That seizure usually must be temporary and limited to preserving evidence until the officer can get a warrant. (Similarly, an officer may *seize* a cell phone incident to arrest, but he may not *search* the cell phone incident to arrest without a warrant. See Riley v. California, 573 U.S. 373 (2014).) Does the *Place* rule mean officers may seize cameras from almost all bystanders who film on the ground that the recordings might reveal criminal activity by either the suspect or the officer? How should courts address such seizures?

In the past, the Supreme Court has raised the bar on reasonable seizures that involve material protected under the First Amendment. See Roaden v. Kentucky, 413 U.S. 496, 504 (1973) ("Seizing a film . . . presents essentially the same restraint on expression as the seizure of all the books in a bookstore. Such precipitate action by a police officer, without the authority of a constitutionally sufficient warrant, is plainly a form of prior restraint and is, in those circumstances unreasonable under Fourth Amendment standards.") What would that mean here?

As for the third approach, you have already seen an example in *Fields*. Police use arrests for minor crimes, or the threat of such arrests, to stop someone from filming or retaliate against them for doing so. As *Fields* suggests, this might violate the First Amendment. Such an arrest could also violate the Fourth Amendment if no probable cause existed.

For another example, watch the May 12, 2011, arrest of Emily Good by a Rochester (N.Y.) police officer, a video of which can be found at RochesterCopwatch, *Rochester Police Arrest Woman in Her Front Lawn for Filming Traffic Stop*, YouTube (Jun. 21, 2011), *https://youtu.be/a7ZkFZkejv8*. Good was charged with second-degree obstructing government administration, defined in New York State by the following statute:

N.Y. Penal Law §195.05. Obstructing governmental administration in the second degree

A person is guilty of obstructing governmental administration when he intentionally obstructs, impairs or perverts the administration of law or other governmental function or prevents or attempts to prevent a public servant from performing an official function, by means of intimidation, physical force or interference, or by means of any independently unlawful act, or by means of interfering, whether or not physical force is involved, with radio, telephone, television or other telecommunications systems owned or operated by the state, or a county, city, town, village, fire district or emergency medical service or by means of releasing a dangerous animal under circumstances evincing the actor's intent that the animal obstruct governmental administration.

If *Fields* and *Gericke* applied in New York, could Emily Good be convicted of this crime? Should she be? What if she had instead been charged with a statute that prohibited refusing to obey a lawful order? Is the First Amendment a license to violate otherwise valid criminal laws?

Emily Good's video went viral on the internet, and prosecutors dropped the charges against her. But when Rochester residents later gathered in a community meeting to discuss police accountability, four police officers showed up with rulers and issued parking tickets to cars parked more than 12 inches from the curb. See brklynmd3, *Revenge on Emily Good by Rochester NY Police*, YouTube (June 28, 2011), *https://youtu.be/DkB89xwVTyA*. What is the legal remedy for *that?* How likely are those who received tickets to receive that remedy?

On one hand, the video of the officers exacting revenge on Emily Good and her compatriots is depressing. How robust is the First Amendment right if officers can easily retaliate on other days and in other ways? On the other hand, you (and many other people) have now seen Rochester officers engaging in that retaliatory behavior, which might create additional pressure on the department to change its practices. As fast as the First Amendment right to record has developed, it has not been as swift as the spread of the technology itself. Any officer who resists being recorded is likely to be recorded resisting, and officers who retaliate might get recorded retaliating. The prevalence of cameras has led officers to come to terms with them: They are simply too common and invisible to avoid. In the end, the right to record has sorted itself out on the street more than in the courts, although perhaps litigation has helped.

Rodney King and the Start of Citizen Video

Historically, most Americans built their view of the police from their own experiences; those of neighbors, families, and friends; and reports they heard in the news. As a result, many Americans, especially white Americans, knew something of the benefits but little about the harms of policing. Even when reports of police violence made it to the media, the public's view was influenced by their take on the charisma and credibility of the people who told their stories.

All of that changed on March 2, 1991.

Late that evening, Rodney King drank beer with a couple of friends before driving while intoxicated from Altadena, California, toward San Fernando. A couple of California Highway Patrol officers tried to pull him over, but King was on parole from a robbery conviction, and he feared returning to prison, so he did not stop. A chase ensued, which other police vehicles joined, before King finally stopped and exited his car. When King failed to follow orders to get down on the ground, Los Angeles Police Department officers took over to arrest King.

George Holliday, who was woken by the police helicopters flying overhead, picked up his new Sony video camera, went onto his balcony, and started taping. For nearly two minutes, Holliday's video shows three police officers kicking and beating Rodney King with batons, as their sergeant supervised. Eventually, King was hogtied and dragged, face down, to the side of the road, where he remained until an ambulance arrived. Nearly a dozen officers stood causally watching, without intervening. Their reaction suggested that perhaps this beating was nothing new. King suffered multiple skull fractures, a shattered eye socket and cheekbone, a broken leg, a concussion, injuries to both knees, and nerve damage that partially paralyzed his face.

A few days later, Holliday offered his tape of the incident to a local police station. They had no interest. He then called local television station KTLA, which showed the video on the local news. When it became clear that the story was a big one, the station paid Holliday $500. Over the ensuing days and weeks, television stations played the tape again and again to stunned audiences, many of whom had never seen (or believed) the kind of police violence it documented.

The state brought criminal charges against Sergeant Stacey Koon and officers Theodore Briseno, Timothy Wind, and Laurence Powell for the beating. In the closely watched trial, the jurors—who were overwhelmingly white—were urged by defense lawyers to consider the video frame by frame, and they were offered explanations for each baton swing and kick. In the end, they interpreted the footage very differently than many members of the public, and they refused to convict any of the officers.

The reaction was swift. Although Mayor Tom Bradley called for peace, within hours residents of Los Angeles set fires, looted stores, and assaulted passersby. The chaos lasted for days, constituting what was arguably the worst urban riot of the twentieth century. Dozens of people died. More than 200 were injured, and more than 1,000 buildings in Los Angeles were destroyed. Reginald Denny was pulled from his truck and severely beaten by a group of men in an attack captured on video by a news helicopter. The governor eventually declared a state of emergency and activated the National Guard. This all happened because the verdict did not condemn police violence, even after everyone had seen King's beating on television.

A year later, federal prosecutors convicted two of the officers, Sergeant Stacey Koon and Officer Laurence Powell, of federal civil rights crimes, and King later reached a civil damages settlement with the city. Nevertheless, the Los Angeles Police Department did not reform easily, and it suffered several subsequent scandals. (See Chapter 15 for additional discussion of the legal ramifications of Rodney King's beating.) Still, the videotape inspired unprecedented public and political attention both locally and nationally to the problem of police violence.

In the three decades since Rodney King was beaten, audio- and video-recording technology has become increasingly available, portable, and inexpensive, and the internet provides unlimited opportunities to share videos with a broader audience. Still, George Holliday's video stands alone in its impact.

See Koon v. United States, 518 U.S. 81 (1996); Seth Mydans, *Los Angeles Policemen Acquitted in Taped Beating*, N.Y. Times (Apr. 30, 1992); Pablo Ximénez de Sandoval, *Meet the Man Who Recorded the World's First Viral Video*, El País (May 25, 2017); *Seven Minutes in Los Angeles—A Special Report; Videotaped Beating by Officers Puts Full Glare on Brutality Issue*, N.Y. Times (Mar. 18, 1991).

Sony Handycam video recorder, like the one used by George Holliday.

Chapter 10

Maintaining Order

When low-level crime and disorder are common in a neighborhood, its residents and visitors feel it. If you walk past graffiti-stained walls, broken glass on the ground, and abandoned cars in the street, or experience aggressive panhandling, open solicitation for prostitution, public intoxication, and rowdy groups of teenagers, you might be less willing to till a community garden, socialize on your front steps, invest in a nice fence, or meet friends at a bar after dark. If you are fearful and unsure of your community's future, you might never get to know your neighbors, which could mean no block party gets organized and no one shovels snow for the older couple down the street. We live in neighborhoods. Our experience of them contributes to the quality of our lives. Disorder therefore matters.

At its worst, disorder also works in tandem with crime to fray a neighborhood's fabric. This is how the California Supreme Court described life in one community in the mid-1990s:

> Rocksprings is an urban war zone. . . . Gang members, all of whom live elsewhere, congregate on lawns, on sidewalks, and in front of apartment complexes at all hours of the day and night. They display a casual contempt for notions of law, order, and decency—openly drinking, smoking dope, sniffing toluene, and even snorting cocaine laid out in neat lines on the hoods of residents' cars. The people who live in Rocksprings are subjected to loud talk, loud music, vulgarity, profanity, brutality, fistfights and the sound of gunfire echoing in the streets. Gang members take over sidewalks, driveways, carports, apartment parking areas, and impede traffic on the public thoroughfares to conduct their drive-up drug bazaar. Murder, attempted murder, drive-by shootings, assault and battery, vandalism, arson, and theft are commonplace. The community has become a staging area for gang-related violence and a dumping ground for the weapons and instrumentalities of crime once the deed is done. Area residents have had their garages used as urinals; their homes commandeered as escape routes; their walls, fences, garage doors, sidewalks, and even their vehicles turned into a sullen canvas of gang graffiti.

People *ex rel.* Gallo v. Acuna, 929 P.2d 596, 601–602 (Cal. 1997).

While lasting social order takes far more than policing, and police-alternatives do less harm, many communities turn to the police to help address disorder—both major and minor. Why? First, there is no bright line between public disorder and public safety threats. Sending a police officer ensures that the person who responds to disorder will have the capacity to do so forcefully, if it becomes necessary. Responding to a call about an abandoned car could easily be handled by a civilian, and responding to an ongoing bank robbery will usually require the special skills of law enforcement, but most situations are not so clear cut. A domestic dispute, a person in crisis, or a group of teenagers hassling passersby could quickly evolve from disorderly conduct to serious criminal behavior. Second, police are already out on the street. When officers patrol the streets, respond to complaints, invoke the law, and make arrests, their actions can serve to address disorder as well as to prevent crime and enforce criminal laws.

Tasking the police with order maintenance has broad consequences for policing. Police often use authority generated by ordinary misdemeanor criminal prohibitions to address disorder, including crimes such as littering, vandalism, blocking roadways, and solicitation. Still, uses of public spaces to which communities object sometimes do not implicate narrowly crafted crimes. Consequently, by long tradition, states and localities empower officers to address unwanted conduct with broader statutes that prohibit disorderly conduct, loitering, and vagrancy, among other petty crimes and violations. As the Supreme Court noted in overturning a vagrancy ordinance in *Papachristou v. City of Jacksonville*, 405 U.S. 156, 165 (1972), "the net cast is large . . . to increase the arsenal of the police."

The laws communities use to empower the police to maintain order solve one problem only to create others. By providing broad power, these laws shift decisions about what conduct justifies intervention from legislatures to officers. This increased discretion brings with it the risk that officers will act on whim or animus instead of reason and public interest, or that officers at the behest of communities will use their power to suppress minority interests and maintain power for elites. Moreover, discretion to invoke the law allows police decision making about when and how much to coerce, and in the absence of a good reason to do so, officers may not minimize the rudeness, intrusiveness, and force they use to maintain order. In these ways, policing to maintain order (helped by the legal tools used to facilitate it) can easily become arbitrary, discriminatory, and unnecessarily harmful.

This chapter considers how the law balances the need to check abusive and unconstrained policing with allowing communities flexibility in pursuing legitimate public order goals. The first part of the chapter considers generally how the Fourteenth Amendment's protection against vague laws has been used to constrain local efforts to assign broad powers to the police. The second part considers vagueness doctrine in the context of one common kind of order-maintenance policing: policing the homeless. The last part of the chapter considers the most common nonconstitutional mechanism for limiting officer discretion: internal departmental rules that guide officer conduct.[1]

As the materials in this chapter demonstrate, there are no easy answers to the challenge of using the police to maintain order while restraining police power. Once you have read the chapter, however, you will understand how vagueness doctrine structures analysis of laws that empower the police, you will see some of the limits of that doctrine as a restraint on police discretion, and you will have an introduction to the internal departmental rules that everyone agrees are essential to effective, accountable policing.

---

[1] This chapter focuses on the police use of legal authority to resolve conflicts over the uses of public spaces that are often labeled disorderly rather than order maintenance strategies, such as broken-windows policing, that primarily address disorder as a means to prevent crime. Broken-windows policing and crime prevention through street policing are addressed further in Chapter 5.

A.   *Vagueness as a Constitutional Limit on Police Discretion*

1.   Vagueness Doctrine and the Police

How vigorously should courts scrutinize state and local efforts to grant the police broad authority to manage the streets? The Court has only rarely addressed this question. In the following case, the Justices do so, vigorously debating the role the Constitution should play in checking legislative efforts to empower officers. As you read the opinions, consider what kind of legislative action the various Justices think is necessary to give the police coercive authority.

CITY OF CHICAGO v. MORALES
527 U.S. 41 (1999)

JUSTICE STEVENS announced the judgment of the Court and delivered the opinion of the Court with respect to Parts I, II, and V, and an opinion with respect to Parts III, IV, and VI, in which JUSTICE SOUTER and JUSTICE GINSBURG join.

In 1992, the Chicago City Council enacted the Gang Congregation Ordinance, which prohibits "criminal street gang members" from "loitering" with one another or with other persons in any public place. The question presented is whether the Supreme Court of Illinois correctly held that the ordinance violates the Due Process Clause of the Fourteenth Amendment to the Federal Constitution.

I

Before the ordinance was adopted, the city council's Committee on Police and Fire conducted hearings to explore the problems created by the city's street gangs, and more particularly, the consequences of public loitering by gang members. Witnesses included residents of the neighborhoods where gang members are most active, as well as some of the aldermen who represent those areas. Based on that evidence, the council made a series of findings that are included in the text of the ordinance and explain the reasons for its enactment.

The council found that a continuing increase in criminal street gang activity was largely responsible for the city's rising murder rate, as well as an escalation of violent and drug related crimes. It noted that in many neighborhoods throughout the city, "the burgeoning presence of street gang members in public places has intimidated many law abiding citizens." Furthermore, the council stated that gang members "establish control over identifiable areas . . . by loitering in those areas and intimidating others from entering those areas; and . . . [m]embers of criminal street gangs avoid arrest by committing no offense punishable under existing laws when they know the police are present. . . ." It further found that "loitering in public places by criminal street gang members creates a justifiable fear for the safety of persons and property in the area" and that "[a]ggressive action is necessary to preserve the city's streets and other public places so that the public may use such places without fear." Moreover, the council concluded that the city "has an interest in discouraging all persons from loitering in public places with criminal gang members."

The ordinance creates a criminal offense punishable by a fine of up to $500, imprisonment for not more than six months, and a requirement to perform up to

120 hours of community service. Commission of the offense involves four predicates. First, the police officer must reasonably believe that at least one of the two or more persons present in a "public place" is a "criminal street gang membe[r]." Second, the persons must be "loitering," which the ordinance defines as "remain[ing] in any one place with no apparent purpose." Third, the officer must then order "all" of the persons to disperse and remove themselves "from the area." Fourth, a person must disobey the officer's order. If any person, whether a gang member or not, disobeys the officer's order, that person is guilty of violating the ordinance.[2]

Two months after the ordinance was adopted, the Chicago Police Department promulgated General Order 92–4 to provide guidelines to govern its enforcement. That order purported to establish limitations on the enforcement discretion of police officers "to ensure that the anti-gang loitering ordinance is not enforced in an arbitrary or discriminatory way." The limitations confine the authority to arrest gang members who violate the ordinance to sworn "members of the Gang Crime Section" and certain other designated officers, and establish detailed criteria for defining street gangs and membership in such gangs. In addition, the order directs district commanders to "designate areas in which the presence of gang members has a demonstrable effect on the activities of law abiding persons in the surrounding community," and provides that the ordinance "will be enforced only within the designated areas." The city, however, does not release the locations of these "designated areas" to the public.

II

During the three years of its enforcement, the police issued over 89,000 dispersal orders and arrested over 42,000 people for violating the ordinance. In the ensuing enforcement proceedings, [trial judges came to mixed conclusions about] the constitutionality of the ordinance. . . .

[Ultimately, t]he Illinois Supreme Court . . . held "that the gang loitering ordinance violates due process of law in that it is impermissibly vague on its face and an arbitrary restriction on personal liberties." . . .

We granted certiorari and now affirm. Like the Illinois Supreme Court, we conclude that the ordinance enacted by the city of Chicago is unconstitutionally vague.

---

[2] The ordinance states in pertinent part:

"(a) Whenever a police officer observes a person whom he reasonably believes to be a criminal street gang member loitering in any public place with one or more other persons, he shall order all such persons to disperse and remove themselves from the area. Any person who does not promptly obey such an order is in violation of this section.

"(b) It shall be an affirmative defense to an alleged violation of this section that no person who was observed loitering was in fact a member of a criminal street gang.

"(c) As used in this Section:

"(d) 'Loiter' means to remain in any one place with no apparent purpose. . . .

"(e) Any person who violates this Section is subject to a fine of not less than $100 and not more than $500 for each offense, or imprisonment for not more than six months, or both. . . ." Chicago Municipal Code §8-4-015 (added June 17, 1992).

III . . .

We are confronted at the outset with the city's claim that it was improper for the state courts to conclude that the ordinance is invalid on its face. The city correctly points out that imprecise laws can be attacked on their face under two different doctrines. First, the overbreadth doctrine permits the facial invalidation of laws that inhibit the exercise of First Amendment rights if the impermissible applications of the law are substantial when "judged in relation to the statute's plainly legitimate sweep." Broadrick v. Oklahoma, 413 U.S. 601, 612–615 (1973). Second, even if an enactment does not reach a substantial amount of constitutionally protected conduct, it may be impermissibly vague because it fails to establish standards for the police and public that are sufficient to guard against the arbitrary deprivation of liberty interests. Kolender v. Lawson, 461 U.S. 352, 358 (1983). . . .

There is no need . . . to decide whether the impact of the Chicago ordinance on constitutionally protected liberty alone would suffice to support a facial challenge under the overbreadth doctrine. For it is clear that the vagueness of this enactment makes a facial challenge appropriate. This is not an ordinance that "simply regulates business behavior and contains a scienter requirement." See Hoffman Estates v. Flipside, Hoffman Estates, Inc., 455 U.S. 489, 499 (1982). It is a criminal law that contains no *mens rea* requirement and infringes on constitutionally protected rights. When vagueness permeates the text of such a law, it is subject to facial attack.

Vagueness may invalidate a criminal law for either of two independent reasons. First, it may fail to provide the kind of notice that will enable ordinary people to understand what conduct it prohibits; second, it may authorize and even encourage arbitrary and discriminatory enforcement. See *Kolender*, 461 U.S. at 357. Accordingly, we first consider whether the ordinance provides fair notice to the citizen and then discuss its potential for arbitrary enforcement.

IV

. . . It is difficult to imagine how any citizen of the city of Chicago standing in a public place with a group of people would know if he or she had an "apparent purpose." If she were talking to another person, would she have an apparent purpose? If she were frequently checking her watch and looking expectantly down the street, would she have an apparent purpose? . . .

The city's principal response to this concern about adequate notice is that loiterers are not subject to sanction until after they have failed to comply with an officer's order to disperse. "[W]hatever problem is created by a law that criminalizes conduct people normally believe to be innocent is solved when persons receive actual notice from a police order of what they are expected to do." We find this response unpersuasive for at least two reasons.

First, the purpose of the fair notice requirement is to enable the ordinary citizen to conform his or her conduct to the law. . . . Although it is true that a loiterer is not subject to criminal sanctions unless he or she disobeys a dispersal order, the loitering is the conduct that the ordinance is designed to prohibit. If the loitering is in fact harmless and innocent, the dispersal order itself is an unjustified impairment of liberty. . . . Because an officer may issue an order only after prohibited conduct has already occurred, it cannot provide the kind of advance notice that will protect the putative loiterer from being ordered to disperse. . . .

Second, the terms of the dispersal order compound the inadequacy of the notice afforded by the ordinance. It provides that the officer "shall order all such persons to disperse and remove themselves from the area." This vague phrasing raises a host of questions. After such an order issues, how long must the loiterers remain apart? How far must they move? If each loiterer walks around the block and they meet again at the same location, are they subject to arrest or merely to being ordered to disperse again? . . .

V

The broad sweep of the ordinance also violates "the requirement that a legislature establish minimal guidelines to govern law enforcement." *Kolender,* 461 U.S. at 358. There are no such guidelines in the ordinance. In any public place in the city of Chicago, persons who stand or sit in the company of a gang member may be ordered to disperse unless their purpose is apparent. . . . It matters not whether the reason that a gang member and his father, for example, might loiter near Wrigley Field is to rob an unsuspecting fan or just to get a glimpse of Sammy Sosa leaving the ballpark; in either event, if their purpose is not apparent to a nearby police officer, she may—indeed, she "shall"—order them to disperse.

. . . [T]he principal source of the vast discretion conferred on the police in this case is the definition of loitering as "to remain in any one place with no apparent purpose."

As the Illinois Supreme Court interprets that definition, it "provides absolute discretion to police officers to decide what activities constitute loitering." City of Chicago v. Morales, 687 N.E.2d 53, 63 (Ill. 1987). We have no authority to construe the language of a state statute more narrowly than the construction given by that State's highest court. . . .

It is true, as the city argues, that the requirement that the officer reasonably believe that a group of loiterers contains a gang member does place a limit on the authority to order dispersal. That limitation would no doubt be sufficient if the ordinance only applied to loitering that had an apparently harmful purpose or effect, or possibly if it only applied to loitering by persons reasonably believed to be criminal gang members. But this ordinance, for reasons that are not explained in the findings of the city council, requires no harmful purpose and applies to nongang members as well as suspected gang members. It applies to everyone in the city who may remain in one place with one suspected gang member as long as their purpose is not apparent to an officer observing them. Friends, relatives, teachers, counselors, or even total strangers might unwittingly engage in forbidden loitering if they happen to engage in idle conversation with a gang member.

Ironically, the definition of loitering in the Chicago ordinance not only extends its scope to encompass harmless conduct, but also has the perverse consequence of excluding from its coverage much of the intimidating conduct that motivated its enactment. As the city council's findings demonstrate, the most harmful gang loitering is motivated either by an apparent purpose to publicize the gang's dominance of certain territory, thereby intimidating nonmembers, or by an equally apparent purpose to conceal ongoing commerce in illegal drugs. . . .

Finally, in its opinion striking down the ordinance, the Illinois Supreme Court refused to accept the general order issued by the police department as a sufficient limitation on the "vast amount of discretion" granted to the police in its enforcement. We agree. See Smith v. Goguen, 415 U.S. 566, 575 (1974). That the police have adopted internal rules limiting their enforcement to certain designated areas in the city would not provide a defense to a loiterer who might be arrested elsewhere. Nor could a person who knowingly loitered with a well-known gang member anywhere in the city safely assume that they would not be ordered to disperse no matter how innocent and harmless their loitering might be.

VI

In our judgment, the Illinois Supreme Court correctly concluded that the ordinance does not provide sufficiently specific limits on the enforcement discretion of the police "to meet constitutional standards for definiteness and clarity." We recognize the serious and difficult problems testified to by the citizens of Chicago that led to the enactment of this ordinance. "We are mindful that the preservation of liberty depends in part on the maintenance of social order." Houston v. Hill, 482 U.S. 451, 471–472 (1987). However, in this instance the city has enacted an ordinance that affords too much discretion to the police and too little notice to citizens who wish to use the public streets.

Accordingly, the judgment of the Supreme Court of Illinois is

Affirmed.

JUSTICE O'CONNOR, with whom JUSTICE BREYER joins, concurring in part and concurring in the judgment.

I agree with the Court that Chicago's Gang Congregation Ordinance . . . is unconstitutionally vague. A penal law is void for vagueness if it fails to "define the criminal offense with sufficient definiteness that ordinary people can understand what conduct is prohibited" or fails to establish guidelines to prevent "arbitrary and discriminatory enforcement" of the law. Kolender v. Lawson, 461 U.S. 352, 357 (1983). Of these, "the more important aspect of the vagueness doctrine 'is . . . the requirement that a legislature establish minimal guidelines to govern law enforcement.'" *Id.* at 358 (quoting Smith v. Goguen, 415 U.S. 566, 574–575 (1974)). I share Justice Thomas' concern about the consequences of gang violence, and I agree that some degree of police discretion is necessary to allow the police "to perform their peacekeeping responsibilities satisfactorily." *Post* (dissenting opinion). A criminal law, however, must not permit policemen, prosecutors, and juries to conduct "'a standardless sweep . . . to pursue their personal predilections.'" *Kolender,* 461 U.S. at 358 (quoting *Smith,* 415 U.S. at 575). . . .

As it has been construed by the Illinois court, Chicago's gang loitering ordinance is unconstitutionally vague because it lacks sufficient minimal standards to guide law enforcement officers. In particular, it fails to provide police with any standard by which they can judge whether an individual has an "*apparent* purpose." Indeed, because any person standing on the street has a general "purpose"—even if it is simply to stand—the ordinance permits police officers to choose which purposes are *permissible.* . . . Any police officer in Chicago is free, under the Illinois Supreme Court's construction of the ordinance, to order at his whim any person standing in a public place with a suspected gang member to disperse. Further, as construed by the Illinois court, the ordinance applies to hundreds of thousands of persons who are not gang members, standing on any sidewalk or in any park, coffee shop, bar, or "other location open to the public, whether publicly or privately owned."

To be sure, there is no violation of the ordinance unless a person fails to obey promptly the order to disperse. But, a police officer cannot issue a dispersal order until he decides that a person is remaining in one place "with no apparent purpose," and the ordinance provides no guidance to the officer on how to make this antecedent decision. . . .

This vagueness consideration alone provides a sufficient ground for affirming the Illinois court's decision, and I agree with Part V of the Court's opinion, which discusses this consideration. Accordingly, there is no need to consider the other issues briefed by the parties and addressed by the plurality. I express no opinion about them.

It is important to courts and legislatures alike that we characterize more clearly the narrow scope of today's holding. As the ordinance comes to this Court, it is unconstitutionally vague. Nevertheless, there remain open to Chicago reasonable alternatives to combat the very real threat posed by gang intimidation and violence. For example, the Court properly and expressly distinguishes the ordinance from laws that require loiterers to have a "harmful purpose," from laws that target only gang members, and from laws that incorporate limits on the area and manner in which the laws may be enforced. In addition, the ordinance here is unlike a law that "directly prohibit[s]" the "'presence of a large collection of obviously brazen, insistent, and lawless gang members and hangers-on on the public ways,'" that "'intimidates residents.'" *Ante* (quoting Brief for Petitioner 14). Indeed, as the plurality notes, the city of Chicago has several laws that do exactly this. Chicago has even enacted a provision that "enables police officers to fulfill . . . their traditional functions," including "preserving the public peace." See *post* (Thomas, J., dissenting). Specifically, Chicago's general disorderly conduct provision allows the police to arrest those who knowingly "provoke, make or aid in making a breach of peace." See Chicago Municipal Code §8–4–010 (1992).

In my view, the gang loitering ordinance could have been construed more narrowly. . . . Nevertheless, we cannot impose a limiting construction that a state supreme court has declined to adopt. See *Kolender*, 461 U.S. at 355–356 n.4. Accordingly, I join Parts I, II, and V of the Court's opinion and concur in the judgment.

[The opinion of Justice Kennedy, concurring in part and concurring in the judgment, is omitted.]

JUSTICE BREYER, concurring in part and concurring in the judgment.

The ordinance before us creates more than a "*minor* limitation upon the free state of nature." *Post* (Scalia, J., dissenting) (emphasis added). The law authorizes a police officer to order any person to remove himself from any "location open to the public, whether publicly or privately owned," *i.e.,* any sidewalk, front stoop, public park, public square, lakeside promenade, hotel, restaurant, bowling alley, bar, barbershop, sports arena, shopping mall, etc., but with two, and only two, limitations: First, that person must be accompanied by (or must himself be) someone police reasonably believe is a gang member. Second, that person must have remained in that public place "with no apparent purpose."

The first limitation cannot save the ordinance. Though it limits the number of persons subject to the law, it leaves many individuals, gang members and nongang members alike, subject to its strictures. Nor does it limit in any way the range of conduct that police may prohibit. The second limitation is, as the Court and Justice

O'Connor, point out, not a limitation at all. Since one always has some apparent purpose, the so-called limitation invites, in fact requires, the policeman to interpret the words "no apparent purpose" as meaning "no apparent purpose except for. . . ." And it is in the ordinance's delegation to the policeman of open-ended discretion to fill in that blank that the problem lies. To grant to a policeman virtually standardless discretion to close off major portions of the city to an innocent person is, in my view, to create a major, not a "minor," "limitation upon the free state of nature." . . .

JUSTICE SCALIA, dissenting.

The citizens of Chicago were once free to drive about the city at whatever speed they wished. At some point Chicagoans (or perhaps Illinoisans) decided this would not do, and imposed prophylactic speed limits designed to assure safe operation by the average (or perhaps even subaverage) driver with the average (or perhaps even subaverage) vehicle. This infringed upon the "freedom" of all citizens, but was not unconstitutional.

Similarly, the citizens of Chicago were once free to stand around and gawk at the scene of an accident. At some point Chicagoans discovered that this obstructed traffic and caused more accidents. They did not make the practice unlawful, but they did authorize police officers to order the crowd to disperse, and imposed penalties for refusal to obey such an order. Again, this prophylactic measure infringed upon the "freedom" of all citizens, but was not unconstitutional.

Until the ordinance that is before us today was adopted, the citizens of Chicago were free to stand about in public places with no apparent purpose—to engage, that is, in conduct that appeared to be loitering. In recent years, however, the city has been afflicted with criminal street gangs. . . . Once again, Chicagoans decided that to eliminate the problem it was worth restricting some of the freedom that they once enjoyed. The means they took was similar to the second, and more mild, example given above rather than the first: Loitering was not made unlawful, but when a group of people occupied a public place without an apparent purpose and in the company of a known gang member, police officers were authorized to order them to disperse, and the failure to obey such an order was made unlawful. The minor limitation upon the free state of nature that this prophylactic arrangement imposed upon all Chicagoans seemed to them (and it seems to me) a small price to pay for liberation of their streets.

The majority today invalidates this perfectly reasonable measure by ignoring our rules governing facial challenges, by elevating loitering to a constitutionally guaranteed right, and by discerning vagueness where, according to our usual standards, none exists.

I

Respondents' consolidated appeal presents a facial challenge to the Chicago ordinance on vagueness grounds. When a facial challenge is successful, the law in question is declared to be unenforceable in *all* its applications, and not just in its particular application to the party in suit. . . .

. . . [U]ntil recently . . . we have—except in free-speech cases subject to the doctrine of overbreadth—*required* the facial challenge to *be* a go-for-broke proposition. That is to say, before declaring a statute to be void in all its applications (something we should not be doing in the first place), we have at least imposed upon the litigant the eminently reasonable requirement that he establish that the statute was *unconstitutional* in all its applications. . . .

When our normal criteria for facial challenges are applied, it is clear that the Justices in the majority have transposed the burden of proof. Instead of requiring respondents, who are challenging the ordinance, to show that it is invalid in all its applications, they have required petitioner to show that it is valid in all its applications. Both the plurality opinion and the concurrences display a lively imagination, creating hypothetical situations in which the law's application would (in their view) be ambiguous. But that creative role has been usurped from petitioner, who can defeat respondents' facial challenge by conjuring up *a single valid application* of the law. My contribution would go something like this[5]: Tony, a member of the Jets criminal street gang, is standing alongside and chatting with fellow gang members while staking out their turf at Promontory Point on the South Side of Chicago; the group is flashing gang signs and displaying their distinctive tattoos to passersby. Officer Krupke, applying the ordinance at issue here, orders the group to disperse. After some speculative discussion (probably irrelevant here) over whether the Jets are depraved because they are deprived, Tony and the other gang members break off further conversation with the statement—not entirely coherent, but evidently intended to be rude—"Gee, Officer Krupke, krup you." A tense standoff ensues until Officer Krupke arrests the group for failing to obey his dispersal order. Even assuming (as the Justices in the majority do, but I do not) that a law requiring obedience to a dispersal order is impermissibly vague unless it is clear to the objects of the order, before its issuance, that their conduct justifies it, I find it hard to believe that the Jets would not have known they had it coming. That should settle the matter of respondents' facial challenge to the ordinance's vagueness.

Of course respondents would still be able to claim that the ordinance was vague as applied to them. But . . . it is doubtful whether some of these respondents could even sustain an *as-applied* challenge on the basis of the majority's own criteria. For instance, respondent Jose Renteria—who admitted that he was a member of the Satan Disciples gang—was observed by the arresting officer loitering on a street corner with other gang members. The officer issued a dispersal order, but when she returned to the same corner 15 to 20 minutes later, Renteria was still there with his friends, whereupon he was arrested. In another example, respondent Daniel Washington and several others—who admitted they were members of the Vice Lords gang—were observed by the arresting officer loitering in the street, yelling at passing vehicles, stopping traffic, and preventing pedestrians from using the sidewalks. The arresting officer issued a dispersal order, issued *another* dispersal order later when the group did not move, and finally arrested the group when they were found loitering in the same place still later. Finally, respondent Gregorio Gutierrez—who had previously admitted to the arresting officer his membership in the Latin Kings gang—was observed loitering with two other men. The officer issued a dispersal order, drove around the block, and arrested the men after finding them in the same place upon his return. Even on the majority's assumption that to avoid vagueness it must be clear to the object of the dispersal order *ex ante* that his conduct is covered by the ordinance, it seems most improbable that any of these

---

[5] With apologies for taking creative license with the work of Messrs. Bernstein, Sondheim, and Laurents. West Side Story, copyright 1959.

as-applied challenges would be sustained. Much less is it possible to say that the ordinance is invalid in *all* its applications. . . .

IV

Finally, I address the . . . the plurality's . . . proposition that the ordinance is vague. It is not. . . . A law is unconstitutionally vague if its lack of definitive standards either (1) fails to apprise persons of ordinary intelligence of the prohibited conduct, or (2) encourages arbitrary and discriminatory enforcement.

The plurality relies primarily upon the first of these aspects. Since, it reasons, "the loitering is the conduct that the ordinance is designed to prohibit," and "an officer may issue an order only after prohibited conduct has already occurred," *ante*, the order to disperse cannot itself serve "to apprise persons of ordinary intelligence of the prohibited conduct." What counts for purposes of vagueness analysis, however, is not what the ordinance is "designed to prohibit," but what it actually subjects to criminal penalty. . . . [T]hat consists of nothing but the refusal to obey a dispersal order, as to which there is no doubt of adequate notice of the prohibited conduct. The plurality's suggestion that even the dispersal order *itself* is unconstitutionally vague, because it does not specify *how far to disperse(!),* scarcely requires a response. If it were true, it would render unconstitutional for vagueness many of the Presidential proclamations issued under that provision of the United States Code which requires the President, before using the militia or the Armed Forces for law enforcement, to issue a proclamation ordering the insurgents to disperse. See 10 U.S.C. §334. . . .

For its determination of unconstitutional vagueness, the Court relies secondarily—and Justice O'Connor's and Justice Breyer's concurrences exclusively—upon the second aspect of that doctrine, which requires sufficient specificity to prevent arbitrary and discriminatory law enforcement. . . .

The criteria for issuance of a dispersal order under the Chicago ordinance could hardly be clearer. First, the law requires police officers to "reasonably believ[e]" that one of the group to which the order is issued is a "criminal street gang member." This resembles a probable-cause standard, and the Chicago Police Department's General Order 92–4 (1992)—promulgated to govern enforcement of the ordinance—makes the probable-cause requirement explicit. Under the Order, officers must have probable cause to believe that an individual is a member of a criminal street gang, to be substantiated by the officer's "experience and knowledge of the alleged offenders" and by "specific, documented and reliable information" such as reliable witness testimony or an individual's admission of gang membership or display of distinctive colors, tattoos, signs, or other markings worn by members of particular criminal street gangs.

Second, the ordinance requires that the group be "remain[ing] in any one place with no apparent purpose." Justice O'Connor's assertion that this applies to "any person standing in a public place," *ante*, is a distortion. The ordinance does not apply to "standing," but to "remain[ing]"—a term which in this context obviously means "[to] endure or persist," see *American Heritage Dictionary* 1525 (1992). There may be some ambiguity at the margin, but "remain[ing] in one place" requires more than a temporary stop, and is clear in most of its applications, including all of those represented by the facts surrounding respondents' arrests described.

As for the phrase "with no apparent purpose": Justice O'Connor again distorts this adjectival phrase, by separating it from the word that it modifies. "[A]ny person standing on the street," her concurrence says, "has a general 'purpose'—even if it is simply to stand," and thus "the ordinance permits police officers to choose which purposes are *permissible.*" *Ante.* But Chicago police officers enforcing the ordinance are not looking for people with no apparent purpose (who are regrettably in over-supply); they are looking for people who "remain in any one place with no apparent purpose"—that is, who remain there without any apparent reason *for remaining there.* That is not difficult to perceive. . . .

V

The plurality points out that Chicago already has several laws that reach the intimidating and unlawful gang-related conduct the ordinance was directed at. The problem, of course, well recognized by Chicago's city council, is that the gang members cease their intimidating and unlawful behavior under the watchful eye of police officers, but return to it as soon as the police drive away. The only solution, the council concluded, was to clear the streets of congregations of gangs, their drug customers, and their associates.

Justice O'Connor's concurrence proffers the same empty solace of existing laws useless for the purpose at hand, but seeks to be helpful by suggesting some measures *similar* to this ordinance that *would* be constitutional. It says that Chicago could, for example, enact a law that "directly prohibit[s] the presence of a large collection of obviously brazen, insistent, and lawless gang members and hangers-on on the public ways, that intimidates residents." *Ante.* . . . The problem, again, is that the intimidation and lawlessness do not occur when the police are in sight. . . .

* * *

. . . [T]he majority's real quarrel with the Chicago ordinance is simply that it permits (or indeed requires) too much harmless conduct by innocent citizens to be proscribed. As Justice O'Connor's concurrence says with disapprobation, "the ordinance applies to hundreds of thousands of persons who are *not* gang members, standing on any sidewalk or in any park, coffee shop, bar, or other location open to the public." *Ante.*

But in our democratic system, how much harmless conduct to proscribe is not a judgment to be made by the courts. So long as constitutionally guaranteed rights are not affected, and so long as the proscription has a rational basis, *all sorts* of per-fectly harmless activity by millions of perfectly innocent people can be forbidden—riding a motorcycle without a safety helmet, for example, starting a campfire in a national forest, or selling a safe and effective drug not yet approved by the Food and Drug Administration. All of these acts are entirely innocent and harmless in themselves, but because of the *risk* of harm that they entail, the freedom to engage in them has been abridged. The citizens of Chicago have decided that depriving themselves of the freedom to "hang out" with a gang member is necessary to elim-inate pervasive gang crime and intimidation—and that the elimination of the one is worth the deprivation of the other. This Court has no business second-guessing either the degree of necessity or the fairness of the trade.

I dissent from the judgment of the Court.

Justice Thomas, with whom The Chief Justice and Justice Scalia join, dissenting. . . .

I

The human costs exacted by criminal street gangs are inestimable. In many of our Nation's cities, gangs have "[v]irtually overtak[en] certain neighborhoods, contributing to the economic and social decline of these areas and causing fear and lifestyle changes among law-abiding residents." U.S. Dept. of Justice, Office of Justice Programs, Bureau of Justice Assistance, *Monograph: Urban Street Gang Enforcement* 3 (1997). Gangs fill the daily lives of many of our poorest and most vulnerable citizens with a terror that the Court does not give sufficient consideration, often relegating them to the status of prisoners in their own homes. . . .

Before enacting its ordinance, the Chicago City Council held extensive hearings on the problems of gang loitering. Concerned citizens appeared to testify poignantly as to how gangs disrupt their daily lives. Ordinary citizens like Ms. D'Ivory Gordon explained that she struggled just to walk to work:

> "When I walk out my door, these guys are out there. . . .
>
> "They watch you. . . . They know where you live. They know what time you leave, what time you come home. I am afraid of them. I have even come to the point now that I carry a meat cleaver to work with me. . . .
>
> ". . . I don't want to hurt anyone, and I don't want to be hurt. We need to clean these corners up. Clean these communities up and take it back from them." Transcript of Proceedings before the City Council of Chicago, Committee on Police and Fire 66–67 (May 15, 1992) (hereinafter Transcript).

Eighty-eight-year-old Susan Mary Jackson echoed her sentiments, testifying: "We used to have a nice neighborhood. We don't have it anymore. . . . I am scared to go out in the daytime. . . . [Y]ou can't pass because they are standing. I am afraid to go to the store. I don't go to the store because I am afraid. At my age if they look at me real hard, I be ready to holler." *Id.* at 93–95. Another long-time resident testified:

"I have never had the terror that I feel everyday when I walk down the streets of Chicago. . . .

"I have had my windows broken out. I have had guns pulled on me. I have been threatened. I get intimidated on a daily basis, and it's come to the point where I say, well, do I go out today. Do I put my ax in my briefcase. Do I walk around dressed like a bum so I am not looking rich or got any money or anything like that." *Id.* at 124–125.

Following these hearings, the council found that "criminal street gangs establish control over identifiable areas . . . by loitering in those areas and intimidating others from entering those areas." It further found that the mere presence of gang members "intimidate[s] many law abiding citizens" and "creates a justifiable fear for the safety of persons and property in the area." It is the product of this democratic process—the council's attempt to address these social ills—that we are asked to pass judgment upon today.

II . . .

B

The Court concludes that the ordinance is also unconstitutionally vague because it fails to provide adequate standards to guide police discretion and because, in the plurality's view, it does not give residents adequate notice of how to conform their conduct to the confines of the law. I disagree on both counts.

1

At the outset, it is important to note that the ordinance does not criminalize loitering *per se*. Rather, it penalizes loiterers' failure to obey a police officer's order to move along. A majority of the Court believes that this scheme vests too much discretion in police officers. Nothing could be further from the truth. Far from according officers too much discretion, the ordinance merely enables police officers to fulfill one of their traditional functions. Police officers are not, and have never been, simply enforcers of the criminal law. They wear other hats—importantly, they have long been vested with the responsibility for preserving the public peace. Nor is the idea that the police are also *peace officers* simply a quaint anachronism. In most American jurisdictions, police officers continue to be obligated, by law, to maintain the public peace.

In their role as peace officers, the police long have had the authority and the duty to order groups of individuals who threaten the public peace to disperse. For example, the 1887 police manual for the city of New York provided:

> "It is hereby made the duty of the Police Force at all times of day and night, and the members of such Force are hereby thereunto empowered, to especially preserve the public peace, prevent crime, detect and arrest offenders, suppress riots, mobs and insurrections, *disperse unlawful or dangerous assemblages, and assemblages which obstruct the free passage of public streets, sidewalks, parks and places*." Manual Containing the Rules and Regulations of the Police Department of the City of New York, Rule 414 (emphasis added).

The authority to issue dispersal orders continues to play a commonplace and crucial role in police operations, particularly in urban areas.[7] Even the ABA Standards

---

[7] For example, the following statutes provide a criminal penalty for the failure to obey a dispersal order: Ala. Code §13A–11–6 (1994); Ariz. Rev. Stat. Ann. §13–2902(A)(2) (1989); Ark. Code Ann. §5–71–207(a)(6) (1993); Cal. Penal Code Ann. §727 (West 1985); Colo. Rev. Stat. §18–9–107(b) (1997); Del. Code Ann., Tit. 11, §1321 (1995); Ga. Code Ann. §16–11–36 (1996); Guam Code Ann., Tit. 9, §61.10(b) (1996); Haw. Rev. Stat. §711–1102 (1993); Idaho Code §18–6410 (1997); Ill. Comp. Stat., ch. 720, §5/25–1(e) (1998); Ky. Rev. Stat. Ann. §§525.060, 525.160 (Baldwin 1990); Me. Rev. Stat. Ann., Tit. 17A, §502 (1983); Mass. Gen. Laws, ch. 269, §2 (1992); Mich. Comp. Laws §750.523 (1991); Minn. Stat. §609.715 (1998); Miss. Code Ann. §97–35–7(1) (1994); Mo. Rev. Stat. §574.060 (1994); Mont. Code Ann. §45–8–102 (1997); Nev. Rev. Stat. §203.020 (1995); N.H. Rev. Stat. Ann. §§644:1, 644:2(II)(e) (1996); N.J. Stat. Ann. §2C:33–1(b) (West 1995); N.Y. Penal Law §240.20(6) (McKinney 1989); N.C. Gen. Stat. §14–288.5(a) (1999); N.D. Cent. Code §12.1–25–04 (1997); Ohio Rev. Code Ann. §2917.13(A)(2) (1997); Okla. Stat., Tit. 21, §1316 (1991); Ore. Rev. Stat. §166.025(1)(e) (1997); 18 Pa. Cons. Stat. §5502 (1983); R.I. Gen. Laws §11–38–2 (1994); S.C. Code Ann. §16–7–10(a) (1985); S.D. Codified Laws §22–10–11 (1998); Tenn. Code Ann. §39–17–305(2) (1997); Tex. Penal Code Ann. §42.03(a)(2) (1994); Utah Code Ann. §76–9–104 (1995); Vt. Stat. Ann., Tit. 13, §901 (1998); Va. Code Ann. §18.2–407 (1996); V.I. Code Ann. Tit. 5, §4022 (1997); Wash. Rev. Code §9A.84.020 (1994); W. Va. Code §61–6–1 (1997); Wis. Stat. §947.06(3) (1994).

for Criminal Justice recognize that "[i]n day-to-day police experience there are innumerable situations in which police are called upon to order people not to block the sidewalk, not to congregate in a given place, and not to 'loiter'. . . . The police may suspect the loiterer of considering engaging in some form of undesirable conduct that can be at least temporarily frustrated by ordering him or her to 'move on.'" Standard 1–3.4(d), p. 1.88, and comments (2d ed.1980, Supp.1986).

In order to perform their peacekeeping responsibilities satisfactorily, the police inevitably must exercise discretion. Indeed, by empowering them to act as peace officers, the law assumes that the police will exercise that discretion responsibly and with sound judgment. That is not to say that the law should not provide objective guidelines for the police, but simply that it cannot rigidly constrain their every action. By directing a police officer not to issue a dispersal order unless he "observes a person whom he reasonably believes to be a criminal street gang member loitering in any public place," Chicago's ordinance strikes an appropriate balance between those two extremes. Just as we trust officers to rely on their experience and expertise in order to make spur-of-the-moment determinations about amorphous legal standards such as "probable cause" and "reasonable suspicion," so we must trust them to determine whether a group of loiterers contains individuals (in this case members of criminal street gangs) whom the city has determined threaten the public peace. In sum, the Court's conclusion that the ordinance is impermissibly vague because it " 'necessarily entrusts lawmaking to the moment-to-moment judgment of the policeman on his beat,' " *ante,* cannot be reconciled with common sense, longstanding police practice, or this Court's Fourth Amendment jurisprudence. . . .

In concluding that the ordinance adequately channels police discretion, I do not suggest that a police officer enforcing the Gang Congregation Ordinance will never make a mistake. Nor do I overlook the *possibility* that a police officer, acting in bad faith, might enforce the ordinance in an arbitrary or discriminatory way. But our decisions should not turn on the proposition that such an event will be anything but rare. Instances of arbitrary or discriminatory enforcement of the ordinance, like any other law, are best addressed when (and if) they arise, rather than prophylactically through the disfavored mechanism of a facial challenge on vagueness grounds.

2

The plurality's conclusion that the ordinance "fails to give the ordinary citizen adequate notice of what is forbidden and what is permitted," *ante,* is similarly untenable. There is nothing "vague" about an order to disperse. While "we can never expect mathematical certainty from our language," Grayned v. City of Rockford, 408 U.S. 104, 110 (1972), it is safe to assume that the vast majority of people who are ordered by the police to "disperse and remove themselves from the area" will have little difficulty understanding how to comply. . . .

* * *

Today, the Court focuses extensively on the "rights" of gang members and their companions. It can safely do so—the people who will have to live with the consequences of today's opinion do not live in our neighborhoods. Rather, the people who will suffer from our lofty pronouncements are people like Ms. Susan Mary Jackson; people who have seen their neighborhoods literally destroyed by gangs and violence and drugs. They are good, decent people who must struggle to overcome their desperate situation, against all odds, in order to raise their families, earn a living, and remain good citizens. As one resident described: "There is only about maybe one or two percent of the people in the city causing these problems maybe, but it's keeping 98 percent of us in our houses and off the streets and afraid to shop." Transcript 126. By focusing exclusively on the imagined "rights" of the two percent, the Court today has denied our most vulnerable citizens the very thing that Justice Stevens, *ante*, elevates above all else—the "'freedom of movement.'" And that is a shame. I respectfully dissent.

NOTES AND QUESTIONS

1. *Vagueness doctrine.* The Justices agree that vagueness doctrine serves two purposes: ensuring that statutes and ordinances give individuals notice about conduct that is prohibited, and ensuring that legislatures guide officers sufficiently to prevent arbitrary and discriminatory enforcement of the law. As Justice O'Connor's concurring opinion notes, the Court focuses more on the second purpose, "the requirement that a legislature establish minimal guidelines to government law enforcement." Kolender v. Lawson, 461 U.S. 352, 357 (1983). Since the 1970s, many vagueness cases have assessed prosecutorial rather than police discretion. *Morales* is one important exception. The Court relied on another, *Kolender*, 461 U.S. 352, in its decision. In *Kolender*, the Court rejected as vague a state statute that permitted officers to arrest any person who did not provide a "credible and reliable" identification because it left too much discretion to officers to determine what suspects had to do to satisfy the statute's requirements. The Court reasoned that, by giving officers the power to determine what constituted an acceptable identification, the law encouraged arbitrary use of the statute. Why, precisely, is the Chicago gang ordinance vague?

2. *Minor crimes vs. serious crimes.* Although vagueness doctrine applies to all criminal laws, vagueness cases about police discretion focus on low-level, street-order offenses, not serious criminal statutes. John Jeffries provides one explanation:

> Laws of this sort are often found vague largely because they lend themselves to informal social control of undesirables. Where enforcement is centralized (and thus likely to be exercised with greater regularity), or where there is an identifiable victim (who is likely to keep track of police action), or where the crime is very serious (and thus likely to attract public monitoring of prosecutorial decisions), the risk of abusive enforcement is reduced, and the tolerance for indefinite standards is increased accordingly.

John Calvin Jeffries, Jr., *Legality, Vagueness, and the Construction of Penal Statutes*, 71 Va. L. Rev. 189, 216 (1985). In this way, vagueness doctrine is closely tied to local efforts to empower the police through ordinances regulating the streets.

3. *Vagueness and public order.* The same discretion that risks making minor street ordinances vague is what allows them to be used to manage public order problems on the street. Some think this justifies such statutes, vagueness be damned:

> The problem with the quest for "rules" in the formulation of public order laws is that the task of maintaining order is itself inherently one of judgment. In many cases, this task cannot be optimally authorized in rules of ministerial character. Consider

noise. . . . Police spend a great deal of time mediating disputes between neighbors about noise or, in some cases, enforcing laws against noise. . . .

So what degree of specificity is appropriate in laws regulating noise? Model Penal Code drafters included . . . a standard aimed at noise constituting a public nuisance. The model law . . . prohibits persons from making "unreasonable" noise "with purpose to cause public inconvenience, annoyance, or alarm, or recklessly creating a risk thereof." . . .

Noise abatement is something that police must be authorized to do. One could imagine, then, an alternative to the Model Penal Code formulation: a rather complicated legal code that would attempt to state volumes (in decibel formulation as measured from specified distances) permissible at different parts of the city, at different times of day, and in different circumstances. . . . Such a code . . . might in theory diminish the necessity of police judgment in enforcement, though it would admittedly still leave the officer with substantial discretion to enforce or not to enforce. It would also be both over and underinclusive, difficult if not impossible to learn and administer, burdensome in localities not already equipped with noise meters, and arguably less immediately accessible to many citizens who might want to know how noisy they can be.

Debra Livingston, *Police Discretion and the Quality of Life in Public Places: Courts, Communities, and the New Policing*, 97 Colum. L. Rev. 551, 613–615 (1997). Is vagueness doctrine counterproductive? Should communities be permitted to grant police the discretion to arrest those who make unreasonable noise? Is noise abatement really something that *police* must be authorized to do?

Livingston seems to trust that police will use this discretion wisely, an assumption that courts mostly share and that Justice Thomas states expressly in his dissent. And indeed many local noise, loitering, and other order maintenance ordinances are upheld in part because courts trust officers to know real violations when they see them. What do you think of that view? If a Model Penal Code–type noise ordinance is overturned on vagueness grounds, what will the police do when residents call the police to complain about their neighbors? Ignore the call?

4. *Applying the Encounter Model.* Review the model of police–citizen interactions in Chapter 1. One way to read *Morales* is by contrasting how the different opinions view the ordinance in terms of the model. Here is how Justice Stevens appears to see things:

[1] **Problem identification.** The ordinance prohibits a problem in the world: remaining in a public place with no purpose.
[2] **Solution imposition.** The ordinance authorizes a particular coercive response to this problem: orders to disperse.
[3] **Citizen reaction.** The ordinance anticipates a particular form of citizen noncompliance: disobeying orders to disperse.
[4] **Officer follow-up.** For that noncompliance, the ordinance authorizes officers a specific coercive response: arrests for violating the ordinance.

To Justice Stevens, the problem with the ordinance is that it inadequately specifies the behavior (the [1] problem) for which officers are granted the coercive power to disperse people from the street (the [2] solution). That problem cannot be corrected by giving the power to arrest (a [4] officer follow-up) only when a person disobeys the order (a [3] citizen reaction), because the officer's coercive order (the initial [2] solution) needs legitimate legislative authority—that is, authority that adequately specifies the behavior (the [1] problem) to which it applies.

Now reread the opinions of Justices Thomas and Scalia. How do they see the components of the statute? What do they say about legislative authority for police orders to disperse? What about legislative authority to arrest? What, in their view, is required for orders to disperse to be enforceable? Looked at this way, *Morales* is a case about whether officers need similar kinds of legislative authorization for *order maintenance* and *criminal law enforcement.* Justice Stevens argues yes. Justices Thomas and Scalia argue that some kind of coercive authority (to impose [2] solutions), including dispersal orders, is simply inherent in the power to police. How do we know who is right?

5. *Vagueness vs. the Fourth Amendment.* If you think about it too much, vagueness doctrine seems odd. In Fourth Amendment cases, the Court has permitted states to grant officers unlimited discretion about whether to make an arrest or issue a citation, see Atwater v. Lago Vista, 532 U.S. 318 (2001), and to allow officers authority to stop any person based on no more than reasonable suspicion of criminal activity, see Terry v. Ohio, 392 U.S. 1 (1968). And yet the Court says those same officers must be given specific guidance to decide, under *Morales*, when someone has "no apparent purpose" and, under *Kolender*, whether identification is "credible and reliable." Why tolerate "expansive street-level discretion conferred on police" under the Fourth Amendment and impose limits on their discretion through vagueness doctrine? Debra Livingston, *Gang Loitering, the Court, and Some Realism about Police Patrol*, 1999 Sup. Ct. Rev. 141, 179–180.

6. *The limits of vagueness.* Vagueness doctrine also does not stop states and localities from giving police considerable discretion and authority, so long as they state criminal prohibitions more precisely. Although *Kolender* rejected as vague a statute allowing police to demand "credible and reliable" identification, a few years after *Morales*, the Court upheld a conviction under a different stop-and-identify statute that permitted officers to demand that suspects state their name. See Hiibel v. Sixth Judicial District Court of Nevada, 542 U.S. 177 (2004). Although Hiibel challenged his conviction on Fourth and Fifth Amendment grounds, the Court suggested that the statute would have survived a vagueness challenge because it was "narrower and more precise" than the one in *Kolender.* Courts have similarly upheld juvenile curfew ordinances that forbid minors from being in a public place unaccompanied by a parent from 11 p.m. to 6 a.m. during the week—which enable police to detain anyone who looks young at night—and traffic laws that almost everyone violates at some point. Moreover, cities can often avoid a vagueness challenge by adding an intent requirement to an ordinance.[2] If Chicago could have achieved much the same policing by saying something more specific or adding a few words to its ordinance, does that indicate that vagueness does not offer any real protection? Or to say it differently, should the Court resolve the apparent tension between *Morales,*

[2] For a twist on this, see *Screws v. United States*, 325 U.S. 91 (1945), which interpreted 18 U.S.C. §242, which is used to prosecute police officers for violating constitutional rights, to have a strong intent requirement to avoid finding it vague. This intent requirement has been a major obstacle in bringing federal criminal civil rights charges against police officers, so perhaps that suggests that intent requirements do constrain discretion. *Screws* is excerpted and discussed in detail in Chapter 14.

which derides discretion, and the various doctrines that otherwise permit discretion to flourish unchecked? How? Get rid of vagueness doctrine? Reconfigure other law to constrain discretion? Some other way?

2.   Race and Chicago's Gang Ordinance

One problem with discretion is that it facilitates discrimination. When a legislature leaves the terms of a criminal prohibition imprecise,

> poor people, nonconformists, dissenters, idlers—may be required to comport themselves according to the life style deemed appropriate by the . . . police. . . . Where . . . there are no standards governing the exercise of the discretion granted by the ordinance, the scheme permits and encourages an arbitrary and discriminatory enforcement of the law.

Papachristou v. City of Jacksonville, 405 U.S. 156, 170 (1972). Are you surprised there is not more talk in *Morales* about discrimination? Although concerns about racism often motivate vagueness challenges, and Chicago police issued its 89,000 orders under the ordinance disproportionately against African Americans, no party in *Morales* alleged racial discrimination. Still, *Morales* and the ordinance produced fierce debate among law professors (especially in the Chicago area) about race.

Dorothy Roberts argues that that broad order-maintenance ordinances like the gang ordinance in *Morales* entrench "the racialized division of Americans into the presumptively lawless whose liberties deserve little protection and the presumptively law-abiding who are entitled to rule over them." Dorothy E. Roberts, *Race, Vagueness, and the Social Meaning of Order-Maintenance*, 89 J. Crim. L. & Criminology 775, 779–780 (1999). They allow police to decide who is likely to commit a crime, and since officers often use race as a proxy for criminal propensity, "[u]pholding the Chicago ordinance would have legitimated the already prevalent practice of police harassment of Blacks on city streets. More ominously, it would have reinforced the view that Blacks are potential criminals for whom police surveillance and even arrest are mundane occurrences, not warranting constitutional concern." *Id.* at 780.

Others disagree. Randall Kennedy argues that "the principal injury suffered by African-Americans in relation to criminal matters is not overenforcement but underenforcement of the laws." *Race, Crime, and the Law* 19 (1997). Courts should therefore be cautious in striking down laws that facilitate policing. Even more so in this case, argue Tracey Meares and Daniel Kahan, because the Black community supported the ordinance, which responded to complaints about crime. See Tracey L. Meares & Dan M. Kahan, *The Wages of Antiquated Procedural Thinking: A Critique of* Chicago v. Morales, U. Chi. Legal F. 197, 205 (1998). They contend that with "the emergence of African American political power in the inner cities, it is no longer plausible to presume that all law enforcement policies adopted by local institutions are designed to oppress minority citizens." *Id.* at 209. When a community bears the freedom costs of the ordinance it passes, as the Black community did in Chicago, courts should allow ordinances that increase police power. In this view, *Morales* was wrongly decided because it made Black communities worse off. See *id.* at 209–210.

Lawrence Rosenthal also thinks *Morales* was wrongly decided, which is perhaps not surprising, as he represented Chicago in the litigation. To him, ordinances such as this one represent a reasonable choice for communities of color fighting crime because the main alternative is aggressive enforcement of drug laws that lead to long criminal sentences. Public order laws instead allow police to target the consequences of "gangs through relatively moderate police tactics" that are less likely to be abused. See Lawrence Rosenthal, *Gang Loitering and Race*, 91 J. Crim. L. & Criminology 99, 100, 105 (2000). Is that an argument for a deferential vagueness standard? Is it possible that an ordinance could give officers enough discretion that, although they are less heavy-handed in each encounter, they make it up in volume, imposing more harm overall? Should that risk invalidate a statute?

Albert Alschuler and Stephen Schulhofer respond that the Chicago gang ordinance was more controversial in the Black community than its advocates admit. The ordinance was emphatically opposed by both the local NAACP chapter and the *Chicago Defender*, the leading African-American newspaper, as well as by many Black politicians. See Albert W. Alschuler & Stephen J. Schulhofer, *Antiquated Procedures or Bedrock Rights? A Response to Professors Meares and Kahan*, U. Chi. Legal F. 215, 216 (1998). Even overwhelming support can hide divisions within "communities." Like all laws, this one was passed by adults, but it mostly affected troublemaking youths, who cannot vote and are often targeted by the police. See *id* at 242–243.

Dorothy Roberts pushes the point further: "Any claim of Black community consensus begs the questions, what defines the community?, who represents the community?, and how are residents' voices counted?" Dorothy E. Roberts, *Race, Vagueness, and the Social Meaning of Order-Maintenance*, 89 J. Crim. L. & Criminology 775, 823 (1999). According to Roberts,

> There is no secure means for determining Black citizens' opinions about aggressive policing, let alone a democratic process for implementing them. It is therefore highly presumptuous to claim that inner-city residents have voluntarily relinquished their civil liberties in exchange for safer streets.

Id. at 852. Does this problem suggest courts should not consider Black support for an ordinance in evaluating vagueness? Who should decide what constitutes a sufficient threat to social order to justify intervention? Or what trade-offs communities may make to maintain order? The "community"? The political process? The courts?

Maybe, if you are genuinely concerned about racial equality in policing to promote social order, fighting over vagueness and officer discretion is a distraction. As Nirej Sekhon points out, racial disparities in policing do not result only—or even primarily—from the individual officer choices with which vagueness doctrine is obsessed. See Nirej S. Sekhon, *Redistributive Policing*, 101 J. Crim. L. & Criminology 1171, 1210 (2013). Recall that the Chicago Police Department determined *where* the ordinance would be enforced. Only within those designated areas did individual discretion matter.

More generally, departmental decisions about allocating resources and setting enforcement priorities may matter more to the racial impact of an ordinance than individual officers' decisions about whether to enforce the ordinance within departmental constraints. Unfortunately, departmental decision making is often hidden and impossible to scrutinize. See *id.* at 1190. This was true in Chicago: The police department did not publicly disclose the designated enforcement areas, much less the department's process for determining those areas. And vagueness doctrine had nothing to say about *that*.

B. *Vagueness Applied: Policing Homelessness*

More than half a million people in the United States are homeless at any time. People experiencing homelessness often have little alternative but to use public spaces in ways to which others object: sleeping on benches, blocking sidewalks, erecting temporary dwellings, and urinating on the streets. Not surprisingly, angry residents often call the police about homeless people in parks and other public spaces. The consequence is an ongoing conflict about the appropriate use of public spaces that is frequently left to the police to resolve. Policing homelessness ends up being a substantial portion of what urban police departments do: In Portland, for example, *more than half of all arrests* in 2017 were carried out against people who were homeless, although they constituted less than 3 percent of the city's population. See Rebecca Woolington & Melissa Lewis, *Portland Homeless Accounted for Majority of Police Arrests in 2017, Analysis Finds,* Oregonlive.com (Jan. 30, 2019).

Police use a variety of tools to manage the conflict between calls for public order and the needs of vulnerable individuals. Departments often aggressively use state criminal statutes and local ordinances largely directed at homeless people, such as rules against panhandling, urinating in public, and sleeping in public parks. However, police can also creatively twist public order statutes designed for other purposes to target behavior that homeless people engage in. Compare the following two federal courts of appeals decisions applying vagueness doctrine to this kind of policing.

1. Los Angeles

DESERTRAIN v. CITY OF LOS ANGELES
754 F.3d 1147 (9th Cir. 2014)

PREGERSON, CIRCUIT JUDGE:

This 42 U.S.C. §1983 case concerns the constitutionality of Los Angeles Municipal Code Section 85.02, which prohibits use of a vehicle "as living quarters either overnight, day-by-day, or otherwise." Plaintiffs include four homeless individuals who parked their vehicles in the Venice area of Los Angeles and were cited and arrested for violating Section 85.02. Defendants are the City of Los Angeles and individual LAPD officers. Plaintiffs argue that Section 85.02 is unconstitutionally vague on its face because it provides insufficient notice of the conduct it penalizes and promotes arbitrary and discriminatory enforcement. We agree.

Factual Background

I. *Section 85.02 and the Venice Homelessness Task Force*

In 1983, the City of Los Angeles enacted Municipal Code Section 85.02:

USE OF STREETS AND PUBLIC PARKING LOTS FOR HABITATION.

No person shall use a vehicle parked or standing upon any City street, or upon any parking lot owned by the City of Los Angeles and under the control of the City of Los Angeles or under control of the Los Angeles County Department of Beaches and Harbors, as living quarters either overnight, day-by-day, or otherwise.

On September 23, 2010, Los Angeles officials held a "Town Hall on Homelessness" to address complaints of homeless individuals with vehicles living on local streets in Venice. Present at the meeting were a member of the City Council, the Chief of the LAPD, the Chief Deputy to the City Attorney, and the Assistant Director of the Los Angeles Bureau of Sanitation. City officials repeated throughout the meeting that their concern was not homelessness generally, but the illegal dumping of trash and human waste on city streets that was endangering public health. To address this concern, officials announced a renewed commitment to enforcing Section 85.02.

Within the week, the LAPD created the Venice Homelessness Task Force (the "Task Force"). The Task Force's twenty-one officers were to use Section 85.02 to cite and arrest homeless people using their automobiles as "living quarters," and were also to distribute to such people information concerning providers of shelter and other social services.

. . . Task Force officers received informal, verbal training, as well as internal policy memoranda, on how to enforce Section 85.02. Supervisors instructed officers to look for vehicles containing possessions normally found in a home, such as food, bedding, clothing, medicine, and basic necessities. According to those instructions, an individual need not be sleeping or have slept in the vehicle to violate Section 85.02. Supervisors directed officers to issue a warning and to provide information concerning local shelters on the first instance of a violation, to issue a citation on the second instance, and to make an arrest on the third.

II. Enforcement of Section 85.02

Beginning in late 2010, the Task Force began enforcing Section 85.02 against homeless individuals. Four such homeless individuals are Plaintiffs in this case. . . .

Los Angeles police officers making conversation with Leona Jackson, 64, during their patrol of Skid Row in 2006. Skid Row is a neighborhood in downtown Los Angeles that has been home to one of the country's densest homeless populations since the 1930s. Earlier the same day, the mayor and police chief announced an initiative intensifying policing of Skid Row, an initiative that led to thousands of citations and arrests in the tiny neighborhood.

Discussion. . . .

II. Section 85.02 is unconstitutionally vague. . . .

A statute fails under the Due Process Clause of the Fourteenth Amendment "if it is so vague and standardless that it leaves the public uncertain as to the conduct it prohibits. . . ." Giaccio v. Pennsylvania, 382 U.S. 399, 402 (1966). A statute is vague on its face when "no standard of conduct is specified at all. As a result, men of common intelligence must necessarily guess at its meaning." Coates v. City of Cincinnati, 402 U.S. 611, 614 (1971) (internal quotation marks omitted).

"Vagueness may invalidate a criminal law for either of two independent reasons. First, it may fail to provide the kind of notice that will enable ordinary people to understand what conduct it prohibits; second, it may authorize and even encourage arbitrary and discriminatory enforcement." City of Chicago v. Morales, 527 U.S. 41, 56 (1999). Section 85.02 fails under both standards.

A. Section 85.02 fails to provide adequate notice of the conduct it criminalizes. . . .

Section 85.02 offers no guidance as to what conduct it prohibits. . . . It states that no person shall use a vehicle "as living quarters either overnight, day-by-day, or otherwise." Yet the statute does not define "living quarters," or specify how long—or when—is "otherwise." We know that under Defendants' enforcement practices sleeping in a vehicle is not required to violate Section 85.02, . . . nor is keeping a plethora of belongings required. . . . But there is no way to know what is required to violate Section 85.02.

Instead, Plaintiffs are left guessing as to what behavior would subject them to citation and arrest by an officer. Is it impermissible to eat food in a vehicle? Is it illegal to keep a sleeping bag? Canned food? Books? What about speaking on a cell phone? Or staying in the car to get out of the rain? These are all actions Plaintiffs were taking when arrested for violation of the ordinance, all of which are otherwise perfectly legal. And despite Plaintiffs' repeated attempts to comply with Section 85.02, there appears to be nothing they can do to avoid violating the statute short of discarding all of their possessions or their vehicles, or leaving Los Angeles entirely. All in all, this broad and cryptic statute criminalizes innocent behavior, making it impossible for citizens to know how to keep their conduct within the pale.

In this respect, Section 85.02 presents the same vagueness concerns as the anti-loitering ordinance held unconstitutional in *Morales*, 527 U.S. 41. . . .

Because Section 85.02 fails to draw a clear line between innocent and criminal conduct, it is void for vagueness.

B. Section 85.02 promotes arbitrary enforcement that targets the homeless.

A statute is also unconstitutionally vague if it encourages arbitrary or discriminatory enforcement. See Papachristou v. City of Jacksonville, 405 U.S. 156, 162 (1972). If a statute provides "no standards governing the exercise of . . . discretion," it becomes "a convenient tool for harsh and discriminatory enforcement by local prosecuting officials, against particular groups deemed to merit their displeasure." *Id.* at 170.

Arbitrary and discriminatory enforcement is exactly what has occurred here. As noted, Section 85.02 is broad enough to cover any driver in Los Angeles who eats food or transports personal belongings in his or her vehicle. Yet it appears to be applied only to the homeless. The vagueness doctrine is designed specifically to prevent this type of selective enforcement, in which a "'net [can] be cast at large, to enable men to be caught who are vaguely undesirable in the eyes of the police and prosecution, although not chargeable in any particular offense.'" *Id.* at 166. . . .

Section 85.02 raises the same concerns of discriminatory enforcement as the ordinance in *Papachristou*, 405 U.S. 156. There, the Supreme Court held that a city ordinance prohibiting "vagrancy"—which was applied to "loitering," "prowling," and "nightwalking," among other conduct—was unconstitutionally vague. *Id.* at 158. The Court viewed the ordinance in its historical context as the descendant of English feudal poor laws designed to prevent the physical movement and economic ascension of the lower class. *Id.* at 161–162. In America, such laws had been used to "roundup . . . so-called undesireables," and resulted "in a regime in which the poor and the unpopular [we]re permitted to stand on a public sidewalk . . . only at the whim of any police officer." *Id.* at 170, 171. The Court concluded that "the rule of law implies equality and justice in its application. Vagrancy laws . . . teach that the scales of justice are so tipped that even-handed administration of the law is not possible. The rule of law, evenly applied to minorities as well as majorities, to the poor as well as the rich, is the great mucilage that holds society together." *Id.* at 171.

The City argues that its enforcement goals were motivated by legitimate health and safety concerns. It notes that some of the plaintiffs were arrested while in cars with garbage, pets, and their personal belongings, and that it was unsafe for plaintiffs to occupy their cars under these circumstances. We do not question the legitimacy of these public health and safety issues, but the record plainly shows that some of the conduct plaintiffs were engaged in when arrested—eating, talking on the phone, or escaping the rain in their vehicles—mimics the everyday conduct of many Los Angeles residents. The health and safety concerns cited by the City do not excuse the basic infirmity of the ordinance: It is so vague that it fails to give notice of the conduct it actually prohibits. As shown by the City's own documents, the different ways the ordinance was interpreted by members of the police department make it incompatible with the concept of an even-handed administration of the law to the poor and to the rich that is fundamental to a democratic society.

Defendants correctly note that they can bring clarity to an otherwise vague statute "through limiting constructions given . . . by the . . . enforcement agency." Hess v. Bd. of Parole & Post–Prison Supervision, 514 F.3d 909, 914 (9th Cir. 2008). Defendants point to their 2008 internal memorandum instructing officers making an arrest to first "establish one of the following— (i) overnight occupancy for more than one night or (ii) day-by-day occupancy of three or more days." This memo is irrelevant. First, Defendant Captain Peters, who heads the Task Force, admitted that he disfavored these instructions. . . . Second, even if Task Force officers had been given the 2008 memo, they did not follow it. Officers did not observe Plaintiffs in their vehicles overnight or for three consecutive days before arresting them.

In sum, Section 85.02 has paved the way for law enforcement to target the homeless and is therefore unconstitutionally vague.

Conclusion

Section 85.02 provides inadequate notice of the unlawful conduct it proscribes, and opens the door to discriminatory enforcement against the homeless and the poor. Accordingly, Section 85.02 violates the Due Process Clause of the Fourteenth Amendment as an unconstitutionally vague statute.

For many homeless persons, their automobile may be their last major possession—the means by which they can look for work and seek social services. The City of Los Angeles has many options at its disposal to alleviate the plight and suffering of its homeless citizens. Selectively preventing the homeless and the poor from using their vehicles for activities many other citizens also conduct in their cars should not be one of those options.

2. New York

BETANCOURT v. BLOOMBERG
448 F.3d 547 (2d Cir. 2006)

KEARSE, CIRCUIT JUDGE.

Plaintiff Augustine Betancourt appeals from so much of a judgment of the United States District Court for the Southern District of New York as dismissed his claims against defendants City of New York ("City"), its mayor, and its police commissioner, brought under 42 U.S.C. §1983, challenging Betancourt's arrest on a charge of violating City Administrative Code §16–122. Betancourt alleged that subsection (b) of that section, which, *inter alia*, prohibits leaving boxes and erecting obstructions in public spaces, is . . . as applied to him, unconstitutionally vague. . . . The district court, John S. Martin, Jr., then-*Judge*, granted defendants' motion for partial summary judgment dismissing th[at] claim[]. . . . [W]e affirm.

I. Background

This case arises out of the 1997 arrest of Betancourt and other homeless persons pursuant to a City program designed to improve the quality of life in the City's public spaces. . . .

A. *The Events*

In 1994, the City undertook a "Quality of Life" initiative designed to reduce a wide range of street crimes including prostitution, panhandling, and drug sales. Betancourt asserted that the initiative was thereafter expanded to, *inter alia*, reduce the number of homeless persons residing in public spaces. The City's Police Department issued a guide for law enforcement officers, listing laws that prohibited conduct targeted by the initiative. Those laws included City Administrative Code §16–122, subsection (b) of which states that

> [i]t shall be unlawful for any person, such person's agent or employee to leave, or to suffer or permit to be left, any box, barrel, bale of merchandise or other movable property whether or not owned by such person, upon any marginal or public street or any public place, or to erect or cause to be erected thereon any shed, building or other obstruction.

N.Y., N.Y., Admin. Code ("NYC Admin. Code") §16–122(b).

In the early morning hours of February 28, 1997, in or around certain parks in lower Manhattan, police officers arrested 25 individuals, including Betancourt. Betancourt had come to the park at approximately 10:30 p.m. on February 27 with some personal possessions, three folded cardboard boxes, and a loose piece of cardboard. He used the three boxes to construct a "tube" large enough to accommodate most of his body; he placed the tube on a park bench, climbed into the tube, covered the exposed part of his body with the loose piece of cardboard, and went to sleep. At approximately 1:00 a.m. on February 28, the police roused Betancourt from his sleep and arrested him. At approximately 5:00 a.m. on March 1, 1997, Betancourt was given a Desk Appearance Ticket, noting that he was charged with violating §16–122, and was released. By that time, the District Attorney's Office had signed a "*DECLINATION OF PROSECUTION*," stating that "*PROSECUTION OF TH[E] CASE* [against Betancourt] *WAS DECLINED* [because the case] Lack[ed] Prosecutorial Merit." . . .

II. Discussion

On appeal, Betancourt principally pursues his claim that §16–122(b) is unconstitutionally vague as applied to him. . . .

A. *The Vagueness Claim*

The Due Process Clause of the Fourteenth Amendment requires that laws be crafted with sufficient clarity to "give the person of ordinary intelligence a reasonable opportunity to know what is prohibited" and to "provide explicit standards for those who apply them." Grayned v. City of Rockford, 408 U.S. 104, 108 (1972). . . .

Regulations need not, however, achieve "meticulous specificity," which would come at the cost of "flexibility and reasonable breadth." *Id.* at 110 (internal quotation marks omitted). . . .

In the present case, §16–122(b) is a criminal statute, and thus is subject to more than a minimal level of scrutiny. But as applied in the present case it does not impinge on constitutionally protected rights. . . . Thus, only a moderately stringent vagueness test was required for a determination of whether §16–122(b) was impermissibly vague as applied to Betancourt.

. . . [T]he second §16–122(b) prohibition forbids a person to "erect [in any public place] . . . any shed, building or other obstruction," and those words have plain dictionary meanings that applied to the conduct of Betancourt. For example, *Webster's Third New International Dictionary* (1976) ("*Webster's Third*") gives one definition of the verb to "erect" as to "put up (as a building or machine) by the fitting together of materials or parts." *Id.* at 770. An ordinary person planning to fashion three boxes into a structure that was sufficiently large for a man to crawl into, and that was designed to give him shelter against the cold, would recognize that he was planning to "put up" something "by the fitting together of materials or parts." *Webster's Third* defines "obstruction" as "something that obstructs or impedes," and defines "obstruct" as to "block up." *Id.* at 1559. An ordinary person would understand that an agglomeration of boxes large enough for a man to fit into would be "something that obstructs or impedes."

Betancourt points out that sheds and buildings are structures that would normally be of some permanence. See, e.g., *Webster's Third* at 2090 (defining "shed" as "a slight structure (as a penthouse, lean-to, or partially open separate building) built primarily for shelter or storage"). . . . He argues that §16–122(b)'s final prohibition concerning "other obstruction[s]" should therefore be interpreted as limited to structures of permanence. We disagree.

An object plainly may "obstruct[] or impede[]" without doing so permanently. Had the lawmakers intended "obstruction" to mean a permanent edifice, they could have simply added that adjective before "obstruction." We think it clear that §16–122(b) was meant to forbid any obstruction, whether permanent or temporary.

In sum, as §16–122(b) forbids a person to "erect" an "obstruction" in a public place, we conclude that the district court properly ruled that that language was sufficient to alert Betancourt, and to provide adequate guidance to law enforcement agents, that Betancourt's conduct was prohibited. Accordingly, §16–122(b) is not unconstitutionally vague as applied to Betancourt. . . .

CALABRESI, CIRCUIT JUDGE, dissenting.

The twilight arrest of Augustine Betancourt, purportedly for "erect[ing] . . . an obstruction" in a public park, presents a textbook illustration of why vague criminal laws are repugnant to the Due Process Clause of the Fourteenth Amendment. It is, as a result, troubling to me that the majority goes to such lengths to find clarity and guidance in a city ordinance that provides little of either. Because I believe the law in question, as applied to Betancourt, is unconstitutionally vague, I respectfully dissent. . . .

The constitutional defects arise from the ambiguous text of the law at issue. On its face, Section 16–122(b) is a bizarre grab bag of loosely-related and imprecise proscriptions. . . . The majority opinion admits that most of [the law's] restrictions are inapplicable to Betancourt. Thus, the majority explicitly disavows the district court's conclusion that Betancourt's conduct was subject to Section 16–122(b)'s prohibition against leaving boxes or other movable property in a public place. Moreover, the majority does not at any point suggest that Betancourt erected a shed or a building. Left only with the language barring individuals from "erect[ing] . . . [some] other obstruction," the majority nonetheless insists that the law is not vague as applied to Betancourt, whose offending conduct was seemingly to lie down on a park bench encircled in a cardboard tube made of two boxes tucked into one another.

The first test for constitutional vagueness is whether "a penal statute define[s] the criminal offense with sufficient definiteness that ordinary people can understand what conduct is prohibited." Kolender v. Lawson, 461 U.S. 352, 357 (1983). As to this, I simply cannot see how one could divine . . . that sleeping on a park bench covered with cardboard is any more unlawful under the ordinance than doing so covered with blankets (which is plainly not illegal under the law at hand). Moreover, the specific words that the majority emphasizes—"to erect" and "obstruction"—do not, with or without the aid of published definitions from Webster's Third New International Dictionary, provide meaningful notice to the ordinary citizen of what is enjoined. Could anyone reasonably believe that "to erect" refers, as the majority would have it, to all acts of "fitting together of materials or parts"? Such a sweeping construction would encompass everything from stitching two blankets together to stuffing one winter jacket into another, or—for that matter—to lacing a silk scarf under the collar of a fur coat on an unusually cold winter day. And, if these activities do not fall within the meaning of "to erect," on what possible basis could a person know that putting one cardboard box into another would be unlawful?

Presumably the majority believes that it is only when one erects an "*obstruction*" that the prohibition of Section 16–122(b) is triggered. But Betancourt's cardboard tube placed on a park bench was no more of an obstruction than his prone body alone. Indeed, had he draped stitched blankets, stuffed jackets, or a warm fur coat over his body before laying down, would Betancourt thereby have created an obstruction? Hardly! . . .

The failure to give fair notice is only the first of the two reasons why Section 16–122(b) flunks the canonical test for constitutional vagueness. To satisfy due process, the legislature must also, in drafting a criminal law, "establish minimal guidelines to govern law enforcement." Smith v. Goguen, 415 U.S. 566, 574 (1974). The majority opinion essentially ignores this constitutional requirement in its analysis. . . . It is . . . well-settled that the second requirement is today the more important one. See *Kolender*, 461 U.S. at 357–358.

As a consequence, I believe that the majority leaves a crucial issue unanswered: what standards, if any, does Section 16–122(b) provide to guide law enforcement, prosecutors, judges, and juries in deciding what conduct violates a law that prohibits "erect[ing] . . . [an] obstruction"? . . .

Ironically, the only guidance on how Section 16–122(b) should be applied came from the New York Police Department itself: in 1994, the NYPD issued a catalog of "enforcement options" to effectuate then-Mayor Rudolph Giuliani's "Quality of Life" initiatives. This type of "guidance" is anything but comforting. The fact that a law against leaving boxes, barrels, and "other movable property" in a public place, on the one hand, and erecting a "shed, building or other obstruction," on the other, was listed, by the police department, as an "enforcement option" to target seemingly unrelated crimes like "prostitution, drug sales, and aggressive panhandling" is evidence of that very unfettered discretion that causes vague texts to give rise to constitutional problems. Cf. City of Chicago v. Morales, 527 U.S. 41, 63 (1999) (deciding that the police's "internal rules limiting . . . enforcement to certain designated areas" fails to rescue a vague ordinance against loitering). Deriving standards as to how a law should be applied not from the text of the ordinance, as drafted by the legislature, but instead from how the police department might use the law to achieve unrelated ends runs contrary to the main reason that vagueness doctrine insists on standards in the first place.

As written, Section 16–122(b) leaves the initial decision as to whether someone's actions constitute a crime not with our elected legislators, but with everyday police. Why doesn't the law apply to a woman who, having wrapped herself in a fur coat and silk scarf, regularly reclines on a park bench to feed the birds? Or to a passing sportsman who, while awaiting his tour bus, takes a nap after lashing together his ski boots, skis, and snowboard? Or to the midnight photographer who mounts his camera onto a tripod and waits patiently for the perfect picture? Or would it apply in these situations, but only if the city administrators or the police were averse to pigeons, snowboarding, or troublesome artists?

Section 16–122(b) is an impenetrable law that could be read to allow police officers to apply the ordinance almost however they want against virtually whomever
they choose. And on the night of February 27, 1997, that is precisely what they
did as part of the mayor's "Quality of Life" campaign against the homeless. But
let me be clear. This case is not about whether the homeless should be allowed to
sleep on park benches. Perhaps they should. Perhaps they should not. The issue
is whether the law that was used to prevent this homeless man from sleeping on a
park gave any guidance whatsoever. Because I, as a citizen, would not know what
I was prohibited from doing, and because I, as an officer of the law, would have
even less of an idea of what I was empowered to stop people from doing, I conclude that the ordinance is unconstitutionally vague. Accordingly, I respectfully
dissent.

NOTES AND QUESTIONS

1. *Aftermath of* Morales. Which ordinance is vaguer New York's or Los
Angeles's? Does the vagueness doctrine as described in *Morales* have predictable
results in these cases? Should these cases have come out the same way, or are the
enforcement efforts they describe meaningfully different? Explain.

2. *What is the problem?* Does something make you uncomfortable about the
police practices described in these cases? Can you articulate what that is? Does
vagueness doctrine capture it? What if officers conducted the same activities under
ordinances that were precise and crystal clear?

3. *Laws against homelessness.* After *Morales*, vagueness challenges sometimes
succeed against broadly framed loitering ordinances and drug exclusion zones,
including those used against homeless people. See, e.g., Johnson v. City of
Cincinnati, 310 F.3d 484 (6th Cir. 2002); NAACP Anne Arundel Country Branch
v. City of Annapolis, 133 F. Supp. 2d 795 (D. Md. 2001); see also Kim Strosnider,
Anti-Gang Ordinances After City of Chicago v. Morales*: The Intersection of Race,
Vagueness Doctrine, and Equal Protection in the Criminal Law*, 39 Am. Crim. L. Rev.
101, 127–143 (2002) (discussing post-*Morales* vagueness challenges). However,
vagueness doctrine does not stop cities from passing or using ordinances that
specifically criminalize activities that people who are homeless can little avoid.
Communities pass bans on camping, sitting, and lying in public; public urina-
tion; and public intoxication; and police use them to roust and arrest people
who are homeless, without much constitutional risk. Courts only sometimes
balk when such laws regulate activity protected by the First Amendment—think
limits on panhandling. Compare Gresham v. Peterson, 225 F.3d 899 (7th Cir.
2000) (upholding an Indianapolis ordinance prohibiting "*aggressive* panhandling"), with Clatterbuck v. City of Charlottesville, 708 F.3d 549 (4th Cir.
2013) (overturning Charlottesville's ban on *all* panhandling near a downtown
pedestrian mall). Does this use of specific ordinances suggest that Fourteenth
Amendment vagueness doctrine has succeeded as a means of constraining police
discretion? Or that it has failed? Why? What other issues do these local ordinances raise? For a rare consideration of issues raised by the proliferation of
local criminal laws, see Wayne A. Logan, *The Shadow Criminal Law of Municipal
Governance*, 62 Ohio St. L.J. 1409 (2001).

A park sign in Orlando, Florida.

4. *Why the Second and Ninth Circuits?* Perhaps it is no coincidence that these two cases arose in New York and California. More than 40 percent of homeless Americans live in these two states. New York City and Los Angeles alone account for nearly a quarter of the total. See U.S. Dept. of Housing and Urb. Dev., *The 2018 Annual Homeless Assessment Report to Congress* 14, 18 (2018). How might population concentration affect community concerns? Policing strategies? Judicial responses?

Tech Bros and Transients: Arbitrating the Use of Public Space

Big-city police departments get many calls complaining about the presence and conduct of people who are unhoused. Consider the dynamics at play in San Francisco. An influx of well-paid technology workers has increased competition for the city's limited housing stock, driving up prices. This gentrification pushes some out of housing. These people are not transient: They are often long-term residents of a community, and they do not intend to leave. Of course, gentrification also brings in new residents, who often have high expectations for order that are violated by people living on the street.

One San Francisco entrepreneur, Justin Keller, vocalized his concerns in an open letter to the city's mayor and police chief, complaining, "Every day . . . I see people sprawled across the sidewalk tent cities, human feces, and the faces of addiction." Keller argued, "The wealthy working people have earned their right to live in the city. . . . I shouldn't have to worry about being accosted. I shouldn't have to see the pain, struggle, and despair of homeless people to and from my way to work every day." Justin Keller, *Open Letter to SF Mayor Ed Lee and Greg Suhr (Police Chief)*, Justin Keller (blog) (Feb. 15, 2016).

It is easy to see why so many people attacked Keller as an insensitive, clueless "tech bro." But Keller was not the first or the last San Franciscan to express such views, and thousands liked his post on Facebook. What should cities do when Keller and his ilk call the police? Are armed police officers with the power to use force really the best way to arbitrate among the competing interests at stake? Can you imagine decriminalizing the activities that homeless people engage in, treating people without housing with respect, and still addressing community concerns? What role should police play in such efforts?

3. Civil Policing Strategies

Morales, Desertrain, and *Betancourt* all consider the vagueness of *criminal* ordinances. Increasingly, law enforcement also leverages *civil* legal tools to manage community spaces. These strategies often pass constitutional muster, but occasionally, the power of these civil tools is so expansive that courts intervene on vagueness or other due process grounds.

For example, until 2019, police officers in Virginia could ask a prosecutor to obtain, in absentia, a civil interdiction order against a person for being a "habitual drunkard." Since Virginia made it a crime for people subject to such an order to possess or attempt to possess alcohol, police used the orders to justify arresting and prosecuting those people for having alcohol or being drunk in public. Some interdicted individuals, especially those who suffered from alcoholism and homelessness, were arrested and prosecuted 25 or 30 times for violating these civil orders. In *Manning v. Caldwell*, 930 F.3d 264 (4th Cir. 2019) (en banc), the Fourth Circuit struck down the "habitual drunkard" statute as vague, noting that the term had no definition in the statute. The majority and dissent split on lines similar to the justices in *Morales*: Judge Wilkinson in dissent argued that Virginia's interdiction framework was simply a civil means of providing notice to individuals about acts that could trigger criminal sanction. See *id*. at 287. The majority countered, "[P]ersons informed that they can no longer possess alcohol because they are an 'habitual drunkard' are not thereby put on notice about what conduct led to that adjudication in the first place." *Id*. at 274.

Somewhat analogously, in St. Petersburg, Florida, a local trespass ordinance allowed officers who discovered someone violating any ordinance or law on public property to issue an exclusionary trespass warning. Someone who received a warning was barred from that space, which meant that, if the police found the person there, they could arrest him, even though he was not violating any law (other than the exclusion). Police used this power to issue warnings to people who were homeless, prohibiting them from continuing to use public parks or rights-of-way and then arrested them, in effect for having nowhere else to go. The Eleventh Circuit ruled that such warnings violated the Fourteenth Amendment by allowing the police to issue instantaneous injunctions against otherwise lawful behavior without due process. See Catron v. City of St. Petersburg, 658 F.3d 1260, 1269 (11th Cir. 2011).

Although both of these schemes were barred by courts, order maintenance policing strategies that leverage civil tools are often more successful, including those that target gangs instead of homelessness. In California and several other states, police departments work with city attorneys to seek a *gang injunction*, a civil restraining order against a group that restricts its members from engaging in specified activities in a limited geographic area. These injunctions issue after a court finds that the gang's activities constitute a public nuisance—that is, a substantial and unreasonable interference with the public's right to safety and peace. Although early gang injunctions were limited in geographic scope, in the number of individuals affected, and in the activities prohibited, courts now routinely impose gang injunctions that reach broadly, include unnamed gang members, and prohibit activities from wearing gang colors to possessing markers that could be used to make graffiti. For cases upholding injunctions, see, e.g., People *ex rel.* Totten v. Colonia Chiques, 67 Cal. Rptr. 3d 70 (Cal. Ct. App. 2007); People v. Englebrecht, 106 Cal. Rptr. 2d 738 (Cal. Ct. App. 2001). Occasionally, courts reject specific gang injunctions. See Vasquez v. Rackauckas, 734 F.3d 1025 (9th Cir. 2013) (inadequate procedures for membership in gang); Youth Justice Coalition v. City of Los Angeles, 264 F. Supp. 3d 1057 (C.D. Cal. 2017) (inadequate notice); Weber County v. Ogden Trece, 321 P.3d 1067 (Utah 2013) (inadequate notice). But more survive scrutiny. What distinguishes gang injunctions from the Chicago ordinance? From the civil tools used in Virginia and St. Petersburg? Does one of these approaches to empowering the police seem more troubling than the other?

Police departments also partner with private actors to fight disorder. For example, a department facing a rash of intoxicated youth might pressure bars to police underage drinking or face liquor license revocation; or a department receiving calls about open drug dealing might press an apartment complex landlord to evict problem tenants or be subject to citations for maintaining a nuisance. Strategies in which the police persuade (or coerce) a nonoffending private party (such as a regulator, property owner, business, or school) to mitigate an order problem are often called *third-party policing*. Such schemes have largely been upheld by courts. In *Virginia v.*

Hicks, 539 U.S. 113 (2003), for example, the Supreme Court upheld against a First Amendment challenge a policy in which the Richmond Redevelopment and Housing Authority authorized the police to serve notice on people who lacked a legitimate reason for being on the premises and to arrest for trespassing any person who remained or returned. Although many third parties are happy to cooperate, others do so only because of the threat of civil fines, license revocations, property forfeiture, and injunctions. Might vagueness doctrine push police departments to look to civil and third-party alternatives? Should the Supreme Court consider the intrusiveness of and lack of regulation for likely alternatives when it evaluates an ordinance for vagueness?

Not all cities take an aggressive approach to the problem of homelessness. Increasingly, some policing leaders are promoting outreach and service provision in place of aggressive policing strategies. See Police Exec. Research Forum, *The Police Response to Homelessness* (2018). Some departments view people experiencing homelessness as members of the community who need compassion, service, and protection from crime and violence, rather than harassment and arrests. In 2019, the Fort Lauderdale Police Department adopted a policy intended "to ensure that personnel are sensitive to the needs and rights of the homeless population . . . and reaffirm that being homeless is not a crime." Fort Lauderdale Police Dept., *Policy 511.0: Homeless Persons* 1 (2019). The policy further states that Fort Lauderdale Police Department personnel should "provide appropriate law enforcement services to the entire community while protecting the rights, dignity and personal property of the homeless." *Id.* It instructs officers:

a. If a police officer observes a homeless person(s) engaged in criminal activity, when practical and prudent to do so, an alternative to a physical arrest shall be used. . . .
b. When encountering a homeless person who has committed a misdemeanor law violation and the continued freedom of the individual would not result in a breach of the peace or a more serious crime, police officers are encouraged to offer services when available in lieu of physical arrest. It must be recognized that such a referral is contingent on the voluntary agreement of the homeless person to accept such referral.

Id. at 3. Given the harms of arrests, what might encourage more departments to take less intrusive approaches? In thinking about appropriate services, some departments recognize that homelessness is not merely a lack of housing. For example, some estimates suggest that up to 40 percent of homeless youths identify as LGTBQ, often homeless because they have been discriminated against or rejected by their families. How can departments address this kind of intersectional concern? Alternatively, can you imagine a world in which police were out of the business of policing homelessness altogether? What would it take for communities to get there? What should we do in the meantime?

Homelessness is only one challenge for policing and public order. Community residents often demand that police address teenagers hanging out on a street corner, prostitutes soliciting customers curbside, men drinking beer in front of a liquor store, and political dissidents occupying a public park. Should police respond to these calls? What tools should they use? How should courts assess police interventions? How much will vagueness law help?

C.   *Beyond Vagueness: Agency Policies and Rulemaking*

As the above cases illustrate, cities look for ways to empower police and give them flexibility to manage problems when informal social controls and community standards fail. But giving police discretion creates problems because the use of that discretion cannot itself be effectively policed by courts. Debra Livingston argues, "Courts have little capacity—very little capacity—to constrain police and to control the discretion that they inevitably exercise on streets, in neighborhoods, . . . and in the administrative offices in which police enforcement policies are hammered out." Debra Livingston, *Police Discretion and the Quality of Life in Public Places: Courts, Communities, and the New Policing*, 97 Colum. L. Rev. 551, 671 (1997). If courts cannot solve the problem, how else might we avoid arbitrary and discriminatory exercises of police discretion?

One traditional approach is through agency policies and rules. Almost all law enforcement agencies have some formal written rules governing officer conduct, collected in a manual for officers. These pronouncements—which are variously labeled policies, rules, directives, standard operating procedures, or general orders—provide a means for higher-ups to communicate and enforce expectations about what officers should do.

Policies or Rules?

In discussions of policing and in state laws, terms like "policy," "directive," and "order" are often treated as interchangeable, and this book treats them the same. But distinctions can be made. Here is one taxonomy that differentiates the different forms of internal standards:

> A *policy* is not a statement of what must be done in a particular situation but it is a statement of guiding principles that must be followed in activities that fall within either specific organizational objectives or the overall police mission. A policy is a guide to thinking.

> A *procedure* is the method of performing a task or a manner of proceeding on a course of action. It differs from policy in that it specifies action in a particular situation to perform a task within the guidelines of policy. A procedure is a guide to action.

> A *rule* is a managerial mandate that either requires or prohibits specified behavior. A rule is a mandate to action. These various control mechanisms are designed to address a multitude of needs, including the need for regulation and uniformity of police activities.

Geoffrey P. Alpert & William C. Smith, *Developing Police Policy: An Evaluation of the Control Principle*, 13 Am. J. Police 1, 3-4 (1994).

According to these authors, policies guide and limit discretion, whereas rules can significantly reduce or eliminate it.

Police policies are not like other legal rules that constrain officer conduct. Internal departmental rules do not provide private rights of action for members of the public, and they are usually unenforceable in court. Still, police policies give officers normative guidance that has significant sway over officers. Policies also set employment expectations. Departments train and supervise officers to follow them, and when officers violate the rules, departments may impose administrative discipline, such as a verbal warning, a written reprimand, suspension without pay, a demotion, or termination.

1.   Calls for Rulemaking

Police departments have long had at least some policies. Three developments in the 1960s and early 1970s stirred new interest in departmental policies as a means to constrain discretion and guide officer conduct.

First, new research, most prominently by the American Bar Foundation, revealed clearly for the first time just how much discretion police officers have in applying criminal law. See Samuel Walker, *Origins of the Contemporary Criminal Justice Paradigm: The American Bar Foundation Survey, 1953–1969*, 9 Just. Q. 47 (1992).

Second, although the Warren Court dramatically expanded the judiciary's supervision of policing practices, the Court's decisions, especially in *Terry v. Ohio*, 392 U.S. 1 (1968), also demonstrated some of the limits of governing police conduct through constitutional doctrine.

Third, the rise of the administrative state, with new federal administrative agencies, illustrated the value of *rulemaking* (as a process) for implementing and interpreting law and the value of *rules* (as the result of that process) as a means for guiding enforcement discretion.

These trends led to a strong call for departmental policies in *The Challenge of Crime in a Free Society*, the 1967 report of President Lyndon B. Johnson's Commission on Law Enforcement and the Administration of Justice. A few years later, the American Bar Association echoed the Johnson Commission and emphasized rulemaking as the way to produce such rules:

> Police discretion can best be structured and controlled through the process of administrative rule making by police agencies. Police administrators should, therefore give the highest priority to the formulation of administrative rules governing the exercise of discretion, particularly in the areas of selective enforcement, investigative techniques, and enforcement methods.

Am. Bar Assn., *Standards Relating to the Urban Police Function* 4.3 (1973).

Perhaps no one is more closely associated with this call than administrative law pioneer Kenneth Culp Davis, whose books *Discretionary Justice* (1969) and *Police Discretion* (1975) applied insights from his administrative law scholarship to criminal justice and advocated rulemaking for police departments. Nevertheless, the classic account in favor of rules and rulemaking to guide police conduct comes from Anthony Amsterdam in his renowned 1974 article, *Perspectives on the Fourth*

Amendment. Amsterdam argued that departmental rules, produced by rulemaking procedures, could improve police performance in four main ways.[3]

> *One. Rulemaking enhances the quality of police decisions.* Vital police policy decisions are now too often left to be made by the individual officer, who usually lacks the expertise, training, resources, time for reflection, and sometimes the dispassion, to do the job properly. Recognizing the police policymaking function and systematizing it in a rulemaking procedure would assure better police decisions in matters of policy than are now possible. . . .
>
> *Two. Rulemaking tends to ensure the fair and equal treatment of citizens.* When unconfined decisionmaking power is placed in the hands of each individual police officer, it is inconceivable that all officers will respond similarly to similar situations. . . .
>
> *Three. Rulemaking increases the visibility of police policy decisions.* Decisionmaking that is diffuse is also thereby invisible; and those who make invisible decisions cannot be held properly accountable for them. When every officer of a department is left to make his own policies, no one in the command structure of the department—and no one in the community which the department serves—knows how the laws are being administered in fact. Bad practices cannot be identified; good practices cannot be instituted; the entire system remains necessarily unresponsive and irresponsible. . . .
>
> *Four. Rulemaking offers the best hope we have for getting policemen consistently to obey and enforce constitutional norms that guarantee the liberty of the citizen.* In particular, the promulgation of police-made rules embodying and conforming to the fourth amendment's guarantees against unreasonable searches and seizures would reinforce those guarantees. . . .

Anthony G. Amsterdam, *Perspectives on the Fourth Amendment*, 58 Minn. L. Rev 349, 423–428 (1973). Can you think of any other way rules might help improve policing?

2.   State Law Requiring Policies

If departmental policies can help constrain discretion, should states require them? Statutes and administrative regulations often demand that police departments adopt policies governing officer conduct in critical areas, such as the use of a surveillance technology or the use of force. Occasionally, states try to be more comprehensive. Here is one example.

ME. STAT. TIT. 25 §2803-B

1. Law enforcement policies. All law enforcement agencies shall adopt written policies regarding procedures to deal with the following:

> **A.** Use of physical force, including the use of electronic weapons and less-than-lethal munitions;
>
> **B.** Barricaded persons and hostage situations; . . .

---

[3] *Ed. note:* Amsterdam's argument is more insightful than it is perspicuous. His four main points are labeled with cardinal numbers (one, two, three, and four). Each of these points has subparts labeled with ordinal numbers (first, second, third, and fourth). Although these labels have been retained from the original, many of the subparts have been removed.

D. Domestic violence, . . .

E. Hate or bias crimes . . . ;

F. Police pursuits;

G. Citizen complaints of police misconduct;

H. Criminal conduct engaged in by law enforcement officers;

I. Death investigations . . . ;

J. Public notification regarding persons in the community required to register [as sex offenders];

K. Digital, electronic, audio, video or other recording of law enforcement interviews of suspects in serious crimes and the preservation of investigative notes and records in such cases;

L. Mental illness and the process for involuntary commitment; and

M. Freedom of access requests. The chief administrative officer of a municipal, county or state law enforcement agency shall certify to the board annually that the agency has adopted a written policy regarding procedures to deal with a freedom of access request and that the chief administrative officer has designated a person who is trained to respond to a request received by the agency. . . .

The chief administrative officer of each agency shall certify to the board [of Trustees for the Maine Criminal Justice Academy] that attempts were made to obtain public comment during the formulation of policies.

2. Minimum policy standards. The board shall establish minimum standards for each law enforcement policy pursuant to subsection 1 with the exception of the freedom of access policy under subsection 1, paragraph M. . . .

3. Agency compliance. The chief administrative officer of each law enforcement agency shall certify to the board annually no later than January 1st of each year that the agency has adopted written policies consistent with the minimum standards established or amended by the board and that all officers have received orientation and training with respect to new mandatory policies or new mandatory policy changes pursuant to subsection 2. New mandatory policies enacted by law must be implemented by all law enforcement agencies no later than the July 1st after the board has adopted the minimum standards.

Is this kind of statute likely to do the trick? Is this the right list of subjects for state law to insist on? Like most statutes that call for policies, this one demands them on particular subjects. What does it say about the process for developing them? About their content? Is there some risk this kind of statute could backfire? After all, a vague, poorly conceived, overly elaborate, or underenforced rule might be worse than no rule at all. How could statutes encourage departments to make policies that are good and effective?

3. How Policies and the Law Interact

a. Law Spurs Policy

Often statutes that mandate departmental policies are narrower than Maine's. For example, a state might require agencies to formulate a policy before adopting a new technology. See, e.g., Cal. Civ. Code §1798.90.51 (requiring a policy before using automated license plate readers) (excerpted in Chapter 2). Or a state might require agencies to adopt a policy to guide a common policing activity that often goes awry. See, e.g., Wis. Stat. §175.50 (requiring agencies to adopt policies on eyewitness identifications) (excerpted in Chapter 3).

Congress has sometimes used grant programs to incentivize police policymaking. For example, one of the largest discretionary grant programs pursuant to the Violence Against Women Act, Pub. L. No. 103-322, tit. IV, 108 Stat. 1902 (1994), offers funding to agencies to improve responses to domestic violence, but only if the agencies first adopt policies favoring arrests for those suspected of domestic violence crimes. See 34 U.S.C. §§10461–10464 (excerpted in Chapter 11).

Less often, courts encourage policymaking. For example, in *Colorado v. Bertine*, 479 U.S. 367, 374 (1987), the Supreme Court upheld as consistent with the Fourth Amendment an inventory search of an impounded car because the search was carried out in accordance with "reasonable police regulations . . . administered in good faith." Effectively, *Bertine* encourages departments to adopt policies governing inventory searches, and departments have complied. Encouraging policymaking, however, is only one way that laws can interact with police policies.

b.   Policies Operationalize the Law

Most police officers do not read the wide variety of federal and state court decisions that might affect what they may do. Nor do officers track every legislative change that affects policing. Instead, police departments use policies to translate the law into a language officers understand and can keep track of. Policies also provide officers an additional incentive to follow the law, the threat of discipline, an important additive given how uncertain and delayed legal remedies are.

c.   Policies Influence the Content of Law

Courts often look to police policies in determining whether new legal rules are likely to produce positive results. In *Miranda v. Arizona*, 384 U.S. 436, 483–491 (1966), for example, the Court invoked Federal Bureau of Investigation practices, embedded in their policies, to defend its new warnings and waiver system as realistic for local law enforcement. In *Tennessee v. Garner*, 471 U.S. 1 (1985), the Court pointed to local agency policies that overwhelmingly restricted force more than the common law rule in defending its interpretation of the Fourth Amendment:

> In light of the rules adopted by those who must actually administer them, the older and fading common law view is a dubious indicium of the constitutionality of the Tennessee statute now before us.
>
> Actual departmental policies are important for an additional reason. We would hesitate to declare a police practice of long standing "unreasonable" if doing so would severely hamper effective law enforcement. But the indications are to the contrary. There has been no suggestion that crime has worsened in any way in jurisdictions that have adopted, by legislation or departmental policy, rules similar to that announced today.

Id. at 19.

Policies also influence the way the law is interpreted in individual cases. For instance, judges and juries sometimes consider whether an officer complied with departmental policies in determining whether his actions were reasonable in a specific case, although, notably, violating a departmental policy does not mean that an officer also has violated the law.

d. Policies Manage Legal Risks

Under limited circumstances, departmental policies that cause constitutional violations can generate civil liability for municipalities under 42 U.S.C. §1983. See City of Canton v. Harris, 489 U.S. 378 (1989); Monell v. Dept. of Soc. Servs., 436 U.S. 658 (1987) (discussed further in Chapter 13). Local governments can mitigate that liability by adopting and implementing legally adequate policies. As a result, police departments often maintain policies for high-litigation-risk activities, such as using force, pursuing suspects, conducting searches and arrests, and handling domestic violence incidents.

Can you think of other ways laws and policies might interact?

4. How Policies Are Made

Those who called for strengthening departmental policies in the 1960s and 1970s often advocated not just *policymaking*, but *rulemaking*, the way administrative agencies make rules. In the intervening decades, commentators have focused less on the process by which policies are made and more on having well-developed policies. And, indeed, contemporary policymaking in police departments looks nothing like administrative rulemaking.

In a midsize department, a chief might instruct an officer to act as policy-manual coordinator (on top of the officer's other responsibilities). That officer might then convene a committee of officers to gather ideas from model policies and other departments and to draft revised policies. Any new policy must harmonize with federal and state constitutional law (as interpreted by the courts); federal and state statutes (also as interpreted); local ordinances; federal and state labor and employment law; collective bargaining agreements or employee contracts; any federal consent decrees entered by the department; intergovernmental agreements; and standards imposed by accreditation agencies. Once written, proposed rules often need little more than sign-off from the chief and the city's legal counsel before they are implemented.

Over the past several years, some scholars, sometimes called "the new administrativists" have renewed calls for rulemaking (rather than simple policymaking) in law enforcement. See Andrew Manuel Crespo, *Systemic Facts: Toward Institutional Awareness in Criminal Courts*, 129 Harv. L. Rev. 2049, 2059 (2016) (bestowing the moniker "new administrativists"). These scholars advocate refining departmental guidance to officers in ways analogous to the way administrative agencies act.

Chris Slobogin is one self-proclaimed member of this club. He argues that "administrative law principles can help ensure that police practices are authorized, rationalized, and transparent, even if the Fourth Amendment has little or nothing to say about them." See Christopher Slobogin, *Policing as Administration*, 165 U. Pa. L. Rev. 91, 118 (2016). Slobogin is most interested in applying rulemaking to police activities that choose targets without individualized suspicion, such as drunk-driving checkpoints, camera surveillance systems, drug testing programs, and DNA collection schemes. He argues these *panvasive* activities look more like what administrative agencies do than the stuff of traditional order maintenance policing, and they should be governed accordingly. See Christopher Slobogin, *Panvasive Surveillance, Political Process Theory, and the Nondelegation Doctrine,* 102 Geo. L.J. 1721, 1771 (2014). This would mean subjecting them to something like notice-and-comment rulemaking and judicial review. Others similarly and more broadly advocate administrative rulemaking (or something like it) to cabin police discretion. See, e.g., Barry Friedman & Maria Ponomarenko, *Democratic Policing,* 90 N.Y.U. L. Rev. 1827, 1832–1835 (2015).

Unlike the calls for rulemaking in the 1970s, which focused on making policing fairer and more rational, new administrativists often seek to make policing more *democratic.* See David A. Sklansky, *Police and Democracy,* 103 Mich. L. Rev. 1699, 1781–1805 (2005). Specifically, they advocate community participation in developing police policies:

> Policing spreads a variety of important social resources across communities, as well as imposing certain burdens of the prevention or investigation of crime. Quite often, it is the police themselves who determine how to apportion those benefits and burdens. They do so by making policy, just as any other administrative agency concerned with resource-allocation might.
>
> Unlike those other agencies, however, police rulemaking is most often not open to public input. Evidence suggests that the police regard themselves as experts in defining both the nature of crime problems and the best means of addressing those problems. Their claim to expertise renders the police particularly prone to make and enforce policing policy free from public interference. The resulting policy is often based solely on their own internal assessment of the appropriate goals and values to pursue, independent of the interests of the community they police. Departmental policy-makers thus remain remote from the community, looking inwards rather than outwards to determine the proposed policy's social and criminological impact. Given this feature of police policy-making, community members lack the ability to participate in—and especially, to challenge—police policy at the front-end during the equivalent of the drafting and comment process.

Eric J. Miller, *Challenging Police Discretion,* 58 How. L.J. 521, 525 (2015).

Scholars have proposed a range of ways to solicit public input, including notice-and-comment opportunities, civilian oversight bodies, and public hearings, to improve the rules governing the police and subject them to democratic norms. See, e.g., Barry Friedman & Maria Ponomarenko, *Democratic Policing,* 90 N.Y.U. L. Rev. 1827, 1886–1887 (2015); Kami Chavis Simmons, *New Governance and the "New Paradigm" of Police Accountability: A Democratic Approach to Police Reform,* 59 Cath. U. L. Rev. 373, 379 (2010); Erik Luna, *Principled Enforcement of Penal Codes,* 4 Buff. Crim. L. Rev. 515, 594–608 (2000).

Community input sounds good, but bringing the public into police policy formation turns out to be complicated:

> [T]here are serious reasons to doubt whether rulemaking—either along the lines of the federal model, or some of the proposed alternatives—is in fact a viable strategy for governing the police. . . . Elsewhere in government, notice-and-comment rulemaking is used primarily to ensure that agencies regulate *us* sensibly. Agencies like the Environmental Protection Agency (or the local board of public health) rely on rules to tell the public what to do. . . . The Administrative procedure Act's

(APA's) notice-and-comment requirements, in turn, require that agencies get public input before these sorts of outward facing (or "legislative") rules go into effect.

Policing agencies do not—and may not—use rules in the same way. . . . When scholars argue in favor of police rulemaking, the sorts of rules they have in mind are rules that tell officers what they can and cannot do in enforcing the law. They are, in short, rules that policing agencies use to regulate *themselves*.

. . . [T]he difference . . . has several implications for the viability of APA-style rulemaking in the policing space. First, policing agencies have far fewer incentives than do traditional administrative agencies to adopt rules. And without rules, there is nothing on which the public can comment. . . . It also is much harder in the policing context to specify when policing agencies would need to obtain public input on the rules they do in fact have. Finally, because police rules regulate internal systems—the workings of which commonly are hidden from public view—it often is more difficult for members of the public to provide input on the substance of those rules.

Maria Ponomarenko, *Rethinking Police Rulemaking*, 114 Nw. U. L. Rev. 1, 5–6 (2019); see also Ronald Allen, *Police and Substantive Rulemaking: Reconciling Principle and Expediency*, 125 U. Pa. L. Rev. 62, 97 (1976) (arguing that "the police perform a very different function from that of a regulatory agency").

Beyond the challenge of getting good public input, public participation in police policymaking encourages departments to develop policies for *public* consumption. That could leave rules that look good on the books but are difficult to administer or do not effectively guide the decisions officers frequently make. Yet without public input, policies that shape police conduct might not take adequate account of the harms of police practices or community preferences about the inevitable trade-offs departments make.

So, should we make policing more *democratic*, such that it better enhances communal self-expression, or more *bureaucratic*, leveraging technical expertise and promoting formal rule compliance? This is a long-standing criminal justice debate. Although the democratizers—focused on increasing public input in policing—have captured public and academic imagination over the past decade, see, e.g., Joshua Kleinfeld et al., *White Paper of Democratic Criminal Justice*, 111 Nw. U. L. Rev. 1693 (2017), bureaucratizers are fighting back, see, e.g., John Rappaport, *Some Doubts About "Democratizing" Criminal Justice*, 87 U. Chi. L. Rev. 711 (2020). Given the disanalogy between archetypal administrative agencies and police departments, how should we think about rules and rulemaking in policing?

Whatever the ideal answer, in most jurisdictions, departmental policies continue to serve primarily as a tool for managing officers rather than democratizing policing, and public input into policing policies is limited. In fact, many agencies have turned hard in the opposite direction: Because many departments lack the capacity to formulate rules well, and because the law changes (sometimes rapidly), departments now frequently buy policies either from nonprofits, such as the International Association of Chiefs of Police, or private companies, such as Lexipol. What do you imagine the advantages and disadvantages of this practice are? How responsive to community preferences and conditions are those rules likely to be? What is the alternative for a small department with limited resources at legal risk if it fails to maintain adequate policies? For a discussion of private rulemaking in police departments, see Ingrid V. Eagly & Joanna C. Schwartz, *Lexipol: The Privatization of Police Policymaking*, 96 Tex. L. Rev. 891 (2018).

5.   Do Policies Guide Discretion?

Do all of these policies actually influence officer conduct? Research is limited, but it seems that departmental rules do affect officer behavior, at least with respect to the use of force. Studies in the 1970s and 1980s found that adopting restrictive deadly force guidelines dramatically reduced police shootings. See, e.g., James J. Fyfe, *Blind Justice: Police Shootings in Memphis*, 73 J. Crim. L. & Criminology 707 (1982); James J. Fyfe, *Administrative Interventions on Police Shooting Discretion: An Empirical Examination*, 7 J. Crim. Justice 309 (1979). More recently, researchers looking at policies on the use of conducted energy devices, including Tasers, have found that officer use of the devices seems to reflect differences in policies. See, e.g., William Terrill & Eugene A. Paoline, *Police Use of Less Lethal Force: Does Administrative Policy Matter?*, 34 Just. Q. 193 (2017) (finding that officers working under restrictive use-of-force policies used less-lethal force less readily than other officers); Frank V. Ferdik et al., *The Influence of Agency Policies on Conducted Energy Device Use and Police Use of Lethal Force*, 17 Police Q. 328 (2014) (finding permissive policies associated with increased usage of conducted energy devices and fewer fatal shootings).

Clearly, those studies are good news for those looking to change the use of force by the police, but there are several reasons to be cautious about drawing conclusions for constraining discretion in order maintenance policing.

First, good rules are hard to write. A good departmental policy would facilitate effective, fair, and minimally harmful policing based on available social science evidence, industry best practices, and community and agency conditions and culture. It would reflect the law, incorporate public input, and earn officer support. As hard as it is to draft such rules on force, it might be harder still to craft good rules that tell officers when they should conduct stops or how to address complaints over aggressive panhandling.

Second, even if policies work, departments might not make policies about some of the activities you care about. President Johnson's Crime Commission complained in 1967 that

> [m]any police departments have published "general order" or "duty" or "rules, regulations, and procedures" manuals running to several hundred pages. They deal extensively, and quite properly, with the personal conduct of officers on and off duty, with uniform and firearms regulations, with the use of departmental property, with court appearances by officers, with the correct techniques of approaching a building in which a burglary may be in progress. They instruct an officer about taking a suspect into custody and transporting him to the station, or about dealing with sick or injured persons, or about handling stray dogs, or about cooperating with the fire department, or about towing away abandoned automobiles—with, in short, dozens of situations in which policemen commonly, or uncommonly, find themselves. What such manuals almost never discuss are the hard choices policemen must make every day: whether or not to break up a sidewalk gathering, whether or not to intervene in a domestic dispute, whether or not to silence a street-corner speaker, whether or not to stop and frisk, whether or not to arrest. Yet these decisions are the heart of police work. How they are made determines to a large degree the safety of the community, the attitude of the public toward the police and the substance of court rulings on police procedures.

President's Commn. on Law Enforcement & the Admin. of Justice, *The Challenge of Crime in a Free Society* 103 (1967). Since then, changes in the interpretation of §1983 have increased litigation risk for agencies. As a result, almost all agencies have policies in areas that pose the greatest litigation risk, such as the use of force, vehicle pursuits, and special operations (think SWAT). Litigation (and the innocence movement) has led some departments to adopt policies on practices that lead to evidentiary exclusion or criminal justice errors, such as eyewitness identification procedures, interrogations, searches and seizures, and evidence handling. But beyond these exceptions, the Commission's observations largely remain true. If agency policies are to effectively cabin discretion on using loitering and disorderly conduct statutes, writing tickets instead of issuing warnings, or deciding when to order a person out of a car, agencies might need more of a push.

Test Your Department

Spend the next five minutes brainstorming the kinds of policies you think a police department should have. Flip through this book for more ideas. Now go on the internet and search for your local police department. See whether its policies are online.

Were they hard or impossible to find? If so, it will not be easy to evaluate (or weigh in) on the guidance officers in your jurisdiction receive. How could you still influence the department's rules?

If they are online, check the department's policies against your list. Does your department have policies in the areas you identified? Can you tell?

Now pick a policy in an area you have listed and read it. If you cannot find another, look at the use-of-force policy. Does the policy adhere to your expectations for your department? How detailed is it? Could you remember it and employ it if you had to? Can you name practices that clearly violate the policy? That clearly comply with it? How does it change your thinking about police policies?

Don't forget that even if a department develops phenomenal policies, that is not enough:

> It is not sufficient . . . for a police department to have a state-of-the-art policy on use of force if it is not reinforced by thorough and accurate training. . . . Similarly, a department can have an excellent policy and training over the handling of mentally ill people but nullify those contributions by having completely inadequate supervision on the street. To understand the interrelatedness of the various elements of the new police accountability, it is useful to think of them in terms of . . . [p]olicy, [t]raining, [s]upervision, and [r]eview.

Samuel E. Walker & Carol A. Archbold, *The New World of Police Accountability* 13–14 (2020).

Good departmental rules could even lead to bad policing if an ongoing disconnect exists between the rules and the rest of the department's practices. An agency's "official organizational messages are selectively affirmed or undermined by informal messages about what kinds of conduct are actually tolerated or rewarded. It is these informal expectations—that officers learn from fellow officers on the street and in the locker rooms—that determine the institutional culture that ultimately governs and shapes the discretionary decisions of street level cops." Barbara E. Armacost, *Organizational Culture and Police Misconduct*, 72 Geo. Wash. L. Rev. 453, 516 (2004).

Those risks hardly counsel against policies. Officers certainly cannot fulfill expectations (or face consequences for failing to do so) if they are never told what those expectations are. Thus, almost every effort to improve policing includes developing and refining departmental policies. But these concerns do suggest more is needed. How can states, cities, and departments ensure that police policies are reinforced with training, culture, and discipline? Are there other ways to reduce police discretion? What about limiting officers' authority *and* responsibilities instead? How might that be done? How should a community decide which path it should follow?

Chapter 11

Federal Influence over Local Policing

By tradition and constitutional doctrine, local policing is fundamentally a state and local enterprise. Nevertheless, all three branches of the federal government participate in regulating local police. As you have learned in earlier chapters, the U.S. Constitution and federal privacy statutes limit what states and localities might otherwise have law enforcement officers do. In these ways, federal courts (who interpret the Constitution) and Congress (which writes statutes) work to limit the harms of local policing. Federal remedies (both statutory and constitutional) help, too. Some of those remedies, discussed in Part Four of this book, are enforced exclusively by the U.S. Department of Justice. When most people think of federal influence over local policing, these mechanisms—constitutional interpretation, privacy statutes, and executive civil rights enforcement—are what they envision.

In fact, the federal government intervenes in local policing far beyond protecting and enforcing rights. Congress has also long sought to make local policing more expansive, more effective, more focused on national priorities, and more cooperative across jurisdictions. To achieve these objectives, however, Congress cannot simply mandate that local police do federal bidding. Constitutional federalism principles include the Anti-Commandeering Doctrine: "The Federal Government may neither issue directives requiring the States to address particular problems, nor command the States' officers, or those of their political subdivisions, to administer or enforce a federal regulatory program." Printz v. United States, 521 U.S. 898, 935 (1997). Instead, Congress must act both within the limits of its enumerated powers and within the principles of federalism to influence what local police do.

So how does Congress influence local policing? One way is by instructing federal agencies to collect information from and distribute information to local police departments, as through the Uniform Crime Reporting Program. The federal government also maintains a newer and more detailed crime reporting mechanism, the National Incident-Based Reporting System (NIBRS); a criminal justice information index, the National Crime Information Center (NCIC); a national fingerprint and criminal history system, the Integrated Automated Fingerprint Identification System (IAFIS); and a national DNA index, the Combined DNA Index System (CODIS), among other databases.

More commonly, though, Congress has created and funded programs that provide billions of dollars, tons of equipment, and considerable power to local law enforcement agencies and officers. Unlike the enforcement of constitutional rights, these programs (mostly) act like carrots rather than sticks, designed to entice local actors into policing in a federally approved way. Far more than federal databases, they change the nature of local policing.

Although federal carrots for local policing provide local resources and serve national ends, they also raise persistent concerns for those interested in the legal regulation of local police. First, federal objectives might conflict with state and local policy preferences. The result is often a tussle in which Congress, states, and localities attempt to impose policy preferences on local policing. Second, unlike constitutional rights and private statutes, which purport to limit the harms of local policing, federal public safety programs often encourage intrusive police conduct. By offering resources that make specific intrusions comparatively more appealing to local communities trying to decide whether a policing practice is worth its harms, federal programs raise questions about how to ensure that local policing helps more than it hurts. Third, federal programs often shift the relative power of different government actors vis-à-vis policing. For example, they sometimes allow local police departments to bypass state or local limits on a policing practice, or they enable police chiefs to secure resources outside of the local budgeting process, empowering chiefs relative to other public officials.

This chapter considers these issues in the context of four controversial policing practices. The first section looks at the federal domestic violence arrest grant program that offers federal funds to local police departments only if they adopt policies and practices that favor misdemeanor domestic violence arrests over nonarrest alternatives. The second section examines federal equitable sharing programs that permit local police departments to seize property and pursue civil forfeiture under federal law. The third section looks at the federal 1033 program that transfers surplus equipment to local police departments, including equipment that militarizes local police. The last section considers federal efforts to strengthen immigration enforcement by leveraging local police interactions with immigrant communities. In each case, the push and pull over local policing adds to our understanding about the complexity of local policing in our federal system.

A.   An Introduction to Federal Programs for Local Policing

This excerpt provides an overview of the federal government's participation in local policing.

Rachel A. Harmon, *Federal Programs and the Real Costs of Policing*
90 N.Y.U. L. Rev. 870, 877–884 (2015)

[There is a] kind of federal involvement in local policing, one that operates on a far larger scale than civil rights enforcement, employee rights litigation, public corruption prosecutions, or national forensic databases: the dozens of federal statutes that authorize federal agencies to give money, equipment, and power to local law enforcement agencies and officers. These programs developed piecemeal over several decades, and they are diverse in scope, concern, and form. Nevertheless, these programs share a core set of means and ends. They seek to improve public safety by expanding local law enforcement, by focusing local law enforcement on national priorities, and by improving coordination among federal, state, and local law enforcement agencies. To reach these goals, these programs provide federal resources and federal power to local police officers and departments. . . .

Local policing in the 1930s had a national problem. By the early 1930s, federal law enforcement had, to a large degree, recovered from the disastrous reputational consequences of failed Prohibition policies. By contrast, local law enforcement was widely perceived as incompetent, if not corrupt. . . .

Congress authorized several new federal programs over the course of the 1930s to mitigate this municipal inefficiency. These federal efforts involved little money. The George-Deen Act and the Works Progress Administration (WPA) together provided a few million dollars in research and training money to police departments, and the FBI used a little money informally to incentivize local cooperation with federal enforcement. But despite early calls for using conditional grants to influence local police work, early public safety programs largely worked through the FBI to provide technical assistance and interstate coordination to police departments, rather than giving financial aid. Thus, the FBI began collecting crime data for the Uniform Crime Reports in 1930. In 1935, it started the National Police Academy, now called the National Academy, which provided a centralized source of training for local police officers from around the country and became an unobtrusive way to promote federal priorities in local law enforcement. By the end of the decade, the FBI was offering a variety of services to assist local law enforcement, such as comparing fingerprints from crime scenes to federal databases, examining forensic evidence collected in local crimes, and providing information on previously arrested criminals.

While federal technical assistance and training opportunities for local law enforcement continue to this day, over time these early programs have been dwarfed by programs that provide resources and power to local policing more directly. This project began in earnest in the 1960s when intensifying public concern about crime led to the Law Enforcement Assistance Act of 1965 (LEAA) and the Omnibus Crime Control and Safe Streets Act of 1968. Together, these statutes provided the first substantial federal financial assistance to local law enforcement, in the form of flexible block grants to states, intended to improve public safety simply by increasing the resources available to state and local law enforcement agencies.

As others have noted, intergovernmental grants to local police departments have waxed and waned with public perceptions about crime and public safety. In short, the block grants of the 1960s faded during the late 1970s in the face of criticisms of their effectiveness and a declining national focus on crime. By the late 1980s, Congress responded to national concern about rising crime with the Edward Byrne Memorial State and Local Law Enforcement Assistance Formula Grant Program, and then more dramatically to the crack epidemic and associated violent crime with the largest crime bill in history, the Violent Crime Control and Law Enforcement Act of 1994. This latter law authorized $10.8 billion over six years for programs to assist state and local law enforcement. Congress dedicated the bulk of that money, $8.8 billion, to fulfill President Clinton's pledge to provide for 100,000 new police officers through the COPS program.

Eventually, like the funding of the 1960s, the monumental funding of the 1990s generated a backlash, and by 2000, some of the key programs of the 1990s decade, such as the COPS Hiring Program (CHP), faced fading support and resources. In 2001, however, after 9/11, terrorism emerged to replace violent crime and crack as a national public safety crisis that justified reenergizing federal funding to local police. Grants of aid once again expanded radically, with tens of billions of dollars spent on new programs for local law enforcement.

Federal public safety programs continue to evolve. Today, they provide not only money, but also equipment and federal power to local law enforcement. They emphasize interstate coordination, fighting terrorism and the war on drugs, and many other goals. They originate not only in the Department of Justice but also in the Departments of Defense, Homeland Security, Treasury, and Agriculture. Together, these federal public safety programs represent a massive intervention into local law enforcement, one that has not been sufficiently assessed.

NOTES AND QUESTIONS

1. *Why?* Does the federal government have legitimate interests in influencing or strengthening local policing? Or, to say it another way, what justifies using one community's tax dollars to support or change local policing in another community? What kinds of problems or crimes justify that kind of interference?

2. *The form of federal intervention.* Why might federal public safety programs take the forms they do: offering technical assistance, running national databases, and providing money and equipment to departments? From the point of view of promoting national goals, what are the advantages and disadvantages of these types of programs?

3. *How much?* There is no comprehensive account of the federal funding that goes to local police departments. Since the mid-1990s, two of the biggest sources of funds have been the CHP and Byrne Justice Assistance Grants mentioned in the excerpt. Byrne Justice Assistance Grants today include both block grants and competitive grants and provide an average of around $435 million per year to state, local, and tribal agencies. In 2019, the program made $264 million available for a wide variety of purposes. The COPS Hiring Program has given away more than $14 billion since it started in 1994. In 2020, it awarded near $400 million to support the hiring of more than 2,700 full-time officers. In addition to these programs, which seek to make local policing bigger and stronger, federal statutes empower agencies to give away money, equipment, and power for more specific purposes. For example, the Department of Homeland Security has given away billions of dollars to local law enforcement agencies for terrorism preparedness since 2002. In 2020, for instance, it provided $90 million for law enforcement agency cooperation on U.S. borders and more than $153 million to law enforcement agencies for urban-area terrorism prevention, among other grants. What criteria would you use to decide whether a program—whether general or specific—is a good idea?

B.   *Domestic Violence Arrests*

1.   Background on Domestic Violence Arrests

Police departments receive nearly three-quarters of a million domestic violence calls each year. See Brian A. Reaves, *Bureau of Justice Statistics, Police Responses to Domestic Violence, 2006–2015*, at 2 (2017). Before the 1990s, police overwhelmingly treated these incidents as family matters that, if anything, necessitated only order-maintenance techniques—such as separating the parties temporarily—rather than formal legal interventions. Officers usually conducted little investigation and rarely arrested suspects. Indeed, the law often permitted no other response: Most states forbid warrantless arrests for misdemeanors that officers had not witnessed, and most domestic violence was considered a misdemeanor. Even when the law permitted a criminal arrest, officers had strong reasons to avoid responding to domestic conflicts when they could and to avoid confrontational approaches when they could not: Domestic violence calls are some of the most unpredictable and dangerous for police officers, who may discover a volatile situation in a closed and unfamiliar environment with angry and armed participants.

Pressure to change this state of affairs began in the late 1970s and early 1980s. Feminists and battered women's advocates fought to increase criminal deterrence and criminal stigma for violence against intimate partners. One high-profile incident especially helped their cause by highlighting the role of law enforcement in maintaining the status quo: In late 1982 and early 1983, Tracey Thurman complained to police repeatedly about a series of threats and violent attacks against her and her son by her estranged husband, Charles Thurman. The police did little in response. In fact, Charles was not arrested until an officer watched him smash her car windshield while she was in the car. Even then, he was charged with breach of the peace and received only a suspended sentence and an order to stay away from Tracey. Charles continued to harass and threaten Tracey, and despite the court order, the police often refused even to take her complaints.

Finally, on June 10, 1983, Charles showed up where Tracey and her son were staying and demanded to see her. She called the Torrington (Conn.) Police Department for help, telling them that he was there, that he was violating his probation, and that she thought he would kill her. Officers had reason to know he was serious: Before the June attack, Charles had bragged to several police officers who frequented the diner where he worked that he intended to kill his wife. Still, the police took 25 minutes to arrive, during which time Charles stabbed Tracey repeatedly. When an officer did appear, he watched without intervening as Charles kicked his bleeding wife several times in the head and dropped her young son on her bleeding body. Even after other officers arrived, Charles was permitted to continue to intimidate Tracey. Only when Charles approached Tracey threateningly again, while she was lying on a stretcher receiving medical attention, was he finally taken into custody. Tracey sued the Torrington Police Department for violating her civil rights and won a $2 million judgment.

The year after the Thurman judgment, prominent criminologists Lawrence Sherman and Richard Berk published the results of the Minneapolis Domestic Violence Experiment. The experiment evaluated different police responses to domestic violence calls and found that arrested offenders reoffended at a lower rate. See Lawrence W. Sherman & Richard A. Berk, *The Minneapolis Domestic Violence Experiment*, Police Found. Rep. (Apr. 1984); Lawrence W. Sherman & Richard

A. Berk, *The Specific Deterrent Effects of Arrest for Domestic Assault*, 49 Am. Soc. Rev. 261 (1984). Although studies replicating the Minneapolis experiment had mixed results, the original study received extensive media attention. Along with cases like Tracey Thurman's, it led to calls for a new approach to policing domestic violence, one that treated domestic violence as a crime.

States began to change their laws to facilitate the new approach, expanding police authority in domestic violence cases. Today, almost every state and the District of Columbia permits officers to make warrantless arrests for some kinds of misdemeanor domestic violence. Police departments also changed their policies and procedures for handling domestic violence calls, encouraging officers to intervene more often and more forcefully.

Nevertheless, officer conduct changed less than statutes and policies. Michael Buerger, a former police officer, has described some of the techniques police used to avoid responding to domestic violence calls:

> [T]he simplest form of resistance was to handle the incident in time-tested fashion (i.e., without an arrest), and radio in (or file a report) officially redefining the event as an argument, no violence involved, and hence no arrest required. Even more blatant was the practice of clearing a call as GOA, "Gone On Arrival," indicating either that there was no suspect at the scene or no complainant with whom to speak, even in cases where both parties were present.

Police Agency Responses to Changes in the Legal Environment, in *Policing and the Law* 105, 121–122 (Jeffrey T. Walker ed., 2002). As Buerger suggests, despite the new powers, police officers often continued to avoid arresting domestic violence perpetrators.

In the face of law enforcement resistance, some states went further, reducing police discretion in domestic violence cases through statutes that mandated or strongly preferred arrests for domestic violence calls. The result was that states diverged in their approaches to domestic violence: Nearly half mandated arrest, at least for some domestic violence crimes; other states preferred arrest but did not require it; and the rest followed the traditional approach of leaving arrests to officer discretion, the same as for other crimes.

2.   Federal Intervention: Domestic Violence Arrest Grants

In the mid-1990s, the federal government joined in. Although a bill to address domestic and sexual violence had been around for several years, it got a boost from public attention to the murder of Nicole Brown Simpson and revelations that she had been battered by her former husband and murder suspect, football star O.J. Simpson. In 1994, President Clinton signed into law the Violence Against Women Act (VAWA) as Title IV of the Violent Crime Control and Law Enforcement Act of 1994, Pub. L. No. 103-322, §§40001–40304, 108 Stat. 1796, 1902-42. Here is one piece of the statute, as amended. As you read, consider what money may be used for and what conditions departments must fulfill to receive a grant.

ARREST GRANT PROGRAM — 34 U.S.C. §10461

(a) Purpose

The purpose of this subchapter is to encourage States, Indian tribal governments, State and local courts (including juvenile courts), tribal courts, and units of local government to treat domestic violence, dating violence, sexual assault, and stalking as serious violations of criminal law.

(b) Grant authority

The Attorney General may make grants to eligible grantees for the following purposes:

(1) To implement proarrest programs and policies in police departments, including policies for protection order violations and enforcement of protection orders across State and tribal lines.

(2) To develop policies, educational programs, protection order registries, data collection systems, and training in police departments to improve tracking of cases and classification of complaints involving domestic violence, dating violence, sexual assault, and stalking. . . .

(3) To centralize and coordinate police enforcement, prosecution, or judicial responsibility for domestic violence, dating violence, sexual assault, and stalking cases in teams or units of police officers, prosecutors, parole and probation officers, or judges.

(4) To coordinate computer tracking systems and provide the appropriate training and education about domestic violence, dating violence, sexual assault, and stalking. . . .

(5) To strengthen legal advocacy service programs and other victim services for victims of domestic violence, dating violence, sexual assault, and stalking, including strengthening assistance to such victims in immigration matters.

(6) To educate Federal, State, tribal, territorial, and local judges, courts, and court-based and court-related personnel in criminal and civil courts (including juvenile courts) about domestic violence, dating violence, sexual assault, and stalking and to improve judicial handling of such cases.

(7) To provide technical assistance and computer and other equipment to police departments, prosecutors, courts, and tribal jurisdictions to facilitate the widespread enforcement of protection orders. . . .

(8) To develop or strengthen policies and training for police, prosecutors, and the judiciary in recognizing, investigating, and prosecuting instances of domestic violence dating violence, sexual assault, and stalking against older individuals (as defined in section 3002 of Title 42) and individuals with disabilities (as defined in section 12102(2) of Title 42).

(9) To develop State, tribal, territorial, or local policies, procedures, and protocols for preventing dual arrests and prosecutions in cases of domestic violence, dating violence, sexual assault, and stalking, and to develop effective methods for identifying the pattern and history of abuse that indicates which party is the actual perpetrator of abuse.

(10) To plan, develop, and establish comprehensive victim service and support centers. . . .

(c) Eligibility

Eligible grantees are—

(1) States, Indian tribal governments[,] State and local courts (including juvenile courts), or units of local government that—

(A) except for a court, certify that their laws or official policies—

(i) encourage or mandate arrests of domestic violence offenders based on probable cause that an offense has been committed; and

(ii) encourage or mandate arrest of domestic violence offenders who violate the terms of a valid and outstanding protection order;

(B) except for a court, demonstrate that their laws, policies, or practices and their training programs discourage dual arrests of offender and victim; . . .

NOTES AND QUESTIONS

1. *Arrest grants.* Pursuant to this statutory authority, the Office on Violence Against Women within the U.S. Department of Justice developed the Grants to Encourage Arrest Policies and Enforcement of Protection Orders Program. In 2016, the program was renamed the Improving Criminal Justice Responses to Sexual Assault, Domestic Violence, Dating Violence, and Stalking Grant Program, but it continues to be commonly known as the Arrest Program. Since 1994, this program has been one of the largest discretionary grants administered by the Office of Violence Against Women, and it has given hundreds of millions of dollars to police departments.

2. *Eligibility criteria.* Notice the grant eligibility criteria. Every grant to a local government for any purpose requires that the local police department "encourage or mandate" arrests. What consequences would you expect from such a requirement? What implications does that have? What does federal policy promote?

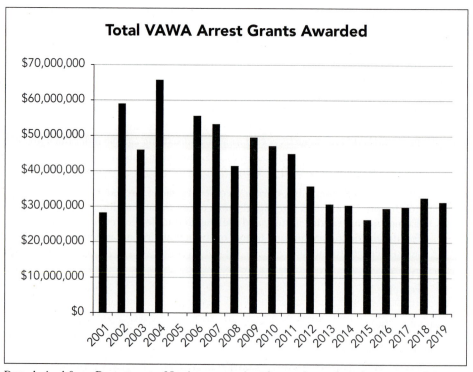

Data derived from Department of Justice summaries of annual awards and reports to Congress. Data are unavailable for 2005.

3. *Are pro-arrest policies a good idea?* When the Arrest Program operates as intended, it increases arrests for domestic violence crimes for which officers might have done nothing or issued a summons. Yet there are costs as well as benefits to arrests:

> An arrest can end ongoing violence. It may deter future crime, even if charges are subsequently dropped. It has symbolic value. And it may increase the chances that prosecutors will pursue the case to conviction. These benefits motivated the Arrest Program, which along with other parts of VAWA, was intended to remedy inadequate protection of women by local law enforcement.

> However, arrests in domestic violence cases can also have substantial marginal costs. For an arrestee and his family, an arrest can lead to lost wages and lost productivity (including childcare and housework); decreased future income; legal costs; forgone education; humiliation; and a decreased quality of life, including from consequences related to housing, child custody, and immigration status. Families may also incur precautionary costs to avoid arrests: Some spouses and children will suffer physical injury and emotional harm because they refrain from calling 911 when attacked to avoid triggering their batterers' arrest.

> . . . Mandatory and preferred arrest policies have the predictable consequence of causing more innocent suspects to be arrested, since the policies reduce officer discretion not to arrest suspects who satisfy the legal standard for arrest but are unlikely to be prosecuted or successfully convicted.

Rachel A. Harmon, *Federal Programs and the Real Costs of Policing*, 90 N.Y.U. L. Rev. 872, 913–915 (2015). When VAWA passed, the federal government was following a wave of pro-arrest sentiment. Since then, concerns about the negative effects of pro-arrest policies on victims have led some advocates to turn away from aggressive policing approaches to domestic violence. See, e.g., Leigh Goodmark, *Decriminalizing Domestic Violence: A Balanced Policy Approach to Intimate Partner Violence* (2018); Aya Gruber, *The Feminist War on Crime*, 92 Iowa L. Rev. 741 (2007).

4. *Who should decide?* Given that favoring arrests as a tool for addressing domestic violence is controversial, who should decide what police officers do? Police departments? States? Congress? Because some states require police officers to favor arrests as a matter of state law, departments in those states can easily adopt a policy consistent with state law and apply for grants under the program. In that case, who is deciding? When states are silent about domestic violence arrests, they may be taking the view either that domestic violence should be treated like other crimes or that localities should determine the appropriate policy. If a police department in either of those kinds of states adopts a pro-arrest policy to secure federal funding for domestic violence programs, whose policy preferences are being vindicated?

5. *Lasting effects.* Funding for the Arrest Program has decreased over time. But even if the Arrest Program were eliminated tomorrow, the policies it has encouraged since 1994 are likely to last. State laws and police department policies are subject to Newton's first law of motion: They operate until a force on them is great enough to change their direction. The Arrest Program was such a force for some departments. What new forces could lead departments and states to change their approaches again?

6. *Idaho.* Here is one possibility. In 2019, in a unanimous opinion, the Idaho Supreme Court ruled that police officers in Idaho cannot, pursuant to the state's

constitution, arrest suspects for misdemeanor offenses without a warrant unless they observed the alleged crime. State v. Clarke, 446 P.3d 451 (Idaho 2019). The case involved drug crimes, not domestic violence, but the court acknowledged that its decision invalidates Idaho Code §19-603(6), which permits police to make warrantless arrests for domestic violence crimes they have not witnessed. Does that mean law enforcement agencies in Idaho can no longer receive grants under the federal program? What would a pro-arrest policy mean if most of the relevant arrests are now forbidden by state law?

7. *The Lautenberg Amendment.* VAWA grant programs are not the only federal intervention into domestic violence that affects local policing. The 1996 Lautenberg Amendment to the Gun Control Act prohibits any individual convicted of a misdemeanor crime of domestic violence from purchasing, transporting, or possessing firearms. 18 U.S.C. §922(g)(9). The law's goal is to get guns out of the hands of domestic abusers, and research suggests that the law reduces domestic gun homicides. See, e.g., Kerri Raissian, *Hold Your Fire: Did the 1996 Federal Gun Control Act Expansion Reduce Domestic Homicides?*, 35 J. Pol'y Anal. & Mgt. 67 (2015).

When police officers are convicted of domestic violence offenses, the Lautenberg Amendment treats them just like everyone else. For officers, however, a gun prohibition has additional implications: Because sworn officers in every state carry guns, the Lautenberg Amendment functions as an employment ban for police officers convicted of domestic violence offenses. Victims of officer–abusers are already more reluctant than others to call the police, and officers seem more reluctant to arrest other officers. Could the Lautenberg Amendment exaggerate both effects? Victims might avoid calling 911 if doing so is likely to have dire financial implications for the family, and even if victims make the call, responding officers might be more reluctant to arrest, knowing that doing so could be career ending for the officer–suspect. Those effects in turn could embolden officer–abusers. How can we tell whether any of this is happening? If it is, what do you think should be done? For discussion of the potential effects of the Lautenberg Amendment on general policing and prosecution practices, see Robert A. Mikos, *Enforcing State Law in Congress's Shadow*, 90 Cornell L. Rev. 1411 (2005).

3.   Resistance to Federal Policy

Many police departments have adopted pro-arrest policies to satisfy local political pressure, to align with state law, or to ensure eligibility for grants. Officers and command staff sometimes oppose those same policies, however, because they force departments to prioritize domestic violence over other public safety threats, and they deny officers discretion in responding to incidents. How does this kind of tension over policing policy play itself out? Consider these two trends in domestic violence policing.

The first is *dual arrests.* Several studies indicate that one way the policies increase arrests is by leading to arrests of both parties to a violent encounter. See David Hirschel et al., *Explaining the Prevalence, Context and Consequences of Dual Arrest in Intimate Partner Cases* (2007). Although some dual arrests result from mutual combat (making them consistent with federal and state policies intending to treat domestic violence as a serious crime), critics argue that dual arrests often arise when officers are unwilling or unable to distinguish the perpetrator from the victim. In this way, police officers may fulfill the mandate and yet undermine the goals of pro-arrest laws: Dual arrests not only punish victims rather than protect them; they also discourage victims from calling 911 in the future, reducing the need for future arrests.

Federal and state actors have long discouraged dual arrests. In fact, discouraging dual arrests is a condition for receiving any Arrest Program grant. See 34 U.S.C. §10461(c)(1)(B). Formally discouraging dual arrests might not be enough, though. Connecticut, for example, has long done so but, as of 2017, decades after the problem was first identified, police still arrested both parties in nearly one in five domestic violence episodes in which arrests are made. See Sarah Smith, *In Connecticut, Calling for Help Carries Risks for Victims of Domestic Violence*, ProPublica (Feb. 16, 2017). The Connecticut legislature responded to ongoing criticism with a statute requiring officers to identify and arrest only primary aggressors. 2018 Conn. Acts 18-5 (amending Conn. Gen. Stat. §46b-38b). Are there any disadvantages to using primary-aggressor arrest laws to steer officers back toward federal and state policy goals? Do such laws address the reasons officers engage in dual arrests? If not, what might?

The second trend is *nuisance ordinances.* Traditional nuisance ordinances prohibit unreasonable interferences with rights common to the general public. See Restatement (Second) of Torts §821B (1979). Some localities have rewritten these ordinances to allow police departments to leverage private actors to help prevent crime, a strategy known as third-party policing. Under such an ordinance, a city may designate a property — often an apartment building — a "nuisance" when a threshold number of emergency calls originate from it, leading police to respond. Property owners are instructed to "abate the nuisance" or face steep fines.

The idea behind these revised nuisance ordinances is to allow police to pressure property owners to mitigate criminogenic conditions, such as poor lighting and inadequate security, that lead, for example, to drug dealing in an apartment building courtyard. However, the ordinances are drafted to permit almost any police response to count toward a nuisance determination, and some police departments issue nuisance notices to landlords when *victims* call 911 from their buildings. See, e.g., N.Y. Civil Liberties Union, *More than a Nuisance: The Outsized Consequences of New York's Nuisance Ordinances* (2018). In response, landlords address the nuisance by threatening to evict the tenants who call for help. Think about who calls 911 repeatedly from their own home. Is it a surprise that this strategy disproportionately affects victims of domestic violence? In a study in one city, nearly one-third of nuisance citations were generated by serious domestic violence incidents, and the majority of tenants threatened with eviction were victims rather than batterers. See Matthew Desmond & Nicol Valdez, *Unpolicing the Urban Poor: Consequences of Third-Party Policing for Inner-City Women*, 78 Am. Soc. Rev. 117 (2013). Like dual arrests, applying nuisance ordinances to calls by domestic violence victims discourages victims from calling the police when violence occurs, allowing police departments to satisfy pro-arrest policies and yet undermine state and federal policy goals.

Just as with dual arrests, some states are fighting this trend. A couple have passed laws prohibiting localities from imposing indirect penalties on domestic violence victims for seeking police assistance or from imposing penalties on landlords who refuse to remove an occupant who does so. See, e.g., 2019 N.Y. Laws ch. 263 (enacting N.Y. Civ. Rights Law §§90-98 (Right to Call Police and Emergency Assistance/Victim Protections)).

What conclusions might one draw from these low-key legal battles over policing domestic violence?

C.   Equitable Sharing

1.   Background on Asset Forfeiture

Both federal and state asset forfeiture laws authorize local law enforcement agencies to seize property connected with criminal activity. Once the property is seized and the asset forfeiture action is brought and completed, the property is usually sold and the proceeds kept by the government, often by the law enforcement agency that carried out the seizure.

Advocates of asset forfeiture argue that forfeitures obtain resources for law enforcement at the same time they "remove the tools of crime from criminal organizations, deprive wrongdoers of the proceeds of their crimes, recover property that may be used to compensate victims, and deter crime." U.S. Dept. of Justice & U.S. Dept. of the Treasury, *Guide to Equitable Sharing for State, Local, and Tribal Law Enforcement Agencies* 1 (2018) [hereinafter *Guide to Equitable Sharing*]. When he was U.S. Attorney General, Jeff Sessions contended that the programs are "an essential component of the Department of Justice's efforts to combat the most sophisticated criminal actors and organizations—including terrorist financiers, cyber criminals, fraudsters, human traffickers, and transnational drug cartels." U.S. Dept. of Justice, *The Attorney General's Guidelines on the Asset Forfeiture Program* 1 (2018). State law enforcement officials make similar arguments.

A Corvette seized by New Braunfels (Tex.) Police Department from an alleged drug dealer and repurposed as Coptimus Prime, a police cruiser.

Critics complain that expansive forfeiture programs have two primary problems. First, most forfeitures are civil forfeitures, which deprive people of property with limited procedural protections. Unlike *criminal* asset forfeitures, which usually are part of a criminal sentence and follow a criminal conviction with its heightened safeguards, *civil* asset forfeitures employ a lower standard of proof, and the government often need not prove the owner knew the property was being used unlawfully. Although property owners can challenge civil forfeitures, they are not entitled to appointed counsel, frequently making it financially infeasible to do so.

Second, forfeiture proceeds often go to the police department that carried out the forfeiture, distorting policing priorities. To see the effect, imagine you are a police chief. If you devote officers to drug crimes, they will seize cars and cash as well as drugs. The additional resources could pay for some new office furniture, a patrol car, and a few new weapons. Devoting more officers to investigating sexual assaults has no such benefit. Might you consider that in allocating resources? And what strategies will you use? Pretextual traffic stops looking for drugs might not dismantle a drug organization, and they might be intrusive (see Chapter 6), but they often result in forfeitures. By contrast, long-term investigations might be more effective but produce no immediate gains for the agency. Or what if you are considering undercover operations? You could send officers to do a *buy–bust* in which they pretend to buy drugs. When the dealer shows up with drugs, the officers can pull drugs off the street and arrest someone who may be up the chain in a drug organization. Or you could have officers do *reverse drug stings*, in which officers pose as sellers rather than buyers. Those catch downstream participants, and the only drugs will be the ones your officers bring. But the criminals will bring cash, which can be forfeited and often kept by your agency. One of these strategies is not always better than the other, but might you favor reverse stings for reasons unrelated to their public safety benefits?

In light of the advantages and concerns about asset forfeiture, states take a range of approaches to it. On the restrictive side, some states ban forfeitures not associated with a criminal conviction, afford procedural protections for owners seeking to keep their property, or restrict local law enforcement agencies from benefiting directly from forfeiture, giving the money instead to general funds or to education. On the permissive side, other states allow forfeitures for a broad range of crimes, permit local agencies to keep 100 percent of the proceeds of forfeitures, and require no more than a preponderance of the evidence to prove property forfeitable. Despite a considerable divide, the trend is clear: More than two-thirds of states and the District of Columbia have made their laws less favorable to forfeiture since 2014. See *Civil Forfeiture Reforms on the State Level*, Inst. for Just., *https://ij.org/activism/legislation/civil-forfeiture-legislative-highlights/* (summarizing reforms).

2. Federal Intervention: Equitable Sharing Program

Now consider the federal intervention into asset forfeiture: In addition to state laws that permit local departments to seize property associated with state criminal violations, and federal law that permits federal law enforcement to confiscate property connected with federal criminal activity, *federal* statutes also permit *local* police departments to seize property associated with federal crimes and to receive a significant share of the proceeds from those seizures. This process is known as *equitable sharing*. Here is one of the statutes that permit it:

21 U.S.C. §881. FORFEITURES

(a) Subject property

The following shall be subject to forfeiture to the United States and no property right shall exist in them:

> **(1)** All controlled substances which have been manufactured, distributed, dispensed, or acquired in violation of this subchapter.
>
> **(2)** All raw materials, products, and equipment of any kind which are used, or intended for use, in manufacturing, compounding, processing, delivering, importing, or exporting any controlled substance or listed chemical in violation of this subchapter.
>
> **(3)** All property which is used, or intended for use, as a container for property described in paragraph (1), (2), or (9).
>
> **(4)** All conveyances, including aircraft, vehicles, or vessels, which are used, or are intended for use, to transport, or in any manner to facilitate the transportation, sale, receipt, possession, or concealment of property described in paragraph (1), (2), or (9). . . .
>
> **(6)** All moneys, negotiable instruments, securities, or other things of value furnished or intended to be furnished by any person in exchange for a controlled substance or listed chemical in violation of this subchapter, all proceeds traceable to such an exchange, and all moneys, negotiable instruments, and securities used or intended to be used to facilitate any violation of this subchapter.
>
> **(7)** All real property, including any right, title, and interest (including any leasehold interest) in the whole of any lot or tract of land and any appurtenances or improvements, which is used, or intended to be used, in any manner or part, to commit, or to facilitate the commission of, a violation of this subchapter punishable by more than one year's imprisonment. . . .
>
> **(11)** Any firearm (as defined in section 921 of Title 18) used or intended to be used to facilitate the transportation, sale, receipt, possession, or concealment of property described in paragraph (1) or (2) and any proceeds traceable to such property.

(b) Seizure procedures

Any property subject to forfeiture to the United States under this section may be seized by the Attorney General in the manner set forth in section 981(b) of Title 18.[1] . . .

(e) Disposition of forfeited property

(1) Whenever property is civilly or criminally forfeited under this subchapter the Attorney General may–

---

[1] *Ed. note:* The relevant parts of 18 U.S.C. §981(b) state that "any property subject to forfeiture to the United States . . . may be seized by the Attorney General . . . the Secretary of the Treasury or the Postal Service," and that forfeitable property may be seized without a warrant if, among other circumstances, "the property was lawfully seized by a State or local law enforcement agency and transferred to a Federal agency."

(A) retain the property for official use or . . . transfer the property to any Federal agency or to any State or local law enforcement agency which participated directly in the seizure or forfeiture of the property;

(B) . . . sell, by public sale or any other commercially feasible means, any forfeited property which is not required to be destroyed by law and which is not harmful to the public . . .

(2) (A) The proceeds from any sale under subparagraph (B) of paragraph (1) and any moneys forfeited under this subchapter shall be used to pay—

(i) all property expenses of the proceedings for forfeiture and sale including expenses of seizure, maintenance of custody, advertising, and court costs; and

(ii) awards of up to $100,000 to any individual who provides original information which leads to the arrest and conviction of a person who kills or kidnaps a Federal drug law enforcement agent . . . at the discretion of the Attorney General.

(B) The Attorney General shall forward to the Treasurer of the United States for deposit . . . any amounts of such moneys and proceeds remaining after payment of the expenses provided in subparagraph (A). . . .

(3) The Attorney General shall assure that any property transferred to a State or local law enforcement agency under paragraph (1)(A) —

(A) has a value that bears a reasonable relationship to the degree of direct participation of the State or local agency in the law enforcement effort resulting in the forfeiture, taking into account the total value of all property forfeited and the total law enforcement effort with respect to the violation of law on which the forfeiture is based; and

(B) will serve to encourage further cooperation between the recipient State or local agency and Federal law enforcement agencies. . . .

NOTES AND QUESTIONS

1. *Equitable sharing.* This statute is one of several laws that authorizes federal forfeitures and permits local agencies to take part in them. Although it is not obvious, close reading indicates that the statute permits two forms of equitable sharing. First, as §881(b) indicates with its reference to 18 U.S.C. §981, a federal agency may accept a transfer of forfeitable property that has been seized by a local agency and bring a forfeiture action. Afterward, the property (under (e)(1)(A)) or the proceeds after expenses are paid (under (e)(1)(B) and (e)(2)) can be given to the local agency in an amount consistent with (e)(3). This is known as an *adoptive forfeiture* because the locals seize the property, and federal actors adopt that seizure and pursue the forfeiture action. Alternatively, a federal agency may seize property itself and bring a forfeiture action, then transfer some of the property or proceeds to a local agency pursuant to (e)(3) because the local agency helped in the seizure. These *collaborative forfeitures* often arise from federally led, multiagency drug task forces. Do you see any different implications from the two options?

2. *An equitable share.* Local agencies may receive up to 80 percent of the proceeds for adopted seizures and less for seizures carried out with other agencies. The Department of Justice Asset Forfeiture Program alone distributes hundreds of millions of dollars a year to state and local law enforcement agencies.

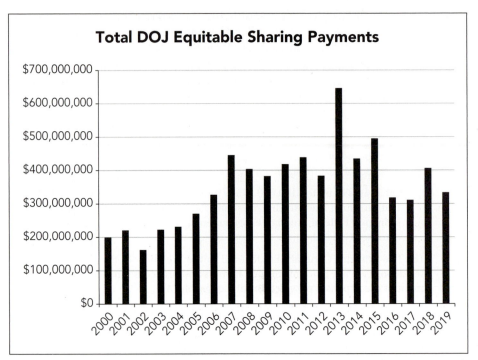

Data based on Justice Department annual reports and Dick M. Carpenter II et al., *Policing for Profit: The Abuse of Civil Asset Forfeiture* 25 (2015).

3. *Purpose.* Why is equitable sharing in the federal interest? How does it help promote national law enforcement goals? Why would local agencies seek an adoption?

4. *Authorized uses for shared funds.* Under federal guidelines, shared funds cannot replace existing budgeted funds. Instead, they "must be used to increase or supplement the resources of the receiving state or local law enforcement agency. . . . The recipient agency must benefit directly from the sharing." *Guide to Equitable Sharing* at 13. In this way, a local agency *always* has a direct stake when it participates in the federal program. Agencies receiving equitably shared funds may spend the money on operations, overtime costs, investigations, training, equipment, or matching grants for federal grant programs, among other uses.

5. *Brief limits.* In the face of harsh criticism of equitable sharing's effects on local police departments, the Obama administration halted federal adoptions of property seized by local law enforcement, although it left collaborative forfeitures intact. See U.S. Dept of Justice, Atty Gen. Order, *Prohibition on Certain Federal Adoptions of Seizures by State and Local Law Enforcement Agencies* (Jan. 16, 2015). But the prohibition was short-lived. The Trump administration reversed course, fully restoring the program. See U.S. Dept. of Justice, Atty. Gen. Order No. 3946-2017, *Federal Forfeiture of Property Seized by State and Local Law Enforcement Agencies* (July 19, 2017).

6. *Local consequences of sharing.* How might these rules affect how police are governed and regulated at the local level? Ordinarily, police departments are answerable in the budget process to local governments for their activities. Even if a department is not banned from engaging in some activities, communities can influence police practices by refusing to fund them. In this way, some communities avoid high-tech surveillance,

the use of payments to informants, buy–bust operations, and military-grade equipment. All of these are permissible uses of federally shared forfeiture funds, however, which the department can secure without going through the local political process.

Similarly, agencies may use seizures and equitable sharing to expand policing resources overall at the same time local governments seek to reduce them. Responding to weeks of protest after George Floyd was killed in Minneapolis in 2020, public officials in more than a dozen major cities, including New York, Chicago, Los Angeles, Philadelphia, Washington, Baltimore, Seattle, Portland, Dallas, and Minneapolis, proposed or pledged to reduce police resources as a means to limit the intrusiveness of policing. See Sarah Holder, *The Cities Taking Up Calls to Defund the Police*, Bloomberg Citylab (Jun. 9, 2020). Equitable sharing cannot fully substitute for money slashed from local budgets: Under federal guidelines, agencies may not "'spend it before you get it'" by planning for shared funds in their budgets. *Guide to Equitable Sharing* at 13. Moreover, because salaries and benefits constitute around 85 percent of most agencies' budgets, "defunding the police" inevitably means cutting the number of officers. Yet agencies are not permitted to use shared funds to pay officer salaries and benefits. *Id.* at 18. Still, an agency could use seizures and equitable sharing to pay overtime to keep remaining officers on the streets more of the time or to buy equipment that expands their reach, countering the intentions of defunding advocates. Presumably, a city could ban its department from participating in equitable sharing, but few have. Does that suggest that equitable sharing is unproblematic? If not, what does it suggest?

7. *Impact on state policy.* Equitable sharing also may undermine state efforts to reduce the harms and distorting effects of asset forfeiture. More than a dozen states' forfeiture laws restrict the percentage of proceeds local agencies may keep from state forfeitures, and laws in eight states (Indiana, Maine, Maryland, Missouri, North Carolina, North Dakota, Ohio, and Vermont) do not allow any forfeiture proceeds to go directly to the agency that carries out the seizure. Local police departments can bypass these state restrictions by seizing property and seeking federal adoption instead. The property can usually be seized either way, depriving alleged criminals, but in restrictive states, only the federal program allows (or increases) direct gain to the agency. Research suggests that agencies are motivated by this benefit: Agencies in states with restrictive forfeiture laws are more likely to participate in the federal program. See Jefferson E. Holcomb et al., *Civil Asset Forfeiture, Equitable Sharing, and Policing for Profit in the United States*, 39 Crim. Just. 273, 280 (2011). Should Congress avoid incentivizing localities to pursue national public safety priorities if doing so limits the effectiveness of state restrictions on a problematic policing practice? How else could criminal problems that cross local and state jurisdictional lines, from human trafficking to terrorism, get adequately addressed? What if the federal program transferred an agency's share of proceeds to state general funds?

3. State Law Responses to Equitable Sharing

Until the mid-2010s, most states did little to respond to equitable sharing. Even states that permitted asset forfeiture only narrowly or without allowing law enforcement agencies to benefit directly allowed local agencies to participate in and benefit from the federal programs. Since then, some states have responded to expansive use of the practice. Here are two examples of state laws responding to concerns about the impact of equitable sharing. How do they differ?

N.M. STAT. ANN. §31-27-11. TRANSFER OF FORFEITABLE PROPERTY TO THE FEDERAL GOVERNMENT

A. A law enforcement agency shall not directly or indirectly transfer seized property to a federal law enforcement authority or other federal agency unless:

   (1) the value of the seized property exceeds fifty thousand dollars ($50,000), excluding the potential value of the sale of contraband; and

   (2) the law enforcement agency determines that the criminal conduct that gave rise to the seizure is interstate in nature and sufficiently complex to justify the transfer of the property; or

   (3) the seized property may only be forfeited under federal law.

B. The law enforcement agency shall not transfer property to the federal government if the transfer would circumvent the protections of the Forfeiture Act that would otherwise be available to a putative interest holder in the property.

WIS. STAT. §961.55(1R). FORFEITURES

(1r) If a law enforcement officer or agency or state or local employee or agency refers seized property to a federal agency directly, indirectly, by adoption, through an intergovernmental joint task force, or by other means, for the purposes of forfeiture litigation, the agency shall produce an itemized report of actual forfeiture expenses, as defined in sub. (5)(b), and submit the report to the department of administration to make it available on the department's website. If there is a federal or state criminal conviction for the crime that was the basis for the seizure, the agency may accept all proceeds. If there is no federal or state criminal conviction, the agency may not accept any proceeds, except that the agency may accept all proceeds if one of the following circumstances applies and is explained in the report submitted under this subsection:

   (a) The defendant has died.

   (b) The defendant was deported by the U.S. government.

   (c) The defendant has been granted immunity in exchange for testifying or otherwise assisting a law enforcement investigation or prosecution.

   (d) The defendant fled the jurisdiction.

   (e) The property has been unclaimed for a period of at least 9 months.

NOTES AND QUESTIONS

1. *Approaches to equitable sharing.* How would you describe these two approaches to equitable sharing? Do they reflect different policy preferences about outcomes or just different mechanisms for achieving their ends? Or can't you tell? What are the advantages and disadvantages of these strategies for mitigating the distorting influence of forfeiture on policing?

2. *New Mexico's law.* The Forfeiture Act of which the excerpted section is a part also requires that to forfeit property under state law, the state must obtain a criminal conviction and prove that the property owner actually knew of the underlying crime. In addition, state forfeiture proceeds go into the state's general fund.

Presumably, these are the protections mentioned in Section B of the statute. What does that mean for New Mexico equitable transfer arrangements?

3. *Wisconsin's law.* Wisconsin's law was also a part of a broader set of reforms. In the same act, Wisconsin prohibited state forfeiture judgments without a criminal conviction, increased the burden of proof, and strengthened defenses. See 2017 Wis. Sess. Laws 812.

4. *Scope of reform.* Only about a quarter of states that have reformed their asset forfeiture laws have also restricted equitable sharing. Why might some states restrict state asset forfeiture—including by disallowing agencies from benefiting directly—but not prohibit agencies from participating in federal equitable sharing that has that effect? By contrast, what might have driven more than half a dozen states that permitted equitable sharing generously in the past to restrict it since 2014?

5. *Alternatives to state restrictions.* Could the federal government obviate the need for state restrictions by responding to some of the concerns these statutes reflect? How could equitable sharing programs be altered to promote democratic values and protect public welfare while still allowing local participation in equitable sharing consistent with national ends?

Preempting Policing Practices

By restricting local police departments from engaging in equitable sharing, the Wisconsin and New Mexico laws effectively preempt local decision making on asset forfeiture. Is that state preemption good or bad?

Long-standing debates exist about where policymaking power best resides. Policymaking at high levels of government increases expertise; ensures uniformity; protects shared values from parochial concerns; and mitigates coordination problems, spillover effects, and other negative externalities of more local decision making. Still, federalists have long argued that empowering states (relative to the federal government) allows innovation, experimentation, and responsiveness to diverse conditions, improving policy outcomes.

"Localist" legal scholars and commentators take the traditional debate one step further: They argue that localities should be empowered relative to state governments. They contend doing so provides "the democratic churn" that improves national policymaking, Heather K. Gerken, *The Supreme Court, 2009 Term—Foreword: Federalism All the Way Down*, 124 Harv. L. Rev. 4, 10 (2010), and effectively increases popular participation in policymaking since local governments are more accessible to citizens, see Richard Briffault, *Home Rule for the Twenty-First Century*, 36 Urb. Law. 253, 258 (2004).

Perhaps not surprisingly, commentators who wish to see localities empowered condemn the wave of state legislative action to preempt local antidiscrimination laws, immigrant protections, sweetened-beverage taxes, and minimum-wage ordinances, calling these efforts an antidemocratic attack on cities. See Richard C. Schragger, *The Attack on American Cities*, 96 Tex. L. Rev. 1163 (2018). Localists have special ire for North Carolina. In 2016, the Charlotte City Council passed an ordinance expanding local nondiscrimination law to include protection on the basis of sexual orientation, gender identity, and gender expression, including in bathrooms. See Charlotte, N.C., Ordinance 7,056 (Feb. 22, 2016). The North Carolina legislature responded immediately with H.B. 2, the Public Facilities Privacy & Security Act, which mandated that individuals use the bathroom correlated with the biological sex specified on their birth certificates so as to prohibit transgender people from using bathrooms correlating with their gender identities. See N.C. Gen. Stat. §143-422.2 (Supp. 2016) (repealed 2017). (North Carolina's law will not be enforced, due to a partial repeal and legal challenges.)

Is there a difference between North Carolina's efforts to rein in localities and New Mexico's or Wisconsin's? Does it matter to you that Charlotte passed an ordinance to achieve its aims, and that police departments use equitable sharing without one? What other factors would you consider in evaluating these laws?

Often, localists' arguments have a political valence: They seek to stop conservative state governments from preempting progressive policies, such as minimum-wage rules, antidiscrimination policies, and local environmental protections. What if localities are not the progressive actors? David Jaros argues that states should aggressively preempt harmful police practices adopted by localities. See David M. Jaros, *Preempting the Police*, 55 B.C. L. Rev. 1149 (2014). You might think of restrictive state asset forfeiture laws in this way. Is your view about whether states or localities should determine policing practices independent of what you think the best policing practices are? Should it be? Can you identify principled bases for deciding whether federal actors, state actors, or local actors should get to determine what local police officers do?

6. *Other challenges to equitable sharing.* Most of the back and forth about equitable sharing has involved Congress (which passed the statutes authorizing the program), federal agency officials (who developed the programs and set their guidelines), state legislatures (which can preempt local participation), and local police departments (which participate in equitable sharing). Might courts also get involved? Here are two ways they might:

a. *Harjo v. City of Albuquerque*, 326 F. Supp. 3d 1145 (D.N.M. 2018). In addition to taking advantage of state and federal forfeitures, some municipalities build their own forfeiture programs with local ordinances, a practice that has received little notice from scholars. (For a rare exception, see Wayne A. Logan, *The Shadow Criminal Law of Municipal Governance*, 62 Ohio St. L.J. 1409, 1432–1433, 1464–1465 (2001)). In 2018, a federal district court ruled that the City of Albuquerque's vehicle forfeiture program violated due process because, in allowing officials to spend whatever they raised in revenue, it gave officials an unconstitutional institutional incentive to forfeit property. See *Harjo*, 326 F. Supp. 3d at 1193–1195. According to the court, Albuquerque could easily fix the constitutional defect by imposing an independent political check on the relationship between funds collected and funds spent: for instance, by placing forfeited revenue into general funds and then appropriating them to agencies, rather than automatically passing forfeited funds back to officials who conducted the seizures. See *id.* at 1197. Might similar arguments be made with respect to equitable sharing?

b. *Timbs v. Indiana*, 139 S. Ct. 682 (2019). After Tyson Timbs pleaded guilty to selling heroin, Indiana brought a state civil forfeiture action against his car, in which he transported the heroin. Timbs argued that the forfeiture was an unconstitutional excessive fine because the car was worth more than four times the maximum fine that could have been imposed for his offense. In its ruling, the U.S. Supreme Court applied the Eighth Amendment's Excessive Fines Clause to states and refused to reconsider a prior decision that treated civil forfeiture as a fine for constitutional purposes. *Timbs* therefore leaves the door open to claims that forfeitures that are grossly disproportionate to the gravity of the connected criminal offense are unconstitutional. The Court did not explain how courts should determine when a forfeiture is grossly disproportionate, a problem that has led many lower courts to reject similar claims in the past. Might *Timbs* nevertheless augur new hope for people whose property has been seized?

7. *How debates about policing policy happen.* Public debate and pressure to change policing programs is often spurred by organizations committed to bringing change. Asset forfeiture is a good example. The Institute of Justice, a national nonprofit committed to reducing the size and scope of government power, embarked on a national campaign against asset forfeiture in 2014. Since then, it has produced numerous research papers and reports, state rankings, and hundreds of editorials advocating reforming or abolishing civil forfeiture. It has brought several major lawsuits, including *Harjo v. City of Albuquerque*, discussed above, and it has lobbied state legislatures, contributing to reform in two-thirds of states. Although the Institute of Justice is not alone in its interest in forfeiture, it is fair to say that concerns about equitable sharing and asset forfeiture would not be nearly as prominent if not for its intense focus and productivity. What are the risks and rewards of having nonprofits fight for police reform in this way?

D. Military Equipment

1. Background on Militarism in Policing

Police militarization can be defined as "the process whereby civilian police . . . draw from, and pattern themselves around, the tenets of militarism and the military model," which includes "the exercise of military power, hardware, organization, operations, and technology as . . . primary problem-solving tools." Peter B. Kraska, *Militarization and Policing—Its Relevance to 21st Century Police*, 1 Policing 501, 503 (2007). Militarization incorporates into policing the view that threatening and using violence is an effective and appropriate way to address public safety challenges. See *id.*

In contrast to today, early police departments were neither organized on military lines nor equipped with military weaponry. That changed over time. When police reformers sought to professionalize police in the early twentieth century, they turned to military command structures and hierarchy. After police departments were forced to rely on the National Guard to respond to urban riots in the 1960s, departments armored up more thoroughly. And when national leaders used the metaphor of war to frame public safety issues such as crime, drugs, and terrorism in the late twentieth and early twenty-first centuries, the result was a further shift toward military thinking, tactics, organizational structures, and equipment in local policing. Although departments vary, today, the military analogy influences every department and many aspects of policing.

Perhaps the most controversial aspect of militarization in police departments has been the use of equipment common to military operations, including high-powered weaponry and armored vehicles. Agencies argue this equipment improves public and officer safety. First, they reason, it ensures that police can respond to extreme violence in hostage situations, high-risk warrant executions, and other dangerous circumstances. Second, they contend the equipment deters that violence by visibly demonstrating that the police are prepared to use overwhelming force if necessary. As these arguments suggest, military equipment works only by making policing more intrusive: by intimidating, by threatening, and ultimately by employing greater violence against those who are policed including, critics complain, in situations in which far less force would be sufficient.

Some think that—in an age of mass shootings and terrorist attacks—the benefits of military equipment outweigh the harms, more so because criminal suspects experience most of the effects. Others think that—in an age of police shootings of unarmed citizens and pervasive racial disparities in criminal justice—using the equipment does more damage than good.

A RAND study in 2017 illustrates how divided Americans are on the issue. When RAND surveyed members of the public about federal programs that provide local law enforcement agencies with excess military equipment, it found that 48 percent were unaware such programs existed, 33 percent thought they were valuable to the community, and 20 percent thought they were detrimental. See Aaron C. Davenport et al., *An Evaluation of the Department of Defense's Excess Property Program* 57 (2018). Once made aware of the programs, respondents divided as to whether there should be any limits: Whereas 41 percent thought transfer should be limited to nonlethal equipment, 38 percent thought there should be no limits. *Id.* at 57–58. In addition, 5 percent thought the transfers should be ended, and 16 percent had no opinion. *Id.*

SWAT training.

2.   Federal Intervention: 1033 Program

The federal government has come down strongly on one side of the militarism debate, including through grant programs that fund military equipment purchases for local police departments. Most controversial, however, is the Department of Defense's 1033 program, which provides surplus military equipment to law enforcement agencies.

10 U.S.C. §2576A—EXCESS PERSONAL PROPERTY: SALE OR DONATION FOR LAW ENFORCEMENT ACTIVITIES

(a) Transfer authorized.—**(1)** Notwithstanding any other provision of law and subject to subsection (b), the Secretary of Defense may transfer to Federal and State agencies personal property of the Department of Defense, including small arms and ammunition, that the Secretary determines is—

> **(A)** suitable for use by the agencies in law enforcement activities, including counterdrug, counterterrorism, and border security activities; and

> **(B)** excess to the needs of the Department of Defense.

(2) The Secretary shall carry out this section in consultation with the Attorney General, the Director of National Drug Control Policy, and the Secretary of Homeland Security, as appropriate.

(b) Conditions for transfer.—The Secretary of Defense may transfer personal property under this section only if—

(1) the property is drawn from existing stocks of the Department of Defense;

(2) the recipient accepts the property on an as-is, where-is basis;

(3) the transfer is made without the expenditure of any funds available to the Department of Defense for the procurement of defense equipment;

(4) all costs incurred subsequent to the transfer of the property are borne or reimbursed by the recipient;

(5) the recipient, on an annual basis, and with the authorization of the relevant local governing body or authority, certifies that it has adopted publicly available protocols for the appropriate use of controlled property, the supervision of such use, and the evaluation of the effectiveness of such use, including auditing and accountability policies; and

(6) . . . the recipient, on an annual basis, certifies that it provides annual training to relevant personnel on the maintenance, sustainment, and appropriate use of controlled property.

(c) Consideration.—Subject to subsection (b)(4), the Secretary may transfer personal property under this section without charge to the recipient agency.

(d) Preference for certain transfers.—In considering applications for the transfer of personal property under this section, the Secretary shall give a preference to those applications indicating that the transferred property will be used in the counterdrug, counterterrorism, or border security activities of the recipient agency.

(e) Publicly accessible website.—**(1)** The Secretary shall create and maintain a publicly available Internet website that provides information on the controlled property transferred under this section and the recipients of such property.

(2) The contents of the Internet website required under paragraph (1) shall include all publicly accessible unclassified information pertaining to the request, transfer, denial, and repossession of controlled property under this section, including—

(A) a current inventory of all controlled property transferred to Federal and State agencies under this section, listed by the name of the recipient and the year of the transfer;

(B) all pending requests for transfers of controlled property under this section, including the information submitted by the Federal and State agencies requesting such transfers; and

(C) all reports required to be submitted to the Secretary under this section by Federal and State agencies that receive controlled property under this section.

(f) Controlled property.—In this section, the term "controlled property" means any item assigned a demilitarization code of B, C, D, E, G, or Q under Department of Defense Manual 4160.21-M, "Defense Materiel Disposition Manual", or any successor document.

NOTES AND QUESTIONS

1. *Background on 1033.* The program started in 1989, when Congress enacted the National Defense Authorization Act for Fiscal Year 1990, Pub. L. No. 101-189, 103 Stat. 1352 (1989). Section 1208 of the Act allowed the Secretary of Defense to transfer military equipment to police departments for counterdrug activities at no cost to the local departments so long as the equipment was suitable for counterdrug activities and no longer needed by the Department of Defense. Six years later, Congress replaced Section 1208 with Section 1033 in the National Defense Authorization Act for Fiscal Year 1997, Pub. L. No. 104-201, 110 Stat. 2422, 2639 codified as amended at 10 U.S.C. §2576a, expanding what is now known as the 1033 program.

2. *Who distributes the equipment.* The program is administered by the Defense Logistics Agency (DLA), a component of the Department of Defense (DOD) that manages the global supply chain for the Armed Forces. Do you find that odd? It might make sense for the DLA to determine that equipment is surplus. Are they equally suited to decide whether equipment is appropriate for local law enforcement? Who should answer that question?

3. *To whom equipment is distributed.* One of the most notable things about the program as implemented is the disconnect between agency size and acquisitions. More than 8,000 law enforcement agencies have participated in the 1033 program, around 30 percent of which have ten or fewer officers. One-third of the Mine Resistant Ambush Protected vehicles (MRAPs) have gone to agencies with fewer than 50 sworn officers, and nearly two-thirds to agencies with fewer than 100 officers. Aaron C. Davenport et al., RAND Corp., *An Evaluation of the Department of Defense's Excess Property Program* 34 (2018). Nor does the DLA consider crime rates or terrorism risk in assessing requests. Should it? Is small-agency participation a signal that tiny police departments are securing equipment better suited for the risks of big-city policing? Or that the program is efficiently transferring resources to communities that otherwise do not have the tax base to properly equip their departments? What else might it mean?

MRAP obtained by the Pueblo (Colo.) Police Department through the 1033 program.

4. *What is distributed.* Much of the surplus equipment distributed under the program is uncontroversial. It includes office furniture, trailers, first-aid supplies, communications equipment, and flashlights. But the program has also distributed dozens of helicopters; nearly 65,000 rifles; more than 5,000 night-vision scopes; and more than 1,000 assault vehicles, armored trucks, and mine-resistant vehicles. See Davenport et al., *supra,* at 31–32. Altogether, more than $6 billion of equipment has been distributed since the start of the program, including more than $1 billion of equipment to state and local law enforcement agencies since 2015. *Id.* at xiv. Although rifles and magazine cartridges are the most frequent items transferred, MRAPs make up nearly a third of the total value of property held by law enforcement agencies as a result of the program.

5. *Managing the program.* Whatever you think of having a surplus military equipment program in the abstract, the 1033 program has been beset by mismanagement, which has been documented in nine reports by the Government Accountability Office (GAO). Among other problems, equipment has been obtained by unauthorized agencies, lost by departments, and sold by police departments in violation of the program's terms. See, e.g., U.S. Govt. Accountability Office, GAO-06-943, *DOD Excess Property: Control Breakdowns Present Significant Security Risk and Continuing Waste and Inefficiency* (2006); see also U.S. Govt. Accountability Office, GAO-17-532, *DOD Excess Property: Enhanced Controls Needed for Access to Excess Controlled Property* 1–2 (2017) (describing prior assessments). In the latest of the investigations, the GAO set up a sting operation against the DLA. Although there are only 83 federal law enforcement agencies (including Offices of Inspectors General), GAO managed to make up a fake federal agency and use it to obtain more than 100 controlled items worth more than $1 million under the program. *Id.* In evaluating federal programs

that promote controversial forms of policing, how should policymakers think about the risk of poor execution?

6. *Controversy over 1033.* The 1033 program received little public attention until 2014. After Michael Brown, an unarmed African-American teenager, was shot and killed by a police officer in Ferguson, Missouri, protests broke out. Responding officers perched on armored vehicles with sniper rifles and used grenade launchers to fire tear gas into crowds. Pictures of camouflaged officers better prepared for a war zone than a political demonstration went viral on the internet. Although no federal equipment was used to manage the protests in Ferguson, the military equipment exacerbated tensions between the police and the community there, generating new opposition to the federal government's role in supporting militarism in policing.

7. *Congressional response.* In 2015, Congress used the National Defense Authorization Act for Fiscal Year 2016 to add subsections (b)(5)–(6) and (e) above. Pub. L. No. 114-92, 129 Stat. 726 (2015). As a result, the DLA now posts on its website a spreadsheet indicating which agencies have requested and received equipment. As a result, those with the wherewithal can check on their departments. If Congress wants to further improve the likelihood that communities get useful equipment without causing undue harm or distrust for the police, are there additional accountability and transparency mechanisms that you would want Congress to consider? What else might be done to address public concerns? There have been several congressional efforts to restrict the equipment available under the program, but none has yet succeeded.

8. *Executive response.* On January 16, 2015, President Obama issued Exec. Order No. 13688, *Federal Support for Local Law Enforcement Equipment Acquisition,* 3 C.F.R. 261 (2016). The order appointed a working group, which made detailed proposals for improving the 1033 program, and President Obama adopted

those recommendations. See Law Enforcement Equipment Working Group, *Recommendations Pursuant to Executive Order 13688* (2015). Most important, the program instituted three categories for equipment. *Prohibited* items, including tracked armored vehicles, grenade launchers, bayonets, and camouflage uniforms, were no longer available to law enforcement agencies. *Controlled* items, including riot batons, wheeled armored vehicles, and aircraft, were available if an agency could justify the need for it and show that it trained officers on proper use and on civil rights. *Uncontrolled* equipment, including office furniture, continued to be distributed freely. DLA also began requiring local law enforcement agencies to get approval from their mayors or city councils before they could acquire controlled equipment under the program.

President Obama said about the change:

> We've seen how militarized gear can sometimes give people a feeling like there's an occupying force, as opposed to a force that's part of the community that's protecting them and serving them. It can alienate and intimidate local residents, and send the wrong message. So we're going to prohibit some equipment made for the battlefield that is not appropriate for local police departments.

President Barack Obama, Remarks in Camden, New Jersey, 2015 Daily Comp. Pres. Doc. 376, 2 (May 18, 2015).

9. *Change in administration.* In President Trump's first year in office, on August 28, 2017, he issued Exec. Order No. 13809, *Restoring State, Tribal, and Local Law Enforcement's Access to Life-Saving Equipment and Resources,* 3 C.F.R. 378 (2018), which revoked the Obama Administration changes to the program and ordered all agencies to take prompt action to reverse them. The order would seem to apply not only to the categorization of equipment and the civilian sign-off requirement, but also other nonpolitical internal controls such as improved inventory tracking and consistent criteria for evaluating requests. Did the Trump Administration really intend to give away more equipment less rationally? Interestingly, despite the order, the DLA has not indicated any significant changes to its process, which the DOD has discretion in administering. What do you make of that?

Two years after his order, President Trump talked about it in a speech to police chiefs:

> To help keep you safe, I have made 600 million dollars' worth of surplus military equipment available to local law enforcement. If you remember, the previous administration didn't want to do that. Nobody knew why. Sitting in warehouses, getting older and dustier. And I—probably, we pay a lot of rent to a lot of landlords all over the country. So someday, I said, you'll explain. Actually, I do know why: Because they didn't want to make you look so tough. They didn't want to make you look like you're a threat. I said, "That's okay. We want to protect our police." And we made it available. . . .

President Donald Trump, Remarks on Signing an Executive Order on the Commission on Law Enforcement and the Administration of Justice at the International Association of Chiefs of Police Annual Conference and Exposition in Chicago, Illinois, 2019 Daily Comp. Pres. Doc. 760, 6 (Oct. 28, 2019).

Homeland Security Grants

Public debate about militarism in policing has focused almost exclusively on the 1033 program. But that program is dwarfed by the Homeland Security Grant Program, which has provided $35 billion in homeland security preparedness grants since 9/11 to states and localities to prevent, protect against, and prepare responses to acts of terrorism. Local law enforcement agencies have received a substantial amount of that money, which they have often used to fund new equipment, such as bomb-detection robots, unmanned aerial vehicles (known as drones), night-vision equipment, and tactical vehicles. Homeland Security grants are also the primary source of funding for helicopters, tactical vehicles, and personal protective equipment for police departments. One especially popular purchase under the program has been BearCats (Ballistic Engineered Armored Response Counter-Attack Trucks). Made by the military supplier Lenco, these armored personnel carriers include ballistic glass, rotating turrets, and gun ports; each costs around $250,000. Here is what that looks like:

A BearCat deployed in Charlottesville, Virginia, during the Unite the Right rally on August 12, 2017.

What might explain why so much less attention is paid to equipment made available to local police departments through Homeland Security grants?

3.   City and State Responses

Despite ongoing controversies, few cities or states have been willing to systematically restrict the equipment agencies obtain under the program. Montana is an outlier.

MONT. CODE ANN. §§ 7-32-401 TO -402

§7-32-401. Limitations on excess property provided to local law enforcement—definitions.

(1) A law enforcement agency may not receive the following property from a military equipment surplus program operated by the federal government:

(a) drones that are armored, weaponized, or both;

(b) aircraft that are combat configured or combat coded;

(c) grenades or similar explosives and grenade launchers;

(d) silencers; or

(e) militarized armored vehicles.

(2) If a law enforcement agency purchases property from a military equipment surplus program operated by the federal government, the law enforcement agency may only use state or local funds for the purchase. Funds obtained from the federal government may not be used to purchase property from a military equipment surplus program.

(3) For purposes of this section, "law enforcement agency" means a law enforcement service provided by a local government as authorized in Title 7, chapter 32.

§7-32-402. Military surplus—public notification

If a law enforcement agency requests property from a military equipment surplus program, the law enforcement agency shall publish a notice of the request on a publicly accessible website within 14 days after the request.

NOTES AND QUESTIONS

1. *What the state requires.* What difference might Montana's laws make in how the 1033 program operates in the state? Look at §7-32-401(2). What implications does that section have?

2. *Enforcement.* The statute does not specify any cause of action or remedy for violations, and no courts have cited the statute since it was enacted in 2015. Does that matter? Do you expect that some laws get followed even without enforcement? Which ones? How and why?

3. *Alternative forms of state influence.* Citing events in Ferguson, Missouri, as motivation, New Jersey passed a law requiring that city councils approve enrollment in the 1033 program and approve by resolution any equipment acquisition by a local police department under the program. See N.J. Stat. Ann. §40A:5-30.2. This seems to duplicate DLA's practice of requiring civilian approval to obtain controlled equipment under the program. Does that explain why other states have not passed similar legislation? Note that the practice of requiring municipal approval, if it still exists, was generated by President Obama's Executive Order, which has now been countermanded.

4. *Opting out.* More than 8,000 agencies have participated in the 1033 program, but that also means that more than 7,000 have not participated. Some used to participate but no longer do so. In Seattle, the police department returned all of the equipment it received under the program, and after that, the City Council passed Ordinance 125472 (Nov. 28, 2017), which prohibited the department from receiving federal surplus military equipment. Why don't more cities address

concerns about military equipment this way? Go to the DLA website and look up whether your city participates in the program. Can you tell what it has received? Are you concerned? If you are, what do you think you can do about it? If your agency does not participate, do you want it to do so? Shouldn't it get free filing cabinets if it can?

E.   Immigration Policing

1.   Background on Local Participation in Immigration Enforcement

Immigration law and policy determine when citizens from other countries may enter and remain in the United States and mandate when they must leave. Serious debates among citizens and policymakers alike exist about how—and how vigorously—the United States should enforce immigration law. One aspect of those debates affects local policing significantly. To mitigate the challenges of having limited resources, information, and reach to find undocumented immigrants, the federal government has tried for several decades to leverage local police officers in fighting illegal immigration.

States and localities have their own interests in how local police treat immigrants. Some jurisdictions strongly support local participation in immigration enforcement because, they argue, illegal immigrants pose a public safety threat and burden schools, hospitals, and social services. Local policing of federal immigration law, they believe, discourages settlement and uproots undocumented people from their communities. Other states and localities oppose police participation in immigration enforcement because, they contend, it alienates immigrant communities, which makes local law enforcement less effective: Victims may avoid calling the police, and witnesses could refuse to cooperate with investigations. It also can lead to racial profiling that corrodes community relations.

As the other examples in the chapter illustrate, the federal government often uses money and equipment to get local actors to pursue federal public safety goals. In the immigration context, the federal government has invited, cajoled, and sometimes coerced localities. In response, localities have often turned programs to their own purposes or resisted federal goals altogether. Sometimes states have stepped in to support one side or the other. Those interested in immigration policy or federalism might be interested in this battle for other reasons: Here, the intergovernmental legal back and forth indicates just how critical local policing is, not just to local public safety, but to the capacity of all levels of government to realize their priorities and goals, raising the stakes of the law of the police.

2.   Round 1: State Resistance and Federal Response

In the 1980s, a rise in unauthorized immigration led to increased federal efforts to discourage immigration, to deport illegal immigrants, and to encourage local governments to participate in federal immigration goals. Most significantly, the Immigration Reform and Control Act, Pub. L. No. 99-603, 100 Stat. 3359 (1986), among its other provisions, banned employing undocumented immigrants and encouraged deporting immigrants who had committed crimes. Some states and cities worried about the effects of expanded immigration enforcement, and they passed ordinances and statutes in response. This is Oregon's statute:

OR. REV. STAT. ANN. §181A.820. ENFORCEMENT OF FEDERAL IMMIGRATION LAWS

(1) No law enforcement agency of the State of Oregon or of any political subdivision of the state shall use agency moneys, equipment or personnel for the purpose of detecting or apprehending persons whose only violation of law is that they are persons of foreign citizenship present in the United States in violation of federal immigration laws.

(2) Notwithstanding subsection (1) of this section, a law enforcement agency may exchange information with United States Immigration and Customs Enforcement, United States Citizenship and Immigration Services and United States Customs and Border Protection in order to:

> **(a)** Verify the immigration status of a person if the person is arrested for any criminal offense; or

> **(b)** Request criminal investigation information with reference to persons named in records of the United States Immigration and Customs Enforcement, United States Citizenship and Immigration Services or United States Customs and Border Protection.

(3) Notwithstanding subsection (1) of this section, a law enforcement agency may arrest any person who:

> **(a)** Is charged by the United States with a criminal violation of federal immigration laws . . . and

> **(b)** Is subject to arrest for the crime pursuant to a warrant of arrest issued by a federal magistrate. . . .

As federal immigration enforcement intensified in the 1990s, the federal government responded to states and localities like Oregon with the following statute:

8 U.S.C. 1373(A)–(B). COMMUNICATION BETWEEN GOVERNMENT AGENCIES AND THE IMMIGRATION AND NATURALIZATION SERVICE

(a) In general

Notwithstanding any other provision of Federal, State, or local law, a Federal, State, or local government entity or official may not prohibit, or in any way restrict, any government entity or official from sending to, or receiving from, the Immigration and Naturalization Service information regarding the citizenship or immigration status, lawful or unlawful, of any individual.

(b) Additional authority of government entities

Notwithstanding any other provision of Federal, State, or local law, no person or agency may prohibit, or in any way restrict, a Federal, State, or local government entity from doing any of the following with respect to information regarding the immigration status, lawful or unlawful, of any individual:

(1) Sending such information to, or requesting or receiving such information from, the Immigration and Naturalization Service.

(2) Maintaining such information.

(3) Exchanging such information with any other Federal, State, or local government entity.

NOTES AND QUESTIONS

1. *Oregon's law.* What does Oregon forbid? What does it command?

2. *Pressure to repeal.* Although Oregon's law remains in effect, it also remains controversial. It has survived several attempts to repeal it, including in 2018 through Ballot Measure 105. In the end, more liberal urban counties in Oregon overwhelmed the largely rural support, and the measure was defeated. On the other side, supporters of the statute have tried to strengthen the law. In 2019, a bill was introduced to amend the statute to permit civil actions for injunctive relief, damages, and reasonable attorney fees against law enforcement agencies that violate it. That bill never got out of committee. See 2019 Or. H.B. 3398 (Mar. 26, 2019). Although more than 30 years have passed since the statute was enacted, no one in Oregon expects that the fight is over.

3. *Federal command.* What precisely does §1373 do? What action does it require of local and state governments? What policies does it prohibit? For example, is it consistent with §1373 for a local agency to adopt a policy prohibiting officers from asking about immigration status?

4. *Oregon and §1373.* Is Oregon's statute still good law after §1373?

3.   Round 2: Federal Enticement and Local Subversion—Section 287(g)

At the same time Congress passed §1373 *prohibiting* some kinds of local resistance, it also attempted to create a carrot, an incentive for locals to cooperate with federal efforts. The Illegal Immigration Reform and Immigrant Responsibility Act of 1996, Pub. L. No. 104-208, div. C, 110 Stat. 3009-546 (1996), added section 287(g) to the Immigration and Nationality Act, codified as 8 U.S.C. §1357(g).

8 U.S.C. §1357(G). PERFORMANCE OF IMMIGRATION OFFICER FUNCTIONS BY STATE OFFICERS AND EMPLOYEES

(1) . . . [T]he Attorney General may enter into a written agreement with a State, or any political subdivision of a State, pursuant to which an officer or employee of the State or subdivision, who is determined by the Attorney General to be qualified to perform a function of an immigration officer in relation to the investigation, apprehension, or detention of aliens in the United States (including the transportation of such aliens across State lines to detention centers), may carry out such function at the expense of the State or political subdivision and to the extent consistent with State and local law.

(2) An agreement under this subsection shall require that an officer or employee of a State or political subdivision of a State performing a function under the agreement shall have knowledge of, and adhere to, Federal law relating to the function, . . .

(3) In performing a function under this subsection, an officer or employee of a State or political subdivision of a State shall be subject to the direction and supervision of the Attorney General.

(4) In performing a function under this subsection, an officer or employee of a State or political subdivision of a State may use Federal property or facilities, as provided in a written agreement between the Attorney General and the State or subdivision.

(5) With respect to each officer or employee of a State or political subdivision who is authorized to perform a function under this subsection, the specific powers and duties that may be, or are required to be, exercised or performed by the individual, the duration of the authority of the individual, and the position of the agency of the Attorney General who is required to supervise and direct the individual, shall be set forth in a written agreement between the Attorney General and the State or political subdivision. . . .

(9) Nothing in this subsection shall be construed to require any State or political subdivision of a State to enter into an agreement with the Attorney General under this subsection.

(10) Nothing in this subsection shall be construed to require an agreement under this subsection in order for any officer or employee of a State or political subdivision of a State—

> **(A)** to communicate with the Attorney General regarding the immigration status of any individual, including reporting knowledge that a particular alien is not lawfully present in the United States; or

> **(B)** otherwise to cooperate with the Attorney General in the identification, apprehension, detention, or removal of aliens not lawfully present in the United States.

NOTES AND QUESTIONS

1. *The statute and a program.* Section 287(g) effectively allows local officers to be trained and deputized as federal immigration officials pursuant to a federal–local agreement. But the section lay largely dormant until after 9/11, when the federal government intensified immigration enforcement in conjunction with its terrorism prevention efforts. Around the same time, a government reorganization replaced the Immigration and Naturalization Service, which had been an agency within the Department of Justice, with Immigration and Customs Enforcement (ICE), in the new Department of Homeland Security. Thus, although the statute refers to the Attorney General, immigration enforcement and §287(g) implementation are now within the control of the Secretary of Homeland Security. Imagine it is 2002 and you are appointed chief of ICE's Office of State and Local Coordination. Your mandate is to build a program to encourage local cooperation with federal immigration enforcement using the authority given to you by §287(g). What would you take to be fixed aspects of the program? What flexibility do you think you have? If you were giving a speech to local police chiefs and sheriffs, what would you say about why they should participate?

2. *How it worked initially.* Although the 287(g) program started in 2002, only a few jurisdictions entered agreements in the first few years. After 2006, funding for the program and participation picked up notably. At the time, ICE used three types of agreements with localities. Under the *jail model*, sheriffs' deputies

or corrections officials working in a jail or prison could use federal databases to determine a person's immigration status and then process aliens for removal, at which time ICE could take them into federal custody. Under the *task force model*, local law enforcement officers participating in joint task forces with federal officers were designated to enforce federal immigration law directly, allowing them to make warrantless arrests of illegal aliens, process them, and transport them to ICE facilities. Finally, some jurisdictions received both powers, under the *joint model*.

3. *Local use of 287(g)*. The program did not go exactly as planned. Advocates of 287(g) claimed that it would help public safety by ridding communities of dangerous terrorists, drug traffickers, and violent criminals. But that was not what local agencies did with their new immigration powers. Instead, although the federal goal was to deport removable aliens who had committed serious crimes, the GAO reported in 2009 that "some participating agencies are using their 287(g) authority to process for removal aliens who have committed minor crimes, such as carrying an open container of alcohol." U.S. Govt. Accountability Office, GAO-09-109, *Immigration Enforcement: Better Controls Needed over Program Authorizing State and Local Enforcement of Federal Immigration Laws* 4 (2009). Moreover, some agencies went crazy with the new authority: One jurisdiction conducted 13,000 arrests in 2008 alone under the program. *Id.* at 5. Even local agencies involved in the program worried that 287(g) was being used to deport people after minor offenses and to engage in racial profiling. See *id.* at 6. Why might local agencies have failed to adhere to federal priorities? Is that an issue of oversight or the structure of the program? What incentives might 287(g) have created for local law enforcement?

4. *How the program changed.* In response to the GAO report and other criticisms of the program, ICE revamped its 287(g) program, reemphasizing the limits of local authority and shifting from task force agreements to jail agreements by which only jail personnel, and not police officers, could check immigration status or process criminal suspects for federal immigration violations. What consequence might these agreements have for policing? Oddly, the results might depend on what patrol officers think of immigration:

> Since patrol officers cannot check immigration status or hold someone for illegal status, the only way for an officer to confirm or dispel suspicion that someone is illegally present in the country is to arrest the suspect—if there is probable cause for a state or local offense—and take him to jail, where such a check can occur. Ordinarily, police officers do not arrest, transport, and book suspects for traffic violations or minor crimes, though those arrests are constitutional and often permitted under state law. Instead, they usually issue a citation or summons to appear for further proceedings. Thus, in order to gain the benefits of increased immigration enforcement pursuant to a 287(g) agreement, jurisdictions must arrest suspects who—absent the 287(g) program—would likely have been released.

Rachel A. Harmon, *Federal Programs and the Real Costs of Policing*, 90 N.Y.U. 870, 916 (2015). What about officers or police departments who are more concerned about their relationships with immigrant communities? What are their incentives if the county sheriff's office that runs the jail has a 287(g) agreement? Can you see that, either way, the program could distort police decision making?

4.   Round 3: Arizona S.B. 1070 and Its Aftermath

The Obama Administration sought to expand immigration enforcement but focus on illegal aliens who posed a national security or public safety risk. States and localities that opposed intensified enforcement responded with new laws like Oregon's. States and localities that disagreed with the narrowing of immigration priorities reacted differently. Consider Arizona.

Arizona has long viewed itself as particularly hard hit by illegal immigration. Before the 287(g) program was revamped in response to the GAO report, several Arizona jurisdictions were among those that used 287(g) powers aggressively to deport removable aliens following minor infractions. Afterward, the agreements became less useful for suppressing the costs of illegal immigration, and many Arizonans decried federal enforcement failure, arguing that state action was necessary. In this spirit, in 2010, Arizona passed S.B. 1070, ch. 113, 2010 Ariz. Sess. Laws 450, to ensure "cooperative enforcement of federal immigration laws throughout all of Arizona," to discourage illegal immigrants from coming to or staying in Arizona. See *id.* §1. Among its other provisions, S.B. 1070 and H.B. 2162, ch. 211, 2010 Ariz. Sess. Laws 1070 (a bill amending S.B. 1070 passed a few days later), revised Arizona law to include the following:

ARIZ. REV. STAT. ANN. §11-1051. COOPERATION AND ASSISTANCE IN ENFORCEMENT OF IMMIGRATION LAWS; INDEMNIFICATION

A. No official or agency of this state or a county, city, town or other political subdivision of this state may limit or restrict the enforcement of federal immigration laws to less than the full extent permitted by federal law.

B. For any lawful stop, detention or arrest made by a law enforcement official or a law enforcement agency of this state or a law enforcement official or a law enforcement agency of a county, city, town or other political subdivision of this state in the enforcement of any other law or ordinance of a county, city or town or this state where reasonable suspicion exists that the person is an alien and is unlawfully present in the United States, a reasonable attempt shall be made, when practicable, to determine the immigration status of the person, except if the determination may hinder or obstruct an investigation. Any person who is arrested shall have the person's immigration status determined before the person is released. The person's immigration status shall be verified with the federal government pursuant to 8 United States Code §1373(c). A law enforcement official or agency of this state or a county, city, town or other political subdivision of this state may not consider race, color or national origin in implementing the requirements of this subsection except to the extent permitted by the United States or Arizona Constitution. . . .

D. Notwithstanding any other law, a law enforcement agency may securely transport an alien who the agency has received verification is unlawfully present in the United States and who is in the agency's custody to a federal facility in this state or to any other point of transfer into federal custody that is outside the jurisdiction of the law enforcement agency. . . .

E. In the implementation of this section, an alien's immigration status may be determined by:

1. A law enforcement officer who is authorized by the federal government to verify or ascertain an alien's immigration status.

2. The United States immigration and customs enforcement or the United States customs and border protection pursuant to 8 United States Code §1373(c).

F. Except as provided in federal law, officials or agencies of this state and counties, cities, towns and other political subdivisions of this state may not be prohibited or in any way be restricted from sending, receiving or maintaining information relating to the immigration status, lawful or unlawful, of any individual or exchanging that information with any other federal, state or local governmental entity for the following official purposes:

1. Determining eligibility for any public benefit, service or license provided by any federal, state, local or other political subdivision of this state. . . .

3. If the person is an alien, determining whether the person is in compliance with the federal registration laws prescribed by title II, chapter 7 of the federal immigration and nationality act.

4. Pursuant to 8 United States Code §1373 and 8 United States Code §1644[2]. . . .

H. A person who is a legal resident of this state may bring an action in superior court to challenge any official or agency of this state or a county, city, town or other political subdivision of this state that adopts or implements a policy that limits or restricts the enforcement of federal immigration laws, including 8 United States Code §§1373 and 1644, to less than the full extent permitted by federal law. If there is a judicial finding that an entity has violated this section, the court shall order that the entity pay a civil penalty of not less than five hundred dollars and not more than five thousand dollars for each day that the policy has remained in effect after the filing of an action pursuant to this subsection.

I. A court shall collect the civil penalty prescribed in subsection H of this section and remit the civil penalty to the state treasurer for deposit in the gang and immigration intelligence team enforcement mission fund established by §41-1724.

J. The court may award court costs and reasonable attorney fees to any person or any official or agency of this state or a county, city, town or other political subdivision of this state that prevails by an adjudication on the merits in a proceeding brought pursuant to this section.

K. Except in relation to matters in which the officer is adjudged to have acted in bad faith, a law enforcement officer is indemnified by the law enforcement officer's agency against reasonable costs and expenses, including attorney fees, incurred by the officer in connection with any action, suit or proceeding brought pursuant to this section in which the officer may be a defendant by reason of the officer being or having been a member of the law enforcement agency. . . .

---

[2] *Ed. Note.* 8 U.S.C. §1644 provides in full: "Notwithstanding any other provision of Federal, State, or local law, no State or local government entity may be prohibited, or in any way restricted, from sending to or receiving from the Immigration and Naturalization Service information regarding the immigration status, lawful or unlawful, of an alien in the United States."

NOTES AND QUESTIONS ABOUT ARIZONA LAW

1. *What does it do?* What does section 11-1051 require police officers to do? What does it permit them to do? What does it forbid them from doing? And how does the enforcement mechanism work?

2. *The rest of the statute.* The above statute comes from section 2 of S.B. 1070. Before the statute took effect, the U.S. Department of Justice filed suit challenging the constitutionality of other parts of the law, and in *Arizona v. United States*, 567 U.S. 387 (2012), the Supreme Court ruled that federal immigration law preempted three sections of S.B. 1070 (not included above): (1) section 3, which made failure to comply with federal alien-registration requirements a state misdemeanor; (2) section 5(C), which made looking for work or working as an unauthorized alien a state misdemeanor; and (3) section 6, which authorized state and local officers to arrest without a warrant any person the officer had probable cause to believe had committed an offense that would make the person removable. The Court also "reject[ed] out of hand any possibility" that local officers could detain individuals for federal civil immigration offenses to facilitate removal "without federal direction." See *Arizona*, 567 U.S. at 455 (Thomas, J., concurring) (describing the majority opinion). The Court upheld section 2(B) — which appears above as section 11-1051(B) — requiring officers to verify immigration status during stops and arrests. The rest of section 2 went unchallenged.

3. *Aftermath of* Arizona v. United States. Although *Arizona v. United States* over-ruled substantial parts of the statute, Arizona Governor Jan Brewer declared the decision a victory because it permitted local officers to continue to check immigration status during traffic stops. In response, the Department of Homeland Security revoked the task force model 287(g) agreements it had with agencies in Arizona, making that check harder to carry out. It also announced that it would not respond to calls by Arizona officers for ICE to take custody of an illegal immigrant, unless the person satisfied federal immigration enforcement priorities. Were these efforts likely to stymie the effect of Arizona's statute?

4. *Other states.* The Arizona law was intended to be, and was in fact, the broadest and strictest anti-illegal immigrant statute passed by any state. Other states, including Indiana, Georgia, South Carolina, Alabama, and Utah, quickly followed with similar laws. Still, in other jurisdictions, including other border states with substantial Latino populations, similar efforts failed.

5. Round 4: Secure Communities and State Reponses

As the problems with the 287(g) program grew, ICE under the Obama Administration ramped up an alternative, the Secure Communities program, which needed no statutory authorization. Under Secure Communities, when local jail officials submit fingerprints to the FBI for criminal-history records checks, those fingerprints are automatically sent to the Department of Homeland Security (DHS) for comparison with DHS's immigration database and evaluation of the arrestee's immigration status. On that basis, DHS determines whether to issue a detainer request, asking the local agency to hold the arrestee for up to 48 hours after his scheduled release to allow federal officials to take the person into custody for removal. Because effectively all local jails submit fingerprints to the FBI for criminal-history record checks, and the federal government made it impossible to submit fingerprints for criminal-history processing without triggering an immigration check, under Secure Communities, an arrest by local police inevitably subjects the arrestee to immigration screening.

Secure Communities was intended by the Obama Administration to avoid some of the problems with 287(g) by automating screening and leaving removal in the hands of ICE, which could make sure that only priority unauthorized immigrants were removed. It turned out, however, that some local law enforcement agencies worried about their relations with local immigrant communities and objected to screening and holding suspects for ICE. Dozens of cities and counties rebelled against the program, passing ordinances or policies that prohibited jail officials from honoring many ICE detainer requests.

In 2013, California passed the first state law limiting local cooperation with Secure Communities.

THE TRANSPARENCY AND RESPONSIBILITY USING STATE TOOLS (TRUST) ACT, CH. 570, 2013 CAL. STAT. 4649

SECTION 1.

The Legislature finds and declares all of the following:

(a) The United States Immigration and Customs Enforcement's (ICE) Secure Communities program shifts the burden of federal civil immigration enforcement onto local law enforcement. To operate the Secure Communities program, ICE relies on voluntary requests, known as ICE holds or detainers, to local law enforcement to hold individuals in local jails for additional time beyond when they would be eligible for release in a criminal matter. . . .

(c) Unlike criminal detainers, which are supported by a warrant and require probable cause, there is no requirement for a warrant and no established standard of proof, such as reasonable suspicion or probable cause, for issuing an ICE detainer request. . . .

(d) The Secure Communities program and immigration detainers harm community policing efforts because immigrant residents who are victims of or witnesses to crime, including domestic violence, are less likely to report crime or cooperate with law enforcement when any contact with law enforcement could result in deportation. The program can result in a person being held and transferred into immigration detention without regard to whether the arrest is the result of a mistake. . . .

(e) It is the intent of the Legislature that this act shall not be construed as providing, expanding, or ratifying the legal authority for any state or local law enforcement agency to detain an individual on an immigration hold.

SECTION 2. Chapter 17.1 . . . is added to Division 7 of Title 1 of the Government Code, to read: . . .

7282.5 (a) A law enforcement official shall have discretion to cooperate with federal immigration officials by detaining an individual on the basis of an immigration hold after that individual becomes eligible for release from custody only if the continued detention of the individual on the basis of the immigration hold would not violate any federal, state, or local law, or any local policy, and only under any of the following circumstances:

(1) The individual has been convicted of a serious or violent felony identified in subdivision (c) of Section 1192.7 of, or subdivision (c) of Section 667.5 of, the Penal Code.

(2) The individual has been convicted of a felony punishable by imprisonment in the state prison.

(3) The individual has been convicted within the past five years of a misdemeanor for a crime that is punishable as either a misdemeanor or a felony for, or has been convicted at any time of a felony for, any of the following offenses: . . . [listing serious, mostly violent, crimes]

(4) The individual is a current registrant on the California Sex and Arson Registry.

(5) The individual is arrested and taken before a magistrate on a charge involving a serious or violent felony, . . . a felony punishable by imprisonment in state prison, or any felony listed in paragraph (2) or (3) other than domestic violence, and the magistrate makes a finding of probable cause as to that charge pursuant to Section 872 of the Penal Code.

(6) The individual has been convicted of a federal crime that meets the definition of an aggravated felony as set forth in subparagraphs (A) to (P), inclusive, of paragraph (43) of subsection (a) of Section 101 of the federal Immigration and Nationality Act (8 U.S.C. Sec. 1101), or is identified by the United States Department of Homeland Security's Immigration and Customs Enforcement as the subject of an outstanding federal felony arrest warrant.

(b) If none of the conditions listed in subdivision (a) is satisfied, an individual shall not be detained on the basis of an immigration hold after the individual becomes eligible for release from custody. . . .

NOTES AND QUESTIONS

1. *Immigration and policing.* In one light, Secure Communities has nothing to do with policing. It simply serves as a way for federal immigration officials to find potential aliens to screen, although in doing so it imposes on jail officials. But in another way, Secure Communities is part of the ongoing battle about who gets to decide how local police officers interact with immigrant communities. What incentives does Secure Communities create for officers in different communities? Specifically, how might it distort custodial arrest practices for crimes where those arrests are discretionary, such as misdemeanor and traffic offenses?

2. *What is the problem?* Secure Communities triggers screening whenever cities check fingerprints against the federal database, something that is important to local policing and hard to avoid. Although local agencies choose whether to respect detention requests, the program requires agencies to opt out of compliance rather than to opt in to cooperation, the way 287(g) and other federal policing programs do. See Trevor George Gardner, *Immigrant Sanctuary as the "Old Normal": A Brief History of Police Federalism*, 119 Colum. L. Rev. 1 (2019) (describing Secure Communities as anomalous in the history of federal relations with local policing). What if the

program were fully *voluntary*? A jurisdiction could trigger immigration screening when making an arrest and detain a removable person, but no jurisdiction would have to do so. Would that make the program unproblematic as a means of soliciting local law enforcement cooperation in federal immigration efforts? Or could it still have a distorting effect on policing?[3]

3. *California Trust Act.* What does the Trust Act require local officers to do? Permit them to do? Forbid them from doing? How is it different from Oregon's law?

4. *The (temporary) death of Secure Communities.* After outright rebellion, with hundreds of communities refusing to participate, the Obama Administration gave up on Secure Communities in late 2014 and replaced it with the Priority Enforcement Program (PEP). PEP was a more voluntary program that solicited local cooperation after instituting deportation priorities. As with Secure Communities, an immigration screening was automatically triggered when a local jail submitted fingerprints to the FBI database. But under PEP, ICE could request a brief detention only with probable cause that the person was removable and fell into a priority category. ICE could also request that the person be transferred to federal custody, but only if the person had been convicted of a priority violent crime, belonged to a criminal gang, or posed a national security threat. Was PEP a victory for states and localities? Do you have any problems with *that* approach? Perhaps it doesn't matter: PEP was short-lived.

6.   Round 5: Executive Order 13768 and Local Resistance

Donald Trump campaigned on a tough approach to immigration. On his fifth day as President, Trump issued an executive order on interior immigration enforcement, Executive Order 13768, 3 C.F.R. 268 (2018). Among other things, this order dictated the administration's policy with respect to local participation in federal immigration enforcement.

ENHANCING PUBLIC SAFETY IN THE INTERIOR OF THE UNITED STATES

By the authority vested in me as President by the Constitution and the laws of the United States of America, including the Immigration and Nationality Act (INA) (8 U.S.C. 1101 et seq.), and in order to ensure the public safety of the American people in communities across the United States as well as to ensure that our Nation's immigration laws are faithfully executed, I hereby declare the policy of the executive branch to be, and order, as follows:

---

[3] Whether or not Secure Communities skews local policing, you might wonder whether it asks local law enforcement to violate the Fourth Amendment. After all, the Fourth Amendment does not permit an arrest except upon probable cause. *Federal* officials may detain an undocumented immigrant on probable cause that the person has violated federal *civil* immigration law but, except under 287(g), *local* officers do not have that authority. When ICE asks local officials to detain a person for removal after he is scheduled to be released, is the agency asking that the person be held without probable cause? Maybe so. See Gonzalez v. Immigration and Customs Enforcement, 416 F. Supp. 3d 995, 1016 (2019) (holding that "ICE violates the Fourth Amendment by issuing detainers to state and local law enforcement agencies in states that do not expressly authorize civil immigration arrests in state statute[s]").

Section 1. Purpose. Interior enforcement of our Nation's immigration laws is critically important to the national security and public safety of the United States. Many aliens who illegally enter the United States and those who overstay or otherwise violate the terms of their visas present a significant threat to national security and public safety. This is particularly so for aliens who engage in criminal conduct in the United States.

Sanctuary jurisdictions across the United States willfully violate Federal law in an attempt to shield aliens from removal from the United States. These jurisdictions have caused immeasurable harm to the American people and to the very fabric of our Republic. . . .

Although Federal immigration law provides a framework for Federal-State partnerships in enforcing our immigration laws to ensure the removal of aliens who have no right to be in the United States, the Federal Government has failed to discharge this basic sovereign responsibility. We cannot faithfully execute the immigration laws of the United States if we exempt classes or categories of removable aliens from potential enforcement. The purpose of this order is to direct executive departments and agencies (agencies) to employ all lawful means to enforce the immigration laws of the United States.

Section 2. Policy. It is the policy of the executive branch to:

(a) Ensure the faithful execution of the immigration laws of the United States, including the INA, against all removable aliens, consistent with Article II, Section 3 of the United States Constitution and section 3331 of title 5, United States Code;[4]

(b) Make use of all available systems and resources to ensure the efficient and faithful execution of the immigration laws of the United States;

(c) Ensure that jurisdictions that fail to comply with applicable Federal law do not receive Federal funds, except as mandated by law; [and]

(d) Ensure that aliens ordered removed from the United States are promptly removed; . . .

Section 8. Federal-State Agreements. It is the policy of the executive branch to empower State and local law enforcement agencies across the country to perform the functions of an immigration officer in the interior of the United States to the maximum extent permitted by law.

(a) In furtherance of this policy, the Secretary shall immediately take appropriate action to engage with the Governors of the States, as well as local officials, for the purpose of preparing to enter into agreements under section 287(g) of the INA (8 U.S.C. 1357(g)).

(b) To the extent permitted by law and with the consent of State or local officials, as appropriate, the Secretary shall take appropriate action, through agreements under section 287(g) of the INA, or otherwise, to authorize State and local law enforcement officials, as the Secretary determines are qualified and appropriate,

---

[4] *Ed. note:* 5 U.S.C. §3331 (2018) states in full:

An individual, except the President, elected or appointed to an office of honor or profit in the civil service or uniformed services, shall take the following oath: "I, AB, do solemnly swear (or affirm) that I will support and defend the Constitution of the United States against all enemies, foreign and domestic; that I will bear true faith and allegiance to the same; that I take this obligation freely, without any mental reservation or purpose of evasion; and that I will well and faithfully discharge the duties of the office on which I am about to enter. So help me God." This section does not affect other oaths required by law.

to perform the functions of immigration officers in relation to the investigation, apprehension, or detention of aliens in the United States under the direction and the supervision of the Secretary. Such authorization shall be in addition to, rather than in place of, Federal performance of these duties.

(c) To the extent permitted by law, the Secretary may structure each agreement under section 287(g) of the INA in a manner that provides the most effective model for enforcing Federal immigration laws for that jurisdiction.

Section 9. Sanctuary Jurisdictions. It is the policy of the executive branch to ensure, to the fullest extent of the law, that a State, or a political subdivision of a State, shall comply with 8 U.S.C. 1373.[5]

(a) In furtherance of this policy, the Attorney General and the Secretary, in their discretion and to the extent consistent with law, shall ensure that jurisdictions that willfully refuse to comply with 8 U.S.C. 1373 (sanctuary jurisdictions) are not eligible to receive Federal grants, except as deemed necessary for law enforcement purposes by the Attorney General or the Secretary. The Secretary has the authority to designate, in his discretion and to the extent consistent with law, a jurisdiction as a sanctuary jurisdiction. The Attorney General shall take appropriate enforcement action against any entity that violates 8 U.S.C. 1373, or which has in effect a statute, policy, or practice that prevents or hinders the enforcement of Federal law.

(b) To better inform the public regarding the public safety threats associated with sanctuary jurisdictions, the Secretary shall utilize the Declined Detainer Outcome Report or its equivalent and, on a weekly basis, make public a comprehensive list of criminal actions committed by aliens and any jurisdiction that ignored or otherwise failed to honor any detainers with respect to such aliens. . . .

Section 10. Review of Previous Immigration Actions and Policies.

(a) The Secretary shall immediately take all appropriate action to terminate the Priority Enforcement Program (PEP) described in the memorandum issued by the Secretary on November 20, 2014, and to reinstitute the immigration program known as "Secure Communities" referenced in that memorandum. . . .

Section 16. Transparency. To promote the transparency and situational awareness of criminal aliens in the United States, the Secretary and the Attorney General are hereby directed to collect relevant data and provide quarterly reports on the following:

(a) the immigration status of all aliens incarcerated under the supervision of the Federal Bureau of Prisons;

(b) the immigration status of all aliens incarcerated as Federal pretrial detainees under the supervision of the United States Marshals Service; and

(c) the immigration status of all convicted aliens incarcerated in State prisons and local detention centers throughout the United States. . . .

DONALD J. TRUMP

THE WHITE HOUSE, January 25, 2017

---

[5] *Ed. note:* 8 U.S.C. §1373 is excerpted above.

NOTES AND QUESTIONS

1. *What it does.* Under President Trump's order, all unauthorized immigrants are prioritized for removal, the Secure Communities and 287(g) programs have new life, and the Priority Enforcement Program ends. What else does the order do that could affect local policing?

2. *Trump Administration and 287(g).* What are the order's specific instructions with respect to 287(g)? After the order, the program expanded, but perhaps not as much as you might expect. First, ICE never revived the task force agreements. Instead, all 287(g) agreements empower jail officials rather than patrol or task force officers. And second, although ICE has signed some additional agreements, as of July 2020, there were only 74 agreements in place in 21 states, all but a few with county sheriff's offices. But there are more than 3,000 sheriff's offices in the United States, and almost none of the largest ones are participating in the program. In fact, few of the agreements include cities of any significant size, and many apply to areas that have very few immigrants. What might be going on?

3. *Sanctuary cities.* President Trump's executive order signaled the administration's intent both to expand local cooperation and to thwart local resistance, including by denying sanctuary cities and counties federal public safety grants. There is no legal definition of a sanctuary city, but it usually refers to cities that adopt policies or ordinances restricting local cooperation with federal immigration enforcement efforts, including some or all of the following:

> a. prohibiting local law enforcement officers from asking about immigration status;
> b. prohibiting participation in 287(g);
> c. limiting compliance with detainer requests under Secure Communities;
> d. prohibiting giving ICE information about potentially removable aliens.
> e. refusing to participate in multiagency task forces that engage in immigration enforcement; and
> f. prohibiting ICE agents from accessing local jails to question immigrants.

No sanctuary city prohibits (or could prohibit) federal immigration enforcement by federal officers within their borders. Despite the order, or maybe because of it, many new cities announced an intention to become sanctuaries after President Trump acted. See Christopher N. Lasch et al., *Understanding "Sanctuary Cities,"* 59 B.C. L. Rev. 1703, 1737–1752 (2018) (describing and citing sanctuary policies).

4. *Legal challenges to Order 13768.* Unlike Congress's efforts with §1373 and 287(g), neither of which required local participation in federal immigration enforcement, Trump's order seems to *demand* local action. Within days of Trump's order, the City of San Francisco, and subsequently the County of Santa Clara, filed suit against the President seeking declarative and injunctive relief on the ground that Section 9(a)'s instruction to the attorney general to enforce §1373(a) impermissibly commandeers state and local governments to enforcement of federal immigration law in violation of the Tenth Amendment. According to the complaint, the executive order denies "a local government's autonomy to devote resources to local priorities and to control the exercise of its own police powers, rather than being forced to carry out the agenda of the Federal government." Complaint at ¶9, City

and County of San Francisco v. Trump, No. 4:17-cv-00485-DMR (N.D. Cal. filed Jan. 31, 2017).

In the fall of 2017, a district judge granted summary judgment for the plaintiffs and issued a permanent injunction against enforcing section 9(a) of the Executive Order. County of Santa Clara v. Trump, 275 F. Supp. 3d 1196, 1202 (N.D. Cal. 2017). The federal government appealed the injunction to the U.S. Court of Appeals for the Ninth Circuit, and the Ninth Circuit upheld the district court's decision on separation-of-powers grounds.

> [T]he Administration has not even attempted to show that Congress authorized it to withdraw federal grant moneys from jurisdictions that do not agree with the current Administration's immigration strategies. Nor could it. In fact, Congress has frequently considered and thus far rejected legislation accomplishing the goals of the Executive Order. The sheer amount of failed legislation on this issue demonstrates the importance and divisiveness of the policies in play. . . . Not only has the Administration claimed for itself Congress's exclusive spending power, it has also attempted to coopt Congress's power to legislate.
>
> Because the Executive Order directs Executive Branch administrative agencies to withhold funding that Congress has not tied to compliance with §1373, there is no reasonable argument that the President has not exceeded his authority. Absent congressional authorization, the Administration may not redistribute or withhold properly appropriated funds in order to effectuate its own policy goals. Because Congress did not authorize withholding of funds, the Executive Order violates the constitutional principle of the Separation of Powers. The district court properly entered summary judgment in favor of the Counties.

City & County of San Francisco v. Trump, 897 F.3d 1225, 1234–1235 (9th Cir. 2018). The Ninth Circuit remanded the injunction for reconsideration of its scope. *Id.* at 1244.

Is Building Trust a Losing Policy?

Imagine West Jefferson is a sanctuary city and wants to resist cooperation with ICE to promote trust with immigrant populations. To facilitate its city's goals, the West Jefferson Police Department forbids officers from cooperating with ICE or asking individuals about their immigration status except as mandated by law. Its neighbor, East Jefferson, wants to intensify immigration enforcement and cooperate with federal efforts. To pursue its city's goals, the East Jefferson Police Department instructs its officers to question all criminal suspects about their immigration status and provide relevant information to ICE. How might East Jefferson's practices affect West Jefferson? How might West Jefferson's practices affect East Jefferson? To put the question another way: What are the potential spillover effects from the different local law enforcement policies on immigration? Would your answer differ if East Jefferson and West Jefferson were 10 miles apart? 100 miles?

7.   Round 6: Challenging Enforcement of Order 13768

After the executive order, the Department of Justice began to insert immigration cooperation requirements into conditions for existing federal grant programs for local law enforcement. Cities responded with lawsuits. Los Angeles brought suit after it was denied funding in an important discretionary Department of Justice program, the COPS Hiring Program. That program funds new officers for local police departments pursuant to a 1994 statute intended to promote public safety through community policing. See Public Safety Partnership and Community Policing Act of 1994, Pub. L. No. 103-322, 108 Stat. 1807. In evaluating grant applications, the Department of Justice gave extra points to applicants that signed a "Certification of Illegal Immigration Cooperation" and indicated an intent to use the funds to combat illegal immigration, which Los Angeles would not do. Perhaps surprisingly, this lawsuit became a battle over what constitutes community policing.

All parties agreed that the Department of Justice could only impose conditions on the program consistent with the statute's purpose. Most conditions on federal grant programs are conditions on the *use* of the funds: Agencies that receive Department of Justice funds under the Bulletproof Vest Program must use the money to purchase vests; and only agencies in Alabama, Florida, Louisiana, Mississippi, and Texas may receive a Gulf States Law Enforcement Technology Initiative grant, and they must use it to improve information sharing across agencies to reduce crime and drug trafficking. Congress also has the power to impose additional conditions on grant recipients, and it frequently does so. The pro-arrest policy requirement in 34 U.S.C. §10461(c)(1)(A)(i), discussed earlier in the chapter, is an example. Still, in *South Dakota v. Dole*, 483 U.S. 203, 207 (1987), the Court indicated that grant conditions could exceed Congress's spending power if they are unrelated to the "particular national projects or programs" to which the grants are directed. In *Dole*, the Court upheld legislation that required states to raise their legal drinking age or lose 5 percent of federal highway funds: Although the condition was not a restriction on how the highway funds were to be used, the condition was "directly related to one of the main purposes" of the funds, highway safety. *Id.* at 208; see also Nat'l Fed'n of Indep. Bus. v. Sebelius, 567 U.S. 519, 580 (2012) (describing the relatedness requirement in *Dole*).

Although federal courts had never before rejected a grant condition for unrelatedness, the City of Los Angeles argued that "entangling local law enforcement with federal immigration enforcement 'undermines the trust and cooperation with immigrant communities'" and is "antithetical to community-oriented policing," the purpose of the statute. Brief of Plaintiff-Appellee at 52, City of Los Angeles v. Sessions, No. 18-55599 (9th Cir. 2018), 2018 WL 3218601 at *45. The administration argued that community cooperation with law enforcement to fight illegal immigration is a form of community policing for public safety. The Ninth Circuit agreed with the administration, recognizing illegal immigration as a public safety issue and finding reasonable the Department of Justice's view that "[t]he public safety issues that arise from illegal immigration can be addressed through collaborative interactions and information flow between law enforcement and the community, just as with any other sort of public safety issue." City of Los Angeles v. Barr, 929 F.3d 1163, 1178 (9th Cir. 2019). As a result, the Ninth Circuit held that the Department of Justice did not exceed its statutory authority, the Tenth Amendment, or the Spending Clause, and it permitted the grant awards to stand.

The degree of discretion an agency has in implementing a grant program depends in part on the type of grant and the terms of the authorizing legislation. Unlike the COPS Hiring Grants, which allow the Department of Justice discretion in distributing its funds to eligible agencies, the Edward Byrne Memorial Justice Assistance Grant (Byrne JAG grant) includes a formula grant program. The formula program is intended to serve as the primary source of federal criminal justice spending to local governments, and it is distributed according to a method specified in the authorizing statute. See 34 U.S.C. §§10151–58.

After cities started to resist Trump's order, the Department of Justice threatened to strip existing grants from several cities, including Chicago, New York, Philadelphia, and New Orleans, and announced that new Byrne JAG grant money would depend on cooperation with federal law enforcement requests. This led several cities and states to bring suit challenging the new conditions. This litigation is ongoing. So far, federal courts of appeals have overwhelmingly concluded that the Department of Justice exceeded its statutory authority by imposing immigration-related conditions on formula grants. Still, a ruling by the Second Circuit has created a circuit split on the issue. Compare Chicago v. Barr, 961 F.3d 882 (7th Cir. 2020); Providence v. Barr, 954 F.3d 23 (1st Cir. 2020); City of Philadelphia v. Attorney Gen. of the United States, 916 F.3d 276 (3d Cir. 2019); City of Los Angeles v. Barr, 941 F.3d 931 (9th Cir. 2019), with New York v. U.S. Dept. of Justice, 951 F.3d 84, 123–124 (2d Cir. 2020).

Informal Enforcement of Order 13768

In addition to litigation, federal authorities have targeted sanctuary cities for intensified immigration enforcement. ICE agents also sometimes pose as local law enforcement officials or claim to be "the police" while making immigration arrests, questioning immigrants, or asking for consent to search. This practice arguably sabotages states or localities that seek to maintain trust in immigrant communities by refusing to participate in federal immigration enforcement. California became so frustrated with this practice that it passed a law just to remind citizens that ICE officers are not California peace officers. See Act of July 24, 2017, ch. 116, 2017 Cal. Stat. 1875 (codified at Cal. Penal Code §830.85). Although trickery in policing is often legal, in *Printz v. United States*, 521 U.S. 898, 930 (1997), the Supreme Court seemed to suggest constitutional disapproval for a federal program that puts state officials "in the position of taking the blame for its burdensomeness and for its defects." Is that what ICE's strategy does?

---

8.   Round 7: State Efforts to Compel Localities

States have taken varying approaches to local decisions about whether to cooperate with federal law enforcement. Many states leave the matter to localities. Increasingly, though, some do not. More than a third of unauthorized immigrants in the United States live in Texas and California. Both states tried to restrict local policies on federal immigration enforcement. Here are their competing approaches:

TEX. GOVT. CODE §§752.053 TO .0565 (SB 4)

§752.053. Policies and Actions Regarding Immigration Enforcement.

(a) A local entity or campus police department may not:

> **(1)** adopt, enforce, or endorse a policy under which the entity or department prohibits or materially limits the enforcement of immigration laws;

> **(2)** as demonstrated by pattern or practice, prohibit or materially limit the enforcement of immigration laws; . . .

(b) In compliance with Subsection (a), a local entity or campus police department may not prohibit or materially limit a person who is a commissioned peace officer described by Article 2.12, Code of Criminal Procedure . . . from doing any of the following:

> **(1)** inquiring into the immigration status of a person under a lawful detention or under arrest;

> **(2)** with respect to information relating to the immigration status, lawful or unlawful, of any person under a lawful detention or under arrest, including information regarding the person's place of birth:

>> **(A)** sending the information to or requesting or receiving the information from United States Citizenship and Immigration Services, United States Immigration and Customs Enforcement, or another relevant federal agency;

>> **(B)** maintaining the information; or

>> **(C)** exchanging the information with another local entity or campus police department or a federal or state governmental entity;

> **(3)** assisting or cooperating with a federal immigration officer as reasonable or necessary, including providing enforcement assistance; or

> **(4)** permitting a federal immigration officer to enter and conduct enforcement activities at a jail to enforce federal immigration laws.

§752.055. Complaint; Equitable Relief

(a) Any citizen residing in the jurisdiction of a local entity or any citizen enrolled at or employed by an institution of higher education may file a complaint with the attorney general if the person asserts facts supporting an allegation that the entity or the institution's campus police department has violated Section 752.053. . . .

(b) If the attorney general determines that a complaint filed under Subsection (a) against a local entity or campus police department is valid, the attorney general may file a petition for a writ of mandamus or apply for other appropriate equitable relief in a district court in Travis County or in a county in which the principal office of the entity or department is located to compel the entity or department that is suspected of violating Section 752.053 to comply with that section. . . .

§752.056. Civil Penalty

(a) A local entity or campus police department that is found by a court of law as having intentionally violated Section 752.053 is subject to a civil penalty in an amount:

   (1) not less than $1,000 and not more than $1,500 for the first violation; and

   (2) not less than $25,000 and not more than $25,500 for each subsequent violation.

(b) Each day of a continuing violation of Section 752.053 constitutes a separate violation for the civil penalty under this section.

(c) The court that hears an action brought under Section 752.055 against the local entity or campus police department shall determine the amount of the civil penalty under this section.

§752.0565. Removal from Office

(a) . . . [A] person holding an elective or appointive office of a political subdivision of this state does an act that causes the forfeiture of the person's office if the person violates Section 752.053.

(b) The attorney general shall file a petition . . . against a public officer to which Subsection (a) applies if presented with evidence, including evidence of a statement by the public officer, establishing probable grounds that the public officer engaged in conduct described by Subsection (a). . . .

(c) If the person against whom an information is filed based on conduct described by Subsection (a) is found guilty as charged, the court shall enter judgment removing the person from office.

CAL. GOVT. CODE §7284.6 (SB 54)

§7284.6. Law Enforcement Agency Personnel or Resources; Investigation or Detainment of Persons for Immigration Enforcement Purposes; Report on Joint Task Forces

(a) California law enforcement agencies shall not:

   (1) Use agency or department moneys or personnel to investigate, interrogate, detain, detect, or arrest persons for immigration enforcement purposes, including any of the following:

      (A) Inquiring into an individual's immigration status.

      (B) Detaining an individual on the basis of a hold request.

      (C) Providing information regarding a person's release date or responding to requests for notification by providing release dates or other information unless that information is available to the public, or is in response to a notification request from immigration authorities in accordance with Section 7282.5. Responses are never required, but are permitted under this subdivision, provided that they do not violate any local law or policy. . . .

      (E) Making or intentionally participating in arrests based on civil immigration warrants. . . .

      (G) Performing the functions of an immigration officer, whether pursuant to Section 1357(g) of Title 8 of the United States Code or any other law, regulation, or policy, whether formal or informal.

(2) Place peace officers under the supervision of federal agencies or employ peace officers deputized as special federal officers or special federal deputies for purposes of immigration enforcement. All peace officers remain subject to California law governing conduct of peace officers and the policies of the employing agency. . . .

(4) Transfer an individual to immigration authorities unless authorized by a judicial warrant or judicial probable cause determination, or in accordance with Section 7282.5. . . .

(e) This section does not prohibit or restrict any government entity or official from sending to, or receiving from, federal immigration authorities, information regarding the citizenship or immigration status, lawful or unlawful, of an individual, or from requesting from federal immigration authorities immigration status information, lawful or unlawful, of any individual, or maintaining or exchanging that information with any other federal, state, or local government entity, pursuant to Sections 1373 and 1644 of Title 8 of the United States Code. . . .

NOTES AND QUESTIONS

1. *Texas's law.* Section 752.053 came about in 2017, when Texas passed SB 4 to prohibit local governments from adopting sanctuary city policies. Although several counties and cities sued to prevent SB 4 from going into effect, the Fifth Circuit upheld the statute, except for the endorsement prohibition in (a)(1), which it held violated the First Amendment when applied to elected officials. See City of El Cenizo v. Texas, 890 F.3d 164 (5th Cir. 2018).

2. *New antisanctuary laws.* Antisanctuary laws are not new, as Arizona's S.B. 1070, passed in 2010 and excerpted above, suggests. Several other states also passed such laws in the early 2010s. Texas's law, however, represents a new trend in such laws, because it is more expansive in its scope, more demanding in its mandates, and more extreme in its penalties. Alabama, Indiana, Mississippi, North Carolina, Ohio, and Tennessee have passed similarly harsh laws. See Pratheepan Gulasekaram et al., *Anti-Sanctuary and Immigration Localism,* 119 Colum. L. Rev. 837, 848–850 (2019) (describing new and harsher antisanctuary laws). As the litigation in Texas suggests, although the federal government may not be able to commandeer local officials, states do not face the same federal constitutional bar on demanding local law enforcement action, although the law in some states might provide other avenues for local challenges. *Id.* at 860–870.

3. *California's law.* Section 7284.6 also came about in 2017, when California passed SB 54. SB 54 amends California's Transparency and Responsibility Using State Tools (TRUST) Act (Cal. Govt. Code §§7282 and 7292.5), and adds the Values Act (Cal. Govt. Code §§ 7824 et seq.). Recall that the TRUST Act limited the circumstances under which a California law enforcement agency could detain an individual past his scheduled release in response to a detainer request from federal immigration authorities. In addition to the above provisions, the Values Act prohibits localities from detaining suspects pursuant to such a request. The Justice Department responded to SB 54 with a lawsuit arguing the statute unlawfully obstructed federal immigration enforcement. In *United States v. California,* 921 F.3d 865, 886–893 (9th Cir. 2019), the Ninth Circuit rejected that argument on the ground that federal

immigration law permits but does not mandate local assistance in immigration enforcement. Although SB 54 prohibits localities from assisting federal authorities, "refusing to help is not the same as impeding." *Id.* at 888. The Court also found SB 54 consistent with 8 U.S.C. §1373, because SB 54 permits localities to share information regarding immigration status as mandated by law. *Id.* at 891.

Illustration by ICE Out of California, a campaign to disentangle California local law enforcement from ICE's immigration enforcement efforts.

4. *Comparing the statutes.* How intrusive is each approach with respect to local policymaking? How is each statute enforced?

5. *Other forms of cooperation and resistance.* These statutes take on federal immigration policy directly. States and localities can also resist each other and support or undermine federal enforcement priorities in more subtle ways. For example, about a dozen states allow unauthorized immigrants to receive driver's licenses. Because driving without a license is a common charge leading to arrest, which in turn triggers notification to ICE under Secure Communities, giving unauthorized immigrants driver's licenses can reduce removals. Alternatively, localities can refrain from making arrests on bases like not having a driver's license, which disproportionately affect unauthorized immigrants. Some cities, including Nashville and Houston, minimize arrests by issuing citations and allowing immigrants to provide an alternate form of identification when they are pulled over. These cities cooperate with ICE and respect detainers. Yet, by avoiding arrests, they can prevent removals. By contrast, Georgia law *mandates* arrests for driving without a license, with the opposite effect. See Randy Capps et al., Migration Pol'y Inst., *Revving Up the Deportation Machinery: Enforcement and Pushback Under Trump* 57 (2018). Can you think of other ways states or localities can use law enforcement practices to undermine or support federal immigration priorities?

6. *State or local control?* Both the California and Texas statutes seek to take control of local police conduct with respect to immigrants. Scholars interested in immigration federalism have often argued that localities should decide such matters instead. See, e.g., Pratheepan Gulasekaram et al., *Anti-Sanctuary and Immigration Localism,* 119 Colum. L. Rev. 837 (2019); Cristina M. Rodriguez, *The Significance of the Local in Immigration Regulation,* 106 Mich. L. Rev. 567, 571 (2008). As a student of the law of the police, do you agree? Do you think these laws are different from state laws you

have read about in other chapters of this book regulating local officer conduct? Can you imagine similar national–state–local fights over local police involvement in terrorism prevention? Drug crime enforcement? Would you view them the same way?

F.   Federal Power and Police Reform

As described in this chapter, federal programs have long sought to strengthen and refocus local policing. Congress has far less often turned its powers to reforming the police. But there are several ways it could do so if it wished.

First, instead of incentivizing intrusive policing, Congress could offer money to police departments to engage in less harmful or more accountable policing. Increasing accountability is one purpose of the Body Worn Camera grants, which since 2015 have given tens of millions of dollars to local agencies to fund cameras. Similarly, although COPS office money overwhelmingly goes to its Hiring Program and antidrug crime programs, the office also offers Community Policing Development microgrants to allow agencies to implement or improve community policing strategies. (In practice, under the Trump Administration, many of these grants support projects that do not fit most conceptions of community policing, such as school safety, officer wellness, and officer recruitment and retention.) Why not grants for training officers in deescalation? Or for implementing alternatives to arrests? Or for strengthening administrative investigations and disciplinary mechanisms in departments? Can you think of other ways Congress might use spending to improve the police?

The main limitation on using grants to promote police reform is practical rather than legal: It costs money. To get around devoting new dollars to police reform, Congress could also use its spending power to impose conditions on existing federal grants to law enforcement agencies. Already, the Byrne JAG grant program bars the basis of race, religion, national origin, or sex "discrimination . . . in connection with any programs or activity funded in whole or in part" with JAG funds. 34 U.S.C. §10228. Similarly, Title VI of the Civil Rights Act prohibits racial discrimination in all programs that receive federal financial assistance. 42 U.S.C. §2000d. (Title VI and other federal discrimination statues are discussed in Chapter 6.) Congress might similarly condition federal funding to law enforcement on policies that prohibit racial profiling or that provide for appointing special prosecutors to police shooting cases, and still adhere to the relatedness requirement for federal grant conditions discussed in *South Dakota v. Dole*, 483 U.S. 203, 208–209 (1987). Such conditions would need to avoid other constitutional limits on program conditions. Thus, a condition could not threaten so much funding that it functions as a "gun to the head" of recipients. Nat'l Fed'n of Indep. Bus. v. Sebelius, 567 U.S. 519, 581 (2012). Moreover, new conditions may not unfairly surprise existing grant recipients. See *Dole*, 483 U.S. at 207. For an example of one proposal in this vein, see Kami Chavis Simmons, *Cooperative Federalism and Police Reform: Using Congressional Spending Power to Promote Police Accountability*, 62 Ala. L. Rev. 351, 381–393 (2011) (proposing an amendment to the COPS program that would withhold 5 percent of funding from states that failed to implement measures to reduce police misconduct).

Congress could also turn back to its more traditional source of authority for regulating the harms of policing: Section 5 of the Fourteenth Amendment. The Fourteenth Amendment bars states and local governments from depriving any person of life, liberty, or property without due process of law and from depriving any person of equal protection of the law. Section 5 of the amendment gives Congress the "power to enforce, by appropriate legislation" those provisions. Congress has used this power in imposing federal criminal and civil liability on individuals who, "under color of law," deprive a person of constitutional or statutory rights in 18 U.S.C. §242 (see Chapter 14) and 42 U.S.C. §1983 (see Chapter 13). It has also given the Department of Justice authority to sue for equitable relief local police departments that engage in a pattern or practice of constitutional violations in 34 U.S.C. §12601 (see Chapter 15).

Might Congress go further using this power?

As the Supreme Court has noted,

> Congress may, in the exercise of its §5 power, do more than simply proscribe conduct that we have held unconstitutional. Congress' power "to enforce" the Amendment includes the authority both to remedy and to deter violation of rights guaranteed thereunder by prohibiting a somewhat broader swath of conduct, including that which is not itself forbidden by the Amendment's text. In other words, Congress may enact so-called prophylactic legislation that proscribes facially constitutional conduct, in order to prevent and deter unconstitutional conduct.

Nevada Dept. of Human Res. v. Hibbs, 538 U.S. 721, 727–728 (2003).

However, although Congress has "wide latitude," valid "prophylactic legislation" must exhibit "congruence and proportionality between the injury to be prevented or remedied and the means adopted to that end." City of Boerne v. Flores, 521 U.S. 507, 520 (1997). Otherwise, Congress exceeds its power to enforce rather than reinterpret constitutional rights. In looking to what satisfies the "congruence and proportionality" test, the Court has noted that "[t]he appropriateness of remedial measures must be considered in light of the evil presented." *Id.* at 530. Thus, the Court has looked for evidence of a "widespread and persisting deprivation of constitutional rights" that would justify preventative efforts. See *id.* at 526; see also *Hibbs,* 538 U.S. at 730 (describing a record demonstrating "long and extensive history" of unconstitutional conduct by the states).

In this vein, Congress might be able to bar the use of chokeholds, which, even if they are not unconstitutional in all circumstances, might sufficiently frequently lead to unconstitutionally excessive force that preventative legislation is justified. It might ban all use of race and national origin in forming reasonable suspicion or probable cause for stops and arrests, given the long and extensive history of racial discrimination in policing, even though the Supreme Court has allowed that use for some purposes and equal protection violations require discriminatory intent. Maybe it would also justify a prohibition on enforcing criminal laws for the purpose of raising revenue rather than promoting public safety, given the widespread abuse of revenue-raising powers. Are there other subjects you think might be appropriate for prophylactic congressional legislation? What would you want to know before deciding?

If Congress were to pass legislation along any of these lines, constitutional challenges would be inevitable. The outcome would depend in part on the record amassed by Congress, which depends in part on what information is available about police practices. What could Congress do to ensure that it (and courts) can assess prophylactic legislation to reduce constitutional violations and improve the police?

PART FOUR

REMEDIES AND REFORMS

As previous chapters of this book indicate, police officers face an array of legal rules that mandate or forbid some conduct. What happens when police break the law? Different rules have different remedies. This part considers some of the major legal consequences of police misconduct, especially constitutional violations, and asks what role these remedies play in encouraging police to follow the law.

- Chapter 12 looks at the exclusionary rule, which excludes evidence obtained through an illegal search or seizure from a defendant's criminal trial.
- Chapter 13 examines civil suits for damages by private actors, which allow victims of police misconduct to seek compensation for any resulting injuries.
- Chapter 14 considers criminal prosecutions of police officers.
- Chapter 15 considers civil suits by both private actors and government officials for equitable relief, such as court-ordered institutional reform, to prevent future legal violations by officers and departments.
- Chapter 16 considers some nonlitigative strategies for preventing police misconduct.

Before considering how each of these remedies works, consider two questions:

1. Why do people—and police officers in particular—break the law?
2. How might possible legal consequences influence their decision to do so?

Standard economic analysis provides one powerful answer to these questions. It suggests that people make (or act as if they make) rational choices that maximize their welfare. Deterrence theory applies this analysis to decisions about complying with rules: Individuals obey the law, the theory goes, when they believe the expected costs of violating it will outweigh the expected benefits of complying. Daniel Nagin, a prominent criminologist and deterrence theorist, summarizes the costs and benefits of engaging in crime in the excerpt below. Lawbreaking by the police looks somewhat different, and it does not always constitute a crime. Still, consider how this list might apply to a police officer's decision to break the law:

Rewards.

Rewards measures the total benefits of victimizing a target. For a crime with a property motive, the value of the property to the perpetrator likely accounts for all or a major share of the total reward. However, the thrill of offending or—in the case of violent crimes without a property motive—the satisfaction of humiliating, physically hurting, or killing the victim may also be relevant to the reward value of a target.

Crime commission cost.

Crime commission cost measures the total cost of committing the crime separate from the sanction cost defined below. Commission cost includes time searching for the opportunity, planning time,if any, and the effort required to commit the crime itself. Importantly, it also includes the potential costs to the perpetrator of victim retaliation or resistance. Finally, commission cost includes Raskolnikov-like feelings of guilt or shame that may affect the perpetrator, whether or not he is apprehended and sanctioned.

Perceived formal sanction cost.

Perceived sanction cost measures the would-be perpetrator's assessment of the formal sanction cost that might be imposed if convicted. These costs include the loss of freedom (if imprisoned) and the unpleasantness of other restrictions on freedom due to conditions of parole or probations and fines.

Perceived informal sanction cost.

The imposition of formal sanctions may also trigger informal sanctions by family, friends, and the community at large, which for some offenders may be even more costly than the formal sanctions. Informal sanction cost may also involve large economic costs due to job loss.

Perceived cost of apprehension.

Apprehension imposes costs that are distinct from formal and informal sanction costs. These include the unpleasantness of the apprehension itself, possible loss of liberty due to pretrial detention, and legal fees. Perceived cost of apprehension also includes the social and economic costs triggered by arrest, even without conviction, such as disapproval of family, friends, and the community at large, as well as job loss.

Daniel S. Nagin, *Deterrence in the Twenty-First Century,* 42 Crime & Just. 199, 209–210 (2013).

Nagin was thinking of traditional criminal activity when he developed this list. Consider these three scenarios:

1. *A use of force.* After pulling Mike Hernandez over for a minor traffic violation, Officer Allen discovered that Hernandez had an outstanding warrant for failure to appear on a prior violation. When Officer Allen attempted to arrest him, Hernandez resisted. Officer Allen wrestled him to the ground, and Hernandez stopped fighting. After Officer Allen placed Hernandez into handcuffs and caught his breath, he kicked Hernandez several times in the ribs.

2. *A search.* After dispatch received a vague anonymous tip that "some punk" had a gun at a city intersection, Officer Baker stopped Willie Johnson, an 18-year-old Black youth waiting for a bus near that corner, pushed him up against the bus stop, and searched him. Officer Baker found an "8 ball" or ⅛ ounce of heroin in Johnson's pocket.

3. *An arrest.* Officer Calvin and his partner were assigned to keep the peace at a march against police misconduct. When protesters walked past shouting,

"Racist cops, you can't hide; we charge you with genocide," Officer Calvin grabbed Andy Lee, who was leading the chant, and arrested him for disturbing the peace.

Each of these acts by the officers is unlawful. Take a minute to jot down some of the things these officers might consider in each of Nagin's categories in choosing what to do. What are the benefits each officer experiences? Crime commission costs? Perceived formal costs? Perceived informal costs? Perceived costs of apprehension, even if no formal remedies are successful? Which things on your list might be different across the three examples?

Now, for each cost or benefit, write down one thing that could affect its magnitude, such as an aspect of the law, an institutional factor, or something individual to the officer.

Can you think of other categories of costs and benefits, beyond those mentioned by Nagin, that influence an officer's decision to break or comply with the law? For example, how about the cost of educating himself about what the law requires? What about the opportunity costs of engaging in a constitutional violation? Or not engaging in one? Some of those are expected *costs* of *following* the law. What about the expected *benefits* of legal compliance, such as personal satisfaction or professional reward?

Note that these are the perceived costs and benefits to each actor, not the social costs and benefits of legal violations all told. Many costs and benefits of misconduct—the suffering of the victim, for example, or the loss of public trust in institutions of government—are little felt by the person who violates the law. Therefore, the officer's cost–benefit analysis will not be socially optimal unless the costs to others are somehow translated into costs for the officer. Legal punishments or consequences imposed on the lawbreakers are one means of doing that.

Often, the legal consequences and other costs and benefits of violating or complying with the law accrue to departments rather than individual officers. How might incentives for agencies get translated into costs and benefits for officers?

Deterrence theorists emphasize three aspects of punishment that can affect a potential lawbreaker's decision: severity, certainty, and celerity. Enforcement mechanisms that are more *severe* in the punishments they impose, more *certain* to impose punishment, and more *swiftly* imposed in relation to the offense are more likely to prevent lawbreaking. Of the three, certainty of punishment is the most important. How do you think the litigation-based legal remedies for police misconduct—the exclusionary rule, criminal prosecution, civil liability, and lawsuits for reform against police departments—stack up on these criteria?

Some critics argue that standard economic analysis is premised on implausible assumptions, including that people act rationally, that they have perfect information, and that they act based solely on self-interest. Instead, *behavioral economics* takes into account that human beings take shortcuts in decision making that can lead to predictable errors in judgment; take short-term actions that conflict with their long-term interests; and care about social norms in ways that affect their assessments of their own welfare. Nagin's list seems to include the last of these. Can you think of ways the first two might be relevant in police decision making?

Other critics of deterrence theory argue that punishments have only a weak effect on behavior. Instead, people are motivated by the broader social meaning of their actions, which contributes to their sense of identity and belonging. If behavior has symbolic as well as material value, is that something that can be captured by assessing costs and benefits? How can the symbolic meaning of officers' choices be guided by legal remedies?

Finally, social psychologists reason that *procedural justice theory* more accurately describes human rule-following behavior. Whereas economic analysis views individuals as maximizing outcomes for their own instrumental ends, procedural justice theory proposes that individuals are motivated by intrinsic preferences for rule-following. These preferences depend not on the consequences of compliance (or noncompliance) but on our perceptions of four characteristics of how the rules were made. We are more likely to comply when we have an opportunity to offer input, when decisions are made neutrally, when the rule maker treats those subjected to the rules with dignity and respect, and when the decision makers act based on objective information and according to reasonable criteria as opposed to personal motivations or biases.

Applying procedural justice theory to police misconduct, then, looks at how police perceive their treatment by courts and police departments, especially when they are accused of wrongdoing. Assuming this theory is right, how might police department policymaking, internal disciplinary processes, and damages lawsuits be carried out to maximize police compliance with the law? See Tom R. Tyler et al., *Armed, and Dangerous(?): Motivating Rule Adherence Among Agents of Social Control*, 41 Law & Soc'y Rev. 457 (2007) (arguing that organizational characteristics lead to self-regulation by police officers).

Chapter 12

The Exclusionary Rule

As earlier chapters demonstrate, the Fourth Amendment is a critical check on contemporary policing. In the past century, the most common and important legal remedy for violations of the Fourth Amendment has been the exclusionary rule, which excludes evidence obtained in violation of the Fourth Amendment from a defendant's criminal trial. This chapter explores exclusionary rule basics, describes how the exclusionary rule has evolved, and discusses how it might affect policing.

A. The Exclusionary Rule and Police Conduct

The U.S. Supreme Court developed the exclusionary rule in *Weeks v. United States*, 232 U.S. 383 (1914). Its ruling forbade evidence seized by federal agents in violation of the Fourth Amendment from being introduced in a federal criminal trial. When the U.S. Supreme Court incorporated the Fourth Amendment against the states in *Wolf v. Colorado*, 338 U.S. 25 (1949), it refused to mandate the exclusionary rule as a remedy for state constitutional violations, reasoning, "Granting that in practice the exclusion of evidence may be an effective way of deterring unreasonable searches, it is not for this Court to condemn as falling below the minimal standards assured by the Due Process Clause a state's reliance upon other methods which, if consistently enforced, would be equally effective." *Id.* at 31. This next case rejected this reasoning and overturned this aspect of *Wolf* merely 12 years later. It is arguably the single most significant Supreme Court case concerning the police.

MAPP v. OHIO
367 U.S. 643 (1961)

Mr. Justice Clark delivered the opinion of the Court.

Appellant stands convicted of knowingly having had in her possession and under her control certain lewd and lascivious books, pictures, and photographs in violation of §2905.34 of Ohio's Revised Code. . . . [T]he Supreme Court of Ohio found that her conviction was valid though "based primarily upon the introduction in evidence of lewd and lascivious books and pictures unlawfully seized during an unlawful search of defendant's home. . . ." 170 Ohio St. 427–428.

On May 23, 1957, three Cleveland police officers arrived at appellant's residence in that city pursuant to information that "a person (was) hiding out in the home, who was wanted for questioning in connection with a recent bombing, and that there was a large amount of policy paraphernalia being hidden in the home." Miss Mapp and her daughter by a former marriage lived on the top floor of the two-family dwelling. Upon their arrival at that house, the officers knocked on the door and demanded entrance but appellant, after telephoning her attorney, refused to admit them without a search warrant. They advised their headquarters of the situation and undertook a surveillance of the house.

The officers again sought entrance some three hours later when four or more additional officers arrived on the scene. When Miss Mapp did not come to the door immediately, at least one of the several doors to the house was forcibly opened and the policemen gained admittance. Meanwhile Miss Mapp's attorney arrived, but the officers, having secured their own entry, and continuing in their defiance of the law, would permit him neither to see Miss Mapp nor to enter the house. It appears that Miss Mapp was halfway down the stairs from the upper floor to the front door when the officers, in this highhanded manner, broke into the hall. She demanded to see the search warrant. A paper, claimed to be a warrant, was held up by one of the officers. She grabbed the "warrant" and placed it in her bosom. A struggle ensued in which the officers recovered the piece of paper and as a result of which they handcuffed appellant because she had been "belligerent" in resisting their official rescue of the "warrant" from her person. Running roughshod over appellant, a policeman "grabbed" her, "twisted (her) hand," and she "yelled (and) pleaded with him" because "it was hurting." Appellant, in handcuffs, was then forcibly taken upstairs to her bedroom where the officers searched a dresser, a chest of drawers, a closet and some suitcases. They also looked into a photo album and through personal papers belonging to the appellant. The search spread to the rest of the second floor including the child's bedroom, the living room, the kitchen and a dinette. The basement of the building and a trunk found therein were also searched. The obscene materials for possession of which she was ultimately convicted were discovered in the course of that widespread search.

At the trial no search warrant was produced by the prosecution, nor was the failure to produce one explained or accounted for. At best, "There is, in the record, considerable doubt as to whether there ever was any warrant for the search of defendant's home." . . .

The State says that even if the search were made without authority, or otherwise unreasonably, it is not prevented from using the unconstitutionally seized evidence at trial, citing *Wolf v. Colorado*, 338 U.S. 25, 33 (1949), in which this Court did indeed hold "that in a prosecution in a State court for a State crime the Fourteenth Amendment does not forbid the admission of evidence obtained by an unreasonable search and seizure." On this appeal, of which we have noted probable jurisdiction, it is urged once again that we review that holding.

I.

. . . [T]his Court, in *Weeks v. United States*, 232 U.S. 383 (1914), . . . concluded:

> If letters and private documents can thus be seized and held and used
> in evidence against a citizen accused of an offense, the protection of the

> Fourth Amendment declaring his right to be secure against such searches and seizures is of no value, and, so far as those thus placed are concerned, might as well be stricken from the Constitution. The efforts of the courts and their officials to bring the guilty to punishment, praiseworthy as they are, are not to be aided by the sacrifice of those great principles established by years of endeavor and suffering which have resulted in their embodiment in the fundamental law of the land.

232 U.S. at 393.

. . . Thus, in the year 1914, in the *Weeks* case, this Court "for the first time" held that "in a federal prosecution the Fourth Amendment barred the use of evidence secured through an illegal search and seizure." *Wolf,* 338 U.S. at 28. This Court has ever since required of federal law officers a strict adherence to that command which this Court has held to be a clear, specific, and constitutionally required—even if judicially implied—deterrent safeguard without insistence upon which the Fourth Amendment would have been reduced to "a form of words." Silverthorne Lumber Co. v. United States, 251 U.S. 385, 392 (1920)....

II.

In 1949, 35 years after *Weeks* was announced, this Court, in *Wolf v. Colorado, supra,* again for the first time, discussed the effect of the Fourth Amendment upon the States through the operation of the Due Process Clause of the Fourteenth Amendment. It said:

"[W]e have no hesitation in saying that were a State affirmatively to sanction such police incursion into privacy it would run counter to the guaranty of the Fourteenth Amendment." 338 U.S. at 28.

Nevertheless, after declaring that the "security of one's privacy against arbitrary intrusion by the police" is "implicit in 'the concept of ordered liberty' and as such enforceable against the States through the Due Process Clause," and announcing that it "stoutly adhere[d]" to the *Weeks* decision, the Court decided that the *Weeks* exclusionary rule would not then be imposed upon the States as "an essential ingredient of the right." *Id.* at 27–29. The Court's reasons for not considering essential to the right to privacy . . . were bottomed on factual considerations.

While they are not basically relevant to a decision that the exclusionary rule is an essential ingredient of the Fourth Amendment as the right it embodies is vouchsafed against the States by the Due Process Clause, we will consider the current validity of the factual grounds upon which *Wolf* was based.

The Court in *Wolf* first stated that "[t]he contrariety of views of the States" on the adoption of the exclusionary rule of *Weeks* was "particularly impressive"; and, in this connection, that it could not "brush aside the experience of States which deem the incidence of such conduct by the police too slight to call for a deterrent remedy . . . by overriding the [States'] relevant rules of evidence." 338 U.S. at 31–32. While in 1949, prior to the *Wolf* case, almost two-thirds of the States were opposed to the use of the exclusionary rule, now, despite the *Wolf* case, more than half of those since passing upon it, by their own legislative or judicial decision, have wholly or partly adopted or adhered to the *Weeks* rule. Significantly, among those now following the rule is California, which, according to its highest court, was "compelled to reach that conclusion because other remedies have completely failed to secure compliance with the constitutional provisions. . . ." People v. Cahan, 292 P.2d 905, 911 (Cal. 1955). In connection with this California case, we note that the second basis elaborated in *Wolf* in support of its failure to enforce the exclusionary doctrine against the States was that "other means of protection" have been afforded "the right to privacy." 338 U.S. at 30. The experience of California that such other remedies have been worthless and futile is buttressed by the experience of other States. . . .

Likewise, time has set its face against what *Wolf* called the "'weighty testimony'" of *People v. Defore*, 150 N.E. 585 (N.Y. 1926). There Justice (then Judge) Cardozo, rejecting adoption of the *Weeks* exclusionary rule in New York, had said that "[t]he Federal rule as it stands is either too strict or too lax." 150 N.E. at 588. However, the force of that reasoning has been largely vitiated by later decisions of this Court. These include the recent discarding of the "silver platter" doctrine which allowed federal judicial use of evidence seized in violation of the Constitution by state agents, the relaxation of the formerly strict requirements as to standing to challenge the use of evidence thus seized, . . . and, finally, the formulation of a method to prevent state use of evidence unconstitutionally seized by federal agents. . . .

It, therefore, plainly appears that the factual considerations supporting the failure of the *Wolf* Court to include the *Weeks* exclusionary rule when it recognized the enforceability of the right to privacy against the States in 1949, while not basically relevant to the constitutional consideration, could not, in any analysis, now be deemed controlling.

III.

. . . Today we once again examine *Wolf*'s constitutional documentation of the right to privacy free from unreasonable state intrusion, and, after its dozen years on our books, are led by it to close the only courtroom door remaining open to evidence secured by official lawlessness in flagrant abuse of that basic right, reserved to all persons as a specific guarantee against that very same unlawful conduct. We hold that all evidence obtained by searches and seizures in violation of the Constitution is, by that same authority, inadmissible in a state court.

IV.

Since the Fourth Amendment's right of privacy has been declared enforceable against the States through the Due Process Clause of the Fourteenth Amendment, it is enforceable against them by the same sanction of exclusion as is used against the Federal Government. Were it otherwise, then just as without the *Weeks* rule the assurance against unreasonable federal searches and seizures would be "a form of words," valueless and undeserving of mention in a perpetual charter of inestimable human liberties. . . . [I]n extending the substantive protections of due process to all constitutionally unreasonable searches—state or federal—it was logically and constitutionally necessary that the exclusion doctrine—an essential part of the right to privacy—be also insisted upon as an essential ingredient of the right newly recognized by the *Wolf* case. In short, the admission of the new constitutional right by *Wolf* could not consistently tolerate denial of its most important constitutional privilege, namely, the exclusion of the evidence which an accused had been forced to give by reason of the unlawful seizure. To hold otherwise is to grant the right but in reality to withhold its privilege and enjoyment. Only last year the Court itself recognized that the purpose of the exclusionary rule "is to deter—to compel respect for the constitutional guaranty in the only effectively available way—by removing the incentive to disregard it." Elkins v. United States, 364 U.S. 206, 217 (1960). . . .

V.

Moreover, our holding that the exclusionary rule is an essential part of both the Fourth and Fourteenth Amendments is not only the logical dictate of prior cases, but it also makes very good sense. There is no war between the Constitution and common sense. Presently, a federal prosecutor may make no use of evidence illegally seized, but a State's attorney across the street may, although he supposedly is operating under the enforceable prohibitions of the same Amendment. Thus the State, by admitting evidence unlawfully seized, serves to encourage disobedience to the Federal Constitution which it is bound to uphold. . . .

Federal-state cooperation in the solution of crime under constitutional standards will be promoted, if only by recognition of their now mutual obligation to respect the same fundamental criteria in their approaches. "However much in a particular case insistence upon such rules may appear as a technicality that inures to the benefit of a guilty person, the history of the criminal law proves that tolerance of shortcut methods in law enforcement impairs its enduring effectiveness." Miller v. United States, 357 U.S. 301, 313 (1958). Denying shortcuts to only one of two cooperating law enforcement agencies tends naturally to breed legitimate suspicion of "working arrangements" whose results are equally tainted.

There are those who say, as did Justice (then Judge) Cardozo, that under our constitutional exclusionary doctrine "[t]he criminal is to go free because the constable has blundered." *Defore*, 242 N.Y. at 21. In some cases this will undoubtedly be the result. But, as was said in *Elkins*, "there is another consideration—the imperative of judicial integrity." 364 U.S. at 222. The criminal goes free, if he must, but it is the law that sets him free. Nothing can destroy a government more quickly than its failure to observe its own laws, or worse, its disregard of the charter of its own existence. As Mr. Justice Brandeis, dissenting, said in *Olmstead v. United States*, 277 U.S. 438, 485 (1928): "Our Government is the potent, the omnipresent teacher. For good or for ill, it teaches the whole people by its example. . . . If the Government becomes a lawbreaker, it breeds contempt for law; it invites every man to become a law unto himself; it invites anarchy." Nor can it lightly be assumed that, as a practical matter, adoption of the exclusionary rule fetters law enforcement. Only last year this Court expressly considered that contention and found that "pragmatic evidence of a sort" to the contrary was not wanting. *Elkins*, 364 U.S. at 218. The Court noted that

> The federal courts themselves have operated under the exclusionary rule of *Weeks* for almost half a century; yet it has not been suggested either that the Federal Bureau of Investigation has thereby been rendered ineffective, or that the administration of criminal justice in the federal courts has thereby been disrupted. Moreover, the experience of the states is impressive. . . . The movement towards the rule of exclusion has been halting but seemingly inexorable.

Id. at 218–219.

The ignoble shortcut to conviction left open to the State tends to destroy the entire system of constitutional restraints on which the liberties of the people rest. Having once recognized that the right to privacy embodied in the Fourth Amendment is enforceable against the States, and that the right to be secure against rude invasions of privacy by state officers is, therefore, constitutional in origin, we can no longer permit that right to remain an empty promise. Because it is enforceable in the same manner and to like effect as other basic rights secured by the Due Process Clause, we can no longer permit it to be revocable at the whim of any police officer who, in the name of law enforcement itself, chooses to suspend its enjoyment. Our decision, founded on reason and truth, gives to the individual no more than that which the Constitution guarantees him, to the police officer no less than that to which honest law enforcement is entitled, and, to the courts, that judicial integrity so necessary in the true administration of justice.

The judgment of the Supreme Court of Ohio is reversed and the cause remanded for further proceedings not inconsistent with this opinion.

MR. JUSTICE DOUGLAS, concurring.

Though I have joined the opinion of the Court, I add a few words. This criminal proceeding started with a lawless search and seizure. The police entered a home forcefully, and seized documents that were later used to convict the occupant of a crime. . . .

When we allowed States to give constitutional sanction to the "shabby business" of unlawful entry into a home (to use an expression of Mr. Justice Murphy), Wolf v. Colorado, 338 U.S. 25, 46 (1949), we did indeed rob the Fourth Amendment of much meaningful force. There are, of course, other theoretical remedies. One is disciplinary action within the hierarchy of the police system, including prosecution of the police officer for a crime. Yet as Mr. Justice Murphy said in *Wolf*, *id.* at 42, "Self-scrutiny is a lofty ideal, but its exaltation reaches new heights if we expect a District Attorney to prosecute himself or his associates for well-meaning violations of the search and seizure clause during a raid the District Attorney or his associates have ordered."

The only remaining remedy, if exclusion of the evidence is not required, is an action of trespass by the homeowner against the offending officer. Mr. Justice Murphy showed how onerous and difficult it would be for the citizen to maintain that action and how meagre the relief even if the citizen prevails. *Id.* at 42–44. The truth is that trespass actions against officers who make unlawful searches and seizures are mainly illusory remedies.

Without judicial action making the exclusionary rule applicable to the States, *Wolf v. Colorado* in practical effect reduced the guarantee against unreasonable searches and seizures to "a dead letter," as Mr. Justice Rutledge said in his dissent. See *id.* at 47.

Wolf v. Colorado was decided in 1949. The immediate result was a storm of constitutional controversy which only today finds its end. I believe that this is an appropriate case in which to put an end to the asymmetry which *Wolf* imported into the law. It is an appropriate case because the facts it presents show—as would few other cases—the casual arrogance of those who have the untrammeled power to invade one's home and to seize one's person. . . .

[The concurring opinion of Justice Black and memorandum of Justice Stewart are omitted.]

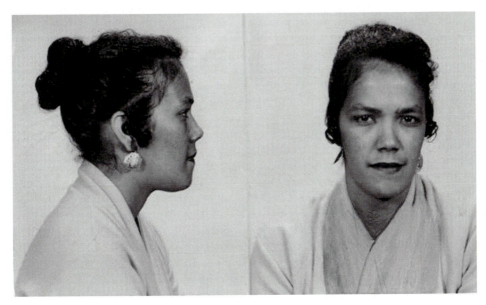

Dollree Mapp, 1957.

NOTES AND QUESTIONS

1. *Court's logic.* The *Mapp* opinion addresses two basic arguments: first, an argument in favor of ignoring the precedential value of *Wolf*, and second, an affirmative argument in favor of mandating evidentiary exclusion on the states by incorporation of the Fourth Amendment. What precisely are those arguments? Are they persuasive?

2. *Exclusionary rule process.* After a prosecutor discloses that a particular piece of physical evidence, information, observation, identification, or statement will be introduced at trial, a defendant may file a pretrial motion objecting to the admission of the evidence because it was discovered during or as a result of a search or seizure that violated the Fourth Amendment. If the government contests the defendant's factual allegations, the court will hold an evidentiary hearing, at which the prosecutor will call at least one law enforcement officer to testify as a fact witness and usually to summarize other aspects of the investigation. If the court finds the officer's testimony credible and the testimony establishes a lawful basis for the search, the court will rule against the motion and admit the evidence at trial. Otherwise, the court will rule the evidence inadmissible at trial. Defendants do not usually testify at these hearings. Why? Probably because they are not likely to be believed if they allege facts substantially different from the officer's; and although their testimony cannot

be introduced against them in the government's case in chief at trial, *Simmons v. United States*, 390 U.S. 377, 393–394 (1968), it can be used to impeach them if they testify at trial.

3. *How does it deter?* As *Mapp* suggests, the Court views the exclusionary rule as primarily prophylactic: It prevents misconduct. What does *Mapp* tell us about how the exclusionary rule might stop constitutional violations from happening? All the Court says in *Mapp* is to repeat from *Elkins*, "'Its purpose is to deter—to compel respect for the constitutional guaranty . . . by removing the incentive to disregard it.'" How, exactly, does excluding evidence influence what police officers do? Returning to the economic principles outlined in the Part Four introduction, to deter, the rule must raise the expected costs of engaging in constitutional violations so that they outweigh the expected benefits of breaking the law, at least for some officers. For this to happen, something like the following must be true:

1. Officers experience positive personal and/or professional consequences when they contribute to convictions in criminal cases.
2. Officers contribute to convictions in part by finding evidence of the defendant's guilt that can be introduced at trial.
3. Officers sometimes find it easier to collect criminal evidence when they violate the Fourth Amendment.
4. Because of the exclusionary rule, evidence resulting from Fourth Amendment violations is more likely to be suppressed in a criminal trial.
5. Without the suppressed evidence, defendants are more likely to receive favorable outcomes by acquittal, conviction on less serious charges, or a lesser sentence.
6. When defendants receive more favorable outcomes as a result of officer conduct, officers experience negative personal and/or professional consequences.
7. Officers are aware of negative consequences of constitutional violations, and are able to comply with constitutional rules to prevent future violations.
8. Officers are more likely to conform to constitutional standards because they believe that, with the possibility of evidentiary exclusion, the costs of those constitutional violations exceed their benefits.

Do you think all of these propositions are likely true most of the time? Which raise the most significant concerns? What kind of information would you need to determine whether they are true in general? In a particular department? What could communities do to ensure that the exclusionary rule works to maximum effect? What about states?

4. *Police departments and police officers.* Police departments impose many of the consequences that police experience—both for discovering evidence and for violating the law. This means that, even if officers do not hear about or think about evidentiary exclusion, they might still comply with the law if the departments that supervise them effectively reward constitutional compliance or punish constitutional violations. To a significant degree, departments also determine how much ongoing training officers receive after they join the force, which helps determine how knowledgeable officers are about what constitutes a constitutional violation and how skilled they are at obtaining evidence other ways. This suggests

that the exclusionary rule might depend on whether police departments care enough about criminal case outcomes to provide the right kind of environment for officers. Where do departmental incentives come from? How can communities strengthen them?

5. *Police perjury.* The exclusionary rule's effectiveness depends both on officers being motivated by penalties for failing to follow the law and officers being willing to tell the truth about breaking the law when they have done so. Does it seem odd to assume that police will sometimes violate constitutional law to get evidence, but also assume that they will not have sufficient incentive to perjure themselves to reap the professional rewards of having obtained that evidence? The incentive to lie might not matter much if trial courts were usually able and willing to reject untruthful officer testimony, but that seems unlikely. Moreover, appellate courts almost never overturn trial courts' determinations about officer credibility except when the testimony is manifestly untrue, physically impossible, or internally inconsistent, and sometimes not even then. What can be done to reduce the incentive to lie without undermining the deterrent value of the exclusionary rule? For a sophisticated discussion of these issues, see Christopher Slobogin, *Testilying: Police Perjury and What to Do About It,* 67 U. Colo. L. Rev. 1037 (1996). Slobogin contends that the best way to stop what is sometimes called *testilying* is to reduce the pressure to do it, including by chucking the exclusionary rule in favor of an easily obtainable damages remedy. Since Slobogin wrote his article, technology has made it much easier to record encounters between officers and members of the public. Might the exclusionary rule work a little better as a result? How could encounter recordings be used to promote constitutional compliance? Are there legal rules that could help?

6. *Advantages.* Although commentators since *Mapp* have often debated whether the exclusionary rule reflects good constitutional law, the more important question for thinking about the legal regulation of the police is this: Is the exclusionary rule a good mechanism for reducing constitutional violations by officers? In thinking about that question, note that, among other advantages, the exclusionary rule has at least two features that other constitutional remedies tend to lack.

a. *It gets used often. Mapp* gave criminal defendants an incentive to challenge police conduct. When the Court, less than two years later, guaranteed many criminal defendants counsel in *Gideon v. Wainwright,* 372 U.S. 335 (1963), it ensured that they would also have a means to bring those challenges. Evidence suppression is far and away the most commonly invoked remedy for constitutional violations, and rulings on motions to suppress have been a critical forum for refining Fourth Amendment law.

b. *It leverages prosecutors and politicians.* The exclusionary rule provides a reason for police chiefs, prosecutors, and politicians to encourage officers to comply with the law (or at least not to get caught breaking it), because when criminals go free, the public can, and often does, hold prosecutors and politicians accountable.

Perhaps these advantages explain why the rule has driven so many changes within agencies. To be sure, the Fourth Amendment is still violated. But far more than before, agencies train officers in Fourth Amendment law and encourage them to follow it. It is no exaggeration to say that understanding and adhering to the Fourth

Amendment was not a major consideration in policing before *Mapp*. *Mapp* has made it a core part of being a police officer today.

7. *Disadvantages.* On the other hand, even assuming that the exclusionary rule works to prevent misconduct, it has some notable limitations and disadvantages.

a. *It reduces accuracy.* Because it works by suppressing otherwise relevant and trustworthy evidence from criminal trials, it can make trials a less reliable mechanism for determining criminal guilt.

b. *It rewards too much (or too little).* When evidence is excluded, the victim of the constitutional violation receives a benefit correlated with the strength of the excluded evidence and the charges against him, not the harm of the constitutional violation. In fact, victims of constitutional violations who have not committed any crime receive no remedy at all under the rule.

c. *It exalts evidentiary searches.* Criminal courts following *Mapp* focus intensely on the details of search-and-seizure law leading to evidence, to the exclusion of other significant problems in policing. Officers broke into Dollree Mapp's house, lied to her, intimidated her, and roughed her up before finding evidence in a trunk in her basement, and yet the only issue before the Court is whether mildly dirty books should be excluded because the officers had no warrant. Does that really vindicate the interests at stake?

d. *It expects improbable behavior from judges.* The exclusionary rule works only if judges do what they are extremely reluctant to do: call officers lawbreakers and liars and exclude good evidence. It asks them to do this in the name of an abstract benefit, future deterrence. As one prominent federal judge noted, "Judges—politicians' claims to the contrary notwithstanding—are not in the business of letting people out on technicalities." Guido Calabresi, *The Exclusionary Rule*, 26 Harv. J.L. & Pub. Pol'y 111, 112 (2003). Given this, is it really so surprising that the exclusionary rule has been watered down over time? Might it also have led to watering down the Fourth Amendment?

8. *Tinkering with (or torpedoing)* Mapp. Whatever its features, the Court has spent the decades since *Mapp* cutting away at the exclusionary rule, purportedly trying to permit the rule's deterrence benefits while minimizing the costs. As you read the following cases and notes, consider whether the Court has succeeded in improving on its original recipe.

9. *No alternative.* The Court argues in *Mapp* that an effective remedy is essential to ensuring Fourth Amendment compliance and that, without the exclusionary rule, no remedy would exist. In his concurrence, Justice Douglas explores this idea more by considering two alternative mechanisms for encouraging police to comply with the Constitution's demands. What does he say is wrong with them? Do you imagine anything has changed? Can you think of any other more workable alternatives?

Why Dollree Mapp?

POLICE DEPARTMENT
CLEVELAND, OHIO
DEPARTMENTAL INFORMATION

Bureau of Special
Investigation

DIST. ZONE.

May 23, 1957

May 24, 1957

EXAMINED BY _____ RANK Lieut.

FROM Carl I. Delau, Sgt.   TO Martin P. Cooney, Lieut.

SUBJECT Daily duty report for Thursday, May 23, 1957.

COPIES TO

Sir:

Reported for duty at 8:30 A.M. this date in company with Patls. Dever #990 and Haney #258, read reports, complaints and performed the following assignments.

At this office requestioned Elijah Abercrombie, 773 E. 93 St. relative to the malicious destruction of property of Donald King, 3713 E. 151 St. Subject again denied that he had ever received money from King and had seen him only about six times in his life. Subject was then booked at the Detective Bureau on the warrant that was issued, this was for violation of R.C. 2901.38, (blackmail-felony). Subject was taken to the statement room but he refused to make a statement.

Made reports which are connected with the investigation of Donald King and the bombing of his home. Report made on the questioning of Sampson Powell, known muscle man and suspected of working for Alex Birns. Report made on the telephone numbers which were confiscated from Elijah Abercrombie.

Went to the residence of Sam Elmore, 3189 E. 132 St., reported clearing house figure who had been given a beating by muscle men of Alex Bi This subject wanted for questioning and possible statement, failed to find this person at home, word was left with his wife for Sam Elmore to come to this office.

On information received from a confidential source, went to 14 05 Milverton Ave., the residence of Dollree Mapp who is known to this offic and has previous arrest for clearing house violations. Information had been obtained that a person was hiding out at this address who was wanted in con nection with the bombing of Donald King and that certain evidence was conve to this address. Dollree Mapp resides on the second floor, subject was at home but refused to let us into her home. After considerable delay a search warrant was obtained and entrance gained. Arrested Dollree Mapp and a Vergi Ogletree for investigation, they were conveyed to the Detective Bureau wher they were booked. Ogletree is known to be connected with a cheating house operation and also the California Gold policy house. In the basement we fou a foot locker which contained a large amount of policy paraphernalia in the form of balls and business from the California Gold and Interstate policy houses. In the second floor residence of Dollree Mapp we found a number of books of a pornographic nature. Special report to be made of this and the prosecutor to be consulted.

Reported off duty at 4:00 P.M.

Respectfully:

What does this report tell you about the investigation that led to *Mapp*? About the decision to charge her?

B.   Is the Exclusionary Rule Necessary?

Decades after *Mapp*, the Court came back to the question of whether the exclusionary rule is essential to vindicate Fourth Amendment interests in the next case, and it reached a different conclusion. This case considers whether the exclusionary rule applies to violations of the Fourth Amendment requirement that officers ordinarily knock and announce their presence before entering a home to search it. Consider how the Court has changed in both substance and tone since *Mapp*.

HUDSON v. MICHIGAN
547 U.S. 586 (2006)

JUSTICE SCALIA delivered the opinion of the Court. . . .

Police obtained a warrant authorizing a search for drugs and firearms at the home of petitioner Booker Hudson. They discovered both. Large quantities of drugs were found, including cocaine rocks in Hudson's pocket. A loaded gun was lodged between the cushion and armrest of the chair in which he was sitting. Hudson was charged under Michigan law with unlawful drug and firearm possession.

This case is before us only because of the method of entry into the house. When the police arrived to execute the warrant, they announced their presence, but waited only a short time—perhaps "three to five seconds," App. 15—before turning the knob of the unlocked front door and entering Hudson's home. Hudson moved to suppress all the inculpatory evidence, arguing that the premature entry violated his Fourth Amendment rights. . . .

. . . From the trial level onward, Michigan has conceded that the entry was a knock-and-announce violation. The issue here is remedy. Wilson v. Arkansas, 514 U.S. 927, 937 n.4 (1995), specifically declined to decide whether the exclusionary rule is appropriate for violation of the knock-and-announce requirement. That question is squarely before us now.

In *Weeks v. United States*, 232 U.S. 383 (1914), we adopted the federal exclusionary rule for evidence that was unlawfully seized from a home without a warrant in violation of the Fourth Amendment. We began applying the same rule to the States, through the Fourteenth Amendment, in *Mapp v. Ohio*, 367 U.S. 643 (1961).

Suppression of evidence, however, has always been our last resort, not our first impulse. The exclusionary rule generates "substantial social costs," United States v. Leon, 468 U.S. 897, 907 (1984), which sometimes include setting the guilty free and the dangerous at large. We have therefore been "cautio[us] against expanding" it, Colorado v. Connelly, 479 U.S. 157, 166 (1986), and "have repeatedly emphasized that the rule's 'costly toll' upon truth-seeking and law enforcement objectives presents a high obstacle for those urging [its] application," Pennsylvania Bd. of Probation and Parole v. Scott, 524 U.S. 357, 364–365 (1998). We have rejected "[i]ndiscriminate application" of the rule, *Leon*, 468 U.S. at 908, and have held it to be applicable only "where its remedial objectives are thought most efficaciously served," United States v. Calandra, 414 U.S. 338, 348 (1974)—that is, "where its deterrence benefits outweigh its 'substantial social costs,'" *Scott*, 524 U.S. at 363 (quoting *Leon*, 468 U.S. at 907).

We did not always speak so guardedly. Expansive dicta in *Mapp*, for example, suggested wide scope for the exclusionary rule. See, e.g., 367 U.S. at 655 ("[A]ll evidence obtained by searches and seizures in violation of the Constitution is, by that same authority, inadmissible in a state court"). . . . But we have long since rejected that approach. . . .

. . . The costs here are considerable. In addition to the grave adverse consequence that exclusion of relevant incriminating evidence always entails (viz., the risk of releasing dangerous criminals into society), imposing that massive remedy for a knock-and-announce violation would generate a constant flood of alleged failures to observe the rule. . . . The cost of entering this lottery would be small, but the jackpot enormous: suppression of all evidence, amounting in many cases to a get-out-of-jail-free card. Courts would experience as never before the reality that "[t]he exclusionary rule frequently requires extensive litigation to determine whether particular evidence must be excluded." *Scott*, 524 U.S. at 366. Unlike the warrant or *Miranda* requirements, compliance with which is readily determined (either there was or was not a warrant; either the *Miranda* warning was given, or it was not), what constituted a "reasonable wait time" in a particular case, United States v. Banks, 540 U.S. 31, 36 (2003), (or, for that matter, how many seconds the police in fact waited), . . . is difficult for the trial court to determine and even more difficult for an appellate court to review.

Another consequence of the incongruent remedy Hudson proposes would be police officers' refraining from timely entry after knocking and announcing. As we have observed, the amount of time they must wait is necessarily uncertain. If the consequences of running afoul of the rule were so massive, officers would be inclined to wait longer than the law requires—producing preventable violence against officers in some cases, and the destruction of evidence in many others. We deemed these consequences severe enough to produce our unanimous agreement that a mere "reasonable suspicion" that knocking and announcing "under the particular circumstances, would be dangerous or futile, or that it would inhibit the effective investigation of the crime," will cause the requirement to yield. Richards v. Wisconsin, 520 U.S. 385, 394 (1997).

Next to these "substantial social costs" we must consider the deterrence benefits, existence of which is a necessary condition for exclusion. (It is not, of course, a sufficient condition: "[I]t does not follow that the Fourth Amendment requires adoption of every proposal that might deter police misconduct." *Calandra*, 414 U.S. at 350.) To begin with, the value of deterrence depends upon the strength of the incentive to commit the forbidden act. Viewed from this perspective, deterrence of knock-and-announce violations is not worth a lot. Violation of the warrant requirement sometimes produces incriminating evidence that could not otherwise be obtained. But ignoring knock-and-announce can realistically be expected to achieve absolutely nothing except the prevention of destruction of evidence and the avoidance of life-threatening resistance by occupants of the premises—dangers which, if there is even "reasonable suspicion" of their existence, *suspend the knock-and-announce requirement anyway*. Massive deterrence is hardly required.

It seems to us not even true, as Hudson contends, that without suppression there will be no deterrence of knock-and-announce violations at all. Of course even if this assertion were accurate, it would not necessarily justify suppression. Assuming (as the assertion must) that civil suit is not an effective deterrent, one can think of many forms of police misconduct that are similarly "undeterred." When, for example, a confessed suspect in the killing of a police officer, arrested (along with incriminating evidence) in a lawful warranted search, is subjected to physical abuse at the station house, would it seriously be suggested that the evidence must be excluded, since that is the only "effective deterrent"? And what, other than civil suit, is the "effective deterrent" of police violation of an already-confessed suspect's Sixth Amendment rights by denying him prompt access to counsel? Many would regard these violated rights as more significant than the right not to be intruded upon in one's nightclothes—and yet nothing but "ineffective" civil suit is available as a deterrent. And the police incentive for those violations is arguably greater than the incentive for disregarding the knock-and-announce rule.

We cannot assume that exclusion in this context is necessary deterrence simply because we found that it was necessary deterrence in different contexts and long ago. That would be forcing the public today to pay for the sins and inadequacies of a legal regime that existed almost half a century ago. Dollree Mapp could not turn to 42 U.S.C. §1983, for meaningful relief; *Monroe v. Pape*, 365 U.S. 167 (1961), which began the slow but steady expansion of that remedy, was decided the same Term as *Mapp*. It would be another 17 years before the §1983 remedy was extended to reach the deep pocket of municipalities, Monell v. New York City Dept. of Social Servs., 436 U.S. 658 (1978)....

Hudson complains that "it would be very hard to find a lawyer to take a case such as this," Tr. of Oral Arg. 7, but 42 U.S.C. §1988(b) answers this objection. Since some civil-rights violations would yield damages too small to justify the expense of litigation, Congress has authorized attorney's fees for civil-rights plaintiffs. This remedy was unavailable in the heydays of our exclusionary-rule jurisprudence, because it is tied to the availability of a cause of action. For years after *Mapp*, "very few lawyers would even consider representation of persons who had civil rights claims against the police," but now "much has changed. Citizens and lawyers are much more willing to seek relief in the courts for police misconduct." M. Avery, D. Rudovsky, & K. Blum, *Police Misconduct: Law and Litigation* v (3d ed. 2005). The number of public-interest law firms and lawyers who specialize in civil-rights grievances has greatly expanded.

Hudson points out that few published decisions to date announce huge awards for knock-and-announce violations. But this is an unhelpful statistic. Even if we thought that only large damages would deter police misconduct (and that police somehow are deterred by "damages" but indifferent to the prospect of large §1988 attorney's fees), we do not know how many claims have been settled, or indeed how many violations have occurred that produced anything more than nominal injury. It is clear, at least, that the lower courts are allowing colorable knock-and-announce suits to go forward, unimpeded by assertions of qualified immunity. As far as we know, civil liability is an effective deterrent here, as we have assumed it is in other contexts.

Another development over the past half-century that deters civil-rights violations is the increasing professionalism of police forces, including a new emphasis on internal police discipline. Even as long ago as 1980 we felt it proper to "assume" that unlawful police behavior would "be dealt with appropriately" by the authorities, United States v. Payner, 447 U.S. 727, 733–734 n.5 (1980), but we now have increasing evidence that police forces across the United States take the constitutional rights of citizens seriously. There have been "wide-ranging reforms in the education, training, and supervision of police officers." S. Walker, *Taming the System: The*

Control of Discretion in Criminal Justice 1950–1990 51 (1993). Numerous sources are now available to teach officers and their supervisors what is required of them under this Court's cases, how to respect constitutional guarantees in various situations, and how to craft an effective regime for internal discipline. Failure to teach and enforce constitutional requirements exposes municipalities to financial liability. See Canton v. Harris, 489 U.S. 378, 388 (1989). Moreover, modern police forces are staffed with professionals; it is not credible to assert that internal discipline, which can limit successful careers, will not have a deterrent effect. There is also evidence that the increasing use of various forms of citizen review can enhance police accountability.

In sum, the social costs of applying the exclusionary rule to knock-and-announce violations are considerable; the incentive to such violations is minimal to begin with, and the extant deterrences against them are substantial—incomparably greater than the factors deterring warrantless entries when *Mapp* was decided. Resort to the massive remedy of suppressing evidence of guilt is unjustified. . . .

[The opinion of Justice Kennedy, in which he concurred in part and concurred in the judgment, is omitted.]

Justice Breyer, with whom Justice Stevens, Justice Souter, and Justice Ginsburg join, dissenting.

. . . [T]he driving legal purpose underlying the exclusionary rule, namely, the deterrence of unlawful government behavior, argues strongly for suppression. See Elkins v. United States, 364 U.S. 206, 217 (1960). . . . Indeed, this Court in *Mapp v. Ohio* held that the exclusionary rule applies to the States in large part due to its belief that alternative state mechanisms for enforcing the Fourth Amendment's guarantees had proved "worthless and futile." 367 U.S. 643, 652.

Why is application of the exclusionary rule any the less necessary here? Without such a rule, as in *Mapp*, police know that they can ignore the Constitution's requirements without risking suppression of evidence discovered after an unreasonable entry. As in *Mapp*, some government officers will find it easier, or believe it less risky, to proceed with what they consider a necessary search immediately and without the requisite constitutional (say, warrant or knock-and-announce) compliance.

Of course, the State or the Federal Government may provide alternative remedies for knock-and-announce violations. But that circumstance was true of *Mapp* as well. What reason is there to believe that those remedies (such as private damages actions under 42 U.S.C. §1983), which the Court found inadequate in *Mapp*, can adequately deter unconstitutional police behavior here?

The cases reporting knock-and-announce violations are legion. See, e.g., 34 Geo. L.J. Ann. Rev. Crim. Proc. 31–35 (2005) (collecting Courts of Appeals cases); Bremer, 85 A.L.R. 5th 1 (2001) (collecting state-court cases); Brief for Petitioner 16–17 (collecting federal and state cases). Indeed, these cases of reported violations seem sufficiently frequent and serious as to indicate "a widespread pattern." *Ante,* at 604 (Kennedy, J., concurring in part and concurring in judgment). Yet the majority, like Michigan and the United States, has failed to cite a single reported case in which a plaintiff has collected more than nominal damages solely as a result of a knock-and-announce violation. Even Michigan concedes that, "in cases like the present one . . . , damages may be virtually nonexistent." Brief for Respondent 35, n.66. . . .

As Justice Stewart, the author of a number of significant Fourth Amendment opinions, explained, the deterrent effect of damages actions "can hardly be said to be great," as such actions are "expensive, time-consuming, not readily available, and rarely successful." *The Road to* Mapp v. Ohio *and Beyond: The Origins, Development and Future of the Exclusionary Rule in Search-and-Seizure Cases*, 83 Colum. L. Rev. 1365, 1388 (1983). The upshot is that the need for deterrence—the critical factor driving this Court's Fourth Amendment cases for close to a century—argues with at least comparable strength for evidentiary exclusion here.

To argue, as the majority does, that new remedies, such as 42 U.S.C. §1983 actions or better trained police, make suppression unnecessary is to argue that *Wolf*, not *Mapp*, is now the law. . . . To argue that there may be few civil suits because violations may produce nothing "more than nominal injury" is to confirm, not to deny, the inability of civil suits to deter violations. And to argue without evidence (and despite myriad reported cases of violations, no reported case of civil damages, and Michigan's concession of their nonexistence) that civil suits may provide deterrence because claims *may* "have been settled" is, perhaps, to search in desperation for an argument. Rather, the majority, as it candidly admits, has simply "assumed" that, "[a]s far as [it] know[s], civil liability is an effective deterrent," *ibid.*, a support-free assumption that *Mapp* and subsequent cases make clear does not embody the Court's normal approach to difficult questions of Fourth Amendment law. . . .

NOTES AND QUESTIONS

1. *Challenging* Mapp. The *Hudson* Court suggests that, at least for knock-and-announce violations, two premises of *Mapp*, that officers have an incentive to violate the law and that victims have no alternative remedies, are not true. Is this reasoning a threat to *Mapp* or a reaffirmation of it?

2. *Privacy vs. security.* In another part of the opinion not excerpted here, the Court concludes that evidentiary exclusion is an inappropriate remedy for knock-and-announce violations because exclusion and the knock-and-announce rule protect different interests. Whereas exclusion is intended to vindicate privacy against unwarranted government searches, the knock-and-announce rule protects "human life and limb, because an unannounced entry may provoke violence in supposed self-defense by the surprised resident," and the elements of privacy and dignity that are preserved by an opportunity to throw on clothes and "collect oneself before answering the door." *Hudson*, 547 U.S. at 594. Is the value of exclusion tied to the suspect's interest in privacy? Could exclusion promote other interests? By what mechanism?

3. *Incentive to violate. Hudson* is a rare case in which the Court expressly considered police incentives to comply with or violate the law. Justice Scalia and Justice Breyer disagreed about whether officers have any interest in violating the knock-and-announce rule. What do they base their views on? Which argument do you find more plausible? According to the prosecutor in the case, one of the officers did not want to wait because he had previously been shot at while executing a warrant. Does that help?

4. *Professionalism as an alternative.* Justice Scalia cites a book by Samuel Walker, one of the country's foremost experts on police accountability, to support the proposition that the exclusionary rule is unnecessary because police departments now "take the constitutional rights of citizens seriously." In the bluntly titled op-ed, *Thanks for Nothing, Nino,* published soon after *Hudson* was decided, Walker argued

back, noting that the point of his book was precisely the opposite of Justice Scalia's conclusion:

> My argument, based on the historical evidence of the last 40 years, is that the . . . Warren court's interventions (*Mapp* and *Miranda* being the most famous) set new standards for lawful conduct, forcing the police to reform and strengthening community demands for curbs on abuse.
>
> Scalia's opinion suggests that the results I highlighted have sufficiently removed the need for an exclusionary rule to act as a judicial-branch watchdog over the police. . . . To the contrary, . . . the results reinforce the Supreme Court's continuing importance in defining constitutional protections for individual rights and requiring the appropriate remedies for violations, including the exclusion of evidence.
>
> The ideal approach is for the court to join the other branches of government in a multipronged mix of remedies for police misconduct: judicially mandated exclusionary rules, legislation to give citizens oversight of police and administrative reforms in training and supervision. No single remedy is sufficient to this very important task. *Hudson* marks a dangerous step backward in removing a crucial component of that mix.

Samuel Walker, *Thanks for Nothing, Nino*, L.A. Times M5 (June 25, 2006).

5. *Civil damages as an alternative.* The authors of the civil rights litigation treatise Justice Scalia cited for the proposition that civil rights litigation provides an accessible and adequate alternative to the exclusionary rule similarly disavowed Justice Scalia's use of their work. They rewrote the first page of the treatise in post-*Hudson* editions to make it clear that though "[i]n certain respects it is now easier to challenge police misconduct in court than it was two decades ago, in other respects, it is far more difficult." In addition, in the book's first footnote, they now say:

> In a highly misleading citation, Justice Scalia quoted this paragraph in *Hudson v. Michigan*, as support for the proposition that the availability of civil remedies against police supports limitations on the application of the exclusionary rule in criminal cases. We invite the reader to judge the honesty of this assertion based on a full review of this book.

Michael Avery et al., *Police Misconduct: Law and Litigation* vii n.1 (3rd ed. 2019). Now what do you think? Do you think that other remedies are not as available as Justice Scalia suggests or that the exclusionary rule might be necessary, even if they are?

6. *The costs in* Hudson. Justice Scalia repeatedly refers to suppressing evidence of guilt as a "massive remedy." What does he mean? There are three perspectives from which the severity of the exclusionary rule might be judged: (1) the perspective of the person who suffered the constitutional injury, the criminal defendant; (2) the perspective of the officer whom the rule is intended to deter; and (3) a societal perspective, including all the costs and benefits of the rule. If you are judging whether the exclusionary rule is a valuable remedy compared to others, you might take a societal perspective by looking at the costs and benefits of using this tool. If you are evaluating whether the exclusionary rule is likely to deter constitutional violations by officers, you might need the second perspective since only from the officer's perspective can we tell whether evidentiary exclusion imposes a penalty substantial enough to change the expected cost of engaging in a constitutional violation. Why

might you care about the perspective of the person who suffered the deprivation? Which perspectives does Justice Scalia consider? What does he use them for?

7. *Cost–benefit analysis and evidentiary exclusion.* As *Hudson* indicates, in an earlier case the Court had advocated restricting evidentiary exclusion when its costs did not outweigh its benefits. In *United States v. Leon*, 468 U.S. 897 (1984), the Court held that the exclusionary rule should not bar the use of evidence obtained by police officers who acted in reasonable reliance on a search warrant issued by a detached and neutral magistrate, even when the warrant was later found to be based on insufficient evidence. In dissent, Justice Brennan commented about this kind of analysis:

> [T]he language of deterrence and of cost/benefit analysis, if used indiscriminately, can have a narcotic effect. It creates an illusion of technical precision and ineluctability. It suggests that not only constitutional principle but also empirical data support the majority's result. When the Court's analysis is examined carefully, however, it is clear that we have not been treated to an honest assessment of the merits of the exclusionary rule, but have instead been drawn into a curious world where the "costs" of excluding illegally obtained evidence loom to exaggerated heights and where the "benefits" of such exclusion are made to disappear with a mere wave of the hand. . . .
>
> A proper understanding of the broad purposes sought to be served by the Fourth Amendment demonstrates that the principles embodied in the exclusionary rule rest upon a far firmer constitutional foundation than the shifting sands of the Court's deterrence rationale. But even if I were to accept the Court's chosen method of analyzing the question posed by these cases, I would still conclude that the Court's decision cannot be justified. . . .
>
> . . . [T]he Court has frequently bewailed the "cost" of excluding reliable evidence. In large part, this criticism rests upon a refusal to acknowledge the function of the Fourth Amendment itself. If nothing else, the Amendment plainly operates to disable the government from gathering information and securing evidence in certain ways. In practical terms, of course, this restriction of official power means that some incriminating evidence inevitably will go undetected if the government obeys these constitutional restraints. It is the loss of that evidence that is the "price" our society pays for enjoying the freedom and privacy safeguarded by the Fourth Amendment. Thus, some criminals will go free *not*, in Justice (then Judge) Cardozo's misleading epigram, "because the constable has blundered," People v. Defore, 242 N.Y. 13, 21 (1926), but rather because official compliance with Fourth Amendment requirements makes it more difficult to catch criminals. Understood in this way, the Amendment directly contemplates that some reliable and incriminating evidence will be lost to the government; therefore, it is not the exclusionary rule, but the Amendment itself that has imposed this cost.
>
> In addition, the Court's decisions over the past decade have made plain that the entire enterprise of attempting to assess the benefits and costs of the exclusionary rule in various contexts is a virtually impossible task for the judiciary to perform honestly or accurately. Although the Court's language in those cases suggests that some specific empirical basis may support its analyses, the reality is that the Court's opinions represent inherently unstable compounds of intuition, hunches, and occasional pieces of partial and often inconclusive data. . . .
>
> By remaining within its redoubt of empiricism and by basing the rule solely on the deterrence rationale, the Court has robbed the rule of legitimacy. A doctrine that is explained as if it were an empirical proposition but for which there is only

limited empirical support is both inherently unstable and an easy mark for critics. The extent of this Court's fidelity to Fourth Amendment requirements, however, should not turn on such statistical uncertainties. . . .

. . . There is no question that in the hands of the present Court the deterrence rationale has proved to be a powerful tool for confining the scope of the rule. In *United States v. Calandra*, 414 U.S. 338 (1974), for example, the Court concluded that the "speculative and undoubtedly minimal advance in the deterrence of police misconduct," was insufficient to outweigh the "expense of substantially impeding the role of the grand jury." *Id.* at 351–352. In *Stone v. Powell*, the Court found that "the additional contribution, if any, of the consideration of search-and-seizure claims of state prisoners on collateral review is small in relation to the costs." 428 U.S. 465, 493 (1976). In *United States v. Janis*, 428 U.S. 433 (1976), the Court concluded that "exclusion from federal civil proceedings of evidence unlawfully seized by a state criminal enforcement officer has not been shown to have a sufficient likelihood of deterring the conduct of the state police so that it outweighs the societal costs imposed by the exclusion." *Id.* at 454. And in an opinion handed down today, the Court finds that the "balance between costs and benefits comes out against applying the exclusionary rule in civil deportation hearings held by the [Immigration and Naturalization Service]." INS v. Lopez–Mendoza, 468 U.S. 1032, 1050 (1984).

Thus, in this bit of judicial stagecraft, while the sets sometimes change, the actors always have the same lines. Given this well-rehearsed pattern, one might have predicted with some assurance how the present case would unfold. First there is the ritual incantation of the "substantial social costs" exacted by the exclusionary rule, followed by the virtually foreordained conclusion that, given the marginal benefits, application of the rule in the circumstances of these cases is not warranted. . . .

At the outset, the Court suggests that society has been asked to pay a high price—in terms either of setting guilty persons free or of impeding the proper functioning of trials—as a result of excluding relevant physical evidence in cases where the police, in conducting searches and seizing evidence, have made only an "objectively reasonable" mistake concerning the constitutionality of their actions. But what evidence is there to support such a claim?

Significantly, the Court points to none, and, indeed, as the Court acknowledges, recent studies have demonstrated that the "costs" of the exclusionary rule—calculated in terms of dropped prosecutions and lost convictions—are quite low. . . .

Id. at 929–950 (Brennan, J., dissenting). Does *Hudson* follow Justice Brennan's script? If insufficient evidence exists to pin down the precise costs and benefits, how should the Court think about the costs and benefits of the exclusionary rule? Is that an argument for ignoring this kind of analysis? What if the costs to public safety of excluding evidence *are* provably high? What else do you need to know?

C. Officer Culpability and the Severity of the Exclusionary Rule

Justice Brennan's argument against a cost–benefit approach to the exclusionary rule came in *United States v. Leon*, 468 U.S. 897 (1984), which created a *good faith exception* to the exclusionary rule. *Leon* ruled that the government may use at trial evidence that police officers discover in reasonable reliance on a search warrant, although the warrant was issued without probable cause. Since *Leon*, the Court has repeatedly extended the good faith exception to other scenarios. In *Illinois v. Krull*, 480 U.S. 340 (1987), the Court held that the exclusionary rule does not apply to evidence found when police officers conducted a search in good faith reliance on a statute later declared unconstitutional. In *Arizona v. Evans*, 514 U.S. 1 (1995), it found the rule inapplicable when officers made an arrest after a court employee's clerical error caused them mistakenly to believe that an outstanding warrant existed for the suspect. In *Herring v. United States*, 555 U.S. 135 (2009), it extended *Evans* to circumstances in which a police error similarly resulted in officers reasonably but wrongly believing that a warrant existed for an arrest. And in the case below, the Court applied the good faith exception to the exclusionary rule to searches conducted in reasonable reliance on binding appellate precedent. In each case, the Court considered the costs and benefits of evidentiary exclusion. As you read *Davis*, consider whether Justice Brennan's dissent in *Leon* could serve as a dissent here, too. Or is something different?

DAVIS v. UNITED STATES
564 U.S. 229 (2011)

JUSTICE ALITO delivered the opinion of the Court.

The Fourth Amendment protects the right to be free from "unreasonable searches and seizures," but it is silent about how this right is to be enforced. To supplement the bare text, this Court created the exclusionary rule, a deterrent sanction that bars the prosecution from introducing evidence obtained by way of a Fourth Amendment violation. The question here is whether to apply this sanction when the police conduct a search in compliance with binding precedent that is later overruled. Because suppression would do nothing to deter police misconduct in these circumstances, and because it would come at a high cost to both the truth and the public safety, we hold that searches conducted in objectively reasonable reliance on binding appellate precedent are not subject to the exclusionary rule. . . .

. . . Our cases have . . . limited the rule's operation to situations in which this purpose is "thought most efficaciously served." United States v. Calandra, 414 U.S. 338, 348 (1974). Where suppression fails to yield "appreciable deterrence," exclusion is "clearly . . . unwarranted." United States v. Janis, 428 U.S. 433, 454 (1976).

Real deterrent value is a "necessary condition for exclusion," but it is not "a sufficient" one. Hudson v. Michigan, 547 U.S. 586, 596 (2006). The analysis must also account for the "substantial social costs" generated by the rule. United States v. Leon, 468 U.S. 897, 907 (1984). Exclusion exacts a heavy toll on both the judicial system and society at large. It almost always requires courts to ignore reliable, trustworthy evidence bearing on guilt or innocence. And its bottom-line effect, in many cases, is to suppress the truth and set the criminal loose in the community without punishment. Our cases hold that society must swallow this bitter pill when necessary, but only as a "last resort." *Hudson*, 547 U.S. at 591. For exclusion to be appropriate, the deterrence benefits of suppression must outweigh its heavy costs. See Herring v. United States, 555 U.S. 135, 141 (2009); United States v. Leon 486 U.S. 897, 910 (1984).

Admittedly, there was a time when our exclusionary-rule cases were not nearly so discriminating in their approach to the doctrine. . . . In time, however, we came to acknowledge the exclusionary rule for what it undoubtedly is—a "judicially created remedy" of this Court's own making. *Calandra,* 414 U.S. at 348. We abandoned the old, "reflexive" application of the doctrine, and imposed a more rigorous weighing of its costs and deterrence benefits. Arizona v. Evans, 514 U.S. 1, 13 (1995). In a line of cases beginning with *Leon,* 468 U.S. 897, we also recalibrated our cost-benefit analysis in exclusion cases to focus the inquiry on the "flagrancy of the police misconduct" at issue. *Id.* at 909, 911.

The basic insight of the *Leon* line of cases is that the deterrence benefits of exclusion "var[y] with the culpability of the law enforcement conduct" at issue. *Herring,* 555 U.S. at 143. When the police exhibit "deliberate," "reckless," or "grossly negligent" disregard for Fourth Amendment rights, the deterrent value of exclusion is strong and tends to outweigh the resulting costs. *Id.* at 144. But when the police act with an objectively "reasonable good-faith belief" that their conduct is lawful, *Leon,* 468 U.S. at 909, or when their conduct involves only simple, "isolated" negligence, *Herring,* 555 U.S. at 137, the "deterrence rationale loses much of its force," and exclusion cannot "pay its way," *Leon,* 468 U.S. at 919, 908, n.6.

The Court has over time applied this "good-faith" exception across a range of cases. . . .

The question in this case is whether to apply the exclusionary rule when the police conduct a search in objectively reasonable reliance on binding judicial precedent. . . .

Under our exclusionary-rule precedents, th[e] acknowledged absence of police culpability dooms Davis' claim. Police practices trigger the harsh sanction of exclusion only when they are deliberate enough to yield "meaningful[l]" deterrence, and culpable enough to be "worth the price paid by the justice system." *Herring,* 555 U.S. at 144. The conduct of the officers here was neither of these things. The officers who conducted the search did not violate Davis' Fourth Amendment rights deliberately, recklessly, or with gross negligence. Nor does this case involve any "recurring or systemic negligence" on the part of law enforcement. The police acted in strict compliance with binding precedent, and their behavior was not wrongful. Unless the exclusionary rule is to become a strict-liability regime, it can have no application in this case. . . .

About all that exclusion would deter in this case is conscientious police work. Responsible law-enforcement officers will take care to learn "what is required of them" under Fourth Amendment precedent and will conform their conduct to these rules. But by the same token, when binding appellate precedent specifically *authorizes* a particular police practice, well-trained officers will and should use that tool to fulfill their crime-detection and public-safety responsibilities. . . . The deterrent effect of exclusion in such a case can only be to discourage the officer from " 'do[ing] his duty.' " *Leon,* 468 U.S. at 920.

That is not the kind of deterrence the exclusionary rule seeks to foster. . . . Evidence obtained during a search conducted in reasonable reliance on binding precedent is not subject to the exclusionary rule.

[The opinion of Justice Sotomayor, concurring in the judgment, and the dissenting opinion of Justice Breyer, joined by Justice Ginsburg, are omitted.]

NOTES AND QUESTIONS

1. *Police culpability and the good faith exception.* In early good faith exception cases, the Court refused to apply the exclusionary rule to police officers who did something reasonable but unconstitutional because of a mistake made by a nonpolice actor: a magistrate in *Leon*, a legislature in *Krull*, and a clerk in *Evans*. These cases followed reasoning in *Leon*, that "the exclusionary rule is designed to deter police misconduct" rather than to punish the errors of others. United States v. Leon, 468 U.S. 897, 916 (1984). *Herring* is different because it extends the exception to mistakes made by police officers themselves, contending that the application of the rule should vary with the "culpability of the law enforcement conduct." Herring v. United States, 555 U.S. 135, 143 (2009). In one way, *Davis* follows obviously from the cases before *Herring*: It eliminates the exclusionary rule when officers violate the law because an appellate court told them they may do so. But in another, *Davis*'s rhetoric emphasizes, more than *Herring*'s, that for the exclusionary rule to apply, it not only must have "real deterrent value," but the officer must *also* be culpable of genuine wrongdoing, rather than engaging in a merely negligent act. How does the *Davis* Court justify this requirement?

2. *Officer culpability and officer incentives.* Is the Court right that intentional conduct is easier to deter? Is that a sufficient argument for refusing to exclude evidence when the conduct is not willful or flagrant? In a dissent in *Herring*, Justice Ginsburg responded that "[t]he exclusionary rule, the Court suggests, is capable of only marginal deterrence when the misconduct at issue is merely careless, not intentional or reckless. The suggestion runs counter to a foundational premise of tort law — that liability for negligence, *i.e.*, lack of due care, creates an incentive to act with greater care." United States v. Herring, 555 U.S. 135, 153 (2009) (Ginsburg, J., dissenting). Can negligent police conduct be deterred? How do you envision that happening? If the Court eliminates the exclusionary rule except when police conduct is egregious, what incentives does that create for officers who know that a search they are about to carry out is close to the constitutional line? Is that a problem?

3. *Proof of officer culpability.* How easy is it for a defendant to establish that an officer violated the Constitution intentionally or recklessly? What evidence would show that unconstitutional conduct is "recurring or systemic"? Where will that evidence come from? Andrew Ferguson argues that the defendants could turn on the police the same technologies that help the police monitor citizens — data mining, video and audio surveillance, and predictive analytics. As he points out, however, jurisdictions do not have the resources or incentives to develop this technological architecture; even if they did, many defense attorneys would not have the resources to use it. Andrew Guthrie Ferguson, *The Exclusionary Rule in the Age of Blue Data*, 72 Vand. L. Rev. 561, 638–642 (2019). By limiting the exclusionary rule to circumstances that defendants cannot usually prove, even if they exist, has the Court undermined the deterrent effect of the exclusionary rule?

4. *Culpability* and *deterrence.* The Court's language suggests that culpability is a requirement *on top of* deterrence. If the point of the exclusionary rule is to deter, and excluding evidence when the officer is not culpable deters future constitutional violations, why should courts care whether the officer is also culpable? By calling exclusion a "harsh sanction," the Court seems to suggest that excluding evidence unfairly impugns officers who have violated the Constitution's labyrinthine rules

only by accident. Is that right? Does that matter to you? Does this reasoning conflict with *Mapp*'s conclusion that the exclusionary rule gives "to the police officer no less than that to which honest law enforcement is entitled"? 367 U.S. at 660.

5. *Procedural justice and culpability.* Although the Court does not consider it, there might be another justification for the culpability requirement. Recall that procedural justice theory suggests that police are likely to obey the Constitution if they believe the courts act legitimately in enforcing it. Might the good faith exception help officers more willingly accept Fourth Amendment regulation and the exclusionary rule? If so, how would we know which effect is more significant, the degree to which the good faith exception undermines deterrence, or the degree to which it promotes compliance with the law by another path?

6. *Officer culpability and departmental deterrence.* In a part of Justice Brennan's *Leon* dissent not quoted above, he argued against the individually oriented view of deterrence taken in cases like *Davis*:

> The key to the Court's conclusion . . . is its belief that the prospective deterrent effect of the exclusionary rule operates only in those situations in which police officers, when deciding whether to go forward with some particular search, have reason to know that their planned conduct will violate the requirements of the Fourth Amendment. If these officers in fact understand (or reasonably should understand because the law is well settled) that their proposed conduct will offend the Fourth Amendment and that, consequently, any evidence they seize will be suppressed in court, they will refrain from conducting the planned search. In those circumstances, the incentive system created by the exclusionary rule will have the hoped-for deterrent effect. But in situations where police officers reasonably (but mistakenly) believe that their planned conduct satisfies Fourth Amendment requirements . . . then such officers will have no reason to refrain from conducting the search, and the exclusionary rule will have no effect.
>
> At first blush, there is some logic to this position. Undoubtedly, in the situation hypothesized by the Court, the existence of the exclusionary rule cannot be expected to have any deterrent effect on the particular officers at the moment they are deciding whether to go forward with the search. Indeed, the subsequent exclusion of any evidence seized under such circumstances appears somehow "unfair" to the particular officers involved. . . .
>
> The flaw in the Court's argument, however, is that its logic captures only one comparatively minor element of the generally acknowledged deterrent purposes of the exclusionary rule. To be sure, the rule operates to some extent to deter future misconduct by individual officers who have had evidence suppressed in their own cases. But what the Court overlooks is that the deterrence rationale for the rule is not designed to be, nor should it be thought of as, a form of "punishment" of individual police officers for their failures to obey the restraints imposed by the Fourth Amendment. Instead, the chief deterrent function of the rule is its tendency to promote institutional compliance with Fourth Amendment requirements on the part of law enforcement agencies generally. Thus, as the Court has previously recognized, "over the long-term, [the] demonstration [provided by the exclusionary rule] that our society attaches serious consequences to violation of constitutional rights is thought to encourage those who formulate law enforcement policies, and the officers who implement them, to incorporate Fourth Amendment ideals into their value system." Stone v. Powell, 428 U.S. 465, 492 (1976). It is only through such an institutionwide mechanism that

information concerning Fourth Amendment standards can be effectively communicated to rank-and-file officers.

> If the overall educational effect of the exclusionary rule is considered, application of the rule to even those situations in which individual police officers have acted on the basis of a reasonable but mistaken belief that their conduct was authorized can still be expected to have a considerable long-term deterrent effect. If evidence is consistently excluded in these circumstances, police departments will surely be prompted to instruct their officers to devote greater care and attention to providing sufficient information to establish probable cause when applying for a warrant, and to review with some attention the form of the warrant that they have been issued, rather than automatically assuming that whatever document the magistrate has signed will necessarily comport with Fourth Amendment requirements.

United States v. Leon, 468 U.S. 897, 952–955 (1984) (Brennan, J. dissenting). Of course, Justice Brennan's argument has not won a majority of the Court. Why does the *Davis* Court reject this kind of thinking? If institutional behavior magnifies the deterrent effects of exclusion, and the exclusionary rule encourages the institutional behavior, are there ways we might avoid exclusion and still get similar agency action?

7. *Exceptions and deterrence. Davis* and other good faith exception cases carve out cases to which the exclusionary rule no longer applies because the Court believes the deterrence benefits do not justify applying the rule. Although the exclusionary rule still applies to many ordinary Fourth Amendment violations, since the 1970s, the Court has also expanded other exceptions to the exclusionary rule. First, it has limited the legal proceedings to which the rule applies, so that the government may introduce illegally seized evidence in civil suits, tax proceedings, deportations, and nontrial criminal proceedings such as grand jury hearings. Second, it has limited the application of the rule in criminal cases in ways other than through the good faith exception. The Court has restricted who may invoke the rule (standing doctrine) and what evidence may be excluded (fruit-of-the-poisonous tree analysis and attenuation). What could these changes mean for the future impact of the rule? Should these carveouts be evaluated one by one? Or might they have an effect greater than the sum of their parts?

8. *Scope of deterrence.* Is the exclusionary rule likely to deter illegal searches that are unlikely to yield evidence? For example, when police officers board intercity buses to question passengers and ask for consent to search, they do not expect to find drugs often. Does the exclusionary rule nevertheless encourage them to comply with the law in case they do find evidence? What if the goal is to prevent crime rather than uncover it? Many cities use aggressive stop-and-frisk practices to *discourage* people from carrying weapons or drugs. Although they arrest and charge people when they find contraband or guns, yields are low and not really the point. How might the exclusionary rule influence whether officers follow the Fourth Amendment in those interactions?

9. *The exclusionary rule and public safety.* Your views about the proper breadth of the exclusionary rule probably depend in large part on how important you think criminal evidence is to public safety, how worried you are about constitutional violations that produce evidence, and how you think we should trade off those two concerns. What do you think about these issues? Where do your views come from?

D. *State Exclusionary Rules*

Every state constitution has a provision analogous to the Fourth Amendment. Although the Fourth Amendment provides a "floor" of protection that local and state law enforcement may not violate, "a State is free *as a matter of its own law* to impose greater restrictions on police activity than those this Court holds to be necessary upon federal constitutional standards." Oregon v. Hass, 420 U.S. 714, 719 (1975). Most states also have their own exclusionary rules, established by state constitutional law, statute, or judicial interpretation.

1. State Exclusion Beyond Federal Exclusion

When the federal approach to both Fourth Amendment rights and remedies was expansive, state constitutional law rarely mattered in criminal cases because its protection was largely redundant. As the Supreme Court has narrowed the exclusionary rule, some states have refused to follow, kicking in to offer a remedy—and therefore perhaps a deterrent—when federal law does not. How does the U.S. Supreme Court's rule and reasoning matter to the Vermont Supreme Court?

STATE v. OAKES
598 A.2d 119 (Vt. 1991)

ALLEN, CHIEF JUSTICE.

The issue presented on appeal to this Court is whether our state exclusionary rule for violations of Article 11 of the Vermont Constitution should be limited by the "good faith" exception articulated by the United States Supreme Court in United States v. Leon, 468 U.S. 897 (1984). We hold that it should not. Accordingly, the trial court's denial of defendant's suppression motion is reversed, and the cause is remanded.

On March 1, 1989, Detective Michael Colgan of the Bennington Police Department applied for and received a warrant to search the residence of defendant's girl friend. That evening Detective Colgan and other officers executed the warrant. Their search uncovered a large plastic bag, inside of which were twelve smaller bags containing marijuana.

Defendant was charged with felony possession of marijuana . . . . Prior to trial, defendant moved to suppress the evidence seized in the search on the ground that there had not been sufficient probable cause for issuance of the warrant, and consequently the search violated Chapter I, Article 11 of the Vermont Constitution[1] and

---

[1] Chapter I, Article 11 provides:

That the people have a right to hold themselves, their houses, papers, and possessions, free from search or seizure; and therefore warrants, without oath or affirmation first made, affording sufficient foundation for them, and whereby by any officer or messenger may be commanded or required to search suspected places, or to seize any person or persons, his, her or their property, not particularly described, are contrary to that right, and ought not to be granted.

the Fourth Amendment of the United States Constitution. . . . We have . . . reviewed the court's determination that the affidavit accompanying the warrant application did not constitute sufficient probable cause for issuance of the warrant. We agree with this determination.

A.

This Court has adopted an exclusionary rule for violations of the Vermont Constitution.

"Evidence obtained in violation of the Vermont Constitution, or as the result of a violation, cannot be admitted at trial as a matter of state law." State v. Badger, 141 Vt. 430, 452–453 (1982). This was not done under compulsion of *Mapp v. Ohio,* 367 U.S. 643 (1961), which worked only to extend to state courts an exclusionary rule for federal constitutional violations. *Id.* at 655. Rather, a state exclusionary rule was adopted because "[i]ntroduction of [illegally obtained] evidence at trial eviscerates our most sacred rights, impinges on individual privacy, perverts our judicial process, distorts any notion of fairness, and encourages official misconduct." *Badger,* 141 Vt. at 453. The State now invites us to follow the Supreme Court's holding in *Leon* and except from our state exclusionary rule evidence seized by a police officer in objectively reasonable reliance on a subsequently invalidated warrant — the so-called "good faith" exception to the exclusionary rule. We decline the invitation.[3]

The United States Supreme Court has distinguished between the rights guaranteed an individual by the Fourth Amendment and the remedy adopted to effectuate those rights. In the thirty years following *Mapp,* a majority of the Supreme Court has consistently treated the federal exclusionary rule as a remedy distinct from the constitutional right itself. . . . When the Supreme Court addresses the scope of the federal exclusionary rule, it does not focus on an individual's constitutional rights; rather it weighs the additional deterrent effect on official misconduct that excluding the unlawfully obtained evidence will achieve against the cost of excluding this evidence.

. . . We point out the distinction made by the Supreme Court simply to clarify the amount of deference we will accord its decision in *Leon.* By treating the federal exclusionary rule as a judicially created remedy rather than a constitutional right, the Supreme Court's decision focuses, not on interpretation of the federal constitution, but on an attempted empirical assessment of the costs and benefits of creating a good faith exception to the federal exclusionary rule. This empirical assessment can inform this Court's decision on the good faith exception only to the extent that it is persuasive. If the assessment is flawed, this Court cannot simply accept the conclusion the Supreme Court draws from it. To do so would be contrary to our obligation to ensure that our state exclusionary rule effectuates Article 11 rights, and would disserve those rights.

---

[3] We are not alone in our rejection of a good faith exception. States rejecting the exception on state constitutional grounds include: State v. Marsala, 579 A.2d 58 (Conn. 1990); State v. Novembrino, 105 519 A.2d 820 (N.J. 1987); People v. Bigelow, 488 N.E.2d 451, 458 (N.Y. 1985); State v. Carter, 370 S.E.2d 553 (N.C. 1988); Commonwealth v. Edmunds, 586 A.2d 887 (Pa. 1991); see also Stringer v. State, 491 So.2d 837, 841 (Miss. 1986) (Robertson, J., concurring). Massachusetts has rejected the exception on statutory grounds. Commonwealth v. Upton, 476 N.E.2d 548, 554 n. 5 (Mass. 1985).

B.

In *Leon* the Supreme Court fashioned a good faith exception to the exclusionary rule by "conclud[ing] that the marginal or nonexistent benefits produced by suppressing evidence obtained in objectively reasonable reliance on a subsequently invalidated search warrant cannot justify the substantial costs of exclusion." 468 U.S. at 922.

The Court's treatment of the "substantial costs" of not adopting a good faith exception is summary:

> The substantial social costs exacted by the exclusionary rule for the vindication of Fourth Amendment rights have long been a source of concern. . . . An objectionable collateral consequence of this interference with the criminal justice system's truthfinding function is that some guilty defendants may go free or receive reduced sentences as a result of favorable plea bargains.

Id. at 907.

In a footnote the Court concedes that many researchers "have concluded that the impact of the exclusionary rule is insubstantial." *Id.* at 907 n.6. Yet the Court answers, without citing empirical data, that the researchers' focus on nonprosecution and nonconviction of felony cases "mask a large absolute number of felons who are released because the cases against them were based in part on illegal searches or seizures." *Id.*

The Court's treatment of the "marginal or nonexistent benefits" of not adopting a good faith exception is more extensive. Taking the possible benefit of the exclusionary rule solely to be deterrence of official misconduct, see *id.* at 906, 921 n.22, the Court attempts to assess the deterrent effect that excluding evidence in this situation will have upon the officials involved: the police and the judicial authorities who issue warrants.

As to the police, the Court reasons that where the individual officer's reliance on a subsequently invalidated warrant is objectively reasonable, there is nothing to deter. . . . The Court dismisses as "speculative" arguments that applying the exclusionary rule in this situation would lessen the incentive for officers to prematurely approach judicial authorities with inadequate facts in the hope that they will get by, and would discourage "magistrate shopping." *Id.* at 918.

As to the judicial authorities who issue warrants, the Court proceeds from the premise that the exclusionary rule does not apply to them to the conclusion that it has no deterrent effect on them. . . .

C.

Criticism of the Supreme Court's cost-benefit approach to the exclusionary rule has been extensive. Voiced by commentators prior to *Leon,* the arguments were forcefully marshalled in Justice Brennan's dissenting opinion. 468 U.S. at 928, 948–959 (Brennan, J., dissenting). A new wave of criticism followed issuance of *Leon,* and has been used by the highest courts of states in their rejection of a good faith exception to their exclusionary rules. We do not find it necessary to recite the full content of this criticism. Consideration of a few basic strands is sufficient to create substantial doubt concerning the Supreme Court's conclusions.

First, there is an inconsistency between the Court's labelling the exclusionary rule's costs as "substantial" and the Court's concession that many of the researchers upon whom it relies have concluded that the costs are "insubstantial." *Leon*, 468 U.S. at 908 n.6. . . .

More fundamentally, we are hesitant to label the nonprosecution or nonconviction of felony arrests a cost of the exclusionary rule as opposed to a cost of the constitutional prohibition itself. As former Justice Stewart wrote:

> Much of the criticism leveled at the exclusionary rule is misdirected; it is more properly directed at the fourth amendment itself. It is true that, as many observers have charged, the effect of the rule is to deprive the courts of extremely relevant, often direct evidence of the guilt of the defendant. But these same critics sometimes fail to acknowledge that, in many instances, the same extremely relevant evidence would not have been obtained had the police officer complied with the commands of the fourth amendment in the first place.
>
> . . . The exclusionary rule places no limitations on the actions of the police. The fourth amendment does.

Stewart, *The Road to Mapp v. Ohio and Beyond: The Origins, Development and Future of the Exclusionary Rule in Search-and-Seizure Cases,* 83 Colum. L. Rev. 1365, 1392–1393 (1983). The same can be said about the relative costs of our state exclusionary rule and Article 11's prohibition on unlawful searches and seizures.

There have also been substantial doubts raised concerning the Court's conclusion that excluding evidence seized by a police officer in objectively reasonable reliance on a subsequently invalidated warrant would be of "marginal or nonexistent" benefit in promoting compliance with the Constitution. The Court's notion that there is nothing to deter if a police officer has acted with objective reasonableness is attractively simple. "Penalizing the officer for the magistrate's error, rather than his own, cannot logically contribute to the deterrence of Fourth Amendment violations." *Leon*, 468 U.S. at 921. The exclusionary rule's deterrent effect, however, does not rest primarily on "penalizing" an individual officer into future conformity with the Constitution. Rather, it rests on "its tendency to promote institutional compliance with Fourth Amendment requirements on the part of law enforcement agencies generally." *Id.* at 953 (Brennan, J., dissenting). It creates an incentive for the police as an institution to train its officers to conform with the Constitution. Consequently, the important question is not whether it is of any benefit to "penalize" the objectively reasonable conduct of an individual officer, but rather whether failure to do so will lower the incentive for institutional compliance. The Court gives no answer to this question.

Nor does the Court effectively address concerns that adoption of a good faith exception will create an incentive for future inadequate presentations and magistrate shopping. The Court rejects these concerns as "speculative." *Id.* at 918. Yet this is no answer, because an assertion that such an incentive will not be created is also "speculative" in the absence of empirical data. These concerns do have the force of logic behind them. Because the good faith exception raises the value of having a warrant and decreases the subsequent judicial inquiry into the basis for the warrant, the benefits to be gained from magistrate shopping and inadequate presentations are heightened, increasing the incentive to engage in such conduct. . . .

The ultimate criticism of the Court's cost-benefit analysis in *Leon* is that it is attempting to do what at this time cannot be done. There simply are insufficient empirical data for the costs and benefits of a good faith exception to be accurately assessed. The benefits of the exclusionary rule are hard to measure because they consist of "non-events." . . . As demonstrated above, there are conflicting interpretations concerning these benefits and the rule's costs. All of these measurement difficulties are further exacerbated when attention turns from the costs and benefits of the exclusionary rule in general to the costs and benefits of an untested exception to the exclusionary rule.

. . . Because of the inability at this time to measure accurately the costs and benefits of the exclusionary rule, we do not find persuasive the Court's conclusions in *Leon* concerning the costs and benefits of a good faith exception to the exclusionary rule.

D.

The good faith exception adopted in *Leon* represents on its face a significant limitation on the exclusionary rule. . . . We will not impose such a significant limitation upon our state exclusionary rule on the basis of the Court's cost-benefit analysis in *Leon*. Nor have we been persuaded that there are other compelling reasons to do so. . . .

Accordingly, the trial court's denial of defendant's suppression motion is reversed.

PECK, JUSTICE, dissenting.

The majority opinion is additional evidence, if any is needed at this point in time, that within the boundaries of the law of search and seizure, the *only* individuals enjoying any constitutional rights recognized by this Court are the criminals. This approach is characteristic of most of the activist-oriented state courts today. . . .

In the real world, the problems, if any, usually faced by noncriminal property owners are not attributable to police action, but to some kind of invasive activity by, or disagreement with, other individual laymen, often neighbors or trespassers, legal proceedings of a civil nature: eminent domain, boundary disputes, mortgage foreclosures and others. On the other hand, the police are charged with protecting the safety and well-being of all of us. They have too much to do and too few resources to spend the limited time available in random invasions of private property without an articulable reason or a shadow of suspicion, "just for the fun of it." The implied concern of the majority for "jack-boots at midnight" kicking in the front door, roving "goon-squads" invading arbitrarily and without the slightest reason, is slick legal demagoguery that provides the pretense of a reason for exaggerating a pimple into an Everest which isn't there. The majority, like the famous Keystone Cops of silent-film comedy, are busy scurrying about in pursuit of paper tigers. We have in the recent past demonstrated that we will act quickly and decisively to strike down arbitrary and clearly unreasonable police action by application of the exclusionary rule.

In rejecting the good-faith exception, the majority dwells almost exclusively on the economic rationale for the Supreme Court's decision in *United States v. Leon*, 468 U.S. 897 (1984); the critique, however interesting, is irrelevant. The underlying concept of a good-faith exception to the exclusionary rule deserves consideration beyond the limited scope of the *Leon* rationale in Article Eleven cases. I submit that *good-faith* reliance on a warrant that seems to the officers proper on its face, even though a reviewing court subsequently finds a defect, is one of the more obvious and workable grounds for application of an exception. "Good faith" is as much a fact as any other; the courts are no less capable, all of a sudden, of resolving that factual question than any other. . . .

I see nothing to render a good-faith search without a warrant necessarily unreasonable under either constitution. The predictions, adopted from dissenting opinions in *Leon*, have no supporting empirical evidence. They are, therefore, pure speculation and unsupported conclusions. They sink to the level of police bashing by the judiciary, so currently in fashion. The police are heroes when they are needed, often putting their lives in jeopardy, or risking serious injury (a number of officers are killed and injured in line of duty every year), but when they are not responding to a need, they are frequently the subject of criticism—bashing, in short; usually generalities inspired by sensational, albeit unfortunate exceptions. . . .

I am not unmindful that "rogue-cops" do surface from time to time. When that happens, their conduct tends to blacken unfairly the police image everywhere. Nevertheless, law enforcement officers at all levels are, on the whole, diligent and sincere; they act, for the most part, in good faith in their efforts to protect our lives, safety and property, when needed. I regret they must be subject to criticism by, of all sources, the courts. . . .

Addressing the final point that admission of the challenged evidence would encourage official misconduct, its application here, and generally, for that matter, is not supported. It is an example of judicial police bashing and speculation. Ultimately it is based on the tiresome question: "How would *you* like a policeman walking into *your* house in the middle of the night without a warrant and start searching the place?" Such a question recognizes that most people do not commit crimes, and that the police have not the slightest reason to suspect the contrary. The question lies at the root of the claim that, in protecting the criminal, the courts are, in reality, protecting the innocent in their right to privacy. In reality, it is a trick question which contains its own self-evident answer: of course I wouldn't like it, no one, guilty of something or not, would like it. . . .

Granting that no one relishes the idea of the police arbitrarily invading their homes, ask also how many, *not* involved in criminal activity, who retire at night, leave their homes unoccupied while at work during the day, or while they are away for some purpose during the evening, or for longer periods on vacations, how many of these are filled with continuing apprehension that the *police* will just drop in unexpectedly for a friendly little search? Ask those who lock their doors at night or when they are away, install alarms and other security devices, why they do so. Ask the same question of banks, stores, and other businesses, and why many of them, who are big enough to justify it, employ their own night watchmen and other security personnel. Will anyone reply that these precautions are taken to secure the premises against unwarranted invasions and searches by the police? Even the majority must acknowledge that no one, other than criminals, fears, or has any reason to fear "official misconduct" in this respect. . . .

The majority concedes that its calamity-howling is speculative, and without empirical support. This can be said of any new rule created by judicial fiat. It is ironic that when new judge-made law serves to relax the burden of criminal defendants and ease the difficulties of committing offenses against the people, they are greeted understandably with great enthusiasm by the defense community. On the other hand, when a new proposal appears on the horizon that will help to *deter* criminal activity, the activist cavalry calls the muster roll, and comes galloping over the ridge to the rescue with sabers drawn, guidon snapping bravely in the wind, and its bugle sounding the charge, all in a manner the unhappy George Custer would have welcomed at the Little Big Horn.

The benefits of a good-faith exception may also be speculative to a degree, but that is no justification for rejecting it, any more than were the dissenting predictions in *Miranda*. The exception could be a breath of fresh air of hope in the war against drugs. . . . In my judgment, any abuses *can* be controlled by this Court.

The failure of the majority to balance, or even consider competing constitutional rights in reviewing this appeal, is an "about face, to the rear march" slap at the progress . . . against the long-standing favoritism on behalf of those who choose, deliberately and intentionally, to violate the laws which are designed to protect the Article One rights of all of us as individuals. In their place, the majority remains firmly entrenched behind an interpretation of the laws which benefits *only* criminal activity. It is little wonder that we hear, increasingly, cries of public outrage at the slavish and unnecessary obeisance of many state courts to technicalities which demean our rights and ease the path of the transgressor. The crime rate is all but out of control and rising. The courts must share the responsibility to a significant degree by their indifference to human suffering, and the impenetrable shield they raise, against common sense and reason, in favor of the "rights" of criminals (many of which are in fact court created), without any recognition or balancing of the rights of society. The courts have much to answer for.

The good-faith exception need not be justified on an economic basis alone, as in *Leon*. It is a desirable and controllable device which would help to deter rather than encourage crime. There should be a balancing of rights. The failure of the majority is contrary to clear precedent and against the public interest. Included in that balancing should be the exception. It should be adopted.

NOTES AND QUESTIONS

1. *Oakes's reasoning.* As a matter of Vermont constitutional law, *Oakes* imposes an exclusionary remedy for a search that violates both state and federal constitutional law. Why? What is the court's disagreement with the Supreme Court about? Is Justice Peck's position that of the U.S. Supreme Court?

2. *Oakes's impact.* If you were advising the Brattleboro (Vt.) Police Chief about what *Oakes* means for his agency and officers, what would you tell him? What do you recommend he do to avoid evidentiary exclusion?

3. *The politics of exclusion.* Is it fair to say that the *Mapp* Court imposed the exclusionary rule in large part because it distrusted state courts to effectively enforce the Fourth Amendment? Yet Justice Peck, dissenting in *Oakes*, takes for granted that today most state courts are "activist-oriented." What has happened in the interim that might explain that change? Are states likely to be better regulators of the police than they used to be? If so, does that help to justify the U.S. Supreme Court's approach to the exclusionary rule? Or is it a product of it? If the Court overturned *Mapp*—not completely inconceivable—what could happen to the evidentiary exclusion in the states?

4. *State remedy for federal (and state) rights.* As *Oakes* suggests, when federal and state rights are coterminous, and the state remedy is broader than the federal remedy, state exclusionary rules effectively provide a remedy for federal rights violations

that the federal exclusionary rule does not address. Is this a form of federal free riding? Does it bother you that the same federal constitutional violation would have no remedy just outside of Brattleboro to the east, across the New Hampshire border?

5. *State remedy for state right.* State exclusionary rules sometimes matter even when they are no broader than the federal exclusionary rule, if the state analog right is more protective than the Fourth Amendment. For example, according to the U.S. Supreme Court, the Fourth Amendment does not apply when an undercover officer dupes a suspect into inviting the officer into his home and then records a conversation the suspect allows the officer to participate in. See United States v. White, 401 U.S. 745, 752 (1971). As a matter of state constitutional law, Pennsylvania disagrees. See Commonwealth v. Rekasie, 778 A.2d 624 (Pa. 2001); Commonwealth v. Brion, 652 A.2d 287 (Pa. 1994). If an officer makes such a recording, he lives up to federal constitutional standards but violates Pennsylvania constitutional law. If the government tries to introduce the recording in a state criminal case, Pennsylvania's exclusionary rule suppresses it. See, e.g., Commonwealth v. Ardestani, 736 A.2d 552, 556 (Pa. 1999) (requiring suppression of evidence taken in violation of *Brion*).

6. *Federal remedy for state right?* By contrast, federal constitutional law does not require state courts to suppress evidence taken solely in violation of state law. See Virginia v. Moore, 553 U.S. 164 (2008). If a state wants state constitutional violations remedied by evidentiary exclusion, it must do so under state law.

2.   Further Interactions Between State and Federal Exclusionary Rules

A few states, such as Maine and Maryland, do not have their own exclusionary rules. Interestingly, some states go further, making the *absence* of an exclusionary remedy a constitutional rule. For example, Michigan prohibits excluding in any criminal proceeding evidence of "any narcotic drug, firearm, bomb, explosive or any other dangerous weapon, seized by a peace officer outside the curtilage of any dwelling house in this state." Mich. Const. art. 1, §11.

The Florida constitution was amended in 1982 to mandate that both the state's right and remedy be coterminous with federal law:

> The right of the people to be secure in their persons, houses, papers and effects against unreasonable searches and seizures, and against the unreasonable interception of private communications by any means, shall not be violated. No warrant shall be issued except upon probable cause, supported by affidavit, particularly describing the place or places to be searched, the person or persons, thing or things to be seized, the communication to be intercepted, and the nature of evidence to be obtained. *This right shall be construed in conformity with the 4th Amendment to the United States Constitution, as interpreted by the United States Supreme Court. Articles or information obtained in violation of this right shall not be admissible in evidence if such articles or information would be inadmissible under decisions of the United States Supreme Court construing the 4th Amendment to the United States Constitution.*

Fla. Const. art. I, §12 (emphasis added).

And California largely abolished the state exclusionary rule by ballot proposition, which, as a means of protecting victims' rights, amended the state constitution to include the following:

> Right to Truth in Evidence. Except as provided by statute hereafter enacted by a two-thirds vote of the membership in each house of the Legislature, relevant evidence shall not be excluded in any criminal proceedings, including pretrial and post-conviction motions and hearings, or in any trial or hearing of a juvenile for a criminal offense, whether heard in juvenile or adult court.

Cal. Const. art. I, §28(f)(2).

Whom do these constitutional rules target? Does it help you to know that, in both Florida and California, law enforcement groups initiated the change because they were dissatisfied with what they saw as state court activism in applying search and seizure law? See Christopher Slobogin, *State Adoption of Federal Law: Exploring the Limits of Florida's "Forced Linkage" Amendment*, 39 U. Fla. L. Rev. 653, 666–672 (1987). What effects are constitutional provisions like those likely have over time?

U.S. Supreme Court decisions interpreting the federal exclusionary rule apply to trials in all states, including states with no exclusionary rule or a rule linked by law to the federal rule. As *Oakes* illustrates, however, each time the U.S. Supreme Court narrows the application of the rule, states with more flexible exclusionary rules have a decision to make. They are forced to determine whether their states' exclusionary rules will follow the federal rule's lead. Although state courts diverge from federal law for a variety of reasons, including distinctive constitutional or statutory language, these state court opinions also function as a kind of ongoing referendum on the persuasiveness of the Supreme Court's reasoning about how best to deter police misconduct, given the costs of the exclusionary rule. Some U.S. Supreme Court exclusionary rule cases fare better than others in this poll. As *Oakes* suggests, *Leon* is a case that many state supreme courts have not found persuasive. As the U.S. Supreme Court has expanded the good faith exception over time, the divergence between state and federal exclusion has expanded accordingly. Are there ways in which state courts might be better positioned to assess the deterrence value of the exclusionary rule? Should the Supreme Court listen to them? Do you see any evidence that it does? How much does it matter that the Supreme Court's rules apply nationwide?

How might divergent state and federal exclusionary rules affect officers day to day? Might it matter to officers whether evidence is excluded under state or federal law? Do you expect they know?

3. Last Thought on the Exclusionary Rule

Today, decades after *Mapp*, some would say that no legal rule has changed policing more than the exclusionary rule. Others would say that no legal rule has so failed to live up to its promise. And some would say that no legal rule has so outlived its usefulness. Do you have a view? Or do you want to know more about other remedies for police misconduct before you form an opinion?

Chapter 13

Suing the Police for Damages

Imagine a police officer detains you on the street just because you look like trouble. Or he arrests you at a political protest because someone near you threw a rock. Or he intentionally bangs your head on the patrol car roof as he places you inside during a legitimate arrest. You decide you want to challenge the conduct and seek a legal remedy, and you hope to discourage the police from similar bad acts in the future.

It turns out that your options are limited. You could invoke the exclusionary rule to exclude evidence the officer found when he arrested you, but only if the officer found evidence *and* the government prosecutes you—and sometimes not even then. You cannot force the government to pursue criminal charges against officers. You could file a complaint with the police department, but then other officers will decide what happens. Even if the police sustain your complaint, the officer might receive little more than a reprimand. In each case, your remedy depends on police officials and prosecutors.

So, what do you do? You might hire a lawyer and bring a civil suit for monetary damages against the police officer and the city. The lawsuit would give you a chance to tell your story, and if you win, you could receive compensation for your injuries and send a message to the police department. When you look for a cause of action, you discover that you might be able to sue the police officer and the city under a federal statute, 42 U.S.C. §1983.[1]

Now imagine that you are a police officer. Your supervisors send you out on patrol each shift, telling you to stop any trouble you see. You know that you will speak to dozens of people, and many will distrust the police or be angry, in crisis, or intoxicated. You know that no one wants to be stopped or arrested, and that sometimes you are expected to use force to get the job done. You know that a lot of subtle

---

[1] Section 1983 is the most important federal civil rights statute, but it is not the only option for individuals seeking money damages against officers. State statutes often also offer similar rights of action. See, e.g., Tom Bane Civil Rights Act, Cal. Civ. Code §52.1 (authorizing private suits when an individual "whether or not acting under color of law" interferes or attempts to interfere "by threat, intimidation, or coercion" with federal or state constitutional rights); Mass. Gen. Laws ch. 12, §11I (authorizing private suits for interference with rights secured under state and federal constitutions). In addition, as the Supreme Court recognized in *Wilson v. Garcia*, 471 U.S. 261, 272–273 (1985), "[a]lmost every §1983 claim can be favorably analogized to more than one of the ancient common-law forms of action." Plaintiffs can therefore often bring claims for assault, battery, wrongful death, false arrest, and malicious prosecution under state law for the same conduct. While state statutory and common law remedies can provide viable avenues for damages against the police, and they are often used alongside federal remedies, the focus in this chapter is on federal law.

legal rules regulate what you do. Those rules change over time, and even the local prosecutors disagree about how to interpret them. You know that some encounters inevitably go awry, and that even if your supervisor, the internal affairs unit, your police chief, and prosecutors all agree that you did your job properly, someone you interacted with for just a few minutes could sue you.

Finally, imagine you are a police chief with 200 officers under you. You run a complicated organization that patrols and responds to calls 24 hours day, with specialized units for criminal investigation, domestic violence, SWAT, and more. You oversee policy development, resource allocation, hiring, training, supervision, and discipline of officers, making a thousand decisions a day. You respond daily to concerns of community members, political leaders, and union officials, and you try to plan for the future. Each day you know that any one of your officers could make a controversial decision on the street that compromises your department's reputation and relationship with the community and inevitably leads to a lawsuit against you and the city.

Section 1983 is the primary avenue by which victims of unconstitutional conduct seek compensation and to deter misconduct. Yet, alongside more traditional bases for interpreting the statute, the Supreme Court has worried that, broadly interpreted, §1983 could do more harm than good. First, the Court has reasoned that, given the complicated legal environment officers operate in, too great a threat of §1983 lawsuits risks discouraging officers from "the unflinching discharge of their duties," which could compromise public safety. Harlow v. Fitzgerald, 457 U.S. 800, 814 (1982). Thus, the Court interprets the statute to limit *officer* liability through qualified immunity doctrine. Second, the Court appears to worry that cities should not be too easily held responsible for the acts of their employees. To mitigate this risk, the Court interprets §1983 to permit municipal liability only for constitutional violations directly caused by the city—unlike liability for private employers, who are vicariously liable for employees' acts through *respondeat superior* doctrine. In this way, the Court has set limits on *municipal* liability for constitutional violations by police officers.

In effect, to weed out insubstantial cases, save officials time and money, and avoid inappropriate interference in local government, the Court has set up an obstacle course for would-be plaintiffs. Every protection the Court gives to officers and departments hampers members of the public in their efforts to hold the police liable. As you read about the barriers plaintiffs must climb over and crawl under, consider how well these legal rules address the Court's concerns; how likely they are to affect how victims, officers, and cities behave; and, thus, how they might affect the power of civil actions to prevent constitutional violations.

A.   An Introduction to 42 U.S.C. §1983

Originally passed as a section of the 1871 Ku Klux Klan Act, 42 U.S.C. §1983 reads in relevant part:

> Every person who, under color of any statute, ordinance, regulation, custom, or usage, of any State or Territory or the District of Columbia, subjects, or causes to be subjected, any citizen of the United States or other person within the jurisdiction

thereof to the deprivation of any rights, privileges, or immunities secured by the Constitution and laws, shall be liable to the party injured in an action at law, suit in equity, or other proper proceeding for redress . . . .

To establish a §1983 claim, a plaintiff must prove:

1. That the defendant deprived the plaintiff of a federal right.
2. That the defendant is a person within the meaning of the statute.
3. That the defendant acted under color of law.

As the first element suggests, §1983 creates no substantive rights for plaintiffs. Instead, it provides a cause of action to vindicate federal rights defined elsewhere, including (most importantly for policing) First Amendment rights, due process and equal protection rights, and Fourth Amendment rights. If the plaintiff cannot prove a constitutional or statutory violation, there is no liability.

The second element determines who can be sued using §1983. Under current doctrine, individual officers, supervisors, chiefs, police departments, and municipalities all are *persons* who can deprive plaintiffs of rights and be named as defendants, so long as they, through their own actions and decisions, have violated the Constitution.

For decades, uncertainty about the third element, what it means for a defendant to act under color of law, discouraged plaintiffs from using §1983. Many thought that an officer only acted under the color of law within the meaning of the statute if state law authorized his actions. In this view, §1983 did not apply to officer conduct that violated state law because such conduct did not take place *under color of law*. Since most constitutional violations also violate state law, this interpretation limited the impact of §1983. In 1961, in *Monroe v. Pape*, 365 U.S. 167 (1961), the Court made clear that §1983 provides a right of action for deprivations of constitutional rights under the cloak of state authority, even if an officer misuses that authority and thereby violates state law. By resolving this issue, *Monroe* made §1983 newly useful to people whose rights are violated by law enforcement.[2]

B.   *Private Suits for Damages Against Officers*

When you sue under §1983 for money damages over having your head banged on the patrol car roof, you will naturally file against the officer who did the deed. In your complaint, you will describe what happened. You will argue that the officer acted under color of state law because he was on duty, in uniform, and carrying out his assigned tasks when he arrested you. You will claim that the officer deprived you

---

[2] The Supreme Court also ruled in *Monroe* that plaintiffs need not exhaust state remedies before filing a §1983 suit and that §1983 imposes no mental state requirement above that required for the deprivation of the underlying right. The *color of law* element of §1983 is discussed further in Chapter 14 because the doctrine is the same for cases involving §1983 and its criminal analogue, 18 U.S.C. §242, the primary federal criminal civil rights statute used to prosecute officers.

of your constitutional right to be free of an unreasonable seizure through excessive force under the Fourth Amendment and that he injured you seriously in the process.

However, even if you allege—and can prove at trial—that the officer acted under color of law and deprived you of your rights, you might not win your lawsuit. In fact, you will not even be permitted to proceed to trial unless the constitutional right you allege was violated was clearly established before the incident. This protection against suit for officers under §1983 goes by the name *qualified immunity*. Even more than the elements of §1983, this defense shapes the course of §1983 litigation. Therefore, to contemplate the impact of civil suits, it is necessary to understand the contours of this defense.

Qualified immunity comes about because the Supreme Court has interpreted §1983 to incorporate some common law immunities against lawsuits. Judges, prosecutors, and legislators receive *absolute immunity* from suit when their actions fall within their ordinary official capacities. While plaintiffs occasionally attempt to name these actors in complaints, such lawsuits almost never proceed past summary judgment. By contrast, police officers receive only *qualified immunity*, which permits lawsuits to move forward against them under limited circumstances. Much of the litigation surrounding §1983 damages actions against individual officers has little to do with §1983's elements. Instead, it concerns when qualified immunity applies, that is, when officers are subject to suit.

1. The Law of Qualified Immunity

When officers face a suit for damages under §1983, they often invoke qualified immunity in a summary judgment motion—or, less frequently, in a motion to dismiss. If recognized, this powerful form of immunity can end litigation against officers, sometimes even before discovery.

The Supreme Court first recognized qualified immunity as a defense against suit under §1983 for police officers in *Pierson v. Ray*, 386 U.S. 547, 555–557 (1967). In *Pierson*, the Court described qualified immunity as adopted from a common law *good faith* defense, which protected officers who reasonably believed their actions constitutional. But the Court subsequently moved qualified immunity doctrine away from the *Pierson* Court's concerns about the good faith of government officials in favor of protecting officers based on an *objective* assessment of their conduct. This contemporary approach to qualified immunity began in earnest in *Harlow v. Fitzgerald*, 457 U.S. 800, 818–819 (1982), which held "that government officials performing discretionary functions, generally are shielded from liability for civil damages insofar as their conduct does not violate clearly established statutory or constitutional rights of which a reasonable person would have known." By moving to an objective standard, the Court hoped that more cases could be resolved without discovery or trial, sparing officials from the costs and burdens of litigation in "insubstantial" cases, without providing "license to lawless conduct." *Id.* at 819 and n.35.

Based on *Harlow*, qualified immunity turns on whether the officer violated a constitutional rule that was *clearly established* at the time of the alleged violation. However, the Court's idea about what constitutes *clearly established* law has evolved since 1982. In 1987, in *Anderson v. Creighton*, 483 U.S. 635, 640 (1987), the Court explained it this way:

> The contours of the right must be sufficiently clear that a reasonable official would understand that what he is doing violates that right. This is not to say that an official action is protected by qualified immunity unless the very action in question has previously been held unlawful, but it is to say that in the light of pre-existing law the unlawfulness must be apparent.

Compare that to the standard articulated by the Court in the following case.

KISELA v. HUGHES
138 S. Ct. 1148 (2018)

Per Curiam.

Petitioner Andrew Kisela, a police officer in Tucson, Arizona, shot respondent Amy Hughes. . . . The question is whether at the time of the shooting Kisela's actions violated clearly established law.

The record, viewed in the light most favorable to Hughes, shows the following. In May 2010, somebody in Hughes' neighborhood called 911 to report that a woman was hacking a tree with a kitchen knife. Kisela and another police officer, Alex Garcia, heard about the report over the radio in their patrol car and responded. A few minutes later the person who had called 911 flagged down the officers; gave them a description of the woman with the knife; and told them the woman had been acting erratically. About the same time, a third police officer, Lindsay Kunz, arrived on her bicycle.

Garcia spotted a woman, later identified as Sharon Chadwick, standing next to a car in the driveway of a nearby house. A chain-link fence with a locked gate separated Chadwick from the officers. The officers then saw another woman, Hughes, emerge from the house carrying a large knife at her side. Hughes matched the description of the woman who had been seen hacking a tree. Hughes walked toward Chadwick and stopped no more than six feet from her.

All three officers drew their guns. At least twice they told Hughes to drop the knife. Viewing the record in the light most favorable to Hughes, Chadwick said "take it easy" to both Hughes and the officers. Hughes appeared calm, but she did not acknowledge the officers' presence or drop the knife. The top bar of the chain-link fence blocked Kisela's line of fire, so he dropped to the ground and shot Hughes four times through the fence. Then the officers jumped the fence, handcuffed Hughes, and called paramedics, who transported her to a hospital. There she was treated for non-life-threatening injuries. Less than a minute had transpired from the moment the officers saw Chadwick to the moment Kisela fired shots.

All three of the officers later said that at the time of the shooting they subjectively believed Hughes to be a threat to Chadwick. After the shooting, the officers discovered that Chadwick and Hughes were roommates, that Hughes had a history of mental illness, and that Hughes had been upset with Chadwick over a $20 debt. . . . Chadwick went outside to get $20 from her car, which is when the officers first saw her. In her affidavit Chadwick said that she did not feel endangered at any time. Based on her experience as Hughes' roommate, Chadwick stated that Hughes "occasionally has episodes in which she acts inappropriately," but "she is only seeking attention."

Hughes sued Kisela under 42 U.S.C. §1983, alleging that Kisela had used excessive force in violation of the Fourth Amendment. The District Court granted summary judgment to Kisela, but the Court of Appeals for the Ninth Circuit reversed.

The Court of Appeals first held that the record, viewed in the light most favorable to Hughes, was sufficient to demonstrate that Kisela violated the Fourth Amendment. The court next held that the violation was clearly established because, in its view, the constitutional violation was obvious and because of Circuit precedent that the court perceived to be analogous. . . . Kisela then filed a petition for certiorari in this Court. That petition is now granted.

In one of the first cases on this general subject, *Tennessee v. Garner*, 471 U.S. 1 (1985), the Court addressed the constitutionality of the police using force that can be deadly. There, the Court held that "[w]here the officer has probable cause to believe that the suspect poses a threat of serious physical harm, either to the officer or to others, it is not constitutionally unreasonable to prevent escape by using deadly force." *Id.* at 11.

In *Graham v. Connor*, 490 U.S. 386, 396 (1989), the Court held that the question whether an officer has used excessive force "requires careful attention to the facts and circumstances of each particular case, including the severity of the crime at issue, whether the suspect poses an immediate threat to the safety of the officers or others, and whether he is actively resisting arrest or attempting to evade arrest by flight." "The 'reasonableness' of a particular use of force must be judged from the perspective of a reasonable officer on the scene, rather than with the 20/20 vision of hindsight." *Id.* And "[t]he calculus of reasonableness must embody allowance for the fact that police officers are often forced to make split-second judgments—in circumstances that are tense, uncertain, and rapidly evolving—about the amount of force that is necessary in a particular situation." *Id.* at 396–397.

Here, the Court need not, and does not, decide whether Kisela violated the Fourth Amendment when he used deadly force against Hughes. For even assuming a Fourth Amendment violation occurred—a proposition that is not at all evident—on these facts Kisela was at least entitled to qualified immunity.

"Qualified immunity attaches when an official's conduct does not violate clearly established statutory or constitutional rights of which a reasonable person would have known." White v. Pauly, 137 S. Ct. 548, 551 (2017) (*per curiam*). "Because the focus is on whether the officer had fair notice that her conduct was unlawful, reasonableness is judged against the backdrop of the law at the time of the conduct." Brosseau v. Haugen, 543 U.S. 194, 198 (2004) (*per curiam*).

Although "this Court's caselaw does not require a case directly on point for a right to be clearly established, existing precedent must have placed the statutory or constitutional question beyond debate." *White*, 137 S. Ct. at 551. "In other words, immunity protects all but the plainly incompetent or those who knowingly violate the law." *Id.* This Court has "repeatedly told courts—and the Ninth Circuit in particular—not to define clearly established law at a high level of generality." City and County of San Francisco v. Sheehan, 135 S. Ct. 1765, 1775–1776 (2015).

"[S]pecificity is especially important in the Fourth Amendment context, where the Court has recognized that it is sometimes difficult for an officer to determine how the relevant legal doctrine, here excessive force, will apply to the factual situation the officer confronts." Mullenix v. Luna, 577 U.S. 7, 12 (2015) (*per curiam*). Use of excessive force is an area of the law "in which the result depends very much on the facts of each case," and thus police officers are entitled to qualified immunity unless existing precedent "squarely governs" the specific facts at issue. *Id.* at 309. Precedent involving similar facts can help move a case beyond the otherwise "hazy border between excessive and acceptable force" and thereby provide an officer notice that a specific use of force is unlawful. *Id.* at 18.

"Of course, general statements of the law are not inherently incapable of giving fair and clear warning to officers." *White*, 137 S. Ct. at 552. But the general rules set forth in "*Garner* and *Graham* do not by themselves create clearly established law outside an 'obvious case.'" *Id.* Where constitutional guidelines seem inapplicable or too remote, it does not suffice for a court simply to state that an officer may not use unreasonable and excessive force, deny qualified immunity, and then remit the case for a trial on the question of reasonableness. An officer "cannot be said to have violated a clearly established right unless the right's contours were sufficiently definite that any reasonable official in the defendant's shoes would have understood that he was violating it." Plumhoff v. Rickard, 572 U.S. 765, 778–779 (2014). That is a necessary part of the qualified-immunity standard, and it is a part of the standard that the Court of Appeals here failed to implement in a correct way.

Kisela says he shot Hughes because, although the officers themselves were in no apparent danger, he believed she was a threat to Chadwick. Kisela had mere seconds to assess the potential danger to Chadwick. He was confronted with a woman who had just been seen hacking a tree with a large kitchen knife and whose behavior was erratic enough to cause a concerned bystander to call 911 and then flag down Kisela and Garcia. Kisela was separated from Hughes and Chadwick by a chain-link fence; Hughes had moved to within a few feet of Chadwick; and she failed to acknowledge at least two commands to drop the knife. Those commands were loud enough that Chadwick, who was standing next to Hughes, heard them. This is far from an obvious case in which any competent officer would have known that shooting Hughes to protect Chadwick would violate the Fourth Amendment.

The Court of Appeals made additional errors in concluding that its own precedent clearly established that Kisela used excessive force. To begin with, "even if a controlling circuit precedent could constitute clearly established law in these circumstances, it does not do so here." *Sheehan*, 135 S. Ct. at 1776. In fact, the most analogous Circuit precedent favors Kisela. See Blanford v. Sacramento County, 406 F.3d 1110 (9th Cir. 2005). In *Blanford*, the police responded to a report that a man was walking through a residential neighborhood carrying a sword and acting in an erratic manner. *Id.* at 1112. There, as here, the police shot the man after he refused their commands to drop his weapon (there, as here, the man might not have heard the commands). *Id.* at 1113. There, as here, the police believed (perhaps mistakenly), that the man posed an immediate threat to others. *Id.* There, the Court of Appeals determined that the use of deadly force did not violate the Fourth Amendment. *Id.* at 1119. Based on that decision, a reasonable officer could have believed the same thing was true in the instant case.

In contrast, not one of the decisions relied on by the Court of Appeals—*Deorle v. Rutherford*, 272 F.3d 1272 (9th Cir. 2001), *Glenn v. Washington County*, 673 F.3d 864 (9th Cir. 2011), and *Harris v. Roderick*, 126 F.3d 1189 (9th Cir. 1997)—supports denying Kisela qualified immunity. As for *Deorle*, this Court has already instructed the Court of Appeals not to read its decision in that case too broadly in deciding whether a new set of facts is governed by clearly established law. *Sheehan*, 135 S. Ct. at 1775–1777. *Deorle* involved a police officer who shot an unarmed man in the face, without warning, even though the officer had a clear line of retreat; there were no bystanders nearby; the man had been "physically compliant and generally followed all the officers' instructions"; and he had been under police observation for roughly 40 minutes. 272 F.3d at 1276, 1281–1282. In this case, by contrast, Hughes was armed with a large knife; was within striking distance of Chadwick; ignored the officers' orders to drop the weapon; and the situation unfolded in less than a minute. "Whatever the merits of the decision in *Deorle*, the differences between that case and the case before us leap from the page." *Sheehan*, 135 S. Ct. at 1776.

Glenn, which the panel described as "[t]he most analogous Ninth Circuit case," 862 F.3d at 783, was decided after the shooting at issue here. Thus, *Glenn* "could not have given fair notice to [Kisela]" because a reasonable officer is not required to foresee judicial decisions that do not yet exist in instances where the requirements of the Fourth Amendment are far from obvious. *Brosseau*, 543 U.S. at 200 n.4. . . .

The panel's reliance on *Harris* "does not pass the straight-face test." 862 F.3d 775, 797 (Ikuta, J., dissenting). In *Harris*, the Court of Appeals determined that an FBI sniper, who was positioned safely on a hilltop, used excessive force when he shot a man in the back while the man was retreating to a cabin during what has been referred to as the Ruby Ridge standoff. 126 F.3d at 1202–1203. Suffice it to say, a reasonable police officer could miss the connection between the situation confronting the sniper at Ruby Ridge and the situation confronting Kisela in Hughes' front yard.

For these reasons, the petition for certiorari is granted; the judgment of the Court of Appeals is reversed; and the case is remanded for further proceedings consistent with this opinion.

It is so ordered.

JUSTICE SOTOMAYOR, with whom JUSTICE GINSBURG joins, dissenting.

Officer Andrew Kisela shot Amy Hughes while she was speaking with her roommate, Sharon Chadwick, outside of their home. The record, properly construed at this stage, shows that at the time of the shooting: Hughes stood stationary about six feet away from Chadwick, appeared "composed and content," and held a kitchen knife down at her side with the blade facing away from Chadwick. Hughes was nowhere near the officers, had committed no illegal act, was suspected of no crime, and did not raise the knife in the direction of Chadwick or anyone else. Faced with these facts, the two other responding officers held their fire, and one testified that he "wanted to continue trying verbal command[s] and see if that would work." But not Kisela. He thought it necessary to use deadly force, and so, without giving a warning that he would open fire, he shot Hughes four times, leaving her seriously injured.

If this account of Kisela's conduct sounds unreasonable, that is because it was. And yet, the Court today insulates that conduct from liability under the doctrine of qualified immunity, holding that Kisela violated no "clearly established" law. I disagree. Viewing the facts in the light most favorable to Hughes, as the Court must at summary judgment, a jury could find that Kisela violated Hughes' clearly established Fourth Amendment rights by needlessly resorting to lethal force. In holding otherwise, the Court misapprehends the facts and misapplies the law, effectively treating qualified immunity as an absolute shield. I therefore respectfully dissent. . . .

II. . .

A

I begin with the first step of the qualified-immunity inquiry: whether there was a violation of a constitutional right. Hughes alleges that Kisela violated her Fourth Amendment rights by deploying excessive force against her. In assessing such a claim, courts must ask "whether the officers' actions are 'objectively reasonable' in light of the facts and circumstances confronting them." *Graham v. Connor*, 490 U.S. 386, 397 (1989). That inquiry "requires careful attention to the facts and circumstances of each particular case, including the severity of the crime at issue, whether the suspect poses an immediate threat to the safety of the officers or others, and whether he is actively resisting arrest or attempting to evade arrest by flight." *Id.* at 396. All of those factors (and others) support the Ninth Circuit's conclusion that a jury could find that Kisela's use of deadly force was objectively unreasonable. . . .

First, Hughes committed no crime and was not suspected of committing a crime. . . .

Second, a jury could reasonably conclude that Hughes presented no immediate or objective threat to Chadwick or the other officers. It is true that Kisela had received a report that a woman matching Hughes' description had been acting erratically. But . . . the record evidence of what the police encountered paints a calmer picture. It shows that Hughes was several feet from Chadwick and even farther from the officers, she never made any aggressive or threatening movements, and she appeared "composed and content" during the brief encounter.

Third, Hughes did not resist or evade arrest. Based on this record, there is significant doubt as to whether she was aware of the officers' presence at all, and evidence suggests that Hughes did not hear the officers' swift commands to drop the knife.

Finally, the record suggests that Kisela could have, but failed to, use less intrusive means before deploying deadly force. For instance, Hughes submitted expert testimony concluding that Kisela should have used his Taser and that shooting his gun through the fence was dangerous because a bullet could have fragmented against the fence and hit Chadwick or his fellow officers. Consistent with that assessment, the other two officers on the scene declined to fire at Hughes, and one of them explained that he was inclined to use "some of the lesser means" than shooting, including verbal commands, because he believed there was time "[t]o try to talk [Hughes] down." That two officers on the scene, presented with the same circumstances as Kisela, did not use deadly force reveals just how unnecessary and unreasonable it was for Kisela to fire four shots at Hughes.

Taken together, the foregoing facts would permit a jury to conclude that Kisela acted outside the bounds of the Fourth Amendment by shooting Hughes four times.

B

Rather than defend the reasonableness of Kisela's conduct, the majority sidesteps the inquiry altogether and focuses instead on the "clearly established" prong of the qualified-immunity analysis. . . . At its core, . . . the "clearly established" inquiry boils down to whether Kisela had "fair notice" that he acted unconstitutionally. See *Brosseau v. Haugen*, 543 U.S. 194, 198 (2004).

The answer to that question is yes. This Court's precedents make clear that a police officer may only deploy deadly force against an individual if the officer "has probable cause to believe that the [person] poses a threat of serious physical harm, either to the officer or to others." Tennessee v. Garner, 471 U.S. 1, 11 (1985). . . . [C]ontrary to the majority's conclusion, Ninth Circuit precedent predating these events further confirms that Kisela's conduct was clearly unreasonable. Because Kisela plainly lacked any legitimate interest justifying the use of deadly force against a woman who posed no objective threat of harm to officers or others, had committed no crime, and appeared calm and collected during the police encounter, he was not entitled to qualified immunity.

The Ninth Circuit's opinion in *Deorle v. Rutherford,* 272 F.3d 1272 (2001) proves the point. In that case, the police encountered a man who had reportedly been acting "erratically." *Id.* at 1276. The man was "verbally abusive," shouted " 'kill me' " at the officers, screamed that he would " 'kick [the] ass' " of one of the officers, and "brandish[ed] a hatchet at a police officer," ultimately throwing it "into a clump of trees when told to put it down." *Id.* at 1276–1277. The officers also observed the man carrying an unloaded crossbow in one hand and what appeared to be "a can or a bottle of lighter fluid in the other." *Id.* at 1277. The man discarded the crossbow when instructed to do so by the police and then steadily walked toward one of the officers. *Id.* In response, that officer, without giving a warning, shot the man in the face with beanbag rounds. *Id.* at 1278. The man suffered serious injuries, including multiple fractures to his cranium and the loss of his left eye. *Id.*

The Ninth Circuit denied qualified immunity to the officer, concluding that his use of force was objectively unreasonable under clearly established law. *Id.* at 1285–1286. The court held, "Every police officer should know that it is objectively unreasonable to shoot . . . an unarmed man who: has committed no serious offense, is mentally or emotionally disturbed, has been given no warning of the imminent use of such a significant degree of force, poses no risk of flight, and presents no objectively reasonable threat to the safety of the officer or other individuals." *Id.* at 1285.

The same holds true here. . . . In fact, Hughes presented even less of a danger than the man in *Deorle.* . . . If the police officers acted unreasonably in shooting the agitated, screaming man in *Deorle* with beanbag bullets, *a fortiori* Kisela acted unreasonably in shooting the calm-looking, stationary Hughes with real bullets. In my view, *Deorle* and the precedent it cites place the unlawfulness of Kisela's conduct " 'beyond debate.' " District of Columbia v. Wesby, 138 S. Ct. 577, 590 (2018).

The majority strains mightily to distinguish *Deorle,* to no avail. It asserts, for instance, that, unlike the man in *Deorle,* Hughes was "armed with a large knife." But that is not a fair characterization of the record, particularly at this procedural juncture. Hughes was not "armed" with a knife. She was holding a kitchen knife — an everyday household item which can be used as a weapon but ordinarily is a tool for safe, benign purposes — down at her side with the blade pointed away from Chadwick. Hughes also spoke calmly with Chadwick during the events at issue, did not raise the knife, and made no other aggressive movements, undermining any suggestion that she was a threat to Chadwick or anyone else. . . .

The majority next posits that Hughes, unlike the man in *Deorle,* "ignored the officers' orders to drop the" kitchen knife. Yet again, the majority here draws inferences in favor of Kisela, instead of Hughes. The available evidence would allow a reasonable jury to find that Hughes did not hear or register the officers' swift commands and that Kisela, like his fellow officers on the scene, should have realized that as well. Accordingly, at least at the summary-judgment stage, the Court is mistaken in distinguishing *Deorle* based on Hughes' ostensible disobedience to the officers' directives. . . .

If all that were not enough, decisions from several other Circuits illustrate that the Fourth Amendment clearly forbids the use of deadly force against a person who is merely holding a knife but not threatening anyone with it. . . .

In sum, precedent existing at the time of the shooting clearly established the unconstitutionality of Kisela's conduct. . . . Because, taking the facts in the light most favorable to Hughes, it is "beyond debate" that Kisela's use of deadly force was objectively unreasonable, he was not entitled to summary judgment on the basis of qualified immunity.

III

For the foregoing reasons, it is clear to me that the Court of Appeals got it right. But even if that result were not so clear, I cannot agree with the majority's apparent view that the decision below was so manifestly incorrect as to warrant "the extraordinary remedy of a summary reversal." Major League Baseball Players Assn. v. Garvey, 532 U.S. 504, 512–513 (2001) (Stevens, J., dissenting). . . .

. . . As I have previously noted, this Court routinely displays an unflinching willingness "to summarily reverse courts for wrongly denying officers the protection of qualified immunity" but "rarely intervene[s] where courts wrongly afford officers the benefit of qualified immunity in these same cases." Salazar-Limon v. Houston, 137 S. Ct. 1277, 1282–1283 (2017) (Sotomayor, J., dissenting from denial of certiorari). Such a one-sided approach to qualified immunity transforms the doctrine into an absolute shield for law enforcement officers, gutting the deterrent effect of the Fourth Amendment.

The majority today exacerbates that troubling asymmetry. Its decision is not just wrong on the law; it also sends an alarming signal to law enforcement officers and the public. It tells officers that they can shoot first and think later, and it tells the public that palpably unreasonable conduct will go unpunished. Because there is nothing right or just under the law about this, I respectfully dissent.

NOTES AND QUESTIONS

1. *The standard.* As *Kisela* indicates, qualified immunity doctrine now requires that precedent place the constitutional question at issue in a lawsuit "beyond debate" so that only those officers who are "plainly incompetent" or who "knowingly violate the law" may be held liable. How different is the *Kisela* Court's application of the "clearly established" standard from the Court's application of the standard in *Anderson*? In *Harlow*?

2. *The application.* As *Kisela* also notes, the Supreme Court has instructed officers that they may, consistent with the Constitution, use deadly force when they have probable cause to believe that a criminal suspect poses a threat of serious physical harm to another person. Officer Kisela did not suspect Amy Hughes of any crime. Nevertheless, he shot her because he believed she posed a threat. What does the Court think a reasonable officer could not have known about the law governing that situation? Do you think a competent officer could have believed under the circumstances that Hughes posed an immediate threat? What precisely do the majority and the dissenters disagree about?

3. *Two dimensions. Kisela* suggests, and other Supreme Court cases reinforce the idea, that two dimensions of prior case law are relevant to determining whether an officer violated a clearly established right: (1) the source and strength of the available precedents; and (2) the closeness of fit between the facts of the prior cases and the officer's conduct. The Court has raised the bar for both dimensions over time, with notable effect. As one scholar pointed out not long before *Kisela* was decided:

> During the past fifteen years, the Court has issued eighteen opinions addressing the question whether a particular constitutional right was clearly established. In sixteen of those eighteen cases, the Court found the governmental defendants were entitled to qualified immunity on the grounds that, whether or not they acted in contravention of the Constitution, they did not violate clearly established law. The Court has not ruled in favor of a §1983 plaintiff on this question in more than a decade.

Kit Kinports, *The Supreme Court's Quiet Expansion of Qualified Immunity*, 100 Minn. L. Rev. Headnotes 62, 63 (2016). The trend has continued since.

4. *What precedent?* Early in qualified immunity law, the Court suggested that obvious constitutional violations could be found to be clearly established, even without a case on point. Subsequently, it required "controlling authority" in the jurisdiction or a "consensus of cases of persuasive authority." Wilson v. Layne, 526 U.S. 603, 617 (1999). In several more recent cases including *Kisela*, the Court goes further still: It demands precedent in the same circuit and at the same time casts doubt on whether even controlling circuit court precedent is always enough. See, e.g., District of Columbia v. Wesby, 138 S. Ct. 577, 591 n.8 (2018) (noting that the Court had not yet decided "what precedents—other than our own—qualify as controlling authority for purposes of qualified immunity"); Taylor v. Barkes, 135 S. Ct. 2042, 2045 (2015) ("Assuming for the sake of argument that a right can be 'clearly established' by circuit precedent despite disagreement in the courts of appeals. . . ."). If the Court of Appeals for the jurisdiction in which a police officer operates specifically declares a practice unconstitutional, how could any competent officer think the practice is okay? What is the Court thinking? What kind of precedent should be sufficient?

5. *Closeness of fit.* The Court's decisions in *Graham v. Connor*, 490 U.S. 386 (1989), and *Tennessee v. Garner*, 471 U.S. 1 (1985), provide primary guidance to lower courts and officers about when police uses of force are reasonable, but the Court has repeatedly cautioned that lower courts should not "find fair warning in the general tests set out in *Graham* and *Garner* [because] *Graham* and *Garner*, following the lead of the Fourth Amendment's text, are cast at a high level of generality." Brosseau v. Haugen, 543 U.S 194, 199 (2004). Instead, they should look for cases that "squarely govern[]" because they were decided on similar facts. *Id.* at 201. If there are no such cases, the officer should receive qualified immunity, and the Court has repeatedly reversed lower courts for failing to provide this result. If Fourth Amendment use-of-force law is too indeterminate to provide fair notice to officers, whose fault is that? Might a more principled constitutional framework for evaluating uses of force be more effective in putting police on notice about whether force is constitutional? See Rachel A. Harmon, *When Is Police Violence Justified?*, 102 Nw. U. L. Rev. 1119, 1142–1143 (2008), arguing that it might.

6. *Do police read cases?* Why is it so important that prior cases be decided on similar facts? The Court suggests that it is essential to give police officers notice about what conduct is illegal. But consider this judge's view:

The Supreme Court's obsession with the clearly established prong assumes that officers are routinely reading Supreme Court and Tenth Circuit opinions in their spare time, carefully comparing the facts in these qualified immunity cases with the circumstances they confront in their day-to-day police work. It is hard enough for the federal judiciary to embark on such an exercise, let alone likely that police officers are endeavoring to parse opinions. It is far more likely that, in their training and continuing education, police officers are taught general principles, and, in the intense atmosphere of an arrest, police officers rely on these general principles, rather than engaging in a detailed comparison of their situation with a previous Supreme Court or published Tenth Circuit case. It strains credulity to believe that a reasonable officer, as he is approaching a suspect to arrest, is thinking to himself: "Are the facts here anything like the facts in *York v. City of Las Cruces*?" Thus, when the Supreme Court grounds its clearly-established jurisprudence in the language of what a reasonable officer or a "reasonable official" would know, Kisela v. Hughes, 138 S. Ct. 1148, 1153 (2018), yet still requires a highly factually analogous case, it has either lost sight of reasonable officer's experience or it is using that language to mask an intent to create "an absolute shield for law enforcement officers," *Id.* at 1162 (Sotomayor, J. dissenting).

Manzanares v. Roosevelt Cty. Adult Det. Ctr., 331 F. Supp. 3d 1260, 1294 n.10 (D.N.M. 2018). Is this a reasonable objection?

The district court in *Manzanares* concluded "that the Supreme Court is . . . crafting its recent qualified immunity jurisprudence to effectively eliminate §1983 claims against state actors in their individual capacities by requiring an indistinguishable case and by encouraging courts to go straight to the clearly established prong." *Manzanares*, 331 F. Supp. 3d at 1294. Many scholars agree. They view the Court's qualified immunity opinions as a "*sub silentio* assault on constitutional tort suits." Kit Kinport, *The Supreme Court's Quiet Expansion of Qualified Immunity*, 100 Minn. L. Rev. Headnotes 62, 64 (2016). Does *Kisela* give you any ideas about why the Court might want to limit constitutional litigation against police officers so severely? If this is what the Court is doing, why not acknowledge it?

7. *The burdens of litigation.* According to the Court, qualified immunity exists not only to protect officers from the burdens of financial judgments against them, but to protect them from all of the burdens of litigation, including discovery and trial. As the Supreme Court put it in *Ashcroft v. Iqbal*, 556 U.S. 662, 685 (2009):

> The basic thrust of the qualified-immunity doctrine is to free officials from the concerns of litigation, including "avoidance of disruptive discovery. . . . Litigation though necessary to ensure that officials comply with the law, exacts heavy costs in terms of efficiency and expenditure of valuable time and resources that might otherwise be directed to the proper execution of the work of the Government.

This purpose informs not only the strength of the doctrine as illustrated in *Kisela* but also leads the Court to protect defendants procedurally. Perhaps most importantly, most litigants may appeal only final judgments, but an officer–defendant may appeal immediately—an *interlocutory appeal*—if a district court denies him qualified immunity in an early stage of a lawsuit it concludes that the law governing his conduct was clearly established. See Mitchell v. Forsyth, 472 U.S. 511, 526–527 (1985).

8. *Qualified immunity's effect.* Clearly, qualified immunity is a powerful defense. But it does not end §1983 cases as cleanly or quickly as you might expect. First, plaintiffs often bring claims that qualified immunity does not resolve such as claims against

municipalities, claims for noneconomic relief, or state law claims. As a result, lawsuits often continue even after a court grants defendant officers qualified immunity. Second, qualified immunity often depends on factual subtleties that are not clear when the defendant files a motion to dismiss. Defendants frequently wait to raise the issue until after discovery, when they file a motion for summary judgment, or at or after trial. Third, courts dismiss lawsuits against officers for many other reasons, whether or not the officers raise qualified immunity, including because the suits are frivolous, the suits are inadequately prosecuted, or complaints fail to properly assert a constitutional violation. The result is that qualified immunity does not resolve most civil rights lawsuits. In fact, in one study of civil rights suits against law enforcement defendants across five federal districts, qualified immunity resulted in dismissal of only 3.9 percent of the cases in which it could be raised. Yet those cases were overwhelmingly dismissed for some reason at some stage of the litigation. See Joanna C. Schwartz, *How Qualified Immunity Fails*, 127 Yale L.J. 2, 45–47 (2017). How might qualified immunity nevertheless affect how victims, lawyers, defendants, and police departments act?

Supervisory Liability Under §1983

In the hierarchy of a police department, a patrol officer's chain of command might easily include a sergeant who supervises him directly, and a lieutenant, captain, major, deputy chief of police, and chief of police above that. When something goes awry, who is responsible?

Section 1983 allows suit against any person who, under color of law, deprives another person of his legal rights. Although the Court ruled in *Monell v. New York City Department of Social Services*, 436 U.S. 658, 691 (1978), that supervisors are not vicariously liable for the actions of their subordinates, they can be liable for constitutional violations that they themselves cause. This is true whether the supervisor is a sergeant or a police chief.

How does a supervisor cause a constitutional violation by a patrol officer? Go back to the officer who banged your head on the car. A supervisor could have ordered him to do that, he could have watched him do it and allowed it to continue,[3] or he might have trained the officer to worry only about speed and his own safety in securing a prisoner in a car. If proven, any of these actions could lead to liability.

Even when a plaintiff can prove that a supervisor caused the violation, supervisory claims pose significant challenges. The legal requirements for establishing supervisory liability vary with the kind of conduct involved, the supervisor's relationship to the violation, and the constitutional violation alleged. Federal courts also disagree about the proper standard. The Supreme Court in *Ashcroft v. Iqbal*, 556 U.S. 662, 676 (2009), compounded the confusion by suggesting that knowledge or acquiescence is insufficient to establish supervisory liability for a constitutional violation that requires discriminatory purpose, without resolving other questions that have plagued lower courts. For discussions of the impact of *Iqbal*, see Karen M. Blum, *Supervisory Liability After* Iqbal: *Misunderstood but Not Misnamed*, 43 Urb. Law 541,

---

[3] Line officers also have a duty to stop other officers from violating a suspect's rights if they are aware of a constitutional violation and have the opportunity to intercede. This duty creates potential bystander liability for police officers for actions of their peers, though judgments on this basis are uncommon.

542 (2011); Kit Kinports, Iqbal *and Supervisory Immunity*, 114 Penn. St. L. Rev. 1291, 1307 (2010). As complex and contested as qualified immunity makes suits against the officer who hit your head, the law of supervisory liability under §1983 makes a suit against his boss even more so.

2.   Qualified Immunity and the Overdeterrence Thesis

Why give officers this strong qualified immunity protection? The Court's interpretation of qualified immunity doctrine is tied to its view about the effects of litigation on policing. As the Court put it in *Harlow*: "[T]here is the danger that fear of being sued will dampen the ardor of all but the most resolute, or the most irresponsible public officials, in the unflinching discharge of their duties." Harlow v. Fitzgerald, 457 U.S. 800, 814 (1982). Some legal scholars have agreed. See, e.g., William J. Stuntz, *The Virtues and Vices of the Exclusionary Rule*, 20 Harv. J. L. & Pub. Pol'y, 443, 445 (1997); Peter H. Schuck, *Suing Our Servants: The Court, Congress, and the Liability of Public Officials for Damages*, 1980 Sup. Ct. Rev. 281, 285–286.

Those who support what might be called the overdeterrence thesis argue something like this:

1. Officers receive limited professional benefit for legal searches and arrests, and they pay substantial personal costs for illegal action if lawsuits against them result in damages.
2. Because the legal standards governing policing conduct, such as *probable cause* and *reasonable force*, are vague, an officer cannot necessarily avoid liability (without qualified immunity) by engaging in only apparently lawful acts.
3. Because officers have discretion over whether to initiate action, for example, by approaching a suspect to question him, they can most easily avoid liability by refraining from *any* action if they have doubts about the lawfulness of their conduct.
4. Officers' inaction threatens public safety.[4]

Qualified immunity purports to solve the risk of overdeterrence by allowing liability when conduct is clearly illegal (and liability is most likely to deter properly) and by eliminating liability when reasonable officers would be uncertain about the legal status of their actions (and liability is most likely to lead officers into doing nothing). In this way, its advocates contend officers can take all but illegal action, the public can benefit from lawful policing, and victims can be compensated when officers commit clearly illegal conduct.

---

[4] Today, you often hear the overdeterrence thesis framed in terms of *depolicing*. Usually, when people talk about depolicing, they are talking about inaction that results from *all* of the expected costs of public scrutiny and legal sanction against officers, not just those arising from civil liability. Whether or not depolicing happens, and scholars debate the point, concern about depolicing is a helpful reminder that civil liability is only one of the expected costs and benefits that a rational police officer would consider in determining whether to act or not to act, and whether to comply with or to violate the law. The rest of the calculus depends on other legal threats, reputational effects, professional costs and benefits, and the consequences experienced as a result of personal values.

Justices and scholars who defend the overdeterrence theory, and qualified immunity to address it, base their arguments largely on intuitions about the actual and perceived costs of officer action, officer inaction, civil liability, and the effects of tweaking immunity rules. Some scholars now contest the empirical basis for the overdeterrence thesis and its judicial solution. For example, police officers virtually never pay anything toward settlements or judgments entered against them. Instead, governments pay effectively all of the damages that plaintiffs recover in lawsuits alleging constitutional violations by officers. See Joanna C. Schwartz, *Police Indemnification*, 89 N.Y.U. L. Rev. 885, 902–912 (2014). That means one basic premise of the overdeterrence thesis—that officers face high financial costs from successful §1983 litigation—is clearly wrong. How should this fact affect qualified immunity doctrine?

The idea of *overdeterrence* inevitably also depends on some conception about the proper trade-off between policing and deterrence. Just how much deterrence of lawful police activity is justified to prevent unlawful conduct? Does this depend on how you view the value of policing? Or how commonly you think officers violate the law? How should courts decide whether and how much to restrict prevention?

3.   Qualified Immunity as Racial Injustice

Qualified immunity doctrine appears race neutral, but in a 2020 opinion, *Jamison v. McClendon*, No. 3:16-CV-595-CWR-LRA (S.D. Miss. Aug. 4, 2020), U.S. District Judge Carlton W. Reeves argues powerfully that the Supreme Court's contemporary qualified immunity doctrine is a form of racial injustice. This is how he started his order granting qualified immunity to a white police officer who stopped and searched a Black man:

Clarence Jamison wasn't jaywalking.[1]

He wasn't outside playing with a toy gun.[2]

He didn't look like a "suspicious person."[3]

He wasn't suspected of "selling loose, untaxed cigarettes."[4]

He wasn't suspected of passing a counterfeit $20 bill.[5]

He didn't look like anyone suspected of a crime.[6]

He wasn't mentally ill and in need of help.[7]

He wasn't assisting an autistic patient who had wandered away from a group home.[8]

He wasn't walking home from an after-school job.[9]

---

[1] That was Michael Brown.
[2] That was 12-year-old Tamir Rice.
[3] That was Elijah McClain.
[4] That was Eric Garner.
[5] That was George Floyd.
[6] That was Philando Castile and Tony McDade.
[7] That was Jason Harrison.
[8] That was Charles Kinsey.
[9] That was 17-year-old James Earl Green.

He wasn't walking back from a restaurant.[10]

He wasn't hanging out on a college campus.[11]

He wasn't standing outside of his apartment.[12]

He wasn't inside his apartment eating ice cream.[13]

He wasn't sleeping in his bed.[14]

He wasn't sleeping in his car.[15]

He didn't make an "improper lane change."[16]

He didn't have a broken tail light.[17]

He wasn't driving over the speed limit.[18]

He wasn't driving under the speed limit.[19]

No, Clarence Jamison was a Black man driving a Mercedes convertible.

As he made his way home to South Carolina from a vacation in Arizona, Jamison was pulled over and subjected to one hundred and ten minutes of an armed police officer badgering him, pressuring him, lying to him, and then searching his car top-to-bottom for drugs.

Nothing was found. Jamison isn't a drug courier. He's a welder.

Unsatisfied, the officer then brought out a canine to sniff the car. The dog found nothing. So nearly two hours after it started, the officer left Jamison by the side of the road to put his car back together.

Thankfully, Jamison left the stop with his life. Too many others have not.

The Constitution says everyone is entitled to equal protection of the law – even at the hands of law enforcement. Over the decades, however, judges have invented a legal doctrine to protect law enforcement officers from having to face any consequences for wrongdoing. The doctrine is called "qualified immunity." In real life it operates like absolute immunity. . . .

. . . Tragically, thousands have died at the hands of law enforcement over the years, and the death toll continues to rise. Countless more have suffered from other forms of abuse and misconduct by police. Qualified immunity has served as a shield for these officers, protecting them from accountability.

This Court is required to apply the law as stated by the Supreme Court. Under that law, the officer who transformed a short traffic stop into an almost two-hour, life-altering ordeal is entitled to qualified immunity. The officer's motion seeking as much is therefore granted.

---

[10] That was Ben Brown.
[11] That was Phillip Gibbs.
[12] That was Amadou Diallo.
[13] That was Botham Jean.
[14] That was Breonna Taylor.
[15] That was Rayshard Brooks.
[16] That was Sandra Bland.
[17] That was Walter Scott.
[18] That was Hannah Fizer.
[19] That was Ace Perry.

Section 1983 was passed as part of The Ku Klux Klan Act of 1871, an expansive statute designed to target the extreme Southern racial violence and the official acts that facilitated it. By invoking recent African-American victims of police violence, Judge Reeves suggests that Black people face an analogous threat today at the hands of the police. Although *Jamison* did not involve the use of force, Judge Reeves notes that race and violence are inevitably in play when a person of color is stopped by the police: "Black people in this country are acutely aware of the danger traffic stops pose to Black lives." *Id.* at 54. Indeed, in his deposition, Jamison indicated that the stop affected him more because he realized that, like Walter Scott, a Black man whose murder by a police officer after a traffic stop had been in the news, Jamison could have been unjustifiably killed during his encounter.

Judge Reeves contends that, just as Supreme Court decisions in the 1870s narrowed the scope of civil rights acts and amendments, helping to end Reconstruction and providing support for white supremacy, the Court's qualified immunity doctrine has cut away at a key civil rights victory of the 1960s, *Monroe v. Pape*, 365 U.S. 167 (1961), which made §1983 a meaningful tool for African Americans to vindicate their rights against police misconduct. In this way, Judge Reeves argues that qualified immunity doctrine presents a pressing civil rights challenge:

> From the beginning, "the Blessings of Liberty" were not equally bestowed upon all Americans. Yet, as people marching in the streets remind us today, some have always stood up to face our nation's failings and remind us that "we cannot be patient." John Lewis, Speech at the March on Washington (Aug. 28, 1963). Through their efforts we become ever more perfect.
>
> The U.S. Congress of the Reconstruction era stood up to the white supremacists of its time when it passed Section 1983. The late Congressman John Lewis stared down the racists of his era when he marched over the Edmund Pettus Bridge. The Supreme Court has answered the call of history as well, most famously when it issued its unanimous decision in *Brown v. Board of Education* and resigned the "separate but equal" doctrine to the dustbin of history.
>
> The question of today is whether the Supreme Court will rise to the occasion and do the same with qualified immunity.

Id. at 62–63.

Popular concern about police violence has placed qualified immunity doctrine under public scrutiny. If the Court does not rethink its approach to qualified immunity soon, Congress may step in. Remember that qualified immunity is an interpretation of §1983, a federal statute. Although the statute is long-standing, it can be changed by Congress at any time. In 2020, after George Floyd was killed by the police, a congressional bill proposed adding the following language.

> It shall not be a defense or immunity in any action brought under this section against a local law enforcement officer . . . that—
>
> (1) the defendant was acting in good faith, or that the defendant believed, reasonably or otherwise, that his or her conduct was lawful at the time when the conduct was committed; or
>
> (2) the rights, privileges, or immunities secured by the Constitution and laws were not clearly established at the time of their deprivation by the defendant, or that at

such time, the state of the law was otherwise such that the defendant could not reasonably have been expected to know whether his or her conduct was lawful.

George Floyd Justice in Policing Act of 2020, H.R. 7120 §102 (2020) (as passed by the House, June 25, 2020). The bill had 133 cosponsors. Is there anything you would want to know before you decide whether to support this amendment? What consequences could it have for policing? If the judge-made doctrine of qualified immunity is a form of racial injustice, as Judge Reeves suggests, is it better to have the Court or Congress fix it?

4. Qualified Immunity and the Order of Operations

Under existing doctrine, an officer can establish a qualified immunity defense *either* by showing that no constitutional right against the alleged conduct exists or by showing that the right was not clearly established at the time of the conduct. In *Kisela*, the majority assumed (while casting doubt on) the existence of a constitutional violation and concluded that the right was not clearly established. Justice Sotomayor's dissent instead began with whether there was a constitutional violation, and only then argued that the right was clearly established.

At one time, the Court insisted that lower courts engage in a merits-first approach, in which they first identified whether the plaintiff had alleged a constitutional deprivation, and only then considered whether the right allegedly implicated had been clearly established at the time of the events. In 2009, however, the Court concluded that to promote efficiency and high-quality decision making, lower courts are "permitted to exercise their sound discretion in deciding which of the two prongs of the qualified immunity analysis should be addressed first in light of the circumstances in the particular case at hand." Pearson v. Callahan, 555 U.S. 223, 236 (2009).

When an officer commits an act that violates the Constitution but that violation has not yet been clearly established under the Court's stringent criteria, the plaintiff is out of luck: If he bothers to bring a suit against the officer, it will founder on qualified immunity. If, under *Pearson*, the court hearing the case exercises its discretion not to decide the constitutional question, then officers on the street may repeat the act, now confident that no civil liability attaches: By ruling the act not clearly established as unconstitutional, the court eliminates any lingering doubt the officer might have had about whether prior cases resolved the issue. The next person to suffer the same (presumptive) constitutional violation may be in a worse situation than the first plaintiff: Now it is clear—if it was not before—that the right is not clearly established. If he sues, the court may again easily avoid the constitutional question. And so on. In this way, a constitutional violation could remain undeclared, unremedied, and undeterred for some time, at least until a plaintiff brings a case and a court decides the issue is worth addressing, despite an officer's immunity, or the issue is decided in another legal arena. Although courts apparently use their discretion to resolve most constitutional questions before them, doctrine develops at a slower rate because courts have the power to grant qualified immunity without clarifying constitutional rights. See Aaron L. Nielson & Christopher J. Walker, *The New Qualified Immunity*, 89 S. Cal. L. Rev. 1, 6 (2015).

To see the impact of *Pearson* on policing, consider the law of Tasers. Conducted energy devices (CEDs), often known by the brand name Taser were invented in 1974 and came into use in policing in the 1990s. They spread rapidly in the early

2000s and now are common throughout the country. When a Taser is used in dart mode, it shoots a pair of aluminum darts tipped with stainless-steel barbs attached by insulated wires up to 35 feet and delivers a 1,200-volt, low-ampere electrical charge through clothing and into a suspect's muscles. If a Taser is deployed properly, it can incapacitate a suspect immediately.

The upside of a Taser is that it permits officers to use less-lethal force when a suspect is beyond the reach of a baton or pepper spray. Previously the officer's options were to (1) get closer—risking his own safety; (2) use deadly force—with potentially terrible consequences for the suspect; or (3) use no force at all—potentially compromising an important law enforcement objective. The downside of a Taser is that it causes intense pain and sometimes serious injuries when the suspect collapses, often onto pavement, without being able to protect his head or soften the impact. Because they do not expect to kill the suspect or get hurt, officers may use a Taser when using less force or no force was possible. Unsurprisingly, CEDs have raised new Fourth Amendment questions about when shocking a suspect constitutes reasonable, as opposed to excessive, force. Such questions are not easy, but they are *Pearson*-avoidable. As a result, the law governing CEDs has developed far more slowly than their use.

A Ninth Circuit case, *Bryan v. MacPherson*, 630 F.3d 805 (9th Cir. 2010), illustrates the issue. This is what happened on July 24, 2005:

> Carl Bryan's California Sunday was off to a bad start. The twenty-one year old, having stayed the night with his younger brother and some cousins in Camarillo, which is in Ventura County, planned to drive his brother back to his parents' home in Coronado, which is in San Diego County. However, Bryan's cousin's girlfriend had accidently taken Bryan's keys to Los Angeles the previous day. Wearing the t-shirt and boxer shorts in which he had slept, Bryan rose early, traveled east with his cousins to Los Angeles, picked up his keys and returned to Camarillo to get his car and brother. He then began driving south towards his parents' home. While traveling on the 405 highway, Bryan and his brother were stopped by a California Highway Patrolman who issued Bryan a speeding ticket. This upset him greatly. He began crying and moping, ultimately removing his t-shirt to wipe his face. Continuing south without further incident, the two finally crossed the Coronado Bridge at about seven-thirty in the morning.

> At that point, an already bad morning for Bryan took a turn for the worse. Bryan was stopped at an intersection when Officer MacPherson, who was stationed there to enforce seatbelt regulations, stepped in front of his car and signaled to Bryan that he was not to proceed. Bryan immediately realized that he had mistakenly failed to buckle his seatbelt after his earlier encounter with the police. Officer MacPherson approached the passenger window and asked Bryan whether he knew why he had been stopped. Bryan, knowing full well why and becoming increasingly angry at himself, simply stared straight ahead. Officer MacPherson requested that Bryan turn down his radio and pull over to the curb. Bryan complied with both requests, but as he pulled his car to the curb, angry with himself over the prospects of another citation, he hit his steering wheel and yelled expletives to himself. Having pulled his car over and placed it in park, Bryan stepped out of his car.

> There is no dispute that Bryan was agitated, standing outside his car, yelling gibberish and hitting his thighs, clad only in his boxer shorts and tennis shoes. It is also undisputed that Bryan did not verbally threaten Officer MacPherson and, according to Officer MacPherson, was standing twenty to twenty-five feet away and not

attempting to flee. Officer MacPherson testified that he told Bryan to remain in the car, while Bryan testified that he did not hear Officer MacPherson tell him to do so. The one material dispute concerns whether Bryan made any movement toward the officer. Officer MacPherson testified that Bryan took "one step" toward him, but Bryan says he did not take any step, and the physical evidence indicates that Bryan was actually facing away from Officer MacPherson. Without giving any warning, Officer MacPherson shot Bryan with his taser gun. One of the taser probes embedded in the side of Bryan's upper left arm. The electrical current immobilized him whereupon he fell face first into the ground, fracturing four teeth and suffering facial contusions. Bryan's morning ended with his arrest and yet another drive—this time by ambulance and to a hospital for treatment.

Bryan sued Officer MacPherson and the Coronado Police Department, its police chief, and the City of Coronado for excessive force in violation of 42 U.S.C. §1983, assault and battery, intentional infliction of emotional distress, a violation of California Civil Code §52.1, as well as failure to train and related causes of action. On summary judgment, the district court granted relief to the City of Coronado and Coronado Police Department, but determined that Officer MacPherson was not entitled to qualified immunity at this stage of the proceedings. The court concluded that a reasonable jury could find that Bryan "presented no immediate danger to [Officer MacPherson] and no use of force was necessary." In particular, it found that a reasonable jury could find that Bryan was located between fifteen to twenty-five feet from Officer MacPherson and was not facing him or advancing toward him. The court also found that a reasonable officer would have known that the use of the taser would cause pain and, as Bryan was standing on asphalt, that a resulting fall could cause injury. Under the circumstances, the district court concluded it would have been clear to a reasonable officer that shooting Bryan with the taser was unlawful.

Id. at 822–823.

The district court denied qualified immunity, and although the Ninth Circuit panel initially affirmed, it subsequently withdrew its initial opinion, and withdrew and superseded its second one, finally concluding that shooting an unarmed, non-dangerous, nonfleeing, and nonconfrontational suspect with a Taser during a traffic stop for a seatbelt violation constituted excessive force. Nevertheless, it reversed the district court's denial of summary judgment on the basis of qualified immunity:

[A]s of July 24, 2005, there was no Supreme Court decision or decision of our court addressing whether the use of a taser, such as the Taser X26, in dart mode constituted an intermediate level of force. Indeed, before that date, the only statement we had made regarding tasers in a published opinion was that they were among the "variety of non-lethal 'pain compliance' weapons used by police forces." San Jose Charter of Hells Angels Motorcycle Club, 402 F.3d 962, 969 n.8 (9th Cir. 2005). And, as the Eighth Circuit has noted, "[t]he Taser is a relatively new implement of force, and case law related to the Taser is developing." Brown v. City of Golden Valley, 574 F.3d 491, 498 n.5 (8th Cir. 2009). Two other panels have recently, in cases involving different circumstances, concluded that the law regarding tasers is not sufficiently clearly established to warrant denying officers qualified immunity. Mattos v. Agarano, 590 F.3d 1082, 1089–1090 (9th Cir. 2010); Brooks v. City of Seattle, 599 F.3d 1018, 1031 n.18 (9th Cir. 2010).

Based on these recent statements regarding the use of tasers, and the dearth of prior authority, we must conclude that a reasonable officer in Officer MacPherson's position could have made a reasonable mistake of law regarding the constitutionality of the taser use in the circumstances Officer MacPherson confronted in July 2005. Accordingly, Officer MacPherson is entitled to qualified immunity.

Id. at 83.

As *Bryan* suggests, several previous cases had been resolved without addressing the constitutionality of Taser use because the matter was not yet clearly established. See also Karen M. Blum, *Qualified Immunity: Time to Change the Message*, 93 Notre Dame L. Rev. 1887, 1897–1899 (2018) (using Taser cases to illustrate the effects of qualified immunity doctrine). If *Bryan*'s tortuous history is anything to go by, lower courts would not have been wrong if they thought answering the legal question could be difficult. One could argue that *Pearson* helped promote good Fourth Amendment law by allowing courts to decide the complicated issues Tasers raised after the issues had ripened for review. Yet the consequence was that for years in the early 2000s, officers in the Ninth Circuit were carrying and using Tasers, a weapon that imposes serious harm, with little constitutional guidance and with legal immunity from civil suit due to the absence of such guidance.

New Force Technologies

It might seem like patrol officers carry only a few basic weapons that do not change very often, so, outside of Tasers, stymying legal development on the use-of-force might not matter that much. Not so. In addition to a handgun and a blunt-force weapon like a baton, most departments equip officers with aerosol pepper spray and CEDs, both of which have been adopted in the last several decades. Agencies also now equip at least some officers with other firearms, including rifles, assault weapons, and shotguns, and with other kinds of projectiles, including tear gas canisters, paintball-style pepper balls, beanbags, and plastic and rubber bullets. Additionally, new force technologies come to market all the time. Whether and how officers use them is determined in part by how courts resolve the constitutional issues they raise.

Want an example? Think about how Spiderman subdues fleeing criminals by shooting webs that wrap around them. Wrap Technologies is now selling Bolawrap 100, "a hand-held remote restraint device that discharges a 7'6" foot bola style Kevlar tether at 513 feet per second to entangle a subject at a range of 10-25 feet." The Kevlar tether is like a projectile lasso that wraps itself around a subject and secures itself with little barbs. Police departments are already purchasing and using this simple new technology, which offers officers a way to secure suspects at a distance without inducing pain. The manufacturer recommends that the wrap only be deployed around a person's legs to avoid injury from an uncontrolled trip or fall.

If BolaWrap works as well as Spiderman's webs and officers use it in place of a Taser, the new technology could reduce harm to suspects. But BolaWrap also raises new legal questions. What if officers shoot a BolaWrap to secure someone who has not ignored verbal commands or attempted to flee? Is that constitutional? Is there a (constitutional) difference between shooting a wrap at suspects' torsos and shooting it at it their legs? Between using it on a standing person and a fleeing one? You can practice the doctrine you learned in Chapter 8 by answering these questions. Given *Pearson* and *Kisela*, however, it could be many years before federal courts do the same. What is likely to happen in the meantime? Is there any way to speed up the process?

C. Private Suits for Damages Against Municipalities

Section 1983 imposes liability only on *persons* who commit constitutional violations. According to the Supreme Court's decision in *Monell v. New York City Department of Social Services*, 436 U.S. 658 (1978), police departments, towns, cities, counties, and other local agencies or governments can be persons within the meaning of the statute.[5] However, based on its interpretation of the statute's text and some indirect legislative history, *Monell* also makes clear that such actors are liable for only their own actions. Cities are not vicariously liable for the conduct of individual officers, just becaue they employ them.

How does a city *cause* a constitutional violation? Cities act through *policy and custom.* One treatise summarizes the following bases for municipal liability:

1. A formally promulgated policy;
2. a well-settled custom or practice;
3. a final decision by a municipal policymaker; or
4. deliberately indifferent training, supervision, or screening of employees.

Martin A. Schwartz, *Section 1983 Litigation* §7.06 (3rd ed. 2014). None of these avenues to proving municipal liability is easy, and few §1983 claims against cities succeed.

---

[5] States, on the other hand, are not subject to suit under §1983. Although plaintiffs frequently name police departments in their suits, most courts do not view them as suable entities and treat suits naming a police department as suits against the municipality. See, e.g., Paige-El v. Herbert, 735 Fed. Appx. 753, 755 (2d Cir. 2018); Best v. City of Portland, 554 F.3d 698, 698 (7th Cir. 2009).

1.   Unconstitutional Policies, Customs, and Decisions

For an unusually clear example of a city acting through an unconstitutional policy and causing a constitutional violation that subjected it to liability, consider *Tennessee v. Garner*, 471 U.S. 1 (1985), and its aftermath.[6] Memphis Police Officer Elton Hymon shot and killed 14-year-old Edward Garner as the teenager fled a suspected burglary. Garner's father brought a §1983 lawsuit against Officer Hymon, the Memphis Police Department, the Department's Director, the City of Memphis, and the Mayor of Memphis.

By the time the case got to the Supreme Court, lower courts had dismissed claims against the individual defendants. They had qualified immunity because they had acted in accordance with Tennessee law, which authorized deadly force against any fleeing felon, not just dangerous ones. In its opinion, the Supreme Court ruled that Officer Hymon's use of deadly force against Garner nevertheless violated the Fourth Amendment because Garner was unarmed and fleeing and did not pose a significant threat of death or serious physical injury to the officer who shot him or to anyone else. The Court remanded the claims against the city and police department back to the district court.

Although it took years of legal wrangling and delays, eventually, the district court granted summary judgment in favor of the remaining defendants. The Sixth Circuit took up the case for the third time in 1993 and reversed. Here is what it said about the liability of the city and the department:

> In *Monell v. New York City Dept of Social Services*, the Supreme Court overruled *Monroe v. Pape*, 365 U.S. 167 (1961), and held that municipalities are "persons" subject to suit under §1983. 436 U.S. 658, 700–701 (1978). Municipalities are not, however, liable for every misdeed of their employees and agents. "Instead, it is when execution of a government's policy or custom, whether made by its lawmakers or by those whose edicts or acts may fairly be said to represent official policy, inflicts the injury that the government as an entity is responsible under §1983." *Id.* at 694. This circuit has stated that to satisfy the *Monell* requirements a plaintiff must "identify the policy, connect the policy to the city itself and show that the particular injury was incurred because of the execution of that policy." Coogan v. City of Wixom, 820 F.2d 170, 176 (6th Cir. 1987). Plaintiff has met this standard.
>
> First, it is clear that the defendants had a policy authorizing use of deadly force when necessary to apprehend a fleeing burglary suspect. Memphis Police Department General Order 5–74(3)(b)(3) provides:
>
> > (3) Other Felonies Where Deadly Force is Authorized.
>
> > After all reasonable means of preventing or apprehending a suspect have been exhausted, DEADLY FORCE is authorized in the following crimes:
>
> > (a) Kidnapping
> > (b) Murder in the 1st or 2nd degree
> > (c) Manslaughter
> > (d) Arson (Including the use of firebombs)
> > (e) Rape

---

[6] *Tennessee v. Garner* is excerpted and discussed in more depth in Chapter 8.

     (f) Assault and battery with intent to carnally know a child under 12 years of age

     (g) Assault and battery with intent to commit rape

     (h) *Burglary in the 1st, 2nd, or 3rd degree*

     (i) Assault to commit murder in the 1st or 2nd degree

     (j) Assault to commit voluntary manslaughter

     (k) Armed and simple robbery

App. 81 (emphasis added). This order was signed by the Director of the Memphis police. The Mayor of Memphis testified in a deposition that he was also involved in the decision to include all types of burglary on the list of felonies justifying use of deadly force: "One of the arguments was to eliminate burglary and this type thing, some kinds of burglary, which I did not do. I did not think it should be done." App. 103. Defendants do not contest that General Order 5–74 represented the official policy of the Memphis Police Department and the City of Memphis. . . .

Having identified the policy and connected it to the defendants, plaintiff need only show that the policy caused the injury complained of, the death of plaintiff's son. See *Coogan*, 820 F.2d at 176. Defendants did not in their briefs or at oral argument contest the causation issue. The Police Department taught Officer Hymon that it was proper to shoot a fleeing burglary suspect in order to prevent escape. That was their policy. Garner v. Memphis Police Dept., 600 F.2d 52, 54 (6th Cir. 1979). As the Supreme Court stated in this case, "Hymon was acting under the authority of a Tennessee statute and pursuant to Police Department policy." Tennessee v. Garner, 471 U.S. 1, 4 (1985). Thus, there is a sufficient link between defendants' deadly force policy and Hymon's actions to establish that the policy was the "moving force of the constitutional violation." See *Monell*, 436 U.S. at 694. Plaintiff has satisfied all of the *Monell* requirements.

Defendants . . . argue that the Police Department and the City should be dismissed from the case because the district court dismissed Officer Hymon, finding that he had not committed a constitutional violation. . . . Defendants rely upon *City of Los Angeles v. Heller*, 475 U.S. 796 (1986), in which the Court upheld the district court's dismissal of the City of Los Angeles and its Police Commission, holding that "[i]f a person has suffered no constitutional injury at the hands of the individual police officer, the fact that the departmental regulations might have *authorized* the use of constitutionally excessive force is quite beside the point." *Id.* at 799.

Defendants' reliance on *Heller* is misplaced. The point in *Heller* was that the city could not be held responsible for a constitutional violation which could have occurred but did not. In the instant case there is no doubt that a constitutional violation occurred. "A police officer may not seize an unarmed, nondangerous suspect by shooting him dead. The Tennessee statute is unconstitutional insofar as it authorizes the use of deadly force against such fleeing suspects." *Tennessee v. Garner*, 471 U.S. at 11. . . .

This court upheld Officer Hymon's dismissal from the case not because he committed no constitutional violation, but because he was protected by the doctrine of qualified immunity. Under the law of this circuit, a municipality may not escape liability for a §1983 violation merely because the officer who committed the violation is entitled to qualified immunity. Doe v. Sullivan County, Tenn., 956 F.2d 545, 554 (6th Cir. 1992).

Garner v. Memphis Police Dept., 8 F.3d 358, 363–365 (6th Cir. 1993). Accordingly, the court entered judgment in favor of the plaintiff on the issue of liability and remanded the case back to the district court to determine appropriate damages.

NOTES AND QUESTIONS

1. *Cities vs. everyone else.* Unlike states, which can invoke sovereign immunity; city council members, who can often invoke absolute immunity as legislators; or individual officers, who can invoke qualified immunity, cities and police departments have no immunity defense under §1983.

2. *City liability absent individual liability.* When does *Garner* suggest cities may be liable for unconstitutional police conduct, even if no one else is liable, including the officer who carried out the conduct? Can you come up with some examples of when else that could occur?

3. *Escaping liability for an unconstitutional policy.* Even if a city has a blatantly unconstitutional policy, *Garner* indicates it can escape liability if there is no constitutional violation by an individual officer. As the Sixth Circuit's opinion suggests, the Supreme Court has said as much: "If a person has suffered no constitutional injury at the hands of the individual police officer, the fact that the departmental regulations might have *authorized* the use of constitutionally excessive force is quite beside the point." City of Los Angeles v. Heller, 475 U.S. 796, 799 (1986).

4. *Why?* Why would a police department adopt an unconstitutional policy? Why did it happen in Memphis?

5. *Formal vs. informal policy.* The policy in Memphis was a formally promulgated one. The Supreme Court recognized in *Monell* that a municipality may adopt a custom or practice that is so widespread that it in effect constitutes a policy, even though it has never been officially approved or written down. *Monell*, 436 U.S. at 694. Although most departments do not formally adopt unconstitutional policies, cities sometimes do have informal, but well-settled, practices that cause constitutional violations. In cases involving formal policies, the challenge may be to establish that the policy was unconstitutional. In cases involving informal practices or customs, the greater hurdle is often to establish exactly what the policy was.

2. Unconstitutional Application of Constitutional Policy

Challenging policies that authorize unconstitutional conduct might seem (almost) straightforward enough. Plaintiffs have more difficulty when they argue that cities caused a violation in a more subtle way, such as by failing to act instead of by acting.

a. Failure to Train

CITY OF CANTON v. HARRIS
489 U.S. 378 (1989)

Justice White delivered the opinion of the Court.

In this case, we are asked to determine if a municipality can ever be liable under 42 U.S.C. §1983 for constitutional violations resulting from its failure to train municipal employees. We hold that, under certain circumstances, such liability is permitted by the statute.

I

In April 1978, respondent Geraldine Harris was arrested by officers of the Canton Police Department. Mrs. Harris was brought to the police station in a patrol wagon.

When she arrived at the station, Mrs. Harris was found sitting on the floor of the wagon. She was asked if she needed medical attention, and responded with an incoherent remark. After she was brought inside the station for processing, Mrs. Harris slumped to the floor on two occasions. Eventually, the police officers left Mrs. Harris lying on the floor to prevent her from falling again. No medical attention was ever summoned for Mrs. Harris. After about an hour, Mrs. Harris was released from custody, and taken by an ambulance (provided by her family) to a nearby hospital. There, Mrs. Harris was diagnosed as suffering from several emotional ailments; she was hospitalized for one week and received subsequent outpatient treatment for an additional year.

Some time later, Mrs. Harris commenced this action alleging many state-law and constitutional claims against the city of Canton and its officials. Among these claims was one seeking to hold the city liable under 42 U.S.C. §1983 for its violation of Mrs. Harris' right, under the Due Process Clause of the Fourteenth Amendment, to receive necessary medical attention while in police custody.

A jury trial was held on Mrs. Harris' claims. Evidence was presented that indicated that, pursuant to a municipal regulation, shift commanders were authorized to determine, in their sole discretion, whether a detainee required medical care. In addition, testimony also suggested that Canton shift commanders were not provided with any special training (beyond first-aid training) to make a determination as to when to summon medical care for an injured detainee. . . .

III

In *Monell v. New York City Dept. of Social Services*, 436 U.S. 658 (1978), we decided that a municipality can be found liable under §1983 only where the municipality *itself* causes the constitutional violation at issue. *Respondeat superior* or vicarious liability will not attach under §1983. *Id.* at 694–695. "It is only when the 'execution of the government's policy or custom . . . inflicts the injury' that the municipality may be held liable under §1983." *Springfield v. Kibbe*, 480 U.S. 257, 267 (1987) (O'Connor, J., dissenting) (quoting *Monell*, 436 U.S. at 694).

Thus, our first inquiry in any case alleging municipal liability under §1983 is the question whether there is a direct causal link between a municipal policy or custom and the alleged constitutional deprivation. The inquiry is a difficult one; one that has left this Court deeply divided in a series of cases that have followed *Monell;* one that is the principal focus of our decision again today.

A

Based on the difficulty that this Court has had defining the contours of municipal liability in these circumstances, petitioner urges us to adopt the rule that a municipality can be found liable under §1983 only where "the policy in question [is] itself unconstitutional." Brief for Petitioner 15. . . . Under such an approach, the outcome here would be rather clear: we would have to reverse and remand the case with instructions that judgment be entered for petitioner. There can be little doubt that on its face the city's policy regarding medical treatment for detainees is constitutional. The policy states that the city jailer "shall . . . have [a person needing medical care] taken to a hospital for medical treatment, with permission of his supervisor. . . ." App. 33. It is difficult to see what constitutional guarantees are violated by such a policy.

Nor, without more, would a city automatically be liable under §1983 if one of its employees happened to apply the policy in an unconstitutional manner, for liability would then rest on *respondeat superior*. The claim in this case, however, is that if a concededly valid policy is unconstitutionally applied by a municipal employee, the city is liable if the employee has not been adequately trained and the constitutional wrong has been caused by that failure to train. For reasons explained below, we conclude, as have all the Courts of Appeals that have addressed this issue, that there are limited circumstances in which an allegation of a "failure to train" can be the basis for liability under §1983. Thus, we reject petitioner's contention that only unconstitutional policies are actionable under the statute.

B

. . . Unlike the question whether a municipality's failure to train employees can ever be a basis for §1983 liability—on which the Courts of Appeals have all agreed—there is substantial division among the lower courts as to what *degree of fault* must be evidenced by the municipality's inaction before liability will be permitted. We hold today that the inadequacy of police training may serve as the basis for §1983 liability only where the failure to train amounts to deliberate indifference to the rights of persons with whom the police come into contact. This rule is most consistent with our admonition in *Monell*, 436 U.S. at 694, and *Polk County v. Dodson*, 454 U.S. 312, 326 (1981), that a municipality can be liable under §1983 only where its policies are the "moving force [behind] the constitutional violation." Only where a municipality's failure to train its employees in a relevant respect evidences a "deliberate indifference" to the rights of its inhabitants can such a shortcoming be properly thought of as a city "policy or custom" that is actionable under §1983. . . .

Monell's rule that a city is not liable under §1983 unless a municipal policy causes a constitutional deprivation will not be satisfied by merely alleging that the existing training program for a class of employees, such as police officers, represents a policy for which the city is responsible. That much may be true. The issue in a case like this one, however, is whether that training program is adequate; and if it is not, the question becomes whether such inadequate training can justifiably be said to represent "city policy." It may seem contrary to common sense to assert that a municipality will actually have a policy of not taking reasonable steps to train its employees. But it may happen that in light of the duties assigned to specific officers or employees the need for more or different training is so obvious, and the inadequacy so likely to result in the violation of constitutional rights, that the policymakers of the city can reasonably be said to have been deliberately indifferent to the need.[10] In that event, the failure to provide proper training may fairly be said to represent a policy for which the city is responsible, and for which the city may be held liable if it actually causes injury.

---

[10] For example, city policymakers know to a moral certainty that their police officers will be required to arrest fleeing felons. The city has armed its officers with firearms, in part to allow them to accomplish this task. Thus, the need to train officers in the constitutional limitations on the use of deadly force, see Tennessee v. Garner, 471 U.S. 1 (1985), can be said to be "so obvious," that failure to do so could properly be characterized as "deliberate indifference" to constitutional rights.

It could also be that the police, in exercising their discretion, so often violate constitutional rights that the need for further training must have been plainly obvious to the city policymakers, who, nevertheless, are "deliberately indifferent" to the need.

In resolving the issue of a city's liability, the focus must be on adequacy of the training program in relation to the tasks the particular officers must perform. That a particular officer may be unsatisfactorily trained will not alone suffice to fasten liability on the city, for the officer's shortcomings may have resulted from factors other than a faulty training program. It may be, for example, that an otherwise sound program has occasionally been negligently administered. Neither will it suffice to prove that an injury or accident could have been avoided if an officer had had better or more training, sufficient to equip him to avoid the particular injury-causing conduct. Such a claim could be made about almost any encounter resulting in injury, yet not condemn the adequacy of the program to enable officers to respond properly to the usual and recurring situations with which they must deal. And plainly, adequately trained officers occasionally make mistakes; the fact that they do says little about the training program or the legal basis for holding the city liable.

Moreover, for liability to attach in this circumstance the identified deficiency in a city's training program must be closely related to the ultimate injury. Thus in the case at hand, respondent must still prove that the deficiency in training actually caused the police officers' indifference to her medical needs. Would the injury have been avoided had the employee been trained under a program that was not deficient in the identified respect? Predicting how a hypothetically well-trained officer would have acted under the circumstances may not be an easy task for the fact-finder, particularly since matters of judgment may be involved, and since officers who are well trained are not free from error and perhaps might react very much like the untrained officer in similar circumstances. But judge and jury, doing their respective jobs, will be adequate to the task.

To adopt lesser standards of fault and causation would open municipalities to unprecedented liability under §1983. In virtually every instance where a person has had his or her constitutional rights violated by a city employee, a §1983 plaintiff will be able to point to something the city "could have done" to prevent the unfortunate incident. Thus, permitting cases against cities for their "failure to train" employees to go forward under §1983 on a lesser standard of fault would result in *de facto respondeat superior* liability on municipalities—a result we rejected in *Monell*, 436 U.S. at 693–694. It would also engage the federal courts in an endless exercise of second-guessing municipal employee-training programs. This is an exercise we believe the federal courts are ill suited to undertake, as well as one that would implicate serious questions of federalism.

Consequently, while claims such as respondent's—alleging that the city's failure to provide training to municipal employees resulted in the constitutional deprivation she suffered—are cognizable under §1983, they can only yield liability against a municipality where that city's failure to train reflects deliberate indifference to the constitutional rights of its inhabitants. . . .

V

Consequently, for the reasons given above, we vacate the judgment of the Court of Appeals and remand this case for further proceedings consistent with this opinion.

It is so ordered.

[Justice Brennan's concurring opinion is omitted.]

Justice O'Connor, with whom Justice Scalia and Justice Kennedy join, concurring in part and dissenting in part. . . .

My single point of disagreement with the majority is . . . a small one. Because I believe, as the majority strongly hints, that respondent has not and could not satisfy the fault and causation requirements we adopt today, I think it unnecessary to remand this case to the Court of Appeals for further proceedings. This case comes to us after a full trial during which respondent vigorously pursued numerous theories of municipal liability including an allegation that the city had a "custom" of not providing medical care to detainees suffering from emotional illnesses. Respondent thus had every opportunity and incentive to adduce the type of proof necessary to satisfy the deliberate indifference standard we adopt today. Rather than remand in this context, I would apply the deliberate indifference standard to the facts of this case. After undertaking that analysis below, I conclude that there is no evidence in the record indicating that the city of Canton has been deliberately indifferent to the constitutional rights of pretrial detainees. . . .

Where, as here, a claim of municipal liability is predicated upon a failure to act, the requisite degree of fault must be shown by proof of a background of events and circumstances which establish that the "policy of inaction" is the functional equivalent of a decision by the city itself to violate the Constitution. Without some form of notice to the city, and the opportunity to conform to constitutional dictates both what it does and what it chooses not to do, the failure to train theory of liability could completely engulf *Monell*, imposing liability without regard to fault. Moreover, absent a requirement that the lack of training at issue bear a very close causal connection to the violation of constitutional rights, the failure to train theory of municipal liability could impose "prophylactic" duties on municipal governments only remotely connected to underlying constitutional requirements themselves.

. . . Section 1983 is not a "federal good government act" for municipalities. Rather it creates a federal cause of action against persons, including municipalities, who deprive citizens of the United States of their constitutional rights.

Sensitive to these concerns, the Court's opinion correctly requires a high degree of fault on the part of city officials before an omission that is not in itself unconstitutional can support liability as a municipal policy under *Monell*. As the Court indicates, "it may happen that . . . the need for more or different training is so obvious, and the inadequacy so likely to result in the violation of constitutional rights, that the policymakers of the city can reasonably be said to have been deliberately indifferent to the need." *Ante*. Where a §1983 plaintiff can establish that the facts available to city policymakers put them on actual or constructive notice that the particular omission is substantially certain to result in the violation of the constitutional rights of their citizens, the dictates of *Monell* are satisfied. Only then can it be said that the municipality has made "'a deliberate choice to follow a course of action . . . from among various alternatives.'" *Ante*, at 389, quoting Pembaur v. Cincinnati, 475 U.S. 469, 483–484 (1986).

In my view, it could be shown that the need for training was obvious in one of two ways. First, a municipality could fail to train its employees concerning a clear constitutional duty implicated in recurrent situations that a particular employee is certain to face. As the majority notes, see *ante*, n.10, the constitutional limitations established by this Court on the use of deadly force by police officers present one such situation. The constitutional duty of the individual officer is clear, and it is equally clear that failure to inform city personnel of that duty will create an extremely high risk that constitutional violations will ensue.

The claim in this case—that police officers were inadequately trained in diagnosing the symptoms of emotional illness—falls far short of the kind of "obvious" need for training that would support a finding of deliberate indifference to constitutional rights on the part of the city. As the Court's opinion observes, this Court has not yet addressed the precise nature of the obligations that the Due Process Clause places upon the police to seek medical care for pretrial detainees who have been *physically* injured while being apprehended by the police. There are thus no clear constitutional guideposts for municipalities in this area, and the diagnosis of mental illness is not one of the "usual and recurring situations with which [the police] must deal." *Ante.* The lack of training at issue here is not the kind of omission that can be characterized, in and of itself, as a "deliberate indifference" to constitutional rights.

Second, I think municipal liability for failure to train may be proper where it can be shown that policymakers were aware of, and acquiesced in, a pattern of constitutional violations involving the exercise of police discretion. In such cases, the need for training may not be obvious from the outset, but a pattern of constitutional violations could put the municipality on notice that its officers confront the particular situation on a regular basis, and that they often react in a manner contrary to constitutional requirements. The lower courts that have applied the "deliberate indifference" standard we adopt today have required a showing of a pattern of violations from which a kind of "tacit authorization" by city policymakers can be inferred.

The Court's opinion recognizes this requirement, but declines to evaluate the evidence presented in this case in light of the new legal standard. . . .

Allowing an inadequate training claim such as this one to go to the jury based upon a single incident would only invite jury nullification of *Monell.* "To infer the existence of a city policy from the isolated misconduct of a single, low-level officer, and then to hold the city liable on the basis of that policy, would amount to permitting precisely the theory of strict *respondeat superior* liability rejected in *Monell.*" Oklahoma City v. Tuttle, 471 U.S. 808, 831 (1985) (Brennan, J., concurring in part and concurring in judgment). As the authors of the Ku Klux Act themselves realized, the resources of local government are not inexhaustible. The grave step of shifting those resources to particular areas where constitutional violations are likely to result through the deterrent power of §1983 should certainly not be taken on the basis of an isolated incident. If §1983 and the Constitution require the city of Canton to provide detailed medical and psychological training to its police officers, or to station paramedics at its jails, other city services will necessarily suffer, including those with far more direct implications for the protection of constitutional rights. Because respondent's evidence falls far short of establishing the high degree of fault on the part of the city required by our decision today, and because there is no indication that respondent could produce any new proof in this regard, I would reverse the judgment of the Court of Appeals and order entry of judgment for the city.

NOTES AND QUESTIONS

1. *Why sue cities?* Cities often have deep pockets, and they have no immunities. Moreover, suing cities might target the problem where it lies: Many experts argue that bad officers are made, not born, and police departments—agencies of municipalities—make them.

2. *Establishing municipal liability.* As *Canton* indicates, to prove a municipality liable for a constitutional violation by a police officer, a plaintiff must show that the officer violated his constitutional rights, that the municipality caused that violation through its actions, and that the municipality acted deliberately. *Canton*[7] applies this framework to arguments that a failure to train officers caused unconstitutional results. What does the majority require to establish liability if the training policy is not unconstitutional on its face?

3. *Establishing deliberate indifference.* Reread footnote 10. The Court suggests two methods for proving deliberate indifference: first, failing to train when an obvious need for training exists to avoid violating constitutional rights, and second, failing to correct training once a pattern of constitutional violations makes obvious the need to provide further training. The first is sometimes referred to as "single-incident" liability, because it permits a city to be held liable for a single violation that was the "obvious" consequence of failing to provide training. The *Canton* Court presents it as exceptional, and the Court has been even more dismissive of this path to liability in subsequent opinions. See, e.g., Connick v. Thompson, 563 U.S. 51, 63–64 (2011) (referring to "the narrow range of *Canton*'s hypothesized single-incident liability"). Thus, most plaintiffs attempting to prove liability for failure to train officers try to establish that a pattern of constitutional violations put the city on notice that its training was deficient.

4. *Causation.* Note that even if the plaintiff can show deliberate indifference, proving causation can be harder than it might seem. Under *Canton*, a city has not caused a violation with its inadequate training if the officer would have committed it even if he had been trained properly or if the officer should have known not to do it, even without instruction. That seems a pretty fine needle to thread.

b. Failure to Screen

In *Board of County Commissioners v. Brown*, 520 U.S. 397 (1997), the Court reiterated and refined the standard established in *Canton*. Jill Brown sued Bryan County, Oklahoma, alleging that a county police officer, Reserve Deputy Stacy Burns, had used excessive force against her. She contended that the county was responsible because Sheriff B.J. Moore had failed to adequately screen Burns, the son of his nephew, before hiring him. If the sheriff had checked, he would have discovered that Burns had previously committed several misdemeanors, including driving infractions, assault and battery, resisting arrest, and public drunkenness, though nothing in Oklahoma law prohibited him from serving as a police officer.

The *Brown* Court recognized the possibility that *inadequate hiring* claims, like *inadequate training* (often called failure-to-train) claims, could represent deliberate municipal policy and cause constitutional violations. But it held inadequate hiring claims to an even higher standard than it recognized in *Canton*.

Brown noted that under *Canton*, a plaintiff could establish that a deficient training program that operated over time and failed to prevent multiple constitutional violations gave municipal actors sufficient notice that continuing the program constituted deliberate indifference to the constitutional violations that resulted. *Brown*, 520

---

[7] Although short forms of case names usually do not refer to geographical names or common litigants, the Supreme Court has referred to *City of Canton v. Harris* as *Canton* in subsequent cases and that use is followed here. See, e.g., Bd. of Cty. Comm'rs v. Brown, 520 U.S. 397 (1997).

U.S. at 407. But this type of claim was irrelevant in *Brown* because the plaintiff did not allege a generally defective hiring scheme—just a single bad decision. As the *Brown* Court read *Canton,* proof that inadequate training had caused a single violation could also serve as the basis of a claim, if it was "accompanied by a showing that a municipality has failed to train its employees to handle recurring situations presenting an obvious potential for such a violation." *Id.* at 409. But the *Brown* Court suggested that it was unlikely that a single violation could similarly establish a defective hiring claim. In doing so, it set a stringent standard for hiring claims:

> As our decision in *Canton* makes clear, "deliberate indifference" is a stringent standard of fault, requiring proof that a municipal actor disregarded a known or obvious consequence of his action. Unlike the risk from a particular glaring omission in a training regimen, the risk from a single instance of inadequate screening of an applicant's background is not "obvious" in the abstract; rather, it depends upon the background of the applicant. A lack of scrutiny may increase the likelihood that an unfit officer will be hired, and that the unfit officer will, when placed in a particular position to affect the rights of citizens, act improperly. But that is only a generalized showing of risk. The fact that inadequate scrutiny of an applicant's background would make a violation of rights more *likely* cannot alone give rise to an inference that a policymaker's failure to scrutinize the record of a particular applicant produced a specific constitutional violation. . . .
>
> We assume that a jury could properly find in this case that Sheriff Moore's assessment of Burns' background was inadequate. Sheriff Moore's own testimony indicated that he did not inquire into the underlying conduct or the disposition of any of the misdemeanor charges reflected on Burns' record before hiring him. But this showing of an instance of inadequate screening is not enough to establish "deliberate indifference." . . . Only where adequate scrutiny of an applicant's background would lead a reasonable policymaker to conclude that the plainly obvious consequence of the decision to hire the applicant would be the deprivation of a third party's federally protected right can the official's failure to adequately scrutinize the applicant's background constitute "deliberate indifference." . . .
>
> . . . [A] finding of culpability simply cannot depend on the mere probability that any officer inadequately screened will inflict any constitutional injury. Rather, it must depend on a finding that *this* officer was highly likely to inflict the *particular* injury suffered by the plaintiff. . . .
>
> Even assuming without deciding that proof of a single instance of inadequate screening could ever trigger municipal liability, the evidence in this case was insufficient to support a finding that, in hiring Burns, Sheriff Moore disregarded a known or obvious risk of injury. . . .
>
> The fact that Burns had pleaded guilty to traffic offenses and other misdemeanors may well have made him an extremely poor candidate for reserve deputy. Had Sheriff Moore fully reviewed Burns' record, he might have come to precisely that conclusion. But unless he would necessarily have reached that decision *because* Burns' use of excessive force would have been a plainly obvious consequence of the hiring decision, Sheriff Moore's inadequate scrutiny of Burns' record cannot constitute "deliberate indifference" to respondent's federally protected right to be free from a use of excessive force. . . .
>
> Cases involving constitutional injuries allegedly traceable to an ill-considered hiring decision pose the greatest risk that a municipality will be held liable for an injury

that it did not cause. In the broadest sense, every injury is traceable to a hiring decision. Where a court fails to adhere to rigorous requirements of culpability and causation, municipal liability collapses into *respondeat superior* liability. As we recognized in *Monell* and have repeatedly reaffirmed, Congress did not intend municipalities to be held liable unless *deliberate* action attributable to the municipality directly caused a deprivation of federal rights.

Id. at 410–415. The Court found the plaintiff's evidence inadequate to meet this standard and therefore concluded that Bryan County was not liable for her injuries.

NOTES AND QUESTIONS

1. *Failure-to-screen claims.* How does *Brown* refine the standards for proving a city's deliberate indifference in the context of failure-to-screen claims? In practice, after *Brown*, plaintiffs alleging inadequate screening almost always must establish a pattern of constitutional violations resulting from a hiring program implemented over time, and they must establish a close connection between the information that would have been discovered or considered in adequate screening and the eventual constitutional violation that occurred.

2. *After* Brown. By extending *Canton* to the failure to screen potential employees adequately, *Brown* also implicitly recognized the possibility of claims for other practices that cause constitutional violations, such as a failure to supervise or to discipline officers properly. But if *Brown* leaves the door open, it is only a crack. It is a rare plaintiff who can meet the standard *Brown* and *Canton* set for establishing deliberate indifference.

3. *High bar.* Commentators frequently point out that the effect of these cases is to establish extreme obstacles to municipal liability. Fred Smith suggests that the bar is so high that municipalities effectively have "local sovereign immunity":

> It has been roughly three decades since the Court has ruled that a municipal policy caused a constitutional violation. . . . While the outcome in lower courts is more mixed, the municipal causation requirement nonetheless often inoculates local governments from accountability, including for conduct that would render them liable for violations of state law.

Fred Smith, *Local Sovereign Immunity*, 116 Colum. L. Rev. 409, 414 (2016).

4. *Practical barriers.* The *legal* barriers to proving municipal liability established in *Canton* and *Brown* also create *practical* obstacles for those who would sue cities. To discover and establish a pattern, plaintiffs usually need extensive discovery. Moreover, to establish that the training or screening was inadequate, they usually need to hire experts who can say what the city should have done. Discovery and experts make municipal liability claims expensive to bring. Although contingency and attorneys' fees are possible for successful claims, they are often insufficient to motivate the investment necessary to take on such a case.

5. *Federalism concerns.* States provide the primary law governing hiring and training in police departments. At the end of the *Brown* opinion, the Court justified its reasoning by arguing, "A failure to apply stringent culpability and causation requirements raises serious federalism concerns, in that it risks constitutionalizing

particular hiring requirements that States have themselves elected not to impose." 540 U.S. at 415. What is wrong with holding police hiring and training unconstitutional even when it complies with state law? How is that different from what the *Garner* Court did in holding Memphis's use-of-force policy unconstitutional, even though it complied with Tennessee law?

6. *Consequences of the municipal liability standard.* If municipal liability is possible in theory but rarely achievable, what effect might that have on the ratio between the costs of constitutional litigation and its benefits? On the likelihood that civil liability will prevent constitutional violations by officers?

7. *Reintroducing* respondeat superior. The barriers to liability in *Brown* are imposed in the name of ensuring that cities are held liable only for the constitutional violations that they cause. Many commentators, and some Supreme Court justices, argue the Court was wrong in rejecting *respondeat superior* liability in *Monell* and that it should reconsider its conclusion. Justice Breyer summarized his argument along these lines (joined by Justices Stevens and Ginsburg) in his dissent in *Brown*:

> The soundness of the original principle is doubtful. The original principle has generated a body of interpretive law that is so complex that the law has become difficult to apply. Factual and legal changes have divorced the law from the distinction's apparent original purposes. And there may be only a handful of individuals or groups that have significantly relied upon perpetuation of the original distinction. If all this is so, later law has made the original distinction, not simply wrong, but obsolete and a potential source of confusion.

520 U.S. at 431.

After all, departments, which is to say cities, strongly influence almost every aspect of an officer's incentives and capacity to comply with the law. They determine policies, hiring, training, equipment, supervision, support, assignments, promotion standards, discipline, and, to a significant degree, culture. Even if not every plaintiff can prove that a city deliberately caused a constitutional violation, it is a rare violation that is not caused in significant part by a department's decisions. Departments are also often better situated to prevent constitutional violations than individual officers, who cannot easily control how much training, backup, or time they have in handling an incident. Is there something wrong with putting liability on the actor that can best avoid the problem? What consequences might introducing *respondeat superior* liability for municipalities have? How could it be done and by whom?

A Problem: Getting Tased in Washington, California

Imagine you are a sole practitioner who occasionally brings civil rights cases. A potential client, Cal Crown, came into your office last week with his face bandaged. He claimed that a Washington (Cal.) Police Department (WPD) officer used excessive force against him during an arrest. Crown admits that on the day he was arrested, he grabbed a cellphone sitting next to a woman on a bench in Washington Park and took off running. WPD Officer Ed Elkins, who was patrolling the area, saw Crown and caught up with him as he left the park. Officer Elkins arrested Crown, handcuffing him behind the back. As they walked to the patrol car, Crown started dragging his feet and refusing to move. Officer Elkins pushed him along and told him to cooperate, and when Crown continued to hang back, Elkins stepped back and shot him with his Taser. Crown broke his nose and an eye socket when he hit the pavement.

In your initial investigation, you learn that two years ago, when crime spiked in Washington, Washington's mayor pressured WPD Chief Steve Schuler to fill empty positions in the department. To expand the hiring pool, Schuler told his command staff to consider candidates with significant criminal records so long as their past crimes did not include felonies. Previously, the only convictions he had allowed for new hires were traffic offenses. The department hired four officers, including Officer Elkins, who had prior convictions for misdemeanor assault. Elkins' conviction resulted from an altercation in a bar. The four officers received standard basic training, including training on the *Graham* and *Garner* standards governing the use of force.

A year ago, the Washington City Council provided funds for Tasers for all WPD officers. Before distributing the Tasers, Chief Schuler arranged for a training session in which the officers were taught how to use a Taser and instructed not to use it against children or pregnant women or to shoot anyone in the chest. Since the Tasers were distributed, two of the other four officers with criminal records have been accused of using them to end nonviolent standoffs with traffic suspects. No other WPD officers have been accused of inappropriately deploying a Taser.

Although you have read the law in this chapter, you have not otherwise had time to research relevant precedent. Crown is coming in again today. Now that you have had a chance to do an initial investigation of the case, he wants you to give him an idea of whom he can sue for damages under §1983, what the obstacles to those claims are likely to be, and whether you think such claims could ultimately be successful. What do you think?

D.   *Special Issues in Civil Liability*

1.   **Federal Officials and *Bivens* Actions**

Section 1983 authorizes suits against state and local officials. That includes the majority of sworn law enforcement officers in the United States, who work for state and local agencies, including municipal police departments, county sheriffs' offices, and state police departments. But it does not reach the more than 100,000 federal law enforcement officers in the United States empowered to carry firearms and make arrests. These officers work on immigration and customs inspections, detain prisoners, and provide security for courts, among other duties. Most work for U.S. Customs and Border Protection, the Federal Bureau of Investigation, the Federal Bureau of Prisons, and U.S. Immigration and Customs Enforcement, but there are also dozens of other federal law enforcement agencies, ranging from the Drug Enforcement Agency and Secret Service to the Amtrak Police and (my personal favorite) the U.S. National Zoological Park Police.

Although §1983 suits are unavailable to plaintiffs whose rights have been violated by federal law enforcement officers, the Supreme Court recognized an implied federal cause of action against federal officers for damages arising from Fourth Amendment violations in *Bivens v. Six Unknown Named Agents of Federal Bureau of Narcotics*, 403 U.S. 388 (1971). The Court subsequently also recognized implied causes of action for Fifth and Eighth Amendment violations by federal officers, Carlson v. Green, 446 U.S. 14 (1980); Davis v. Passman, 442 U.S. 228 (1979), and it has assumed without deciding the availability of an implied damages remedy for First Amendment violations, see, e.g., Ashcroft v. Iqbal, 556 U.S. 662 (2009). Although the Court has shown significant reluctance to expand *Bivens* to new contexts or new categories of defendants, see Ziglar v. Abbasi, 137 S. Ct. 1843 (2017), *Bivens* actions remain an important analog to §1983 in the federal law enforcement context, and the doctrine governing these actions closely mirrors the law arising from §1983 actions.

Since *Bivens*, some states have recognized *Bivens*-type causes of action arising from their own constitutions when state tort law and statutory remedies are unavailable. These implied causes of action provide an additional mechanism for holding state and local officials accountable when officers violate state constitutional law.

2. Attorneys' Fees

One obstacle to bringing a §1983 suit is finding a lawyer. To encourage plaintiffs to enforce §1983, Congress addressed this issue in the Civil Rights Attorney's Fees Award Act of 1976, codified as 42 U.S.C. §1988(b). Section 1988, as this statute is usually known, grants federal courts discretion to award reasonable attorneys' fees to the prevailing party in a §1983 lawsuit. To determine appropriate fees, courts start by calculating the number of hours attorneys reasonably expended. They then multiply that number by a reasonable hourly rate and adjust for other attorney- and case-specific factors. See City of Riverside v. Rivera, 477 U.S. 561 (1986).

When a plaintiff has a winning high-value claim, he usually will not need a fees statute to find a lawyer. The possibility of contingency fees will be incentive enough. An attorneys' fees regime such as §1988 provides an incentive for accepting strong cases that offer little prospect of financial gain, either because the damages are low or because the plaintiff seeks equitable rather than monetary relief. (Suits for equitable relief are discussed further in Chapter 15.) Although the statutory availability of attorneys' fees has helped expand the pool of skilled lawyers willing to bring civil rights cases, the Court has narrowly interpreted what it means for a party to prevail, limiting the availability of fees and therefore the availability of attorneys in low-damages cases.

3. Release-Dismissal Agreements

Section 1983 litigation is intended to deter constitutional violations by making those violations expensive for those who commit them. But reducing constitutional violations is not the only way for local governments to limit the financial impact of §1983 litigation and judgments. The next case considers another method: "paying" potential plaintiffs not to sue by dismissing criminal charges against them.

TOWN OF NEWTON v. RUMERY
480 U.S. 386 (1987)

JUSTICE POWELL announced the judgment of the Court and delivered the opinion of the Court with respect to Parts I, II, III–A, IV, and V, and an opinion with respect to Part III–B, in which THE CHIEF JUSTICE, JUSTICE WHITE, and JUSTICE SCALIA join.

The question in this case is whether a court properly may enforce an agreement in which a criminal defendant releases his right to file an action under 42 U.S.C. §1983 in return for a prosecutor's dismissal of pending criminal charges.

I

In 1983, a grand jury in Rockingham County, New Hampshire, indicted David Champy for aggravated felonious sexual assault. Respondent Bernard Rumery, a friend of Champy's, read about the charges in a local newspaper. Seeking information about the charges, he telephoned Mary Deary, who was acquainted with both Rumery and Champy. Coincidentally, Deary had been the victim of the assault in question and was expected to be the principal witness against Champy. The record does not reveal directly the date or substance of this conversation between Rumery and Deary, but Deary apparently was disturbed by the call. On March 12, according to police records, she called David Barrett, the Chief of Police for the town of Newton. She told him that Rumery was trying to force her to drop the charges against Champy. Rumery talked to Deary again on May 11. The substance of this conversation also is disputed. Rumery claims that Deary called him and that she raised the subject of Champy's difficulties. According to the police records, however, Deary told Chief Barrett that Rumery had threatened that, if Deary went forward on the Champy case, she would "end up like" two women who recently had been murdered in Lowell, Massachusetts. Barrett arrested Rumery and accused him of tampering with a witness in violation of N.H. Rev. Stat. Ann. §641:5(I)(b) (1986), a Class B felony.

Rumery promptly retained Stephen Woods, an experienced criminal defense attorney. Woods contacted Brian Graf, the Deputy County Attorney for Rockingham County. He warned Graf that he "had better [dismiss] these charges, because we're going to win them and after that we're going to sue." After further discussions, Graf and Woods reached an agreement, under which Graf would dismiss the charges against Rumery if Rumery would agree not to sue the town, its officials, or Deary for any harm caused by the arrest. All parties agreed that one factor in Graf's decision not to prosecute Rumery was Graf's desire to protect Deary from the trauma she would suffer if she were forced to testify. . . . Rumery . . . signed the agreement. The criminal charges were dropped.

Ten months later, on April 13, 1984, Rumery filed an action under §1983 in the Federal District Court for the District of New Hampshire. He alleged that the town and its officers had violated his constitutional rights by arresting him, defaming him, and imprisoning him falsely. The defendants filed a motion to dismiss, relying on the release-dismissal agreement as an affirmative defense. Rumery argued that the agreement was unenforceable because it violated public policy. . . .

II

. . . The agreement purported to waive a right to sue conferred by a federal statute. The question whether the policies underlying that statute may in some circumstances render that waiver unenforceable is a question of federal law. . . . The relevant principle is well established: a promise is unenforceable if the interest in its enforcement is outweighed in the circumstances by a public policy harmed by enforcement of the agreement.

III

The Court of Appeals concluded that the public interests related to release-dismissal agreements justified a *per se* rule of invalidity. . . . [A]lthough we agree that in some cases these agreements may infringe important interests of the criminal defendant and of society as a whole, we do not believe that the mere possibility of harm to these interests calls for a *per se* rule.

A

Rumery's first objection to release-dismissal agreements is that they are inherently coercive. He argues that it is unfair to present a criminal defendant with a choice between facing criminal charges and waiving his right to sue under §1983. We agree that some release-dismissal agreements may not be the product of an informed and voluntary decision. The risk, publicity, and expense of a criminal trial may intimidate a defendant, even if he believes his defense is meritorious. But this possibility does not justify invalidating *all* such agreements. In other contexts criminal defendants are required to make difficult choices that effectively waive constitutional rights. For example, it is well settled that plea bargaining does not violate the Constitution even though a guilty plea waives important constitutional rights. We see no reason to believe that release-dismissal agreements pose a more coercive choice than other situations we have accepted. . . .

In many cases a defendant's choice to enter into a release-dismissal agreement will reflect a highly rational judgment that the certain benefits of escaping criminal prosecution exceed the speculative benefits of prevailing in a civil action. Rumery's voluntary decision to enter this agreement exemplifies such a judgment. Rumery is a sophisticated businessman. He was not in jail and was represented by an experienced criminal lawyer, who drafted the agreement. Rumery considered the agreement for three days before signing it. The benefits of the agreement to Rumery are obvious: he gained immunity from criminal prosecution in consideration of abandoning a civil suit that he may well have lost.

Because Rumery voluntarily waived his right to sue under §1983, the public interest opposing involuntary waiver of constitutional rights is no reason to hold this agreement invalid. Moreover, we find that the possibility of coercion in the making of similar agreements insufficient by itself to justify a *per se* rule against release-dismissal bargains. If there is such a reason, it must lie in some external public interest necessarily injured by release-dismissal agreements.

B

As we noted above, the Court of Appeals held that all release-dismissal agreements offend public policy because it believed these agreements "tempt prosecutors to trump up charges in reaction to a defendant's civil rights claim, suppress evidence of police misconduct, and leave unremedied deprivations of constitutional rights." 778 F.2d at 69. We can agree that in some cases there may be a substantial basis for this concern. It is true, of course, that §1983 actions to vindicate civil rights may further significant public interests. But it is important to remember that Rumery had no public duty to institute a §1983 action merely to further the public's interest in revealing police misconduct. Congress has confined the decision to bring such actions to the injured individuals, not to the public at large. Thus, we hesitate to elevate more diffused public interests above Rumery's considered decision that he would benefit personally from the agreement. . . .

The vindication of constitutional rights and the exposure of official misconduct are not the only concerns implicated by §1983 suits. No one suggests that all such suits are meritorious. Many are marginal and some are frivolous. Yet even when the risk of ultimate liability is negligible, the burden of defending such lawsuits is substantial. Counsel may be retained by the official, as well as the governmental entity. Preparation for trial, and the trial itself, will require the time and attention of the defendant officials, to the detriment of their public duties. In some cases litigation will extend over a period of years. This diversion of officials from their normal duties and the inevitable expense of defending even unjust claims is distinctly not in the public interest. To the extent release-dismissal agreements protect public officials from the burdens of defending such unjust claims, they further this important public interest.

A *per se* rule invalidating release-dismissal agreements also assumes that prosecutors will seize the opportunity for wrongdoing. . . . Our decisions . . . uniformly have recognized that courts normally must defer to prosecutorial decisions as to whom to prosecute. The reasons for judicial deference are well known. Prosecutorial charging decisions are rarely simple. In addition to assessing the strength and importance of a case, prosecutors also must consider other tangible and intangible factors, such as government enforcement priorities. See Wayte v. United States, 470 U.S. 598, 607(1985). Finally, they also must decide how best to allocate the scarce resources of a criminal justice system that simply cannot accommodate the litigation of every serious criminal charge. Because these decisions "are not readily susceptible to the kind of analysis the courts are competent to undertake," we have been "properly hesitant to examine the decision whether to prosecute." *Id.* at 607–608. . . . [T]radition and experience justify our belief that the great majority of prosecutors will be faithful to their duty. Indeed, the merit of this view is illustrated by this case, where the only evidence of prosecutorial misconduct is the agreement itself.

Because release-dismissal agreements may further legitimate prosecutorial and public interests, we reject the Court of Appeals' holding that all such agreements are invalid *per se.*

IV

Turning to the agreement presented by this case, we conclude that the District Court's decision to enforce the agreement was correct. As we have noted, it is clear that Rumery voluntarily entered the agreement. Moreover, in this case the prosecutor had an independent, legitimate reason to make this agreement directly related to his prosecutorial responsibilities. The agreement foreclosed both the civil and criminal trials concerning Rumery, in which Deary would have been a key witness. She therefore was spared the public scrutiny and embarrassment she would have endured if she had had to testify in either of those cases. Both the prosecutor and the defense attorney testified in the District Court that this was a significant consideration in the prosecutor's decision.

In sum, we conclude that this agreement was voluntary, that there is no evidence of prosecutorial misconduct, and that enforcement of this agreement would not adversely affect the relevant public interests.

V

We reverse the judgment of the Court of Appeals and remand the case to the District Court for dismissal of the complaint.

It is so ordered.

[Justice O'Connor's opinion, concurring in part and concurring in the judgment, is omitted.]

JUSTICE STEVENS, with whom JUSTICE BRENNAN, JUSTICE MARSHALL and JUSTICE BLACKMUN join, dissenting.

The question whether the release-dismissal agreement signed by respondent is unenforceable is much more complex than the Court's opinion indicates. . . . Even an intelligent and informed, but completely innocent, person accused of crime should not be required to choose between a threatened indictment and trial, with their attendant publicity and the omnipresent possibility of wrongful conviction, and surrendering the right to a civil remedy against individuals who have violated his or her constitutional rights. Moreover, the prosecutor's representation of competing and possibly conflicting interests compounds the dangerous potential of release-dismissal agreements. . . .

I . . .

. . . By simultaneously establishing and limiting the defendant's criminal liability, plea bargains delicately balance individual and social advantage. This mutuality of advantage does not exist in release-dismissal agreements. A defendant entering a release-dismissal agreement is forced to waive claims based on official conduct under color of state law, in exchange merely for the assurance that the State will not prosecute him for conduct for which he has made no admission of wrongdoing. The State is spared the necessity of going to trial, but its willingness to drop the charge completely indicates that it might not have proceeded with the prosecution in any event. No social interest in the punishment of wrongdoers is satisfied; the only interest vindicated is that of resolving once and for all the question of §1983 liability.

. . . Although the outcome of a criminal proceeding may affect the value of the civil claim, as a matter of law the claims are quite distinct. Even a guilty defendant may be entitled to receive damages for physical abuse, and conversely, the fact that a defendant is ultimately acquitted is entirely consistent with the possibility that the police had probable cause to arrest him and did not violate any of his constitutional rights.

. . . Experience teaches us that *some* §1983 suits in which release-dismissal agreements are sought are meritorious. Whatever the true value of a §1983 claim may be, a defendant who is required to give up such a claim in exchange for a dismissal of a criminal charge is being forced to pay a price that is unrelated to his possible wrongdoing as reflected in that charge. . . .

Thus, even though respondent's decision in this case was deliberate, informed, and voluntary, this observation does not address two distinct objections to enforcement of the release-dismissal agreement. The prosecutor's offer to drop charges if the defendant accedes to the agreement is inherently coercive; moreover, the agreement exacts a price unrelated to the character of the defendant's own conduct.

II

When the prosecutor negotiated the agreement with respondent, he represented three potentially conflicting interests. His primary duty, of course, was to represent the sovereign's interest in the evenhanded and effective enforcement of its criminal laws. In addition, as the covenant demonstrates, he sought to represent the interests of the town of Newton and its Police Department in connection with their possible civil liability to respondent. Finally, as the inclusion of Mary Deary as a covenantee indicates, the prosecutor also represented the interest of a potential witness who allegedly accused both respondent and a mutual friend of separate instances of wrongdoing. . . .

. . . There is . . . an obvious potential conflict between the prosecutor's duty to enforce the law and his objective of protecting members of the Police Department who are accused of unlawful conduct. The public is entitled to have the prosecutor's decision to go forward with a criminal case, or to dismiss it, made independently of his concerns about the potential damages liability of the Police Department. It is equally clear that this separation of functions cannot be achieved if the prosecutor may use the threat of criminal prosecution as a weapon to obtain a favorable termination of a civil claim against the police.

In negotiating a release-dismissal agreement, the prosecutor inevitably represents both the public and the police. When release agreements are enforceable, consideration of the police interest in avoiding damages liability severely hampers the prosecutor's ability to conform to the strictures of professional responsibility in deciding whether to prosecute. In particular, the possibility that the suspect will execute a covenant not to sue in exchange for a decision not to prosecute may well encourage a prosecutor to bring or to continue prosecutions in violation of his or her duty to "refrain from prosecuting a charge that the prosecutor knows is not supported by probable cause." ABA Model Rules of Professional Conduct, Rule 3.8(a) (1984). . . .

It may well be true that a full development of all the relevant facts would provide a legitimate justification for enforcing the release-dismissal agreement. In my opinion, however, the burden of developing those facts rested on the defendants in the §1983 litigation, and that burden has not been met by mere conjecture and speculation concerning the emotional distress of one reluctant witness.

III

Because this is the first case of this kind that the Court has reviewed, I am hesitant to adopt an absolute rule invalidating all such agreements.[22] I am, however,

---

[22] It seems likely, however, that the costs of having courts determine the validity of release-dismissal agreements will outweigh the benefits that most agreements can be expected to provide. A court may enforce such an agreement only after a careful inquiry into the circumstances under which the plaintiff

persuaded that the federal policies reflected in the enactment and enforcement of §1983 mandate a strong presumption against the enforceability of such agreements and that the presumption is not overcome in this case by the facts or by any of the policy concerns discussed by the plurality. The very existence of the statute identifies the important federal interests in providing a remedy for the violation of constitutional rights and in having the merits of such claims resolved openly by an impartial adjudicator rather than *sub silentio* by a prosecutor whose primary objective in entering release-dismissal agreements is definitely not to ensure that all meritorious §1983 claims prevail. The interest in vindication of constitutional violations unquestionably outweighs the interest in avoiding the expense and inconvenience of defending unmeritorious claims. Paradoxically, the plurality seems more sensitive to that burden than to the cost to the public and the individual of denying relief in meritorious cases. In short, the plurality's decision seems to rest on the unstated premise that §1983 litigation imposes a net burden on society. If that were a correct assessment of the statute, it should be repealed. Unless that is done, however, we should respect the congressional decision to attach greater importance to the benefits associated with access to a federal remedy than to the burdens of defending these cases. . . .

Accordingly, although I am not prepared to endorse all of the reasoning of the Court of Appeals, I would affirm its judgment.

NOTES AND QUESTIONS

1. *Holding.* What is the holding of *Rumery*? What does *Rumery* indicate about when release-dismissal agreements may be invalid? Would this agreement have been invalid if there had been no testimony that the prosecutor wanted to spare Deary from testifying?

2. *No advantage?* The dissent suggests that criminal defendants do not benefit much from release-dismissal agreements. So why do they enter them? Imagine that when the officer banged your head on the car roof, as described in the introduction to the chapter, you were being arrested for driving under the influence. It was your second offense, so conviction likely would mean losing your driver's license for one year, and you know you are guilty. Because you were aggressive and pretty obnoxious when the officer arrested you, you think you might not appear sympathetic to a civil jury in a damages action. Do you think you would benefit from a release-dismissal agreement? Do you want that option?

---

signed the agreement and into the legitimacy of the prosecutor's objective in entering into the agreement. This inquiry will occupy a significant amount of the court's and the parties' time, and will subject prosecutorial decisionmaking to judicial review. But the only benefit most of these agreements will provide is another line of defense for prosecutors and police in §1983 actions. This extra protection is unnecessary because prosecutors already enjoy absolute immunity and because police have been afforded qualified immunity. See Harlow v. Fitzgerald, 457 U.S. 800 (1982). Thus, the vast majority of "marginal or frivolous" §1983 suits can be dismissed under existing standards with little more burden on the defendants than is entailed in defending a release-dismissal agreement. . . . In most cases, if social and judicial resources are to be expended at all, they would seem better spent on an evaluation of the merits of the §1983 claim rather than on a detour into the enforceability of a release-dismissal agreement.

3. *Protecting the public interest?* Do release-dismissal agreements harm the public interest even if they benefit the individuals who enter them? Does it matter to you that no victim is required to bring a §1983 suit? Is it different when a potential plaintiff with a legitimate §1983 claim does not bring a suit because (a) he got a deal in a criminal case not to do so pursuant to an agreement; (b) no lawyer would take the case; or (c) it was not worth the hassle given the damages involved? What kinds of cases might fall into each category?

4. *Challenging agreements.* Imagine a potential criminal defendant signs a release-dismissal agreement, and wants to adhere to it, because he believes it serves his interests in avoiding conviction. However, the agreement reflects prosecutorial misconduct and arguably disserves the public interest. Who could challenge the agreement? On what basis?

5. *Prosecutorial misconduct?* Both the majority and the dissent seem to agree that prosecutorial misconduct should invalidate an agreement. What do they mean by prosecutorial misconduct?

6. *Before charges.* What about a release/nonprosecution agreement before charges are brought? Should that be treated as valid under *Rumery?* Does that kind of agreement raise different concerns?

7. *Who pays?* Both the majority and the dissent seem to assume that these agreements protect police officers and departments. But if officers are always indemnified, then cities pay both the cost of a §1983 suit and the price of crime undeterred by dropped charges. Should cities (or individual prosecutors) get to choose whether they pay the costs of police misconduct in dollars paid out to plaintiffs or in lost criminal deterrence from release-dismissal agreements? If not, and courts continue to allow these agreements, should state legislatures step in? In what way?

8. *A remedy for misconduct?* Could you argue that release-dismissal agreements are a good thing? City officials might pressure a prosecutor to enter a release-dismissal agreement to avoid paying the costs of litigation and damages for a §1983 claim. Prosecutors receive no direct benefit from a §1983 claim release, and they are professionally harmed (if just a little) by dropping criminal charges. So maybe prosecutors would pressure police officers to stop engaging in constitutional violations to avoid having to enter such agreements. What needs to be true for this argument to work? If you wanted to maximize their potential to work this way, what regulations would you impose on release agreements and prosecutors?

E.   Does §1983 Liability Deter Police Misconduct?

We don't know much about whether the risk of §1983 litigation reduces constitutional violations. Here are some reasons why §1983 suits might not work as well as one might hope.

1.   Constitutional Violations Do Not Reliably Lead to Damages

As this chapter suggests, the law stymies many would-be §1983 plaintiffs. Section 1983 only addresses police misconduct that violates the Constitution. Individual officers are entitled to qualified immunity for many unconstitutional actions. Suing supervisors and chiefs requires establishing at least deliberate indifference or reckless action rather than negligence—and maybe more. Suing a city or department requires showing that the city had a deliberate municipal policy or custom that caused the misconduct. As a result of the legal barriers, many people who believe their rights were violated by the police never bring suit, and many of those who do lose. In either case, the police may commit misconduct and no one pays.

2. Departments and Officers May Not Reform When Judgments Are Paid

Some plaintiffs win at trial or settle favorably, costing some cities millions of dollars each year. Still, civil suits for damages might do little to change future police conduct. Officers and departments do not like to be sued, but neither officers nor departments suffer direct financial consequences from lawsuits, which instead are borne by cities (and insurers). See Joanna C. Schwartz, *How Governments Pay: Lawsuits, Budgets, and Police Reform*, 63 UCLA L. Rev. 1144 (2016).

If city officials paid a high *political* price for judgments that affect the municipal budget, they might pressure police chiefs and, through them, officers to comply with the law. But only in high-profile cases and perhaps in small jurisdictions—where civil judgments are visible enough to voters—do civil damages judgments translate easily into costs for political actors. In other cases, a city may pay without ramification for politicians or police chiefs, in part because the public is unlikely to notice. See Daryl J. Levinson, *Making Government Pay: Markets, Politics, and the Allocation of Constitutional Costs*, 67 U. Chi. L. Rev. 345 (2000). Thus, departments often do not bother to track common causes of litigation. See Joanna C. Schwartz, *Myths and Mechanics of Deterrence: The Role of Lawsuits in Law Enforcement Decisionmaking*, 57 UCLA L. Rev. 1023 (2010). Nor do they usually consider lawsuits or judgments when evaluating officer performance. Under these circumstances, it is hard to see how the threat of civil suits could create strong incentives for departments to adopt reforms or for individual officers to take steps to avoid violations.

3. Reform Efforts May Not Be Effective

Even when judgments create an incentive to reform, for reform to occur, the benefits of reducing §1983 judgments would have to exceed the costs of reform. Unfortunately, reducing police misconduct often requires a major departmental overhaul to change policies, training, supervision, recordkeeping, and complaint and disciplinary systems. Such reform can be costly and protracted, and it does not always work. In addition, civil service laws and collective bargaining can impose significant additional burdens on police departments that try to reform by managing, disciplining, or firing officers who commit misconduct. The consequence is that the costs of real reform may be greater than its benefits for a department and its leaders, even factoring in liability.

To make matters worse, many of the costs of reform are immediate, whereas the benefits take place in the future. Given elections for political actors and short average tenures for police chiefs, both politicians and police chiefs may discount future costs and benefits more than the public interest would warrant. After all, if they lose their jobs, future benefits of reform will not accrue to them.

These conditions might make it attractive to public officials to make superficial reforms. Superficial reforms can help reduce the political costs that arise from §1983 payouts, by making officials look like they are doing something, without requiring the kind of investment that would be politically costly now and likely to yield benefits in reduced misconduct and liability awards mostly in the future, if at all.

For these reasons and others, §1983 actions for damages under current law may fail to deter misconduct by the police much of the time. What should we make of this fact? Given what you have read, what reforms might improve the situation?

F.   Final Note: Do Civil Damages Achieve Justice?

In July 2014, New York Police Department officers tried to arrest Eric Garner in Staten Island for selling cigarettes unlawfully. When Garner refused to be handcuffed, officers took him to the ground, with one, Daniel Pantaleo, holding Garner by the neck. On the ground, officers held Garner down and handcuffed him, while he repeatedly said, "I can't breathe." He lost consciousness and was pronounced dead an hour later at the hospital. A video of the incident went viral on the internet within hours.

Many were outraged by the incident, and several thousand people participated in protests and rallies to condemn the police use of force against Garner. Critics were further enraged several months later when a Staten Island grand jury refused to indict Officer Pantaleo for using what many viewed as an illegal chokehold. A year after the incident, Garner's family reached a civil settlement with the City of New York, the police department, and several officers. They received $5.9 million in damages to resolve a wrongful-death claim over Garner's killing, the largest settlement ever paid out by the City of New York for a death at the hands of police officers.

Eric Garner and several of his children.

In evaluating the meaning of civil damages actions, consider these responses to the settlement:

- "Financial compensation is certainly not everything, and it can't bring Mr. Garner back. But it is our way of creating balance and giving a family a certain closure." (New York City Comptroller Scott M. Stringer)
- "No sum of money can make this family whole, but hopefully the Garner family can find some peace and finality from today's settlement." (New York City Mayor Bill de Blasio)
- "[T]his settlement is one step of many that our city must take to ensure that no more families need suffer this pain." (City Council Speaker Melissa Mark-Viverito)
- "[H]aving to pay out all that money isn't good. The city is paying that $5.9 million out, but it's not coming outta their pocket—it's coming out of our taxes." (New York City resident Bea Arroyo)
- The settlement is "a slap in the face to the New York Police Department." (State Conservative Party Chairman Mike Long)
- "In my view, the city has chosen to abandon its fiscal responsibility to all of its citizens and genuflect to the select few who curry favor with the city government." (Head of the Sergeants Benevolent Association Ed Mullins)
- "It's not 'mission accomplished,' but at least it brings a measure of justice to the family." (Lawyer for the Garner family, Jonathan C. Moore) Although the settlement included no admission of wrongdoing, Moore also noted that the amount demonstrated "an appreciation by the city that there was wrongdoing."
- "[J]ustice is measured by money going from the bank account of the City of New York to your bank account." (Civil rights lawyer Andrew G. Celli, Jr.)
- "Money is not justice. Money is a recognition of the loss of the family, but it does not deal with the criminal and other wrong done to this family and other families." (Civil rights activist and lawyer Al Sharpton, Jr.)
- "It's a buyout without justice. . . . Where's the justice at?" (Jewel Miller, the mother of Garner's youngest daughter, an infant at the time of his death)
- "Don't congratulate us; this is not a victory. The victory will come when we get justice. . . . We're asking the federal government, which we've been asking them for a whole year, to come and take Eric Garner's case." (Garner's mother, Gwen Carr)
- "Justice is when somebody is held accountable for what they do." (Garner's daughter, Emerald Snipes)

These quotes were reported in J. David Goodman & Nikita Stewart, *Eric Garner's Family Says Settlement Will Not Stall Push for Police Reform,* N.Y. Times (July 14, 2015); Frank Rosario et al., *Taxpayers' Response to Garner Settlement: He "Isn't a Martyr,"* N.Y. Post (July 14, 2015); Associated Press, *The Latest: De Blasio: Garner's Death Could Bring Change,* Wash. Times (July 14, 2015); J. David Goodman, *Eric Garner Case Is Settled by New York City for $5.9 Million,* N.Y. Times (July 13, 2015); Joe Tacopino et al., *Union Head Blasts City's $5.9M Settlement in Eric Garner Case,* N.Y. Post (July 13, 2015); *City Announces $5.9 Million Settlement for Eric Garner's Family,* CBS N.Y. (July 13, 2015).

With whom do you agree? How should we think about the relationship between compensating the victim, changing police practices, and "justice"?

Chapter 14

Prosecuting the Police

Imagine a police officer near the end of his shift stops in a bar, has several stiff drinks, and then drives his patrol car back to the station house to finish his paperwork. Or an officer sexually assaults a young runaway he picked up before taking him home. Or an officer accepts a $200 bribe during a traffic stop and lets the speeder off without a ticket. All too often, an officer is not arrested, is not prosecuted, or is not convicted. Still, no one—including the offending officers—doubts that when the officer drives under the influence, commits a sexual assault, or accepts a bribe, he commits a punishable crime.

This chapter focuses on a different kind of crime. If someone pushed you against a wall and took everything from your pockets, you would report a robbery. If you saw someone grab your neighbor from his driveway, tie his hands behind his back, throw him into a car, and drive away, you would report a kidnapping. If you saw the neighbor killed while struggling to escape, you would report a murder. The very thing that makes a police officer a police officer is that states authorize him to take actions that would be criminal under different circumstances. Yet police power is not unlimited: Police are sometimes prosecuted for acts that, in other contexts, they are permitted to do. This chapter will help you understand the legal standards that determine when and how the criminal justice system decides that officers have broken the law. Because police officers are prosecuted under both state and federal law, the chapter considers each in turn.

As you read, consider that criminal prosecution represents more than simply one more remedy for police misconduct. When in 2014 an officer in Ferguson, Missouri, shot and killed Michael Brown, an 18-year-old Black man, demonstrators took to the streets in the small St. Louis suburb. Protests quickly spread to other cities, becoming a flashpoint for pent-up anger about race and police violence. Protesters condemned the shootings of Black men with signs reading, "Hands Up. Don't Shoot." They also demanded justice. For many of those protesters, justice did not mean that the Ferguson Police Department chief should step down, or that the city should reform the department, or that the city should pay damages to Brown's family—although many wanted and expected all of those things. Instead, in Ferguson, in St. Louis, and beyond, demonstrators demanded that the officer who shot Brown, and other officers in other cities involved in other killings, be arrested and prosecuted. Something similar happened in May 2020 after George Floyd was killed by Minneapolis Police Officer Derek Chauvin, who knelt on Floyd's neck, and again in June when Rayshard Brooks was shot twice in the back by an Atlanta police officer. Protesters specifically demanded criminal charges. As one writer put it, "It's not the killings alone. It's the denial of justice, over and over, that follows. . . . In case after high-profile case, cops who kill black people aren't convicted—or, often, even indicted—when the visual evidence, and common sense, strongly suggest that they should be." Lolis Eric Elie, *It's Not Just Police Shootings That Spark Protests. It's the Denial of Justice,* Wash. Post (July 14, 2016).

In reading these materials, consider why people value criminal prosecutions so much, how the law determines who to prosecute, how we can evaluate decisions to prosecute, and whether and how you think the law governing prosecutions should be changed.

A.   State Criminal Law

When police activities satisfy the elements of criminal law, police officers are guilty of a crime unless state law provides a criminal defense. Police officers often use the same defenses available to other criminal defendants, defenses such as self-defense and mistake of fact. In addition, police officers are given special defenses. Below are some examples of state law defenses available to the police.

As you read the statutes, you might think about how Garrett Rolfe, the Atlanta officer who shot Rayshard Brooks, would fare in each state. According to video, witnesses, and reports, Officer Devin Brosnan responded to a call that a man had fallen asleep in his car in a Wendy's restaurant drive-through lane. That man was Rayshard Brooks. Brosnan woke Brooks and encouraged him to move his car. Brooks cooperated, and Brosnan called the department to send another officer to the scene. Officer Rolfe soon arrived, proceeded to question and frisk Brooks, and then performed field sobriety tests on him. Brooks cooperated and offered to leave his car and walk to his sister's home nearby. Instead, after conducting a breath test, Officer

Rolfe told Brooks that he had too much to drink to drive and started to handcuff him. Brooks resisted, and the officers struggled with him on the ground. During the struggle, Officer Brosnan pulled his Taser. Brooks struck Officer Rolfe, grabbed Brosnan's Taser, and took off running. Officer Rolfe discharged his own Taser at Brooks, and Brooks turned and fired the stolen Taser wildly in Officer Rolfe's direction. Officer Rolfe drew his handgun and fired three times at Brooks after Brooks turned and continued to run away. Rolfe hit Brooks twice in the back. Brooks was taken to a nearby hospital and died after surgery. See Malachy Browne et al., *How Rayshard Brooks Was Fatally Shot by the Atlanta Police*, N.Y. Times (June 14, 2020).

1.   The Statutes

a.   *Georgia*

Ga. Code. Ann. §16-3-20

The fact that a person's conduct is justified is a defense to prosecution for any crime based on that conduct. The defense of justification can be claimed:

(1) When the person's conduct is justified under Code Section 16-3-21, 16-3-23, 16-3-24, 16-3-25, or 16-3-26;[1] . . .

(4) When the person's conduct is reasonable and is performed in the course of making a lawful arrest; . . .

Ga. Code Ann., §16-3-21(a)

A person is justified in threatening or using force against another when and to the extent that he or she reasonably believes that such threat or force is necessary to defend himself or herself or a third person against such other's imminent use of unlawful force; however, . . . a person is justified in using force which is intended or likely to cause death or great bodily harm only if he or she reasonably believes that such force is necessary to prevent death or great bodily injury to himself or herself or a third person or to prevent the commission of a forcible felony.

Ga. Code Ann. §17-4-20(b)

Sheriffs and peace officers . . . may use deadly force to apprehend a suspected felon only when the officer reasonably believes that the suspect possesses a deadly weapon or any object, device, or instrument which, when used offensively against a person, is likely to or actually does result in serious bodily injury; when the officer reasonably believes that the suspect poses an immediate threat of physical violence to the officer or others; or when there is probable cause to believe that the suspect has committed a crime involving the infliction or threatened infliction of serious physical harm. Nothing in this Code section shall be construed so as to restrict such sheriffs or peace officers from the use of such reasonable nondeadly force as may be necessary to apprehend and arrest a suspected felon or misdemeanant. . . .

---

[1] *Ed. note:* Section 16-3-23 provides a justification defense for the use of force in defense of a habitation. Section 16-3-24 provides a justification defense for the use of force in defense of property. Section 16-3-25 makes entrapment a defense. Section 16-3-26 provides a defense for coerced actions.

b.   *Hawaii*

Haw. Rev. Stat. §703-307 (1)-(3)

(1) Subject to the provisions of this section and of section 703-310,[2] the use of force upon or toward the person of another is justifiable when the actor is making or assisting in making an arrest and the actor believes that such force is immediately necessary to effect a lawful arrest.

(2) The use of force is not justifiable under this section unless:

> **(a)** The actor makes known the purpose of the arrest or believes that it is otherwise known by or cannot reasonably be made known to the person to be arrested; and

> **(b)** When the arrest is made under a warrant, the warrant is valid or believed by the actor to be valid.

(3) The use of deadly force is not justifiable under this section unless:

> **(a)** The arrest is for a felony;

> **(b)** The person effecting the arrest is authorized to act as a law enforcement officer or is assisting a person whom he believes to be authorized to act as a law enforcement officer;

> **(c)** The actor believes that the force employed creates no substantial risk of injury to innocent persons; and

> **(d)** The actor believes that:

>> **(i)** The crimes for which the arrest is made involved conduct including the use or threatened use of deadly force; or

>> **(ii)** There is a substantial risk that the person to be arrested will cause death or serious bodily injury if his apprehension is delayed.

c.   *Alabama*

Ala. Code §13A-3-27 (a)-(c)

(a) A peace officer is justified in using that degree of physical force which he reasonably believes to be necessary, upon a person in order:

> **(1)** To make an arrest for a misdemeanor, violation or violation of a criminal ordinance, or to prevent the escape from custody of a person arrested for a misdemeanor, violation or violation of a criminal ordinance, unless the peace officer knows that the arrest is unauthorized; or

---

[2] *Ed. note:* This reference is to Hawaii's provision that, following the Model Penal Code, an actor who recklessly or negligently forms the belief that force against another is necessary cannot use a justification defense for an offense requiring recklessness or negligence:

(2) When the actor is justified under sections 703-303 to 703-309 in using force upon or toward the person of another but the actor recklessly or negligently injures or creates a risk of injury to innocent persons, the justification afforded by those sections is unavailable in a prosecution for such recklessness or negligence toward innocent persons.

(2) To defend himself or a third person from what he reasonably believes to be the use or imminent use of physical force while making or attempting to make an arrest for a misdemeanor, violation or violation of a criminal ordinance, or while preventing or attempting to prevent an escape from custody of a person who has been legally arrested for a misdemeanor, violation or violation of a criminal ordinance.

(b) A peace officer is justified in using deadly physical force upon another person when and to the extent that he reasonably believes it necessary in order:

(1) To make an arrest for a felony or to prevent the escape from custody of a person arrested for a felony, unless the officer knows that the arrest is unauthorized; or

(2) To defend himself or a third person from what he reasonably believes to be the use or imminent use of deadly physical force.

(c) Nothing in subdivision (a)(1), or (b)(1) . . . constitutes justification for reckless or criminally negligent conduct by a peace officer amounting to an offense against or with respect to persons being arrested or to innocent persons whom he is not seeking to arrest or retain in custody.

NOTES AND QUESTIONS

1. *So?* An officer is not criminally prosecutable for using force if he has a justification defense. Could Officer Rolfe be prosecuted in his home state of Georgia? Why or why not? What additional facts or law might you want to know? What about in Hawaii or Alabama?

2. *Differences.* What are the circumstances in which each state provides a justification for officers who have used deadly force? What other differences do you see between the states' laws?

3. *Two justifications.* Officers commonly use force in two circumstances: to carry out a stop or arrest successfully and to defend themselves. Some states provide officers with a defense for both activities in the same police-specific statute. Other states provide a police-specific justification statute for force used to seize a suspect and allow officers to use self-defense laws or other justification statutes for force to protect themselves or others. Recognizing that you do not have all the justification statutes for these states, can you tell in which category they each fall? Even if a state provides a single defense covering both purposes, the protection it offers may differ depending on why the officer used force. Look again at Ala. Code §13-A-3-2 (including (c)) for an example.

4. *Authorized or justified?* Do you see that Georgia authorizes force differently than the other two states? It authorizes force in one statute and provides justification defenses for force under some circumstances in others. The other two states effectively authorize force by prohibiting officers from being held liable for using it. Use-of-force law (discussed in Chapter 8) and criminal defenses to prosecution for using force are closely connected. Indeed, states often do not clearly distinguish between authorizing conduct and eliminating criminal liability for it. Still, states may protect officers from prosecution for acts that are not expressly authorized. For instance, a state may allow force only when it is *reasonably necessary* to carry out an arrest or protect the officer or another from harm, but it might provide a legal defense to any officer who *believed* that his use of force was necessary, even if that

belief is mistaken and unreasonable. Given the complexity and variety of state law, and the lack of legal development around the statutes, whether a use of force is authorized, justified, or both is not always clear.

Violent Crimes

When police officers commit acts that constitute state crimes, they can be criminally liable unless they have a legal defense. Here are some of the crimes an officer's use of force might implicate:

> *Assault*: threatening or attempting to physically touch someone else against their will;
> *Aggravated assault*: making threats of physical harm with a weapon or in circumstances that suggest particularly severe harm;
> *Battery*: touching or striking someone else against their will, offensive touching, or causing actual bodily injury;
> *Aggravated battery*: causing serious injury or causing injury to particularly vulnerable victims such as children or the elderly;
> *Murder*: the intentional killing of a human being in cold blood (often referred to as an "intentional" killing or a killing "with premeditation" or "with malice aforethought") or the unintentional killing of a human committed with callous disregard of the risk to human life (often referred to as "depraved heart murder");
> *Manslaughter*: the intentional killing of a human being in hot blood (often referred to as a killing after "adequate provocation") or the unintentional killing of a human being resulting from recklessness or criminal negligence;
> *Kidnapping*: restricting another person's movement or forcing them to move from one location to another against their will;
> *Attempt*: intending and actually trying, unsuccessfully, to commit some underlying crime. For example, planning and attempting to kill another person would not constitute the crime of murder because it did not result in a death, but it could constitute the crime of *attempted* murder; and
> *Conspiracy*: entering into an agreement to commit some underlying crime. For example, planning with another person to kill someone could constitute the crime of conspiracy to commit murder.

Seth W. Stoughton et al., *Evaluating Police Uses of Force* 64–65 (2020).

Officers are often authorized to take other actions that would constitute crimes as well. Think about a SWAT team that uses a battering ram to breach a home, enters without permission, shoots an approaching dog, ransacks the house for evidence, and shoots and kills a homeowner who reaches for a gun. Can you think of crimes not listed above that the officers might be committing if they have no defense? Of course, these actions are often authorized by state law and by search warrants issued pursuant to that law. What about when officers exceed their authority? Have you ever heard of an officer prosecuted for damaging property or for trespassing?

5. *Mistakes.* If an officer uses necessary, nondeadly force to make a lawful arrest, or uses necessary deadly force to save his own life, he behaves legally. If an officer intentionally uses too much force, he has committed a crime. What if an officer mistakenly uses excessive force in carrying out an arrest? There are three basic kinds of mistakes an officer can make: mistakes as to *whether the arrest is legal* (e.g., whether there is probable cause), mistakes about *whether any force is necessary* (e.g., whether the suspect will harm the officer unless force is used), and mistakes about the *amount of force* that is appropriate under the circumstances (e.g., whether the threat to the officer is one of serious bodily harm or the suspected crime involved violence). States take three basic approaches to these mistakes (although they do not always take a uniform approach to all three types). A few states disallow mistakes as a defense. Many more allow *reasonable* mistakes. Finally, some states consider it a defense that an officer *believed* an arrest is lawful, *believed* that force was necessary, or *believed* that the suspect posed an immediate danger of serious bodily harm or death to the officer or a member of the public, even if the officer was both mistaken and unreasonable. What approach do these statutes take? Does it matter?

6. *Burden of proof.* Overwhelmingly, states require the prosecution to disprove justification defenses beyond a reasonable doubt, so long as the defendant provides enough evidence to make the defense an issue in the case. Imagine an officer on trial for murder in Alabama, who claims he shot the suspect because it looked like the suspect was pulling a gun from his jacket, making him afraid for his life. If his belief was reasonable, he has a defense under Alabama law. If no gun, cellphone, or wallet was found on the suspect, how might the officer attempt to establish his reasonable belief? How can the government disprove it sufficiently to satisfy its burden of proof?

7. *Proving a crime.* As this example suggests, if an officer claims he thought a criminal suspect was reaching for a weapon, the government may have a hard time mustering physical evidence or witnesses to persuade the jury otherwise. As a result, even when such officers are tried for shootings, they are often acquitted. For example, in 2005, Hartford (Conn.) police officer Robert Lawlor approached the car 18-year-old Jashon Bryant was riding in because it matched the description of a car involved in a homicide. Lawlor claimed he shot and killed Bryant because he thought Bryant was reaching for a weapon and posed a threat to Lawlor's partner. The partner testified that he was in no danger. Lawlor was tried for and acquitted of first-degree manslaughter. Similarly, in 2008, Baltimore police officer Tommy Sanders stopped Edward Lamont Hunt to question him about drug transactions. Sanders alleged that he believed Hunt was reaching into his pocket for a gun when he shot him twice in the back. Sanders was also charged and acquitted of voluntary manslaughter, and he stayed on the force. See *Police Officers Prosecuted for Use of Deadly Force,* Wash. Post (Apr. 11, 2015). Knowing this, what might an officer be tempted to say after a fatal encounter?

8. *General or police-specific crimes.* Police officers are mostly prosecuted using general criminal statutes prohibiting murder or assault. Some states, however, have crimes on the books that only public officials can commit. Here is California's law:

> Every public officer who, under color of authority, without lawful necessity, assaults or beats any person, is punishable by a fine not exceeding ten thousand dollars

($10,000), or by imprisonment in a county jail not exceeding one year, . . . or by both that fine and imprisonment.

Cal. Penal Code §149. Normatively, which approach do you prefer? Why? (Neither approach precludes the other.)

9. *State law and constitutional law.* Federal constitutional law sets limits on what states may authorize officers to do, but states are not obliged to impose a criminal remedy against officers who violate federal constitutional law. As a result, a state may impose criminal liability on officers who comply with constitutional law, and it may provide a defense (against state prosecution) to officers who violate it. Nevertheless, as these statutes suggest, states often are influenced by federal constitutional standards governing the use of force in formulating justification defenses. Thus, many states criminalize only force that violates constitutional law. A few states criminalize force that federal law permits, and around a quarter of states permit a criminal law defense for some kinds of force that violate federal constitutional law. Recall that *Tennessee v. Garner,* 471 U.S. 1, 11 (1985), permits police officers to shoot fleeing felons in the back as they run away "if the suspect threatens the officer with a weapon or there is probable cause to believe that he has committed a crime involving the infliction or threatened infliction of serious physical harm." Can you identify how constitutional law intersects with these statutes? For a list of state statutes and a discussion of states that do not criminalize some force that would violate *Tennessee v. Garner,* see Chad Flanders & Joseph Welling, *Police Use of Deadly Force: State Statutes 30 Years After Garner,* 35 St. Louis Pub. L. Rev. 109 (2015). See also Stoughton et al., *Evaluating Police Uses of Force* 81 (2020) (recategorizing states).

10. *Does the law matter?* In the face of protests about police violence that goes unprosecuted, many states are reconsidering their justification defenses governing the use of force. Given how few officers are prosecuted for using force, how much do you expect the details of the statutes to matter compared to prosecutorial preferences and jury receptiveness? If your answer is "probably not that much," then why fight over the law? If you were asked to design a study to determine whether the language of justification defenses matters to what officers or prosecutors do, how would you propose testing the question?

2. Police Crime

The limited data available on charges against police officers for using excessive force confirms what civil rights prosecutors will tell you: When officers are charged, they go to trial more often than other defendants, and they fare better at those trials. In a 2015 study, Washington Post and Bowling Green State University researchers led by Philip Stinson found that although police officers killed approximately 10,000 people between 2005 and 2015, prosecutors charged only 54 officers with homicide offenses. Most of those officers went to trial, and most of those officers were not convicted. The six who were convicted after going to trial in state court received prison sentences averaging 3.5 years. According to the Washington Post/ Bowling Green analysis, the cases that were prosecuted tended to have at least one of four factors: the officer shot a victim in the back, someone recorded the incident, one or more officers gave incriminating testimony, or the defendant officer tried to cover up the incident. See Kimberly Kindy & Kimbriell Kelly, *Thousands Dead, Few Prosecuted,* Wash. Post (Apr. 11, 2015).

Stinson and his team have updated the data since, and as of June 2020, 110 officers have been charged with murder or manslaughter for fatal on-duty shootings since 2005. Of those, 42 were convicted, often of a lesser charge, and 18 had charges still pending. The rest were not convicted. Although it seems like public pressure on prosecutors to bring charges against officers has increased, and some high-profile trials have taken place since the original study, according to Stinson, the uptick in charges after 2014 is not statistically significant. See Amelia Thomson-DeVeaux, *Why It's So Rare for Police Officers to Face Legal Consequences*, FiveThirtyEight.com (Jun. 4, 2020).

The Stinson team focuses on killings, as do most commentators and prosecutors. State cases against police officers for excessive force often involve a death and serious criminal charges. In this way, prosecutions for excessive force seem to be a high-impact, low-volume affair. What if instead of focusing on charges in high-profile death cases, prosecutors focused on bringing frequent simple assault and battery charges against officers who used excessive force during arrests, as established by video or witnesses?[3] How might those cases be different? What might the impact of such charges be?

Philip Stinson and colleagues have also tried to identify every police officer arrested for *any* crime from 2005 to 2011. From news sources and court records, they found 6,724 arrests involving 5,545 officers. Forty percent of the crimes took place while the officer was on duty. Some additional off-duty offenses relied on the officer's law enforcement status in some way: They involved brandishing an official weapon, flashing a badge, or some other invocation of police power. The rest had no apparent relationship to the defendant's status as a police officer. The most common charges, across both on-duty and off-duty offenses, were simple assault, driving under the influence, and aggravated assault. Serious sex crimes, including forcible rape, forcible fondling, and sodomy, made up approximately 13 percent of the arrests, and half of the known victims of those crimes were children.[4] See Philip Stinson et al., Nat'l Inst. of Justice, *Police Integrity Lost: A Study of Law Enforcement Officers Arrested* (2016).[5] The data do not indicate how many arrests were for civil rights offenses. An arrest for an assault, aggravated assault, manslaughter, or a murder *might* reflect a use of excessive force while the officer was on duty, but it also could be an off-duty bar fight or domestic assault. A sex crime could mean an officer coerced an arrestee to have sex or it could mean the officer molested a child in his family. What conclusions would you be willing to draw from such data?

Interestingly, in the study, two-thirds of officer arrests were made by agencies other than the arrestees' employers. One innocent explanation is that officers often do not live where they work, which could lead other agencies to catch off-duty conduct. A less innocent explanation is that agencies are especially reluctant to arrest their own officers. Compared to arrests of civilians, a far higher proportion of arrests for drunk driving in the study took place after an accident or other incident. Because officers have little choice but to arrest someone who is intoxicated and

---

[3] This prosecution strategy was suggested by my research assistant Alec Ward while he was a student in my *Law of the Police* course.

[4] The high proportion of child victims may represent fellow officers' greater reluctance to ignore crimes against children rather than the actual proportion of child victims in police crimes.

[5] Stinson and his colleagues have continued to update the data since this study, though they have not yet published further analysis. As of 2019, the database covers the years 2005 to 2014 and includes information for more than 10,000 arrests involving nearly 8,500 officers employed by close to 3,500 agencies. See Henry A. Wallace, Police Crime Database, *https://policecrime.bgsu.edu*.

involved in a car accident, those data might suggest that officers are letting go other officers they discover driving under the influence when they can, such as when no one else is present, and especially so when the drunk officer is from the same agency. Given that victims and witnesses likely underreport crimes by police officers because they believe such reports are futile and they fear retaliation, if officers also sometimes refuse to arrest officers they catch in the act of committing crimes, it might turn out that these thousands of arrests understate dramatically the number of crimes police officers commit.

Another interesting finding in the study is that many officers continue to serve after convictions, even though they no longer meet state qualifications for officers. Most states disqualify felons and some misdemeanants from serving in police departments. In addition, even when a conviction does not disqualify an officer, most sworn positions require carrying a gun, and the federal Gun Control Act of 1968 forbids felons from possessing a firearm. The Lautenberg Amendment to the act extends that prohibition to those convicted of misdemeanor domestic violence offenses. See 18 U.S.C. §922(g). However, because most departments carry out background checks on only new hires, and two-thirds of the officer arrests were conducted by an agency other than the one that employed the officer, departments might never discover that their officers have been arrested or convicted (although they could easily find out that if they checked). How could we solve this problem? Better federal enforcement of the gun laws? State laws requiring annual background checks by police departments? Something else?

Notice what we do not know about police crime. All of this is *arrest* data. The National Crime Victimization Survey does not ask victims whether their crime was committed by a police officer so we cannot compare *reported* crimes against arrests the way we do for other offenses. We do not have data that allow us to assess trends over time. And the arrest data Stinson gathered are insufficiently detailed to identify characteristics about victims of police crime, including race. Can you imagine ways to help improve what we know? What else do you want to know about police crime?

B. State Investigative and Charging Process

1. Risking Bias in Investigating and Charging the Police

States vary in how they charge crimes. In some states, a prosecutor brings charges directly by filing an information or a complaint. In other states, a prosecutor must prepare and present an indictment to a grand jury, which then determines whether to return a true bill of indictment to the court. And in some states, prosecutors choose between these approaches. Whatever the system, most police officers accused of using excessive force never face criminal charges. In recent years, critics have argued that prosecutors have failed to charge police officers when they should have been charged, especially when officers have shot and killed unarmed African-American men.

The grand jury investigation after Officer Darren Wilson killed Michael Brown on August 9, 2014, in Ferguson, Missouri, illustrates some of the concerns about how prosecutors handle police uses of force. St. Louis County Prosecutor Bob McCulloch and his assistants presented months of testimony and physical evidence to a grand jury, which in the end failed to indict Wilson for any crime. When the grand jury materials and transcripts became public, many blamed the prosecutors' approach to the case.

Indeed, the grand jury transcripts provide support for the argument that prosecutors worked hard to demonstrate Darryl Wilson's innocence rather than his guilt. When Wilson testified, prosecutors failed to follow up on ambiguous and self-serving statements, and they did not treat him like a potential criminal defendant. Instead, they encouraged him to detail the injuries Brown caused him before the shooting and the threat that Brown posed, sometimes seemingly feeding him his defense. By contrast, prosecutors closely questioned witnesses who suggested Wilson's guilt.

Whether Wilson was actually guilty of a state crime, the prosecutors' approach undermined public faith that the grand jury reached the right outcome. Moreover, McCulloch's use of the grand jury seemed to some to avoid responsibility for a decision not to prosecute Wilson that, in effect, he made:

> . . . St. Louis County prosecutor Bob McCulloch had two legitimate options following Wilson's killing of Brown, neither of which he chose. The first would have been simply to decline to indict Wilson for the reasons McCulloch's defenders posit—that the law would have made it very difficult to secure a conviction. The second legitimate option would have been to obtain an indictment against Wilson from the grand jury, which McCulloch almost certainly could have done had he sought one. But McCulloch chose a third option—using the grand jury process to establish Wilson's innocence—which is deeply unfair. . . . McCulloch's team essentially cherry-picked evidence . . . accept[ing] Wilson's account at face value, even leading him toward exculpatory statements through their questioning, while going out of their way to point out flaws and contradictions in alternative accounts from other witnesses.

> . . . [W]hen the prosecutor stage-manages a grand jury into affirming his view of the defendant's innocence, that's it. That's the only trial we get.

> . . . He gets to wrap his preference for not indicting Wilson in the legitimacy of a trial-like process . . . [b]ut as a matter of justice, it's outrageous.

Noam Scheiber, *St. Louis Prosecutor Bob McCulloch Abused the Grand Jury Process,* New Republic (Nov. 25, 2014). Do you agree? Other prosecutors have faced similar criticism for bringing before grand juries that then decline to indict.

Even when prosecutors do not use grand juries, critics contend that prosecutors are biased against charging officers because they have an inherent conflict of interest. "When prosecuting an officer, the prosecutor must switch from her reliance on the police as allies to the position of an adversary. . . ." Kate Levine, *Who Shouldn't Prosecute the Police,* 101 Iowa L. Rev. 1447, 1470 (2016). That is not an easy switch to make:

> [P]rosecutors—the very ministers of justice we rely upon for accountability— work with and depend upon law enforcement officers in the discharge of their duties. Police officers are the front-line representatives of the law enforcement complex of which prosecutors are a part. Police officers exercise discretion, gather evidence, apprehend individuals so that they can face justice, and bring cases for prosecution. In most criminal cases, law enforcement officers work hand in hand with prosecutors toward a shared goal of bringing criminal offenders to justice. Thus, it is no surprise that some express doubts about the ability of prosecutors' offices to fairly evaluate and prosecute allegations against police officers in their jurisdictions.

Roger A. Fairfax, Jr., *The Grand Jury's Role in the Prosecution of Unjustified Police Killings—Challenges and Solutions,* 52 Harv. C.R.-C.L. L. Rev 397, 398 (2017). Political considerations could also factor into prosecutorial decision making:

> The police . . . are well-informed and interested in the outcome of elections, and their support matters. . . . [A] district attorney . . . must contend with the real possibility that she will not be reelected if she crosses the powerful police unions. It is hard to fathom that even the most well-intentioned politician is able to completely separate herself from such unfettered pressure from a highly mobilized and well-informed electorate in her jurisdiction.

Levine, *supra,* at 1476–1477.

Although critics most often identify *prosecutors* as the obstacles to charging, poor *investigation* before prosecutors get involved also stymies criminal prosecutions of officers. If officers at the scene fail to collect evidence, inadequately canvass for witnesses, or influence witness accounts through their questioning, they could affect the outcome of the criminal case, as well as any non-criminal efforts to determine what happened.

Again, the incident in Ferguson is instructive. Initial interviews with Officer Wilson immediately after the shooting were not taped. Investigators did not take measurements at the crime scene because they decided the scene was "self-explanatory." Officer Wilson was also treated unlike any ordinary homicide suspect: He was not photographed immediately; he was allowed to handle the weapon he used to shoot Brown and place it in an evidence bag himself; he drove himself back to the station house; and he washed Michael Brown's blood off of his hands without supervision. Deficient investigation could be a result of bias, or it could just be sloppiness. Does the difference affect how you would address the problem?

When confronted with a potential crime by an officer, some agencies routinely use criminal investigators from other jurisdictions. But many police officers are investigated by officers from their own agency. That might not be a good idea:

> [S]elf-policing will necessarily and unavoidably produce a biased result[.] . . . [E]ven reasonable, honest, and well-intentioned police investigators simply cannot overcome the pressures from all sides that come to bear. . . . The pressure . . . may come from superiors within the police organization who do not want an embarrassing incident publicly exposed, or who fear the credibility and authority of the police will be undermined. . . . Pressure may come from the police union, which may be inclined to vigorously defend even bad officers. A mayor or city council may not want to hear bad news about the police department, and may encourage suppression of it. Finally, fellow officers may not want to see one of their peers held up to withering scrutiny.
>
> . . . [B]ias may show up in many ways. For example, the investigation may be half-hearted, wherein not all relevant witnesses are interviewed . . . particularly those witnesses who might give testimony unfavorable to the officer. Interviews of the officer himself may be tainted: investigators may simply pitch softball, open-ended questions to the officer, allowing him to give a narrative answer that is not given rigorous cross-examination. More troubling still, investigators, at times, may use leading questions . . . : "You were in fear for your life, weren't you?" or "You thought your partner was about to be shot, correct?" or "You saw the suspect reach for his waistband and withdraw a black, shiny object you thought was a gun, right?" . . .
>
> There is a natural, predictable, human impulse involved; even in the absence of external pressures, no law enforcement officer can examine an officer-involved shooting without saying at some level, "There but for the grace of God go I."

Merrick Bobb, *Civilian Oversight of the Police in the United States*, 22 St. Louis Pub. L. Rev. 151, 156–157 (2003).

2.   Preventing Bias in Investigating and Prosecuting the Police

In light of these criticisms, public officials and reformers argue that investigations and prosecution decisions concerning police officers should not be made by local officials in the same jurisdiction. Instead, they advocate independent investigations and prosecutions of police officers to improve public perceptions about the legitimacy of decisions whether to prosecute and, for some critics, to increase those prosecutions.

President Obama's Task Force on 21st Century Policing echoed these calls, advocating as action items in its Final Report departmental policies that "mandate external and independent criminal investigations" and "mandate the use of external and independent prosecutors" whenever an officer shoots someone resulting in injury or death or otherwise uses force resulting in death. *Final Report of the President's Task Force on 21st Century Policing* §§2.2.2, 2.2.3 (2015). The report mentioned three possible mechanisms for achieving independence: creating a multiagency task force with local and state investigators; using neighboring jurisdictions to handle investigations and prosecutions; and moving investigations and prosecutions up to state agencies, such as state attorney generals' offices. Do you prefer one of these options? Why?

a. Legal Solutions

Although the President's Task Force encouraged police departments to facilitate this kind of independent investigation of officers through their own policies, less timid reformers have advocated mandating independence under state law. Some states have heeded their call. In New York, Governor Andrew Cuomo did it by executive order, appointing the New York State Attorney General as a special prosecutor to "investigate, and if warranted, prosecute certain matters involving the death of an unarmed civilian, whether in custody or not, caused by a law enforcement officer. . . ." N.Y. Exec. Order No. 147 (July 8, 2015). Other states have passed statutes. For example, in 2019, New Jersey similarly mandated that the state Attorney General investigate and prosecute police-involved deaths. Act of Jan. 30, 2019, ch. 1, 2019 N.J. Laws. Here are two more laws:

WIS. STAT. §175.47(2)-(5)

(2) Each law enforcement agency shall have a written policy regarding the investigation of officer-involved deaths that involve a law enforcement officer employed by the law enforcement agency.

(3) **(a)** Each policy under sub. (2) must require an investigation conducted by at least two investigators, one of whom is the lead investigator and neither of whom is employed by a law enforcement agency that employs a law enforcement officer involved in the officer-involved death. . . .

(c) Each policy under sub. (2) may allow an internal investigation into the officer-involved death if the internal investigation does not interfere with the investigation conducted under par. (a). . . .

(5) (a) The investigators conducting the investigation under sub. (3) (a) shall, in an expeditious manner, provide a complete report to the district attorney of the county in which the officer-involved death occurred.

(b) If the district attorney determines there is no basis to prosecute the law enforcement officer involved in the officer-involved death, the investigators conducting the investigation under sub. (3) (a) shall release the report, except that the investigators shall, before releasing the report, delete any information that would not be subject to disclosure pursuant to a request under §19.35 (1) (a).

UTAH CODE ANN. §76-2-408(2)-(5)

(2) When an officer-involved critical incident occurs:

(a) upon receiving notice of the officer-involved critical incident, the law enforcement agency having jurisdiction where the incident occurred shall, as soon as practical, notify the county or district attorney having jurisdiction where the incident occurred; and

(b) the chief executive of the law enforcement agency and the county or district attorney having jurisdiction where the incident occurred shall:

(i) jointly designate an investigating agency for the officer-involved critical incident; and

(ii) designate which agency is the lead investigative agency if the officer-involved critical incident involves multiple investigations.

(3) The investigating agency under Subsection (2) may not be the law enforcement agency employing the officer who is alleged to have caused or contributed to the officer-involved critical incident.

(4) This section does not preclude the law enforcement agency employing an officer alleged to have caused or contributed to the officer-involved critical incident from conducting an internal administrative investigation.

(5) Each law enforcement agency that is part of or administered by the state or any of its political subdivisions shall, by December 31, 2015, adopt and post on its publicly accessible website:

(a) the policies and procedures the agency has adopted to select the investigating agency if an officer-involved critical incident occurs in its jurisdiction and one of its officers is alleged to have caused or contributed to the officer-involved incident; and

(b) the protocols the agency has adopted to ensure that any investigation of officer-involved incidents occurring in its jurisdiction are conducted professionally, thoroughly, and impartially.

NOTES AND QUESTIONS

1. *Compare and contrast.* One of the most obvious differences between the statutes is that Utah's is not limited to cases involving deaths. Why do New York, New Jersey, and Wisconsin limit independence to those cases? Is bias likely to be more extreme when the stakes are higher and subject to scrutiny or when the stakes are

lower and perhaps invisible? Do you see other differences between the Wisconsin and Utah statutes? How are they different from what New York and New Jersey are doing?

2. *Are they sufficient?* According to Walter Katz, a longtime police watchdog,

> Independent investigative bodies must exhibit a number of common characteristics to be effective. First and foremost is the ability to investigate potential criminal wrongdoing by officers and to make recommendations for prosecutions that are then evaluated by special prosecutors. The independent investigative agency should be open and transparent, independent of any other law enforcement agency, but with unrestricted access to officers and agency records. It must be given a sufficient budget, the power to issue subpoenas, search warrants and a well-defined jurisdiction and mandate. Investigators should be granted all the powers of peace officers.

Walter Katz, *Enhancing Accountability and Trust with Independent Investigations of Police Lethal Force*, 128 Harv. L. Rev. F. 235, 244 (2015). To what degree do these statutes ensure Katz's minimum conditions for independence? Are there other options? What about requiring that a public defender be appointed to evaluate charges?

3. *Should Congress intervene?* The Police Training and Independent Review Act was first introduced in 2015 and then again in 2017 and 2019 with dozens of members of Congress signing on. Here is an excerpt from §2 of the bill:

H.R. 125, Police Training and Independent Review Act of 2019

SEC. 3043. Independent Review of law enforcement use of deadly force.

In the case of a State that fails by the end of a fiscal year to enact or have in effect an independent prosecution of law enforcement law, that State is not eligible for a grant under this part.

The grant mentioned is the Edward Byrne Memorial Justice Assistance Grant, a program that provides hundreds of millions of dollars each year in flexible funding to states and local police departments. If this law passed, it would provide an important incentive for local governments to do things differently. If the federal government is so enthusiastic about using independent prosecutors to charge police officers, why not expand its own investigations and prosecutions instead? One response is that federal criminal law does not favor such prosecutions. Why not change *that*? Which approach is a greater intrusion on traditional state functions: federally prosecuting state agents or using federal grant programs to punish states for not prosecuting state agents the way the feds want them to? Which is more likely to yield positive results? What counts as positive?

4. *Evaluating the law.* What is independence for? Does the argument in favor of these laws turn on whether more police officers are prosecuted? If not, what does it turn on?

Is Independence All It's Cracked Up to Be?

In Minnesota, the state Bureau of Criminal Apprehension (BCA) typically investigates or oversees investigations of police shootings, but it has been frequently criticized for its officer-friendly approach. For example, in 2017 when Minneapolis police officer

Mohamed Noor shot and killed 911 caller Justine Ruszczyk, the BCA oversaw the crime scene. It failed to document conversations with Noor at the scene. It failed to collect or preserve evidence from the car Noor was sitting in when he fired the fatal shots, instead returning it to Minneapolis police, who washed it within hours. It did not interview the only witness to the shooting—Noor's partner—for several days. It failed to follow up on the original 911 call made by Ruszczyk. For months it failed to interview other officers who had been on the scene. At trial, a former police chief who testified as an expert *for the prosecution* called some of these lapses " 'pretty disturbing.' " Jon Collins & Riham Feshir, *Noor Trial: Questions Resurface Over BCA's Cop-Friendly Approach*, MPRnews.org (Apr. 25, 2019). Noor was charged and convicted anyway, but what if he had never been charged or had been acquitted?

That is what happened when officers shot and killed Lori Jean Ellis in her own home. Like most police shootings in South Carolina, it was investigated by the South Carolina Law Enforcement Division (SLED), a state agency. The officers who killed Ellis (with a bullet to the back of the head) were executing an arrest warrant for her failure to appear in court on an open-container violation. They claimed that she fired a high-powered rifle at them, but the only weapon found in her house was a BB gun with no prints on it. SLED investigators allowed the officers to sit in a room together unmonitored before they took the officers' statements; they failed to question the officers about their unusual tactics or critical inconsistencies between the statements and other evidence; they failed to assess relevant physical evidence; and they failed to canvass the area or speak to neighbors. The SLED nevertheless cleared the officers, determining that they were in reasonable fear for their lives. Why? Maybe this deposition exchange between an attorney representing Ellis's estate and the SLED captain who supervised the investigation helps to explain:

Lawyer:	Let's assume these cops aren't telling the truth [about whether Ellis fired her weapon].
SLED Captain:	But they are telling the truth.
Lawyer:	How do you know that?
SLED Captain:	Because they're police officers and I believe what they're telling me . . .

Radley Balko, *South Carolina's Poisonous Police Culture: The Death of Lori Jean Eillis,* Wash. Post (May 6, 2016).

Is independence enough to guarantee a fair investigation? Or is a state agency that works closely with local law enforcement not independent?

As you think about those questions, consider that deficient investigations sometimes result from law rather than bias. As a result of collective bargaining agreements and Law Enforcement Officers' Bills of Rights protections, officers involved in a shooting are often allowed to delay questioning and review evidence before giving a statement. Imagine a convenience store owner who shoots someone he claims was attempting to rob the store. Even if the police find a Bowie knife in the shooting victim's hand and conclude that the shooting was likely lawful, they are not going to suggest that the store owner spend a few days thinking about it, get himself a lawyer, and review the security-camera footage before he speaks to the police about what happened. Yet that often happens in police investigations of police officers. What might help *that*?

b.   Political Solutions

One argument in favor of independent investigation and prosecution assumes that local political pressure, the usual tool for ensuring fair prosecutions, does not work in policing because majoritarian politics cut against prosecuting police officers. This is often true, and prosecutors are celebrated for *not* charging the police. In some communities with high-profile police shootings, however, prosecutors have paid a high political price for failing to bring charges against police officers. Here are two examples.

Timothy McGinty

Tamir Rice, a 12-year-old African-American boy living in Cleveland, was killed in November 2014 after a 911 caller reported seeing a male pointing a gun at people. Although the caller also indicated that the gun might be fake and that the male was probably a juvenile, dispatch did not relay those details to the responding officers, Timothy Loehmann and Frank Garmback. A video of the incident revealed that Officer Loehmann fired two shots at Rice within seconds of arriving on the scene, one of which hit the boy. Elahe Izadi & Peter Holley, *Video Shows Cleveland Officer Shooting 12-Year-Old Tamir Rice Within Seconds*, Wash. Post (Nov. 26, 2014). Though Rice was not holding a weapon when shot, Loehmann and his partner said, and the video did not contradict, that Rice reached toward his waistband. Rice died the following day from his injuries. Rice's gun was a toy.

Cuyahoga County Prosecutor Timothy McGinty presented evidence about the shooting to a grand jury, which declined to indict either officer. When he announced the grand jury's decision, McGinty called Rice's death a "perfect storm of human error, mistakes and miscommunications." He said, "The death of Tamir Rice was an absolute tragedy. But it was not, by the law that binds us, a crime." Rice's family and other critics alleged that McGinty had manipulated and mishandled the grand jury to exonerate the officers. Jeff Noble, a former deputy chief with 28 years of policing service (and a law degree) was an expert in the case. He has said that in the more than 300 cases in which he has been retained since retiring from law enforcement, he never saw a prosecutor trying as hard to avoid an indictment. When McGinty faced reelection in 2016, the year following the grand jury's decision, the Cuyahoga County Democratic Party endorsed his challenger and McGinty lost his office.

Anita Alvarez

The same month that McGinty lost, Cook County State's Attorney Anita Alvarez was unseated for her handling of the prosecution of Officer Jason Van Dyke in the October 2014 shooting of Laquan McDonald, an African-American teenager in Chicago. McDonald repeatedly failed to comply with Van Dyke's instructions and was armed with a knife when he was shot. Nevertheless, Van Dyke fired the first shot as McDonald walked away from him and fired at him several more times as McDonald lay on the ground. See *Chicago Dashcam Video Shows Police Killing of Laquan McDonald*, Guardian (Nov. 24, 2015).

Although Van Dyke was charged with first-degree murder and official misconduct, Alvarez was widely criticized for refusing to release a video showing the incident until the threat of a court order forced her hand, and for taking more than a year to charge Van Dyke. She resoundingly lost a primary battle to Kim Foxx, a former prosecutor whose criticisms of Alvarez's handling of the case were a centerpiece of her campaign.

NOTES AND QUESTIONS

1. *Elections.* Does throwing out a prosecutor change subsequent charging decisions? If it does, does it do so by *deterring* decisions or by *replacing* decision makers? Does there have to be an election to create political pressure on prosecutors to reconsider how they make charging decisions? How could we develop well-informed answers for some of these questions?

2. *Risks.* Community input into prosecutorial priorities seems like a good thing. Should prosecutors also respond to political pressure in charging specific cases? Could that lead to *overcharging* some police defendants (as well as undercharging others)? Some say that overcharging is what happened in Baltimore. Baltimore state attorney Marilyn Mosby ran on a promise to aggressively prosecute police officers. When protests rocked Baltimore in the days after Freddie Gray's death from injuries he sustained in the back of a police van, Mosby quickly brought charges against the six police officers involved. In announcing the charges, she said, "To the people of Baltimore and the demonstrators across America, I heard your call for 'No Justice, No Peace.'" Alan Blinder & Richard Pérez-Peña, *6 Baltimore Police Officers Charged in Freddie Gray Death,* N.Y. Times (May 1, 2015). The first officer's trial ended in a hung jury, a judge acquitted three more officers, and Mosby then dropped all remaining charges. (See *Nero v. Mosby,* 890 F.3d 106 (4th Cir. 2018), excerpted in section C.2 below.) How can we know if she brought charges too quickly because of political pressure? Or if she just had a hard time proving a complicated case?

3. *What do voters know?* In high-profile cases, prosecutors sometimes announce and explain decisions not to prosecute. In most cases, however, the public never learns about charging decisions, much less why they were made. How big an obstacle is that to electoral accountability? Some prosecutors release information about decisions not to prosecute police officers to signal their commitment to fairness in policing cases. The Baltimore City State's Attorney's Office under Mosby, for example, publishes a declination report for every decision it makes not to charge officers accused of using excessive force. See *Police Use of Force Declination Reports,* Office of the State's Atty. for Baltimore City, *https://www.stattorney.org/policy-legislative-affairs/policy/police-use-of-force-declination-reports.* Read one or two of these reports. Should more advocates for victims of police misconduct ask for this kind of explanation? Is there something special about police cases, or might you also like to see declination reports for other serious crimes?

4. *Election, redux.* Elections are rarely determined by only one issue. Take Alvarez. Although her handling of charges against Jason Van Dyke dominated the election, her critics voiced other concerns as well. Activists organizing under the hashtags #AlvarezMustGo and #ByeAnita produced a zine titled *Ten Things You Hate About Anita,* that was widely distributed before the election. Although first on the zine's list was, "She waited 400 days to charge the officer who murdered Laquan McDonald," and items two through four also concerned police misconduct, items five through nine concerned broader complaints about her use of prosecutorial discretion. Item five was, "She has contributed to the hyperincarceration of black people," and item six was, "Because she punishes prosecutors who pursue justice over convictions." What lessons should her successor take from the election?

C. *Judicial Review of Prosecutorial Decisions*

Decisions about whether to charge police officers for uses of force are almost inevitably controversial. Some criticize prosecutors when they do not bring charges, and others criticize them when they do. Can the judiciary ever serve to check prosecutorial discretion?

Yes, at least in one direction and for one reason: Courts can stop prosecutors who bring charges against officers based on inadequate evidence. A trial court will dismiss charges at the preliminary hearing (if there is one) if probable cause is lacking. It will enter a judgment of acquittal (either before or after a jury hears the case) if the evidence is insufficient to sustain a conviction. An appellate court will overturn a conviction if it is based on insufficient evidence.

Beyond dismissing charges based on inadequate evidence, however, courts rarely have the power to regulate prosecutorial exercises of discretion. Here are two cases to illustrate the point, one about the failure to bring charges, and one looking for a remedy (beyond acquittal) when unsuccessful charges were brought. Why do these courts refuse to step in?

1.   Civil Litigation to Force Prosecution

INMATES OF ATTICA CORRECTIONAL FACILITY
v. ROCKEFELLER
477 F.2d 375 (2d Cir. 1973)

MANSFIELD, CIRCUIT JUDGE:

This appeal raises the question of whether the federal judiciary should, at the instance of victims, compel federal and state officials to investigate and prosecute persons who allegedly have violated certain federal and state criminal statutes. Plaintiffs . . . are certain present and former inmates of New York State's Attica Correctional Facility ("Attica"), the mother of an inmate who was killed when Attica was retaken after the inmate uprising in September 1971, and Arthur O. Eve, a New York State Assemblyman. . . .

The complaint alleges that before, during, and after the prisoner revolt at and subsequent recapture of Attica in September 1971, which resulted in the killing of 32 inmates and the wounding of many others, the defendants . . . either committed, conspired to commit, or aided and abetted in the commission of various crimes against the complaining inmates and members of the class they seek to represent. It is charged that the inmates were intentionally subjected to cruel and inhuman treatment prior to the inmate riot, that State Police, Troopers, and Correction Officers (one of whom is named) intentionally killed some of the inmate victims without provocation during the recovery of Attica, that state officers (several of whom are named and whom the inmates claim they can identify) assaulted and beat prisoners after the prison had been successfully retaken and the prisoners had surrendered, that personal property of the inmates was thereafter stolen or destroyed, and that medical assistance was maliciously denied to over 400 inmates wounded during the recovery of the prison.

The complaint further alleges that Robert E. Fischer, a Deputy State Attorney General specially appointed by the Governor to supersede the District Attorney of

Wyoming County and, with a specially convened grand jury, to investigate crimes relating to the inmates' takeover of Attica and the resumption of control by the state authorities, "has not investigated, nor does he intend to investigate, any crimes committed by state officers." . . .

With respect to the sole federal defendant, the United States Attorney for the Western District of New York, the complaint simply alleges that he has not arrested, investigated, or instituted prosecutions against any of the state officers accused of criminal violation of plaintiffs' federal civil rights, 18 U.S.C. §§241, 242, and he has thereby failed to carry out the duty placed upon him by 42 U.S.C. §1987, discussed below.

. . . The motions of the federal and state defendants to dismiss the complaint for failure to state claims upon which relief can be granted, were granted by Judge MacMahon without opinion. We agree that the extraordinary relief sought cannot be granted in the situation here presented. . . .

The Insufficiency of the Complaint

Claim Against the United States Attorney

With respect to the defendant United States Attorney, plaintiffs seek mandamus to compel him to investigate and institute prosecutions against state officers, most of whom are not identified, for alleged violations of 18 U.S.C. §§241 and 242. Federal mandamus is, of course, available only "to compel an officer or employee of the United States . . . to perform a duty owed to the plaintiff." 28 U.S.C. §1361. And the legislative history of §1361 makes it clear that ordinarily the courts are " 'not to direct or influence the exercise of discretion of the officer or agency in the making of the decision,' " United States ex rel. Schonbrun v. Commanding Officer, 403 F.2d 371, 374 (2d Cir. 1968), cert. denied, 394 U.S. 929 (1969). More particularly, federal courts have traditionally and, to our knowledge, uniformly refrained from overturning, at the instance of a private person, discretionary decisions of federal prosecuting authorities not to prosecute persons regarding whom a complaint of criminal conduct is made.

This judicial reluctance to direct federal prosecutions at the instance of a private party asserting the failure of United States officials to prosecute alleged criminal violations has been applied even in cases such as the present one where, according to the allegations of the complaint, which we must accept as true for purposes of this appeal, serious questions are raised as to the protection of the civil rights and physical security of a definable class of victims of crime and as to the fair administration of the criminal justice system.

The primary ground upon which this traditional judicial aversion to compelling prosecutions has been based is the separation of powers doctrine. . . .

In the absence of statutorily defined standards governing reviewability, or regulatory or statutory policies of prosecution, the problems inherent in the task of supervising prosecutorial decisions do not lend themselves to resolution by the judiciary. . . . In the normal case of review of executive acts of discretion, the administrative record is open, public and reviewable on the basis of what it contains. The decision not to prosecute, on the other hand, may be based upon the insufficiency of the available evidence, in which event the secrecy of the grand jury and of the prosecutor's file may serve to protect the accused's reputation from public damage based upon insufficient, improper, or even malicious charges. *In camera* review would not be meaningful without access by the complaining party to the evidence before the grand jury or U.S. Attorney. Such interference with the normal operations of criminal investigations, in turn, based solely upon allegations of criminal conduct, raises serious questions of potential abuse by persons seeking to have other persons prosecuted. Any person, merely by filing a complaint containing allegations in general terms (permitted by the Federal Rules) of unlawful failure to prosecute, could gain access to the prosecutor's file and the grand jury's minutes, notwithstanding the secrecy normally attaching to the latter by law.

Nor is it clear what the judiciary's role of supervision should be were it to undertake such a review. At what point would the prosecutor be entitled to call a halt to further investigation as unlikely to be productive? What evidentiary standard would be used to decide whether prosecution should be compelled? How much judgment would the United States Attorney be allowed? Would he be permitted to limit himself to a strong "test" case rather than pursue weaker cases? What collateral factors would be permissible bases for a decision not to prosecute, e.g., the pendency of another criminal proceeding elsewhere against the same parties? What sort of review should be available in cases like the present one where the conduct complained of allegedly violates state as well as federal laws? With limited personnel and facilities at his disposal, what priority would the prosecutor be required to give to cases in which investigation or prosecution was directed by the court?

These difficult questions engender serious doubts as to the judiciary's capacity to review and as to the problem of arbitrariness inherent in any judicial decision to order prosecution. On balance, we believe that substitution of a court's decision to compel prosecution for the U.S. Attorney's decision not to prosecute, even upon an abuse of discretion standard of review and even if limited to directing that a prosecution be undertaken in good faith would be unwise. . . .

Claims Against the State Officials

With respect to the state defendants, plaintiffs also seek prosecution of named and unknown persons for the violation of state crimes. However, they have pointed to no statutory language even arguably creating any mandatory duty upon the state officials to bring such prosecutions. To the contrary, New York law reposes in its prosecutors a discretion to decide whether or not to prosecute in a given case, which is not subject to review in the state courts. Yet the federal district court is asked to compel state prosecutions and appoint an "impartial" state prosecutor and state judge to conduct them, as well as to require the submission of a plan for impartial investigation and prosecution of the alleged offenses. . . . The very elaborateness of the relief believed by the plaintiffs to be required indicates the difficulties inherent in judicial supervision of prosecutions, federal or state, which render such a course inadvisable.

Plaintiffs point to language in our earlier opinion, *Inmates of Attica Correctional Facility v. Rockefeller*, 453 F.2d 12, 20 (2d Cir. 1971), to the effect that "the State has the duty to investigate and prosecute all persons, including inmates, who may have engaged in criminal conduct before, during and after the uprising." But the statement does not support their present demands. The existence of such a duty does not define its dimensions or imply that an alleged failure to perform the duty completely or equally, as between inmates and state officials, will support federal judicial supervision of state criminal prosecutions. The serious charge that the state's investigation is proceeding against inmates but not against state officers, if shown to be accurate, might lead the Governor to supplement or replace those presently in charge of the investigation or the state legislature to act. But the gravity of the allegation does not reduce the inherent judicial incapacity to supervise. . . .

The order of the district court is affirmed.

NOTES AND QUESTIONS

1. *In the Court's view.* The Supreme Court has never ruled whether prosecutors may be compelled to prosecute, but its reasoning in other cases on prosecutorial discretion indicate its view:

> In our criminal justice system, the Government retains "broad discretion" as to whom to prosecute. United States v. Goodwin, 457 U.S. 368, 380 n.11 (1982). "[S]o long as the prosecutor has probable cause to believe that the accused committed an offense defined by statute, the decision whether or not to prosecute, and what charge to file or bring before a grand jury, generally rests entirely in his discretion." Bordenkircher v. Hayes, 434 U.S. 357, 364 (1978). This broad discretion rests largely on the recognition that the decision to prosecute is particularly ill-suited to judicial review. Such factors as the strength of the case, the prosecution's general deterrence value, the Government's enforcement priorities, and the case's relationship to the Government's overall enforcement plan are not readily susceptible to the kind of analysis the courts are competent to undertake. Judicial supervision in this area, moreover, entails systemic costs of particular concern. Examining the basis of a prosecution delays the criminal proceeding, threatens to chill law enforcement by subjecting the prosecutor's motives and decision-making to outside inquiry, and may undermine prosecutorial effectiveness by revealing the Government's enforcement policy. All these are substantial concerns that make the courts properly hesitant to examine the decision whether to prosecute.

Wayte v. United States, 470 U.S. 598, 607–608 (1985). Do you agree? Could courts feasibly review decisions made on these bases? Even if they cannot generally do so, might cases against law enforcement officers be different? If so, how? What if a prosecutor adopts a policy against charging *any* police officers?

2. *Good for the goose, good for the gander?* After reform-minded Suffolk County (Mass.), District Attorney-Elect Rachael Rollins indicated that she would not generally prosecute some low-level offenses, including trespassing, shoplifting, larceny under $250, disorderly conduct, disturbing the peace, and drug possession, many criticized her, including other district attorneys. Here is what one said:

> [D]istrict attorneys do not make laws. That is the job of the Legislature. It is true that district attorneys have the power of nolle prosequi — that is, to end a prosecution in the interests of justice or not to prosecute a case at all for the same reason. However, those decisions are made based on the facts and circumstances of an individual case. A district attorney does not have the power to nullify an entire class of criminal conduct. . . . The idea that we should exempt groups of people from having to obey the law is an insult to them and a destructive form of pandering, because it suggests that these people are lesser beings than those we expect to obey the law.

Michael D. O'Keefe, *The True Role of the District Attorney*, Boston Globe (May 28, 2019). Can the same arguments be made about prosecutors who consistently fail to bring charges against police officers accused of misconduct? If so, does that mean that shoplifters in Boston and corrections officers in Attica should both be charged?

3. *More on Attica.* For a detailed account of the uprising at Attica, the retaking of the prison, the retaliation against inmates, and the subsequent decisions not to prosecute public officials, see Heather Ann Thompson, *Blood in the Water: The Attica Prison Uprising of 1971 and Its Legacy* (2016). The story of the uprising and its aftermath is a remarkable one, and it illustrates some of the significant obstacles to law enforcement accountability.

Can the Failure to Prosecute Be Unconstitutional?

Although prosecutorial discretion is broad, it is not unlimited. The Constitution forbids some bases for government decisions. "In particular, the decision to prosecute may not be deliberately based upon an unjustifiable standard such as race, religion, or other arbitrary classification, including the exercise of protected statutory and constitutional rights." Wayte v. United States, 470 U.S. 598, 608 (1985).

Those same constitutional rules also apply to decisions *not* to act. See DeShaney v. Winnebago County Dept. of Soc. Servs., 489 U.S. 189, 197 n.3 (1989). Relying on this principle, in 2014 the Obama Administration's Civil Rights Division accused the Missoula County, Montana, Attorney's Office (MCAO) of failing to adequately pursue women's sexual assault allegations thereby discriminating against the victims on the basis of their gender. See Letter to Fred Van Valkenburg, County Attorney, Missoula, Montana, from Jocelyn Samuels, Acting Assistant Attorney General, Civil Rights Division, and Michael W. Cotter, U.S. Attorney, District of Montana (Feb. 14, 2014). According to the Civil Rights Division,

> Our investigation to date has revealed substantial evidence suggesting that MCAO's response to allegations of sexual assault and rape discriminates against women and that this discrimination is fueled, at least in part, by gender bias. This bias erodes public confidence in the criminal justice system, places women in Missoula at increased risk of harm, and reinforces ingrained stereotypes about women. It also undermines sexual assault investigations in Missoula from the outset, impairing the ability of both police and prosecutors to uncover the truth in these cases and hold perpetrators of sexual violence accountable.
>
> In addition, our investigation indicates that the County Attorney's Office has often failed to take the steps necessary to develop sexual assault cases properly so that informed and fair prosecutorial assessments may be made. As a result, female sexual assault victims in Missoula are deprived of fundamental legal protections and often re-victimized by MCAO's response to their reports of abuse.
>
> Specifically, our investigation has uncovered evidence indicating that the County Attorney's Office engages in a pattern or practice of gender discrimination in violation of the Equal Protection Clause of the Fourteenth Amendment to the United States Constitution and relevant statutes. In particular, there are strong indications that the decisions of the County Attorney's Office regarding the investigation and prosecution of sexual assaults and rape, particularly nonstranger assaults and rapes, are influenced by gender bias and gender stereotyping and adversely affect women in Missoula.

Id. at 2.

Although the MCAO entered a Memorandum of Understanding with the U.S. Department of Justice, resolving the claims, the agreement was far from favorable to the Department of Justice. MCAO not only continued to deny any constitutional violations, it also denied that the Department of Justice had authority to bring suit to challenge the office's handling of sexual assault cases, and it was joined by the Montana Attorney General on that issue. See Memorandum of Understanding Between, the Montana Attorney General, The Missoula County Attorney's Office, Missoula County, and the United States Department of Justice (Jun. 10, 2014). Because the case never reached a court, the legal authority to bring this kind of suit against prosecutors' offices remains uncertain.

If the Department of Justice was right that prosecutors' offices can violate the Constitution by failing to bring cases vigorously enough, could it also sue prosecutors' offices that fail to bring criminal charges against police officers because of the race of the victims or in retaliation for victims' exercise of First Amendment rights?[6] Should it? What would the practical obstacles to such lawsuits be?

If the Department of Justice was right that prosecutors' offices can violate the Constitution by failing to bring cases vigorously enough, if they do so for an unconstitutional reason, then can private plaintiffs also bring suit against those offices for the same claim under 42 U.S.C. §1983? Does that suggest that, if the plaintiffs in Inmates of Attica could establish racial discrimination, they could have sued the prosecutors for damages or injunctive relief for failing to bring the cases against law enforcement officers? What about the court's arguments against such lawsuits in Inmates of Attica? If a nonprofit came to you for advice about how to develop the basis for such a lawsuit, what would you say?

2. Civil Litigation to Punish Prosecution

The plaintiffs in *Inmates of Attica* sued prosecutors because they did not prosecute law enforcement officers. The plaintiffs in the next case sued a prosecutor because she did. In reading the case, consider whether the Fourth Circuit's reasoning has anything in common with the Second Circuit's reasoning in *Inmates of Attica*.

---

[6] The Department of Justice has made analogous claims against police departments. For instance, it sued the Town of Colorado City, Arizona, and Hildale City, Utah, alleging that both towns violated the constitutional rights of residents in part by refusing to provide policing services to those who were not members of the Fundamentalist Church of Jesus Christ of Latter Day Saints based on their religion. The towns litigated the case and lost. Among its factual findings, the district court concluded that officers failed to provide effective police services to some residents based on their religion in violation of the Equal Protection Clause. United States v. Town of Colorado City, Arizona, No. 3:12-cv-8123-HRH, slip op. at 20–21 (D. Ariz. 2017), *aff'd*, 935 F.3d 804 (9th Cir. 2019). The defendants did not challenge this finding or its legal basis on appeal.

NERO v. MOSBY
890 F.3d 106 (4th Cir. 2018)

GREGORY, CHIEF JUDGE:

Freddie Gray, Jr., suffered fatal injuries while handcuffed and shackled in the custody of the Baltimore City Police Department. The Baltimore State's Attorney's Office, led by State's Attorney Marilyn Mosby, conducted an investigation into Gray's death. After the State Medical Examiner ruled Gray's death a homicide, Major Samuel Cogen of the Baltimore City Sheriff's Office criminally charged six of the police officers involved in Gray's arrest and detention. The same day, State's Attorney Mosby announced the charges and read the supporting probable-cause statement to the public at a press conference. A grand jury subsequently indicted the officers on substantially similar counts, but ultimately, none was convicted.

Five of the charged officers . . . now seek to make State's Attorney Mosby stand trial for malicious prosecution, defamation, and false light invasion of privacy. They claim that her role in independently investigating their conduct strips her of absolute prosecutorial immunity and that their bare allegations of malice or gross negligence overcome Maryland's statutory immunity protections. We resoundingly reject the invitation to cast aside decades of Supreme Court and circuit precedent to narrow the immunity prosecutors enjoy. And we find no justification for denying Mosby the protection from suit that the Maryland legislature has granted her.

I.

A.

Because this appeal comes to us at the motion-to-dismiss stage, we recount the facts as alleged by the Officers and must accept them as true for purposes of this appeal.

The morning of April 12, 2015, Lieutenant Rice encountered Freddie Gray, Jr., and another person walking along North Avenue in Baltimore City. After making eye contact with Rice, Gray and his companion ran. Rice pursued them and called for backup. Officers Miller and Nero responded; Miller chased Gray, and Nero chased Gray's companion. While pursuing Gray, Miller yelled that he had a taser and instructed Gray to get on the ground. Gray voluntarily surrendered with his hands up. Miller brought him to the ground and handcuffed him in a prone position. When Miller searched Gray, he found a knife and informed Gray that he was under arrest.

A police van arrived to transport Gray to the police station. Nero, who had failed to apprehend Gray's companion, and another officer placed Gray inside. Because a crowd of citizens was forming, the van and the officers—including Rice, Miller, Nero, and Officer Porter, who had arrived on the scene—reconvened one block south to complete the paperwork for Gray's arrest. At this second stop, Rice and Miller removed Gray from the van, replaced his handcuffs with flex cuffs, shackled his legs, and placed him back in the van. The van departed, and the officers returned to their patrol duties.

Shortly thereafter, Porter received a call from the van driver requesting assistance at another location several blocks away. Porter met the van at this third location, assisted the driver with opening the van's rear doors, and observed Gray lying prone on the floor of the van. Gray asked for medical assistance. Porter informed the driver that Gray should be taken to the hospital, and then he left.

Meanwhile, Miller and Nero returned to North Avenue, where they arrested another person and called for a police van and additional units. The van carrying Gray responded to this fourth location, as did Porter and Sergeant White, who had already "received supervisor complaints" about Gray's arrest. J.A. 169. The second arrestee was placed in the van. Gray again communicated to Porter that he wanted medical assistance. White separately attempted to speak with Gray, but Gray did not respond. Porter and White returned to their vehicles and followed the van to the Western District police station.

At the police station, Gray was found unconscious in the back of the van. An officer rendered emergency assistance, and Porter called a medic. White confirmed that a medic was en route. Gray was taken to the University of Maryland Shock Trauma Unit, where he died due to a neck injury on April 19, 2015. The State Medical Examiner ruled Gray's death a homicide.

On May 1, 2015, Major Cogen executed an application for Statement of Charges for each of the five Officers, plus the driver of the van. Each application contained the same affidavit, sworn by Major Cogen, reciting the facts supporting probable cause. The affidavit explained that Rice, Miller, and Nero illegally arrested Gray without probable cause because the knife found on him was legal. . . . The affidavit further stated that the officers repeatedly failed to seatbelt Gray in the back of the van, contrary to a Baltimore City Police Department General Order. It noted that Porter observed Gray on the floor of the van, but "[d]espite Mr. Gray's seriously deteriorating medical condition, no medical assistance was rendered to or summonsed for Mr. Gray at that time." And, the affidavit asserted, "White . . . spoke to the back of Mr. Gray's head. When he did not respond, she did nothing further despite the fact that she was advised that he needed a medic. She made no effort to look, assess or determine his condition."

A Maryland district court commissioner approved the applications and issued warrants for the Officers' arrests. Nero and Miller were each charged with two counts of assault in the second degree, two counts of misconduct in office, and false imprisonment. Rice was charged with manslaughter, two counts of assault in the second degree, two counts of misconduct in office, and false imprisonment. Porter and White were each charged with manslaughter, assault in the second degree, and misconduct in office.

Later that day, State's Attorney Mosby held a press conference to announce the charges and call for an end to the riots that had erupted in Baltimore following Gray's death. . . .

During the press conference, Mosby emphasized that she and her office independently investigated Gray's death. . . . Mosby concluded her speech by calling for peace in Baltimore as she moved forward with the charges. . . .

On May 21, 2015, a grand jury indicted all six officers on charges substantially similar to those listed in the Statements of Charges. Porter was tried before a jury, and after the jury could not reach a unanimous verdict, the judge declared a mistrial. Nero and Rice underwent bench trials, and the judge ultimately found them not guilty on all counts. Thereafter, Mosby dismissed all outstanding charges against Miller, White, and Porter.

B.

While the criminal charges against all of the Officers were still pending, the Officers sued State's Attorney Mosby. The Officers claimed that she violated their rights by bringing charges without probable cause and defamed the Officers by making false accusations against them at the May 1, 2015 press conference. . . .

Mosby moved to dismiss the Officers' claims, asserting various immunities. She asserted absolute prosecutorial immunity, or alternatively qualified immunity, for the §1983 malicious-prosecution claim; absolute prosecutorial immunity under Maryland common law and statutory immunity under the Maryland Tort Claims Act (MTCA) for the state malicious-prosecution claims; and MTCA immunity and common-law public-official immunity for the defamation and false-light claims. . . .

After a hearing, the district court allowed the three malicious-prosecution claims, the defamation claim, and the false-light claim to proceed.). . . . Mosby timely appealed. . . .

II.

We begin with the Officers' §1983 malicious-prosecution claim and State's Attorney Mosby's assertion of absolute prosecutorial immunity. . . .

Absolute immunity protects "the vigorous and fearless performance of the prosecutor's duty" that is so essential to a fair, impartial criminal justice system. *Imbler v. Pachtman*, 424 U.S. 409, 427–428 (1976). As representatives of the people, prosecutors have a responsibility to enforce the laws evenhandedly and to exercise independent judgment in seeking justice. . . . Without immunity from suit, this threat of retaliatory litigation would predispose prosecutors to bring charges based not on merit but on the social or political capital of prospective defendants. . . .

Mosby's alleged wrongs fall squarely under the umbrella of absolute immunity. Mosby correctly argued that the specific conduct the Officers challenge was within her role as an advocate. Therefore, the district court should have dismissed the §1983 malicious-prosecution claim.

The gravamen of the Officers' complaints is that Mosby and her office conducted an investigation into Gray's death, and despite finding no evidence of criminal wrongdoing, Mosby either instructed Cogen to file false charges or erroneously advised him that probable cause supported the charges. The Officers contend that Mosby brought charges against them "for the purpose of stopping the riots rather than prosecuting charges supported by probable cause."

The Officers also allege that Mosby misrepresented facts in the applications for Statement of Charges that Cogen executed and filed. . . .

At bottom, the Officers take issue with Mosby's decision to prosecute them and her role in preparing the charging documents.

These claims are barred by settled Supreme Court and circuit precedent. In *Kalina* [*v. Fletcher*, 522 U.S. 118 (1997)], the Supreme Court held that a prosecutor's "selection of the particular facts to include in the certification" of probable cause, "her drafting of the certification, her determination that the evidence was sufficiently strong to justify a probable-cause finding, her decision to file charges, and her presentation of the information" to the court are all entitled to absolute immunity. *Id.* at 130. And, in *Springmen*, we held that a Maryland Assistant State's Attorney enjoyed absolute immunity for reviewing an application for Statement of Charges prepared by a police officer and for advising the officer that the facts were sufficiently strong to proceed with filing the application. *Springmen v. Williams,* 122 F.3d 211, 212 (4th Cir. 1997).

We see no material difference between the conduct protected in *Kalina* and *Springmen* and the acts the Officers allege here. . . .

We also reject the Officers' argument that Mosby's involvement in the investigation of Gray's death strips her of absolute immunity. Certainly, prosecutors enjoy only qualified immunity for their actions before securing probable cause for an arrest. *Buckley v. Fitzsimmons,* 509 U.S. 259, 274 (1993). And Mosby apparently began investigating before she had probable cause. But conducting an investigation is not actionable—in fact, it was Mosby's *responsibility* to investigate—and the Officers make no specific allegation that Mosby engaged in misconduct during that investigation.

To the extent the Officers ask us to create a new rule that participation in an investigation deprives a prosecutor's subsequent acts of absolute immunity, we balk at the proposition. Such a rule would . . . effectively eliminate prosecutorial immunity in police-misconduct cases. Most jurisdictions, including Baltimore, charge prosecutors with independently investigating cases of criminal behavior by police. Per the Officers' theory, whenever a prosecutor takes on one of these cases, her actions—even those intimately tied to the judicial phase—no longer enjoy absolute immunity. This approach torpedoes the fundamental premise of absolute prosecutorial immunity: ensuring a fair, impartial criminal justice system, in which prosecutors have the independence to hold even powerful wrongdoers accountable without fear of vexatious litigation. And we refuse to sanction it. . . .

IV.

Finally, we address the Officers' state-law defamation and false-light claims, which arise from Mosby's press-conference statements. . . . We . . . hold that the MTCA bars the Officers from bringing suit based on Mosby's press-conference statements. . . .

. . . The Officers allege that, at the press conference, Mosby defamed them and invaded their privacy by placing them before the public in a false light. The MTCA bars these claims if Mosby's press-conference statements were "within the scope of [her] public duties" and "made without malice or gross negligence." Md. Code Ann., Cts. & Jud. Proc. §5-522(b). . . .

. . . Mosby's press-conference statements clearly fell within the scope of her employment. As Baltimore City's State's Attorney, Mosby was elected by the people of Baltimore to lead the city's State's Attorney's Office, a key agency in Maryland's state government. The State's Attorney's Office houses Baltimore's Police Integrity Unit and prosecutes crimes on behalf of the public. At the press conference, Mosby informed the public that her Police Integrity Unit had conducted an investigation into Freddie Gray's death, found probable cause to believe that the Officers had committed numerous crimes, and initiated criminal prosecutions against them. . . .

The Officers allege that Mosby used their arrests "for her own personal interests and political agendas" and thus acted outside the scope of her employment. But their argument is entirely devoid of support. The statements they cite—"I heard your call for 'No justice, no peace,'" "your peace is sincerely needed as I work to deliver justice," and "I will seek justice on your behalf"—simply do not give rise to a reasonable inference that Mosby acted for reasons other than furthering the operations of the State's Attorney's Office. The people of Baltimore elected Mosby to deliver justice. A young African-American man had been killed in the custody of the Baltimore City Police Department, and the city was rioting. Pursuing justice—i.e., using the legal system to reach a fair and just resolution to Gray's death—was not a political move. It was Mosby's duty. And Mosby was well within her role to tell the people of Baltimore, and the nation, that she was carrying out that duty. The viability of a democratic government requires that the channels of communication between citizens and their public officials remain open and unimpeded. That Mosby may gain some future career advantage for doing her job well does not take her actions outside the scope of her employment. . . .

V.

In conclusion, none of the Officers' claims can survive the motion-to-dismiss stage. That the Officers disagree with Mosby's decision to prosecute—as most defendants do—or with the information in the application for Statement of Charges—which inherently contains defamatory information—does not entitle them to litigate their disagreement in court, and much less recover damages.

The Officers' malicious-prosecution claims epitomize the "vexatious litigation" that absolute prosecutorial immunity is designed to preclude. See Pachaly v. City of Lynchburg, 897 F.2d 723, 727–728 (4th Cir. 1990). Having "transform[ed] [their] resentment at being prosecuted into the ascription of improper and malicious actions to the State's advocate," see Imbler, 424 U.S. at 425, the Officers ask us to depart from well-settled law so that they can force Mosby to defend her decision to seek justice on behalf of Freddie Gray. We find their arguments both meritless and disconcerting. . . .

The Officers' defamation and false-light claims are equally bereft of support. The Officers cite no facts showing that Mosby spoke at the press conference with malice or gross negligence, as required by the MTCA. Their allegations, accepted as true, do not even negate that Mosby had probable cause to charge them. And the Officers' contention that Mosby acted outside the scope of her employment by telling the public that she would pursue justice borders on absurd.

Perhaps to the Officers' chagrin, they must accept that they are subject to the same laws as every other defendant who has been prosecuted and acquitted. Those laws clearly bar the type of retaliatory suits that the Officers brought here. The district court therefore erred in allowing their claims to proceed.

Reversed.

WILKINSON, CIRCUIT JUDGE, concurring:

I am pleased to join Chief Judge Gregory's fine opinion. . . .

I wish only to underscore my colleague's concern about the perils of appellees' defamation claim. State's Attorney Mosby is an elected official. After the death of Freddie Gray, her community, her constituents, and her city faced a crisis of confidence. Baltimore's citizens had their faith shaken, not only in the police, but in the very ability of government to administer justice. As any of us would expect of our political leaders, Mosby responded to a crisis. And as all of us should demand from our political leaders, Mosby explained her actions to the public. At a press conference, she read from a charging document, praised investigators, and explained the basis of the prosecution. To say that an elected official exposes herself to liability by discharging her democratic duty to justify the decisions she was elected to make is to elevate tort law above our most cherished constitutional ideals. . . .

This is not to say that a prosecutor can never face consequences for reckless public remarks. But the proper avenue for regulating prosecutorial statements is a state's ethical code governing attorneys, not private tort suits. . . .

By advancing a theory of tort liability for explanations of official acts, the officers here strike at the very heart of the democratic dialogue. Courts must repel such attacks. In doing so, we honor our "profound national commitment to the principle that debate on public issues should be unlimited, robust, and wide-open" on all sides. New York Times Co. v. Sullivan, 376 U.S. 254, 270 (1964).

Defamation law unbound is inimical to free expression. I thought the principle of *New York Times v. Sullivan* secure. But no. As the saying goes, the censors never sleep. Here they come again.

NOTES AND QUESTIONS

1. *Punishing decisions to prosecute. Mosby* involves a damages action against a prosecutor. Should decisions to prosecute ever be subject to this kind of collateral litigation? Would you feel differently if the *victims* of police misconduct rather than the police officers were involved? What if a suspect against whom excessive force was used was charged with resisting arrest?

2. *The criminal cases.* This civil suit was filed after the charges Mosby brought against the officers involved in Freddie Gray's death failed spectacularly. Circuit Judge Barry G. Williams declared a mistrial in the trial of Officer William Porter, after the jury deliberated for three days but could not come to a verdict. Judge Williams subsequently found Officer Caesar Goodson, Officer Edward Nero, and Lieutenant Brian Rice not guilty of all charges, each in a separate bench trial. After that, prosecutors dropped charges against the other officers. Mosby's experience has been a caution to other prosecutors. See, e.g., *Minnesota Attorney General, "I Anticipate There Will Be Charges,"* CNN (May 29, 2020) (explaining delays in charging police officers involved in George Floyd's death, noting "we have seen cases that seem so clear go south"). Interestingly, Judge Williams, who is African American, has both worked with police officers as a state's attorney in Baltimore and prosecuted them as a trial attorney in the U.S. Department of Justice, Civil Rights Division's Criminal Section. It would have been hard to find a judge with more credibility to hear such cases.

3. *Constitutional challenges to decisions to prosecute.* Although the primary mechanism for scrutinizing criminal charges is to bring them to trial, in limited circumstances, defendants may challenge a prosecutor's decision to bring charges on the ground that it violates the Constitution. For example, in a *selective prosecution* claim, a defendant may argue that he was chosen for prosecution on the basis of his race or in retaliation for First Amendment activity. In practice, however, the standards set by the Supreme Court for bringing selective prosecution claims make them exceptionally rare. See, e.g., United States v. Armstrong, 517 U.S. 456 (1996); Wayte v. United States, 470 U.S. 598 (1985). Does the court in *Mosby* explain why?

4. *And there's more.* In addition to the civil suit against her, and the political fallout both for bringing and for losing the criminal cases, Mosby had a bar complaint filed against her by a law professor uninvolved in the case. The complaint alleged that Mosby violated ethical rules by bringing the charges because " 'charges

were clearly unwarranted by the evidence'" and "'not even supported by probable cause.'" *Grievance Against Md. Prosecutor in Gray Cases,* Courthouse News (Jun. 30, 2016). If so, why did Judge Williams hold a trial? Isn't dismissal the proper remedy for overcharging? Is this kind of bar complaint liable to deter other prosecutors from bringing charges against police officers? But what if a prosecutor *does* bring politically motivated charges unsupported by the evidence? What remedy should there be?

In a widely reported case in 2006, Durham County, North Carolina, District Attorney Mike Nifong brought rape charges against several Duke University men's lacrosse players based on exceptionally weak evidence in an apparent attempt to help himself in a tight election. He continued to pursue the charges after evidence undermined the alleged victim's accusations; he also withheld exculpatory DNA evidence from defense lawyers in the case, and then lied in court about having done so. Nifong was disbarred, forced from office, and convicted of criminal contempt. See *Nifong Guilty of Criminal Contempt; Sentenced to 1 Day in Jail,* WRAL (Aug. 31, 2007). How is Nifong's conduct different from Mosby's? Can you articulate a principle for when prosecutors should face collateral consequences for charging decisions?

Why Prosecute the Police?

Why is criminal prosecution of police officers so important to so many people?

Some argue that criminally prosecuting police officers will deter future offenders, but right now, the threat of criminal charges is probably not a strong deterrent. Criminal prosecutions take at least months, and often years, to resolve; sentences are often short; and although it is hard to say what proportion of officers who commit crimes are convicted, most commentators think it is not high. How much of that can be changed to strengthen the deterrent effect?

Note also that criminal prosecutions focus on the individual officer. Most experts believe that excessive force is best prevented by institutional changes, including training, supervision, policies, and disciplinary processes, matters that are within the control of police chiefs and command staff, rather than the officer on the street. Is convicting an officer likely to encourage departmental reform? How might such a cause-and-effect operate? If not, should criminal prosecutions still be pushed as a deterrent?

Of course, deterrence is not the only reason to prosecute criminals. This chapter started with calls for justice in Michael Brown's death. Those calls rarely focused on stopping future bad acts. Instead, they emphasized retribution—imposing harm on the perpetrators to balance the scales of justice. State-imposed retribution can seem especially important when a *police officer* commits a crime, because—unless punished—a police officer's crimes seem to signal the state's contempt for the victims as citizens. Criminally prosecuting the officers counteracts that disrespect and recognizes the political status of victims and their communities.

Some go further and argue that punishing police officers is a way to reinforce new values. "If the criminal justice system in America tends to tell the story of dangerous black men plaguing society with brutal crimes, the prosecution of the police can offer a new narrative." Rebecca Roiphe, *The Duty to Charge in Police Use of*

Excessive Force Cases, 65 Clev. St. L. Rev. 503, 517 (2017). In this view, criminal prosecutions should be used to push new societal norms as well as to punish clear violations of old ones. This strategy of prosecuting crimes to shift social attitudes has been successful with respect to driving while intoxicated and domestic violence crimes. Could that happen with police violence? Should it? Is it fair to put people in prison to "offer a new narrative"?

Are there other reasons you think police officers who break the law should be prosecuted?

D. *Federal Criminal Prosecution*

When accused police officers escape prosecution or conviction locally, critics inevitably call for federal action. When people talk of federal criminal prosecution of police officers, they are usually talking about the work of the Criminal Section of the U.S. Department of Justice, Civil Rights Division. The Criminal Section works with the FBI and U.S. Attorney's Offices around the country to investigate and charge cases involving excessive force, sexual assault, theft, false arrest, and other crimes by law enforcement officials. Although the Criminal Section prosecutes other civil rights crimes, including hate crimes and human-trafficking cases, violence by police officers and other government officials has long been the mainstay of the Section's work.

The Criminal Section started in an early form more than 80 years ago. In February 1939, just one month after he was appointed U.S. Attorney General, Frank Murphy established the Civil Liberties Unit in the U.S. Justice Department (DOJ). It was dedicated to "the aggressive protection of fundamental rights inherent in free people," including by "a program of diligent action in the prosecution of infringement of these rights."[7] The Unit—soon renamed the Civil Rights Section to avoid confusion with the American Civil Liberties Union—later evolved into the contemporary Civil Rights Division, which continues to include the Criminal Section, devoted to prosecuting civil rights offenses, including criminal constitutional violations by police officers.[8]

Unlike many state decisions about police prosecutions, federal decisions are largely made by committed civil rights prosecutors based on independent investigations by the FBI. Yet no more than a few dozen law enforcement officers are prosecuted federally each year. The following sections suggest some reasons why.

1. Primary Statute

Federal prosecutors use this federal statute most often when they prosecute police officers.

---

[7] Murphy served only a year as Attorney General. In January 1940, he was nominated by President Franklin D. Roosevelt to the U.S. Supreme Court and was confirmed 11 days later.

[8] *Ed. note:* I served as a prosecutor in the Criminal Section from 1998 to 2006.

18 U.S.C. §242

Whoever, under color of any law, statute, ordinance, regulation, or custom, willfully subjects any person in any State, Territory, Commonwealth, Possession, or District to the deprivation of any rights, privileges, or immunities secured or protected by the Constitution or laws of the United States, or to different punishments, pains, or penalties, on account of such person being an alien, or by reason of his color, or race, than are prescribed for the punishment of citizens, shall be fined under this title or imprisoned not more than one year, or both; and if bodily injury results from the acts committed in violation of this section or if such acts include the use, attempted use, or threatened use of a dangerous weapon, explosives, or fire, shall be fined under this title or imprisoned not more than ten years, or both; and if death results from the acts committed in violation of this section or if such acts include kidnapping or an attempt to kidnap, aggravated sexual abuse, or an attempt to commit aggravated sexual abuse, or an attempt to kill, shall be fined under this title, or imprisoned for any term of years or for life, or both, or may be sentenced to death.

Section 242 is hard to parse. The Supreme Court has interpreted it to create two different criminal offenses. The first clause prohibits the willful deprivation of constitutional rights, which is the one used today against police officers. It does not require proving discrimination or racial injustice—although the cases often take place in the context of the historically fraught relationship between the police and people of color. The second offense prohibits courts and legislatures from formally imposing different punishments, pains, or penalties on the basis of alienage, color, or race. United States v. Classic, 313 U.S. 299, 327 (1941). That almost never happens, so this part of the statute is effectively a dead letter. In summary, then, §242 makes it an offense to willfully deprive a person of a constitutional right while acting under color of law.

As it is used today, §242 creates a crime with three elements:

1. that the defendant acted under color of law;
2. that the defendant acted willfully; and
3. that the defendant deprived the victim of a right secured by the Constitution or laws of the United States.

The next sections consider these elements in more detail.

Misdemeanors vs. Felonies Under 18 U.S.C. §242

Reread §242. Without *bodily injury*, use of a *dangerous weapon*, or another aggravating factor, a §242 violation is a misdemeanor. That means that an officer who plants evidence on a suspect, deliberately makes a false arrest, or coerces someone to have sex without force or the threat of force is subject to no more than one year in prison. Yet, one punch, kick, or slap to an arrestee in the heat of the moment can be a felony, if it causes injury, as can almost any use of a weapon.

Prosecutors sometimes have discretion to choose whether to charge a felony or a misdemeanor. For example, *bodily injury* has been construed broadly by the courts. Especially when an injury is minor, a prosecutor can bring a felony charge, but no one would look twice if the prosecutor instead charged a misdemeanor. On what basis do you think prosecutors make such choices?

Whatever might shape charging decisions in ordinary cases, prosecutors have another factor to consider in charging police officers: A felony conviction ends an officer's career. Under federal law, felons may not possess firearms, and states both expect officers to carry weapons and prohibit felons from serving as officers.[9] By contrast, a misdemeanor conviction might not be definitive: Some states allow misdemeanants to serve as officers, even if they have been convicted of a civil rights violation.

Should these employment consequences factor into a prosecutor's charging decisions? Federal prosecutors are generally permitted to consider collateral consequences in determining whether a charge would serve federal interests. See U.S. Dept. of Justice, *Justice Manual* §9-27.230 (calling "[t]he probable sentence *or other consequences* if a person is convicted" a relevant consideration in initiating charges). In ordinary criminal cases, prosecutors often take into account whether a defendant will end up as a registered sex offender or suffer immigration consequences as result of a criminal charge. Is this different? If prosecutors do consider that an officer will no longer be able to serve after a felony conviction, which way should it cut?

The DOJ purports to limit federal prosecutors' discretion to charge misdemeanors in place of felonies. Under the Department's Charging and Sentencing Policy, prosecutors are required to charge the "most serious, readily provable offense," except under exceptional circumstances. Memorandum from Jefferson B. Sessions, Attorney Gen., U.S. Dept. of Justice, to All Federal Prosecutors (May 10, 2017). In practice, it is hard to enforce such a missive. In many instances only prosecutors working directly on a case can discern the most serious, readily provable offense, including in circumstances like the ones presented by police cases.

2.   Interpreting Willfulness

Section 242 requires that officers prosecuted for violating constitutional rights act *willfully*, and many see that as the most significant legal obstacle to federal civil rights prosecutions for excessive force. What does willfulness mean in this context? The Supreme Court decides in the next case.[10]

---

[9] Not every state enforces its criminal history rules for officers fully. See, e.g., Kyle Hopkins, *Dozens of Convicted Criminals Have Been Hired as Cops in Rural Alaska. Sometimes, They're the Only Applicants,* Anchorage Daily News (July 18, 2019).

[10] Section 242 was originally enacted in the Civil Rights Act of 1866. It was joined by §241, a conspiracy statute enacted in the Enforcement Act of 1870 (discussed *infra*). The two laws became Rev. Stat. §§5508 and 5510 in 1873; then Criminal Code §§19 and 20 in 1909; and 18 U.S.C. §§51 and 52 upon adoption of the U.S. Code in 1926. They finally moved to 18 U.S.C. §§241 and 242 with the recodification of Title 18 in 1948. Besides the addition of *willfully* as described in *Screws*, and the addition of the death penalty, only minor alterations have been made to the text of either law. In *Screws*, the statutes are referred to as 18 U.S.C. §§51 and 52. Although statute numbering is preserved within the cases, for simplicity, the text of this chapter refers to the statutes as §241 and §242, even when discussing their precursors.

SCREWS v. UNITED STATES
325 U.S. 91 (1945)

MR. JUSTICE DOUGLAS announced the judgment of the Court and delivered the following opinion, in which the CHIEF JUSTICE, MR. JUSTICE BLACK and MR. JUSTICE REED concur.

This case involves a shocking and revolting episode in law enforcement. Petitioner Screws was sheriff of Baker County, Georgia. He enlisted the assistance of petitioner Jones, a policeman, and petitioner Kelley, a special deputy, in arresting Robert Hall, a citizen of the United States and of Georgia. The arrest was made late at night at Hall's home on a warrant charging Hall with theft of a tire. Hall, a young negro about thirty years of age, was handcuffed and taken by car to the court house. As Hall alighted from the car at the court house square, the three petitioners began beating him with their fists and with a solid-bar blackjack about eight inches long and weighing two pounds. They claimed Hall had reached for a gun and had used insulting language as he alighted from the car. But after Hall, still handcuffed, had been knocked to the ground they continued to beat him from fifteen to thirty minutes until he was unconscious. Hall was then dragged feet first through the court house yard into the jail and thrown upon the floor dying. An ambulance was called and Hall was removed to a hospital where he died within the hour and without regaining consciousness. There was evidence that Screws held a grudge against Hall and had threatened to "get" him.

An indictment was returned against petitioners—one count charging a violation of §20 of the Criminal Code, 18 U.S.C. §52, and another charging a conspiracy to violate §20 contrary to §37 of the Criminal Code, 18 U.S.C. §88. . . .

The case was tried to a jury. . . .

The jury returned a verdict of guilty and a fine and imprisonment on each count was imposed. The Circuit Court of Appeals affirmed the judgment of conviction, one judge dissenting. . . .

We are met at the outset with the claim that §20 is unconstitutional, in so far as it makes criminal acts in violation of the due process clause of the Fourteenth Amendment. The argument runs as follows: It is true that this Act as construed in *United States v. Classic,* 313 U.S. 299 (1941), was upheld in its application to certain ballot box frauds committed by state officials. But in that case the constitutional rights protected were the rights to vote specifically guaranteed by Art. I, §2 and §4 of the Constitution. Here there is no ascertainable standard of guilt. There have been conflicting views in the Court as to the proper construction of the due process clause. . . .

. . . [T]he decisions of the courts are, to be sure, a source of reference for ascertaining the specific content of the concept of due process. But even so the Act would incorporate by reference a large body of changing and uncertain law. That law is not always reducible to specific rules, is expressible only in general terms, and turns many times on the facts of a particular case. Accordingly, it is argued that such a body of legal principles lacks the basic specificity necessary for criminal statutes under our system of government. . . .

. . . Those who enforced local law today might not know for many months (and meanwhile could not find out) whether what they did deprived some one of due process of law. The enforcement of a criminal statute so construed would indeed cast law enforcement agencies loose at their own risk on a vast uncharted sea.

If such a construction is not necessary, it should be avoided. . . .

Sec. 20 was enacted to enforce the Fourteenth Amendment. It derives from §2 of the Civil Rights Act of April 9, 1866, 14 Stat. 27. . . . The requirement for a "willful" violation was introduced by the draftsmen of the Criminal Code of 1909. And we are told "willfully" was added to §20 in order to make the section "less severe". 43 Cong. Rec., 60th Cong., 2d Sess., p. 3599.

We hesitate to say that when Congress sought to enforce the Fourteenth Amendment in this fashion it did a vain thing. . . . Only if no construction can save the Act from this claim of unconstitutionality are we willing to reach that result. We do not reach it, for we are of the view that if §20 is confined more narrowly than the lower courts confined it, it can be preserved as one of the sanctions to the great rights which the Fourteenth Amendment was designed to secure.

II.

We recently pointed out that "willful" is a word "of many meanings, its construction often being influenced by its context." Spies v. United States, 317 U.S. 492, 497 (1943). . . .

An analysis of the cases in which "willfully" has been held to connote more than an act which is voluntary or intentional . . . make clear that if we construe "willfully" in §20 as connoting a purpose to deprive a person of a specific constitutional right, we would introduce no innovation. . . . [W]here the punishment imposed is only for an act knowingly done with the purpose of doing that which the statute prohibits, the accused cannot be said to suffer from lack of warning or knowledge that the act which he does is a violation of law. . . . We think [such] a . . . course is appropriate here. . . .

Once the section is given that construction, we think that the claim that the section lacks an ascertainable standard of guilt must fail. . . .

It is said, however, that this construction of the Act will not save it from the infirmity of vagueness since neither a law enforcement official nor a trial judge can know with sufficient definiteness the range of rights that are constitutional. But that criticism is wide of the mark. For the specific intent required by the Act is an intent to deprive a person of a right which has been made specific either by the express terms of the Constitution or laws of the United States or by decisions interpreting them. . . . He who defies a decision interpreting the Constitution knows precisely what he is doing. If sane, he hardly may be heard to say that he knew not what he did. Of course, willful conduct cannot make definite that which is undefined. But willful violators of constitutional requirements, which have been defined, certainly are in no position to say that they had no adequate advance notice that they would be visited with punishment. When they act willfully in the sense in which we use the word, they act in open defiance or in reckless disregard of a constitutional requirement which has been made specific and definite. When they are convicted for so acting, they are not punished for violating an unknowable something. . . .

. . . The fact that the defendants may not have been thinking in constitutional terms is not material where their aim was not to enforce local law but to deprive a citizen of a right and that right was protected by the Constitution. When they so act they at least act in reckless disregard of constitutional prohibitions or guarantees. Likewise, it is plain that basic to the concept of due process of law in a criminal case is a trial—a trial in a court of law, not a "trial by ordeal." Brown v. Mississippi, 297 U.S. 278, 285 (1936). . . . Those who decide to take the law into their own hands and act as prosecutor, jury, judge, and executioner plainly act to deprive a prisoner of the trial which due process of law guarantees him. And such a purpose need not be expressed; it may at times be reasonably inferred from all the circumstances attendant on the act.

The difficulty here is that this question of intent was not submitted to the jury with the proper instructions. . . . [I]n view of our construction of the word "willfully" the jury should have been further instructed that it was not sufficient that petitioners had a generally bad purpose. To convict it was necessary for them to find that petitioners had the purpose to deprive the prisoner of a constitutional right, e.g. the right to be tried by a court rather than by ordeal. And in determining whether that requisite bad purpose was present the jury would be entitled to consider all the attendant circumstance — the malice of petitioners, the weapons used in the assault, its character and duration, the provocation, if any, and the like. . . .

III.

It is said, however, that petitioners did not act "under color of any law" within the meaning of §20 of the Criminal Code. We disagree. We are of the view that petitioners acted under "color" of law in making the arrest of Robert Hall and in assaulting him. They were officers of the law who made the arrest. By their own admissions they assaulted Hall in order to protect themselves and to keep their prisoner from escaping. . . .

. . . He who acts under "color" of law may be a federal officer or a state officer. He may act under "color" of federal law or of state law. The statute does not come into play merely because the federal law or the state law under which the officer purports to act is violated. It is applicable when and only when some one is deprived of a federal right by that action. The fact that it is also a violation of state law does not make it any the less a federal offense punishable as such. Nor does its punishment by federal authority encroach on state authority or relieve the state from its responsibility for punishing state offenses.[10]

. . . We are not dealing here with a case where an officer not authorized to act nevertheless takes action. Here the state officers were authorized to make an arrest and to take such steps as were necessary to make the arrest effective. They acted without authority only in the sense that they used excessive force in making the arrest effective. It is clear that under "color" of law means under "pretense" of law. Thus acts of officers in the ambit of their personal pursuits are plainly excluded. Acts of officers who undertake to perform their official duties are included whether they hew to the line of their authority or overstep it. If, as suggested, the statute was designed to embrace only action which the State in fact authorized, the words "under color of any law" were hardly apt words to express the idea. . . .

Since there must be a new trial, the judgment below is reversed.

Reversed.

[Mr. Justice Rutledge's opinion, concurring in the result, is omitted.]

---

[10] The petitioners may be guilty of manslaughter or murder under Georgia law and at the same time liable for the federal offense proscribed by §20. The instances where "an act denounced as a crime by both national and state sovereignties" may be punished by each without violation of the double jeopardy provision of the Fifth Amendment are common.

Mr. Justice Murphy, dissenting.

I dissent. Robert Hall, a Negro citizen, has been deprived not only of the right to be tried by a court rather than by ordeal. He has been deprived of the right of life itself. That right belonged to him not because he was a Negro or a member of any particular race or creed. That right was his because he was an American citizen, because he was a human being. As such, he was entitled to all the respect and fair treatment that befits the dignity of man, a dignity that is recognized and guaranteed by the Constitution. Yet not even the semblance of due process has been accorded him. He has been cruelly and unjustifiably beaten to death by local police officers acting under color of authority derived from the state. It is difficult to believe that such an obvious and necessary right is indefinitely guaranteed by the Constitution or is foreign to the knowledge of local police officers so as to cast any reasonable doubt on the conviction under Section 20 of the Criminal Code of the perpetrators of this "shocking and revolting episode in law enforcement."

. . . We are unconcerned here with state officials who have coerced a confession from a prisoner, denied counsel to a defendant or made a faulty tax assessment. Whatever doubt may exist in those or in other situations as to whether the state officials could reasonably anticipate and recognize the relevant constitutional rights is immaterial in this case. Our attention here is directed solely to three state officials who, in the course of their official duties, have unjustifiably beaten and crushed the body of a human being, thereby depriving him of trial by jury and of life itself. The only pertinent inquiry is whether Section 20, by its reference to the Fourteenth Amendment guarantee that no state shall deprive any person of life without due process of law, gives fair warning of state officials that they are criminally liable for violating this right to life.

Common sense gives an affirmative answer to that problem. . . . There is nothing vague or indefinite in these references to this most basic of all human rights. Knowledge of a comprehensive law library is unnecessary for officers of the law to know that the right to murder individuals in the course of their duties is unrecognized in this nation. . . . To subject a state official to punishment under Section 20 for such acts is not to penalize him without fair and definite warning. Rather it is to uphold elementary standards of decency and to make American principles of law and our constitutional guarantees mean something more than pious rhetoric.

. . . Too often unpopular minorities, such as Negroes, are unable to find effective refuge from the cruelties of bigoted and ruthless authority. States are undoubtedly capable of punishing their officers who commit such outrages. But where, as here, the states are unwilling for some reason to prosecute such crimes the federal government must step in unless constitutional guarantees are to become atrophied.

This necessary intervention, however, will be futile if courts disregard reality and misuse the principle that criminal statutes must be clear and definite. Here state officers have violated with reckless abandon a plain constitutional right of an American citizen. . . . We should therefore affirm the judgment.

Mr. Justice Roberts, Mr. Justice Frankfurter and Mr. Justice Jackson, dissenting.

Three law enforcement officers of Georgia, a county sheriff, a special deputy and a city policeman, arrested a young Negro charged with a local crime, that of stealing a tire. While he was in their custody and handcuffed, they so severely beat the lad that he died. . . . Of course the petitioners are punishable. The only issue is whether Georgia alone has the power and duty to punish, or whether this patently local crime can be made the basis of a federal prosecution. The practical question is whether the States should be relieved from responsibility to bring their law officers to book for homicide, by allowing prosecutions in the federal courts for a relatively minor offense carrying a short sentence. The legal question is whether, for the purpose of accomplishing this relaxation of State responsibility, hitherto settled principles for the protection of civil liberties shall be bent and tortured. . . .

In subjecting to punishment "deprivation of any rights, privileges, or immunities secured or protected by the Constitution and laws of the United States", Section 20 on its face makes criminal deprivation of the whole range of undefined appeals to the Constitution. Such is the true scope of the forbidden conduct. Its domain is unbounded and therefore too indefinite. Criminal statutes must have more or less specific contours. This has none. . . .

. . . "Willfully" doing something that is forbidden, when that something is not sufficiently defined according to the general conceptions of requisite certainty in our criminal law, is not rendered sufficiently definite by that unknowable having been done "willfully". It is true also of a statute that it cannot lift itself up by its bootstraps. . . .

. . . There can be no doubt that this shapeless and all-embracing statute can serve as a dangerous instrument of political intimidation and coercion in the hands of those so inclined.

We are told local authorities cannot be relied upon for courageous and prompt action, that often they have personal or political reasons for refusing to prosecute. If it be significantly true that crimes against local law cannot be locally prosecuted, it is an ominous sign indeed. In any event, the cure is a re-invigoration of State responsibility. It is not an undue incursion of remote federal authority into local duties with consequent debilitation of local responsibility. . . .

NOTES AND QUESTIONS

1. *Historical context of* Screws *prosecution.* Before *Classic* and *Screws*, 18 U.S.C. §§241 and 242 had not been used for decades. When Attorney General Murphy created the Civil Rights Section in 1939, he did so without a clear legislative mandate. To pursue its mission, the Section attempted to jury-rig prosecutions using existing statutes. Initially, the Section used §§241 and 242 cautiously and attacked only official acts that violated express constitutional provisions, as in *Classic*. When those cases succeeded, the *Screws* prosecution was brought to test whether §242 could be used to address a broader array of civil rights complaints, including those involving individual acts of police misconduct. See Frederick M. Lawrence, *Civil Rights and Criminal Wrongs: The Mens Rea of Federal Civil Rights Crimes*, 67 Tul. L. Rev. 2113, 2170–2171 (1993).

As the dissenting opinions in *Screws* might suggest, critics at the time attacked federal prosecutions of police officers from two directions. Some saw the DOJ's efforts as unwarranted interference into local control of law enforcement. To others, the Section's efforts were inadequate and impotent, given the challenge of protecting civil rights nationally. Those dual criticisms continue today, although the first of them is more often levied against the Civil Rights Division's civil suits against police departments, discussed in Chapter 15, rather than its criminal prosecutions.

2. *The Legacy of* Screws. *Screws* has a mixed legacy. On one hand, *Screws* ensured the survival of the Civil Rights Section and enabled federal police prosecutions. "Without such a statute, this fundamental civil rights protection would have become meaningless. Since it is unlikely that Congress would have enacted a new law, the Department of Justice could not have functioned in this area." Harry H. Shapiro, *Limitations in*

Prosecuting Civil Rights Violations, 46 Cornell L.Q. 532, 536 (1961). Because *Screws* upheld the Civil Rights Section's use of the statute, the Section lived on. It became the Civil Rights Division, grew in importance, and prosecuted police officers, not only for brutality, but also other kinds of unconstitutional conduct, highlighting the federal commitment to civil rights. For more on the background on *Screws* and an optimistic view of its significance in civil rights history, see Hon. Paul J. Watford, Screws v. United States *and the Birth of Federal Civil Rights Enforcement*, 98 Marq. L. Rev. 465 (2014).

On the other hand, Justice Douglas's Delphic decision on *willfulness* has often stymied federal police prosecutions, which number only a few dozen each year. The Civil Rights Division acts cautiously in initiating federal prosecutions, and even with that caution, unsympathetic judges and juries sometimes reject convictions in the face of seemingly clear civil rights violations—in part, it seems, because the *willfulness* instruction mandated by *Screws* allows them to do so.

Section 242 and Constitutional Rights

When commentators talk about problems with §242, they almost inevitably focus on willfulness. However, a §242 prosecution also requires that the defendant have deprived the victim of a right under the laws or Constitution. As the statute suggests and *Screws* confirms, §242 does not confer rights. Instead, it provides a way to vindicate existing rights when officers violate them. The rights, incorporated by reference, must come from elsewhere, almost always from the U.S. Constitution.

As earlier chapters in this book suggest, constitutional rights are interpreted based on text, history, and institutional concerns that have nothing to do with whether police officers should engage in the conduct. As a result, many forms of objectionable, harmful conduct are not unconstitutional, or are not clearly so; and under existing law, police officers cannot usually be federally prosecuted for such conduct. When protesters' calls for federal criminal prosecutions of police officers go unmet, it is often because the officer's conduct—as terrible as it seems—did not violate the Constitution, rather than because the officer did not act willfully.

Recall, for instance, that *Tennessee v. Garner*, 471 U.S. 1, 11 (1985), permits police officers to shoot fleeing felons in the back as they run away "if the suspect threatens the officer with a weapon or there is probable cause to believe that he has committed a crime involving the infliction or threatened infliction of serious physical harm." In the context of non-deadly force incidents, some circuits hold that so-called *de minimis force* during a lawful arrest does not violate the Fourth Amendment, even if it is clearly unnecessary. Moreover, they construe *de minimis* force broadly. In *Nolin v. Isbell*, 207 F.3d 1253, 1255 (11th Cir. 2000), for example—a case that has been cited approvingly many times—the Eleventh Circuit applied this rule when an officer grabbed an unresisting suspect "from behind by the shoulder and wrist, threw him against a van three or four feet away, kneed him in the back and pushed his head into the side of the van, searched his groin area in an uncomfortable manner, and handcuffed him." The *Nolin* Court suggested that a chokehold could similarly be *de minimis*. See *id.* at 1256 (citing *Post*). Relatedly, other federal courts have held that chokeholds are not always unconstitutional. See, e.g., Thompson v. City of Chicago, 472 F.3d 444, 446 (7th Cir. 2006).

If these acts are constitutional, they cannot be prosecuted with §242 or, in most cases, any other federal statute. Can you imagine reasons Congress might want to

> criminalize unnecessary force or chokeholds even when federal courts do not con-
> sider them unconstitutional? Should it pass laws to achieve those ends?
>
> To be sure, Congress's power to criminalize police conduct is not unlimited, but
> it is not restricted to criminalizing constitutional violations either. Congress has wide
> latitude to enact prophylactic legislation that prohibits *constitutional* conduct to pre-
> vent and deter *unconstitutional* conduct, so long as the legislation is congruent and
> proportional to the harm it seeks to avert. See Nev. Dept. of Human Res. v. Hibbs,
> 538 U.S. 721, 727–728 (2003); City of Boerne v. Flores, 521 U.S. 507, 520 (1997).
> Could you argue that criminalizing chokeholds and intentionally unnecessary force is
> necessary to prevent constitutional violations? Might that kind of statutory interven-
> tion matter more than solving the problem of willfulness?

3. *Applying* Screws. Can you figure out what precisely *Screws* requires the government to prove to establish *willfulness*? The opinion is hardly a paragon of clarity,
and in the 75 years since it was decided, lawyers and courts have never stopped
struggling to figure out what it means. The result is that definitions and jury instructions on *willfulness* vary, sometimes significantly. Here are three examples.

The Fifth Circuit has approved this instruction:

> The word "willfully," as that term has been used from time to time in these instruc-
> tions means that the act was committed voluntarily and purposely with the specific
> intent to do something the law forbids. That is to say, with a bad purpose either to
> disobey or to disregard the law.

United States v. Garza, 754 F.2d 1202, 1210 (5th Cir. 1985) (cited approvingly in United
States v. McRae, 795 F.3d 471, 479 n.36 (2015); United States v. Sipe, 388 F.3d 471, 479–
480 n.21 (2004)). Pursuant to the Fifth Circuit's pattern instructions, courts often add:

> To find that the defendant was acting willfully, it is not necessary for you to find
> that the defendant knew the specific Constitutional provision or federal law that his
> [her] conduct violated. But the defendant must have a specific intent to deprive the
> person of a right protected by the Constitution or federal law.

Instruction 2.12, in Committee on Pattern Jury Instructions, District Judges
Association Fifth Circuit, *Pattern Jury Instructions (Criminal Cases)* 123 (2019). Is this
true to *Screws*? What does it mean to "have a specific intent to deprive the person of
a right," but not know the right that was violated?

The Fourth Circuit has held:

> To satisfy the element of "willful" conduct, the government must prove that the
> defendant acted "with the particular purpose of violating a protected right made
> definite by the rule of law or recklessly disregard[ed] the risk that [he] would do so."

United States v. Cowden, 882 F.3d 464, 474 (4th Cir. 2018) (quoting United States v.
Mohr, 318 F.3d 613, 619 (4th Cir. 2003)). Can you make sense of that?

The Seventh Circuit in 2019 approved a district court instruction that stated
that the defendant acted willfully if he "intended to deprive" either victim of his
right to be free from unreasonable force and continued:

> The defendant acted intentionally if he used force knowing that the force he used was more than what a reasonable officer would have used under the circumstances. The defendant did not act intentionally if he did not know that the force he used was more than what a reasonable officer would have used under the circumstances.

United States v. Proano, 912 F.3d 431, 442 (7th Cir. 2019).

How different are these instructions from each other? Are they all reasonable applications of *Screws*? Are juries likely to understand them? Does it matter?

Postscript to *Screws*

After the Court reversed the convictions in *Screws*, the government reprosecuted the defendants. At the end of the second trial, District Court Judge Louie Strum rambled on about the two-count indictment. His confusing instructions took up more than 35 pages in the trial transcript, and his second crack at willfulness is sprinkled throughout. Early in his description of *willfulness* he said this:

> Doing a thing knowingly and wilfully implies, not only a knowledge of the thing, but a determination to do it with bad intent, or with an evil purpose or motive. It means, not something done voluntarily, merely voluntarily, but with a bad purpose, or as signifying an evil intent without a justifiable excuse. When it is a question of whether or not an act was willfully done or omitted, the gravamen of the offense consists in the evil design with which such act is done and it is a question here whether this was willfully done. That is one of the questions for you gentlemen to consider.

Charge of the Court 12, United States v. Screws, No. 1300 (M.D. Ga. Nov. 1, 1945). Putting aside how the jury was supposed to parse all that, it doesn't seem to contradict *Screws*, right? What about the way Judge Strum ended his willfulness discussion?

> And so, gentlemen, that I think gives you a pretty clear picture of what is charged in this second count. The gravamen of the count is that the defendants willfully, for the purpose and with the intent, not merely of working their own personal spleen on this man for some private grudge, for the willful and deliberate purpose of depriving him of a trial by due process of law in the courts of the State of Georgia, assaulted and beat him and brought about his death. That is the charge that is brought in this second count.

Id. at 19.[11] Is this part true to *Screws*? In this view, would an officer who angrily beat a man to death for mouthing off during an arrest be acting willfully?

In the context of the labyrinthine instructions, Judge Strum's declaration of clarity sounds almost ironic. But it is an apt reminder. In 1945, as today, no matter how carefully the Supreme Court refines legal standards, the law in a criminal trial is what the jury understands it to be, and that understanding comes from the trial court.

---

[11] These instructions come from the court transcript of the second trial, obtained from the National Archives. The only previously published account of these instructions comes from Harry H. Shapiro, *Limitations in Prosecuting Civil Rights Violations*, 46 Cornell L.Q. 532, 535 (1961). Shapiro's account has been quoted repeatedly since, including in several recent law review articles on *Screws*. However, Shapiro's heavily edited paragraph from the instructions does not fairly reflect the original character of the court's charge. The full charge of the court is too long to reproduce in its entirety here.

In the second trial, Screws' lawyers argued that he did not act willfully. After the instructions, the jury acquitted Screws and his fellow officers of both counts of the indictment. All three continued to serve as police officers. Screws won reelection as sheriff even while being prosecuted, and he was later elected state senator. All told, M. Claude Screws served as sheriff of Baker County for 20 years, including 14 years after he beat Robert Hall to death and was convicted by a jury of doing so.

3.   Practicing Willfulness

Are the following officers acting willfully within the meaning of *Screws*?

Problem 1: Spit and Party

Officer Eli Ellison is interrogating Uri, who is seated in a chair with his hands cuffed behind the back of the chair. Uri cannot stand up or move much, but when he gets mad about the direction of the questioning, he spits at Ellison instead of answering. Officer Ellison knows that officers have gotten sick from suspects before, and he warns Uri angrily, "If you spit again, we're gonna party." When Uri does, Ellison punches him in the face several times.

Problem 2: Ignoring Complaints

Officer Ira Ickowitz arrests Xavier following an undercover buy–bust drug operation. After Xavier is handcuffed, he tells Ickowitz that he has asthma and is having trouble breathing. Officer Ickowitz ignores his pleas to retrieve his inhaler from his pocket. Although Ickowitz is aware that he has an obligation to address legitimate medical needs, he thinks Xavier is exaggerating and figures that Xavier will soon be assessed back at the station house, just a few minutes away. By the time Officer Ickowitz tries to take Xavier out of the car, Xavier is unconscious, and he dies a short time later.

Problem 3: Jumping the Gun

Detective Hal Hanson stops Will on the street after observing a suspicious bulge in his coat that Hanson suspected was an illegal gun. Forgetting his training, Hanson demands to see Will's identification before patting him down for weapons. When Will reaches quickly into his coat and starts to pull out a black object, Hanson shoots him. The object turns out to be just a leather wallet, and no gun is found on Will's body. In the ensuing investigation, Hanson swears that he believed the object was a gun when he fired.

Problem 4: Ending the Confrontation

Sergeant Dan Daniels, a shift supervisor, responds to a standoff situation in which a fleeing driver, Tom, has crashed into a fence and refuses to exit his car or show his hands. The car is blocked in by several patrol cars, and officers are aiming guns at the car. As Daniels arrives, Tom briefly accelerates toward the officers in reverse. The officers are about to fire, but the car stops before getting dangerously close to them. Several minutes later, the driver again begins to reverse toward the officers, but very slowly. Impatient with the standoff, Daniels says, "Time to end this," and he fires ten shots from his pistol through the rear windshield of the car. The driver is struck in the head and killed.

Obviously, these are simplified scenarios. In real life, there would usually be far more evidence. What kind of evidence would you want to help you determine what the officer believed about the situation and what he intended by his actions?

4. Proving Willfulness

Some kinds of misconduct are *always* willful. An officer cannot plant evidence on a suspect or commit a sexual assault, unaware that he is breaking the law. If the government can prove what happened, the intent requirement takes care of itself. Willfulness comes up most often in cases about the use of force. An officer might argue that, even if the conduct violated the Constitution, the officer believed the force was reasonable, and therefore that he did not act willfully.

How do prosecutors overcome this defense and establish willfulness? Here are some options in a use-of-force case:

1. Introduce statements by the defendant that show callousness or disregard for legitimate law enforcement goals.
2. Demonstrate that the defendant had a motive for using excessive force, for example, by showing that the victim provoked him.
3. Prove that the defendant violated his training or departmental policy.
4. Introduce prior bad acts that show motive or a pattern of conduct.
5. Establish that the defendant attempted to cover up his actions.
6. Argue that the egregiousness and nature of the acts, such as force against someone who was already handcuffed and under control, indicate the requisite intent.

What investigative steps would you undertake to discover such evidence? How might a defense attorney show an act was *not* willful?

In determining and establishing willfulness, especially pursuant to the last strategy, civil rights prosecutors often rely on testimony from other officers. If other officers describe what happened and indicate that they knew the conduct was unreasonable, it is easier for a jury to infer that the defendant knew that, too. Without another officer saying so, juries, sympathetic to the difficulties of police work, are often reluctant to label actions "willful." This strategy poses its own challenges, though: In police cases, as in ordinary criminal prosecutions, government cooperators and whistleblowers can be problematic witnesses.

In *United States v. Reese*, 2 F.3d 870 (9th Cir. 1993), for example, drug suppression task force officers of the Oakland Housing Authority Police Department made illegal arrests, searched illegally, engaged in excessive force, stole, lied in reports and testimony, made racist comments to members of the public, planted evidence, and more. Three task force members and former members cooperated with the federal prosecution: One was disliked by his colleagues. He was labelled "not a team player" almost as soon as he arrived, and he quickly left the task force. The second was fired for lying on a report before federal charges were brought. The third pled guilty to conspiring with the officers he testified against. None of that is unusual.

Police departments value loyalty and conformity, which officers frequently view as preconditions for trust in dangerous, high-stress situations. Prosecutors find cooperators in two basic ways. They offer deals to officers who are least culpable but nevertheless vulnerable to prosecution, and they identify officers who are least loyal and conformist, including those who have not been at the agency long, those who have already left it, and those whose personalities prime them to subvert group norms. These strategies frequently produce unappealing witnesses, subject to inevitable lines of cross-examination.

Fixing *Screws*

Many people have argued that *willfulness* in the form required by *Screws* constrains use of force prosecutions under §242 too much. How might this be fixed?

In the George Floyd Justice in Policing Act of 2020, H.R. 7120 §101(1) (2020) (as passed by the House, June 25, 2020), introduced in the days after Minneapolis police officers killed George Floyd and protests rocked the country, Congress proposed to solve the problem "by striking 'willfully' and inserting 'knowingly or recklessly.'" Does that work? What about the vagueness problem the Court identified in *Screws*? Would the bill fix the willfulness problem in use-of-force cases by making the statute unconstitutional in all cases? Or has something changed since *Screws*?

What if, instead of amending §242, Congress passed this imaginary alternative?

§1. Excessive Force

Whoever, acting under color of law, causes bodily injury to another through the intentional use of excessive force shall be imprisoned for not more than ten years and if death results, shall be sentenced to a term of years to life.

Whoever, acting under color of law, causes bodily injury to another through the reckless use of excessive force shall be imprisoned for not more than seven years and, if death results, shall be sentenced to not more than twenty years.

What would be the advantages and disadvantages of this approach?

Creating an alternative to §242 for use-of-force cases is not a new idea. Eighteen months after *Screws* was decided, President Truman issued an Executive Order establishing the President's Committee on Civil Rights, the primary mission of which was to "inquire into and to determine whether and in what respect current law-enforcement measures and the authority and means possessed by Federal, State, and local governments may be strengthened and improved to safeguard the civil rights of the people." Exec. Order 9808, 11 Fed. Reg. 238 (Dec. 5, 1946). Among other recommendations, the Committee proposed that Congress supplement §242 with "a new statute . . . specifically directed against police brutality and related crimes," that spelled out federal rights more clearly to overcome the handicap imposed by *Screws*. *To Secure These Rights: The Report of the President's Committee on Civil Rights* 157 (1947).

Nor is the George Floyd Justice in Policing Act the first congressional effort to fix *Screws* in the 75 years since it was decided. Since the 1940s, dozens of Congress members have introduced legislation to amend §242 or to add new statutes that would permit more prosecutions. None has passed. For as long as some have called for more aggressive prosecutions of police officers, others have remained skeptical either that police misconduct is a serious problem or, if it is, that federal intervention is the best solution.

Would you support a new statute? What would it contain? What arguments would you make on its behalf?

5. Acting Under Color of Law

If *Screws* caused one problem in criminal prosecutions of officers by making it difficult to prove *willfulness*, it mitigated another by making it easier to prove the first element of a §242 violation, that the defendant acted *under color of law*. In *Screws*, the defendants argued they could not violate §242 if they violated state law when they beat the defendant. In their view, *under color of law* meant *pursuant* to state authority, which would require that an officer's actions were authorized by state law to be criminal under §242. The *Screws* plurality makes plain that "[a]cts of officers who undertake to perform their official duties are included whether they hew to the line of their authority or overstep it." 325 U.S. at 111. As a result, §242 applies to officers who willfully deprive individuals of their constitutional rights, whether or not state law permits the constitutional violation.

The Court reaffirmed the *Screws* plurality's interpretation of *under color of law* a few years later in *Williams v. United States*, 341 U.S. 97, 99 (1951). *Williams* concerned an incident in which a lumber company suffered several thefts and hired a private detective to find the culprits. Williams, the detective, and several others beat confessions out of four men for the thefts.

> A rubber hose, a pistol, a blunt instrument, a sash cord, and other implements were used in the project. One man was forced to look at a bright light for fifteen minutes; when he was blinded, he was repeatedly hit with a rubber hose and a sash cord and finally knocked to the floor. Another was knocked from a chair and hit in the stomach again and again. He was put back in the chair and the procedure was repeated. One was backed against the wall and jammed in the chest with a club. Each was beaten, threatened, and unmercifully punished for several hours until he confessed.

Id. at 98–99. Although a private citizen, Williams was qualified as a "special police officer" with a local department, and he flashed his department badge repeatedly during the interrogations. Moreover, a local police officer joined him "to lend authority to the proceedings." *Id.* at 99. The *Williams* Court noted that even private actors, such as security guards or detectives, when vested with police powers, can act under color of law.

The Court later reaffirmed *Williams* in *United States v. Price*, 383 U.S. 787 (1966), better known as the Mississippi Burning case. In *Price*, local law enforcement officers collaborated with members of the Ku Klux Klan to lynch three civil rights workers who had come to Philadelphia, Mississippi, in 1964 to register African-American voters during Freedom Summer. The federal district court initially dismissed the §242 charges against the private individuals (including the Klan Imperial Wizard) on the ground that they were not acting *under color of law*. The Supreme Court reversed the dismissal of the indictment, noting that

> To act "under color" of law does not require that the accused be an officer of the State. It is enough that he is a willful participant in joint activity with the State or its agents.
>
> In the present case, according to the indictment, the brutal joint adventure was made possible by state detention and calculated release of the prisoners by an officer of the State. This action, clearly attributable to the State, was part of the monstrous design described by the indictment. State officers participated in every phase of the alleged venture: the release from jail, the interception, assault and murder. It was a joint activity, from start to finish. Those who took advantage of participation by state officers in accomplishment of the foul purpose alleged must suffer the consequences of that participation. In effect, if the allegations are true, they were participants in official lawlessness, acting in willful concert with state officers and hence under color of law.

Id. at 794–795. At the subsequent trial, seven men were convicted, including the Imperial Wizard. Nine defendants were acquitted, and the jury was unable to reach a verdict on three.

Today, to determine whether evidence is sufficient to show that a private person acted under color of law, courts consider whether the person was deputized, was given arrest power, or otherwise exercised a public function, as well as whether the actions were compelled, endorsed, or encouraged by or in concert with public officers. Prosecutors therefore use these kinds of facts to help establish color of law for nonofficers.

Just as private individuals sometimes act as officers, police officers sometimes act as private individuals. Sometimes they assault a family member, commit a rape, or drive while intoxicated in ways that have little to do with their jobs. Just because a police officer is off duty, though, does not mean that he is not using his authority. To figure out whether an officer's actions were carried out as a private person or under the cloak of authority, courts consider whether the defendant was on duty, was in uniform, used official equipment, flashed a badge or otherwise identified himself as an officer, gave commands, invoked his office, or purported to arrest someone, and whether the conflict originated from a personal or professional encounter. See, e.g., Bustos v. Martini Club Inc., 599 F.3d 458, 465–466 (5th Cir. 2010) (officers who assaulted plaintiff at a bar held to not be "under color of state law" because they were not on duty, not in uniforms, did not have duty weapons, and did not invoke their authority).

Former Officers and Police Pretenders, or What Is §242 For?

Most defendants in §242 prosecutions are on-duty officers. A few are private individuals or off-duty officers. However, courts have rejected §242 prosecutions against either *officers stripped of powers* or *people pretending to be the police,* finding that such people cannot act under color of law. In *Gibson v. City of Chicago*, for example, the Seventh Circuit held that a suspended officer could not act under color of law because "we have found no authority for expanding this concept of 'pretense' of law to compass the actions of an official who possessed absolutely no authority to act but nonetheless assumed the position of an imposter in pretending that he did." 910 F.2d 1510, 1518 (7th Cir. 1990). Seems reasonable, right? Still, the rule has some odd implications.

Consider Abe, a police officer; Bob, a guy who hangs around with Abe; and Cal, a law enforcement wannabe.

Imagine Abe pulls over Yanni in a traffic stop and beats him for talking back. Bob is riding along in the car, in violation of departmental policy and unknown to anyone else in the department. Bob joins Abe in kicking Yanni, just for fun. Yanni knows that Bob is not an officer.

At the same time, Cal, who purchased a police siren on the internet, pulls over Zack in a purported traffic stop and beats him. Zack thinks Cal is a police officer.

Under cases such as *Gibson*, along with the Supreme Court's decisions in *Williams* and *Price* above, Abe can be prosecuted under §242 for beating Yanni. Bob might be prosecuted under §242 by virtue of his connection to Abe, even without any other connection to the department, although Yanni never thought Bob was acting with state authority. Cal cannot be prosecuted under §242, although Zack believed he was an officer.

Does that make sense to you? What is §242 for?

If the statute attempts to punish those who abuse state power, one might think there are two basic options for deciding what to do about pretenders:

- Option 1: Punish only those who abuse others with state authority. In this case, Cal would not be prosecuted under §242, but maybe Bob would not be either and, for that matter, maybe not the Klansmen in *Price*, given the informal nature of their relationships.
- Option 2: Punish those who abuse others while professing to exercise state authority. If this is the right answer, Bob might not be prosecuted under §242, but Cal would be.

What principle are the courts using that leads to Bob being prosecuted but not Cal? Or are the courts compromising incoherently? Does it affect your thinking that, whatever federal prosecutors are permitted to do, state prosecutors will sometimes fail to prosecute Abe and Bob, but they almost always go after guys like Cal?

6. Depriving a Victim of a Constitutional Right

A §242 prosecution requires that the defendant have deprived the victim of a right under the laws or Constitution. Under *Screws*, prosecutors cannot bring criminal cases challenging conduct as unconstitutional to help develop constitutional law regulating the police. Instead, the *Screws* plurality dictates that an act cannot be willful within the meaning of §242 unless the right at issue has been previously "made specific either by the express terms of the Constitution or laws of the United States or by decisions interpreting them." Screws v. United States, 325 U.S. 91, 104 (1945). How well delineated must a right be to justify a §242 prosecution? The U.S. Supreme Court took up this question in the next case.

UNITED STATES v. LANIER
520 U.S. 259 (1997)

JUSTICE SOUTER delivered the opinion of the Court.

Respondent David Lanier was convicted under 18 U.S.C. §242 of criminally violating the constitutional rights of five women by assaulting them sexually while Lanier served as a state judge. The Sixth Circuit reversed his convictions on the ground that the constitutional right in issue had not previously been identified by this Court in a case with fundamentally similar facts. . . .

. . . We now vacate and remand. . . .

The general language of §242 . . . is matched by the breadth of its companion conspiracy statute. . . . [I]n lieu of describing the specific conduct it forbids, each statute's general terms incorporate constitutional law by reference, and many of the incorporated constitutional guarantees are, of course, themselves stated with some catholicity of phrasing. The result is that neither the statutes nor a good many of their constitutional referents delineate the range of forbidden conduct with particularity.

The right to due process enforced by §242 and said to have been violated by Lanier presents a case in point, with the irony that a prosecution to enforce one application of its spacious protection of liberty can threaten the accused with deprivation of another: what Justice Holmes spoke of as "fair warning . . . in language that the common world will understand, of what the law intends to do if a certain line is passed. To make the warning fair, so far as possible the line should be clear." McBoyle v. United States, 283 U.S. 25, 27 (1931). . . . [T]the touchstone is whether the statute, either standing alone or as construed, made it reasonably clear at the relevant time that the defendant's conduct was criminal.

We applied this standard in *Screws v. United States*, 325 U.S. 91 (1945). . . . Accordingly, *Screws* limited the statute's coverage to rights fairly warned of, having been "made specific" by the time of the charged conduct. See also United States v. Kozminski, 487 U.S. 931, 941 (1966) (parallel construction of §241).

The Sixth Circuit, in this case, added two glosses to the made-specific standard of fair warning. In its view, a generally phrased constitutional right has been made specific within the meaning of *Screws* only if a prior decision of this Court has declared the right, and then only when this Court has applied its ruling in a case with facts "fundamentally similar" to the case being prosecuted. None of the considerations advanced in this case, however, persuade us that either a decision of this Court or the extreme level of factual specificity envisioned by the Court of Appeals is necessary in every instance to give fair warning.

First, contrary to the Court of Appeals, we think it unsound to read *Screws* as reasoning that only this Court's decisions could provide the required warning. . . .

Nor have our decisions demanded precedents that applied the right at issue to a factual situation that is "fundamentally similar" at the level of specificity meant by the Sixth Circuit in using that phrase. To the contrary, we have upheld convictions under §241 or §242 despite notable factual distinctions between the precedents relied on and the cases then before the Court, so long as the prior decisions gave reasonable warning that the conduct then at issue violated constitutional rights.

But even putting these examples aside, we think that the Sixth Circuit's "fundamentally similar" standard would lead trial judges to demand a degree of certainty at once unnecessarily high and likely to beget much wrangling. This danger flows from the Court of Appeals' stated view that due process under §242 demands more than the "clearly established" law required for a public officer to be held civilly liable for a constitutional violation under §1983 or *Bivens*. This, we think, is error.

In the civil sphere, we have explained that qualified immunity seeks to ensure that defendants "reasonably can anticipate when their conduct may give rise to liability," by attaching liability only if "[t]he contours of the right [violated are] sufficiently clear that a reasonable official would understand that what he is doing violates that right," Anderson v. Creighton, 483 U.S. 635, 640 (1987). So conceived, the object of the "clearly established" immunity standard is not different from that of "fair warning" as it relates to law "made specific" for the purpose of validly applying §242. The fact that one has a civil and the other a criminal law role is of no significance; both serve the same objective, and in effect the qualified immunity test is simply the adaptation of the fair warning standard to give officials (and, ultimately, governments) the same protection from civil liability and its consequences that individuals have traditionally possessed in the face of vague criminal statutes. To require something clearer than "clearly established" would, then, call for something beyond "fair warning."

This is not to say, of course, that the single warning standard points to a single level of specificity sufficient in every instance. In some circumstances, as when an earlier case expressly leaves open whether a general rule applies to the particular type of conduct at issue, a very high degree of prior factual particularity may be necessary. But general statements of the law are not inherently incapable of giving fair and clear warning, and in other instances a general constitutional rule already identified in the decisional law may apply with obvious clarity to the specific conduct in question, even though "the very action in question has [not] previously been held unlawful," *Anderson*, 483 U.S. at 640. . . . In sum, as with civil liability under §1983 or *Bivens*, all that can usefully be said about criminal liability under §242 is that it may be imposed for deprivation of a constitutional right if, but only if, "in the light of pre-existing law the unlawfulness [under the Constitution is] apparent," *Anderson*, 483 U.S. at 640. Where it is, the constitutional requirement of fair warning is satisfied.

Because the Court of Appeals used the wrong gauge in deciding whether prior judicial decisions gave fair warning that respondent's actions violated constitutional rights, we vacate the judgment and remand the case for application of the proper standard.

NOTES AND QUESTIONS

1. *After* Lanier. The Sixth Circuit never resolved the fair-warning issue on remand because Lanier, who was free pending his appeal, went on the lam instead of showing up to court. As a result, the Sixth Circuit dismissed his appeal with prejudice. Two months later, Lanier was caught in Mexico and deported back to the United States to start serving his 25-year sentence. Still, in subsequent cases, the constitutional right to be free from sexual assaults committed under color of law has

been consistently recognized, including against police officers. See, e.g., Fontana v. Haskin, 262 F.3d 871, 878–881 (9th Cir. 2001); Rogers v. City of Little, 152 F.3d 790, 793–796 (8th Cir. 1998). David Lanier was released from prison in 2018.

2. Lanier *and* Screws. What precisely is the issue in *Lanier*? How does *Lanier* relate to *Screws*? Is *Lanier* an interpretation of an element of §242 or a constitutional constraint on prosecutions that is independent of the elements?

3. *Criminal and civil cases against officers.* Police officers who violate constitutional law may be sued civilly under 42 U.S.C. §1983 by victims as well as prosecuted under 18 U.S.C. §242 by the government. The language and history of the statutes makes it clear that they are analogous, and Supreme Court doctrine indicates that some elements, such as what it means to act under color of law, are the same in both statutes, allowing the law to be used interchangeably. Proving a violation of either statute requires establishing that the defendant engaged in a *deprivation of rights,* and constitutional rights are constitutional rights, whether they are articulated in civil cases or criminal ones. *Lanier* does not expressly equate criminal and civil cases; instead it determines that criminal cases require no more than civil cases in the specificity of the right. A subsequent case, *Hope v. Pelzer,* 536 U.S. 730, 739 (2002), made clearer that officers have the same due process right to fair notice when they are sued civilly or charged criminally. As a result, a right that is sufficiently *clearly established* to overcome qualified immunity under §1983 has also been *made specific* within the meaning of *Screws.*

4. *Changes in qualified immunity. Pelzer* also reiterated that fair notice does not require a case involving "fundamentally similar facts," noting that "officials can still be on notice that their conduct violates established law even in novel factual circumstances." *Id.* at 741. Since *Lanier* and *Pelzer,* however, the Court has notably changed its tone on qualified immunity. It has raised the standard both for what it means to be *clear* and for what it means to be *established.* The Court reiterated the clarity standard this way in 2015:

> A clearly established right is one that is sufficiently clear that every reasonable official would have understood that what he is doing violates that right. We do not require a case directly on point, but existing precedent must have placed the statutory or constitutional question beyond debate. Put simply, qualified immunity protects all but the plainly incompetent or those who knowingly violate the law.
>
> We have repeatedly told courts not to define clearly established law at a high level of generality. The dispositive question is whether the violative nature of particular conduct is clearly established. This inquiry must be undertaken in light of the specific context of the case, not as a broad general proposition. Such specificity is especially important in the Fourth Amendment context, where the Court has recognized that it is sometimes difficult for an officer to determine how the relevant legal doctrine, here excessive force, will apply to the factual situation the officer confronts.

Mullenix v. Luna, 136 S. Ct. 305, 308 (2015) (per curiam).[12] What might this mean for §242 prosecutions? Is it possible that *willfulness* is now a higher standard than *Screws* ever meant it to be?

---

[12] *Ed. note:* Internal quotations, omissions, alterations, and citations are removed without notation throughout the book in accordance with the preface, but those changes have especially extreme effect in the context of qualified immunity cases, including this one. Although the quote as presented is far more readable, those who wish to understand qualified immunity law fully should look to the original. Qualified immunity is discussed further in Chapter 13.

Conspiracies and Obstruction

In addition to §242, federal prosecutors bring a variety of other charges against police officers. For example, 18 U.S.C. §241 makes it an offense to conspire to deprive a person of a constitutional right while acting under color of law. To establish a §241 violation, the government must prove that the defendant agreed to injure, oppress, threaten, or intimidate a person for the purpose of interfering with a specific right guaranteed by federal law or the Constitution. Anderson v. United States, 417 U.S. 211, 222–228 (1974). The *agreement* required for a §241 prosecution is the same as that required by 18 U.S.C. §371, the general federal criminal conspiracy statute. Although §241 contains no overt act requirement, as §371 does, in practice prosecutors always charge overt acts in furtherance of the conspiracy, and it is hard to imagine a successful prosecution without them. As with §242, the *right* conspirators under §241 seek to interfere with must be one established by federal civil law or constitutional law. Although the text of §241 does not appear to limit prosecution to those acting *willfully* or to those acting *under color of law*, the U.S. Supreme Court has applied both requirements to §241 prosecutions. *Anderson*, 417 U.S. at 223; United States v. Price, 383 U.S. 787, 806 (1966).

Given that proving a §241 violation requires proving that a defendant willfully agreed to deprive a person of his rights, just as a §242 violation does, and conviction also effectively demands proving an overt act that often amounts to a violation or an attempt to violate §242, you might wonder why prosecutors ever use this statute. One reason is that a conspiracy charge often enables prosecutors to combine multiple defendants into a single trial, which can often help the government's case. Another relates to the sentencing provisions of the statutes. Whereas §242 is sometimes a misdemeanor, §241 is always a felony. Can you imagine the circumstances in which §241 charges might be especially important to prosecutors who want to prevent future violations?

It is also not uncommon for prosecutors to charge officers with obstruction for falsifying reports, 18 U.S.C. §§1501–1519; or with making false statements in a federal investigation for lying to FBI agents or federal prosecutors, 18 U.S.C. §1001. Sometimes prosecutors bring (or threaten to bring) these charges against marginal players in a civil rights incident to pressure them to testify against their colleagues. Evidence that an officer lied or covered up the incident can also often be used to establish that the officer acted *willfully* in a §242 or §241 trial.

E.   U.S. Department of Justice Policy and Civil Rights Prosecutions

1.   Grounds for Initiating a Federal Prosecution

Although victims and commentators call strongly for prosecuting accused officers, as this chapter suggests, evidentiary, legal, and practice obstacles abound. When should a prosecutor initiate a criminal prosecution? Here is what the Department of Justice tells its lawyers:

JUSTICE MANUAL §9-27.220 (2018)

Grounds for Commencing or Declining Prosecution

The attorney for the government should commence or recommend federal prosecution if he/she believes that the person's conduct constitutes a federal offense, and that the admissible evidence will probably be sufficient to obtain and sustain a conviction, unless (1) the prosecution would serve no substantial federal interest; (2) the person is subject to effective prosecution in another jurisdiction; or (3) there exists an adequate non-criminal alternative to prosecution.

Comment. Evidence sufficient to sustain a conviction is required under Rule 29(a) of the Federal Rules of Criminal Procedure, to avoid a judgment of acquittal. Moreover, both as a matter of fundamental fairness and in the interest of the efficient administration of justice, no prosecution should be initiated against any person unless the attorney for the government believes that the admissible evidence is sufficient to obtain and sustain a guilty verdict by an unbiased trier of fact. . . .

Where the law and the facts create a sound, prosecutable case, the likelihood of an acquittal due to unpopularity of some aspect of the prosecution or because of the overwhelming popularity of the defendant or his/her cause is not a factor prohibiting prosecution. For example, in a civil rights case or a case involving an extremely popular political figure, it might be clear that the evidence of guilt—viewed objectively by an unbiased factfinder—would be sufficient to obtain and sustain a conviction, yet the prosecutor might reasonably doubt, based on the circumstances, that the jury would convict. In such a case, despite his/her negative assessment of the likelihood of a guilty verdict (based on factors extraneous to an objective view of the law and the facts), the prosecutor may properly conclude that it is necessary and appropriate to commence or recommend prosecution and allow the criminal process to operate in accordance with the principles set forth here.

NOTES AND QUESTIONS

1. *Popularity and credibility.* How easy is it to decide whether "the law and the facts create a sound, prosecutable case" under this rule? Let's say Officer Joe Friday, accused of excessive force, is unlikely to be convicted because he is an effective, credible witness without a criminal history, and Jean Valjean, the victim of the alleged misconduct, initially lied about the encounter and served 19 years in prison. If Friday is likely to be acquitted, is a prosecutor to assume that is because of his popularity? Or is credibility what determines whether a case is provable? What consequences might that difference have?

2. *Overenthusiastic rule-following.* Section 9-27.220 is not crime-specific. In every federal criminal case, a grand jury may indict if there is probable cause to believe a person committed an offense, but the prosecutor is instructed by §9-27.220 to pursue the charge only if convinced that the government could prove crime beyond a reasonable doubt at trial. Critics allege that prosecutors seem to take this rule to heart more in cases against police officers than they do when charging drug crimes. You will frequently hear critics argue, contrary to §9-27.220, that if there is probable cause, prosecutors should bring civil rights charges and let the jury sort it out. Should the rules be different for prosecuting police officers than they are for other crimes? Why or why not? What about the critics' complaint that prosecutors are too scrutinizing in these cases compared to others?

Police Misconduct and Jury Nullification

Consider the killing of Billy Ray Stone:

> In July 2001, Billy Ray Stone kidnapped Charlene Wright, a fifty-five-year-old woman, in Tupelo, Mississippi. During a high-speed chase that followed, Stone pushed Wright—naked and bound—out of his car, causing the popular Lee County Sheriff Harold Ray Presley to run her over. She died the following day from her wounds. When Presley and his deputies caught up with Stone a few hours later, a gun battle ensued, in which Stone shot Sheriff Presley six times, killing him. Deputies subdued Stone, who had been shot once during the fight. According to overwhelming evidence at the federal criminal trial of two of the sheriff's deputies, these and other deputies kicked Stone and hit him with a flashlight repeatedly while he lay handcuffed, suffering from a gunshot wound to the chest. Emergency personnel also testified that the charged deputies prevented them from treating Stone, who died at the scene of massive head trauma and his gunshot wound. Nevertheless, a federal jury acquitted the officers accused of using excessive force against Stone in three hours.

Rachel A. Harmon, *When Is Police Violence Justified?*, 102 Nw. U. L. Rev. 1119, 1164 n.209 (2008).

Criminal cases against officers are hard for prosecutors. It can be difficult to prove what happened, much less that an officer acted wrongly. Some officers are fairly acquitted, despite using what appears to the public to be egregious force, because the evidence at trial does not establish a crime beyond a reasonable doubt. But how can we tell those cases from cases in which the jury nullifies, refusing to convict a defendant–officer despite strong evidence of guilt under the law?

A not-guilty verdict does not explain *why* a jury acted. We do not know whether the jury acquitted the officers for killing Stone because of their view of the evidence or because they could not sympathize with the likes of a Billy Ray Stone. Is there any way to build trust for a verdict, whichever way it goes? Or are people likely to see injustice whenever a case turns out differently than their assessment of the incident?

---

2.   *Petite* Policy: Prosecuting When the State Has Already Done So

Under the Department of Justice's policy on dual and successive prosecutions, known as the *Petite* policy, the Department defers to local prosecutors in the first instance, even when the facts support a federal criminal charge. According to this policy, the Department of Justice will charge a local officer only if the state first declines to prosecute or if special circumstances exist.

JUSTICE MANUAL §9-2.031 (2018)

Dual and Successive Prosecution Policy ("Petite Policy")

. . . This policy precludes the initiation or continuation of a federal prosecution, following a prior state or federal prosecution based on substantially the same act(s)

United States v. Schmidgall, 25 F.3d 1523, 1528 (11th Cir. 1994); United States v. North, 920 F.2d 940, 942 (D.C. Cir. 1990). As a result, an administrative investigation that compels statements can seriously complicate subsequent criminal investigation. The Ninth Circuit made this point in its decision upholding the convictions of officers involved in beating Rodney King in 1991.

> [I]mmunity attaches in the *Garrity* context when a threat of the loss of employment forces a public employee to respond to questioning by another public employee. In this context, the individuals who question the employee are concerned about potential misconduct, and their goal is generally to learn the facts of a situation as quickly as possible. They do not necessarily act with the care and precision of a prosecutor weighing the benefits of compelling testimony against the risks to future prosecutions; indeed, they may not even have the prospect of prosecution and the requirements of the Fifth Amendment in mind. In addition, because statements may be compelled soon after the event in question, it is far more likely that these statements will be circulated before there is an opportunity to can testimony. Although this may occur out of a legitimate desire to ascertain the truth of the matter, it may also occur out of a desire to protect one's colleagues. Thus, in the context of internal affairs investigations, police officers could protect each other by compelling testimony and disseminating it widely, placing any criminal prosecution at serious risk and possibly barring prosecution altogether.

United States v. Koon, 34 F.3d 1416, 1433 n.13 (9th Cir. 1994), *rev'd on other grounds,* 518 U.S. 81 (1996).

4. Garrity *as a sword.* Notice the last point in the quote from *Koon. Garrity* can be used as a sword as well as a shield. Police departments—and not prosecutors—control whether officers are compelled to give statements in an administrative investigation under the threat of firing. A department that is hostile to criminal prosecution can use that power to compel strategically, to generate *Garrity* material, which then may be shown to other witnesses (making their potential testimony for the prosecution not "wholly independent") or provided to the media (so that investigators, prosecutors, and witnesses are unknowingly tainted). Similarly, once statements are compelled, anyone with access to them—such as a defendant or his surrogates—can similarly release them. And, of course, there *are* accidents: Imagine an internal affairs investigator asks a witness, Officer Smith, "What would you say if I told you Officer Jones claims the victim approached him with a knife in his hand?" If Jones gave a statement after a *Garrity* warning and is subsequently criminally prosecuted, has Smith's testimony about whether he saw a knife been tainted?

5. *The state in* Garrity. *Garrity* worries about the state controlling the levers both of criminal prosecution and of employment, which enables it to "use the threat of discharge to secure incriminatory evidence against an employee." 385 U.S. at 499. Police misconduct cases are usually more complicated: The government often will not be unified against an officer. In many cases, command staff in the police department oppose criminal prosecution of officers (and can use *Garrity* to sabotage it); state prosecutors (who work closely with the police department) prefer to stay out of the matter; and the federal government is the only actor pursuing the officer. Should the Court consider this context in interpreting the constitutional principles at stake? Should it consider the role the federal government has long played in ensuring that local policing meets constitutional standards?

6. *Self-Garritizing.* Not only can police officers sometimes control the dissemination of *Garrity* statements, they can sometimes control whether a court will treat a statement as compelled. In *Garrity*, the officers were expressly threatened with firing in a formal hearing. Since then, courts have extended the consequences of *Garrity* to informal situations in which the officer has a subjective belief that he must give a statement or lose his job, so long as that subjective belief is objectively reasonable under the circumstances. See, e.g., United States v. Camacho, 739 F. Supp. 1504 (S.D. Fla. 1990). Thus, for example, if a supervisor tells an officer that if the officer tells the supervisor what happened, he will not be fired or prosecuted, that officer could have a reasonable belief that his statements were compelled. See, e.g., United States v. Sayes, 49 F. Supp. 2d 870 (M.D. La. 1999). There are limits: Ordinarily, courts do not apply *Garrity* to situations in which a supervisor at an incident scene simply asks an officer what happened or to routine incident and arrest reports. See, e.g., United States v. Rios Ruiz, 579 F.2d 670, 675–676 (1st Cir. 1978). But in ambiguous circumstances, union officers and policing lawyers sometimes recommend that officers "self-invoke" *Garrity*'s protection by writing on any report or statement after an incident: "I have been commanded to give this statement and do so only because I believe that I may be terminated if I refuse to cooperate and provide this information." If a supervisor accepts a report with such a statement written on the top, does that make an officer's fear objectively reasonable? If so, can a police officer secure the protections of *Garrity* at will so long as his superiors go along?

7. *Preventing* Garrity *violations.* To prevent *Garrity* from interfering with its criminal prosecutions, federal prosecutors sometimes take two steps. First, they discourage departments from compelling statements in internal administrative investigations against police officers who could be defendants or witnesses in a federal prosecution. But federal investigations are often slow, and prosecutions are rare. What are the pros and cons for police accountability of honoring such a request? If you were a chief, how would you decide?[14]

Second, if an internal administrative investigation has taken place, federal prosecutors sometimes set up procedures to ensure that the criminal investigators and prosecutors are not exposed to compelled statements as they investigate. In a simple case, this might mean having a paralegal redact compelled statements before the prosecutor examines personnel files. In more complex cases, it might involve creating a *dirty* team of lawyers and paralegals in addition to the *clean* team. The dirty team identifies all statements by potential targets that have been compelled within the meaning of *Garrity*. Before a clean prosecutor looks at *any* evidence or even the newspaper, the dirty team screens it and redacts compelled statements and material that might be derived from compelled statements. The clean team can thereby direct the investigation and draw conclusions without taint. This process is expensive and

---

[14] Critics sometimes assume that any limit on interrogations of officers pursuant to union contracts or state LEOBRs undermines efforts to hold officers accountable for their actions. But the interplay of local administrative interrogations and federal criminal prosecution suggests that the picture might be more complicated. In some cases, policies that delay interrogations or inhibit them may increase the opportunity for criminal investigations to get started before the department compels statements. In cases in which criminal prosecutions are unlikely, perhaps limiting administrative investigations is more costly than it is beneficial. But in cases of serious misconduct, LEOBRs and contractual provisions limiting departmental access to the officers might, at least sometimes, improve the prospects for untainted criminal prosecution.

slow, however. Is that simply a price we pay to protect the constitutional rights of officers? Or is it a tax put on vindicating the constitutional rights of their victims?

G.   Federal Law Applied: The Death of Michael Brown

Department of Justice Report Regarding the Criminal Investigation into the Shooting Death of Michael Brown by Ferguson, Missouri Police Officer Darren Wilson
(Mar. 4, 2015)

I. Introduction

At approximately noon on Saturday, August 9, 2014, Officer Darren Wilson of the Ferguson Police Department ("FPD") shot and killed Michael Brown, an unarmed 18-year-old. The Criminal Section of the Department of Justice Civil Rights Division, the United States Attorney's Office for the Eastern District of Missouri, and the Federal Bureau of Investigation ("FBI") (collectively, "The Department") subsequently opened a criminal investigation into whether the shooting violated federal law. The Department has determined that the evidence does not support charging a violation of federal law. . . .

The Department conducted an extensive investigation into the shooting of Michael Brown. . . .

Based on this investigation, the Department has concluded that Darren Wilson's actions do not constitute prosecutable violations under the applicable federal criminal civil rights statute, 18 U.S.C. §242, which prohibits uses of deadly force that are "objectively unreasonable," as defined by the United States Supreme Court. The evidence, when viewed as a whole, does not support the conclusion that Wilson's uses of deadly force were "objectively unreasonable" under the Supreme Court's definition. Accordingly, under the governing federal law and relevant standards set forth in the USAM, it is not appropriate to present this matter to a federal grand jury for indictment, and it should therefore be closed without prosecution.

II. Summary of the Evidence, Investigation, and Applicable Law

A. Summary of the Evidence

. . . The encounter between Wilson and Brown took place over an approximately two-minute period of time at about noon on August 9, 2014. Wilson was on duty and driving his department-issued Chevy Tahoe SUV westbound on Canfield Drive in Ferguson, Missouri when he saw Brown and his friend, Witness 101, walking eastbound in the middle of the street. Brown and Witness 101 had just come from Ferguson Market and Liquor ("Ferguson Market"), a nearby convenience store, where, at approximately 11:53 a.m., Brown stole several packages of cigarillos. As captured on the store's surveillance video, when the store clerk tried to stop Brown, Brown used his physical size to stand over him and forcefully shove him away. As a result, an FPD dispatch call went out over the police radio for a "stealing in progress." The dispatch recordings and Wilson's radio transmissions establish that Wilson was aware of the theft and had a description of the suspects as he encountered Brown and Witness 101.

As Wilson drove toward Brown and Witness 101, he told the two men to walk on the sidewalk. According to Wilson's statement to prosecutors and investigators, he suspected that Brown and Witness 101 were involved in the incident at Ferguson Market based on the descriptions he heard on the radio and the cigarillos in Brown's hands. Wilson then called for backup, stating, "Put me on Canfield with two and send me another car." Wilson backed up his SUV and parked at an angle, blocking most of both lanes of traffic, and stopping Brown and Witness 101 from walking any further. Wilson attempted to open the driver's door of the SUV to exit his vehicle, but as he swung it open, the door came into contact with Brown's body and either rebounded closed or Brown pushed it closed.

Wilson and other witnesses stated that Brown then reached into the SUV through the open driver's window and punched and grabbed Wilson. This is corroborated by bruising on Wilson's jaw and scratches on his neck, the presence of Brown's DNA on Wilson's collar, shirt, and pants, and Wilson's DNA on Brown's palm. While there are other individuals who stated that Wilson reached out of the SUV and grabbed Brown by the neck, prosecutors could not credit their accounts because they were inconsistent with physical and forensic evidence, as detailed throughout this report.

Wilson told prosecutors and investigators that he responded to Brown reaching into the SUV and punching him by withdrawing his gun because he could not access less lethal weapons while seated inside the SUV. Brown then grabbed the weapon and struggled with Wilson to gain control of it. Wilson fired, striking Brown in the hand. Autopsy results and bullet trajectory, skin from Brown's palm on the outside of the SUV door as well as Brown's DNA on the inside of the driver's door corroborate Wilson's account that during the struggle, Brown used his right hand to grab and attempt to control Wilson's gun. According to three autopsies, Brown sustained a close range gunshot wound to the fleshy portion of his right hand at the base of his right thumb. Soot from the muzzle of the gun found embedded in the tissue of this wound coupled with indicia of thermal change from the heat of the muzzle indicate that Brown's hand was within inches of the muzzle of Wilson's gun when it was fired. The location of the recovered bullet in the side panel of the driver's door, just above Wilson's lap, also corroborates Wilson's account of the struggle over the gun and when the gun was fired, as do witness accounts that Wilson fired at least one shot from inside the SUV.

Although no eyewitnesses directly corroborate Wilson's account of Brown's attempt to gain control of the gun, there is no credible evidence to disprove Wilson's account of what occurred inside the SUV. . . .

After the initial shooting inside the SUV, the evidence establishes that Brown ran eastbound on Canfield Drive and Wilson chased after him. The autopsy results confirm that Wilson did not shoot Brown in the back as he was running away because there were no entrance wounds to Brown's back. . . .

Brown ran at least 180 feet away from the SUV, as verified by the location of bloodstains on the roadway, which DNA analysis confirms was Brown's blood. Brown then turned around and came back toward Wilson, falling to his death approximately 21.6 feet west of the blood in the roadway. Those witness accounts stating that Brown never moved back toward Wilson could not be relied upon in a prosecution because their accounts cannot be reconciled with the DNA bloodstain evidence and other credible witness accounts.

As detailed throughout this report, several witnesses stated that Brown appeared to pose a physical threat to Wilson as he moved toward Wilson. According to these witnesses, who are corroborated by blood evidence in the roadway, as Brown continued to move toward Wilson, Wilson fired at Brown in what appeared to be self-defense and stopped firing once Brown fell to the ground. Wilson stated that he feared Brown would again assault him because of Brown's conduct at the SUV and because as Brown moved toward him, Wilson saw Brown reach his right hand under his t-shirt into what appeared to be his waistband. There is no evidence upon which prosecutors can rely to disprove Wilson's stated subjective belief that he feared for his safety.

Ballistics analysis indicates that Wilson fired a total of 12 shots, two from the SUV and ten on the roadway. Witness accounts and an audio recording indicate that when Wilson and Brown were on the roadway, Wilson fired three gunshot volleys, pausing in between each one. According to the autopsy results, Wilson shot and hit Brown as few as six or as many as eight times, including the gunshot to Brown's hand. Brown fell to the ground dead as a result of a gunshot to the apex of his head. With the exception of the first shot to Brown's hand, all of the shots that struck Brown were fired from a distance of more than two feet. . . .

Although there are several individuals who have stated that Brown held his hands up in an unambiguous sign of surrender prior to Wilson shooting him dead, their accounts do not support a prosecution of Wilson. As detailed throughout this report, some of those accounts are inaccurate because they are inconsistent with the physical and forensic evidence; some of those accounts are materially inconsistent with that witness's own prior statements with no explanation, credible for otherwise, as to why those accounts changed over time. Certain other witnesses who originally stated Brown had his hands up in surrender recanted their original accounts, admitting that they did not witness the shooting or parts of it, despite what they initially reported either to federal or local law enforcement or to the media. Prosecutors did not rely on those accounts when making a prosecutive decision. . . .

IV. Legal Analysis

. . . The evidence is insufficient to establish probable cause or to prove beyond a reasonable doubt a violation of 18 U.S.C. §242 and would not be likely to survive a defense motion for acquittal at trial pursuant to Federal Rule of Criminal Procedure 29(a). . . . Witness accounts suggesting that Brown was standing still with his hands raised in an unambiguous signal of surrender when Wilson shot Brown are inconsistent with the physical evidence, are otherwise not credible because of internal inconsistencies, or are not credible because of inconsistencies with other credible evidence. In contrast, Wilson's account of Brown's actions, if true, would establish that the shootings were not objectively unreasonable under the relevant Constitutional standards governing an officer's use of deadly force. Multiple credible witnesses corroborate virtually every material aspect of Wilson's account and are consistent with the physical evidence. Even if the evidence established that Wilson's actions were unreasonable, the government would also have to prove that Wilson acted willfully, i.e. that he acted with a specific intent to violate the law. As discussed above, Wilson's stated intent for shooting Brown was in response to a perceived deadly threat. The only possible basis for prosecuting Wilson under Section 242 would therefore be if the government could prove that his account is not true—i.e., that Brown never punched and grabbed Wilson at the SUV, never struggled with Wilson over the gun, and thereafter clearly surrendered in a way that no reasonable officer could have failed to perceive. Not only do eyewitnesses and physical evidence corroborate Wilson's account, but there is no credible evidence to disprove Wilson's perception that Brown posed a threat to Wilson as Brown advanced toward him. Accordingly, seeking his indictment is not permitted by Department of Justice policy or the governing law.

A. Legal Standard

To obtain a conviction of Darren Wilson at trial for his actions in shooting Michael Brown, the government must prove the following elements beyond a reasonable doubt: (1) that Wilson was acting under color of law; (2) that he acted willfully; (3) that he deprived Brown of a right protected by the Constitution or laws of the United States; and (4) that the deprivation resulted in bodily injury or death. . . . In this case, Wilson had attempted to stop and possibly arrest Brown. The rights of an arrestee are governed by the Fourth Amendment's prohibition against unreasonable searches and seizures, which includes the right to be free from excessive force during the course of an arrest. See Nelson v. County of Wright, 162 F.3d 986, 990 (8th Cir. 1998). Under the Fourth Amendment, an officer's use of force must be "objectively reasonable" under the facts and circumstances known to the officer at the time he made the decision to use physical force. *Id.* Establishing that the intent behind a Constitutional violation is "willful" requires proof that the officer acted with the purpose "to deprive a person of a right which has been made specific either by the express terms of the Constitution or laws of the United States or by decisions interpreting them." See United States v. Lanier, 520 U.S. 259, 267 (1997) (citing Screws v. United States, 325 U.S. 91 (1945)). While the officer need not be "thinking in Constitutional terms" when deciding to use force, he must know what he is doing is wrong and decide to do it anyway. *Screws,* 325 U.S. at 106–107. Mistake, panic, misperception, or even poor judgment by a police officer does not provide a basis for prosecution under Section 242. See United States v. McClean, 528 F.2d 1250, 1255 (2d Cir. 1976) (inadvertence or mistake negates willfulness for purposes of 18 U.S.C. §242).

There is no dispute that Wilson, who was on duty and working as a patrol officer for the FPD, acted under color of law when he shot Brown, or that the shots resulted in Brown's death. The determination of whether criminal prosecution is appropriate rests on whether there is sufficient evidence to establish that any of the shots fired by Wilson were unreasonable given the facts known to Wilson at the time, and if so, whether Wilson fired the shots with the requisite "willful" criminal intent, which, in this case, would require proof that Wilson shot Brown under conditions that no reasonable officer could have perceived as a threat.

B. Uses of Force

Under the Fourth Amendment, a police officer's use of physical force against an arrestee must be objectively reasonable under the circumstances. Graham v. Connor, 490 U.S. 386, 396-397 (1989). . . .

The use of deadly force is justified when the officer has "probable cause to believe that the suspect pose[s] a threat of serious physical harm, either to the officer or to others." Tennessee v. Garner, 471 U.S. 1, 11 (1985). An officer may use deadly force under certain circumstances even if the suspect is fleeing. ". . . [I]f the suspect threatens the officer with a weapon or there is probable cause to believe that he has committed a crime involving the infliction or threatened infliction of serious physical harm, deadly force may be used if necessary to prevent escape, and if, where feasible, some warning has been given." See Garner, 471 U.S. at 11-12.

. . . [W]e must examine whether the available evidence shows that Wilson reasonably believed that Brown posed a threat of serious bodily harm to Wilson himself or others in the community, or whether Brown clearly attempted to surrender, prior to any of the shots fired by Wilson. . . .

Shots Fired After Brown Turned to Face Wilson

The evidence establishes that the shots fired by Wilson after Brown turned around were in self-defense and thus were not objectively unreasonable under the Fourth Amendment. The physical evidence establishes that after he ran about 180 feet away from the SUV, Brown turned and faced Wilson, then moved toward Wilson until Wilson finally shot him in the head and killed him. According to Wilson, Brown balled or clenched his fists and "charged" forward, ignoring commands to stop. Knowing that Brown was much larger than him and that he had previously attempted to overpower him and take his gun, Wilson stated that he feared for his safety and fired at Brown. Again, even Witness 101's account supports this perception. Brown then reached toward his waistband, causing Wilson to fear that Brown was reaching for a weapon. Wilson stated that he continued to fear for his safety at this point and fired at Brown again. Wilson finally shot Brown in the head as he was falling or lunging forward, after which Brown immediately fell to the ground. Wilson did not fire any additional shots. Wilson's version of events is corroborated by the physical evidence that indicates that Brown moved forward toward Wilson after he ran from the SUV, by the fact that Brown went to the ground with his left hand at (although not inside) his waistband, and by credible eyewitness accounts.

Wilson's version is further supported by disinterested eyewitnesses Witness 102, Witness 104, Witness 105, Witness 108, and Witness 109, among others. These witnesses all agree that Brown ran or charged toward Wilson and that Wilson shot at Brown only as Brown moved toward him. Although some of the witnesses stated that Brown briefly had his hands up or out at about waist-level, none of these witnesses perceived Brown to be attempting to surrender at any point when Wilson fired upon him. To the contrary, several of these witnesses stated that they would have felt threatened by Brown and would have responded in the way Wilson did. . . . These witnesses' accounts are consistent with prior statements they have given, consistent with the forensic and physical evidence, and consistent with each other's accounts. Accordingly, we conclude that these accounts are credible.

Furthermore, there are no witnesses who could testify credibly that Wilson shot Brown while Brown was clearly attempting to surrender. The accounts of the witnesses who have claimed that Brown raised his hands above his head to surrender and said "I don't have a gun," or "okay, okay, okay" are inconsistent with the physical evidence or can be challenged in other material ways, and thus cannot be relied upon to form the foundation of a federal prosecution.[28] The two most prominent witnesses who have stated that Brown was shot with his hands up in surrender are Witness 101 and Witness 127, both of whom claim that Brown turned around with his hands raised in surrender, that he never reached for his waistband, that he never moved forward toward Wilson after turning to face him with his hands up, and that he fell to the ground with his hands raised. These and other aspects of their statements are contradicted by the physical evidence. Crime scene photographs establish that Brown fell to the ground with his left hand at his waistband and his right hand at his side. Brown's blood in the roadway demonstrates that Brown came forward at least 21.6 feet from the time he turned around toward Wilson. Other aspects of the accounts of Witness 101 and Witness 127 would render them not credible in a prosecution of Wilson, namely their accounts of what happened at the SUV. Both claim that Wilson fired the first shot out the SUV window, Witness 101 claims that the shot hit Brown at close range in the torso, and both claim that Brown did not reach inside the vehicle. These claims are irreconcilable with the bullet in the SUV door, the close-range wound to Brown's hand, Brown's DNA inside Wilson's car and on his gun, and the injuries to Wilson's face.

Other witnesses who have suggested that Brown was shot with his hands up in surrender have either recanted their statements, such as Witnesses 119 and 125, provided inconsistent statements, such as Witness 124, or have provided accounts that are verifiably untrue, such as Witnesses 121, 139, and 132. Witness 122 recanted significant portions of his statement by acknowledging that he was not in a position to see what either Brown or Wilson were doing, and . . . [s]imilar to Witness 128, Witness 122 told Brown's family that Brown had been shot execution-style. Witness 120 initially told law

---

[28] The media has widely reported that witness testimony stated that Brown said "don't shoot" as he held his hands above his head. In fact, our investigation did not reveal any eyewitness who stated that Brown said "don't shoot."

enforcement that he saw Brown shot at point-blank range as he was on his knees with his hands up. Similar to Witness 138, Witness 120 subsequently acknowledged that he did not see Brown get shot but "assumed" he had been executed while on his knees with his hands up based on "common sense" and what others "in the community told [him.]" There is no witness who has stated that Brown had his hands up in surrender whose statement is otherwise consistent with the physical evidence. For example, some witnesses say that Wilson only fired his weapon out of the SUV (e.g. Witnesses 128, 101, and 127), or that Wilson stood next to the SUV and killed Brown right there (e.g. Witnesses 139, 132, 120). Some witnesses insist that Wilson shot Brown in the back as he lay on the ground (e.g. Witnesses 128 and 139). Some witnesses say that Wilson shot Brown and he went to the ground immediately upon turning to face Wilson (e.g. Witnesses 138, 101, 118, and 127). Some say Wilson went to the ground with his hands raised at right angles (e.g. Witnesses 138, 118, and 121). Again, all of these statements are contradicted by the physical and forensic evidence, which also undermines the credibility of their accounts of other aspects of the incident, including their assertion that Brown had his hands up in a surrender position when Wilson shot him.

When the shootings are viewed, as they must be, in light of all the surrounding circumstances and what Wilson knew at the time, as established by the credible physical evidence and eyewitness testimony, it was not unreasonable for Wilson to fire on Brown until he stopped moving forward and was clearly subdued. Although, with hindsight, we know that Brown was not armed with a gun or other weapon, this fact does not render Wilson's use of deadly force objectively unreasonable. Again, the key question is whether Brown could reasonably have been perceived to pose a deadly threat to Wilson at the time he shot him regardless of whether Brown was armed. Sufficient credible evidence supports Wilson's claim that he reasonably perceived Brown to be posing a deadly threat. First, Wilson did not know that Brown was not armed at the time he shot him, and had reason to suspect that he might be when Brown reached into the waistband of his pants as he advanced toward Wilson. While Brown did not use a gun on Wilson at the SUV, his aggressive actions would have given Wilson reason to at least question whether he might be armed, as would his subsequent forward advance and reach toward his waistband. This is especially so in light of the rapidly-evolving nature of the incident. Wilson did not have time to determine whether Brown had a gun and was not required to risk being shot himself in order to make a more definitive assessment.

Moreover, Wilson could present evidence that a jury likely would credit that he reasonably perceived a deadly threat from Brown even if Brown's hands were empty and he had never reached into his waistband because of Brown's actions in refusing to halt his forward movement toward Wilson. The Eighth Circuit Court of Appeals' decision in *Loch v. City of Litchfield*, 689 F.3d 961 (8th Cir. 2012), is dispositive on this point. There, an officer shot a suspect eight times as he advanced toward the officer. Although the suspect's "arms were raised above his head or extended at his sides," the Court of Appeals held that a reasonable officer could have perceived the suspect's forward advance in the face of the officer's commands to stop as resistance and a threat. . . . *Id.* at 966.

Were the government to prosecute Wilson, the court would instruct the jury using *Loch* as a foundation. Given the evidence in this matter, jurors would likely conclude that Wilson had reason to be concerned that Brown was a threat to him as he continued to advance, just as did the officer in *Loch.*

In addition, even assuming that Wilson definitively knew that Brown was not armed, Wilson was aware that Brown had already assaulted him once and attempted to gain control of his gun. Wilson could thus present evidence that he reasonably feared that, if left unimpeded, Brown would again assault Wilson, again attempt to overpower him, and again attempt to take his gun. Under the law, Wilson has a strong argument that he was justified in firing his weapon at Brown as he continued to advance toward him and refuse commands to stop, and the law does not require Wilson to wait until Brown was close enough to physically assault Wilson. Even if, with hindsight, Wilson could have done something other than shoot Brown, the Fourth Amendment does not second-guess a law enforcement officer's decision on how to respond to an advancing threat. The law gives great deference to officers for their necessarily split-second judgments, especially in incidents such as this one that unfold over a span of less than two minutes. . . . An officer is permitted to continue firing until the threat is neutralized. See Plumhoff v. Rickard, 134 S. Ct. 2012, 2022 (2014).

For all of the reasons stated, Wilson's conduct in shooting Brown as he advanced on Wilson, and until he fell to the ground, was not objectively unreasonable and thus not a violation of 18 U.S.C. §242.

C. Willfulness

Even if federal prosecutors determined there were sufficient evidence to convince twelve jurors beyond a reasonable doubt that Wilson used unreasonable force, federal law requires that the government must also prove that the officer acted willfully, that is, with the purpose to violate the law. Screws v. United States, 325 U.S. 91, 101–107 (1945). The Supreme Court has held that an act is done willfully if it was "committed" either "in open defiance or in reckless disregard of a constitutional requirement which has been made specific and definite." *Screws,* 325 U.S. at 105. The government need not show that the defendant knew a federal statute or law protected the right with which he intended to interfere. *Id.* at 106–107. However, we must prove that the defendant intended to engage in the conduct that violated the Constitution and that he did so knowing that it was a wrongful act. *Id.*

"[A]ll the attendant circumstance[s]" should be considered in determining whether an act was done willfully. *Id.* at 107. Evidence regarding the egregiousness of the conduct, its character and duration, the weapons employed and the provocation, if any, is therefore relevant to this inquiry. *Id.* Willfulness may be inferred from blatantly wrongful conduct. See *id.* at 106. Mistake, fear, misperception, or even poor judgment do not constitute willful conduct prosecutable under the statute. See United States v. McClean, 528 F.2d 1250, 1255 (2d Cir. 1976).

As discussed above, Darren Wilson has stated his intent in shooting Michael Brown was in response to a perceived deadly threat. The only possible basis for prosecuting Wilson under section 242 would therefore be if the government could prove that his account is not true — *i.e.*, that Brown never assaulted Wilson at the SUV, never attempted to gain control of Wilson's gun, and thereafter clearly surrendered in a way that no reasonable officer could have failed to perceive. Given that Wilson's account is corroborated by physical evidence and that his perception of a threat posed by Brown is corroborated by other eyewitnesses, to include aspects of the testimony of Witness 101, there is no credible evidence that Wilson willfully shot Brown as he was attempting to surrender or was otherwise not posing a threat. Even if Wilson was mistaken in his interpretation of Brown's conduct, the fact that others interpreted that conduct the same way as Wilson precludes a determination that he acted with a bad purpose to disobey the law. The same is true even if Wilson could be said to have acted with poor judgment in the manner in which he first interacted with Brown, or in pursuing Brown after the incident at the SUV. These are matters of policy and procedure that do not rise to the level of a Constitutional violation and thus cannot support a criminal prosecution.

Because Wilson did not act with the requisite criminal intent, it cannot be proven beyond reasonable doubt to a jury that he violated 18 U.S.C. §242 when he fired his weapon at Brown.

VI. Conclusion

For the reasons set forth above, this matter lacks prosecutive merit and should be closed.

NOTES AND QUESTIONS

1. *Is the report persuasive?* Are you convinced? Why or why not?

2. *Does the report make a difference?* Since the report was issued, Darren Wilson's killing of Michael Brown has continued to be spoken about as a travesty of justice that should have been prosecuted. Why? If an independent investigation by the Civil Rights Division during a sympathetic administration is not enough to persuade people, what would be? What does that say about the role of criminal prosecutions for police misconduct? Or is what happened in Ferguson *sui generis*?

3. *Accelerating a movement.* Whatever you think of the Department of Justice's decision as a legal matter, there is little doubt that concern about the failure to charge Wilson helped accelerate a movement. The hashtag #BlackLivesMatter was born in a Facebook post by Alicia Garza in 2013 after George Zimmerman was acquitted for killing 17-year-old Trayvon Martin in Florida. But use of the hashtag and the movement it sparked grew dramatically after Brown's death and the state prosecutor's decision not to bring criminal charges. While the Department of Justice's decision not to charge Wilson drew less attention, it is fair to say that many have been spurred to write, march, and organize in response to the government's failure to

bring charges against officers who have killed Black people. The #BlackLivesMatter hashtag has been used nearly 50 million times on Twitter, often in association with a decision not to prosecute an officer. Now that you have learned more about criminal prosecutions of police officers, what do you make of the gap between the demands of activists and the decisions of prosecutors? What, if anything, should be done?

Chapter 15

Suing for Reform

Imagine Hill Valley, a fast-growing suburb of 105,000 people. When Hill Valley was smaller, its police department was staffed by a few full-time officers and a chief. Faced with increased crime, the Hill Valley Police Department (HVPD) went on a hiring spree, and it now has 130 officers.

You are a lawyer in Hill Valley, and you sometimes do criminal defense. Although most of your friends seem satisfied with the HVPD, you hear differently from your clients. Several have complained about HVPD's 12-officer Crime Suppression Unit (CSU). According to the HVPD website, CSU officers are expected to engage in "highly proactive enforcement" to stop illegal drug activity, weapons violations, and prostitution. Some of your clients report that language translates like so: CSU officers rove downtown at night in two marked cars. When they see young men who catch their eye, they jump out, throw everyone in the group against a wall, and start searching. If they find drugs, they make arrests, claiming they saw a hand-to-hand drug deal. Otherwise, they let everyone go. Clients who have been charged with prostitution tell this version: When CSU officers find them alone and arguably engaged in solicitation, the officers demand sex and cash. If the women refuse, they are arrested; during the search incident to arrest, the officers intentionally grope their breasts and genitals, sometimes encouraging other officers to join in.

You have moved to suppress drug evidence resulting from the "jump outs," but judges seem reluctant to find no probable cause. You have raised the extortion and sexual assaults defending clients charged with solicitation, but local judges consider the complaints extraneous to whether the women committed the offenses. You have helped several clients file administrative complaints with HVPD, but in response, they received form letters indicating that the matters were under investigation. Months later, letters arrived stating that each complaint is "not sustained because evidence was insufficient to prove the allegation." None of the complainants was ever interviewed. You have brought several §1983 suits for damages, but you have never received more than a few thousand dollars in a settlement, which did not seem to trouble the city attorney or police department much. Hill Valley juries, on the rare occasion that you have appeared before them, are not sympathetic to the damages claims of purported drug dealers and prostitutes picked up by the CSU. In any case, you know that none of these strategies would be enough to bring CSU under control. Unless the unit is disbanded, or retrained and properly supervised, and future complaints are taken seriously and officers disciplined, you believe that things will go on much as they have.

What can be done about Hill Valley?

You might file a lawsuit describing the constitutional violations your clients regularly face and demanding that HVPD make changes to prevent them, or you might ask the government to file such a lawsuit. This chapter explores those possibilities.

A.   Private Suits for Police Reform

Private individuals who want a remedy for constitutional violations by the police often bring lawsuits under 42 U.S.C. §1983 seeking damages. Sometimes, though, damages are not enough. As you saw in Chapter 13, politicians and police chiefs do not always feel the pain when cities pay civil damages. For this reason, among others, even successful damages actions do not always generate effective reform:

> Compensation is imperfect. It operates only after violations have occurred, and so it can prevent violations only through the rough and inexact medium of deterrence. Compensation also faces the problem of the impecunious defendant. . . .
>
> And compensation is imperfect for another reason. It offers no way to compel any behavior except payment. Of course there is and has always been bargaining in the shadow of the compensation required by law, and the bargain struck by the parties might well involve other kinds of conduct. But as long as the offending party is willing to pay, a legal system that has only compensatory, substitutionary remedies will struggle to regulate conduct directly.
>
> The solution to these problems is fairly obvious: There must be some way for courts to compel action or inaction. In contemporary American law, this is usually done by means of an equitable remedy.

Samuel L. Bray, *The System of Equitable Remedies*, 63 UCLA L. Rev. 530, 552-553 (2016).

Section 1983 gives plaintiffs whose rights have been violated another option. By authorizing "suit in equity," the statute permits plaintiffs to seek what are known as equitable remedies as well as or instead of damages.

The most common equitable remedies are declaratory relief—court orders stating the parties' rights—and injunctions—court orders instructing defendants to act or refrain from acting. Plaintiffs may seek one or both. A simple equitable remedy in a §1983 suit might state that the plaintiff's constitutional rights are being violated and order the defendant to stop the acts that violate them. Often, however, constitutional violations result from complex and systemic institutional dysfunction. Merely telling the department not to violate constitutional rights may not be enough. In those cases, plaintiffs—often represented by a nonprofit organization and collected into a class action—may seek more elaborate injunctions specifying the organizational changes the department must make. Parties sometimes settle by entering a consent decree, agreeing to a negotiated set of reforms under the supervision of a court. Suits for significant institutional reform are known as structural reform litigation.

Remaking public institutions through court orders has long been controversial: Supporters see no other way to address systemic problems; critics doubt judicial capacity and decry federal intrusion into local concerns. The law has developed to allow, yet limit and guide, appropriate remedies in civil rights cases. But most cases against police departments seeking equitable relief never get that far.

1. Standing as a Barrier to Equitable Relief

In the 1970s and 1980s, the U.S. Supreme Court imposed limits on civil suits for equitable relief. Although these legal constraints apply to cases against all public institutions, they have formed especially powerful checks on lawsuits against police departments. The following case explains the most important of these limits.

CITY OF LOS ANGELES v. LYONS
461 U.S. 95 (1983)

JUSTICE WHITE delivered the opinion of the Court.

The issue here is whether respondent Lyons satisfied the prerequisites for seeking injunctive relief in the federal district court.

I

This case began on February 7, 1977, when respondent, Adolph Lyons, filed a complaint for damages, injunction, and declaratory relief in the United States District Court for the Central District of California. The defendants were the City of Los Angeles and four of its police officers. The complaint alleged that on October 6, 1976, at 2 a.m., Lyons was stopped by the defendant officers for a traffic or vehicle code violation and that although Lyons offered no resistance or threat whatsoever, the officers, without provocation or justification, seized Lyons and applied a "chokehold"—either the "bar arm control" hold or the "carotid-artery control" hold or both—rendering him unconscious and causing damage to his larynx. . . . Count V, with which we are principally concerned here, sought a preliminary and permanent injunction against the City barring the use of the control holds. That count alleged that the city's police officers, "pursuant to the authorization, instruction and encouragement of defendant City of Los Angeles, regularly and routinely apply these choke holds in innumerable situations where they are not threatened by the use of any deadly force whatsoever," that numerous persons have been injured as the result of the application of the chokeholds, that Lyons and others similarly situated are threatened with irreparable injury in the form of bodily injury and loss of life, and that Lyons "justifiably fears that any contact he has with Los Angeles police officers may result in his being choked and strangled to death without provocation, justification or other legal excuse." Lyons alleged the threatened impairment of rights protected by the First, Fourth, Eighth and Fourteenth Amendments. Injunctive relief was sought against the use of the control holds "except in situations where the proposed victim of said control reasonably appears to be threatening the immediate use of deadly force." . . .

. . . The District Court found that Lyons had been stopped for a traffic infringement and that without provocation or legal justification the officers involved had applied a "department-authorized chokehold which resulted in injuries to the plaintiff." The court further found that the department authorizes the use of the holds in situations where no one is threatened by death or grievous bodily harm, that officers are insufficiently trained, that the use of the holds involves a high risk of injury or death as then employed, and that their continued use in situations where neither death nor serious bodily injury is threatened "is unconscionable in a civilized society." The court concluded that such use violated Lyons' substantive due process rights under the Fourteenth Amendment. A preliminary injunction was entered enjoining "the use of both the carotid-artery and bar arm holds under circumstances which do not threaten death or serious bodily injury." An improved training program and regular reporting and record keeping were also ordered. The Court of Appeals affirmed in a brief per curiam opinion stating that the District Court had not abused its discretion in entering a preliminary injunction. We granted certiorari, and now reverse.

II

Since our grant of certiorari, circumstances pertinent to the case have changed. Originally, Lyons' complaint alleged that at least two deaths had occurred as a result of the application of chokeholds by the police. His first amended complaint alleged that 10 chokehold-related deaths had occurred. By May, 1982, there had been five more such deaths. On May 6, 1982 the Chief of Police in Los Angeles prohibited the use of the bar-arm chokehold in any circumstances. A few days later, on May 12, 1982, the Board of Police Commissioners imposed a six-month moratorium on the use of the carotid-artery chokehold except under circumstances where deadly force is authorized. . . .

In his brief and at oral argument, Lyons has reasserted his position that in light of changed conditions, an injunctive decree is now unnecessary because he is no longer subject to a threat of injury. . . . The City, on the other hand, . . . asserts that the case is not moot because the moratorium is not permanent and may be lifted at any time.

We agree with the City that the case is not moot, since the moratorium by its terms is not permanent. Intervening events have not "irrevocably eradicated the effects of the alleged violation." County of Los Angeles v. Davis, 440 U.S. 625, 631 (1979). We nevertheless hold, for another reason, that the federal courts are without jurisdiction to entertain Lyons' claim for injunctive relief.

III

It goes without saying that those who seek to invoke the jurisdiction of the federal courts must satisfy the threshold requirement imposed by Article III of the Constitution by alleging an actual case or controversy. Plaintiffs must demonstrate a "personal stake in the outcome" in order to "assure that concrete adverseness which sharpens the presentation of issues" necessary for the proper resolution of constitutional questions. Baker v. Carr, 369 U.S. 186, 204 (1962). Abstract injury is not enough. The plaintiff must show that he "has sustained or is immediately in danger of sustaining some direct injury" as the result of the challenged official conduct and the injury or threat of injury must be both "real and immediate," not "conjectural" or "hypothetical." See, e.g., Golden v. Zwickler, 394 U.S. 103, 109-110 (1969).

In O'Shea v. Littleton, 414 U.S. 488 (1974), we . . . reversed for failure of the complaint to allege a case or controversy. . . . [W]e observed that "[p]ast exposure to illegal conduct does not in itself show a present case or controversy regarding injunctive relief . . . if unaccompanied by any continuing, present adverse effects." Id. at 495-496. Past wrongs were evidence bearing on "whether there is a real and immediate threat of repeated injury." Id. at 496. But the . . . most that could be said for plaintiffs' standing was "that if [plaintiffs] proceed to violate an unchallenged law and if they are charged, held to answer, and tried in any proceedings before petitioners, they will be subjected to the discriminatory practices that petitioners are alleged to have followed." *Id.* at 497. We could not find a case or controversy in those circumstances: the threat to the plaintiffs was not "sufficiently real and immediate to show an existing controversy simply because they anticipate violating lawful criminal statutes and being tried for their offenses. . . ." *Id.* at 496. It was to be assumed "that [plaintiffs] will conduct their activities within the law and so avoid prosecution and conviction as well as exposure to the challenged course of conduct said to be followed by petitioners." *Id.* at 497. . . .

Another relevant decision for present purposes is *Rizzo v. Goode,* 423 U.S. 362 (1976), a case in which . . . [t]he Court reiterated the holding in *O'Shea.* . . . The claim of injury rested upon "what one or a small, unnamed minority of policemen might do to them in the future because of that unknown policeman's perception" of departmental procedures. *Id.* This hypothesis was "even more attenuated than those allegations of future injury found insufficient in *O'Shea* to warrant [the] invocation of federal jurisdiction." *Id.* The Court also held that plaintiffs' showing at trial of a relatively few instances of violations by individual police officers, without any showing of a deliberate policy on behalf of the named defendants, did not provide a basis for equitable relief. . . .

IV

No extension of *O'Shea* and *Rizzo* is necessary to hold that respondent Lyons has failed to demonstrate a case or controversy with the City that would justify the equitable relief sought. Lyons' standing to seek the injunction requested depended on whether he was likely to suffer future injury from the use of the chokeholds by police officers. . . . That Lyons may have been illegally choked by the police on October 6, 1976, while presumably affording Lyons standing to claim damages against the individual officers and perhaps against the City, does nothing to establish a real and immediate threat that he would again be stopped for a traffic violation, or for any other offense, by an officer or officers who would illegally choke him into unconsciousness without any provocation or resistance on his part. The additional allegation in the complaint that the police in Los Angeles routinely apply chokeholds in situations where they are not threatened by the use of deadly force falls far short of the allegations that would be necessary to establish a case or controversy between these parties.

In order to establish an actual controversy in this case, Lyons would have had not only to allege that he would have another encounter with the police but also to make the incredible assertion either, (1) that *all* police officers in Los Angeles *always* choke any citizen with whom they happen to have an encounter, whether for the purpose of arrest, issuing a citation or for questioning or, (2) that the City ordered or authorized police officers to act in such manner. Although Count V alleged that the City authorized the use of the control holds in situations where deadly force was not threatened, it did not indicate why Lyons might be realistically threatened by police officers who acted within the strictures of the City's policy. If, for example, chokeholds were authorized to be used only to counter resistance to an arrest by a suspect, or to thwart an effort to escape, any future threat to Lyons from the City's policy or from the conduct of police officers would be no more real than the possibility that he would again have an encounter with the police and that either he would illegally resist arrest or detention or the officers would disobey their instructions and again render him unconscious without any provocation. . . .

Of course, it may be that among the countless encounters between the police and the citizens of a great city such as Los Angeles, there will be certain instances in which strangleholds will be illegally applied and injury and death unconstitutionally inflicted on the victim. As we have said, however, it is no more than conjecture to suggest that in every instance of a traffic stop, arrest, or other encounter between the police and a citizen, the police will act unconstitutionally and inflict injury without provocation or legal excuse. And it is surely no more than speculation to assert either that Lyons himself will again be involved in one of those unfortunate instances, or that he will be arrested in the future and provoke the use of a chokehold by resisting arrest, attempting to escape, or threatening deadly force or serious bodily injury. . . .

Our conclusion is that . . . the District Court was quite right in dismissing Count V.

V

. . . As we noted in *O'Shea,* 414 U.S. at 503, withholding injunctive relief does not mean that the "federal law will exercise no deterrent effect in these circumstances." If Lyons has suffered an injury barred by the Federal Constitution, he has a remedy for damages under §1983. Furthermore, those who deliberately deprive a citizen of his constitutional rights risk conviction under the federal criminal laws. Ibid. . . .

Reversed.

JUSTICE MARSHALL, with whom JUSTICE BRENNAN, JUSTICE BLACKMUN and JUSTICE STEVENS join, dissenting.

The District Court found that the City of Los Angeles authorizes its police officers to apply life-threatening chokeholds to citizens who pose no threat of violence, and that respondent, Adolph Lyons, was subjected to such a chokehold. The Court today holds that a federal court is without power to enjoin the enforcement of the City's policy, no matter how flagrantly unconstitutional it may be. Since no one can show that he will be choked in the future, no one—not even a person who, like Lyons, has almost been choked to death—has standing to challenge the continuation of the policy. The City is free to continue the policy indefinitely as long as it is willing to pay damages for the injuries and deaths that result. I dissent from this unprecedented and unwarranted approach to standing. . . .

The Court's decision removes an entire class of constitutional violations from the equitable powers of a federal court. It immunizes from prospective equitable relief any policy that authorizes persistent deprivations of constitutional rights as long as no individual can establish with substantial certainty that he will be injured, or injured again, in the future. . . . Under the view expressed by the majority today, if the police adopt a policy of "shoot to kill," or a policy of shooting one out of ten suspects, the federal courts will be powerless to enjoin its continuation. The federal judicial power is now limited to levying a toll for such a systematic constitutional violation.

NOTES AND QUESTIONS

1. Lyons *as a standing case.* Pursuant to Article III of the Constitution, federal courts hear only cases and controversies. A plaintiff has a "case" only if he has a "personal stake in the outcome of the litigation," Bender v. Williamsport Area Sch. Dist., 475 U.S. 534, 543–544 (1986). To demonstrate standing, a plaintiff must show that

> 1. [he] has suffered an "injury in fact" that is (a) concrete and particularized and (b) actual or imminent, not conjectural or hypothetical;
> 2. the injury is fairly traceable to the challenged action of the defendant; and
> 3. it is likely, as opposed to merely speculative, that the injury will be redressed by a favorable decision.

Friends of the Earth, Inc. v. Laidlaw Envtl. Servs. (TOC), Inc., 528 U.S. 167, 180–181 (2000).

Lyons is largely about the third requirement for standing. It dictates that redressability varies with the form of relief requested. Just because a plaintiff has standing to bring a damages action by establishing past injury does not mean he may also seek injunctive relief. Instead, according to the Court, a plaintiff must demonstrate that the defendant has an official policy and that the plaintiff "is likely to suffer future injury" as a result of that policy to move forward with a suit for an injunction. Lyons's allegations did not fulfill this requirement to the Court's satisfaction.

2. *LAPD's policy.* The analysis in *Lyons* is hard. It might be easier when you realize the Court did not evaluate standing in the abstract. Instead, it evaluated it in relation to the specific policy that Lyons was challenging. Although Lyons claimed that he did *nothing* to provoke *his* chokehold, his description of the department's *policy* was different: He alleged that the city routinely encouraged and permitted chokeholds when officers faced no threat of *deadly* force. The Court took that to be an allegation that the department authorized chokeholds when officers faced at least some resistance, but not otherwise. You might call that a *low-resistance chokehold* (LRC) policy in contrast to a hypothetical *no-resistance chokehold* (NRC) policy, which allows chokeholds by officers facing no resistance or threat. The Court assessed Lyons's standing only in relation to the LRC policy.

3. *Threat to Lyons under LRC.* The Court reasoned that, although the LRC policy might be unconstitutional (because it allowed deadly force in response to nonserious resistance), it did not pose a significant future threat to Lyons. Because an officer acting *pursuant* to the policy would use a chokehold only against someone who resisted arrest, to be choked again, Lyons would have to do something to justify an arrest or detention and then resist. He could avoid that scenario simply by refraining from illegal conduct or refraining from resisting. Of course, some officers might *violate* the policy and do illegal arrests and no-resistance chokeholds, and Lyons could not easily avoid those officers by his own choices. But to suffer that fate, Lyons would have to encounter such an officer. As Lyons provided little reason to believe the department had a rampant problem of policy-violating officers, it was exceptionally unlikely that Lyons, one random man among the 3 million residents of Los Angeles, would fall victim to one of the few policy-violating officers. Given the department's LRC policy and the absence of evidence of widespread policy violations, in the Court's view, Lyons could easily avoid the only probable constitutional violations likely to befall him.

4. *Hill Valley.* Might your Hill Valley clients, either the young men who have suffered jump outs or the women who are targeted as prostitutes, have standing to sue HVPD for injunctive relief? What would you want to investigate further to decide?

5. *Stopping before the start.* Because standing is a threshold issue in a lawsuit, *Lyons* imposes a considerable burden on would-be plaintiffs early in the litigation. In effect, "evaluation of a complaint under the *Lyons* standard, when the plaintiff has had no opportunity to develop a factual record demonstrating the appropriateness of injunctive relief, forces a court to make a remedial decision before the litigation truly has begun." MacIssac v. Town of Poughkeepsie, 770 F. Supp. 2d 587, 599–600 (S.D.N.Y. 2011). Some view this as a critical barrier to protect defendants from the burdens of litigation in suits that should never happen. Others think it "unfair to those plaintiffs for whom discovery or trial would have unearthed the appropriateness of injunctive relief." *Id.*

6. *The consequences of* Lyons. Is Justice Marshall right? Under *Lyons,* would anyone have standing to sue for injunctive relief a police department that required officers to shoot every tenth driver in traffic stops on sight?

7. *Constitutional development.* Because *Lyons* ends lawsuits early in litigation, it often prevents courts from elaborating on the contours of constitutional rights in question. Recall from Chapters 13 and 14 that constitutional rights are not easily developed in federal civil damages actions or criminal civil rights prosecutions against police officers: To bring a civil damages action under §1983 against an officer, plaintiffs must show that a right is already "clearly established." See Harlow v. Fitzgerald, 457 U.S. 800 (1982). Although a plaintiff may not need to demonstrate a previously articulated right to sue a municipality, courts often escape resolving the nature of the right by finding that, even if the right exists, the plaintiff cannot meet the high bar for establishing the city caused its violation. Cf. City of Canton v. Harris, 489 U.S. 378 (1989). Similarly, to bring a federal criminal prosecution against an officer under 42 U.S.C. §242 for violating a constitutional right, the government must prove that a right has already been "made specific." See Screws v. United States, 325 U.S. 91, 104–105 (1945). Should the Court, as it considers the standard for establishing standing, keep in mind that some constitutional rights are likely never to be articulated (or remedied) as a result of this combination of doctrines? See MacIssac v. Town of Poughkeepsie, 770 F. Supp. 2d 587, 599–600 (S.D.N.Y. 2011).

8. *Explaining the high bar.* Why is the Court so exacting in *Lyons?* Judge Frank Easterbrook explained it this way:

> Damages are a normal, and adequate, response to an improper search or seizure, which as a constitutional tort often is analogized to (other) personal-injury litigation. Erroneous grants of injunctive relief that hamper enforcement of the criminal law have the potential to cause havoc, while erroneous awards (or denials) of damages to a single person have more limited ability to injure the general public. Judges are fallible, so the costs of false positives always must be considered when choosing among remedies. When the costs of false negatives are low—and this is what it means to say that the remedy at law is adequate—there is correspondingly slight reason to incur the risk of premature or overbroad injunctive relief. . . . Once . . . litigation has run its course, the decision will have precedential effect even if the only remedy is monetary. If [a] court decides that the City's practice is unconstitutional then it must cease whether or not a formal injunction issues (for the prospect of damages paid to thousands of suspects would bring the City into line). If, however, the City prevails in the end, or suffers only a partial defeat, then avoiding premature injunctive relief will prove to have been a wise exercise of restraint.

Campbell v. Miller, 373 F.3d 834, 835–836 (7th Cir. 2004). Is Judge Easterbrook right that injunctive relief is special? Does that explain *Lyons*?

9. *Policing-specific impact.* Although *Lyons* applies to all §1983 suits for injunctive relief, including suits to desegregate schools or reform public housing, it has had an especially strong impact on suits alleging unconstitutional policing. Why? Lyons is focused on how foreseeable violations are. Consider the difference between the way psychiatric hospitals, schools, public housing complexes, and prisons interact with people and the way a police department does. How predictably do individuals encounter each kind of agency?

10. *Mootness.* Consistent with ordinary mootness principles, *Lyons* concludes that a lawsuit against a police department does not become moot just because the department eliminates an unconstitutional policy or orders its officers to stop violating the law. It must also be clear that the conduct will not begin again. See Already, LLC v. Nike, Inc., 568 U.S. 85 (2013). Can you see why this might be important? Why was the *plaintiff* the party arguing this case was moot?

11. *Chokeholds after* Lyons. Because *Lyons* did not have standing, the Supreme Court did not clarify how the Fourth Amendment applies to chokeholds.[1] Some major departments have banned or restricted chokeholds, as the LAPD did during the litigation. Several states have banned them, at least when deadly force is not justified, and more are considering doing so. Finally, the George Floyd Justice in Policing Act of 2020, H.R. 7120, 116th §363 (as passed by the House, June 25, 2020), proposed prohibiting any police department from receiving funds under the Edward Byrne Memorial Justice Assistant Grant program or the COPS grant program — the two largest sources of federal funds for police departments — unless they have in effect a policy that prohibits all chokeholds and carotid holds. In the meantime, chokeholds continue to be used and continue to be controversial in policing.

Other Rules Governing Structural Reform

The Supreme Court considers injunctions an extraordinary remedy. As a consequence, even if a plaintiff establishes standing, a district court may not enter an injunction unless it also finds that the plaintiff has suffered irreparable injury; that the injury cannot be relieved by traditional legal remedies; that in comparing the hardships each party will suffer, the injunction is nevertheless warranted; and that the injunction serves the public interest. See eBay Inc. v. MercExchange, L.L.C., 547 U.S. 388, 391 (2006). Moreover, any injunction binds only the parties, and it must state the reasons why it was issued, state its terms specifically, and describe in detail the acts it prohibits or requires. See Fed. R. Civ. P. 65(d).

---

[1] Departments sometimes use the term *chokeholds* to include both chokeholds and carotid restraints. In a carotid restraint, an officer induces unconsciousness by putting pressure on the sides of a victim's neck, restricting blood flow to the brain. A chokehold (in its more precise meaning) refers to pressure applied to the front of the neck and trachea that restrict a person's ability to breathe. Chokeholds can fracture or damage structures in the neck as well as cause death by cutting off a person's oxygen supply. For this reason, departments that distinguish between them tend to regulate chokeholds more stringently.

An injunction must also be narrow enough in scope. Specifically, it "must directly address and relate to the constitutional violations itself. . . . [F]ederal-court decrees exceed appropriate limits if they are aimed at eliminating a condition that does not violate the Constitution or does not flow from such a violation." Milliken v. Bradley, 433 U.S. 267, 282 (1977). Not only must it be directed at appropriate harms, it must be no broader than necessary to achieve legal relief.

Even after an injunction is issued, the defendant may seek relief from an injunction when enforcing the order is "no longer equitable," Fed. R. Civ. P. 60(5), and courts have no choice but to modify or terminate the decree if changed circumstances warrant it. See Agostini v. Felton, 521 U.S. 203, 215 (1997). In 2009, the Supreme Court indicated that courts should be especially generous in modifying and terminating structural reform injunctions because they raise special federalism concerns. See Horne v. Flores, 557 U.S. 433 (2009).

What do you take away from these limitations? Do they help you make sense of *Lyons*?

2.   Digging Deeper into *Lyons*

Dust off your analytic skills for the next few subsections. Plowing through them is challenging, but it will help you apply *Lyons* to future cases.

a.   The Lyons *Ratio*

Reread Part IV of the Court's opinion. One way to see what the Court is saying is that the likelihood of future injury from an alleged constitutional violation can be calculated by comparing the number of reasonably likely departmentally caused constitutional violations (assuming the allegations in the lawsuit are true) with the set of potential victims of those violations into which the plaintiff falls not as a result of his own choices.

One way to represent this idea is as a ratio:

$$\frac{likely\ violations}{group\ of\ potential\ victims\ including\ plaintiff}$$

This is the *Lyons* ratio.

In *Lyons*, the Court considered whether Lyons had standing given two possible versions of the ratio. One assumed that officers complied with the policy, conducting chokeholds against people who resisted arrest:

$$\frac{policy\text{-}compliant\ low\text{-}resistance\ chokeholds}{people\ who\ are\ detained\ and\ resist}$$

The other assumed that some officers violated the LRC policy and used force against individuals who neither committed crimes nor resisted, something that could happen to anyone encountering such an officer:

$$\frac{policy\text{-}violating\ no\text{-}resistance\ chokeholds}{people\ encountering\ police\ in\ LA}$$

The Court found that both versions fell "far short of the allegations that would be necessary to establish a case or controversy between these parties." In the Court's view, *Lyons* could avoid being in the first version's denominator, and he did not allege the second version's numerator was high enough to threaten him. In this way, the Court suggested that lower courts should reject standing when complaints describe ratios similar to *Lyons*, and they should distinguish *Lyons* when the fraction of likely constitutional violations to potential victims is higher, that is, much closer to one.

For comparison, the fraction would be (at least) one for policy-compliant officers if the department's policy were: "Go out and find Adolph Lyons and carry out a chokehold on him, no matter what he does." In that case, any officer complying with the policy might find Lyons and impose a chokehold. Lyons would be the only likely victim. That ratio would therefore be 1:1, or higher if Lyons encountered more than one officer. In that case, Lyons would have standing.

b. The **Lyons** *Ratio Denominator*

In *Lyons*, the Court gave two instructions about calculating the *Lyons* ratio's denominator. First, a threat that someone will suffer a constitutional violation as a result of a city's policy is not "real and immediate" if a plaintiff could avoid the constitutional violation simply by complying with the law. In that case, the plaintiff does not unavoidably fall into *any* group against which the policy causes violations. The denominator is zero, making the fraction undefined. There is no standing. This is the first of the two applications of the ratio above.

Second, if the relevant set of likely victims includes everyone in a city with whom the police interact, the denominator is likely too large to justify standing. To establish standing, then, it is better for plaintiffs to define a subset of the city's population that is likely to be targeted by the unconstitutional conduct. Otherwise, the ratio will be trivially small, and according to *Lyons*, there is unlikely to be standing. This is true in the second of the two applications.

Lower courts following *Lyons* take both points to heart. First, they tend to refuse to find standing where a plaintiff must engage in illegal conduct to be targeted, unless that illegal conduct is common and nonculpable, such as the conduct necessary to put a plaintiff in the class of all traffic-law violators. Second, they are more permissive with standing if plaintiffs identify a class of likely future victims that is a subset of the total population identifiable to the police. Still, this guidance can be difficult to apply. What about a police department like Hill Valley's that targets suspected prostitutes? Or one that targets suspects against whom there is reasonable suspicion of criminal activity but not probable cause?

c. The **Lyons** *Ratio Numerator*

The *Lyons* Court's comments on the numerator in the *Lyons* ratio are more puzzling: "In order to establish an actual controversy in this case, Lyons would have . . . to make the incredible assertion either, (1) that *all* police officers in Los Angeles *always* choke any citizen with whom they happen to have an encounter, whether for the purpose of arrest, issuing a citation or for questioning or, (2) that the City ordered or authorized police officers to act in such manner." *Lyons*, 461 U.S. at 105–106. In this way, the Court suggests that the only possible adequate numerator for standing would be the set of all police interactions, either because a formal policy permitted no-resistance chokeholds, or because, even in the absence of a formal policy, police officers *always* carried out chokeholds during encounters.

Why isn't a *high risk* that officers will violate policy and engage in unconstitutional chokeholds enough to establish standing? Why must every officer always do so? After all, *Monell v. Department of Social Servs.*, 436 U.S. 658 (1978), holds that a city may be sued under §1983 for unconstitutional actions that implement informal policies or customs, so long as the custom is sufficiently "persistent and widespread" as to have the force of law. This rule applies to §1983 cases no matter what relief is sought. See Los Angeles County v. Humphries, 562 U.S. 29 (2010). Why might the Court believe a different rule is needed for standing than for establishing that a policy existed for the purposes of municipal liability under §1983? The Court does not say.

Use the cases in the next section to test yourself. What does the *Lyons* ratio look like in each of the cases below? Can you see why the courts did what they did?

3. Through the *Lyons* Gate

Many cases against police departments founder (or are never brought) because of *Lyons*. Still, some suits for structural reform against law enforcement agencies survive, and they help reveal the effect *Lyons* has had on equitable relief as a remedy for police misconduct. Below are excerpts from five cases, two in which the courts found standing, and three in which they did not. As you read them, see whether you can identify what factors help plaintiffs achieve standing. Then, consider what this means about the kinds of misconduct that private suits for structural relief can address.

a. Plaintiffs Without Standing

MACISSAC v. TOWN OF POUGHKEEPSIE
770 F. Supp. 2d 587 (S.D.N.Y. 2011)

[O]n March 1, 2008 . . . MacIssac was operating his vehicle on a public highway in the Town [of Poughkeepsie]. The Officers . . . stopped MacIssac's vehicle and arrested him on suspicion of driving while intoxicated ("DWI"). MacIssac admits that both the stop and the arrest were undertaken with "arguable probable cause."

. . . He contends that, after he was handcuffed, the Officers used a Taser stun gun on him three times; bent his back, arms, and legs in a manner that caused significant pain; and otherwise used excessive force beyond that needed to control him. He denies that he was resisting arrest. . . .

. . . In his prayer for relief, he seeks, in addition to compensatory and punitive damages, to . . . enjoin the Town's police officers from using Taser stun guns when making otherwise peaceful arrests. He lacks standing to bring this claim under *Lyons,* however, because he has failed to allege facts demonstrating with any credibility that he himself will suffer the same injury again. As an initial matter, MacIssac has not alleged in the complaint that he will have another encounter with the Town's police. In responding to the Town's motion for partial dismissal, MacIssac argues that "an act as mundane as driving in the Town of Poughkeepsie, an everyday occurrence, brings [him] into contact with poorly trained and supervised Town of Poughkeepsie police officers, employed by a Town indifferent to his constitutional rights." But he ignores the fact that he was stopped not for innocently driving his vehicle but on suspicion of DWI, an offense to which he later pled guilty. This distinguishes his case from those in which the plaintiffs had standing to sue for injunctive relief in part because their likelihood of suffering the same harm again did not depend on them willfully breaking the law.

More importantly, even assuming that MacIssac faces a realistic threat of being stopped on suspicion of DWI again, nothing in the complaint suggests a reasonable likelihood that, during such a stop and possible arrest, the Town's officers again will use a Taser stun gun. As the Supreme Court in *Lyons* held, a claim by MacIssac that the Town's officers always use such excessive force on anyone who is stopped or arrested, regardless of that person's conduct in response to the stop or arrest, would be "untenable." . . . Rather, MacIssac alleges that the Town's failure to train and supervise its officers caused his injury and that the Town's failure to discipline the individual defendants in this case after he filed a complaint demonstrates its condonement of conduct in violation of his constitutional rights. Whether these allegations, if proven, would give rise to municipal liability under *Monell* is irrelevant because they do not confer standing to sue for injunctive relief under *Lyons*. . . . Thus, taking all the allegations in his complaint as true, MacIssac has not established an actual case or controversy with respect to his claim for an injunction.

CHANG v. UNITED STATES
738 F. Supp. 2d 83 (D.D.C. 2010)

This case is one of several which arose from events on September 27, 2002, during demonstrations in the District of Columbia protesting the policies of the World Bank, the International Monetary Fund, and the United States government. On that date, plaintiffs, seven students from George Washington University, were . . . observers for the National Lawyers Guild or . . . journalists or photographers for *The Hatchet*, a George Washington University student newspaper. Plaintiffs allege that they were not engaged in any unlawful activity. Nevertheless, police officers surrounded them and hundreds of others in Pershing Park, gave them no warning or order to disperse, and arrested them. Plaintiffs allege they were subsequently handcuffed, held on buses for up to 13 hours, and later detained at the Metropolitan Police Academy for up to 18 hours with one wrist cuffed to the opposite ankle. . . .

[P]laintiffs fail to create a genuine issue of material fact that they, personally, face a likelihood of additional injury similar to that alleged in their complaint. In their opposition to the motion for partial summary judgment, plaintiffs provide a declaration from only one of the remaining plaintiffs, Chris Zarconi. . . . He states that he is "often required to photograph events that take place throughout the District . . . ." He then describes one of his current assignments.

> I was recently hired to photograph the university view book for The George Washington University. For this job, I will be required to take photographs of 4–6 students over an extended period of time. Each of the students is involved politically, socially, academically, and otherwise with the university and the community extensively. I expect to be out on assignment with them in the early spring [2010] at demonstrations or rallies for causes they support or with which they are involved. . . .

The kinds of assertions offered by Mr. Zarconi have been rejected by *Lyons* and its progeny as insufficient to establish standing. His assertions regarding his presence at additional demonstrations as a professional photographer require the occurrence of several contingent, future events: that Mr. Zarconi will be working as a photographer, that his clients will attend demonstrations or rallies and ask him to accompany them, and that he will be trapped and arrested without committing any illegal activity or being afforded an opportunity to disperse. This sequence of hypothetical future events is indistinguishable from that found insufficient to establish standing in *Lyons*.

b.   Plaintiffs with Standing

THOMAS v. COUNTY OF LOS ANGELES
978 F.2d 504 (9th Cir. 1992)

The plaintiffs, predominately black and hispanic residents of the City of Lynwood, California, brought this section 1983 class action alleging that deputy sheriffs at the Lynwood station of the Los Angeles County Sheriff's Department . . . use excessive force in detaining minority citizens and employ unlawful procedures in searching residences occupied by minorities. . . .

The misconduct as described by the plaintiffs is both malicious and pervasive. Affidavits . . . charge that black and hispanic men have been repeatedly arrested without cause and severely beaten. . . . Guns, flashlights, fists, clubs, boots, a brick wall, and an electric Taser gun were just a few of the weapons allegedly used to injure individual plaintiffs. Many of the victims required medical treatment after being "apprehended" by Lynwood deputies, and some were hospitalized. . . . Affidavits recount instances where deputies placed the muzzle of a firearm in a suspect's ear, mouth or behind his head, and threatened to pull the trigger, or actually fired the gun without discharging a bullet. The plaintiffs also cite ten incidents where deputies allegedly illegally forced entry into residences, searched and ransacked the premises, and then left without arresting anyone. Many of the incidents described by the plaintiffs involved racial slurs and obscene language directed at the victim of the beating or search. . . .

As a threshold matter, appellants challenge plaintiffs' standing to pursue this action in which they seek to represent a class of residents and visitors to the Lynwood area who have been or may be mistreated by Lynwood Sheriff's deputies on account of their race, color, national origin, age, or economic class. . . .

The majority of the incidents alleged by the plaintiffs are said to have occurred within a six by seven block area within the jurisdiction of the Lynwood station. Seventy-five plaintiffs allege that they were victims of police misconduct, many within this small section of the City. A number of the class members are alleged to have been repeatedly subject to police brutality and harassment. . . .

Also significant is the fact that members of the plaintiff class have been subjected to retaliatory attacks in response to the filing of this action. . . . Repeated instances of violence and retaliatory confrontations are "continuing present adverse affects" and cause the threatened injury to be "sufficiently real and immediate to show an existing controversy." O'Shea v. Littleton, 414 U.S. 488, 496 (1974).

. . . The Court held that Lyons, one citizen in a very large city, could not credibly allege that he would again be detained by the police and again be the victim of a police chokehold. In contrast, the record before this court indicates that numerous instances of police misconduct have occurred in a small six by seven block area, some minority residents of the area have been mistreated by deputies more than once, and many victims purportedly did nothing to warrant detention or apprehension prior to the mistreatment. Moreover, plaintiffs have alleged that the misconduct is purposefully aimed at minorities and that such misconduct was condoned and tacitly authorized by department policy makers. We conclude that the plaintiffs have alleged a "real and immediate threat of injury" and consequently have presented a justiciable controversy. City of Los Angeles v. Lyons, 461 U.S. 95, 103 (1983).

NATIONAL CONGRESS FOR PUERTO RICAN RIGHTS v.
CITY OF NEW YORK
75 F. Supp. 2d 154 (S.D.N.Y. 1999)

This case involves alleged constitutional violations by a unit of the New York City Police Department (the "NYPD") known as the Street Crime Unit (the "SCU"). The SCU is an elite squad of police officers whose purported mission is to interdict violent crime in New York City and, in particular, remove illegal firearms from the streets. It is alleged that SCU officers subject residents of high crime areas, particularly Black and Latino men, to stops and frisks based not on reasonable suspicion but on their race and national origin.

The named individual plaintiffs are six Black and Latino men between the ages of 23 and 31 years old who reside in the boroughs of the Bronx and Brooklyn. Each plaintiff alleges that he has been stopped and frisked by police officers believed to be members of the SCU without reasonable suspicion and on the basis of his race and national origin. . . .

Defendants contend that the present case is on "all fours" with *Lyons* which compels dismissal of plaintiffs' claims for injunctive and declaratory relief. . . .

Lyons is distinguishable from the present case on a number of grounds. First, there is the difference in the number of alleged constitutional violations resulting from the challenged policies. In *Lyons,* in addition to himself, the plaintiff alleged in his first amended complaint that 10 chokehold-related deaths had occurred as a result of defendant's official policies. Here defendants' policy, evidenced by a pervasive pattern of unconstitutional stops and frisks, has allegedly affected tens of thousands of New York City residents, most of whom have been black and Latino men. Courts have not been hesitant to grant standing to sue for injunctive relief where numerous constitutional violations have resulted from a policy of unconstitutional practices by law enforcement officers.

A second distinguishing factor is that here at least three of the named individual plaintiffs claim they have been victimized by these unconstitutional practices repeatedly. . . . [T]his alone establishes that plaintiffs face a realistic threat of future harm. Unlike the situation presented in *Lyons,* here there is no chain of contingencies making the threat of future harm speculative. This is especially true in light of the fact that, unlike the plaintiff in *Lyons,* plaintiffs do not have to break the law to be exposed to the alleged constitutional violations. The fact that plaintiffs were stopped while engaging in everyday tasks further illustrates a realistic risk of future harm. Courts have distinguished *Lyons* and found standing where innocent individuals are victims of unconstitutional police conduct.

MARYLAND STATE CONFERENCE OF NAACP BRANCHES v.
MARYLAND DEPT. OF STATE POLICE
72 F. Supp. 2d 560 (D. Md. 1999)

On April 10, 1998, plaintiffs Maryland State Conference of NAACP Branches and several named individuals filed a class action lawsuit against the Maryland State Police, Col. David Mitchell, and several supervisory and individual members of the Maryland State Police ("MSP") alleging constitutional and statutory violations in connection with an alleged pattern of racially discriminatory stops, detentions and searches of minority motorists traveling on I–95 in the state of Maryland.

The defendants assert that the individual plaintiffs lack standing to seek injunctive relief, relying on *City of Los Angeles v. Lyons,* 461 U.S. 95 (1983), and *O'Shea v. Littleton,* 414 U.S. 488 (1974)....

Lyons, however, is distinguishable from this case. Not only do the plaintiffs allege a pattern and practice of racially discriminatory stops, but also the Court has found, in the *Wilkins* case, that for a period of time prior to April 1997 the plaintiffs "clearly have made a reasonable showing that there was a pattern and practice of stops by the Maryland State Police based upon race" on a portion of I–95. The *Lyons* complaint, on the other hand, did not assert that there was a pattern and practice of applying chokeholds without provocation or, if it did state such a claim, the Court found it was not supported by the record. Moreover, in *Lyons,* the likelihood that the plaintiff would again be subjected to a chokehold depended on his having "an encounter with the police [in which] either he would illegally resist arrest or detention or the officers would disobey their instructions and again render him unconscious without any provocation." *Lyons,* 461 U.S. at 106.

Here, the plaintiffs' likelihood of injury depends only on their status as a member of a minority group and their need to travel on I–95. Any "illegal" action on their part associated with the future stop need be no more than a minor, perhaps unintentional, traffic infraction; indeed, according to their allegations, they may be stopped even if no traffic violation has been committed. The plaintiffs also have reason to expect they will continue to travel on I–95. This combination of alleged past injury, an earlier pattern and practice finding, and the plaintiffs' likely future travel is sufficient to confer standing.

NOTES AND QUESTIONS

1. *What is the difference?* Can you see the differences between these two sets of cases? Based on this sample, plaintiffs are less likely to survive motions to dismiss when violations are infrequent, when no formal departmental policy authorizes them, and when those who risk injury are suspected of committing crimes or resisting the police. By contrast, plaintiffs more easily establish a risk of future injury when the challenged conduct is common, deliberate, or repeated, or when it targets an identifiable and largely innocent segment of the population. Can you think of the kinds of cases that might fall into each category?

2. *Excessive force.* Clearly, some important kinds of policing practices, including cases involving allegations of excessive force, will mostly fall into the first category. Plaintiffs suffering these harms will not usually be plausible plaintiffs. Therefore, such conduct will not be addressed by equitable relief and will not be deterred by the threat of equitable litigation. How problematic is that? On one hand, excessive force seems like exactly the kind of problem that might have systemic origins and institutional solutions. See Barbara E. Armacost, *Organizational Culture and Police Misconduct,* 72 Geo. Wash. L. Rev. 453 (2004). On the other hand, excessive force claims tend to do better in damages actions than other kinds of claims, in part because force causes visible injuries. In that light, what you think of *Lyons* may depend on how well you think damages actions deter the kinds of misconduct barred from injunctive relief.

3. *Racial profiling.* By contrast, racial discrimination and Fourth Amendment violations in traffic or street stops of Black and Latino men appear more likely to succeed in demonstrating standing. This important set of civil rights violations leads to cases that are not easily or well addressed by the exclusionary rule, criminal prosecution of police officers, or damages actions under §1983, the major alternatives. In this way, assuming plaintiffs could overcome other obstacles, could *Lyons* be said—at least very roughly—to protect local governments from intrusive reform by federal courts when alternative remedies exist and to allow reform when they don't? If so, is that a satisfactory justification for the Court's rule?

4. Imposing a Remedy: *Floyd v. City of New York*

When courts get into the business of imposing injunctive relief on big police departments, they face an immense challenge. They must dictate reforms for complex bureaucracies to prevent unconstitutional policing, but without undermining public safety or bankrupting a city. Most parties take over this process themselves, agreeing on remedies and seeking approval from the court. But when they do not, and a court finds widespread constitutional violations, the task can be overwhelming. Nowhere has this challenge been greater in policing than in New York City.

New York is the most populous city in the United States with more than 8.5 million people. Its police department is the country's largest law enforcement agency with more than 35,000 officers. It patrols the city's streets, subways, and public housing. And it is organized into a Byzantine arrangement of offices, bureaus, boroughs, precincts, units, and squads.

The Center for Constitutional Rights filed a class action suit, *Floyd v. City of New York*, to challenge the constitutionality of 4.4 million stops carried out between January 2004 and January 2012.[2] Following a nine-week trial, U.S. District Court Judge Shira Scheindlin found the New York Police Department liable for discriminating against Black and Latino New Yorkers and stopping many without sufficient cause. In a separate remedial opinion, Judge Scheindlin found injunctive relief against the NYPD justified.

Though Judge Scheindlin encouraged the parties to cooperate in developing reforms to prevent further constitutional violations, the NYPD refused to participate, leaving remedies to the court. Judge Scheindlin ordered some immediate remedies and appointed an independent monitor to oversee them. The implementation of those reforms continues. According to the monitor's tenth report, significant changes have occurred in policies, training, auditing, and performance evaluation in the department, and stops have gone down dramatically. But the department is not yet in substantial compliance, and many reforms are left to go. See Tenth Report of the Independent Monitor: Corrected Report Filed: January 7, 2020, Floyd v. City of New York, 959 F. Supp. 2d 540 (S.D.N.Y. 2013) (No. 08-CV-1034).

In addition to the limited immediate reforms Judge Scheindlin imposed, she intentionally left other more substantial remedial measures unspecified, on the ground that "[i]t would be unwise and impractical for this Court to impose such

---

[2] The liability opinion in *Floyd v. City of New York* is excerpted in Chapter 5.

reforms at this time." Instead, Judge Scheindlin set up a "Joint Remedial Process" to design additional reforms:

> Drawing on this Court's broad equitable powers to remedy the wrongs in this case, I am ordering that all parties participate in a joint remedial process, under the guidance of a Facilitator to be named by the Court. I hereby order the following specific relief:
>
> 1. All parties shall participate in the Joint Remedial Process for a period of six to nine months to develop proposed remedial measures (the "Joint Process Reforms") that will supplement the Immediate Reforms discussed above. The Joint Process Reforms must be no broader than necessary to bring the NYPD's use of stop and frisk into compliance with the Fourth and Fourteenth Amendments.
>
> 2. The Joint Remedial Process will be guided by the Facilitator, with such assistance as the Facilitator deems necessary and in consultation with the Monitor.
>
> 3. The initial responsibility of the Facilitator will be to work with the parties to develop a time line, ground rules, and concrete milestones for the Joint Remedial Process. The Cincinnati Collaborative Procedure and subsequent DOJ consent decrees and letters of intent may be used as models.
>
> 4. At the center of the Joint Remedial Process will be input from those who are most affected by the NYPD's use of stop and frisk, including but not limited to the people and organizations noted above. Input from academic and other experts in police practices may also be requested.
>
> 5. The Facilitator will convene "town hall" type meetings in each of the five boroughs in order to provide a forum in which all stakeholders may be heard. It may be necessary to hold multiple meetings in the larger boroughs in order to ensure that everyone will have an opportunity to participate. . . .
>
> 8. When the parties and the Facilitator have finished drafting the Joint Process Reforms, they will be submitted to the Court and the Monitor. The Monitor will recommend that the Court consider those Reforms he deems appropriate, and will then oversee their implementation once approved by the Court.
>
> 9. In the event that the parties are unable to agree on Joint Process Reforms, the Facilitator will prepare a report stating the Facilitator's findings and recommendations based on the Joint Remedial Process, to be submitted to the parties, the Monitor, and the Court. . . .
>
> 10. The City will be responsible for the reasonable costs and fees of the Facilitator and the Joint Remedial Process.

Floyd v. City of New York, 959 F. Supp. 2d 668, 687–688 (S.D.N.Y. 2013). Judge Scheindlin noted that community input would be essential:

> The communities most affected by the NYPD's use of stop and frisk have a distinct perspective that is highly relevant to crafting effective reforms. No amount of legal or policing expertise can replace a community's understanding of the likely practical consequences of reforms in terms of both liberty and safety.

Id. at 686.

Because New York City withdrew its appeal, Judge Scheindlin's unusual approach to reform was never assessed by the Court of Appeals. The *Floyd* case was subsequently reassigned to Judge Analisa Torres, who then appointed a facilitator to guide the Joint Remedial Process Judge Scheindlin ordered. At the end of the process, the facilitator issued a report recommending that the court order additional reforms.

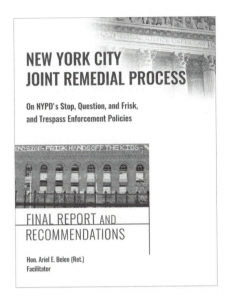

Here is a summary of the facilitator's recommendations:

1. Create permanent structures for feedback regarding officer conduct.
2. Publish monthly reports chronicling findings of misconduct and discipline.
3. Develop and publish disciplinary standards.
4. Develop permanent body-worn-camera practices and policies with stakeholder input.
5. Keep data on all low-level police–citizen encounters.
6. Make stop reports accessible to members of the public on request.
7. Establish permanent mechanisms for engaging with youth, the LGBTQ community, and department critics, and establish a board to offer feedback from affected communities on court-ordered reform.
8. Educate the public about citizens' rights and obligations of officers during street encounters and changes to NYPD policing policies.
9. Survey the community annually regarding community relations, perceptions of street encounters, and experience with court-ordered reforms, and use those surveys in command staff evaluation.
10. Stop using pedestrian stops to coerce young people to act as confidential informants.
11. Train officers on stopping and frisking people with mental, physical, or developmental disabilities or mental illness.
12. Train officers on engaging with LGBTQ communities in street encounters and on deescalation.
13. Use civil rather than criminal summonses for trespass.
14. Train officers on trauma and the implications of trauma for public safety.

See Ariel E. Belen, *New York City Joint Remedial Process on NYPD's Stop, Question, and Frisk and Trespass Enforcement Policies: Final Report and Recommendations* 218 (2018). In the end, the parties could not agree on any of those reforms. Instead, the facilitator used the final report to submit findings and recommendations to the court. Since then, the court has issued several orders consistent with recommendations by the facilitator.

You might think this process raises three issues. The first is *timing*. Given the time it takes for complex litigation to work its way through the courts, for remedies to be developed, and for remedies to be adopted and assessed in a big organization, it might be inevitable that injunctive relief takes time. Still, are you comfortable with the fact that new remedies are still being ordered and implemented in response to a report issued in 2018 to prevent constitutional violations found by a judge in 2013 to have occurred between 2004 and 2012? Is that an argument against injunctive relief? Is there any way to mitigate timing concerns?

The second issue is *community input*. The facilitator received input from dozens of organizations and thousands of individuals during the process. Assume, as most experts do, that community and officer input is critical to identifying effective reforms and building sufficient support for them to succeed. How exactly are the facilitator and the judge to weigh the preferences of various stakeholders? Isn't aggregating policy preferences what we have elections for? On the other hand, would it make sense to reform the NYPD without asking affected communities about what is needed?

The third issue is *scope*. Recall that Judge Scheindlin found that the city was liable for violating plaintiffs' Fourth and Fourteenth Amendment rights because:

> The City acted with deliberate indifference toward the NYPD's practice of making unconstitutional stops and conducting unconstitutional frisks. . . . In addition, the City adopted a policy of indirect racial profiling by targeting racially defined groups for stops based on local crime suspect data. This has resulted in the disproportionate and discriminatory stopping of blacks and Hispanics in violation of the Equal Protection Clause.

Floyd v. City of New York, 959 F. Supp. 2d 540, 562 (S.D.N.Y. 2013). In her liability decision, Judge Scheindlin made no findings about the police department's interactions with youth, the LGBTQ community, people with mental illness, or people with developmental or physical disabilities, all mentioned in the facilitator's recommendations. Yet these groups have disproportionate contact with police in street encounters, and the remedial process revealed many problematic interactions with them. Do you think the report goes too far in recommending reforms regarding these groups? Or is it more efficient to include them than to encourage another similar and costly lawsuit for further injunctive relief against similar police practices?

As is suggested by *Floyd v. City of New York*, *negotiated* and *litigated* remedies for structural reform freely borrow provisions from each other. But court-imposed injunctions like the one in *Floyd* are not interchangeable with negotiated remedies reflected in consent decrees. Unlike an injunction, a consent decree has characteristics of a contract as well as characteristics of a judicial decree. See Firefighters v. Cleveland, 478 U.S. 501, 519 (1986). It is treated as an agreement between the parties that they expect to be enforceable against them. See Rufo v. Inmates of Suffolk

County Jail, 502 U.S. 367, 378 (1992). Courts enter consent decrees more freely than litigated injunctions, and consent decrees may include provisions that a court could not impose by injunction. Cases, like *Floyd*, in which parties cannot agree on remedies, therefore present especially difficult questions for federal courts.

5. Winning by Losing

Suits for equitable relief are lengthy, expensive, and uncertain ventures. Given the obstacles to and expense of structural reform litigation, you might wonder why so many plaintiffs continue to pursue it. The controversy over stops and frisks in New York City illustrates some potential side benefits for plaintiffs of equitable relief suits.

Rachel A. Harmon & Andrew Manns, *Proactive Policing and the Legacy of* Terry
15 Ohio St. J. Crim. L. 49, 66–70 (2017)

Constitutional litigation can obviously spark changes when plaintiffs are able to win on the merits. But it can also prompt change through settlements, especially those for injunctive or declaratory relief, even when . . . the law seemingly provides limited leverage for plaintiffs. . . .

Constitutional litigation is also surprisingly powerful at facilitating the political process. Specifically, lawsuits can be used to generate additional data about what the police are doing. For example, pre-*Floyd* litigation against the NYPD settled in a consent decree that committed the NYPD to collecting and making available the UF-250s—the forms on which police recorded *Terry* stops and frisks. Those UF-250s became the basis for Jeffrey Fagan's expert report in *Floyd*, which declared SQF unconstitutional. But equally important, because the settlement also made the data public, it allowed a much richer public debate about stops and frisks and their value. For example, the data made possible the *New York Times*'s interactive map, which allowed residents to see how many stops occurred on their block and to see the density of stops in the city overall. As a result, both the justifications for the NYPD's stops and their distributional effects were far better understood.

In New York City, the litigation led to data, which in turn, led to public debate. In other localities, constitutional litigation has led to legislative action, including the passage of statutes mandating data collection and placing restrictions on police authority to engage in certain kinds of activities. In *Chavez v. Illinois State Police*,[3] for example, the American Civil Liberties Union challenged a practice of traffic stops alleged to be in violation of the Fourth and Fourteenth Amendments. . . . The Illinois State legislature passed laws mandating data collection on traffic stops and requiring police officers to record reasons for their stops. Laws such as these help to facilitate future accountability by making practices more visible and the coercive costs of the activities more apparent to the voting public. A similar suit in

---

[3] *Ed. note. Chavez v. Illinois State Police*, 251 F.3d 612 (7th Cir. 2001), appears in Chapter 6.

Maryland led not only to a state law mandating data collection, but also to substantive prohibitions on the use of racial profiling by state police.

In addition, litigation—again, even when not entirely successful—can strengthen the salience of a policing practice, giving it a sufficient public profile to ensure scrutiny of the costs of that program and possible electoral consequences as a result. In this way, litigation facilitates political accountability and makes the costs of policing an important part of the local political process. This appears to have happened in New York City, at least to some degree. The plaintiffs won in *Floyd*, and the decision is influential, but that decision would not have been the last word in the expected litigation. Given the issues, it is not clear that either the liability decision or the remedy would have fared well on appeal. That question was never answered because political events overcame legal ones. In the presence of intense public and media debate following the *Floyd* decision, Bill de Blasio, a long-shot candidate, bet his political future on opposing the SQF policy, and won that bet. After he took office, he withdrew the appeal, ending further litigation of the merits; agreed to the City's participation in the court-run remedial process; and has substantially changed NYPD's practices with respect to stops and frisks in New York City. . . . At the end of the day, politics, not law, decided what was best for the City of New York. But law helped.

NOTES AND QUESTIONS

1. *Strategic litigation.* When is it legitimate to bring a lawsuit to gather information? To promote political change? See also Model Rules of Prof. Conduct 3.1 ("A lawyer shall not bring or defend a proceeding . . . unless there is a basis in law and fact for doing so that is not frivolous, which includes a good faith argument for an extension, modification or reversal of existing law."). What about maximizing the political benefits of a lawsuit underway?

B.   Public Suits for Police Reform

The most influential suits against police departments for equitable relief have been by the U.S. Department of Justice rather than private plaintiffs. This section describes federal enforcement efforts that have led to structural reform.

1.   The History of the Pattern-or-Practice Statute

In other civil rights arenas, the federal government has long played an important role in driving structural reform litigation. In policing, that role is more recent. In the 1970s, many big cities were known for police violence. Philadelphia was especially problematic. In 1978, just after several investigations highlighted claims of beatings and threats by Philadelphia police officers, the police blockaded the residence of MOVE, a Black liberation group, leading to a shootout in which an officer died. Soon afterward, U.S. Attorney General Griffin B. Bell ordered the Justice Department's Civil Rights Division and the U.S. Attorney's Office in Philadelphia to investigate the Philadelphia Police Department for police brutality.

After an eight-month investigation, the Department of Justice filed a complaint against the city, its mayor, and the department, among others, claiming that Philadelphia officers engaged in rampant unconstitutional violence. The complaint accused the department of deliberately encouraging illegal conduct through its training, policies, and disciplinary procedures. As a remedy, the suit sought an order enjoining further illegal violence and ordering federal funds withheld from the city if it failed to comply. The complaint represented the first Department of Justice attempt to sue a police department for injunctive relief, but it was not intended to be the last: The Department had ongoing investigations in Houston, Memphis, and Mobile when it filed the Philadelphia suit.

The Department of Justice based its complaint on what it argued was an implied right of action. The district court rejected this argument and dismissed the suit, and the Third Circuit affirmed: "Congress has by explicit legislation established a comprehensive and detailed remedial structure for the protection of constitutional rights, and it has repeatedly refused to sanction federal executive intervention in local affairs in order to protect those rights." United States v. City of Philadelphia, 644 F.2d 187, 198 (3d Cir. 1980). The court rejected the lawsuit as "an attempt by the federal executive to intervene on a grand scale in the workings of a local government, an area that is manifestly the concern of the states and not the federal government." *Id.* It summarized its view of the implied right-of-the action argument this way:

> [T]he Attorney General argues that he possesses implied authority under the Civil Rights Acts and under the fourteenth amendment to request far-reaching mandatory injunctions, notwithstanding three separate refusals of Congress to grant him this authority and a widely-shared understanding that the authority does not exist. He also has looked to the courts, and applications similar to this have been rejected in the fourth, seventh, and ninth circuits. Unabashed, he has continued to shop for a forum that will lend its ear. He will not find it here.

Id. at 203. The decisive rejection of the Department of Justice's theory killed any further attempts to bring suits for injunctive relief under then-existing legal authority. And that is how the situation remained for more than a decade.

Then, on March 2, 1991, the California Highway Patrol (CHP) tried to pull Rodney King over for speeding. King took off, leading officers and the Los Angeles Police Department (LAPD) on a high-speed chase that ended when the police cornered King. LAPD officers attempted to subdue King. Although he initially resisted, officers continued to stomp, kick, and strike him with batons repeatedly, even after he remained on the ground. Three officers and a supervisor were directly involved in the beating. Eight others stood by. The beating was captured on video by George Holliday, and it generated enormous public outrage, in part because it corroborated long-standing complaints about the LAPD. Many thought that the video and subsequent legal actions would change the LAPD forever.

Instead, the aftermath of the King incident reinforced how inadequate existing remedies for police misconduct could be. Despite the apparent illegality of the conduct, the state's prosecution resulted in no convictions, leading to a riot that left Los Angeles burning for days. A subsequent federal prosecution resulted in convictions for two officers, both of whom received light sentences, and acquittals for two more. The Christopher Commission, an independent commission established to review the

LAPD's practices after the beating, issued a blunt report describing management failures in the LAPD, including a pervasive failure to hold officers accountable for repeated acts of excessive force. The Commission recommended substantial changes to the department to prevent further excessive force. Overwhelmingly, they were not adopted. King received $3.8 million in damages from a civil jury more than two years after the incident, but that verdict did not seem to make the city more open to reform. Given *Lyons*, private actors were unlikely to have standing to sue the LAPD for court-ordered reform, at least to stop excessive force. And given *United States v. City of Philadelphia*, 644 F.2d 187 (3d Cir. 1980), which held that the United States had no authority to sue a police department for equitable relief, the federal government was sure not to sue either. All told, neither legal interventions nor the political process reformed the LAPD. And although Rodney King's beating became the most visible manifestation of departmentally tolerated police violence in the United States, no one thought the LAPD was unique.

Congress responded to this series of events by including new authority for the Department of Justice in the Violent Crime Control and Law Enforcement Act of 1994, the largest crime bill in U.S. history. Passed when violent crime was high, and fear was even higher, the act gave a vast amount of new money and power to law enforcement through $30 billion in funding for crime prevention and enforcement and dozens of new federal crimes. It also expanded the federal death penalty, lengthened federal sentences, and mandated state sexual offender registries. Through it, Congress also created the Office of Community Oriented Policing Services in the Department of Justice and provided more than $1 billion a year to fulfill President Bill Clinton's promise to place 100,000 new police officers on the street. Only one tiny corner of the law was devoted to police accountability. That corner included §12601.[4]

34 U.S.C. §12601: Cause of Action

(a) Unlawful conduct

It shall be unlawful for any governmental authority, or any agent thereof, or any person acting on behalf of a governmental authority, to engage in a pattern or practice of conduct by law enforcement officers or by officials or employees of any governmental agency with responsibility for the administration of juvenile justice or the incarceration of juveniles that deprives persons of rights, privileges, or immunities secured or protected by the Constitution or laws of the United States.

(b) Civil action by Attorney General

Whenever the Attorney General has reasonable cause to believe that a violation of paragraph (1) has occurred, the Attorney General, for or in the name of the United States, may in a civil action obtain appropriate equitable and declaratory relief to eliminate the pattern or practice.

This statute is often referred to either by its *pattern-or-practice* language or as *14141* because it was originally codified as 42 U.S.C. §14141. It was recodified as 34 U.S.C.

---

[4] The other police accountability provision, §14142, now codified as 34 U.S.C §12602, mandated that the Department of Justice "acquire data about the use of excessive force by law enforcement officers" and "publish an annual summary of the data." However, Congress never required that state and local agencies provide the data to the Department of Justice, and it soon stopped allocating money to pay for federal data collection entirely. The Department of Justice issued only a couple of early reports, and since then the section has become nearly a dead letter.

§12601 effective September 2017, as part of the new U.S. Code title 34, Crime Control and Law Enforcement. More than most statutes, this one has depended on political support for enforcement, and the Trump Administration did not meaningfully enforce the statute after (or before) its recodification. Thus, although the following notes call it the *pattern-or-practice* statute or *§12601*, the cases and secondary materials mostly use *§14141*.

2. The Constitutionality of the Pattern-or-Practice Statute

Section 12601 is enforced against law enforcement agencies by the Special Litigation Section, a unit of the Civil Rights Division within the Department of Justice. Because most investigations initiated using the statute are resolved without litigation, there are few reported cases involving the law. Still, one of the first departments targeted by the Department of Justice challenged the constitutionality of the statute, resulting in the only decision on the issue, an unreported opinion by a federal magistrate.

The case arose when the Department of Justice sued Columbus, Ohio, alleging that the Columbus Division of Police engaged in a pattern of excessive force and false arrests. The city, along with the local Fraternal Order of Police, moved to dismiss the suit, arguing that Congress had exceeded its constitutional authority in promulgating §12601. In her report and recommendation, the magistrate disagreed:

> The United States takes the position that Congress "had ample authority under the Commerce Clause to enact §14141 given the substantial effect on interstate commerce of the consequences of police misconduct. . . ." There is no indication, however, that, in enacting §14141, Congress intended the statute to effect a regulation of interstate commerce. More important, the United States Supreme Court has recently held that Congress may not regulate "non-economic [mis]conduct . . . based solely on that conduct's aggregate effect on interstate commerce." United States v. Morrison, 120 S. Ct. 1740, 1754 (2000). This Court concludes that §14141 cannot be justified as a valid exercise of congressional authority under the Commerce Clause.
>
> In their memoranda, all parties also discuss, in comprehensive fashion, whether §14141 reflects a valid exercise of congressional power under §5 of the Fourteenth Amendment. . . . Congressional power under §5 to enforce the Fourteenth Amendment includes the authority both to remedy and to prevent the violation of rights guaranteed by the amendment. However, it does not include the power "to decree the substance of the Fourteenth Amendment's restrictions on the states." City of Boerne v. Flores, 521 U.S. 507, 519 (1997). "Congress does not enforce a constitutional right by changing what the right is." Id. . . .
>
> The distinction between remedial measures properly taken by Congress pursuant to §5 and substantive changes to the Fourteenth Amendment forbidden to Congress is, as the Supreme Court has recognized, "not easy to discern." Id. at 519. Critical to the distinction is the existence of "congruence and proportionality between the injury to be prevented or remedied and the means adopted to that end." Id. at 520. . . . Moreover, where congressional action would prohibit conduct not otherwise unconstitutional, it cannot be said, in the absence of a significant pattern of unconstitutional misconduct by state officials, that the action is congruent and proportional to the authority conferred upon Congress by §5 of the Fourteenth Amendment. Where legislation "is so out of proportion to a supposed remedial or preventive object that it cannot be understood as responsive to, or designed to prevent, unconstitutional behavior," the statute may be characterized as attempting to effect "a substantive change in Constitutional protections." City of Boerne, 521 U.S. at 532. . . .

Without doubt, the Fourteenth Amendment offers substantive protection from various forms of misconduct on the part of state law enforcement officials. Moreover, the legislative history referred to by all parties in this action makes clear that the House Committee perceived the problem of police misconduct in constitutional terms and described the problem in its report as "serious," "real," and "not limited to Los Angeles." This Court has no doubt that, in enacting §14141, Congress intended to respond, by both remedial and preventative measures, to a widespread pattern of violations of the Fourteenth Amendment by police officials acting under color of state law. The first test of the "congruence and proportionality" test . . . has been met.

The movants argue that any remedy under §14141, and particularly the far-reaching relief sought by plaintiff in this action, is disproportionate to any claimed Fourteenth Amendment violations in light of the availability of private civil actions under §1983 and the possibility of criminal prosecutions under 18 U.S.C. §§241, 242. However, as the House Committee report noted, some forms of unconstitutional police misconduct will, by operation of current judicial law, fall beyond the reach of private litigants and the possibility of remedy. The fact that Congress has previously promulgated 42 U.S.C. §1983 and 18 U.S.C. §§241, 242 does not transform §14141 into an incongruent and disproportionate method of enforcing Fourteenth Amendment violations.

Once a Fourteenth Amendment violation has been identified, Congress is entitled to "much deference" in determining "whether and what legislation is needed to secure the guarantees of the Fourteenth Amendment." *City of Boerne*, 521 U.S. at 536. That the method of enforcement selected by Congress in the lawful exercise of its authority under §5 may be unprecedented and even severe does not necessarily militate a finding of incongruity and disproportionality. *Id.* at 526. As the United States Supreme Court has cautioned, "Difficult and intractable problems often require powerful remedies, and we have never held that §5 precludes Congress from enacting reasonably prophylactic legislation." Kimel v. Florida Bd. of Regents, 120 S. Ct. 631, 648 (2000).

United States v. City of Columbus, No. 2: 99-CV-1097, 2000 (S.D. Ohio Aug. 3, 2000). No other court has ruled on the matter. Still, it seems hard to disagree.

3.   The Scope of Liability Under the Pattern-or-Practice Statute

After ruling on the constitutionality of the statute, the magistrate in *City of Columbus* went on to interpret the statute. The United States had argued that the statute imposed vicarious liability on cities for the actions of police officers. The court disagreed, concluding that §14141 should be interpreted as having the same limits on municipal liability as §1983, as articulated in *Monell v. Department of Social Services of the City of New York,* 436 U.S. 658, 691 (1978). Thus, the court ruled, a city should be held liable for the actions of its officers only if that conduct was a product of the city's "policy or custom." See also United States v. Johnson, 122 F. Supp. 3d 272, 347–349 (M.D.N.C. 2015) (taking a similar approach to §12601 in interpreting "pattern or practice").

As Chapter 13 discusses, *Monell's* controversial rejection of vicarious liability has severely hampered private suits against municipalities for police misconduct. Demanding similar proof for suits by the United States could have significantly limited enforcement of §12601. Both sides filed objections to the magistrate's report, but the parties settled before the district court ruled. Since the *City of Columbus* litigation, the Civil Rights Division's complaints and findings letters inevitably emphasize policy deficiencies that helped cause the constitutional violations identified in the jurisdiction, but they do not cite *City of Columbus*. Instead, the Division maintains that §12601 permits cities to be held vicariously liable for officer conduct.

In 2019, the Ninth Circuit agreed. The case involved two of the smallest jurisdictions targeted under the statute, the Town of Colorado City, Arizona, and Hildale City, Utah. These adjoining communities, which straddle the Arizona–Utah border, are primarily populated by members of the Fundamentalist Church Community of Jesus Christ of Latter-Day Saints (FLDS), under the leadership of Warren Jeffs.[5] The 2012 complaint alleged that the towns engaged in a pattern or practice of violating the First, Fourth, and Fourteenth Amendment rights of non-FLDS residents. In effect, the government alleged that the towns acted as an arm of the church and systematically discriminated against non-FLDS members in providing policing services, including by refusing to investigate crimes against them, refusing to arrest FLDS members who committed crimes against non-FLDS members, and destroying and trespassing on property of non-FLDS members. After a 44-day trial in 2016, the towns were held liable under §12601. Colorado City appealed, arguing among other things, that the district court incorrectly interpreted §12601. The Ninth Circuit ruled on the issue in *United States v. Town of Colorado City*, 935 F.3d 804, 808-811 (2019):

> Colorado City argues that the district court erred by construing the statute as imposing liability on governments for patterns of constitutional violations committed by their officers and agents. It asserts that §12601 requires the United States to demonstrate that the Towns "instituted an official municipal policy" of violating residents' constitutional rights. The United States, on the other hand, contends that the statute "imposes liability on municipalities for patterns of constitutional violations [that] their law enforcement officers commit, without requiring an additional showing that the municipality's policy or custom caused those violations." This issue—whether §12601 imposes *respondeat superior* liability[3]—is one of first impression in our circuit.
>
> Colorado City relies on the premise that, by including "pattern or practice" in §12601, Congress used "language with a well-defined meaning [] developed under [*Monell v. Department of Social Services*, 436 U.S. 658 (1978)] for municipal liability." That contention, however, confuses the relationship between general liability rules in civil rights statutes and the Supreme Court's decision in *Monell*.
>
> "[T]he general rule regarding actions under civil rights statutes is that *respondeat superior* applies." Bonner v. Lewis, 857 F.2d 559, 566 (9th Cir. 1988). In *Monell*, the Court carved out an exception to this general rule by holding that a municipality may not be held liable pursuant to 42 U.S.C. §1983 for the actions of its subordinates. Instead, to establish municipal liability, a plaintiff must show that a local government's "policy or custom" led to the plaintiff's injury. *Monell*, 436 U.S. at 694. In reaching its holding, the Court relied on "the language of §1983, read against the background of the [statute's] legislative history." *Id.* at 691. Because

---

[5] Warren Jeffs was sentenced to life in prison in 2011 for sexual assault of a 12-year-old girl and 20 additional years for the sexual assault of a 15-year-old girl. He has remained the spiritual leader of FLDS while in prison.

[3] *Respondeat superior* is "[t]he doctrine holding an employer or principal liable for the employee's or agent's wrongful acts committed within the scope of employment or agency." *Black's Law Dictionary* (11th ed. 2019).

§1983 imposes liability only where a state actor, "under color of some official policy, 'causes' an employee to violate another's constitutional rights," the Court reasoned that Congress did not intend to impose vicarious liability on municipalities "solely on the basis of the existence of an employer-employee relationship with a tortfeasor." *Id.* at 692. Moreover, in the Civil Rights Act of 1871—the predecessor statute to §1983—Congress "did not intend municipalities to be held liable unless action pursuant to official municipal policy of some nature caused a constitutional tort." *Id.* at 691.

Monell's holding remains the exception to the general rule. We have declined to bar *respondeat superior* liability in other contexts. In *Bonner*, for example, we held that *respondeat superior* liability applies to claims pursuant to §504 of the Rehabilitation Act of 1973. . . . And, in *Duvall v. County of Kitsap*, we held that *respondeat superior* liability applies to claims brought pursuant to Title II of the Americans with Disabilities Act, 42 U.S.C. §12132. 260 F.3d 1124, 1141 (9th Cir. 2001).

We likewise decline to extend *Monell's* holding to claims pursuant to §12601. Several features of the statutory text lead us to that conclusion.

First, §12601, unlike §1983, does not include the words "under color of any law, statute, ordinance, regulation, custom or usage." That difference is important because, by including "custom" in §1983, Congress expressly contemplated imposing liability on actors who violated constitutional rights under an official policy. The absence of that language from §12601, therefore, suggests that Congress did not intend to limit liability to those acting under an official law or policy. . . .

Second, §12601 does not limit liability to those who "cause [citizens or persons] to be subjected" to a deprivation of their constitutional rights. The *Monell* Court interpreted that language, which appears in §1983, as imposing liability "on a government that, under color of some official policy, 'causes' an employee to violate another's constitutional rights." *Monell*, 436 U.S. at 692. The lack of that causal phrase in §12601 suggests that Congress did not intend to limit local governments' liability to situations when "the action that is alleged to be unconstitutional implements or executes a policy statement, ordinance, regulation, or decision officially adopted and promulgated by that body's officers." *Id.* at 690. Taken together, these statutory clues persuade us that Congress intended to allow for *respondeat superior* liability against local governments pursuant to §12601. . . .

We acknowledge that Congress used "pattern or practice" in both statutes, and are mindful that "[a] basic principle of interpretation is that courts ought to interpret similar language in the same way, unless context indicates that they should do otherwise." Shirk v. United States ex rel. Dep't of Interior, 773 F.3d 999, 1004 (9th Cir. 2014). That principle, however, does not necessarily support Colorado City's argument, for Congress has also used "pattern or practice" literally, rather than as a term of art, in several statutes. See, e.g., 42 U.S.C. §2000e-6(a) (authorizing the Attorney General to pursue injunctive relief in cases alleging a pattern or practice of employment discrimination); 42 U.S.C. §3614(a) (authorizing the Attorney General to bring civil action in cases involving a pattern or practice of Fair Housing Act violations); 42 U.S.C. §10101(e) (authorizing courts to find a pattern or practice of voting rights deprivations). Under those statutes, the United States must demonstrate only that the conduct alleged "was not an isolated or accidental or peculiar event." United States v. Ironworkers Local 86, 443 F.2d 544, 552 (9th Cir. 1971). It need not show the existence of an official policy or custom.

For this reason, Congress's use of "pattern or practice" in §12601 does not support the weight that Colorado City wishes to place upon it. Congress could have used the phrase to refer to an official policy or custom, as in §1983, but it also could have used the phrase to refer to a regular event, as in the statutes cited above. . . .

. . . Section 12601 provides a civil cause of action to the United States Attorney General when a local government's agents "engage in a pattern or practice of conduct . . . that deprives persons of rights, privileges, or immunities secured or protected by the Constitution or laws of the United States." 34 U.S.C. §12601. Because the statutory language does not demonstrate that Congress intended to exclude local governments from *respondeat superior* liability, we hold that §12601 imposes liability based on general agency principles. Accordingly, the district court did not err in its construction of §12601.[5]

NOTES AND QUESTIONS

1. *Vicarious liability.* Are you persuaded that cities should be vicariously liable for a pattern or practice of constitutional violations by its officers?

2. *Patterns and practices.* Do you now know what constitutes a "pattern or practice" under the statute? How many constitutional violations are sufficient to establish a pattern? How pervasive does a pattern have to be within a department? Over what period of time do incidents have to take place to constitute a pattern or practice of constitutional violations?

3. *Thin law.* Does it surprise you that the statute has been enforced dozens of times since the original decision in *City of Columbus* with so little clarification? Why do you think this is?

4. Enforcement of the Pattern-or-Practice Statute

There are several steps in a pattern-or-practice case:

1. intake and initial screening;
2. preliminary investigation;
3. justification and approval for full investigation;
4. full investigation and findings;
5. negotiation and settlement; and
6. implementation.

---

[5] We reject Colorado City's argument that our interpretation of 34 U.S.C. §12601 violates §5 of the Fourteenth Amendment. It argues that the district court violated the Supreme Court's decision in *City of Canton v. Harris* because it "interpreted [§12601] to impose vicarious liability upon the Towns without requiring the United States to show that the Towns were responsible for the alleged misconduct." 489 U.S. 378 (1989). Not so. The Court's decision in *City of Canton*, which stated that permitting *respondeat superior* liability against local governments under §1983 "would implicate serious questions of federalism," was limited to that statute. *Id.* at 392. The Court did not hold that it was unconstitutional to permit *respondeat superior* liability against local governments in any context.

a.   Initial Steps in §12601 Enforcement

The Civil Rights Division receives more than a thousand referrals, complaints, and reports alleging police misconduct each year. They come by email, phone calls, and letters from community members and families of victims, advocacy groups, prosecutors and defense attorneys, public officials, and police officers. Section attorneys also identify potential subjects for investigation in many other ways, including other activities of the Department of Justice, such as criminal prosecutions of police officers. They have been alerted by sources as diverse as a "petition for grievances" by the American Civil Liberties Union in Newark; a series of investigative news articles about deadly police force in Washington, D.C.; and public protests in Baltimore and Ferguson. In the end, unlike criminal investigations of police officers by the Civil Rights Division, most civil investigations of police departments do not arise from complaints.

Once a preliminary investigation is opened, Special Litigation Section attorneys collect easily available information to assess initially whether the law enforcement agency appears to be engaged in systemic misconduct. If the facts support it, the Special Litigation Section may seek approval from the Assistant Attorney General to open a full investigation. The Special Litigation Section provides no formal guidance to attorneys on selecting cases for full investigation from its complaints and referrals, and it does not explain its decisions to target one alleged violator and not another. Attorneys report considering the following:

1. Whether the allegation meets the requirements of the statute as interpreted by the Section.
2. The strength and credibility of the evidence supporting the allegation.
3. Whether the allegation helps to ensure that the Section represents all geographic regions, community and police force sizes, and protected classes.
4. The availability of attorneys to work on the case.
5. Whether the resources required would prevent opening future complex or urgent cases.
6. Whether there is an immediate threat to public order or safety, including that which arises from public interest and media coverage.

Office of the Inspector General, U.S. Dept. of Justice, *Audit of the Department of Justice's Efforts to Address Patterns or Practices of Police Misconduct and Provide Technical Assistance on Accountability Reform to Police Departments* 13 and tbl. 4 (2018).

A full investigation is a resource-intensive undertaking that can consume several attorneys and last for several years. Because the Section has never had more than 30 lawyers working on policing cases, the decision to open a full investigation necessarily includes consideration of resource constraints and substantive priorities. Because the Assistant Attorney General for Civil Rights ultimately decides whether a full investigation is warranted, the administration's commitment to promoting civil rights through pattern-or-practice litigation also inevitably influences decisions to investigate.

Many of the investigations have been against major city police departments with high-profile problems, but some such departments have never been sued, and some less obvious targets have been. Given that there are approximately 18,000 law enforcement agencies in the United States, without information about the selection process, the Civil Rights Division's targets can seem arbitrary, at least to the cities themselves. When Steubenville, Ohio, was investigated, City Manager Gary Dufour commented, "We're an awfully small community. You see all these problems that have come up at the police departments in Los Angeles and New York and New Orleans, and you've got to wonder, why us?" See Eric Lichtblau, *U.S. Low Profile in Big-City Police Probes Is Under Fire*, L.A. Times A1 (Mar. 17, 2000). Should it make him feel better that Los Angeles and New Orleans were subsequently investigated? When the Missoula (Mont.) Police Department was investigated for discriminating against women in its response to sexual assaults, Police Chief Mark Muir similarly said, "I've got to tell you, Missoula, Montana, is not one of the worst of the worst in any respect." Erica Goode, *Some Chiefs Chafing as Justice Department Keeps Closer Eye on Policing*, N.Y. Times (July 28, 2013).

Should the United States Sue the "Worst of the Worst"?

By its own criteria, the Special Litigation Section does not expressly compare misconduct in its target agencies to that in similar departments. In this respect, the Section operates more like a prosecutor's office evaluating each complaint on its merits rather than like a regulator considering how best to influence the conduct of those it regulates. If the goal is to *prevent* misconduct, is that how it should be?

> With existing resources, it is impossible to imagine that §14141 could be used to force change in more than a handful of departments each year. Even if the Special Litigation Section's budget were doubled or tripled, the Section still could not be expected to examine more than a tiny fraction of large police departments. Assuming that a significant number of large American police departments need reform, no plausible allocation of resources will allow the Justice Department to sue many of those departments.

Rachel A. Harmon, *Promoting Civil Rights Through Proactive Policing Reform*, 62 Stan. L. Rev. 1, 5 (2009). Given how few departments will ever be sued, and how intense and costly an investigation and suit can be both for a city and for the Department of Justice, the process seems potentially both arbitrary and inefficient as a means of achieving reform. An ungenerous observer might compare it to a prosecutor's office in a high-crime city that ignores all but a few violent crimes and then spends enormous resources seeking life without parole for those unlucky perpetrators.

If the Department of Justice cannot reform all or most departments engaged in constitutional violations, is there a way to use the limited resources most fairly and to best effect? I have argued that the Justice Department could use suits to induce reform in police departments that are engaged in substantial misconduct, even if it does not sue them, by making the proactive adoption of reforms a less costly alternative for these departments than risking suit. To induce reform, I proposed a three-prong strategy:

> The first prong requires the Justice Department to adopt a "worst-first" policy that prioritizes suing the worst large departments. Such a policy raises the

expected costs of a §14141 suit for the worst departments in the nation by raising the probability of suit for those departments. . . .

The second prong requires the Justice Department to announce a "safe harbor" policy. Such a policy would shield from investigation or suit any department that officially commits itself to adopting proactively a preset array of reforms and then makes substantial, verifiable progress toward their implementation. A police department that receives the safe harbor would avoid the litigation costs associated with a §14141 suit. In addition, the set of reforms that a department would be required to adopt in order to receive the safe harbor, though still beneficial, would be less extensive and costly than the reforms imposed as a result of a suit. The safe harbor policy would therefore raise the net expected benefit of proactively adopting reforms. . . .

The third prong requires using Justice Department resources to refine and disseminate information about institutional deficiencies that breed police misconduct, remedial measures that will reduce misconduct, and means for effectively implementing those measures. This technical assistance effort would make reform more cost-effective for police departments by lowering the information costs of adopting reform.

Id. at 4–7.

"Worst-first" is not the only way to focus resources, and some suggest it might not be the best. Leigh Osofsky, talking mainly about tax enforcement, commented:

"Worst-first" methods do not necessarily maximize overall compliance. While "worst-first" methods . . . can, under certain circumstances, incentivize all regulated individuals to increase their compliance, so as not to be the "worst," they can also convey the relative safety of engaging in moderate levels of evasion with little likelihood of getting caught. This dynamic can be particularly problematic when compliance is very low, because, in such cases, regulated individuals can safely engage in high noncompliance, without attracting attention.

Leigh Osofsky, *Concentrated Enforcement*, 16 Fla. Tax Rev. 325, 337–338 (2014). Do we know whether compliance with constitutional law among police departments is high or low? Could a safe harbor mitigate concern about evaders? Osofsky instead favors other methods of concentrating enforcement, including "focusing on nodes of noncompliance," the way hot-spots policing focuses on very small high-crime areas. *Id.* at 362. What might concentrated enforcement look like in this context? What is a node of police misconduct?

All this targeting talk might sound good, at least if you think the primary purpose of pattern-or-practice litigation is to achieve widespread policing reform. Most proposals for rational enforcement choices, however, depend on articulating criteria for misconduct and obtaining good enough data to evaluate and compare alleged violators. What are the chances of that in policing? Not very good. Right now, there is little national data collection on lawful police conduct. There is even less basis to compare departments' illegal activities.

b.   Constitutional Violations Targeted

From the beginning, the Department of Justice focused its enforcement of the statute on a few core constitutional concerns: excessive force; unlawful stops, searches, and arrests; and discrimination based on race and national origin, especially in traffic stops. Around 2010, however, the Division under the Obama Administration started to look at several additional issues. The suit against Colorado City and Hildale City for discrimination on religious grounds illustrates one. Here are some other examples.

- In the Missoula Police Department, Missoula County Attorney's Office, and the University of Montana Office of Public Safety, the Division found gender bias in handling sexual assault complaints.
- In New Orleans, the Division found that officers discriminated based on LGBTQ status in interacting with suspects and based on gender by failing to respond adequately to violence against women.
- In Puerto Rico, Ferguson (Mo.), and Baltimore, the Division found that officers interfered with efforts to observe and record police activity in violation of the First Amendment.
- In Ferguson, the Division criticized the agency's focus on revenue generation at the expense of both public safety and constitutional policing.
- In Newark, the Division considered theft by officers, gender bias, discrimination against members of the LGBTQ community, and the failure to protect suspects from physical harm in police detention.
- In the Ville Platte Police Department and Evangeline Parish Sheriff's Office in Louisiana, the Division found that officers illegally jailed witnesses and suspects to coerce testimony and confessions.

On one hand, focusing narrowly enabled the Division to build expertise, to concentrate resources on core issues that affect public trust in law enforcement, and to send a clear message to agencies nationwide. On the other, focusing narrowly left constitutional concerns of some vulnerable populations unaddressed. Which is better: a narrow, consistent focus or a wide-ranging, inclusive one?

c.   Full Investigations

If the Assistant Attorney General agrees that an investigation is warranted and authorizes an investigation, the Division notifies the jurisdiction's chief executive officer and chief legal officer of the Division's intent to open an investigation, generally in advance of any public announcement. That notice will generally identify the specific areas of inquiry to define the scope of the investigation. Following that notification, the Division makes the existence of the open investigation public.

Civil Rights Division, U.S. Dept. of Justice, *The Civil Rights Division's Pattern and Practice Police Reform Work, 1994–Present* 8 (2017). Here is how the Division described its investigations at the end of the Obama Administration:

The Division's pattern-or-practice investigations examine not only whether there is a pattern or practice of police misconduct, but also why such a pattern or practice exists, in order to identify the right reform steps to eliminate it. . . .

Attorneys, investigators, paralegals, and community outreach specialists from the Civil Rights Division and, often, local United States Attorney's Offices, alongside policing experts retained for purposes of the investigation, typically spend significant time meeting with people face-to-face, listening to the concerns of the police and the communities they serve, and directly observing how policing works in that location

Although the precise contours of an investigation will vary . . . almost all pattern-or-practice investigations involve the following steps:

- Immediately following the opening of an investigation, meeting with the law enforcement leadership, local political leadership, police labor unions and affinity groups, and local community groups to explain the basis for the investigation, preview what the investigation will involve, and explain the next steps in the Division's process;
- Reviewing written policies, procedures, and training materials relevant to the scope of the investigation, through requests for documents shared with the law enforcement agency;
- Reviewing systems for monitoring and supervising individual officers, and for holding individual officers accountable for misconduct, including the handling of misconduct complaints; systems for reviewing arrests, searches, or uses of force; and officer disciplinary systems;
- Observing officer training sessions; ride-alongs with officers on patrol in varying precincts or districts, to view policing on the ground and obtain the perspective of officers on the job; and inspections of police stations, including lock-up facilities;
- Analyzing incident-related data (i.e., arrest and force reports, disciplinary records, misconduct complaints and investigations, and data documenting stops, searches, arrests and uses of force), often using sampling methods depending on the size of the data set, as well as an analysis of the adequacy of the law enforcement agency's system for collecting and analyzing data to identify and correct problems;
- Interviews with police command staff and officers at all levels of rank and authority in the department, both current and former; representatives of police labor organizations and other office affinity groups; community representatives and persons who have been victims of police misconduct; and local government leadership, including members of the local executive branch, legislators, judges, and prosecutors.

Id. at 9–10.

Investigations can take years to complete, and they depend heavily on the cooperation of the agency because the Special Litigation Section has no power to subpoena documents in its pattern-or-practice investigations.

Concluding a Pattern-or-Practice Investigation

If the Division determines that there is insufficient evidence to support a finding of a pattern or practice of conduct in violation of the Constitution or federal law, the Division will notify the jurisdiction of that finding and close the investigation.

Of 69 total investigations since Section 14141's enactment, the Division has closed 26 investigations without making a formal finding of a pattern or practice. Since 2008, the Division has concluded six investigations of law enforcement agencies without finding a pattern or practice of police misconduct.

If, on the other hand, the Division determines that there is reasonable cause to believe that there is a pattern or practice of conduct in violation of the Constitution or federal law, the Division will send a letter or report (sometimes referred to as a "Findings Letter" or "Findings Report") notifying the jurisdiction of the Division's determination and setting forth the specific conclusions underlying the Division's determination. . . . The Division's findings are public documents and are posted on the Division's website.

A Findings Letter or Report represents the culmination of the evidence the Division gathered in the course of its investigation. It lays out the basis for the Division's findings, linking those findings to specific problems within a law enforcement agency or between that agency and other parts of local government. The document also sets forth the steps the Division took to complete its investigation, so that the community and the law enforcement agency understand the sources and evidence on which the Division based its conclusions. It is both a diagnosis of a law enforcement agency's problems and the foundation for a plan to treat the root causes of those problems.

Id. at 15-16.

d. *Reaching Agreement*

Once the Special Litigation Section issues findings that include a pattern or practice of constitutional violations, it attempts to negotiate with the law enforcement agency about appropriate remedies. The Obama Administration expanded these negotiations to include not only the parties, but also union representatives, community groups, and other stakeholders.

In all but a handful of pattern-or-practice cases, the Department of Justice and the law enforcement agency have reached agreement without the need for litigation.

[O]f the many dozens of cases in which the Division has found a pattern or practice of police misconduct, all but six have resulted in a reform agreement without the need for civil litigation. In Colorado City, Arizona, the Division obtained a verdict at trial. In Alamance County, North Carolina, the Division did not prevail at trial, but appealed and entered into a settlement reform agreement while the appeal was pending. In Maricopa County, Arizona, litigation was required to enforce a court order requiring reforms, resulting in an order of contempt. In Meridian, Mississippi, the Division entered into a consent decree shortly after filing suit, after the City initially declined to negotiate. Likewise, in Columbus, Ohio, the Division filed litigation but later reached an agreement resolving its claims. And in Ferguson, Missouri, the City initially rejected a proposed consent decree resolving the Division's findings but later accepted it shortly after the United States filed suit in federal court. In a seventh case, in New Orleans, the Division was forced to litigate to compel the City of New Orleans' compliance with a consent decree to which it had previously agreed.

Id. at 18-19.

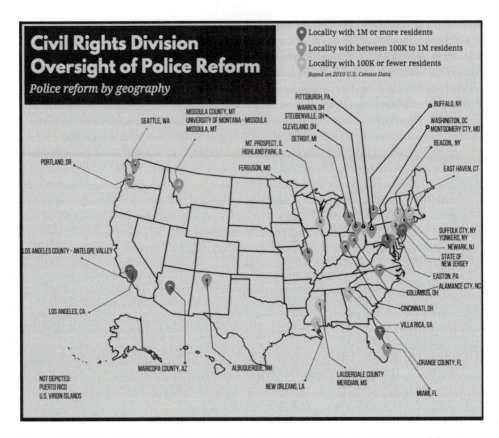

Source: Civil Rights Division, U.S. Dept. of Justice, *The Civil Rights Division's Pattern and Practice Reform Work, 1994–Present*, 9 (2017). This map shows the location of police reform driven by the Civil Rights Division's pattern-or-practice investigations through January 2017. That month, President Trump took office. His administration ended efforts to investigate and reform additional law enforcement agencies.

e.   *Implementing Reforms and Independent Monitors*

In settlements with the Department of Justice, most cities agree to take on substantial reforms and appoint an independent monitor to assist with implementation and to report on progress to the Department and to the court. In a statement of interest in *Floyd v. City of New York*, a private suit for equitable relief, the Department of Justice discussed the value of a monitor this way:

> [I]t is the view of the United States, based on decades of police reform efforts across the country, that the appointment of a monitor to guide implementation of that injunctive relief may provide substantial assistance to the Court and the parties and can reduce unnecessary delays and litigation over disputes regarding compliance.

> An independent monitor can be essential to ensuring that complex institutional reform is achieved. . . . A monitor provides the independence and expertise necessary to conduct the objective, credible analysis upon which a court can rely to determine whether its order is being implemented, and that gives the parties and the community confidence in the reform process. . . .

If the Court finds here that a pattern or practice of civil rights violations has occurred, it faces substantially similar considerations as judges handling other police reform matters: measuring compliance; early detection of any non-compliance; and entry of relief to correct any barriers to implementation of the order. Without an independent monitor, the Court will be forced to depend on motions practice between the parties to assess progress; a costly, contentious, inefficient, and time-consuming process. An independent monitor, by contrast, gives the Court access to necessary information to ensure that its injunction, and the underlying goal of constitutional policing, is being met. Equally important is the monitor's ability to diagnose and explain barriers to implementation of any remedial measures the Court may order.

Statement of Interest of the United States, Floyd v. City of New York, No. 08 Civ. 1034, 11–16 (S.D.N.Y. 2013).

As for what monitoring looks like:

Sometimes the named monitor is a person, who works with a team; other times it may be an organization, firm, or corporate entity. Monitoring teams generally include diverse perspectives, including team members with real-world policing experience reflecting both a management and rank-and-file perspective. . . . The independent monitoring team is generally the agent of the court overseeing the reform agreement and is independent from the Department of Justice and the local jurisdiction, although . . . most monitoring teams are jointly agreed upon by the Division and the local jurisdiction before being appointed by the court.

Civil Rights Division, U.S. Dept. of Justice, *The Civil Rights Division's Pattern and Practice Police Reform Work, 1994–Present* 21 (2017).

Early consent decree monitoring teams focused almost exclusively on assessing implementation. Over time, their role expanded to providing the city advice about implementation. Teams also began to be part of the reform itself, meeting with community groups and officer groups to solicit input.

Although most chiefs involved in consent decrees report that their monitoring teams were both expert and helpful, critics complain that monitors cost too much and slow down the process of winding up consent decrees. The Obama Administration sought to address these concerns in its later decrees. See *id.* at 23. Still, monitoring can easily cost a city more than $1 million a year beyond the expense of implementing reforms in the agency. Presumably, expanding the responsibilities of a monitoring team increases that cost. Of course, a community pays a high price for an ongoing pattern of constitutional violations, and without a monitor, a city might waste reform dollars by engaging in ineffectual reform. What is the appropriate role of a monitor in a pattern-or-practice case? Can that question be answered only on a case-by-case basis? Are there roles monitors should not play? Costs a city should not have to bear?

5. The Civil Rights Division's Model of Reform

Although each decree is specific to the problems and conditions of the law enforcement agency and community, the Department of Justice has also used its settlements to articulate and promote a consistent, if evolving, model of policing reform. Under the Obama Administration, the most active administration in enforcing §12601, this model had the following five basic components.

a.   Policies and Training

Agreements require that target agencies adopt detailed policies in areas of concern to set clear and specific expectations for officer conduct. They also require that agencies develop policy-specific training to ensure that officers understand these rules.

b.   Supervision and Discipline

Agreements require increased supervision of officers and additional training for supervisors. In addition, they demand strengthened civilian complaint and internal investigation and disciplinary mechanisms to ensure officers are accountable for failing to follow policies and procedures.

c.   Monitoring Officers

Agreements require additional use-of-force, stop, search, and arrest reporting by officers and other mechanisms, such as community-wide surveys, to enable agencies to ensure that officers are complying with new rules and that policing is improving in the community.

They also require developing early intervention systems (EIS). An EIS is a computerized system that collects data on key indicators of abnormal behavior by officers, such as a high number of complaints or excessive use of sick leave, that are thought to identify problematic officers before they engage in serious conduct. Supervisors are then expected to provide additional training or counseling in order to prevent that conduct.

d.   Engaging the Community

Agreements emphasize developing mechanisms for engaging with community groups and rewarding positive officer interactions with the community. Some require agencies to create community councils or civilian review boards. Many require reporting some kinds of data to the community.

e.   Implementing Reform

The agreements contain provisions designed to ensure that required reforms are effectively implemented. Most require the appointment of an independent monitor, who heads a team of experts to aid the agency in adopting reforms and reports back to the Department of Justice and the district court on the agency's progress.

In its broad strokes, the Department of Justice has promoted much of this model for decades: It sought a version of it in *United States v. City of Philadelphia.* 644 F.2d 187, 198 (3d Cir. 1980). Nevertheless, the Division's refined, consistent, and detailed articulation of what practices cause misconduct and how the reforms should be implemented to fix them may be the most significant legacy of the Division's two decades of pattern-or-practice enforcement. The consent decrees have become a benchmark for best practices in policing, expanding the impact of the Division's efforts far more than its limited resources could otherwise allow. The result is that, as the Division is keenly aware, when it resolves a case, it has two audiences: the city being reformed and all other police departments and communities.

Might this create some questions about the right form for the Division's agreements? The Division might send a clear message to departments far afield by developing reforms that are commonly needed and easily mimicked. But constitutional rights might be best protected in any one jurisdiction by reforms that are closely tailored to local conditions and concerns, which after all justify imposing equitable relief in the first place. It also may be that remedies designed to fix broken departments are not the most effective or efficient models for improving unbroken ones. How should the Division balance these competing concerns?

Finally, although the outlines of this reform model have been accepted by experts for decades, these reforms should not be taken for granted. If §12601 litigation has demonstrated anything, it is that changing a broken department is a massive, long-term undertaking, with uncertain reward. The costs of that undertaking can divert resources from other projects, including improving housing, job, and educational opportunities. Those services might improve individual life and racial equity in ways that could themselves mitigate police misconduct both by reducing the need for policing and by empowering those who are subjected to its excesses but presently lack adequate voice in the community. Can you imagine how bitter a pill it is to have been subject to discriminatory and predatory policing for years, have the Department of Justice sue to vindicate your rights, and then be told that your taxes will go up and your social services down because it is necessary to hire, train, and equip better (and more) police officers?

Moreover, even assuming an adequate reform model, the parties may find it nearly impossible to translate that model into specific consent decree provisions that ensure meaningful change. Getting out from under a consent decree requires proving substantial compliance with the decree's provisions. To have objective measures of compliance for the court, monitors and departments build metrics for various provisions, but those metrics might not be good measures of actual change. One consent-decree auditor illustrated this point in criticizing reforms in New Orleans:

> New Orleans's consent decree obligates the police to improve its relationship with the city's Black majority and other communities that the DOJ found the department was illegally targeting. One metric I saw auditors and monitors use to assess progress was the provision that precincts had to show auditors two photographs per month depicting officers interacting with city residents. I examined these photos, and could not decipher how they could be used as evidence that police were gaining people's trust. When looking at the photographs, which included children and teenagers, it appeared to me that some of those who appeared in them may have been unaware of the right to say no when asked to stand next to an officer and smile. They certainly seemed unaware that police officials and consent decree monitors would use the images to claim that the NOPD is improving community relations.

> Another metric used to determine trust building is whether police district precincts are holding regular public meetings. But in the dozens of these meetings that I attended, people spent most of the time griping that there were not enough police, or that officers were not sufficiently aggressive toward young people or Section 8 renters and did not prioritize "quality of life" crimes. No one asked about police bias or abuse. Residents who mistrust police—the people with whom the department was supposed to build trust under the consent decree—largely did not attend.

Matthew Nesvet, *My Year as a New Orleans Consent Decree Insider*, The Appeal (July 30, 2019). Nesvet's assessment is that New Orleans's police commissioner and compliance chief embarked on an intentional strategy: "carrying out small reforms and creating the appearance of improvement while preventing larger, structural changes." Is that an inevitable risk of police reform efforts? Or a special risk of consent decrees?

Should these challenges make the Department of Justice cautious about intervening to stop widespread patterns of constitutional violations? Or rethink its approach to reform? What is the alternative? Perhaps, at least, it should remind us that, in a healthy community, good policing is unlikely to be best achieved by litigation.

6.   Special Issues in Pattern-or-Practice Enforcement

a.   *Department Selection: Should Departments Be Able to Self-Select?*

Although most investigations and suits arise when complaints are made, several big cities, including Miami, Washington, and Baltimore have referred themselves for investigation. Mayor Stephanie Rawlings-Blake of Baltimore, for instance, invited in the Department of Justice after Freddie Gray, Jr., died in police custody in April 2015 and unrest followed. The Civil Rights Division opened a formal investigation almost immediately and, a year later, found that the Baltimore Police Department was engaged in a pattern or practice of unlawful stops, searches, and arrests, excessive force, and intentional discrimination against African Americans. Negotiations and a consent decree followed, and implementation is ongoing.

Baltimore's invitation suggests that the Baltimore Police Department had serious problems, and the city was committed to fixing them. Given limited resources, should the Department of Justice investigate such a department? Is such an invitation evidence that Department of Justice involvement in reform is likely to be efficient and effective? Or is it evidence that outside intervention is probably unnecessary to achieve change? Or is it evidence of something else entirely? Does it matter that the mayor invited the Department of Justice, but it is the police chief who is largely responsible for implementing reform? Does it matter that the Department of Justice has sometimes offered alternative, noncompulsory technical assistance for cities interested in police reform?

b.   *Rights Targeted: Should the Division Investigate Violations of Developing Rights?*

Some of the constitutional rights addressed by the Division during the Obama Administration are undeveloped or newly recognized rights. For example, some commentators believe that gender bias in responding to, classifying, and investigating sexual assault complaints violates the Equal Protection Clause. Still, because equal protection violations require proving intentional discrimination, something plaintiffs seeking to establish underenforcement of sexual assault laws have had difficulty proving, courts have not considered what the Equal Protection Clause demands of police departments in responding to allegations of violence against women. See Deborah Tuerkheimer, *Underenforcement as Unequal Protection*, 57 B.C. L. Rev. 1287, 1306 (2016).

Perhaps because of the underdeveloped nature of the law, the Division started to address this kind of gender discrimination by expressing "serious concerns" in Puerto Rico and Newark about gender bias in police responses, without actually finding a pattern or practice of constitutional violations. In Missoula, however, the Division went further, finding that the Missoula Police Department's "failures in responding to sexual assault, together with statements by MPD officers, reflect sex-based stereotypes, and thus constitute discrimination barred by the Equal Protection Clause of the Fourteenth Amendment." See Letter from Thomas E. Perez, Asst. Atty. Gen., Civil Rights Div. and Michael W. Cotter, U.S. Atty., Dist. of Mont. to John Engen, Mayor, Missoula, Mont. 6 (May 15, 2013).

As one commentator described it,

> Missoula is a landmark intervention. It introduces a novel way of catalyzing the enforcement of rape law. . . . Missoula also represents a significant conceptual breakthrough because it is premised on an understanding of gender-based under-policing as an equal protection violation; one demanding a federal response.

Tuerkheimer, *supra*, at 1324.

Because the parties have so far settled in all of the pattern-or-practice cases involving gender discrimination due to underenforcement, including in Missoula, the matter has never been litigated by the Division.[6] Still, the Department of Justice's views might be influential among police departments or, perhaps, among courts. Not long after the Missoula investigation, the ACLU and antidomestic violence groups cited the Division's findings in an amicus brief to the Federal Circuit in support of a similar claim. See Corrected Brief of the ACLU et al. as Amici Curiae in Support of Petitioners at 29, Service Women's Action Network v. Secretary of Veterans Affairs, 815 F.3d 1369, 2015 WL 227422 (Fed. Cir. Jan. 7, 2015) (No. 14-7115).

What are the advantages and disadvantages of the Division using its pattern-or-practice authority to articulate and promote undeveloped rights? Should the Division be promoting "conceptual breakthroughs" in civil rights? If you are skeptical about the practice, would it matter to you that the reforms the Division has advocated using this strategy are recognized as best practices in policing? That civil rights advocates have long engaged in impact litigation designed to strengthen rights development?

c. Negotiating Reform: What Role Should Stakeholders Play?

During the Obama Administration, the Civil Rights Division treated community and officer input as critical in negotiating reforms with police departments.

> Beyond the specific impacts engaging community leaders, line officers and police unions have on the content of the Division's reform agreements, engagement with all stakeholders is itself the cornerstone of the Division's reform process. . . . Communities must be invested for the long-term sustainability of reform. Individual officers who, day-to-day, will carry out the reforms must be invested for the long-term durability of reform. And police and local leadership must be invested to provide the leadership and support a long-term commitment reform requires.
>
> Thus, although the Division negotiates resolutions to its pattern-or-practice cases with representatives of the agency or government under investigation, it does so equipped with the information gathered from community representatives, rank-and-file officers, police union leadership, and other stakeholders, and with a commitment to ensuring that the input of those stakeholders remains a part of the process.

---

[6] Even if Missoula had contested the issue and won as a matter of equal protection, the lawsuit might have proceeded on the theory that the same discrimination violated the Safe Streets Act, which does not require intentional discrimination to establish a claim.

Civil Rights Division, U.S. Dept. of Justice, *The Civil Rights Division's Pattern and Practice Police Reform Work, 1994–Present* 18 (2017). The Department of Justice is not alone its view about the importance of bringing communities into reform efforts.

> Democratic theorists have emphasized that "citizens should participate in the design and implementation of the policies that affect them." Adhering to these values may create not only better substantive reforms, but may also increase the legitimacy of the ultimate police reforms implemented in a particular jurisdiction. . . . Specifically, the tension experienced between police officers and communities, especially poor, minority communities, can be traced to the political disenfranchisement these community members have historically experienced.
>
> The opportunity for police officers and community members to deliberate about police conduct and police-citizen interactions is key to dismantling the "us versus them" mentality. Active deliberation also encourages citizens "to take a broader perspective on questions of public policy" and consider the claims of other citizens, including the police. . . . Although the benefits of deliberation in the context of police reform may be obvious, the lack of opportunity for stakeholders to participate and discuss the implementation of new policies threatens the success of the reforms, because the lack of participation in police reforms may exacerbate the alienation and distrust that police officers and citizens already harbor toward each other.

Kami Chavis Simmons, *New Governance and the "New Paradigm" of Police Accountability: A Democratic Approach to Police Reform*, 59 Cath. U. L. Rev. 373, 409 (2010).

Some find it counterintuitive to include officers in the process of developing reforms intended to remedy their own unconstitutional practices. After all, unions frequently attempt to block decrees and resist changing collective bargaining agreement provisions that prevent implementing reform. Still, as one article put it, without officer participation, reform efforts may be fruitless:

> [T]he way that power is exercised within departments can influence whether rank-and-file officers view reforms as legitimate and entitled to deference, or whether they attempt to undermine them through acts of resistance. Policymakers should recognize that when they work solely with the top command levels of police departments, they might unintentionally exacerbate rank-and-file frustrations with existing power arrangements, leading to resistance to any new policies that might be enacted. Thus, although reformers may believe they have achieved success because police management has enacted new policies and procedures in response to their concerns, their failure to engage the rank-and-file may ultimately doom their efforts. . . . Because street officers operate primarily out of sight of management, they have numerous opportunities to engage in covert resistance to reform-oriented policies. When resistance is subtle rather than overt, management and reformers may be unaware that the new policy is not being implemented.

Catherine L. Fisk & L. Song Richardson, *Police Unions*, 85 Geo. Wash. L. Rev. 712, 775 (2017); see also David A. Sklansky & Monique Marks, *The Role of the Rank and File in Police Reform*, 18 Policing & Soc'y 1 (2008) (highlighting the benefits of involving officers in efforts to improve policing). It isn't just line officers that reformers need to worry about:

Resistance does not just come from the bottom of police organizations; revolts by mid-level managers have defeated community-policing projects in several cities. Managers near the middle of the organizational hierarchy saw authority being taken from them and pushed to lower levels in the organization, as part of decentralization schemes. Opportunities for promotion for middle managers may be limited by shrinking management layers and the flattening of the formal rank structure that sometimes goes along with efforts to decentralize for neighborhood-oriented policing.

Wesley G. Skogan, *Why Reforms Fail*, 18 Policing & Soc'y 23, 24 (2008). Similarly,

Sergeants have direct control over what street officers do on a day-to-day basis. One observer identified sergeants as most officers' "real employer." Herman Goldstein notes, "However strongly the head of an agency may elicit a different style of policing, the quality of an officer's daily life is heavily dependent on how well the officer satisfies the expectations and demands of his or her immediate supervisor." Sergeants interpret the operational meaning of official policies at the street level, so when roles and rules are up for grabs, they have to have a clear vision they can support if change is really going to occur there.

Id. at 25–26.

Does this suggest that negotiated reform, with stakeholder input, has a better chance of achieving change, even if it mandates the same remedies a court would have imposed? What if, as seems likely, getting all stakeholders to buy in requires compromising some of the strength or coherence of the reforms?

d. *Negotiating Reform: Do Consent Decrees Risk Collusion?*

Given that the bargaining over consent decrees happens, as lawyers like to say, "in the shadow of the law," Robert H. Mnookin & Lewis Kornhauser, *Bargaining in the Shadow of the Law: The Case of Divorce*, 88 Yale L.J. 950 (1979), and rules governing civil rights liability disadvantage plaintiffs, you might expect consent decrees to heavily favor defendants. But many include significant and expensive reforms. Why?

The ordinary litigation incentives favoring settlement operate strongly for parties and judges in structural reform cases. Settlement saves the enormous expense and uncertainty of trial and appeal, and it gives the parties augmented control over the specifics of a remedy. More speculatively, defendants who agree to a decree may transform themselves in the eyes of the public, and even in their own eyes, from "lawbreakers to law implementers." And there are also more situation-specific incentives. Plaintiffs or their counsel, and judges, may push especially hard for settlement if they believe that necessary institutional change requires the cooperation of the defendants, which is more easily obtained by consent than by judicial fiat. Another frequently remarked dynamic favoring settlement in institutional reform cases . . . is the high level of cooperation by defendants. The explanation seems clear: defendants, who are government officials operating under fiscal and political constraints, frequently win by losing. The result of a consent decree can be more resources and freedom from entrenched restrictions on changes in policy and practice. "The court is making me do it" trumps many ordinary political considerations.

Margo Schlanger, *Beyond the Hero Judge: Institutional Reform Litigation as Litigation*, 97 Mich. L. Rev. 1994, 2011–2012 (1999) (book review).

Avoiding the expense, uncertainty, and reputational costs of trial seem well recognized as a reason to settle a lawsuit, but when Schlanger writes that government officials "win by losing," she is describing a phenomenon that some think undermines the legitimacy of structural reform litigation. The worry is that public officials might effectively collude with plaintiffs — public or private — to use consent decrees to sidestep the political process.

First, consent decrees can lock in the policy preferences of present-day local officials, immunizing them from subsequent electoral defeat. As the Supreme Court put it in *Horne v. Flores*, 557 U.S. 433, 448–449 (2009):

> Scholars have noted that public officials sometimes consent to, or refrain from vigorously opposing, decrees that go well beyond what is required by federal law. Injunctions of this sort bind state and local officials to the policy preferences of their predecessors and may thereby "improperly deprive future officials of their designated legislative and executive powers." Frew v. Hawkins, 540 U.S. 431, 441 (2004).
>
> States and localities "depen[d] upon successor officials, both appointed and elected, to bring new insights and solutions to problems of allocating revenues and resources." *Frew*, 540 U.S. 442. Where "state and local officials . . . inherit overbroad or outdated consent decrees that limit their ability to respond to the priorities and concerns of their constituents," they are constrained in their ability to fulfill their duties as democratically-elected officials.

In *Horne*, the Court cited this muffling of the democratic process as reason for courts to be flexible about modifying and terminating consent decrees, perhaps more so than injunctions.

Second, consent decrees secure desirable resources in the competitive budget process. In *Horne*, the Court framed the concern this way.

> Institutional reform injunctions often raise sensitive federalism concerns. . . . Federalism concerns are heightened when . . . a federal court decree has the effect of dictating state or local budget priorities. States and local governments have limited funds. When a federal court orders that money be appropriated for one program, the effect is often to take funds away from other important programs.

557 U.S. at 448.

Those involved in structural reform litigation readily acknowledge this consequence. As one jail administrator put it in talking about jail reform:

> To be sure, we used "court orders" and "consent decrees" for leverage. We ranted and raved for decades about getting federal judges "out of our business" but we secretly smiled as we requested greater and greater budgets to build facilities, hire staff, and upgrade equipment. We "cussed" the federal courts all the way to the bank.

Mark Kellar, *Responsible Jail Programming*, Am. Jails (Jan.–Feb. 1999), at 78, 79 (also quoted in Margo Schlanger, *Beyond the Hero Judge: Institutional Reform Litigation as Litigation*, 97 Mich. L. Rev. 1994, 2012 n.68 (1999) (book review)).

What's true in prison litigation is also true in policing. As Philadelphia Commissioner Charles Ramsey put it in talking about pattern-or-practice suits by the Department of Justice:

> The process of having a consent decree can actually be a benefit to your department. You can leverage the Justice Department to get some things that you desperately need. When I was chief at the Metropolitan Police Department in Washington, we would not have been able to make the changes we made without the consent decree. We would have encountered pushback from the union, and we would not have obtained the funding needed to develop an early intervention system and underlying technology infrastructure to support it.
>
> The end result was very positive. Shootings dropped by 80 percent and have remained low. And it gave us credibility with the public.

Police Executive Research Forum, *Civil Rights Investigations of Local Police: Lessons Learned* 34 (2013).

How problematic is this type of strategic conduct? On one hand, public officials are securing public money necessary to provide public services in a lawful manner. On the other, a consent decree that ensures that a police department stops constitutional violations might prevent the city from adequately addressing child abuse or mitigating rampant homelessness. Is it always better to prevent constitutional violations by the police than to allow them?

Beyond enshrining political preferences against electoral change and securing scarce resources outside the budget process, can you think of any other reasons public officials might be especially favorable to consent decrees that mandate reforms? What countervailing factors might lead police executives to resist settlement?

e. *Reforms: How Innovative Should Settlement Reforms Be?*

The core set of reforms promoted by the Department of Justice has been stable and uncontroversial, but the Division has also incorporated innovations in policing into its decrees. For example, the Division's early settlements mandated Early Intervention Systems, a form of computerized accountability that was new at the time and turned out to be far harder to implement than parties expected. Decrees have also mandated body-worn cameras, implicit bias training, officer wellness practices, and training designed to improve officer interactions with vulnerable populations such as immigrants and the LGBTQ community. All of these relatively new practices in policing have limited research to draw on, and yet they are often recognized as best practices. What level of confidence should the Division have that a reform will prevent constitutional violations before it embeds it in a consent decree? Should the Division consider intrusiveness and expense in making that calculation?

For years, the Division focused on changing policies and practices rather than strategies or philosophies. Toward the end of the Obama Administration, however, the Division began to demand that departments commit to community and problem-oriented policing. Problem-oriented policing refers to a specific analytic method for targeting crime by an iterative strategy of identifying crime problems, analyzing them, responding, assessing, and adjusting the response. The idea is to address recurrent problems that lead to police intervention proactively rather than merely send officers when community members repeatedly call the police. Community policing (also called community-oriented policing) engages the public as "coproducers" of crime control. Its implementation varies, but it usually includes neighborhood groups in identifying public safety and order maintenance priorities and tasks community based officers to work with citizens to solve them. According to the Obama Administration's final-days report on its pattern-or-practice enforcement, "The Division's promotion of community and problem-oriented policing strategies helps make policing safer and more effective. Officers can only police safely and effectively if they maintain the trust and cooperation of the communities they serve." Civil Rights Division, U.S. Dept. of Justice, *The Civil Rights Division's Pattern and Practice Police Reform Work, 1994–Present* 26 (2017).

The National Academies of Sciences was decidedly more mixed when it reviewed the evidence available in favor of these strategies in its 2018 report on proactive policing.[7] On whether these strategies make communities *safer*, the panel found that neither strategy was well studied. Problem-oriented interventions showed positive short-term crime prevention impacts, but long-term studies did not exist. Studies on community policing were inconsistent in approach and often combined it with other strategies. The committee "did not a identify consistent crime-prevention benefit for community-oriented policing programs." Nat'l Acads. Of Scis., Eng'g & Med., *Proactive Policing: Effects on Crime and Communities* 6–8 (David Weisburd & Malay K. Majmundar eds., 2015). With respect to the *community effects* of these strategies, the panel found that problem-solving strategies show small-to-moderate short-term impacts on community satisfaction with the police and that "community-oriented policing contributes modest improvements to the community's view of policing and the police in the short term," with little evidence about long-term impacts for either strategy. *Id.* at 9–10. Finally, the panel found empirical evidence insufficient to draw *any* conclusions about whether the strategies reduce (or cause) constitutional violations. *Id.* at 5.

The National Academies report was not released after agreements in Albuquerque, Newark, and Baltimore mandated these strategies, although most of the research on which the report was based was already available. Given what we know now, should the Division include community-oriented and problem-oriented policing in future settlements? What if a community group demands the inclusion of such provisions as a precondition for supporting the agreement? Conversely, what should the Department of Justice do when experts agree that evidence supports a reform, such as increasing training or salaries for officers, but community members are strongly against it?

f.   Reforms: Are the Justice Department's Agreements Too Onerous?

Each reform agreement signed by the Civil Rights Division mandates specific institutional changes the Division views as necessary to stop systemic misconduct. The Puerto Rico agreement runs more than 100 pages and has more than 300 provisions with which the police department must comply. In New Orleans, there are nearly 500 provisions in 124 pages. The Baltimore consent decree is more than 200 pages long with more than 500 provisions. Of course, if reforms were

---

[7] *Ed. note*: I served on the Committee on Proactive Policing: Effects on Crime, Communities, and Civil Liberties that authored the National Academies of Sciences report.

less detailed and less comprehensive, then compliance might not achieve the systemic change necessary to prevent future violations. On the other hand, the exacting nature of the agreements often means that the Division's consent decrees are costly and difficult to implement, leading to many years of court-monitored reform. Take, for example, Los Angeles. The City of Angels took longer than almost any other city sued for a pattern-or-practice violation to come out from under court supervision — 12 years[8] — and some estimate the cost of reform there at around $300 million.

However, many think Los Angeles is also the Division's greatest success. Before getting sued by the Department of Justice, the LAPD had resisted reform despite report after report documenting its failings. Yet, even before the decree was lifted, a study in 2009 credited it with transforming the department:

> Public satisfaction is up, with 83 percent of residents saying the LAPD is doing a good or excellent job; the frequency of the use of serious force has fallen each year since 2004. Despite the views of some officers that the consent decree inhibits them, there is no objective sign of so-called "de-policing" since 2002; indeed, we found that both the quantity and quality of enforcement activity have risen substantially over that period. The greater quantity is evident in the doubling of both pedestrian stops and motor vehicle stops since 2002, and in the rise in arrests over that same period. The greater quality of stops is evident in the higher proportion resulting in an arrest, and the quality of arrests is evident in the higher proportion in which the District Attorney files felony charges.

> Our analysis confirmed what others have previously reported: that serious crime is down substantially in Los Angeles over this same period. Indeed, recorded crime is down in every police division in the city. A majority of Los Angeles residents no longer rate crime as a big problem, substantially down from only four years ago, and that is true among Black and Hispanic as well as White and Asian residents.

Christopher Stone et al., Harvard Kennedy School, *Policing Los Angeles Under a Consent Decree: The Dynamics of Change at the LAPD* i–ii (2009).

When the decree was finally lifted by the federal court, Police Chief Charlie Beck, who had both a daughter and son on the force at the time, commented, "The consent decree has made this a department that I am proud to hand over to my children. It has been the catalyst for incredible change in my Police Department. We've become accountable, we've become transparent and we've become more effective than we've ever been." More surprisingly, Hector Villagra, Executive Director of the ACLU of Southern California, said, "The reform package, accomplished its purpose by and large. This is no longer your father's Los Angeles Police Department. The LAPD has made serious culture changes." Joel Rubin, *LAPD Is Finally Free of Federal Decree*, L.A. Times (May 17, 2013).

In the face of criticisms of its settlements for being too onerous, the Civil Rights Division during the Obama Administration worked to reduce the expense and length of reforms and help departments with grants and technical assistance. Moreover, if reform is successful, some of the costs should be reclaimed in lower

---

[8] Detroit took 13 years. It entered two consent decrees with the Department of Justice in 2003 and was released from oversight in 2016. Other long efforts to comply with mandated reforms are ongoing.

payouts in civil damages actions and other benefits of reduced misconduct. Still, it looks like meaningful reform takes years and costs millions, and most reform efforts are not as successful as Los Angeles's was. Of course, pervasive constitutional violations harm individuals and fray the fabric of a community. Was reform worth it in Los Angeles? Who should decide? How should the Division think about the trade-offs between thoroughness and cost in reform?

g.   Settlements: Why Do §12601 Parties Settle So Often?

Most agencies settle with the Civil Rights Division. Yet, Alamance County, one of the few jurisdictions to litigate to judgment, won at trial. Moreover, even if a jurisdiction loses at trial, it is unlikely that a judge will impose a hundred-page order on the department. Why don't more departments fight? Maybe because investigations by the Special Litigation Section are thorough, the legal standard for establishing a pattern or practice is vague, and most major departments are complex organizations with multiple constitutional violations. Might cities conclude that litigation is not worth the expense and reputational harm of fighting the government to defend conduct that is already controversial in the community? Although the cost of litigation usually pales in comparison to the cost of reform, spending on reform might at least help the department and improve its relationship with the community. Moreover, when a jurisdiction loses in court, it spends extra years doing so and pays both the cost of litigation *and* the cost of subsequent reform. What about the political incentives public officials might have to reach a settlement?

The Department of Justice also benefits from avoiding litigation. Given the political sensitivity of federal intervention in local policing and the limited resources available to the Special Litigation Section, the Department cannot fight many all-out legal wars against police departments, especially major ones. Does that help explain why several of the smallest jurisdictions investigated by the Special Litigation Section have ended up litigated in court? The combined population of Colorado City, Arizona, and Hildale City, Utah, is less than 8,000 people. About 21,000 people live in Ferguson, Missouri. Meridian, Mississippi, has fewer than 40,000 residents.

Let's say a jurisdiction fights to the end and the Division wins. Given the complexity of preventing constitutional violations, something even committed agencies have trouble doing, how likely is it that an agency beaten in court is going to reform successfully and create institutional mechanisms and a culture that supports constitutional policing? Should that affect the Special Litigation Section's willingness to compromise?

Are there other reasons each side in a pattern-or-practice suit might be highly motivated to reach agreement?

h.   Settlements: Informal Agreements or Formal Decrees?

Although the Department of Justice has usually won at trial, or reached some kind of settlement, some resolutions have been far less decisive than others. The Special Litigation Section's investigation of Columbus was one of its first, opened early in 1998. Columbus initially resisted but eventually settled, at least sort of: The litigation ended when the Columbus Mayor sent a letter in 2002 summarizing in general terms its ongoing efforts to improve the police department's policies and practices and promising to continue reform and send documentation about it to the Department of Justice in exchange for the Division dismissing the lawsuit without prejudice. The Division accepted the proposal and dismissed the suit. Is that a win or a loss for the Department of Justice? What does it say about its bargaining position? About politics? Although the Columbus investigation and litigation occurred during the Clinton Administration, the matter was resolved in 2002, after George W. Bush became president.

As the Columbus litigation suggests, the Department of Justice has resolved pattern-or-practice investigations and suits in a range of forms. Most agreements have been memorialized in consent decrees, ensuring that implementation and enforcement are supervised by a federal court. Others have taken the form of out-of-court settlements, sometimes documented in a memorandum of agreement, enforceable only by suing the department for a breach of contract. In a few cases, the Justice Department issued a technical assistance letter recommending reforms or entered an agreement that has no means of enforcement or monitoring.

The Bush Administration especially favored informal resolutions to pattern-or-practice investigations. According to R. Alexander Acosta, Assistant Attorney General of the Civil Rights Division, this practice represented an alternative vision of how reform is best achieved rather than a lack of commitment to reform:

> [W]e have adopted a more transparent approach for achieving solutions and remedying problematic practices. The Special Litigation Section thus strives to keep target agencies fully informed as to its findings and potential violations as the investigation proceeds. And, as the process unfolds, we work hard to resolve complaints without litigation. Our response is a graduated one, which considers the potential violations. By working with law enforcement agencies, rather than appearing only as a litigation opponent, we can achieve greater, in less time, results which are longer lasting, and with less cost and rancor. In short, we have expanded our effort to affect not only a prosecutorial, but also an instructive, role.

> Let me give you [an example]: . . . [W]e recently entered both a consent decree and a memorandum of understanding with Prince George's County Police Department. Through these, the Department agreed to sweeping reforms. . . .

> This structure was unique in its use of both a consent decree and memorandum of understanding. We insisted on the consent decree where court involvement was essential, and employed a memorandum of understanding where flexibility and the ability to work with the Department to craft solutions were necessary. Our approach was sufficiently creative and effective that the agreements were applauded by the city, the police force, the Fraternal Order of Police, and community groups alike. To ensure the effective implementation of the agreements, the Justice Department will continue to monitor the Prince George's County Police Department for the next three years. But, we will not be present solely as a watchdog; we also will remain involved to offer technical assistance.

> The agreements resolved investigations that had been open since July 1999 and October 2000. By working with the jurisdiction towards these goals, rather than simply investigating with an eye to civil litigation, I believe we have come farther much faster than we otherwise would have.

Reauthorization of the Civil Rights Division of the United States Department of Justice: Hearing Before the Subcomm. on the Constitution of the H. Comm. on the

Judiciary, 108th Cong. 13–14 (2004) (prepared statement of R. Alexander Acosta, Assistant Attorney General, Civil Rights Division).

The following year, Acosta declared the new approach a roaring success. "Local police agencies are fully the Division's partner in developing constitutional norms for policing. By including them in the process, local agencies are more likely to 'buy in' to the solution, making lasting change more likely." Reauthorization of the Civil Rights Division of the United States Department of Justice: Hearing Before the Subcomm. on the Constitution of the H. Comm. on the Judiciary, 109th Cong. 27 (2005) (prepared statement of R. Alexander Acosta, Assistant Attorney General, Civil Rights Division).

By contrast, the Special Litigation Section at the end of the Obama Administration said this about its preferred approach:

> Although the Division has pursued several different approaches to the structure of its settlement agreements in the two decades since Section 14141 enforcement began, its experience demonstrates that court-enforceable consent decrees are most effective in ensuring accountability, transparency in implementation, and flexibility for accomplishing complex institutional reforms. Federal court oversight is often critical to address broad and deeply entrenched problems and to ensure the credibility of the reform agreement's mandates.

Civil Rights Division, U.S. Dept. of Justice, *The Civil Rights Division's Pattern and Practice Police Reform Work, 1994–Present* 20–21 (2017). Is it clear who was right? How could we tell?

When the Trump Administration took office, it made clear that it opposed new pattern-or-practice litigation and had little enthusiasm for enforcing existing settlements. To a significant degree, however, agreements that resulted in consent decrees and court-imposed judgments have continued to be implemented under the supervision of courts with the help of independent monitors. Out-of-court settlements might not have fared as well. In this way, a consent decree or injunction is a buffer against changing political winds. Is that an argument in their favor or against them?

i. Implementation: What Can Go Wrong? The Twisted History of Maricopa County

In thinking about why agencies settle, it might be worth thinking about an agency that did not. During his 20-year tenure as chief executive of the Maricopa County Sheriff's Office (MCSO), Joe Arpaio made national headlines for his colorful—and brutal—practices: housing convicted prisoners outdoors in a large tent encampment in temperatures as high as 118°F, routinely feeding detainees substandard food, clothing inmates in purposely emasculating uniforms, and engaging a host of other tactics to reinforce Arpaio's self-professed status as "America's toughest sheriff." See Joe Arpaio & Len Sherman, *America's Toughest Sheriff: How to Win the War Against Crime* (1996). However, it was the MCSO's racial profiling strategies in service of Arpaio's anti-immigration agenda that made the MCSO the target of a decade-long battle in federal court.

Invoking its immigration authority as part of a program with Immigration and Customs Enforcement in 2007, MCSO began conducting routine sweeps of predominantly Latino neighborhoods, stopping Latino drivers at a far higher rate than similarly situated people of other national origins and often without reasonable suspicion or probable cause. The ACLU filed a §1983 suit, *Melendres v. Arpaio*, No. 2:07-cv-02513 (D. Ariz. filed Dec. 12, 2007), on behalf of Latino residents of Maricopa County against Arpaio and Maricopa County, alleging that the tactics violated their Fourth and Fourteenth Amendment rights. In June 2008, the Department of Justice initiated a parallel §14141 pattern-or-practice investigation into the MCSO.

In December 2011, the Civil Rights Division issued a report on Maricopa County detailing unconstitutional racial profiling and retaliation against those who complained about MCSO's policies and practices. When negotiations failed to produce a settlement, the Division filed suit against Maricopa County. In May 2013, Judge G. Murray Snow issued Findings of Fact and Conclusions of Law in *Melendres v. Arpaio*, concluding that "MCSO's use of Hispanic ancestry or race as a factor in forming reasonable suspicion that persons have violated state laws relating to immigration status violates the Equal Protection Clause of the Fourteenth Amendment." 989 F. Supp. 2d 822, 899 (D. Ariz. 2013). Later that year, Judge Snow permanently enjoined the defendants from using race or national origin in law enforcement decisions pertaining to immigration. In 2015, the court in *United States v. Maricopa County* granted partial summary judgment for the government on the discriminatory policing allegations. 151 F. Supp. 3d 998 (D. Ariz. 2015).

In what seemed like the final chapter of the saga, the Civil Rights Division reached a settlement with Maricopa County shortly after the order. But Arpaio disregarded the *Melendres* injunction: MCSO deputies continued to stop and detain Latino drivers despite the absence of reasonable suspicion for any state charges, and the department failed to meaningfully implement any of the reforms the settlement required. See Melendres v. Maricopa County, 897 F.3d 1217, 1220 (9th Cir. 2018). So, in May 2016, after 21 days of evidentiary hearings on the matter, Judge Snow held that the defendants willfully failed to implement the preliminary injunction. He imposed an extensive supplemental injunction to remedy the MCSO's misconduct and prevent further constitutional violations, an injunction upheld by the Ninth Circuit. See 897 F.3d 1217 (2018). Judge Snow also held Arpaio in civil contempt and referred him for criminal contempt proceedings. The case was assigned to District Judge Susan Bolton, who asked the Department of Justice to prosecute Arpaio. It agreed.

Arpaio was convicted of criminal contempt on July 31, 2017, following a five-day trial. But he was never sentenced. In another sharp turn in events, on August 25, President Donald Trump issued Arpaio a full and unconditional pardon for his criminal contempt conviction and for any other Title 18 offenses "that might arise, or be charged, in connection with *Melendres v. Arpaio*." Donald. J. Trump, U.S. President, Executive Grant of Clemency (Aug. 25, 2017). In a Tweet announcing the pardon, Trump called Arpaio a "patriot" who "kept Arizona safe!" Donald J. Trump (@realDonaldTrump), Twitter (Aug. 25, 2017, 7:00 p.m.). The criminal contempt case was then dismissed with prejudice.

Despite the litigation's abrupt end, change nevertheless came to Maricopa County. Two weeks after the pardon, the Maricopa County board of supervisors established a $1 million fund to compensate victims of Arpaio's illegal detentions. Paul Penzone defeated Joe Arpaio in the 2016 election for Maricopa County Sheriff, running on a reform platform. In April 2017, Penzone reported that MCSO was closing its tent encampment and ending its discriminatory policing practices in compliance with the court orders. Still, monitoring for *Melendrez v. Arpaio* remains ongoing, and Penzone has been hauled back into court on occasion to answer for the pace and adequacy of reform.

In the end, Maricopa County paid around $9 million in legal fees to go to trial against the Department of Justice and fight the contempt proceedings arising from the case. It then spent more than $50 million more in damages and reforms. Some estimate the total cost of litigation and monitoring for the county will reach more than $70 million. Is this litigation an object lesson for other departments? For the Justice Department? Or is Maricopa County under Sheriff Arpaio *sui generis*?

7.   The Politics of Pattern-or-Practice Enforcement

Because structural reform litigation is a tool by which plaintiffs seek to leverage federal courts to regulate local government institutions, reactions to it are deeply political, driven in large part by beliefs about the appropriate role of litigation and views about federalism and the separation of powers. Structural reform litigation directed at policing is more political still because it implicates ongoing debates about potential trade-offs between public safety and policing's harms and about the federal role in enforcing civil rights. It should hardly be surprising §12601 enforcement rises and ebbs with political tides.

a.   *Clinton Administration*

After the statute was passed in 1994, the Clinton Administration took a couple of years to get the program up and running, opening its first investigation in Pittsburgh in 1996. From then to the end of the Clinton presidency in January 2001, the Civil Rights Division developed its initial investigation practices and a model of reform and pursued several cases under the new law. Although the Division enthusiastically enforced the statute, given the challenges of starting the program and the scope of the initial cases, when President Clinton left office, the Division had only a few settlements in place.

b.   *Bush Administration*

Even before he was elected, President George W. Bush announced that he favored a less aggressive approach to pattern-or-practice suits, contending that the Department of Justice should not "routinely seek to conduct oversight investigations, issue reports or undertake other activity that is designed to function as a review of police operations in states, cities and towns." Eric Lichtblau, *Bush Sees U.S. as Meddling in Local Police Affairs*, L.A. Times (June 1, 2000). Consistent with that view, the Bush Civil Rights Division often provided advice to police departments or entered informal agreements, rather than insisting on consent decrees or injunctions. Still, by the end of the Bush Administration, the Division had investigated some departments, reached some enforceable settlements, and refined some elements of the investigations and reform strategies.

c. Obama Administration

The Obama Civil Rights Division dramatically ramped up the program. It brought more investigations, reached more settlements, and targeted a broader range of constitutional rights violations than ever before. By early 2017, when President Obama left office, the Division had increased the number of departments subject to reforms supervised by a federal court severalfold.

This graph illustrates the Division's efforts through the end of the Obama Administration:

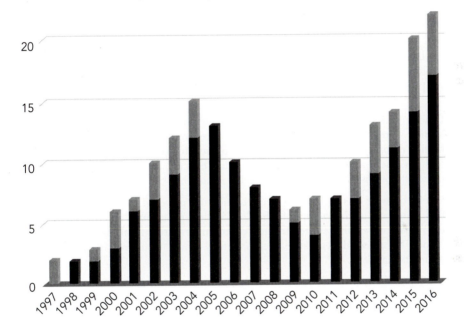

Police Reform Over Time:
The Civil Rights Division's Reform Agreements by Year

■ Existing Reform Agreements ■ New Reform Agreements

Source: Civil Rights Division, U.S. Dept. of Justice, *The Civil Rights Division's Pattern and Practice Police Reform Work, 1994–Present* 19 (2017).

d. Trump Administration

When President Donald Trump took office, he immediately reversed course. Both the President and his new Attorney General Jeff Sessions expressed deep skepticism about any federally guided policing reform. Sessions announced that no new investigations would occur, he ordered ongoing negotiations in cases to a screeching halt, and he raised doubts about the status of existing reform agreements.

In April 2017, after ferocious criticism of the Department's approach to civil rights, Attorney General Sessions defended the administration's approach in a newspaper editorial. He argued that "surging" violent crime justified more aggressive policing of criminals, rather than a counterproductive focus on "a small number of police who are bad actors" that discourages good police officers from doing their jobs. Jeff Sessions, *Avoid Harmful Federal Intrusion*, USA Today (Apr. 18, 2017). Moreover, Sessions argued that ending pattern-or-practice litigation serves the cause of racial equity: "When proactive policing declines and violent crime rises, minority communities get hit the hardest. We will not sign consent decrees for political expediency that will cost more lives by handcuffing the police instead of the criminals." *Id.* No one was surprised when, just before he left office, Sessions signed a memorandum severely restricting the use of consent decrees against police departments. See U.S. Attorney General, Principles and Procedures for Civil Consent Decrees and Settlement Agreements with State and Local Governmental Entities (Nov. 7, 2018). The memorandum remained in effect under Sessions's successor, William Barr, and the Trump Administration has not entered into any consent decrees against police departments under either Attorney General.

At the same time that the Department of Justice refrained from enforcing §12601, Attorney General Barr and other Justice officials became increasingly vocal in criticizing reform-minded local prosecutors for picking and choosing which criminal laws to enforce. In several speeches and editorial opinions, Deputy Attorney General Jeffrey A. Rosen said some version of the following:

> It doesn't take a law degree . . . to understand the principle that the legislative branch writes the law; the judicial branch interprets the law; and the executive branch enforces the law. . . . By refusing to prosecute broad swaths of core criminal offenses, social-reform DAs are ignoring duly-enacted laws in favor of their own personal notions of what they think the law should be.

> Several of these DAs aren't even trying to hide this power grab. . . . These prosecutors, who swore an oath to uphold the Constitution, proclaimed that they "don't see the role of prosecutors elected by their communities through this narrow lens" and "proud[ly]" rejected "legislative decisions" they found "troubling" in light of their own personal views.

> . . . There is no question that prosecutors have discretion to decide what cases to prosecute and how to spend their limited resources. But these DAs are not making individualized decisions based on the facts and circumstances of particular cases. They are predetermining whole categories of offenses for non-enforcement. They are effectively legislating through inaction. And the offenses they are unilaterally striking from the books are not antiquated or rare; they are basic criminal laws directed at maintaining public safety. These DAs' decriminalization strategies go far beyond prosecutorial discretion and fly in the face of the fundamental concept that no one part of the government exercises total control of our legal system. If you believe in the rule of law, that is a problem.

> As concerning as that is, it is not the only problem. Another real tragedy of the social reform DAs' non-prosecution strategy is its lack of respect for victims. The refusal to enforce entire categories of criminal laws ignores the often tragic harm exacted upon innocent victims.

U.S. Department of Justice, Deputy Attorney General Jeffrey A. Rosen Delivers Remarks at Wake Forest School of Law (Nov. 8, 2019). Are the same criticisms fairly leveled at the Trump Administration's (non-)enforcement of §12601? Aren't there victims of patterns and practices of police misconduct, too? Or are the two situations different?

e. Chicago and Baltimore: Down the Rabbit Hole

When Attorney General Jeff Sessions promised to "pull back" from investigating police departments just days after taking office, his statements not only boded ill for future enforcement, they also left existing negotiations in doubt. Two cities were especially affected by the transition.

Chicago

The Civil Rights Division began an investigation in Chicago in 2015 in the aftermath of the shooting of Laquan McDonald by a Chicago police officer. Although the police initially claimed that the officer shot McDonald in self-defense when McDonald lunged at him with a knife, a video subsequently showed that McDonald, a Black teenager, was walking away at the time, and the knife he was carrying was found to be closed. On January 13, 2017, just days before the end of the Obama Administration, the Division issued its findings, concluding that Chicago Police Department officers engaged in a pattern or practice of using unreasonable force and that the pattern was attributable to systemic deficiencies in the department and the city. At the same time the findings were announced, the city and the Division released an agreement in principle, stating their intention to negotiate a consent decree. Despite frantic work, no consent decree was signed before the administration changed, and under the Trump Administration, the Division dropped the matter.

A private civil rights lawsuit was filed by community groups, but that suit was quickly overtaken when the Illinois Attorney General Lisa Madigan initiated a §1983 lawsuit against the city in federal court seeking injunctive relief based on the Civil Rights Division's findings, saying:

> The new administration at the Department of Justice has made it clear it will no longer seek a consent decree in Chicago. We are essentially stepping into the shoes of the Department of Justice, shoes that DOJ has abandoned at this point.

Matt Zapotosky, *Illinois Files Suit to Force Police Reform in Chicago*, Wash. Post (Aug. 30, 2017). In doing so, Attorney General Madigan had the full support of Mayor Rahm Emanuel, who enthusiastically appeared at her press conference announcing the suit, along with Police Superintendent Eddie Johnson.

Then, the state and the city negotiated a consent decree. Illinois v. City of Chicago, No. 17-cv-6260, 2019 WL 398703 (N.D. Ill. Jan. 31, 2019). Despite Chicago's willing participation, both President Trump and Attorney General Sessions publicly opposed the consent decree. The United States filed a statement opposing it in court on the ground that "the safety of the people of Chicago is paramount," and the consent decree was a bad idea because it "will not permit local leaders the flexibility they need to proactively adjust law enforcement strategies to address the crime wave across the City." United States Statement of Interest Opposing Proposed Consent Decree 1, 5, Illinois v. City of Chicago, No. 17-cv-6260 (N.D. Ill. Oct. 12, 2018). According to the federal government, "There may be times when ongoing federal court oversight is necessary to ensure that a recalcitrant local government agency comes into compliance with federal law. But this is not such a time." *Id.* at 4. In elaborating why, the United States expressed concern about how the consent decree would supplant the role of the city's democratically accountable local officials. The consent decree is now in effect.

Just to be clear, the federal government found the city police department rampantly violating federal law and decided to do nothing. The state took over as plaintiff and—with the defendant—joyfully announced a lawsuit. When that lawsuit reached a settlement, the federal government—which purports to oppose unwarranted federal intrusion into local affairs—attacked it as bad for the city. Is this what police reform looks like in a second-best (or maybe seventh-best) world?

Baltimore

In Baltimore, the Department opened up an investigation in 2015, in the aftermath of the death of Freddie Gray, Jr., a 25-year-old Black man, who was arrested by Baltimore Police Department officers for allegedly carrying an illegal knife. Gray received injuries to his spinal cord during transport and died days later. In August 2016, the Department of Justice issued findings that the Baltimore Police Department engaged in a pattern or practice of a variety of constitutional violations, including illegal stops, searches, and arrests; intentional discrimination; excessive force; and suppressing speech. On January 12, 2016, the Division reached agreement with the city on a consent decree and filed a complaint and a joint motion to enter the decree.

Eight days later, on January 20, 2017, the day of President Trump's inauguration, lawyers for the Department of Justice asked the district court for a short delay before entering the decree to allow them to consult with the new leadership of the Department. That delay was granted, and two weeks later, after President Trump had taken office but before Jeff Sessions was confirmed, attorneys for both the Department of Justice and Baltimore reaffirmed their commitment to the consent decree in court. Two months later, following an executive order directing federal agencies to "prioritize crime reduction," the Department of Justice sought a further 90-day delay in entering the consent decree to allow the Department of Justice to "review and assess" the reforms. The city strongly objected to any delay, and District Judge James K. Bredar denied the motion, indicating that it was untimely and burdensome to those involved. United States v. Baltimore Police Dept., No. JKB-17-0099 (D. Md. Apr. 5, 2017).

During a hearing on the decree the same week, the Department of Justice told Judge Bredar that it had "grave concerns" that the decree would increase crime. Federal attorneys again asked the Judge to hold off, this time for 30 days, arguing that police reform was "really the job of local officials." Kevin Rector, *DOJ Doubtful About Decree*, Balt. Sun (Apr. 7, 2017). Judge Bredar refused to delay and approved the consent decree, concluding that it was in the public's interest and that the time for negotiations was over. United States v. Baltimore Police Dept., 249 F. Supp. 3d 816 (D. Md. 2017). Jeff Sessions immediately spoke out against the order. See Kevin Rector, *Judge OKs Consent Decree*, Balt. Sun (Apr. 8, 2017). Baltimore's mayor and police chief continued to support the consent decree, and the decree went into effect. The Judge selected a monitoring team and reform is ongoing.[9]

---

[9] *Ed. note:* I served on the Baltimore monitoring team in 2017 and 2018.

Just to summarize, the Baltimore lawsuit's plaintiff reached a tentative settlement with the defendant, giving the plaintiff almost everything it wanted. Not satisfied, the plaintiff then tried to get out of that agreement, preferring to get nothing. The defendant objected, though, insisting it had the right to be forced to remedy the harm at the cost of millions of dollars. The judge agreed and wouldn't let the plaintiff withdraw. Wait, what?

f. How Much Do Politics Matter?

Obviously, politics determines how (and whether) the pattern and practice statute will be enforced. But, even at its most aggressive, the Division opened and negotiated no more than a handful of new pattern-or-practices cases each year. In 2016, the last year for which the Obama Administration had budget influence, the police practices program cost $6.7 million and had only 22 staff attorneys, five supervising attorneys, and two investigators working on policing cases. These individuals were responsible for selecting cases, investigating them, litigating and negotiating settlements, and monitoring existing agreements, although they were aided by local United States Attorney's Offices and outside experts. That $6.7 million represented nearly half of the expenditures of the Special Litigation Section that year, but less than .003 percent of the Department of Justice's $28.7 billion budget. In the light of how tiny the program has been, even at its zenith, how much do political winds really matter? Should we ask the people most affected by policing in cities that have been sued and in cities that have not?

8. State Pattern-or-Practice Enforcement

One possible response to federal pullback from civil rights enforcement is to increase state pressure on local police departments. State attorneys general in several states already occasionally investigate or sue police departments for injunctive relief, often using 42 U.S.C. §1983. Illinois's lawsuit and settlement with the City of Chicago building on the U.S. Department of Justice investigation provides an example. See Illinois v. City of Chicago, No. 17-cv-6260, 2019 WL 398703 (N.D. Ill. Jan. 31, 2019).

New York has engaged in similar investigations. In 2001, for example, then-Attorney General Eliot Spitzer sued the town of Wallkill, New York, for failing to train, supervise, or discipline officers, who sexually harassed women during traffic stops and arrests, solicited bribes, threatened citizens, and suppressed free speech in violation of the First, Fourth, and Fourteenth Amendments, see Complaint, People v. Wallkill, No. 01-0365 (S.D.N.Y. Jan. 18, 2001). The resulting consent decree led to changes in the department. See Final Judgment, People v. Wallkill, No. 01-0364 (S.D.N.Y. Feb. 28, 2006).

Some scholars have argued that states should be doing more: for instance, that states should pass pattern-and-practice statutes analogous to §12601, especially in the face of federal inaction. See Samuel Walker & Morgan Macdonald, *An Alternative Remedy for Police Misconduct: A Model State "Pattern or Practice" Statute*, 19 Geo. Mason U. C.R. L.J. 479 (2009). California already has such a statute, which has been in effect since 2000:

CAL. CIV. CODE §52.3

Law enforcement officers; prohibitions against conduct depriving persons of Constitutional rights, privileges, or immunities; civil actions

(a) No governmental authority, or agent of a governmental authority, or person acting on behalf of a governmental authority, shall engage in a pattern or practice of conduct by law enforcement officers that deprives any person of rights, privileges, or immunities secured or protected by the Constitution or laws of the United States or by the Constitution or laws of California.

(b) The Attorney General may bring a civil action in the name of the people to obtain appropriate equitable and declaratory relief to eliminate the pattern or practice of conduct specified in subdivision (a), whenever the Attorney General has reasonable cause to believe that a violation of subdivision (a) has occurred.

Section 52.3 was passed in the aftermath and in response to what is known as the Rampart Scandal. Dozens of Los Angeles Police Department officers in the Rampart Division stole and dealt drugs, used excessive force, and made illegal arrests. The Rampart Scandal also led the Civil Rights Division to (finally) investigate the LAPD.[10] The city settled with the U.S. Department of Justice the same year California's pattern-or-practice law took effect, so the city that inspired the statute was an unlikely target of it. Although there are more than 500 law enforcement agencies in California, some of which have been repeatedly accused of misconduct, Cal. Civ. Code §52.3 has been used only against a few. Why might enforcement be so limited?

Even as California's pattern-or-practice statute remained relatively dormant, controversy over police shootings led lawmakers to seek repeatedly to pass laws to make it easier to prosecute officers in California. Most experts think consent decrees inspire more reform than prosecutions do. What does that tell us? Is individual accountability better politics than institutional reform? Is structural reform litigation too challenging even for a big state? Are legislatures looking to just do something? Or is there another lesson to learn here? What advantages might state attorneys general have over the U.S. Department of Justice when they investigate patterns of misconduct and seek reform? What if §12601 were amended to allow states to bring suit?

You might wonder why states need pattern-or-practice authority at all. States can influence local policing by setting hiring and training standards, by decertifying officers for misconduct based on agency-provided information, and by setting standards for agency accreditation, including accountability, recordkeeping, and transparency requirements. Why not just mandate through legislation and regulation that all agencies take the steps necessary to prevent police misconduct? Are there reasons why you want state attorneys general also to have the power to sue police departments for equitable relief?

9.   Other Department of Justice Tools for Reducing Police Misconduct

The pattern-or-practice statute is not the only civil authority the Department of Justice has to enforce civil rights against police departments or promote civil rights within them. Here, briefly, are a few others.

---

[10] *Ed. note:* As a Department of Justice prosecutor, I was involved in the Division's criminal investigation into aspects of the Rampart Scandal. I was not involved in the civil investigation of the LAPD.

a. Antidiscrimination Statutes

Both Title VI of the Civil Rights Act of 1964 and the Omnibus Crime Control and Safe Streets Act of 1968 (discussed further in Chapter 6) prohibit law enforcement agencies receiving federal funds, training, or technical assistance from discriminating on the basis of race, color, national origin, sex, or religion. Most police departments receive some federal assistance, so these statutes can be used to prevent discrimination by police departments. The statutes permit enforcement by injunctive relief or termination of federal funding.

In practice, the Special Litigation Section brings investigations for violations of Title VI and the Safe Streets Act almost exclusively in conjunction with §12601 pattern-or-practice investigations. This has two advantages from the government's perspective. First, Title VI can capture forms of discrimination that §12601 cannot. Unlike the Equal Protection Clause, which is enforced through §12601 pattern-or-practice suits, Title VI and the Safe Streets Act prohibit practices that have discriminatory effects, even without evidence of discriminatory intent.

Second, the Department of Justice has subpoena power under Title VI, but not under §12601. Bringing a Title VI claim with a §12601 action ensures that the Department of Justice can engage in thorough investigations against noncooperative departments.

These statutes can also be enforced by the Office of Civil Rights in the Office of Justice Programs, which responds to complaints about Title VI violations by law enforcement agencies receiving grants from the Department of Justice. In theory, local law enforcement could lose federal funding for discrimination. In practice, the statutes and implementing regulations seem designed to discourage aggressive enforcement. They tell the Department of Justice to pursue termination of funding only once it has thoroughly exhausted efforts to obtain voluntary compliance from the target agency. Even without such cautions, federal agencies, including the Department of Justice, rarely end federal funding because of discrimination in funded programs. You can probably imagine reasons why. Is the Department of Justice likely to deprive a city of antiterrorism funding because its department discriminates on the basis of national origin? Or deprive a city of community policing funds because it discriminates on the basis of race? Should it? Are there other ways to use these laws to change departments?

b. COPS Office

Many agencies know they have a problem and welcome reform, but they fear the length, expense, and intrusion of pattern-or-practice litigation. In 2011, the Department of Justice developed a nonadversarial method for helping departments, run out of the Office of Community Oriented Policing (COPS). Unlike the Civil Rights Division, the COPS office seeks to expand and strengthen law enforcement and is led by former law enforcement officials.

The new approach was first used in Las Vegas, after a series of controversial police shootings. With the help of outside consultants, COPS spent six months reviewing the Las Vegas Municipal Police Department's policies and practices and then recommended changes in training, policy, supervision, and accountability designed to reduce police shootings. See Community Oriented-Policing Services, Dept. of Justice, *Collaborative Reform Process: A Review of Officer-Involved Shootings in the Las Vegas Metropolitan Police Department* (2012). The Las Vegas report was used by the police department to leverage political will to secure investment in reform, and shootings went down. The project was widely hailed as a success.

The COPS office's efforts expanded and evolved into two programs. The Critical Response Technical Assistance Program addressed high-profile events, and the broader Collaborative Reform Initiative for Technical Assistance made focused, expert, nonadversarial assistance available to a range of agencies. Through both, the COPS office offered departments detailed analysis and nonbinding recommendations, although the Collaborative program eventually included monitoring of agency reforms. Agencies had to apply to receive assistance, and many did. By 2017, more than two dozen law enforcement agencies had participated or were participating in the two programs.

Collaborative reform allows the Department of Justice to address problems in policing that do not violate the Constitution, such as the excessive use of *legal* force against suspects. Moreover, it allows the Department of Justice to help improve policing without aggressive federal intrusion: Communities actively sought the technical assistance. In this way, collaborative reform encourages good policing by lowering the cost of engaging in best practices as opposed to raising the cost of engaging in constitutional violations.[11]

Nevertheless, in 2017, the Trump Administration declared the program inconsistent with its goals of promoting "officer safety, officer morale, and public respect for their work," and ensuring that public safety remains under "local control and local accountability." U.S. Attorney General, Memorandum for Heads of Department Components and United States Attorneys (Mar. 31, 2017). To the surprise of departments waiting for reports, the administration ended the program, replacing it instead with new grants for technical assistance to law enforcement agencies on subjects such as reducing violent crime and gun violence and expanding proactive policing. Although some critics saw the COPS programs as pattern-or-practice lite, many cities were counting on the aid. In thinking about why the Trump Administration might have ended the efforts, consider that the COPS office, which was created under President Bill Clinton, had long been unpopular with some Republicans. In addition, Hillary Clinton, President Trump's Democratic Party rival

---

[11] It is not surprising that I look favorably on this approach because it is what I have argued the Department of Justice should do:

> Some costs of reform are difficult to mitigate. The information technology and data collection required for an early intervention system, the costs of training officers on a use-of-force continuum or de-escalation techniques, and the costs of establishing an independent internal affairs component in a department are not easy to reduce. The Justice Department, however, has substantial control over one aspect of the costs of reform. Police departments must identify misconduct, determine what problematic practices contribute to the misconduct, choose reform measures, tailor those measures for the department's circumstances, and implement and monitor reforms. Each of these tasks requires expertise that police departments are unlikely to possess. Thus, the Justice Department can most easily reduce the costs of reform by reducing information costs for police departments. Lowering the information costs of reform requires two tasks: (1) developing the relevant information on what causes and cures misconduct and (2) disseminating it to police leadership in a manner that facilitates departmental reform.

Rachel A. Harmon, *Promoting Civil Rights Through Proactive Policing Reform*, 62 Stan. L. Rev. 1, 48-49 (2009).

for the presidency, celebrated COPS collaborative reform as an alternative to litigation and had promised to expand the program during her campaign.

c.   Grant Programs and Coordination Concerns

Beyond the various Department of Justice units engaged in *reform*, there are massive grant and equipment programs in the Department of Justice, the Department of Defense, the Department of Homeland Security, and other federal agencies that are intended to *support* policing. See Chapter 11 (discussing federal grant and equipment programs). A few of these programs seek to increase accountability or promote civil rights. That is, for example, one purpose of body worn camera grants, available to law enforcement agencies to fund cameras since 2015.

Overwhelmingly, however, federal grant programs administered by the Department of Justice focus on crime control. These programs sometimes influence policing in ways that undermine rather than strengthen civil rights and that contravene reforms recommended by the Civil Rights Division. Yet, no one coordinates federal programs on policing across agencies or even within the Department of Justice, and they sometimes reflect competing agendas. For drug control policy, an area of similar complexity, we have the Office of National Drug Control Policy in the Executive Office of the President, created in 1968 to lead and coordinate U.S. policy. Its head is often known as the federal drug czar. Does the White House need a czar for policing?

10.   Comparing Private and Public Litigation for Equitable Relief

Both private and public suits for equitable relief seek to reduce misconduct and build institutional capacity for constitutional policing. Not surprisingly, throughout the history of pattern-or-practice litigation, the Department of Justice has drawn lessons from the work of private plaintiffs, and private plaintiffs have invoked the Department of Justice's efforts, and courts facing either type of suit have drawn from both contexts. Still, there might be important differences between public and private litigation seeking reform.

Here is one: The Department of Justice's efforts mark a deep national commitment to protecting individual rights, one that many believe more than justifies infringing on the American tradition of local political control over the police. The pattern-or-practice program also represents a rare opportunity to articulate a credible national message about what local policing should look like, even to agencies that are not being investigated or sued. As such, the Department of Justice might justifiably compromise some level of tailoring consent decrees to local priorities and conditions to send a clear and consistent message to other agencies.

By contrast, §1983 suits represent an avenue for private parties to use federal courts to ensure that local governments do not unfairly sacrifice the interests of the few for those of the many. Private plaintiffs cannot as easily set usable national standards or coordinate to promote similar aims across agencies. And no matter how publicly minded private plaintiffs are, they do not represent the public interest. In fact, §1983 suits for injunctive relief can be viewed as a form of private consumption of public resources.

This difference suggests that the legitimacy of §1983 suits depends more heavily than the legitimacy of pattern-or-practice suits on a close connection between the constitutional violations at stake and the reforms. It might also raise concerns about mandating stakeholder participation in developing reforms in §1983 suits, as Judge Scheindlin did in *Floyd v. City of New York*, 959 F. Supp. 2d 668, 686–688 (S.D.N.Y. 2013), that do not come up in pattern-or-practice litigation. When the monitoring team runs community meetings pursuant to a Department of Justice–led consent decree in Baltimore, one might see the federal government ensuring that a federal court-monitored process meets local needs. In private plaintiff suits, though, might the same activity look more like substituting private political processes for local government by election?

How should differences between the two kinds of cases be reflected in the law governing equitable remedies? Or is the difference not significant enough to justify the distinction?

Assessing What You Have Learned: Suing Hill Valley

Go back to the introduction to this chapter. A woman who was sexually assaulted by a police officer during a traffic stop comes into your office and asks what can be done to stop Hill Valley officers from continuing their patterns of unconstitutional conduct, given local intransigence to reforming the department. She asks you: What more do you need to know to evaluate the possibility of a private suit for equitable relief? How likely do you think it is that the state or federal government might get involved in seeking to force reform? What good could a lawsuit do?

---

11.   Do Pattern-or-Practice Suits Prevent Police Misconduct?

It is hard to know how well structural reform litigation works to prevent future constitutional violations by police departments. Most experts applaud the Civil Rights Division's pattern-or-practice program. Anecdotally, many police chiefs and community members say their departments are better for having been through investigation and settlement with the Civil Rights Division. Los Angeles and Cincinnati (which involved a private-public partnership) are often cited as the Division's most successful efforts. However, the program has hardly been an unvarnished success. Even cities considered reformed struggle with backsliding and communities who remain alienated from the police. Other agreements have never seemed to yield the promised rewards: In Portland, after a settlement with the Civil Rights Division and implementation of a consent decree, public opinion viewed police treatment of the mentally ill—the primary focus on the agreement—as worse than it was before.

Only a few studies evaluate the effects of the Civil Rights Division's pattern-or-practice suits across departments, and those look only at early decrees. Largely, those studies have found that agencies subject to Civil Rights Division consent decrees developed "a stronger, more capable accountability infrastructure, more robust training, and a set of policies that reflect national best practices." Joshua M. Chanin, *Examining the Sustainability of Pattern or Practice Reform*, 18 Police Q. 163, 185 (2015). The research has mostly asked narrow questions, however, such as whether reforms were effectively implemented and whether communities were happier with their departments. It is much harder to figure out whether consent decrees reduce constitutional violations, and no research has yet satisfactorily answered that question. The Civil Rights Division has tried to improve assessment of the program by introducing into consent decrees outcome measures that can help determine whether the reforms are having the intended effects. Right now, though, there is a lot that is unknown about the consequences of consent decrees. How should we think about the value of public equitable litigation in the face of this uncertainty?

Even if reforms by consent decree achieve their aims, they may have down-sides. Here are some of the concerns that have been raised about the Civil Rights Division's efforts.

a.   Depolicing

Although studies have found that officers felt disaffected under early consent decrees, most research does not support officer claims that reform pursuant to consent decrees discourage police activity, what is often called *depolicing.* See Robert C. Davis et al., Vera Inst. of Just., *Turning Necessity into Virtue: Pittsburgh's Experience with a Federal Consent Decree* (2002); Christopher Stone et al., Harvard Kennedy School, *Policing Los Angeles Under a Consent Decree: The Dynamics of Change at the LAPD* (2009); Joshua Chanin & Brittany Sheats, *Depolicing as Dissent Shirking: Examining the Effects of Pattern or Practice Misconduct Reform on Police Behavior*, 43 Crim. Just. Rev. 105 (2018). These studies did not stop Attorney General Jeff Sessions from repeatedly claiming that the investigations and consent decrees not only reduce officer morale, but also make cities unsafe by increasing crime. What if federal investigations do increase crime? Would that be a decisive argument against stopping constitutional violations?

b.   Sustainability

Several commentators have raised doubts about whether the Division's reform efforts last. Joshua Chanin's analysis of Pittsburgh's experience with reform under the consent decree, for example, found considerable backsliding after the consent decree lifted. See Chanin, *Examining the Sustainability, supra.* Since Pittsburgh, the Civil Rights Division has revised its remedial efforts to improve long-term outcomes. Perhaps that is why Chanin's study also found that Cincinnati maintained its reforms. Overall, there is not yet enough data to know whether agencies undo reforms and begin to commit additional constitutional violations after court supervision and monitoring ends. How important is sustainability? If reforms do lapse, is that an argument for ending the program? Or changing it? Say you know that a department would reform only temporarily. Is that enough to justify the Division's expenditure of resources in securing that reform? How could you tell?

c.   Cost-effectiveness

Given constrained resources and competing public goals, good public policies must be cost-effective as well as effective. Assume that Congress wants fewer constitutional violations to be committed by police departments. How should it spend money to make that happen? Should it invest more in the Civil Rights Division's reform efforts? Provide additional technical assistance to departments? Incentivize reforms with federal grants? The best answer to those questions requires knowing something about the relative costs and effects of each alternative, something about which we have very little evidence. How should Congress act in the face of that uncertainty?

d.   Superficiality

Some worry that federal investigations and settlements merely tinker with a system of policing that is far more broken than current institutional reform efforts acknowledge.

> [F]ederal investigations work, some of the time, to reduce police violence and to improve community perceptions about the police. They are expensive and the benefits may be only short term. But, in the jurisdictions where the federal intervention is successful, fewer people are killed or beat up by the police, and that is a good thing.

> Reform does not, however, do the work of transformation. It does not bring about the kind of change that the radical critics are seeking. . . .

> Because the law is not neutral or objective but actually perpetuates white supremacy, seeking change through liberal legal reform will result in "ephemeral" victories and "substantial" risks. Incremental progress through reform can lead to a backlash and further repression, a phenomenon highlighted by Kimberly Crenshaw. In addition, reforms are often inadequate because reformers often underestimate the pervasiveness of racism and other biases ingrained in the law: "While mainstream civil rights reformers assume that racism is a product of ignorance and can be overcome by education, critical race theorists insist that racism is pervasive and immutable. . . ." Given reformers' misunderstanding of the centrality of race in society, incremental reforms are unlikely to fundamentally alter an institution like the criminal justice system, which has racialized control at its core.

Paul Butler, *The System Is Working the Way It Is Supposed to: The Limits of Criminal Justice Reform*, 104 Geo. L. J. 1419, 1461–1462 (2015).

Amna Akbar has explored in more depth the ways the Civil Rights Division's ideas of reform fall short as a tool for fundamental change in policing. According to Akbar, the Division's investigations and settlements "expose a central dilemma of liberal law reform projects, caught between a commitment to the rule of law and status quo arrangements on the one hand, and the desire for substantive justice and social, economic, and political transformation on the other." Amna A. Akbar, *Toward a Radical Imagination of Law*, 93 N.Y.U. L. Rev. 405, 411 (2018). She contrasts the Division's investigation reports in Ferguson and Baltimore with the 2016 policy platform of the Movement for Black Lives, "A Vision for Black Lives: Policy Demands for Black Power, Freedom, and Justice," to illustrate the limits of the Department of Justice's approach. In short form, she argues:

> The Vision and DOJ reports offer alternate conceptualizations of the problem of policing and the appropriate approach to law reform. Reflective of liberal law reform projects on police, the DOJ reports identify policing as a fundamental tool of law and order that serves the collective interests of society, and locate the problems of police in a failure to adhere to constitutional law. As a corrective, the DOJ reports advocate for investing more resources in police: more trainings, better supervision, community policing. In contrast, the Vision identifies policing as a historical and

violent force in Black communities, underpinning a system of racial capitalism and limiting the possibilities of Black life. As such, policing as we now know it cannot be fixed. Thus, the Vision's reimagination of policing—rooted in Black history and Black intellectual traditions—transforms mainstream approaches to reform. In forwarding a decarceral agenda rooted in an abolitionist imagination, the Vision demands shrinking the large footprint of policing, surveillance, and incarceration, and shifting resources into social programs in Black communities: housing, health care, jobs, and schools. The Vision focuses on building power in Black communities, and fundamentally transforming the relationships among state, market, and society. In so doing, the movement offers transformative, affirmative visions for change designed to address the structures of inequality.

Id. at 410.

Can the Civil Rights Division take these critiques seriously? What effect would doing so have on the program? Imagine if, when the Department of Justice finds that a police department has engaged in a pattern or practice of constitutional violations, it were to seek a consent decree that attempts to reshape the city's public safety efforts rather than reform its police department. A decree might require a city to invest in housing, employment, and mental health services to prevent unconstitutional uses of force against people in crisis. Or it could require civilianizing or automating traffic enforcement to prevent suspicionless stops or racial profiling. Or it might demand that the city fund community-led antiviolence initiatives and bar most arrests in order to prevent illegal, discriminatory, or excessively forceful seizures. After all, the Department of Justice sues cities, not the police. What are the potential risks and rewards of mandating these kinds of reforms? Of rethinking the purposes of the program?

e.   Deterrence

Assuming you think law enforcement in this country would be better if more agencies adopted the reforms promoted by the Civil Rights Division, you might wonder whether the Civil Rights Division's efforts have improved policing outside of the departments it has targeted for investigation.

If the question is whether the Civil Rights Division's efforts deter constitutional violations, the answer is "It is hard to say." Given the tiny number of police departments that have been targeted, most agencies that have not yet been investigated should rationally consider the future risk minimal, at least in the absence of a critical event that could draw the Civil Rights Division's attention. Still, the public nature of the lawsuits and their dramatic impact on cities may make city officials wary and willing to reform, at least some, even if getting sued is unlikely. We simply do not know whether municipalities adopt reforms to reduce the risk of an investigation and suit.

If the question is instead whether the program has had a positive impact on policing nationwide, the answer is almost certainly "Yes." Law enforcement agencies frequently turn to consent decrees for guidance about best practices. In fact, it would be fair to say that this small program has done more to set national standards for protecting constitutional rights and improving accountability than any other effort in decades.

Chapter 16

Changing the Police: Beyond Litigation

As you have seen throughout this book, law molds policing, but the casting process is messy. Law does not always have its intended consequences. It often has unintended consequences. And many other forces shape the final product.

Still, in reading earlier parts of this book, you have found both reason for despair and cause for hope. You have seen that policing remains a flawed enterprise, and the law sometimes contributes to its problems—or at least, does not always mitigate them. Yet you have also seen the power of the law to mandate—and signal a commitment to—policing that promotes public safety less harmfully and more fairly.

In reading about legal remedies, however, you probably feel mostly frustration. Standard legal remedies burden victims, officers, and cities, and yet they remain dramatically imperfect tools for encouraging police to follow legal rules. You might wonder what else can be done to push policing in desired directions.

To help you think about additional ways the law might help change policing, this chapter starts with a summary proposal for legal reforms to reduce misconduct and promote accountability. Most of the reforms it mentions touch on topics you have studied in prior chapters. The chapter then considers a few reform mechanisms that are not discussed in depth elsewhere in the book: hiring, training, civilian oversight, and body-worn cameras. These sections are not comprehensive: The number of law reform options seems almost infinite, and many promising ways of improving policing—such as community–police reconciliation efforts or treating police violence as a public health issue—are not primarily legal. Nevertheless, considering a few of the common legal means communities use to change policing might help illustrate some of the promise and challenge of law reform.

For those who want the CliffsNotes version, here it is: There is no silver bullet for the problems in policing.

A. Changing the Law

Now that you have learned about the law of the police, what would you do to make it better? Spend a few minutes brainstorming legal changes that you now believe could improve policing. What are they intended to do? Are they national, state, or local changes? How difficult would they be to achieve? Who might have the incentive to bring them about? What unintended consequences or risks might they have?

In the days immediately after George Floyd was killed by Minneapolis police officers in 2020, a small group of law professors active in police reform put together the following set of proposals.

Barry Friedman, et al.,[1] *Changing the Law to Change Policing: First Steps* (2020)

Recent events have brought to the fore longstanding concerns about the nature of policing in the United States and how it undermines racial equity. As an institution, policing needs significant reconsideration. It is time to rethink the structure and governance of policing. It is also time to engage in a deeper conversation about the meaning of public safety. In the meantime, however, the following is a list of urgently-needed reforms, compiled by a small group of law school faculty, each of whom runs or is associated with an academic center devoted to policing and the criminal justice system. The reforms are not intended as an entire agenda for what ought to happen around policing, or what American policing should look like. Rather, they offer immediate, concrete steps federal, state, and local governments can take to address enduring problems in policing. The authors are scholars who are also deeply involved in the daily practice of policing, and included among them are the Reporters for the American Law Institute's *Principles of the Law: Policing*, which works with advisers from across the ideological spectrum in drafting high-level principles to govern policing, though the recommendations here go beyond the scope of the ALI project. . . .

Federal Reforms

1. Enforcing Constitutional Rights and Ensuring Adequate Remedies for Constitutional Violations:

Qualified Immunity—Federal legislation should eliminate qualified immunity. Widespread indemnification would ensure that municipalities rather than officers bear the primary burden of increased liability, putting pressure to reform on actors who most influence officers. In addition, eliminating qualified immunity would force courts that now sometimes avoid constitutional questions to reach decisions that clearly establish the constitutional standards governing policing.

Municipal Liability—The Supreme Court has interpreted the federal civil rights statute, 42 U.S.C. §1983, to shield municipalities from liability for the actions of police officers that violate statutory or constitutional rights, unless what the officer did was official municipal policy. This likely is a misinterpretation of the original statute, and in any event should be reversed. Municipalities should be responsible for the actions of their officers, to ensure that individuals who are harmed are compensated properly, to provide an incentive to improve training programs, and to facilitate the injunctive relief necessary for meaningful agency-wide police reform.

---

[1] *Ed. note.* I am one of the authors.

Federal and State Enforcement to Remedy Patterns or Practices of Police Misconduct—34 U.S.C. §12601 should be amended in three respects: first, to grant enforcement authority to states' attorneys general. This will amplify enforcement authority and provide a buffer against a dramatic shift in enforcement when priorities at the federal level shift. Second §12601 should be amended to provide for subpoena power. This will mitigate the extent to which pattern or practice investigations are stalled or compromised by jurisdictions unwilling to provide documents and other information voluntarily during an investigation. Third, the statute should be modified to clarify that state and local prosecutors are "law enforcement officers," within the meaning of the statute. Although the Department of Justice has taken this position in the past, its explicit adoption would facilitate protection of constitutional rights against infringement by prosecutors' offices.

Protection of First Amendment Rights—The Department of Justice should promote a national commitment to protection of the First Amendment right to protest by law enforcement, and it should use its authority under 18 U.S.C. §242 to prosecute willful violations of the First Amendment, including at political protests. Federal law enforcement agencies should promote and model First Amendment protections by ensuring that all federal law enforcement officers on duty at protests are trained in policing public protests and that their agency and individual identity is made clear via uniform, nameplates, and other descriptors.

2. Regulating Specific Policies or Practices:

National Use of Force Standard—One of the areas of greatest concern in the country is police use of force, which typically is regulated at the state and local level. But Congress has power to enact laws to enforce the guarantees of the 14th amendment. The federal government could establish national standards for the use of force through statutes creating new criminal and civil actions for excessive force that impose liability beyond the very minimal constitutional floor, by making clear that use of force must be proportionate and necessary and that lethal force should be a last resort (see state level reforms, #1). Alternatively, Congress could impose conditions on federal spending grants and withhold funds to state and local agencies that do not meet federal standards on the use of force, or advance national use of force standards through a federal accreditation body.

No Knock Entries—Unless police knock and announce their presence before they enter a residence to search it or make an arrest, occupants may mistake the police for intruders and unnecessary harm to them or to the police can, and often has, resulted. Police should dispense with the constitutional knock-first requirement only when there is reason to believe doing so would allow evidence destruction or endanger the police, and even in that event, they should announce their presence upon entry. Although technically the standard for law enforcement action, this rule is regularly honored in the breach.

3. Promoting Uniform Standards, Recordkeeping, and Information Sharing:

Decertification Database—The federal government should ensure that all policing agencies have access to accurate and timely information about officers who have been decertified by their states. If modeled after the National Practitioner Database, it would include other derogatory information, including firings, civil judgments, and criminal convictions that do not require decertification.

Data Collection—Congress should mandate data collection, including demographic information, for all enforcement actions, by any policing agency in the United States, including federal agencies.

Uniform Data Standards—In its legislation regulating data collection, Congress should require the Department of Justice to develop national standards for collecting data on the use of force and other policing practices, just as it has done with respect to crimes for nearly a century with the Uniform Crime Reporting program. National classifications and compatible formats will allow agencies and communities to better assess and monitor the use of force and will improve research efforts.

4. Institutional Reforms:

Reconsider DOJ's Conflicting Roles in Policing—Many U.S. Department of Justice components play a role in local policing, including working with local law enforcement on crime and terrorism, providing grants and technical assistance, enforcing civil rights laws, and funding research. DOJ entities playing these various roles sometimes take conflicting positions, do not coordinate adequately, and promote mixed messages. Congress should consider ways to rationalize policing policy, perhaps through a policing czar or Assistant Attorney General, to ensure that DOJ reduces harm and improves fairness, even as it works to make policing throughout the country more effective. Relatedly, some federal entity should have the authority to conduct pattern or practice investigations and undertake enforcement actions against federal law enforcement agencies.

Federal Grant Programs—Police departments should not be permitted to participate in any federal grant or equipment program without formal approval by the governing body of the jurisdiction. Otherwise, federal programs may serve to bypass usual political and budgetary decision-making about the amount and kind of policing that best will serve that community. In addition, in measuring the success or productivity of policing, federal programs should focus on improvements in public safety or welfare, not outcomes that measure intrusions such as arrests or property deprivations. The federal government should also end federal equitable sharing programs that encourage local and state law enforcement to engage in civil asset forfeiture.

National Accreditation Body—Congress should create a federal accreditation body to motivate state and local adoption of a number of measures described below. In order to be accredited, agencies should have to demonstrate both policies and compliance consistent with a number of substantive baselines, such as minimum use of force standard, use of tactical teams, and policies to ensure facilitation of community members' first amendment rights. Also critical to receiving accreditation should be conformity with the data collection measures described above and a provision tying future federal accreditation standards to evidence. . . .

State-Level Reforms

Some of these reforms, such as use of force policies and data collection, also could be pursued nationally. But in the absence of federal reform, the proposals below should be adopted at the state level.

1. Regulating Specific Policies or Practices:

For many policing policies or practices, it does not make sense to have every single agency develop its own policies from scratch, in part because the way the police interact with the public on fundamental issues ought not to fall below an acceptable floor from jurisdiction to jurisdiction (although jurisdictions could exceed these floors). One important role that states can play is in setting baseline requirements with which all police department policies must comply. States should consider:

Use of Force—States should regulate the use of force by statute and set minimum requirements for all agency use of force policies. State-level policies should incorporate principles of necessity and proportionality, impose strict limits on the use of lethal and less-lethal weapons and techniques, and require de-escalation where possible, prior to resorting to force. (See ALI Principles on the Use of Force; Camden County Police Department Use of Force Policy.)

Use of Tactical Teams—Although tactical teams (e.g. SWAT) can play an important role in safely diffusing certain dangerous situations, which was their original purpose, they also have the potential to seriously increase the risk of injury or death, and should therefore only be used in situations that cannot be resolved using less intrusive means. Today tactical teams are overused. States should set minimum standards regarding the training, equipment, and deployment of tactical teams, and require agencies to maintain and report data on all deployments.

Use of Invasive Surveillance Techniques—Police increasingly rely on invasive surveillance techniques, including technology that monitors social media, tracks public travels, scans and mines databases, detects objects through walls, and records public activities. The information obtained through these techniques often is retained indefinitely by the police or by private companies under contract with the police department. State and local governments need to ensure that collection, maintenance, access, analysis and use of information obtained through surveillance technology is governed by policies that clearly delineate when it may occur, safeguard privacy, certify accuracy, prevent abuse, and require even-handed, non-discriminatory application of the rules.

Stops and Searches—States should consider measures to limit or regulate the use of traffic and pedestrian stops, as well as consent searches. Examples of possible measures include: limiting the use of reasonable suspicion stops for certain categories of offenses; requiring officers to inform individuals that they have a right to refuse consent to search; prohibiting the use of consent searches in the context of routine traffic stops absent reasonable suspicion to believe that the search will turn up evidence or contraband.

Arrests—Arrests impose substantial harm and are often unnecessary to promote public safety, even when criminal charges are appropriate. States should restrict arrests for low-level offenses and discourage arrests for other offenses where summonses and citations could replace them adequately. States should set standards for arrests, and demand that departments set standards for arrests, that clarify the circumstances under which arrests are appropriate and limit officer discretion to make arrests that do not serve public safety goals.

Body Cam Footage Release Policy—The country has spent a fortune on body cameras. Body cameras were adopted for police accountability, but quickly have become yet one more tool for surveillance and collecting evidence for prosecution. Body cameras fail entirely as an accountability mechanism without a sound policy for release of the video to the public after critical incidents. (See Chicago's Video Release Policy, or LAPD's Video Release Policy as examples.)

Interrogations—In the absence of a recording, accounts of interrogation, by either the police or the suspect, cannot be corroborated and courts cannot fully evaluate the legality of the process. Just as depositions of litigants in civil cases always are transcribed, police interrogations always should be recorded, from start to finish, preferably with video capturing both the questioner and the person being questioned. Agencies should adopt interrogation policies that promote reliability, eliminate undue coercion, and treat persons with dignity and fairness.

2. Institutional Reforms:

Special Independent Investigators and Prosecutors for Critical Incidents—Independent investigations and prosecutions of officers engaged in critical incidents are necessary to reduce conflicts of interest and promote public faith that officers are being held to the legal standards that the state has set for them. It is especially critical that states and agencies prepare in advance for independent investigators to respond quickly to the scene of critical incidents. Only this quick response can promote trust in subsequent state assessments about the lawfulness of police conduct.

Decertification—Officers who engage in serious misconduct or fail to meet ongoing requirements for certification and yet continue to serve pose a risk to the public, erode faith in government self-regulation, and undermine standards in policing. All states should decertify officers under these circumstances and should report those decertifications to the national decertification database. States should not limit decertifications to officers who have been convicted of a crime, because criminal convictions are too rare and limited in scope to serve as the sole professional licensing standard for police officers.

Unions—Police officers are entitled to unionize like all workers, but at least two related problems have emerged. First, bargaining sometimes leads to inappropriate limits on accountability for misconduct that affects the public safety of the community as a whole. Second, unions have sometimes used their power to promote statutory protections for officers, including Law Enforcement Bills of Rights, that interfere with accountability, for instance, mandating time delays before officers can be questioned after critical events such as officer-involved shootings. The law governing union contracts, including the appropriate subjects of collective bargaining, should be reexamined, with unions participating in the conversation.

3. Data and Transparency:

Transparency—States should consider requiring agencies to make certain kinds of information available to the public on the department's website, including: department policies, information regarding the agency's use of various surveillance technologies, collective bargaining agreements, complaint data, and crime/call for service data.

Data Collection/Reporting—States should mandate data collection and reporting, including demographic information, for all enforcement actions, including stops, arrests, citations, searches, and uses of force.

4. Substantive Criminal Law and Enforcement Discretion:

Policing practices also are shaped profoundly both by the scope of substantive criminal law, and the authority that officers are given to take someone into custody (as opposed to issuing a citation, etc.). Too often, the machinery of criminal law is deployed to deal with social problems that are best addressed through other means. States should review their criminal codes and consider decriminalizing low-level offenses for which arrests and criminal penalties are inappropriate; adopt least intrusive intervention policies, by restricting arrests and overcharging; and discourage the excessive use of police stops to harass individuals or deter criminal activity, rather than to investigate it.

Local-Level Reforms

Although many of the various reforms discussed above should be adopted at the national or state levels, local agencies and legislatures can and should ensure in the meantime that their own policies and practices are consistent with the principles above on everything from data collection and transparency, to the use of force.

In addition, local legislatures should consider the following:

Accountability Systems—Local legislatures should ensure robust front-end and back-end accountability. Typically accountability has meant "back-end" accountability, which involves holding individual officers accountable for misconduct. Back-end accountability is all too often lacking around policing, and local jurisdictions should ensure there are adequate systems in place to investigate and adjudicate allegations of misconduct, and to proactively review all serious uses of force to ensure compliance with department policy.

Just as important, however, local jurisdictions should ensure that policing agencies are held accountable at the front-end (i.e., before things go wrong), which means formulating police department policies and priorities in a way that is transparent, evidence-based, and provides an opportunity for public input and debate. A number of jurisdictions have created regulatory bodies designed to promote front-end accountability in policing, including Inspectors General who can review existing policies and practices and identify shortfalls, as well as Commissions that can help facilitate greater community participation in police decision-making. Jurisdictions should ensure that these bodies are adequately resourced and staffed to actually regulate policing and ensure that the community has a voice in how it is policed.

Budgets—Local officials should review municipal and county budgets to ensure that there are adequate resources in place to pursue a holistic vision of public safety, and to address social problems—such as poverty or substance abuse—through mechanisms other than the criminal law. Legislatures also should ensure that cities and counties, not law enforcement agencies, control funding related to policing—for example funding that comes from federal grants. Legislative bodies should not simply approve police budgetary items in a pro forma fashion, but should invite public comment and debate, especially when things like surveillance technologies are the issue. And police should not be acquiring technologies or equipment off budget without legislative approval.

Municipal and County Codes—Local government leaders should review municipal and county codes and remove provisions that contribute to over-criminalization and encourage police involvement in situations that may be better handled by other agencies of government. Jurisdictions should pay special attention to provisions that may result in criminalization of poverty or status, or reflect anachronistic views or concerns.

Consolidation—One of the great obstacles to sound, quality policing is the sheer number of policing agencies in the country, many of them quite small. There simply is no way this many small agencies can adhere to the range of requirements that ought to govern policing agencies. One solution under consideration in a number of places is consolidating agencies so that they meet a minimum threshold of size and budget to operate in a safe fashion.

NOTES AND QUESTIONS

1. *The list.* Do you agree with this list? What is missing? What should be cut? What problems do these reforms try to solve?

2. *Grading.* Imagine you received a call from a U.S. Senator's senior legislative assistant. Recognizing that you have limited information, the staffer asks you to quickly grade these proposals (A to F) on three criteria:

- How likely is it to significantly improve policing if it is adopted?
- What could go wrong?
- How likely is the reform to happen?

Do any reforms get A's in all three categories? Why have they not been carried out already? Which proposals fail these tests? What more do you want to know before you are willing to testify in a legislative hearing about promising reforms? What research would you do?

3. *Strategy.* Pick a proposal you favor. If a nonprofit organization came to you and asked you to sketch a strategy to achieve it, what would you say? Do you think that litigation, legislative proposals, lobbying, public education, activism and

organization building, or something else would help? Which stakeholders might have views about the reform? How might those views be incorporated into the process? What are the likely obstacles? Inertia? Information? Intransigence? Expense?

B. Training

The Berkeley (Calif.) Police Department adopted the first formal training program in the United States in 1908 under the leadership of August Vollmer, Berkeley's first police chief and the country's most important early twentieth-century innovator in policing and academic policing studies. He intended the training as a means for modernizing and professionalizing the police. New York followed by developing its own training academy the next year, with other departments close behind, also hoping to make policing more effective and less corrupt. Today, advocates for police reform often turn to training to make policing less harmful.

Police receive four kinds of training.

1. Preservice Training

Before they start on the job, police officers receive initial *preservice training*, often at a multiagency regional academy, an academy hosted by an educational institution like a two-year college, or a department-run academy. These preservice programs vary substantially in both length—from about 12 to 25 weeks—and in style—with some more like boot camp and others more like college.

In an average training academy, about a quarter of the training is devoted to teaching police operations such as patrol procedures, investigations, and report writing. Another 20 percent of the training hours are devoted to training on using force. Legal training and self-improvement each take up another 10 percent of the hours. Less than 5 percent of training time is devoted to topics related to community policing, including identifying and solving community crime and disorder problems, and less than 2 percent is devoted to domestic violence and mental illness. Brian A. Reaves, Bureau of Justice Statistics, U.S. Dept. of Justice, *State and Local Law Enforcement Training Academies, 2013*, 5–7 (2016).

2. Field Training

Once officers are trained and certified and they start working, they receive *field training* on practical aspects of the job and agency-specific practices, usually by working for some period of time under the direct supervision of a field training officer within their agencies.

3. In-Service Training

For the rest of their careers, officers receive both mandatory and optional *in-service training*, which can include anything from a brief talk by a supervisor at the start of a shift to days of classroom sessions with an outside expert.

4. Specialized Training

Finally, officers with particular assignments, such as those on a SWAT team or crisis intervention team, will receive *specialized training* for that work. Like in-service training, specialized training is offered by a range of providers, including officers within the agency, state-approved trainers, and private vendors.

However much training officers receive, almost everyone who advocates for change in policing also calls for additional training to make it happen. Such calls are not new. In 1931, for example, the Wickersham Commission advocated for additional training to give officers effective alternatives to brutal interrogation tactics, known as the "third degree." Zechariah Chafee, Jr. et al., *The Third Degree*, in U.S. Nat'l Commn. on Law Observance & Enforcement, *Report on Lawlessness in Law Enforcement* 86 (1931) ("Policemen and detectives are not so likely to go after the other and better kinds of evidence unless they are well trained and energetic . . . .").

Here is the 2015 call for training from the Final Report of the President's Task Force on 21st Century Policing. What goals are its training recommendations intended to achieve?

Final Report of the President's Task Force on 21st Century Policing
51–59 (2015)

As our nation becomes more pluralistic and the scope of law enforcement's responsibilities expands, the need for more and better training has become critical. Today's line officers and leaders must meet a wide variety of challenges including international terrorism, evolving technologies, rising immigration, changing laws, new cultural mores, and a growing mental health crisis. All states and territories and the District of Columbia should establish standards for hiring, training, and education.

The skills and knowledge required to effectively deal with these issues require[] a higher level of education as well as extensive and ongoing training in . . . a wide variety of areas:

- Community policing and problem-solving principles
- Interpersonal and communication skills
- Bias awareness
- Scenario-based, situational decision making
- Crisis intervention
- Procedural justice and impartial policing
- Trauma and victim services
- Mental health issues
- Analytical research and technology
- Languages and cultural responsiveness . . .

The need for understanding, tolerance, and sensitivity to African Americans, Latinos, recent immigrants, Muslims, and the LGBTQ community was discussed at length at the listening session, with witnesses giving examples of unacceptable behavior in law enforcement's dealings with all of these groups. . . .

The need for realistic, scenario-based training to better manage interactions and minimize using force was discussed by a number of witnesses. Others focused more on content than delivery: Dennis Rosenbaum suggested putting procedural justice at the center of training, not on the fringes. Ronal Serpas recommended training on the effects of violence not only on the community and individual victims but also on police officers themselves, noting that exposure to violence can make individuals more prone to violent behavior. And witnesses Bruce Lipman and David Friedman both spoke about providing officers with historical perspectives of policing to provide context as to why some communities have negative feelings toward the police and improve understanding of the role of the police in a democratic society.

Though today's law enforcement professionals are highly trained and highly skilled operationally, they must develop specialized knowledge and understanding that enable fair and procedurally just policing and allow them to meet a wide variety of new challenges and expectations. Tactical skills are important, but attitude, tolerance, and inter-personal skills are equally so. And to be effective in an ever-changing world, training must continue throughout an officer's career. . . .

5.7 Recommendation: POSTs [Peace Officer Standards and Trainings] should ensure that basic officer training includes lessons to improve social interaction as well as tactical skills.

These include topics such as critical thinking, social intelligence, implicit bias, fair and impartial policing, historical trauma, and other topics that address capacity to build trust and legitimacy in diverse communities and offer better skills for gaining compliance without the use of physical force. Basic recruit training must also include tactical and operations training on lethal and nonlethal use of force with an emphasis on de-escalation and tactical retreat skills.

5.8 Recommendation: POSTs should ensure that basic recruit and in-service officer training include curriculum on the disease of addiction.

It is important that officers be able to recognize the signs of addiction and respond accordingly when they are interacting with people who may be impaired as a result of their addiction. Science has demonstrated that addiction is a disease of the brain—a disease that can be prevented and treated and from which people can recover. . . .

5.9 Recommendation: POSTs should ensure both basic recruit and in-service training incorporates content around recognizing and confronting implicit bias and cultural responsiveness.

As the nation becomes more diverse, it will become increasingly important that police officers be sensitive to and tolerant of differences. It is vital that law enforcement provide training that recognizes the unique needs and characteristics of minority communities, whether they are victims or witnesses of crimes, subjects of stops, or criminal suspects. . . .

5.9.1 Action Item: Law enforcement agencies should implement ongoing, top down training for all officers in cultural diversity and related topics that can build trust and legitimacy in diverse communities. This should be accomplished with the assistance of advocacy groups that represent the viewpoints of communities that have traditionally had adversarial relationships with law enforcement.

5.9.2 Action Item: Law enforcement agencies should implement training for officers that covers policies for interactions with the LGBTQ population, including issues such as determining gender identity for arrest placement, the Muslim, Arab, and South Asian communities, and immigrant or non-English speaking groups, as well as reinforcing policies for the prevention of sexual misconduct and harassment.

5.10 Recommendation: POSTs should require both basic recruit and in-service training on policing in a democratic society.

Police officers are granted a great deal of authority and it is therefore important that they receive training on the constitutional basis of and the proper use of that power and authority. Particular focus should be placed on ensuring that *Terry* stops are conducted within constitutional guidelines.

NOTES AND QUESTIONS

1. *Legal status.* The President's Task Force targeted its recommendations at two different actors: state POSTs and police departments. Although states sometimes provide minimum training requirements for officers by statute, generally legislatures task state commissions known as POSTs to promulgate detailed training standards. See, e.g., Cal. Penal Code §13510; see also 50 Ill. Comp. Stat. 705/6 (granting powers to a training board); Mass. Gen. Laws ch. 6, §116G (establishing the municipal police training committee). Telling POSTs to make a change suggests that the training change should be required for all departments in a state and should be a matter of law. Telling police departments to make a training change suggests that it should be a matter for internal policy or practices.

2. *State law.* Although legislatures overwhelmingly leave detailed training standards to POSTs, they weigh in in two ways: first, by setting broad minimum standards, such as the number of weeks in basic training, or setting a number of hours and mandatory subjects for in-service training. Second, they weigh in ad hoc, adding new training on specific topics in policing, often in response to a critical incident. For example, just months after an officer shot a caregiver who was trying to help an autistic man in 2016, Florida passed a state law requiring departments to train officers on how to identify autism spectrum disorder and respond to people who display its symptoms. See Fla. Stat. Ann. §943.1727; see also Ark. Code Ann. §12-9-113 (domestic violence); Ark. Code Ann. §12-9-116 (persons with disabilities); Colo. Rev. Stat. Ann. §24-31-313 (abuse and exploitation of elders); Ky. Rev. Stat. Ann. §15.334 (mandatory training on HIV, bias in policing); Minn. Stat. Ann. §626.8455 (community policing). What effects might ad hoc training legislation have on police training over time?

3. *The constitutional law of training.* In *City of Canton v. Harris*, the U.S. Supreme Court recognized that municipalities may be held liable for failing to train employees when the inadequate training causes a constitutional injury and amounts to "a policy for which the city is responsible." 489 U.S. 378, 389 (1989). This can happen if "in light of the duties assigned to specific officers or employees the need for more or different training is so obvious, and the inadequacy so likely to result in the violation of constitutional rights, that the policymakers of the city can reasonably be said to have been deliberately indifferent to the need." *Id.* at 390. Supervisors can be also held liable for inadequate training if they show callous or reckless indifference

with respect to the failure to train, see, e.g., Febus-Rodriguez v. Betancourt-Lebron, 14 F.3d 87 (1st Cir. 1994), but perhaps only when the training was so deficient as to make a constitutional violation inevitable, see Elkins v. District of Columbia, 690 F.3d 554 (D.C. Cir. 2012). In theory, civil liability for failure to train should encourage departments to ensure adequate training, but the standard is such that successful suits are uncommon. See Chapter 13 for more on suing municipalities for failure to train officers adequately.

4. *More calls.* Innumerable advocacy groups argue for more or different police training. Some are specific: Mothers Against Drunk Driving calls for more training in enforcing laws against impaired driving, and the National Alliance on Mental Illness advocates more training on crisis intervention. Others advocate a range of training reforms: To reduce police violence, Campaign Zero recommends at least quarterly scenario-based training on some of the same topics as the President's Task Force, as well as additional training on appropriate engagement with many of the communities with whom police frequently interact but might not understand.

5. *#NoCopAcademy.* Not everyone wants more training. Training requires resources that some community groups would instead invest in community-based social services. In Chicago, for example, a coalition of grassroots organizations known as #NoCopAcademy tried to halt the city's plan to build a new $95 million police and fire training facility, arguing that the money should be devoted to education and mental health services rather than "the racist and violent police." Alienated communities are understandably reluctant to invest in problematic departments. Other communities have advocated cutting police budgets substantially, often under the catchphrase "defund the police," which would almost inevitably necessitate less training for officers. How can a police department improve without training on new policies, practices, and means of interacting? How can a community struggling with problematic policing be expected to invest more?

6. *Community involvement.* Some commentators, including Campaign Zero, also call for community involvement in designing and implementing training. What should that look like? What benefits and risks might community involvement entail?

7. *Does training work?* Calls for training assume that training works. More specifically, they seem to assume that officers will do their jobs better if they are told more about the situations and individuals that they are likely to confront and given skills to make those encounters less harmful and more trust-inspiring. That seems commonsensical. But how, exactly, and how well does training achieve its ends? Does it have to change hearts, minds, or hands? How do we know whether it works? Research about training effectiveness is exceptionally limited. But it does indicate that at least some carefully constructed programs can alter officer attitudes or improve officer performance. See, e.g., Emily Owens et al., *Can You Build a Better Cop: Experimental Evidence on Supervision, Training, and Policing in the Community*, 17 Criminology & Pub. Pol'y 41 (2018); Scott Wolfe et al., *Social Interaction Training to Reduce Police Use of Force*, 687 Annals Am. Acad. Pol. & Soc. Sci. 124 (2020). Overall, though, we know next to nothing about how well contemporary training prepares officers for duty or changes their behavior once they are on the job. Nor do we know what style of training, what evaluation methods, or what frequency of training are best. See Nat'l Research Council, *Fairness and Effectiveness in Policing: The Evidence* 141 (Wesley Skogan & Kathleen Frydl eds., 2004). Additionally, most training programs are carried out with no effort to assess their effects on officer behavior. What should states, cities, and departments do, given limited evidence?

8. *Are calls for training realistic?* Assuming that well-conceived and well-executed training can improve policing, are contemporary calls for additional training likely to get us there? How sustainable is it to add new training for every concern raised about policing? Training is expensive for agencies, which pay trainers and pull officers off the street (which might mean paying overtime to other officers) to train them. Where should training money come from? Is training, as one leading policing researcher put it, "a popular but overworked cure for just about anything that ails the police in America"? Stephen D. Mastrofski, Police Foundation, *Policing for People* 6 (1999). Assuming better training makes better policing, what is the best way to ensure that police officers receive comprehensive and effective training, that is tailored both to local conditions and changing circumstances, both at the beginning of their career and throughout?

9. *Training as counterprogramming.* Not all training is true to its goals. For example, where officers are trained by state providers or in regional academies, they receive generic training that provides little, if any, introduction to agency-specific values, practices, and policies. Field training rectifies this gap, but field training also often undermines both preservice training and agency policies. Field training officers commonly tell new officers to forget everything they learned at the academy. This type of training might overemphasize the importance of informal norms in policing, including norms that could be radically inconsistent with community expectations and formal rules. (An exaggerated version of this problem was famously fictionalized in the movie *Training Day* (Village Roadshow Pictures, Outlaw Productions 2001).) Can law do anything to mitigate the very real problem of training that contradicts, rather than reinforces, official mandates?

10. *Training as politics/training as punishment.* Training sometimes serves more as reform theater than reform. When confronted with a crisis in policing, cities and their police departments sometimes impose training on officers to demonstrate immediate action. For example, just one day after a grand jury refused to indict the officer who killed Eric Garner on Staten Island in 2014, and community groups reacted strongly, the mayor and police commissioner of New York announced a substantial (but vague) retraining of the city's officers—details to come. See Marc Santora, *Mayor de Blasio Announces Retraining of the New York Police*, N.Y. Times (Dec. 4, 2014). In Virginia, after white Alcoholic Beverage Control officers violently arrested a Black student from the University of Virginia, the governor quickly signed an executive order mandating retraining on cultural diversity and interacting with young people. See T. Rees Shapiro & Jenna Portnoy, *McAuliffe Orders Va. ABC Officers to be Retrained in Use of Force, Diversity*, Wash. Post (Mar. 25, 2015). Officers often view such training cynically as a form of politically motivated public relations, or even as a form of collective punishment. That cynicism might be reinforced when training is poorly executed or designed more for external audiences than for officers. How likely is training to achieve its ends under those conditions?

Communities might be equally skeptical. In Chicago, critics were outraged when it was discovered that many of the officers responsible for providing procedural justice and implicit bias training had been previously accused of using excessive force and mistreating people of color. See Debbie Southorn & Sarah Lazare, *Officers Accused of Abuses Are Leading Chicago Police's "Implicit Bias" Training Program*, Intercept (Feb. 3, 2019). Is there any way to help ensure that additional training is meaningful?

11. *Training alone.* Even if training can work, training alone will do little to improve policing unless reinforced through policy, supervision, promotions,

discipline, and informal norms. Yet calls for training—above and apart from other changes in policing—keep coming. Why?

12. *Untrained officers.* If more training is not always better, *no* training seems worse. In January 2020, Jackson Ryan Winkeler was working as an officer in South Carolina when he was killed while conducting a traffic stop. Although he was working for one police agency and volunteering for another, he had not yet gone through preservice training or received field training at the time he was killed. See Jeffrey Collins, *SC May End Untrained Officers on Regular Patrols*, Associated Press (Feb. 23, 2020). State law allowed—and continues to allow—untrained individuals to "perform any of the duties of a law enforcement officer, including those involving the control and direction of members of the public and exercising the powers of arrest" for up to one year so long as they go through a short "firearms qualification program" (and even that requirement may be waived). S.C. Code Ann. §23-23-40. South Carolina is not alone; several other states also permit officers to work without or before they fully satisfy preservice or recruit training requirements for sworn officers. See, e.g., 2013 A.R. Reg. 132.00.13 (allowing individuals to serve as officers for up to 12 months without formal training); 250 Ind. Admin. Code 2-2-1 (allowing officers to serve for a year prior to basic training). Others permit individuals to serve as reserve deputies, conservators of the peace, or other positions in which they have some of the core powers of sworn officers, such as the arrest power, but need not *ever* receive the training or certification required for other officers. See, e.g., Va. Code Ann. §15.2-1734, Okla. Stat. tit. 19 §547. Why might these laws exist? In light of calls for additional training, should they be revisited?

C.   Hiring

Commentators frequently call for hiring different officers to improve policing. Calls for more racial diversity in police forces are especially loud: Communities confronting racial disparities in stops, arrest, and force cannot help but notice when departments fail to reflect the demographics of their communities. They often see more diverse police forces as a solution to problems of violence and trust, on the theory that different officers would police differently. The reality is more complicated, something acknowledged in this excerpt from the U.S. Department of Justice's report on the Ferguson (Mo.) Police Department. The report found that the Ferguson Police Department engaged in a pattern or practice of violating both statutory law and the First, Fourth, and Fourteenth Amendments by intentionally discriminating against African Americans and by using policing as a revenue-generating scheme. This is the section of the report on diversity and hiring:

U.S. Department of Justice, Civil Rights Division Investigation of the Ferguson Police Department
88–89 (2015)

Ferguson's Lack of a Diverse Police Force Further Undermines Community Trust

While approximately two-thirds of Ferguson's residents are African American, only four of Ferguson's 54 commissioned police officers are

African American. Since August 2014, there has been widespread discussion about the impact this comparative lack of racial diversity within FPD has on community trust and police behavior. During this investigation we also heard repeated complaints about FPD's lack of racial diversity from members of the Ferguson community. Our investigation indicates that greater diversity within Ferguson Police Department has the potential to increase community confidence in the police department, but may only be successful as part of a broader police reform effort.

While it does appear that a lack of racial diversity among officers decreases African Americans' trust in a police department, this observation must be qualified. Increasing a police department's racial diversity does not necessarily increase community trust or improve officer conduct. There appear to be many reasons for this. One important reason is that African-American officers can abuse and violate the rights of African-American civilians, just as white officers can. And African-American officers who behave abusively can undermine community trust just as white officers can. Our investigation indicates that in Ferguson, individual officer behavior is largely driven by a police culture that focuses on revenue generation and is infected by race bias. While increased vertical and horizontal diversity, racial and otherwise, likely is necessary to change this culture, it probably cannot do so on its own.

Consistent with our findings in Ferguson and other departments, research more broadly shows that a racially diverse police force does not guarantee community trust or lawful policing. See Diversity in Law Enforcement: A Literature Review 4 n.v. (U.S. Dep't of Justice, Civil Rights Division, Office of Justice Programs, & U.S. Equal Employment Opportunity Commission, Submission to President's Task Force on 21st Century Policing, Jan. 2015). The picture is far more complex. Some studies show that Africa[n]-American officers are less prejudiced than white officers as a whole, are more familiar with African-American communities, are more likely to arrest white suspects and less likely to arrest black suspects, and receive more cooperation from African Americans with whom they interact on the job. See David A. Sklansky, *Not Your Father's Police Department: Making Sense of the New Demographics of Law Enforcement*, 96 J. Crim. L. & Criminology 1209, 1224–1225 (2006). But studies also show that African Americans are equally likely to fire their weapons, arrest people, and have complaints made about their behavior, and sometimes harbor prejudice against African-American civilians themselves. *Id.*

While a diverse police department does not guarantee a constitutional one, it is nonetheless critically important for law enforcement agencies, and the Ferguson Police Department in particular, to strive for broad diversity among officers and civilian staff. In general, notwithstanding the above caveats, a more racially diverse police department has the potential to increase confidence in police among African Americans in particular. See Joshua C. Cochran & Patricia Y. Warren, *Racial, Ethnic, and Gender Differences in Perceptions of the Police: The Salience of Officer Race Within the Context of Racial Profiling*, 28(2) J. Contemp. Crim. Just. 206, 206–227 (2012). In addition, diversity of all types—including race, ethnicity, sex, national origin, religion, sexual orientation and gender identity—can be beneficial both to police–community relationships and the culture of the law enforcement agency. Increasing gender and sexual orientation diversity in policing in particular may be critical in re-making internal police culture and creating new assumptions about what makes policing effective.[60] Moreover, aside from the beneficial impact a diverse police force may have on the culture of the department and police–community relations, police departments are obligated under law to provide equal opportunity for employment. *See* Title VII of the Civil Rights Act of 1964, 42 U.S.C. §2000e et seq.

Our investigation indicates that Ferguson can and should do more to attract and hire a more diverse group of qualified police officers.[61] However, for these efforts to be successful at increasing the diversity of its workforce, as well as effective at increasing community trust and improving officer behavior, they must be part of a broader reform effort within FPD. This reform effort must focus recruitment efforts on attracting qualified candidates of all demographics with the skills and temperament to police respectfully and effectively, and must ensure that all officers — regardless of race — are required to police lawfully and with integrity.

NOTES AND QUESTIONS

1. *Ferguson investigation.* After Ferguson police officer Darren Wilson killed Michael Brown on August 9, 2014, Ferguson exploded. Protests continued for more than a week and recurred with every new legal turn in the case. The Civil Rights Division of the Department of Justice carried out two investigations, one into the death of Brown, which concluded that Darren Wilson could not be prosecuted federally for using excessive force against Brown, and the second into whether Ferguson's municipal court and police practices constituted a pattern or practice of constitutional violations against the city's residents. The first investigation is excerpted at the end of Chapter 14. This excerpt is from this second investigation, which concluded, first, that Ferguson's police department was more focused on revenue generation than public safety, leading to unconstitutional policing, and, second, that both police and municipal court practices in Ferguson were racially biased against African Americans, resulting in community distrust of law enforcement, especially among African Americans. This section on the demographics of the police departments is only one small piece of what was wrong in Ferguson according to the Department of Justice, but it is one that members of the community and the media raised again and again. What do you take away as the primary benefits and limitations of changing the demographics of policing?

2. *Beyond Ferguson.* Not every city faces as great a gap between the racial makeup of the police department and the community. As of 2016, about one in

---

[60] While the emphasis in Ferguson has been on racial diversity, FPD also, like many police agencies, has strikingly disparate gender diversity: in Ferguson, approximately 55% of residents are female, but FPD has only four female officers. *See* 2010 Census, U.S. Census Bureau (2010). During our investigation we received many complaints about FPD's lack of gender diversity as well.

[61] While not the focus of our investigation, the information we reviewed indicated that Ferguson's efforts to retain qualified female and black officers may be compromised by the same biases we saw more broadly in the department. In particular, while the focus of our investigation did not permit us to reach a conclusive finding, we found evidence that FPD tolerates sexual harassment by male officers, and has responded poorly to allegations of sexual harassment that have been made by female officers.

four local police officers was Black or Hispanic, and racial minorities make up half or nearly half of officers in many of the largest urban police departments. Still, while police departments have become more diverse over time, the change is uneven. Departments lag especially in communities where recent demographic shifts have increased minority residents, including in departments in California, Connecticut, Nevada, and New Jersey—some of the most diverse states in the country. What could be done to help departments diversify?

3. *Stopping violence and discrimination?* Although many argue hiring more African-American officers will decrease violence and discrimination in policing, as the Department of Justice suggests, the evidence is mixed at best. Devon W. Carbado and L. Song Richardson have proposed some reasons why "racialized policing" is not "solely a white officer phenomenon."

> First, . . . like white officers, black officers can draw on Fourth Amendment law . . . to target other African Americans. Second, conscious or unconscious racial biases might lead black police officers to aggressively police other African Americans. Think of these biases as "same-race biases" or "intraracial biases," because both the victims and the perpetrators of these biases have the same racial identity. Third, black police officers, like white police officers, might experience a set of anxieties or vulnerabilities that increase the likelihood that they will mobilize violence against other African Americans. An example of what we mean is "masculinity threat." A relatively new body of research demonstrates that police officers who feel that their masculinity is being challenged or undermined in the context of a particular interaction are more likely to use violence than officers who do not experience that masculinity threat. Another example is . . . that police officers who worry that they will be perceived as racist in particular interactions are more likely to use force against black citizens than officers who do not experience racial anxiety.
>
> . . . If police officers are specifically deployed to proactively police communities in which African Americans live—and if their performance evaluations, pay increases, and promotions are tied to, among other measures, the number of stops and frisks they conduct, the number of citations they issue, and the number of arrests they effectuate—black police officers, like white police officers, will end up having significant contact with African Americans.
>
> A final reason . . . is this: to fit into and become a part of the law enforcement community of "blue," black police officers may have to marginalize the concerns of and disassociate themselves from the community of "black."

Devon W. Carbado & L. Song Richardson, *The Black Police: Policing Our Own*, 131 Harv. L. Rev. 1979, 1990–1991 (2018).

4. *Other arguments for diversity.* Whatever racial diversity among officers does for violence and bias, there are other good arguments for diversifying police departments. For example, the Justice Department suggests that, although diversifying a department alone might not increase community confidence, a community is unlikely to trust a police department that does not reflect the community it serves. Diversity might also increase openness to reform and new perspectives. It could also disrupt insular and pathological subcultures inside a police department. Can you see how? What other benefits might diversity bring?

5. *Obstacles to diversity.* The project of diversifying a police department is neither easy nor quick. As Sherrilyn Ifill, President of the NAACP Legal Defense Fund, told the President's Task Force, describing youth in poor communities, "By the time

you are 17, you have been stopped and frisked a dozen times. That does not make that 17-year old want to become a police officer." *Final Report of President's Task Force on 21st Century Policing* 11 (2015). Troubled departments find it especially difficult to achieve racial and gender diversity. But difficult does not mean impossible: Few departments are as notoriously troubled as Ferguson's. Still, as of mid-2019—five years after a Ferguson officer shot Michael Brown, four years after the Department of Justice issued its report, and three years after the city and the federal government entered a consent decree—more than half of the officers and the police chief in Ferguson were African American. See Jim Salter, *Ferguson: 5 Years Later, Racial Tension Lingers Nationally*, Associated Press (Aug. 8, 2019).

6. *Gender.* Although some major police departments are as racially diverse as their communities, no major police department can say that about gender. Nationally, only about one in eight police officers is female. Shelley S. Hyland & Elizabeth Davis, Bureau of Justice Statistics, U.S. Dept. of Justice, *Local Police Departments, 2016: Personnel* 5 (2019). Less research is done about gender in policing than about race, but some evidence suggests that women officers use less force and generate fewer complaints than their male counterparts. When a department has more women officers, victims of domestic violence and sexual assault are also more likely to report the crimes against them. See, e.g., Joshua Chanin & Reynaldo Rojo-Mendoza, *Does Gender Matter? Using Social Equity, Diversity, and Bureaucratic Representation to Examine Police-Pedestrian Encounters in Seattle, Washington*, 42 Admin. Theory & Praxis 133, 136–137 (2020) (summarizing existing research). Why are there not more calls for women officers? The Department of Justice does not collect national data about other kinds of diversity, such as sexual orientation, gender identity, religion, or life experience. Thus, there are no national data, and even less research exists about whether those kinds of diversity matter. Does that mean departments should not worry about them?

7. *Hiring alone.* Although commentators focus on *hiring* more diverse officers, the obstacles to diversity in police departments do not end once officers are in the job: Diversity is not the same as inclusion. Officers from groups underrepresented in an agency may lack opportunities for advancement or mentoring, and their perspectives might not be treated as valuable. They might also be harder to retain. How can communities and departments evaluate and change obstacles to making diversity matter?

8. *Other hiring objectives.* Rather than focus on diversity, some commentators advocate higher standards for all officers, for example, by requiring some college education. But the evidence about whether educational requirements and other hiring standards improve policing is as mixed as the evidence on racial diversity. Some research shows that college-educated officers use less force and generate fewer complaints. See, e.g., Eugene A. Paoline & William Terrill, *Police Education, Experience, and the Use of Force*, 34 Crim. J. & Behavior 179 (2007). Other studies, however, indicate that more educated officers are more aggressive in stopping and arresting people for minor offenses. See Richard Rosenfeld et al., *Are College-Educated Police Officers Different? A Study of Stops, Searches, and Arrests*, 31 Crim. Just. Pol'y Rev. 206 (2018). Should we raise educational standards in policing or not? Can you propose an explanation for the apparent inconsistency in those findings?

9. *Collateral consequences of raising the bar.* Imposing educational or other requirements can have unintended effects. Many departments face substantial staffing shortages and are unable to generate enough qualified applicants to fill the pipeline.

Given that recruiting crisis, adding requirements can result in unfilled positions, less diversity, or other hiring compromises. For that reason, many departments are going in the opposite direction: They are eliminating education requirements and other employment barriers. For example, some departments are accepting applicants who have used illegal drugs recreationally, who have juvenile criminal records, or who have visible tattoos, all of which have traditionally disqualified officer candidates. Every employment standard represents a trade-off: Communities might want a residency requirement to ensure that officers understand and are committed to the community they serve. That same requirement, though, could dramatically limit the potential applicant pool for officer positions. As a result, the quality of candidates is likely to decrease. Who should participate in balancing these competing concerns? What role should communities have in setting hiring standards?

10. *State law.* State laws fix minimum hiring standards for officers by stating qualifications for certification, including minimum age, education standards, and criminal record limitations. Like agency hiring requirements, state standards can limit the pool of available applicants. For example, 30 states forbid departments from hiring noncitizens, laws that the Supreme Court has upheld as constitutional. See Foley v. Connelie, 435 U.S. 291 (1978). This type of state-law requirement can deprive agencies of qualified candidates who would add racial diversity and language skills to departments. As a result, some police chiefs advocate eliminating such restrictions. In 2015, Tennessee reversed its citizenship requirement, at least in part in response to calls from the Nashville police chief. The state now allows noncitizens who have served in the military to work as police officers. See Act of May 20, 2015, 2015 Tenn. Pub. Acts ch. 498. After Tennessee changed its law, however, several major police departments, including the Memphis Police Department, maintained a citizenship requirement for applicants. Are there qualifications that should be decided by states rather than cities? Why?

11. *Federal discrimination law.* Next to state law, the primary legal rules that constrain agency hiring standards are federal laws that prohibit discrimination in hiring. These laws have been used to invalidate some physical fitness tests for discriminating against women, some written promotion tests for discriminating against African Americans, and some prehiring psychological testing for discriminating against people with disabilities.

12. *Federal liability for hiring.* Agencies can also be held liable under 42 U.S.C. §1983 for hiring officers who subsequently commit constitutional violations—but not easily. To succeed, a plaintiff must show that adequate scrutiny of the officers' backgrounds would have led a reasonable policymaker to conclude that the "plainly obvious consequence" of the department's decision to hire those officers would be the specific constitutional violations that resulted. Bd. Commrs. of Bryan County v. Brown, 520 U.S. 397, 411 (1997). A single bad hire probably cannot generate liability. *Id.* Lower federal courts have permitted some inadequate screening claims when police departments have repeatedly hired officers with histories of excessive force complaints, see, e.g., Montes v. City of El Paso, Tex., No. EP-09-CV-82-KC (W.D. Tex. May 18, 2010), or of sexual harassment, Birdwell v. Corso, No. 3:07-0629 (M.D. Tenn. May 21, 2009), or a history of criminal charges of assault and corruption of minors, M.C. v. Pavlovich, No. 4:07-CV-2060 (M.D. Pa. July 25, 2008). Still, liability for hiring officers who commit constitutional violations is rare enough that it is hard to imagine that departments consider it enough of a threat to significantly change their hiring practices.

D. Community Oversight

Another common response to controversial uses of force in a city is to call for civilian oversight. Although many small towns and cities do not currently have any form of oversight board, most large cities and some smaller ones do. These boards are created by municipal ordinances and vary enormously from jurisdiction to jurisdiction. Consider this excerpt from the National Association for Civilian Oversight of Law Enforcement (NACOLE) that summarizes different approaches for communities considering adopting an oversight structure. NACOLE is a non-profit organization that helps communities develop and maintain effective civilian oversight.

Joseph DeAngelis et al., *NACOLE Civilian Oversight of Law Enforcement: A Review of the Strengths and Weaknesses of Various Models* (2016)

Introduction and Overview

Over the last several decades, issues of trust and accountability have moved to the forefront of community–police relations, and a great deal of scholarship has been devoted to enhancing police performance including strengthening police accountability and oversight functions. During this same period, the creation of organizational mechanisms for reviewing and improving officer conduct has also increased.

One such mechanism for increasing accountability is civilian oversight of law enforcement. Sometimes referred to as citizen oversight, civilian review, external review and citizen review boards, this accountability tool utilizes citizens (non-sworn officers) to review police conduct. . . .

Common Goals of Civilian Oversight Programs

1. Improving public trust
2. Ensuring accessible complaint processes
3. Promoting thorough, fair investigations
4. Increasing transparency
5. Deterring police misconduct . . .

Contemporary Models of Civilian Oversight

While almost no two civilian oversight agencies in the US are identical, the literature offers several initial observations about characteristics of contemporary forms of civilian oversight. These include:

- *High Variability in Organizational Structure.* There is currently a tremendous amount of variation in the structure of different oversight agencies. Some agencies are operated almost completely by a small number of community volunteers while others have a large number of paid professional staff. Some oversight agencies have no operating budget while other agencies have multi-million-dollar budgets.

- *Wide Differences in Organizational Authority.* There is substantial variation in the role that oversight agencies play in relation to the intake of complaints, the relationship they have to the complaint investigation process, their level of access to police records, whether they can make recommendations as to findings and discipline, their ability to make policy recommendations and a long list of other characteristics.
- *Organizational "Hybrids" Are Common.* While early forms of oversight tended to operate as "citizen review boards," and focused on reviewing and commenting on completed internal affairs investigations, many contemporary oversight agencies combine different organizational forms and types of organizational authority in relatively complex ways.

Classifying Contemporary Models of Civilian Oversight

Over the years, there have been multiple attempts to classify approaches to civilian oversight of law enforcement. . . .

This report . . . groups oversight agencies into three categories based on the core agency functions: (1) Investigation-focused; (2) Review-focused; and (3) Auditor/monitor-focused.

Three Categories of Civilian Oversight Models

Investigation-Focused Model

The investigation-focused agency operates separately from the local police or sheriff's department. . . . These oversight agencies may either completely replace the police internal affairs function or they may conduct investigations that supplant, parallel or duplicate the work of internal affairs. . . .

The organizational structure of investigative agencies can vary significantly. In some cases, an investigative agency may be governed by a volunteer board and supported by a professional staff of investigators. In small jurisdictions, an investigative agency may be staffed by a single investigator or consultant.

The available literature on investigation-focused agencies identifies a common set of organizational functions, including:

- Serving as the intake point for public complaints against police officers
- Reviewing and classifying the nature of the complainants' allegations
- Conducting independent interviews of complainants, officers and witnesses

- Being staffed by non-police "civilian" investigators, although some agencies may employ retired or former police officers
- Being headed by a community board or commission that may hold hearings, issue subpoenas or make findings on investigations conducted by professional non-police investigative staff

Potential Strengths of the Investigation-Focused Model

An investigation-focused agency with appropriately trained staff can complete thorough and impartial investigations. . . . [W]here investigation-focused agencies are sufficiently resourced, have well-trained, competent staff and are granted sufficient access to department personnel and records, they may be able to improve the quality of internal investigations. . . .

A related potential strength of the investigation-focused model is its ability to increase public faith in the integrity of the investigations process, especially in the aftermath of significant public scandals involving the police. . . .

Potential Limitations of the Investigation-Focused Model

One potential limitation of the investigative model is the significant costs and resources necessary to conduct competent, timely investigations, including large staffing requirements and complex organizational issues that can accompany the implementation of a stand-alone investigative oversight agency. Full investigative agencies are more expensive than other models of oversight, largely due to the increased personnel costs that accompany the hiring of professional investigators.

Another potential weakness is that investigation-focused agencies tend to generate significant resistance from police unions and their allies. Unions have routinely argued that civilian investigators do not have the technical background or professional experience to conduct competent investigations into allegations of officer misconduct. Arguing that they will be biased against police officers, police unions have often opposed the implementation of full investigatory oversight agencies. . . .

Independent investigation-focused agencies in large cities have also been plagued with budgetary and personnel limitations that have resulted in untimely investigations. The New York City CCRB has often been criticized for lack of timely investigations as well as efforts taken by that agency to reduce its workload through re-allocation of resources.

Some researchers argue that while the community may have great confidence in full investigative models initially, community confidence can wane over time if these models are perceived as not leading to the reforms promised during implementation. For example, the public may expect that more citizen complaints will be sustained and stronger punishments imposed after full investigative oversight models are implemented. However, there is currently no systematic evidence to support this expectation, and it is currently unclear what impact full investigative models have on patterns in findings and discipline for police officers alleged to have engaged in misconduct. . . .

Review-Focused Model

Review-focused agencies examine the quality of internal investigations, primarily those conducted by internal affairs. Many review agencies take the form of volunteer review boards or commissions and are designed around the goal of providing community input into the internal investigations process. . . . As with investigation-focused agencies, review-focused agencies vary in their organizational structure and can perform a range of functions.

The available literature on review-focused agencies indicates they:

- Receive complaints from the community
- Review completed police investigations of externally generated complaints
- Make recommendations to the police executive on individual investigations
- Hear appeals
- Gather, review and report on public concerns.

Potential Strengths of the Review-Focused Model

Some researchers argue that review boards and commissions may be perceived by the public as more representative of the community than programs that are staffed by full-time professionals. As such, community members may be more likely to perceive the review-focused model as supporting and protecting community interests.

Beyond public perception, review-focused agencies have the benefit of allowing community representatives to bring an outsider's perspective to the complaint investigations process, which may help jurisdictions identify and correct deficiencies within individual complaint investigations. . . . With respect to the review of policy and officer conduct, review-focused agencies have the ability to identify deficiencies in policy or training as they apply to individual cases being reviewed. A diverse board will have the ability to provide different perspectives on police policy and training and make recommendations for change that could result in improved police–community relations.

Finally, review-focused agencies tend to be the least expensive form of oversight. They are often operated by volunteers and may have no standalone budget. As a result, this type of oversight is popular in smaller jurisdictions that have limited resources.

Potential Limitations of the Review-Focused Model

Review-focused agencies tend to have limited authority and, like investigation-focused agencies, typically focus on individual case investigations. As a result of such a reactive focus, their ability to promote large-scale systemic organizational change may be limited. Moreover, review-focused agencies may not have the authority to systemically evaluate police policies or procedures, make policy recommendations, or examine aggregate patterns in officer conduct.

Depending on the structure of the review agency, they may be less independent from the police than other oversight models. These types of oversight agencies may be more likely to report to the police chief, have a small or no stand-alone budget, have limited or no staff support and board members tend to be political or police chief appointees. Moreover, they may have to rely on the police or sheriff's department for meeting space, administrative support and training. Since review-focused agencies do not always have the power to conduct independent investigations, they are also more likely to rely on the police or sheriff's department for information.

Since review-focused agency board members are generally volunteers drawn from a range of professional backgrounds, they may have less expertise than paid professional oversight staff and have limited time to perform oversight functions. This aspect may reduce the efficiency of a jurisdiction's oversight function and lead to a shallow impact on the quality of internal investigations.

Auditor/Monitor-Focused Model

One of the newest forms of police oversight can be found in the auditor/monitor-focused model of oversight. Civilian oversight agencies that follow this model can also be referred to by several different names including police monitor or inspector general. This model of civilian oversight began to develop in the 1990s and generally emerged as a type of political compromise to satisfy police and community concerns about bias and professionalism. While local community and civil rights activists tended to argue in favor of citizen review boards or full investigative models, police unions tended to be strongly opposed to those models. As a result, the auditor/monitor-focused model emerged partly as a mechanism for bridging the disparate goals held by the different stakeholders to the complaint process.

While there can be variation in the organizational structure of this type of civilian oversight, auditor/monitor agencies tend to focus on promoting large-scale, systemic reform of police organizations. . . .

The available literature on auditor/monitor-focused agencies identifies a core set of functions which include:

- Ensuring a jurisdiction's processes for investigating allegations of misconduct are thorough, complete and fair
- Conducting evaluations of police policies, practices and training
- Participating in open internal affairs investigations
- Robust public reporting

Potential Strengths of the Auditor/Monitor-Focused Model

Since these agencies tend to focus on exploring patterns in complaints, auditor/monitor-focused models may have broader access to police and sheriff's department records, case files and electronic databases than review-focused agencies. While review-focused agencies tend to have only limited access to individual closed internal affairs files, auditor/

monitor-focused models tend to be granted more expansive access to police department records. Moreover, auditor/monitor-focused agencies tend to be (or become) policing experts, have larger budgets and may have more extensive training than might be found in volunteer-based oversight agencies.

It is possible that the auditor/monitor-focused model may be more effective at promoting long-term, systemic change in police organizations, in part because [it] can focus on broader trends and patterns in complaints and make public recommendations for how the police department can improve. . . . Auditor/monitor-focused agencies also have the ability to track whether police departments implement their recommendations and whether those changes have resulted in organizational improvements over time. . . .

Potential Limitations to the Auditor/Monitor-Focused Model

Local civil rights or community activists may oppose this type of civilian oversight because they may view this model's reliance on full-time, paid staff with skepticism. Some community members and civil rights activists may be left dissatisfied, since they may desire that discipline be imposed in specific cases of officer misconduct versus the auditor/monitor agencies' focus on aggregate patterns in complaints and other metrics within law enforcement agencies. In fact, the very nature of the auditor/monitor-focused model concept may put the police auditor/monitor at odds with community demands or expectations in high profile and controversial cases. . . .

Like other models of oversight, most auditor/monitor-focused agencies can only make recommendations and cannot compel law enforcement agencies to make changes. In situations where the law enforcement agency regularly declines to accept recommendations or continues to engage in activities contrary to the expectations of certain members of the public, the oversight agency may be perceived as ineffective. . . .

Considerations When Implementing or Reforming a Civilian Oversight Program

Over the past 30 years, local experimentation with different types of oversight models, to include hybridization of these different models, has resulted in a complex, heterogeneous organizational field. And while the data included in this report explores organizational variation across different oversight agencies, it does not answer two fundamental questions:

- Which forms of oversight are the most effective?
- Under what circumstances should a jurisdiction implement a review-focused model of oversight as opposed to an investigative or auditor/monitor-focused model? . . .

*Jurisdictions Should Focus on the "Best Fit" Rather Than the "Best Practices"
When Considering How to Structure Civilian Oversight*

A key lesson that can be learned from the history of oversight in the US is that there is not necessarily any "best practice" in the creation of a civilian oversight of law enforcement program. Rather, a jurisdiction should look for a "best-fit" model of oversight. Every jurisdiction has its own social, cultural and political issues, and every police agency has its own unique organizational history, traditions and sub-cultural characteristics. While some police agencies may be proficient at holding their officers to account with respect to certain types of conduct, other police agencies may struggle. Some large jurisdictions have ample financial resources to implement highly professionalized, organizationally complex forms of oversight while smaller jurisdictions may have far fewer resources with which to implement and sustain police oversight. . . .

Oversight Should Employ the "Least Force" Necessary to Accomplish Its Goals

Even though law enforcement resistance to the concept of police oversight has diminished over time, it can still be argued that "the least intrusive means of oversight" necessary to achieve police accountability is the best means of approaching the oversight function in the long term. Just as the police are expected to only use that amount of force that is proportionate, necessary, and reasonable to accomplish their task, so it can be argued that jurisdictions creating or reforming an oversight function should similarly accomplish the feat of ensuring police accountability. In other words, a jurisdiction seeking to create or update an oversight function should choose the least intrusive model of oversight necessary to accomplish the task. . . . Each jurisdiction must evaluate its own police agency; its culture, its leadership, its overall current capacity to police itself and its future potential in that regard before choosing the most appropriate form of oversight that will have the highest likelihood of success over time. . . .

NOTES AND QUESTIONS

1. *Why?* To figure out what kind of community oversight is appropriate, is it necessary to determine what community oversight is for? You might think community oversight is important because of the intrinsic value of community participation in governing the police. Or you might think community oversight is necessary because internal disciplinary mechanisms in police departments do a poor job of fairly, thoroughly, and transparently holding officers to account for legal and policy violations. Might those two goals suggest different structures?

2. *What?* Several experts on policing have favored the auditor model based on the belief that it can serve to assess the need for policy and administrative changes in a police department and therefore achieve significant reform. Is an inspector general or auditor really a form of *community* oversight, though, or is it just a form of *external* review? Is that a feature or a bug? What about a board made up only of former law enforcement officers (something some communities call civilian review)? What about civilian police commissions (elected or appointed by mayors)

that govern chief selection and policy development in some big cities, including Los Angeles, Chicago, and Detroit. Is that civilian review or just governance?

3. *Oversight and its alternatives.* Communities that are heavily affected by policing increasingly want to participate in policymaking and priority-setting as well as in complaint investigations. Are these models adequate to address their concerns? If not, what might a mechanism for more substantial citizen participation in governing the police look like? Who should get to participate? What should they get to do? If a group of appointed unelected citizens gets special power to weigh in on policing, is that antidemocratic or extrademocratic? For two views on designing institutions that move beyond civilian review, see K. Sabeel Rahman & Jocelyn Simonson, *The Institutional Design of Community Control*, 108 Calif. L. Rev. 679 (2020), and Maria Ponomarenko, *Rethinking Police Rulemaking*, 114 Nw. U. L. Rev. 1 (2019).

4. *Who?* One challenge in building civilian oversight boards is determining who should be on them. Overwhelmingly, boards have members appointed by a city's mayor or city council (although Detroit elects its members). Many ordinances require members with specific skills, such as experience in criminal law, investigation, mediation, community outreach, or data analysis. Does this make civilian oversight more like a layer of bureaucratic review? Other ordinances require that some members be residents of low-income housing or historically disadvantaged communities. Because the boards are small, no board can incorporate representatives from all of the groups in a jurisdiction who have disproportionate contact with the police or complaints about how they are treated by officers. Moreover, some of the groups most affected by policing—such as youth, people with mental disabilities, people experiencing homelessness, and immigrants without documentation—are highly unlikely to be asked to serve. Is that a problem or just an inevitability? Does it matter that some communities will be represented and others will not? Are members really *representative* at all?

5. *Least intrusive?* NACOLE endorses the idea that communities should adopt the "least intrusive" structure that is "necessary," just as officers should minimize their use of force. Is the analogy between oversight and the use of force really apt? Is oversight harmful to its subjects the way force is because boards often alienate officers and command staff? What exactly is *intrusive?* Transparency? Community engagement? And *necessary* to do what? What about the strategy of starting weak and then strengthening? Could ineffectual boards reduce community confidence in the police (and the government)?

6. *How?* Although several major cities have had review boards since the 1960s, civilian oversight boards have expanded notably in the twenty-first century. Communities are also now pushing for more powerful oversight, including boards with subpoena power, full access to the department's records and files, the power to impose rather than recommend discipline or policy, and even a role in hiring and firing the police chief. Following a charter amendment in 2017, for example, Honolulu expanded its police commission's powers to include not only investigating complaints independently, subpoenaing records and witnesses, imposing discipline, and hearing appeals, but also removing the police chief. Honolulu, Haw., Revised Charter of the City and County of Honolulu 1973 §6-1603 (2017). As boards get more powerful, do they raise additional concerns about whether they are representative of the community, whether they are fair to officers, and whether they have sufficient experience and expertise? Is there any power you think civilian oversight boards should *not* have?

7. *How well?* How should we measure the success of a civilian oversight structure? Timely investigations carried out? Changes in the proportion of sustained complaints? The number of complaints? Reductions in the use of force? Reductions in crime? Community sentiment? Something else?

8. *Procedural justice and community oversight.* Would you want an untrained skeptic of your industry with no experience in investigations or expertise in your field deciding whether you should be disciplined for how you do your job? If not, is policing different in some respect? If the goal is to change police conduct, should the architects of civilian oversight mechanisms consider that police officers, like other people, will most likely respond better to discipline and policy changes that they believe give them a voice, treat them fairly, and are impartial? Can you envision an oversight board that earns the trust of both the public and the police?

9. *Legal constraints on civilian oversight.* Collective bargaining agreements and state law often constrain civilian review. For example, the Department of Justice's consent decree with the Baltimore Police Department recommended that civilians serve on the police trial boards that review officer misconduct, see Consent Decree, United States v. Baltimore Police Dept., No. JKB-17-99 (D. Md. approved Apr. 7, 2017), but the officers' collective bargaining agreement barred civilian participation in discipline, see Memorandum of Understanding between Baltimore City Police Dept. and the Baltimore City Lodge No. 3 Fraternal Order of Police, Inc. Unit 1, at 19 (2004). In New York City, the Civilian Complaint Review Board may bring administrative charges against New York Police Department officers, but under the state's Civil Service Law §75(4), those charges must be served within 18 months of the alleged violation, which can stymie some prosecutions. See N.Y. Civ. Serv. Law §75(4). Most states limit or prohibit access to police disciplinary records, which can hinder boards in their efforts to investigate, recommend discipline and policy changes, or achieve transparency. Should these state laws or bargaining agreements be revised *because* they inhibit community review? Or should community oversight operate within the boundaries of whatever laws and rules constrain the systems in which they attempt to intervene?

10. *Weak boards or none at all?* Although a few communities view their oversight boards as successful, most civilian review boards fail to generate community trust and instead are widely perceived as ineffectual. Communities commonly complain that boards fail to address complaints in a timely manner, that they leave many complaints uninvestigated, or that they merely affirm departmental findings. Perhaps this is not surprising: Civilian oversight boards are often created in response to a crisis in policing, and the political will to form a board does not always translate into adequate power, staffing, funding, and independence, especially over time. See Stephen Clarke, *Arrested Oversight: A Comparative Analysis and Case Study of How Civilian Oversight of the Police Should Function and How It Fails*, 43 Colum. J. L. & Soc. Probs. 1 (2009). Whatever the reasons, given that most efforts at building effective civilian oversight fail, why do so many communities continue to clamor to create new boards? Why do advocacy groups, such as Campaign Zero, the Movement for Black Lives, and the American Civil Liberties Union, as well as scholars (see, e.g., Joshua Kleinfeld et al., *White Paper of Democratic Criminal Justice*, 111 Nw. U. L. Rev. 1693, 1700 (2017)), continue to insist that civilian oversight structures are essential for police accountability? Is the hope that if civilian oversight is created in just the right way, it will succeed? Is weak civilian oversight better than none at all? Are you sure?

E. Decertification

Police misconduct can undermine community trust in law enforcement, but it does so far more when it is predictable, such as when an agency allows an officer to commit misconduct repeatedly or when a police officer who commits misconduct is let go by one agency, only to be hired by another. Civilian review is intended as a partial solution to the first problem. Decertification is often promoted as a solution to the second. The first decertification statute was passed by New Mexico in 1960. Here are two more recent examples.

1. Georgia

GA. CODE ANN. §35-8-7.1

§35-8-7.1. Authority of council to refuse to grant certificate or to discipline officer; restoration and reissuance of certificates

(a) The council shall have authority to refuse to grant a certificate to an applicant or to discipline a council certified officer . . . upon a determination by the council that the applicant, [or] . . . officer has:

> **(1)** Failed to demonstrate the qualifications or standards for a certificate provided in this chapter or in the rules and regulations of the council . . . ;

> **(2)** Knowingly made misleading, deceptive, untrue, or fraudulent representations in the practice of being an officer or in any document connected therewith or practiced fraud or deceit or intentionally made any false statement in obtaining a certificate to practice as an officer;

> **(3)** Been convicted of a felony in the courts of this state or any other state, territory, country, or of the United States. . . . ;

> **(4)** Committed a crime involving moral turpitude, without regard to conviction. The conviction of a crime involving moral turpitude shall be conclusive of the commission of such crime. . . . ;

> **(6)** Engaged in any unprofessional, unethical, deceptive, or deleterious conduct or practice harmful to the public; such conduct or practice need not have resulted in actual injury to any person. As used in this paragraph, the term "unprofessional conduct" shall include any departure from, or failure to conform to, the minimal standards of acceptable and prevailing practice of an officer;

> **(7)** Violated or attempted to violate a law, rule, or regulation of this state, any other state, the council, the United States, or any other lawful authority without regard to whether the violation is criminally punishable, so long as such law, rule, or regulation relates to or in part regulates the practice of an officer;

> **(8)** Committed any act or omission which is indicative of bad moral character or untrustworthiness;

> **(9)** Been adjudged mentally incompetent by a court of competent jurisdiction, within or outside this state;

> **(10)** Become unable to perform as an officer with reasonable skill and safety to citizens by reason of illness or use of alcohol, drugs, narcotics, chemicals, or any other type of material or as a result of any mental or physical condition; or

(11) Been suspended or discharged by the officer's employing law enforcement unit for disciplinary reasons.

(b)(1) When the council finds that any person is unqualified to be granted a certificate or finds that any person should be disciplined pursuant to subsection (a) of this Code section, the council may take any one or more of the following actions:

> **(A)** Refuse to grant a certificate to an applicant;
>
> **(B)** Administer a public or private reprimand, provided that a private reprimand shall not be disclosed to any person except the officer;
>
> **(C)** Suspend any certificate for a definite period;
>
> **(D)** Limit or restrict any certificate;
>
> **(E)** Revoke any certificate; or
>
> **(F)** Condition the penalty, or withhold formal disposition, upon the officer's completing such care, counseling, or treatment, as directed by the council. . . .

(c) In its discretion, the council may restore and reissue a certificate issued under this chapter or any antecedent law to an officer and, as a condition thereof, may impose any disciplinary or corrective measure provided in this chapter. . . .

GA. CODE ANN. §35-8-7.2

§35-8-7.2. Proceedings to issue certificate or discipline peace officer

(a) Except as otherwise provided in subsection (b) of this Code section, proceedings of the council in the exercise of its authority to issue any certificate or discipline any peace officer under the terms of this chapter shall be conducted in accordance with Chapter 13 of Title 50, the "Georgia Administrative Procedure Act." In all such proceedings the council shall have authority to compel the attendance of witnesses and the production of any book, writing, or document upon the issuance of a subpoena therefor. In any hearing in which the fitness of a peace officer or applicant is in question, the council may exclude all persons from its deliberation of the appropriate action and may, when it deems necessary, speak to the peace officer or applicant in private. All final determinations, findings, and conclusions of the council under this chapter are final and conclusive decisions of the matters involved.

(b) Proceedings for review of a final decision of the council shall be instituted by filing a petition within 30 days after the service of the final decision of the council or, if a rehearing is requested, within 30 days after the decision thereon. The petition shall be filed in the superior court of the county of residence of the petitioner.

2. Alabama

ALA. CODE 1975 §36-21-52

§36-21-52. Revocation of certification or authority of law enforcement officer upon conviction of felony.

(a) The certification or authority of any law enforcement officer certified by the Alabama Peace Officers' Standards and Training Commission . . . shall be revoked by the commission when a law enforcement officer is convicted of a felony. If the conviction is reversed or a new trial granted, the certification or authority of the law enforcement officer shall be restored.

(b) Any law enforcement officer whose certification or authority is revoked pursuant to this section may request a hearing before the commission concerning the revocation. The only issue at the hearing shall be whether the revocation was based on a felony conviction of the officer.

NOTES AND QUESTIONS

1. *What?* Although local police officers are hired and paid by local governments, they depend on the state to provide them with their power. In 45 states, including Georgia and Alabama, the same agency that certifies an officer can also deprive the officer of his state certification. Once a state decertifies an officer, no agency may decide that the officer is good enough for government work. In this way, decertification is a state intrusion into local affairs.

2. *Why?* Officers who are fired for misconduct by one agency sometimes wander to another town and get hired there. In the largest study to date, Ben Grunwald and John Rappaport looked at the employment records of all 98,000 full-time officers in Florida over a 30-year period. They found that in any given year, around 1,100 officers who had been previously fired were working for other Florida agencies. These officers represented nearly 3 percent of officers employed in Florida. Moreover, wandering officers may be more prone to misconduct than unfired peers: They were more likely to be fired (again) than other officers, and they received more state licensing board complaints. See Ben Grunwald & John Rappaport, *The Wandering Officer*, 129 Yale L.J. 1676, 1687 (2020). Why do agencies hire officers who have resigned under a cloud or been fired by agencies? There are three basic reasons: They do not know, they do not care, or they have limited alternatives. Decertification solves the first two. What does it do with the third?

3. *When?* Compare the extent of decertifiable conduct in the two states. Many states take Alabama's approach, limiting decertification to convictions. In those states, decertification depends on prosecutors who are willing and able to pursue criminal charges against officers, a matter discussed in Chapter 14. Other states allow a broader range of decertifiable conduct, although few as broad as Georgia does. These states use administrative hearings to determine whether an officer is decertifiable. A few additional states decertify based solely on an officer's termination or resignation in lieu of termination from an agency. Roger Goldman, *A Model Decertification Law*, 32 St. Louis U. Pub. L. Rev. 147, 150–153 (2012) (describing approaches). Given the difference between the two laws above, it might not surprise you that Georgia decertifies wildly more officers than Alabama does: In a study of all state decertifications for 2015, Georgia represented 30 percent of the country's total; Alabama 1 percent. See Matthew J. Hickman, *POST Agency Certification Practices, 2015* (2016).

4. *How often?* Although Alabama's and Georgia's results seem predictable given the statutes, the scope of a state's decertification law does not always correlate strongly with how many officers a state decertifies. Of the 45 states that permit decertification, just two, Georgia and Florida, account for more than half of the officers decertified in most years. See, e.g., Loren T. Atherley & Matthew J. Hickman, *Officer Decertification and the National Decertification Index*, 16 Police Q. 420, 425 (2013). Other states with seemingly broad decertification almost never use it. One reason

is that states never learn about some decertifiable conduct. Georgia's POST has issued a regulation requiring that agencies notify the state about suspensions of more than 30 days, disciplinary discharges, and resignations in lieu of termination. See Rules of Georgia Peace Officer Standards and Training Council §464-3-.06. Fewer than half of states require agencies to report conduct that could lead to decertification, and even where such requirements exist, they are sometimes unenforced. Why else might a state not decertify an officer who has committed decertifiable conduct?

5. *Carpetbaggers.* State decertifications only prevent an officer from being hired in the state in which he has been decertified. Some officers wander beyond state boundaries. What can be done about them? The National Decertification Index (NDI) is a repository of information about officers who have been decertified nationally. Agencies can consult the NDI to determine whether an officer they are considering hiring has been decertified in another state. However, the NDI is a voluntary enterprise. Some states contribute regularly, but others do not participate at all or are incomplete or untimely in reporting decertifications. Georgia, for example, the most active decertifier, does not report its activities to the NDI. Even if states do contribute, remember that they have dramatically different standards for decertification, and some are far more consistent about the practice than others. Given all these qualifications, what does an entry in the NDI mean? Should an agency ever hire an officer who has been decertified in another state? Why or why not? What legal changes might lead to a more effective national tool?

6. *Recertification.* Should officers who have been decertified ever be permitted to be recertified? What should the conditions be? For comparison, some states permit disbarred attorneys to be readmitted, but overwhelmingly they make readmission a long and difficult process. See G.M. Filisko, *Disbarred Lawyers Who Seek Reinstatement Have a Rough Road to Redemption*, ABA J. (Aug. 1, 2013). Does a recertification process recognize the human capacity for personal growth? Or does it undermine the public's faith in law enforcement?

7. *Alternatives to decertification.* You could argue that decertification does more than prevent wandering. It also promotes the legitimacy of policing and maintains professional standards. If we put those goals aside, are there other ways to prevent wandering officers? If departments hire officers with histories of misconduct because they have inadequate information or because they perceive the benefits of doing so outweigh the costs, can you imagine legal interventions that would help address those issues? What are the advantages and disadvantages of decertification over other reforms you think are important?

F. Body-Worn Cameras

Perhaps no intervention has been more enthusiastically advocated in recent years as a solution to problems in policing than body-worn cameras (BWCs), small video and audio recording devices mounted to officers' eyeglasses or uniforms that capture police interactions with the public. Activists have demanded them, a few states have required them, the federal government has funded them, and departments have adopted them in droves. Around half of departments now use them. From an accountability perspective, however, BWCs might not be all they are cracked up to be.

Many states do not yet have statutes on police body cameras. Those that do take a range of approaches to the subject. Below are two examples. The statutes are detailed. As you read, consider whether and how the statutes deal with the following persistent questions:

- Should police officers be required to wear cameras?
- If they do, when should officers record?
- How should BWC recordings be used within an agency?
- Under what circumstances should BWC recordings be accessible to officers, supervisors, and those outside the agency?
- How long should recordings be kept?

1.   New Hampshire

N.H. REV. STAT. ANN. §105-D:2 USE OF BODY-WORN CAMERAS.

I. This chapter shall apply to any law enforcement agency that elects to equip its law enforcement officers with body-worn cameras. All BWCs shall be operated in a manner consistent with the provisions of this chapter. Every law enforcement agency that elects to equip its officers with BWCs shall adopt policies and procedures relating to the use of BWCs and the retention and destruction of data consistent with this chapter. . . .

III. Officers who are assigned BWCs shall successfully complete an agency-approved training program to ensure proper use and operations.

IV. Officers shall only use BWCs while in uniform.

V. Officers shall activate the video and audio components of BWCs and start recording upon arrival on scene of a call for service or when engaged in any law enforcement-related encounter or activity, or, if so required by local policy, upon activation of lights and siren; provided, however, that in those cases set forth in subparagraphs VII(d) and (e), and paragraph IX in which an individual has a right not to be recorded, officers shall inform an individual of this option. If a citizen then declines to be recorded, the officer shall deactivate the audio and video functions. The officer shall document the reason why the camera was not activated in the associated police report. If exigent circumstances exist which prevent the BWC from being activated as set forth above, the device must be turned on as soon as practicable.

VI. Recordings shall be specific to an incident. Officers shall not indiscriminately record entire duties or patrols.

VII. A BWC shall not be used to record any of the following:

(a) Communications with other police personnel except to the extent such communications are incidental to a permissible recording.

(b) Encounters with police personnel or individuals whom the officer knows are acting in an undercover capacity or as confidential informants respectively, unless expressly directed to be included as part of the investigation.

(c) Intimate searches, when otherwise permitted by the agency's strip-and-body-cavity search policy.

(**d**) An interview with a crime victim unless his or her express consent has been obtained before the recording is made. . . .

(**e**) Interactions with a person seeking to report a crime anonymously. In such an instance, the law enforcement officer shall, as soon as practicable, ask the person seeking to remain anonymous if the person wants the officer to use the officer's BWC. If the person responds negatively, the law enforcement officer shall deactivate the audio and video functions.

(**f**) While on the grounds of any public, private, or parochial elementary or secondary school, except when responding to an imminent threat to life or health or a call for service.

(**g**) When on break or otherwise engaged in personal activities.

(**h**) In any instance when it is believed that an explosive device may be present and electrostatic interference from the BWC may trigger the device.

VIII. Officers shall inform an individual that he or she is being recorded as soon as practicable. When notification is not made, the recording officer shall note the reason for non-notification within the associated report.

IX. In locations where an individual has a reasonable expectation of privacy, such as a residence, a restroom, or a locker room, a citizen may decline to be recorded unless the recording is being made while executing an arrest warrant, or a warrant issued by a court, or the officer is in the location pursuant to a judicially-recognized exception to the warrant requirement. Officers shall inform an individual of this option. If a citizen then declines to be recorded, the officer shall deactivate the audio and video functions, and any images shall, as soon as practicable, be permanently distorted or obscured. The officer shall document the reason why the camera was not activated in the associated police report.

X. Once activated, the BWC shall remain activated until the event is completed in order to ensure the integrity of the recording unless otherwise provided in this section.

XI. If an officer fails to activate the BWC, fails to record the entire contact, interrupts the recording, or if the BWC malfunctions, the officer shall document why a recording was not made, was interrupted, or was terminated as part of the associated police report.

XII. Except as authorized in this section, no person, including without limitation officers and their supervisors, shall edit, alter, erase, delete, duplicate, copy, subject to automated analysis or analytics of any kind, including but not limited to facial recognition technology, share, display, or otherwise distribute in any manner any BWC recordings or portions thereof. This paragraph shall not apply to the sharing of a still image captured by the BWC to help identify individuals or vehicles suspected of being involved in a crime.

XIII. Recorded images and sound made from an agency-issued BWC shall be for law enforcement purposes only. All access to this data shall be audited to ensure that authorized users only are accessing the data for law enforcement purposes only. All access to BWC data shall be authorized by the head of the law enforcement agency and only for the purposes set forth in this chapter.

XIV. If an officer is suspected of wrongdoing or involved in an officer-involved shooting or other use of deadly force, the agency may limit or restrict an officer from viewing the video file.

XV. All recordings shall be securely stored no later than the end of each shift, or as soon thereafter as is reasonably practicable. . . . Recordings shall not be divulged or used by a law enforcement agency for any commercial or other non-law enforcement purpose. Where a law enforcement agency authorizes a third party to act as its agent in storing recordings, the agent shall not independently access, view or alter any recording, except to delete videos as required by law or agency retention policies. Neither the agency nor its agent shall subject any recording to analysis or analytics of any kind, including without limitation facial recognition technology and data mining.

XVI. Recordings made by a BWC shall be permanently destroyed by overwriting or otherwise no sooner than 30 days and no longer than 180 days from the date the images were recorded, except that such recording shall be retained by the law enforcement agency that employs the officer whose BWC made the recording, or an authorized agent thereof, for a minimum of 3 years if:

> **(a)** The recording captures images involving any of the following:
>
>> **(1)** Any action by a law enforcement officer that involves the use of deadly force or deadly restraint.
>>
>> **(2)** The discharge of a firearm, unless for the destruction of an animal.
>>
>> **(3)** Death or serious bodily injury
>>
>> **(4)** An encounter about which a complaint has been filed with the police department within 30 days after the encounter.
>
> **(b)** The recording is being retained by the law enforcement agency as evidence in a civil or criminal case or as part of an internal affairs investigation or as part of an employee disciplinary investigation. . . .

§91-A:1 Preamble.

Openness in the conduct of public business is essential to a democratic society. The purpose of this chapter is to ensure both the greatest possible public access to the actions, discussions and records of all public bodies, and their accountability to the people.

§91-A:4 Minutes and Records Available for Public Inspection.

I. Every citizen . . . has the right to inspect all governmental records in the possession, custody, or control of such public bodies or agencies . . . and to copy and make memoranda or abstracts of the records or minutes so inspected, except as otherwise prohibited by statute or RSA 91-A:5. . . .

V. In the same manner as set forth in RSA 91-A:4, IV, any public body or agency which maintains governmental records in electronic format may, in lieu of providing original records, copy governmental records requested to electronic media using standard or common file formats in a manner that does not reveal information which is confidential under this chapter or any other law. If copying to electronic media is not reasonably practicable, or if the person or entity requesting access requests a different method, the public body or agency may provide a printout of governmental records requested, or may use any other means reasonably calculated to comply with the request in light of the purpose of this chapter as expressed in RSA 91-A:1. Access to work papers, personnel data, and other confidential information under RSA 91-A:5, IV shall not be provided. . . .

§91-A:5 Exemptions.

The following governmental records are exempted from the provisions of this chapter: . . .

X. Video and audio recordings made by a law enforcement officer using a body-worn camera pursuant to RSA 105-D except where such recordings depict any of the following:

> **(a)** Any restraint or use of force by a law enforcement officer; provided, however, that this exemption shall not include those portions of recordings which constitute an invasion of privacy of any person or which are otherwise exempt from disclosure.
>
> **(b)** The discharge of a firearm, provided that this exemption shall not include those portions of recordings which constitute an invasion of privacy of any person or which are otherwise exempt from disclosure.
>
> **(c)** An encounter that results in an arrest for a felony-level offense, provided, however, that this exemption shall not apply to recordings or portions thereof that constitute an invasion of privacy or which are otherwise exempt from disclosure. . . .

2. Washington

WASH. REV. CODE §10.109.010 POLICIES

(1) A law enforcement or corrections agency that deploys body worn cameras must establish policies regarding the use of the cameras. The policies must, at a minimum, address:

> **(a)** When a body worn camera must be activated and deactivated, and when a law enforcement or corrections officer has the discretion to activate and deactivate the body worn camera;
>
> **(b)** How a law enforcement or corrections officer is to respond to circumstances when it would be reasonably anticipated that a person may be unwilling or less willing to communicate with an officer who is recording the communication with a body worn camera;
>
> **(c)** How a law enforcement or corrections officer will document when and why a body worn camera was deactivated prior to the conclusion of an interaction with a member of the public while conducting official law enforcement or corrections business;
>
> **(d)** How, and under what circumstances, a law enforcement or corrections officer is to inform a member of the public that he or she is being recorded, including in situations where the person is a non-English speaker or has limited English proficiency, or where the person is deaf or hard of hearing;
>
> **(e)** How officers are to be trained on body worn camera usage and how frequently the training is to be reviewed or renewed; and
>
> **(f)** Security rules to protect data collected and stored from body worn cameras. . . .

§10.109.020 Ordinance or resolution—Community involvement process.

For a city or town that is not deploying body worn cameras on June 9, 2016, a legislative authority of a city or town is strongly encouraged to adopt an ordinance or resolution authorizing the use of body worn cameras prior to their use by law enforcement or a corrections agency. Any ordinance or resolution authorizing the use of body worn cameras should identify a community involvement process for providing input into the development of operational policies governing the use of body worn cameras.

§42.56.240 Investigative, law enforcement, and crime victims.

The following investigative, law enforcement, and crime victim information is exempt from public inspection and copying under this chapter: . . .

(14) Body worn camera recordings to the extent nondisclosure is essential for the protection of any person's right to privacy . . . including, but not limited to, the circumstances enumerated in (a) of this subsection. A law enforcement or corrections agency shall not disclose a body worn camera recording to the extent the recording is exempt under this subsection.

> **(a)** Disclosure of a body worn camera recording is presumed to be highly offensive to a reasonable person under RCW 42.56.050 to the extent it depicts:
>
> > **(i)(A)** Any areas of a medical facility, counseling, or therapeutic program office . . .
> >
> > **(ii)** The interior of a place of residence where a person has a reasonable expectation of privacy;
> >
> > **(iii)** An intimate image;
> >
> > **(iv)** A minor;
> >
> > **(v)** The body of a deceased person;
> >
> > **(vi)** The identity of or communications from a victim or witness of an incident involving domestic violence . . . or sexual assault . . .; or
> >
> > **(vii)** The identifiable location information of a community-based domestic violence program. . . .
>
> **(b)** The presumptions set out in (a) of this subsection may be rebutted by specific evidence in individual cases. . . .
>
> **(d)** A request for body worn camera recordings must:
>
> > **(i)** Specifically identify a name of a person or persons involved in the incident;
> >
> > **(ii)** Provide the incident or case number;
> >
> > **(iii)** Provide the date, time, and location of the incident or incidents; or
> >
> > **(iv)** Identify a law enforcement or corrections officer involved in the incident or incidents.
>
> **(e)(i)** A person directly involved in an incident recorded by the requested body worn camera recording, an attorney representing a person directly involved in an incident recorded by the requested body worn camera recording, a person or his or her attorney who requests a body worn camera recording relevant to

a criminal case involving that person . . . has the right to obtain the body worn camera recording, subject to any exemption under this chapter or any applicable law. In addition, an attorney who represents a person regarding a potential or existing civil cause of action involving the denial of civil rights under the federal or state Constitution, or a violation of a United States Department of Justice settlement agreement, has the right to obtain the body worn camera recording if relevant to the cause of action, subject to any exemption under this chapter or any applicable law. . . .

(j) A law enforcement or corrections agency must retain body worn camera recordings for at least sixty days and thereafter may destroy the records in accordance with the applicable records retention schedule; . . .

NOTES AND QUESTIONS

1. *Describe the statutes.* What does each state's law do? How would you characterize each state's response to BWCs?

2. *Form of regulation.* Look at how each law regulates. Washington requires public input and leaves decision making largely in local hands. New Hampshire's law is more prescriptive. What are the advantages and disadvantages of each approach? In thinking about these alternatives, consider this: There are fewer than 3,000 officers in New Hampshire in just over 200 agencies. Fewer than a dozen of those departments have BWCs. By contrast, Washington is many times the size of New Hampshire. Although it has one of the lowest officer-to-citizen ratios in the country, it still has more than 11,000 officers in more than 250 agencies, and more of those agencies have cameras.

3. *The limits of law.* Remember that just because an agency requires an officer to record does not mean that a recording will happen. Research suggests that officers violate rules and laws governing BWC use more frequently than other rules. Why might that be? What should be done about it?

4. *What should officers record?* New Hampshire limits recording to specific incidents. This means that officers will not capture many casual encounters. So when a department receives complaints that an officer was disrespectful to racial minorities, it will not be able to use BWCs to monitor officer conduct or reassure the public. Other states and agencies require officers to record more (for example, to turn on cameras whenever they are on duty) or less (for example, to record only high-risk activities such as warrant execution). Can you see why policymakers might favor one approach over others? Is there a way to avoid trading off comprehensiveness and consistency against privacy?

5. *Access to recordings.* Imagine Samir Singh, an Indian-American resident of New Hampshire, is arrested for assault on a law enforcement officer after he is pulled over in a traffic stop. He filed a complaint with the department alleging that the arresting officer fabricated the charge to cover up a racially motivated traffic stop. He wants access to the BWC footage showing the stop. Is he entitled to it? May the officer review it before being interviewed by his internal affairs unit about the stop? Would the agency's internal affairs unit be allowed to use it in evaluating the complaint? May the local paper request and post on its website a copy of the video? Could the chief show the recording in a press conference in response to public concern? What if the same incident happened in Washington?

6. *Recordings and complaints against officers.* Should officers be allowed to review BWC recordings of an event before they write reports or respond to questions that could subject them to discipline? Only a few states have legislated on the issue. They largely either give agencies discretion or require that agencies allow officers access to the footage. See, e.g., Fla. Stat. §943.1718(2)(d). When states give agencies discretion, most agencies allow officers access to recordings they have made. See Shelley S. Hyland, Bureau of Justice Statistics, U.S. Dept. of Justice, *Body-Worn Cameras in Law Enforcement Agencies, 2016* 7 (2018). What are the implications of such review? Would you want to look at available video if you were asked questions about your conduct? Would you be more likely to distrust the testimony of an officer permitted to do so? Should the nature of the incident matter? See Seth W. Stoughton, *Police Body-Worn Cameras*, 96 N.C. L. Rev. 1363, 1418–1419 (2018) (arguing that prereport review should not be permitted in use-of-force incidents that turn on the reasonableness of the officer's perceptions and actions in response to those perceptions).

7. *Public access.* All states have laws that facilitate some public access to government records. Nearly half of states also specify how BWC data should be treated under these laws. Some states, including Connecticut, Nevada, North Dakota, Oklahoma, and Texas, treat the data as public records but set caveats on public release. Others, including Florida, Georgia, Illinois, Oregon, and South Carolina, exclude body-worn camera footage from open record requests, but authorize access to specific individuals under some circumstances. In other states, the question has wound up in court. See, e.g., Patrolmen's Benevolent Association of City of New York v. De Blasio, 101 N.Y.S.3d 280 (N.Y. App. Div. 2019) (concluding that BWC footage is not a "personnel record" under NY §50-a and could be publicly released). Should there be a public right of access to BWC footage? For what purposes? What do you think of a rule that disallows direct public access but allows officers or citizens who appear in a video to access the footage and release it to the public? One complication for public access is that gathering, redacting appropriately, and providing footage is burdensome for departments. Should that be a consideration in deciding what the public has a right to see?

8. *States or agencies?* Around half of states have laws specifically addressing BWCs, including a few states that require agencies to adopt them. Around half of police departments have adopted cameras, including almost all major city departments. Who should set what rules for BWC use? States can drive policymaking and impose consistent standards, but they have trouble keeping up with technology and research. States may also find it difficult to account for resource inequality among agencies in formulating rules. On the other hand, local policies cannot force data standards for BWCs, they may be more deferential to officers, and not all will engage in policymaking without a state push: By last count, one in seven departments that has adopted BWCs has no formal policy regarding their use. See Shelley S. Hyland, Bureau of Justice Statistics, U.S. Dept. of Justice, *Body-Worn Cameras in Law Enforcement Agencies, 2016* 5 (2018).

9. *Why?* Commentators disagree on the primary purpose of recording officer encounters with the public. Communities often hope videos will encourage lawful and respectful policing, promote accountability for misconduct, and increase community trust. By contrast, law enforcement experts often claim they can resolve citizen complaints and lawsuits, generate evidence in criminal cases, and provide material for training. See, e.g., Brett Chapman, *Body-Worn Cameras: What the Evidence Tells Us*, 280 Nat'l Inst. Justice J. 48, 49–50 (2019). Seth Stoughton suggests that BWCs

have three kinds of advantages: symbolic benefits—promoting trust by showing a commitment to openness; behavioral benefits—reducing rule violations, incivilities, and violence; and informational benefits—by producing evidence about police–citizen interactions. Seth W. Stoughton, *Police Body-Worn Cameras*, 96 N.C. L. Rev. 1363, 1378–1393 (2018). What do you think BWCs should be expected to do?

10. *How?* Step back for a minute and think about *how* BWCs achieve these goals. For example, for BWCs to reduce misconduct, they likely have to deter it. To deter conduct, they need to change the perceived cost of engaging in that conduct. To do that, officers would have to believe that the information on camera would be used to impose consequences on them, perhaps through administrative discipline, evidentiary exclusion, or civil damages actions. Does that mean that for BWCs to work, institutional or legal remedies already have to be effective at addressing known misconduct? What are the obstacles to *that?* Perhaps BWCs could instead induce legal compliance by facilitating informal consequences for committing misconduct? How might that work? What are the mechanisms by which BWCs might build community trust?

11. *Do they work?* Researchers who study the effectiveness of BWCs have mostly focused on whether BWCs reduce force, reduce civilian complaints, or improve community relations. The first major study took place in 2012 in Rialto, California, after a series of scandals plagued the police department. Researchers randomly assigned cameras to some officers and found that, over the course of a year, uses of force and citizen complaints declined dramatically among those assigned cameras compared to their unrecorded peers. See Barak Ariel et al., *The Effect of Police Body-Worn Cameras on Use of Force and Citizens' Complaints Against the Police: A Randomized Controlled Trial*, 31 J. Quantitative Criminology 509 (2015). The Rialto study was small, involving only 54 officers, but it was widely cited, including by Axon, the most prominent company selling BWCs to police departments, and by Judge Scheindlin in imposing a pilot program in New York City. See Floyd v. City of New York, 959 F. Supp. 2d 668, 686 (S.D.N.Y. 2013). Its findings helped spur enthusiasm for cameras and their consequent spread. Dozens of studies have followed since but with far more variable results. At this point, it is fair to say that the evidence that BWCs change officer behavior is, at best, "modest and mixed." Cynthia Lum et al., *Research on Body-Worn Cameras: What We Know, What We Need to Know*, 18 Criminology & Pub. Pol'y 93, 111 (2019). Nor do studies suggest that BWCs significantly improve police–community relations. See *id.* at 110.

Cameras do better at resolving individual disputes, but even there, they have not had the results that advocates expected. Unlike dash cams, which take a third-party view of interactions, BWCs take the first-person perspective of the officer. Initial research suggests that when viewers watch BWC footage and take the view of the officer, they perceive the officer's actions to be less intentional and less worthy of punishment than those who see the same incident from other perspectives. See Kristyn A. Jones et al., *Look There! The Effect of Perspective, Attention, and Instructions on How People Understand Recorded Police Encounters*, 37 Behav. Sci. & L. 711 (2019); Broderick L. Turner et al., *Body Camera Footage Leads to Lower Judgments of Intent Than Dash Camera Footage*, 116 Proc. Nat'l Acad. Sci. U.S. 1201 (2019).

Most of the other benefits of BWCs, such as reducing litigation risk and increasing effectiveness in proving crimes, have not yet been adequately studied, though research suggests that fears that BWCs would lead to depolicing have not been realized. See Lum et al., *supra*, at 110. Now what do you think of cameras?

12. *Budgetary costs.* Whatever the benefits of BWCs, those benefits should be assessed in relation to their costs, and those costs are substantial. It usually costs a law enforcement agency a few thousand dollars per camera per year to purchase, maintain, and replace cameras and to store the data and respond to data requests. Most agencies that have not acquired BWCs cite these costs as their primary reason for reframing. See Shelley S. Hyland, Bureau of Justice Statistics, U.S. Dept. of Justice, *Body-Worn Cameras in Law Enforcement Agencies, 2016* 9 (2018). The costs are often a greater burden for small departments.

13. *Privacy costs.* By their nature, BWCs increase surveillance and decrease privacy. Victim and witness privacy present a special problem. As Mary Fan notes, "We call the police because of intimate partner violence, sexual assaults, fights, home invasions, hurt loved ones, and much more. Police see us when we are battered and bleeding, drunk and disorderly, distraught, traumatized, enraged, hopped up on drugs or stoned, and worse." Mary D. Fan, *Privacy, Public Disclosure, Police Body Cameras: Policy Splits*, 68 Ala. L. Rev. 395, 399 (2016). New Hampshire's law is cited by some as a model for protecting privacy while promoting transparency and accountability. (South Carolina's law, which mandates broad use of BWCs but precludes the public from accessing recordings except in limited circumstances, is often cited as an example of the opposite. See S.C. Code. Ann. §23-1-240(G). Is it better to prohibit sensitive recordings, as New Hampshire does, or restrict access to such recordings, as Washington does? Or should we handle these concerns another way? Fan wants agencies to redact and release recordings, though doing that efficiently will require improvements in redaction technology. See Fan, *supra*, at 431–437. Are there other ways the law can maximize the benefits and minimize the harms of cameras?

14. *Public demand.* Despite the research, critics of policing continue to call for BWCs to improve accountability. How should police chiefs and political leaders respond, knowing that the cameras will be expensive and might well not achieve that result? See Howard M. Wasserman, *Moral Panics and Body Cameras*, 92 Wash. U. L. Rev. 831, 843 (2015) (arguing for more nuanced public debate about body cameras).

15. *Civilian recordings.* Even when BWCs are adopted by agencies, civilian recordings of police conduct, discussed further in Chapter 9, might provide an important supplement to the video BWCs provide. Civilian recordings offer different perspectives on encounters, which can mitigate the "camera perspective bias" that occurs when viewers watch police BWC footage from the first-person perspective of the officer. Moreover, civilians do not have to depend on agency decisions about when to record or what to do when officers "forget" to activate their cameras. Civilian recordings also shift control over access to video footage from departments to the public, potentially allowing greater access to video evidence of an encounter. See Jocelyn Simonson, *Beyond Body Cameras: Defending a Robust Right to Record the Police*, 104 Geo. L.J. 1559 (2016); see also Mary D. Fan, *Democratizing Proof: Pooling Public and Police Body-Camera Videos*, 96 N.C. L. Rev. 1639 (2018) (arguing that pooling civilian recorded videos and incorporating them into the official record of an incident "democratizes proof so that members of the public can help shape and contest the official story").

16. *Federal law.* Federal law has little to say about the use of BWCs. When police record encounters in which they are involved, they conduct neither a search nor a seizure within the meaning of the Fourth Amendment and therefore do not implicate constitutional law. See, e.g., Lopez v. United States, 373 U.S. 427 (1963); United States v. Mancari, 463 F.3d 590 (7th Cir. 2006); see also United States v. White, 401

U.S. 745 (1971) (holding that recording a conversation using a radio transmitter worn by confidential informants does not implicate the Fourth Amendment). Nor are recordings of conversations in which an officer is a party covered by federal laws governing wiretapping and electronic recording of conversations. See Electronic Communications Privacy Act of 1986, 18 U.S.C. §§2510–2520. Nor does the federal Freedom of Information Act, 5 U.S.C. §552 et seq., apply to local governments and agencies. Instead, the primary federal intervention with respect to BWCs is through the U.S. Department of Justice Bureau of Justice Assistance. It has provided technical assistance to departments on BWCs since 2015 and administers tens of millions of dollars of grants through the Body Worn-Camera Policy and Implementation Program, authorized and funded by Congress. In addition, the Civil Rights Division has mandated body-worn cameras in several of its consent decrees with police departments engaged in a pattern or practice of misconduct. See Consent Decree at 52–57, United States v. City of Ferguson, No. 4:16-cv-000180-CDP (E.D. Mo. Mar. 17, 2016); Consent Decree at 38–39, United States v. City of Newark, No.2:16-cv-01731-MCA-MAH (D.N.J. May 5, 2106).

17. *Anecdote or data.* Consider how New Hampshire restricts the production of video in N.H. Rev. Stat. Ann. §105-D:2 IV and the way Washington restricts public access to the data in Wash. Rev. Code §42.56.240(14)(d). These requirements, which other states share, indicate that states think BWC recordings are useful to better understand specific incidents. But over time, BWC recordings could lead to large indexed and searchable data sets about police conduct. With machine learning, such troves could enable an individual agency to detect problems in officer conduct and allow researchers to compare conduct across jurisdictions. In this way, BWC recordings could revolutionize our understanding of police–citizen encounters. Of course, changing technology affects communities, too: BWC recordings combined with advanced facial recognition and other biometric technologies could radically expand surveillance of the public (and perhaps disparities in policing—at least until biometric technologies get better). Should we write laws to address the near future? How?

G. Final Word

Now that you have learned about the laws through which communities create, govern, and hold accountable the police, what is your takeaway? What laws seem most important in shaping police conduct that you care about? What actors seem best suited to promoting good policing? To preventing bad policing? What laws help or stand in the way? What legal reforms do you most want to see carried out?

Producing public safety through policing is complex, and it is an enterprise shaped by a web—a sometimes tangled web—of laws. Understanding *policing* requires examining those laws, the choices we make about them, and how those choices might affect what officers and departments do. By the same measure, understanding the *law of the police* requires taking seriously how officers and departments work, examining the benefits and harms of policing to individuals and communities, and judging the capacities and incentives of government actors that participate in making that law. If this book has helped you to better understand both policing and the law of the police better, it has fulfilled its aim.

The history of policing in the United States is troubled, and its future path uncertain. Ensuring that everyone feels safe both from others and from the government is a moral imperative. Yet too often policing has been violent, abusive, ineffectual, or unfair. Even as communities explore alternatives to coercion to generate public safety, they are likely to continue to depend on the police to make them safer and stronger. As long as there is policing, the law will play a role in shaping it. The law will give the police their power, structure how they are governed, set limits to the harm they may do, determine the information they provide, hold them accountable, and ensure that affected stakeholders have a voice in how order and safety are maintained. Each of us has a role to play in uncovering that law, assessing it, and working to make it better so that communities and the police can find the best ways forward.

Table of Cases

Principal cases are indicated by italics.

Table of Authorities

ARTICLES and REPORTS

BOOKS

Index